Story of My Life

SUNY Series, Women Writers in Translation

Marilyn Gaddis Rose, Editor

Story of My Life

The Autobiography of George Sand

A Group Translation
Edited by Thelma Jurgrau

Critical Introduction by Thelma Jurgrau

Historical Introduction by Walter D. Gray

State University of New York Press

Published by
State University of New York Press, Albany

For information, address State University of New York
Press, State University Plaza, Albany, N.Y., 12246

Production by M. R. Mulholland
Marketing by Theresa A. Swierzowski

Library of Congress Cataloging-in-Publication Data

Sand, George, 1804–1876
    [Histoire de ma vie. English]
    Story of my life: the autobiography of George Sand: a group
translation / edited by Thelma Jurgrau; critical introduction by
Thelma Jurgrau; historical introduction by Walter D. Gray.
       p. cm.—(SUNY Series, Women writers in translation)
    Translation of: Histoire de ma vie.
    Includes bibliographical references.
    ISBN 0-7914-0580-X (alk. paper). —ISBN 0-7914-0581-8 (pbk.:
alk. paper)
    1. Sand, George, 1804–1876—Biography. 2. Novelists, French—19th
century—Biography. I. Jurgrau, Thelma, 1930– . II. Title.
III. Series.
PQ2412.A2E5 1991
843'.7—dc20
    [B]
                                                   90-35172
                                                      CIP

10 9 8 7 6 5 4 3 2

Contents

Editor's Foreword 1

Critical Introduction 7

Historical Introduction 31

Story of My Life 53

Author's Notes 1119

Editor's Notes 1139

Editor's Foreword

The idea of a group translation was born in a workshop held at a George Sand conference about ten years ago. The French and History Departments of Hofstra University had marked the centennial of Sand's death, 1976, with several events: the first American conference devoted to Sand's work and her circle; the keynote address of the eminent Sand scholar, Georges Lubin; and the founding of the Friends of George Sand under the energetic leadership of Natalie Datlof. It was high time, considering the response to those events and the resurgent interest in this nineteenth-century French novelist, that her work was revived.

Sand's oeuvre had almost disappeared from print in France. In this country, one could occasionally find Victorian-sounding translations of a handful of her novels in second-hand bookstores. But for all practical purposes, the voluminous literary opus that had been acclaimed by her contemporaries was no longer available to readers. True, Sand as a notorious figure had never completely vanished from the public eye. Biographies such as André Maurois' *Lélia* still found an audience. Yet Sand's own five-volume autobiography, *Histoire de ma vie,* had, until Gallimard saw fit to produce it again in 1970, not been reprinted since 1876. And no translation of that work had appeared in English since the turn of the century.

A discrete portion of the autobiography, covering the two-and-a-half years during which the future George Sand received her only formal education at the English Convent of Augustinian sisters in Paris, remained accessible in an 1893 translation called *My Convent Life.* In fact, Academy Press reprinted that version in 1977. A year later, alert to the new, growing readership, Harper & Row published *My Life,* a version of *Histoire de ma vie* shortened from the original of almost 1,600 pages to 240. The translation and adaptation by Dan Hofstadter is an evocative rendering of the compassionate woman who evolves from the tormented young girl, but it omits the broad historical, political, and social context that makes Sand's an exceptional work in the annals of men's and women's autobiography.

Looking back now to the early nineteen sixties, when Garnier began publication of Lubin's edition of the first volumes of her massive correspondence, one could already have predicted a renaissance of interest in Sand and her work. And when Lubin's edition of Sand's autobiographical works appeared in 1970 (in addition to *Histoire de ma vie,* it includes a number of short pieces: *Voyage en Espagne, Mon grand-oncle, Voyage en Auvergne, La Blonde Phoebé, Nuit d'hiver, Voyage chez M. Blaise, Les Couperies, Sketches and hints, Lettres d'un voyageur, Journal intime, Entretiens journaliers, Fragment d'une lettre écrite de Fontainebleau, Un hiver à Majorque, Souvenirs de mars-avril*

1848, Journal de novembre-décembre 1851, Après la mort de Jeanne Clésinger, Le Théatre et l'Acteur, and *Le Théatre des marionnettes de Nohant*), it quickly became evident that the autobiography per se deserved a full translation into English, all 1,585 pages. The convergence of these events—Lubin's new edition, revival of interest in Sand's work, and the growing network of people willing to devote time to studying and translating it—led to the present translation.

It seems fitting for a writer with a strong sense of herself as part of a human collective to inspire a cooperative translation effort. I do not clearly remember whose idea it was to distribute the seventy-two chapters of *Histoire de ma vie* among interested Sandistes, but I assumed responsibility for coordinating that task and editing the work of each contributor for accuracy and consistency. The nucleus of four or five grew, in five years, to sixty-five. Translators were recruited through the publications of the Modern Language Association, the American Literary Translators Association, and the Friends of George Sand.

There have not been many examples heretofore of so large a group participating in the translation of a single work. Obviously, there are numerous cases of collaboration by two, or several, translators; and there exist books of poems or other short works by a single author which contain translations by various people; the remarkable Bollingen edition of Plato's *Dialogues* as translated by fourteen different scholars, edited by Edith Hamilton and Huntington Cairns, also comes to mind. But aside from the *Bible,* I know of no other single work of such magnitude where a group translation has been attempted. And probably for good reason. Strictly speaking, the potential benefits of mutual exchange and revision have not applied in this case. I was the recipient of all the translators' work, but I did not attempt to conduct discussions of my revisions with each of them. I corresponded with the group by sending progress reports, and I received letters of encouragement, or letters expressing pleasure at the experience of translating Sand.

A major concern of those who heard about the project was stylistic consistency. Could so many disparate workers bring forth a unified product? Clearly that would depend on the skills of the editor, and to this editor's mind, the narrative style and voice of George Sand was sufficiently strong to withstand a multitude of translators. What I found more problematic was to differentiate my role as lead translator from that of editor. It meant limiting my tolerance for awkwardness, sharpening my ability to distinguish accidental from intended ambiguity, and becoming more stringent in my standards for a readable translation.

Readability became as important a criterion as accuracy and consistency. And within the purview of readability the intolerance of a modern audience for effusive rhetoric and extended sentences had also to be considered. The liberties I took were few: I omitted one adjective in a series of four or five, when it seemed redundant; or I limited Sand's repeated reference to a beloved individual as "My poor, dear So-and-So," only to "So-and-So." My aim was to use Sand's own advice as a guide, when she warns translators that their work "is a form of subjection and dependence which it would be rash to want to set free from its natural shackles. . . . The [writer of the original] will have a right to oppose . . . free translation, and if he is wrong in fact, he will always be right in theory, because for every intelligent translator, he can find ten who aren't, and ruin things thinking to make them better" (V, vi, 999).

All contributors agreed that the work should be translated and published in its entirety, in spite of the anticipated difficulty of finding a publisher for such a lengthy work. Considering that Sand begins her autobiography with a history of her family prior to her birth, which is, for the most part, devoted to her presentation of her father's letters to his mother, a reader could conceivably argue that these be condensed, as they do not always pertain to the story of Sand's own life. Argument might also be made that Maurice Dupin, her father, was not writing for publication. However, that would be in contradiction to Sand's expressed concept of herself as a link in the great chain of humanity, or her concept of history as made up of the trivial documents left by insignificant individuals. As she says early in her work, "Everything converges in history; *everything is history* [Sand's italics], even novels that do not seem to be related in any way to the political circumstances that bear witness to their birth. It is therefore true that the actual details of each human existence are like brush strokes on the larger picture of the collective life" (I, iv, 119). Thus, she introduces the letters of her father—whom we first meet as an adolescent writing to his mother in prison under the Terror, and later as a young officer from various stations in Napoléon's campaigns—by way of proving her thesis that history is best told by obscure human beings.

Some of the contributing translators felt that the 420 pages of notes Georges Lubin had provided for his French edition—the text which served as our source—should also be included in our translation, and indeed many of the group translated Lubin's notes along with Sand's text. Ultimately, it was my decision not to include these, mainly because I felt that American readers would find the information laden with details of French history and culture excessive for their needs and uses. Walter D. Gray, Chairman of the History Department at Loyola University in Chicago, has provided an introduction that keys its presentation of French history to the events George Sand refers to in her autobiobraphy. I have provided additional historical notes with the "common" reader in mind. In a number of cases my notes do refer explicitly to M. Lubin's. The translation also contains the notes George Sand had occasion to add as she wrote her autobiography over a seven-year span and subsequently went through it again for a new edition. The reader will find Sand's notes indicated by numbers within parentheses and the editor's notes simply numbered. Both sets of notes follow the text of *Story of My Life*.

As stated, being privy to a variety of translations of a work by a single author is problematic, but the very spectrum of translations becomes advantageous. Hearing the variations in Sand's voice resulting from the work of different translators was helpful in forming the more unified one that I trust emerges from the edited whole. By the same token, my having access to versions of other translators provided me with interpretations against which to check my own. Often one translator's fortuitous solution was applicable in another chapter. Having a sense of the whole made me more aware of recurrent themes and thus facilitated consistent terminology.

Behind this translation was the impulse to put a neglected, but worthy, work, in its entirety, into the hands of the reading public. The effort was made out of admiration for the original and a desire to correct the undeserved decline into which Sand's reputation as a writer had fallen since her lifetime. Those who contributed to this translation all did so voluntarily; they come from several different countries and many states in this country. There were some who collaborated on a particular chapter, including mothers and daughters, husbands and wives, and friends. Most were content to translate a single chapter, but there was one who was glad to do five. The majority of the group have academic affiliations; a few are professional translators. I regret to say that two of the group have died since translating their chapters; I am elated that another has recovered from a nearly fatal illness. The names of the translators follow:

Tamara Alvarez-Detrell, Allentown College of St. Francis de Sales, Center Valley, Pennsylvania; Kristine Anderson, New York City; Sandra Beyer, University of Texas at El Paso; Mary E. Biggs, Ottawa, Ontario (Canada); Bernadette Archer Bielitz, Clifton, New Jersey; Sarah Burd, New York City; Peter Byrne, Venice (Italy); Anne Callahan, Loyola University of Chicago, Illinois; Robert T. Cargo, University of Alabama at Tuscaloosa; Joyce Carleton, Connecticut State University at New Britain; Janet Holmes Carper, Sacopee Valley High School, Cornish, Maine; Elaine L. Corts, Port Crane, New York; Margaret Cullen, Framingham, Massachusetts; Pierrette Daly, University of Missouri at St. Louis; Michael Danahy, University of Wisconsin at Stevens Point; Henriette Moullot Deering, Indian Head Beach, Florida; Andrée Demay, Professor Emeritus, Smith College, Northampton, Massachusetts; Sergine Dixon (née Dosne), Dorset, Vermont; Sherry A. Dranch, Provincetown, Massachusetts; Maria Espinosa, Oakland, California; Lee Fahnestock, New York City; Adèle Mosonyi Fahssis, Paris (France); Richard Gentile-Berthaume, Hicksville Senior High School, Hicksville, New York; Janis Glasgow, San Diego State University, California; Robert Godwin-Jones, Virginia Commonwealth University at Richmond; Sylvia Glass Goldfrank, Santa Cruz, California; Estelle R. Green, Brooklyn College of the City University, New York City; David A. Griffith, University of Victoria, British Columbia; Richard I. Harper, Houston Public Library, Houston, Texas; Sue Ann Huseman, Illinois Wesleyan University at Bloomington; Ilene Ilton (deceased); JoAnn James, Florida State University at Tallahassee; Thelma Jurgrau, Empire State College of State University of New York at Hartsdale; Frederick Kluck, University of Texas at El Paso; Ursula Korneitchouk, Gallery Director, Cleveland Institute of Art, Ohio; Helen Laird, Huntington Library, San Marino, California; Alvin E. Lundquist, Oxford (England); Margaret McCallion, Londonderry, New Hampshire; Alba McKeon, State University of New York at Farmingdale; Ann F. Miller, Shawnee Mission, Kansas; Constantina Mitchell, Gallaudet University, Washington, D.C.; Myriam Mason Mosonyi, London (England); Elena B. Odio, Darton College, Albany, Georgia; Janis L. Pallister, Distinguished University

Professor, Bowling Green State University, Bowling Green, Ohio; Carole Deering Paul, Port Edwards, Wisconsin; Michael G. Paulson, Kutztown University, Kutztown, Pennsylvania; Palomha Paves-Yashinsky, York University at Toronto, Ontario (Canada); Lynn Kettler Penrod, University of Alberta at Edmonton (Canada); Bernard Pohoryles (deceased); David A. Powell, Hofstra University, Hempstead, New York; Annabelle M. Rea, Occidental College, Los Angeles, California; Sylvie L. F. Richards, University of Missouri at Kansas City; Carol L. Robinson, Calgary, Alberta (Canada); Marilyn Gaddis Rose, State University of New York at Binghamton; Virginia A. Schubert, Macalester College, Saint Paul, Minnesota; Lucy M. Schwartz, University of North Dakota at Grand Forks; Gloria M. Smolenski, New York City; Robert Stanley, University of Tennessee at Chattanooga; Mary Street, Nevada City, California; F. M. Swensen, California State University at Long Beach; Alex Szogyi, Hunter College of the City University, New York City; John VanEerde, Professor Emeritus, Lehigh University, Bethlehem, Pennsylvania; Erdmute Wenzel White, West Lafayette, Indiana; Paule A. Wilson, University of Tennessee at Knoxville; Sylvie Charron Witkin, Colby College, Waterville, Maine.

In the summers of 1985 and 1986, at the first and second annual workshops devoted to translating women writers, organized by Marilyn Gaddis Rose for the National Resource Center for Translation and Interpretation at SUNY Binghamton, I led a workshop whose members were helpful directly or indirectly in solving some translation problems; those who attended were Kristine Anderson, Elaine Corts, Sylvia Goldfrank, Cecilia Grenier, Saul Levin, and Marilyn Rose. I believe the idea for the present SUNY Press series, Women Writers in Translation, emerged in some measure from these workshops; as editor of the series, Marilyn Gaddis Rose deserves special gratitude for recommending this work for publication, as does Carola F. Sautter of SUNY Press.

Notwithstanding all the participants, responsibility for any errors in the translation must be mine, as editor.

Besides the aid of numerous translators, I received help through conversations with family, friends, and colleagues during which a linguistic problem was often resolved; these included Vinnie-Marie D'Ambrosio, Stephanie Goldenthal, Alice Paul, Mary Regan, and Andrea, Maura, and Robert Jurgrau. I specifically consulted some people to help solve technical problems; these included Herbert Beller, Jill Haworth, Pierre Mosonyi, Maria Pyron, and Ruth Z. Temple. Special assistance was requested from two bilingual friends: Adèle Mosonyi Fahssis and Muriel Rosenblitt Albert, who were most generous with their time. Early in this effort, Charlotte Hirst provided valuable secretarial support; later Diane Germano assisted in the daunting task of putting the text on a computer disk. Several colleagues, Mayra Bloom, Vinnie-Marie D'Ambrosio, Alan Mandell, and Mickie S. Grover, read the editor's introduction and offered suggestions that considerably improved the form and content. My husband, David, provided an editorial standard beyond my own and helped me aspire to it during months of truly collaborative labor. I am grateful to him, and to our mothers, Rose and Ethel, for encouragement and support. Without leave time from teach-

ing granted me by Empire State College, I would not have been able to finish
editing this work.

While George Sand's words provided the inspiration, it was the scholar-
ship of Georges Lubin which provided the invaluable source text. These collective efforts are dedicated to him.

Note: Translators' initials appear at the end of each chapter.

Critical Introduction

Gender Positioning in *Story of My Life*

I

The comprehensive story George Sand tells in her autobiography is that of a woman making her way into a man's world. Reading with that story in mind, we necessarily highlight the shifts in gender the author engages in to arrive at her goal. Readers who emphasize the pain and struggle of her journey may overreact in their sympathy and come to defend her as a suffering woman; those who view her journey as a triumph over great odds may exaggerate the extent of her escape from the confines of a woman's life. Thus, reading for gender has its pitfalls. On the other hand, if we concentrate on the way the gender shifts take place, their origins and subtle effects, and the extent to which they were imposed on Sand rather than willed by her, we discover that *Story of My Life* is not simply the story of a woman making her way into a man's world, but a tale of gender in flux: the story of a female child subjected, from an early age, to conflicting family pressures, who finds, as she grows up, more psychic comfort in associations that are typically considered masculine, although her ties to her sex are binding.

Gender questions have always intrigued Sand's readers. In her lifetime, she inspired extreme reactions that attest the fact that her gender obscured the fair consideration of her work. As Paul Blount tells us, some Victorians judged that, as a novelist and a woman, she was "a dangerous enemy of marriage and morality" (56); while others, according to Elaine Showalter, saw her as heroic and "involved in the turbulence of womanly suffering" (103)."[1] Contrasting images of Sand are still with us, notwithstanding the sharpening focus of gender criticism in our time. For example, Carolyn Heilbrun is especially intrigued by the cross-dressing Sand engaged in from childhood and by the fact that admiring contemporaries referred to her as a "great man" (33–36). By contrast, the picture that stays most in Ellen Moers' mind is that of a typical country evening at Nohant. "At the center is Madame Sand, with the needlework she loved in her hands, surrounded by a houseful of friends, children, lovers, guests, neighbors" (11).

Not only contrasting images, but conflicting impressions still abound. For example, as to the legacy of Sand's life and work, Moers' impression, in the Introduction to Joseph Barry's *George Sand: In Her Own Words*, is that "Today Sand's social thought sustains her love stories rather than the other way around, for her pairings of lovers of different ages and places and classes still convey that aspiration toward a new, humane social order which lifted the

hearts of her contemporaries and still has the power to move even our own"
(xx). Simone de Beauvoir, quoted by her biographers in an interview, dis-
agrees: "George Sand did not write well. She refused any type of solidarity
with women. She was always giving stupid names to her lovers, 'my child, my
little one.' She was a landowner. She settled down and became a conservative"
(398).

Allowing for personal bias, such disparate views become easier to understand in light of the shifting gender alliances that emerge in Sand's life story.
Sand was aware that her unconventional woman's life unsettled her readers,
and she uses the autobiography to clarify what being female means to her and
her contemporaries when she discusses her unusual upbringing and education,
her relations to women, her marriage and motherhood, and her entry into the
world of male writers.

However, a proliferation of images of herself was not quite what Sand
had in mind. Her intentions vis-à-vis the reader of *Story of My Life* may be
summarized as twofold: a desire to reflect on her past in order to inspire others
to reflect on theirs; and a hope to entertain the reader along the way, for that is
her métier. Unspoken are two other motives: the first is money; Sand has
promised a substantial dowry to her daughter, Solange, an expense over and
above the usual drain of supporting herself, her children, needy friends, and
residences in Paris and the country. The second is self-justification. Having a
chance, finally, to reach the public in her own voice instead of through created
characters, Sand makes a calculated effort to alter contemporary readers' perceptions of her from the notorious transvestite novelist to a dedicated mother,
who almost became a nun. Sand wants to assure her readers that the woman
who made her way into a man's world never forgot her "true" sex. It is surely
ironic that one of Sand's unspoken intentions in writing her life story was to
"come out of the closet" as a woman.

Given the fact that Sand herself seems to wish to slant the picture, it will
not be easy to find the "real" George Sand in her autobiography, if indeed there is
only one. However, reading for gender can clarify the complex nature of Sand's
femininity. In addition to what Sand tells, the reader can make inferences, considering current insights into the effects of gender difference, about what she
unwittingly reveals. Furthermore, Sand's stated motives and apparent approaches
to the autobiographic form can be examined to determine how substantial was
the mask of masculinity by which she came to be recognized as a writer.

Nancy K. Miller, in "Writing Fictions: Women's Autobiography in
France," focuses on the problems Sand and other women have had in writing
their life stories which make reading for gender necessary. One problem is revelation. Women's ability to be truthful is affected by their knowledge that "they
are being read as women" (49). Exposure to the public eye is risky; they have
their reputations to protect. What Miller calls "anxiety of gender identity" (58)
also forces women to make sense of their written lives and shape the autobiographic form in ways that skew the truth. Readers must read "for difference";
that includes a "commitment to decipher what women have said (or, more
important, left unsaid) about the pattern of their lives" (55).[2]

Elaine Showalter, in *A Literature of Their Own*, proposes that, historically, the literature of women novelists has gone through developmental phases. The first, or Feminine phase, includes the work of those who, like George Sand, came of age in the mid-nineteenth century. The sexual "double bind" (21) Showalter ascribes to Feminine writers also explains how and why to read for gender: such writers imitate traditional modes as well as internalize dominant standards of art and prevailing views on social roles (13), behavior that induces a conflict in their image of themselves as females. As in the case of Sand, they adopt male pseudonyms and, at the same time, show strong anxiety over the possibility of appearing unwomanly. Some tactics they use for coping with their anxiety are to picture themselves as helplessly female, deprecate their own abilities, and subvert the accepted masculine paradigms they are imitating.

The experiences of womanhood to which Sand herself directs us in *Story of My Life* are a primary source of evidence of gender anxiety, for they give readers a sense of the unusual origins and development that explain her inability to adapt to the typically constrained life of a woman of her time, a weakness that ultimately became a strength and allowed for the uncommonly flexible gender adjustments visible in her autobiography.

II

Already on page one we are aware of a gap between Sand's expressed intention in writing her autobiography and the result. With her first stated reason, "a sincere study of my own nature and a careful examination of my own existence" (I, i, 71),[3] Sand makes a pact with the reader to pursue a traditional course in presenting her life story.[4] In her original phrasing, Sand had called it a "swift (*rapide*) examination," which she later changed to "careful" (*attentive*).[5] Yet it takes a great many pages before she confronts that study and examination, threading the way to her eventual birth through many digressions and chapters of family history.[6]

One reason for this delaying tactic could be that Sand is aware that, in her role of autobiographer, she will have to revise the concept of truth she has held as a novelist. She acknowledges discomfort when she says, "I know of nothing more difficult than to define and sum oneself up as a person" (I, i, 71). It seems likely that her reluctance stems from the fact that she is finally openly writing as herself.

Prior to writing *Story of My Life* [1847–1854], Sand was accused of airing her own problems in her novels. Some readers had chosen to see the author herself as the disconsolate wife in *Indiana* [1832], the insatiable heroine of *Lélia* [1833], the maternal lover to a Chopin-like hero in *Lucrezia Floriani* [1846], among other characters. Sand denies such identifications with simple reasoning that probably persuaded no one: "Nature does not create things the way art does. . . . Nature has caprices and inconsistencies. . . . Art corrects these inconsistencies only because it is too limited to convey them" (V, xiii, 1107). If Sand is preparing to follow nature instead of art in her coming work, it seems likely that she intends to convey the truth of her development in all its "caprices and inconsistencies," meaning to supply the reader with origins, sources, documents—all the "natural" evidence, so to speak—if only to dispel the superficial resemblances of herself to her heroines. By writing as herself, she can set the record straight, but the record will have to be voluminous. Thus, she begins to subvert her original intention of writing a "swift examination."

Wittingly or not, Sand goes on to subvert prevailing paradigms of autobiography by inventing her own form and by employing other strategies of indirection typical of woman autobiographers.[7] She will *not*, she claims, be following in the mainstream of those autobiographers whose current selves are always in agreement with their selves of yesterday; she will *not* contemplate herself unrealistically in the heroic guise of a Werther, Manfred, Faust, or Hamlet; she will *not* follow the confessional example of Rousseau, because she feels the rest of the world is not morally better than she and thus should not hear her confessions. Nevertheless, Sand steadily, though indirectly, asserts her gender by expressing concern for others and telling her story through others. In addition, Sand claims she is fulfilling the painful duty of telling her story as an inspiration for others to do the same: "Such personal impressions or attempts to voyage into the abstract world of intelligence and feeling, told by a serious soul, might be a prod, an encouragement, even a counsel or guide, for other souls in the labyrinth of life" (I, i, 74).

By taking the female prerogative of portraying others to define herself, she grants herself permission to avoid her own story, for the time being, and focus on other members of her family. She thereby also affords herself the opportunity to discover one who might be "a prod, or guide," for her. For example, from the array of ancestors on her father's side, she chooses Mme. Dupin de Chenonceaux—second wife of Sand's great-grandfather and protectress of his secretary, Jean-Jacques Rousseau—a "remarkable woman who never took her rightful place in the republic of serious writers" (I, ii, 94). Sand tells us that M. and Mme. Dupin de Chenonceaux were writing a work on the merits of women when the husband died; also that her ancestress, being a disciple of Abbé de Saint-Pierre (early proponent of the emancipation of women and author of a plan for world peace), was more advanced than most other eighteenth-century thinkers. Discovering this forebear serves to justify Sand's coming story in three ways: her choice of writing as a profession, her belief in an ideal marriage where the partners share a life of the mind, and her conviction that a woman can be a politically enlightened and still merit society's respect.

So we see her, from the time she starts writing her autobiography, beset by the problems of gender and resolving them as women were wont to do: her first expressed intention, the conventional one of studying her nature and examining her existence, is subverted, at least temporarily, by her need to provide the public with a semblance of the mighty family tree from which she grew; this, in order to counter their impressions of her notoriety and questionable origin. Her second intention, of fulfilling the writer's duty to inspire others to do the same, has a conventionally altruistic ring but also is a permit to begin work, and writing is her livelihood.

From letters written to friends during her first year of writing, 1848, we learn that, in spite of the volatile political situation in which she is directly involved, and in spite of devastating personal problems, she is looking forward to a change from novel writing, for it leaves her free to follow her own chronology, to meditate on life, and to bask in the fullness of her recollections.[8] She had signed a contract in December 1847, to produce a five-volume autobiography, for the grand sum of 130,000 francs. Not only does she want to write, she *has* to write! And the method she resorts to involves her quickly enough in erecting barriers, detours, diversions away from herself, engaging the reader in a game equally intriguing as the fictional one: she creates her own myth.

III

Sand may have rationalized that, by threading her way through a maze of past lives that preceded her own, she was giving her readers a historical bonus, but it served her needs as well. By writing her family history she could, in a sense, "right" the illegitimacy of her father's noble line as well as the poverty of her mother's. She could re-create the father who died when she was four—the first of her natural protectors she claims she was doomed to lose. She could, furthermore, construct a series of chambers that would simultaneously serve to protect and to channel, that would allow the author to go through a gestation and labor, as it were, finally culminating, after twenty-two chapters, in her birth.[9]

It should be pointed out that, by imputing a pretext to Sand's uses of history, I am reflecting not only the ideas of gender theorists but also some recent developments in the study of autobiography. James Olney comments that the awakening of literary theorists to the subject of autobiography in the past twenty years has been characterized by a shift in focus from *bios* (the historical life) to *autos* (the "I" or self); so that now when we read an autobiography, we do so with the realization that the "I" writing "half-discovers, half-creates" (11) itself. Olney is a disciple of Georges Gusdorf, whose influential study, "Conditions and Limits of Autobiography," ascribes to autobiographers the burden of being separate and isolated from their social groups. The interest in the self common to autobiographers, he claims, is peculiar to our civilization, indicating a shift from a cyclical to a linear view of history, whereby humanity can no longer foresee its common goals, hence individuals focus inward.

One can argue that Sand's hopefulness that her work may benefit others and her often-expressed vision of human communality contradict Gusdorf's emphasis on the isolated individual. Indeed Susan Sanford Friedman questions whether Gusdorf's individualistic concept of the autobiographical self can be applied to any women autobiographers, concluding her essay, "Women's Autobiographical Selves: Theory and Practice," with the comment that "The autobiographical self does not oppose herself to all others, does not feel herself to exist outside all others, and still less against others, but very much *with* others [Friedman's emphasis] in an interdependent existence that asserts its rhythms everywhere in the community" (56). But a counterargument to

Friedman's can also be made, that Sand's hopes and visions are masks of optimism covering a deeper despair, mere recitals of faith in humanity that need to be made public precisely because that faith is crumbling. There is sufficient evidence to make such a counterargument in Sand's portrayal of herself, at times, as separate and melancholy.

In any case, following Gusdorf may be fruitful for the moment: he considers all autobiographers powerless to reveal their true selves; their only power is to reveal their self-imagined aspect. He thus gives a distinct edge to literary artists, for whom, he claims (as Nancy K. Miller does, in the case of women writers), life and work—fiction and autobiography—cannot be split. The prerogative of autobiographers, therefore, consists only in "the effort of a creator to give meaning to *his own* [Gusdorf's emphasis] mythic tale" (48), while the reader can look forward only to find traces of the author's struggle with a shadowy self.

In Sand's case, the struggle is not so shadowy; in fact it is the mythic tale itself, patterned in the many images having to do with the threat of separation from her mother. The earliest ones go back to age four, when Sophie is giving birth to a sickly infant and the daughter is overcome with fear for the mother's life (II, xiii, 448). Shortly after, Sand recalls her mother's fear when father, mother, daughter, and infant, on the way to France from Spain via the Bay of Biscay, are in danger of shipwreck (II, xiv, 454). The death of Sand's father comes soon after to cancel any hope for a truce between his aristocratic mother and his wife of the Parisian streets. After his death, the girl is sporadically threatened with separation from her mother, a threat realized when she is thirteen. At that time, Sand recalls her grandmother telling her the "terrible story [of her mother's disreputable life before she met Sand's father] calculated to destroy my respect and love for my mother" (III, x, 633).

There is, in addition, a particular image that Sand presents as transcending her personal experience, which takes on a mythic proportion. She recalls a story told to her by two classmates at the English convent, sisters who were separated from their Indian mother and sent to Europe for reasons of health and schooling: " . . . Élisa and Lavinia had vague recollections of their mother writhing in despair on the Indian shore as the boat moved away at full sail" (IV, i, 715). This image of physical separation became emblematic for Sand. Not focusing directly on herself, she can more readily freeze, as in a tableau vivant, the pain pervading her development, and thereby create a distance between herself and the suffering creature to whom her contemporaries responded.

The suffering portrayed in *Story of My Life* is indeed very vivid, and certainly felt. For the condition in which Sand felt herself most a woman was precisely the one in which women feel themselves most in need of protection—as mothers. She saw her own mother as thoroughly vulnerable with respect to class and money. This was compounded in the small girl's mind when she saw Sophie afflicted, first, by the death of her six-month-old son and, then, by the accidental death of her husband. Later, the girl became sharply aware of her grandmother's suffering after the same event. The struggle between grandmother and mother for her custody, and her grandmother's victory, further added to Sand's sympathy on behalf of her mother. Germaine Brée, who is concerned with the use and prominence of the mother motif in Sand's autobiographical writing, calls that victory "shattering" in its exclusion of the mother (443).

While the birth of her own son is heralded as "the most beautiful moment of my life" (IV, ix, 838), not long afterward, Sand suffers a severe and prolonged postpartum depression and then, periodically, a certain panic when the child is out of her sight for longer than a day. During his residence at boarding school, mother and son exhibit classic symptoms of what we today commonly refer to as "separation anxiety." By the end of her autobiography, Maurice Sand (who took his mother's pen name as his own surname) emerges as his mother's source of life; witness Sand's words in the Conclusion: "Be blessed filial friendship, friendship of my son, who has responded to every fiber of my maternal feeling!" (V, xiii, 1117).

She has less to say about her daughter's birth, which she claims was premature. But as Georges Lubin's notes inform us, Sand is disguising an obvious discrepancy regarding the date of Solange's conception, which, if ascertained, would prove her father to be someone other than Sand's husband, Casimir. Solange is usually depicted in contrast to Maurice, who can sit for hours making cutouts or coloring. As a child, she is hyperactive, hard-to-control, domineering, manipulative, rebellious, and spoiled; we hear little about her as an adult. Sand may have felt "the less said the better" about this failure to raise a daughter she was proud of, but the reader for gender is bound to find Solange's absence provocative. Simone de Beauvoir, who herself chose not to have children, concluded, after reading eight volumes of correspondence, that Sand was unable to give Solange any more than a "'conditional' love—a terrifying thing for children, for whom emotional security is so necessary" (169).

Germaine Brée offers further food for speculation as she postulates a crucial threesome in Sand's development whereby Sand became the mediating child between grandmother and mother, the older ultimately coming to represent the good and peaceful mother; the younger, by contrast, eventually assuming the role of the ill-willed and unstable mother—a pattern, Brée claims, Sand repeats with others at different times in her life. Such a pattern could explain her intolerance of Solange, assuming Sand saw herself in the role of the wise, older mother; Maurice as the mediating child; and Solange as the destructive, younger mother who has to be banished. Whatever the true story of their relationship, it is clear from *Story of My Life* that Sand's assumption of the mother role as a suffering one left her liable to interpret her daughter's independent nature as calculated to give her pain.

Sand's maternal point of view was of the kind that required a certain docility on the part of its object of focus. She often took on the role of nurse from the time her grandmother was suffering the after-effects of a stroke. She nursed Michel de Bourges, her first mentor in revolutionary politics, during his frequent bouts of exhaustion. Later, she kept the consumptive Chopin in reasonably good health for seven years. Speaking of herself in the nursing capacity, she wryly observes: "A woman's friendship has a great deal of the maternal in it, and that sentiment dominated my life more than I would have liked" (V, ix, 1053). Sand does not often confess to shortcomings in her behavior vis-à-vis others, so this remark reveals a side of her that usually remains silent. Motherhood—the aspect of being female that came most naturally to her who had two mothers overseeing her and no fathers to mediate—fused nurturing, in her mind, with vulnerability and suffering. The mother role could well satisfy her psychic need to unload a bounteous affection on someone, if that someone did not threaten her will—struggling since childhood to control its destiny—and leave *her* on the shore, writhing in despair.[10]

IV

Sand's two-and-a-half-year stay in the convent of English sisters, in the company of the daughters of the nobility, was unusual in that it represented a happy time in her life. This was possibly due to a strong sense of shared equality among the adolescents, for whom other attributes than money and class had value. In that all-female setting she found calmer "mothers" to console her and peers to befriend. Yet, for all of the fondness this time in her life evokes, Sand comes to a critical conclusion: "... we had the childish and absurd tradition of drawing up lists of friends and adhering to the order of affections thus established. We all demanded this of each other, which proves that women are born jealous, and insist on their rights in the domain of friendship, as they lack any power to command respect in society" (III, xiii, 685).

As already mentioned, being a woman had painful associations for Sand, and being raised by women had had unhappy results. Furthermore, as a child, she had observed, through her mother's democratic eyes, the coquetry of aging female aristocrats and found it ridiculous; she later resisted all attempts on the part of her grandmother to train her in the social graces of the old nobility. Thus, at an early age, aristocratic women were associated in Sand's mind with feminine behavior at its most artificial, and working-class women with victimization. Looking back later, she sees all women as lacking the respect of society. It would seem she had no choice, in light of her strong impulse to control her life, but to reject, with rare exceptions, the company of women. It would further seem, paradoxically, that the very strength of that impulse in some way derived from the separations she had been forced to sustain. I think it fair to say that such a complex set of associations with being female had promoted an ambivalence in Sand regarding her alliance to her sex. (It will become apparent later that Sand's gender formation was additionally complicated by a strong identification with her father.)

Sand devotes an entire chapter, in the last part of her autobiography, to her friendship with the actress Marie Dorval. She prefaces this account by stating: "With very few exceptions, I cannot stand the company of women for long, not because I feel they are inferior to me in intelligence... but woman is, in general, a nervous, anxious being who communicates to me her eternal confusion about everything, in spite of myself" (V, iv, 963). Dorval was a woman as exceptional as herself, six years older, a working artist, who captivated her despite being an expression of feminine agitation at its height. Sand's portrait shows her friend as a version of the suffering mother; indeed, the actress's turbulent personality attracted and repelled Sand not unlike the way her mother's did. Dorval's plight and Sophie's were similar: poor, unsheltered girls forced to sacrifice respectability in order to support themselves. Sand feels called upon to defend Dorval, as she does her mother, against a society that is unwilling to forgive actions committed for survival.

By the same token, both Sand and her friend were raising ungrateful, rebellious daughters who became their rivals, so that many observations in the chapter about Dorval may be read as a gloss to events in Sand's life at the time she started to write her autobiography (see note 8). By presenting a lengthy dialogue during which she elicits her friend's fuller responses, Sand uses a strategy of self-revelation typical of women autobiographers, with one variation—she sounds as if she were speaking to an immature part of herself:

"'Are you hiding something from me?' I said to her.

"'Not at all!' she exclaimed. 'You know very well I have the opposite fault, that of piling all my troubles on you, and that it's always you whom I ask for courage. But don't you understand boredom? Boredom without apparent cause, because if one knew the cause, one might find the cure.... I would like to be you,' she resumed, in response to the reflections which hers had suggested to me.

"'I love you too much to wish that on you,' I said to her. 'I've been bored, in the sense you mean, not since today or yesterday, but since the hour I came into the world.'

"'Yes, yes, I know that,' she exclaimed, 'but it's a grand boredom, or a powerful boredom, if you prefer. Mine is feeble; it's disheartening. You unearth the reason for your sadness, and when you grasp it, your course is set. You take yourself in hand by saying: "That's the way it is, it can't be otherwise." That is what I'd like to be able to say. And then, you believe that there is a truth, justice, and happiness somewhere; you don't know where; it doesn't matter to you. You believe one has only to die to enter something better than life. I feel all that in a vague way, but I desire it more than expect it'" (V, iv, 971).

Thus, her dialogue with her friend allows Sand indirectly to reveal a similar battle with mental weariness and yet set a distance of experiential superiority between them.

Sand begins her autobiography with a lengthy history, and she closes with a set of final chapters portraying her contemporaries. But Marie Dorval is the only woman Sand focuses on in any depth. Other gifted women, whose performing talent or political action move her, come in for words of praise—Charlotte Marliani, Pauline Viardot. Regarding women writers, however, Sand is less forthright. She describes Hortense Allart, among other celebrities she admires, through the gender lens of her time: " . . . a woman's compassion and a man's firmness" (V, xiii, 1103). Marie d'Agoult, who had been a close friend for several years, is passed over in several cordial paragraphs wherein Sand seems coolly obliging in her praise. The similarities between them—D'Agoult was the lover of Franz Liszt and wrote under the pen name of Daniel Stern—probably promoted rivalry instead of friendship. Sand does not mention Flora Tristan, whose exposé of life among the London work-ing-class she was certainly familiar with. Nor does she mention Louise Colet, who had earned a reputation as a poet and tried to enlist Sand's friendship on more than one occasion. Relationships with women like herself, who had established reputations in male-dominated fields, or under the auspices of men, and earned a measure of independence, were problematic.

Taking stock of her masculine and feminine qualities as she embarks on her entry into the writing profession, we see her fluctuating in her gender alliance. Sand admits that she does suffer from an essentially female constitu-tion, subject to alternating moods of action and passivity, "dependent, nervous, prey to my imagination, childishly susceptible to the emotionalism and anxi-eties of motherhood." Yet she insists on her exceptionality from other women for having had an atypical education that left her with more strength of mind, as well as a scorn for vanity and a suspicion of the desire to please all men. Thus, she protests against being relegated to "secondary standing in artistic and family life." But more interesting, a further reading on the gender scale is still in favor of the injured female. "What man," she asks, "could have set me an example for a secret heroism to which God was the only confidant, hearing my protests against a slighted dignity?" (IV, xiii, 899).

V

Just as a pattern of female suffering pervades *Story of My Life*, so does the quest for education; just as Sand stands to gain sympathy for the suffering, she stands to gain respect for her forays into the patriarchy of learning. However, writing about her education was more than a means to establish her standing in the eyes of the public: it was to reiterate the quest for mental and spiritual suste-nance whose periodic resolutions relieved anxiety throughout her life, and helped her forge an identity. As Sand looks back to her return to Nohant at age seventeen, after her stay at the convent, in time to help care for her dying grand-mother, she comments, "If destiny had made me pass immediately from my grandmother's control to that of a husband or the convent, it is possible that, always subject to accepted influences, I would never have become myself" (IV, iv, 752). The unusual influences to which Sand is alluding are her first serious readings, which made her aware of her intellect for the first time.

Lessons with her grandmother prior to those readings had provoked in her "the same mood of inert submissiveness and secret disgust as the one in which I found myself in the face of studies imposed on me in the convent. At Nohant, aspiring to become a worker with my mother, I had despised study as being too aristocratic. In the convent, thinking only of becoming a servant with Sister Hélène, I despised study as being too worldly" (IV, i, 716). Studies in French, Latin, and botany—where her tutor took a dry, pedantic approach —had ended in the conviction that these subjects were sterile. Now, at age sev-enteen, reading Chateaubriand for the first time, she is struck by the contradic-tion between his contemporary appreciation of the aesthetics of Christianity and the self-effacing approach with which she had been imbued at the convent.

Encouraged by her Jesuit advisor not to fear intellectual questioning, she goes on to read the philosophers—Mably, Locke, Condillac, Montesquieu, Bacon, Bossuet, Aristotle, Leibnitz, Pascal, Montaigne—and then the poets or moralists—La Bruyère, Pope, Milton, Dante, Virgil, Shakespeare—"all without order and method, as they fell to my hand, and read with intuitive ease that I have never regained since and that was even beyond my normally slow ability to comprehend" (IV, iv, 763-4). She finds her belief in God affirmed, yet she feels herself drifting further from conventional religious practice and prayer. In other words, when Sand discovered the authorities contradicting one another, she was able to make better use of them and her self was strengthened. At this point, she discovers Rousseau, whose language and manner "took hold of me like glorious music lighted by a huge sun. I compared him to Mozart; I understood everything! What pleasure for an awkward and obstinate pupil finally to happen to open her eyes fully and see no more clouds before her! . . . From that intoxicating reading on, I indulged in the poets and eloquent moralists with no more worries about transcendent philosophy" (IV, iv, 770).

Like so many women, Sand expresses feelings of inadequacy with regard to her abilities when confronting the barrage of male authorities, but in coming to Rousseau when she did, she was fortunate to meet an intellect compatible with hers. She not only found a way to unite ideas and feelings, but also a confirmation of her "feminine" mode of thinking from the founding father of Romanticism. Sand entitles this chapter on her reading "From Mysticism to Independence"; it could just as well be entitled "From Chateaubriand to Rousseau," for it was reading itself that enabled her first step toward independence, tantamount to what she equated with becoming herself.

Predictably, this road to liberation would make her measure her solidarity with other women as she came across sexist slurs in her readings. For example, in her early twenties, when reading Montaigne's comments regarding the moral inferiority of women, Sand claims she protested inwardly: "This ineptitude and frivolity that you throw up to us is the result of the bad education to which you have condemned us, and you compound the evil by putting it in writing. Improve our lot; allow men to share it; make them virtuous, mature, and strong-willed, and you will see very well that our souls emerged equal from the hands of the Creator'" (IV, xiii, 899).

At the age of seventeen, Sand was bound to learn from authorities in books. But her later education took place in the many conversations with thinkers in the realms of theology, philosophy, politics, science, and the arts, to whom her position as a successful novelist gave her access. Without exception, these were all men—Delacroix, Balzac, Sainte-Beuve, Lammenais, Pierre Leroux, among the better known. Obviously, she was accepted in their company. She generally deferred to these experts, many of whom were older than she. Although she often expressed how inferior she felt in their presence, she was clearly able to follow their ideas, which are amply paraphrased in the later chapters of her autobiography. Still, taking her cue from Rousseau, Sand is always insistent, when reminded of the strength of her intellect, that there is nothing strong in her but her feelings. By that she means us to understand her need to love others and her ability to love God (independent of religion)—assurances, perhaps, to herself as well as the reader, of her basic ties to femininity, which she could never afford to disown.

VI

Yet the broad lines of Sand's development are ever aimed toward strength and independence, qualities associated rather with males, whose prejudices about females Sand has internalized. She has externalized them as well, as she surrounds herself with the young men friends from Berry who support her efforts to become a writer, and as she dons male clothing and assumes a man's name. This strategy worked for her in several ways: it gave her freedom to move and share in daily experiences common to male writers, and it allowed her entry into the world of the working artist, long idealized by Sand as a classless middle-ground between rich and poor. But mainly, it established her professional identity—"George Sand" was negotiable—and once earning money, she could justify her outward liberation from femininity. It is also well to remember that the strategy was probably assumed partly by default rather than wholly by desire in order to compensate for her real inability to adjust to the typically constrained life of a woman.

In Sand's younger years, the male mantle was not worn easily. It took her a while to harden to the ambivalence of the public, who bought her books but abused her as a female upstart. The heroine of *Indiana* [1832], for example, was seen as her protest against the lack of equality in marriage; the heroine of *Lélia* [1833], against the lack of equality in sexual freedom. For her own survival, Sand finally acceded to the prevailing inequality of the sexes. In doing this she temporarily bought a certain peace of mind; her "shrill" fictional protests on behalf of women came to a halt, and she limited her sights to her own liberation.

Here is an example of how Sand's hopes for sexual equality were dampened by the subtleties of role playing. On her return from Italy, already an established novelist, she was beginning to sense an inclination toward politics, and published a fictionalized "little tirade" (*Le Prince*) against Talleyrand, which, from the vantage point of *Story of My Life*, she regrets. In 1834, at the time she wrote it, Talleyrand's long and somewhat morally questionable career as minister and diplomat under each of the rapidly shifting forms of French government was nearing its end: "But although that old duffer was hardly sacred; although he had one foot in the grave and already belonged to history, I felt sorry—justifiably or not—for not having better hidden his personality in my critique. . . . I knew my vocation did not oblige me to attack the living, first of all because I did not have enough talent in this field to produce a useful work of destruction, and, finally, because I was a woman, and battles between the sexes are not equal; the man who insults a woman commits a wanton act of cowardice, while a woman who wounds a man first, without provocation, abuses her impunity" (V, iii, 961).

Writing at a distance of approximately fifteen years, she still recalls the risk she ran by momentarily forgetting that she was not writing as a man, but only as a woman assuming a man's role. Sand is expressing her remembered anxiety of appearing unwomanly to her male colleagues, who evidently believed that her mask of masculinity was more transparent than she did.

The kind of sexism she was subject to even before adopting male credentials is related to us as Sand seeks advice from her compatriots. She receives the suggestion from a deputy from the Berry district, an older man, that if she wants to be a novelist she must consult a colleague of his in the Chamber, M. de Kératry, who writes popular novels. Sand describes with humor an incident where Kératry delivers his theory on the inferiority of women, informs her that women shouldn't write, and finally declares, " . . . don't make books, make babies! " (IV, xv, 915).

Nor was joining the enemy, as it were, protection from the sexism of her colleagues. Sand was already an accepted novelist when Balzac remarked to her, regarding his literary penchant toward realism and hers toward idealism, "Idealize what is pretty and what is beautiful; that is a woman's job." Sand excused him: "Balzac's speech had no disdain or causticity behind it. His brotherly feeling for me was sincere; he has idealized woman too often for anyone to ever accuse him of holding the Kératry theory" (IV, xv, 923). Evidently, Sand's awareness of sexism had been sufficiently present for her to realize that Balzac's remark was suspect and required her defense, just as she had felt it necessary to laugh off Kératry's earlier misogyny.

From her account, the sources of Sand's creativity were not bounded by gender. Corambé, the fantasy god she had invented as a child—focal character of her endless daydreams and precursor to her concept of an ideal hero or heroine—was androgynous; he shifted easily from male to female, as she herself seemed able to do when narrating her novels. Such flexible regard for sexual boundaries undoubtedly helped her to adopt male credentials for her debut in the world of letters.

A subtler sign of gender hedging may be seen in the fact that, in spite of the satisfaction and independence Sand achieved by becoming an artist, and in spite of the admiration she expressed for a few men she considered geniuses—Balzac, Chopin, and Delacroix, for example—from her very first attempts at writing, she claims superiority for nature: "No art form can render the charm and freshness of the impression produced by the beauty of nature, just as no artistic expression can equal the force and spontaneity of our intimate feelings. In the soul is something more than in the form. Enthusiasm, passion, reverie, pain do not find adequate expression in the domain of the arts, whatever the art, whoever the artist."

And lest anyone accuse her of being disrespectful to the male world of artists by subordinating them to nature, she continues: "I beg the masters to forgive me; I venerate and cherish them, but they have never rendered to me what nature has given me; what I myself have felt, a thousand times, to render for others was impossible. Art seems to me an eternally impotent and imperfect aspiration—along with other human manifestations" (III, viii, 601). It is possible that Sand speaks here solely as a representative of the Romantic school enamored of Nature's infinite variety, but could she be covertly expressing the superior power of women as mother/creators over that of artist/creator men? True, she has distanced herself from the world of women, but her connection to the world of men was still more tenuous and less secure. While grateful for male acceptance, she may well have harbored an understandable resentment of the effort it cost her.

VII

We learn from her autobiography that suicide entered Sand's mind on several occasions. She does not go into detail about one of the most desperate, when, returning from the trip to Italy she had made with Alfred de Musset, she was unable to put an end to her masochistic affair; but she does say that this led her to think of leaving the country once again and planning elaborately for her children's welfare—in case she failed to return. At this point in her story, her friends from Berry introduce her to Michel de Bourges, the attorney and revolutionary activist who undertakes her political education.

When Sand informs Michel that she has had enough "of all your republics" and has decided to leave France a second time, he argues with her in the predictably sexist way she has come to accept as her due: "I am making a discovery—souls have a sex, and yours is female. . . . I see well—and you remind me—that you have the ambition and imperiousness of undeveloped minds, of beings of pure feeling and imagination—of women, in short. . . . But the logic of pure feeling is not sufficient in politics. . . . [P]erfect harmony between the demands of action and those of our sensibility . . . would be ideal, but it is still unrealizable on earth; so, you conclude that one should stand by with folded arms, and let it happen by itself" (V, viii, 1038).

Won over by an argument that reinforces her exceptionality from other women, Sand does not leave; she stays to become active in politics and on her own behalf, by successfully suing her husband for separation, thus beginning her marital liberation.

Sand's involvement, under Michel's guidance, in the study of marital law allows her to recognize her inequality as confluent with that of other women. Indeed, the whole tenor of her argument becomes a concern for every family member. As Sand reflects on the existent legal conditions that put the wife of an unhappy marriage in an untenable position, she criticizes the law that requires public debate, forcing one of the pair to heap blame on the other in public. If the wife resists, she will be forced to "choose between respecting her husband or protecting her children. One of these duties will stand in opposition to the other" (V, x, 1065). Sand points out that for the wife to cite love affairs of her husband is more painful to her self-esteem than it is to his reputation, for "according to the prejudices and customs of our society, the more a man is known for his many conquests, the more he is met with congratulatory smiles" (V, x, 1065). But if the husband petitions for separation, his task is more appalling still, for being physically stronger he cannot bring injury or bad treatment as complaints. "He must invoke adultery, and morally kill the woman who bears his name" (V, x, 1066). Even worse, she goes on to say, he can "condemn her to return, in subordination to him, to submit to his pardon and his caresses" (V, x, 1066).

To remedy such injustice, Sand emphasizes the need for privacy, suggesting that counsel should be called in when there are grounds for discontent which have not yet reached the level of irreconcilable complaint, and a decision made "solely on incompatibilities that are certain in the judges' minds, unattested by judicial formalities, and unknown to the public" (V, x, 1067). In this way, society would honor its obligation to protect all parties to the marriage, especially women and children, from the pain of publicity.

Her point is that "The marital bond is broken from the moment it becomes unbearable to one of its members" (V, x, 1066). And yet, given her prior comment that men are not the ones to whom the bonds of marriage become unbearable, I assume she is talking about the female member of the marriage. The thrust of the comment is as a plea that society acknowledge the kind of freedom to conduct one's private life with which Sand has been trying for years to conduct hers—again a plea on behalf of women, since men already have that freedom. Sand may not be verbally specific, but the identification with women is clear: since society still treats Sand as a woman, exceptional or not, she must respond as such, and acknowledge herself opposed to men. Thus, by bringing her private pain into a public arena through the institution of legal action, she clarifies her understanding of her problem in terms of societal injustice, thereby gaining a sense of control over her life and diminishing her personal suffering and impotence, to some degree. But she does it through the prevailing institutions, and always with the help of men.

VIII

Sand assures her readers in the very first chapter of her autobiography that she has no intention of republicizing the sensational trial by which she acquired a favorable separation settlement from Casimir Dudevant. Yet she devotes portions of several chapters in the last part of *Story of My life* to doing just that. By this point in her life story, however, Sand is using the events of the public trial to reveal the moral position she reached and the unique road that took her there. Her confidence grows as her life story develops. Her self-protectiveness declines as she takes a stand on public issues.

Therefore, while the autobiography is full of private lacunae to which I have already alluded (such as her relations with Solange or with Alfred de Musset), Sand provides unexpected areas of frankness, one of them being sex and love. Attempting to explain the serious differences that have arisen between her and Casimir by the time she is in her early thirties, she relates a conversation with a family friend who advises her that "by becoming my husband's mistress I could become mistress of my situation." Sand is appalled at the suggestion. "A woman who courts her husband for the purpose of subduing his will is doing something analogous to what prostitutes do for bread and courtesans do for luxuries" (V, vii, 1009).

Nor is her friend's suggestion (that she invoke her love for her children and concern for their future to help her to submissiveness) a viable one in Sand's mind; for duty, as important as it may be, can never serve to rationalize a woman's sexual concessions to a man. "When a chaste young girl makes the decision to marry, she knows nothing at all about what marriage consists of, and can mistake love for what is not love. But at thirty, a woman can no longer entertain vague illusions; if she has courage and intelligence, she knows the price. And here I am speaking not so much of her physical being—which could resign itself to humility, if it could give itself up separately, as an object—but rather of her complete, indivisible being" (V, vii, 1010).

Sand goes on to articulate the importance of the integration of mind and body with regard to the sex act, not least for the sake of the race: "The true human being will only emanate from true love. Two bodies can join to produce a third, but thought alone can give life to thought." Hence most of us are passive beings, "because for the most part we are born of a passive act.... " Sand insists that the mind, by nature, plays an ethical role in relation to the senses: "When a human being, male or female, arrives at the understanding of perfect love, it is no longer possible ... to slide back and commit a purely animal act. ... the conscience must say No, even though the appetite may say Yes." Her conclusion is that sex without love is a mortal sin: "One must love with one's being, or live in complete chastity, no matter what the consequences" (V, vii, 1012).

Sand might seem naïvely idealistic in these comments addressed to a male friend were it not for a final remark which, by alluding to the double standard, makes it clear that the words of the original dialogue have been reformulated in her autobiography into a message intended for women: "This will not impress men at all, I am well aware, but women, who have at their disposal a sense of shame and propriety, can accept this doctrine, no matter what their station in life, when they feel they are worthy of complying with it. For those women who have not the least pride, I am at a loss what to say" (V, vii, 1012).

No one can accuse Sand of leading women into sexual rebellion with such advice; her words may even strike some readers as moralistic. But considering her argument mainly as a plea for women to reject the role of sex object, this can certainly be read as a revolutionary statement.

IX

Sand's political education began with an awareness of her mother's inferior class status, evolved into empathy for female victims of society, and then broadened beyond the boundaries of gender to make her a strong proponent of class equality. Political action could, therefore, have relieved both her pain on behalf of the victims and her guilt at distancing herself from their plight. She maintained her connection with forces for political reform by co-founding journals, writing for them, and ultimately becoming active in the Revolution of 1848 through a series of "bulletins," one of which was considered particularly inflammatory and brought about a reaction against her in her own village. Recall De Beauvoir accusing Sand of settling down and becoming a conservative, but the fact is that all factions of the republican party were subdued under the reign of Napoleon III.

By the time Sand began writing her autobiography, she had emerged in the public spheres of art and politics, become financially independent as a writer, and freed herself from a mismatched marriage, retaining custody of her children and her property. She had not only challenged the oppressive qualities of life common to women but gained enough strength from her quasi-masculine freedom to balance the hypersensitivity and inclination to despair she had been prone to earlier. It is probably more than mere coincidence that she begins writing her autobiography at the same time as she becomes politically active, for to some extent, Sand identified her life with the history of France.

While Sand describes her active role in politics as dating only from the time in her life recorded toward the end of the autobiography—the 1840's, the theme of political liberation runs through the entire work, including the time before her birth. Her family history coincides with the French Revolution and the rise and fall of Napoléon, while her own history touches the major political events that followed. She sees the path her spiritual education took toward enlightened belief as inevitable; she demonstrates for us how her early, intuitive belief in the democratic ideals of the Revolution was later affirmed through experience.

By beginning her autobiography with a history of her family and her country prior to her birth, Sand establishes the link between her life and the political life of France. This is especially true as she arrives at the focal point of her family history—her father, whose letters to his mother take up a sizable portion of this history. (The family history of her mother, Sand points out, has been lost due to the marginality of her class.) As Sand presents these letters, and comments on them, it is important for her to identify her grandmother and father as on the side of the Revolution in spite of the fact that they were aristocrats. In the case of her grandmother, this was perhaps true before Mme. Dupin's imprisonment under the Terror, considering that her intellect had thrived on the ideas of Voltaire and Rousseau. However, no matter how liberal Mme. Dupin was in theory, she bitterly objected to her son's liaison with the lower class woman he was to marry.

The impression one gets from Maurice Dupin's letters to his mother when he first meets Sophie Delaborde is that he is having a fling. Even though Sand has refined some of her father's expressions, it seems clear he is alert to the dangers of entrapment by this seductive young woman who is able to supplement his ever-dwindling finances with resources she has gathered from previous liaisons with other, richer officers in Napoléon's army. Sand has edited her father's letters and slanted the correspondence to emphasize the romantic nature of the involvement, probably irresistible for the novelist in her, and for the autobiographer as well, if Sand indeed believes that "the true human being will emanate only from true love" (see p. 22).

Sand would have readers believe, and is persuasive here too, that Maurice was passionately in love with Sophie and sufficiently enlightened in his political beliefs to overcome the prejudices of his class against such a misalliance. We know that he had been able, with his mother's help, to extricate himself from other love affairs in the past, including one which had produced a son, Sand's half-brother Hippolyte. Indeed, had Maurice wanted to escape Sophie's grip, he would have been grateful for his mother's intervention instead of resisting it. So, in spite of Sand's tampering with the text of her father's letters, we have no reason to disbelieve either the sincerity of his passion or his political liberalism.

Sand also gives convincing evidence of the maturation of her father's character. Maurice was fifteen when his mother was taken to prison for hiding valuables from the revolutionary search committees. At that time, he was a spoiled young man, whose letters to his mother are a continual whining protest about how his life has been disrupted. But by the time he writes his last letter, at the age of almost thirty, he has advanced to the rank of captain on his own merit, been decorated for bravery in battle, and become a responsible family man. Now he is writing to inform his mother that he, his wife, and two children are returning from war-ravaged Spain to the ancestral home, where he hopes for a "reunion" that represents the "complete happiness" he has been wanting for so long (II, xiv, 450). His accidental death occurred several weeks after the reunion took place, three months after he had written his last letter. The longed-for reconciliation of differences that separated his mother and his wife was thus postponed forever.

Sand was in many ways the reincarnation of her father in the eyes of her grandmother. Indeed both mother and grandmother shifted much of their feeling for Maurice to his daughter. For several years she was the link that held them together, and she would remind them of him when they were at odds. But the child did not have the power of reconciliation her father would have had, and ultimately she became a pawn in their struggle.

Napoléon's power, at its apex in 1808 when Maurice Dupin died, was steady during the years when Sand's two mothers were sharing her in relative peace (1808–1812). As the emperor embarked on a fatal war with Russia (1812–1814), Sand's decisive break with her mother was approaching. Her description of Napoléon's declining fortunes triggers Sand's memories of childhood visions of herself flying over the vast icy stretches of Russia, her mission being to lead Napoléon and his lost armies back to their homeland. By imagining herself France's savior, the child seems to have assumed the mantle of her father's heroism and first aligned her own destiny with that of her country. Her own and France's history figuratively merge in the person of her father when she later re-creates him as a figure in the autobiography. Thus, Sand's reasons for including her father's letters in the early chapters of *Story of My Life* go beyond a desire to romanticize her parent's love story and idealize her own origins: she is attempting to reintegrate herself into the mainstream of French history, and from there into its dominant society, from which she was, in effect, expelled when her first protector died.

Naomi Schor indicates that reconciling the class differences that presided over her birth was a perpetual concern for Sand (268). Sand's attempt to re-create her lost father is surely evidence of one such attempt at class reconciliation.

Schor hypothesizes further that "Sand's sexual oscillation was the psychic act-ing out of the impossibility for her of surmounting the irreconcilable class dif-ferences . . . " (268). The many instances of gender "oscillation" evident in Sand's autobiography may indeed be symptoms of a deeper class malaise. At the very least, they are reactions to the particular social and psychological pres-sures that shaped her identity.

Simone de Beauvoir, in *The Second Sex*, was one of the first gender theo-rists to make clear that woman is "defined and differentiated with reference to man and not he with reference to her" (xvi) and that most women develop their sense of themselves as women through an awareness of sexual otherness. Obviously, from the time her father died when she was four, Sand was not reacting very much to the presence of the dominant sex, but rather to its absence; this peculiar condition allowed her more freedom to re-create the masculine, or imagine it, and even act it out. But her visions have little basis in reality; in her immature daydreaming they took on vaguely androgynous, vaguely neuter, always heroic, always idealistic proportions.

Thus, in one sense, her father's death left Sand free to re-create him in accordance with her own image, when she undertook to write the story of her life.[11] In another sense, however, the claim can be made that we owe the cre-ation of "George Sand" to the death of her father, for if he had lived, his pres-ence could easily have arrested the development of the exceptional woman we today think of her as being. Her curiosity, her intellect, her imagination were all sparked by the dead father; yet the bedrock of her nature was the two moth-ers, whose reconciliation she may still have been trying to effect at age forty-three when she began to write her autobiography and they were both dead.

X

Sand's autobiography, on the surface the story of a woman making her way into a man's world, is more aptly read as a tale of tenuous gender. From early on, Sand's femininity was never left to settle into a conventional mold, owing partly to her taking on aspects of her dead father's identity in the eyes of her mother and grandmother, and partly to the tug of their opposing class affili-ations. The fluctuation between masculine and feminine tendencies kept up during her youth. The two-and-a-half-year stay in the convent may have seemed particularly peaceful to her because, in that bastion of femininity, the gender issue for once came to rest.

Thereafter, her philosophical education began, mandating that she inter-nalize male values and paradigms for it to be successful. At the same time she was being trained to manage her grandmother's estate in the country, which further reinforced the sense of masculine identification. When, at her grand-mother's death, her mother arrived to claim custody, Sand tried to submit and could not. The conflict of wills between mother and daughter was particularly painful for Sand because her deepest desires were to please her mother, but she had already felt the threat to her own social integration posed by the class her mother represented.

To extricate herself from her mother's legal rights, Sand sought protection in another legal institution—marriage. Becoming a mother, Sand was again able to steady her gender identity for a while, but she found she could not submit to the authority of her husband. She again used the legal authority to break the bonds of marriage, but the bonds of motherhood remained.

By the time of her legal separation, Sand was openly making her way into the male world of writing, less difficult for her than for a woman of more conventional upbringing, as she had been adopting the attitudes, guises, and strategies since late adolescence. It is extraordinarily difficult to explain the finely-tuned mechanism by which these gender shifts take place, but such flexible orientation was invaluable in the creation of fictional characters of both sexes and of narrators that continue to defy classification by gender. In writing her autobiography, however, she was forced to characterize *herself*, that is, the creature of shifting gender she had become. Of course she knew she was unusual and could not hide it; her public expected that. She herself was quite at ease with her "unwomanly" life; it is on the womanly side that defense was required. Portraying that side of herself on paper was not simple, for she had to reveal and protect at the same time. Hence the plea for sympathy for the suffering female, the telling of her story through others, the historical couching at both ends of the story, and the discrepancies between expressed intention and actual practice.

The contradictions between what she says about herself and the evidence that is her created story must have been visible to Sand herself: she apologizes for "bothering" the reader with a nonentity like herself, yet writes for over a thousand pages; she deprecates her intellect, yet discusses complex political, religious, esthetic, and scientific theories of her day; she gives the impression that she became a writer by chance, yet the story she tells is the story of a writer's genesis. Is she herself not telling us to read her "for difference?" *Story of My Life* offers ample evidence that Sand understood the complex nature of her femininity and hoped that her readers would understand it as well, by calculating for themselves the invisible mean between her shifting positions on the gender scale.

—*Thelma Jurgrau*

Notes

1. The events in George Sand's life that account for her notoriety are fairly well known by now: she separated from her husband, Casimir Dudevant, to become a writer; wearing men's clothing, she pursued that goal, imbibing Parisian culture among a band of young men, some of whom became her lovers; she exposed her two children to this bohemian lifestyle, and left them behind to travel in Italy with the rising star of romantic poetry, Alfred de Musset; he returned to Paris while she stayed on in Venice having an affair with the doctor who had cured the poet of typhoid fever; her third novel, *Lélia*, shocked the public by portraying a woman disappointed in male lovers

consoled by a female; she sued her husband for separation in a public trial and won; among her lovers was the acclaimed Chopin, who died not long after she ended their affair; during all this "private" turmoil, she became financially independent and a respected novelist.

2. Obviously, we can know better what Sand is leaving unsaid by reading sources other than the autobiography. Miller suggests that we try to use a woman writer's fiction, with her autobiography, in an "intratextual practice of interpretation," or as she also calls it, "a double reading" (59). This will not be possible in my introduction, but I direct the reader to the following of Sand's novels available in translation: *Indiana, Valentine, Lucrezia Floriani, Fanchon the Cricket, The Bagpipers,* (Academy Press); *Lélia,* (Indiana UP); *Mauprat, Consuelo,* (Da Capo Press); *Marianne,* (Carroll & Graf); *Lavinia, The Haunted Pool,* (Shameless Hussy Press); *The Country Waif,* (Univ. of Nebraska Press). Other helpful books in English are Joseph Barry's *George Sand: In Her Own Words,* which portrays Sand via excerpts from her novels, letters, journals, and political writings; *George Sand/Gustave Flaubert Letters,* (Academy Press); and *Lettres d'un Voyageur,* (Penguin).

3. References in parentheses to part, chapter, and page follow all further citations from the present translation of *Story of My Life.*

4. By terming Sand's expressed intention a "pact" I allude to the title of the first chapter, "The Autobiographical Pact," in Philippe Lejeune's, *On Autobiography.* His definition of traditional autobiography encompasses Sand's: "Retrospective prose narrative written by a real person concerning his own existence, where the focus is his individual life, in particular the story of his personality" (4). Lejeune's starting point is from the position of the reader, who, he claims, always looks for "breaches of contract" (14). If the pact purports to be fictional, the reader will try to find resemblances between author and text; if autobiographical, the reader will look for disparities. Thus, Lejeune's reader may also be a reader for gender.

5. Georges Lubin fully documents all variants of *Histoire de ma vie* in his edition of Sand's autobiographical works. The variant referred to in this note may be found in Volume One, p. 1,134.

6. Other readers, too, have noted the quantity of space Sand devotes to the history of her family. At the 1986 George Sand conference at Hofstra University, three panelists on the "Poetics of Autobiography" addressed this issue. Gita May attributed it to Sand's inability, as a novelist, to resist the true romance of her parents' early relationship; Marilyn Yalom considered Sand's use of family history as enabling her to bridge the personal and public aspects of her existence; Peter Christensen judged that Sand had placed herself in a familial, literary, and historical frame of reference "to decenter the self from the life lived" (1).

7. Recent studies of autobiography find inherent gender differences in that genre stemming from the fact that women are saddled with a problem men do not have: since writing about one's life implies *ipso facto* a sense of self-importance, and since women's roles have traditionally subsumed that sense, women autobiographers have had to come up with strategies to deal with the contradiction. For example, Patricia Meyer Spacks confirms that women use autobiography "paradoxically, partly as a mode of self-denial" (132). Examining the lives of five political activists—Roosevelt, Pankhurst, Goldman, Meir, and Dorothy Day—Spacks finds that, even as these women

describe their unique accomplishments, they avoid asserting themselves. Mary G. Mason has a more sanguine view of women's strategies; she claims that the women whose written lives she studied as examples of their contribution to the tradition of spiritual autobiography—Dame Julien of Norwich, Margery Kempe, Margaret Cavendish, and Anne Bradstreet—managed *successfully* to "record and dramatize self-realization and self-transcendence through another..." (235).

8. For example, in February 1848, Sand wrote to Pierre-Jules Hetzel: "It is almost a miracle how my memories of childhood are awakened as I near the time to speak of myself" (264). Again in October: "I'm working on my memoirs with great energy. It is the only distraction I find from my unhappiness, for what's going on around me is sad and ugly" (642). To Pauline Viardot in December: "... while writing my memoirs with a great serenity of mind and a great forgiveness of heart, I feel ever more detached from myself, ever more disposed to accept work or death with equal tranquility" (728); and again to Hetzel about writing about her life: "It is work that pleases and does not tire me" (757). Among the "sad and ugly" personal problems besetting her at this time were her daughter's rebellious marriage to a man Sand detested, the death of her daughter's first child, and the definitive break with Chopin, to an extent due to her daughter's behavior.

9. Béatrice Didier is of the opinion that the "very object" of the entire autobiography is Sand's own birth, i.e., it is a "story of a birth to writing" (quoted by Miller, 54).

10. While acknowledging the emphasis Sand gives to maternity in her life, Nancy K. Miller concludes that, in the life stories of Sand, Stern and De Beauvoir, the impulse toward writing transcends that of motherhood (53). My impression is that, for the reasons I have given, maternity is a deeper bond for Sand than Miller allows. The maternal played an important role also in her sexual relationships, as Sand's comment implies.

11. I was glad to find confirmed the importance of Sand's father in her genesis as a writer in Katherine Crecelius's *Family Romances: George Sand's Early Novels*, the first study in English in which Sand's work takes precedence over her life. Crecelius makes a convincing case that the early death of Sand's father was the catalyst for her becoming a writer because it allowed her to internalize his image as well as free herself psychologically from paternal constraints. She states specifically that the autobiography "invites the reader to seek the absent father" (19).

Works Cited

Barry, Joseph, ed. *George Sand: In Her Own Words*. Garden City, NY: Anchor Press/Doubleday, 1979.

Blount, Paul. "The Reputation of George Sand in Victorian England (1832–1886)." Diss. Cornell U, 1961.

Brée, Germaine. "The Fictions of Autobiography." *Nineteenth-Century French Studies* 4 (1976):438–449.

Christensen, Peter. "Positioning the Self in Autobiographical Writing: George Sand as Model for Marguerite Yourcenar." Panel on Poetics of Autobiography, George Sand Conference, Hofstra University, Hempstead NY, 18 Oct. 1986.

Crecelius, Katherine J. *Family Romances: George Sand's Early Novels.* Bloomington and Indianapolis: Indiana UP, 1987.

De Beauvoir, Simone. *All Said and Done.* Trans. Patrick O'Brian. 1974. Middlesex: Penguin, 1987.

———. *The Second Sex.* Ed. and trans. H. M. Parshley. 1952. New York: Bantam, 1961.

Francis, Claude and Fernande Gontier. *Simone de Beauvoir: A Life . . . A Love Story.* Trans. Lisa Nesselson. New York: St. Martin's Press, 1987.

Friedman, Susan Sanford. "Women's Autobiographical Selves: Theory and Practice." *The Private Self: Theory and Practice of Women's Autobiographical Writings.* Ed. Shari Benstock. Chapel Hill, NC: Univ. of North Carolina Press, 1988. 34–62.

Gusdorf, Georges. "Conditions and Limits of Autobiography." Trans. James Olney. Olney 28–48.

Heilbrun, Carolyn G. *Writing a Woman's Life.* New York: W. W. Norton, 1988.

Lejeune, Philippe. *On Autobiography.* Trans. Katherine Leary. Minneapolis: Univ. of Minnesota Press, 1989.

May, Gita. *"The Story of My Life:* George Sand and Autobiography." Panel on Poetics of Autobiography, George Sand Conference, Hofstra University, Hempstead NY, 18 Oct. 1986.

Mason, Mary G. "The Other Voice: Autobiographies of Women Writers." Olney 207–35.

Miller, Nancy K. "Writing Fictions: Women's Autobiography in France." *Life/Lines: Theorizing Women's Autobiography.* Eds. Bella Brodzki and Celeste Schenck. Ithaca: Cornell UP, 1988. 45–61.

Moers, Ellen. *Literary Women.* New York: Oxford UP, 1976.

Olney, James. "Autobiography and the Cultural Moment: A Thematic, Historical and Bibliographical Introduction." *Autobiography: Essays Theoretical and Critical.* Ed. James Olney. Princeton: Princeton UP, 1980. 2–27.

Sand, George. *Correspondance.* Ed. Georges Lubin. Vol. 8. Paris: Garnier, 1971. 101–784. 22 vols. to date. 1964–1988.

———. *Histoire de ma vie* in *Oeuvres autobiographiques.* Ed. Georges Lubin. Vol. 1 and part of vol. 2. Paris: Gallimard, 1970.

Schor, Naomi. "Reading Double: Sand's Difference." *The Poetics of Gender.* Ed. Nancy K. Miller. New York: Columbia UP, 1986. 248–269.

Showalter, Elaine. *A Literature of Their Own: British Women Novelists from Brontë to Lessing.* Princeton: Princeton UP, 1977.

Spacks, Patricia Meyer. "Selves in Hiding." *Women's Autobiography: Essays in Criticism.* Ed. Estelle Jelinek. Bloomington: Indiana UP, 1980. 112–132.

Yalom, Marilyn. "L'Art poétique de l'autobiographie selon George Sand." Panel on Poetics of Autobiography. George Sand Conference. Hofstra University, Hempstead NY, 18 Oct. 1986.

Historical Introduction

The period covered by George Sand's *Histoire de ma vie* is one of the most significant periods in French History, extending from before the French Revolution to the later years of the July Monarchy. Sand begins her autobiography with a description of the tranquil aristocratic world of the Eighteenth Century that formed the attitudes of her family, and moves into the tempestuousness of the revolutionary years of the 1790's, which saw the imprisonment of her grandmother during the Terror. She then recounts her father's life from his early military career in the service of Napoleon, when he was an eyewitness to some of Napoleon's greatest victories, until his accidental death in 1808. Finally, she narrates recollections of her childhood and young adulthood years in a changing world, one marked by major economic changes, urban and rural prosperity and distress, revolutionary movements, and a ferment of ideas concerning social, political, and aesthetic solutions to Europe's problems. In this later period treated in *Histoire de ma vie,* George Sand grapples with the influences of the the three upheavals which form a key to any understanding of the Nineteenth Century: the French Revolution, the beginnings of the Industrial Revolution in France, and the Romantic Movement.

George Sand was born in 1804. However, *Histoire de ma vie* treats her family history for the years well before her birth. She calls the first part of her memoirs, "The History of My Family from Fontenoy to Marengo," that is, from the Battle of Fontenoy (1745)—one of the great victories her illustrious great-grandfather, the Maréchal de Saxe, won in the War of the Austrian Succession to the Battle of Marengo (1800)—at which her father was present—which marked Napoleon's decisive defeat of the Austrian forces in Italy a few months after his coup d'état. George Sand views this period of family history principally through her great grandfather, the Maréchal de Saxe (1696–1750), her grandmother, Marie-Aurore de Saxe (1748–1820), and her father and mother, Maurice Dupin (1778–1808) and Antoinette-Sophie-Victoire Delaborde (1773–1837). Thus her *Histoire de ma vie* covers events of more than a century, ending as it does around 1840, although Sand herself was an adult for only the last two decades of the period covered by the autobiography. The century treated in this book is a most remarkable one in French history and one which requires some historical explanation and clarification.

The France before 1789 which George Sand described was a France where one travelled from place to place by stagecoach over rough, dusty roads, whereas by the 1840's, when the events in *Histoire de ma vie* come to an end, travel was often over the new railroad lines. Before 1789, France was a semi-feudal country where the clergy and nobility still possessed vast rights and privileges which existed in law until the Declaration of the Rights of Man and

the Citizen of 1789 instituted the sacred trinity of Liberty, Equality, and Fraternity. Before 1789, rural France was certainly in a pre-industrial age, whereas
by the 1840's industrialism and its resultant ups and downs in the business
cycle of prosperity and recession were evident throughout the country and also
in Sand's beloved province of Berry. In politics, France experienced the
monarchy of Louis XVI (1774–1792), the Convention and the Reign of Terror
(1792–1795), the Directory (1795–1799), the Consulate (1799–1804), the
Empire of Napoleon (1804–1814), the Bourbon Restoration (1814–1830), and
the July Monarchy (1830–1848). Although many looked back with nostalgic
passivity to the period before 1789, George Sand was one who did not hesitate
to grapple with the chief intellectual currents and trends of her time.

Sand's sources for the first two parts of *Histoire de ma vie*, (some five
hundred-odd pages in the Pléiade Edition are devoted to the history of her family prior to her birth or to when she was a very young girl) are family documents, letters, and the memoirs of her grandmother. For example, her father's
letters to his mother (her grandmother) end with his death in 1808 when Sand
was only four years and three months old.

Sand's Ancestors

Maurice, Comte de Saxe, Duc de Courlande et de Semigalle, Maréchal-
Général des Armées de Sa Majesté très Chrétienne, was according to his biographer, "... the most brilliant adornment of a brilliant age."[1] In writing about
her illustrious great-grandfather George Sand said, "I was raised with a blind
respect for his glory (I, vi)." Maurice de Saxe was the illegitimate son of
Frédéric-Auguste de Saxe (1670–1733), Elector of Saxony and also King of
Poland, and Marie-Aurore de Koenigsmarck (1662–1728), the daughter of a
prominent Swedish noble family. Hence, Maurice de Saxe was the illegitimate
son of a king, and throughout his life he desired to be a monarch as well. He
was raised a Lutheran, and he died in that faith. When twelve years old, he
entered military service and saw action in the War of the Spanish Succession.
He served in one capacity or another in various European armies. Eventually,
he devoted his full service to the French king, Louis XV. He was widely known
in Europe and counted such eminent men as Louis XV, Voltaire, and Frederick
the Great among his friends. He aspired to become tsar of Russia, a desire
which he never realized. His military career reached its greatest heights when
he commanded the armies of Louis XV in the Wars of the Austrian Succession.
He was accorded the highest military rank possible in France, that of
Maréchal-Général, a rank only held once before by Louis XIV's great general,
Turenne. Louis XV expressed his gratitude to Saxe by giving him the Château
of Chambord and its domain as his residence.

Maurice de Saxe was, then, one of the greatest military leaders of his time;
he was also a writer on military topics; *Mes Rêveries,* published posthumously
in 1757, reveal him as a brilliant and original military thinker. One of the foremost military writers, Captain Liddell Hart, writes of Maurice de Saxe, "... as a
military thinker and prophet his outlook was so original, his expression so unfet-

tered by convention, that his writings enjoy a perennial freshness and appeal to the modern spirit of scientific inquiry."[2] The Battle of Fontenoy, fought in 1747, was perhaps his greatest victory. His adversary and host, Frederick the Great, wrote in a letter to Voltaire of Maurice de Saxe in 1749: "I have been entertaining the hero of France, the Turenne of the Age of Louis XV. I have derived much information from my conversation with him, not in speaking French but in the art of war. The Marshal should be the tutor of every general in Europe."[3] Saxe's military career, in fact, can be compared in brilliance to only two other eighteenth-century captains, Frederick the Great and the Duke of Marlborough.

Marie-Aurore de Saxe, George Sand's grandmother, was only two years old when her father died. She was, befitting her station, educated at Saint-Cyr, the foremost school for the education of young girls of the noble class. Marie-Aurore subsisted on an annual pension from the Dauphine, Marie-Josèphe, who was her father's niece and, thereby, her cousin. She considered the pensions inadequate for her needs. After the death of the Dauphine in 1767, when Marie-Aurore was nineteen, her pension was increased by the Minister of War, the Duc de Choiseul, but only after repeated requests. The Parlement de Paris, the chief appellate court in France, had taken the necessary steps to allow her birth certificate to indicate that she was the daughter of the Maréchal de Saxe and Marie Rainteau instead of *"fille naturelle de père et mère inconnus."* This act of the Parlement made it possible for Marie-Aurore to have a respectable marriage, but although she was a cousin of Louis XVI, she could not be presented at court because of her illegitimate birth. At the age of eighteen she married Captain Antoine de Horne, a marriage which ended six months later with Horne's accidental death. It was in her youthful widowhood that she met her second husband, Louis-Claude Dupin de Francueil.

M. Dupin de Francueil was a wealthy tax farmer who had purchased his office in order to collect the taxes from the area around Chateauroux. The office of tax farmer was a lucrative one under the ancien régime. Consequently, when Marie-Aurore, at the age of twenty-nine, married M. Dupin de Francueil, who was fifty-one, she married a wealthy, established, and prosperous gentleman. M. Dupin was something of a *bon vivant.* He was rich, and in addition to his chateau at Chateauroux, he provided Marie-Aurore with a Parisian townhouse. After nine years of marriage, M. Dupin died leaving his wife an annual income of 75,000 francs—a not inconsiderable sum in the eighteenth century. Nevertheless, Marie-Aurore felt that she had been ruined financially. In 1793, seven years after the death of her husband, Marie purchased a small territory and château at Nohant in Berry, a property which has long been associated with her and her granddaughter.

When the events of the French Revolution began to unfold, Mme. Dupin de Francueil witnessed the fall of the Bastille, since her Parisian house was near the prison. In fact, some of her servants participated in its capture. Although her sympathies during the Revolution probably leaned toward the Monarchy rather than the Republic, she did not choose the path of emigration, as did many nobles. She remained in Paris. On one occasion she loaned her cousin, the Comte d'Artois, the brother of the executed Louis XVI, 75,000 francs. This was illegal, and if it had been found out, she could have been tried and executed. Fortunately for her, she managed to conceal this loan from the revolutionary authorities. Both Louis XVI and the Comte d'Artois were her cousins, although not in the legitimate line. After the death of the King and the proclamation of the Republic, she was able to purchase the property of Nohant in 1793, which was only twenty miles from Chateauroux, a place associated with happier times. Her ability to purchase property and to reside in Paris is evidence that until 1793 she had avoided suspicion regarding both her Royalist sympathies and any reservations she might have had concerning the policies of the revolutionaries.

Mme. Dupin de Francueil's good fortune in avoiding arrest ended during the Terror, as she had been persuaded to hide some of her valuables in a wall, and she was reported to the authorities. In fact, in 1793–1794 a series of laws were directed against nobles, which made the hiding of jewels, gold, silver, and other valuables illegal and punishable by imprisonment and possibly death. When the authorities searched Mme. Dupin's apartment, they found the valuables hidden in a wall, but they did not find evidence of her loan to the Comte d'Artois. She was imprisoned in the former Convent of the English Augustinians, on the Montagne Sainte-Geneviève, today near the Panthéon. Her son, Maurice, who was fifteen, was forced to leave Paris, as the Convention had decreed that former nobles could not live there. He moved with his tutor, Deschartres, to Passy, which in the 1790's was outside the city gates. He could not visit his mother, as he could not enter Paris. The two could only communicate by letter as is evident from the touching exchange in the *Histoire de ma vie* (I, iv). With the execution of Robespierre in July 1794, the Terror ended, and Mme. Dupin de Francueil was released from prison in August 1794.

Maurice Dupin's Early Military Career

The hundreds of pages George Sand devotes to her father's letters to his mother, as well as some letters of her grandmother to her father, are of extreme interest for the history of Sand's family and for a description of life in the army between 1798 and 1808. Maurice Dupin enlisted in the French Army in September, 1798. Universal military conscription was one of the contributions of the French Revolution to the modern world, and it was believed to embody the principle of equality as well as to proclaim to Europe the principle of the "nation in arms." Although it was possible legally to escape conscription by hiring a replacement, a method surely open to someone of Maurice Dupin's economic status, he did not elect to follow this course of action. Instead he entered active service. No doubt some of his inspiration for a military career was due to his adulation of his grandfather, the Maréchal de Saxe. The young Maurice Dupin was clearly influenced by his lineage, as is evident in a letter to his mother in the first year of his military service. He wrote on 2 July 1799: "The title of grandson of the Maréchal de Saxe, which I avoid taking advantage of, by which I am announced and introduced everywhere, is certainly in my favor...but also gives me a responsibility; and if I were a boor or an impertinent fellow, my birth, far from saving me, would condemn me and make me hated ever more (I, xi)."

When Maurice entered the army in September 1798, the government of the Directory was engaged in fighting the War of the Second Coalition. In this coalition France was at war with Great Britain, Russia, Austria, and several smaller states. While Napoleon was engaged in his ill-fated Egyptian Campaign from May 19, 1798 to October 9, 1799, the war in Europe was marked by a three-pronged Allied attack on the French forces. First, an Anglo-Russian amphibious expedition under the command of the Duke of York was to land in Holland. Second, the Archduke Charles was to lead the Austrian armies across Germany to the Rhine. Third, a joint Russian and Austrian army under the Russian General Aleksandr Suvorov was to drive the French out of Italy and to conquer the Parthenopian Republic, the Roman Republic, and the Cisalpine Republic. In the summer of 1799 several decisive battles were fought, the most important being the Battle of Zurich on August 26-27, when the French General André Masséna defeated the Austro-Russian forces under the incompetent Russian General Rimsky-Korsakoff. Before the Battle of Zurich, the victorious Austro-Russian forces had invaded Switzerland, after driving the French out of most of the Italian States. Shortly after the Battle of Zurich, the Anglo-Russian forces in the Netherlands were defeated by the French General Guillaume Brune. The campaigns of the Archduke Charles in Central Germany saw the defeat of the French forces commanded by General Jean-Baptiste Jourdan. Jourdan's forces were driven back to the Black Forest and the Rhine. Thus when Bonaparte left Egypt and landed at Fréjus on October 9, 1799, the military situation on the European continent was grave, although there had been some recent victories in the Netherlands and Switzerland. French conquests had been lost in the Italian States and in the German States. An advantage for the French was that there were major disagreements among the Allies. Suvorov, the Russian commander-in-chief, returned with his forces to Russia, and the Russians, in effect, left the war. Thus Austria and Britain remained as the chief active opponents of France in the Second Coalition.

It is within the context of the above military events that Maurice Dupin entered military service as an ordinary soldier in October 1798. His first assignment was to serve in the Army of the Rhine at Cologne, and he was to remain on garrison duty in the environs of Cologne most of the time until June 1799. Cologne was at the center of two of the allied thrusts in 1799, namely, the Anglo-Russian invasion of Holland and the advance of the Archduke Charles across Germany. Although Maurice was not committed to action during his assignment in Cologne, he was surely aware of the threats to the French army stationed there. In July he was posted to Thionville in Lorraine. From there he engineered a transfer to a unit in the Canton of Thurgau and the area around Zurich. This unit was destined for combat, and as he wrote his mother after the battle, the only way to become an officer was to have been in active combat. He wished to fulfill his cherished dream as a grandson of the Maréchal de Saxe to serve with distinction. His desire to become an officer underscores one of the legacies of the French Revolution: promotion in the French Revolutionary and Napoleonic armies was based on talent and ability and not on birth or noble status. Hence, in order to merit promotion, he had to distinguish himself in battle.

It was near Zurich that he witnessed his first active combat and was present at Masséna's victorious Battle of Zurich over Rimsky-Korsakoff. After his initiation into combat, Maurice took part in several minor battles and remained for several months in Switzerland on what would be termed today the front lines, facing the Austrian forces near the Rhine. He served in the Armée du Danube. After the victorious campaigns of August and September 1799, Maurice informed his mother, "A harvest of laurels, glory, victories; the Russians beaten and chased out of Switzerland in twenty days, our troops ready to enter Italy, the Austrians repulsed to the other side of the Rhine [i. e., Switzerland]—there you have without a doubt great news of wondrous deeds (I, xii)."

While Maurice was serving in Switzerland, Napoleon Bonaparte returned to France on October 9, 1799. Upon his return to Paris, Napoleon became involved in a series of negotiations and plots to overthrow the government of France. This government was the Directory, which comprised a plural executive of five members and a legislative branch comprising a two-chambered legislature, the Council of Elders and the Council of Five Hundred. For various reasons the Directory had become unpopular, especially in the areas of governmental corruption, fiscal matters, recent military defeats, and the inherent difficulties of a plural executive. Also, the presence in 1799 of a brilliant, young, charismatic general served as a rallying point for opponents of the Directory. On the 18th of Brumaire (November 9, 1799), Napoleon and his associates successfully staged a coup d'état and set up the Consulate with Napoleon as First Consul. Shortly after the establishment of the Consulate, Maurice was permitted to travel to Paris, where he spent the winter with his mother, who travelled to Paris to be with him. Sand wrote of Maurice's presentation to the First Consul, "The introduction to Bonaparte took place, resulting in promises and minor encouragements, on the condition that he take part in the fighting and do so with distinction. The young man could ask for nothing better. (I, xiii)."

The year 1800 was a fateful one for Napoleon and France. Napoleon considered it necessary to defeat the Austrian forces, the only major continental army then at war with France. The Austrian forces were concentrated in Italy and in the German States; consequently, the French had a two-pronged attack against the Austrians—a campaign in Italy and a campaign across the German States—to bring the Austrians to the peace table. Napoleon personally led his forces across the Saint Bernard Pass, a passage made forever memorable by David's painting, and decisively defeated the Austrians at the Battle of Marengo on June 14, 1800. This decisive battle fought between Genoa and Milan epitomized Napoleon's penchant for the rear maneuver. The Austrians were driven from all of Italy except the Province of Venetia, which they were to retain according to the armistice agreement signed at Alessandria. In short, Austria was to occupy territories east of the Mincio River. The armistice was to end on November 22, 1800. Later that year General Moreau decisively defeated the Austrian forces at the Battle of Hohenlinden on December 3rd. Shortly thereafter, on February 9, 1801, a peace treaty was signed with Austria at Lunéville. General peace was to come a year later when Great Britain signed the Treaty of Amiens with France in April 1802.

Maurice Dupin took part in Napoleon's campaign in Italy during the year 1800. He participated in the crossing of the Saint Bernard Pass, and he was received by the First Consul after the crossing of the Saint Bernard at Aosta. In this brief conversation Napoleon asked him if he were the grandson of the Maréchal de Saxe. Maurice replied in the affirmative and then informed Napoleon that he was now receiving battle experience by serving as an aide in the headquarters staff of General Dupont de l'Étang, the commander of the Army of the Reserve (I, xiii). Maurice continued on the campaign and was present at the Battle of Marengo, a battle in which the headquarters to which he was attached played a key role in the victory.

Maurice Dupin complained to his mother of his poverty in these early campaigns and also, at times, that there was no food. His remarks underscore several basic problems inherent in the French armies at this time. First, pay was usually in arrears and troops often went for considerable lengths of time without it, hence Maurice's requests to his mother and also his gratitude for receiving money. Second, when advancing on campaign the French armies lived off the land by requisitioning food supplies from villages and towns that they passed through. This practice meant that when large military units passed through a certain area it was depleted of food both animal and vegetable. The story is often told of Napoleon's personal chef who, when able to find only a chicken and a few vegetables after the Battle of Marengo, concocted chicken Marengo—remembered still on various restaurant menus. This anecdote merely points out the scarcity of food when an army did not have a large supply train carrying foodstuffs. After the Battle of Marengo, General Dupont informed Maurice that he would recommend him for a battlefield commission as a lieutenant. In fact, Maurice served during the battle as the General's aide-de-camp when the General's aide was wounded. As Maurice wrote his uncle, the Abbé de Beaumont, he was promoted on the battlefield of Marengo. In this battle, he was grazed by a cannon-ball, thrown off his horse by another cannon-ball, and wounded slightly in the chest. His reward for valor on the battlefield was his commission as a lieutenant, and he eagerly awaited his next promotion to captain (I, xiv).

An armistice concluded at Alessandria after the Battle of Marengo lasted until November 22, 1800. During the period of the armistice, Maurice was sent on various assignments in Italy, including missions to Bologna, Florence, Rome, and Padua. At the conclusion of these missions, he rejoined the division of General Dupont de l'Étang on the Mincio River, which formed the truce line between the French and Austrian forces. When the armistice expired, General Brune, who assumed command of the Army of Italy after the Battle of Marengo, was ordered by Napoleon to cross the Mincio with an army which numbered approximately 90,000 men. General Brune committed several errors in commanding this operation. One of the divisions which suffered the most was the division commanded by General Dupont de l'Étang. During this operation Maurice Dupin was captured by the Austrians and was marched on foot in the dead of winter over the Alps, eventually reaching Hungary in early February. His release came shortly after the signing of the peace treaty at Lunéville on February 7, 1801. This peace ended ten years of war on the European continent.

With the conclusion of peace on the continent, Napoleon as First Consul turned next to making peace with Great Britain. The result was the signing of a peace treaty at Amiens in April 1802. Although this treaty signaled the beginnings of a general peace, it was, in reality, a truce lasting only a little over three years. Hostilities broke out once more in the fall of 1805. However, these years of peace witnessed the consolidation of some of the basic domestic reforms of Napoleon, the influence of which is still evident in our own time.

Napoleon had several goals in domestic affairs when he came to power in the coup d'état of 1799. He wished to end the bitter civil war, centered in the Vendée, which had divided France since 1792, and this he did by offering the Vendéans amnesty. Napoleon also wished to end the religious schism which began with the adoption of the Civil Constitution of the Clergy in 1790. The Civil Constitution made the French head of state head of the Catholic Church in France. The schism began with the papal condemnation by Pius VI of the Civil Constitution. France was divided between those who accepted the Civil Constitution and those who did not. Napoleon, who was a political realist, understood that France required religious unity, that is to say, the end of the schism. Consequently, a Concordat was negotiated with the Pope, which settled some of the outstanding difficulties between church and state in France. The Concordat was signed in 1801, but it went into effect on Easter Sunday, 1802. The official ceremony was a Te Deum held at the Cathedral of Notre Dame in Paris, which not only commemorated the Concordat but also the Treaty of Amiens.

Napoleon also recodified the laws of France and considered himself the new Justinian. The Code Napoléon became his proudest achievement; it was promulgated in 1804. In this Code he set down the property rights of husband and wife in marriage. The Code reflected Napoleon's personal view toward women and family stability by making wives inferior to their husbands in matters of property, adultery and divorce (the effects of which would cause great anguish to Sand, when she separated from her husband). Napoleon also established the Bank of France to bring financial stability after a decade of turbulence in France. His most lasting reforms were in the area of administration of the departments; the establishment of the office of prefect has had a lasting influence on French centralization. In yet another area of reform the French educational system was centralized in the University. It is no exaggeration to say that the years before the outbreak of hostilities in 1805 were remarkable ones for reform in France.

Between Campaigns

During the years of peace, Maurice Dupin spent most of his time in France serving in the Ardennes and other areas of northeastern France and also in Paris. He made frequent trips to Nohant to visit his mother, who was hostile to his liaison and eventual marriage in 1804 to Antoinette-Sophie-Victoire Delaborde (1773–1837). Mme. Dupin de Francueil considered it a misalliance because Sophie-Victoire was the daughter of a bird merchant on the Quais of Paris and, in her view, certainly not a match for a grandson of the Maréchal de

Saxe. Although the French Revolution had established the principles of liberty and equality, they did not extend in Mme. Dupin de Francueil's mind to her son marrying a woman of the lower classes. Her views were consistent with most people of her class in the nineteenth century, who believed that marriage should be to someone of the same or higher social class but never, if it could be avoided, to someone of a lower class.

Maurice Dupin's activities in Paris and elsewhere led him to meet with Ercole Cardinal Consalvi, the papal secretary of state, who was negotiating the Concordat with Joseph Bonaparte, the brother of Napoleon. Maurice Dupin was also present in the Cathedral of Notre Dame on Easter Sunday, 1802, at the solemn Te Deum celebrating the signing of the Concordat and the Peace of Amiens. He and General Dupont occupied seats immediately behind the First Consul.

Maurice's duties in the garrisons of northeastern France bored him. He wrote his mother, "Here is my plan: to go to war or to stay in Paris, for life in the garrison is odious (II, vii)." He made efforts in vain to become an officer in the guard of the First Consul, so that he could be in Paris. In late 1803, Maurice was stationed near Boulogne on the English Channel—the reason being that Napoleon was collecting a large force on the Channel in order to invade England. For by late 1803 it was obvious to Napoleon that the Peace of Amiens was only an armistice, that hostilities would soon resume, and that the only way to deal a mortal blow to England was to invade that country.

The year 1803 marked the gradual evolution of France from a Republic to an Empire. Signs of an impending change were evident when the First Consul allowed himself to be voted a large civil list (an appropriation for the personal and household expenses of the First Consul) and to be surrounded by attendants and an etiquette which was usually reserved for royalty. In the summer, the Senate (which had the power to change the Constitution) proposed that Napoleon accept the hereditary title of Emperor of the French. The proposal was submitted to a plebiscite, and Napoleon was overwhelmingly elected Emperor of the French. Napoleon's coronation took place on December 2, 1804 in the Cathedral of Notre Dame, in the presence of Pope Pius VII. Maurice Dupin was present at the ceremony at which Napoleon crowned himself and then crowned the Empress Josephine. The Pope's presence horrified European conservatives, as it seemed to them to signify the Church's approval of the French Revolution. Joseph de Maistre expressed the conservative view when he wrote of the Pope's presence at the coronation, " . . . the crimes of Alexander Borgia are less revolting than this hideous apostasy by his weak-kneed successor."[4] For others, the ceremony served to dramatize the end of the French Revolution and also the reconciliation of the Church and France. The coronation was, however, the beginning of imperial government in France, with the Emperor's family becoming princes and princesses; later some became kings and queens. An imperial nobility was set up, and successful generals became marshals of France as well as dukes and princes.

In June 1804, Maurice Dupin and Sophie-Victoire Delaborde were married in Paris in a civil ceremony. George Sand, Amantine-Aurore-Lucile

Dupin, was born on July 5, 1804, scarcely a month later. This marriage was without Mme. Dupin de Francueil's permission and without her knowledge. When she did hear about it, she wrote several letters to the mayor who performed the ceremony to ask him for details concerning the ceremony, because according to French law, she had to give her consent to the marriage to make it legal. In due time she sent the Abbé d'Andrezel to Paris to look into the matter of an annulment. After investigating, he concluded that the marriage was indissoluble, as the mayor who performed the ceremony acted in good faith. This did not satisfy Mme. Dupin de Francueil who travelled to Paris and consulted the leading Royalist lawyer, Romain de Sèze, who had defended Louis XVI. After reflecting on his advice and also after having held her grandaughter in her arms, through a ruse of Maurice, she abandoned her thoughts of legal procedures against the marriage.

The central preoccupation of Maurice Dupin in 1804 was to get promoted to captain. He was eventually told by General Dupont that Napoleon said he would have to wait until his fifth year, which would be in 1805. Maurice tried to get Caulaincourt, the Grand Ecuyer of the Empire; Mme. Caroline Murat, Napoleon's sister; and the Empress Josephine's ecuyer to intercede on behalf of his promotion, but to no avail. As he wrote his mother, he would only obtain it "as a special favor of the Emperor (II, viii)." He did receive the honor of being named a chevalier of the Légion d'Honneur in late 1805. He also received what was to be commonplace advice, from General Duroc, namely, "Quit your generals and return to line units (II, ix)." This echoed advice given him earlier by Napoleon himself.

The Wars of the Third Coalition

Although active hostilities broke out on the Continent only late in 1805, the Peace of Amiens had been shattered in 1803 by the English, when they withdrew their ambassador from Paris. According to international law at the time, this was tantamount to a declaration of war, although war had not been formally declared. Since England was primarily a naval power, hostilities on land did not really begin until autumn in 1805. And since the French did not at that time have a navy capable of defeating the English navy, there were only skirmishes and minor engagements at sea until the Battle of Trafalgar in October 1805.

Two factors influenced the Continental Powers to form a coalition against Napoleon. The first was the kidnapping on March 14, 1803 by the French of the Duc d'Enghien from the neutral territory of the Grand Duchy of Baden. Enghien's kidnapping took place in Baden, a few miles across the Rhine from Alsace. Enghien, who was a Bourbon prince and the last of the Condé line, was taken to French territory and later to Paris, where he was tried and executed at the Château de Vincennes and charged with plotting against the life of the First Consul. Enghien reached the Château of Vincennes at 5 o'clock in the afternoon, he was tried at 11 o'clock in the evening, and executed at 2 o'clock in the morning.[5] This flagrantly illegal act of violating neutral territory and executing a prince who was not only improperly tried but also probably innocent offended Royalists within France and outraged many European courts. For example, the Court at Saint Petersburg went into official mourning for Enghien. Napoleon certainly was implicated in his execution, and the charges that Enghien was plotting to overthrow or assassinate Napoleon, whether true or false, did not justify either his arrest in neutral territory, his trial, or his execution. Many years later at St. Helena, Napoleon commented on this affair, saying: "I had the Duc d'Enghien arrested and sentenced because it was necessary to the safety, the interest and the honour of the French people, at a time when the Comte d'Artois by his own account was maintaining sixty assassins in Paris. Under similar circumstances, I would act in the same way."[6] The most significant defection from Napoleon's admirers over the Enghien affair was Châteaubriand. The great French historian Georges Lefebvre summed up the Enghien Affair in the following words, "Had he [Enghien] been arrested on French soil or in enemy territory, the law would have prescribed the death penalty. But by kidnapping him on neutral soil, Bonaparte blatantly compromised the interest of France and provided the Continental Powers with the pretext for which they were searching."[7]

The second event was Napoleon's coronation. The coronation and the establishment of the Grand Dignitaries and the Grand Officers of the Crown were viewed quite simply as a threat to Europe's peace and harmony; also the use of the term "empire" implied an expansiveness which would only be accomplished at the expense of some other power or powers. The true legacy of Napoleon's coronation was war. Lefebvre argues, "Napoleon had seduced the French nation with the promise of peace—he had finished by installing himself, while fanning the flames of war. Now there was nothing to restrain him from fulfilling his real desires. Imperial conquest, despotism, and the aristocratic principle would have their day, while the nation, stunned and troubled, was compelled to follow, lest it perish, the chariot of Caesar triumphant (176)."

Tsar Alexander of Russia (1801–1825) gradually formed an alliance with Britain, Austria, and several smaller states against Napoleon. His efforts to persuade Prussia to join this offensive alliance were, for the most part, futile. Prussia would enter a defensive alliance after Napoleon's coronation, and an offensive alliance in 1806, only after the defeat of Austria and Russia at Austerlitz. As the coalition was being formed, Napoleon gathered a large army on the English Channel coast for an invasion of England. French troops were chiefly concentrated in the vicinity of Boulogne, but the construction of boats to ferry this large army across the Channel became the chief industry of almost every French channel port. Maurice Dupin was stationed in the Boulogne area during these preparations for a Channel crossing.

In the summer of 1805, it was obvious that Austria and Russia were gathering their forces for an invasion of France. Napoleon abandoned his plan for an invasion of England and ordered his troops to assemble in Alsace in order to cross the Rhine into the South German States. The French armies advanced across the Rhine into the South German States, and at Ulm in Western Bavaria they decisively defeated the Austrians on October 15, 1805. French troops then advanced into Austria proper and eventually occupied Vienna. The Austrian and Russian forces under the personal command of Tsar Alexander and the Emperor Francis were concentrating their forces north of Vienna, in Moravia. Napoleon engaged them in battle at the Moravian village of Austerlitz on December 2, 1805, the anniversary of his coronation. In this battle, sometimes known as the Battle of the Three Emperors, Napoleon won what he always considered his most decisive victory—a verdict shared by most military historians. In this battle he managed to split the Russian and Austrian forces and thereby inflict a crushing defeat upon them. After the battle, the Tsar left for Russia and the Emperor Francis signed a humiliating peace treaty at Pressburg. The division of General Dupont was engaged in battle in the vicinity of Austerlitz, and Maurice Dupin saw enough action to be promoted to the rank of captain on December 20, 1805. He also was awarded the Cross of the Legion of Honor.

Almost contemporaneous with Napoleon's great victory at Austerlitz, the French suffered a crushing defeat at sea. On October 21, 1805, the combined French and Spanish fleets (Spain was France's ally) were defeated at the Battle of Trafalgar by an English force commanded by Lord Nelson. England now had command of the seas, and no longer had to fear an invasion. From this point on, Napoleon's empire was restricted to land warfare on the European continent.

In 1806, hostilities broke out with Prussia. Napoleon deployed his forces once again across the Rhine and into the German states. On October 14, 1806, Napoleon's forces met the Prussians near Jena, and in the ensuing battle, the Prussians were severely defeated at what is known as the Battle of Jena-Auerstädt. Napoleon then led his forces in pursuit of the Prussians towards Berlin, capital of Prussia, which he and his army entered on October 27, 1806. From material he uncovered in the Prussian archives in Berlin it was evident that there was an entente between Prussia and Russia, and it became obvious to him that Russia would reenter active combat to aid Prussia. Napoleon steadfastly refused to sign a separate peace treaty with Prussia until there was a general peace treaty which would include Russia.

While in Berlin, Napoleon issued the so-called Berlin Decrees on November 21, 1806. In these decrees, Napoleon established a policy of economic warfare against England by attempting to close the continental European ports to English trade and imports. The establishment of the Continental System was to prove disastrous for Napoleon; it was unenforceable because of his lack of sea power, and it led him into two unfortunate campaigns which were to be his undoing, namely, the Spanish Campaign and the Russian Campaign.

During the winter of 1806-1807, Napoleon's forces occupied a line along the Vistula and Bug Rivers, a position roughly between Danzig and Königsberg in East Prussia. In their operations to reach the Vistula and occupy Warsaw, the Polish Question was reopened as the Poles in Prussian Poland revolted against their Prussian masters. Once again the Poles desired their independence from foreign rule. Napoleon's armies reached Warsaw on November 27, 1805. Maurice Dupin took part in the campaigns of 1806, as his division was in the rear in the vicinity of Auerstädt, but apparently it was not in action in the main battle. His unit later was on the Bug-Vistula line, and he also was in various places in Poland. Russian forces began to move into East Prussia as well as to cement their positions in Russian Poland. Eventually Napoleon engaged the Russians under General Levin Bennigsen on February 8, 1807, at Eylau, in a battle fought in a blinding snowstorm. Napoleon was victorious, but he was unable to pursue the Russians because of the intense cold. In June, he encountered the Russians once again at Friedland on June 18, 1807, and in this decisive battle, fought on the anniversary of the Battle of Marengo, he decisively defeated Bennigsen. Tsar Alexander sued for an armistice shortly thereafter. Napoleon's troops were now on the very borders of Holy Mother Russia.

Napoleon and Tsar Alexander met on a raft in the River Niemen, at Tilsit, between June 25, 1807 and July 9, 1807. Napoleon's secretary, L. A. F. de Bourienne, said somewhat enthusiastically of Tilsit, "The interview at Tilsit is one of the culminating points of modern history, and the waters of the Niemen reflected Napoleon at the height of his glory."[8] The meeting at Tilsit turned Tsar Alexander into an ally of Napoleon against England. At this prototype of the modern summit meeting, the first words of the Tsar to Napoleon were: "I hate the English as much as you do yourself." Napoleon replied, "If that is the case, then peace is already made (586)." The real victim of the meeting was the Kingdom of Prussia, which saw much of its territory annexed to the French satellite states of the Kingdom of Westphalia, ruled by Napoleon's brother, Jerome, and the Grand Duchy of Warsaw, ruled by the King of Saxony. Napoleon at Tilsit was indeed at the zenith of his power. The only marshal of France present at Tilsit was Marshal Joachim Murat with his aide-de-camp, Maurice Dupin (II, x).

After Tilsit, Murat and Maurice Dupin returned to Paris for a few months until they accompanied Napoleon on a visit to Northern Italy during November and December 1807. Napoleon paid this visit to Northern Italy in his capacity as King of Italy, a crown he had received in Milan on May 26, 1805. On this visit to Italy, he also visited Eugène de Beauharnais, the son of the Empress Josephine, who served as Napoleon's viceroy of Italy. Two letters from Maurice Dupin to his wife from Venice and Milan attest that he accompanied Napoleon on this trip (II, x).

The Spanish Campaign

In 1808, Napoleon's attention turned to Spain, a fateful decision that would later return to haunt him. Throwing aside his concepts of statecraft, he was determined to enforce his policy of economic blockade against England, known as the Continental System. David Chandler, one of the foremost students of Napoleon, says of his Spanish campaign, "In 1808, however, it was his instinct as a soldier that overruled his prudence as a statesman, and led him into an unanticipated large-scale struggle. He badly misjudged both the moment for action and the caliber of his intended victims (601-2)." Earlier his forces under General Junot had invaded Portugal for not enforcing the Continental System. On February 20, 1808, Marshal Murat, Grand Duke of Berg, was appointed lieutenant-general in command of the French forces invading Spain. He successfully led French troops into Madrid on March 25, 1808, but on May 2, 1808, the celebrated *dos de Mayo* in Spanish history, the citizens of Madrid rose up against the French. Murat put down the insurrection in a harsh manner captured for posterity in the paintings of Goya. A few days after the insurrection, Napoleon succeeded in getting the Spanish King Charles IV and his son, Ferdinand, the Prince of Asturias, to abdicate. Their abdication took place on May 6, 1808, at Bayonne, France, where Napoleon had assembled members of the Spanish royal family. On the same day of the abdication of Charles IV and his son, Ferdinand, Napoleon named his brother Joseph to be King of Spain and the Indies. Napoleon named Marshal Murat as King of Naples to replace Joseph on that throne. From George Sand's *Histoire de ma vie* (II, xiii and xiv), it is evident that she and her mother left for Madrid, arriving there in May, and that they were housed with her father, Maurice Dupin, Murat's aide-de-camp, in the same palace as the Murat family. They remained there two months and returned to France amid the chaos of battles fought between the French and the Spanish. A few weeks after the family's return to Nohant her father's tragic death occurred in October 1808; he was thrown from a horse given to him by King Charles IV. The Spanish Campaign dragged on until the end of the Empire in 1814; French forces were drained as a result of numerous retreats and defeats. The Campaign also marked a series of brilliant victories of the English forces under Sir Arthur Wellesley, the Duke of Wellington, who pushed the French out of Spain and eventually invaded southwestern France in 1814. The Spanish Campaign was indeed a fiasco for Napoleon.

The Last Years of the Empire

After recounting her father's death, George Sand recounts the events of her childhood and her early education, which took place in the later years of the Napoleonic Grand Empire. These final years of the Grand Empire were marked by increasing stress and strain not only on the French military machine but also on Napoleon's political system, which was attempting to rule a large portion of the European continent. His efforts to enforce the Continental System led him not only into Spain but also into the Italian and the German States to annex sizeable territories to the French Empire. He also had to deal with the numerous satellite states such as Naples, Westphalia, the Confederation of the Rhine, Bavaria, Saxony, and Denmark. Eventually his efforts to establish a hereditary empire led him to a marriage alliance with the House of Hapsburg and in 1810 he married the Archduchess Marie-Louise, the daughter of the Emperor Francis of Austria. The marriage was one of the benefits of the peace treaty of 1809 which was signed after the crushing Austrian defeat at Wagram. Prior to the marriage, Napoleon had to secure the annulment of his marriage to Josephine; Marie-Louise bore him a son, who at birth was declared the King of Rome. In history, he is better known as L'Aiglon, the Eaglet.

In the five years following Tilsit the relationship between Napoleon and Tsar Alexander changed from that of ally to enemy. The reasons for this change of affairs were: Alexander's desire for Constantinople which Napoleon thwarted; Alexander's distrust of Napoleon's satellite state, the Grand Duchy of Warsaw; also Alexander resumed trade relations with England in violation of the Continental System. All of these factors were exacerbated by Napoleon's limitless ambition.

Napoleon's greatest military disaster was his campaign against Russia which began in 1812. Commanding the largest land force ever assembled up to that time, he embarked on his invasion of Russia on June 21, 1812. Less than half of his forces were recruited from metropolitan France. The majority were drafted from the satellite states in non-French speaking regions of the French Empire. Napoleon reached Moscow on September 14, 1812, and he remained there for six weeks, or just long enough for the severe Russian winter to make his retreat turn from an orderly one into a debacle. He returned to Paris on December 29, 1812, but the remnants of his army were scattered across the Russian steppes, and only a small proportion of his forces crossed the Niemen River out of Russia. Of the half-million men who entered Russia in the French army, scarcely 100,000 managed to get out safely. Irreparably lost in Russia were the horses of the Grand Army as well as its artillery and the cadres of officers and non-commissioned officers which would be so desperately needed in the future, especially in 1813 and 1814.

In 1813, Napoleon had just enough time to gather together an army and give it a modicum of training in order to take to the campaign trail once more. Although Napoleon won several brilliant victories, his armies were crushed at the decisive battle of Leipzig, October 16-20, 1813. As Sand describes France's declining fortunes, it was a battle which Talleyrand considered "the beginning of the end (III, v)." The Allies, chiefly the Austrian, Prussian, and Russian forces, pursued Napoleon through the German States across the Rhine into France. The Campaign of France took place in the early months of 1814 and marked a series of brilliant retreats by Napoleon which culminated by the Allies occupying Paris on April 5, 1814. A few days later on April 14, Napoleon abdicated. The Allies ironically allowed him to become Emperor of the island of Elba off the west coast of Italy. During the Campaign of 1814, numerous deserters and soldiers who had lost their regiments wandered about France seeking food and shelter. George Sand vividly recounts the near starvation of these troops wandering through the Sologne and Berry, where many freed prisoners of war also wandered and begged in the areas adjacent to Nohant (III, v). Berry was a severely economically depressed area at the end of the Empire and during the Restoration.[9]

The Bourbon Restoration

With Napoleon's abdication, the Allies agreed to permit Louis XVI's brother, the Comte de Provence, to return to France and to rule as Louis XVIII, and the Senate asked him to assume the throne on April 6, 1814, the very day that Napoleon signed his act of abdication. The restoration of the Bourbon dynasty represented a compromise between the ideas of the ancien régime and the French Revolution. This compromise was not pleasing to everyone; as George Sand said of her grandmother, "My grandmother . . . has not become a Royalist, but a partisan of the ancien régime (III, vii)." This also reflects the deep divisions that took place within France and within French families on the question of Bonapartists and Bourbons, the tricolor cockade and the white rosette.

Louis XVIII, breaking with the tradition of the ancien régime, issued a Constitutional Charter on June 4, 1814, which preserved the principal political and social gains of 1789: " . . . equal access for all to state offices, the right of the people to consent to taxes and to participate through their representatives in the making of laws, individual liberty, freedom of expression, and freedom of religion, with the added novelty that Catholicism was proclaimed the state religion."[10]

Before the Bourbon Restoration could deal effectively with the aftermath of the Napoleonic Wars, it had to contend with a major threat to its political stability. Napoleon escaped his realm on the island of Elba and reached the southern French Coast the night of March 1, 1815. He arrived in Paris on March 20, 1815. Along the way from Southern France the troops sent to arrest him rallied to his cause. These included Marshal Ney, whom Napoleon once called the "bravest of the brave," and who had told Louis XVIII a few days before that he would arrest Napoleon and bring him back to Paris in a cage. Louis XVIII left Paris for Belgium the night before Napoleon arrived at the Tuileries Palace. Napoleon soon had to face the allied armies, and he met them in Belgium, where between June 15 and 18 he engaged in the Battle of Waterloo, which marked his final defeat. On June 22, he abdicated in favor of his son. Napoleon went to Rochefort and eventually surrendered to the British. He died on the island of St. Helena, in the South Atlantic, on May 5, 1821. Louis XVIII returned to the Tuileries Palace on July 8, 1815, just 100 days after he had fled.

After Napoleon's abdication, the Anglo-Prussian forces occupied Paris. The Paris garrison numbering 100,000 men under the command of Marshal Davout retreated south of the Loire River, and the remnants of this force, the Army of the Loire, were stationed in the vicinity of Nohant. George Sand describes the flurry of entertainments at Nohant for the officers commanding these troops that were stationed near her grandmother's château. She also recounts in several moving passages how discharged soldiers had to make their way home on foot and beg for their food. She summed up her view of the political situation in 1815 by writing, "Thus I was disillusioned with the Empire and resigned to the Restoration (III, vii)." This is something of a simplification, as the grandmother became a fervent Royalist while the grandaughter maintained her sympathies to Napoleon. She wrote, when recalling a time somewhat later than 1815, "I remained a Bonapartist and I did not hide it . . . (IV, ii)."

After the Hundred Days, the government of the Restoration devoted itself to governing France and maintaining order. The basic economic and social gains of the French Revolution were preserved, and above all, the revolutionary land settlement was maintained. The Church enjoyed a period of favoritism, as Louis XVIII wished to reestablish the ancien régime's concept of the union of throne and altar. The renewed esteem in which religion was held was evident in the future George Sand's educational experiences at the Couvent des Anglaises, where she was enrolled in 1818. It is ironic that the place where Aurore Dupin received her formal education was the very same place where her grandmother, Mme. Dupin de Francueil, had been imprisoned during the Terror.

The political climate in Restoration France was characterized by the staunch supporters of the Bourbons, called the Ultras, a group whose political world view harkened back to the days before 1789 and which did not wish to preserve the political and social gains of the Revolution. Their political opponents, the Doctrinaires, looked with favor on most of the French Revolution's gains and did not wish to turn the clock back to the days before 1789. At first, Louis XVIII chose moderates for his chief ministers, but an event occurred which changed all hope of moderation, the assassination of the Duc de Berry in 1820.

The Duc de Berry was the eldest son of the Comte d'Artois, the future Charles X; as such he was an heir to the throne and really the hope of the Bourbon family, since his uncle, Louis XVIII, and his father were advanced in years. In fact, Louis XVIII died scarcely four years after his nephew's assassination, in 1824. The future George Sand was present in the Basilica of Saint Denis for the lengthy funeral ceremonies of Louis XVIII. She had married Casimir Dudevant in 1822 and given birth to her son Maurice, the following year. Her description of the royal funeral is remarkable (IV, ix).

After the young duke's assassination, the Ultras gained control, and their influence was to be paramount during the reign of Charles X (1824-1830), a king whom the poet Béranger characterized as "Charles le simple." Charles' short reign ended with the July Revolution of 1830. In the view of the foremost historian of the Bourbon Restoration, Guillaume de Bertier de Sauvigny, the regime was badly served by its ministers and no men of great talent were present in the government. He wrote, "Not one of them had the qualities of a great minister who could have dominated the princes, elicited the support of the nation's elite, and given a life-saving dynamism to the regime."[11]

The July Monarchy, 1830–1848

In 1830, a three-day revolution in Paris toppled the reactionary regime of Charles X, and he abdicated. In this revolution the Parisian workers played a major role. The Duc d'Orléans, a cousin of the three previous kings, Louis XVI, Louis XVIII, and Charles X, was proclaimed King of the French, in a civil ceremony. He took the name Louis Philippe I, rather than the title of Louis XIX or Charles XI. Louis Philippe was King of the French and not King of France. By making this distinction he emphasized that the new national monarchy of the French was a break with Bourbon monarchical tradition. The French royal house was henceforth the House of Bourbon-Orléans, and the ceremony of proclamation was devoid of all the trappings of divine right or traditional French monarchical coronations. Although the Charter of 1814 was kept in force, the voting age was lowered from thirty to twenty-five, and the eligibility requirements for office holding were reduced. The Catholic Church was no longer the state religion but only the religion of the "majority of the French." During the July Monarchy, the aristocracy of birth which had ruled France during the Bourbon Restoration was replaced by the aristocracy of wealth as the most influential in ruling France. Most of the aristocracy of birth who had served Charles X refused to take the oath of allegiance to Louis Philippe and thereby lost their offices, one reason why the July Monarchy is often called the Bourgeois Monarchy.

In politics, Louis Philippe expressed the hope that his government would follow the *juste milieu,* or the middle-of-the-road, and thereby avoid the extremes of the conservative supporters of Charles X and the French revolutionary tradition as expressed in republican, socialist, or Jacobin political aims. The first decade of the July Monarchy was a turbulent one and comprised a series of insurrections, strikes, and assassination attempts on the life of Louis Philippe. George Sand, who was twenty-six in 1830, and on the verge of a personal uprising, makes numerous references to these events as well as to some of the leading thinkers of the 1830's, notably those whom she deemed influential in her life. Also, her mature political views were formed during this crucial decade.

During the decade of the 1830's, socialist thought began to emphasize the plight of the workers and also to envision utopias which would create a perfect society based on harmony, equality, and fraternity. Many socialist theorists sought to restructure society in such a manner as to alleviate hunger, poor housing, long working hours in the factories (where a twelve or fourteen hour day was common), and to provide for the education of the children of workers.

Socialist thought and the desire to establish a republic came together in a series of uprisings in the 1830's. In 1831 there was an insurrection in Lyon which was crushed with great severity. The *canuts,* or silkweavers, of Lyon were strongly influenced by republican thought, namely to set up a republic, as well as a desire to alleviate their miserable plight. The republican idea conjured up in the minds of the Royalists the Reign of Terror and the Jacobin dictatorship of the Committee of Public Safety under Robespierre's leadership in 1793–1794, as well as the horrors of the uprising of Gracchus Babeuf and Buonarroti in March 1796, which had aimed at setting up a dictatorship of the proletariat establishing perfect equality. (This first communist uprising had its followers in the 1830's, known as Babouvists). Revolution from the left was not only the fear of the conservatives but also that of the bourgeois government, with its advocacy of the *juste milieu.* The insurrection of 1831 was followed by another and more serious one in April 1834, whose epicenter was Lyon. Once again it was led by the *canuts.* This insurrection also broke out in several provincial cities as well as in Paris. There were even disturbances in the army at Lunéville. All over France the insurrection was subdued ruthlessly, and in Paris the crushing of the revolt, known as the Massacre of the Rue Transnonain, immortalized in a lithograph of Daumier, became a permanent frame of reference in political debates.

The government of Louis Philippe gathered the accused leaders of the insurrection from all over France for a trial in Paris in May 1835. In this monster trial, or *procès monstre,* as it was called at the time, there were 164 defendants, 558 witnesses for the prosecution, 261 for the defense, and a judicial inquiry of 17,000 documents. The case was tried before the Chamber of Peers, and the Chancellor of France, Etienne-Denis Pasquier, presided.

The leading specialist on the revolts of 1834 notes the resemblance in the contest between judges and defendants to trials in more recent times.[12] For the first three days of the trial the proceedings were disrupted by the shouts and demonstrations of the prisoners. The court then ordered a police officer to sit next to each defendant, and when these measures failed to bring decorum to the courtroom, the Court of Peers decided that each defendant would hear accusations against him read to him in his cell rather than in court. This was a major break with French law. "There was pandemonium when this controversial decision was announced. A few peers withdrew from the trial in disgust, the influential liberal deputy Odilon Barrot thundered that such tactics resembled those used by the Jacobins during the trial of the Girondists, and Daumier drew a cartoon of a smiling judge leaning over the bench to tell a bound and gagged defendant, *Accusé, parlez, la défense est libre!* (188)."

George Sand attended one of the sessions of this *procès monstre*. The verdicts were handed down in stages; the earliest ones on August 13, 1835. Some of the accused were acquitted, some were sentenced to deportation, and others to imprisonment. Sand was sympathetic to the accused, and she made no secret of her views when she said that the government had provoked the people to revolt; she also sympathized with the speech of Jules Favre in defense of the accused (V, viii). Another renowned speech for the defense was made by Michel de Bourges, an avowed republican and intimate friend of George Sand, to whom she devoted more than one chapter of her autobiography (V, viii and ix). Michel de Bourges had to spend a month in prison for a manifesto he wrote attacking the judicial process of the trial. In *Histoire de ma vie* Michel de Bourges is known as Éverard.

While the monster trial was in progress on July 28, 1835, Louis Philippe left the Tuileries Palace to review the troops drawn up in formations from the Rue Royale to the Bastille. As the King and his sons passed the Boulevard du Temple, firing was heard. Although the King and his sons escaped injury, forty people were dead or wounded from this so-called infernal machine (twenty-four muskets mounted on a slanting frame and firing together). Giuseppe Fieschi (1790–1836) was charged with the crime, tried, found guilty and executed. The monster trial and the Fieschi attempt resulted in more repressive laws, known as the September Laws, against the press, especially against those newspapers favorable to the republicans; and these laws also simplified court procedures when trying insurgents. George Sand reflected on the trial, the Fieschi attempt, and the repressive September Laws and wrote, "Not that the April lawsuit had given me cause for great hopefulness; but however realistic or pessimistic we were at the time, there had been in the air some ineffable breath of life that suddenly died down with a chill. The Republic was vanishing beyond the horizon for yet another stretch of time (V, x)." A year later, on June 25, 1836 an assassin by the name of Louis Alibaud shot at Louis Philippe at close range with a firearm in the form of a walking stick. The bullet lodged in the King's hair, but he was unhurt. George Sand also expressed sympathy for Alibaud, who was tried and executed (V, xi).

The last insurrection of the 1830's, organized by the Société des Saisons, broke out on May 12, 1839. Its leaders were Auguste Blanqui (1805-1881) and

Armand Barbès (1809–1870). The revolt was suppressed on the day it began.
This uprising, supported by some of the popular elements in Paris, saw few
bourgeois taking part compared to earlier uprisings. Many of the participants in
this rebellion wished for a radical revision in the principle of private property.
George Sand was more critical of the uprising of the Société des Saisons and
declared that their leaders had made errors, but at the same time she expressed
great admiration for Barbès and the sublimity of his error (V, xii).

According to George Sand, two of the "greatest intellects of our century"
were Pierre Leroux (1797–1871) and Felicité de Lamennais (1782–1854) (V,
ix). In this crucial decade of the 1830's, which was so important to George
Sand's intellectual development, she was strongly influenced by the thought of
these two men who also became her friends. Pierre Leroux, an early French
socialist, was in his younger years an editor of the Saint-Simonian newspaper,
Le Globe, and is usually considered the first writer in France to have used the
term "socialism." Leroux published the *Revue Indépendante* (1841–1848) in
collaboration with George Sand, who proclaimed herself a disciple of Leroux's
philosophical religion of progress. A republican and deeply concerned with
social issues of the day, Leroux wrote extensive analyses of the social question.
On one occasion he noted that French capital was controlled by 196,000 heads
of families who also controlled political rights. One author says of Leroux, "he
perhaps came closest to expressing in systematic fashion the humanitarian,
progressivist, and partly pantheistic 'religion' that was embraced—with individual variations—by some of the leading members of the romantic literary
movement—as their affection and admiration help to affirm."[13]

Félicité de Lamennais was, until his condemnation by Pope Gregory
XVI, the leading apologist of the Catholic Church in Europe and certainly one
of the most widely read. He deservedly earned the nickname, *"Le prophète
Féli."* Lamennais, writing in the 1820's, was convinced that the close alliance
between Church and State during the Bourbon Restoration was undesirable,
and he concluded that there would only be a revival of Catholicism when it
was freed from dependence on the Bourbon state. He opposed the Gallican
view of church-state relations and advocated Ultramontanism, or close ties
with Rome. In other writings he urged the Church to abandon its privileged
position and to be content with those liberties guaranteed in the Charter of
1814. The Revolution of 1830 confirmed Lamennais in his views, and he
founded the newspaper *L'Avenir* with a distinguished group of collaborators. It
became the mouthpiece for the liberal Catholic point of view with its motto,
"God and Liberty." The paper advocated religious liberty, freedom of the press
and association, freedom for the Church in education, universal suffrage, and
decentralization of the government. Although many of these views would be
accepted by the Catholic Church in the twentieth century, *L'Avenir* was condemned in 1832 by Pope Gregory XVI. Lamennais accepted the condemnation; however, he abandoned his priestly functions two years later.

The insurrections of 1831 and, especially, 1834 in Lyon and the subsequent monster trial had a profound influence on Lamennais as they had on
George Sand. His thought turned to the plight of the workers; his friend Franz

Liszt wrote at this time the piano piece, *Les années de pèlerinage: Lyon,* and dedicated it to Lamennais. Liszt's epigraph for the piece was the motto of the *canuts:* "To live working or to die fighting."[14]

Fernand Rude states, "The insurrection of April 1834 and the trial which followed rallied Lamennais once and for all to the democratic and social Republic . . ."(101). Lamennais henceforth was an ardent defender of the poor, and after publishing *Le Pays et le gouvernement* in 1840, he was sentenced to a year's imprisonment in Sainte Pélagie, the prison for political offenders. His writings were widely read and were usually sold out within a few days; for example, eight editions of his *Paroles d'un croyant* (1834) were sold out within a year, and Sainte-Beuve reported that the workers who set the type were "roused and transported" by the book. Hence, Lamennais' writings reached a people that was alienated from the Church.

From her two great intellects of the century, Leroux and Lamennais, George Sand drew much that was to form the views she held on government, religion and society until her dying days. Her republicanism certainly stems from this period, when she opposed the July Monarchy, and her joy was great when it fell in 1848, to be replaced by the Second Republic. Her views on religion and society were reflected not only in her literary works but also in her correspondence; her circle of friends in the 1830's and 1840's certainly included many who were on the political left: one need only cite the socialist Louis Blanc, and the historians Henri Martin, Edgar Quinet, and Jules Michelet. The period covered in the *Histoire de ma vie* really ends about 1840, although Sand does make certain references to the Revolution of 1848. Thus Sand covers a time span of more than a century in this monumental work that presents an unforgettable portrait of her family, a fascinating account of her intellectual development, as well as a unique commentary on French history.

—*Walter D. Gray*

Notes

1. White, John Manchip, *Marshal of France, The Life and Times of Maurice, Comte de Saxe [1696–1750]* (London: 1962), p. xi.

2. Liddell Hart, Captain B. H., *Great Captains Unveiled* (Freeport, New York: 1967), p. 37.

3. Voltaire, *Oeuvres complètes de Voltaire* (Paris: 1880), XXXVII, 32.

4. Joseph de Maistre as quoted in Adrien Dansette, *Religious History of Modern France* (New York: 1961), I, 151.

5. Pasteur, Claude, *Le Duc d'Enghien, ou la mauvaise destinée* (Paris: 1984), pp. 156–172.

6. Tulard, Jean, *Napoleon, The Myth of the Saviour* (London: 1984), p. 382.

7. Lefebvre, Georges, *Napoleon from 18 Brumaire to Tilsit, 1799–1807* (New York: 1969), p. 182.

8. Bourienne, *Memoirs of Napoleon* (London: 1836), II, 18, as quoted in David G. Chandler, *The Campaigns of Napoleon* (New York: 1966) p. 585.

9. Bertier de Sauvigny, Guillaume de, *The Bourbon Restoration* (Philadelphia: 1966), p. 11.

10. G. de Bertier de Sauvigny and David H. Pinkney, *History of France* (Rev. ed., Arlington Heights, Ill.: 1983), p. 258.

11. Bertier de Sauvigny, *The Bourbon Restoration,* p. 458.

12. Bezucha, Robert J., *The Lyon Uprising of 1834, Social and Political Conflict in the Early July Monarchy* (Cambridge, Mass.: 1974), p. 188.

13. Charlton, D. G., *Secular Religions in France, 1815–1870* (London: 1963), p. 83.

14. Fernand Rude, *"Les insurrections ouvrières Lyonnaises de 1831 et de 1834 et 'l'engagement de Lammenais,'"* in *L'Actualité de Lammenais: Colloque de La Tourette, 2–4 juin 1978* (Strasbourg: 1981), p. 83.

Story of My Life

Charity toward others;

Dignity toward oneself;

Sincerity before God.

Such is the epigraph of the book I undertake.

April 15, 1847.

Contents of *Story of My Life*

Part I

Family History, from Fontenoy to Marengo

Chapter i   71
Why this book? —It is a duty to let others profit from one's own experience. —*Lettres d'un voyageur.* —*Les Confessions* of J.-J. Rousseau.
—My name and my era. —Reproaches to my biographers. —Antoine
Delaborde, master of tennis courts and master bird handler. —Mysterious affinities. —In praise of birds. —The story of Agathe and Jonquille. —The bird handler of Venice.

Chapter ii   82
On birth and free will. —Frederick Augustus. —Aurora von Königs-
marck. —Maurice de Saxe. —Aurore de Saxe. —Comte de Horn.
—Mlles. Verrières and the eighteenth-century wits. —M. Dupin de
Francueil. —Mme. Dupin de Chenonceaux. —Abbé de Saint-Pierre.

Chapter iii   99
An anecdote about J.-J. Rousseau. —Maurice Dupin, my father.
—Deschartres, my tutor. —The curé's head. —"Liberalism" before the
Revolution. —The domiciliary visit. —Incarceration. —The devoted-
ness of Deschartres and my father. —Nérina.

Chapter iv   114
Sophie-Victoire-Antoinette Delaborde. —At the town hall with Mother
Cloquart and her daughters. —The Convent of the English Sisters.
—On adolescence. —Behind a nation's official history, there is a more
personal story. —Collection of letters under the Terror.

Chapter v   143
After the Terror. —The end of prison and exile. —Deschartres' ill-fated
idea. —Nohant. —The bourgeois terrorists. —The moral state of the
privileged classes. —A musical passion. —Paris during the Directoire.

Chapter vi   159
Maréchal de Saxe.

Chapter vii   169
Continuation of my father's story. —The persistence of philosophical
ideas. —*Robert, chef de brigands.* —Description of La Châtre.
—Schiller's *Die Raüber* —The bourgeois theater of La Châtre in 1798.
—Conscription. —La Tour d'Auvergne, First Grenadier of France.

Chapter viii   187
Letters continued. —Voluntary enlistment. —Military flair of the youth
of 1798. —Letter from La Tour d'Auvergne. —Mess. —Cologne.
—Général Harville. —Caulaincourt. —Capitaine Fleury. —Love of
one's country. —Durosnel.

Chapter ix   204
Letters continued. —New Year's Day in Cologne. —Sleigh rides.
—The German baronesses. —The canoness. —The review. —Ice on
the Rhine. —Carnival. —A burlesque duel. —The red hussar. —Portrait of my father. —The appetite of German ladies. —The billeting
order. —Serious concerns of the young men on the general staff.

Chapter x   220
Letters continued. —Maulnoir. —Saint-Jean. —Garrison life. —An
excursion. —The Egyptian campaign. —An adventure. —The Little
House. —Departure from Cologne.

Chapter xi   234
Letters continued. —The escort. —Ehrenbreitstein. —Along the Rhine.
—Thionville. —Arrival at the depot. —The friendliness of the officers.
—The quartermaster sergeant as teacher of good manners. —The drill.
—The first promotion. —A peculiar custom in Thionville. —A white lie.

Chapter xii   244
Letters continued. —Joining the campaign. —The first cannon shot.
—Crossing the Linth River. —The battlefield. —A good deed.
—Glarus. —Meeting M. La Tour d'Auvergne on the Lac de Constance.
—Ordener. —Letter from my grandmother to her son. —The
Rheinthal.

Chapter xiii   256
Letters continued. —Général Brunet. —Disappointment. —Comman-
der Lochet. —Oath of allegiance to the constitution of Year VIII taken
by the troops. —Letters of my grandmother after 18 Brumaire. —Letter
of La Tour d'Auvergne. —Return to Paris. —Introduction to Bonaparte. —Italian campaign. —Saint-Bernard Pass. —The fort at Bard.

Chapter xiv   271
A short résumé. —The battle of Marengo. —Turin and Milan in 1800.
—Robbers on the roads. —The mission.

Part II

My Early Years (1800–1810)

Chapter i   283
The mission. —La Tour d'Auvergne. —Parma. —Bologna. —The
occupation of Florence. —Georges La Fayette.

Chapter ii   289
Rome. —An interview with the Pope. —A simulated attempt at assas-
sination. —Monsignor Consalvi. —Asola. —First passion. —The eve
of the battle. —Crossing the Mincio. —Maurice taken prisoner.
—Deliverance. —A love letter. —Rivalries and resentments between
Brune and Dupont. —Departure for Nohant.

Chapter iii   303
Romantic incidents. —Deschartres' unfortunate action. —The Inn of
the Black Skull. —Family sorrows. —Trips to Le Blanc, Argenton,
Courcelles, Paris. —Continuation of the romantic novel.
—Général——. —Uncle Beaumont. —The Year IX in brief.

Chapter iv   318
Extracts of letters. —Society's swains. —Plans for marriage. —Musical studies. —Englishmen in Paris. —The return of luxury. —Celebrating the Concordat. —The ceremony at Notre Dame. —What the generals think. —Deschartres in Paris. —Leaving for Charleville. —Wild
animals. —Masonic initiation and acceptance. —Recurrence of aristocratic prejudices in certain minds. —Reply to Deschartres. —Life Consulate. —Frustrations of an aide-de-camp in peacetime. —Disgrace and
discontent at headquarters.

Chapter v   336
Summary of the Year X. —The Concordat and M. Thiers. —Religious
sentiment during the Republic. —Napoléon's religious skepticism.
—The cult of the Supreme Being. —The Concordat and the Restoration.
—Vote on the Life Consulate. —My father. —The religion of love.

Chapter vi   347
The love story continued. —Meeting with the Turks. —M——'s
adventure. —A painful separation. —The general's idiosyncrasies.
—Return to Paris. —Caulaincourt, Ordener, Harville. —The eminent
ladies. —High society. —The favor. —M. de Vitrolles, M. Cambacérès, M. Lebrun. —M. Hékel. —Eugène Beauharnais and Lady
Georgina. —April Fool. —My aunt on my father's side.

Chapter vii   361
The stay in Nohant, return to Paris, and departure for Charleville.
—Bonaparte in Sedan. —Général Dupont's attitude in the presence of
Bonaparte. —The camp at Boulogne. —A squall at sea. —An
exchange of gunfire with the English. —Général Bertrand. —A party
given for Mme. Soult in the camp at Ostrohow. —Général Bisson.
—Outbursts against Deschartres. —A speech in which the army begs
Bonaparte to accept the imperial crown. —My mother in the camp at
Montreuil. —The return to Paris. —My father's marriage. —My birth.

Chapter viii   375
The date of this work. —My physical description. —My mother's

naïve stance on civil and religious marriage. —Mme. Murat's corset.
—The general staff in complete disfavor. —Heartbreak. —Maternal
diplomacy.

Chapter ix   385
Letters continued. —The coronation. —An exchange of letters between
my grandmother and a civil official. —Abbé d'Andrezel. —Letters
continued. —Marquis de S——. —A passage from Marmontel's
Mémoires. —My first meeting with my grandmother. —My mother's
character. —Her church marriage. —My Aunt Lucie and my Cousin
Clotilde. —My first stay at Chaillot.

Chapter x   401
The campaign of 1805. —Letters from my father to my mother. —The
Haslach Affair. —Letter from Nuremberg. —Heroic feats of the Gazan
and Dupont divisions on the banks of the Danube. —The honorable
conduct of Mortier. —Letter from Vienna. —Général Dupont. —My
father passes into the line with the rank of captain and receives the
Cross. —The campaign of 1806 and 1807. —Letters from Warsaw and
Rosemberg. —Continuation of the 1807 campaign. —The Tilsit raft.
—Return to France. —Trip to Italy. —Letters from Venice and Milan.
—End of the correspondence with my mother and beginning of my
own story.

Chapter xi   418
Earliest memories. —First prayers. —Children's silver egg. —Father
Christmas. —J.-J. Rousseau's theory. —The laurel woods. —Pulcinella
and the street lamp. Novels-among-four-chairs. —Military games.
—Chaillot. —Clotilde. —The Emperor. —Butterflies and gossamer.
—The King of Rome. —The flute.

Chapter xii   431
My parents' home life. —Our friend Pierret. —Departure for Spain.
—Dolls. —The Asturias. —The bindweed and the bears. —The blood-
stain. —The pigeons. —The talking magpie.

Chapter xiii   441
The Queen of Etruria. —Madrid. —Godoy's palace. —The white rabbit. —The toys of the Spanish Infantes. —Prince Fanfarinet. —I pass
muster as Murat's aide-de-camp. —His illness. —The fawn. —Weber.
—Early solitude. —The Mamelukes. —*Orblutes* —The echo. —The
birth of my brother. —They realize he is blind. —We leave Madrid.

Chapter xiv   450
My father's last letter. —Recollections of a bombardment and a battlefield. —Misery and illness. —Supper with candles. —Embarkation and
shipwreck. —Leopardo. —Our arrival at Nohant. —My grandmother.
—Hippolyte. —Deschartres. —The death of my brother. —The old
pear tree. —The death of my father. —The ghost. —Ursule. —A duel

to settle a question of honor. —Early notions of wealth and poverty. —Portrait of my mother.

Chapter xv   472
My mother. —A river in a room. —My grandmother. —Deschartres. —His medical practice. —Hieroglyphic writing. —First readings. —Fairy tales, mythology. —The Nymph and the Bacchante. —My great uncle. —The Canon of *Consuelo*. —The difference between "truth" and "reality" in the arts. —My grandmother's birthday. —Early musical studies and impressions.

Chapter xvi   483
Mme. de Genlis. —*Les Battuécas* —Fairy-tale kings and queens. —The green fire screen. —The grotto and the waterfall. —The old château. —First separation from my mother. —Catherine. —The fear my grandmother's age and imposing manner caused me.

Part III

From Childhood to Youth (1810–1819)

Chapter i   495
Trip to Paris. —The four-wheeled berlin. —The Sologne. —The Forest of Orléans and the hanged. —My grandmother's apartment in Paris. —Promenading with my mother. —My Chinese hair-do. —My sister. —First case of violent upset. —The Negro doll. —Being ill and hallucinating while delirious.

Chapter ii   503
Rose and Julie. —My grandmother's maternal diplomacy. —I rediscover my true home. —The interior of my great uncle's apartment. —"The eyes alone own." —My great uncle's gourmet dinners, his snuffboxes. —Mme. de la Marlière. —Mme. de Pardaillon. —Mme. de Bérenger and her wig. —Mme. de Ferrières and her lovely arms. —Mme. de Maleteste and her dog. —The Abbés. —First signs of a talent for observation. —Five generations at Rue de Gramont. —The children's ball. —Acquired grace. —The literary reactionaries of our time.

Chapter iii   520
The idea of a moral law to regulate one's affections. —Return to Nohant. —La Brande. —Bivouac in a rattletrap. —The haven. —A year of happiness. —The Emperor's power at its apex. —First betrayals. —Gossip and calumny overheard in the salons. —My brother's first communion. —Our old curé, his housekeeper, his sermons. —The thief who robbed him, his mare, his death. —Childhood pranks. —Deschartres' imposter. —My mother's piety. —I study French and Latin.

Chapter iv   540
The tyranny and weakness of Deschartres. —Fischer's minuet. —The

magic book. —We conjure the devil. —The seeker of affection. —My brother's first loves. —Pauline. —Masters Gogault and Loubens. —Disinclination for the social graces. —Maréchal Maison. —The apartment on Rue Thiroux. —Great sadness at age seven on anticipating marriage. —The army's departure for the Russian campaign. —Nohant. —Ursule and her sisters. —How games affected me. —My old friends. —Czar Alexander's war strategies. —Moscow.

Chapter v 557
Army and Emperor lost for fifteen days. —A vision. —A word from the Emperor on my father. —The German prisoners. —The Tyroleans. —Separation from Ursule. —Familiar address. —The big yellow bed. —My father's tomb. —Talleyrand's bon mot. —The politics of the old contessas. —A patriotic child. —Another vision. —Mme. de Bérenger and my mother. —Starving soldiers in the Sologne. —The Jacobin innkeeper. —My grandmother's illness. —Mme. de Bérenger destroys our garden. —The corset. —"Lorette de Bérenger." —The Allies enter Paris. —My grandmother's opinion of the Bourbons. —The cannonball. —Lovely ladies and the Cossacks.

Chapter vi 568
The domestic struggle is embittered. —I come to know real grief. —A discussion with my mother. —My entreaties, her promises, her departure. —First night of sleeplessness and despair. —The deserted room. —First deception. —Liset. —An adventurous plan. —My treasure. —My grandmother is stricken. —I abandon my plan. —Thoughts on the relationship one should have with servants in order to make equality habitual. —My grandmother is forced to neglect me. —Lessons by Deschartres. —Botany. —My contempt for what is taught me.

Chapter vii 582
My relationship with my brother. —Similarities and incompatibilities in our characters. —My maid's violence toward me. —Moral tendencies developed in me by her tyranny. —My grandmother becomes a royalist of sorts. —The portrait of Czar Alexander. —Return from the Isle of Elba. —More fantasies. —My mother comes back to Nohant. —I forgive my maid. —The Army of the Loire passes through. —Général Subervie's cockade. —Général Colbert. —How Nohant almost provided the fuel and setting for a patriotic Vendée. —The army is disbanded. —Colonel Sourd. —Brigands of the Loire. —Deschartres' peaches. —My father's regiment. —Our cousin visits us. —Mme. de la Marlière's piety. —My mother leaves Nohant. —My brother leaves Nohant. —Alone.

Chapter viii 597
How history is taught. —I study it like a novel. —A tutor "unteaches" me music. —First literary attempts. —Art and feeling. —My mother makes fun of me, and I give up the life of letters. —My great unpub-

lished novel. —Corambé. —Marie and Solange. —Plaisir the swine-herd. —The hidden ditch. —Demogorgon. —The secret temple.

Chapter ix   611
Liset's ambition. —The energy and listlessness of adolescence. —The gleaners. —Deschartres turns me into a communist. —He spoils Latin for me. —A storm during haying. —The Beast. —Story of the altar boy. —The hempworkers' evenings. —The sacristan's stories. —My brother's visions. —Beauties of winter in the country. —The Brother-hood of Lark Trappers. —The Corambé novel gets along without the essential ingredient. —First communion. —The traveling players. —The mass and the opera. —Brigitte and Charles. —For some people childhood is never over.

Chapter x   628
Recital of a profound unhappiness that everyone will understand. —An act of spite. —Mlle. Julie's denunciation. —Penitence and solitude. —Autumn evening in the doorway of a thatched cottage. —My heart is broken. —I harden myself to my affliction and become, once and for all, an enfant terrible. —I rejoin my mother. —Disappointment. —I enter the Convent of English Sisters. —The origin and appearance of this monastery. —The Mother Superior. —New heartbreak. —Mother Alippe. —I begin to assess my situation and resign myself. —Total seclusion.

Chapter xi   643
Description of the convent. —The lower class. —The pain and sadness of children. —Miss D., Class Mistress. —Mary Eyre. —Mother Alippe. —Limbo. —The sign of the cross. —The "devils," the "sages," and the "beasts." —Mary Gillibrand. —Escapades. —Isabelle Clifford. —Her strange creations. —Sophie Cary. —The convent's mystery. —Searches and expeditions for liberating the "victim." —The under-ground passageways. —The mysterious impasse. —A walk on the rooftops. —A comical accident. —Whiskey and the lay sisters. —The cold. —I become a devil. —My relations with the sages and the beasts. My leave days. —Great uproar against me. —My correspondence is intercepted. —I move to the upper class.

Chapter xii   663
Louise and Valentine. —The Marquise de La Rochejaquelein. —Her memoirs. —Her salon. —Pierre Riallo. —My classmates in the lower class. —Héléna. —Convent wit and humor. —The Countess and Jacquot. —Sister Françoise. —Madame Eugénie. —Single combat with Miss D. —The storage closet. —Solitary confinement. —Poulette. —The nuns. —Madame Monique. —Miss Fairbairns. —Madame Anne-Augustine and her silver stomach. —Madame Marie-Xavier. —Miss Hurst. —Madame Marie-Agnes. —Madame Anne-Joseph. —On intellectual incapacity. —Madame Alicia. —My adoption.

—Conversations at a quarter to nine. —Sister Teresa. —The distillery.
—The ladies of the choir and the lay sisters.

Chapter xiii   683
Isabelle's departure for Switzerland. —Sophie's protective friendship
for me. —Fannelly. —The friendship roll. —Anna. —Isabelle leaves
the convent. —Fannelly consoles me. —A look backward. —Misunderstood measures of the nuns. —I write verse. —I write my first
novel. —My grandmother comes back to Paris. —M. Abraham.
—Serious preparation for presentation at court. —I relapse into family
grievances. —I am presented to suitors. —Visits to the old contessas.
—I am given a cell. —Description of my cell. —I begin to tire of deviltry. —*The Lives of the Saints.* —Saint Simeon Stylites, Saint Augustine, Saint Paul. —Christ in the Garden of Gesthemane. —The Gospel.
—I enter the church one evening.

Chapter xiv   697
Tolle, lege. —The sanctuary lamp. —Religious fervor takes me
unawares.

Part IV

From Mysticism to Independence (1819–1832)

Chapter i   703
The reactions of Anna, Fannelly, and Louise. —Mary's return and her
jibes. —General confession. —Abbé de Prémord. —Jesuitism and
mysticism. —Communion and rapture. —The last nightcap. —Sister
Hélène. —Enthusiasm and calling. —The reaction of Marie-Alicia.
—Élisa Anster. —The pharisee and the publican. —Feelings and
instincts run parallel.

Chapter ii   718
The cemetery. —A mysterious outrage against Sister Hélène. —My
first instinctive doubts. —Mother Alippe's death. —Élisa's fears.
—My second bout with discontent. —Listlessness and fatigue. —The
sickness of scruples. —My confessor orders me to have fun by way of
penance. —Perfect happiness. —Devotions of a cheerful kind.
—Molière at the convent. —I become author and director of theatricals. —Unprecedented success for *Le Malade imaginaire* performed
for the whole community. —Jane. —Rebellion. —The death of the Duc
de Berry. —My departure from the convent. —The death of Madame
Canning. —Her administration. —The election of Madame Eugénie.
—The decline of the convent.

Chapter iii   737
Paris, 1820. —Marriage plans postponed. —A daughter's saddened
love. —Mme. Catalani. —Arrival at Nohant. —Spring morning. —An

attempt at working. —Pauline and her mother. —Plays at Nohant. —New inner strife. —My brother. —Colette and Général Pépé. —Winter at Nohant. —A February evening. —Misfortune and sorrow.

Chapter iv   752
Sorrows, strolls, and dreams. —Fighting sleep. —My first serious reading. —*Le Génie du Christianisme* and *L'Imitation de Jésus-Christ*. —Absolute truth and relative truth. —Scruples of conscience. —Wavering between mental development and regression. —The solution. —Abbé de Prémord. —My opinion of Jesuit thought. —Readings in metaphysics. —The war in Greece. —Deschartres sides with the Grand Turk. —Leibnitz. —My brain's great impotence, my heart's victory. —Relaxation of devotional practices, with an increase in faith. —Country and provincial churches. —Jean-Jacques Rousseau, *Le Contrat social*.

Chapter v   771
The son of Madame d'Épinay and my grandfather. —A strange system of proselytism. —My grandmother's commendable attitude. —She orders me to hear her confession. —She receives the sacraments. —My thoughts and the Archbiship's sermons. —A serious quarrel with my confessor. —The old parish priest and his servant. —The unreasonable behavior of a skeleton. —Claudius. —Deschartres' goodness and simplicity. —The spirit of charity among the people of La Châtre. —The village festival. —Discussions with my tutor, thoughts on scandal. —The definition of public opinion.

Chapter vi   789
My grandmother's illness worsens. —Extreme fatigue. —René, Byron, Hamlet. —A morbid state of mind. —Suicidal thoughts. —The river. —Deschartres' lecture. —The classics. —Correspondence. —Excerpts from a young girl's letters. —My grandmother's last days. —Her death. —Christmas night. —The cemetery. —The next night's vigil.

Chapter vii   803
My guardian. —The arrival of my mother and my aunt. —A strange change in relationships. —The reading of the will. —An illegal clause. —My mother's resistance. —I leave Nohant. —Paris, Clotilde. —1823. —Deschartres in Paris. —My vow. —A break with my father's family. —My cousin Auguste. —A divorce from nobility. —Domestic trials.

Chapter viii   816
My mother's peculiarity, magnanimity, and turbulence. —A night of revelations. —Parallels. —Le Plessis. —My father James and my mother Angèle. —Country happiness. —Return to health, youth, and high spirits. —The children of the household. —Opinions of the time. —Loïsa Puget. —M. Stanislas and his mysterious quarters. —I meet my future husband. —His prophecy. —Our friendship. —His father. —More

bizarre behavior. —My brother's return. —Baroness Dudevant. —The dotal system. —My marriage. —Return to Nohant. —Autumn 1823.

Chapter ix   834
Retreat to Nohant. —Needlework and its moral usefulness to women. —The desirable balance between effort and leisure. —My robin. —Deschartres leaves Nohant. —The birth of my son. —Deschartres in Paris. —Winter of 1824 at Nohant. —Changes and improvements which plunge me into melancholy. —Summer at Le Plessis. —The children. —The ideal in their society. —Aversion for the positivist view of life. —Ormesson. —The funeral of Louis XVIII at Saint-Denis. —The deserted garden. —Montaigne's *Essaies* —We return to Paris. —Abbé de Prémord. —Retreat to the convent. —Aspiration to monastic life. —Maurice at the convent. —Sister Hélène hastens our departure.

Chapter x   848
Émilie de Wismes. —Sidonie Macdonald. —M. de Sémonville. —The Desmoiselles Bazouin. —The mysterious death of Deschartres, perhaps a suicide. —My brother gets a head start toward a disastrous habit. —Aimée and Jane at Nohant. —Trip to the Pyrenees. —Fragments of a journal written in 1825. —Cauterets, Argelès, Luz, Saint-Sauveur, the Marboré, etc. —The shepherds come down from the mountains. —The passage of the flocks. —A dream of pastoral life takes possession of me. —Bagnères-de-Bigorre. —Spelunking at Lourdes. —Retrospective fear. —Departure for Nérac.

Chapter xi   863
Guillery, my father-in-law's "château." —Fox-hunting. —Peyrounine and Tant-belle. —The Gascons, fine folk, though much maligned. —Peasants, bourgeois, and nobles: hearty eaters, magnificent idlers, good neighbors and friends. —Trip to La Brède. —A few words about premonitions. —Return by way of Castel-Jaloux at night, on horseback, in the thick of the woods, escorted by wolves. —Pigon devoured by wolves. —They come to our very windows. —A wolf eats away at my bedroom door. —My father-in-law attacked by fourteen wolves. —The Spaniards, nomadic shepherds and bandits in the Landes. —The growing and collecting of cork. —The charm of winter in this region. —The death of my father-in-law. —A portrait and character study of his widow, Baroness Dudevant. —Her woeful situation. —Return to Nohant. —Comparison of Gascony and Berry. —Blois. —Mont-d'Or. —Ursule. —Duris-Dufresne, the deputy from Indre. —A song. —A memorable scandal in La Châtre. —A rapid summary of various short trips and the reasons for them, up to 1831.

Chapter xii   877
A retrospective glance over the several years sketched in the preceding chapter. —Troubled home. —Vanished dreams. —My religion. —Does freedom of worship include the freedom to abstain from worship?

—The quiet death of a fixed idea. —The death of Cricri. —Vague, but persistent, plans for a future to my liking. —Why these plans? —Managing a year of my income. —I resign. —In fact, I am suspended. —My brother and his troublesome addiction. —Salty winds, salty faces. —Trying out a modest profession. —The museum of painting. —Art makes revelations without assuring me any speciality. —No aptitude for the natural sciences, despite a love of nature. —I am granted an income and freedom. —I leave Nohant for three months.

Chapter xiii 888
By way of a preface to a new phase of my narration. —Why I do not mention everyone who influenced my life either through persuasion or persecution. —A few lines by J.-J. Rousseau on the same subject. —My feeling is completely the opposite of his. —I do not know how to assail the lives of others, and due to inveterate Christianity, I have not been able to throw myself into the politics of personalities. —I resume my story. —The garret on Quai Saint-Michel and the eccentric life I led for a few months before settling down. —A disguise that was extraordinarily successful. —Singular errors. —M. Pinson. —Émile Paultre. —Mlle. Leverd's bouquet. —M. Rollinat, Sr. —His family. —François Rollinat. —A rather long digression. —My chapter on friendship, less beautiful but as heartfelt as Montaigne's.

Chapter xiv 903
A last visit to the convent. —My eccentric life. —Deburau. —Jane and Aimée. —Baroness Dudevant forbids me to compromise her name in the arts. —My pseudonym. —Jules Sand and George Sand. —Karl Sand. —Cholera. —Saint-Merry's cloister. —I change garrets.

Chapter xv 913
Four men of letters from Berry. —Delatouche and Duris-Dufresne. —My visit to M. de Kératry. —My dream of an income of fifteen hundred francs. —*Le Figaro*. —A walk in the Latin Quarter. —Balzac. —Emmanuel Arago. —Balzac's first luxury. —His contrarieties. —Delatouche's aversion for him. —Dinner and a whimsical evening at Balzac's. —Jules Janin. —Delatouche encourages and inhibits me. —*Indiana*. —Those who said it was about me and my own story were wrong. —Theory of Beauty. —Theory of Truth. —What Balzac thought. —What the critics and public thought. —Corambé. —The apparitions fly away. —Work saddens me. —Alleged manias of artists.

Part V

Literary and Private Life (1832–1850)

Chapter i 931
Delatouche changes abruptly from critical to enthusiastic. —*Valentine* is published. —The impossibility of planned collaboration. —*Le Revue*

des Deux Mondes. —Buloz. —Gustave Planche. —Delatouche is displeased and breaks with me. —Summary of our relationship afterward. —Maurice goes to school. —His unhappiness and mine. —The sadness and harshness of the school routine. —An "execution" at Henri IV. —Love knows no reason. —Maurice makes his first communion.

Chapter ii   936
What I gained by becoming an artist. —Organized begging. —Swindlers of Paris. —Begging for employment and for fame. —Anonymous letters and those which should have been. —The visits. —The English, the curious, the loafers, the advice-givers. —The millstone. —Reflections on charity and on the use of one's goods. —Religious and social duty in flagrant opposition. —Future problems and present law. —Material and intellectual inheritance. —The obligations of family, justice, and probity, in actual society, versus renunciation according to the Gospel. —Inevitable conflict within oneself. —What I had to conclude for my own conduct. —Doubt and pain. —Reflections on human destiny and the workings of Providence. —*Lélia.* —Criticism. —Troubles that pass and those that last. —The malady at large. —Balzac. —Departure for Italy.

Chapter iii   951
Monsieur Beyle (Stendhal). —The cathedral at Avignon. —Trip to Genoa, Pisa, and Florence. —Arrival in Venice by way of the Apennines, Bologna, and Ferrara. —Alfred de Musset, Géraldy, Léopold Robert in Venice. —Financial distress. —Pretty picture of an Austrian officer. —Catullus the Elder. —Dilemma. —Punchinello. —A strange encounter. —Departure for France. —Carlone. —Bandits. —Antonino. —Meeting with three Englishmen. —Theater in Venice. —La Pasta, Mercadante, Zacometto. —Standards of equality in Venice. —Arrival in Paris. —Return to Nohant. —Julie. —My friends from Berry. —The ones from the garret. —Prosper Bressant. —*Le Prince.*

Chapter iv   962
Mme. Dorval.

Chapter v   980
Eugène Delacroix. —David Richard and Gaubert. —Phrenology and magnetism. —Saints and angels.

Chapter vi   996
Sainte-Beuve. —Luigi Calamatta. —Gustave Planche. —Charles Didier. —Why I do not say anything about certain others.

Chapter vii   1009
I take up my narrative again. —I succeed in saying some extremely delicate things, and I expressly say them without delicacy, thus finding them more properly stated. —The opinion of my friend Dutheil on marriage. —My opinion on love. —Marion Delorme. —Two of Balzac's

women. —Women's pride. —The pride of humanity in general. —*Lettres d' un voyageur*: my plan at the beginning. —How the traveller was me, and how he was not. —Physical and emotional illnesses reacting on each other. —The self-concern of youth. —The detachment of maturity. —Religious arrogance. —My ignorance still depresses me. —If only I could relax and improve my mind! —I love, therefore I believe. —Catholic arrogance, Christian humility. —Leibnitz again. —Why my books have boring passages. —New horizon. —Coming and going. —Solange and Maurice. —Planet. —Departure plans and clauses of a will. —M. de Persigny. —Michel (de Bourges).

Chapter viii   1023
Éverard. —His head, his face, his manners, his habits. —Patriots: enemies of cleanliness. —A nocturnal conversation on foot. —Sublimities and contradictions. —Fleury and I have the same dream at the same time. —From Bourges to Nohant. —Letters from Éverard. —The April lawsuit. —Lyon and Paris. —The lawyers. —A philosophical and political Pleiades. —Planet asks the social question. —The bridge of Saints-Pères. —A celebration at the royal palace. —Babouvist phantasmagory. —My morale. —Sainte-Beuve pokes fun. —An eccentric dinner. —A page from Louis Blanc. —Éverard sick and hallucinating. —I decide to leave. —A crucial conversation. —Éverard wise and true. —Another page from Louis Blanc. —Two different points of view in the defense: I agree with Jules Favre.

Chapter ix   1040
An incriminating letter in the monster trial. —My draft rejected. —The defection of the republican bar. —Trélat. —Éverard's speech. —His condemnation. —Return to Nohant. —Plans for a settlement. —The empty house in Paris. —Charles d'Aragon. —The Fieschi affair. —Maurice's political opinions. —Lammenais. —Pierre Leroux. —I am seized by homesickness. —The deserted house in Bourges. —Éverard's contradictory nature. —I come back to Paris.

Chapter x   1056
Indecision. —I do not go to La Chênaie. —My brother's letter. —I do go to Nohant. —Great resolve. —The Vavray woods. —A dash to Châteauroux and Bourges. —The prison at Bourges. —The break in the wall. —A quarter hour in the dungeon. —Consultation, decision, and return. —Let's kidnap Hermione! —The Duteil family. —The Inn of La Boutaille and the gypsies. —First ruling. —The deserted house at Nohant. —Second ruling. —Reflections on separations. —The deserted house at La Châtre. —Bourges. —The Tourangin family. —Pleas. —Settlement. —Final return and possession of Nohant.

Chapter xi   1072
Travelling in Switzerland. —Mme. d'Agoult. —Her salon at the Hôtel de France. —Maurice gets sick. —Struggles and sorrows. —I take him

back to Nohant. —Letter from Pierret. —I go to Paris. —My mother's illness. —Review of our relationship since my marriage. —Her last moments. —Pierret. —I fly to Maurice. —I run after Solange. —The Sub-Prefecture at Nérac. —Return to Nohant. —New disputes. —Two fine children for fifty thousand francs. —Work, weariness, and will. —The role of parents.

Chapter xii   1084
The death of Armand Carrel. —Émile de Girardin. —Éverard summed up. —Departure for Majorca. —Frédéric Chopin. —The monastery at Valldemosa. —*Les Préludes*. —Rainy day. —Marseille. —Dr. Cauvières. —Sea voyage to Genoa. —Return to Nohant. —Maurice's illness and recovery. —May 12, 1839. —Armand Barbès. —His flaw and his transcendence.

Chapter xiii   1098
I try the teaching profession and fail. —Indecision. —My brother's return. —Our quarters in Rue Pigalle. —My daughter at boarding school. —Square d'Orléans and my acquaintances. —A big meditation in the little Nohant woods. —Chopin's character developed. —Prince Karol. —Causes of suffering. —My son consoles me for everything. —My heart forgives everything. —My brother's death. —A few words about those who are gone. —Heaven. —The untold sorrows. —The future of the century. —Conclusion.

Part I

Family History
From Fontenoy to Marengo

I

Why this book? —It is a duty to let others profit from one's own experience. —*Lettres d'un voyageur*. —*Les Confessions* of J.-J. Rousseau. —My name and my era. —Reproaches to my biographers. —Antoine Delaborde, master of tennis courts and master bird handler. —Mysterious affinities. —In praise of birds. —The story of Agathe and Jonquille. —The bird handler of Venice.

I do not think there need be vanity or impertinence in writing the story of one's own life, still less in choosing from among the memories that life has left us those which seem worth saving.[1] From my point of view, I feel as though I am fulfilling a duty, painful at that, for I know of nothing more difficult than to define and sum oneself up as a person.

The study of the human heart is such that the more one is absorbed by it, the less clearly one sees it, and for certain active minds, to know oneself is a fastidious, never-ending study. However, I intend to discharge this duty; I have always had it in view; I have always promised myself not to die without having done what I have always advised others to do for themselves: a sincere study of my own nature and a careful examination of my own existence.

An insurmountable laziness (malady of preoccupied minds, hence that of youth) has made me defer this task until today, and perhaps to my own detriment, I have allowed a fair number of biographies to be published about me, which erred in both directions—praise and blame. In certain of these biographies, first published in foreign countries and then reproduced in France with further fanciful modifications, my name is about the only thing left that is not fiction. Questioned by the authors of such works, called on to furnish information at my own discretion, I have pushed apathy to the point of refusing the slightest guidance to those well-meaning people. I confess I felt it distasteful to bother the public with my personality, which has no striking features, while my head and heart abound with personalities that are stronger, more logical, more ideal—types superior to myself; that is to say, with characters for novels. I feel one must speak about oneself to the public only once in a lifetime, very seriously, and not return to it again.

The habit of speaking about ourselves seems easily to lead to self-praise, and that, doubtless quite involuntarily, by a law instinctive to the human mind, which cannot keep from embellishing the object of its contemplation. There is even a naïve kind of vaunting that need not be considered a pitfall when it is cloaked in lyricism like that of the poets, who have a special privilege in this area. But the self-enthusiasm which inspires such audacious surges toward heaven is not the milieu in which the soul can settle in order to speak of itself to humankind. In that mood, it loses the sense of its own weaknesses. It identifies with the godhead, with the ideal that it embraces; if it finds itself inclined toward regret and repentance, it exaggerates them to the point of poetic despair and remorse; it becomes Werther, or Manfred, or Faust, or Hamlet—sublime types from art's point of view, but types which, without the aid of philosophical detachment, have sometimes become morbid examples or ideals beyond our reach.

May these great portraits of the most powerful emotions of the poetic soul nevertheless remain forever blessed! And let us very quickly agree to forgive great artists for having draped themselves in thunderclouds or rays of glory. It is their right, and in giving us such renderings, they have accomplished their mission. But let us also agree that, in more humble circumstances and under more vulgar wraps, we may fulfill a serious duty more immediately useful to our fellow-creatures by communicating ourselves to them without symbol, halo, or pedestal.

It is surely impossible to believe that the penchant of poets for idealizing their own existences and making of them something abstract and impalpable is a lesson complete in itself. Useful and vivifying it is without doubt, for everyone's spirit is uplifted with those of the inspired dreamers; everyone's sentiments are purified by following them across those rapturous regions, but what is missing in this subtle balm spread by them over our failings is very important—reality.

Naturally, it takes something for an artist to mirror reality; those who get their pleasure this way are really very generous! As for me, I cannot carry the love of duty that far, and it is not without great effort that I am going to descend into the prose of my subject.

I have always found it in bad taste not only to speak a great deal about oneself, and worse, to do so with only oneself for any length of time. There are few days, few moments in the lives of ordinary beings which are interesting or useful to contemplate. But I have sometimes felt at such times like anyone else, and then I have taken up my pen to vent some vivid suffering I could not contain, or some violent anxiety that was working in me. The majority of these fragments have never been published and will serve me as markers for the examination of my life that I am undertaking. Only a few of these have assumed semi-confidential or semi-literary form in letters published from time to time and postmarked from diverse places. They have been collected under the title, *Lettres d'un voyageur* [1836]. At the time I wrote those letters, I did not feel too alarmed at speaking about myself, because it was neither overtly nor literally of myself that I spoke. That "traveller" was a sort of fiction, a convenient character, masculine as is my pseudonym, old though I was still young, but into the mouth of that sad pilgrim, that semi-fictional hero, I put impressions and reflections more personal than those I would have risked in a novel, where the conditions of the art are more stringent.

I needed then to rid myself of certain anxieties, not to attract my readers' attention to myself. Today I have that need still less than before—a need which in ordinary people is merely childish, but in artists is a risk, to say the least. I shall explain why I do not have it and also why I am, nevertheless, going to write about my life as if I did have it, as we eat because we know we should, without feeling any appetite.

I do not need to attract attention, because I have arrived at an age of tranquility, where my personality has nothing to gain by exhibiting itself and where I would aspire only to have it forgotten, indeed to forget it myself, if I were only following my instincts and good taste. I no longer try to solve the enigmas which tormented my youth; I have resolved many of the problems which used to keep me awake. I had help, for left on my own I would very likely have clarified nothing.

My century has set off sparks of truth and is keeping them alive; I have seen them, and I know from whence their main fires emanate. That is sufficient. In days gone by I looked to the facts of psychology for enlightenment. That was pointless. When I understood that such enlightenment lay in moral principles and that those principles were in me though not necessarily having originated from me, I was able to enter a peaceful state of mind without too much effort. Peacefulness of the heart has by no means been achieved and never will be. For those who were born compassionate there will always be something to love on this earth, consequently to lament, to serve, to suffer for. So, we need not seek the absence of pain, fatigue, or fear, no matter how old we are, for that would mean insensitivity, impotence, premature death. We can better cope with an incurable disease once we have accepted it.

My mind being at peace and my feelings resigned, I should not resent the human race for deluding itself, nor be enamored of myself who was for so long deluded. So, neither the attraction of a struggle nor the need for self-aggrandisement brings me to speak of my present and my past.

As I have said, I rather regard it as a duty, and here is why: many human beings live without taking serious account of their existences, without understanding, and almost without seeking God's design with respect to them as individuals as well as to the society of which they are part. They pass among us unrevealed, because they vegetate in unawareness, and although their destiny, undeveloped as it is, always has its usefulness in the eyes of Providence, it is as sure as fate that any disclosure of their lives remains morally barren for the rest of us.

The source of progress for the human mind which is most alive and serious is, in the language of today, the idea of "solidarity."[2] People of all eras have felt it vaguely or distinctly, and every time an individual found himself invested with a somewhat developed gift for disclosing his own life, he was led into doing it by the wishes of those close to him, or by an interior voice no less persuasive. Then it seemed to him to be the fulfillment of an obligation, as indeed it was, whether he had to relate historic events to which he had been witness, or whether he had frequented important individuals, or finally, whether he had travelled and appreciated people and things beyond the ordinary.

Another kind of personal writing exists which has been more rarely accomplished and which, in my opinion, has as great a usefulness: relating the interior life, the life of the soul—that is to say, the story of one's mind and heart—with a view toward teaching one's peers. Such personal impressions or attempts to voyage into the abstract world of intelligence and feeling, told by a serious soul, might be a prod, an encouragement, even a counsel or guide for other souls in the labyrinth of life. It is like an exchange of trust and sympathy which elevates the thought of the one who talks as well as the one who listens. In our private lives we are naturally moved toward this kind of exposition at once humble and proud. When a friend, a brother, approaches us to confess the trials and perplexities of his situation, we have no better arguments with which to strengthen him than those taken from our own experience, so sure are we then that the life of a friend resembles our own, just as the lives of each resemble those of all. "I have suffered the same ills, I have crossed the same reefs, and I have survived; so you, too, can be healed and conquer." That is what one friend says to another, what human beings teach each other. And which of us in those moments of despair, when the affection and help of another are indispensable, has not received strength from the outpourings of that soul to whom we went to pour out our own?

Certainly then, it is the most tried spirit that has the greatest influence over another. Under stress we rarely look to the support of a mocking skeptic. It is toward an unlucky one of our species, even unluckier than we, that we look and reach out. If we catch him in a moment of pain, he will be versed in pity and will weep with us. If we call to him during the fullness of his strength and sanity, he will advise us and perhaps save us; but surely he will influence us most by his understanding, and in order to be understanding, he will be compelled to confide in us in turn.

The recital of struggles in the life of each is, therefore, a lesson for all; it would mean health for all if each of us could analyse the cause of our suffering and realize what has saved us. It is with this sublime intention and under the influence of a passionate faith that Saint Augustine wrote his *Confessions*, which were the ones for his century and effectively rescued several generations of Christians to come.

There is a gulf between *Les Confessions* of Jean-Jacques Rousseau and those of the Church father. The purpose of the eighteenth-century philosopher seems more personal, hence less serious or useful. He accuses himself in order to clear himself, he reveals his private crimes for the right to reject public slander. Furthermore, his is a monumental confusion of pride and humility, which sometimes repels us by its affectation and sometimes touches us by its sincerity. As pervasively flawed and occasionally blameworthy as this famous work may be, it carries with it serious lessons, and the more the martyr abases himself and wanders from the pursuit of his ideal, the more the same ideal beckons to us.

But *Les Confessions* has been judged for too long as a purely individual apology. Jean-Jacques is partly responsible for provoking this negative response by injecting in his work personal preoccupations. Now that his friends and enemies no longer exist, we judge the work to be of greater value. We are no longer so concerned to know to what extent the author was unfair or deluded, to what extent his detractors were lying or cruel. What does interest us, what enlightens and influences us is the spectacle of an inspired human being at grips with the errors of his time and the obstacles in his philosophical destiny; his is a genius imbued with austerity, independence, and dignity in a struggle with the frivolous, disbelieving, corrupt environment through which he passed and which, reacting on him constantly either by seduction or tyranny, either dragged him into the pit of despair or propelled him toward sublime protestations.

If the intention behind *Les Confessions* was a good one; if it was Rousseau's mission to seek out childish mistakes and relate failures, I am not among those who shrink from such public penance. I think my readers know me well enough, at least as a writer, not to accuse me of cowardice. But in my opinion, that manner of self-accusation is not humble, and public sentiment is not taken in by it. It is not useful, it is not edifying to know, for example, that Jean-Jacques stole three livres, ten sous from my grandfather, still more so because it may not even be true.[3] As for me, I recall as a child having taken ten sous from my grandmother's purse in order to give it to a beggar, and even to have done it secretly and with pleasure. I do not find that at all a subject worth praising or blaming myself for. It was simply a misjudgment, because I could have had the money by asking.

Well, the majority of our faults, at least for us decent folk, are nothing more than misjudgments, and we would do well to accuse ourselves of them in front of the dishonest folk who commit evil artfully and with premeditation. The public is composed of both. We would be paying the public a little too much homage to reveal ourselves worse than we are in order to placate or please it.

I suffer mortally when I see the great Rousseau humiliate himself this way and imagine that by exaggerating or even inventing such sins he clears himself of the vices of the heart which his enemies ascribe to him. He certainly did not disarm them with his *Confessions*; and isn't it enough, in order to believe him good, to read the parts of his life where he forgets to accuse himself? It is only there that he is unselfconscious, and one is well aware of it.

Whether we are good or evil, young or old, it is always vanity, childish and miserable vanity, to undertake our own justification. I have never understood how an accused person could take the stand in his own defense. If guilty, he becomes more so by lying, and his lie, exposed, adds humiliation and shame to the rigor of his punishment. If innocent, how can he lower himself to wish to prove it?

And furthermore, it all has to do with honor. In the ordinary course of existence, it is necessary either to love oneself dearly or have a serious commitment to repulse the calumny which reaches even the best of us and to wish absolutely to prove one's worth. This is sometimes a requirement of public life, but in private life you do not prove your loyalty with speeches, and since no one is able to prove that he has reached perfection, we must leave to those who know us the care of absolving us from our failings and appreciating our virtues.

In the long run, since we are all responsible for one another, there is no such thing as an isolated fault. There is no error to which someone is not the cause or accomplice, and it is impossible to accuse ourselves without accusing the next one, not only the enemy who denounces us, but even sometimes the friend who defends us. That is what happened to Rousseau, and that is unfortunate. Who can excuse him for having implicated Mme. de Warens in his own confession?

Forgive me, Jean-Jacques, for blaming you when I finished your admirable *Confessions*! In blaming you, I pay you greater tribute, because this blame does not obviate my respect and enthusiasm for the whole of your oeuvre.

I am not making a work of art here, I even forbid myself to do so, because such subjects as these have value only through spontaneity and abandon, and I would not want to tell my life like a novel. The content would be overwhelmed by the form.

I shall, therefore, be able to speak without order or sequence, and even fall into many contradictions. Human nature is but a tissue of inconsequences, and I do not for a moment believe those who pretend to find themselves always in accord with their selves of yesterday.

Thus, the form of my work will feel the effects of this relaxation of my mind, and to begin, I shall not belabor the usefulness of these memoirs but simply show it by the account itself that I embark on, as it unfolds.

Let none of those who have done me harm take fright, I do not remember them; let no scandal mongers rejoice, I do not write for them.

I was born the year Napoléon was crowned, Year Twelve[1] of the French Republic (1804). My name is not Marie-Aurore de Saxe, Marquise de Dudevant, as several of my biographers have "discovered," but Amantine-Lucile-Aurore Dupin, and my husband, M. François Dudevant, claims no title. He has never been more than a second lieutenant in the infantry, and he was twenty-seven when I married him. In making him out as an old colonel of the Empire, they have confused him with M. Delmare, a character in one of my novels.[2] It is really too simple to write the biography of a novelist by transporting the fiction of her stories into the reality of her existence. Such expenses of the imagination are small.

They have perhaps also confused us with our forebears. Marie-Aurore de Saxe was my grandmother; my husband's father was a colonel in the cavalry during the Empire. But he was neither boorish nor peevish, as they claimed; he was the best and gentlest of men.

In this connection, and I beg the pardon of my biographers, but at the risk of quarreling with them and repaying their good will with ingratitude, I find it neither tactful nor honest that, in order to excuse me for having given up living under the conjugal roof and having obtained a legal separation, they accuse my husband of wrongs which I have absolutely stopped complaining about since I regained my independence. It cannot be helped if the public, in its spare time, discusses its souvenirs of a trial of this kind and if it has kept an impression more or less favorable to one or the other of us; there should be no cause for concern on either side if we have had to confront and suffer such publicity. But writers who devote themselves to relating the life of another writer, especially those who are prejudiced in her favor and who wish to inflate or rehabilitate her in public opinion, ought not to act contrary to her feelings and thoughts by parrying and thrusting around her. A writer's task in such a case is the same as a friend's, and friends should not lack respect, after all, for what concerns public morality. My husband is still alive and reads neither my writings nor those that are done on my account, which is another reason for me to disavow the attacks of which he is the object apropos of me. I was not able to live with him, our characters and our ideas being essentially different. He had motives for not consenting to a legal separation, of which he nevertheless felt the need, since we were already separated. Imprudent counsels committed him to public debates which forced us to accuse each other—unhappy result of an imperfect legal system that the future will amend. Since the separation was decreed and upheld, I hastened to forget my grievances, to the extent that all public recrimination against him seems to me in bad taste and could lead to the belief that resentments persist, which is not so in my case.

This said, it should be apparent that I am not going to transcribe the documents of my trial into my memoirs. It would make my task too painful to give space to childish grudges and bitter memories. I have suffered greatly from all that, but I am not writing to complain and give myself consolation. The sufferings I would have to relate in connection with purely personal action would not be generally useful. I shall relate only that suffering with which you all can identify. Once again, therefore, scandal lovers, close my book. It is not made for you.

The above is probably all I shall have to declare about my marriage, and I have said it quickly to obey a decree of my conscience. It is not prudent, I know, to disavow biographers who are well disposed in your favor, and who can threaten you with a revised and corrected edition, but I have never been prudent no matter what was at stake, nor have I observed that those who bother to be are spared more than I. When the chips are down, one must follow the impulse of one's true character.

There I leave the fact of my marriage, for the time being, and return to that of my birth.

This birth, for which I have been reproached so often and so singularly by both sides of my family, is a fact curious enough in actuality, and has every now and then given me pause to reflect on my ancestry.

I especially suspect my foreign biographers of an aristocratic bias, for they have all bestowed on me (those who ought to have been better informed) an illustrious origin while ignoring a very visible stain on my blazon.

One is not only the offspring of one's father, one is also a little, I believe, that of one's mother. It seems to me that the latter is even more the case, and that we are attached to the entrails of the one who gave birth to us in the most immediate, powerful, and sacred way. Hence, if my father was the great-grandson of Augustus II, King of Poland, and if on that side I find myself the illegitimate, but nevertheless very real, next of kin to Charles X and Louis XVIII,[3] it is no less true that my bloodlines are tied to the people in a way as intimate and direct; and what's more, there is no bastardy on this side.

My mother was a poor child of the old streets of Paris; her father, Antoine Delaborde, was a "master of tennis courts"[4] and a "master bird handler," that is to say, he sold canaries and finches on Quai aux Oiseaux, after having run a small tavern with billiards in some corner or other of Paris, where as a matter of fact he did not do much business. My mother's godfather did indeed have an illustrious name among members of the bird trade—Barra—and this name is still legible at Boulevard du Temple, above an edifice of cages of all sizes, where flocks of winged creatures which I look on as so many godfathers and godmothers—mysterious patrons with whom I have always had a peculiar affinity—always sing joyously.

Let whoever wishes explain these attractions between humans and lesser beings in creation. They are quite as real as the overwhelming antipathy and terror that certain inoffensive animals inspire in us. As for me, the sympathy for birds is so deeply ingrained that my friends have often reacted to it as though it were some prodigious feat. I have, in this regard, done some miraculous training, but birds are the sole beings in creation on which I have ever exerted a power, and if there is conceit in bragging about it, I owe them my apology.

I come by this gift through my mother, even more gifted than I, who always walked in our garden accompanied by cheeky sparrows, nimble warblers, chattering finches, which lived in the trees in total freedom but would come to peck with confidence at the hands that always fed them. I would safely wager that she came by that talent through her father, and that he did not become a bird seller simply by accident but through a natural attraction to those creatures with which instinct had put him in touch. No one has denied Martin, Carter, and Van Amberg a particular power over the instincts of wild animals. I hope no one will contest too much my savoir faire and savoir vivre with these feathered bipeds, which perhaps played a role in my former lives.

Joking aside, it is certain that each of us has a marked, even violent, predilection for or against certain animals. Dogs play an exorbitant role in people's lives, and there is indeed some mystery there that we have not entirely fathomed. I once had a servant who had a passion for pigs and who swooned from despair when she saw them pass into the hands of the butcher; whereas I, raised in the country—even, one might say, as a rustic—and destined to see numerous of these animals fed at our house, always had an infantile terror of them, insuperable, to the point of losing my head if I envisioned myself surrounded by that unclean species; I prefer a hundred times over to be in the midst of lions and tigers.

Perhaps for each human type, corresponding traits may be found among the animal families. The physiognomists have established physical resemblances; who can deny the psychological ones? Aren't there among us foxes, wolves, lions, eagles, beetles, flies? Human coarseness is often as vile and ferocious as the appetite of a pig and is precisely what causes me the greatest terror and disgust among my fellows. I like dogs, but not all dogs. I even have marked aversions to certain traits of particular members of that species. I prefer them a little rebellious, plucky, scolding, and independent. Their invariable greed distresses me. They are excellent creatures, wonderfully gifted, but incorrigible along certain lines where animal grossness reasserts its rights excessively. The dog-man is not a likable type.

But the bird, I insist, is the superior being in all creation. The way it is made is admirable. Its flying ability places it substantially above man and has endowed it with a power that our genius has not yet been able to acquire for us. Its beak and claws possess unparalleled dexterity. It has instincts for conjugal love, for domestic foresight and industry; its nest is a masterpiece of skill and scrupulous comfort. It is the principal species where the male helps the female with family chores and where the father is occupied, as with man, with building a home and protecting and nourishing the offspring. The bird is a singer, it is beautiful, it has grace, vivacity, affection, spirituality. That it is often made to typify inconstancy is certainly unjust. To the extent that an instinct for fidelity is given to animals, it is the most faithful. In the highly-touted canine family, the female alone loves her progeny, which renders her superior to the male; in birds, both sexes, endowed with equal virtue in this respect, offer us examples of ideal marriage. Hence, let no one speak lightly of birds. They would have to be less endowed for them to deserve us, and like musicians and poets, they are better endowed by nature than we. The bird-man is the artist.

As I am on the subject of birds (and why not exhaust it, since I am once and for all allowing myself unlimited digressions?), I shall mention a trait I have witnessed and which I would have wanted to relate to Buffon,[5] that discreet poet of nature. I raised two warblers from different nests and of different vari-eties—one yellow-breasted, one gray. The yellow chest, which was called Jonquille, was a fortnight older than the gray, which was called Agathe. Fifteen days for a warbler (the most intelligent and precocious of our small birds) is equivalent to ten years for a person. Jonquille was therefore a very nice little girl, still thin and poorly feathered, knowing how to fly only from one branch to another, but not yet feeding herself; for birds that are raised in captivity develop much more slowly than those which grow up in the wild. Mother sparrows are much stricter than we, and Jonquille would have fed herself fifteen days sooner if I had had the wisdom to force her by leaving her on her own and not giving in to her pleas.

Agathe was an unbearable little baby. All she could do was fidget, squeak, shake her nascent feathers, and torment Jonquille, who was beginning to use her brain and pose problems for herself, one foot drawn under the down of her dress, her head buried in her shoulders, her eyes half-shut.

However, she was still a very little girl, very greedy, and striving to fly to as far as where I was, in order to eat her fill, as soon as I was imprudent enough to glance at her.

One day I was writing some novel or other which intrigued me a little; I had placed at some distance the green branch on which my two pupils perched and existed on good terms. It was a bit chilly. Agathe, still half-nude, was snuggled up and nestled into Jonquille's belly, who lent herself to the mother role with generous compliance. They remained quiet for a half hour, from which I profited to write, for it was rare that they gave me that much leisure during the day.

But, finally, appetite won out, and Jonquille, landing on a chair, then on my table, came to obliterate the last word at the end of my pen, while Agathe, not daring to leave the branch, beat her wings at my side and stretched her wide-open beak with desperate cries.

I was in the middle of the dénouement and for the first time got cranky with Jonquille. I pointed out to her that she was old enough to feed herself, that she had under her nose an excellent mash in a pretty saucer, and that I was resolved no longer to close my eyes to her laziness. A little piqued and stubborn, Jonquille made up her mind to sulk and returned to her branch. But Agathe, not so resigned, turned toward her and demanded to be fed with unbelievable insistence. Undoubtedly, she addressed her with great eloquence, or if she did not yet know how to express herself well, she had in her voice accents to break a sensitive heart. Barbarous me, I looked and listened without budging, studying the visible emotion of Jonquille, who seemed to hesitate and undergo a most extraordinary internal conflict.

At last she arms herself with resolution, flies in a single swoop as far as the saucer, lets out a single cry, hoping the food will come by itself to her beak; then she makes up her mind and bites into the mash. But, miracle of sensitivity! she does not dream of appeasing her own hunger, she fills her beak, returns to the branch, and gives the food to Agathe, with as much skill and tidiness as if she were already a mother.

From that moment, Agathe and Jonquille no longer bothered me, and the little one was fed by the older, who did the job better than I, for she rendered her clean, shining, plump, and able to help herself much more quickly than I ever could have. Thus, the poor little thing had made of her companion an adoptive daughter while she herself was still only a child, and she had learned to feed herself only when pushed and overcome by a feeling of maternal charity towards her companion.[4]

A month later, Jonquille and Agathe, always inseparable although of the same sex and different breeds, were living freely among the tall trees of my garden. They did not fly far from the house, and their chosen domicile was atop a giant pine. They were quite long, lithe, and glistening. Each day, as it was summer and we ate outdoors, they winged swiftly down to our table and hovered around us like amiable guests, sometimes on a nearby branch, sometimes on our shoulders, sometimes flying in front of the servant who carried the fruit, in order to taste them on the platter before we did.

Despite their trust in all of us, they did not allow themselves to be caught and held except by me, and no matter what the time of day, they came down from the height of their tree at my call, which they knew very well and never confused with that of other people. It was a great surprise to one of my friends who arrived from Paris to hear me call to birds seemingly lost in the high branches and see them fly down immediately. I had just told him that I could make them obey, and as he had not been present during their training, for a moment he believed some witchcraft was at work.

I also had a red-throat which was a miracle of memory and intelligence, a royal kite, ferocious to everyone, which lived with me in such an intimate rapport that he perched on the edge of my son's cradle and, with his large beak, sharp as a razor, delicately lifted with a smart, little, tender cry the flies which alighted on the baby's face. The bird did this with such skill and caution that it never woke him. However, this fellow had so much strength and will that he flew away the day after he had had rolled under him and broken out of an enormous cage in which he had been put because he was becoming dangerous to people whom he did not like. There was no chain whose links he could not break quite easily, and the largest dogs had an insurmountable fear of him.

There would be no end to the story of birds I have had as friends and companions. In Venice, I lived tête-à-tête with a charming starling which, to my great despair, drowned in the canal; then with a thrush that I had to leave there and parted from with pain. Venetians have a talent for raising birds, and there was on a street corner a young chap who did marvels in this line. One day he bought a lottery ticket and won more sequins than he could count. He squandered them on a great feast for his beggar friends. The next day he sat down again at his corner, on the steps of a landing, with his cages full of completely tame magpies and starlings that he sold to passers-by and with whom he discoursed lovingly from morning till night. He had not a worry, not a single regret for having wasted his money on his friends. He had lived too long among birds not to have become an artist. That was the day he sold me my lovable thrush for five sous. To have a beautiful, good, cheerful, trained companion, who asks only to live with you for a day to love you all its life, for five sous! It is really too cheap! Ah, birds! how poorly we value them!

I have lived through the writing of a novel where birds play an important role and where I tried to say something about occult propensities and influences. I send my reader to *Teverino* [1845], which is what I shall often do when I do not wish to repeat what I have developed better elsewhere. I am quite aware that I do not write for all mankind. The human race has a few other things on its mind than to keep abreast of a collection of novels or read the story of an individual out of step with the official world. People in my profession always write only for a limited number of persons, who happen to be in situations or lost in dreams analagous to those which preoccupy the writers. I, therefore, shall not worry about being presumptuous if I ask those who have nothing better to do to reread certain of my pages in order to augment those they have before them.

Thus, in *Teverino*, I depicted a girl who, like Eve, had power over all the birds in creation; let me say here that that was not pure fantasy, no more than the same kind of marvels they relate about the poetic and wonderful "imposter" Apollonious de Tyane are fables contrary in spirit to Christianity. We are living at a time when we cannot quite explain the natural causes of what have heretofore passed for miracles, but when we can already assert that nothing on earth is a miracle and that the laws of the universe are no less conforming to an eternal order for having as yet been undiscovered and undefined.

But it is time to close this treatise on birds and return to the one on my birth.

T.J.

II

On birth and free will. —Frederick Augustus. —Aurora von Königsmarck. —Maurice de Saxe. —Aurore de Saxe. —Comte de Horn. —Mesdemoiselles Verrières and the eighteenth-century wits. —M. Dupin de Francueil. —Mme. Dupin de Chenonceaux. —Abbé de Saint-Pierre.

So, the blood of kings was mixed in my veins with that of the poor and lowly. And just as what is said to be fate is really an individual's character; just as one's character amounts to one's constitution; just as what constitutes each one of us is the result of a mixture, or a parity, of bloodlines, and the continuation, ever modified, of a succession of types that are linked to one another; so I have always concluded that the principle of natural heredity, which pertains to body *and* soul, was grounds for a sufficiently important bond between each one of us and each of our ancestors.

For we all have ancestors, high and low, plebian and patrician; ancestors signifies *patres*, that is to say, a succession of fathers, for the word is not used in the singular. It is amusing that the nobility has appropriated this word to its own advantage, as though the artisan and peasant are presumed not to have any lineage, as though one could not bear the sacred title of father without having a coat of arms, as if legitimate forefathers would indeed be found more commonly in one class than another.

What I think of racial superiority was stated in *Le Piccinino* [1847], and I probably wrote that novel only in order to present the three chapters where I expressed my feelings on nobility. The way people have understood it until now is tantamount to a monstrous prejudice wherein it hoards for the benefit of a class of rich and powerful people the sacredness of family, a principle which must be dear to all mankind. This principle is inalienable in and of itself, and I find lacking the following Spanish maxim: *Cado uno es hijo de sus obras* [Each of us is the son of his works]. The idea of being the son of one's works and as worthy in terms of one's virtues as the patrician is by his titles is a grand and generous one. That was the idea which engendered our great revolution, but it was inspired by reaction, and reactions only take into account one side, the one that people had grossly misunderstood and sacrificed. Thus, it is very true that each is the son of his works, but it is equally true that each is the son of his fathers, of his ancestors, *patres et matres*. We carry within us from birth instincts which are only the result of the blood that has been transmitted to us and which would govern us as a terrible fate were it not for the fact that we possess a certain measure of will-power, that individual gift granted to each one of us through divine justice.

In this respect (and this will be yet another digression), I say that, in my opinion, we are not absolutely free, and those who have conceded the dreadful dogma of predestination should, in order to be logical and not insult the kindness of God, be obliged to suppress the atrocious fiction of hell, as I myself suppress it in my soul and conscience. But neither are we absolutely enslaved by our instincts. God has given us all a certain rather powerful one to combat the others by giving us the power to reason, to compare, to profit from experience, to be "saved" ultimately, whether through a well-intentioned love of oneself or through the love of absolute truth.

To raise as objections idiots, madmen, and homocides would be in vain, for these examples, being under the influence of an uncontrollable monomania, consequently revert to the category of madmen and idiots. Every rule has its exception by which it is confirmed; every combination, no matter how perfect, has its accidents. I am convinced that, with the progress of societies and better education of humankind, these disastrous accidents will disappear; and likewise the measure of possibilities that we bring with us at birth, resulting from a better combination of transmitted instincts, will become our strength and the natural support of our acquired logic instead of creating interminable struggles between our inclinations and our principles.

It is perhaps a bit rash to try to resolve questions that have throughout the centuries been the concern of philosophy and theology when one admits to, as I dare to do, both a degree of bondage and a degree of liberty. Religions have believed that they could not be established without admitting or rejecting free will in an absolute manner. The church of the future will understand, I believe, that it has to take into account an element of fate—in other words, some drive of instinct, some pull of passion. The church of the past had already divined it, inasmuch as it had provided for a purgatory, a middle term between eternal damnation and eternal beatitude. The perfected theology of humankind will concede the two principles, fate and freedom. But as I trust we are done with Manichaeism, it will admit a third principle, grace, which will be the solution to the antithesis.

Nor will it invent this principle, it will only preserve it; for in its ancient heritage, that is what will be the best and most beautiful to exhume. Grace is divine action, always fecund and always ready to come to the aid of the one who pleads for it. That is what I believe, and I would not know how to believe in God without it.

The old theology had outlined this dogma for the use of people more naïve and ignorant than we, and also as a consequence of the limited enlightenment of the times. To conquer Satan it had preached, "temptations of Satan," "free will," and "succor of grace." Thus, we have three terms which are not in balance, two against one: absolute freedom of choice and succor from the Almighty pitted against fate, the devil's temptations, which must yield and be easily brought down. If that had been true, how therefore explain the imbecility of human beings who continued to satisfy their passions and give in to the devil, in spite of the certainty of eternal hellfire, when all the while it was so easy for them, with all their free will and support from God, to take the road to eternal happiness?

Apparently this dogma of eternal damnation never thoroughly convinced them; this dogma that stemmed from austere, exalted, courageous sentiment; this dogma that was rash to the point of arrogance and marked by the passion for progress, but that did not take into account the very essence of man; this dogma so grim in its effect and tyrannical in its decrees, since it logically condemns to the eternal wrath of God the mindless one who has freely chosen the cult of evil; this dogma has never saved anyone; saints never gained access to heaven except by love. Fear has not prevented the weak from tumbling into the Catholic hell.

In separating absolutely the soul from the body, and mind from matter, the Catholic Church was obliged to misunderstand the power of temptation and to decree that it had its seat in hell. But if temptation is within ourselves, if God has permitted it to be there in setting forth the law that joins son to mother, or daughter to father, all children to one or the other, at times as much to one as the other—at times also to a grandfather, or an uncle, or a great-grandfather (for all these phenomena of resemblance, whether physical or moral, or whether physical and moral at the same time, can be observed daily in families)—it is certain that temptation is not determined a wicked element in advance and that it is not the influence of an abstract principle placed outside ourselves in order to test us and torment us.

Jean-Jacques Rousseau believed we were all born good, capable of self-improvement; thus, he eliminated the factor of fate; but then how was he to explain the general perversity that took possession of every man from the cradle, effectively corrupting and injecting him with a love of evil? Nevertheless, he too believed in free will! It seems to me that when we concede this absolute liberty of man and when we see the bad use he makes of it, we must come to doubt God absolutely—or else proclaim His inaction, His indifference—and re-immerse ourselves, out of a final consequence of desperation, into the dogma of predestination; this is somewhat the history of theology during the last few centuries.

If one concedes that the educability or the barbarousness of our instincts is, as I have claimed, a heritage that is not ours to reject and quite useless to deny, then eternal evil, as a principle, is destroyed; for progress is not bound up in the type of fate I take into consideration. It is a fate always modifiable, always being modified, sometimes excellent and sublime because one's heritage is at times a magnificent gift to which the goodness of God is never opposed. The human race is no longer a multitude of isolated beings going at random, but a coming together of lines which are connected to one another and which are never absolutely broken even when the names happen to perish (this latter being an accident of little importance and of embarrassment only to the nobility); the intellectual conquests of the time always exert an influence on the free part of the soul, and as for divine action, which is the very soul of this progress, it always aims toward revitalizing the mind, which thus frees itself little by little from the bonds of the past and from the original sin of one's ancestry.

In this way, the physical evil little by little leaves our blood, as the spirit of evil abandons our soul. As long as our imperfect generations continue to struggle against themselves, philosophy can be indulgent and religion compassionate. Neither has the right to destroy man for an act of madness, nor condemn him for a false point of view. When the time comes for philosophy and religion to outline a new dogma for stronger and purer beings, Satan the stoker—inquisitor of the darkness, eternity's executioner—will have only a minor part. Fear will no longer have any effect on men (indeed, it already has none). Grace will suffice; for what people have called grace is the action of God as manifested, through faith, in men.

Faced with this dreadful dogma of hell, which the human spirit rejects, faced with the tyranny of a belief which would sanction neither pardon nor hope beyond this life, the human conscience has rebelled. It has broken its shackles. It has severed society from the church, the tomb of its forebears from the altars of the past. It has taken flight, it has gone astray momentarily, but it will get back on its course, never fear.

Here I am once again quite some distance from my subject, and my story runs the risk of resembling that of the King of Bohemia and his seven castles. Ah, well! what is the difference, my good readers? My story in itself is of rather slight interest. The facts play the minor role in it, the reflections round it out. No one has dreamed more and acted less than I in her life; would you expect otherwise from a novelist?

Listen! My life is yours, for you who read me are not immersed in the fracas of interests of today's world, otherwise you would push me aside out of boredom. You are dreamers like me. From the outset, everything that has stopped me on my way has stopped you too. You have sought, as I have, to give meaning to your existence, and you have come to some conclusions. Compare yours with mine. Weigh them and pronounce judgment, for the truth is only revealed by examination.

We shall, therefore, stop at each step, and we shall examine each point of view. Just now a truth has come to me, which is that the idolatrous cult of family is false and dangerous, but that respect and solidarity in the family are necessary. In antiquity the family played a big role. Then the role took on an exaggerated importance, with entitlement to noble rank being transmitted as a privilege. In the Middle Ages the barons acquired such a high opinion of their family origins that they might have held the august patriarchal families in scorn had not religion consecrated and sanctified their memory. The philosophers of the eighteenth century upset the cult of nobility, the Revolution overthrew it; but the religious ideal of the family disappeared in this destruction, and the people who had suffered from hereditary oppression, the people who laughed at blazons, got used to regarding themselves solely as the sons of their works. In this the people were mistaken, for they have their ancestors just as kings do. Each family has its nobility, its glory, its titles—work, courage, virtue, or intelligence. Every man who is endowed with some natural distinction owes it to some man who preceded him, or to some woman who gave birth to him. Every descendant of any lineage whatsoever would therefore have some examples to follow, if he could look back over his family's history. He would even find some examples to avoid. Families of illustrious lineage are filled with them; and it would not be a bad idea for children to learn from the lips of their wet-nurses the old family traditions that used to make up the education of a young noble ensconced in his castle.

Thus, you artisans who are beginning to understand all things, you peasants who are learning to write, don't forget your departed ones any longer. Hand down the life of your forefathers to your sons, make up the titles and coats of arms if you wish, but do it for all! The trowel, the pickaxe, or the pruning hook are just as beautiful symbols as the horn, the tower, or the bell. You can treat yourselves to this entertainment if you are so inclined. Financiers and men of industry take to it very well!

But you are more serious than those folks. Well then, may each one of you seek to retrieve and rescue from oblivion the fine deeds and useful works of your ancestors, and may you each behave in such a way that your descendants give you the same honor. Oblivion is a stupid monster which has devoured too many generations. How many heroes forever unknown because they have not left the wherewithal to erect a tomb! How many luminaries extinct in the past because the nobility insisted on being the sole guide and history of by-gone centuries! Escape from oblivion, all of you who have something more in your mind than the limited notion of the isolated present. Write your stories, all of you who have understood your lives and probed your hearts. For no other reason do I write mine and am I about to tell you the story of my forebears.

Frederick Augustus, Elector of Saxony and King of Poland, was the most astonishing debauchee of his time. It is no extraordinary honor to have a bit of his blood in one's veins, for he had, they say, several hundred bastard offspring. He had, by the beautiful Aurora von Königsmarck, that great and clever coquette before whom Charles XI withdrew leaving her to regard herself as more formidable than an army,[5] a son who surpassed him greatly in nobility although he was never more than a field marshal of France. This son was Maurice de Saxe, victor of Fontenoy, clever and brave like his father, but no less debauched, more knowledgeable in the art of war, also more fortunate and better supported.

Aurora von Königsmarck was granted, in her old age, a position in the Protestant Abbey of Quedlinburg, the same one in which Princess Amelia of Prussia (sister of Frederick the Great and mistress of the celebrated, unfortunate Baron von Trenk) was also to become the abbess. La Königsmarck died at the abbey and was buried there. A few years ago, the German newspapers published a report on excavations in the vaults of Quedlinburg Abbey, where the remains of Abbess Aurora were found perfectly embalmed and intact. She was attired in a sable-lined, velvet cloak over a dress of brocade embroidered with precious stones. As a matter of fact, I have hanging in my room in the country a portrait, strikingly beautiful in color, of this lady when she was still young.

One can readily see that she was made up to pose for the painter. Her complexion is quite swarthy, which does not at all fit our conception of a beauty from the north. Her jet-black hair is lifted behind by ruby clasps, and her smooth, exposed forehead has no trace of modesty; her thick, loose tresses fall over her bosom; she is wearing the gown of gem-covered, gold brocade and the red velour mantle with sable lining she had on when found in her coffin. I confess that this bold and smiling beauty does not appeal to me, and since learning the story of the exhumation, the portrait makes me even a bit fearful on evenings when it looks at me with its glittering eyes. It seems, then, as though she is saying to me, "With what nonsense do you confound your poor brain, degenerate offspring of my proud stock? With what chimera of equality do you fill your dreams? Love is not what you believe it to be; men will never be what you hope for. They are only created to be deceived by kings, by women, and by themselves."

Next to her is a handsome pastel of her son, Maurice de Saxe, done by Latour. He has a dazzling breast-plate and powdered hair, a handsome and good face which seems ever to be saying, "Onward to the beating drum, the cannon fuse is lit!" and shows little concern about learning French to justify his admission to the Academy. He resembles his mother, but he is blond, with a rather delicate skin tone; his blue eyes are softer and there is more frankness in his smile.

However, what was written under the heading of his passions often detracted from his glory, as in the affair he had, among others, with Mme. Favart, which Favart's correspondence reports with such dignity and sensitivity. One of his last loves was Mlle. Verrières,[6] a *dame de l'opéra* [courtesan], who lived with her sister in a "little country hideaway" still extant today and located in the new center of Paris, in the middle of Chaussée d'Antin. Mlle. Verrières had a daughter, who was not recognized as that of Maréchal de Saxe until fifteen years later and who was then authorized to bear his name by official decree. As a picture of the customs of the period, this story is a rather curious one. Here is what I found on the subject in an old work of jurisprudence:

"The demoiselle Marie-Aurore, illegitimate daughter of Maurice, Comte de Saxe, field marshal general of the French armies, had been baptized under the title of 'daughter of Jean-Baptiste de La Rivière, Paris citizen, and Marie Rinteau, his wife.' Since Mlle. Aurore was about to be married, M. Montglas had been named as her guardian by judgment of the Châtelet court, on May 3, 1766. There was difficulty with the publication of the bans inasmuch as Mlle. Aurore was unwilling to agree to being identified as the daughter of M. de la Rivière and still less as the daughter of 'father and mother unknown.' Aurore submitted a petition to the court tribunal appealing the Châtelet judgment. Before the court, Attorney Thétion, in behalf of Mlle. Aurore, furnished the complete proof through the deposition of M. Gervais, who delivered her, as well as through evidence of individuals who had held Aurore at the baptismal font, etc., that she was the illegitimate daughter of Comte de Saxe, and that he had always acknowledged her as his daughter; M. Massonet, in behalf of the first guardian, who left the matter to legal determination, and in accordance with the consistent conclusions of M. Joly de Fleury, advocate general, rendered June 4, 1766, a decree which invalidated the judgment of the preceding third of May. As amended, it named Attorney Giraud, agent of the court, as Mlle. Aurore's guardian, and declared her 'as having the status of illegitimate daughter of Maurice, Comte de Saxe,' and maintained and kept her in said status and as a ward of the aforementioned court. This being the case, it ordered that the notice of baptism inscribed in the registry of the parish of Saint-Gervais and Saint-Protais in Paris, dated 19 October 1748, containing the said extract: 'Marie-Aurore, daughter, presented on said day for baptism by Antoine-Alexandre Colbert, Marquis de Sourdis and by Geneviève Rinteau, godfather and godmother, respectively,' will be amended, and that instead of the names Jean-Baptiste de la Rivière, Paris citizen, and of Marie Rinteau, his wife, there will be added after the name of Marie-Aurore, daughter, these words: '*Illegitimate daughter of Maurice, Comte de Saxe*, field marshal general of the armies of France, and of Marie Rinteau'; this to be carried out by the bailiff of our said court, bearer of the present decree, etc."[7]

Another irrefutable proof that my grandmother might have been able to put before the public was the fact of the obvious resemblance she bore to Maréchal de Saxe and the manner in which she was virtually adopted by the Dauphine, who was the daughter of King Augustus, niece of the field marshal, mother of Charles X and of Louis XVIII. This princess enrolled her in Saint-Cyr, assuming responsibility first for her education and then for her marriage, and advising her not to see or associate with her mother.

At fifteen, Aurore de Saxe left Saint-Cyr to be married to Comte de Horn,[8] illegitimate son of Louis XV, and king's lieutenant at Schelestadt. She saw him for the first time on the eve of their wedding and became very frightened, as she believed she saw in him a likeness to the late king, whom he resembled to an alarming degree. He was taller, more handsome, yet he had the same severe and insolent air. On the evening of their wedding day, which my great-uncle, Abbé de Beaumont, attended (he was the son of Duc de Bouillon and Mlle. Verrières), a devoted valet came to ask the young abbé, who was then still quite young, to prevent the young Comtesse de Horn by all means possible from spending the night with her husband. The doctor of Comte de Horn was consulted, and the count himself listened to reason.

The result was that Aurore de Saxe was the wife of her first husband in name only, for they saw each other only at the princely festivities given in their honor at Schelestadt in Alsace—presentations of arms, cannon salutes, keys to the city presented on a gold plate, speeches by magistrates, illuminations, grand balls at the town hall, and whatever else made up the vain, noisy display with which people seemed to want to console this poor little girl for belonging to a man she did not love, whom she did not know, and whom she had to avoid like the plague.

My grandmother often told me how impressed she was with the pomp of the reception she received on leaving the convent school. She was taken in a big golden carriage drawn by four white horses, while her husband, attired in magnificent full regalia, rode on horseback. The noise of the cannon frightened

Aurore as much as her husband's voice. Only one thing delighted her: their bringing for her signature royal papers authorizing pardon of some prisoners. And thereupon about twenty prisoners left the prisons of the state and came to thank her for it. Then she began to cry, and perhaps the naïve joy she experienced was taken into account by Providence when she herself left prison after 9 Thermidor.[7]

But a few weeks after her arrival in Alsace, in the very middle of a grand ball—the governor having departed, while his wife continued to dance until three in the morning—Aurore was told in a whisper that her husband would be grateful if she came to see him for a moment. She went at once, but at the entrance to the count's chamber she stopped suddenly, recalling how her young brother, the abbé, had advised her never to enter his room alone. She took courage as soon as the door was opened and she could see people there in the lighted chamber; the same valet who had spoken to the abbé on her wedding day was holding Comte de Horn in his arms. They had laid him out on a bed, and a doctor was in attendance. "Monsieur le Comte has no more to say to Madame la Comtesse," exclaimed the valet on seeing my grandmother appear. "Do take Madame away!" She saw only the count's large, white hand that hung down over the edge of the bed and that they quickly lifted to give the body a more seemly appearance. Comte de Horn had just died from a severe blow sustained in a duel with swords.

My grandmother never knew any more about it. There was little she could do to fulfill her duty to her husband other than wear mourning; living or dead, he had always inspired her with fear.

I believe, if I am not mistaken, that the Dauphine was still living at this time and that she had Marie-Aurore placed in a convent. Whether this was done right away or shortly afterward, it is certain that the young widow quickly gained the liberty of seeing her mother, whom she had always loved, and that she was keen to benefit from this experience.[(9)]

The Mlles. Verrières continued to live together comfortably and even led a rather luxurious life, for they were still attractive and yet sufficiently mature to be favored with disinterested homage. The one who was my great-grandmother was the more intelligent and likeable. The other was haughtily proud; I no longer know who provided her support. I heard it said that they used to be called the Beauty and the Beast.

They lived pleasantly, with a degree of insouciance in keeping with the period's easy manners, "cultivating the muses," as they were wont to say in those days. Plays were put on at their house, M. de La Harpe[8] coming there himself to act in his as yet unpublished plays. Aurore played the title role in *Mélanie*, with well-deserved success. They busied themselves exclusively with literature and music. Aurore possessed angelic beauty and showed superior intelligence and training equal to that of the most enlightened minds of her time; her intelligence was further cultivated and developed through her association with members of her mother's circle. She had, in addition, a magnificent voice, and I have never known a better female musician. They would also put on comic operas at her mother's place. She played Colette in *Le Devin du vil-*

lage, Azémia in *Les Sauvages*, as well as all the principal roles in the operas of Grétry and the plays of Sedaine.[9] I have heard her a hundred times in her old age sing the airs of the old Italian masters, from whom she had subsequently gained greater sustenance: Leo, Porpora, Hasse, Pergolese, etc. Her hands were paralyzed, and she would accompany herself with only two or three fingers on an old discordant harpsichord. Though her voice was tremulous, it was always on pitch and reached to its full range; she never lost her technique or her tone. She would sightread all the scores with ease, and never since have I heard better singing or better accompaniment. She had that large manner, that unadorned simplicity, that purity of taste and distinguished pronunciation that no one has any more, that no longer exist today. In my childhood she would have me say with her a little Italian duet by some master whose name escapes me:

Non mi dir, bel idol mio [Don't tell me my beautiful idol],
Non mi dir ch'io son ingrato [Don't tell me you find me ungrateful].[10]

She would take the tenor part, and on a number of occasions, although she was then about sixty-five years old, her voice rose to such a power of expression and charm that once I stopped short and burst into tears while listening to her. But I shall have to come back later to these first musical impressions, which were the dearest of my life. Now I am going to retrace my steps and take up the story of my "grandmama" in her youth.

Among the famous men who used to frequent her mother's house, she knew Buffon especially well and found in his conversation a charm that remained forever fresh in her memory. Her life at this period was happy and sweet as well as brilliant. She inspired love or friendship in everyone. I have a number of love epistles, in rather bland verse, addressed to her by the wits of the day, one of which by La Harpe was expressed in these words:

All the respect of the Caesars I place at your feet.[10]
Accept then this gift that Friendship does treat,
But do not tell Love what you have just heard . . .
For I fear he'll deny every word!

This is a sample of the gallantry of the time. But Aurore was able to cope with the temptations of this society and its host of compliments without swerving from her goal of cultivating the arts and developing her mind. She never had a passion other than that of maternal love, nor did she have any idea of what a love affair was. She was, however, possessed of a tender, generous nature and had an exquisite sensibility. Piety was not what restrained her. She had no religion other than the one of the eighteenth century, the deism of Jean-Jacques Rousseau and Voltaire. But hers was a firm, perceptive soul and particularly attracted to a certain ideal of pride and self-respect. She was ignorant of coquetry, for she was too gifted to have need for it, and that method of provocation offended her idea of dignified behavior. She survived a very liberal epoch in a very corrupt world without suffering the slightest blemish to her character, and condemned as she was by a strange destiny never to know love in marriage, she resolved this great problem in her life by managing to live with composure and to escape all malevolence and slander.

I believe she was about twenty-five years old when she lost her mother. Mlle. Verrières died one evening just as she was about to retire, without being ill in any way, and complaining only that her feet were a bit cold. She was seated before the fire, and while her maid was warming her slippers, she passed away without saying a word or uttering a sigh. When the maid put her slippers on, she asked her if she was feeling warmer, and not receiving any answer, looked at her face and saw that eternal sleep had closed her eyes. I believe, in those days, for the few who by nature found themselves in complete harmony with the mood and customs of their philosophical milieu, everything was pleasant and easy, even dying.

Aurore went into the convent. That was the custom if you were a young girl or a young widow who did not have relations to guide you through the world. There you would quietly settle with a certain degree of elegance, you would receive visits, go out in the morning and even at night, with a suitable chaperone. It was somewhat of a precaution against slander, a matter of etiquette and good taste.

However, for my grandmother, who had serious interests and orderly habits, this cloistered life was both useful and valuable. There she read prodigiously and amassed volumes of extracts and quotations I still keep and which are for me a testimony of the strength of her mind and the good use of her time. Her mother had left her only a few old clothes, two or three family portraits, including the one of Aurora von Königsmarck (purposely left with her by Maréchal de Saxe), many madrigals and pieces of unpublished verse from her literary friends (which were well worth publishing), the seal of the field marshal and his snuffbox, which I still have and which are of very fine workmanship. As for her house, her theater, and all the luxurious embellishments of a charming lady, it can be assumed that her creditors were ready to pounce on them, but until the calm and carefree hour of her departure, the lady had had too much trust in their good breeding to be concerned. The creditors in those days were, in fact, very well brought up. My grandmother never had the least unpleasantness to suffer from that quarter, but she was reduced to a very small pension from the Dauphine, and even it suddenly stopped one day. It was on that occasion that she wrote to Voltaire, who replied with a charming letter which she used in contacting Duchesse de Choiseul. Here is my grandmother's letter and the reply:

To. A. M. de Voltaire   24 August 1768.

It is to the Bard of Fontenoy that the daughter of Maréchal de Saxe is writing in order to obtain her daily bread. I have been acknowledged as his daughter; Madame la Dauphine took care of my education after the death of my father. She removed me from Saint-Cyr in order to have me married to M. de Horn, Chevalier de Saint-Louis and Capitaine in the Royal Bavarian

Regiment. For my dowry she caused him to be made Lieutenant du Roi of Schelestadt. It was in the midst of the festivities they gave us on our arrival that my husband died suddenly. Since then, death has taken away also my protectors, the Dauphin and his wife, the Dauphine.

Fontenoy, Raucoux, Laufeld are forgotten. I am forsaken. I have thought that he who immortalized the victories of the father would be interested in the misfortunes of the daughter. It is for him to adopt the children of the hero and to be my support, just as he has done for the daughter of the great Corneille. With the eloquence that you have devoted to pleading the cause of unfortunate persons, you will make the cry of pity reverberate in all hearts, and you will gain every bit as much right to my gratitude as you already possess of my respect and admiration for your sublime talents.

(Reply) 2 September, 1768, at Château Ferney

Madame,

I shall soon be going to join the hero, your father, and I shall inform him with indignation of the condition his daughter finds herself in. I had the honor of associating a great deal with him, and he condescended to show me kindness. One of the misfortunes that afflict me in my old age is to discover that the daughter of France's hero is not happy in France. In your place, I should present myself to Duchesse de Choiseul. My name will assure your welcome at her door, and Madame la Duchesse, whose soul is just, noble, and charitable, will not let this opportunity pass to do some good deed. It is the best advice I can give you, and I am sure that you will be successful, if you speak to her. You have, without doubt, done me too much honor, Madame, in thinking that a dying old man, persecuted and retired from the world, would be fortunate enough to be of assistance to the daughter of Maréchal de Saxe. You have done me justice in not doubting the keen interest I must take in the daughter of such a great man.

> I have the honor of being respectfully, Madame,
> your very humble and very obedient servant,
> Voltaire, Gentleman, Order of the King's Chamber.

It is probable that this approach to the duchess did not succeed, for Aurore decided when she was about thirty to marry M. Dupin de Francueil, my grandfather, who was then sixty-two.

M. Dupin de Francueil, the very same person whom Jean-Jacques Rousseau in his memoirs, and Mme. d'Epinay in her correspondence, identify simply as Francueil, was the consummate "charmer," as this expression was understood in the last century. He was not of the upper nobility, being the son of Monsieur Dupin, a financier who had abandoned military life for that of estate management. He himself was a tax collector at the time of his marriage to my grandmother. His was a very old family of many branches, with several folio-size pages of lineage well-supported by heraldic gibberish and very pretty, colored vignettes. Nevertheless, my grandmother hesitated a long time before making this alliance, not because M. Dupin's age was an obstacle but because her entourage regarded him as too minor a personage to be a match for Mlle. de Saxe, Comtesse de Horn. Prejudice gave way to financial considerations, for M. Dupin was quite wealthy at this time. For my grandmother, the boredom of being secluded in the convent during the prime of her life and the assiduous attentions, the grace, wit, and amiable nature of her aging admirer were of greater importance than the attraction of riches; after two or three years of hesitation, during which he never let a day pass without coming to the parlor to dine and chat with her, she rewarded his love and became Madame Dupin.[11]

She often spoke to me of this marriage so carefully weighed, and of the grandfather I never knew. She told me that during the ten years they lived together, he and her son were the greatest attachments of her life, and although she never used the word love, and in fact never did I hear the word from her lips with respect to him or to anyone, she would smile when she heard me say that it seemed impossible to love an old man. "An old man feels more deeply than a young man," she would say, "and it is impossible not to feel affection for one who is devoted to you so completely. I used to call him my old husband and my papa. He liked it that way, and he always referred to me as his daughter, even in public." And then she added, "Was anyone ever really old in those days! It was the Revolution that brought old age into the world. My dear, your grandfather was handsome, elegant, soigné, gracious, scented, cheerful, kind, affectionate, and even-tempered until his last hour. In his younger years, he had been rather too sociable to think of settling for such a quiet life, and perhaps I might not have been so happy with him—rivals would have sought to take him from me. I am convinced that I had the best years of his life and that never has a young man made a young woman as happy as I was; we never left each other for a moment, and I never felt the slightest boredom in his company. His mind was an encyclopedia of ideas, knowledge, and skills that for me would never be exhausted. He had the gift of always knowing how to spend his time so that he would please others as much as himself. During the day, we would make music together; he was an excellent violinist and made his own instruments; in addition he was also a clock and watch maker, architect, turner, painter, locksmith, decorator, cook, composer of music, joiner, and he could embroider marvellously. I do not know anything he could not do. The unfortunate thing is that he went through his fortune in order to satisfy his urge to try everything. But I was dazzled by it all, and we went to our ruin in the most pleasant way imaginable. In the evenings, if we did not go out to a party, he would sit next to me and draw, while I unravelled gold thread,[11] and we would take turns reading to each other. Sometimes a few charming friends would join us and engross his sharp and fertile mind with their witty conversation. My friends were young women who, though they had made more brilliant marriages, never tired of telling me how much they envied me my old husband.

"Those were the days when they knew how to live and die," she would continue. "We never had tiresome illnesses. If you had the gout, you would still carry on without making a wry face; good breeding demanded that you hide your pain. People did not have those business worries that spoil their home life and dull their wit. We knew how to face ruin without letting it show, like first-class gamblers who can lose without a trace of concern or annoyance. Better to be carried to the hunt half dead than miss it. And it was better to die at the ball or the theater than in bed, between four candles and dreadful men in black. We were philosophical, we did not entertain austerity, although sometimes we felt it without letting it show. When one displayed wisdom, it was done with good taste, without being pedantic or prudish. People savored life, and when the time came to leave it, they did not want to spoil its pleasure for others. In his farewell words, my old husband made me promise to survive him for many years and create a happy life for myself. To show such generosity of spirit is truly the way to make yourself missed."

It certainly was pleasant and attractive, this philosophy of affluence, of independence, of tolerance, of amenity, but it would require five or six hundred thousand francs annually to support it, and I fail to see how the poor and oppressed could ever have benefited from it.

This philosophy broke down in the face of revolutionary vengeance, and the fortunate ones of the past retained little but the art of knowing how to mount the scaffold with good grace, which was no mean feat, I grant you, but what helped them show this final bravery was their profound distaste for a way of life in which they no longer saw the possibility of amusement and their dread of a social environment where they would have to concede, at least in principle, everyone's right to well-being and leisure.

Before going further, I shall speak of an illustrious person from the family of M. Dupin, a true and authentic character from whom, however, neither I nor my grandfather can lay claim to honor and intelligence. This personage was Mme. Dupin de Chenonceaux, with whom I have no connection by blood, since she was the second wife of M. Dupin, the financier, consequently the stepmother of M. Dupin de Francueil. This is no reason not to speak of her. I am all the more obliged to do so, for in spite of the reputation she had for wit and charm and the praise accorded her by her contemporaries, this remarkable woman never took her rightful place in the republic of serious writers.

She was Mlle. de Fontaines, acknowledged daughter of Samuel Bernard,[12] at least according to Jean-Jacques Rousseau. The dowry she brought to M. Dupin was considerable; I do not remember which of the two personally owned the Chenonceaux estate, but together they possessed an immense fortune. They had as a *pied-à-terre* in Paris the Lambert mansion, and thus they could pride themselves on occupying two of the most beautiful residences in the world.

We know that Jean-Jacques Rousseau became M. Dupin's secretary, lived at Chenonceaux with them, and that he fell in love with Mme. Dupin, who was of angelic beauty. We know also how he rashly declared his love without success. Nevertheless, he remained on good terms with her and her stepson, Francueil.

Mme. Dupin devoted herself without pretension to the study of literature and philosophy, and did not venture to link her name to the works of her husband; however, I am certain that she could have laid claim to the best ideas in most of his works. Their extended critique of *L'Esprit des lois* is a very fine work, little known and little appreciated. It is inferior in form to Montesquieu's work, but superior in many respects as to substance; and by the very fact that it made available to the world more advanced ideas, it inevitably went unnoticed alongside the genius of Montesquieu, who was in tune with all the tendencies and political aspirations of the time.[12]

M. and Mme. Dupin were writing a work on the merits of women at the time Jean-Jacques was living with them. He helped them with note-taking, did research, and accumulated a considerable amount of material on the subject, which still exists in manuscript form at the château of Chenonceaux. The work was never completed due to the death of M. Dupin; and Mme. Dupin, out of modesty, made it a practice never to publish *her* work. However, some summaries of her opinions, written in her own hand under the humble title of *Essais*, would be worth publishing, even if only as a historical document to accompany the philosophic history of the last century. This amiable woman belongs to that family of clever and well-meaning people of her time, and we perhaps have much to regret that she did not devote her life to developing and spreading the wisdom she carried within her.

What gives her a very special and very original aspect in the midst of all these thinkers is the fact that she was more advanced than most of them. She was not a follower of Rousseau, she did not have his talent; but he himself lacks the courage of his convictions. She proceeds from another doctrine, a bolder and more profound one, more ancient in the history of humankind and more novel, apparently, in the eighteenth century. She is the friend (pupil or master, who knows?) of an old man reputedly eccentric, of limited genius, with little gift for form, and yet whom I believe to be more inwardly enlightened by the spirit of God than Voltaire, Helvetius, Diderot, and Rousseau himself. I speak of the Abbé de Saint-Pierre, whom the world then called the "famous" Abbé de Saint-Pierre, an ironic designation for which it can be forgiven now that he is scarcely known, if not forgotten.

He is one of those unfortunate geniuses who are unable to express themselves and who, for lack of a Plato to interpret them to the world, leave pale outlines in the night of time and carry into the tomb the secret of their intelligence, the "unrevealed essence of their meditation," as a member of that great family of illustrious mutes or stutterers, Geoffroy Saint-Hilaire, called it.

Their ineffectuality appears as inescapable as the fact that the ability to make the seemingly clearest and most fortunate presentation is often found distributed among men of limited vision and indifferent feeling. As far as I am concerned, I understand quite well that Mme. Dupin may have preferred the utopian ideas of Abbé de Saint-Pierre to Montesquieu's professed anglomania. The great Rousseau did not have as much moral courage and freedom of spirit as this generous woman. When Rousseau was commissioned by her to summarize Abbé de Saint-Pierre's plan for perpetual peace through international councils called "polysynods," he accomplished it with his usual clarity and beauty, but he confessed that he felt obliged to pass over the most daring features of the author's work, and he advises readers with the necessary courage to examine the text for themselves.

I admit that I do not care very much for the kind of irony adopted by Jean-Jacques Rousseau with respect to the utopias of Abbé de Saint-Pierre, nor for the discretion he believed he had to use in the face of the powerful men of his time. Besides, his pretense is either too clever or too clumsy; either his irony is not obvious enough and thus loses its power, or it is not disguised enough and thus loses a degree of prudence and power. There is no unity, no consistency in Rousseau's judgments on the philosopher of Chenonceaux; he treats him as "great" or "poor," depending on how much anguish his own persecution caused him in different periods of his life. In parts of *Les Confessions*, one would say he is blushing for having admired the abbé. Rousseau is wrong. One is not "poor" for lack of a "gift." Genius comes from the heart and does not have a set form. And, therefore, the principal criticism he makes of him, like all the Abbé's critics at the time, is that of not being practical and of believing in the possibility of his social reforms. It seems to me, however, that this dreamer saw much more clearly than all his contemporaries and that he was much closer to revolutionary, constitutional, Saint-Simonian ideas, and even to those we call humanitarian ones today, than his contemporary Montesquieu and his successors Rousseau, Diderot, Voltaire, Helvetius, et al.

For there was everything in that vast brain of Abbé de Saint-Pierre, and inside that seeming chaos of his thought, one finds piled up pell-mell all the ideas which have since individually occupied the attention of very able men for an entire lifetime. Certainly Saint-Simon[13] stems from him, Mme. Dupin, his pupil, and M. Dupin, who, in their *Critique de l'Esprit des lois*, are avowed "emancipators" of woman. The various essays on government published in the past hundred years, the principal documents of European diplomacy, as well as the shams of royal agreements called alliances, have borrowed from Abbé de Saint-Pierre's theories on government a semblance, albeit a tendentious one, of wisdom and morality. As for his philosophy of perpetual peace, it is in keeping with the spirit of the latest philosophic schools.

It would, therefore, be quite ridiculous today to devalue Abbé de Saint-Pierre or speak disrespectfully of him, for even his detractors have called him "man of good will" par excellence. Had he merely kept that title as his sole claim to posterity, it would be more than many a great man of his time could claim.

Mme. Dupin de Chenonceaux had a fervent devotion to this man of good will, shared his ideas, enhanced his old age in touching solicitude, and witnessed his last breath, at Chenonceaux. I have seen there, in the very room where this generous soul departed, a portrait of him done shortly before his death. His fine face, at one and the same time sweet and austere, resembles somewhat that of François Arago. But the expression is different, for in fact the shadows of death have already invaded his big dark eyes made hollow through suffering, and his pale cheeks emaciated by time.[(13)]

Mme. Dupin left at Chenonceaux some very brief writings that nevertheless abound with clear ideas and noble sentiments. They are, in general, discrete thoughts, yet they make a very logical sequence. A little treatise entitled *Du bonheur*, though only a few pages long, seemed a masterpiece to us. And in order to convey its philosophic tenor, only the first words of it need be transcribed, "All men have an equal right to happiness," or to quote her literally, "All men have an equal right to *pleasure*." But the word "pleasure," which has its fixed locale, like the mantelpiece mirror, must not be taken equivocally and as an expression of Regency thinking. No, its true sense is material happiness, enjoyment of life, well-being, distribution of wealth—as we would say today. The title of the work, the chaste and solemn spirit with which its writing is imbued, leave no doubt as to the present-day significance of that egalitarian formula which corresponds to this one, "To each according to his needs." It is a rather "advanced" idea, I believe, so much so that even today it is too advanced for the cautious minds of the majority of our thinkers and politicians; it took a certain courage on the part of the illustrious historian, Louis Blanc, to proclaim this idea and to develop it.[14]

Beautiful and charming, modest, strong, and calm, Mme. Dupin ended her days at Chenonceaux at a very advanced age. The style of her writing is as limpid as her soul, as delicate, and fresh as the features of her face. That style is her own, and the elegant correctness of her writing does not detract from its originality. She writes the language of her time, but she can turn a phrase like Montaigne, or drive a shaft like Bayle,[14] and one can see that this fine lady does not shrink from dusting off the old masters. She does not imitate them, but she did assimilate them, like a sound system fed on sound nourishment.

I must pay her yet another tribute: of all the old friends whom Rousseau came to abandon and suspect in his sorrowful old age, she is perhaps the only one he treats justly in his *Confessions*, and he admits her generosity without bitterness. She was kind even to Thérèse Levasseur and her undeserving family. She was kind to everyone and was held in great esteem; for the Revolutionary furor that entered the royal manor of Chenonceaux respected the white hair of that old lady. Of all the austerity measures, she suffered only the confiscation of a few historic paintings which she sacrificed in good grace to the exigencies of the moment. Her tomb, in its simple, good taste, reposes in the cool and melancholy shadows of the Chenonceaux park. Know you, O visitor, when you devotedly gather the cypress leaves without any other motive than to render homage to that virtuous beauty loved by Jean-Jacques, she is entitled to respect for more than that. She consoled the old age of *the* man of good will of her era; she was his disciple; she inspired in her own husband the principle of respect for her sex, and this was no small homage to the sweet and modest superiority of her intelligence. She went still further. She who was rich, beautiful, and powerful understood that all men had a right to happiness. Therefore, may honor go to her who was as beautiful as the mistress of a king, as wise as a matriarch, as enlightened as a true philosopher, and as good as an angel!

A noble friendship that was slandered, like everything which is natural and good in this world, served as a bond between Francueil and his stepmother. Indeed, this attachment must have been one more reason for the affection and esteem my grandmother felt for her old husband. The association with a stepmother like the first Mme. Dupin, and then one with a wife like the second, must inevitably illuminate the youth and old age of a man. Men owe more to women than to other men for whatever they may possess of good or bad in the lofty regions of the soul, and it is in this context that we should say to them: Tell me whom you love, and I shall tell you who you are. A man is able to live more easily in society when faced with the scorn of women than with that of men, but before God, before the decrees of Justice that sees and knows all, the scorn of women would be much more prejudicial. This point would perhaps be the pretext for a digression, for I could cite a few excellent pages from M. Dupin, my great-grandfather, on the equality of status between man and woman in God's design and nature's order. But I shall return to this subject at greater length and with more relevance in the account of my own life. *A.E.L.*

III

An anecdote about J.-J. Rousseau. —Maurice Dupin, my father.
—Deschartres, my tutor. —The curé's head. —"Liberalism" before
the Revolution. —The domiciliary visit. —Incarceration. —The
devotedness of Deschartres and my father. —"Nérina."

Since I have mentioned Jean-Jacques Rousseau and my grandfather, I
shall include at this point a charming anecdote from the papers of my grandmother, Aurore Dupin de Francueil.

"I saw him only once (she is speaking of Rousseau), and he remains
ever fresh in my memory. He was already living in a withdrawn and unsociable manner, a victim of that misanthropy which his shallow friends mocked so
cruelly.

"From the time of our marriage, I had not stopped hounding M. de
Francueil to arrange for me to see him; and this was not easy. He went there
several times without being received. Finally, one day he found him throwing
some bread out of his window at some sparrows. His sadness was so great that
he said to Dupin while watching them fly away, 'Now they're restored, do you
know what they're going to do? They're off to the highest rooftops to speak ill
of me, to say my bread is worthless.'

"Prior to my seeing Rousseau, I had just finished reading, without putting
it down, *La Nouvelle Héloïse*, and in the final pages I felt so moved that I
began to sob. M. de Francueil made fun of me gently for it. I wanted to make
fun of it myself, but that day, from morning to night, I did nothing but weep. I
could not think of Julie's death without breaking into tears. It made me ill, it
made me unsightly.

"Meanwhile, M. de Francueil, with the wit and grace he applied to all he
did, ran to look for Jean-Jacques. I do not know how he did it, but he carried
him away, he brought him, without informing me of what he was doing.

"Jean-Jacques agreed most ungraciously, without asking about me at all,
not even my age; from what I understand, he expected only to satisfy a
woman's curiosity and did not lend himself to it willingly.

"Unaware that anything was in store, I did not hurry to finish dressing. I
was with my friend, Mme. d'Esparbès de Lussan, the nicest woman in the
world and the prettiest, even though she was slightly cross-eyed and deformed.
She was teasing me about my recent fancy to study osteology and was both
laughing and shrieking terribly, because she had found, while passing me some
ribbons from a drawer, a large and ugly hand of a skeleton caught on them.

"M. de Francueil had come two or three times to see if I was ready. He had an 'air,' according to the 'marquis,' (which is what I called Mme. de Lussan, who had nicknamed me her 'dear baron'). I myself did not notice my husband's 'air' and continued my toilette, not suspecting for a moment that Rousseau was there, the sublime bear, in my salon. He had come in looking half-sheepish, half-surly, and had sat down in a corner, showing marked impatience for nothing other than dinner, so that he could be off again very quickly.

"Finally I was dressed, and I went to the salon with my eyes still red and swollen; I saw a little man, poorly dressed and somewhat scowling, who got up awkwardly while mumbling some indistinct words. I looked at him and guessed who he was; I screamed, I tried to speak, I burst into tears. Jean-Jacques, stunned by this greeting, wanted to thank me and burst into tears. Francueil, wanting to restore our tranquility with a joke, burst into tears. We could not say a thing to each other. Rousseau shook my hand and did not utter a word.

"We tried to have dinner as a way to put a stop to all the sobbing. But I could not eat anything. M. de Francueil failed to be witty, and Rousseau slipped away as soon as he got up from the table without having said a word, unhappy, perhaps, that someone had once again given the lie to his assertion that he was the most persecuted, the most hated, and the most slandered of men."

I hope my reader will not be annoyed by the inclusion of this anecdote or by the style in which it is reported. For a person brought up at Saint-Cyr, where they did not teach spelling, it is not badly done. It is true that at Saint-Cyr, instead of grammar, they learned Racine by heart and put on his best plays. I regret very much that my grandmother did not leave me more of her personal remembrances in her own writing. But they are confined to a few sheets. She spent her life writing letters—which were, I must say, almost as good as those of Mme. de Sévigné—and copying, for the sustenance of her mind, a host of passages from her favorite books.

Now I resume her story.

Nine months to the day after her marriage to M. Dupin, she gave birth to a son, who was to be her only child and who received the name of Maurice, in memory of the Maréchal de Saxe.[15] She wanted to nurse him herself, of course; it was still considered a little eccentric, but she was one of the women who had read *Émile* religiously and wanted to set a good example. Aside from that, her maternal feelings were extremely pronounced, and this was a passion that supplanted all others.

But nature did not second her desire. She had no milk, and for several days, while she insisted on nursing her baby in spite of excruciating pain, she could feed him only with her blood. She had to give it up, which was a fierce disappointment, and she took it as a somewhat sinister omen.

As chief tax collector for the duchy of Albret, M. Dupin spent, with his wife and son, part of the year at Châteauroux. They lived in the old château which today houses the prefecture's offices, and whose picturesque mass overlooks the Indre and the vast meadows it waters. M. Dupin, who had dropped the name Francueil after the death of his father, set up some cotton mills at

Châteauroux and spread a great deal of wealth around the district through his activity and largess. He was lavish and led the life of a prince. He had on his payroll a company of musicians, cooks, parasites, lackeys, horses, and dogs, liberally spending it all on pleasure and benefaction, wanting to be happy and wanting everyone to be happy with him. His was a different style from that of the financiers and industrialists today. They do not waste their fortunes on pleasure, on a love for the arts, and on the imprudent generosity of an outdated sentiment for being aristocratic. They follow the prudent ideas of their time, as my grandfather followed the easy routine of his. But let no one praise these times more than the others; men still do not know what they are doing or what they should do.

My grandfather died ten years after his marriage, leaving behind great disorder in his accounts with the state and in his personal affairs. My grandmother showed good sense by surrounding herself with wise counsellors and actively taking charge. She promptly liquidated her assets, and when she had paid all her debts to the state as well as to individuals, she found herself "ruined," that is to say with an annual income of only seventy-five thousand francs.[16]

The Revolution would soon limit her resources even more, and she did not immediately resign herself so easily to this second stroke of bad luck; but in the first instance, she conducted herself bravely, and although I cannot understand how one is not immensely rich with seventy-five thousand francs income, since everything is relative, she accepted this "impoverishment" valiantly and philosophically. In doing that, she obeyed an old principle of honor and dignity which corresponded to her beliefs, whereas she could never consider the confiscations of the Revolution as anything other than theft and pillage.

After leaving Châteauroux, she lived on the Rue du Roi-de-Sicile, in a "small apartment," in which, judging by the quantity and size of the furniture which decorates my house today, there was still enough room to turn around. She engaged, for the education of her son, a young man whom I knew when he was old and who was also my tutor. This personage, serious and comic at the same time, occupied too large a place in our family life for me not to make special mention of him.

His name was François Deschartres, and since he had worn a clerical collar in his role as teacher in the Collège du Cardinal Lemoine, he entered into my grandmother's services with the costume and title of abbé. But at the time of the Revolution, which soon came to quibble over all sorts of titles, Abbé Deschartres prudently became Citizen Deschartres. Under the Empire, he was Monsieur Deschartres, mayor of the village of Nohant; during the Restoration, he would readily have recovered his title of abbé, since he retained his love for the customs of the past. But he had never been in a religious order; besides, he could not rid himself of a nickname I had attached to his universal competence and his air of importance, since which no one has ever called him anything but "great man."

He had been a handsome lad, and still was when my grandmother engaged him—neat, clean-shaven, with bright eyes and impressive calf muscles. Indeed, he was formed exactly like a tutor should be. But I am sure that even in his best days no one could ever have looked at him without laughing, for he had the word "pedant" written all over him, in the lines of his face as well as in all the movements of his body.

To make the portrait complete, he should have been ignorant, gluttonous, and cowardly. But far from it, he was very knowledgeable, extremely moderate, and insanely brave. He had all the great virtues of the soul, joined to an unbearable disposition and a self-satisfaction which exceeded the boundaries of reason. He had the most absolute ideas, the rudest manners, the most presumptuous language. But what devotion, what zeal, what a generous soul! Poor great man, how I've pardoned your persecutions! Pardon me, in turn, in the next life, for all the mean tricks I played on you, all the detestable mischief by which I avenged myself for your suffocating despotism. You taught me very little, but there is one thing which I owe you and which has served me well—how to succeed, despite the boiling over of my natural independence, in enduring for a long time the least tolerable personalities and the most outlandish ideas.

My grandmother, in placing her son's education in Deschartres' hands, did not at all suspect that she was purchasing a tyrant, a savior, and a lifelong friend.

During his free time, Deschartres continued to take courses in physics, chemistry, medicine, and surgery. He was very attached to M. Desault, and became, under the guidance of that remarkable man, a very skillful practitioner of surgical operations. Later on, when he was in charge of my grandmother's estate and the mayor of the village, his knowledge made him very useful to the people of the region, all the more so as he practiced for the love of God, without any compensation. He was so big-hearted that there was no night too black or stormy, no heat or cold, nor time too inconvenient to keep him from running, often very far, on forsaken roads, to bring help to the thatched cottages. His devotion and unselfishness were truly wonderful. But as he was destined to be ridiculous as well as sublime in all things, he pushed the integrity of his function to the point of beating those of his patients who returned cured, bringing him money. Nor was he more reasonable when it came to presents, and I have ten times seen him push some poor devil down the stairs, hitting him over the head with the duck, the turkey, or the hare he had brought in homage to his savior. Humiliated and mistreated, these worthy folk went away with heavy hearts, saying, "He's so mean, that dear, good man!" A few of them would add, "I'd kill him, if he hadn't saved my life!" And Deschartres would shout from the top of the stairs in a stentorian voice, "What, you rabble, you ignoramus, you churl, you wretch; I did you a favor, and you want to pay me! You don't want to feel grateful! You want to be quits with me! If you don't get out of my sight fast, I'll beat you black and blue and put you in bed for a fortnight. And then you'll indeed be obliged to send someone to look for me!"

In spite of his good deeds, the poor great man was as hated as he was admired, and his temper sometimes got him into unpleasant encounters that he did not boast about. The Berrichon peasant is tolerant up to a point, after which it is a good idea to watch out.

But here I go again, advancing the chronology of my story. Please forgive me. I wanted to include at this point an anecdote not exactly rose-colored on the subject of Abbé Deschartres' anatomical studies. It will still be out of sequence by a few years, but my memories come to me somewhat haphazardly, leave me in the same way, and I am afraid I shall forget anything I leave for later.

During the Terror, although he was diligent in looking after my father and the interests of my grandmother, it would seem that his passion pushed him again and again toward hospital rooms and dissection amphitheaters. There were quite enough bloody dramas going on in those times, but his love for science prevented him from reflecting too philosophically on the heads that the guillotine dispatched to medical students. One day, however, he had a little shock that greatly disturbed his scientific observations. Several human heads had just been thrown on a laboratory table, accompanied by the comment of a student who was quite resigned to his task, "Freshly cut!" They were preparing a hideous caldron where the heads were to be boiled in order to be stripped of skin and studied later on. Deschartres took the heads one by one and was going to immerse them. "This one's the head of a curé," the student said, passing him the last of them. "It's tonsured." Deschartres looked at it and recognized one of his friends whom he had not seen for two weeks and who he did not know was in prison. He himself told me this horrible tale. "I didn't say a word; I looked at that poor head with white hair. It was calm and still beautiful; it looked like it was smiling at me. I waited for the student to turn his back before giving it a kiss on the forehead. Then, I put it in the pot with the others, and I worked on it myself. I kept it for awhile, but there came a time when it became too dangerous a relic. I buried it in a corner of the garden. This encounter was so upsetting that for a long time I couldn't concentrate on science."

Let us move on quickly to more cheerful tales!

My father took very poorly to his lessons. Deschartres would not have dared mistreat him, and although he was a fervent advocate of the old school of discipline—the strap and the rod—the extreme love my grandmother had for her son forbade him from using these efficient methods. He tried to replace the whip, which he called "that potent lever of intelligence," with zeal and tenacity. He took, along with his student, lessons in German, in music, or in any other subject which he could not himself teach him, so that he could help him study in the absence of the teachers. He even took up fencing out of devotion to his student, and helped him practice his passes between lessons with the instructor. My father, who was lazy and in languishing health at that time, awoke a little from his torpor when in the fencing room, but whenever Deschartres got involved—poor Deschartres, who had the gift of making the most interesting things boring—the child would yawn and fall asleep on his feet. "Monsieur l'Abbé," he asked him one day, in all innocence and without any malice, "will it be more fun when I'm truly fighting?"

"I don't believe so, my friend," answered Deschartres, but he was mistaken. My father very quickly acquired a love for war and even a passion for battle. Never did he feel so calm, so at ease, so sweetly roused, as in the midst of a cavalry charge.

But this future hero was first a sickly and terribly spoiled child. They brought him up literally wrapped in cotton, and as he suffered growing pains, they permitted him to become so indolent that he would ring for his servant to pick up his pencil or his pen. He changed completely, thank God, and he was one of the first to be consumed by France's fervor as she rushed to her frontiers, making his swift transformation one miracle among thousands.

When the rumblings of the Revolution began, my grandmother, like the enlightened aristocrats of her time, viewed its approach without fear. She had been fed too much Voltaire and Jean-Jacques Rousseau not to hate the abuses of the court. She was even among the most ardent opponents of the Queen's coterie, and I have found cartons full of couplets, madrigals, and stinging satires against Marie-Antoinette and her favorites. Quite proper people copied and spread this libel. The most civil verses are in my grandmother's handwriting, perhaps she even authored some of them; for it was in the best of taste to compose epigrams about the bruited scandals, and it was the philosophical opposition of the time which took this very French form. Some of the epigrams were really very daring and quite unusual. They put into popular phrases and rhymed in the argot of the marketplace unbelievable songs about the parentage of the Dauphin, about the love affairs and prodigality of "that German woman"[15]; they threatened mother and child with the whip and the pillory. But let no one think that these songs emerged from the common people. They went from the salons to the streets. I burned some that were so obscene I would not have dared read them to the end; and the ones written in the hands of abbés whom I knew in my youth, and coming from the minds of marquis of good families, left me no doubt about the profound hatred and raving indignation of the aristocracy at that period. I believe that the people could have avoided involvement, and if, in fact, they had, the family of Louis XVI would have come to the same end without gaining the status of martyrs.

At any rate, I deeply regret the attack of prudishness at age twenty which made me burn the majority of those manuscripts. Coming from a person as chaste, as saintly as my grandmother, they scalded my eyes; however, I should have reminded myself that they were historical documents and could have genuine value. Several were perhaps unique, or at least very rare. The ones I have left are well known and have been quoted in several works.

I think my grandmother must have had great admiration for Necker and, later, for Mirabeau.[16] But I lose the thread of her political ideas in the period when the Revolution became an overwhelming fact and personal disaster for her.

Among all those of her class, she was perhaps the one who least expected to be hit by this great catastrophe; and indeed, how could her conscience have warned her that she deserved, as one of her class, to undergo social punishment? She had adopted the tenets of equality as much as it was possible in her situation. She was abreast of all the advanced ideas of her time. She accepted the social contract along with Rousseau; she hated superstition along with Voltaire; she even accepted the ideas of the generous utopias; the word "republic" did not phase her at all. She was by nature loving, helpful, agreeable, and readily saw as her equal every lowly person. Could the Revolution have been accomplished without violence and without confusion, she would have followed it to the end, without regret and without fear, for she was a noble soul, and all her life she had loved and looked for justice.

But one must be more than sincere, more than just, to accept the inevitable shocks attached to an immense upheaval. One must be enthusiastic, adventurous, heroic, even fanatic about the reign of God. It is necessary that the "zeal of His house devour us,"[17] if we are to witness the horrifying details of such a crisis. Each of us is capable of consenting to an amputation to save our lives; few of us can smile during the anguish.

From my point of view, the Revolution is one of the active phases of the evangelical life—a tumultuous, bloody life, terrible at certain times, full of convulsions, delirium, and sobs. It is the violent struggle for the principle of equality preached by Jesus, and it passes, sometimes like a radiant flame, sometimes like a blazing torch, from hand to hand, up to our time—a struggle against the old pagan world which has not been destroyed, which will not be for a long time, in spite of the mission of Christ and so many other missions, in spite of so many burnings at the stake, so many scaffolds and martyrs.

The history of the human race is complicated by so many bizarre, mysterious, and unforeseen events; the ways of truth branch out into so many strange and precipitous roads; the pervasive shadows are so frequent and so thick on this eternal pilgrimage; the storm uproots so persistently the markers along the way, from the inscriptions left on sand to the pyramids; so many disasters disperse and mislead the pale travelers, it is not surprising that we have not yet had a true and definitive history, and that we move through a labyrinth of errors. The events of yesterday are as obscure for us as the epics of legendary times, and only today do serious studies permit a little light to penetrate this chaos.

What, then, is so astonishing about the giddiness which took possession of every mind at the time that France precipitated herself into that inextricable fray in '93? When reprisals were the order of the day, when each was, in fact or by intention, victim and executioner in turn, and when one did not have the time to reflect or the liberty to choose between being oppressed and oppressing others, how could passion have been cut off from action and how could impartiality have handed down tranquil edicts? Impassioned souls were judged by impassioned souls, and the human race cried out as in the times of the old Hussites, "The day has come for mourning, ardor, and wrath."

What faith would it then have taken joyfully to resign oneself, whether rightly or wrongly, to being a martyr? To be one wrongly, as a result of one of those fatal mistakes that turmoil makes inevitable, would be more difficult to accept; for faith was lacking sufficient enlightenment, and the social climate was too murky for the sun to appear to an individual conscience. However, all classes of society were enlightened by the revolutionary sun, up to the day of the meeting of the Estates General. Marie-Antoinette, the first head to fall in the Counter-Revolution of '92, was revolutionary in her own household and for her own profit at the Trianon in '88,[18] as Isabella is today on the throne of Spain, and as Victoria of England would be, if she were forced to choose between absolutism and her personal liberty. Liberty! Everyone called for it, everyone wanted it with a passion, with a fury. Kings demanded it for themselves, as well as for the people.

But then came those who demanded it for everyone, and who as a result of the collision of so many opposing passions, were not able to make it possible for anyone.

They did try. May God forgive them for the methods they were reduced to using. It is not up to us, for whom they were working, to judge them from the height of our fruitless inaction.[17]

In that bloody epoch in which each party claimed for itself the deserts of martyrdom, we must surely recognize that there were, in effect, martyrs on both sides. One group suffered for the cause of the past, the other for the cause of the future; still others, situated to the side of these two principles, suffered without understanding what they were being punished for. Had the reactionary forces of the past prevailed, they would have been persecuted by the men of the past just as they were by the men of the future.

This was the odd position in which the noble and sincere woman whose story I here unfold found herself. It had not occurred to her to emigrate; she continued to bring up her son and absorb herself in this sacred task.

She even accepted the considerable reduction which the public crisis had brought about in her resources. From the debris of what *she* had called the debris of her first fortune, she bought for approximately three hundred thousand francs the estate of Nohant, not too far from Châteauroux; her relations and habits kept her in the Berry region.

She yearned to retreat to this peaceful province, where the passions of the moment were as yet little felt, when an unforeseen event came knocking.

At that time she lived in the house of a certain M. Amonnin, a disbursement official, whose apartment, like almost all of those occupied at that period by well-off people, contained several secret hiding places. M. Amonnin proposed that she hide a rather large quantity of silver and jewels belonging to him as well as to her in the panels of the woodwork. In addition, a certain M. de Villiers hid his titles of nobility there.

But these secret hiding places, cleverly fitted into the thickness of the walls, could not elude the searches often made by the very workers who had put them in and who were the first to inform the police about them. The 5th of Frimaire, in Year Two [Nov. 26, 1793], by virtue of a decree which prohibited the secreting of such wealth taken out of circulation, a police raid was made on the home of M. Amonnin.[18] An expert carpenter sounded the panels, and as a result everything was discovered; my grandmother was arrested and incarcerated in the convent of English nuns, on Rue des Fossés-Saint-Victor, which had been converted into a jail.[19] Seals were affixed to her home, and the confiscated objects, as well as the apartment, were entrusted to Citizen Leblanc, a corporal. Young Maurice (my father) was permitted to live in his apartment, which was, as they say, under separate lock and key, and which Deschartres occupied also.

The young M. Dupin, who was then scarcely fifteen years old, was as stunned by the separation as though he had been dealt a staggering blow. He had not expected anything of the kind, he who had also been brought up on

Voltaire and J.-J. Rousseau. The gravity of the situation was kept from him, and the gallant Deschartres secreted his own worries. But the latter sensed that Mme. Dupin would be lost if he did not accomplish an undertaking that he conceived without hesitation and executed with as much luck as courage.

He knew perfectly well that the most compromising items among all of those hidden in the panels of the house had escaped notice during the first searches. These were papers, titles, and letters affirming that my grandmother had voluntarily contributed to a loan secretly collected on behalf of the Comte d'Artois, who had then emigrated and was later to return as King of France, Charles X. What motives or influences prompted this action, I do not know. Perhaps a reaction was beginning against the revolutionary ideas to which she had energetically adhered until the storming of the Bastille. Perhaps she had let herself be taken in by impassioned counsels, or by a secret feeling of pride in her royal blood. For actually, in spite of the barrier of illegitimate birth, she was the cousin of Louis XVI and his brothers, and she believed she owed alms to these princes who had, nonetheless, left her in poverty after the death of the Dauphine. I believe she had nothing else in mind, and this sum of seventy-five thousand francs, which in her situation had been a serious sacrifice, did *not* represent, for her, as it did for many others, an investment in future favors and rewards. On the contrary, from that period on, she considered the princes as a lost cause. She had neither sympathy nor esteem for the dishonest character of "Monsieur" (Louis XVIII), nor for the shameful and debauched life of the future Charles X. She talked to me about that sad family at the time of Napoléon's fall, and I remember perfectly what she said about them. But let us not move ahead of our story. I shall simply say that it never crossed her mind to take advantage of the Restoration to demand her money back from the Bourbons in order to be repaid for a service which almost sent her to the guillotine.

Whether these papers had been hidden in another opening in the wall which had not been sounded, or whether they had escaped the first investigation of the commissioners because they were mixed in with M. de Villiers' papers, Deschartres was certain they had not been mentioned in the report of proceedings, and it was important to protect them from the new investigation which would take place when the seals were removed.

That meant risking his life and liberty. Deschartres did not hesitate.

However, to make the gravity of his resolution quite understandable in parallel circumstances, it is helpful here to quote the report of proceedings related to the discovery of incriminating objects. It is a detail which has its color and which I shall transcribe faithfully in its own spelling and style:

"Revolutionary committees of the Bon Conseil and the Bondy section called to order.

"This day the 5th of Frimaire, in the Year Two, of the Republic, one and indivisible and imperishable, we Jean-François Posset and François Mary, commissioners of the revolutionary committee of the Bon Conseil section, were transported to the revolutionary committee of the Bondy section, for the purpose of requesting the members of said committee to be transported with us to the domicile of Citizen Amonnin disbursement official, dwelling at Number

12 Rue Nicolas, and there came with us Citizen Christophe and Gérôme, members of the committee of the Bondy section, and Feuilloys, *idem*, where we were transported to the aforementioned domicile, went in, went up to the third floor and entered an apartment and from there into a dressing room three steps down, in the company of Citizeness Amonnin, her husband not being there, where we challenged her to declare to us if there was not anything hidden in her house; she declared to us that she knew of nothing. And then the said Amonnin took ill and lost her senses. After that we continued our search and summoned Citizen Villiers being in the said house, dwelling at Number 21 Rue Montmartre in the Brutus section, to be witness to our searches, that he did as well as Citizen Gondois *idem* in the said house, and from there proceeded to the opening, through the talents of Citizen Tartey, dwelling at Number 90 Rue du Faubourg Saint-Martin, and in addition in the presence of Citizen Froc, porter of the said house, all present at the opening of the panel giving access to an armoire opposite the door to the right. And then we made an opening for the purpose of discovering what was in the said panel, and thence the opening having been made, still in the presence as above, made the discovery of a quantity of silver and many chests and different papers, and thence made the inventory in the presence of all the abovenamed. —*1*. a sword in sculptured steel, —*2*. a blunderbuss, —*3*. a tooled leather box containing teaspoons, sugar spoons and mustard spoons in silver-gilt, all with coats of arms, etc. . . ."

A detailed inventory follows, always indicating the pieces and jewels with coats of arms, for that, as we all know, was one of the principal grounds for complaint.

". . . . And thence Citizen Amonnin arrived and we had him summoned to remain with us to be present for the rest of the proceedings.

"And thence, had summoned the said Amonnin to declare to us the contents of a packet of papers wrapped in white linen and on which there was a seal.

"And thence, had read different letters addressed to Citizen de Villiers, employed at the national constituent assembly, which Citizen de Villiers, named as present at the proceedings in the absence of Citizen Ammonin, declared to us to belong to him as well as the correspondence which we found wrapped in white linen, and the said Citizen Amonnin declared to us not to know they were there, and not to have knowledge of them, to which Citizen de Villiers agreed. Thence challenged Citizen Amonnin to declare to us how long the said silver and jewels had been hidden, and he answered that they were there at the time of the flight of the former king for Varenne.

"Asked him if the said silver and jewels belonged to him, and he answered part belonged to him and part to Citizeness Dupin dwelling on the second floor beneath him.

"Thence had Citizeness Dupin appear for the purpose of giving us a note for the silver which was found hidden in the home of M. Amonnin, which the citizeness did promptly . . . . thence went on to the verification of the letters and their content, always in the presence of Citizen Villiers, which letters verified, found some copies of letters of nobility and coats of arms which we put under seal with a stamp of a heart crossed by a bar, and a stamp forming the watch-winding key of said commissioner, all enclosed in a sheet of white paper, for said letters to be examined by the committee of public security, in order for them to decide as shall seem fit. And thence seized, as this report of proceedings indicates, all the said silver and jewels, in order for the terms of law to decide as shall seem fit, and closed the present report of proceedings on the 6th day of Frimaire at two o'clock."

And so you see that these searches usually took place at night and without warning, for this report was begun on the 5th and ended on the 6th of Frimaire at two o'clock in the morning. The commissioners then and there declared the arrest of M. de Villiers, whose offense apparently seemed to them the most serious, and issued no orders concerning Mme. Dupin or M. Amonnin, her accomplice, except that seals were to be placed on the trunks, chests, and boxes of jewels and silver "in order, during the day, to be transported to the national Convention and left in attendance under the guard and responsibility of Citizen Leblanc, a corporal, in order to be produced by him complete and untouched at the first request, and he declared unable to sign his name."

It appears that, at first, the event did not cause much concern in the household, or perhaps they believed that the danger was past; in truth, now that the confiscation had taken place, with hope of restitution (for they took careful notes of all the objects seized, and a good part was returned intact, as indicated by notes in Deschartres' handwriting in the margin of the inventory contained in the report of proceedings), the charge of hiding valuables was not well-supported in the case of Mme. Dupin. She had entrusted or lent the seized objects to M. Amonnin, who thought it appropriate to hide them. That was her plan of defense, and at that moment they did not yet believe that things would come to the point where no defense was possible. The fact is they were imprudent enough to leave the dangerous papers I mentioned above in a piece of furniture on the second mezzanine, which we shall discuss presently.

The 13th of Frimaire, that is, seven days after the first search at the Amonnins', a second raid took place in the same house, and this time in the apartment of my grandmother, who was to be arrested. There was a new report of proceedings more laconic and less flowery than the first.

"The 13th of Frimaire, Year Two of the French Republic one and indivisible, we, the members of the surveillance committee of the Bondy section, by virtue of the law and a decree by the said committee, dated the 11th of Frimaire, stating that seals will be affixed at the home of Marie Aurore, widow Dupin, and the said citizen put under arrest. For this purpose, we were transported to her domicile, Number 12 Rue Saint-Nicolas. Went up to the second floor, the door on the left, there having made known to the aforementioned our mission, and affixed seals to the windows and doors of the said apartment, as well to the entry door which opens onto the staircase to Number 10, which seals left in the care of Charles Froc, porter of the said house, who recognized them after they were read to him.

"And thence, we went into the doorway across the hall, on the said landing occupied by Citizen Maurice François Dupin, son of the said widow Dupin, and by Citizen Deschartre, his tutor. After verifications made of the papers of said citizen, we found nothing contrary to the interest of the Republic, etc."

And so, my grandmother was arrested and Deschartres assumed the burden of saving her; for at the moment she was led away to the English convent, she had had time to tell him where those cursed papers were which she had neglected to get rid of. She had, in addition, a great many letters which proved her relationships with people who had emigrated, very innocent relationships, certainly, on her part, but relationships which could cause her to be accused of crimes against the state and treason to the Republic.

The last report of proceedings which I quoted—and God knows with what scorn and indignation the purist Deschartres must, in his soul, have reacted to documents written in such bad French!—whose every spelling error gave him gooseflesh, did not attest to the existence of a little mezzanine situated above the second floor, which adjoined my grandmother's apartment. One gained access to it by a staircase concealed in the dressing room.

Seals had been affixed to the doors and windows of this mezzanine, and it was there he had to go to get the papers. Thus, it was necessary to break three seals before entering—one on the door on the second floor, opening onto the stairway of the house; one on the door of the dressing room, giving access to the concealed staircase; and one on the door of the mezzanine at the top of the same staircase. The quarters of the citizen porter, a ferocious republican, were located directly below my grandmother's apartment, and Caporal Leblanc, an incorruptible citizen, assigned to guard the seals on the third floor, slept on a camp bed in the room beside M. Amonnin's apartment, that is, directly above the mezzanine. There he was, armed to the teeth, with orders to fire on anyone who might enter either apartment. And Citizen Froc, who, though a porter, slept lightly, had a bell placed *ad hoc* in the corporal's window; he had only to pull its cord to wake him in case of an emergency.

Thus, the undertaking was sheer madness on the part of a man who had no skill in breaking and entering, which knowledge is acquired only by dint of special study by Messrs. Burglars and Company. But devotion works miracles. Deschartres equipped himself with everything necessary and waited until everyone was asleep. It was already two in the morning before the house was silent. Then he gets up, gets dressed without a sound, fills his pockets with all the tools he has procured at risk. He removes the first seal, then the second, then the third. There he is on the mezzanine. Now he must open a cabinet of inlaid wood used to store records and go through twenty-nine cartons filled with papers, for my grandmother could not tell him precisely where the ones which compromised her were.

He does not get discouraged. There he is examining, sorting, burning. The clock strikes three. Nothing is moving—ah, but wait! light footsteps make the parquetry creak faintly on the second floor; maybe it's Nérina, the prisoner's favorite dog, who sleeps beside Deschartres' bed and could have followed him. For he has been forced, in any case, to leave the doors open behind him; the porter is the one with the keys, and Deschartres got in with the help of a pick-lock.

When one listens carefully with one's heart thumping in one's chest and one's blood ringing in one's ears, there comes a moment when one can no longer hear anything. Poor Deschartres stands immobile, petrified; for either someone is coming up the steps of the mezzanine, or he is having a nightmare. And it is not Nérina, these are human steps. Someone is approaching cautiously; Deschartres has armed himself with a pistol; he loads it, he goes straight to the door of the little staircase—but he drops his arm, which was already raised to shoulder level, for the person who is coming to join him is my father, Maurice, his beloved pupil.

The child, from whom he has tried in vain to hide his project, has surmised it, watched for it; he comes to his aid. Deschartres, terrified to see him share such dreadful danger, wants to speak, to send him back. Maurice puts his hand over his mouth. Deschartres understands that the smallest noise, one word exchanged between them, could destroy them, and anyway, the expression on the child's face proves to him that he would not give in.

Thereupon the two of them, in utter silence, go to work. The examination of the papers continues and progresses rapidly. They burn as they go. But what was that! the clock strikes four! It will take more than an hour to lock up the doors and replace the seals. Half the task is still to be done, and Citizen Leblanc never fails to rise at five o'clock.

There is no time to lose. Maurice makes his friend understand by signs that they will have to return the following night. Besides, that miserable little Nérina, whom he carefully locked in his room and who is sad to be alone, is beginning to whine and howl. They shut everything up, they leave the seals broken on the inside, and make do with replacing only the seal on the main door which opens onto the central stairway. My father holds the candle and hands his tutor the wax. Deschartres, who has taken a print of the seals, carries out the operation with the speed and dexterity of a man who has done other delicate surgical operations. They return to their apartment and go to bed, at ease on their own behalf, but not assured of the success of their undertaking, for someone could come during the day to remove the seals without warning, and everything was left in disarray in the apartment. Besides, the most incriminating pieces of evidence have yet to be found and destroyed.

Luckily that terrible day of waiting passed without a catastrophe. My father took Nérina to a friend's house, Deschartres bought a pair of cloth slippers for my father, oiled the doors of their apartment, put his tools in order, and did not try to alter the heroic resolution of his pupil. When he told me this story twenty-five years later: "I know very well," he said, "that if we were caught, Mme. Dupin would never forgive me for having let her son put himself in such danger, but did I have the right to keep a good son from risking his life to save his mother? That would have been contrary to every principle of a good education, and I was an educator above all."

The following night they had more time. The guards went to bed earlier; they could begin their work an hour earlier. The papers were found and reduced to ashes; then they gathered these harmless ashes in a box, which they carefully closed and carried away to dispose of the next day. As they had looked into all the cartons and purged them, they destroyed many jewels and signets with coats of arms; they even removed shields from the corners of beautifully bound books. When the task was finally finished, they replaced all the seals, restored the imprints to perfection; the bands of paper appeared intact; the doors were closed soundlessly, and the two accomplices, having completed a generous action with all the mystery and emotion attendant on the perpetration of a crime, retired to their apartment within the allotted time. There, they threw themselves into each other's arms and without a word mingled their tears of joy. They believed they had saved my grandmother. But they had to live a great deal longer fearing the worst, because her detention continued until after the catastrophe of 9 Thermidor,[19] and right up to that time, the revolutionary courts became more easily offended and more terrifying each day.

The 16th of Nivose, that is, about a month later, Mme. Dupin was removed from the house of detention and returned to her apartment under the guard of Citizen Philidor, a very humane commissioner, who showed himself more and more disposed in her favor. The report of proceedings, written under his direction and signed by him, attests that the seals were found intact. The citizen porter would not have looked the other way; thus, we may believe that nothing betrayed the infraction.

Let me say in passing, for I do not want to forget it, that the brave Deschartres only told me this story when pressed by my questions; furthermore, he told it rather poorly; and I never would have known all the details except through my grandmother. Moreover, I have never met a more prolix, more finicky, more pedantic narrator, or anyone so vain about his role in little things, or so enamored of the sound of his own voice than that honorable man. He never failed to repeat each evening a series of anecdotes and deeds of his life, which I knew so well that I would correct him if he missed one word. But he—like others who have no idea of the true nature of their greatness: when it came to showing the heroic side of his character, he, who became truly and comically pretentious over trivialities—was as naïve as a child, as humble as a true Christian.

My grandmother had been released from prison only to be present at the removal of the seals and the examination of her papers. Of course, they found nothing contrary to the "interest of the Republic," even though this examination lasted nine hours. It was a day of joy for her and her son because they could spend it together. Their mutual tenderness touched the commissioners very much, especially Philidor, who was, if I remember correctly, a former wigmaker, a very good patriot, and an honorable man. He developed a great friendship for my father in particular and was ceaseless in his efforts to have my grandmother brought to trial, in the hope that she would be acquitted. But his efforts were unsuccessful until the reaction set in.

The evening of 16 Nivose, he accompanied his prisoner back to the

English convent, and she remained there until 4 Fructidor [August 22, 1794]. For a while, my father was able to see his mother an instant every day, in the parlor of the convent. It was during an icy spell that he awaited this happy moment, and God knows it was cold in that cloister, where for three years of my life I strode about in every direction, for I was educated in that same convent. Sometimes he would wait for her for several hours, since especially in the beginning, the hours changed from day to day, according to the whim of the concierges, and perhaps in accordance with the desire of the revolutionary government, which feared too frequent and easy communications between those detained and their families. In another era, the thin and sickly child would have caught pneumonia. But strong emotion can transform our health and our constitution. He did not even have one cold, and he learned quickly to stop coddling himself, to stop complaining to his mother about his minor pains and annoyances, as he had been in the habit of doing. He became, all of a sudden, what he should have been all along, and the spoiled child disappeared forever. When he saw his mother arrive at the barred window, completely pale and terrified because of the time he had spent waiting to see her, ready to melt into tears when she touched his cold hands and beg him not to come again rather than expose himself to such suffering, he was ashamed of the indolence in which he had been cradled; he reproached himself for having yielded to this overly solicitous upbringing, and finally knowing firsthand what it meant to tremble and suffer for someone he loved, he denied that he had waited; he assured her he had not been cold, and by an effort of will, he succeeded in no longer feeling the cold.

His studies had been completely interrupted; there were no more teachers of music, dance, or fencing. The good Deschartres himself, who was so fond of teaching, no more had the heart to give lessons than his student had to take them. But that education was worth as much as the other, and the times which formed the heart and conscience of the man were not a waste for the child.

L.M.S.

IV

Sophie-Victoire-Antoinette Delaborde. —At the town hall with
Mother Cloquart and her daughters. —The Convent of the English
Sisters. —On adolescence. —Behind a nation's official history, there
is a more personal story. —Collection of letters under the Terror.

I shall momentarily suspend the history of my paternal lineage in order to
introduce a new individual who was, by some unlikely circumstance, placed in
the same prison at the same period as my grandmother.

I have spoken of Antoine Delaborde, "master of tennis courts" and "master
bird handler," which is to say that after having run a billiard parlor, my maternal
grandfather sold birds. If I have not said any more on his behalf, it is because I do
not know any more. My mother hardly spoke of her parents because she scarcely
knew them at all; they died when she was still a child. Who was her paternal
grandfather? She knew nothing of him, nor did I. And of her grandmother?
Likewise. This is a clear case where the genealogies of ordinary people cannot
compete with those of the rich and powerful. Both may have produced the best or
the worst of beings, but the latter have impunity; the former, ingratitude. No title,
no escutcheon, no painting preserves the memory of these obscure generations
who spend time on this earth without leaving a trace. The poor man dies in totality; scorning him, the rich man seals his tomb and walks over it, without knowing
whether it is even on human dust that his disdainful foot is treading.

My mother and aunt have spoken to me of a maternal grandmother who
raised them, a good and pious woman. I do not think they were "ruined" by the
Revolution; they had nothing to lose. But like the rest of the working class,
they did suffer from the scarcity and costliness of bread. This grandmother was
a Royalist—Lord knows why—and kept her two granddaughters in mortal fear
of the Revolution. As a matter of fact, they did not have an inkling of what it
was about. One fine morning, the older one, who was then fifteen or sixteen
and who was called Sophie-Victoire (as well as Antoinette, like the Queen),
was dressed up in white, powdered, crowned with roses, and taken to the town
hall. She herself did not know what it all meant, but the plebeian dignitaries of
the quarter, just recently returned from the Bastille and from Versailles, said to
her, "Little citizeness, you are the prettiest girl in the district; they're going to
make you a heroine; here is Citizen Collot-d'Herbois, an actor with the
Théâtre-Français, who is going to teach you a verse compliment with gestures;
here is a wreath of flowers; we shall conduct you to the town hall where you
will present these flowers and say your piece to Citizens Bailly and La

Fayette,[20] and you will have indeed earned the respect of your country."

Victoire went off gaily to perform her role in the midst of a chorus of other pretty girls, apparently all less attractive than she, for they had nothing to recite nor to present to the heroes of the day; they were only there for viewing.

Mother Cloquart (Victoire's grandmama) followed her granddaughter with Lucie, the younger sister, both happily and proudly picking their way through an immense crowd, and managed to enter the town hall and see with what grace the pearl of the district recited her piece and presented her wreath. M. de La Fayette was quite moved by it all, and accepting the wreath, gallantly and paternally placed it on Victoire's head, saying, "My dear child, these flowers suit your face more than mine." Everyone applauded and took their places at the banquet in honor of La Fayette and Bailly. Dances were forming around the tables, and the young beauties were led there; the crowd became so dense and noisy that good Mother Cloquart and little Lucie, on losing sight of their Victoire in her moment of triumph, feared they would be unable to rejoin her and would be crushed, so they went out into the square to wait for her. But the crowd pursued them there. The shouts of exultation frightened them. Mother Cloquart was not a heroine; she believed that Paris was collapsing all around her, and she and Lucie escaped in tears, exclaiming that Victoire would be smothered or massacred in this gigantic farandole.

It was toward nightfall when Victoire, escorted by a band of patriots of both sexes, rejoined them in their poor little abode. She had been so well protected and respected that her white dress was not even wrinkled.

What political event was the occasion for this celebration at the town hall? I have no idea. Neither my mother nor my aunt were ever able to tell me; they probably knew nothing more than the role they played. As far as I can presume, this was when La Fayette came to declare before the Commune that the king had decided to return to his good city of Paris.

The young Citizenesses Delaborde probably found the Revolution charming at that period. But later on, they were to see paraded in the street a beautiful head with long blond hair, mounted on a pike, which was that of the unfortunate Princesse de Lamballe. This spectacle made such a horrible impression on them that they no longer judged the Revolution except in the light of this dreadful scene.

They were then so poor that Lucie worked as a seamstress and Victoire played minor roles in a little theater. My aunt later denied this second fact, and since she was honesty personified, her denial must be taken in good faith. It is possible that she was unaware of it, because in that storm which carried them off and whirled them about like two little leaves, they lost their bearings; in that confusion of mishaps, of frightening and misunderstood emotions violent enough to have destroyed my mother's remembrance of certain periods, it is possible that the sisters were separated for some time. It is possible that, afterward, Victoire, who feared reproaches on the part of her devout grandmother, as well as the dread of prudent and hardworking Lucie, might not have dared admit to what extremes poverty or her youthful lack of foresight had reduced her. But the fact is not open to question, because Victoire, my mother, told me so, and under circumstances that I shall never forget. I shall tell it for her, but I beg the reader not to come to any conclusions before I have finished.

I do not know where it came to pass that, during the period of the Terror, my mother sang a seditious song against the Republic. The next day they came to search her place. There they found the manuscript of this song which had been given to her by a certain Abbé Borel. The song was, in fact, seditious; but she had sung only a single couplet, which was a very little bit. She was arrested on the spot with her sister Lucie (Lord knows why!), and incarcerated first in the Bourbe prison, then placed in another, and finally transferred to the English convent, where she probably was at the same period as my grandmother.

Thus, two poor young girls of the working class found themselves on a par, so to speak, with the most esteemed ladies of the court and the town. Mlle. Contat[21] was there too; and Madame Canning, Mother Superior of this English convent, became personally acquainted with her. The celebrated actress manifested a tender and exalted piety. Never did she meet Madame Canning in the cloisters without going on bended knee before her and asking for her blessing. The kindly nun, who was full of wit and savoir vivre, would console and strengthen her against the terrors of death, would take her into her cell and preach to her without fostering her dread, finding her soul beautiful and good, with nothing shocking about it. Madame Canning herself told this to my grandmother, in my presence, when during my stay at the convent, they reminisced in the parlor about their recollections of this bizarre epoch.

In the midst of such a great number of detained persons, frequently renewed by the departures (for the guillotine) of some and the arrests of new ones, there can be nothing remarkable in Marie-Aurore de Saxe and Victoire Delaborde not being acquainted with each other nor even aware of each other's presence. The fact is that their mutual memories did not date from that period. But let me indulge here in something of a novelistic sidelight. I imagine Maurice walking in the cloister, stiff with cold and stamping the soles of his shoes against the wall while awaiting the hour for embracing his mother; I imagine also Victoire wandering in the cloister and noticing this handsome child; she was already nineteen; she might have said, if someone had apprised her that he was the grandson of the Maréchal de Saxe, "He's a pretty lad; but as for the Maréchal de Saxe, I'm not acquainted with him." And I imagine further someone saying to Maurice, "Behold this poor pretty girl who has never heard of your ancestor and whose father used to sell birds in cages; she is to be your future wife...." I do not know what he might have replied, but there you have the makings of a novel.

However, let no one be taken in. It is unlikely that they ever met in the cloister; yet it is not impossible that they exchanged glances or greeted each other in passing, even if only on one occasion. The young lady would not have paid much attention to a schoolboy; the young man, so preoccupied with personal worries, would perhaps have seen her, but he would have promptly forgotten her. The fact is that neither one nor the other had any recollection of such a meeting when they actually became acquainted some years later in Italy, under other tumultuous circumstances.

At this point my mother's life becomes a complete blank for me, just as it had vanished from her own recollections. She only knew that she left prison as she had entered it, without understanding how or why. Grandmother Cloquart believed that her granddaughters were dead, not having heard anything for over a year. She was very feeble by the time she saw them again, for instead of thrusting herself right into their arms, she got frightened and took them for ghosts.

I shall take up their story again at the proper place. I now return to the account of my father, who, thanks to his letters, is seldom lost to my view.

The hurried meetings which were a consolation to both mother and son came to an abrupt end. The revolutionary government instituted a mandatory measure against the close relatives of those detained by which they were prohibited from setting foot in the Paris confines until further orders. My father went with Deschartres to live in Passy and remained there for several months.

This second separation was yet more devastating than the first. It seemed more absolute; it destroyed the little hope they had been able to salvage. My grandmother was heartbroken, but she managed to conceal from her son the anguish she felt when she gave him a parting embrace and believed it was for the last time.

As for him, he had no such gloomy forebodings, but he was despondent. This poor child had never left his mother, had never known sorrow nor expected to feel it. He was lovely as a flower, chaste and sweet as a maiden. He was sixteen, his health was still delicate, his soul exquisite. At that age, a boy brought up by a loving mother is a creature quite apart from other beings. One might say that he does not belong to any sex; his thoughts are as pure as an angel's; he has not a trace of that immature coquetry, that anxious curiosity and over-sensitivity which so often disturb the onset of womanhood. He loves his mother in a way a daughter never does and is forever incapable of doing. Immersed as he is in the happiness of being exclusively cherished and lovingly pampered, the mother becomes for him something of a goddess. It is love minus the trials and errors into which the love of another woman will lead him later on. Yes, it is ideal love, and it exists for only a short spell in a man's life. The previous moment, he was oblivious and lived in the torpor of pure instinct; the moment after, his love will be disturbed or distracted by other passions, or may come in conflict with the overpowering attraction of a mistress.

A world of new emotions will then be revealed before his dazzled eyes, but if he is capable of loving this new idol wholly and nobly, it will be because he will have already experienced the divine initiation into true love with his mother.

I find that neither poets nor novelists have availed themselves of the source of knowledge which that fleeting and unique moment in the life of man offers. It is all too true that in our present, sad world, the essential adolescent is almost unknown to us, or is someone raised in an exceptional manner. What we see daily is the unkempt schoolboy, rather ill-informed, contaminated by some crude element which has already destroyed in his being the sanctity of the first and ideal love. Or, if by some miracle the poor child has escaped that scourge of student life, you can be sure the purity of his imagination and sacred innocence of his age have not been preserved. In addition, he harbors a masked hatred for his comrades who have sought to lead him astray and for the jailors who oppress him. He is ugly even when nature has endowed him with beauty; his clothing is dirty, he has an air of shame, and does not look you straight in the face. He devours vicious books on the sly, and yet the sight of a woman frightens him. His mother's caresses make him blush. One would say that he considers himself unworthy. The most beautiful languages of the world, the greatest poems ever created are for him a boring pursuit to be despised and rejected; given the purest nourishment in a brutal way and without understanding, his taste has been warped and aspires only to the inferior. It will take him years to overcome the effects of such a detestable education, to learn his own language (while forgetting Latin, of which he knows little, and Greek, which he knows not at all) in order to develop his taste, to have a just conception of history, to lose that mark of ugliness that an embittered childhood and the degradation of slavery have imprinted on his forehead, before he can look at the world squarely and carry his head high. Only then will he love his mother; but already the passions are taking hold of him, and he will never have known that angelic love of which I just spoke and which gives the male soul pause in the shelter of an entrancing oasis between childhood and puberty.

This is not at all my definitive stance against a university education. In principle, I recognize that communal education has its advantages. In fact, however, as it is practiced today, I do not hesitate to say that anything else is better as far as education is concerned—even spoiling children at home.

Moreover, this is not the place to draw a conclusion from a specific case. An education like the one my father received would not do as an example of a type. It was both too refined and too deficient. Twice interrupted—first by a malady of listlessness, second by the traumas of the revolutionary Terror and the resulting necessity of living a precarious and chaotic existence—his education was never completed. But such as it was, it produced a man of incomparable candor, bravery, and kindness. This man's life was out of a novel of war and romance, brought to an end by an unforeseen catastrophe when he was thirty years old. His premature death left him forever young in the minds of those who knew him, and a young man endowed with heroic sentiment, whose entire life was enclosed within an equally heroic period of history, cannot help but be a figure of interest and charm. What a wonderful subject for a novel this life would be for me, if the principal characters had not been my father, mother, and grandmother! But whatever one may do, notwithstanding, in my opinion, that nothing may be of higher seriousness than certain novels I have written with love and devotion, one must not put in a novel either those whom one loves or those whom one detests. I shall have a great deal to say on this subject, and I hope to make a frank reply to a few persons who have accused me of wanting to portray them in my books. But this is not the right place, and I limit myself to saying that I would not have dared make my father's life the subject of a novel; later on you will understand why.

Besides, I do not think his existence would have been rendered more interesting with literary embellishment. Told the way it happened, it has more meaning and sums up by means of a few very simple facts the moral history of the society which was its milieu.

This preamble has no other purpose than to explain why I am going to present a series of letters which, without seeming to have any great historical dimension, nevertheless have a very real one. Everything converges in history; *everything is history*, even novels that do not seem to be related in any way to the political circumstances that bear witness to their birth. It is, therefore, true that the actual details of each human existence are like brush strokes on the larger picture of the collective life. Which of us, on finding a fragment of writing from the past, whether it be a dry procedural document or an insignificant letter, has not scrutinized it, turned it over and over, annotated it, in order possibly to gain some insight into the conduct and customs of our ancestors! Each century, each period has its style, sentiment, preference, preoccupation. The history of legislation is made out of old documents; the history of social custom is made out of old letters.

My son[22] wrote—not, of course, for publication, but for his own amusement—a burlesque novel with "scientific" commentary, rather more burlesque than scientific. In the middle of this novel, in a letter of high intrigue, one of the characters writes to another, "Oh, heavens! Do send me twenty-seven lengths of green velvet." We had a good laugh around the fireside about this green velvet, although the author assures us there is some deep significance in his character's apostrophe. So be it! But what if this were in fact a genuine letter—the only addition being that it was dated in the reign of Louis XIV—which happened to fall into our hands? We would immediately be very curious about this velvet. What did they make in those days with twenty-seven lengths of velvet? An article of clothing, furniture upholstery, a door-hanging? Was it something luxurious, or an item in common usage? How much did it cost? Where was it made? What social classes in particular would have used it? It is regrettable not to have any other details, for if we had them, we could speculate on a whole range of things: the business conditions, the lot of the workers, the luxurious habits of some, and the differences in affluence. Indeed, one could draw a scale that reached from lowest to highest on the economic ladder; one could compare the past to the present and perhaps draw some conclusions that would inform our present social problems.

History thus makes use of everything: a merchant's bill, a cookbook, a laundry list; that is how twenty-seven lengths of green velvet can inform the history of humankind. This, then, may serve as a footnote to the worthy work from which I have drawn the example.[20]

I am, therefore, going to cite word for word[23] a series of letters written by my father when he was sixteen years old, addressed to his mother, who was held in the English convent during the Terror, and I warn the reader that there is nothing dramatic or out of the ordinary in the personal circumstances these letters attest to. On the contrary, they merely verify the dismal situation of two souls racked with sorrow. But they are dated 1794, wherein lies their historic value. And as for their moral value, one can judge that after having read them.

They are a monument of innocence, of filial love, and of that angelic condition of the soul that characterizes the true adolescent.

Letters of 1794

Letter I   (no date).

Exiled! Exiled at fifteen, and for what crime? Oh, if I could have foreseen that they would take such action against relatives of detained persons, I would have had myself imprisoned with you. To be separated from you, not to see you anymore! Oh, yes, it is indeed exile! My dear mother, take courage if you can; I am no longer able; I have wept so much, I can no longer see clearly. I was as if dazed when I left Paris, I didn't know where I was going, and if not for Citizen Deschartres, who led me by the arm, I would have curled up on the ground when going out of Porte Maillot. I dare not write anything further, lest my letter not get through. What have we done to be so unhappy? I must surely have committed some great crime not to deserve to see you any more and, my God, I've done nothing! Oh, my mother, my mother, give me back my mother soon!

At this point there is a lacuna. Those first, missing letters were doubtless the most heartrending, the most impassioned. Perhaps they contained some complaints against the revolutionary government, and, fearing the consequences, my grandmother would have burned them as soon as she had read them.

Letter II   Passy, 8 Floréal, Year II of the Republic (April 1794).

We certainly must have "met"[24] when looking at the Panthéon, because I stayed quite some time at my vantage point. My dear mother, what a sad expedient this is! If I were two hundred fathoms higher, with a telescope, I could have made out the English convent.

This evening after our "meeting" (at a distance of one league!), I took a walk around the Bois de Boulogne, where I had the pleasure of being caught in a storm. Not a drop of rain nor a grain of hail missed me. Don't let that worry you, I have never felt better. I arrived at the town hall in the midst of tempestuous winds and torrential downpours, where the officials were very courteous. Just as one was saying that he believed we would be moved further away, another assured us to the contrary. They were *very* polite and said they would be *very* sorry if that happened. I would rather be sent back to Paris covered with insults than be condescended to in that way.

Goodnight, my dear and loving mother. I embrace you with all my heart. Six days have passed since I had that pleasure; how long and searing it is!

Letter III (after a second lacuna)   Passy, 19 Floréal, Year II (May 1794).

If my exile is a great distress for me, my dear mother, because it deprives me of seeing you, it may also be very useful in that it leaves me an immense void which I am forced to fill with work. In Paris I was distracted all day long. I had to run here and there, visit this one and that, and all my time was wasted. Now, isolated as I am and not knowing anyone here, I have no other alternative but to study in order not to perish from boredom during these long and solitary days. I work from the time I wake up until three o'clock, and since I'm alone and there is no noise, I can devote myself more completely and seriously than I have ever done. Citizen Deschartres comes, gives me a letter from you which I read at the same time that you are reading mine. In the afternoon, we go out, we take a walk in the Bois de Boulogne, we read, and thus the day is taken up. This evening I was at the town hall to get a good-conduct pass, and they gave me trouble in granting it because my baptismal certificate was not notarized. However, I shall have it tomorrow, and I shall be conducting myself better than ever.

Goodnight, my dear mother, Citizen Deschartres is tired, we came home late from the town hall, and he wants to retire. Pardon the brevity of my letter as due to his weariness. I embrace you very tenderly.

Letter IV   Passy, 20 Floréal.

I am writing you, dear mother, while seated by the fire. I do not know what I have done to Messrs. Éole, Borée and company for them to keep pursuing me in this place. This morning, at our "rendez-vous" on the terrace, I believe they would have taken me off to Paris if I had been a bit more transparent; and I would have been grateful to them for it, I assure you. If I am ever permitted to visit you, the thirty-two winds would be like thirty-two turtles compared to me. Oh, it has been a long time, my dear mother, since I embraced you! Work can indeed make one forget boredom and solitude, but nothing in the world can console me for not being permitted to see you. It is a gnawing worm that destroys all species of pleasure, even the sight of these charming woods whose long lanes of tender green are bathed in sunlight, or of the darker woods whose trunks are covered with moss and have fresh turf at their foot. I take walks, I quickly derive some sense of pleasure, but as soon as I come across one of the lanes where you and I walked together, my sadness descends as before. Since I need no reminding to think of you, even when I am savoring some lovely spectacle of nature, I savor it sadly.

My headache has not come back. The country air is most healthful, and I haven't heard from my migraines since I am here; I am very weary. Perhaps I will dream again, as I did last night, that I am with you. That was very sweet; but on awakening, happiness ended.

Goodbye, my dear and loving mother, I embrace you with all my soul.

Maurice.

Letter V   Passy, 23 Floréal of Year II.

.... Does the loving interest you take in everything I do give you a clue as to how I spent my morning? I reread the fables of La Fontaine, after having talked to my friend from the mount,[21] who had dozens of comical and charming anecdotes to tell me about him. Anyone who had judged him by his conduct, would have taken him for a madman. I now find that these fables I formerly skimmed so rapidly are actually filled with a beauty I hadn't suspected. What lovely, rare simplicity!

Martin has just arrived and brings me the chocolate you sent. How generous you are to have thought of it! I'm sorry that you deprived yourself for me; I could easily have done without it! I would have liked to have had it to give to you. Being far from you is painful for me. If only I knew you were happy!

. . . . I really need to receive news from you. It feels like I am forty more leagues removed from you since I no longer have a letter from you every day. I have heard that you're feeling well, but it is quite different hearing it from you. I am well aware of the reasons that prevent you from writing to me, but that does not prevent me from being worried without knowing why. In short, I need a letter to calm my nerves. I look forward to it like the thirsty traveller who seeks a spring after a long trek on the burning sands. There is no doubt that writing, that is to say, the art of giving substance and color to one's thoughts, was invented by persons such as we, who are separated by insurmountable obstacles. What a consolation it is to get a letter during such a long and painful absence! How sweet it is to be able to talk to one another, answer questions, chat together! One must have savored this consolation as I have done, and then lost it, to know how priceless it is. I hope that by the time you receive this letter, my dear mother, we will be able to exchange letters. This hardship has lasted four whole days, and I have been disoriented all that time. Before, when Citizen Deschartres was the bearer of your letters, he could not come soon enough to allay my impatience; I counted the seconds. Now I no longer look at the time, he comes when he wants, it doesn't matter to me. But I hope I will soon regain my impatience and again devote myself to counting the seconds. Do inform me, I beg you, what has happened on your side, my impatience to hear it is extraordinary. They say that as soon as the police agents have finished their work, the people's Commissions will begin to operate. I cannot wait for that to be decided, for the time I spend is quite long and quite sad. Last summer was still so happy for us that I do not recall the time when we were all living together without feeling a thrill; our daily lives were so sweet! Though these memories bring a certain element of pleasure, they bring bitterness as well, I assure you! Anyway, my dear mother, if we recapture that happy time, we will be able to sing our duet:

> And every day, we both do bless
> The happy hour that reunites us.

Goodbye, my dear mother, I embrace you with all my soul, with all my heart, with all my strength, with all the love I have for you.

Maurice.

Letter VI   24 Floréal.

I really did need, my dear mother, to receive a letter from you. This pleasure has become all the greater since I have had to do without it. I hope this will be the only set-back our correspondence suffers, or rather I hope it will soon be over and I will be able to tell you in person all that I feel for you. See how one is never content with one's lot! When I was prevented from writing to you, I aspired only to having this liberty restored; now that it is mine again, it only increases my desire to be reunited with you.

They say that all these measures were taken only until the Commissions could be made operational. I do not know how all this will come about, but justice cannot fail to triumph in the decrees passed by honest magistrates.

This morning I saw Citizen Beaumont,[22] as well as my friend from the mount. We took a long, long walk, and I do not need to tell you whom it was we talked about. If your ears were not ringing all during that time, then the old saying deceives me.

I escorted my visitors back to the barrier, and I can tell you that I find it so strange not to be able to go through as before, not even as far as the revolutionary demarcation; that was the way I used to go to the Bois de Boulogne with you, or on horseback. When I pass by these same places and when I arrive at that barrier, I can hardly keep from running to embrace you at the place where you live. . . . But I am restrained by a few small considerations: I can see the guillotine from there, and with a spyglass, I could read the newspaper someone left on one of the tables of the Café de la Terrasse des Feuillants. . . . Oh! if heaven only grants my prayer, I assure you we will soon be together, never more to part. Oh! that will be the height of happiness for me.

Goodbye, my dear mother, I hug you to my heart.

Maurice.

Letter VII   (no date).

You always date your letters at six o'clock in the morning. Such an early hour shocks me, my dear mother, for you retire very late and therefore you are not getting enough sleep. I fear that this may damage your health. . . .

This evening, while walking along reading on the road to Versailles, we heard someone calling; it was Feuilloys, of the Revolutionary Committee. He was very friendly and inquired about you. As he was in a carriage, we could not talk to him for very long.

They say that if the Commissions are not activated in a month's time, it will be up to the Committee on General Security to decide the fate of those detained, based on the rosters of the different sections. Everyone has his bit of news whether true or false. . . .

I too do much pondering on our fate, my dear mother, but my reasoning is a bit different from yours. You say that the further you advance, the more your hope fades. It is certain that all suffering comes to an end, and therefore the further we advance, the sooner we arrive at the desired end. If we miss the happy hours we have had, we must also rejoice that the unhappy ones have passed and we can look back on them as so much medicine swallowed. . . . Ah! if only the doctor would send you to Passy and thus effect two remarkable cures. Would that he really could heal the deep wounds we have suffered for the past six months! . . . This evening I took a walk along the river going toward Meudon. How lovely it was! Tree-covered hills and delightful country houses as far as the eye can see. Whichever way one looks, the view is charming; Paris on one side with its majestic buildings, and on the other, the smiling countryside. How I miss you on my walks! These pleasures really leave something to be desired when I partake of them without you.

I came back by way of Auteuil. I asked where Boileau's house was. Everyone knew it. It is supposed to be the oldest one. Nowadays the house is occupied by a character who hasn't shown it proper respect. He has had it whitewashed, he's given it a new shape, and hasn't failed to destroy the boxwood and the clipped yew trees once cared for by "Antoine."[25] Those shady walks where Boileau once composed his verse and where such geniuses of France as D'Aguesseau, Lamoignon, Racine, Molière and La Fontaine gathered have become an English garden! I did however find one lone path that has by chance been spared. It is there perhaps that Boileau would meditate by choice, it is there that he would bring to trial the failings and foibles of humankind.

If that house had belonged to me, I would have left all its old ornamentation, I would have restored only what was needed to keep it standing. The gardens would have been maintained according to the original plan, and my gardener would have been called "Antoine." This dwelling would have been wholly consecrated to the memory of the great poet.

On our return, since we always imagine that your detention cannot last much longer, we visited some housing that could suit you. There is one that has a view of all of Paris; but it has a tree like Rousseau's, which would hide from your sight all of Montagne Sainte-Geneviève, the accursed place that would revive sad memories. Oh, how I would like you to come choose for yourself! How happy I would be! I hope we are in for better times.

I embrace you with all my soul, all my affection.

Letter VIII   Passy, 27 Floréal, 8 o'clock in the evening.

I have just come in. Your Antoine is here to find out my news. He has given me a little reassurance; I was afraid that the privilege of writing to you might be withdrawn. All the news is quite sad. Sometimes one cannot see you, sometimes one cannot write to you. When will these torments be over? Goodbye, my dear mother, Antoine wants to get back; it is late, and I have not yet signed in at the town hall.

Letter IX   28 Floréal.

I have followed your advice, my dear mother, I have been to see Boileau's house again this afternoon; but since I found the gates closed, I could only see it from the outside this time. I can well believe that you would not be in favor of restoring the yews and boxwood. You prefer trees with long branches waving in the breeze to those hedges, to those clipped trees that have assumed the iron stiffness of the tool that trims them. But it was not my intention to restore them in the "romanesque" manner. It was a case of my being mentally transported to the time when Boileau lived, just as in the theater we are shown Greeks and Romans with their costumes, their buildings, their furnishings. Thus, lest nothing be omitted, you might have seen me strolling in my garden in a full-bottom wig and sleeve ties.... But now I must leave "my" garden at Auteuil and return to the present. From what I hear, the Commissions have not been named, although the Convention had decreed that they would be in operation by the 15th of Floréal.... Here it is the 28th, and there is no doubt that they do not yet exist in any of the prisons. When I learned that a tribunal would be named to judge the cases of the ones detained, I looked upon this as your deliverance, knowing as I do the fairness of the people's representatives and the justice of your case. But we are again frustrated in our hopes from this quarter. However, some people say it will be the Committee on General Security who will hand down the decisions.

Goodnight, my dear mother, I embrace you as I used to do at this same hour, when we were together. How I miss those times! How happy they were for us! Here we are scattered like leaves in the wind and have no idea why!

Letter X   29 Floréal.

It is three weeks ago today since I saw you and have been here at this "pleasure" spot, far from you, far from hearth and home, from my friends; I am as weary physically as spiritually. A very long walk is the cause of my physical fatigue; but it will take more than one good night to rest my spirit. I would need to be with you and everything else would be as nothing. You compare me to a rose, my dear mother, I assure you that for six months now I have darkened in my ideas as well as my complexion. Another slight gradation, and I'll be the equal of Othello. For that, I must approach the fair Apollo. As for the color of my thoughts, in my situation I no longer see the world through rose-colored spectacles.... I do not think the hail, snow, and thunderstorms that fall on Nohant need bother us very much; as for the income from that property, it does not belong to us for the moment. How happy we are to be in the hospital! We needn't worry at all about keeping up our possessions! And how trivial is such worry compared to the privation I am now experiencing! I say:

Of all the earthly goods of mine you've seized,
Great gods! she's the only one I ask for back.

That is my refrain. Let them give me back my mother, I ask for nothing more.

Goodbye, always goodbye! When will we be able to say hello as often?

Maurice.

Letter XI   Passy, 1 Prairial, Year II [May 20, 1794].

At last we can base our hopes on something tangible! If you read the newspapers, you know how the Commissions will decide. There will be three categories, one of which will be referred to the Revolutionary Tribunal. Those that the Commissions judge to have been detained on less serious grounds will be referred to the Committee on General Security. Some will be condemned to exile or to detention until peace is restored, but no one will be released on the spot. Which hardly matters; once you are sent to the Committee on General Security, you are sure to be free! This good news has made my day quite different from previous ones. I dined at M. de Vézelay's, and later I was at M. de Serennes' place. There was a young man there, a pupil of Krumpholz, who played the harp to perfection. That did me a world of good, for it has been a long time since I've listened to any music. You are right, that certainly lifts the spirits, and especially being able to abandon myself to the sweet hope of seeing you again, of embracing you, of being with you. I jump for joy when I think of it. How sweet it will be after this long, cruel absence! Once I have you back again, nothing will upset me, I'll long for nothing more, all my wishes will be satisfied.

Goodnight, my dear mother, I am going to sleep on these joyful thoughts; every night I dream that you have been set free, that we are together; yesterday, in my sleep, I believed we were all reunited. It was in your former home; Victor, all our friends were there; we had all been allowed to go back to our homes. Joy reigned supreme, everything was fine, until an irksome demon woke me up. Goodnight again, my dear mother, I press you quite tenderly in my arms.

Letter XII   2 Prairial.

I write you, my dear mother, from my corner by the fire; I came home icy, frozen, chilled to the bone. My friend from the mount came to see me. We wanted to do him the honors of our dew-laden meadows, but the north wind cooled our enthusiasm. It felt like January. You cannot imagine how bored I am at not being able to see you; when I compare my sad and monotonous life to the even more dismal one you lead, I am reproachful of the air I breathe; everything is spoiled for me. What used to give me pleasure is now only a subject of regret. The other day when I listened to the overture from *Oedipe à Colone*, I cannot tell you the pain it gave me, having heard it so often with you. To think it was only last summer that together we savored the sweetness of freedom! I could embrace you morning and evening, I lived by your side. Oh! I was too happy, I was oblivious to my good fortune. All these memories drag me down. I envy the children I see playing by the roadside. Free from worry, they have no notion of exile, of arrest, of the pain of separation; they do not tremble for their loved ones; dark thoughts do not interrupt their sleep....

I have dined as the guest of Citizen Vézelay Senior. Both he and his wife showered me with friendship. He is the most courteous man imaginable. As for his son, I believe him to be very shallow. He doesn't live at Passy with his father, but at Neuilly. That is not the way you and I will arrange our lives, is it!

Goodnight, my dear mother. I embrace you a thousand times with all the tenderness of my love!

Maurice.

Letter XIII   3 Prairial.

I always see you in my dreams, my dear mother, and did again last night! You never leave my thoughts, even when I'm asleep. If sleep is the image of death, and if being dead I could always see you in my dreams, I would very quickly lay me down to the long sleep in order to revel in that happiness. . . .

Besides, I live as much as I can with the departed, for I read without a stop, I have spent my whole day with them; the bad weather has kept me in. You ask me to devote time to my violin. I have only had it since this morning. I promise you faithfully, since it is your wish, that I will keep at it; and when you can hear me again, you will find me advanced. We are always in the future, I am conceiving a strong aversion to it! That goes for the present, too; I pursue the past: "I was" and "I have been" lead me back to hurtful memories. "I used to be" with you! We have to change all that.

The following letter and fragments are not dated, but all of them are from the Prairial period of Year II (May-June 1794).

Letters XIV, XV, and XVI   (undated fragments).

How grateful I am, my dear mother, for the chain and the lock of hair that you sent me! How precious they are to me! I will always keep them with me! When I felt your hair, I believed for a moment that I was with you! I recalled the dressing table in Paris, the times when I was happy! And today I will have your portrait! From now on it will be worn around my neck and never removed. I will talk to it, it will never be out of my sight. But it will not console me for no longer seeing the original!. . .

Therefore, I am going to try to approach you, with the aid of my telescope. Everyone here does likewise. Every exile is equipped with a spyglass, so as to be able to look out on Paris. . . . Perhaps this too will be prohibited!

My God! when will our troubles be over? Goodbye, my dear mother. I haven't words strong enough to express my love for you. . . .

You are suspended from my neck, my dear mother. You are reposing both in and above my heart. . . . This evening I had a rather amusing experience. Citizen Deschartres and I were near the window, playing the overture from *Oedipus*; when we were finished, we heard applause behind us.[23] On turning around, we saw a man dressed in the old style, who asked us not to take him for a spy and to please allow him to remain and listen. Since he looked well bred, after exchanging a few remarks, we asked him to come in. He accepted eagerly. We played several pieces for him. Finally, he picked up a violin, and there we were, going through the opera scores, making wonderful music, for he was an excellent musician, a very good violinist, and that really did my ears good. I had needed to hear some good music; in spite of his good heart and good intentions, Citizen Deschartres cannot manage to play in tune. To further assure us that he was not a spy, our newfound friend told us his name was Gaviniès, composer of the music for several comic operas that were performed at the Italiens. He was first violinist at the Opéra for a long time. It turned out he had had a special acquaintance with my father—whom he always referred to as Franceuil—and that he had played a lot of music with him at the time *Devin*[24] and such works were popular. And so you see, he knew me very well without ever having seen me. Finally, after playing quite a while, he took his leave, saying that if he weren't living in Paris, it would be his pleasure often to help me with the violin. As for my instrument, he recognized it and even remembered its number, which he told me before he checked it. This was the most extraordinarily pleasant experience!

That encouraged me to work even harder. I love music with a passion, and although I do not have a master to study under, I can become a musician, for this evening I found myself playing some second violin parts that I had never seen, and I was going through them without hesitation, with technique and feeling. It would give me so much pleasure to become proficient! How I would work if you were here to enjoy my progress! Ah! I see it all so clearly, I didn't realize my good fortune, I didn't appreciate it enough.

Nérina[25] is here by my side with her little pup whom I love so much. If he becomes tired while we are out walking, we put him in a handkerchief. His head sticks out of one corner; he acts like he is being borne on a litter, or else he becomes a ball and falls asleep. It was thus he made the trip from Paris. He is so wonderful and affectionate. He has all of his mother's mannerisms and jumps over our hands they way she does; he is a superb animal. He does not have a name, and I would like for you to give him one; that would make him even more dear to me. Please find one for him. Take suggestions from every quarter—the Office of Inquiry, for example—and entertain various counsels. "From the clash of contrary opinions, the spark of truth is born."

> You hardly thought you'd hear
> The words of Young in this affair.[26]

In short, I await your supreme decision.

Goodbye, my dear mother. I am the arch babbler ... I have let myself run on. ... My God, it seemed like I was with you. Ah, my dear mother, I embrace you a thousand times with all my soul!

Maurice.

Letter XVII   ... Floréal.

We are negotiating to move up to the fifth floor; for just four francs more per month, we will have a magnificent view. Our ground floor quarters are unbearably damp. Citizen Deschartres' room is so unhealthy that he sleeps in mine; for a bed, he puts his mattress on some chairs; every evening he plays the part of M. d'Asnières. ... And since we are going to be located so high up, I plan to borrow a spyglass from M. de Vezelay and make my observations of Montagne Sainte-Geneviève. If only I can make out the English convent! At least I will get close to it. I was hoping to surprise you, my dear mother, with my sketch of Meudon and its environs before you had suggested it to me. I am now hurrying to complete it. At least you will have an idea of the view I boast about so much. ... As for my height, it is coming along. I am now as tall as

Citizen Deschartres. Oh, how I need to see you again! It seems almost a year since I saw you!

Goodbye, my dear mother, I embrace you as tenderly as I love you.

Letter XVIII   . . . Floréal.

You fear that the chain is not long enough to be doubled. You are right, but I loop it twice around my neck in such a way that it crosses and does not annoy me. I get so much pleasure from having your portrait! I appreciate this fine present so much that I cannot find words to thank you for it. Every evening I go to work on the landscape for you. How difficult an entire scene from nature is! But I hope to succeed, I am devoting all my time to it. However, please do not set your expectations too high; I am doing my best, and you will at least have a reasonably accurate idea of the view we enjoy every evening when we walk along the banks of the river. Looking at this drawing at the time I take my walk, you will be able to say that we both see the same scenery at the same time. You must admit that we manage to exhaust every means of getting closer in our imagination. What a sad apprenticeship we engage in! How right you are! Destiny has not parted mothers and sons who are indifferent to one another and would willingly have gone their separate ways, such as Mme. de W——— and ———. And it makes a point of keeping those apart who cannot live without each other! Our misfortunes have succeeded one another for a year without interruption. There is a proverb which says quite truly that rain falls on him who is already wet. . . . We hear the thunder rumbling overhead, never a serene sky. A view always hidden by dark clouds. . . . My God, what weather! And such seas that no one has ever crossed! Providence is leading us to the devil. Oh, how sweet will be the calm after such a storm! I can find that calm only by being with you. Let us hope it will come. . . .

Yes! The name you want to give to Nérina's little one—by all means, Tristan—it made me think of that prince who was born into misfortune, that son of Saint-Louis, who came into the world in Palestine when his father was imprisoned and was thus named Tristan.

This poor little animal is charming. This evening, while I was sketching, he slipped under my portfolio. He was annoying me, so Citizen Deschartres called to him, but he paid no attention and kept coming closer to me and showing his affection. When I go in one direction and Deschartres in the other, it is I whom he follows. He does not leave my side. He is spotted all over in brown and white. He has a square head with long ears, which gives him a very dignified look. I can tell you that I am very fond of him and that he keeps me from being bored on my long walks.

M. de La Madelaine came to see me this morning, by chance. He was not aware that I was here. M. Deschartres met him near our door, which gave me the greatest pleasure. When one has no circle, it is delightful to meet people one used to know. He is so hard up that he told us he was writing vaudeville plays in order to have enough to live on. Where would he be if he were some witless fool? Since he often comes to the Bois de Boulogne, he promised to come see us. Exile makes one cognizant of pleasures previously unappreciated! The sages, however, tell us that we must learn how to be sufficient unto ourselves. That would seem very easy for me if I were with you, but without you I need extraordinary strength of character!

Letter XIX   Passy, 1 Prairial (May 1794).

Citizen Deschartres did not go to Paris yesterday; you probably were worried, not having received news from me. And I, for the same reason, was deprived of your news. Furthermore, my day was wearisome, unlucky, the worst ever. I hope that you weren't worried! Well perhaps I will receive two letters today, for you will have done as I did since I didn't want to forego the pleasure of chatting with you. I still have magnificent plans for observations. If I move to the fifth floor, M. Vézelay has promised to lend me a telescope of his, the one with which you can read the time on the clock tower at seven leagues distance. Imagine how easily I'll locate the mountain! Not a single house will escape my observation, including the English convent; can you perceive my joy?

Letter XX   3 Prairial.

You were very likely worried and thought I was ill. That very morning when you failed to receive my news, we had lunch with Philidor and Lefèvre. They were on their way to Versailles, and they didn't want to pass by here without giving us the "fraternal kiss." We spoke to them of our idea to tell the Commission that you were a farmer. They strongly approved and told us that we should speak about it to the Revolutionary Committee now in session. Philidor took responsibility for the petition, as he feared it might go astray if we addressed it to the committee as a whole. They both have the highest regard for you; if it were up to them, you'd be free in no time. They are speaking to everyone on your behalf. What has made them so well disposed toward you are the favorable comments everyone in the section has made about you. Less than a month ago they were again at the information office to see someone they thought might give your case his blessing. We made it quite clear to them that you were not of the nobility. They found laughable the chain of circumstances which kept me confined here; so much so that, if ever a judgment is made, you will undoubtedly be set free. You should certainly be at peace on that score.

Goodbye, my dear mother. Let us hope that our troubles soon come to an end; I feel yours much more than my own. I embrace you as I love you.

Letter XXI   7 Prairial.

Your description of the refectory gave me a good idea of the fare they serve you. The schedule, especially, is nothing if not convenient! My greatest regret is that I cannot be there to share your troubles. I assure you that, had I known I would be exiled and that all means of working in your behalf would be denied me, I would have requested your Revolutionary Committee to have you transferred to Saint-Lazare or another location where I could have been imprisoned with you. I would have been the happiest man in the world, and that would have made your long detention more bearable; but I thought that by being free, I would be able to help you; I did not foresee that they would keep me from doing so! The place where I live seems sadder and sadder. Admittedly, without you I would find paradise as wearisome as what they call being under "house arrest." Since I am poorly housed—and it is quite noisy too, surrounded as I am by stone masons who risk knocking senseless the people who come and go—I am going to change my "apartment," which is the name with which I enhance my room. . . . "In the good old days," when I awakened, my clothes were brushed, my breakfast ready. My bed was made promptly and my room swept. It seemed so natural to be served that I didn't even notice it. . . . All that has been completely changed, and yet that is hardly what bothers me. It is quite all right to learn how to serve oneself; but when I make comparisons, I start remembering, and when I remember, I see myself near you, where I can embrace you from the morning on, every morning! Ah, it is now clear to me that I was too happy!

Goodbye, my dear mother. I beg of you not to let sorrow defeat you. I embrace you and press myself to your heart for a long time.

Maurice.

Letter XXII

8 Prairial.

Well, it seems quite impossible to enjoy a moment of tranquility! Our letters could give us a bit of consolation, were it not that this means of communication is under constant threat! For more than six months now that we have been separated, I have led this uncertain life, always hoping and always frustrated, sometimes a bit more at ease for a day, and then, as if in expiation of that moment of peace, upset for a month! They say one must fortify oneself with strength. It is sound enough advice but hard to carry out. I am so worried about your kidney ailment. As if your soul isn't burdened enough without your being beset with physical problems! I hope we get some good weather, so you will be able to take some exercise. As for me, whether it rains or shines is all the same. I am just as weary when the barometer is steady as when it forecasts a storm. Yesterday, I stayed in all day with my books, which are a great resource. Tell me whether you can take baths and if our correspondence will be able to continue. That does indeed worry me! But don't let it lower your spirit, take good care of yourself for my sake.

I embrace you the way I will when we see each other again. May this happen very soon!

Letter XXIII

9 Prairial.

I loathe this bad weather! It keeps you from taking the exercise you must have. All day long it hardly left me enough time to go to the town hall, and since everyone else chose the same interval, there were over a hundred persons gathered to sign in. Those who were not in a hurry crowded the entrance; but in spite of my patient nature, I wormed my way through and entered. There were many people gathered around the table who were all busy setting their spectacles on their noses and taking them off again. This was indeed a rather time-consuming ritual, but finally my turn came. —My neighbor from Rue Bondy has been summoned. I just received the news. He should be coming to see me, and that will give me much pleasure, for I have not seen him since the day I left Paris. Ah! I will remember that sad day as long as I live. I said "adieu" to you and in turn took leave of everything that is dear to me. As I walked off, I felt completely crushed. My legs were shaking. Each acquaintance I met was a source of renewed distress. Twenty times I was on the verge of turning back from the barrier to see you again. I was saying to myself that I still had the chance and that, in several more moments, I would regret not having done so. Had I been alone, I assure you I would have returned. . . . But what is the use recalling these sad moments? Let us rather hope for happy days and may this hope give us the courage to put up with our misfortune!

Goodbye, my dear mother; I embrace you a thousand times.

Maurice.

Letter XXIV   (no date).

Finally the dawn of a happier day is about to break. The Commissions are now in session. Citizen Deschartres has sent you his findings. He made me jump for joy when he told me they had released eighty persons from La Force in one day. I do not yet know the names of those they set free. He will find out more and give you news about it; it is important for us to know.

Saint-Lambert says, "To hope is to be joyful." I do not quite share his opinion and could sooner say, as in the ludicrous sonnet from *Le Misanthrope*: "To be ever hopeful means ever to despair." Not really! The thought of soon being reunited with you is a very sweet one. Only it cannot be compared to how I will feel when I have you back. I beg you not to become discouraged, not to look at the dark side. Have faith that there is a Providence which sometimes punishes the wicked and rewards the good. The justice of your case gives me reason to hope for the best, and hope, they say, is the order of the day. For my part, my dear mother, I am getting down to work in earnest. I want to leave Passy quite different from when I came. We find ourselves in circumstances where we must rise above material fortunes. One is happy just to be able to say, like Bias, "*Omnia mecum . . . ,*" which is what the rest of "us learned folks" translate as, "I carry with me all I have." Now one must abandon the old trodden paths and clear a new road for oneself. I want to become someone, do something important, be worthy of my grandfather. When I am alone this ambition comes over me. In company, I had never thought about it. Boileau was right in saying to reserved people:

Tell me, don't you ever feel those powerful desires
Which a divine buoyancy of spirit inspires?

I don't know whether I told you that Couthon was here to visit a doctor who promises to restore the use of his legs. He is living next door to M. de

Serennes. Goodnight, my dear mother, I embrace you with all my heart, and I hope that soon it will no longer need to be by letter, for I am quite weary of that means. The wind carries it away, and I have nothing left.

Letter XXV   10 Prairial.

You see, my dear mother, that everything is coming along rather well at the moment. Your case is now before the Revolutionary Committee. They have indeed realized that, should they not rescind your prison custody, they would find themselves in a self-contradiction, since your warrant charged you unjustly, and in all their allegations they said that you had conceded to the demands of Citizen Amonnin. They have had one meeting with the Commission, and will be talking to them again. It appears that they will pass judgment on those detained and that they will set them free without warning. This will be done in closed session. The detainees will not be present. Thus you see that we will be spared the earlier formalities. They will look at the sectional rosters in particular and make their decisions accordingly. It is a bit like a secret tribunal that sentences or absolves the accused without a hearing. But after all, nothing could be more in your favor than that procedure. The roster from your section is tantamount to a certificate of good citizenship, the way it reads. And so, my dear mother, we may be permitted to wear our rose-colored spectacles. What joy to be together again, to take up our former pursuits! To really savor happiness, one must have been deprived of it. Do tell me whether my unsealed letter has reached you. I'm going to write to our good old friend Marolles to tell him how happy I am that he obtained his papers. Goodbye, my dearest mother; I beg you, share my hopes! Oh, how lovely it will be to trade good and veritable kisses for the paper ones I give you every day!

Maurice.

Letter XXVI   Passy, 14 Prairial, Year II (June 1794).

I am extremely tired; I walked quite some distance this evening, my dear mother. At last the weather has become bearable, and I hope you are taking advantage of it to stride about the gardens of the English convent. I assure you I would prefer that to all my fine walks in the country. I would regard it as the pinnacle of happiness to be confined with you. I sometimes build castles in Spain; I dream of a prison house where we would be with all our friends. This would be delightful, and my liberty would be of little concern to me. I have such a great need to see you! It is so long that we've been separated! Perhaps it won't be much longer. My friend has sent you word that they took testimony on your behalf and in how satisfactory a manner all those who knew you were eager to reply. Is there anyone who wouldn't find you lovable! You are like Zaïre: "To know you is to love you." I am quite plagued by that tooth that is giving you pain and that acts up when you drink hot or cold liquids. Mine has gotten better by itself and no longer causes me the least discomfort. If it should flare up again, I would have it extracted and replaced, for by this method you end up with better teeth than you had before, a clear profit.

Goodbye, my dear mother; do not write me any more after you have dined. I know how tiring it is for you, and I fear you may become flushed and suffer a headache. You see, I am meddling and scolding you!

Letter XXVII   15 Prairial.

We are looking forward to attending the Festival of the Supreme Being,[27] albeit at a distance, and this is how we shall do it: Citizen Vézelay has a window that looks out toward the Champ de Mars. He will have his telescope set up there, as well as his pretty little nine-foot spyglasses. We should make it our business to be there. And I assure you we won't forget to focus on the Panthéon and its environs. I will very likely be able to see the clock at the Saint-Étienne church, which is but ten steps from the English convent. Oh, heavens! if you could be standing on an elevated vantage point, I would see you! And if you had a spyglass, we would see each other, just as if we were talking face to face! . . . but I still would not be satisfied. I would like to really be able to talk to you, and then afterward I would want to embrace you, and then never leave you. There you have the *nec plus ultra* of my dreams. To live with you and never leave you! My eternal refrain! Our friend Marolles wrote me a charming letter. The province of Berry is for him too the promised land.

Letter XXVIII   23 Prairial.

Exile is going to make an artist out of me. I have done a drawing for my friend from the mount, and he liked it. I shall continue. Nature is all around me, and it is the best model. Also, I am reading through Pleyel's quartets almost effortlessly, which gave me great pleasure yesterday, for I was going into things I had never seen before. You see, my dear mother, I do not wait for others to boast about my achievements, but I don't have to observe the niceties with you.

Again I am about to move, for the third time in two months. In your case, alas, you are spared that bother.

Couthon has asked for news regarding us at the town hall. They gave him a satisfactory report. He is of the opinion that we will not only be restricted to the parish, but that we may not even be allowed to go to the Bois de Boulogne. And so a decree may well be issued to the effect that every exile will not be permitted to move away from the village in which he is detained. I can assure you that would be all the same to me! When one is in a constant state of misery, a bit more or less makes no difference.

Here there is another lacuna. Their hopes for freedom were not realized, and new restrictions, probably regulations for the internal policing of the prisons, affected the correspondence of those detained.

Letter XXIX   Passy, 9 Messidor (June 1794).

Finally, my dear mother, I can write you more than three lines. I could hardly accommodate myself to such brevity. Three lines are very soon used up, and since I have no other pleasure than chatting with you, my pleasure was sharply curtailed.

Well, the hot weather is beginning again. How are you getting along in your little garden room, you who do not like the heat? How wearying you must find it! It is indeed difficult to be punished when one is innocent and everyone knows it! Socrates said to his friends who grieved over seeing him die an innocent man: "Would you have preferred that I die guilty?" And as for us, we can surely say, as on the day after the Battle of Pavia: "We have lost all save honor."

If this heat continues, I am going to throw myself into the river. That is where I finish my days. What long days they are! I can't stand the Bois de Boulogne, I'm fed up with all the walking, while *you* are not even permitted to take a walk!

Letter XXX   10 Messidor (July 1794).

Here we are having such fine weather, and yet I am exceedingly sad. Everything wearies me without you. Ah, how charming these dull walks would become if we were together! When, then, will I be reunited with you? I won't leave you for more than a day, for more than an hour! Oh, I'm obsessed with concerns! My only remedy is work. I stayed in until seven this evening. Your drawing is progressing. This will be my little token of welcome. I find it incredibly difficut; but everything I do for you is transformed into pleasure. Goodbye, my dear mother. Please do take care of yourself. I embrace you with all my soul.

Maurice.

Letter XXXI   Passy, 11 Messidor, Year II (July 1794).

My friend did not get to Paris today, my dear mother, which means that I have received no news from you and that I am a hair more depressed than usual. However, I am working hard. I'm up to my neck in dead writers. I am living with the greatest minds the centuries have produced. I am particularly excited reading of the great achievements of your father. I'm going to get maps of his battles; I want to study them, become familiar with them. Perhaps one day you will see my own battle maps. I regret that circumstances do not permit me to study them at the very places where they were waged. That would well be worth all the hay in Nohant! My ambition is to do big things, and in saying this, my dear mother, I am a bit like "M. de l'Empyrée."[28] The fact is that I love what is grand, what is beautiful; men are distinguished on the soil of freedom by their talent and their courage. Our revolution

...has avenged humble virtue against arrogant wealth

And the worthy footman, who bears the litter of the worthless.[29]

In the past, a man's talent was stifled by plotting and intrigues. Nowadays the most brilliant career is open solely on basis of merit. There are no longer pompous titles spawned by pride. There is one greater one, that of citizen. One must try to be worthy of it in every respect; this is what I aim for and to which I wish to apply myself.

Goodbye, my dear mother; I am so impatient to receive news from you. I embrace you a thousand times with all my soul.[26]

Letter XXXII   12 Messidor.

Yesterday a bit of news was confirmed that could be quite good, namely that the Revolutionary Committee will have the power to grant exiles one-day passes to Paris to take care of their affairs, but not to stay overnight. I could diminish the distance between us, which would be a little consolation. But it may be only a rumor!

I did a lot of swimming yesterday, and I am a bit tired. Just as we were diving in, a brisk wind developed, causing high waves that had to be dodged to avoid getting water up our noses—which is very unpleasant—and finding ourselves rather more under than above the water. I exercised all my ingenuity in this perilous situation and came out successful. Do not for a moment think, however, that I was running any risk; I am only boasting, that is all. I am totally discouraged, as usual. If I were with you, everything would seem delightful to me, but considering the position we both find ourselves in, by what means are we to combat sadness? I embrace you with all my soul, oh my dear mother!

Maurice.

Letter XXXIII   14 Messidor (July 1794).

I must explain, my dear mother, why my arms were so strained after I went swimming. It is not at all that my arms have become weaker, nor that I swam for too long; but you surely recall that I did very little swimming last year, and I am a bit out of practice. I will soon get back in shape. I plan to go again this afternoon, and I will give you a report tomorrow. My friend Citizen Deschartres always dives in as well, and I am trying to teach him to swim on his back; but he is quite thick-skulled and doesn't listen to what I tell him.

My little dog wants to swim too, and he is so plump that all he can do is roll. I would be sorry to upset him, I love him so much. In order to get him accustomed to the water and give him confidence, I did not let him get knocked over at the beginning; I carried him in my arms and put him back on the ground without getting him wet. Yet, although the water hadn't touched him, he thought he was wet and ran, shaking himself, to dry off in my clothing. Now he joins me for a swim, despite my cautions; for I do not think he is strong enough yet to brave it, and I have to lift him up whenever he begins to sink. Now, my dear mother, I have finished with my dog stories.

Goodbye, I embrace you with all the tenderness of my love.

Letter XXXIV   13 Messidor.

Several days ago, my dear mother, I was reading the history of my grandfather, written by Baron d'Espagnac, former governor of the Invalides; but having no map on hand, I could get only a rough idea of his campaigns. It so happens that the maps which just appeared are by the same D'Espagnac and were made at the same time as the two volumes that I have, but they had not been published. Thus I do have a complete work. The battles are described as if one were there. The smallest unit, the smallest cannon battery can be identified. But we are spared the rain of bullets, the cannon balls and clouds of smoke that must have caused the battlefield observer some anxious moments. It was, however, in the middle of such a battle din that your father, at the time only a colonel, stationed himself in order to make his assessment. He would calmly seek out the most dangerous posts to gain intelligence. You realize that within the confines of my room I unfortunately cannot get a complete overview, but I avail myself of what I can.

What a hot spell we're having, quite nice in fact, but it tires you and I almost condemn it. Oh, if only we were together! (my constant refrain), I would be at the height of happiness.

Goodbye, my beloved mother, I hold you in my arms with all the tenderness of my love.

Dupin.[27]

Letter XXXV

15 Messidor.

Nérina is neither dead nor missing; rest assured, she is livelier, more insane than ever. Yesterday, she stayed in Paris, where my friend takes her every day, but she returned this morning; and every evening she goes out running with her pup. You have no idea how brutal she is to him. Poor Tristan is overturned and jostled, and he seems to find it all very much fun. But Nérina has so little judgment that I worry about him. The other day, we were on the banks of the Seine along a steep embankment; she didn't realize that in making him roll over she would send him into the river, and if I hadn't leaped promptly and blocked his roll to the river with my body, the poor little animal would have sunk into the mire, for that side of the river is very polluted.

Today it is quite hot enough to go swimming. I hope that by the time I get into the water we do not have another squall like the one we had the other day, and that I can plough through the tranquil waters at my leisure. —The military encampment is here in our district. We will go to see it one of these days; they say it is superb.

Goodbye, my dear mother, keep well. I embrace you with all the tenderness of my love.

Maurice Dupin.

Letter XXXVI

16 Messidor.

My solitary days go on and on, and weigh me down. My friend is off to Paris every day, which takes up almost the whole day; I am left completely to myself, and if I did not work with ardor, I would go mad. I cannot tell you that

I suffer boredom, because I keep busy; but what I do say is that I suffer weariness, which means that I miss you, that I do not see you, and that I cannot get used to it.

However, it is not through any lack of things to do that I am saddened, for yesterday I worked from eight in the morning until seven in the evening without interruption, except for lunch and dinner. I am reviewing in depth your father's battles, and I have returned to the one at Malplaquet, which is the first, to work through it and learn it by heart. I now know the number of batteries, how many cannon in each, what factor was decisive in winning the battle, the location of the cavalry, the infantry, the encampment, the village, the farm, the forest, the river, the gap opened up by the cannon, and the number of men fallen, etc. Thus I feel much better here in my own quarters than outside, where reflection depresses me. My God, if we were together, how your presence would give me encouragement to get on with my work! So when will this moment come?

Goodbye, I embrace you as I love you.

Dupin.

Letter XXXVII   The 17th.

I found your letter of yesterday rather short, my dear mother, and perhaps someone will have found mine too long. Is this yet another pleasure that we will have to forego? The further we advance, the longer our misery seems to stretch, the more our unhappiness increases. Oh, how hard it is, when one is innocent, to be treated as guilty!

If the Austrian, English, Spanish, and all the other nations that wage war with us could be eliminated, we would have peace and, consequently, liberty. We are already beginning to put them in their place. And what am I doing here? What is the point of my being exiled? The study of war that I pursue in this little room does nothing to advance our cause. Let us have hope, however!

I embrace you with all my strength.

Dupin.

Letter XXXVIII   18 Messidor.

Nérina will join my friend today, and you will have her tomorrow. But I advise you to keep an eye on her, for she doesn't stay still. Two days ago, my friend left her in Paris so that she could become accustomed to it; but she missed not seeing us, and she turned up here again, alone, at eight o'clock yesterday morning. The first thing she did was to go look for her pup. After she had fondled him, she came and said hello to us.

These days, because of the extremely hot weather, I still live down below and am in no hurry to move out. When it gets a bit more temperate, I'll soar up to the fifth floor; perhaps I will feel better there, since I'll be able to look out on the mountain where you live. Oh, God, my dear mother, what a difficult and long separation this is! Just think, it has been three months since I saw you!

Never has anything like this happened to me, and I would never have believed it could have happened to me! I let it bother me as little as possible. Yesterday again I worked from eight in the morning until seven in the evening; I do not take my walk until late, and I find that when I have racked my brains over my books all day long, at least I can derive some pleasure from being out in the fresh air. Right now, I'm at the seige of Belgrade. During the last attack, we thoroughly defeated the Turkish cavalry and infantry, for the Turks had wanted to blockade us in our lines of encirclement and entrenchment. I think they'll give up their position.

Goodbye, my dear mother. I play the role of hero in my imagination. I embrace you a thousand times with all my heart.

Maurice Dupin.

Letter XXXIX   The 20th.

I found the letter you wrote yesterday quite short, my dear mother, and I hope that today's will be longer. Your letter influences my whole day; yesterday's was bitterly sad for me. I lose half my courage when, at the usual time, I fail to see the lengthy letter I was counting on. If that were to happen again today, my day would be completely dismal. We are at a low in our misfortunes. Ordinarily sorrow comes as punishment for some fault. What then can ours be? Nevertheless, I consider a guilty person who is free as far more to be pitied than an innocent one in chains. A clear conscience is an invaluable asset, something that I possess and that I assure you will never leave me. It will give me strength in my unhappiness ... but will never make our separation more bearable. Moral lessons and maxims are to no avail; I cannot rationalize it.... Your letter just arrived, but only three lines! What on earth is going on? I am overwhelmed with sorrow and all I see every day is that it becomes worse! Oh, I would forget all my troubles if I were near you, if I could at least see you! But none of that is possible!

Letter XL   22 Messidor.

Even as I write, I fear that my letters are no longer reaching you. The weather is quite hot, but I am oblivious to it. I am so discouraged that I am in a stupor.

Goodbye, my dear mother, I embrace you with the tenderness of my love.

The following letter is from my grandmother; it is, unfortunately, the only one of hers that remains from this correspondence. It is very likely dated 22 Messidor.

For My Son,

I have just heard that they arrested everyone at Villiers yesterday and that tonight they will go to Neuilly. Alas! Passy is quite close to Neuilly! Do not let yourself be arrested; watch out and avoid being taken. I understand that no one is left in Villiers, that they took away everyone over nine years of age. My son, preserve your freedom, if you want to save my life. It is a pretext for arresting all the nobles, a sort of round-up that they have been planning. Get out of Passy, so that your friend can save you! I am frightfully upset. My God, suppose you were to be arrested tonight! I shudder, I tremble at the thought of it! How painful is my existence!

Adieu, adieu, your poor mother presses you to her heart.

The reply is from Deschartres, who apparently thought he should not leave my father that day to visit the English convent.

23 Messidor.

I realize, my friend, that you are giving in to despair. Whatever may be the causes of your distress, we commiserate with you in the most feelingful way. Like you, we deplore the misfortune that overwhelms us. But must you banish all hope from your heart? That misfortune would be the most terrible for us. Do try, my friend, to keep up your courage. The cause of your dejection undoubtedly comes from the fear you are experiencing about the safety of our young friend. I can, however, give you complete reassurance. In our parish, they made inquiries of the kind that the circumstances would seem to mandate with regard to the exiles, and they had no reproaches to make them. We are perfectly at ease, of that you may be sure. I have it from our friend from the mount,[28] who has gathered some definite information. Furthermore, I will not hide the fact that I would like to obtain an enlistment for our young friend. If I do not succeed in this, our efforts will not have been in vain, since we will have obtained the necessary affidavits from our committee. If I am successful, and if our friend is engaged at once, I shall shoulder his burden, and he will pursue his normal work. We will not be separated from each other. I believe it is unnecessary to reiterate my devotion, as nothing is more sacred to me. I would be amply compensated, if I could believe you would find in it a small source of consolation.

You may well sense the tears I shed in spite of myself. They are a tribute which unhappiness wrests from friendship; but let us not despair, my friend, of seeing our tears dry up one day, no matter how distant it may seem.

There is yet another lacuna which ends 9 Thermidor,[30] a day that will live in our memories forever. The note that follows is in a small, squeezed handwriting on a tiny square of paper. Doubtless, Deschartres made a desperate attempt to get it through to the English convent.

Letter XLI Passy, 9 Thermidor.

I went swimming yesterday. The weather was marvelous. Today it is raining, the sky is all clouded over, just like my spirits. Being far away from you makes it impossible for me to live tranquilly. For me there is no longer any happiness!

Maurice.

Letter XLII   10 Thermidor, Year II (July 1794).

You have certainly read yesterday's decree which orders the release of all those not included under the law of suspect persons. We obtained a copy of that law. You are in no way included, especially as your Revolutionary Committee has rightly vouched for your patriotism. Thus, if ever we should have hope, it is right now. Yes, my dear mother, we will be reunited, of this I can have no doubt. A great many people have already been released. The painter, Robert, was set free. They say that it was David who, out of jealousy, had him incarcerated. How horrible! We owe our salvation to the Convention. Without it, they say, all patriots might have become victims of Robespierre's tyranny.[29]

It is today that disposition will be made of patriots from our section who have been detained. Ah, there is nothing else that interests me! My friend will be there, and you can have no doubt that, as soon as they pronounce your name, he will rise to claim you. We have nothing more to fear. My God, how much pleasure you gave me in sending a lock of your hair! I hope that I shall soon see you in your entirety. Goodbye, my dear mother, courage is all we need. I embrace you with all the tenderness of my love.

                                                                        D.

P.S. I have your letter. Do keep calm. We are like devils in a holy water font, and we must do whatever we must.

Letter XLIII   (No date).

Do have a bit of patience. There is nothing in the decree issued yesterday that should upset you. They will do justice to oppressed innocence. The facts of your case are with the Committee on General Security. My friend went there again this morning with the Commission. Tallien has said that if they were considering establishing another government like Robespierre's, he would sooner die. In one more moment you will be free. Goodbye, my dear mother, I can't tell you anything further. Antoine is leaving. I embrace you.

Letter XLIV   16 Thermidor.

Keep calm, my dear mother, your freedom is a certainty. The Revolutionary Committee has lodged a petition on behalf of four or five patriots with the Committee on General Secruity, and your name is one of them. The facts of your case are in the hands of the Commission, the very one which reviews the cases and grants freedom. The truth is that at any moment you may be set free without our knowing it. That could happen tomorrow, today, or this evening! Oh, how I gasp for joy at the thought of it! All our troubles of the past are now over!

I have excluded several notes filled with details on the activities of Deschartres and his friends in the section. They reveal a succession of hope, fear, impatience, and dejection.

you may be set free without our knowing it. That could happen tomorrow, today, or this evening! Oh, how I gasp for joy at the thought of it! All our troubles of the past are now over!

I have excluded several notes filled with details on the activities of Deschartres and his friends in the section. They reveal a succession of hope, fear, impatience, and dejection.

Letter XLV   Passy, 22 Thermidor (August 1794).

You are quite right, my dear mother, all the innocent persons were set free, and your turn is coming up. It is almost impossible that you should remain more than several days on that wretched mountain where you've been languishing for eight months. We are going to be reunited, of that there can no longer be any doubt. I am already waiting for you at the barrier. What a moment it will be when I see you again! I am like a madman, I can't sit still for an instant. My God, how happy we're going to be!

Letter XLVI   The 24th.

They are now working on your case. Just a bit more patience, that is what I really need. My friend is away in Paris constantly. My God, if you could only be free on your birthday! When I think of my happiness, it seems like a dream!

Letter XLVII   28 Thermidor.

This day, which was formerly such a happy one for me, when I could hold you in my arms and wish you happy birthday, today I find quite sad, as I am such a distance from you! But I no longer want to look back. I am sending you my drawing, my dear mother. Not one pencil stroke did I make without thinking of you. Oh, when will you come and compare it with the actual scene from nature? How much fun I shall have in taking you on my regular walks along the banks of the Seine! How beautiful that whole scene will become for me again! Well, your birthday arrives under the most felicitous auspices, for we will soon have no more tears to shed. I embrace you with all my soul.

Maurice.

A.E.L.

V

After the Terror. —The end of prison and exile. —Deschartres' ill-fated idea. —Nohant. —The bourgeois terrorists. —The moral state of the privileged classes. —A musical passion. —Paris during the Directoire.

And finally, on the 4th day of Fructidor (August 1794), Mme. Dupin was reunited with her son. The terrible drama of the Revolution receded a moment from view. Entirely absorbed by the happiness of finding each other again, the tender mother and excellent child, forgetting all they had suffered, all they had lost, all they had seen, all that might yet occur, looked on this day as the most beautiful of their lives.

In her haste to go and embrace her son in Passy, Mme. Dupin, not yet in possession of the certificates which would allow her to cross the Parisian barrier and afraid of being spotted at Porte Maillot, dressed up as a peasant woman and duly proceeded to board a boat going toward Quai des Invalides, in order to cross the Seine and arrive at Passy on foot. It was a prodigious trip for her to take, considering she had never walked in her life. Whether due to idleness or to an organic weakness in her legs, she had never reached the far end of the garden without being exhausted; nevertheless, she was shapely, pert, in excellent health, and of a fresh and calm beauty that had all the earmarks of strength.

She walked on without giving it a thought and at such a speed that Deschartres, whose costume matched hers, could hardly keep up. But at the boat passage, an unforeseen circumstance threatened to bring more misfortune on them. The boat was filled with working-class people who noticed the whiteness of my grandmother's hands and complexion. A brave volunteer of the Republic made mention of it out loud. "There," said he, "is a nice looking little mother who hasn't done much work in her life." Deschartres, quick to take offense and not easily silenced, answered him with a "What business is it of yours?" which was not well received. At the same time, one of the women on board placed her hands on a blue package which protruded from Deschartres' pocket, raising it high in the air, "Look at this!" she said. "They're aristocrats on the run. If they were the likes of us, they wouldn't be burning wax." And another woman knavishly continued the inventory of the poor pedagogue's pockets, snatching a roller of Cologne water, which brought down a storm of alarming abuse on the two fugitives.

Good old Deschartres, who, despite his gruffness, was full of delicate attentiveness—too delicate, under the circumstances—thought he had worked miracles by acquiring for my grandmother, without her being aware of it, all those little civilized refinements that she could never have found in Passy or could never have procured for herself without arousing the neighbors' suspicions.

He cursed his ingenuity, seeing that it was threatening to become dangerous to the object of his good intentions; but unable to bide his time, he stood up in the middle of the boat, shouting at the top of his voice, brandishing his fists, and threatened to throw anyone into the sea who might venture to insult "his crony." The men only laughed at his bravado, but the boatman said in a dogmatic tone of voice, "We'll clear this matter up at the landing." The women shouted "bravo" and continued vigorously to threaten the disguised aristocrats.

The revolutionary government had already openly relaxed its recently rigid system, but the people had not yet renounced their rights and were quite ready to take justice into their own hands.

It was then that my grandmother, taken with one of those inspirations of the heart which are so powerful in women, went and sat down between two real cronies who were insulting her roundly and took their hands into hers. "Aristocrat or not," said she to them, "I am a mother who has not seen her son for six months, who believed she would never see him again, and who is going to embrace him at the risk of her life. Do you wish to destroy me? Well then, denounce me, kill me, if you wish, on the return trip, but do not prevent me from seeing my son today; I put my fate in your hands."

"There, there, Citizeness," these decent women immediately responded, "we don't wish you any harm. You're right to trust us, we also have children and we love them."

They landed. The boatman and the other crew members, who couldn't stand Deschartres' attitude, tried to make difficulties to keep him from going any farther, but the women had taken my grandmother under their wing. "None of that," they said to the men. "Respect for the female sex! Don't upset this Citizeness. As for her valet (that was how they described poor Deschartres), let him go with her. He makes a big fuss, but he's as harmless as you are."

Mme. Dupin embraced those good cronies with tears in her eyes, Deschartres decided to laugh off his adventure, and they arrived without further ado at the little house in Passy where Maurice, who was not expecting them yet, nearly died with joy at embracing his mother. I no longer recall the day the decree against exiles was revoked, but it was almost immediately thereafter; my grandmother's status was regularized; I still have her certificates of residence and good citizenship, the latter principally due to her servants—footman Antoine in the lead—having behaved, as everyone around testified, with bravery during the storming of the Bastille. These were great lessons in pride for the "aforementioned."[31]

But my grandmother, without entirely admitting the social consequences of her philosophical convictions, nurtured no prejudices that would make her blush to owe her civic reintegration to the good conduct of her servant. She left for Nohant at the beginning of Year III, with her son, Deschartres, Antoine, and Mlle. Roumier, a good old soul who had raised my father and who always ate "with the masters." Nérina and Tristan were certainly not left behind.

The other day, while I was writing the story of Nérina into this collection of memories, my son Maurice found buried in the attic of our house the nameplate from the collar of that interesting little animal, bearing this inscription, "My name is Nérina, I belong to Madame Dupin, at Nohant, near La Châtre." We greeted this object as a sacred relic. In '96, I discovered in my father's letters Nérina's line of descendants, consisting of Tristan, poor child of the Terror and companion in exile, and then Spinette and Belle, his younger sisters. Nérina had ended her days in her mistress' lap. She was buried in our garden under a rose bush: "Incaved," as our old gardener said, who in his pure Berrichon way, would never have applied the verb "interred" to any creature who was not a "baptized Christian."

Nérina died young due to an agitated existence, but Tristan enjoyed extraordinary longevity. By an odd coincidence, his tender and melancholy character matched his name, and as active and anxious as his mother had been, he was calm and collected. My grandmother preferred him to all of Nérina's progeny, and one can imagine that after having gone through such mighty crises, one can become attached to every being, even to the animals with whom one went through them. Tristan was therefore particularly cherished and lived through almost all the rest of my father's life, for he was alive in the days of my first childhood, and I remember having played with him, although he did not play willingly and habitually wore the face of a dog who is absorbed in the contemplation of the past.

I am no longer sure of the dates of the story I am relating; but I see that on 1 Brumaire, Year III (October 1794), my grandmother received from the administrators of the district of La Châtre a letter with the following epigraph: *Unity, Indivisibility of the Republic, Liberty, Equality, Fraternity or Death.* (The Republic was morally dead, but its slogans were maintained.):

> To Citizeness Dupin,
>   We are sending you a copy of the contract of sale that Péaron has consented to give you last August 3rd (old calendar), and the official account of the requests he has made of you, etc.
>
>   Salutations and brotherhood.
>   (Followed by three signatures of important bourgeois.)

How delighted they were—those good bourgeois, those great emancipated children of only a day ago—to use the familiar form with the modest owner of the château of Nohant, and to call an ex-lord just plain Péaron, he whom they had formerly called M. le Comte de Serennes! My grandmother smiled at all that and did not feel offended in the least. But she noticed that the peasants did not use the familiar form with these gentlemen, and she was grateful to her carpenter for using, with utter ingenuousness, the familiar form with her. She saw it as a friendly preference, which she enjoyed a little maliciously.

One day, when she was with her son in the small house of this carpenter—at that time tax collector for his parish, a hardy and intelligent republican who was all his life our devoted friend and whose last breath I witnessed—two bourgeois from La Châtre passed in front of the door, highly intoxicated, and thought it just the thing to insult a woman and child, threaten them with the guillotine, and take on the airs of small-time Robespierres, the very ones who, with their entire caste, had just spiritually killed Robespierre and the Revolution. My father, who was only sixteen years old, threw himself on them, seized one of their horses by the bridle, challenging them to dismount and fight with him. Godard, the carpenter-tax collector, came to his aid, armed with a great caliper with which he wished, said he, to measure these men. The men did not respond to the challenge and spurred their horses. They were drunk, that was their only excuse. Today[30] they are ardent conservatives and Royalists—but they are old, which absolves them.

Moreover, there was a motive behind their anger. One of them, named by the district administrator of revenues of Nohant during the enforcement of the law on suspects, had deemed it proper to help himself generously to those revenues and to present false accounts to the Republic as well as to my grandmother. She took him to court and exacted restitution. But the trial lasted two years; she received during all that time only the revenue from Nohant, which then did not even amount to four thousand francs. Having to pay back monies borrowed in '93 to defray the so-called "voluntary" required loans and patriotic gifts, my grandmother saw herself reduced to extreme poverty. For more than a year, we lived only on the income from the garden, which brought to market twelve or fifteen francs worth of vegetables each week. Little by little her debt was liquidated and her position improved, but from the time of the Revolution, her income never again went up to fifteen thousand francs.

Thanks to an admirable sense of order and acceptance of the modest habits she had to espouse, she was able to face everything, and I often heard her say, smiling, that she had never been so rich as since she was poor.

I shall say a few words about this land of Nohant where I was raised, where I spent almost all my life, and where I would wish to be allowed to die.

The income from it is not considerable; the residence is simple and commodious. The countryside is devoid of beauty, though situated at the center of the Vallée Noire, a vast and admirable site. But it is precisely this central location in the most level and least elevated part of the country, in a wide vein of wheat land, that deprives us of the varied terrain and extended views one enjoys on the heights and slopes. We do, nevertheless, have great blue horizons and some variation of terrain nearby. Compared to Beauce or Brie, we have a magnificent view, but compared to the ravishing little details we find when we go down to the hidden river-bed a quarter of a league from our door, and to the smiling vistas we behold when climbing the hills which look down on us, this is a bare and limited landscape.

Be that as it may, it pleases us and we like it. My grandmother liked it as well, and my father went there to seek sweet hours of repose from the agitations of life. The furrows of dark, rich land, the great round walnut trees, the little shady paths, the untidy thickets, the cemetery full of grass, the small tile-covered belfry, the porch of rough wood, the great dilapidated elms, the small peasant houses surrounded by pretty enclaves, with vine arbors and green hemp fields—all become pleasant to contemplate and dear to one's thoughts when one has lived so long in this restful, humble, and silent milieu.

The château, if it can be called that (for it is only a mediocre abode of the time of Louis XVI), touches the hamlet and is situated beside the rustic square, with no more ostentation than a village dwelling. The hearths of the parish, two or three hundred in all, are quite dispersed throughout the countryside, but there are about twenty of them grouped around the house, door to door one might say, and you must live at peace with the peasant, who is well off, independent, and who enters your home as he would his own. We always benefited from this, and although well-to-do proprietors generally complain about the proximity of day laborers, there is less to complain about the children, hens, and goats of these neighbors than there is to praise their obliging ways and their good character.

The people of Nohant, all peasants, all small home owners (I take the option of speaking of them and saying good about them, since I make the claim, by no means universal, that the peasant can be both good neighbor and good friend), all possess a waggish humor hidden beneath a serious air. They have high principles, a trace of piety free of fanaticism, a genuine decency in their behavior and their manners, a slow but steady way of going about things, a sense of orderliness and extreme cleanliness, natural wit, and they are frank. With one or two exceptions, I have had only agreeable exchanges with these good people. I have, however, never paid court to them, nor have I demeaned them with what are called "gratuities." I have rendered them services and they have acquitted themselves with me according to their abilities, totally willingly and in the measure of their goodness and intelligence. Consequently, they owe me nothing; for some small service, a good word, some small proof of true devotion is worth as much as we can ever do. They neither flatter nor do they grovel, and each day I have seen them take on more well-placed pride, more well-intentioned boldness, without ever abusing the confidence placed in them. Nor are they ever vulgar. They have more tact, reserve, and politeness than I have ever seen among those who have the reputation of being well bred.

That was also the opinion my grandmother held. She lived among them twenty-eight years and never regretted it. Deschartres, with his irritable nature and prickly pride, did not have as easy a time, and I always remember him declaiming against the wiles, the roguery, and the stupidity of the peasant. My grandmother repaired his blunders, and he, with the zeal and humanity which abided in the depths of his heart, was pardoned for the ridiculous pretentiousness and unjust outbursts of his temperament.

I shall come back often to the subject of the "country folk," as they refer to themselves, for since the Revolution, the epithet "peasant" has become injurious, a synonym for the uncouth and ill-bred.

My grandmother spent several years at Nohant, busy helping Deschartres to educate my father and putting in order her economic situation. As for her moral state, it is nicely summed up in a page of her writing I have come upon which refers to this period. I do not guarantee that these are her very own words. She had the habit of copying extracts from her readings. Be that as it may, the thoughts that follow give a very good picture of the moral state of an entire stratum of society after the Terror.

"We are right to contest the rigorous judgment of Europe, which, when seeing all the horrors that have been visited on France, allows itself to attribute them to the particular nature and innate perversity of a numerous portion of a great people. May God preserve the other nations from ever being subjected to the experience of the furors to which all men of all countries are subject when they are no longer held back by any bond, when the wheel of society has received such a violent shock that no one knows where he is any more, no longer witnesses the same things, and can no longer hold to his old beliefs! Everything will perhaps change if the government becomes better, if it settles down, and if it stops playing on the weaknesses of men. Alas! let us seek out hope, since our memories destroy us. Let us chase the future since the present is without consolation. And you who must guide the judgment of posterity, you who often fix it forever, writers of history, suspend your recitals so that you may soften its impressions by the heralding of a rebirth and a repentance. At least do not conclude your picture without noting the first glimmer of dawn in the darkness of this terrible night. Speak of the courage of the French, speak of their gallantry, and cast, if you can, a veil over the actions which have soiled their glory and tarnished the brilliance of their triumphs!

"The French are all experiencing the fatigue of misfortune. They have been broken or bent by the events of a supernatural force, and after having experienced the rigors of a heavy oppression, they can no longer formulate any of the wishes which belong to a different situation. Their yearnings are curbed, their desires are restrained, and they are content if they can believe in the suspension of their anxieties. A terrible tyranny has prepared them to count safety among the goods of life.

"The public spirit has weakened and will languish for a long time, the inevitable result of an unheard-of catastrophe and a persecution without precedent. They have lived so much with their troubles that they have lost the habit of associating themselves with the common good. Personal dangers, when they go beyond a certain limit, upset all other rapports, and the loss of hope almost changes our very natures. One must have a little happiness to allow oneself to love the community. There must be a little overflowing of the self to be able give something of oneself to others. . . ."

Whoever the author of this fragment may be, it is not without its own beauty, and my grandmother was quite capable of having written it. It was, at any rate, the expression of her thoughts, even if she had only taken the trouble to copy it. There is also some truth in this picture of an era and a relative justice in the complaints of those who suffered for no apparent reason. At least there is a sort of grandeur in their reproaching the revolutionary government for the loss of their souls rather than their material existences.

But there is also a clear contradiction, as one always finds in judgments which have a personal motive. It says the French were great because of their courage and their victory, which supposes a great emphasis given to patriotism: then almost immediately the author presents a picture of the despondency and selfishness which take hold of these very Frenchmen who have become insensitive to the pain of others because they have suffered too much themselves. The answer is they were no longer the same Frenchmen. The fortunate ones of yesterday, those who had long disposed of the happiness of others, had to expend great efforts to accustom themselves to a precarious fate. The best of them, my grandmother for example, trembled at having nothing left to give and at seeing the suffering which they could no longer alleviate. Having had their function as benefactors taken away, they were profoundly saddened, and the benefits accruing to the renewed society were not yet noticeable, even less so because this renewal was aborted at birth; the bourgeoisie was already taking power, and at the time my grandmother was judging society, she was witnessing without realizing it the death throes of the rights and hopes of the people.

As for the Frenchmen in the army, they were necessarily the friends of all who had remained in France. They were the defenders of everyone—people, bourgeoisie, and patriotic nobility. Heroic martyrs of freedom, they had an incontestable and glorious mission for all times and from all points of view—that of safeguarding the national territory. Doubtless the sacred fire had not been lost over this land of France which could produce such armies in the blink of an eye.

In contrast with the eloquent lamentation I have just reported, I shall cite new fragments from the correspondence of my father, where the period reveals itself such as it was on the surface, just after the severe regime of the Convention. This picture contradicts the sad predictions of the previous fragment. We now see the frivolousness, intoxication, insouciant boldness of youth avid to seize again the pleasures from which it had for so long been deprived; the nobility returning to Paris half-dead, half-ruined, but preferring the austere life of the châteaux to the spectacle of the bourgeoisie triumphant; luxury exploited by the newly powerful as a means of reaction; the people itself losing its head and giving its hand to the return of the past.

Moreover, France at that moment presented the strange spectacle of a society which wishes to leave anarchy behind and does not yet know whether it will make use of the past or bank on the future to regain the forms which guaranteed order and individual safety. Public spirit was gone. It only lived in the military. The Royalist reaction, as cruel and bloody as the excesses of Jacobinism, began to subside. The Vendée[32] had breathed its last in the Berry region, during the Palluau affair (May '96). A Royalist chief by the name of Dupin, who was not related to us as far as I know, had organized this last attempt. My father would have been old enough then to have gotten involved in it, if he had wished to, and he would not have lacked the bravery for a desperate last effort. But my father was not a Royalist and never had been. Whatever the future would bring (and at this time, despite the victories of Bonaparte in Italy, no one could foresee the return of despotism), this youth condemned and renounced the past without reservation or regret. He and his mother, innocent of any secret participation or sympathy with the furors of the parties and their special vengeances, allowed themselves to be lulled by the ever restless flow of the latest popular tremors. They took note of events, she, judging them with philosophic impartiality; he, yearning for the independence of the homeland and the magnanimous reign foretold in the theories of eighteenth-century writers. Soon he would go and seek the last breath of this democratic life in the army, and as his mother was sometimes frightened by the aspirations which he harbored, she sought to distract him from them with the sweet pleasures of art and the lure of permissible distractions.

Some words now about the personality of my father before making him speak as he did in '96. Since 1794, he had studied a great deal with Deschartres, but he had not become strong in classical studies. He was by nature an artist and had only the lessons of his mother to profit from. Music, living languages, oratory, drawing, literature held passionate attractions for him. He did not really take to mathematics or Greek, and hardly to Latin. Music always won out over the rest. His violin was the companion of his life. In addition, he had a magnificent voice and sang wonderfully. He was all feeling, impulse, courage, trust—loving all that was beautiful and throwing himself into it without a thought for the outcome or the reason. Much more a republican than his mother—by instinct, if not by principle—he personified the chivalrous phase of the Empire's early battles. But in '96 he was still just an artist, and here is a letter which recalls the musical delirium so often and so well described by Hoffmann:[33]

24 July 1796.

I am in Argenton, my dear mother. I let one writing day go by without writing to you, for the purposes of sleep. Imagine that the day of my arrival I found all the musicians of Châteauroux at M. de Scévole's home. The Prior of Chantôme, who is quite a good cellist and an amiable man, was also there; after supper, eight of us went off to a pavilion at the end of the garden, where we played the symphonies of Pleyel until three o'clock in the morning. The orchestra was complete: a good cello, good wind instruments, good music; it was charming. The next day we went visiting to Mme. Ligondais. At six o'clock the concert began with a symphony which I led at the first violin, with an open score and without a single mistake, because M. Thibault, the virtuoso of these parts, had not yet arrived. He did finally come, and I gave him his place with great pleasure, for it was getting difficult and could have compromised my reputation. Then I played a quartet by Pleyel; I never played so well in my life. At each transition, I was interrupted by loud applause. My triumph was complete. I was standing before fifty persons, with such audacity, such impudence! trembling no more that a bass fiddler. Once the concert was over, all the musicians had supper at M. de Scévole's house. During dessert, enlivened by the excellent champagne, the fat prior brought his cello to the table and made us swear on it not to leave each other until the next morning. We removed our jackets and ran to the pavilion. We were as if possessed! And there we made music until daybreak. The prior took turns at the cello with a fellow from Châteauroux, M. de Scévole at the viola with one of his neighbors, but I never left my place all night long. I sightread like a demon, nothing could stop me. I was a little drunk; I was flying into clouds of notes without missing a single one. We quit at five o'clock and had a little meal; there was noise, there was laughter! . . . I slept until noon and I feel marvelous. Farewell, my dear mother; they're calling me to start all over again. I love you and I embrace you with all my heart.

Maurice.

Autumn of the same year, my grandmother sent her dear Maurice to Paris, either for the distraction of a long stay, or for other reasons that were more serious, which their letters seem to imply, but which I know nothing about. No matter, we will now deal with the physiognomy of Paris during the Directoire.[34]

Before arriving there, let us take a glance at the route. Today we go from Nohant to Paris in ten hours; at that time it took eight to ten days. The coaches from Châteauroux to Orléans were awful rattletraps, so badly cared for that it was more efficient to make the voyage on horseback in short stages. The road from Issoudun to Vierzon was the most direct; my father and Deschartres took it; but it consisted only of ravines, precipices, unfordable streams, "all manner of quagmire," so that in one of his letters (for I will only cite a few), Maurice begged his mother to send him back his horses by the longest route, which was a little more negotiable. From Orléans to Paris, it was only possible to find carriages twice a week, and what carriages! "At least," my father said, "one can walk on that road! *It only takes eighteen hours to go from Orléans to Paris!*" (He was wrong, it took him twenty-four.)

But let him tell it:

Here I am finally in Orléans, my dear mother, and I realize that it has been a long time since I've seen you. Deschartes has gone ahead to get us some seats, and I am remaining here to talk to you. I am hardly tired. Between La Ferté-Saint-Chaumont and La Ferté-Lowendal, we almost returned to you. The route is bordered with windmills, and when my mare first spotted them in the distance, she reared and turned right around toward Berry. I was tempted to let her do it. Deschartres persisted with his steed, which was mimicking the stupidities of mine. He thought of blindfolding them, but that was far worse; and we had to set off through the fields. Here at least we're beginning to see some humanity. Outside the town, I came across a Royalist dandy in a gig! I hope we'll soon see more of the same. I admire Orléans, I admire the bridge, I admire the houses, I admire the passersby! I'm in a daze. What will it be like in Paris? . . .

Paris.

We spent the night in Orléans, Deschartres not having been able to find seats in the coach. I told you, my dear mother, that I admired the bridge, the passersby; it was quite something else when I entered Rue Royale; it was ecstasy! Feeling more like myself, I went to see young Orsanne, and we were delighted to meet again. He took me for a walk on the mall, by the port, on the bridge, then to the theater. They were doing *Les Amours de Bayard* and *La Fausse Magie*. Never was drama performed, I do believe, in a more comical manner. La Palisse was played by Gascon, Bayard by a big buffoon who put on his hat with both hands, Sotomajor was gilded and decked out like an old marionnette. I held my sides, and in the most tragic parts, I burst out laughing, to the great shock of my neighbors, who found the performance superb. Finally we arrived here in twenty-four hours, safe and sound, I was ninth out of the cab, drawn by three trotting horses. They are wild animals of the first order. The coachman, wilder even than they, thought it fun, going down the mountain at Étampes, to let them run. The carriage pursued them and would have been as fast without them. We weren't rolling along, we were hurtling. Some of the passengers were swearing, others wanted to get out. An elegant lady in a blond wig vowed she would die of fear. I personally enjoyed riding in this fashion, and I yelled, "Use your whip, coachman!" —"But, Sir, do keep quiet! We'll all be killed." —"No, gentlemen, we'll simply arrive with more verve. It's the only way to travel."

And the carriage cleaved the air, everyone holding on to his neighbor for dear life. And I enlisted the carriageful of people to contribute toward a tip for the coachman when we arrived. Finally the impetuous course relented, and we stopped not far from an inn where everyone, during supper, recovered from his fright.

You won't believe the joyous manner in which I made my entrance into Paris. Immediately, I ran to Mme. de Jassaud's place. The pleasure of seeing each other after such a long time was mutual. From there, I went to the Café de la Régence to find M. Hékel; I entered running and singing, but all I saw were people deeply absorbed in their chess games, who looked at me askance as if to say, "What is this barbarian doing here?" Not finding my friend, I bounded right out of that boring place. I went to the Café Valois, where I again hoped to find him. The first person I saw was M. de Préville, who informed me that M. and Mme. de La Roche-Dragon had been in Paris for two days. Not yet finding the one whom we were seeking, we went to his restaurant . . . not there either! But finally, on Rue des Petits-Champs, we met face to face. Transported by joy, we went back to the Palais-Royal, we crossed the Cour des Fontaines, constanty talking to, smiling at, and hugging each other, till we landed in some unrecognizable spot. Finally, M. Hékel, the first to stop, asked where we were going. "I haven't the slightest idea," was the unanimous response. His reply was serious: "We're mad, we must go and have dinner." No sooner said than done. After dinner, we went to see *Abufar* and *Le Dédit*. As I had spent the night wide-awake in the coach, I fell deeply asleep in the last act. On the way home, I found a note at the porter's: "We arrived this evening, and you this morning. We shall finally see other again! We are still on Rue d'Angoulême; see you tomorrow."

It was M. de La Blottais and his son. What an astonishing coincidence! At seven in the morning I was already there, and already he had gone out; but I did find Amand, and I shall tell you in person all that he told me. I then saw Amédée. Then I had lunch at M. Hékel's. In the evening we went to see *Didon* and the *Psyché* ballet. I didn't miss a note or a step. My god, my dear mother, how I thought of you, how I missed you! A magnificent hall, a world of people, a sublime spectacle! Lainé outdid himself; always a little trembling in the voice, but what nobility! what soul! what acting! he is a man...who...oh! a man, after all!... I couldn't stop applauding. Didon was played by a young actress making her debut, who has a great deal of talent and sings marvellously.

The ballet of *Psyché* is beautified to an astonishing degree. The décor of the second act has been changed completely. It is no longer that awful red palace. It is a superb portico, an immense perspective. Everything has been embellished. Amour no longer enters his palace through the door, but arrives on a cloud. Zéphyre is a young and charming dancer, made to order, who shall perhaps equal Vestris.[35] All in all, no spectacle was ever more completely wonderful. This morning I went to see Mme. de Ferriéres, then to Mme. de Jassaud with M. de Pernon. We ate oysters and drank champagne. Our laughter and joy were only interrupted by our regret at your absence. We drank to your health and spoke about you, ah!... I have returned from Mme. de Bérenger's, who for a moment didn't recognize me. She finds me changed from head to foot. I dropped in at Mme. de Vézelay's, and now I am back here. I will tell you all the details *viva voce*; but we all love you, you know, and how glad we are to see one another! it is like a dream! How I thank you for sending me to Paris! How I would like to be near you in Nohant! How happy I am! How I miss you!

I embrace you a thousand times with all my heart.

Maurice.

From Deschartres to Madame Dupin   3 Vendémiaire, Year V [Sept. 24, 1796].

Finally, I can hear you say, here is some news! How can they wait so long before writing! What are they doing? What is happening to them? You are right to scold us, and to scold us thoroughly. Your son is a scatterbrain; he has let the time for the last mail go by. Aside from that, he seems quite reasonable. I do not doubt that people shall sing his praises to you. Many people do not recognize him at first; everyone finds him charming. There must be some truth to it; but he is not yet all that he shall be, and what *he should be*. I will not recount any news. There is none other than what is reported in the newspapers, which is to say, a fourth defeat for Jourdan.[(31)] As disastrous as it is, it makes no impression here. No one bothers about it. Never have I seen Paris so indifferent to the destiny of France.

Everything is very expensive here. You would never believe what the trip from Orléans to Paris cost us. Saint-Jean will have to bring back our steeds, for there are no more coaches, strictly speaking. You have to reserve a month in advance to have seats, which is to say that at this present moment, and while Paris is the center for every comfort and luxury, one can only cross France on foot or on horseback.

Goodbye, Madame; may the absence of your son not cause you any worries which may be harmful to your health. Take care of that above all! etc.

From Maurice to His Mother   2 October 1796.

. . . I went to a beautiful concert yesterday, which was given at the Louvois theater. Guénin and old Gaviniès were conducting the orchestra. You remember our old Gaviniès, who knew my father so well and Rousseau at the time of *Le Devin du village*, and who met me in such a singular way at Passy during my exile. Well, the audience made him play his romance again, and he acquitted himself so well that he was literally covered with applause. For a man of seventy-five, that's not bad! It gave me such pleasure!

You will never guess whom I met and recognized at that concert. Dressed in the latest fashion, with casual shoes and *oreilles de chien* [dog ears],[36] I saw the sansculotte Soubielle, and I spoke to him. He is a *merveilleux*.[37] One could die laughing at such encounters. He asked a great deal about you. He was not so gallant in the Year II!

Goodbye, my dear mother, time hurries me along, I am going to the Opéra. I miss you at every moment. All the pleasures I have far from you are imperfect ones. I kiss you a thousand times.

And a thousand hellos to my *stupid* maid. . . .

8 Vendémiaire.

Don't worry so much, my dear mother. You cannot imagine how bad the postal service is. Sometimes letters take six days to travel eighty leagues, sometimes a fortnight, and sometimes more; for M. de La Dominière received only yesterday the one you wrote him a month ago. There is no logic to it. . . .

The day before yesterday, I went to see *Oedipe* and the ballet of *Psyché*. I was in the absolute center, ten steps from the stage, and I was on the parterre, for the place is now a magnificent amphitheater which goes from the orchestra up to the first tiers. We are seated as if in your big armchair. We have a perfect view, we hear even better; in short, they are the best seats in the house. I thought of you so much! How I regretted your absence while listening carefully to the opera! I didn't miss a single part of the orchestra. Yesterday, I went with Messrs. Hékel and Heuzé to see *L'Intérieur des comités révolutionnaires*. The Jacobins are so well disposed there!

Everyone I see asks me if you wish to remain in the provinces again this winter, and when I say yes, there are exclamations and endless astonishment. They don't understand at all our point of view. As for me, alas! I understand it only too well. . . .

3 October.

I left you the other day to go to the Opéra. They were to have played *Corisandre*, instead they played *Renaud*. But nothing fazes a provincial. I listened from beginning to end with the greatest pleasure. I was in the orchestra. M. Hékel knows Ginguené, director of the arts council, and every opera day Ginguené makes him a present of two orchestra tickets. It is there that those who are now called "quality" sit. One sees charming-looking women, marvellously elegant; but if they open their mouths, all is lost. One hears, "Jesus, how well they dance!" or "It's hot as hell in here." On leaving, this high society get into shiny and noisy carriages, while the good folk return home on foot, taking out their revenge in sarcasm for the splashing they receive. They can be heard shouting, "Make way for Monsieur the prison caterer!" or "Step aside for Monsieur the seal breaker!"

But they go anyway and make fun of it all. Although everything is reversed, one can still say, as in the old days, "The gentleman goes on foot, and the scoundrel on a litter." They are different scoundrels, that's all.

Farewell, my dear mother. Once again this evening I am going to the Opéra. This coming morning, M. Hékel is having me dine with M. le Duc. I embrace you with all my love.

5 October.

. . . . I had lunch with M. le Duc, who heaped on me kindness and attention. Tomorrow I go with my friend and his to dine in the country. This acquaintanceship can only do me good. I went back to see *Oedipe* in the evening; Chéron, who believes he has lung trouble, no longer sings in it; those who replace him are second-rate. Lainé always gives me pleasure. Yesterday, I went to the Italiens to see *Rose et Colas* and *Arnill*. . . .

Tell my maid that my pigtail suffers a lot without her attention; it sends her best regards.

8 October.

How terribly unhappy I am to cause you anxiety! However, I do write to you every mail day. I take too much pleasure in talking with you to lose the opportunity. But the post plays us awful tricks! So calm down, my dear mother, I am marvellously well, I run around like a sleek cat. The day before yesterday, I dined in the duke's quarters; he is staying with Mme. Delage, who has the most beautiful house in Suresnes; today I shall be at the home of the magistrate of Frelon, at a dinner for "important" people. . . .

The 9th.

Cursed mail! I was hoping for a letter from you today. I came back yesterday at three o'clock, counting on it; I didn't find any, and I was sad all the rest of the day. I went to the Salon this morning; there were three paintings of

Swebach, two of Bidault, some Van Spaedoncks, and many tavern signboards. I do not miss a day at the Opéra; I have seen *Iphigénie en Aulide*. Lainé outdid himself; it was perfection. I have seen *Bélisaire* and *Philidor* at the Italiens; there were enough things of beauty to behold.

Yesterday I got my hussar boots, now very much in fashion; they are the last word, also my trousers; my frock-coat is in the latest mode. Nowadays people dress as if they were wearing sacks—little collars stitched down on one side, big lapels, enormous waists, side pockets, and hands inside them—a style which is extremely prudent in times like these. In short, my dear mother, in me you will see the finest flower of dandyism; you will see! you will see! You will die laughing.

Goodbye, my dear mother, I will make my rounds in my new clothing. I embrace you with all my heart. Above all, be well!

A nice strong fisticuff on the head of my maid, and I whiten her face with a powderpuff. How is the three-headed watchdog, Tristan-Belle-Spinette? Is it still rolled up like a ball on the big armchair? ...

The 11th.

I finally saw *Corisandre*. The quintet in the second act is performed to perfection; I was there with my friend, who always has his pockets full of tickets. I was in the orchestra, and from my seat I had the pleasure of reading Guénin's score; I almost imagined I was playing the first violin.

I went yesterday to Mme. de Nanteuil's, and she heaped upon me kind favors. I thought I would stay only five minutes, but her eldest daughter was seated at the piano; on the piano was a good violin; I took hold of it and got to accompany her from noon to three o'clock; she played accurately the prettiest sonatas of Pleyel, those in which I accompanied M. de Scévole. I know them by heart, so I went right along without a stop! I made the passages sparkle! And the most glorious part of it was that some visitors dropped in who quickly formed a considerable audience; it was the rage, and now today invitations are pouring in on me, I don't know where to go first.

The 13th.

.... I just received your two letters at once. The postal service decided that they would be bored travelling alone, and they placed them together. You ask me so many questions, my dear mother, I could never answer in a letter. There are a host of things I am saving for our wonderful evening chats. I have made all my visits and done all your errands. Yesterday I dined with Mme. de Ferrières, and in the evening she sent me to Mme. de Bar's box, with D'Heuzé, her sister, and two other young people. It was an infinitely serious group, and we talked more nonsense than I would normally hear in six months. I saw Master Guilloteau; I found him at home, looking fresh-faced, fat, and feisty, his lips cherry red from having just taken a preventive medicine. I have had my hair attended to; they found it too short, and instead of cutting all of it, they only exposed the ear. They leave the hair long in front and behind to fall over the neckline of one's outfit. The perfection of the dog ear, when it is long enough, is to put some curlers at the ends without letting the hair frizz. As for the plaits and the pigtail, there is nothing to change. May my maid be consoled and expect to see me with my ear showing. In addition, I send her a thousand words of grace, friendship, and nonsense. Farewell, my dear mother, I embrace you, and I love you with all my heart. . . .

The 15th.

On foot or not, the gentleman thumbs his nose at Parisian bad weather! There are so many things to do and to see! In the morning, I go to the Salon; from three to six I dine leisurely and in splendid company; in the evening, I go to the theater. I dined at Mme. de Ferrières with all your friends; I was received with open arms! Oh, how they spoke of you! The dinner was delicious, served on beautiful silver. The Republic did not take everything. The wines were perfect. There were some very gay young people, and we even made M. de La Dominière laugh out loud! In the evening I was at Rue Feydeau to see *L'École des pères* and *Les Fausses Confidences*. This last play is performed exactly as it was before '93. Fleury wore the same costume; Dazincourt as well. . . .

The 17th.

How good you are to continue being bored in your solitude, in order to let me have several more days in Paris! What a too good mother! If you were here with me, I would enjoy myself so much more. Today I joined the useful to the pleasurable, and it seems to me that I am transported. My friend M. Hékel read me two works of morality, one on the immortality of the soul, the other on true happiness. Everything in them is admirable, profound, swift, clear, eloquent; he composed them last winter, and he assures me that he had no other aim in writing than to develop the principles of virtue in me.

Yesterday I had extraordinary success singing *Oedipe* at the home of Mme. de Chabert. But to whom do I owe these successes? To my good mother, who took such pains to teach me and who knows more about it than all the professors in the world! After the music, we all danced; we were all in boots, don't be scandalized, it's the style now; but how badly one dances in boots! After that, we all took a fancy to take tea, which is the blandest and most economical kind of supper. Goodbye, my dear mother, I embrace you with all my heart, and I send thirty-three regards to my maid. . . .

The 19th.

You ask me whether M. de La Blottais has received your letter. I have no idea; he is in the country and comes here only secretly, because he is on the list of émigrés. The duke pays me many attentions, I often take lunch with him, and if he goes to Spain, he will pass by way of Nohant. I told him that it wasn't at that price that we would wish to see him. I am absolutely like a Panurge[38] here. Everyone invites me, and I cannot dine at everyone's home. Tell Saint-

Jean to bring my mare in from the field and feed her oats, so she'll be in a travelling mood. It is still the fastest and cheapest way to travel....

This morning I lunched again with M. le Duc and my friend Hékel. We ate like ogres and laughed like lunatics.... And imagine that as all three of us walked to the Pont Neuf, the fishwives surrounded us and embraced the duke as if he were the son of their good king! You can see for yourself if the spirit of the people has changed! But I will "speak to you verbally," as Bridoison[39] says.

I am running to say my goodbyes. I will not regret Paris because I will have you again.

A thousand brutalities to my maid; let her get ready to shave me, for here they gave me tusks, which frightened everyone and are now growing out with a vengeance....

Deschartres has been searching in vain for a tutor for Mme. de Chandaire's son; he sees it as an impossibility in these times. It is a lost species. All the young people who were destined for education aim to become doctors, surgeons, lawyers. The most robust have been employed in the offices of the Republic. For six years, no one has studied, it must be said, and books were held to be wrong. All you see are people who are looking for tutors for their children and not finding them. There will therefore be many donkeys some years from now, and I would be one as well, were it not for Deschartres; what am I saying? Were it not for my dear mother, who would always have been sufficient to mold my mind and my heart.

The 13th.

We leave tomorrow. Deschartres finally decided to place his esteemed legs into boots. There is no way to struggle against the current! They are fine on horseback, but not at the ball. They slow you down in the quadrille. Tell my maid that I am going to be repaid by making her do leaps and pirouettes, whether she wants to or not. Farewell, Paris ... and hello to you soon, my dear mother! I leave here crazier than when I arrived because everyone here is also a little crazy. It is enough to have your head on your shoulders to believe you are happy. The parvenus give themselves up to it with all their hearts, and the people seem indifferent to everything; never has luxury been so dazzling.... Bah! bah! farewell to all these vanities, my dear mother is bored and awaits me; too bad for my mare. I am finally going to embrace you! Perhaps I shall arrive before this letter!

Maurice.

A. S.

VI

Maréchal de Saxe.[40]

Those of my friends who are reading these pages as they appear in print have come to me with questions and observations that are more or less justifiable. Here is one I believe I should pause at for a moment before going further.

Why, they ask me, have you said so little concerning Maréchal de Saxe? Was he not a most remarkable figure and was his destiny not the most notable in that past which you are evoking as a basis for your story? Don't you know something of particular interest regarding this hero which may have escaped history? Didn't your grandmother have some household tales that might throw some light on this character whom posterity still finds foreign and quite mysterious?

No, in truth, on the subject of her father, my grandmother had no particular knowledge that she wished or was able to impart. She was only two years old when he died, and somewhere in her vague memories or in her mother's stories, she had recoiled from her father's caresses during a dinner because the odor of rancid butter offended her already refined sense of smell. Her mother explained to her that the hero was passionately fond of this kind of butter and that they could never find it putrid enough to satisfy him. When it came to food, all his tastes were in keeping with this one. He liked stale bread and vegetables served nearly raw. This was permitted considering he had spent three-quarters of his life on the battlefield.

My grandmother also seemed to remember that he had brought her an enormous sheep threaded with gold; when the sheep was later shown to her, she was told it was a gift from the famous Comte de Lowendahl, that the marshal had brought it at the count's behest; moreover, that it had cost two or three thousand francs, of which the gold thread itself was worth five or six hundred.[(32)] A strange form of extravagance this indirect giving to women or children some sum or other, paid for at three or four times its value, to demonstrate that one had money to waste on pleasing them.

That is all my grandmother saw of her father, and it is not of any great interest.

Maurice de Saxe belongs henceforth to history, which exalted and flattered him during his lifetime to such a degree that it can well afford to be severe with him today. But is such severity in good taste coming from me? Have I the right, even considering the distance that time has placed between us (already one hundred years since his death), to judge him totally free of constraint? I was raised with a blind respect for his glory. Since the time I read about that grand existence, I must admit my respect has been tainted with a kind of dread and my conscience absolutely refuses to be blind to the entrapments of such an era.

I recognize great personal qualities in Maréchal de Saxe, but if I set out to make them emerge without showing the shadows alongside the highlights, won't I be indulging in what I condemn as antiquated ideas of ancestral prejudice? These ideas consist, as I have said, of pride in rank or success, in the blind cult for dazzling things; whereas real respect, which must supersede all others, should inhere especially to humble virtues and to unrecognized merit.

I am told that my scruples are not founded on legitimate descent. But it is, nonetheless, real and direct. I agree that it lacks the sanction of the exclusive fidelity which renders adoptions serious and familial with or without an official stamp.

But not having a particular concept of Maréchal de Saxe, I would only have to tell what everyone knows about him anyway—that he was named Arminius-Maurice, born in 1696 in Goslar, in the Harr region;[33] that he was raised with his brother, the future Prince Elector who became Augustus III, King of Poland; that at the age of twelve he fled from his mother's house and journeyed through Germany on foot in order to join the allied army commanded by Prince Eugene of Savoy and of Marlborough, then beseiging Lille.

Perhaps the young adventurer sang, "Marlb'rough goes off to war," as he marched along. We do know that he boldly climbed to the front lines several times and received from the French, who were his enemies at the time, his first baptism by fire. At the age of thirteen, he took part in the siege of Tournay, where his horse was shot from under him and his hat pierced by bullets. At the siege of Mons, the following year, he was among the first to jump in the river, carrying a wounded infantryman on the rump of his horse, and he killed with a single pistol shot an enemy who believed he would be easily taken prisoner; and leaving himself open to all manner of danger with a kind of fury, he was admonished by Prince Eugene, personally, for his excessive temerity.

We know that in 1711, he fought against Charles XII; that in 1712, at the age of sixteen, he led a cavalry regiment, had another horse shot from under him, and launched three consecutive charges with a regiment that had been virtually destroyed.

Married at seventeen to the Countess Loeben, a father at twenty of a son who survived only briefly, ever warring with a passion—sometimes against Charles XII, whom he admired so ingenuously that ten times he risked being killed or captured in order to get close enough to see him; sometimes against the Turks, in the capacity of a volunteer and for the love of war—he would return home to his wife only to meet her just reproaches for his unfaithfulness. He had expressed a great aversion for marriage, and his mother, in betrothing him as he emerged from childhood, had not taken it to heart. He was so truly a child of his time that after having obstinately resisted his mother's wishes, he suddenly decided to favor them when he learned that the young Miss Loeben was called Victoire.

He left her in 1720 to come to France, where the regent gave him the rank of field marshal. Maurice annulled the marriage a year later. His wife cried a great deal and married again soon after. Everything that surrounded that young man—the manners at the regency court, the ease in breaking ties that were formed without credence and without love, the circumstances of his own birth, the terrible examples of his father's debauchery and those of all the courts at which his education took place—are quite sufficient causes of disorder and early demoralization. Elected duke by the people of Courland and Sémigalle, loved and encouraged by the Duchess Anna Ivanovna, who went on to become Czarina of Russia, he fought energetically to preserve this principality against the aggressive intentions of its neighbors. His ambition and willpower retained this position for him, not to mention the protection of the duchess. But he soon lost Anna's protection through his own fault. Incapable of fidelity, one night he was crossing the courtyard of the duchess' palace, carrying a woman on his shoulders; he came upon an old lady wielding a lantern, who cried out in fear. He gave the lantern a kick, slipped, and rolled into the snow with the old woman and the young one. A sentry came running, the news spread. The future czarina was unforgiving and later took revenge by saying about him, "He could have been emperor of Russia. That woman cost him dearly!"

But I realize I am digressing, and I do not wish to pad my book with useless parts. The campaigns of Maurice de Saxe in France are too well known for me to have to speak of them. If I am forced to find a place in this work for an appreciation of his character and mission, I can only extract and convey the judgment consigned to divers places in Henri Martin's *Histoire de France*, the most beautiful of histories published until now, because it is the most complete:

"(1741) A methodical siege of Prague was unthinkable. The Elector of Bavaria received the audacious advice of attacking this large city by means of a military escalade. The author of this advice was a general officer who already enjoyed great military renown, although he had not yet been commander in chief; it was Comte Maurice de Saxe, illegitimate son of the late King Augustus II, an adventurer filled with flaming passions, violent ambitions, and high military aspirations. After having been elected Duke of Courland by the estates of that sovereignty in 1726, and having defended his duchy with heroic temerity again Russia and Poland, he came to offer his services to France, distinguished himself during the war of 1733, and led a division of the Army of the Danube. The Elector had at least the good sense to listen to Maurice. The author of the plan became its executor. Maurice chose as second in command a man who had nothing in common with him except courage, the Lieutenant Colonel Chevert, an officer born in the ranks of the people, who was the epitome of virtue in a corrupt time, as Maurice was the epitome of unbridled passion. The town had only one surrounding bastion and dry ditches. During the night of December 25th, Chevert quietly led his grenadiers up one of the bastions, repulsed the enemy who had come running at the sentries' cries, took possession of a nearby gate, and opened it to the French cavalry of Maurice.... The generals saved the city from sacking and pillage, which was thought to be a considerable advance in military manners....

"(1744) ... The principal French army, eighty thousand strong, entered

Flanders in mid-May. The king himself led them, accompanied by the Maréchal de Noailles and the Comte Maurice de Saxe, who had just received the baton of marshal, in spite of his being a Huguenot. This victory over intolerance, an odd contradiction considering the escalation of persecution against French Protestants, was due in great measure to Noailles and had cost the king a great deal by way of his petty prejudice and superstition. Noailles had managed to convey to Louis the military superiority of this foreigner and the need to tie him definitively to France, so bereft of generals.

"(1745) —The Maréchal de Saxe, who had showed himself a truly great general in 1744, and who, with very inferior forces, had prevented the enemy from besieging Lille or attempting any other enterprise, became commander in chief by 1745, at a moment when he seemed threatened by a death other than that of a hero. In the grips of a dropsy that obliged him to submit to painful punctures, he succumbed under the excesses that had ruined the prodigious vigor of his constitution. It was doubtful whether he would be in condition to rejoin his army. Voltaire could not help but ask him, one day, how he would be able to do it, in his state of weakness. 'It is not a question of survival, but of departure!' replied the marshal. That is an impressive statement; in certain natures, the height of courage so resembles virtue as to be mistaken for it. The effect is the same, and the difference is only in the motive. . . .

"(Fontenoy.) The turn of events did not look promising. The Maréchal de Saxe, overseeing everything and dragging himself everywhere on horseback or in a little wicker cart, began to prepare for retreat, in case the last effort was not successful. The presence of the king and of the dauphin, the duty of assuring their safety, was becoming an enormous burden and impelled him to make timid decisions, although it must be added that they both put on a brave front. . . . That victory at Fontenoy keenly flattered the national spirit, and it has remained a popular event. . . . Its true glory belonged to the general who had conquered at death's door.

"(1746) The Maréchal de Saxe, somewhat recovered from his illness, had suddenly stormed Brussels in the middle of winter, and this beautiful capital of the Austrian Netherlands had capitulated at the end of three weeks. At the beginning of May . . . the king's presence was not only useless, but prejudicial. The burden of a 'court army' inhibited Maurice from pressing the enemy as sharply as he might have. . . ."

Let us interrupt the historian and allow the marshal to speak for himself. The only thing that people who are not engaged in the military arts know about his style is from his famous letter to Maréchal de Noailles concerning the invitation that had been made him (in 1746, to be precise) to become a member of the Académie Française, the letter in which he alleges and proves so well that he has no idea how to spell. "I replide that it wood fitt me like a ringe on a catte." But this fantastic spelling did not prevent the marshal from having a feeling for writing nor from belonging, considering some examples of his written ideas, to the literary movement of the eighteenth century. His letters—concise, clear, quick—have, through their very limitations, a truly historical scope, and through their humor and playfulness, a mark of grandeur and frankness. They have undergone a certain amount of translation in the editing process, but they have been neither altered nor rearranged in their form, which one can easily sense. Here is what he wrote to the Chevalier de Folard:

> Camp at Bouchout, 5 May 1746.

> I have received, my dear chevalier, the letter that you have done me the honor of writing to me on ———, and I note with pleasure that we think alike about what had to be done after the enemy abandoned its position behind the Nèthe, and I would have done it if I had been alone; other circumstances prevented me from pursuing them and throwing them into the sea, which could not have failed to happen, given their disorder, our superiority, and our position. I don't know if you know what a court army means, and all the inconveniences it entails. I have detached from this army forty battalions and fifty squadrons for the investiture at Mons. The siege will be led under the direction of M. le Prince de Conti, and may God bless his operations! . . . As for the politics, I'm not the one to talk to; cleverer folks than I are involved in that! . . .

Several days later, he wrote to Frederick II:

> Your Majesty knows very well that the military party always submits to politics. Thus, I flatter myself that Your Majesty will not blame me for the errors that may be made in the course of this campaign. My present situation will persuade you of this truth; for I sense very clearly that a march on our right would place the allies' army in a highly critical position.

On July 6th of the same year, he wrote to the Comte d'Argenson:

> You do me honor to tell me that the king expects me not to make any retrograde movement except as a last resort. One cannot, without high risk, make any kind of retreat when one expects the last resort; but one must always situate oneself in a way to not be obliged to retreat. . . . I am not naturally inclined, sir, to movements of retreat; it seems to me I have given you proofs of my constancy, and perhaps of something further, when military requirements invited me to. Only political considerations can authorize a different conduct; I will not enter into a discussion here of how to know to which one owes preference, but I think that the first is fruitless—I mean politics—concerning good wartime conduct.

Nearly all of Maurice's letters bear witness to the difficulties that were created for him, the blunders he was exposed to, and the terrible responsibility they burdened him with, all the while limiting the absolute authority he would have needed in such grave circumstances. While the king flatters the opinion of the French—who love their kings chivalrous—by displaying his sangfroid on the battlefield, whose ease and verifiability the general in charge had to guarantee even at the expense of his army's honor; while the king writes to him, "My dear cousin, I write you this letter to express my intention that you be present at the *Te Deum* with the officers of my army, etc." the Huguenot marshal must think only of how to avoid or repair the mistakes that he is well aware are always on the verge of being committed; and in the way in which he expresses himself, one can see not only the sharp eye of a military leader, but the openness—rare in that era of fawning and indulgence—of a man who wishes to perform his duty at all costs. Complaining to Argenson on the subject of Conti's deplorably poor orders, he writes as follows: "You will further note, sir, that instead of conceivably sending me reinforcements, he warns me that he will send M. le Comte d'Estrées—where to I don't know—to beat the bushes in places where the enemy is not. . . . I am too good a servant of the king to render to M. le Prince de Conti what he does to me. However, I want to frighten him with it, by threatening to make my way back to the camp at Louvain."

In 1747, he wrote a luminous memoir on the condition of the army, in which he included some reflections that reveal that genial frankness and that inner suffering of the frustrated *artist*:

"Any man of wisdom must be alarmed to see his judgment meet with general disapproval. If uncertainty and changeability are an evil in one's private life, it can be said that they are fatal on the battlefield; and whoever changes his mind lightly or against his judgment throws all parts of an army into disorder and confusion, because changes in operation can be regarded as accidental to the plan conceived,[34] which is based solely on a meditation made at leisure, and which embraces every objective, including its related parts. Persons of wit, and especially eloquent ones, are very dangerous in an army, because their ideas make converts; and if the general is not an opinionated person and headstrong in that opinion, which is a mistake,[35] it can cause him uncertainties that may make him commit serious errors; this is my case. . . . My conduct has appeared too plainly, and it has been judged as effecting and provoking events. . . . Berg-op-Zoom has become an affair beyond human powers, so to speak, or at least beyond any previous example. It may be that politics, our losses, and our pride have fired us up over this enterprise to the point where we are ready to sacrifice the army, our military glory, and that of the king. Tempers are running high, the general is blamed for being slow; he is loathe to leave too soon to rush into a labyrinth that he foresees. People are talking, writing memoirs, and communicating ideas as if the one in charge of conducting this campaign was not doing his job. They want to make him move at last, they plot and they scheme to that end. . . . Meanwhile, they will permit me to do as doctor's do—always defer to a consultant's decision, to cover myself from any blame. In war, one must often act on inspiration; if one always was obliged to account for why one makes one decision over another, one would often meet contradiction. Circumstances are better sensed than explained, and if war smacks of inspiration, that should not trouble the fortune teller."

We can glean from all these letters how Maurice chafed at the yoke of the court and what disdain he had for the politics of that same inept and frivolous court, where war was regarded as a sort of amusement, as an opportunity to shine without any concern for soldiers' blood or country's honor. Each young officer dreamed of his individual glory, if one can call it glorious to get one's regiment and oneself hacked up, not only for no reason, but moreover to the great detriment and peril of the campaign. Maurice had committed such follies at fifteen. He had heard Eugene say, "Learn not to confuse temerity with valor," and while still a child, he had reflected on this piece of advice; he had matured early, and from then on, no one could have been more sparing of the blood of the men he commanded. Beyond the fact that he was really very humane, he used his reputation and knowledge to avert the evils of war and prevent those striking incidents into which the nobility—eager to return to its pleasures—wished to dash headlong in order to win their spurs and be gone. Frederick the Great wrote to Maurice in 1746:

"Your letter could well instruct any man who has been charged with the conduct of any army. You give precepts; you support them with examples. In the first flush of youth, when we live only through the vivacity of our imagination as yet unchecked by experience, we sacrifice everything for the sake of brilliant actions and singular choices, which make a splash. At the age of twenty, Boileau esteemed Voiture. At thirty, he rather chose Homer. When I first took command of my army, I was all for spearheads; but too many events which I have seen come to pass, in which I have even taken part, have cooled my ardor for them. It was those spearheads that made me lose the campaign of 1744. . . . The great art in war is to anticipate all events. . . . The chapter of events is vast, but foresight and competence can stave off misfortune."

Since I am immersed in quotation—having resolved not to do otherwise—I shall transcribe yet another fragment of a letter from Maréchal de Saxe to Frederick. His expression of appreciation for the bravery and intelligence of the French troops is worth noting:

"The French are what they were at the time of Caesar, and such as he depicted them: excessively brave, but changeable; steady to the point of letting themselves all be killed at their post, once the first moments of panic are passed; for they get intensely excited over matters of post, if one can make them hold out for only a few minutes; they are poor at maneuvers in the open country. . . . Hence one must have recourse to positions that cannot be chosen too carefully. The simple soldier is a judge of this, and when they are well posted, then one becomes aware of their gaiety and their chatter."

I have said that the marshal was far from being a courtier. As the son of a king, ever aspiring to be king himself, he had immense pride. Had he been only a bold adventurer, who needs must make do with the rubric of a great general, his independence of character could have been very detrimental to him. Here are the terms in which he asked, in 1734, for an advancement from the king of France, in a letter addressed to the Comte de Noailles and dated from the camp at Graben:

"Although beautiful actions speak for themselves, I find myself in a position of having to praise myself. I have neither relatives nor friends at court, and

false modesty degenerates into stupidity. . . . For fourteen years I have had the
honor to be of service to the king, in the rank of field marshal; I am almost
forty, and I am not the kind to submit to rules or to attain promotion by growing old. Besides, I have paid less heed to what is due to blood or to my own
interests than to the honor that has bound me to the king's service. If you add
to that the title of foreigner, you will find sufficient reasons to promote me and
to influence the king to accord me this grace, adding thereto the charm that
puts a price on things."

Let us compare this estimation of his own situation with that of M. Henri
Martin:

"There was something not quite flattering to national pride in owing its
success to a foreigner. In addition, this foreigner, this bastard of Saxony, had as
his chief lieutenant another foreigner, a bastard of Denmark, the Comte de
Lowendahl, who had been trained by commanding Russian armies under the
Maréchal de Münich. The fact is that generals were no longer being created
among the French, the major reason being the disappearance of advanced military studies and theorizing among the upper nobility."

After having recounted the campaigns of Maréchal de Saxe, the details of
which were admirably summed up, but which were linked to too many general
events to find a place here, the superior historian whom I cite tackles the personality of Maurice de Saxe, in his book, *Des moeurs et des idées en France
depuis la mort de Louis XIV jusqu' au milieu du dix-huitième siècle*:

" . . . Richardson . . . in his famous novel, enlivened with so powerful and
poignant a reality . . . makes us see vice raised to tragic proportions, systematic
seduction pursuing with cold and violent treachery what still subsists in the way
of virtue and true sentiment in the heart of woman, seducer transformed into a
kind of hero in a halo of infernal glory: *Lovelace* is the *Antichrist* of love.
Models for this unusual figure were not lacking. Lovelace is but a Richelieu
made taller and more serious in the business of evil. Maurice de Saxe expresses
a particular nuance of this figure. He has not that serpent's coldness; impetuous
in vice as in battle, he is Homer's Ajax, bereft of a moral sense and thrown into
the midst of a refined civilization, capable of acting odiously or generously, following wherever his ardor leads him. But whether, in the real world, Lovelace is
called Richelieu or Maurice de Saxe, the end result is the same, though the character and means may differ. . . . Contrary to the opinion of Montesquieu and others, Voltaire does not think that the human race has diminished in number. He
believes that the world population neither increases nor decreases. . . . The
Maréchal de Saxe wrote a curious treatise on this subject, which was published
at the end of his *Rêveries*. He suggests, by way of remedy for the supposed
depopulation, that marriages ought to last only five years and that no one should
be able to marry the same woman twice, if no children have been born after the
first five years. —A strange philosopher, this Maurice de Saxe.— Montesquieu,
in *L'Esprit des lois*, also would like laws, less bizarre of course, to favor population growth. He would have been quite astonished to find out that in one century
the population throughout almost all of Europe had doubled, and tripled in certain countries, despite the wars and enormous revolutions."

In the fourth volume of *La France sous Louis XV*, M. Henri Martin concludes his sketch of Maréchal de Saxe:

"The Maréchal de Saxe has just died (November 30, 1750), his head full of plans for reform and carrying with him all we had left of the science of war on a grand scale. It was recognized, via one of Maurice's letters to the minister of war, that he foresaw the consequences of that state of indiscipline and ignorance into which the army had fallen. . . . He would probably have found the solution, that is to say, exposed the secret of Frederick II, if his excesses had not snatched him from France prematurely. . . . In his letter to the Comte d'Argenson, Maurice states that the French army should avoid tactical maneuvers on the plains and try to restrict themselves to auxiliary thrusts and stationary tactics. He was only too good a prophet. His military works, *Rêveries, notes,* etc., published in 1757, are very interesting to study. He would have wished to render the equipment of the soldier cleaner and more convenient, have the majority of the cavalry resume using defensive armor and the lance, have the infantry march in the cadenced step of the Prussians, have combat decided by use of the bayonette rather than firing arms, create a staff officers' school and see to it that higher ranks be given for merit rather than seniority; have war machines in constant readiness for the defense of seaports, from which underwater retrenchments could be formed at the port's entry to stop vessels and fire ships; create a light infantry closely analogous to our 'Chasseurs de Vincennes.' Very preoccupied with protecting the life and health of the soldier, he mourned the defensive weapons of days gone by. He sprinkled his vices with some sentiments for humanity. He tried to have the cruel practice abolished of burning the suburbs of threatened cities. He had spies put in chains instead of hanging them. He sometimes philosophizes more seriously than in that bizarre *Mémoire sur la population*, which we have mentioned elsewhere. 'What spectacle do nations present us today? We see a few rich, lazy, voluptuous men who take their pleasure at the expense of a multitude . . . whose existence depends on ceaselessly furnishing them with new luxuries. This assemblage of men, oppressors and oppressed, forms what is called society, and this society gathers its vilest and most despicable and makes them soldiers. It is not with such mores nor with such members that the Romans conquered the universe.' That is neither Montesquieu nor Rousseau speaking; it is Maurice de Saxe in his *Rêveries*. Maurice wanted every Frenchman without exception to serve five years as a soldier. . . . Illustrious generals vanished with Maurice de Saxe and Lowendahl, who survived his companion in arms by only a few years. The government sank to ever new depths under the hand of the Pompadour, etc."

We can see that, while rendering him justice, the renowned historian treats Maréchal de Saxe with much severity. That severity is respectable on the part of such a judge, and I would not know how, were my grandmother here to urge me, to counter the condemnation brought to bear by such a beautiful and honest talent, a talent that is the essence of patriotism at the same time as that of conscience and virtue.

All that is allowed me is to recall that the transgressions of the hero were those of his era and his upbringing. After all is said and done, his soul was beautiful and great, his character habitually kind and generous. In another milieu, and sustained by other counsels, principles, and examples, this Homeric Ajax would have captured his military fame untainted by the blemishes of his private life. "If he was steeped in vice," says another historian of his life, "there were the women who most willingly participated and did their best to help him to it." That is likely, but Mme. Favart is a great sin in his life, a sin that only God could pardon him for, no matter what Grimm had to say in his *Correspondance*.[41] The efforts on the part of that writer to stigmatize the victim and rehabilitate the guilty party are almost as awful as the sin itself. Such were the times and the customs.

Maurice really loved his soldiers and abhorred the members of the court army, witness his response to a lieutenant general who, while proposing that he attack a post, added, "You risk to lose a dozen soldiers at most." "Only," the general replied, "if they were all lieutenant generals,"and turned his back on him.

He met his death without fear, saying to his doctor, "Life is a dream. Mine has been short, but it was beautiful." This sums up the man and the century.

His was, on the whole, a very exalted temperament whose flaw lay in its very exaltation. His destiny was inadequate for his energy. He needed to be sovereign, and as he had no right to be at that time, his friends often had to defend him against the reproach of folly which his contemporaries levelled at him. If he had attained the age of fifty at a later time in history, he might have sought and realized, perhaps to some extent, his dream of royalty, unless France had stifled his ambition on the scaffold. The destiny of Napoléon is like an expanded fulfillment of Maurice's ardent dreams. We know that the fiery Saxon dreamed of ruling Tabago, then Corsica, then finally the homeland of the Jews. He was a reformer insufficiently enlightened, but if he had been engaged in a vaster task than securing for corrupt France a futureless moment of glory, his remarkable practical sense—which always reemerged in action, despite his physical and moral debilities—would perhaps have preserved him from the errors that he hatched in solitude. He might have found counsel, he might have been enlightened, and as Adrienne Lecouvreur[42] had initiated him, savage and fierce as he was, into the arts of delight, some serious mind might have been able to initiate him into more just ideas. One should never doubt that a great but compromised intelligence would have taken the good road, if he had found it accessible. A life of intoxication is not the aim of the high faculties God gives to certain men. It is the jutting rock on which their mission runs aground by fault of circumstance. It is the malady of a boredom and despair which are not always acknowledged but could perhaps be bravely shaken if, instead of the pollution of libertine courts, a purer and freer air came to revive and retemper those powerful chests.   *S.D.*

VII

Continuation of my father's story. —The persistence of philosophical ideas. —*Robert, chef de brigands.* —Description of La Châtre. —Schiller's *Die Räuber.* —The bourgeois theater of La Châtre in 1798. —Conscription. —La Tour d'Auvergne, First Grenadier of France.

Prefatory Note

Certain reflections inevitably come to mind with the flow of the pen when one speaks of the past: one compares it to the present, and this present, the moment one is writing, is already the past for those who read a few years after the words were written. Writers have also sometimes envisioned the future. Their predictions may have been realized or belied by the time their work appears. I have not wanted to change in any way the reflections and forecasts that came to me in these last years. I believe they are already part of my story and of all our history. I shall limit myself to noting their dates.

I continue the history of my father, since he is, no pun intended, the real author of the story of my life. This father whom I hardly knew and who has remained in my memory like a shining apparition—this artistic young man and warrior has remained wholly alive in the flights of my fancy, in the pitfalls of my constitution, in the features of my face. My being is a reflection—weakened no doubt, but rather complete—of his. The milieu in which I have lived has brought about modifications. My faults are, therefore, not absolutely of his making, and my good points benefit from the instincts he has passed on to me. My exterior life has differed as much from his as the period in which it developed; but had I been a boy and had I lived twenty-five years earlier, I know and I sense that I would have acted and felt in all things like my father.

What were, in '97 and '98, my grandmother's plans for the future of her son? I believe they were not settled in her mind and that this was true regarding all young people of a certain class. All available careers in favor at the time of Louis XVI were, under Barras,[43] suspect. Nothing had really changed in all that except the cast of characters, and my father had really only to choose between the camps and the fireside. From his point of view, the choice had never been in doubt, but from '93 onward there arose in my grandmother a rather understandable reaction against the acts and leading figures of the Revolution. A very remarkable thing, however, was that her faith in the philosophical ideas which had produced the Revolution had not been shaken, and in '97 she wrote a fine letter to M. Hékel, which I have found again. Here it is:

From Madame Dupin to M Hékel

You detest Voltaire and the philosophers, you believe they are the cause of the evils which beset us. But do all revolutions which have desolated the world therefore have to have been instigated by foolhardy ideas? Ambition, vengeance, the furor of conquests, the dogma of intolerance have toppled empires much more often than the love of liberty and the cult of reason. Under a king such as Louis XIV, all those ideas could exist without anything being overthrown. Under a king such as Henry IV, the ferment of our Revolution would not have led to the excesses and transports that we have seen, and which I impute above all to the weakness, the unfitness, and the lack of righteousness of Louis XVI. That pious king offered his sufferings up to God, and his strict resignation saved not his partisans, nor France, nor himself. Frederick and Catherine have retained their power, and you admire them, Monsieur; but what have you to say about their religion? They have been protectors and extollers of philosophy, and there have been no revolutions in their lands. Therefore let us not attribute the misfortune of our times and the fall of the monarchy in France to new ideas, for one could say that the sovereign who rejected them has fallen and the ones who supported them have remained standing. Let us not confuse irreligion with philosophy. Atheism has been used to excite the people to fury, just as at the time of the *Ligue*[44] they were made to commit the same horrors in the name of religion. Everything can serve as a pretext for the unleashing of wicked passions. The Saint-Bartholomew massacres bear sufficient resemblance to the September ones. The philosophers are likewise innocent of both these crimes against humanity.

My father had always dreamed of a military career. We have seen him, during his exile, studying the battle of Malplaquet in his little room at Passy, in the solitude of those days so long and overwhelming for a child of sixteen; but his mother would have wanted, by way of seconding her inclinations, the return of the monarchy or the assurance of a moderate republic. When he found her contrary to his innermost desires, since he did not then conceive of acting without her complete backing, he spoke of being an artist, composing music, putting on operas or performing symphonies. We shall find this desire keeping company with his military ardor, just as his violin often campaigned with his saber.

In 1798, a situation emerges in the life of my father which is trifling in appearance but important in reality, as are all those vivid impressions of youth which are to have an impact on the rest of our lives and which sometimes even make use of us without our knowledge.

He had allied himself with the society of the neighboring town, and I must say that this little city of La Châtre, in spite of the failings and faults characteristic of the provinces, has always been remarkable for the quantity of very intelligent and educated people numbered among its population, bourgeois as well as proletariat. In a body, however, they are very stupid and nasty, because they are subject to those prejudices which reign everywhere but more naïvely and overtly in small localities than large. The bourgeoisie is well off without being opulent, it has no battle to wage with an arrogant nobility and rarely with a needy proletariat. Hence, the milieu there is very favorable for developing the intelligence, although perhaps too tranquil for the heart and too cool for the imagination.

An old city, emancipated long ago, La Châtre is situated in a charming, fertile little valley, which opens completely to view on reaching the edge of the surrounding plateaus. Going by way of Châteauroux, hardly has one left behind a thatched cottage romantically named the Devil's House, than one goes down a long highroad bordered with poplars, with a gully of vineyards and prairies to the right and left, and from there one can take in at a single glance the small town, somber against the greenery, dominated on one side by an old square tower which was the seigniorial château of the Lombauds and which is presently used as a prison; on the other by a belltower with a heavy, quite shiny bell which sits atop a very handsome piece of antique and massive architecture that serves as a porch to the church.

One enters the city by an old bridge over the Indre, where a rustic grouping of old houses and old willows presents a picturesque composition.

But before describing the city, I shall permit myself a short digression in the form of an apostrophe.

Oh, my dear compatriots! Why are you so unclean? I reproach you in all seriousness, with some hope of correcting you. You live in the healthiest climate, and in the midst of the rustic population of the Vallée Noire, which is exquisitely clean, and yet you seem to take pleasure in making your city a reeking cesspool where one does not know where to step and where you inhale at all hours fetid miasmas, while behind the precinct of your houses the fragrant countryside flourishes, and above your dropped roofs a mass of free and pure air wafts, of which you seem to have a horror. It is really difficult to maintain clean and healthy cities like Lyon and Marseille, but La Châtre! a group of little houses cast into an oasis of perfumed meadows and flowering orchards! Really, the corruption of the sense of smell, the affront to the sense of sight inherent to the population of small, interior cities are vices which poverty in no way excuses; which, here, poverty cannot even explain, since this population is prosperous; and where, moreover, the richest bourgeois have no more sense of decency than the workers of limited means to remove the dirt from their unwelcoming doorsteps. Apparently the town officials are unconcerned that no one observes the rules, even the easiest ones to enforce. However, decency as well as salubrity should demand it. To be unclean is indecent; it reveals an absence of self-respect in one's manners and a shameful habit of sluggishness in one's mind. Shame on La Châtre in this regard! In some little-known, out-of-the-way corner of the Vallée Noire, you sometimes find under the shrubbery a miserable cottage built of mud, dried by the sun, and held together by a few old worm-eaten planks. If, by exception, the housewife is only a lazy runaround, the interior will correspond with the exterior, but be assured that this will be an exception. Ten times out of twelve, you will find the tiny house well-swept, the dishes shining on the sideboard, the bed made, the hearth spotless, not a speck of dust on the smoke-blackened beams—-profound poverty, sometimes heart-rending to see, yet always respectable and never repugnant. Yes, cleanliness is the dignity of the poor, by which they show themselves superior to their destiny and worthier to live in palaces than the idlers who own them. I believe I have said this often, and I shall repeat it untiringly. The indigent who give up and become listless and discouraged deserve pity; the ones who fight against destitution, who wash their rags, who sweeten and cleanse their poor dwelling, deserve respect and friendship. But gratuitous and voluntary filth inspires only disgust. It is nothing more than depravity and disgrace.

Barring that frightful uncleanness, La Châtre would be a pleasant sojourn. The handsomest street, Rue Royale, is in reality the ugliest; it has no character. But the old quarter is picturesque and preserves several of those wooden houses from the Renaissance, which are so elegant and have such a beautiful color. The town, laid out on an incline, rises steadily toward the prison, and some of the narrow streets which snake between the rows of uneven gables overrun with moss and pigeons serve to shore up the flank of the old city against an abrupt ravine at whose bottom the Indre traces its cool meanderings in a confined but ravishing landscape. That side is remarkable, and when you leave the city by the abbey's walk in order to follow the little sandy road of La Renardière, you arrive at the Couperies, one of the region's most delightful sites, beyond which you can get lost in a terrain mined by surfacing waters, broken up by charming gullies, and strewn with picturesques irregularities.

I have described La Châtre—I have sermonized on it—because at heart I love it, and I love it because my father had friends there whose children are my friends.

In 1798, my father, socially linked with about thirty young people of both sexes, and personally linked with several, put on plays with them. That pastime is an excellent form of study, and I shall say elsewhere all I think about what makes it useful and important for the intellectual development of youth. True enough, amateur groups, like professional acting companies, are divided most of the time by ridiculous pretensions and petty rivalries. It is the fault of the individuals and not of the art. And as, in my opinion, the theater is the art which encompasses all the others, there is no more interesting occupation for the leisure of a group of friends than that. Two things would be needed to make the pleasure ideal—true benevolence, which would impose silence on all jealous vanity; and a true feeling for the art, which would render these endeavors successful and instructive.

One can believe that these two conditions were united at La Châtre in the period I speak of, for the efforts were very well received and the impromptu actors remained friends. The play that had the most success and sparked a spontaneous and irresistible talent for acting in my father was a detestable drama very much in vogue then, the reading of which affected me strongly as a specimen of historical color, *Robert, chef de brigands* [*Robert, the Robber Chieftain*].

This drama, "taken from the German," is only a poor imitation of Schiller's *Die Räuber* [*The Robbers*]; nevertheless this imitation has some interest and importance, for it implies an entire doctrine. It was performed in Paris in 1792. It portrays the Jacobin system in essence; Robert is the ideal Montagne[45] leader, and I urge my readers to re-read it as a very curious monument to the spirit of the times.

Schiller's *Die Räuber* is and signifies something completely different. It is a great and noble work, filled with the exuberant defects of youth (for, as we know, it was achieved by a child of twenty-one), but if it is full of chaos and extremism, it is also a creation of great import and profound meaning. Permit me to remind you of it with the following abstract.

A weak and kindly old man has two sons, energetic and terrifying characters, whose kinship with this good-natured, credulous soul is hardly comprehensible. One would like to meet the lioness who bore them, or hear about some trait of hers which could explain the origin of the violent passions of these two formidable types. But that did not occur to Schiller at all. We are free to suppose what we like; this omission is a defect of the richly endowed, who contain too much to show it all, and a work that leaves much to be supposed and invented beyond the frame that encloses it is already a work full of fire and life.

Karl, the older of these two sons of Graf von Moor, is a generous and brave lion; Franz, the younger, is a cowardly and perfidious wolf. The first is a force for good, the second for evil. Both of them have genius, both vie for the affection of the father, who is to be the victim of this unnatural struggle.

Karl, left to the aberrations of youth, slandered by his brother, embittered, desperate, wants nevertheless to abandon his friends, the students who draw him into a disorderly life, in order to return to his father's side, whom he deeply loves and respects. He writes to him to ask pardon for his mistakes and to express sincere repentance. He awaits a reply with impatience; he is filled with the memory of his early years and a pure love which he bitterly regrets having neglected. The play opens at that point. Karl wants to return to virtue. Will he be able to? Has vice merely grazed this superior soul? Could such an impetuous character have plunged with impunity into the delirium of wicked passions? Yes, without a doubt, unless fate, which adheres like a punishment to the destiny we have taken for granted, comes to oppose its conversion and transform these tender and pious longings into fury.

The reply of the old Moor arrives, transmitted by the intermediary of Franz; it is a rejection, it is the paternal curse. Franz has intercepted Karl's letters. He has substituted forgeries which consign Karl to the wrath of his father, as an incorrigible, menacing scoundrel plunged in dishonor and dangerous to the very life of the old count.

Exasperated, Karl swears allegiance to the Furies. Love is changed to hate, despair, blasphemy, in his heart and on his lips. He curses God and humanity. He wants to shed the blood of all masters, all oppressors, in revenge for the shame and neglect of all the disinherited. He becomes the furious and implacable enemy of the society which rejects and condemns him. His companions, immersed in debt and rejected like him by the official world, group around him and utter frightful oaths.

But what are they going to do with all this anger, with all this need for vengeance? One of them, a cowardly, cynical, and cunning creature, has introduced the idea of practicing highway robbery, and he has conceived this plan under the influence of his greedy and contemptuous preoccupations. The others have only seen it as a way to separate themselves from society and to take their revenge by exacting a ransom from its members. Karl Moor latches forcefully onto this idea, because at that particular moment it appears very grand and logical to him. He shall become an awesome power for punishing the wicked and avenging their victims. He shall be the right arm of divine justice. He shall revive the bloody decrees of the secret tribunal of Old Germania. He takes command of the enterprise. He pronounces anathema on all his past and all his future. He leads his companions into the forests and the mountains.

This resolution, however romantic and sudden it may seem, is not at all hard to believe in Schiller's work. Its explanation lies in the violent situation in which the overly stimulated minds of these young people, too learned and too ignorant at the same time, find themselves; various types, but all real and profound, bitterly skeptical, and in a frightening state of moral disarray. Their animated conversations are full of an exaggeration where bad taste mingles with the sublime and which admirably depicts the era of transition in which humanity found itself at the end of the eighteenth century. Faith in the past was dead, there was nothing to provide hope in a new faith. The evil which reigned in customs and institutions appeared in all its ugliness. The abuses were monstrous, and enthusiastic youth, caught in a dream of liberty and reform, did not have enough strength, belief, or real power to oppose this fall of the old world which would engulf them despite their cries and protestations.

German youth in 1781 was much sicker in this respect than French youth. Having rallied around Voltaire and Jean-Jacques Rousseau, our fathers, children then, were creating the revolution in their dreams, with no awareness of its course and its results, but impelled by a fatality in our national logic. Now, Voltaire and Rousseau were not at all suitable to the tastes of the Germans then, and it would be fruitless for them to imagine that those ideas are any more suitable today. Aside from the fact that such harking back is an anachronism in the order of progress, the positivist mind of Voltaire, the ardent and troubled soul of Jean-Jacques do not have the wherewithal to satisfy the bent of the Germans, which is more enthusiastic and colder at the same time.[(36)] Young Schiller revealed their sickness, the greatness and the weakness of that generation, which he painted and brandished in his drama, *Die Räuber*, with so much power and naïveté. This revelation was so spontaneous for him that he was not aware of it and did not understand his work at all. Witness the preface he wrote in 1781, which is nothing but a lie told in good faith.

In this preface, he wishes to prove that his play is highly moral and that the official world ought to accept it as an edifying lesson. No doubt his play is moral, as is all that is vividly felt, as is any cry from the soul, complaint or act of grace, reproach or benediction, blasphemy or prayer. No matter whether the emotion of the soul thus shaken is bitter or tender, the poet renders oracles in which, as in those of the ancient sibyls, error becomes relative truth and revelation equally relative fiction. But in the eyes of the official world, the audacious frankness of young Schiller was immoral and deadly. The effect it produced well proved it, since after the brilliant success of his drama, one could see students turning into highwaymen-reformers of Germany, in their desire to realize the chimera of Moor.

Such is the gist of Schiller's drama, and all parts of the action only tend to augment it. Karl Moor wants to punish a guilty society, but by placing himself outside it, he has cast himself outside humanity, and he can accomplish his acts of justice only with the aid of murder and violence. The end justifies the means, which is Jesuit morality, the morality of the Terror, and which we are going to see proclaimed more naïvely in the French drama of 1792, *Robert, chef de brigands*, an imitation of Schiller's *Die Räuber*, but a free imitation, in which each modification is significant, as we shall presently show.

While pursuing his work of ferocious repayment, Karl Moor perceives his fatal error at every step. It is completely impossible for him to lecture his highwaymen-philosophers and render the instrument worthy of the cause. In order to punish one guilty person, they sacrifice one hundred innocent victims; in order to strike one impure heart with their daggers, they must walk on the cadavers of women and children. These men have, in their own eyes, certain particular virtues: heroic audacity, unlimited devotion to one another, chivalrous loyalty in their dealings with their leader. But their blind passions can only be sated in murder and pillage. Their thoughts are a bloody nightmare, their conversations a desperate blasphemy. One of them, the one who initiated this strange form of protest, is a cowardly scoundrel whose contact further sullies this impious and disastrous work and who, finding Karl Moor too scrupulous, threatens his days and brings to mind the likes of Carrier and Fouquier-Tinville,[46] monsters that emerge inevitably in the trauma of revolution.

On its side, official society, by dint of its infamies and heinous crimes, pushes Karl's indignation to the limit. His brother, Franz Moor, personifies the evil which eats away at and destroys that corrupt, atheistic society. Franz believes in nothing, and in his dream of nothingness, he is one hundred times more odious than poor Karl in his dream of fatality. Karl has believed in good, and he would believe in it again, if he saw God's justice reigning here on earth. He protests against the power of Satan, he dares to reproach the Divine Principle for being too indifferent to the evils of the world, and he substitutes himself for this too slow, too roundabout action. Franz believes neither in Satan nor God. Nothing is good, nothing is evil according to him; he smothers the feeble cry of his conscience, he mocks the beliefs of humankind. He is almost stronger in his perversity than Karl in his bewilderment. He assassinates his father, he overburdens and tortures his vassals, he steals the patrimony, he shrinks from no betrayal, no cruelty. At the approach of death he is assailed by superstitious visions and cowardly fears, but he is not converted by that. He escapes his enemies through suicide. It is as though a perverted and accursed society were to swoop down on itself and take its own life before revenge had the time and daring to strike it.

Karl Moor, in the presence of so many abuses, detests evil with a growing rage, and his friends horrify him as much as his enemies. He goes mad, he kills his mistress, he abandons his accomplices, he delivers himself to the executioner's hands; he has cursed and repudiated his work; he ends in despair, in a sort of insanity.

All this is logical and contains a great lesson, which is that society is lost and that it is not the role of despair to revive it; that something other than the sword and the torch is needed to purify it; that, in a word, the end does not justify the means, and that not one living work can emerge from the hands of the executioner, whether his axe be blessed by the Inquisition or by Calvin, Richelieu, or Marat, by faithless power or by ruthless revolt.

About ten years after this drama of Schiller's had stirred Germany and forecast a terrible upheaval in the old society, France pronounced the fall of its government and sent its rulers to the scaffold. Louis XVI and his German wife awaited their sentences in the Temple prison. The theaters, however, did not shut down. Popular life, far from being suspended by the emotions of this too real drama, was still seeking food for its anger in scenic fictions, a redoubled intensity of that febrile life that agitated it. A Monsieur Lamartellière (was he descended from the famous lawyer, passionate enemy of the Jesuits?) conceived of furnishing the passions of the mob with an extract from Schiller's *Die Räuber*. But in summarizing this drama and in adapting it to the uses and customs of the French stage, it happened, very innocently no doubt, that he radically altered its spirit and meaning; that is to say, out of a work of skepticism or pain, he made, without a qualm, a work of faith and triumph. It was no longer the cry of agony from expiring Germany, it was the war chant of France renewed. The student thinkers and fanatics of Germania became the philosophers of Parisian clubs, and while conserving their German names, even transporting them from the eighteenth to the fifteenth century of the Germanic empire, the author made idealized Jacobins out of them, benevolent Septembrists. The result of this amalgam (fundamentally more credible that one would believe) was a completely bizarre drama, at times sublime, at times ridiculous, but never venomous, which is the amusing side of the business.

As a matter of fact, the Jacobin robbers of *Robert* do not at all foreshadow on stage the aberrations and crimes which their system brought about. Robert is a rose-water Karl Moor. He is pure of all crime, and if he reigns through terror, it is because he likes to be feared and to have a big red mustache. Besides, he is a lamb, and even though he threatens to break the heads of his comrades at the least misdeed, he has trained them so well that there is not one among them who has not deserved the Montyon prize[47] ten times over. Whereas the robbers in Schiller throw into the flames a poor little child "who felt cold," Robert's robbers singe their beards to extract the child from blazing ruins, and they hire a clean, healthy nursemaid for him. They give pensions to the old; they as much as offer a hand to help the ladies step down from the carriage, while they mete out justice to their husbands or fathers. In a word, they only attack criminals—the scoundrels the official world has forgotten to judge and send to the gallows; they protect the widow and the orphan, they wage war on the partisans of despotism, but they do it with wonderful fairness; the innocent never pay for the guilty; innocent bystanders are never drawn into the scuffle; every bullet reaches its mark, and when the pockets of the usurers and extortionists have been emptied, it is to fill the hands of the poor. All that is hardly true to life, as you can see, but it would be pointless to criticize such a bad play. What is worth examining is the doctrine it contains.

This doctrine is nothing less than that of the Montagne, such as pure and generous hearts could conceive it, without any prescience of the excesses to which their system of horror and hostility would lead them. There is one scene in which Robert asks his accomplices to account for their conduct; they have just assassinated a powerful personage steeped in crime, and they accomplished it almost without striking a blow. "What?" said the leader, "Nobody defended him? His friends?" "Tyrants do not have any," answer the robbers. "But how about his courtiers?" "Courtiers are cowards," etc. Everything takes on this tone, and the audience bursts into applause, as you can imagine. Unfortunately, tyrants need not be surrounded by virtuous men and faithful friends for blood to flow in comparable struggles, and the blood of men divided in opinion is not always necessarily impure on one side or the other, but from the moment it had organized for terror, the Revolution could disregard these catastrophes, and while conjuring up this terrorist system, it had no desire to foresee them.

It is not here that I shall judge this system. Anyway, I doubt that one can judge it well no matter what one does; until now[37] historians have not resolved the questions that it raises. Perhaps the time has not yet come when the friends of humanity can put the Montagne on trial, because the power to do it resides in the hands of humanity's enemies, those who condemn guilty passions in the name of passions still more guilty.[38]

For thirty years the question has been put to us in this way: Would you have been a Royalist, a Girondist, or a Jacobin? Assuredly, I answer that I would have been a Jacobin, for probably my intelligence would not have been raised beyond the level of ideas which gave birth to the deeds. At present, no matter what happened, I would not be a Jacobin, but neither would I be a Girondist nor a Royalist. You can see that it is an insoluble problem when one poses it other than in the past. When we are more intelligent as well as more humane than the Montagne, we shall condemn the Montagne. We are already humane enough to detest the guillotine and the proscriptions. Are we clever enough to save a revolution that followed the same stages and encountered the same obstacles? I doubt it. What reassures the conscience with regard to the future is that revolutions do not copy each other, and that humanity never passes by the same road twice. In vain would it want to; the law of life is opposed.

Let us then leave to others the task of concluding on a hypothesis which will never come to pass. Everything that has been said, everything that will be said, observed, recounted, analyzed concerning the events of our history, will be useful to those who, one day, will have to pronounce on its errors and its benefits.

What concerns me at this moment, the little literary fact that I am analyzing, is not unworthy of occupying my readers for an instant. Let them remember—or find out, if they do not know—the travestied conclusion of Schiller's *Räuber*. As a historic invention, the shift of the dénouement into the fifteenth century is really hilarious, but as a revolutionary portent it is very interesting. Karl Moor, that is to say, Robert, the robber chieftain, covers himself with so much glory and does so many lovely things, that society becomes reconciled with him; the Germanic Kaiser extends his arms to him, his mistress perseveres in her love and marries him; his father blesses him, the populace are about to carry him in triumph, and henceforth regenerated Germany is going to adopt the principles of Robert's robbers and place these elite men at the head of its armies and government. In other words, the Montagne wins, Robespierre will reign; the world has returned from its erring ways. The Terror has passed over the earth like a cloud filled with salutary dew. The blade of the guillotine has purified humanity. These misunderstood men who yesterday were treated as thieves and assassins tomorrow shall be the archangels of the Revolution. They have floored the devil, they open the road to heaven to the reconciled people. "Hercules" has sanctioned their works.[39] The end has justified the means. That is the terrorist doctrine, not mine, but what are all of you complaining about, you who have done service for despotism? Isn't it also your doctrine?

Errors of our fathers, I do deplore you and do not curse you! But here is a more curious fact: our fathers were playing *Robert, chef de brigands* in 1798! The Terror had passed, its cloud having burst on their very heads; it had spewed up appalling calamities; they already knew, alas! that the end does not justify the means. Robert's robbers had tried in vain to purify humanity. It was waking up in the midst of smoking ruins, it was hastily wiping up the blood it had just spilled; it had killed Robert and his accomplices, henceforth hated and stigmatized as cannibals. The Directoire was an anarchy sullied with more vices than the Committee for Public Safety had crimes for which to blame itself. The world was not to be renewed, for the enemy was at our gates and we were calling for a dictator to save us. The men whose rigors and suspicions had exceeded those of Robespierre had assassinated Robespierre, and they were trying in vain to make it appear meritorious for the nation, which scorned and mistrusted them. Our fathers' consciences cried out to them the formula implicitly proclaimed by Schiller: "No, the end will never justify the means." And Bonaparte, moreover, was coming to power by means of this doctrine; they were going to submit to it once more; they were not at all worried about it; they laughed, our young parents, they were gay, they were in a hurry to live and forget their sufferings; they played with the debris of this awful idea, they dressed up as robbers, they conceived a passion for the role of reformers; they still said, with emphasis, "Tyrants have no friends, their death is a benefit to their subjects; courtiers are cowards," etc., etc., but the tyranny of the genius was approaching. The "subjects" of Napoléon were going to perish by the thousands for his glory, and the reign of the courtiers was going to flourish anew, more brilliantly and more insolently than under the former monarchy! Was Robespierre, the robber chieftain, therefore mistaken? Yes, alas! In reality, hadn't he ended the same as Karl Moor, detesting his work and delivering himself up to the blows of his enemies?

The illusion which had carried him so high, the prestige of the idea which had made him so strong, outlived him then, since after having cursed and sacrificed him, people were once again starting to believe in the world's salvation under another form! It is because faith is imperishable. The Republic had adorned itself with this title and did not wear it long, but the instinct for the true and the just was not destroyed along with fleeting forms. These forms were there like old theater costumes that one freshens up to be used for other roles, for new inventions. Joyfully my father buckled the belt that held the pistols of the robber chieftain, his young friends (several had already served the Republic as volunteers) enrolled in his troupe, and all together, forgetting they were performing a Jacobin play, dreamed of combat and wondrous events. These robbers were no longer the sansculottes of the future, they were budding field marshals of France. Robert was going to be called Bonaparte.

These theatrical performances filled the leisure of La Châtre's society for several months and fired my father's imagination more than his mother could foresee. Soon the action on stage would no longer satisfy him, and he would exchange his saber of gilded wood for a Hussar's.

I have just read this analysis of *Robert* to one of my childhood friends, the son of a friend of my father. The mother of my friend Charles Duvernet played the role of Sophie, the heroine of the play, and she played it very well, although (or, rather, because) she followed no method and no tradition. She was then not quite grown up, just recently married, never having left her province, and not only never had been in a play, but never had seen one performed. The first performance she attended was, therefore, the very one in which she resolutely played this tearful and difficult role. She played it with inspiration that to her was quite justified. That intelligent lady has retained down to the smallest detail memories of the incident which I am relating, and her son hands me a very curious note from her. M. Duvernet, father of my friend, and M. Delatouche, father of my other friend and compatriot, the author of *Fragoletta*,[40] were also playing important roles in the play.

Here is the note they eagerly passed on to me, in which will be found some unusual details that reveal an era unique in history:

"Near the church of the Carmelites at La Châtre (presently the town hall theater), stood, in the middle of the garden of the Carmelites, the dwelling of those religious, a vast and grandiose building (entirely destroyed in 1816). In the period of the Revolution, a long time after the closing of the church, the 'Société populaire,' corresponding to the Jacobin Society, chose for the site of its meetings the refectory of the Carmelite monks, a vast square room under a beamed ceiling, with windows facing the garden, and a large arched doorway. In that room they built graded rows of seats for members, probably also to represent the Montagne. But these rows of seats took up only a third of the room. They brought the pulpit from the Carmelite church, and they placed it at one end of the room to serve as a platform for speeches. The public took up the rest of the space, standing, and on tenth days[49] there was dancing.

"The Thermidor reaction came, then the Directoire. We took a deep breath, 'we got married,' we wanted to laugh and have fun. A drama society was formed. The monks' refectory, that is, the clubroom with its graded seats, was chosen as the theater site. They took out the pulpit and brought the stage forward in its place; opposite, behind the wall which backed the graded seats, an immense staircase led to the dormitories, which had become the offices of different administrations. On the first landing of this staircase, they cut out a doorway which led directly to the upper rows of seats. This was the entrance to the 'loges.' The parterre and the orchestra naturally took up the free space between the graded seats and the stage.

"Alongside the refectory extended the immense kitchen of the Carmelites. This was the foyer and at the same time the actors' dressing room; they hung curtains to separate the sexes.

"During the series of performances, M. Deschartres asked to join the orchestra with his pupil M. Maurice Dupin, then about eighteen or nineteen years old. The following year, M. Dupin wanted to quit the orchestra and become part of the troupe. There was a great debate and surprisingly it was the ladies who proved to be recalcitrant. M. Duvernet was, as a friend, the natural partisan of the postulant, and the majority of the men lined up on his side. The feminine faction made a lot of noise protesting against the 'grand seigneur'—but when the ballots were counted, it was clear that their aversion had not influenced their voting. We voted with white beans or red.

"Once admitted, M. Dupin brought his youthful fire to bear, which more than once nonplussed the classical traditions of the director, M. Delatouche, Senior. Finally, a play was chosen which had been avoided because of the difficulties of the principal role and the setting. It was *Robert, chef de brigands*. M. Dupin assumed the role of Robert and took charge of the sets. New scenery was made, extras were signed up, and the Hungarian-Croatians, who were in France as prisoners of war and who had been billeted at La Châtre, became Robert's soldiers. They had them simulate combat. They made clear to them that after the battle, they had to appear wounded; they were so well disciplined and conscientious that at the performances you could see them leaving the fray all limping on the same foot.

"Robert's costume consisted of a hussar's pelisse attached at the neck by a diamond clasp, tight red pants, a knitted belt outfitted with an awesome set of pistols and daggers, Louis XIII boots, an ample cloak of red wool edged with marten, and a fur bonnet. Maurice de Molda (Schiller's Franz Moor), played by M. Delatouche, Senior, was dressed in a no less curious costume: Louis XIV coat, cloak of white satin embroidered with silver, short trousers, silk hose, scarf and hat in the Henry IV style. Mme. Duvernet (Sophie) had a gown with a train held up by a brilliant spangled belt, and a long white veil reaching to the ground."

Thus, my father, robber chieftain on the boards where the monks had made merry and where the Montagne had held its meetings, was in charge of Hungarian and Croatian prisoners. Two years later, he was taken prisoner himself by the Croatians and Hungarians, who did not give him plays to perform and who treated him much more harshly. Life is a novel that each of us carries within, past and future.

But in the midst of my grandmother's indecisiveness concerning her son's career came that famous law of 2 Vendémiaire, Year VII (September 23, 1798), proposed by Jourdan, which proclaimed every Frenchman a soldier by right and duty during a specific period of his life.

War, asleep for a moment, threatened to break out anew on all fronts. Prussia was hesitating in its neutrality, Russia and Austria were zealously arming. Naples was enlisting its entire population. The French army was decimated by battles, sickness, and desertion. Once conceived and adopted, the conscription law was put into practice immediately by the Directoire, by ordering the raising of two hundred thousand conscripts. My father was twenty years old.

For a long time his heart had been leaping with impatience; inaction weighed on him, the young man was restless and prayed that a "stable" government, as his mother expressed her longing, would permit him to serve. He himself placed no great value on stability. When the mandated requisitions came to take away his only horse, he stamped his foot and said, "If I were a soldier, I would have the right to be a horseman; I would take horses for France from the enemy instead of submitting to going on foot like a useless, weak creature." Whether it was his instinct for adventure and chivalry, whether the seduction of new ideas, whether his insouciant temperament, or rather whether, as his letters prove on every occasion, it was the good sense of a clear and calm mind, he never missed the old regime or the opulence of his early years. Glory was for him a vague, mysterious word which kept him from sleeping, and when his mother persisted in proving to him that there was no true glory in serving an "unjust cause," he did not dare argue, but he sighed deeply and told himself that every cause is just, provided one could defend one's country and repel the foreign yoke.

Probably my grandmother felt the same way, for she strongly admired the great feats of arms of the republican army, and she had the battles at Jemmapes and Valmy at her fingertips, as well as Fontenoy and the earlier Fleurus, but she could not reconcile her logic with the fear of losing her only child. She would have been willing to see him provided with a regiment on condition that there would never be a war. The idea that he might one day eat in the mess and sleep in the open made her hair stand on end. At the thought of a battle, she felt like dying.

I never saw a woman so courageous in her own right, so weak when it came to others; so calm in facing personal dangers, so faint-hearted in facing the dangers to those she loved. When I was a child, she indoctrinated me so well with stoicism that I would have been ashamed to cry out in front of her if I hurt myself, but if she had been witness to it, it was she then, dear woman, who uttered loud screams. Her whole life was spent in this touching contradiction; and as everything good produces something good, as everything which comes from the heart always reacts on the heart, her weak spot did not affect her children in a way contrary to her teachings. We derived more courage from the will to spare her grief and fright by hiding our little pains than we perhaps would have if she had not given way when she saw them.

My mother was just the opposite. Rough on herself and others, she had a precious coolness, a wonderful kind of presence of mind which brings succor with it and inspires confidence.

Apparently both ways of behaving are useful although diametrically opposed. From which we may conclude whatever we wish. I personally have not found theories helpful in raising children. They are such changeable creatures that if you do not change along with them (when you can), they elude you at every stage of development.

My father had been called to Paris during the last days of the Year VI in order to settle some business, and in the first days of Year VII, that terrible conscription law struck him like an electric shock and was decisive in his life. I have sufficiently outlined the agitation of the mother and the secret wishes of the child. I shall now let him speak for himself.

Letter I   No date. Sometime during the last days of Year VI
                                          (September 1798), Paris.

To Citizeness Dupin, at Nohant

I have finally received a letter from you, my dear mother. It took eight days to arrive, which is expeditious all the same. How good of you to miss me! So, you are both fearful that I might succeed and that I might not? You pose a peculiar dilemma. I myself am rather calm as to the family business we have on our hands. To that end, I am busy with Uncle Beaumont, don't torment yourself. We'll come out of it all right. But as to current circumstances, I find your worries distressing. My poor mama, be brave, I beg you. It is impossible, under any pretext whatsoever, to be exempt from the latest law, and it concerns me absolutely. Generals can only take aides-de-camp from the ranks of officers. Public institutions such as the École polytechnique, the Conservatoire de musique, etc., have received orders not to admit any student considered to be in the first class. So you see, one must serve, and there is no way out of being a soldier. Beaumont has knocked on every door, and everywhere the same response. One no longer begins by being an officer, one ends up there, if one can. Beaumont knows all Paris, he is on particularly good terms with Barras and Rewbell. He introduced me to the good M. de La Tour d'Auvergne,[50] who by virtue of his fearlessness, his talents, his modesty, is worthy of being a Turenne for our times. After having questioned me carefully for some time, he said to me, "Could the grandson of Maréchal de Saxe be afraid to see active service?" These words caused me neither to pale nor to blush, and I answered him, "Certainly not," looking him straight in the eye. And then I added, "But I have some education, I have the ability to acquire some skills, and I believe I can serve my country better in a graded position, or at headquarters, rather than in the anonymous ranks of the simple soldier." "Well," he said, "it's true, and one must aspire to an honorable post. However, one must begin by being a soldier, and that is what I think you should be for the shortest possible time and the least severe. I have a close friend, a colonel in the 10th light cavalry regiment. You must enter his regiment; he will be delighted to have you. He is a man 'high-born of yore.' He will shower you with friendship. You will remain a plain infantryman for the time necessary to perfect your horsemanship. The colonel is on the list for promotion to general. If he is appointed, he will contact you personally at my recommendation; if he is not, I will have you go into engineering. But no matter what happens, you mustn't aspire to any grade until you have fulfilled the prescribed conditions; that is the nature of things. We must manage to combine glory and duty, the pleasure of brilliant service to our country and the laws of justice and reason." There you have almost word for word his speech.

Well, mother, what have you to say? There is no answer to that! Isn't it nice to be a man, a brave one like La Tour d'Auvergne? Doesn't one have to pay for that honor with some sacrifices, and would you want it said that your son, the grandson of your father, Maurice de Saxe, was afraid to see active service? The career is open. Should one prefer endless and shameful repose to the painful path of duty? And that is not the only consideration. Remember, mama, that I am twenty years old, that we are in financial straits, that I have a long course to run, you also, thank God! and that I can render you a little of the comfort you have lost by becoming something. It is my duty, it is my ambition. Beaumont is happy to see me with these ideas. He says that I must make up my own mind. It is very obvious that a man who doesn't wait for his number to come up, like delivered merchandise, but who, on the contrary, voluntarily presents himself to run to his country's defense, has more right to benevolence and advancement than one who is dragged by force. This conduct won't be approved by people in our class? They will be committing a grave error, and I for one shall disapprove of their disapproval. Let us let them talk, they would do better to imitate me. I see others who play the role of patriot and "handsome Titus" more than I, and who do not feel at all impelled to go to rejoin their flag.

Here one has little faith in peace, and Beaumont doesn't advise me at all to count on it. M. de La Tour d'Auvergne has already taken me under his wing. He said to Beaumont that he likes my calm demeanor, and the manner in which I answered him made him feel I was a man. You will say to that, dear mother, that he saw me at my best moment! But really one can often have such moments; one only needs the occasion. Our fortunes are reversed; should we let ourselves be discouraged because of that? Isn't it more beautiful to rise above our own reverses than to fall by our failings from the top of the heights where chance had placed us? The beginnings of this career can appear repugnant only to a common mind; but you, you will not be ashamed of being the mother of a good soldier. Armies are very well disciplined nowadays, officers are all people of merit, don't be afraid. It is not a question of going to battle immediately but of spending some time studying horsemanship. It will be all the less disagreeable since you made me learn perhaps more than they are going to show me. I don't need to brag about that, but I won't be serving an apprenticeship which endangers my bones or gives rise to laughter among the onlookers. You can at least rest easy on that score.

Goodbye, mama, give me your opinion on all my reflections, and remember that from the sorrow of our separation may result a great good for both of us. Goodbye again, my dear mother, I embrace you with all my soul.... Ah! here is the ham arriving in wonderful condition. We shall slice into it at dinner; it will be perfect. Yesterday, I went to the Italiens, I almost forgot to tell you; they were giving *Zoraïme et Gulnare*, a subject taken from *Gonzalve de Cordoue*. The music is in very new taste. It is M. de Florian's version of Arab. All in all, it is very pretty. Martin and Elleviou sing wonderfully in it. Chenard plays a mulatto jailor; he is terrifying and, as always, causes outbursts of laughter. He is an excellent comic. The sets are a realization of dreams of the Alhambra and the beautiful countryside of Andalusia. I was in the parterre, and during the intermission, having seen Rodier and his family arrive in the balcony, I planted myself behind them, surreptitiously, and while they were chatting, I blended into their conversation. They were quite astonished, and turning around, they saw me. This caused laughter and nonsense for the whole rest of the evening. On leaving, I felt someone clasp me on the shoulders in the lobby. It was D'Auberjon. "Oh! hello!" "Oh! hello to you!" "Oh! my friend!" "Oh! my comrade!" We noticed we were giving the spectators a show, and we went to eat a Bavarian cream together.

I do pay my respects to the eminent ladies. Ceaselessly "do I take pen to paper" to prove to Mme. de La Marlière how much...how much more than... that's enough! she shall see my style. I pray that Mlle. Fanny is making more progress at reversi[51] than I am. I waltz my maid, I embrace Deschartres, and I urge him to put a little more rosin on his bow to avoid the squeaks and the squawks. Come now, laugh, my dear mother!

The lives of modest great men go largely unpublished. How many wonderful gestures have had only God and conscience for witnesses! The letter you have just read contains such a gesture which profoundly stirs me. There is La Tour d'Auvergne, the First Grenadier of France, that unassuming and gallant hero, who himself departed shortly afterward as a plain soldier although his white hair did not render the new law applicable to him. This deed that several people have perhaps forgotten needs to be recalled. He had an octogenarian friend who lived only from the labor of his grandson. The conscription law strikes this young man—no means in such a case to buy his way out. As a special favor from the government, in reward for a glorious life, La Tour d'Auvergne obtains permission to report as a simple soldier, in place of his friend's grandson. He reports, he is covered with new glory, he dies on the field of honor, without ever having wished to accept any reward, any rank! Well, here is this man, with such feelings, perhaps with the plan already decided to have himself conscripted (at the age of fifty-five) in place of a poor young man, who finds himself in the presence of another young man, one who hesitates before the necessity of becoming a soldier. He examines attentively this spoiled child whom a fearful mother would want to shield from the rigors of discipline and dangers of war. He questions his look, his attitude. One feels that, if he discovers a cowardly heart, he will no longer take an interest in him and will make him blush to be the grandson of an illustrious military man. But one word, one look from this child suffices for him to sense a man in him; and immediately he accepts him in friendship, he speaks to him with sweetness, he condescends, through generous promises, to the solicitude of the mother. He knows that not all mothers are heroines; he guesses that this one cannot adore the Republic, that this young man has been reared with infinite delicacy, that people are ambitious for him, and that they could not accept the antiquated loyalty of a La Tour d'Auvergne as a model; but this La Tour d'Auvergne seems unaware of the sublimity of his own role. He draws from it so little vanity that he does not remind others of it; he exacts from no one else the same degree of virtue. He can love, even esteem those who aspire to the comfort and honors that he scorns. He takes part in their projects, he indulges their hopes, he will work to make them come true, just as an ordinary man would, who values the pleasures of life and the smiles of fortune. And as if he were talking to himself in order to diminish his merit in his own eyes and preserve himself from pride, he sums himself up by saying: "One can reconcile glory and duty, the pleasure of brilliantly serving one's country and the laws of justice and reason."

For me, this benevolent and simple language is thrice great, thrice holy, on the lips of a hero. What one sees, what one knows of an illustrious life can always be ascribed to a hidden subtlety of pride. It is in the detail, in the apparently insignificant deeds that one grasps the secret of the human conscience.

If I had ever doubted innocence in heroism, I would see proof of it in this sweetness of the First Grenadier of France. Anyone else in his place might well have said to my father, "My boy, you are descended from Maurice de Saxe, I am descended from Turenne; you are leaving the nest where a loving mother has gently hatched you, I have turned white on the fields of battle, and I count more than thirty years of active service; I believe therefore that my existence is as precious as yours; nonetheless, you fear being forced to become a soldier, and I am going to be one by my own accord. Tell that to your mother, and reflect on it a little yourself."

Such language would have been very wise, quite legitimate, and irrefutable. Well, it just did not occur to La Tour d'Auvergne to think of setting himself as an example and drawing a parallel which could make the young man blush. Sensitive and generous, he guessed what was going on in this poor child's heart; he saw the struggle that his youthful ardor was waging with filial love, the fear of devastating an adored mother. For an instant, the old soldier himself had a mother's heart to console and encourage this child for whom it seems he would have wished to be able to remove the thorns from along the path.

My father did not analyze this touching conduct, at least not when reporting it to his mother. But it is certain that his interview with this man who had commanded the "infernal column"[52] and who had so tender a heart and such gentle language made a profound impression on him. From that day on, his mind was made up, and he discovered he had a certain skill for deceiving his mother as to the dangers which were going to surround his new existence. One already sees that, by speaking to her about studies of horsemanship, he tries to divert her thoughts from the imminent eventuality of battles. Later on, you will see him still more ingenious in sparing her the torments of anxiety, until the moment when, indifferent himself to feelings of peril, he seems to think she

has accustomed herself to the fortunes of war. But she never resigned herself to
the inevitable, and a long time afterward, she wrote to her brother, Abbé de
Beaumont: "I detest glory, I would like to reduce to ashes all the laurel wreaths
on which I always expect to see the blood of my son. He loves what for me is
torture, and I know that, instead of protecting himself, he is always, and even
needlessly, at the most perilous post. He drank from that inebriating cup from
the day he saw M. de La Tour d'Auvergne for the first time; it is that accursed
hero who turned his head!"

I take up again the transcription of these dear letters, and I cannot convince myself that my reader finds them too long or too numerous. For my part,
when I realize that by publishing them I now and then extract from oblivion
some detail which honors humanity, I feel reconciled to my task, and I taste a
pleasure that the fictions of the novel have never given me.   *A.M.*

VIII

Letters continued. —Voluntary enlistment. —Military flair of the youth of 1798. —Letter from La Tour d'Auvergne. —Mess. —Cologne. —Général d'Harville. —Caulaincourt. —Capitaine Fleury. —Love of one's country. —Durosnel.

Letter II   Paris, 6 Vendémiaire, Year VII (September 1798).

I am writing to you, dear mother, from the home of our "man from Navarre"[41] The conscription law, which went into effect this morning ordering us to join up within the next twenty-six days, prevents me from waiting for your reply and impels me to take the action I spoke to you about. This morning we are both going to see the cavalry captain in order to settle this question. Don't worry, mother dear, it is a matter of being stationed in Brussels, not of going to face enemy fire. I will probably have a leave or an order "forcing" me to come home soon to embrace you. All the young men here don't know if they're coming or going. All the pretty women and the dear mothers are beside themselves; but it is uncalled for, I assure you. I am going to don the green dolman, take up the big saber, and let my mustache grow. And voilà, you'll be the mother of a defender of the nation who has a right to the milliard in pay; it will be clear profit. There, there, dear mother, don't torture yourself, you will be seeing me soon. After two or three months of service, I will obtain orders through our friend to go to Nohant, you can be sure of it; so just regard all this as an enforced trip for business. I have only one regret, which is being away from you for a while. Having to sign up as a simple soldier is nothing; and as for you, rest assured that you must not have the slightest worry on my account. Goodbye, my dear mother, I embrace you with all my heart; don't grieve, I beg you!

Letter III   Paris, 7 Vendémiaire (September '98).

I can't understand, my dear mother, why you didn't hear from me sooner. I sent a letter regularly in every mail. Day after day I have been waiting for your response to my new circumstances, but it hasn't yet reached me. The notice of conscription and call-up of young men is posted in all the streets. It is rumored that this call-up consists of bundling young men off to prison and forcing them to rejoin their corps. You mustn't let that frighten you. I am no longer subject to conscription, I am a volunteer. I have the big saber, the red toque, and the green dolman. As for my mustache, it is not yet as long as I would like, but that will come. Already "they tremble at the sight of me"; at least I hope so. So there, my dear sweet mother, do not worry; I shall come to see you at Nohant, if you want, before going off to camp. My captain offered me this. He is a very nice person, as cold as a well rope, but he knows how to treat people. I am certain I will receive a promotion soon. I have always aspired to be in the military; I would have, in any case, been obliged to be away from you. After all, you know, I must choose a profession in life. With a bit of willpower and courage, I may succeed in this one. I am just a soldier; but didn't the Maréchal de Saxe voluntarily serve as one for two years? You yourself admitted that I was old enough to pursue a career. I equivocated over the decision because you were too afraid of war, but deep down I wanted to be forced by circumstances to follow my own inclinations. That has happened. I would be happy about it, except for the pain of leaving you and of your worrying, which tears me apart; but I assure you, mother dear, that where I am going there is no fighting and that I will often have leave to go see you. Anyway, your cavalryman embraces you with all his heart and sends his respects to the eminent ladies. There is a vacancy in our regiment for a trumpeter; suggest it to old man Deschartres. A hug to my maid. Goodbye, goodbye, I love you.

Letter IV   Paris, 11 Vendémiaire (September '98).

Your two letters arrived at the same time, my dear mother. In the first one you are afraid that I will act too quickly; in the second, that I won't get to it on time. Do calm youself. The proclamation decided me, and as I have already written you, I am a soldier of the Republic. I have very good recommendations, and in spite of what you say about my desire to go to war, here I am, condemned to six months of camp. You can therefore sleep soundly for six months, and that is a lot. I will give you my news in detail; I am to be in Brussels on the 19th of this month, and I have no more than five days to return, for I will need three days to reach my post. My captain, who is cold but obliging, has said to me, however, that if my affairs were to keep me here a few days longer, he would extend my travel order. I shall hurl myself into the coach and thus arrive like a prince. The government gives us three sous per league, which adds up to nine or ten pounds from Paris to Brussels; which is, I hope, enough to travel magnificently. But I will not take advantage of this magnificence, and in accord with your wishes, I will go find M. Le Fournier, who will advance me six louis. He has already offered me more, if I need it. There is no one more decent and obliging than he.

Speaking of stopovers, I gave them quite a fright the other day at Épinay. I arrived with Rodier at nine in the evening. He went in first without saying I was with him. I went in through the kitchens. I announced myself to the housemaid, who arrived all flustered in the middle of the salon where the guests were, Mme. de Montagu and a few other elegant ladies. The housemaid tells Mme. de Montcloux that there's a drunken Hussar in the kitchen who claims he has a billeting order, who's breaking everything in sight, and they don't know what to do with him. Thereupon, all the men of the house are summoned, and they advance on me en masse. I go ahead of them into a dark corridor, swearing and disguising my voice. With the light coming from behind me and revealing only my plume and my toque, the confusion gave rise to the funniest questions and answers. Rodier, my buddy, came forward with a furious air and tried to throw me down, but the others held him back. I swore even more mightily, and they held me back. Finally, they recognized me and had a good laugh. But those ladies had such a nice scare that it made them all rather indisposed. Now there you have a lovely way to gain entrance to a house! If you had been there, my dear mother, you would have laughed at their frightened expressions. . . . But I can see your sad face, at home, and that breaks my heart in the middle of my gaiety. Take courage, all this is only momentary, and I will not give you cause for worry. Goodbye, my dear mother, I embrace you with all my heart. Don't forget to give my regards to the grapepicker Deschartres, worthy rival of Bacchus and Noah. A hug to my maid.

Letter V   Paris, 13 Vendémiaire, Year VII (October 1798).

I am writing to you just before going to see Général Beurnonville. A friend of M. Perrin, who is a close friend of the general, is introducing me. Beurnonville is the general of the Army of England, to which I belong, and through his resources I hope to advance quickly. It would be fitting if you wrote to him. You can tell him that you did not send me to defend my country any sooner because the law forbade it, what with my being classed with the nobles; that finally the conscription decree permitted me to join, and that you are asking for his support of me. There is only half a lie in all that—your eagerness to send me off to war. Anyway, you will manage it beautifully, I have no doubt. There is once more talk of peace here, and all my efforts are probably going to be spent in parades.

Yesterday I went to see the elephants, the lions, and the entire wild community at the Jardin des Plantes. There is a dog the size of Tristan locked up with the lioness. He bites her like Tristan bites La Belle, and makes her howl. However, that kind beast lifts him with her claws into her formidable jaws without doing him the slightest harm, for she loves him to distraction. A fine example of magnanimity for us members of mankind!

Goodbye, my dear mother, I am flying off to Beurnonville's. I will fill you in on how it went in the next mail. Rodier is leaving one of these days for Berry, I will have him bring you your wig and old Deschartres his shoes. Won't his feet be pretty in those shoes! I embrace you with all my heart.

Letter VI   16 Vendémiaire.

I was at Beurnonville's, he received me very warmly. Since five or six people had spoken to him of me, among them Mme. de Bérenger, I hardly needed to identify myself. He told me to return tomorrow, that he would give me a letter of recommendation for the commanding general of the Army of Mainz, to which I belong (for I was wrong in writing you that I was with the Army of England); that soon, on his recommendation, I would be assigned to this general; that in six weeks he would come to Brussels to pass us in review, that I had only to come see him, and that as soon as I was familiar with cavalry maneuvers, steps would be taken to have me promoted. Goodbye, my dear mother, I am off to my captain to extend my travel order. I embrace you as I love you. I hope you aren't worried any more?

Letter VII   17 Vendémiaire, Year VII (October '98).

Beurnonville has given me two letters of recommendation, one for the brigade chief commanding the 10th regiment, to which I belong; the other for Général d'Harville, inspector general of the cavalry of the Army of Mainz. He recommends me to them as the grandson of the Maréchal de Saxe, "a model for us all," he says; he requests employment for me, at first as clerk, then as whatever they find me good for. He recommends me just as highly to the brigade chief, saying that he will take note of any consideration the chief will have for me. You can see that my affairs are on the right track and that with such recommendations I won't moulder away in the barracks. He tells them, for example, that my family is supporting me and that I will not need a salary. That is not exactly what pleases me the most, for we aren't rich and I'm going to cost you some money. Let's hope, however, that it won't be long before I can live off my own work! Do not worry any more, my dear mother, and believe that you will perhaps be hearing about me soon.... I am going to visit Murinais, who has promised to teach me in less than a week how to do charting and use the mapping board. That could be useful to me in the future.

Goodbye, I embrace you with all my heart.

Letter VIII   19 Vendémiaire, Year VII (October '98).

This morning I am going to visit my captain "Coussaud" (as he is called), and I shall go with him to the war office to have my travel orders extended in order to arrive in Brussels around the 30th. If I wanted to recruit here, I would make a fortune; for young men continually approach me everywhere—in the streets, at the theater—wanting to know the name of my regiment and what to do to join it. There is nothing like a good example. At the beginning everyone trembled with fear; now everyone wants to sign up. My uniform, which is extremely handsome, tempts a good number of them. It consists of a green dolman with all manner of piping, braid, and buttons; the collar and lapels are scarlet, the toque is a tall one in black and red, ditto for the plume. I have bought a fine, curved saber in the Hussar's style, which cost me thirty-three pounds. Today I dine at Mme. de Nanteuil's in full dress; she wants to have me meet a young man who wishes to join my regiment. We shall leave for Brussels together, and I shall have a traveling companion. The newspaper has been saying lately that the most important families in Brussels have been eager to get their sons into the 10th regiment stationed in that city. Thus you see, mother dear, that I shall be in merry company and that I am not the only person to have found that course the right one. Don't be upset, mother dear, I shall not suffer, and I shall have leaves to go to see you. And furthermore you know perfectly well it is only the stupid ones who can't make do and aren't good at anything. Mme. La Marlière writes to M. Perrin that old man Deschartres is still the rage with his violin, which does not prevent me from embracing him with all my heart, and you, my dear mother, I squeeze you tenderly in my "soldierly" arms. I am off to M. Coussaud's—for you know that you may

> Keep your mistress
> Waiting at the church

but

> ...never leave your
> Captain in the lurch.[42]

Letter IX   20 Vendémiaire, Year VII (October '98).

I still plan to leave on the 27th and am hurrying to say my goodbyes. At Mme. de Ferrières' I saw the De Fargès daughters, the elder of whom is Mme. de Brosses. The duke and others are going to give me letters of recommendation for Brussels, for with no passport other than my uniform, I shall not be invited anywhere. I myself will take your letters to Beurnonville and to my captain; I am to go charting with the latter in a few days; I should tell you that he does not know how to use the graphometer, and that now, thanks to Murinais, I know how to chart as if I had done it all my life. Please send me, my dear mother, my case of drawing instruments, my violin, and my graphometer.

My God, yes, upon arriving I shall be put up in the barracks and fed at the mess. Well, so what? There are worse things in life. To prove to you that I have no desire "to destroy myself," I am going out to purchase a good heavy green coat to wear this winter while I am doing patrol and sentry duty on the ramparts of Brussels. The regimental ones are half-coats, which cover only part of you, and are made of material that's good for fishing for minnows. I'll find a stray one somewhere and will come by it cheaply, I hope. My entire outfit, a sketch of which I am sending you, has cost me seventy-one pounds. But since M. Le Fournier has had to pay that debt for you (you know what I mean), I hardly dare ask him to advance me six louis. I hope you find the hat good-looking; it is like the one worn by the hussars, from whom we differ only slightly.

You tell me that you don't want people in Berry to know in what capacity I serve; but, dear mother, it will have to come out some time. First of all, what imbeciles are going to take offense at seeing your son a soldier of the Republic? Furthermore, so that you will not be bothered in my absence, I shall have to send to the town hall a certificate attesting to my activity in the military service, otherwise I shall be considered a fugitive and an émigré, which hardly suits me. M. de La Tour d'Auvergne is out in the country; I shall give him your letter when he returns. The coach takes only forty-eight hours to go from Paris to Brussels, so I shall arrive at my post punctually. Goodbye, dear sweet mother, I embrace you with all my heart.

Letter X   23 Vendémiaire, Year VII (October '98).

Ah! my poor dear mother! How good you are to send me your diamonds! Not possessing the wherewithal for my equipment, you do as the women of Rome, you sacrifice your jewels for the needs of the country; I shall have them appraised and sold as advantageously as possible.

Letter XI   25 Vendémiaire, Year VII (October '98).

Yesterday I dined with M. de La Tour d'Auvergne at the home of M. de Bouillon. Ah! my dear, what a man M. de La Tour is! If you could chat with him for only an hour, you would no longer have so much chagrin at my being a soldier! But I see that this is not the time to prove to you that I am right; your grief prevents me from convincing you. I gave him your letter; he found it charming, admirable, and he was touched; that is because he is as kind as he is courageous. Let me confess to you that if there had only been men such as he in the Revolution, I would be even more revolutionary than I am . . . that is to say, barring your imprisonment and your hardship, I would be.

From there I went to the Italiens to see *Montenero*; it was awful. It consists of several scenes from *The Mysteries of Udolpho* very badly strung together; silly words, insignificant music. The sets were magnificent. The audience applauded thunderously and called for the author; I shouted for the set designer. At the end of an interminable and boring song in five couplets, as the parterre were applauding furiously and the boxes were yawning with mouths agape, I shouted, "Bis!" That proposition revolted the boxes, and they did me the honor of hissing at me as I stood my ground. All the elegant ladies of Paris were there: Mme. Tallien, Mlle. Lange, and a thousand others—as many Greeks as Romans—all of whom did not prevent me from being bored. Tomorrow M. Perrin will give me tickets for the République, where they are playing a new tragedy by Ducis, entitled *Les Comédiens*. Goodbye, dear mother, I love you with all my heart.

Letter from La Tour d'Auvergne to My Grandmother

Passy, 25 Vendémiaire, Year VII of the French Republic.

Madame, I received only this very moment the extremely flattering letter that you did me the honor of sending. You owe me no thanks for what I was able to do for your son in the awkward situation in which he found himself. The people who owed me a true debt of gratitude were his officers and his fellow comrades. They too have not failed to make known to me their every thought and feeling concerning the favor I had done them by procuring young Maurice as their comrade in arms, who already has every promise of one day fulfilling the great destiny of his immortal grandfather. Every precaution and all possible steps have been taken to assure that his service will be pleasant and comfortable. Set your mind at ease, Madame, concerning the first steps in his career at arms. Peace, in which I still believe in spite of appearances to the contrary, might send him back to you earlier than you dare hope. Therefore, make a place for this thought amidst all those reasons for being alarmed, which a mother's affection so easily finds deep in her heart whenever her son is separated from her for the first time. I shall not attempt, Madame, to arrest the first impulses of your sensibility; they are only too legitimate. I do not have the good fortune to be a father, but I feel that I deserve to be one, judging from the effect your letter had on me.

I beg you, Madame, to accept my most respectful homage,

Citizen La Tour d'Auvergne,
Infantry Captain Corret.

Letter XII   27 Vendémiaire in the evening, Year VII (October '98).

I am leaving at daybreak, dear mother. I have just taken leave of my captain, who was charmed by your letter and who in turn gave me one for the squadron commander; then he embraced me effusively. I don't know what I've done to him, but cold as he is, that worthy man seems to love me like his own son. Beurnonville has recommended me everywhere; he has heaped kindnesses on me; he calls me his "Saxon." I think that I owe all this to the letters sent by my dear mother rather than to my own doing. I am sending you a duplicate of my enlistment papers. Beaumont took me to his district and had me registered. That step was necessary; otherwise, in spite of my presence in the corps, I would have been liable to the penalties prescribed by law. You are going to read that I practice the profession of light cavalryman and that my height is "one meter seven hundred thirty-three millimeters," which you won't understand, and you will perhaps imagine that during this past month I have grown seven hundred thirty-three cubits, but that still makes only five feet, three inches. Yesterday, after reserving my seat in the coach, I left the office with the clerk who had put my name on the list. "Ah, Monsieur! I am subject to conscription; your uniform suits you well, will you take me to your captain?" "Certainly, comrade, I'm going to see him, come with me." A young man who had also come to reserve a seat overheard us and followed; soon I'll be taking along the driver and the horses.

So you see, mother dear, I am not the only one who has a taste for the military, for everyone is going off happy and proud. I take my leave, I embrace you, I love you; I exhort old Deschartres, my maid, and even also Tristan, to distract you, to reassure you, to take care of you. I shall soon be back, be sure of that, and I shall be happy!

Maurice.

Letter XIII   Cologne, 7 Brumaire, Year VII (October '98).

Here I am in Cologne. Bah! How did I get so far away? Envision that, on arriving in Brussels, I entered the quarters of the 6th company. They were about to sit down to dinner, which is to say, line up around the mess kettle. I was politely invited to dine, I took a spoon, and there I was gorging myself with the rest. But for a slight smoky taste, the soup was indeed very good, and

I assure you that no one can die from that cooking. Afterwards, I offered a few pitchers of beer and some ham all around. We smoked a few pipes, and there we were, as friendly as if we had spent ten years together. Suddenly, the call is sounded; we go down into the courtyard. The squadron leader comes forward, I go to meet him, hand over my letter from the captain, and he shakes my hand; but he informs me that the brigade commander and the general are at the outposts of the Army of Mainz with the rest of my regiment. I see instantly that there is nothing for me to do in Brussels and say so point blank to the squadron leader, who unhesitatingly agrees. He expedites a travel order for me to the outposts, and after eighteen hours of friendship with my leader and my comrades, I'm gone!

But destiny, dear mother, serves me better than prudence. I was passing through Cologne on my way to the outskirts of Frankfurt, where my regiment is, when I learned that Citizen d'Harville, general in charge and inspector of the Mainz cavalry, was going to arrive here in two days. I halt my course, I await him. Everyone tells me that with the recommendation of Beurnonville, his friend, I will at once be employed on his staff as a clerk. I will therefore be more active—if not in body, at least in mind—than if I were forced to remain on orders as a barracks soldier. Thus my affairs are going well, rest assured.

You will learn from the newspapers that there has been trouble in Brabant over the conscription. For a few hours the insurgents held the city and the citadel of Malines; but the French, against whom resistance is impossible, drove them out and killed three hundred of them. Twenty-seven were brought to Brussels while I was there, and I saw people of all ages among them, including two Capuchin monks. The conscription was only a pretext, and the plan of the insurgents was to promote an invasion of the English, for they are spreading out from the coast at Ostend and from Ghent. Our coach broke down and we were forced to spend eight hours in Louvain; at all the towns en route, people came out to meet us in a mood of great emotion. Rumors had spread that Brussels was in a state of insurrection because no one saw any coaches arrive. The alarm had reached a point where this was the biggest news in the area, and people found it hard to believe me when I said that, when I left, Brussels was quite calm. Many units from the Army of Mainz have been called down, and they hope soon to have Brabant pacified. More and more I bless the benefits you heaped on my childhood, dear mother. German is of the greatest use here; during the whole trip I served as interpreter for my fellow passengers. They were very sorry to leave me in Cologne and thus lose their go-between. You are going to spend a very sad winter, mother dear, and the very thought of it pains me. But I hope to be given orders of some kind for the department of Indre. I shall again come to take care of you, to hug you, and to make you laugh. Your pain is my only worry, for I don't care about what can happen to me and I'm sure that I'll come out of it all right.

While waiting for Général d'Harville, our cavalryman took walks along the Rhine, and in spite of his joy at being a soldier, he could never resign himself to the absence of his mother. "The banks of the Rhine remind me of the banks of the Seine at Passy," he wrote on the 9th of Brumaire, "and I suddenly find myself sad, thinking of you and calling out to you, as in the days when we were so unhappy." He meets one of Général Jacobé's aides-de-camp; they talk music, they play some together, they become friends. Général d'Harville finally arrives and instantly chooses Beurnonville's protégé as his clerk. He promises a handsome horse, completely equipped, as soon as possible, for horses were hard to come by then, and they had to wait a long time for the one in question.

This general, who at the time called himself August Harville, was the Comte d'Harville who has since been a senator and a lord-in-waiting to Josephine; he had been a field marshal before the Revolution; then, under the command of Dumouriez, he had been a little indifferent or hesitant at the battle of Jemmapes. Brought before the revolutionary tribunal following the latter's betrayal, he had the good fortune to be acquitted. The rest of his life was spent enjoying favors rather than fighting for glory. In 1814, he voted for the deposition of the emperor and was made a peer of France. This could have been a fine, gallant man, but the sum of these lives which have served every cause does not leave a very heartwarming impression on the memory of mankind, and one is always a bit suspicious of their sincerity. This general was very sensitive to influence from the highborn. His aide-de-camp and relative, the young Marquis de Caulaincourt, pushed him toward snobbishness and conservatism. The aristocratic nature of these two characters is well drawn in my father's letters, which I shall again cite, for they furnish a rather original picture of the reactionary spirit which was growing each day in the ranks of the army. There we shall see that the equality of rights established by the Revolution was in fact already no longer equality at all.

Letter XIV   Cologne, 26 Brumaire, Year VII (November '98).

The general's aides-de-camp, one of them being Citizen Caulaincourt, invited me to dinner yesterday. It was a very gay, very friendly meal. Afterward, we went to his room to visit with the general, who has an erysipelas infection on his leg. I remained alone with him for half an hour. He spoke to me with the leisure and affability of a personage of days gone by, worrying over the way I was housed and fed; then he asked a thousand questions about my past, my birth, my connections. On learning that the wife and daughter of Général de La Marlière had spent the summer with you, that the daughter of Général de Guibert had married my nephew, that Mme. Dupin de Chenonceaux had been my grandfather's wife, he became more and more gracious, and it was evident that he was not indifferent to all that. After that, there was some music. Many of Cologne's elegant men and women were there, who were rather well turned out, for Germans. Everyone asked the general, "Who, pray, is that cavalryman?" For in Germany, it is not customary for clerks to socialize formally with superior officers, and that breach of etiquette unsettled them a bit; I could care less, and I go about my business as if it were nothing, all the more so because after the concert came a magnificent collation of which not a single dish found me squeamish. Then some punch . . . and then there were waltzes. And then the aides-de-camp invited me to supper with Général Trigny, the resident commander. We drank some of the greatest champagne, then some more punch, then we were a bit tipsy, and then we each went our own way at midnight.

You see that, even if I don't have a sou, I am living like a prince. The general staff is very well chosen. The aides-de-camp are all very personable young men, and "Citizen" de Caulaincourt has told me the general thinks that in three or four months I'll be an officer.

They are still fighting the rebels; several villages between Mons and Brussels have been burned. Cologne is quiet. . . .

Tell my maid that there are several vacancies here for canteen keepers and that I am offering her one. I embrace *il signor* Fugantini[53] Deschartres. Are they still prattling on in the neighborhood about my absence? Have they come to the realization that I did not emigrate but am a soldier? Are all our good peasants leaving to join up? Do they ask you where I am? Crowds of conscripts are arriving here. They are counted, regimented, and led around like sheep. Every morning, the street around general headquarters is full of them; some of them sing; a few, poor things, have tears in their eyes. I would like to be able to console them or give them my gaiety.

I now know the city as if I had always lived here. It is a very sad and solemn pile of churches, convents, and old brick houses. The Rhine is very wide here and carries small merchant ships coming from Holland. There is a flying bridge that crosses the river in six minutes. It is attached by a single rope, placed in the middle of the Rhine, and as a result of the current pushing in different directions against the sides of the ships, the rope describes a circle and carries the bridge from one bank to the other.[54] It can hold a cavalry unit. Since soldiers and dogs can use it gratis, I often give myself the pleasure of a crossing.

Letter XV   7 Frimaire, Year VII (November '98).

. . . I cannot understand the slowness of the mail. I am consumed with impatience. Every day I go looking for a letter, every day I return empty- handed. Being utterly deprived of news from you makes everything else intolerable. I am unable to find anything to distract me, nor can I concentrate on a thing. I cannot stay in one place very long; I prefer being outdoors in the rain or the cold than shut up in my little room, thinking that you might be ill, or angry with me, or sad! . . .

The 11th.

Finally, mother dear, a letter from you! It had been lying in the military post office for a week, while I kept going to the German post office. That damned German post office! They'll never catch me there again. Ah! how I needed to hear from you! When one is in a foreign country for the first time in his life, cut off from everything he has known, far from everything he loves, he has moments of dread. It does no good to steel myself to events and try to make light of them; there are times when our separation depresses me and my courage fails. But I fight it, and I regain my strength of mind by thinking of the moment which will reunite us. I don't want to be as childish any more as I was at Passy, when I did not have enough sense to hide my pain from you. True enough, there was no way then to forget oneself, and here at least I have an active life which saves me.

By dint of rushing around in order to escape my somber thoughts, I came down with a cold and a fever; but that lasted only two days; now that I have your letter, now that I know you are well, that I still have your blessing and your approval in spite of your worry, I am well again. I feel marvelous this evening; don't start worrying, please. I feel like crossing out the word fever, which is going to frighten you; just know that it was a very little fever, a tiny dwarf of a fever. And whenever a few days have gone by without news of me, think of the thousand insignificant circumstances which can delay a letter. This is a folly—an awful harm we inflict on ourselves when we insist on getting a letter on such and such a day, at such and such a time. If it doesn't come, our minds can conceive of nothing short of the death of our loved ones; we then become sick, real maniacs; I have just experienced it.

Don't think I am preaching this lesson to prepare you for any irregularity on my part. I will do my best to write at every mail. It gives me so much pleasure to chat with you, dear mother, that I can think of no other that could entice me from it.

You ask me for details about the "functions of my office." Just between us, they come down to warming myself from time to time at an excellent German stove, to making conversation with those gentlemen, the secretaries, who don't seem to me any more weighed down with work than I am. From there, we go to dinner together or for a walk....

Do tell Saint-Jean that I dreamed I was galloping on my mare. If they give me a good horse, he'll have a share in it. So, M. de G. thinks I occupy an important post? Rest assured he is not that stupid, that he doesn't think such a thing at all, and that it is the bantering sarcasm of a "gentleman."

Goodbye, my dear mother; how I do love you!

Letter XVI   Cologne, 14 Frimaire, Year VII (December '98).

. . . . By special favor, the general has ordered the remount at Namur to send me, via a reliable man, one of their best horses, completely equipped. I am thus going to be well mounted, which already makes me stand out in the general's stables. Ever since they learned that he sent a messenger sixty leagues in order to bring me a horse, the squires and grooms look at me in veneration, and even if I should sit like a pair of tongs on an old nag, they consider me in advance as the handsomest rider in the world; my horse will be fed at the expense of the Republic, and in that he'll be ahead of me; for I haven't yet heard a word about my pay—which is six sous a day—owing to the fact that the copy of my enlistment has not yet arrived. I am practicing the strictest economy; but the 200 pounds you sent me did me a world of good. I was boarded very expensively and very badly with a Herr Badorf, whom I could not leave because I was unable to pay him and who would have ruined me, if my general hadn't had the extreme kindness to wrest me from his clutches by paying my bill. I am now at the home of a good bourgeois where the fare isn't sumptuous; but we are surviving, and that's all that counts. I'm getting used to the Flemish beer which, in spite of its reputation, is horrible. German cuisine isn't worth a damn either; in France we are spoiled children when it comes to what pertains to physical existence.

At the theater I met a cavalry captain called M. Fleury. He is the one whom I saw at La Châtre last spring, the one with whom I did some fencing. He is the best of men. We embraced like old friends. It is such a pleasure to meet someone from home in a foreign land! He is stationed at Mulheim, on the right bank of the Rhine. He made me promise to visit him, and I shall, as soon as my horse arrives. I have never seen anyone so surprised to see me. How happy he was to be able to talk about La Châtre with someone from La Châtre! We had supper together and drank to the health of Berry with two bottles of Rhine wine. Please, mother dear, let all his relatives know about this happy meeting. Moreover, tell them he's well, and still as strong as a Turk. And such a nice fellow! But this encounter made me so think of you that I believed I was "at home," and now I'm quite sad!

The Captain Fleury under discussion here was indeed a worthy and excellent military man. A volunteer at age sixteen, he had already fought in all the campaigns of the Army of the Rhine in '92. He distinguished himself in '98, at the time of Moreau's crossing of the Danube, the very same year my father had met him in Cologne. At the head of his squadron, he withstood the onslaught of four squadrons of Austrian cuirassiers. That magnificent resistance gave his regiment time to cross the river. He was decorated in 1807, and left the service with the rank of major in the 10th regiment of Cuirassiers. His son Alphonse Fleury is my childhood friend.[43]

At this point in the collection of letters, so preciously conserved by my grandmother, is one from Général d'Harville which is rather curious. In it he speaks in completely paternal terms of his young cavalryman and apprises her of the dangers he should be guarded against. The first one is his lack of economy, and there the general is perfectly right; for with the best resolutions in the world and with the naïve conviction that he was prudent and steady, my father was completely improvident, and abandoning himself to all things and all people with the ease of an artist, he managed all his life to leave behind him debts to be paid. I shall let pass in silence the details of these minutiae, even though they take up a large part of his letters. He was not one of those who, to use a soldier's phrase, "wangle money" out of their parents. Always sincere with his dear mother, always in despair at not being able to support her instead of being supported by her, he goes into great detail, he makes painful efforts to explain to her what has become of the scarce and diabolical commodity called money, which melts in his hands he knows not how. The fear of not keeping his word makes him decide to confess at the earliest opportunity, and his confessions are touching. In sum, his filial love, the pain of seeing his mother deprive herself for his sake, the consciousness of his honor wage such battle with the carefree and liberal side of his character (which he got from his father) that he did succeed in becoming as prudent and sober as it was given him to be. In the long run, his whole adventurous and agitated existence did not cause too serious a deficit in the family's modest means.

Général d'Harville's second warning has less foundation and was underlined in his letter by my grandmother, who probably found it very strange. "I fear for him his liking for music, which can too easily cause him to drift into bad company." What a barbarian the good general was! In the eyes of my grandmother, as in those of her son, I am sure there was not a more ridiculous blasphemy. But in all likelihood she abstained from reporting this to her dear Maurice and nonetheless sent him his violin.

Letter XVII   Cologne, 20 Frimaire, Year VII (December '98).

I have not received any news from you in the last two mails, dear mother! My friend, the secretary at staff headquarters, who usually brings me your letters, arrived at the theater empty-handed, and as soon as he saw me from afar he sadly shook his head. They say that the post office has gone bankrupt and that this can interrupt epistolary communications for some time, if the government doesn't take over the service. That is all I'd need! Being far from you is already very hard; not hearing from you would drive me to despair....

Yesterday I was at the cathedral to hear a rather beautiful benediction set to music. All the lovely and elegant women of the city were there. As I went in, with my Hussar's uniform, and my saber hitting the stone floor, they all thought the devil was on their tail. They looked at me wide-eyed with fright. For them a Frenchman of the Republic is the Antichrist. I scare them rather often that way, for they have very good organists, and whenever I pass by a church and hear it filled with beautiful harmonies, I enter as if drawn by some irresistible force.

On leaving the benediction, I went to the theater to hear *Nina*. At the moment I least expected it, I heard them sing the duet that you taught me when I was a child, "He calls me his good friend," etc. And the whole piece came back to me immediately, every last word, and I thought I had forgotten it. I found myself back with you once again on the Rue du Roi-de-Sicile, in your pearl gray boudoir! It is uncanny how music can plunge you in memories! Just like smells. The perfume of your letters takes me back to your room at Nohant, and my heart leaps at the thought that I am going to see you open the little inlaid cabinet which smells so good and which reminds me of such grave things of a time now gone by.[44]

.... After the play, that devil of a fellow (my friend, the secretary) took me out to supper. I didn't want to drink any wine because it is too expensive here and I'd like to get out of the habit. I hadn't tasted any for six days; but seeing it on the table, and urged on by my comrade, I couldn't resist.

So, here I am this morning, detesting beer again. Ah! what a drunkard's resolution that was! "What, you've become a drunk!" you're going to exclaim. No, my dear mother, I am not and will not become one, but I now understand that privation can make a man intemperate, and that the poor devil who is short of bread can lose his senses "in his cups," whenever he gets the chance. Besides, good wine is certainly the great comforter of mankind. Yesterday I was sad and as homesick as a Swiss, and this morning I feel myself capable of braving all the strokes which fate may have in store, no more or no less than Alexander or Caesar, who most certainly did not drink Louvain beer. But were I to swallow all the wine in Greece and Italy, it wouldn't console me for our separation. You recently asked for news of my mustache. It is as black as ink and can be seen at least a hundred feet away. Goodbye, my dear mother, I embrace you with all my heart. I toss my maid thirty feet into the air and bang my fist down on old Deschartres' head. These are "military" customs, very pretty indeed!

Letter XVIII   Cologne, 23 Frimaire, Year VII (December '98).

Upon my word, dear mother, if I dared I would scold you, for I do not hear from you, and I cannot get used to it. Once more I have come back from digging through the general's dispatches, and once more I have come back sad. The day before yesterday, I went to see my good compatriot, Capitaine Fleury;[(45)] I went there with another captain from his regiment. We took a sailing launch down the Rhine as far as Mulheim in a wind which whipped our faces and sent us along at a good clip. He gave us a very good dinner of which I was in great need; for that bloody wind had given me a huge appetite. The good man welcomed us with open arms, and we did nothing but talk about Berry. The sentiment that one calls love of country is of two kinds. There is the love of the land itself, which you feel as soon as you set foot on foreign soil, where nothing pleases you, neither the language, the faces, the customs, nor the types of people. Mixed in with that is a certain national pride which makes you think that everything is nicer and better at home than elsewhere. Military pride is mixed up in it too, God knows why! But childish or not, I can suddenly be overcome by it, and a passing joke at my uniform or my regiment would make me as angry as an old soldier whose saber or mustache was being ridiculed.

And then beyond that attachment for the land and that esprit de corps, there is love of nation, which is something else and can hardly be defined. No use for you to say, my dear mother, that I'm building a mythical case, I feel I love my country like Tancrède:

Be it worthy or not, I give it my life!

We all felt these deep loyalties through the haze of our Rhine wine as we furiously clinked glasses and drank, Fleury and I, to Berry and to France.

How is your poor tenant farmer? Are his children leaving to join up? Does old Deschartres persist in his miraculous cures? Does he ride my mare? Is he still scratching away on his violin? Tell my maid that my shirts are in a sorry state since they are no longer her business. It was very good of her to suggest that I send her my linen so she could mend it! The cost of sending it back and forth would be more than the linen is worth.

Letter XIX   Cologne, 27 Frimaire, Year VII (December '98).

Since you insist, I shall try to buy some shirts and handkerchiefs, but the uniform they require of us uses up all our money. The general is going to pass us in review, and M. de Caulaincourt ordered me to have some boots made, because mine do not have the required two seams, nor spurs screwed on to the heel, according to regulations. They are sticklers for things like that. My toque wasn't trimmed in velvet, my plume wasn't the required eighteen inches. Fortunately my dolman has the six rows of little silver buttons. But I had to get a pair of green cashmere trousers all tricked out with goatskin piping. There you have the "perquisites" of ordinance. One has to be in dazzling dress to accompany generals. If I had your beautiful martens, I would have made an Ulan cap, for that's all the rage now, and it would enhance my image in the regiment. But don't go sending them to me. I don't want to use them until I'm an officer. I am quite "handsome" enough as it is, and when I go out in full dress, the conscripts on duty take me for a general and present arms. On the other hand, the old whiskers who stand guard for the general are not taken in, and present nothing whatsoever. No, I did not take your portrait; I gave it to Uncle Beaumont for safekeeping. I would have feared that others might fall in love with it and steal it from me. But I still have the chain around my neck, as in the Passy days. It doesn't show, and don't worry, I would rather eat dirt than sell it. I am truly sorry about the death of your poor tenant farmer. Give my friendly greetings to all our good peasants. What! Old Deschartres thinks he too has to be ill? I prescribe warm water and an emetic, the great remedies he is so good at administering to others, but which I don't think he would bother about for himself. However, I wouldn't joke about this if it were serious and if you hadn't told me at the end of your letter that he is better. Goodbye, my dear, my excellent mother, I embrace you with all my heart.

Letter XX   Cologne, 3 Nivôse, Year VII (December '98).

For days we have been on the verge of leaving on the general's tour of inspection. But now we are not leaving at all, and there will be no inspection; we'll be here yet another month or longer. Since our troops have just been ordered to cross over the left bank again, the divisions are changed. The general no longer has the same number of regiments under his command. I am very disappointed by these changes; I would have traveled and seen something of the country. My horse has not yet arrived, but I would have taken the one belonging to my fellow clerk, the red Hussar, who is in the hospital. Don't worry about the new law, it does not apply to me but to public servants working in offices. They, in effect, must be incorporated in those regiments to which they will be assigned; but as for me, I am doing "double" military service, since my being employed by the general doesn't stop my belonging to my regi-

ment. They owe me my pay, my clothes, my horse, just like the rest of the soldiers. True enough, I never hear anything about all that, but I have to hope that
the order will be complied with. My duty counts double, as does that of the
others. So don't worry about these things.

What! The chimney caught fire and I was not to blame? That is an outrage, for you know how nicely I acquit myself of such things. If my violin has
not left, please do not send it; for if the general should change headquarters, I
would be afraid my dear instrument might fall into profane hands, and that
would be wishing it dead. Suggest to our virtuoso Deschartres that he play it
often, so that it doesn't get rusty. Now there's a nice errand for you! But make
sure that he plays it far from your earshot. So you're still playing out your
hands of patience? Do you remember how impatient your "patiences" made
me? They have no sense, those cards, since they didn't tell you I was still in
Cologne.

Letter XXI   Cologne, 8 Nivôse, Year VII (December '98).

I have just been apprised of very good news, my dear mother. My regiment, which was on the way to Italy, is coming back to Deutz, which is only on
the other side of the Rhine. It might be there right now, as I write. It is consequently under the inspection of my general. At the theater I met an adjutant
general named Guibal, who asked if my general intended to make me an officer. I said that he had given me to hope so. A few days later he spoke to him
about me, and the general replied that in the beginning he feared I might be a
scatterbrain, but that now he knew me better and took a strong interest in me,
that he was going to keep an eye on me, and that his plan during his inspection
tour was to choose the depot best equipped in instructors and horses and send
me there, so that I could master cavalry maneuvers as soon as possible. Except
that we're back where we started: as to the last item, somewhat indefinitely
postponed.

A splendid ball was given the day before yesterday; the general was there
with his aides-de-camp. I went up to greet him, and he was very pleasant to
me. He asked me if I knew how to waltz, and I quickly proved to him I did. I
noticed that he was watching me and speaking about me to one of his aides-de-
camp with an air of satisfaction. You don't like war, my dear mother, and I
don't want to say anything bad about the old regime; but nonetheless I would
rather prove myself on a field of battle than at a ball.

You ask me if I have neglected Caulaincourt. He is not a man to feel
neglected by me, I assure you; for in the general's office, what he says goes. I
always pay him all the respect and attention expected of me; but he is an odd
person of whom I cannot be terribly fond. One day he is warm and gracious,
the next he greets you coldly. He uses kind expressions with the brusqueness of
Deschartres. He scolds his secretaries as if they were schoolboys, and in the
most insignificant conversation, he takes the tone of a man who is teaching the
whole world a lesson. He personifies the love of command. He tells you that
the weather is hot or cold the same way he would tell his servant to bridle his

horse. I am much fonder of Durosnel, the other aide-de-camp. He is truly likable, kind, and unaffected. He always speaks in an open and friendly way, and is not capricious. He too was at the ball day before yesterday, and we were lined up to waltz according to our rank. First of all Citizen de Caulaincourt, then Durosnel, then myself, so that the adjutant, the aide-de-camp, and the clerk went through their rotation like the planets.

All your thoughts on matters touching my situation are very true, mother dear. I shall keep them in mind and will profit from them. Your letter is charming, and I am not the first to tell you that you write like Sévigné, but you are wiser than she about the vicissitudes of this world.

Happily for our noses, we did not leave on the inspection tour, for we would have left them behind in the snows of Westphalia. It is not exactly warm here; yesterday the thermometer was thirty-four degrees below freezing. The poor sentries are dying like flies. It would therefore be ungracious of me to complain about going to bed in a room without a fire and waking up in the morning with icicles on my mustache. The fact is that this is the most rigorous winter I have experienced, but I don't give it any more thought than if I'd never seen a fire in my life. *J.C.*

IX

Letters continued. —New Year's Day in Cologne. —Sleigh rides.
—The German baronesses. —The canoness. —The review. —Ice on
the Rhine. —Carnival. —A burlesque duel. —The red hussar.
—Portrait of my father. —The appetite of German ladies. —The
billeting order. —Serious concerns of the young men on the general
staff.

Letter XXII   Cologne, January 1, 1799 (Nivôse, Year VII).

This is the first time in my life, my dear mother, that I've spent this day
without kissing you! I see all these good Germans, full of joy, coming together,
kissing, enjoying themselves with their families, while I feel my heart breaking! Today I went to the home of some rich merchants who are in the general's
social circle. I stayed there part of the evening. The father was surrounded by
his eight children. The eldest son is quite talented. He had done a pretty
gouache that morning, which the good father showed me with delight. His sister played a sonata by Pleyel fairly well. Joy and happiness reigned in their
midst. I alone was sad. They perceived this and could see that they were
reminding me of happy moments. They took a greater interest in me and treated me with real friendship. I too felt somehow more at ease with them. Yet it
was just the second time I'd seen them. But I was grateful to them for having
read my mood and, by trying to share their happiness with me, having relieved
my feeling of loneliness.

There is a form of gallantry here which is unknown in our country. It
consists of firing off rifles on the first day of the year beneath the window of
the person to whom you want to show proof of affection. In preventing her
from sleeping, you show her that you are not sleeping either, and that you are
thinking of her while milling about in the street. Who cares about the neighbors! I was on alert all night, since no one had warned me about a thing, and I
was sure "the robbers" had arrived. My hostess has a rather pretty sister, whose
admirers took turns firing under her window all night long. There were hourly
rounds of shots which woke me with a start. I really did want to sleep, too,
since I had gone on foot to Mulheim that morning in order to see my regiment.
I went to look for the quartermaster, who received me very well indeed and
took me to see the major in charge of the squadron. The latter showered me
with kindness and accompanied me out to the street. They are on their way to
Deutz, which is just across the Rhine from Cologne, and they have invited me

to come dine there with them often. The rest of the regiment will be arriving soon. They are still detained by the ice covering the river toward Düsseldorf. Don't you applaud the happy coincidence which brings me, just when I least expected it, to the division in Cologne? No one will be able to reproach me for having been consistently away from my regiment.

You are quite astounded, my dear mother, at the respect which you are shown by certain people owing to your status as Mother of a Defender of the Nation. Yes, you have penetrated through to the real reason. They understand that I might return with arms and booty, and that one shouldn't get on the bad side of the chasseurs, who as far as manners go, are first cousins to the hussars. No one more wary than those fellows in authority!

You made me very happy by telling me that the lemonade agreed with you. So there is finally something which does you some good! If that is the case, may the devil take all the pellitory, doradilla, and *uva ursi*,[55] and may heaven send us lemons! Goodbye, my dear mother! Be trusting and happy, and may you not suffer: that is the prayer I say for you every day of my life. I embrace you with all my heart.

I wish the virtuoso Deschartres some deaf and dumb players who can neither hear nor criticize him, and to Citizeness Roumier, my respectable maid, some slightly more republican sentiments. Tell them I love them both.

Letter XXIII   Cologne, 18 Nivôse, Year VII (January 1799).

... The general had M. de Caulaincourt invite me to dinner. He made me speak of Jean-Jacques Rousseau, of his adventures with my father, and he listened to me in a way which would have turned my head, if I were a fool. But I was on my guard not to babble and to speak only to the point. After dinner, the general and M. Durosnel got into a splendid sleigh in the form of a green and gold dragon pulled by two charming horses. I got into another with Caulaincourt; my comrade, the red hussar, seeing that I had eaten with the general and was getting into one of his sleighs, opened his eyes as wide as saucers. He thought he was dreaming. The general drove his sleigh all over town, handing out invitations to a big party which was to take place the next day. He wanted me to accompany him on all his visits, and at Mme. Herstadt's, when asking her to let her daughter come to the party, the general jokingly went down on his knees and said, "Will you suffer me to remain at length in this position, in the presence of my aides-de-camp and my orderly, the grandson of the Maréchal de Saxe?" The ladies opened their eyes wide, not comprehending probably why I wasn't in exile. ...

The next day there was a superb outing. They left from the general's house at six in the evening. All the grooms were on horseback with six feet long torches. There were fifteen sleighs. The 23rd regiment band, dressed all in red with gold braid, were in the lead, sounding the charge. It was truly beautiful. I was in the courtyard watching the sleighs and the horses: the general came to inspect them and said to me, "You shall come with us, and from there you shall come to the ball to be held afterward." He is really very nice to me, and he would be even more so, if he weren't flanked by his Caulaincourt. But the latter is an intermediary who puts a chill on everything. Monsieur has his little intrigues in the town, and monsieur is jealous. The other day, I took it into my head to say that Mlle. P——— was very pretty. As I said it, I could see from his face that he was upset, and that same evening I saw that he had given her the order not to dance with me. He's not generally liked, not by a long shot. Yet I don't think he is either stupid or malicious, but there is no man who is more imperious or has a drier and more unpleasant voice. When he is working with the secretaries, he remains alone with them for days at a time without talking to them at all. If anyone comes, he makes a show of giving them order after order and reprimanding them as if they were errand boys. However, for the last two days he has been very nice to me and calls me, simply, Dupin. But that won't last, his temperament is too changeable.

Goodbye, dear mother. How charming your last letter was!

Letter XXIV   Cologne, 23 Nivôse, Year VII (January '99).

What! Our house really did almost burn down? Your description of the event made me shudder. That is just what we needed! However, I did have this scrap of consolation, namely that you would have come to live in my room in Cologne; truly the hovel of a starving poet, although there is a mirror, a dresser, and a stove; but the mirror is broken, the dresser wobbles, and as for the stove, my hosts claim that it cannot be lit. There is also a carpet of unidentifiable color, somewhere between black, brown, yellow, etc. But yet, if I saw you here in this gloomy room, instantly it would be lit up, heated, decorated, sparkling, magnificent, and preferable to any palace....

We have a very posh subscription ball, which is attended by all high-ranking officers and the better members of local society. You won't believe it, but a little idiot of a German baroness, who takes her daughters to it, disapproved of my being there and forbade her daughters to dance with me. A cavalry captain who is billeted in their house told me this. He was furious over it and wanted to move out then and there. His anger was comically excessive, and I had to calm him down; but I couldn't prevent him last night from spreading the word to all the Frenchmen, military and civilian, who are here; and as I arrived at the ball with my quartermaster and squadron leader, with whom I had just dined, other officers came up to us and said, "The order is given and honor pledged that no Frenchman will dance with the daughters of Baroness ———, and I hope, gentlemen, you will keep this commitment as well." I asked why, and was told that the baroness had forbidden her daughters to dance with plain soldiers, and thus I learned that I was the cause of this conspiracy....

My regiment is leaving for Siegbourg, which is six leagues from here. My quartermaster and my squadron leader are extremely kind to me. They told me they would ask the general to have me join them. The brigade leader absolutely wants me in the regiment. Tell all the millers along the Indre that I drink to their health and thank them for their friendship.

Letter XXV   Cologne, 28 Nivôse, Year VII (January '99).

We leave tomorrow for Düren; we are going to inspect the 25th cavalry regiment, formerly the dragoons of the Republic, the worst regiment in the whole army, word has it. My horse has not yet arrived, but I will be riding the red hussar's horse; she's a young filly who behaves with no rhyme or reason, who goes left when told to go right and who will only obey instructions which are as far removed as possible from the laws of common sense and equitation. My hussar comrade has told me the particular procedures he himself invented to make her obey, without which I would never have gotten anywhere. I complimented him on his effectiveness in education....

I am tempted to bless the famous baroness who wants the orderlies to wait in the courtyard while the officers are at a ball. This has resulted in the friendliest words and most delightful glances imaginable from Mlle.———, and we have expressed our mutual interest and regard in a way which gives me much hope. This young person is a canoness and virtually in charge of herself. She is charming, and by my faith, if a canoness of the Electoral Chapter isn't put off by my dolman, I can snap my fingers at the old baroness and her shrews of daughters....

Düren, 28 Nivôse.

I had gotten that far, my dear mother, when suppertime forced me to leave you. I put my letter in my pocket, and I left the next day. First thing in the morning I put on my boots and went to headquarters to learn the departure time. Sire Caulaincourt, who was in a rare mood, told me that the order he had given me to leave need only be carried out if I so desired; if I preferred remaining there, that was up to me. There was a ball that evening at which I was to see my charming canoness again, and more than that, the piercing cold, which did not incline me toward going out. I was very tempted to take advantage of the offer, to put my horse back in the stable, and to go warm myself by the secretary's red hot stove while waiting for the happy hour to arrive. However, I thought I could see in the wicked eye of Caulaincourt that he expected me to accept his offer eagerly, and I wasn't anxious to have only the title of orderly without fulfilling its functions. His benevolence seemed too much like permission to be useless. I took the order, jumped on my horse, and was about to leave with the regimental carabineers. Thereupon Caulaincourt, putting on a very charming demeanor, called me back and said, "This will be a sorry campaign. Most of the lodgings are dreadfully dirty." Was this a test of my mettle, or had he noticed that I was falling head over heels in love with Mlle.———, which allayed his fear of seeing me please Mlle. P———? Or does he want the general to think I'm a wet noodle? I have no idea; but seeing that he wanted to have me stay, I wanted all the more to leave; and I told him that I would try to have clean lodgings or manage to get by without any. Then he added in a paternal tone, "Well, if you have the misfortune of being assigned to lodgings which are too unpleasant, go find the quartermaster and tell him for me to give you something different, and that if he doesn't, *I'll box his ears.*" What do you think of such instructions given to a simple cavalryman for an officer who could just as well give back the order as accept it? "You're too kind," I said to Caulaincourt; and then I was off on my mare, or rather on the red hussar's red mule, which I admit I would have been extremely vexed not to be able to control while the Citizen aide-de-camp was watching me. I acquitted myself honorably and rode the eight leagues from Cologne to Düren, with the carabineers, in one stretch.

Upon my arrival, I took my orders to the commandant, led to the stables the general's six horses, which the grooms had brought along behind us, and then went to find my lodging. It was a miserable hole from which I would not have emerged with a drop of blood left; the insects in this country do not mind the cold. I didn't let it worry me at all, but went to see the quartermaster and very seriously and with the coolness of someone who knows what he's doing delivered the message I had been given. He began to roar with laughter. All the officers who were there working did the same. He bowed down to me almost to the ground, took me by the arm, led me to the town hall, and had me lodged in a good house. You can think what you like of this adventure. As for me, I prefer to believe that Caulaincourt acted in good faith, but I am not totally convinced. In any case, it turned out for the best, as you see, and I am lodged with people who are steeped in religion. The hostess is a widow of forty years of age, who blesses you each time you sneeze, and her brother wears a wig and says his benediction before eating his soup. They eat very well, have a nice snug house, well-heated stoves, and soft beds; and they welcome you with as much good will as if you had been invited. They made me think of the *Paysan parvenu* by Marivaux, and there I was, a tired, famished chasseur, just like the hero of the book. What a godsend, I said to myself, and I responded solemnly with an "amen" after grace had been said. There is no one like the pious for knowing how to live! That morning I had eaten in Cologne with another quartermaster, the one from my regiment, who is the best lad on the face of the earth. He had arrived the night before from Siegbourg, and waking at daybreak, had sent the baggagemaster to search the town for me before I had gotten out of bed. He had filled me with oysters and chops for the trip; but all that seemed far away by the time I arrived at the home of my observant ones. So I did justice to their sauerkraut and turkey stuffed with prunes and dried pears. If anyone at Nohant had spoken of such a dish, I would have turned up my nose at it, but in Düren it seemed marvelous and prepared by the hands of the gods. It appears that I have scarcely any accent, for they insist on taking me for a German, and I did not insist too strongly on the fact that I am French, inasmuch as hunger made me not want to lose their good graces and their good food all at once. At any rate, they were not any the less friendly for it, and they are decent people. The general will arrive this morning. After all this chatter by the stove of my blessed hosts, I only have time left to embrace you. I am using their pens and their seal, which bears a coat of arms, by my faith! Three birds, Lord have mercy! They are chickens, or perhaps, three stuffed turkeys. What a lovely emblem!

Letter XXVI Cologne, 7 Pluviôse, Year VII.

I received your letter in Düren, my dear mother, where it arrived just in time to assure me a pleasant evening. It was in the general's dispatches, which were brought from Cologne by special courier. That morning (I believe it was 30 Nivôse) we had inspected the dragoons of the Republic, now the 25th cavalry. The general, in his grand uniform covered with gold, his red satin scarf with gold tassels, was riding a magnificent white mare. The two aides-de-camp followed him; Durosnel had on his grand chasseur's uniform, Caulaincourt was followed by a cuirassier, and I was behind Durosnel,[46] which I much preferred. We were preceded by a captain of the 25th, who took us to the site of the review. The sun was shining brightly. All the banners, all the plumes sparkled and waved. We cantered across the city of Düren. When we were face to face with the regiment, all the trumpets sounded in the fields. We rode past the ranks. Then the general had the companies break ranks and passed the regiment in review, which lasted four hours. It began to rain and got very cold; the weather was not nearly as nice as when we started. Finally, we returned chilled and wet. In my days as a dandy, all this would have given me a cold; but now cold, hot, dry, wet, it's all the same to me.

You asked me if my hair style is in fashion. No one in the regiment wears it similarly, but you do see some congenial officers who comb their hair that way, and several, my quartermaster among them, think that it goes very well with a chasseur's uniform. However, I have promised everyone to let my hair grow so I can wear it in a pigtail, and from now until it gets to that length I'll have time to wash my head. So, you've been told that if I become an officer, the uniform would cost a fortune, and already you're worried about the twelve hundred pounds it will take to equip me. Set your mind at ease, my dear mother. First of all, I am not an officer yet, and I will be quite content to start by being a sergeant; for the further we go, the less possible it becomes to rise all at once to another level. My general can tell that he won't be able to keep the promises he has made, for he does not mention them to me anymore. As for the twelve hundred pounds, reduce that in your calculations to one hundred fifty. The regular officer's uniform consists of a green dress coat with a shoulder strap and a large revers on the chest. The full-dress dolman, which is trimmed and piped in silver, would be a bit more expensive. But if it all amounts to two hundred pounds, that would be a lot.

My colonel is named Ordener; he's a German and a very good fellow, according to what everyone says. I will soon get to see him when we go to inspect the division regiments. My regiment is now in Coblenz.

You surely know already that Ehrenbreitstein has surrendered. The Rhine is working great havoc here. The port of Cologne is full of Dutch merchant ships. First they were heavily bound by the ice, then the river overflowed and carried them to the level of the second floor of the houses in the port. It froze over again at that level; then suddenly the Rhine flowed back into its bed, so that there no longer was any water underneath the ice; the ice broke, and the ships, which had been lined up against the houses on a par with the second story casement windows, fell back into the harbor from a height of thirty feet and were mostly smashed to pieces. This was a unique occurrence, perhaps never seen before. Yesterday, I spent all afternoon on the bastions of the Rhine, observing its movement with an artillery officer, a bright young fellow for whom I have developed an affection, which he reciprocates. We had a four-pounder, and at each movement of the ice, we alerted the men at the port by firing a cannon shot. It brought me back to my games in the Rue du Roi-de-Sicile, and setting off the gun I felt was still a source of amusement. No matter what you say, my dear mother, there is nothing as nice as noise. I wish I could still bother you with my ruckus! . . . but they're calling me to dinner. There are yells, laughter, and so much noise that you cannot hear yourself think, and although I like a racket, I would gladly do without it when I am chatting with you. Well, I will have to leave you abruptly, but before I do, I embrace you as I love you.

Before transcribing the next letter, I should perhaps beg the pardon of some readers for reporting my father's lively criticism of M. de Caulaincourt. It seems to me, however, that it contains nothing serious or distressing for relatives and friends of that figure. When it is a question of a man as distinguished as was the Duc de Vicence, his characteristics, his manner, and the details of his life belong, in a sense, to history, and the correspondence I am publishing is already part of history. It adds color, as one says today. That is true, yet I must admit there is more at stake: I know we should respect the dead and especially the relatives of the dead. That is why I shall report, with no omissions, the good my father will later have to say of the man who inspired him in his youth with such naïve antipathy. This antipathy, which was instinctive and had no hidden motive, is understandable on the part of a young man as open and outgoing as the young soldier of the Republic, put in a subservient position under the orders of a serious and reserved man. It is merely a matter of the confrontation of two opposing personalities.

Letter XXVII   Cologne, 16 Pluviôse, Year VII (February '99).

I won't tell you, my dear mother, like the cobbler in the fable, "Please give me back my songs and my sleep, and take back your hundred crowns." No, the arrival of the hundred crowns will give me back my songs and sleep, although they haven't really suffered much, I must confess, from the emptiness of my purse. For the past week I have been penniless, and I far prefer going without to asking my general for money. I am not afraid of him at all, but I could not bear to have M. de Caulaincourt as an intermediary. That "Citizen" puts on airs of being so important, and is so patronizing; I so little desire and, indeed, dread his attention that I avoid it as much as possible. You asked me to sketch his portrait for you. Caulaincourt is a man of about twenty-five. He is an inch taller than I. He stands fairly solid on his legs, although he's a bit knock-kneed. He has a square face, a large nose, and small eyes. He would have a noble manner, if he were not so insolent. Whether he is walking or dancing, he pushes out his backside and lifts his head with affectation, which gives him a strange enough profile.

Yesterday evening, at the ball, he invited me to a costume party. At first I thought he was ordering me to saddle up, his intonation was so unsuited to the topic of conversation. It wasn't until I heard the word mask repeated several times that I understood it was a party he was inviting me to. This party was supposed to take place after a German comedy that the barons are giving this evening and for which I received a ticket from a grand lady whom I've never met and from whom I hadn't requested one. This morning, at headquarters, from where I'm writing you, Caulaincourt came to tell me, still in the same tone of voice, that the party will perhaps not take place, because the comedy will last too long. That'll be gay!

Durosnel is a very good fellow, the son of a secretary of the war ministry under Louis XV. He is very well turned out, quite a handsome officer.

Today is Mardi gras, than which no day should be less sad. Yet it saddens me almost as much as New Year's Day. Those days when families come together make me aware of my isolation. At certain periods, the soul is used to expanding, and suffers twice as much when, instead of opening up to others, it is forced to retire within itself. But yet I find consolation in imagining that you are thinking of me in Nohant, that someone in Nohant loves me, and that the wishes which I hear all around me and in which I have no part are made for me in Nohant.

The 17th.

.... The comedy was dreadful, pitiful, unbearable. But that doesn't matter; one only goes for appearances, since only generals and barons receive tickets. Between the two plays, Caulaincourt came to get me. Again I thought he was going to give me an order. But no, he came to do the costumes. I was dressed as a woman ten feet tall. In one hand I held a parasol and in the other I held under my arm a large *danois*[56] belonging to Durosnel. There were three coachfuls of people in costume. Caulaincourt played the role of my husband, and I was called Mme. Pont-Volant [Flying bridge]. With my enormous fan and height, I was a caricature of the old regime. We went thus to all the important homes in the city, which was rather cheeky. We also went to the general's house; he actually took me for a woman and tried to kiss me. I was forced to call M. Pont-Volant to my rescue.

Letter XXVIII   Cologne (no date).

Your letter with the news of the earthquake makes me shudder. That is all we need now, a volcanic eruption. The German newspapers have preached a long sermon on that subject, which is quite comical. They threaten us with punishment from heaven. However, the city of Cologne, which is very pious and calls itself the city of the three kings and the eleven thousand virgins, was handled far more roughly by the ice than our fine French towns by the earthquake.

You would not believe, my dear mother, that for the past four days every-one here has been talking about me. I was a second in an affair which caused quite a stir in the city among both the Germans and the French. I met a young conscript who is in the 23rd cavalry regiment and who remained in Cologne on Caulaincourt's account. We were recently at an all-night ball which was held at the theater and for which the general had given me a ticket. A young German, who is a rival for love with my chasseur friend, rudely interrupted a conversa-tion which the latter was having with the beauty in question. Of course they picked a quarrel, and the German called my comrade a wretch and a jackass. A great hubbub arose around them. Seeing that the chasseur is surrounded, I go up to him, and without making a fuss, we take the German into a corner and promise him another interview for the next day. Our man stays there with his mouth open and seems unwilling to understand what we're saying. The next morning, on leaving the ball, we go to his house, and the chasseur asks if the German still considers him a wretch. "Yes, sir," says the German, "you are." "In that case, sir, find a second and we shall duel." "I will not, gentlemen, I never duel." To that pretty response, my comrade gives him a slap on the face. The German yells and calls for help. In an instant, all the people in the house fill the staircase. I stand in front of the door and refuse to let anyone in. Germans are notoriously slow. While they're debating what to do, my comrade gives the man a good box on the ears. He screams, and the whole house starts to cry out for help and for the police. We leave the room. We come tearing down the stairs in the middle of the consternated Germans, and make off.

Our battered man gets dressed and runs to Général Jacobé, who is in charge of administrative affairs, and files a long written complaint with him in which he accuses us of trying to murder him. The general sends for the chas-seur, who gives an honest account of the affair. Fearing a major scandal in town, the general, while siding with my comrade, wants him to leave immedi-ately. Jacobé's aide-de-camp, who is a friend of mine, pleads my comrade's case and wins.

In the meantime, the episode has quickly become the talk of the town. All of us Frenchmen have no trouble condemning the conduct of the battered German; his own compatriots find it embarrassing, and talk him into accepting the duel. A Frenchman even generously offers to be his second. No longer able to back out, he writes our chasseur a challenge, on fancy paper, in a grand Germanic style, which makes us want to die laughing. It was like Roland chal-lenging Charlemagne's twelve peers. We give our solemn acceptance, and there we are, one morning, on the banks of the Rhine. The German, still hoping that the affair can be settled by other means, hasn't brought any weapons. I lend him my saber. The chasseur charges at him in good French fashion. The German parries as well as he can and retreats almost into the water. Then the chasseur, who only wanted to frighten him, sends half the handle of my saber flying with a backhand blow, which the German almost throws into the Rhine in his haste to lay down his arms. He asks to capitulate. We are slow to accept. He offers to withdraw his complaint. Not having been at all winded by the duel, I give him a good sermon (à la Deschartres). I demand that he not only withdraw his complaint, but that he tell the general that no one ever wanted to murder him.

He agrees, and begs us to accept his invitation to a lunch. He runs to Jacobé to fulfill our conditions, he comes back to report to us what he has done, takes us to eat, and treats us to a royal feast. From there he takes us to the theater. Finally, we end up spending the entire day in enemy territory. I told the whole story to Caulaincourt and to Général Harville, who laughed till they cried.

But that is not all. The German now considers me his life's saviour and overwhelms me with favors; twice yesterday at the ball he gave me his partner; he wanted me to drink all the punch there was at the buffet; he adores the French military and would willingly address me as "monseigneur." I told the whole story to my canoness, who with a forced laugh, said that it was "very schtupid to fight like zat for nozink, and to haff almost killt zat poor man," that we had only wanted to hurt him because he was German, and that we didn't like Germans. I assured her that, by way of compensation we did very much like German women. She accepted that, and we struck a truce.

You long for peace, my dear mother, and I tremble at the thought. War is my only means of advancement. If the war starts up again, I can become an officer easily and honorably. If you conduct yourself well in battle, you can be commissioned on the battlefield. What pleasure! What glory! My heart soars just thinking of it. Isn't that when one gets leave, when one comes back to spend some happy moments in Nohant, and in that way is well rewarded for the little one has done?

I am now studying the organization of the squadron and am learning all the commands, so that with a little practice, I will soon be up to date.

You tell me that your letters are too long; I just wish they were longer. Getting one I can read for an hour constitutes my greatest happiness. . . . No one here is using "citizen" or "citizeness" as a form of address anymore; everyone in the military is using "monsieur" more each day, and ladies are still "madame." Tell old Deschartres that he's a lazy bum for sleeping so much.

Goodbye, my dear mother, I embrace you with all my heart.

Letter XXIX   Cologne, 20 Pluviôse, Year VII.

Happy is he who has his mother still, and can bask in her tenderness! He is blessed, for he will have known that happiness of having been loved for himself alone!

Your letter, my dear mother, has arrived to complete my day in a very pleasant fashion. I received it on my way back from a walk which I took on the other side of the Rhine with Lecomte (that is the name of the chasseur for whom I served as second). He took me to see the ship of a merchant friend of his. This vessel had no damage from the ice; it is very pretty, the rooms are perfectly clean; we went through the whole ship. It was full of goods. The merchant and his crew were busy loading it for Holland. Foremen and workmen were swarming over the deck. The weather was absolutely beautiful; we alone, the chasseur and I, did nothing in the midst of all those busy-looking faces. As for me, leaning on my saber, pipe in mouth, my eyes vacantly fixed on the spectacle before me, I said to myself, "I was born into a higher and richer class than these merchants who have houses in town, ships in the harbor, and gold in their coffers; but I, a soldier of the Republic, my sole belongings are my saber and my pipe. But ice, fire, thieves, and customs agents do not keep me from sleeping; all these worries I am spared! Should the town collapse and the port and all that is in it be swallowed up, I don't care—in fact, I would even say, as do the hussars, I don't give a damn. Work for yourselves, you rabble, hoard your money; we shall work for our country and reap all the glory; my trade is just as good as yours."

Thereupon, leaving my chasseur friend on board busy emptying several bottles with his merchant friend, I went back to meet my canoness, who had promised to have a bad headache which would allow her to forego the theater and to remain "alone" at home all evening.

You ask me who this great lady is who obtained a ticket for me to the baron's comedy without my requesting it. She is a canoness friend of my canoness, called Frau Augusta de Frenchen. She is tall, beautiful, and has the bearing of an empress. At the ball the other day, the general gave her his arm. He was wearing his full-dress uniform and red scarf with gold tassels; they made the noblest, the most dignified, the most stately couple imaginable. Yet her proud appearance does not inspire the love and trust that do the eyes of my canoness. Those are eyes which look at you with feeling and intelligence, which can tell from the other side of the room if you are sad and why, which continually meet your eyes, showing they understand you, and at times light up and at other times soften; and when a fool in epaulets struts in front of her, those eyes tell you clearly, "It's you, soldier, whom I prefer."

You ask me also to describe Général Harville. You will recognize him in a minute. Five feet five, on the heavy side, very solid on his legs, white hair, exposed forehead, Roman nose, jutting chin, an extremely noble appearance and gait, the ease of a courtier, which makes him extremely polite to his inferiors. He makes a three-quarter bow, his tone is curt and loud, yet good-natured; asks questions often without listening to the answers; makes you feel, when he wants to, that he is making a great exception by speaking to you, of which you mustn't take advantage. Inferiors are captivated by his politeness because he readily speaks to them, and some take this mark of superiority for approachability and cordiality, whereas nothing is more a sign of power than this manner of addressing those who would not dare to approach you first.

He treats me much better in private than in public, as can well be imagined. He is generally well thought of, and he likes to do favors. In short, he's a good man, and he'd be even better without his nephew Caulaincourt.

This dear nephew is leaving in three days. May heaven guide him and not lead him back for a long time! The other day what did he do but scold the red hussar for having lent me his horse! That surely proves that he has it in for me, and that he didn't like my going to the review; for I would have been on foot if I hadn't had that animal. The hussar has hurt his leg, and for the past month his horse would have languished in the stables, if I hadn't exercised him. But Caulaincourt, who had seen me go by on the ramparts and hadn't said a word to me, went and gave him a lecture, screaming at the top of his lungs that I wasn't riding the horse for the horse's sake but for my own, since you don't exercise horses with a saddle but with a blanket. So there! And why doesn't he say anything to me instead of humiliating my poor comrade? Is it because I'm from a good family? Well, I am certainly not indebted to him. Maulnoir, the young officer in the dragoons and secretary, described this tirade to me and shrugged his shoulders over it. It is astonishing that with such intelligence and ability one can be so petty.

Speaking of horses, I am still waiting for mine. A chasseur from the depot was supposed to bring him to me, but the remounts have been changed. In short, I have nothing to do, and I am on foot. It is true that I love and am loved. That is a lot, but after all I didn't enlist in order to make love.

How sad everything is that happens on that poor farm! All those poor people who are dying one after the other! I miss them as you do....

They're really stupid to pronounce me crippled that way in La Châtre and cause you so much worry. I would like to thrash whoever is giving you such a scare. Do remember, my dear mother, that I am invulnerable, and that I could fall from the top of the Cologne cathedral, as I did from the top of the château in Châteauroux, without being hurt....

My father is referring here to a childhood incident. When he was only three years old, he fell from a window just under the roof, into the moat of the old château at Châteauroux, in which château M. de Francueil, his father, was living, at that time, as the general revenue collector. The child was found covered with blood; but when he had been washed, it was apparent that he was not hurt at all. He had fallen onto a pile of organs from some butchered animals which the cooks had thrown into the moat just moments earlier and which had served to cushion his fall and save his life. But he was destined to die a violent death, and his poor mother had a terrible foreboding of it ever since that terrifying and miraculous accident.

In the following letter, there is mention of a portrait, and since I have this portrait here in front of me, I want to describe the young man whose correspondence reveals such a good and pure heart and a mind so honest, lively, and just! In order to portray him in a few words, I shall use the form which we have just seen him employ for his general and M. de Caulaincourt.

Five feet, three inches; a thin, elegant, and well-porportioned figure; pale complexion; slightly Roman nose of admirable contour; good intelligent mouth; eyebrows and mustache as black and clear as if outlined in ink; large black eyes, soft and shining at the same time, the most beautiful eyes imaginable; thick, powdered hair falling casually over his forehead, which it covers almost entirely without clinging to it. This mass of jet-black, powdered hair, almost touching his jet black eyebrows, is very becoming and brings out the brilliance of his eyes. In short, my father's appearance at the period was extremely delicate, and it is easy to understand that, despite his size, Général

Harville mistook him for a woman. In addition, he had small feet and perfectly beautiful hands.

The portrait is nicely painted. The chasseur's uniform is a dark green verging on black, and the dark-red striped collar lends him a simple, severe appearance, which goes very well with his expression, where dreamy melancholy is habitually at odds with innate gaiety.

Later on, my father gained some weight without losing the elegance of his appearance. His figure filled out and his features became more angular. He became one of the handsomest officers in the army. Yet for me, his ideal beauty and most devastating charm reside in the small portrait I have been discussing and which he will speak of now.

Letter XXX   Cologne, 26 Pluviôse, Year VII (February '99).

Well, my dear mother, did I arrive safe and sound? What do you think of me? Am I a good resemblance? Everyone here thought it was, as they say, *striking*. As soon as I saw myself in this one, I personally, who never in my life thought a portrait looked like me, recognized myself. It was begun quite a long time ago, and I would have liked to have surprised you with it for New Year's, but halfway through his work the painter left for Coblenz, from where he returned just a few days ago.

I received the money, paid for my shirts and handkerchiefs, and here I am all furnished. It was high time that the carnival was over, because every evening for the past week, I have been plunking down six or eight pounds out of my own pocket. German women like to eat, and when you've danced with them, you're obliged to offer them something to eat or drink. As soon as they have had something to drink, they head for the tarts. Their mamas arrive: "Oh, mama, you'll surely take a few of these darioles, won't you?" Then the brother arrives: "By God, my dear friend, let's drink a glass of punch together." If the dog came, you would have to feast him as well. After all, that is the custom. If you go to someone's house at five in the evening, you are served, by way of refreshment, wine and a slice of ham. You should be able to tell from that what a slight effect sweets produce on such stomachs.

I have left the merchant's and the sad room I described to you. I now have marvelous lodgings. I have a pretty room with a fire, and every morning I am brought tea with bread and butter. Though I'm here under billeting order, it is a very hospitable house. My host is a likeable doctor with a very pretty daughter who plays the piano quite well. Général Laborde's secretary lived in this good man's house, and when he left, he passed his lodgings on to me, which I had the right to take by going and turning mine in at the town hall. I went to move in with my saber under my arm and my billeting order in my hand, like Count Almaviva,[57] and like he, I said, on entering: "Doesn't here live the house of Doctor . . . ?" "No, not Bartholo," my friendly host gaily replied, "but Daniel, and delighted to welcome you." You see that my luck follows me everywhere. I find friends all over, or people ready to become my friends.

There have been a lot of changes in our general staff. Durosnel is leaving, more's the pity! And Caulaincourt as well, all the better! Durosnel was only a supernumerary squadron leader; he is going to join the 10th hussar regiment as active squadron leader. Caulaincourt is ordered back to his unit; what a pleasure! The general will be without any aides-de-camp. A young officer of the dragoons arrived here two weeks ago. The general likes him very much and acts as his protector. He is a lad of eighteen years of age whom the general had commissioned as an officer. But the Directoire would not confirm his commission, and so the young man, despite having spent a year at that rank, was forced to leave his post and lose his rank. You see that it is no longer so easy to be promoted and that even patronage is useless. You just have to make the best of it, since it is fair, and try to win your spurs like the knights of old, by true feats of valor. This young man is waiting here, like all of us, for a lucky turn of events. He still wears his officer's epaulets, however, and the general uses him as the corresponding officer; but this is all going on rather covertly and may not last. It would be a shame, though, if the lad couldn't stay with us and were held back in his career because of having begun too well, since he is quite likeable, and we have struck up a strong friendship. When we are in the office in the evening with the secretary, and the general and his aides-de-camp have left to pay their calls, the three of us are like children freed from the teacher; we wrestle and have pillow fights, which makes a dust storm and a wonderful din; and when someone comes, we blow out the candles and hide in the large wardrobe. They think no one is there and leave, and we start in again.

You send me very bad news about our crops. Here they are doing splendidly, even though it is a lot colder than back home. Perhaps they have not actually frozen and it is just one of Deschartres' bad dreams, for he is a pessimist, if ever there was one.

My regiment has left for Haguenau. It is being burdened with marches and countermarches, heaven only knows why. Good night, my dear mother, don't worry about me, I'm fine and am not suffering from the cold. I have only had one migraine since I've been here. I embrace you with all my heart. I embrace old Deschartres and my maid. When she claims that I've forgotten her, tell her from me it's a lie.

Letter from My Grandmother to Général D'Harville

Nohant, 7 Ventôse, Year VII.

You were kind enough, Citizen Général, to sympathize with my grief and ease my pain. This remembrance is so constantly present in my heart and mind that whatever disturbs your happiness elicits my concern. My son has told me that you are going to lose your aides-de-camp, one of whom, namely Citizen de Caulaincourt, you are specially sorry to see leave, as he is a relative of yours. I wish my son could replace him, not in the high position he held at your side, toward which I feel that Maurice is still too new a soldier to aspire, but in some way which would ease you of your burden of work. If you were kind enough to take notice of him, he would learn under your orders. He would do all he could to please you and to earn the mark of esteem you would be giving him. He is still new to the army, but he has done all he can to make himself useful, and he would carry out zealously and intelligently anything you told him to do. You made me very happy by indicating to me that he was behaving well and that you were trying to teach him to be more frugal. This desire on your part shows me that he is sometimes on your mind. I thank you for that, and I know you will value a mother's thanks, since you have such a fond memory of the one who gave birth to you.

I invoke her memory in order to awaken in you a little friendship for my Maurice. Oh, Général! Twenty-five years ago, you would have been a poor conscript yourself. What wouldn't your loving mother have done to soften your fate! What gratitude wouldn't she have felt for the one who, like you, had taken her son under his wing! She would have thought she had found a second father for him and a noble friend for herself. If I had the same hope, Général, would you think me wrong?

All the flattering things you have been kind enough to tell me are profoundly touching to me; you assure me that my letters do not importune you, and that is another consolation which I owe you, to be able to speak with assurance of the dear object of my affection. I send you anew, Citizen Général, the gratitude and affection with which, etc. . . .

Reply of Général Harville to Citizeness Dupin, Née De Saxe

Cologne, 20 Ventôse, Year VII.

I have just this moment received your letter of the 7th, Citizeness, and I won't worry about importuning you with my quick reply, since I do so in order to send you news of your Maurice, whom I had come to me immediately to talk to him about you and, at the same time, try to interest him in keeping busy. It is true that at the moment he cannot be very useful to me. The bureaucratic side of inspection needs men who are somewhat experienced in military details and whose handwriting is rapid and neat, and useful for that purpose; well, he told me that he has neglected his handwriting, and furthermore he does not even seem to me to want to do this kind of work, which indeed would not very well fulfill his proposed aim of activity and distinction. He is dining with me today; we will be *en famille*, and I'll be able to talk with him more. I will try to find useful ways for him to fill his time; unfortunately, in the purely military line, there is necessarily a good deal of wasted time.

The details I have given you will prove the interest which I take in the being who is so dear to you and will answer, in a way which will go straight to your heart, the phrase in your letter, "She would have thought she had found a second father for him and a noble friend for herself. If I had the same hope, Général, would you think me wrong?" Oh, surely not, Citizeness, answers a caring friend. Your affection for your son, the sensitivity of your letter, and the gratitude which you show me for such a simple procedure, all give me the greatest desire to know you and to earn your kindness. Excuse my scribbling, I write so much that I am no longer able to write. Accept my deepest and most sincere homage, which you well deserve.

    Yours respectfully,

Auguste Harville.

R. G. -J.

X

Letters continued. —Maulnoir. —Saint-Jean. —Garrison life. —An excursion. —The Egyptian campaign. —An adventure. —The Little House. —Departure from Cologne.

Letter XXXI   Cologne, 24 Ventôse, Year VII (March '99).

From My Father to His Mother

Caulaincourt has finally gone. I wished him good health and a safe trip. He answered with deeply respectful bows, colder even than usual. I did not shed a tear, which is unusual; neither did the secretary, nor the little officer of the dragoons, nor anyone to my knowledge, not even his mistress, whom he bored royally, I am sure. He is missed only by the good general. And by the way, my dear mother, have you written to him again? How good of you to trouble yourself this way for me! He said nothing to me about receiving your letter, but I surmised from his manner at the dinner to which he invited me that very day that something like that had happened. He asked me if I thought I could do office work; I told him, word of honor, that my handwriting resembled chicken scratchings; aside from that fact, I feel no inclination at all toward the fastidious profession of copyist, which teaches you nothing and leads nowhere. He asked many questions about your means, your connections, your style of living, and he was so interested in all that, that damned if I don't think he's in love with you without ever having met you. He asked me if I looked like you, and I told him *yes*; I am too proud to deny it. Then he said, by way of a compliment, that you must have been very beautiful; and I could not help answering that, Good Lord, you certainly still were and always would be. Thereupon, he said that he really would like to pay his respects to you. Take care, my dear mother, that his interest in you does not make him lose sight of me entirely; I know that is not your intention and, if you could have played the coquette a single day of your life, it is on my behalf and for my welfare that you would have done it. But let us be serious. The general cannot really do a great deal for me under the circumstances. His command is too tranquil, and I am not inclined to grow moldy in office dust. I must wait. The general tells me that I do not keep busy enough; but what does he want me to do, since he assigns me no work, since I do not even have a horse to ride, and since our time here is spent in paying visits, going to balls, and to the theater? If I didn't love music, I would be bored to death, for I am obliged to study the regulations and squadron maneuvers in my room, which does not teach me very much. Since I have been living with my doctor, I have been his daughter's escort. At my request, my beautiful canoness has resumed her study of music, which she knows wonderfully well. She has had a piano brought from Mainz, and she plays with much delicacy and taste. I also often go to play the violin and sing at the home of Mme. Maret, wife of the commissioner-in-chief of warfare, at Cologne. She receives the best of French society here, and the general sometimes comes.

We had a very beautiful review enhanced by magnificent weather. For once the plumes and braiding shone in all their glory. There was one truly superb moment. After the inspection, the mount for maneuvers was sounded. In a flash the regiment was on horseback. I was some five hundred feet away from the general. I rode toward him at full speed with the horses following, led by his equerry. Thus we ran through all the ranks at a gallop. Then the regiment paraded past us, playing the Tartar's march from *Lodoïska*. The music was powerfully good, and the whole scene was intoxicating. I was so happy.... But all that does is whet, not satisfy, the military appetite. True, the war seems to be starting up again, albeit undeclared. This will be, I hope, the signal for my advancement. Don't let this hope frighten you; remember that replacements will have to be made in the various units, and of necessity, my turn will come. Have you ever heard of anything as ludicrous as the Rastadt negotiations? Both sides make a great show of courtesy, and they cannonade each other while loudly proclaiming their friendship. Well done!

Those grandiose, disdainful airs disappeared from headquarters along with Caulaincourt. Disobliging and discouraging words no longer sadden our ears. Durosnel has taken on the workload. He is not leaving yet, thank God! What a different character! He is gentle, amiable, speaks to you gladly, gives orders with precision but without harshness. He is squadron chief only on review days, and not, as was the case with the other one, from the moment he gets up until the time he goes to bed. I do truly believe that Caulaincourt took it into his head to imitate the manner and authority of Bonaparte, whom he talks about constantly and of whom he surely falls far short. I do not know whether his style would be tolerable even in a commander-in-chief. The trappings of power must at least be accompanied by great talent, but although Caulaincourt does have some ability, he will never be endowed with enough to allow him to imitate gracefully those who are first rate.

My friend, the little officer of the dragoons, is named Maulnoir. He is the son of a notary from Coulommiers, in Brie. The refusal of the Directoire to promote him is not the fault of the general per se, but rather that of Augereau, who had recommended his nomination, and all of whose nominations were quashed by the Directoire.

Goodbye, my dear mother, I'll be so happy when you go to spend some time in Néris; it will be a distraction for you. You could also go to see our friends in Argenton and Bourges. Those trips would be very good for you. You were wise to give up your apartment in Paris. This savings will allow you to be more comfortable in Nohant. What you tell me about the next harvest, however, is not very promising; but in my optimistic wisdom, I have told myself that, if wheat were more scarce, it would cost more and you would thereby lose nothing. It is true that the responsibility for the poor, who will suffer for it, will revert to you, and you will have to provide for them more than usual. Well, I see that I am optimistic to a fault and that kind hearts are not destined to be wealthy. . . . I hear them coming to call me to dinner. It is the general's secretaries; they make such a racket that the neighbors are at their windows. I must join them to put an end to this scandal. I embrace you with all my heart.

Tell Saint-Jean that a rumor is circulating through the army that there is to be a draft of all men from forty to fifty-five, and that I will try to get him assigned to my regiment as a cook, so that the only fire he'll be exposed to will be in the kitchen, for I believe he would not at all like that of the artillery.

Saint-Jean, the frequent object of my father's good-natured teasing, was the household coachman and husband of Audelan, the cook. This old couple died at our place, the husband a few months before my grandmother, who was never told of his demise, her paralysis enabling us to conceal it from her. Saint-Jean was a very comical drunkard. He had been an atrocious coward, and especially when drunk, he was assailed by ghosts, by "Georgeon," the devil of the Vallée Noire, by "the pale greyhound," by "the big beast," by the whole fantastic cast of regional superstitions. Charged with the responsibility of going to collect the mail in La Châtre on delivery days, he always took solemn precautions when making this one-league trip, especially in winter, when he would not return until nightfall. Early in the morning, after having fortified himself with several pints of local wine, he put on a pair of boots which dated at least from the time of the Fronde; he donned an article of clothing of undefinable shape and color, which he called his "roquemane," God only knows where he got the name! Then he embraced his wife, who respectfully brought him a chair, by means of which he climbed onto an ancient and phlegmatic white horse, which in "less than two short hours" (his expression) would carry him into town. There he forgot himself in the tavern for two or three more short hours, before and after his errands; and finally, night coming on, he started back home, where he rarely arrived without some mishap: sometimes he would meet a band of thieves who would beat him black and blue; sometimes, seeing an enormous ball of fire coming to meet him, his "spirited" horse would carry him off over the fields; sometimes the devil in any number of guises would get under his horse's belly and prevent it from advancing; finally, sometimes the devil would leap on behind, and the added weight would force the poor animal to the ground. Having left Nohant at nine in the morning, he nevertheless succeeded in returning home toward nine at night; and while slowly unfolding his satchel to hand the letters and newspapers over to my grandmother, he would relate, in the gravest fashion, the account of all his hallucinations.

One day, he had a rather amusing adventure that he did not brag about. Lost in the profound meditations that wine brings on, he was returning on a dark and foggy evening, when, before he had time to get out of their away, he found himself face to face with two armed horsemen, who could only have been thieves. By one of those inspirations of courage that fear alone is capable of inducing, he stopped his horse and decided to frighten them off by pretending to be a thief himself and by shouting in a threatening voice, "Stay where you are, messieurs, your money or your life!"

The horsemen, a little taken aback by so much bravado, and thinking themselves surrounded by bandits, drew their sabers. Ready to do poor Saint-Jean in, they recognized him and burst out laughing. They did not let him go, however, without giving him a little lecture and threatening, should he do it again, to conduct him to prison. He had called "halt" to the police.

In his youth he had been something akin to an apprentice helper in the stables of Louis XV, from whence he had retained some solemn and dignified ideas and manners, as well as an obstinate respect for rank. Having thereafter become a postilion, a small difficulty arose when, after the Revolution, my grandmother took him on as a coachman; he never wanted to climb into the driver's seat nor abandon his jacket with red lapels and silver buttons. My grandmother, who was unable to gainsay anyone, let him have his way; and all his life he drove her around postilion-style. Since he had the habit of going to sleep on horseback, she had many a spill. At any rate, he served her in an intolerable manner for twenty-five years, without this incredibly patient and easy-going woman ever having the very natural idea of letting him go.

It seems that he took seriously my father's teasing about the pretended draft of fifty-year-old men and that he married Audelan at that time only to escape the eventual demands of the Republic. Twenty years later, when someone asked him if he had been in the army, he answered, "No, but I almost had to go." The first time my father came home on leave, after Marengo and the Italian campaign, Saint-Jean did not recognize him and took flight. But seeing that he approached my grandmother's apartment, he ran to Deschartres' place to tell him that a dreadful-looking soldier had entered the house "in spite him" and that Madame was surely going to be killed.

All that notwithstanding, he had his good side, and once, knowing that my grandmother was without money and worried at being unable to send any right then to her son, he joyfully brought her his year's salary, which by some miracle, he had not yet spent on drink. Perhaps he had received it the day before. But anyway the idea did come to him, and for a drunkard, that was something. He pardoned my father for driving the horses a little fast, but in his old age, he became less tolerant of me, and in order to go riding I was often obliged to bridle and saddle the horse myself, and other times to ride slowly to the first village, in order to have a shoe put back on my mount that he had been malicious enough to remove, to prevent me from making the horse run.

My father had made him a present of a pair of silver spurs. He lost one, and for the rest of his life used only one spur, stubbornly refusing to replace the other. He never failed to say to his wife each time she got him ready for a trip, "Madame, do not forget to put on my silver spur."

All the while calling each other "Monsieur" and "Madame," not a single day of their sweet union went by without a fight, and finally old Saint-Jean died drunk, as he had lived.

Here are a few more letters out of the batch.

Letter XXXII   Cologne, 1st Germinal, Year VII (March '99).

I am leaving for M————. My general absolutely insists on getting me a horse, and having run into too many difficulties in getting one sent from the regiment, he is sending me to the remount depot. He is giving me a letter of introduction to Général Ferrand, in order to have them give me the very best animal available, and I am leaving by coach with my saddle. I expect to come back at a leisurely pace. But this upsets my plans for economy. It is true the general advanced me sixty pounds, and on the return trip, the government provides stables and forage. But the coach alone costs fifty pounds, and as far as soldiers' lodgings are concerned, considering the great turnover, one invariably catches scabies in those places. Therefore, I am going to borrow one hundred francs from the general and repay him on my return, which will coincide with my monthly pay-period.

When I get back, I believe I will find the general getting ready to move, because we are supposed to go to Coblenz or Mainz, since having headquarters in Cologne makes it too far from the army of the Danube. I shall really be sad to leave Cologne, for here I am, as they say in regimental style, *en pied*: in other words, here I am in love with a charming woman who makes my life very pleasant. She has seen to it that all her lady friends have made me welcome, sometimes by means of music or by outings, sometimes by platters of cakes or bowls of cream. They have indulged me abominably; how now can such a coddled rooster go and catch scabies! Farewell to my pride and my pleasure! And if we go to Mainz, farewell to laughter, pastimes, love affairs; to hell with gentleness and little niceties! But anyway, a soldier is a migratory bird, and I should not have been smitten by my canoness, though of course I know I am not the first and won't be the last. She has a weakness for Frenchmen, and I cannot hold that against her, no more than the fact that she had Hoche's head turned in her direction for so long, who gave a magnificent party in her honor when he left Cologne. That celebration, which began with the maneuver of two regiments and ended with a ball, is something that people in this region still talk about with awe. It is only human to be a little jealous of the past, but reason dictates that I should be grateful to have such a beautiful, celebrated lady respond to me, a simple chasseur who doesn't have the means to offer her the most modest ball or the smallest cavalry maneuver. If I don't have the right to be jealous of the past, neither do I have the right to be jealous of the future; yet I have all I can do to restrain myself from falling in love to the point of losing my philosophy.

You ask me what this charming woman looks like. That is quite easy. Open your big volume on the antiquities of Herculanum, in *Le Voyage de Naples et Sicile*. At the top of the page, look for two women dancing against a background of clouds. That is not it; look below; there is a woman putting a section of her gown over her shoulder—that is not it either; look beside her: there, wearing a crown of reeds, is a woman holding a kind of platter or paten in one hand and an ewer in the other. Well, she has the shape, the size, the grace of my canoness; that is her portrait; it is as if you were looking at her in person.

As for her personality, she is spiteful and cutting to excess—sensitive and gentle, but spiteful! Only she is capable of making me behave like a fool. When she wants to find out something I am trying to conceal from her, she envelops me in traps; she misses not my slightest gesture nor glance; finally she forces me to admit everything. I believe she can read my thoughts. I am caught like an animal; so now I have decided to tell her everything, without undergoing the interrogation. If I am made too welcome in someone's house, she forbids me to go there, except on those days when she will be there. Really, I would never finish if I told you all her cunning ways and her charming displays of jealousy. It would be a sad thing to leave behind so much happiness to go take up the life of a loyal soldier in a garrison, to sleep two in a bed with a mangy friend, to groom the horses and become saturated with the smell of manure and other sweetnesses of the profession! If the general asks me, I will plead with him to send me to the squadrons at war, because there, in case of trouble, one can at least be useful and find honor; and, truth be told, I am not too eager to have trouble without honor. You amuse me, my dear mother, with your horror of conquerors. You would willingly proclaim:

> I detest all heroes, from the Grand Cyrus
> To that brilliant king who created Lentulus.
> Of their wondrous pursuits, I will not hear tell,
> I flee from them all; let them go to hell.[58]

The general is truly a fine man, humane, kindly, a man whom I like in spite of his somewhat cool and vague sermons. The other day, the wife of a man who had worked with the forage people came to request him to initial a memorandum that she had had drawn up for the re-instatement of her husband, who had been discharged. Not knowing her, the general could not give her his signature; but since she seemed to be in need, he sent her four louis via Durosnel. The woman accepted them with much gratitude and came with great dignity a week later to repay the debt.

Something further about Caulaincourt. He had gained so much influence over the general that, once, the latter came to the office to bring a work order for the day, broken down into hours; finding this paper on the table, Caulaincourt entered the general's office furious, tore up the order before his eyes, and told him that he knew very well how to handle his work and that he would wash his hands of it, if the general interfered. That is a bit strong! He was telling Maulnoir that he should not get too friendly with me and let himself be called simply "Maulnoir" by a plain cavalryman. Maulnoir responded that, outside of military contact, I was his friend and comrade and that he knew I had enough discretion not to shout out "Maulnoir" when we were in the field leading the regiment, he alongside the general, and I behind. Caulaincourt persuaded the general to promote to quartermaster an office secretary who delivered his love letters and repeated to him everything we said, for he is as curious as a woman! So the general is indeed going to nominate to a nice position this fellow, spy and love messenger of Monsieur Caulaincourt. Thus, all day long, Maulnoir, the other secretary, and myself made him the butt of many mean tricks and jokes. He must be pleased to be rid of us.

Goodbye, my dear mother, I embrace you with all my love; I am leaving for M————. There, as everywhere, your great lout of a son will be thinking of you.

Letter XXXIII   8 Germinal.

I am in M————, my dear mother, feeling generally out of sorts. In Brussels, I met the chief of the regimental squadron in charge of the remount. He told me that, in accordance with the general's orders, he has chosen me an excellent horse, one that was selected from among the very best, that I had only to saddle up and be off.

I arrive in M————, delighted by this preamble—all the more so since I did not have the wherewithal to remain there, my crowns having been diminished by twenty sous each in Brabant, due to the rate of exchange. Hence I rush to the remount, where I find the damned horse dying from the strangles. Général Ferrand, for whom I had a letter from Général Harville, is in Paris, which means that I cannot have any other horse and that I have to take this one, dead or alive, and then wait and see if he will be in any condition to ride, since I don't have enough money to return by coach.

Fortunately, Lady Luck, who goes everwhere with me, has shown me a way to keep from being bored. A young man who works in Cologne had given me a letter of introduction to his sister, who is married to a M. V———— here, and who has another sister with her, also very pretty. The older one is tall, beautiful, friendly; the younger one small, pretty, witty. These ladies love music with a passion. I am required to have lunch there every day, then dine, then spend the evening at the theater. The husband has taken a liking to me, so much so that once again I am the coddled rooster. If my canoness only knew! And, oh, when she does find out! For I am sure she will make me tell her everything. At any rate it is not my fault if they stuff me with delicacies; I am forced to accept, since I cannot go away.

My penury does not diminish my store of ideas, however. Tomorrow I will go to Jemmapes to study the battle plan, so as to be able to talk about it knowledgeably with Général Harville, who was there. Those fields of Flanders are sown with great military memories. I am not far from Fontenoy, and I shall try to push on to there. If my poor devil of a horse can walk, in a few days I should traverse and get acquainted with all those illustrious places where your dying father beat back the enemy and saved France. I would only have to write the general for permission, and he surely would not deny it, for if there was ever a country where the marshal's name is popular and everyone knows his slightest accomplishments, it is here.

Goodbye, my dear mother, I love you. Continue writing to me in Cologne. I will be there as soon as possible.

Letter XXXIV   Hervé, 25 Germinal, Year VII (April '99).

Heavens, how long it has been, my dear mother, since I've heard from you. This scarcity was my source of greatest annoyance all the time I was forced to remain in M————. If I had not expected to leave from one day to the next, I would have asked you to send your letters to me there. Now I am starving to reach Cologne, in order to get them and devour three or four. As I told you, I was forced to stay in M———, not being able to ride my sick horse and not having the money to take the coach, for I didn't know a soul I could borrow from. It is quite true that I quickly made the intimate acquaintance of someone, but you will see that this someone was the last person in the world from whom I could honorably make such a request.

I told you that M. V———, to whose wife I had brought a letter of introduction, had become quite friendly with me and no longer wanted to let me leave his home, where I was like a duck in water. He is very light-hearted and amiable; but having had his fill of the theater in Paris, he has no desire to go to the one in M——— and would always put me in charge of conducting his wife and his sister-in-law. The residents, little impressed with my soldier's uniform, wracked their brains to figure out how a lowly chasseur could be the escort of two Parisian *merveilleuses*,[59] who are highly esteemed in the provinces. M. V———, who is a great tease, told the provincials that, though I was but a simple soldier, I had already been covered with glory; that I was coming from the Egyptian campaign, where I had been severely wounded; that I had made the return trip with Bonaparte's aide-de-camp; that I was on my way, on behalf of that general, to join Masséna at the Rhine, but that en route my wounds had opened again and I had been forced to stop at his place. These turkeys then came to question me with awe about the campaign in Egypt, so I was forced to tell other-worldly tales, without hesitating and without laughing. I gave them descriptions of the Sinai desert as if I had lived there all my life, and I fabricated a story about the death of one of my horses that the crocodiles had devoured right before my eyes, a story that met with incredible success and that I had to retell ten times a day. When I came to the part about my wounds, they wanted to see them, and I was obliged to take refuge behind the presence of the ladies, so as not to re-enact Mascarille's famous scene.[60] Anyway, there was one member of my audience who was moved to tears and who one day asked me to allow him to embrace me. This would have the makings of good vaudeville, as would the rest of my tale, as you shall see.

Several times the two ladies had great stomach pains from restraining their laughter within hearing distance of my audience. My tall tales led them to believe I was quite witty; add to that, music, youth, and what have you! . . . and there I am between the two sisters, not knowing which one to turn to, and thoughts of my canoness coming to crown all the rest in my poor heart. I could not resist the temptation of two present beauties for one absent one. I yielded to the beautiful eyes of Mme. V———. She had asked me to make her a drawing on her ivory writing-tablets, a caricature of my return to Cologne on my sick horse. And I did in fact do it, reluctantly crossing a bridge into hell; leaving behind me flowers and trees, going toward a barren shore and snow-covered rocks, turning my back on springtime to return to the Cologne winter. Oh, my canoness! I committed this blasphemy and deception without giving it a thought, and yet, if you had been there, I would have thrown myself at your feet, I would have sung to you: "How timely you come to finish my pain!"[61]

Finally, my cursed drawings, my sung romances, my tales of Egypt, my plume, my dolman brought about my downfall, and to make matters worse, M. V——, friendlier toward me than ever, almost wept upon seeing my horse on its legs and offered to open his purse to me at my departure, worrying that I might be delayed by some accident on the road and that I might happen to be short of money. No doubt about that, I was already short, and my horse could barely drag itself along; but you understand that I could not impose on his friendship to that extent. I assured him that my pockets were full, and I left with twelve francs to cover sixty leagues on a broken-down horse.

Well, I will come through all right, for here I am in Hervé, between Aix and Liège, and I still have some money. There is nothing like having to do things, to make you aware you can do them. The trip is a bit harsh, it is true, but I am neither sick, nor tired, nor do I have a cold. By all appearances, I have a good mount; my horse is a fine specimen, but he is only four years old, runs at the nose, and can scarcely go six leagues a day at a walk; I would rather go completely on foot, because I am obliged to lead him along roads like those from Nohant to Saint-Chartier. The roads are impassable, it snows, it rains, it freezes; the poor animal fell down three times yesterday, and then I was forced to spend a day here to give him some treatment and rest, unless I want him to die on the road. At times I give him up to the devil; how I would like to have my old mare here! But I console myself for this wretched stopover by writing to you.

Passing back through Brussels, I found Jacquin, the squadron chief, the one who had received me when I first made my debut at the regiment mess hall. He insisted that I have lunch and dinner with him, and he informed me that the regiment had suffered a great deal recently. You have seen that we have drawn back our army of observation. Our outposts have not yet budged. They are at Siegbourg, Kaiserwerth, and Elberfeld, on a line ten leagues beyond the Rhine. On that point, we are impervious to attack, having under our control all the redoubts of the Rhine, the fort at Ehrenbreitstein, and so many other impregnable positions. Therefore the emperor[62] is directing his attacks against Schaffhouse and Basle. It would not be difficult for him to penetrate through there, but his army's tactics are so stupid that they won't be able to profit from their advantages. Unlike us, they don't know how to make breaches in enemy lines, and they never advance except in a long, flaccid line.

The headquarters of the army of observation will now be in Cologne, which will make this city very lively. Don't be worried about me, my dear mother; we are living an easy life in the army. Goodbye, I embrace you with all my heart. I could really use my maid at my stopovers to pass the bedwarmer between the sheets. But I don't need Deschartres' discoursing to put me to sleep. Fatigue does the job.

Letter XXXV   Cologne, 4 Floréal.

At last, my dear mother, I have seen the walls and fortifications of Cologne again. And the sight is not free of pain, believe me! For me it is what land is to the ship's pilot after a long and difficult navigation. I would have far preferred a vessel to row into port than to ride this wretched horse into the stable. At any rate, here he is, with a new abscess under his jaw. One more day of travel and he would have died in my arms.

The cold, rainy weather, which did not let up during the entire trip, brought back the strangles, and I am a pedestrian once again, as I was at the time of my departure, poorer by one hundred francs and richer by a pain in the knee. I believe it is rheumatism; it is as if I have a wooden leg; but I will soon be my old self again, cured before the warm stoves of Cologne. Having left M——— with my twelve pounds, I succeeded in reaching Cologne, after travelling sixty-three leagues, with twenty-four sous in my pocket. I used vouchers for my lodgings, which were at times tolerable, at other times "so-so." I went looking for forage from the local stores, carried it back on my shoulders, rubbed down my horse, cared for him like a little child; I fed myself like a hussar, with bread, cheese, and beer; consequently, I slept like a baby, and it all could have been worse.

Moreover, good fortune, my faithful companion, led me to a few good resting places. At Saint-Trond, I slept in the bed of Général Lacroix. My hosts, wealthy and likable people, offered me an excellent supper that I had the good sense to accept. At Aix and at Berghem, I met residents of Cologne, who offered me the hospitality of their cities. Anyway, the most wretched pallets and the harshest fatigues were still less painful to me than any pleasure I would have derived from the money of good M. V———. It seemed to me that I would have been degraded by taking it.

The weather here is superb; I am suddenly passing from winter to summer, from poverty to opulence, from stable to salon; say what you like, my dear mother, I don't smell too much of the stable. To groom a horse is the least of troubles. All it takes is an old smock, and if a little of that fragrance does indeed adhere to your person, our ladies don't seem to take much notice of it. Besides, they will just have to get used to it. If we were really at war, we would smell worse. Let me say, dear mother, that I must reject your idea of increasing my allowance so I might get a manservant. I do not want that, first because you are not wealthy enough now to make this sacrifice, and then because a simple cavalryman having a servant shine his boots and stand in line for him would become the laughing stock of the whole army. I confess that I laughed at the idea of seeing myself with a valet given my present circumstances, but I was still more touched by your concern. If the idea of seeing me with currycomb and pitchfork in hand disturbs you, please let me say, to reassure you, that it would be very easy for me, if I wished, to have my horse cared for by one of the general's grooms for six francs a month.

Since my return, the general has been charming to me. It is clear that Caulaincourt is no longer here. As I was coming back into Cologne on horseback, he saw me through his window, tapped on the pane to attract my attention, and gave me a friendly wave. I was afraid he might reproach me for my long absence, but he saw the condition of my horse and pitied my tribulations, laughing, as I related them to him. Mind you, I don't know what he wants to do with me and for me. He wished to have me in the office, and he insisted on it with such benevolence that, in spite of my dislike for this kind of work, I began today, and under his orders have taken on the title of secretary of acknowledgments. But he is going to leave for his estates, and he told Durosnel and Maulnoir that he would take me along, that I came too highly recommended for him not to concern himself with me, in short that he loved me dearly. But on the other hand, he told his servant that he would leave me in Cologne; the result being that now I know nothing about his plans for me, that he perhaps does not know them himself, and that I am left hanging.[47]

Berry is decidedly the land of obliging souls. I am deeply touched by the friendship of good Saint-Jean, who is willing to postpone receiving his wages to allow you to send money to me. The general's servant is also from Berry, from Châteauroux. His name is Barilier. He is more like a friend than a servant. During the general's arrest concerning the Dumouriez affair, Barilier displayed extraordinary devotion. He likes me too, as a compatriot, and whenever I dine at the general's house, he stuffs me with food, and he keeps my glass filled, exactly the way Saint-Jean used to do, to the point where he would get me drunk, if I were not paying attention. Farewell, my dear mother, I leave you to go have dinner at Mme. Maret's.

Letter XXXVI   Cologne, 27 Floréal (April '99).

You scold me, my dear mother, and I do not deserve it. For by this time, you must have received the letters that I wrote you from M——— and Hervé, on the way back to Cologne. A pox on the postal service for causing you to worry. So be assured, once and for all, that these delays can never be of my doing, that I am incapable of "forgetting" to write to you, and as concerns accidents, remember that I am *invulnerable*, that nothing can ever happen to me, and that a soldier of my size cannot be lost like a pocket handkerchief.

The general is true to the promise he made you and is giving me so much work that I don't know which way to turn. I am now his jack-of-all-trades— "To whom does the general wish to speak? To his orderly, or to his secretary?"—doing double duty, and like M. Thibaudier, am trained to both fur and feather.[63] What with men-friends, women-friends, correspondence, and errands, I do not have a minute to breathe. The general is "enraptured" with my handwriting. He is really not demanding. Besides, I am doing my best, since you insist that I do this kind of work, but I prefer delivering letters to writing them. The other day, he sent me to Bonn, six long leagues from here, to carry a dispatch to Général Wirion. I came back the same day. I had had terrible weather all morning; I was done up like the devil, with my carbine, my cartridge-pouch, my sabretache, all covered with mud, as I was myself, up to the ears. In this outfit, I met the general, who was out walking with the ladies of the chapter, the solemn Mme. Augusta on his arm. As soon as he saw me, he signaled me to approach. I came up to him at a trot, gave him the reply, and left after having paid my respects. I noticed that the ladies, seeing me harnessed with military equipment, were looking at me with interest. My canoness happened to be there, a little behind the others, trying to hide her emotion. I saw her eyes become red and moist, and I forgot my fatigue. Although beset just a moment earlier, I would now have run like a hare and leapt like a goat. Women were born to console us for all the earth's woes. Only in women are to be found these charming and attentive solicitudes which make grace and sensitivity so prized. You introduced me to them, my dear mother, when I was at your side, and now you are trying to make amends for my misdeeds.[64] Oh! if all mothers were like you, never would families have been forsaken by peace and happiness! Each of your letters, each day that goes by increases my gratitude and love for you. Oh, no, we must not abandon that little creature. I am sure you won't. Let us not be among those members of the human species who deserve the terrible pronouncment delivered by some writer through the mouths of young birds:

> Our mothers shall raise us,
> Every chick, as many as we are.
> Had we been born to humankind,
> We might be left at someone's door.[65]

Your reflections, my dear mother, have moved me deeply. I should have come to them myself, earlier. If your behavior in this instance had not repaired the unforeseen consequences of my rashness, I would perhaps have been reduced to coming to only fruitless, grievous ones. To profess and practice virtue is your custom and your lot. Farewell, my dear mother, my excellent and cherished mother. I am wanted at the general's house. I have only time left to embrace you with all my heart.

Maurice.

Here is the explanation of the preceding letter. A young woman attached to the household service had just given birth to a fine boy who was later to be my childhood companion and friend of my youth. This pretty woman had not been the victim of seduction. She had yielded, as had my father, to the temptations of youth. My grandmother dismissed her with no reproach, provided for her livelihood, kept the child, and raised him.

She placed him with a wet-nurse, under her very eyes, at the home of an extremely clean peasant woman who lived almost next door to us. We see, in subsequent letters from my father, that his mother sent him news about this child and that they alluded to him privately with the code name, the Little House, though this should hardly bring to the reader's mind the "little hideaways" of those debauched noblemen of the good old days. A small, rustic maisonette does indeed figure in this story, but there are no rendezvous, except between a loving grandmother, an honest village wet-nurse, and a strapping baby, who was not placed in a foundling home but who was brought up with as much care as a legitimate son. The rashness of a single day will be redressed by a whole life's solicitude. My grandmother had read and valued Jean-Jacques—she had profited from his verities and errors; for to turn evil to the path of virtue is to make use of a bad example to set a good one.

Letter XXXVII   Cologne, 19 Prairial, Year VII (June '99).

The general is not turning in his resignation, my dear mother, rest assured. He customarily goes each year to spend a month or two on his estates. He is not losing sight of me. He has just spoken to me with much affection to say that he had to transfer me to the supply depot, that I needed to be trained for cavalry maneuvers, and that it would not be for long, since Beurnonville was proceeding, along with him and Beaumont, to obtain a promotion for me from the Directoire. He told me he was well aware that you would be vexed to know I was at the depot but that, on the other hand, you wanted him to keep an eye on me, and this was the only way, since the depot is at Thionville, and the general is going to Metz or its environs. He will advance me the money I need for the trip. So don't worry, don't grieve. I will be fine no matter where I am, provided you are not distressed. Remember that if you make yourself unhappy, then of necessity, I am too—were I loaded with riches and rolling in luxury. One fine day, you shall see me return, an officer, decorated from head to foot, and then you will have the potentates of La Châtre bowing and scraping before you. Come now, be patient, my dear mother, travel, go to the spas, amuse yourself, try to find some distraction, try to forget me for a while, if thinking about me disturbs you. I don't really mean that; don't forget me, and do give me courage. I need it too. I have farewells to make which are going to cost me dearly! As yet she knows nothing about my departure. I must tell her this evening, and tears must replace happiness. I shall think of you in pain as I always have in exultation. I shall write a longer letter for the next mail. The general wants me to write Beurnonville before the latter leaves.

All your decisions on behalf of the Little House are excellent. You are protecting my self-esteem, which is not pride, I assure you. I reproach myself more on that score than you ever could! You protect the weak, you ward off misfortune! How good you are, mother, and how I love you!

Letter XXXVIII   Cologne, 26 Prairial (June '99).

You are sad, my dear mother, and so am I—but your sorrow is the only reason. For myself I have courage, and I have always told myself that love would not make me forget duty, but faced with your suffering, I have no strength. I see that your life is poisoned by excessive, continuous worries. My God, how you invent frightening demons! So open your eyes, my dear mother, and recognize that there is nothing so ominous in all this. Why such a fuss? I am leaving for Thionville, an interior city, the most peaceful in the world, carrying with me the friendship and protection of the general, who is recommending me to the squadron chief. I shall therefore be able to leave from there only on his orders, and I shall not be free to go confront those dangers that you dread so.[48] Would that I could make you a hussar for a little while, so you could see how easy it is and what a provision of unconcern for oneself is attached to that uniform! Do you know how I am going to leave Cologne? In tears? No—they must be shelved, and I must go off in the din of a celebration. When I announced my departure to my friends, they all cried out, "We must give him an honorable send-off. We must get drunk with him at his first stopover and part from each other intoxicated, because to keep our sangfroid would be too difficult." Consequently, they are preparing three cabriolets, two *birouches*,[66] and five saddle horses, for Bonn. Not only will I be escorted by all those who have shared my dining table, but also by a young officer of the light infantry, a charming Parisian, who has received an excellent education; also by Maulnoir, by the general's secretaries, by a guard of the rations warehouse, and by a young warrant officer, who will lend an aura of respectability to the joyous band and prevent it from being stopped because of all the noise it plans on making. In truth, it is nice to be loved, and as you can see, rank and wealth have nothing to do with it. Affection does not take those things into consideration, especially in youth, which is the age of true equality and fraternal love.

We already number some twenty, and my escort is constantly recruiting new participants. This city serves as the gathering point for all members of the left flank of the army of the Danube, among whom there are a host of excellent young men. I am on good terms with them all; we swim together, we fence, play ball, etc. As one who has shared in their pleasures, they don't want me to leave them without formal farewells. Even the man who is in charge of coach rentals, a very affable young man, wishes to be included and is lending his carts and carriages free of charge. I shall be seated gravely on horseback, and I think that if Alexander made a glorious entry into Babylon, my entry into Bonn shall be more joyous.

Concerning the swimming, I have twice swum across the famous Rhine. It was quite cold and very swift. Thus I have faced it under all conditions, for not long ago, I crossed it on ice.

I leave the day after tomorrow. I am up to the sad subject of farewells. Tomorrow, I shall see her for the last time! That is the moment I dread! After that, a band of wild friends will expect me for supper, to work out the details of the procession on the following day. A thousand absurd things will be said; they will make fun of my air of consternation, and I shall be forced to laugh to hide my secret. So let us get on with it! My will-power will come to aid me, and with the help of wine, I'll be numb to my sorrow. But yours will remain in my heart, as long as you don't make an effort to console yourself. I will write you en route. I love you and embrace you with all my heart. All best wishes to Deschartres and to my maid. *R.T.C.*

XI

Letters continued. —The escort. —Ehrenbreitstein. —Along the Rhine. —Thionville. —Arrival at the depot. —The friendliness of the officers. —The quartermaster sergeant as teacher of good manners. —The drill. —The first promotion. —A peculiar custom in Thionville. —A white lie.

Letter XXXIX   Lutzerath, 2 Messidor, Year VII (June '99).

I left Cologne, my dear mother, as I had informed you, escorted by vehicles and horses carrying a quantity of noisy and spirited young men. The procession was headed by Maulnoir and Leroy, the general's aides-de camp, and I was between the two of them, cartridge pouch and carbine at my back, mounted on my stripped-down Hungarian. Our passage was acknowledged by the sentries' snapping to attention, and whoever saw those plumes in the wind and those wagons on the move could hardly guess that all they were doing was escorting a mere private.

Instead of proceeding to Bonn as planned, we left the main road and headed for Brühl and its magnificent castle, formerly the regular residence of the elector. This place was much more appropriate for saying goodbye than the town of Bonn. The joyous group had lunch and then went on to visit the castle, an imitation of Versailles. The dilapidated apartments still have their beautiful frescoes on the ceilings. The staircase, of vast proportions and highly polished, is supported by caryatids and decorated with bas-reliefs. But despite its richness, it all bears the ineffaceable imprint of German bad taste. They cannot help but overdo it when they copy us, and instead of merely copying, they ape us. I wandered around the palace at length with the cavalry officer, who is a passionate lover of the arts, as I am.

Then we went back to the others in the park, and after crisscrossing it in every direction, somebody suggested playing ball. We were on a beautiful lawn surrounded by a magnificent forest of tall trees. The weather was gorgeous. Jackets are off, heads up, eyes fixed on the ball, each one struggling to outdo the other. Banquet preparations can be seen arriving at the far end of a shaded pathway. The game is abandoned, we run, we rush. The little patties are devoured before even being put out on the table. At the end of the dinner, where high spirits were mingled with affection, I was assigned to carve a hunting horn and saber, with my initials in the middle, on the bark of the huge tree that shaded our banquet. I had barely finished when they all came to put their names around it, with this motto, "Our longings go with him." We formed a circle around the tree, sprinkled it with wine, and took turns drinking from my shako, which they had named the cup of friendship.

As it was getting late, someone brought me my horse, they embraced me before letting me mount, they embraced me again when I was mounted, and we parted with tears in our eyes. I rode away at a fast trot, and soon I had lost sight of them.

So there I was, all alone, sadly proceeding along the road to Bonn, bereft of friends and mistress all at once, just as gloomy at the end of my stay as I had been bright-eyed at the beginning. Truly this method of parting by way of frenzied activity is the most painful one I know. It makes no provision at all for bringing our courage to bear, and it chases away our powers of reflection, which could bring it to bear. We sit down to a banquet, image of an eternal association, and suddenly we find ourselves all alone and desolate, as if emerging from a dream....

Arriving in Bonn, I called on a young man, secretary to a war commissary, whom I had met in Cologne. The next day he invited me to an excursion to Poppelsdorf, another of the elector's castles, and to the spa at Godesberg, an earthly paradise. After our return to Bonn, we visited the palace that the elector had built in this pretty little town. The gardens are delightful: sparkling waters, avenues of orange trees with a view of the Rhine and the mountains rising from it. These beautiful sights did not console me, but they sweetened the bitterness of my thoughts. The next day, in order to get to Coblenz, I took the road parallel to the Rhine, which is bordered by menacing rocks and sheer mountains throughout this whole area. Several pretty islands rose from the water's depths like bouquets of flowers. The road is everchanging and presents unexpected tableaux at each step. Here a monastery, there a village, then flocks of animals, fleets of large sailboats, and, in the distance, retrenchments and bastions.

Having arrived in Coblenz, I was aimlessly wandering around the streets when I met the brother of the war commissary in charge of the Ehrenbreitstein service. A nice opportunity to visit this famous fortress so talked about in recent days! We renewed our acquaintance, he took me to his place for dinner, and at sunset we went up to see the fort. Just imagine, my dear mother, Mount Pelion piled on top of Mount Ossa—in other words, the handiwork of the Titans. Enormous bastion-covered rocks, bristling with two hundred cannon; storehouses of bombs and cannonballs; quartered stones at all the slopes, destined to crush the assailants. On the rocky plateau is a courtyard surrounded by eight rows of ramparts, from where you have a birdseye view of Coblenz, and the Rhine is like a ribbon winding around the shoreline of rocks. Never before had this place changed masters. We are the first to have seized it. I went four leagues out of my way to see it, and it was well worth it.

You are surprised at the great number of people who know me; in faith, I was so myself last night. Crossing one of those gorges of Hunsrück, where you descend as into a precipice, it was almost night; the thickness of the forest added to the darkness; passing alongside a *birouche*, I heard someone call my name. I turn around and in the cart I see, next to a young woman, an officer whom I had met several times at the balls in Cologne. There we were, engaged in conversation, astounded at the coincidence that had first made us meet at balls in order then to reunite us at this terrifying stop; for all the scenic hells at the opera are nought compared to these gorges. There are nothing but forests that end in mid-air, black torrents, or arid flats. Finally, we separated after having wished each other a good trip, and it was quite late when I arrived at a cluster of huts called Kaisersech. Oh, my dear mother, how I blessed you there again for having made me learn German! I knock at every door. The inhabitants peep through their dormers; but at the sight of my uniform, they doublelock and hasten to barricade themselves. They give us shelter only when they have no choice, and fear us like the devil. As for me, I would sooner have slept outdoors than in those shanties, but my poor horse, which is not yet fully recovered from his sickness, was half dead from hunger and fatigue. Thus, on reaching the far end of the village, I had the idea to pass myself off as an ulan and announce the arrival of the imperial troops. I make up German names, I talk about a Colonel Baron von Stromberg, about some prince or other, and a good-natured peasant opens his door and receives us, my horse and me, with a great deal of respect. He will be undeceived later on, if he has a mind to; that is his business. I left at dawn. I am writing you from Lutzerath; tomorrow I shall be in Treves. Very soon I shall see Général Harville, who is supposed to come to Thionville to inspect his troops. He said goodbye to me in a most amiable way, told me where I should write to him, and promised to write to the quartermaster and to the commander of the depot on my behalf. Adieu, my dear mother, I embrace you, and take to the road again.

Letter XL   Thionville, 14 Messidor, Year VII (July '99).

Really! my dear mother, you must stop worrying once and for all, because I am happy here, or in any other place; things always turn out for the best for me. The first thing I did upon entering town was to fall literally into a wigmaker's shop, while my horse fell at the door. As usual, I am not hurt in the least. I pick myself up more quickly than my horse. I look on this happening as a good omen, and get back on my horse, which didn't get hurt either. I arrive at headquarters. I go to find the quartermaster, Boursier, who receives and embraces me with his usual cheery frankness. He tells me that the general's letters have not yet arrived but that I should be good enough to introduce and recommend myself, and he takes me to see the commander of the depot, by the name of Dupré, an officer of the old regime who resembles our friend M. de La Dominière. I tell him who I am and where I am coming from. He too embraces me! he invites me to supper, gives me permission to sleep off post, and tells me that he hopes I will live with the officers. In fact, I dine with him and with them every day, at a table costing thirty-six francs a month. My lodgings cost me fifteen; that is not expensive, and I'm very comfortable there. Except for my rank, I'm an officer. All of them are very pleasant, and the officer in charge of the drill is very good to me; I participated for the first time yesterday, and he paid me a lot of compliments. I had never been in the middle of a squadron, and I assure you it is not a soft job. I was in the first row, and when one moves forward into battle formation, the two wings draw closer together and one is pressed from right and left by the weight of fifty horses. We shall do it again tomorrow. The bones and muscles have got to get used to it, and I'm confident I'll get to that point quickly.

I spend my days at the quartermaster's, and I am writing you from his office. We have another young recruit at our table, a cavalry private like me. He comes from one of the best families in Liège and plays the violin as well as Guénin or Mestrino. Furthermore, he is friendly and witty, and the commander likes him a lot because he himself plays the flute, adores music, and sets great store by talent and a good education. This, in my opinion, is the distinction which will always survive the disappearance of ancient privileges, abolished for good reason, and the equality dreamed of by our philosophers will only be possible when all men will have been granted a culture that makes them sociable and pleasant to one another. You were frightened to see me become a soldier, thinking that I would be forced to live with unrefined people. First of all you ought to realize that there are not as many unrefined people as we think, that it is a matter of temperament, and that education does not always destroy rudeness in people who are born rude and disobliging. I even think that a veneer of politeness enables these characters to be still more offensive than those who have the excuse of a total lack of education. Thus, I would prefer to live with fieldhands conscripted from behind their plough than with M. de Caulaincourt, and I much prefer the behavior of our Berrichon peasants to that of certain great German barons. Stupidity is shocking on every level; geniality, on the other hand, makes up for everything. I agree that I would not for long enjoy the company of people without culture; a lack of ideas in others provokes a need for ideas in me that verges, I sense, on a craving. In this respect you spoiled me, and if I had not had the resource of music, which intoxicates me enough to make me forget everything else, I would surely die of boredom in certain social situations. But, coming back to your chagrin, you see that it is not justified, and that everywhere I go, I meet pleasant people who receive me well and who live with your soldier on equal terms. The title of grandson of Maréchal de Saxe—which I avoid taking advantage of, but by which I am announced and introduced everywhere—certainly is in my favor and opens many doors; but it also gives me a responsibility, and if I were a boor or an impertinent fellow, my birth, far from saving me, would condemn and make me hated ever more. It is therefore only on our own that we have some merit, or to express it better, because of the principles that education has instilled in us; if I am worth something, if I inspire some sympathy, it is because you, my dear mother, took a great deal of trouble so that I would not disgrace you.

You may add to that my good fortune, which thrusts me in among friendly people, for the Schomberg regiment of dragoons, which is here now, in no way resembles ours. The officers are very arrogant and keep their young non-commissioned soldiers at a distance, no matter how well brought up they may be. With us, it is the opposite: our officers are our comrades and companions, if they like us. They take us by the arm and have a beer with us, and we are only the more obedient and respectful for it when they exercise their functions and we ours.

By the way, there is one officer in the Schomberg dragoons to whom the general particularly recommended me, who is an exception, the Quartermaster M. Favé. The general told me to consider him as I would the general himself and to ask him to advance me money, if I should need it. This M. Favé, having not yet received the general's letter, welcomed me most kindly on faith, introduced me to his wife, who is charming, and took me to visit his father in the country.

I don't know who on earth here could have spread the word that I was rich; this morning my host wanted to borrow ten louis from me, and M. Dupré wanted to sell me a horse. The truth is, however, that I possess one single louis. I arrived with two, and the first has already found its way into the stomachs of my quartermaster sergeant and my arms sergeant, since it was indispensable to make their acquaintance by way of a splendid treat. Of course, they now like me to the point of adoration, which is very convenient for me. They heard tell that I was a protégé of the general, and they asked me to intervene for them with him. They are bringing me their service records, and as often as I tell them that I would very much like a promotion myself, they stubbornly cling to the belief that I can obtain it for them and that I am a private merely for my personal pleasure.

They attend to my littlest chores and are spoiling me as if I were their superior. They have the right to give me orders, even give me company punishment, and yet they serve me as if they were my grooms. I always have the best horse for the drill, all saddled and reined in, held in check by those good men, who would almost venture so far as to give me a boost. When the drill is over, they relieve me of my horse and won't let me give it another thought. With all of that, they are so droll that they make me double up with laughter. My quartermaster especially believes in educational principles, and he acts like Deschartres with his recruits, who are good little peasants whose manners he wishes to polish at all costs. He doesn't let them play quoits with stones, because that "smacks too much of the farm." He also takes pains with their language. Yesterday, one of them came to tell him that "the horses were all of them saddled." "What's that!" he says to him indignantly, "Haven't I told you a hundred times that you mustn't say 'all of them?' You simply say, 'My sergeant, it's done, and what's more, I'm taking off myself.'" And after this nice lesson, he takes off.

I would surely hope you were on your way,[67] what with this beautiful weather. The heat here is stifling, but I am not complaining. Last winter I was so cold that it seems to me I haven't totally thawed out yet. What did old Deschartres select for a mount to make the trip to Néris? Could it be he chose a donkey? Tell me more about Nohant, my dear mother. Everything that did not interest me when I was there now has great value, since you take care of it and find pleasure in it. I embrace you with all my heart.

Letter XLI   Thionville, 16 Messidor (July '99).

I am now well established in the society of Thionville, just as I was in Cologne, my dear mother. Hardy, the young virtuoso recruit I mentioned to you in my last letter, made his debut with me in a concert organized weekly by our commanding officer, which takes place at the home of a captain in the engineering corps, who is married and lives in town. We were showered with applause. The commandant introduced us in another home where we had a sumptuous meal. There were some very pretty women there, and we all played parlor games. The commandant, who is full of wit and mischief under his cold and serious appearance, was making the funniest comments; and taking me to task after I had held my own with him rather amusingly, he addressed such flattering and friendly remarks to me, I was truly touched.

The general wrote to say I would be nominated for corporal, if there was a vacancy, and in fact there is one, because the holder of that post has been retired for reasons of health. I expect my nomination any day, and in the meantime I am getting acquainted with the facts in the manual of details as quickly as possible; every morning I go to drill. The commandant ordered that I be put on the flank, in the corporal's position, in order to get me used to the pivoting and wheeling flank maneuvers. This is not very difficult, and the exercises you had me learn in my childhood stand me in good stead for easy handling of my carbine on horseback. My quartermaster, whom I cram with food quite regularly, is crazy about me. He calls me "my chasseur" as if he were saying "my general," and at the squadron session he makes it a point to whisper to me what I have to do. So I shall soon be acquainted with my duties and wear stripes on my sleeve. I owe my promotion to Beurnonville, because Général Harville, a fine man in every other way, cannot get himself to do anything unless he is continuously prodded. Beurnonville even had written to him to have me made sergeant, but it seems that this was not possible. He wrote me a charming letter, to which I shall reply today. This is why I leave you, my dear mother, while embracing you with all my heart.

Letter XLII   Thionville, 20 Messidor, Year VII (July '99).

If I had known how to read, says Montauciel,[68] I would have been a corporal ten years ago; and knowing how to read and write, here I am, my dear mother, exercising my functions after my promotion to this brilliant rank by order of the general, at the head of my company, which—lined up, saber in hand—received orders to "obey me in anything I might command." Since that great day, I have been wearing two braided chevrons on my sleeves. I am a section leader in charge of twenty-four men, and "general" inspector of their uniform and headdress. On the other hand, I no longer have a moment for myself. From six in the morning till nine in the evening, I do not have time to sneeze. From six to seven-thirty, the horses are groomed. From eight to eleven-thirty, there is drill. At noon we dine. At two, the recruits are taught how to saddle and bridle a horse. Grooming again at three until four-thirty. At five, dismounted drill until seven-thirty. At eight we have supper. Retreat is called at nine. At ten we go to bed very tired, and the next day it starts all over again. Into the bargain, I am on a rotating ten-day work detail, which means that I have to be in the supply room from four in the morning to supervise the distribution of oats for the horses and bread for the troops. As a result, for the last nine days that I've had the honor of being corporal, I haven't had a single moment to write to you. Fortunately, my ten days are coming to an end, and I shall no longer be so overburdened. I have been to Metz, in charge of six cavalrymen, to bring in some conscripts who had gone into hiding in order to avoid their fate. I congratulated myself for having blindly devoted myself to mine and to be riding a good horse, giving orders, instead of being dragged along by my ears. But I felt badly for those poor devils on foot, in the dust, on an atrociously hot day. We had them march in front of us like a flock of sheep, and they were so unhappy! I made their journey as easy as possible, leading them at slow speed and allowing them to stop when they were tired.

I won't tell you anything about Metz; the fortifications are superb, you know them. But what you don't know is how much the inhabitants "love" us. My chasseurs were billeted in a big beautiful house. While they were eating their bread and meat ration, they asked for something to drink. A bucket of water was brought for them into the middle of the room, but no one would give them any kind of vessel to pour it out. In other words, they were treated like animals. The oldest of the soldiers took the bucket and threw it in the face of the cook who had brought it and who now was the recipient of every last drop. I arrived in the middle of the ruckus. The cook was shouting and came to me with his complaint, but after hearing both sides, I judged him to be at fault for his boorishness and advised him to change his clothes or stay wet.

The general seems to feel he would be compromising himself by promoting me more quickly, and in spite of Beurnonville's urging, it was indeed difficult for him to have me made corporal. He wrote to the commandant, Dupré, to address a request to him; at the same time he wrote to me that he nominated me on the strength of this request. It is all very well and good for him to want to make others believe it was not he who promoted me, but if he wants to convince me of it when I have in my hand Beurnonville's letter containing the notification, that is a little too much. In any event, I am now a corporal. However, you can see that it is not at all that easy to get over the first hurdle. They are sounding the trumpet, a very quick goodbye to you, my dear mother. Here they wait for no one.

Letter XLIII   Thionville, 25 Thermidor (August '99).

I believe, my dear mother, that I haven't told you anything about the dwarfish town of Thionville. The fortifications are very ingenious and beautiful. The interior town is very well constructed; but how tiny it is! One can walk around the ramparts in seven minutes. "Society" meets every Sunday at the house of a certain M. Guiot, a relative of the commandant. It is what is called here, as in La Châtre, the "first" society. It comprises four or five rather pretty women, any number of old chatterboxes, three or four old newsmongers, and two young fellows of provincial cast, who haven't stepped outside the walls of their city since the day they were born. I tell them absurd and silly stories, which they swallow hook, line, and sinker.

They have a very bizarre custom here. When a family loses a boy or girl under the age of sixteen, they bury him, as they do everywhere else, but here it is an occasion for laughter. After the funeral, they invite all their friends and relatives and serve a copious meal, where they all drink as much as they can. It is quite similar to what our peasants do in Berry, but there the meal after the burial can be justified by the necessity of feeding those who come from a distance, and it has a certain ancestral aspect. Here, the custom has something savage about it; people are merry, they needs must be, and after the meal they dance all night; I would not have believed it, if I hadn't seen it with my own eyes, yesterday. It happened in a shoemaker's family. There was a ball and as much noise and high spirits as at a wedding.

The officers of the garrison recently gave a very nice ball to which I received a written invitation. Since I did some high stepping on that occasion, I am considered another Vestris here, and my footwork apparently caught the eye of a very pretty lady whom I already had had my eye on for some time and who hadn't paid me any attention. It was during this ball that I got to break the ice with her by means of the esteem my rigadoon had won for me. Unfortunately, I don't have a moment of leisure to ingratiate myself; I spend all my time with my horses and my men. The little free time at my disposal I use for studying the drill manual and learning the commands, so as not to commit any blunders when I have a platoon in my charge. It wouldn't be worth it to have something else on my mind, and I already am only too distractable by nature. The other day, for example, when I was told to take my place at the right flank of the squadron, I don't know what devil possessed me to go directly to the left. Fortunately, the officer was busy elsewhere or distracted himself; I realized my mistake before he did, and I had the time to correct it.

My rank of corporal exempts me from having to groom my horse, but I gain nothing thereby in terms of greater leisure, because it takes more time to have the officers' orders carried out and see to it that it is done properly than do it myself. I marvel at the difficulty that men have in learning the simplest things. However, it seems to me that we should at least adjust easily to those things we are forced to learn. The discipline is very strict, and in spite of the consideration of our officers, the subordination is perfect. The team spirit is excellent. Blabbermouths and barracks lawyers are heartily detested. Service is performed obediently, promptly, and respectfully. Wartime conditions have now made us like the Prussians. Speaking of the Prussians, are you aware that there lives no Corporal Schlag[69] with a more beautiful pigtail than mine? For a long time I wore a false one, attached with false plaits, but my hair has grown back, and today my pigtail is my own. I have been wearing my hair cut above the ear, powdered white, with the braid exactly two inches down from the head. To be all snapped and strapped like a portmanteau, with stick in hand, is one of the attributes and advantages of my rank. Who could have told me a year ago that I would be a Corporal Schlag? One year ago, my dear mother, I was at your side; it is almost a year that we've been apart! At that time, I was chanting your name, thinking up verses and good wishes for your name day. I make those wishes for your happiness every day of my life, and I shall make them come true when I come back to you, worthier of your tender love than when I let myself be spoiled like a big baby. Our separation is a painful one, but I owed it to myself to make some effort to escape that delicious life where my insouciance, plus a bit of natural laziness, would have rendered me selfish. You loved me so much that you would perhaps not have noticed it. You would have believed, seeing me accept the happiness you gave me, that your own happiness was my doing, and I would have been an ingrate, without suspecting it and without being aware of it. I had to be torn away from my nullity by imperious external circumstances. There was a little destiny in all that. The same fatality that crushes weak and fearful souls may be the salvation of those who accept it. Christiana of Sweden took for her motto, *Fata viam inveniunt.* "The Fates guide my path." I myself prefer Rabelais' oracle, *Ducunt volentem fata, nolentem trahunt.* "Fate wafts the willing and drags the reluctant." You will see that this career is right for me. In a revolution, differences are resolved with sabers, and here we are, battling the enemy in order to defend our philosophical conquests; our sabers will prevail. Your good friends, Voltaire and Rousseau, my dear mother, now need our swords. Who would have told my father, when he was chatting with Jean-Jacques, that some day he would have a son who would not grow up to be a farmer general or a revenue collector, neither wealthy, nor witty, nor even very much of a philosopher, but who would be, out of choice as much as out of necessity, a soldier of a republic, and that the republic would be France? Thus do ideas become facts and take us further than we imagine.

Goodbye, dearest mother. On the crest of these fine reflections, I am off to give out the oats and carry away their end result.

Letter XLIV   Thionville, 13 Fructidor, Year VII (September '99).

Still in Thionville, my dear mother, from four in the morning to eight in the evening engaged in exercises on foot and on horseback, and in my capacity as corporal, bringing up the rear in either case. I come back at night worn out, without having been able to devote a single moment "to muse or to amuse." I miss the nicest parties, neglect the prettiest women, I hardly even play music any more. I am a corporal to the letter, I immerse myself in tactical theory, and am petrified to think I have become a model of energy and punctuality. And the funniest part of this whole affair is the fact that I like it this way and in no way miss my free and easy life. I am hopeful, according to Beurnonville's promises, soon to move up to the rank of sergeant, in which event I shall most decidedly become "Mr. Do-as-I-say." No one can be more obliging than Beurnonville. He wrote me twice since my arrival here, he wrote on my behalf to the brigade chief, and to the commandant, Dupré. He isn't waiting for others to ask him to obtain advancement for me, and he, for one, is not afraid to compromise himself. I have no doubt that Général Harville wishes me well, but he becomes paralyzed when it's a question of putting himself out for whatever it is. Perhaps the Terror and the prisons left an unfortunate mark on him, but one would be tempted to say that he wants to be forgotten by the government and to go unnoticed. I learned today that my regiment was no longer under his inspection. He will set up headquarters in Strasbourg. At the moment he probably is in Paris, and I really no longer know where to write to him. It must have been your letters that influenced him so greatly. He took such a liking to me that he wouldn't have hesitated to put me in a jar to preserve me, had he been able. But he ought not push his solicitude to the point of preventing me from pursuing my career. How good of you to take care of the Little House that way! Ah, if all mothers were like you, an ungrateful son would be an imaginary monster!

I received the money and paid all my expenses. I am up to date in my affairs, which is to say that I don't have a sou, but I no longer owe anybody anything. Don't send me anything before the end of the month. I get everything here on credit, and I want for nothing. Goodbye, my dear mother, I love you with all my heart and embrace you as I love you. My greetings to old Deschartres and to my maid.

The letter you have just read, which bears a date from Thionville, was written from Colmar. That date is a white lie which will be explained in the following letter. The burst of ill humor against Général Harville will also be explained. In case the reader's interest has been caught up in this correspondence, I do not wish to spoil the surprise by telling him what went on in the young corporal's mind during this fortnight.   *B.P.*

XII

Letters continued. —Joining the campaign. —The first cannon shot.
—Crossing the Linth River. —The battlefield. —A good deed.
—Glarus. —Meeting M. de La Tour d'Auvergne on the Lac de
Constance. —Ordener. —Letter from my grandmother to her son.
—The Rheinthal.

Letter XLV

Weinfelden, Canton Thurgau, 20 Vendémiaire, Year VIII (October 1799).

A harvest of laurels, glory, and victories; the Russians beaten and chased
out of Switzerland, in twenty days; our troops ready to enter Italy; the
Austrians repulsed to the other side of the Rhine—there you have without a
doubt great news of wonderful deeds! Well, my dear mother, your son has had
the satisfaction of sharing in this glory, and within two weeks he has taken part
in three decisive battles. He is in extremely good form. He drinks, he laughs,
he sings. He jumps three feet off the ground when he thinks about what a joy it
will be to bring you a kiss next January and place at your feet in your room at
Nohant whatever meager laurels he will have earned.

I picture you surprised and confused by my words and asking a hundred
questions, demanding a thousand explanations: how is it that I am in Switzerland? Why have I left Thionville? I will answer all that, and I shall recount the
circumstances in detail, as well as the reasoning behind my actions. It was the
fear of worrying you needlessly that prevented me from keeping you informed
of my whereabouts.

I am a military man, and that is the career I want to pursue. My personal
destiny, my name, the way in which I reported for duty, my honor and yours,
all require that I conduct myself well and earn the favors which have been
granted to me. You especially want me not to remain an unknown face in the
crowd and to become an officer. Well, my dear mother, in the French army
today it is just as impossible to become an officer without having fought in a
war as it would have been, in the fifteenth century, to make a bishop out of a
unbaptized Turk. You simply have to realize this fact. Any man, whoever he is,
arriving as an officer in any corps, without having been under fire, would be
the laughingstock not so much of his peers, who would be capable of appreciating his other talents, but of his own men, who would be unable to evaluate
his ability and who respect and esteem physical courage only. Struck by these
two facts—the need to have fought in a war in order to be made an officer on

the one hand, and the need to have fought in a war to serve honorably as an officer on the other—I concluded that I had to participate in a campaign as soon as possible. Do you think I left Nohant with the intention of spending my life being sociable in the garrisons and indispensable in the depots? No, certainly not. I have always dreamed of battles, and if I have lied to you a little about this, forgive me, my dear mother, it was your loving fears that forced me into it.

Before the general could say anything to me about leaving him, and from the moment the hostilities resumed, I went and asked if I could join the battle squadrons. At first this request pleased him. Then, influenced by your letters, he was afraid of displeasing you by taking the responsibility for my fate. So he called me back to tell me to report to the depot because you didn't want me to fight, but when I pointed out to him that all mothers were more or less like you and that this is the only kind of disobedience a man is permitted and even obliged to commit, he acknowledged that I was right. "Report to the depot," he said, "and from there you will be able to leave with the first detachment destined for the battle squadrons; and your esteemed mother can't reproach me for what was your own decision."

I arrive at Thionville, and my first concern is to find out if a detachment is leaving soon. I cannot hide my eagerness to join the regiment. I wait anxiously for a month. Finally a detachment is formed, I'm part of it, I train with them every day, I talk war with the most experienced chasseurs, they can see how anxious I am to share their fatigue, their labor, and their glory. And that, my dear mother, is the secret of their friendship for me, far more than all the drinks I buy them. Finally, a date was set for departure. There was only a week to wait. I was writing to you about things of no importance, but how could you believe that I'd be so interested in dressings and ammunition, if I wasn't thinking about going into battle?

Just when I least expect it, I receive a letter from the general in which he tells me—very kindly, it's true, but very firmly—that he wants me to remain at the depot until further notice. Just look at the unpleasant role he was making me play! How was I to explain and convince the whole regiment that it wasn't my fault if I didn't leave with them? I was in despair. I showed that fatal letter to all my friends; the officers could easily see what an impossible position I was in and how much it grieved me, but the illiterate and unthinking soldier didn't believe it. I heard people say behind my back, "I knew all along he wouldn't go. Daddy's boys are scared. Privileged people never go," etc. Sweat formed on my brow, and I felt dishonored. I couldn't sleep in spite of the fatigue of military duties; death was in my soul, and I didn't write to you very often, as you must have noticed. How could I tell you all that? You would never have wanted to believe it!

At last, in desperation, I go off to see the commander, Dupré, I show him that confounded letter, and I tell him that I'm resolved to disobey the general, to desert the regiment if I have to, and go serve as a volunteer in the first army corps I meet up with, even if it means losing my rank of corporal, etc. I was wild. The commander embraces me and approves of my resolve. He had pointed me out and recommended me to the brigade chief and to several other officers of the regiment, and he could easily see that if I didn't seize the opportunity to distinguish myself in this campaign, my future was compromised, perhaps even ruined. He told me he would take it upon himself to announce my departure to the general and that even if I were to lose his kindness and protection thereby—which was not at all likely—I shouldn't hesitate. Delighted with this outcome, I mount my horse along with the others in the detachment on the morning of our departure. All the officers come and embrace me, and to the great astonishment of all the soldiers, I set out with them on the road to Switzerland. Not wanting to inform you of my decision until after I had justified it by the baptism of a first encounter with the enemy, I wrote you a letter from Colmar with a dateline of Thionville, and I sent my letter to our virtuoso friend, Hardy, for him to mail. We traveled for twenty days, and after having gone through Canton Basel, we rejoined the regiment in Canton Glarus. It is there that you begin to see the steep mountains covered with dark pines. Their summits, snowbound all year long, are lost in the clouds. You hear the torrents thundering out of the rocks and the wind as it whistles through the forests. But now the songs of the shepherds and the bleating of the flocks were no more. The chalets had been hurriedly abandoned. Everything had fled at the sight of us. The inhabitants had retreated into the mountains with their herds. Not a living soul in the villages. The canton presented a picture of the dreariest desert. Not a single piece of fruit or a glass of milk. We lived for ten days on the terrible bread and even more terrible meat that the government issues. For the other ten days that we were in transit, we ate potatoes that were nearly raw, as we didn't have time to cook them, and drank brandy when we could get any.

The hostilities began on 3 Vendémiaire (September 25). We attacked the enemy on all flanks. They were entrenched behind the Limmat and Linth Rivers. The order to attack was given at three o'clock in the morning. I had heard so much about the first cannon shot! Everyone talks about it and no one succeeds in conveying an impression of it. I wanted to experience it on my own, and believe me, far from a punishment, it was pleasurable. Try to imagine a solemn moment of silence, and then a sudden, magnificent roar. It is like hearing the opening chord at the opera, when you've momentarily collected yourself in anticipation of the overture. But what a wonderful overture is a proper cannonade! The cannon fire, the rifle fire, at night, amidst the cliffs, which amplify the noise (you know how I love noise!)—it was splendid, and when the sun lighted up the scene and gilded the spirals of smoke, it was more beautiful than all the operas in the world.

At dawn, the enemy abandoned its left flank and withdrew all its forces to Uznach, on the right. We followed. We didn't give way at all that day. We remained at the front, behind the infantry, which was preparing to cross the river that separated us from the enemy. We built a bridge under their very fire. It was the Russians with whom we were involved. Those folks know how to fight. When the bridge was finished, three batallions came forward to cross it. But they had just barely reached the other side when the enemy advanced with considerable force and in greater numbers than ours, and the troops which had crossed the bridge rushed back onto it in total disorder, trying to get back across. Half of them had reached the left bank when the overloaded bridge collapsed. Those who were still on the right bank had not been able to make their retreat, and seeing the broken bridge behind them, found their only hope in a desperate burst of courage. They held their fire until the Russians were twenty paces away and then made a terrible carnage of them. I shuddered, I admit, to see so many men fall, in spite of my admiration for this heroic defense by our batallions. A twelve-pounder which we had on the promontory gave them the cannon support they needed. The bridge was quickly repaired, we flew to the aid of our brave comrades, and the battle was over. If the bridge hadn't collapsed, the enemy would have taken advantage of our disorder, and we would have lost. Since the marshy terrain did not allow the cavalry to advance, we camped on the battlefield. They had to go through our encampment to bring the wounded to the ambulance station. The huge fires we had built made everything as bright as day. At that moment I would have liked to get hold of those who decide the fate of nations for just one hour. Those who have in their hands the power to make peace or war and decide on war, not for sacred causes but for the base reasons of personal gain, should have this sight constantly before them as their punishment. It is horrible, and I didn't expect that it would cause me so much pain.

That evening I had the satisfaction of saving a man's life. He was an Austrian. The body of a man was lying beside our fire. I watched him. He was only wounded in the leg, but he was overcome with fatigue and hunger, and he was hardly breathing. I brought him around with a few drops of brandy. All our men were asleep. I went to ask them to help me carry this poor wretch to the ambulance. They too were overcome by fatigue, and they refused me. One of them offered to finish him off for me. That idea revolted me. Pushed to the breaking point myself with fatigue and hunger, I don't know where I found the words to say what I did; I was stirred, I spoke to them with indignation and with anger, and I reproved them for their cruelty. Finally, two of them got up and came to help me transport the wounded man. We made a stretcher with a board and two rifles. A third chasseur, inspired by our example, joined us; we picked up our man and carried him through the marshes, in water and mud up to our knees, to the ambulance station more than a mile away. On the way they complained a lot about the load and debated about leaving me to struggle with my invalid as best I could, and I kept yelling, "Courage!" and delivering all the greatest maxims of the philosophers, in soldier's terms, about the mercy one owes to the vanquished and how much we would want someone to do the same for us in similar circumstances. Men are good at heart, for it was a rough task, and yet my poor comrades let themselves be convinced. At last we arrive, we put the unlucky man in a place where he can be helped, I myself make sure he's noticed, and I return with my three chasseurs, a hundred times happier and more satisfied in my soul than if I had just been to the most splendid ball or the finest concert. I get back, I stretch out on my coat in front of the fire, and I sleep peacefully until daybreak.

Two days later we caught up with the enemy at Glarus. Général Molitor, who commanded this attack, asked for an intelligent man from the company. I was sent to him. That evening he went out to reconnoiter the enemy position, and I accompanied him. The next day we attacked and pushed the enemy out of the city. During all this I acted as the general's aide-de-camp, which I thoroughly enjoyed. I carried nearly all his orders to the different units under his command. The enemy retreated twelve miles and burned all the bridges on the Linth River. Two days later, as the enemy was advancing forcefully to our right, Général Molitor sent me to Zurich with a letter for Général Masséna, in which he was probably requesting reinforcements. I travelled by stagecoach. It is a good sixty miles from Glarus to Zurich, and it took me nine hours. The next day I returned via the lake in a rowboat. I got off twenty miles from Zurich, at Richtersville. Try to guess who was the first person I saw after setting foot on the shore! M. de La Tour d'Auvergne! He was with Général Humbert. He recognizes me, throws his arms around my neck, and I too embrace him joyously. He introduced me to Général Humbert as the grandson of Maréchal de Saxe. The general invited me to have supper with him and to stay overnight in his house; I needed it, for I was worn to a frazzle. The next day, M. de La Tour d'Auvergne, who was getting ready to return to Paris soon, chatted with me about you and approved of my not having been overly influenced by your worries or by the cautiousness of Général Harville. He added that nothing would be easier for me than to get thirty day's leave this winter, to go and see you, that the Directoire had the power to appoint fifty officers a year, and I could be one of them. He will talk to Beurnonville about it. He himself has some influence with the Directoire, and he will take care of my leave. So, my dear mother, it is to your least favorite hero that I shall owe the privilege of bringing you my kisses! If I indulge in that daydream, I envision myself arriving at Nohant and falling into your arms. Beurnonville might appoint me to his staff, which would give me time to see you more often. We will work it all out this winter, my dear mother. The first steps are always hard, but one must go through them; rest assured that I did the right thing.

We left Glarus four days ago for Constance. It is a nineteen-league stretch of land that would be equal to twenty-five in France. [A league is equivalent to about three miles.] We covered it in pouring rain without stopping and arrived only to camp in fields of water. But extreme fatigue makes it possible to sleep anywhere. We arrived during the battle, and by evening, the city was in our hands. The hostilities seemed to be coming to an end. We went into the village to rest up from twenty days of bivouacking, and it is from there that I am writing to you. It is the first place I have had the chance to do so. The objective they had set is fulfilled. The enemy has left Switzerland. We are now going to recuperate. You mustn't worry about me, my dear mother. I'll write you as often as possible. Don't be too angry with me especially for not telling you sooner than today of my whereabouts. But if I had told you I was going to war, you would never have consented, or else you would have spent all this time worrying your heart out. War is only a game, and I don't know why you make such a monster out of it; it is really nothing. I give you my word of honor that I thoroughly enjoyed seeing the Russians clamber up the mountains during the attack on Glarus. They go about it very gracefully. Their grenadiers wear hats like those of the soldiers in *Caravane*.[70] Their cavalry, which include a great many Tartars, wear pleated knickers like Othello's, a little dolman, and a pillbox hat; I am enclosing a sketch. There were six thousand of them in Canton Glarus. Their horses, most of them without shoes, collapsed on the roadways. Fatigue destroyed nearly all of them.

Just now I received two letters from you dated 6 and 9 Fructidor (August 24 and 27). Ah, my dear mother, what pleasure they bring, and what worlds of good they do me! I had already received one dated 25 Thermidor (August 14); it arrived six days ago, while we were encamped on the banks of the lake at Wallenstadt. I read it sitting on an outcropping of rock overhanging the beautiful lake. The weather was splendid and before me were some enchanting vistas. I was basking in having done my duty serving my country, and I held a letter from you in my hand! It was one of the happiest moments of my life.

What the devil does M. de Chabrillant mean by "my services rendered to the Gargilesse family"? I haven't seen them for more than a year. Somebody is inventing stories that don't make any sense.

Would you like to hear about the brigade chief? His name is Ordener. He's a forty-year-old Alsatian, tall, brusque, very serious, fierce in battle, an excellent corps leader, expert in his job, and well-versed in history and geography. At first glance, he looks like Robert, the Robber Chieftain. On the strength of Beurnonville's recommendation, he received me very kindly.

As I mentioned, I received the hundred fifty francs you sent me at Thionville, and before leaving, I paid for everything except two months' worth of wine, which comes to thirty pounds. That, I shall pay to Hardy, who settled my account. As you can see, the drinks I bought my comrades haven't ruined me; I preferred to depart without a sou than to leave debts behind me. It is true that I haven't made my fortune in the wars, as the troops haven't been paid in four months. But I don't know where to ask you to send me money; you may be sure I can get along without it, just like the others. If you can, send me Général Harville's address. I don't know where to reach him.

Goodbye, my dear mother. This is, I hope you'll agree, a long letter. God knows when I'll get time to write another like it; but rest assured that I won't let any opportunity go by. Don't be worried. I send you a thousand kisses with all my heart! What a pleasure it will be to see you again! Tell Deschartres that I thought about him during the cannonade, and I thought of my maid, who really should have come to "tuck me in" at the bivouac.

I wonder if the reader really needs to have recalled the situation in Europe that serves as background for this episodic recital of the well-known Swiss campaign. A few words will suffice. Our plenipotentiaries at the congress of Rastadt had been vilely assassinated. War broke out again. In the space of twenty-five days, Masséna saved France at Zurich by clearing the enemy out of Switzerland. Suvarov retreated with some difficulty to the other side of the Rhine, leaving many of his Russian troops battered or crushed in the Helvetian mountains. At the same period, Bonaparte had just landed in France, having left Egypt. On the same day that my father wrote the letter you have just read (25 Vendémiaire — October 17), Napoléon presented himself before the Directoire in Paris, and already the rumblings of what were to be the events of 18 Brumaire (November 10) were already beginning to be heard.

Unfortunately, I have very few letters from my grandmother to her son. Here is one, however. It is very worn and smudged. The young soldier carried it next to his heart through the rest of the campaign, and he succeeded in bringing it back as a family heirloom.

Nohant, 6 Brumaire (Oct. 29), Year VIII.

Ah, my child, what have you done! You have decided your future, your life and mine, without even asking me! You made me suffer unspeakable torment by your six weeks of silence; your poor mother nearly died. I dared not talk about you anymore. Mail days became days of agony, and I was almost calmer on the days when there was no hope of any news from you. But each time Saint-Jean returned to the house, it was terrible. Just hearing him at the door made my heart pound. He would not say a word, poor man, and I was ready to die. My son! I hope you never have to suffer like that!

At last, yesterday, I received your good long letter. Ah, how I pounced on it! How long I pressed it to my heart without having the strength to open it! I found myself bathed in tears which blinded me when I tried to read. My God, what had I not imagined! I was afraid they had sent you to Holland. I hate that country and that army, I don't know why. All those dead, all those wounded made me numb with terror. But I said to myself that you would have written to me about leaving, and I was certainly a long way from thinking that you might have been with Masséna's victorious army. I could hardly believe such a successful campaign, until I read your letter. It is because you were there, my son; you brought him luck, and it is to you he owes his glory. You were in three battles in two weeks! And you are alive and well, thank Heaven! Lord be praised! My God, if only it were over! Like you, I would laugh and sing; but peace is not here yet. You say that we are ready to advance into Italy; if that is true, there will be no end to our woes, and it is time we gave up butchering ourselves on territory that will never be ours. My child, I understand the reasons which made you play a part in it. It is clear that M. Harville told you to stay behind only out of concern for me. He made you a corporal only with great caution, and he will stop there. He did his duty by Général Beurnonville. He was a help to you for a time; you have to be grateful to him for that. He owed you nothing, and he is not the man to bestow favors openly any more than he would openly refuse them. You understood him well. His relation to Caulaincourt put him on a footing where he had all the haughtiness of the old regime and the severity of the new one. M. de La Tour d'Auvergne will know how to make your experience count for you. What good luck that you met him as you got out of that rowboat at Richtersville! He will be able to confirm that you took part in this campaign, that he saw you, and he, as someone who never asks any favors for himself, can really put himself out to show others in a good light. But I am afraid that your leave has to come from Général Harville, and if that is true, in spite of the influence you think I have over him, we will not get it easily. However, I shall begin again right away taking steps, writing letters, making inquiries. For one long month, I was dead. Hope will bring me back to life. But I am in despair knowing that you have no money and not knowing how to send you any. I shall try to get some sent to the commander, Dupré, or to your friend, Hardy. Since they succeeded in getting my letters to you, perhaps they will be able to get some money to you. But in the meantime, you are in a devastated and deserted country without a penny in your pocket! If you could ask the paymaster of the regiment or the brigade chief to advance you some, I would certainly manage to reimburse them. Your unconcern about that really dismays me. Living on potatoes and brandy! What kind of nourishment is that after such exhaustion, after forced marches in terrible weather and nights out in sopping wet fields! My poor child, what awful conditions, what an awful profession! Horses and dogs get better care in peace time than men do in war. And you stand up under such terrible fatigue! You forget all about it to save the life of some poor unfortunate whom fate brought into your vicinity! Your good deed touched me deeply; your sensitivity, your eloquence reached those ruffians who wanted to finish him off, and you brought him aid with your own arms and with your own waning strength! And you came back to sleep on your coat, more satisfied than you would have been after any pleasures that my love could have obtained for you! Only virtue can bring that sort of joy, my child; unfortunate is he who doesn't know it! You found it in your heart, for in your deed there was no ostentation, no public recognition, not even a desire to emulate. God alone saw you do it, and only your mother was to hear the story of it. It is your love of goodness which led you. You are always talking about your lucky star; rest assured that it is your good deeds which bring you good fortune, and in the eyes of God they are never wasted. I believe, because I have to believe, that the course you have chosen is the wisest one; those unexpected victories convince me of it. You want to serve in the army, that is your wish, it is your most important goal. You can make faster progress in your career with the present government, I know, than you could have in the past. Men of today will want to acknowledge the sacrifices of a hero publicly. It will not be a case of nobility but of public gratitude, and I am not being unjust when I say that humble people are more capable of that gratitude than those in high places were in the past. Throughout my life I have found it so. The former, at least in my experience, kept before them only the memory of a great man whose services to the people were greatly appreciated. The latter, quick to forget individual favors, preferred to diminish his glory in their jealousy and ingratitude. They saw me impoverished, without influence, all alone; and they were totally indifferent. Even my lady the Dauphin's wife, who owed her marriage arrangements to my father, disapproved of my signing with his family name and wanted to prevent me from bearing it as well; that is how unjust and ungrateful vanity is.

So, my son, you do well to choose a direction where you will not meet obstacles of this kind. You have energy, courage, and virtue. You have no errors to make up for, and no suspicious relatives. Your first steps are in the direction of public life, the road is clearly marked; follow it, my son, harvest your laurels, bring them to Nohant, and I shall clasp them to my heart and water them with my tears. Those tears won't be as bitter as the ones which I shed for the past two weeks!

In January, you say, I shall be able to put my arms around you. Goodness, that is two months away! I can hardly believe it, but I am going to make that the unique object of my attentions. I am strong, from three battles! I am going to talk in a loud voice. Everyone will know that you have seen the enemy and that you defeated him. They will love you at La Châtre. Everyone there shared in my consternation, and there was rejoicing when they saw the little packet from you. Saint-Jean carried it triumphantly, and he was stopped in the streets. They equated you with Bonaparte—at least in La Châtre!

So you read my letter on the shore of a beautiful Swiss lake, and, you say, it put the finishing touch on the most beautiful day of your life? My lovely child, how grateful my heart is for that sweet sensibility! How dear you are to me, and how I envy you that moment of joy that I could not share with you! What happiness it gives me to imagine you in those circumstances, entirely devoted to your mother and to your tender recollections! How right I am to love only you and to have placed in you all the happiness, all the joy, and all the affection of my life! Never will my whole soul be big enough to welcome you, to kiss you, to press you against my heart; I shall die of joy.

Tell me right away where I can send you money. There is no way I can send it to that village of Weinfelden, because you won't be staying there long. If your regiment is anywhere for long enough, I would send you by return mail whatever you ask me for. In the meantime, you will receive, I hope, the forty écus which I shall send to M. Dupré today. It would be too bad if they got lost. Money is so scarce that six louis is a fortune nowadays. I do not know where M. Harville is. I am going to write him immediately to ask for your leave, and I shall send the letter to Paris, Rue Neuve-des-Capucins, number 531.

Goodbye, my child, preserve your life, as mine is a part of it. Don't sleep in wet places, for I too endure every one of your hardships. You were not shaken by that first cannon fire. My Lord, it goes right through my heart. I am sure that it is mothers who have given cannon fire such a terrible reputation. As for you, you laughed to see the poor Russians flee into the mountains, and the noise of the shooting delighted you as when you were a child. But that evening, what did you see by the light of those huge fires? It was all very well to veil those horrors in your letter to me; my imagination lifts up a corner of that veil nonetheless, and like you, I shudder.

Are you going to get some rest? Alas, I do hope so! But don't forget to write to me, just a note to say, "I'm alive." That is all your poor mother asks of you, for my wild joy in response to your long letter will soon diminish, I know, in the face of new worries, and if I have to wait another six weeks for news of you, my torture will begin anew. I shall end my letter the way you ended yours. "How happy I will be to see you this winter!" Here in my room, next to my fire! All the delicacies we are now preparing, I tell myself over and over they are for you. Your old maid says, "This if for Maurice, I know what he likes."

Deschartres is making some wine that is not very good, but he thinks it is wonderful, and he claims you will think it is excellent. He cries when he talks about you. Saint-Jean screamed in terror when I told him you had been in three battles, and he cried out, "Ah! how brave he is, that one!" Anyway, everyone here goes crazy with joy at the thought of your return. I send you my kisses, my child. I love you more than life itself. My health is about the same. I drink Vichy water, which sometimes helps. I would like to be completely well for your return because I do not want to have anything to complain about while you are with me. You must get assigned to the general's staff, that is my firm wish. Our poor friend from the Rue de l'Arcade is in terrible trouble: her eldest son is still in irons, and the other one has not come back. It is killing her, and I don't dare talk about you. Gallepie, the fat priest, was killed when a chest fell off a wagon and crushed him. He was returning to our area for the fourth time, pursued as always by the bailiffs and leaving debts wherever he went.

The Little House is doing fine. He is enormous. He has a charming laugh. I look after him every day, and he recognizes me perfectly; I shall introduce him to you. Goodbye, goodbye; my letter is the second volume to yours. It is getting too dark to see. Have you ridden the horse you went to get at Mons? Is he fine and handsome? They are going to take my colt away again, and all I shall have left is my donkey. . . . They just brought me a light, so I can write you a little more. I shall have to hide from some people the haste with which you threw yourself into this war, because after all, you could have found yourself face to face with Pontgibault, D'Andrezel, Termont, etc.,[71] and been obliged to fight them. My role will be to say that you were forced to go along, because with your family background, people will say that you ought not have shown so much zeal for the Republic. It is an awkward situation, because with some people I have to shout very loudly the very things I must hide from others. You cut through all these difficulties with your saber, and yet the future offers us no security! You see it as your duty to serve your country against foreign forces, without worrying about the consequences. And I think only of your future and your best interests, but I see that I can resolve nothing and that we have to leave everything to fate.

Letter XLVI   Canton Appenzell, 28 Vendémiaire (October 20), Year VIII,
Army of the Danube, Third Division.

I write you today, my dear mother, from the home of fogs and freezing rain, from the Rheinthal, at the foot of these mountains whose sparkling summits are lost in the clouds. If a country exists that is uninhabitable, miserable, and detestable in its sublimity, it is this one, certainly. The inhabitants are practically savages, having no belongings other than a chalet and several animals. They have no idea of agriculture or of commerce; they subsist on roots and cheese; they keep to their cliffs all year long and almost never have any contact with the cities. They were astonished the other day to see us making soup, and when we let them taste the broth, they thought it was terrible. Personally, I thought it was delicious, as we had gone two days without bread or meat, and we had been forced to put ourselves on their shepherds' diet, which, at my age and with my appetite and profession, I can say quite heartily can go straight to the devil.

On the same day I wrote you last, we left Weinfelden for Saint-Gallen, which is about sixty leagues from there. We were then sent into these mountains, and for two days I've been at Gams, to the south of Alstätten, serving temporarily, with two chasseurs, as orderly to Général Brunet; and since one does not go hungry as a member of the general's staff, I don't hesitate to make up for the mountain diet and the shepherds' frugal ways. Yesterday, we were on horseback all day with the general. He visited the camps on the Rhine ahead of us. The river is no wider here than the Indre in Châteauroux, and I could say that the river and I are old friends, since we "kept company" for a rather long time at Cologne. Today is a quiet day, and I am using the opportunity to chat with you and re-read your two letters. The one you wrote to Sergeant Ordener I had sent on to him. You reproach me for not having written to M. Hékel. It's true my mind was so unsettled it prevented me from doing so. I did write him twice from Cologne, but lately all I've had time for is to write to you, my dear mother. You are well aware that I lost my heart to a charming woman whom I had to leave behind, and who didn't want to see me go to war any more than you do. Opposing the wishes of one's mother and of the mistress of one's heart, leaving the one and disobeying the other, feeling that such was one's duty and that death on the battlefield would be preferable to a life of ease lived in shame—all that was a great struggle for me, and I am only twenty, my dear mother! I beg you not to make my struggle even more difficult by your grief and worrying. To get back to my friend—yes, of course, I should have written him. He would have responded with only encouragement and good advice. But would he have kept my secret from you? Anyway, since I have been in battle, I have decided I deserve forgiveness, and I wrote him before I received your letter.

As for the one M. Dulourdoueix says he received from me, he must be wrong about the date, because I haven't written him since I left you. I will write to Général Harville, even though I cannot help but be annoyed at him, as the more I see, the more I realize that a soldier who asks to be promoted without having fired a shot is a poor fool, and I would have looked pretty silly if I had not disobeyed him. As it is now, I can realistically request promotion to officer's rank. I've shot at the enemy, I've heard his bullets whistling around my ears, and I can talk with experienced military men without blushing. It happens that I wasn't ungrateful to Général Harville because, as I must tell you now, I did have the opportunity to leave him and fight in somewhat less difficult circumstances than I am in now. I had written to Beurnonville from Cologne to tell him that I was determined to join the battle squadrons, and he had answered that he approved of that, and he offered to put me with Général Hautpoul or Général Klein, whomever I chose. I thanked him but said I didn't want to leave Général Harville to go to another general, and if I was to be separated from him, I would want it to be for the sole reason of going into battle with my own regiment and enduring all the hardships of a soldier. True, I am far from being in luxury right now. I get all the dirty work, all the guard duty, all the camp detail, and I have to answer all the roll calls like everybody else. I groom my horse, I get him his hay, I eat at the mess, when we're lucky enough to have any! But even if it were ten times worse, I wouldn't be sorry I chose this, because I know that I have nothing to be ashamed of, and if Général Harville is angry with me, he shouldn't be. In any case, Beurnonville and M. de La Tour d'Auvergne approve, and they support me. They have all the more reason to do so now that I am no longer just the grandson of Maréchal de Saxe, but a soldier of the Republic, for good and all, and I have tried with everything I possess to justify their interest in me. Even you, my dear mother, you can no longer be considered an untrustworthy lady from the old regime, but the mother of an avenger of our country's wrongs. Yes, mother, you have to see it in that light in France these days, because any other point of view is false and untenable. I haven't exactly become the Jacobin of the regiment, but I have found out that you have to stick to the straight and narrow and serve your country without a backward glance; you have to willingly forgo any rank and fortune the Revolution took away, and you have to feel lucky that we must now earn by ourselves whatever we used to have by virtue of our birth. Come, come, Father Deschartres, you must pose as Cato of Utica[72] and stop talking to me about the past. I have not succumbed to the rigors of military life; instead I am visibly growing, and everybody who hasn't seen me for a month or so is immediately aware of it. I certainly haven't gotten any thinner; I have filled out more, and I am in stronger and better shape with each day that goes by. You will soon be able to judge my progress in length and girth. You asked me if I designed my new seal.[(49)] Yes, my dear mother, I drew it and had it made at Thionville. I am glad you like it and that you prefer it to the coats of arms that were taken away from us.

Tomorrow I am going to Mels, four leagues to the south, with Général Brunet. It is the headquarters of Général Soult. The regiment of my dear Maulnoir is in that town, and I hope to see him.

Everyone here believes that Bonaparte's arrival will decide who gets what in the peace treaty. The Russian back is broken. The Austrians detest them. The same hatred exists between them as in '92 with the Prussians. They are just opposite us, on the other side of the Rhine. They are defending the Grisons mountains, and we have no desire to go after them there, as they have nothing to subsist on but snow, and the devil take me if I can figure out how they manage it. We could perhaps pass on the left bank at Rheineck, which is at the tail end of the beautiful Lac du Constance. Look at the map and you will see all our positions from Rheineck to Mels; if we went by Rheineck, we would go into Swabia. But there is no possibility of that yet; both sides are equally unable to move. They sent us some negotiators a few days ago. Our trumpets made it their duty to drown out the Austrian trumpets, which joined in as gallantly as possible. Goodbye, my dear mother, don't worry about me, I cannot say it often enough. I send you my kisses and I love you with all my soul.

J.H.C.

XIII

Letters continued. —Général Brunet. —Disappointment.
—Commander Lochet. —Oath of allegiance to the constitution of
Year VIII taken by the troops. —Letter of my grandmother after 18
Brumaire. —Letter of La Tour d'Auvergne. —Return to Paris.
—Introduction to Bonaparte. —Italian campaign. —Saint-Bernard
Pass. —The fort at Bard.

Letter XLVII   Altstätten, 7 Brumaire, Year VIII (October 29, 1799),
                                               Army of the Danube, 4th division.

A turnabout in my adventures! A lucky stroke of fate! "Fortune often
outdoes prudence," that's my refrain, my dear mother, and the sum total of all
that I am about to tell you. Eight or ten days ago, as fate would have it, I was
detailed to the general of the brigade, Brunet. I was with him at Soult's headquarters where another stroke of fate resulted in my meeting Général Mortier,
whom I had met in Cologne at Général Harville's. He recognized me even
though from quite a distance and through a window. Maulnoir, who was at
headquarters at the time with a detachment from his regiment, told him that I
had been with Général Brunet for two days and recounted to him how I had
disobeyed Général Harville. The result was that during dinner they talked
about me, and Général Mortier informed Général Brunet who I was and what I
had done. Maulnoir, like a good friend, joined in with praise and said that I
knew German perfectly; he did such a good job of it that upon leaving the dinner table, Général Brunet sent for me and told me that we would do the campaign together, that I would share no one's table but his own, that he would put
in a request for me to my brigade chief, and that if the latter should refuse, he
would indicate to him in no uncertain terms that he was keeping me with him,
that my knowledge of German would be very useful to him, and that if he had
known sooner who I was and how I had acted, he would have treated me as I
deserved from the start. Finally, after profuse expressions of gratitude on my
part and very obliging comments on his, we all got back on our horses, very
satisfied with each other. He did, in fact, put in a request for my presence to my
brigade chief, and the latter having declined the request under the pretext that
regimental orders required all men on detail to be relieved every ten days, the
general rather dryly informed him in writing that in his brigade he was only
familiar with the orders that he gave, and that he was keeping me. I am sorry
that things could not have been arranged amicably, for if the general should

change divisions, the brigade chief, perhaps out of pique, would demand that I return. On the other hand I do not doubt that his refusal derives only from his interest in me, due to the letters that were sent to him recommending me for his consideration. Now is the time I need someone to say, "Take care of my friend," for it would be ironic if, as a result of the protection of two division generals, I would be forced to stay in the company—the center for all miserable and exhausting chores. I shall do all I can, I assure you, not to go back there, for in spite of my resolution to put up with anything rather than shirk my duty, I would far prefer to go into battle with a general. After all is said and done, I don't care a bit about the good eating and the niceties of life, but when you are properly informed about all the army's operations and about all the enemy's movements, war becomes attractive as an art or as a science and inspires you with emotions that you would seek in vain in a regiment, where you're transformed into a brainless machine. I am not hard to please—I just want to experience the best the profession has to offer.

The day before yesterday, I took part in negotiations with the Austrians, along with the general's aide-de-camp and a trumpeter. We advanced along the banks of the Rhine while sounding the appeal, to keep them from pitching a few cannon balls our way. The officer of the Austrian post gave us an impressive greeting, telling us they were going to come find us. Sure enough, their ferry came to fetch us, and we crossed to the other side. The idea was to transmit to the adjutant Général Latour, prisoner of the Austrians, a letter and verbal riga-marole about the sale of one of his properties, which had quite a different mean-ing. The meeting took place between an officer of the hussars from Granitz, Général Brunet's aide-de-camp, and myself, who acted as interpreter. When our business was finished, we took to chatting and laughing most heartily. The Austrian hussar officer offered us something to drink. We toasted and drank to the health of Bonaparte, Prince Charles, the Directoire—all with great bursts of laughter. After shaking hands all around most cordially, we took leave of each other as the best of friends.

I am constantly with generals and brigade chiefs, eating well and drinking good wine, but without a sou in my pocket, which does get to be inconvenient because in such brilliant company you must be powdered, pomaded, laundered, etc. Whenever you can send me something, address it to Citizen Brunet, Brigadier General, Third Division. If he were willing to make me a sergeant, that would be a big step! But above all, I have to have a leave. What a pleasure it would be to embrace you, my dear mother, and console you for all the suffer-ing my absence has caused you! I feed on that idea with delight. I can see my arrival, the household confusion, my joy and yours, old Deschartres dropping his serious expression, my maid screaming at the top of her lungs, the dogs barking their heads off, my poor Tristan hardly recognizing me, and endless questions; it will undoubtedly be the most beautiful day of my life, second only to the day I saw you emerge from your prison. How you're going to look me over! You will find some noteworthy changes in my outfit; you will no longer have the ugly, shapeless cut to complain about, for now we're fitted, tucked, and shortened in the elegant manner. Once back in Nohant, I won't leave the house;

I will stay locked inside, tête-à-tête with you, answering all your questions, telling you every little detail of my adventures, and losing not a single one of the moments I'll have to spend with you. What bliss!

Goodbye, my dear mother, it has been a long time since I've received anything from you; I live in impatient expectation, and I re-read your old letters.

I embrace you from afar, over many mountains and valleys, but in a short while I hope, from very close by.

When naming a military leader of that period, we love to let our memories encompass his whole life before and after the events where we see him in action. The names of Masséna, Soult, and Mortier recall the whole history of the wars of the Republic and the Empire, but other names have perhaps left fewer traces in the memory of many readers. Therefore, it will not be unhelpful to recall that, after some brilliant campaigns, Général Humbert, whom they in the army referred to as "the handsome general," fell into disfavor with Napoléon. In '94 he had distinguished himself in the Vendée; in '98 he had commanded our expeditionary forces in Ireland and had beaten the English there; in 1802 he had chased the blacks from Port-au-Prince; in 1814 he went to join the insurgents of Buenos Aires. Général Brunet, too, was a most distinguished superior officer. His father, a general of the Republic, had perished on the scaffold in '93. Colonel and general in '94, the younger Brunet was, in 1801, a member of the expeditionary forces in Saint-Domingue, and in 1802, captured Toussaint L'Ouverture.

Letter XLVIII   Altstätten, 3 Frimaire, Year VIII (November 24, 1799).

As of four o'clock, my dear mother, I am no longer with Général Brunet, and here is why. The brigade chief sent him word to return me to my company because he was going to make me a sergeant-major. In spite of my reluctance to take leave of this general, in spite of his kind regrets, I did leave him this evening after having been embraced by him, his aides-de-camp, his secretary, and right down to his servants, who exclaimed at my departure, "What? Our corporal is leaving us? And who's going to waltz us around now? He, who told such funny stories and who made our general laugh so!" The truth is that I had a way of putting the general into a good mood. He's a very fine man, a bit irascible, unpredictably rude to strangers, but truly a father to those in his circle, and I knew I was too happy in his company for it to last. When I took leave of him, making a very deep bow, as I had the habit of doing in Cologne with Général Harville, he didn't give me time to finish my obeisance, and cordially taking hold of both my hands, he embraced me saying, "My dear Dupin, it is with extreme regret that I see you go. I am agreeing to let you go only because your promotion requires it. But you won't be gone long, I hope. The important thing for you is to get promoted quickly to sergeant. As soon as you've got the rank, I'm going to work to get you back. Your regiment is no longer under my orders, but I'm going to ask the commanding general of the division for your squadron, and if I can't get it, I'm going to have that same general request you from your brigade chief." That is what is called really caring for people, and you are really quite right: one finds more cordiality among people of humble origin than among the high and mighty.

So here I am, back in the company, camping out again, and roughing it, but before long I shall get back again with that good general in whose company I met several kind people with whom I've also become good friends. There are two whose names you have certainly seen in the newspapers, in articles about our Helvetian success. One is Citizen Godinot, commander of the 25th light cavalry, and the other is Citizen Lochet, commander of the 94th regiment of the line. It was the latter who rallied the troops and got them to confront the enemy when the bridge was broken at the crossing of the Linth River. He is five feet, ten inches tall, a veritable Hercules, who likes nothing better than to laugh and play at being what they call here the "teaser." A few words of honest praise that I could not help saying to his face about his heroic action caused him to notice me at the general's table. He said to me, with a serious expression, putting his hand to his forehead as soldiers do when saluting, "So, my corporal, you were there?" "Yes, my commandant." And since then he knows me only as his corporal. At table, he solemnly toasts the health of his corporal. He stops in the street whenever I pass and doffs his hat almost down to the ground. It is enough to make one die laughing, and the name corporal has stuck to me; Général Brunet himself no longer calls me anything but "my corporal."

The other day, the Austrians suddenly take a notion to cross the Rhine while we're eating dinner. Someone comes to tell the general, and right away the drums beat a general alarm, the trumpets sound the call to horse, the dogs bark, the people of the town shut their doors, the women and children begin to shout. It was a devil of a confusion. Losing no time, I saddle my horse and return to the general, who orders me to run posthaste to the outpost that was being attacked and tell Commander Lochet, who was defending it, to topple the Austrians back into the Rhine until we could rush him some reinforcements. I take off; it was about two leagues away; I could hear the firing of the cannon and the muskets; my horse went like the wind. I think I would have gone through hell to get there. I arrive out of breath. Commander Lochet sees me, comes over to me, and doffing his hat with his usual gravity, says, "What can I do for you, my corporal?" "My commandant, I've come to tell you to topple the Austrians back into the Rhine." "It's done, my corporal. Do me the honor of accepting a glass of wine." "With great pleasure, my commandant." And while we were drinking, he tells me that the enemy had disembarked, but that he had forced them to re-embark after having taken some of them prisoner and killing several of their men.

I bring back this news, but my horse—already worn out from the preceding runs, having left the depot too young to stand up under the strains of war—refused to serve me and, done in by that last stretch at full gallop, went completely lame. With a great deal of difficulty, I led him back by the bridle. By evening his legs swelled up, and it was impossible to use him. Most fortunately, we were not obliged to retreat, for I would have been captured by the Cossack gentlemen positioned across from us, who have the bad habit of keeping no prisoners. It is not at all pleasant to fall into their hands. Being always on alert, it would have been very unwise to remain without a mount. The general realized this and very graciously offered me some money to buy a horse. It was absolutely necessary, my dear mother; these are the misfortunes of war. I accepted six louis, which I used to buy from a captain in the regiment a pretty little Tartar horse captured from our Cossack friends, as light as the wind and fiery as gunpowder. With saddle and bridle thrown in, it really was a bargain, but I always feel it's too much, whenever you have to pay for it. However, since I sent my mount back to the small depot, the one that I bought really belongs to me, and I shall be able to resell it when, at the next distribution of horses, I will have picked out another. So now I'm in debt for six louis, which I beg you, my dear mother, to send to Général Brunet.

Yesterday, I rode up and down our whole battle line to administer the new oath of allegiance to the troops. Everyone here is very happy about these recent events.[50]

I finally got two letters from you at the same time; I have been deprived of that joy for quite a long time. But I was only deprived, whereas you were worried along with being deprived. Excuse me for having caused you this suffering! You may be right, that I am making you suffer, and yet! . . . But whenever you complain, it always seems to me that I'm in the wrong.

Ordener, the brigade chief, is not, as you believe, a friend of M. de La Tour d'Auvergne. He doesn't even know him. The only one in my regiment whom M. de La Tour knows is Coussaud, my captain, the one who received my enlistment in Paris and who, in spite of his cool manner, has always shown me so much good will. He has become an adjutant general, attached to this army. He came to dinner recently at the general's, and we were delighted to see each other again. As for my leave, it in no way depends on Général Harville. It is to the minister of war or to the commanding general, Masséna, that you would have to apply to obtain it, and it is through the intervention of Beurnonville or M. de La Tour d'Auvergne that you will obtain it. If I manage to become an officer, I shall request an assignment to the 3rd Hussars; I am very keen on leaving my regiment when I can, for the brigade chief seems to be convinced that once you're here, you should stay here. He doesn't care for those who are attached to the general staff, and since that is my aim, he would always be a stumbling block; I can see it coming.

So that I can see you without being rushed, try to get an order from the minister for me to report to Paris. That is much better than a regimental leave with a routing order that limits the time and rigidly outlines how you have to travel.

Goodbye, my dear mother, I hope to be a sergeant by the time I come to see you. Seeing you is all I think and dream about. Goodbye, goodbye. I love you with all my heart.

From My Grandmother to My Father

Nohant, 22 Brumaire, Year VIII (November 13, 1799).

If you had not written me from your post, my child, I would have died of sorrow and worry, because M. Dupré, to whom I had written to inquire as to your whereabouts, has not yet replied. God grant that he has at least sent you the money which I had M. Lefournier send on to him for you! It was not without difficulty that I managed to procure those six louis; the poor man had no currency with which to pay me, and without saying anything about it, he sold his belongings in order to send you exactly that sum. Of all the people to whom I wrote, I received a reply only from M. de La Tour d'Auvergne, but it is a charming letter, full of feeling and concern for you and for me. He tells me that your superb bearing, your politeness, your discretion, the responsiveness of your character have earned you the approval of all the generals to whom you have been introduced. That is wonderful, my child, these praises go straight to my heart, but what upsets me is that he adds that Général Humbert wanted to make you promise to follow him to Ireland. You did not say yes, my son? You could not have said so! This Général Humbert does not know that you have a mother whose only son you are. You don't have the mania for warring that he does, I hope. You like the service, but you also like peace, which brings happiness to us all and which your sad mother so longs for. . . .

Once again we find the whole Directoire thrown off course, what with Bonaparte having been given command of the city and the army. It was not chance that made him come back from Egypt just when they thought he was lost in the deserts of Syria. It is another revolution, one which can conceivably lead to great events. Peace and security would be the most interesting for me. If your Capitaine Coussaud, who wrote me a very kind letter and who seems to be a fine man, wanted to be helpful to you with Masséna (and M. de La Tour d'Auvergne does not doubt it), Masséna could make you an officer, because as far as the Directoire is concerned, it is hopeless. Sieyès is the only one left. Those who are still to be appointed (if they take any others), will be committed to the new leader. How many plans and hopes deceived! The leave I am requesting for you won't be affected, I hope. . . .

Goodnight, my child; you advise me to remain calm. Alas! I shall be able to do that only when I hold you in my arms, but you will be here so little that I shall not have time to reassure myself. I embrace you with the keenest affection, my son, and I love you a thousand times more than my life.

I did not get the newspapers this evening, but those who have them say that the councils have been dismissed, that there are only fifty members left, that an officer in Bonaparte's retinue took a shot at him in the chamber, which fortunately missed its mark, and that he was arrested on the spot. Everyone hopes to be better off; it seems to me that we could not be worse. Anyway, I am a bit relieved. Perhaps our troubles are going to be over. They say that Prussia was privy to this event; it is the obverse of what happened on 18 Fructidor.[74] Members of the Directoire and the chambers are now in the same boat.

Letter XLIX   Altstätten, 13 Frimaire (December '99).

Alas! my dear mother, I am not yet promoted, and in order to pursue those devilish stripes, I left Général Brunet; I see all my plans upset, for he writes me just now that he is leaving for the fighting in Italy. I find that devastating; I would have had such a nice trip with him! He was certainly right at first to refuse to let that damned brigade chief have me back, and to tell him, "You shall not have my corporal. I contended with Général Mortier over him, and that wasn't just to give him back to you. He is mine, and I want to keep him, absolutely." And when he does acquiesce in consideration of the promise that they would make me sergeant major, now that he is leaving for Italy, a lovely thought occurs to Citizen Ordener. He tells me that he is afraid of making others jealous and that he cannot keep his promise. However, at the request of the doctor, who has a lot of influence over his thinking, he is consenting to appoint me quartermaster sergeant. How nice! Oh well, I will just have to be satisfied with it. I am no longer required to carry a carbine, and that means a good deal less weight. I am no longer bound to groom my horse, I am no longer eligible for special details, inspections of horses, weapons, saddles, or to do all those other wearisome little chores that are regretfully inflicted upon the poor harassed soldier in time of war. Thus I am a little better off, but I am furious at having been duped by that fierce-looking Alsatian, who didn't seem as sly as all that, and whom I, stupidly enough, was quite disposed to like.

I am impatiently looking forward to your being able to send me something, because I didn't get any richer by buying myself a new mount at your expense. I no longer have a handkerchief, my neckties are in rags, my boots have holes in them, my jacket is worn through at the elbow; I don't even have the wherewithal to buy a ribbon for my pigtail! However, you mustn't suffer over all that, and don't take these misfortunes too seriously. I'm young, strong, not too delicate in my physical habits, and I couldn't care less when I think that you have everything you need. I sometimes see our former opulence as if in a dream. How different it is now for me! Well, when I wonder how it would affect me if I saw you in the state in which I now am, I have the feeling I would go mad, and then when I think that I am the one who is suffering a bit, I find that I am almost happy. You see that I can come up with some baroque reasoning to console myself.

I haven't seen the Devil's Bridge. For that, I would have had to go as far as Saint-Gothard. But I recognized a good number of sights from our big book at Nohant: the lake at Zurich, the one at Constance, etc. I saw glaciers in the vicinity of Glarus. In the Muttenthal, I saw a bridge suspended about fifteen hundred feet, over a falls. The bridge is twelve feet wide. Our army passed over it beating a retreat, during one of the last encounters, and a large number of our soldiers took a fatal plunge. I scaled horrifying mountains overlooking valleys that were the image of desolation, the horizon bounded by hideous crags wherever you looked. Not a hut, not a living creature, just a dreadful silence! ...

I am very happy that our friend Pernon is going to spend the winter in Nohant. That company will distract you. Would that I could soon come to make a fourth! But everything is now in such a state of confusion that it is impossible to arrange anything. Do try anyway. I would be so happy to see you! I embrace you and I love you with all my heart.

Letter from M. de La Tour d'Auvergne to My Grandmother

Passy, 23 Frimaire, Year VIII (December 14, 1799).

To Citizeness Dupin, née de Saxe

Madame,

On my return from Montreuil, where I went to spend a few days, I received the kind letter which you graciously sent me. You repay me with too many flattering rewards for the happiness of being of service to you. Those of us who aspire to such service and who find themselves in competition with Général Beurnonville, deserve only a very small share of merit. You repay with a thousand graces all those that this general displayed in showing you how much he cares about what happens to your son.

Placed on the list of men cherished by our country, whose names never come to mind without our admiration and gratitude paying them just tribute, one can hope, without compromising one's judgment, that the grandson of the great Maurice will be honored by the government upon his return from the front. In this regard, my hope is further strengthened by that which Général Beurnonville has given you. I also learned that M. d'Épernon had seen Général Harville, and that the latter had written that very day to the division general, Mortier (who commands Général Brunet), in order to expedite a provisional leave of absence for your son. What a triumph, Madame, for friendship, and what a disappointment for envy!

I cannot tell you how indignant I was to learn of the conduct of the brigade chief toward his corporal. It is urgent that he be separated from this uncivilized individual, from whom one can expect only crude behavior. You portray him in the darkest colors, but my indignation multiplies his deformities even further in my eyes. I hasten to divert them from this awful sight. It is more soothing to let them contemplate the vision of you with outstretched arms waiting to embrace your cherished son! I anticipate with relish the happiness you are to experience.

My only desire is to see you both happy.

Madame, I fear I have already overly abused your kindness by the length of my letter. I should like, however, that you permit me not to end it without thanking you for your precious remembrance, nor without assuring you that the feelings you have inspired in this captain are so filled with respect and admiration that nothing further can be added.

La Tour d'Auvergne-Corret.

Receive with indulgence my excuses for a scribbling that does not conform to the standards of good breeding, but were I to rewrite my letter, I would lose the opportunity of posting it with the courier, who is hurrying me and is on the verge of leaving.

You can see from this letter that the leave was not obtained without powerful interventions, and it is clear, despite the naïve magniloquence of the letter you have just read, that the brigade chief, Ordener, was hardly well-disposed toward the corporal. At any rate, the campaign was over, and my father was able to leave the craggy cliffs of Switzerland and hasten to Paris, from where he wrote his mother the following letter:

Letter L   Paris.

I find myself, my dear mother, signed, sealed, and delivered to Paris, until I have my introduction to Bonaparte. Such is the express desire of M. de La Tour d'Auvergne, and since he wants us to follow his advice exactly, we would have run the risk of falling out with him if we had not complied with it. He wants me to embrace you as an officer. That is hard to reconcile with my impatience! But it must be done. I am to be introduced to Bonaparte in three or four days. This step will determine our expectations and future conduct. I surely wish you would carry out your plan to come to Paris! All your friends are clamoring to see you. They have spoken to you about staying at Mme. de Maleteste's. She made the offer to me most graciously, but I doubt that it would suit you. I have found for you, in the same house where the Rodiers live, a very nice apartment on the third floor, consisting of two bedrooms, salon, boudoir, dining room, etc., for three hundred pounds, on Rue Saint-Honoré near Rue Royale. If we could soon have access to our income, that would be just right for you. It would really be nice if, on your arrival here or my arrival in Nohant, I had my commission! My last resort, if we don't get that, would be to change regiments and have nothing more to do with that devil of an Ordener. Général Lacuée gives me good reason to hope. Your presence here, my dear mother, would perhaps help matters along quite a bit for me, because I have never seen anyone resist your ways and persuasiveness. In any case, I can hardly wait to kiss you, and there are times when I am ready to let everything go to the devil and run away to see you. It does me no good to be here in the midst of all these delights and comforts, which to me, fresh from my rough campaign life, seem like a dream, when the most precious thing in the world to me is missing, which is you. Come, come, or else I am leaving to come and see you.

I may be an eligible young man, as you call it, but you needn't fear that marriage fancies will capture me so soon. How could you expect a quartermaster sergeant of the light cavalry, the most nimble man in the world, to tie himself down with a household and become a family man? Damn it! The way women are these days, I'd sooner take off on an expedition that would ruin my hair-do for good! . . . No thanks! Goodbye, my dear mother, I'm dying to take you in my arms.

"My dear mother" did indeed go to Paris. The introduction to Bonaparte took place, resulting in promises and minor encouragements, on condition that he take part in the fighting and do so with distinction. The young man could ask for nothing better. Général Lacuée requested on his behalf that he be attached to the army's general staff. We shall see what it meant to be on one of those general staffs, which so appealed to the ambition of young men, and which, in this first stage, were hastily composed of those whom one wanted to make happy. My young father spent the winter in Paris with his mother, constantly occupied with music and visiting numerous friends. Bonaparte's power was taking hold with magical rapidity, and yet most naturally, that is, by satisfying all those interests which had been hurt by ten years of formidable struggle and disruptive anarchy. Everyone knows all about what this man of genius did to consolidate the mental and material state of France in the course of the year 1800, which had just begun. The alliance with Russia and with Spain was accomplished and strengthened; the line along the Rhine was made secure by the skillful campaigns of Moreau and the gallant exploits of Lecourbe and Richepanse; under them our army pushed on to the very gates of Vienna; the Saint-Bernard Pass was crossed and the Austrians beaten at Montebello and Marengo; Masséna reentered Genoa victoriously two weeks after having left it, as a result of the most glorious of sieges; Tuscany was occupied by the French; an alliance was formed with the Pope; Naples was reduced to pleading for mercy; the Mincio was crossed; Austria was forced to break with England and accept the conditions of a peace she had so stubbornly resisted; then, in Egypt, there was the striking revenge of Kléber at Heliopolis; the United States was reconciled with us and joined, along with Sweden and Russia, the maritime league against England. Such were the spectacular and marvellous events which—thanks to Napoléon, and with the help of several illustrious generals—distinguished that memorable year. I sum them up here without any particular order, and it does not really matter. I am not writing history with a capital H, but rather traversing it from the viewpoint of an eye witness to a number of these famous events. And this witness, who perceived them with the energy of his youth, will continue to narrate them with a simplicity and charm that is rarely found in narrations intended for the public.

The year 1800 witnessed the fall of three heroes: Kléber, Desaix, and La Tour d'Auvergne; the first two were known for their genius in massive military operations; the third was cast, by inclination and by choice, into a life just as turbulent but less dazzling, a modest glory that verged on the ideal by reason of the disinterestedness and collectedness of the scholarly, studious life he pursued in the midst of the turmoil of military camps. The First Grenadier of the Armies of the Republic perished on the field of honor on June 28, 1800, before Neuburg, in a heroic battle. He was mourned by the entire army; my father mourned him in Italy, a few days after the battle of Marengo.

At the end of Floréal, having managed a transfer to the 1st light cavalry regiment, with the promise of doing active service as a staff assistant under Général Dupont, my father left to report to that general and present him his letters of recommendation.

Letter LI   Lyon, 25 Floréal, Year VIII (May 1800).

I arrived yesterday evening, my dear mother, after such a bumpy ride that even the courier was ill. As for myself, I assure you that I was no more tired than when I left Paris. Before going to bed, I fortified myself with an ample supper, and like a worthy disciple of Roger Bontemps,[75] I am waiting here until tomorrow, at a good inn, for the departure of the Geneva post. However, the night that I just passed seemed long to me. I repeatedly woke, thinking I was still with you and saying goodbye to you. And suddenly I was far away, very far away, and I wanted to return because it seemed to me that I hadn't kissed you goodbye. Indeed, I am already far away and on the verge of going even farther. The imagination does not adjust immediately to these great changes, especially when the pleasant memories are still a living reality!

Everyone here assures me that the general staff is no longer in Geneva but in Lausanne. That makes no difference to me, for Geneva is on my way, and I shall simply have to carry my letters of recommendation a little bit farther.

So far, I don't care too much for Lyon. The quays along the Rhône are quite picturesque, but the interior of the town, with its tall houses and narrow streets, is sad, somber, and dirty. There are as many people, proportionately, and as much activity as in Paris, but it is sad activity, hectic, the bustle of labor, not pleasure. Anyway, I may be seeing the dark side, my mind is all filled with our goodbyes; I can no longer embrace you morning and evening, I cannot see you any more, and deprived of your presence, what place would make me happy?

I thank you for having agreed to go to the Italiens for a little diversion. What did they perform? Did you pay attention? Talking about diversion and music, just imagine that during the trip, my travelling companion, the courier, a pious man, began to make me Christian exhortations, and in the intermissions sang me litanies and a few little selections from the high mass. And he sang just like Deschartres. What finally rendered him purely entertaining was that he was as deaf as a post, to the extent that he had no reason to fear being interrupted by an argument. So I just let him talk and sing to his heart's content, and I thought of you, our friends, the present, the future, and at the end of my thoughts, I kept coming back to you. That will always be the best I can do to give me courage and console me.

Goodbye, my dear mother, I embrace you with all my heart.

Letter LII   Lausanne, 28 Floréal (May 1800).

My dear mother, there was no general staff in Geneva. They are on their way across the mountains. In fact, I think they have already crossed. I am in pursuit. In Geneva, we formed a caravan of six officers who are rejoining the general staff at headquarters. We are leaving tomorrow morning, and I think that we'll be having supper with the monks on Mont Saint-Bernard. Right now I'm in Lausanne and I'm writing you on the corner of a table. There's the devil of a confusion here. The Consul[76] left this morning, but the administrative units are still around. So, I am really going to see the great Saint-Bernard, and I shall tell you whether the stage setting at the Feydeau[77] looks like the real thing and whether the monks sing as well as Chérubini has them singing in Paris.

Goodbye, my dear mother, I embrace you a thousand times with all my heart and go to rest up from today's exertions, on a rather poor bed that it took me a while to find.

Letter LIII   Headquarters at Verres, 4 Prairial.

Finally, I'm here! It is no small matter to travel across the mountains without horses, through a ghastly wilderness and ruined villages. Each day I missed the general staff by a day. They have finally halted before the stronghold at Bard, which is preventing our entry into Italy; we are now in the heart of the precipitous slopes of Piedmont. I reported yesterday, immediately upon my arrival, to Général Dupont. He received me very well. I am attached to his staff, and this morning I shall receive my assignment and certification papers. I am establishing this fact for you at the outset in order to relieve you of any worry or suspense, which would have made any preliminary narration unbearable for you. So here I am, in a country where we are dying of hunger. The characters who make up this staff, except for the three generals, all seem rather preposterous to me. I have noticed, however, in the twenty-four hours I've been here, that the aides-de-camp and the adjutant general show more respect to me than to all the others. I think I know why. I will tell you later, when I have had a closer look at things.

I crossed Mont Saint-Bernard. The descriptions and painted renderings don't really measure up to the horror of the real thing. The night before, I had slept in the village of Saint-Pierre, which is at the foot of the mountain, and I left before breakfast in order to reach the monastery, which is located three leagues up the slope, which is to say, in the region of ice and perpetual frost. These three leagues are climbed through snow, over craggy rocks. Not one plant, not one tree, caverns and canyons at every step. Several avalanches which had fallen the day before managed to make the road impassable. Several times we fell into snow up to our waist. Well, then! Across all of these obstacles, a demi-brigade carried its cannon and caissons on its shoulders, hoisting them from rock to rock. The work, the determination, the shouting, and the singing of that army presented the most extraordinary sight you can imagine. Two divisions were united in those mountains. Général Harville was in command. It seemed, for the moment, he was frozen! On arriving at the monastery, he was the first person I met. He was very surprised to find me way up there and, shivering, received me quite kindly, still making no mention of my disobedience nor expressing either approval or blame. Perhaps he would have gotten to it at another time, but he only had lunch on his mind, and he invited me to have lunch with him. However, not wishing to leave my travelling companions, I refused with thanks. I chatted with the prior during the very frugal meal he had brought to us. He told me that his monastery was the highest inhabited spot in Europe, and showed me the big dogs which help him find people swallowed up by avalanches. Bonaparte had just petted them an hour before, and with no hesitation, I did as Bonaparte. I was quite surprised, upon telling the good prior that the virtuous hospitality of his monks was being offered to public admiration in our theaters, to learn that he was familiar with the play. After having cordially taken leave of him, we descended seven leagues, in order to get to the valley of Aosta in Piedmont. Thus I walked for ten leagues, having my baggage carried by mules. Once in Aosta, I ran to the palace of the Consul to see Clerc. The first person I encountered there was Bonaparte. I went up to him to thank him for my nomination. He abruptly interrupted me to ask me who I was. "The grandson of Maréchal de Saxe." "Oh, yes!, Well, good! In what regiment are you?" "First Light Cavalry." "Well, fine! But it isn't here now. You must be attached to the general staff." "Yes, Général." "That's fine, so much the better. I'm very happy to see you here." And then he turned away.... Now admit that I'm always lucky and that, if I had arranged it on purpose, I couldn't have done it better. Right off, I am attached to the general staff, and with the blessing of Bonaparte, without having to wait the "infamous" three months. To make sure your letters reach me, address them to Citizen Dupin, Member of the General Staff of the Reserve Army, at Headquarters, without designating the place. They will be forwarded.

The fort[51] we have before us has been preventing our passage into Italy, but the decision has been made to go around it, so that headquarters will be set up in Ivrea. I am quite pleased about that, because here we are reduced to a half ration of food, and my devil of a stomach simply refuses to give in to a half ration of appetite. You certainly did well to fatten me up in Paris, for I don't think they're going to give it much thought around here.

Goodbye, my dear mother; I kiss you most tenderly. I would surely like it if this new separation were less cruel for you than the others. Remember that it won't be for long and that it's for a good cause.

Letter LIV   Prairial, Year VIII (no date).

Whew! We're here, we're here! Let's take a breath! So where are we? In Milan, and if we keep on going at this rate, pretty soon we'll be in Sicily, I think. Bonaparte has transformed the venerable general staff into the nimblest of vanguards. He has us running like hares, and that is all to the good! Since Verres, we haven't had a minute's rest. At any rate, we got here yesterday, and I am taking advantage of it to chat a bit with you. I will recapitulate our advance since leaving the aforementioned Verres. I believe I've already mentioned the fort at Bard, the only obstacle preventing us from entering Italy. The moment he arrived, Bonaparte ordered the attack. He passed six companies in review. "Soldiers," he said, "we must go over the top tonight, and the fort will be ours." A few moments later, he went and sat down on the edge of a rock. I followed and positioned myself behind him. All the division generals surrounded him: Loison raised strong objections about the difficulty of climbing up through the rocks under the fire of the enemy, who were fortified in such a way that they merely had to light the bombs and shells and let them roll down, to prevent us from getting closer. Bonaparte did not want to hear it, and going by again, he repeated to the soldiers that the fort was theirs. The attack was ordered to begin two hours after midnight. Not having any mount, and since the fort was two leagues away from headquarters, I was not under orders to go there. Hence I went back to Verres with my walking companions. After supper, I wish everyone good evening and, without saying anything, I set out again for the fort at Bard. The way to this fort is through a long, cypress-covered valley bordered by immense, rocky cliffs. It was a dark night, and the silence which reigned in this wild place was interrupted only by the sound of a rushing torrent in the shadows and the muffled and distant thunder of the cannon of the fort. I move forward at a brisk pace. I can already hear the cannon more distinctly, shortly I can see the gunfire. Soon, I am within range. I see two men lying behind a rock next to a good fire. Assuming that Général Dupont had to be with the commanding general, I go over to them to ask whether they had seen the latter pass. "Here he is," one of them says to me, rising; it was Berthier himself. I told him who I was and whom I was looking for. He informed me where Général Dupont was—on the bridge in the town of Bard; I go there and find him surrounded by grenadiers who were awaiting the moment of the attack. I join his retinue, and just as he turns his head around, I wish him a good evening. "What?" he says to me, in amazement, "You are here without orders and on foot?" "If it's all right with you, sir." "Marvellous! The attack is about to begin, and you come just in time."

It was decided to bring up six guns and caissons to the foot of the fort. The general's aides-de-camp accompanied them, and I followed, still on foot. Half way up to the town, three shells came toward us at the same time. We went into a house which was open, and after waiting for them to explode, we continued our trek, and came back down again, ever escorted by a few grenades or cannon-balls. The attack was not successful. We climbed as far as the last entrenchment, but the bombs and shells which the enemy fired and rolled down into the cliffs, the ladders which turned out to be too short, and the generally insufficient precautions resulted in total failure; and we had to withdraw with losses.

The following morning we left for Ivrea. We circumvented the fort by climbing—men and horses—over the rocks, by means of a narrow trail on which the local inhabitants had never even dared to bring their mules. And several of ours plunged into the depths. One of Bonaparte's horses broke a leg. After arriving at a certain point which overlooks the fort, Bonaparte halted and, in a foul mood, directed his field glasses at that unimpressive pile which had just daunted him. After a lot of strenuous going, we came into the plains, and since I was still on foot, Général Dupont, pleased with my stroll of the night before, gave me one of his horses to mount. I rode along with his aides-de-camp, with those of Bonaparte and those of Berthier, and in the midst of this distinguished company, one of Général Dupont's aides-de-camp named Morin began to speak, saying: "Gentlemen, out of the thirty officers attached to the general staff, M. Dupin, who just arrived the evening before last and is still without mount, is the only one to have been with the general at the attack on the fort. The others remained prudently in bed." Now I must tell you what I had guessed from the very beginning, and that is that this general staff is a bunch of totally undisciplined loafers. The title of associate staff member is handed out and attached to anyone who happens to be without a unit and without any particularly distinguishing characteristics. However, there are eight or ten of us who are better than the others and who stick together. The general staff improves in quality as we advance: the blockheads and bores are left to take care of the different places we pass through. Lacuée was quite mistaken when he extolled to you the advantages of my job. We are much less well thought of than the aides-de-camp. We run around like orderlies, without knowing anything about the messages we are carrying. We don't associate at all with the general, and we certainly don't eat with him.

When we were in Ivrea, I realized that by advancing constantly I would not receive my horses very soon. I made up my mind to go fleet-footedly over to the outposts. Horses had been captured the day before. An officer of the 12th hussars sold me one for fifteen louis, which would be worth thirty in Paris—a wild Hungarian stallion that belonged to an enemy captain. He is dapple gray. He has incomparably fine and handsome legs. He has a fiery look, a tender mouth, and in addition to all those advantages, the manners of a ferocious animal. He bites everyone he doesn't know and allows himself to be mounted only by his master. He gave me a lot of trouble before I managed to mount him: the rascal just didn't want to serve France. By dint of bread and kisses, I brought him around. But for the first few days, he reared and bit like a demon. Once you mount him, he's calm and peaceful. He runs like the wind and bounds like a deer. When my other two get here, I shall be able to sell him.

Here comes the post. Goodbye, my dear mother, I have only time to send you a hug. Goodbye, goodbye.   *F.M.S.*

XIV

A short résumé. —The battle of Marengo. —Turin and Milan in 1800. —Robbers on the roads. —The mission.

If I continue my father's story, perhaps it will be said that I am putting off keeping the promise I made to tell my own story. Need I recall here what I said at the beginning of my book? Every reader has a short memory, and at the risk of repeating myself, I shall sum up once more my thinking on the work I have undertaken.

All existences are linked to one other, and human beings who would present their own, separately, without connecting it to those of their fellow creatures, would only be offering us an enigma to decipher. The interconnections are still more evident when they are direct, as in the case of children to parents, friends to friends of the past and present, contemporaries to contemporaries of then and now. As for myself (just as for all of you), my way of thinking, my beliefs and my aversions, my instincts as well as my feelings would be mysteries even for me—and I would only be able to ascribe them to chance, which has never explained much in this world—were I not to reread in the universal book the page that precedes the one on which my individual self is inscribed. That individual self, by itself, has neither meaning nor importance of any kind. It takes on meaning only by becoming part of all creation, by blending with the individual selves of each of my fellow creatures, and through this blending it becomes history.

In addition to this obvious truth, which I imagine no one will dispute, I have acknowledged the great influence I attribute to biological heredity, which seems to me just as obvious a truth as the other. I have not concluded, and I would certainly be careful not to conclude, that heredity absolutely entails fatality, but it has enough influence on us to keep our freedom from being absolute. The same instincts, the same tendencies produce different results, because the milieu we traverse is never identical to the milieu traversed by those who have preceded us. There is a further distinction to be made; that is, that any tendency, even a seemingly dangerous one, can be directed toward good; that the instinct for violence can become either viciousness or bravery, depending on education or circumstances, just as the instinct for tenderness can take the form of devotion or debility. A sameness of elements, but an infinite diversity in the combination of those elements—that is the invariable law that presides over all things in the universe, without which nothing is comprehensible. The role of human reason and conscience is to find a balance and harmony between these two terms—sameness and diversity. It is God's motive in universal creation; it is the key to man's logic in governing his own existence.

That stated, and in order not to come back to it any more, I affirm that I shall not be able to relate or explain my life without having related and made comprehensible my parents' lives. This is just as necessary for the story of individuals as it is for the story of humankind. If you read by itself a page on the Revolution or on the Empire you will not understand a thing, unless you know all the history prior to the Revolution or the Empire; and in order to understand the Revolution and the Empire, you will still have to know the whole history of humanity. Here, I am relating a personal history. Humanity has a personal history in every person. Hence, I have to include a period of about a hundred years in order to tell the story of forty years of my own life.

Without that, I cannot coordinate my memories. I have lived through the Empire and the Restoration. I was too young at the beginning to understand by myself the history that was being made before my eyes and coming into play around me; then, my understanding came—sometimes in the form of conviction, sometimes by way of reaction—through the impressions of my parents. They themselves had lived through the old monarchy and the Revolution. Without their impressions, mine would have been much more vague, and it is doubtful that I would have preserved from the beginnings of my own life a memory as clear and distinct as the one I have. Well, those first impressions, when they have been vivid, have enormous importance: the whole rest of our lives is often only the rigorous consequence of them.

My Father's Story Continued

I left my young soldier departing from the stronghold at Bard, and to remind the reader of his situation, I shall quote a few fragments concerning the same events from a letter dated at Ivrea and addressed by him to his nephew René de Villeneuve.

But first of all, I shall tell how my father, who was twenty-one years old, happened to have a nephew, his friend and comrade, who was one or two years older than he. M. Dupin de Francueil was sixty when he married my grandmother. His first marriage had been to Mlle. Bouilloud, with whom he had had a daughter. That daughter had married M. de Villeneuve, nephew of Mme. Dupin de Chenonceaux, and had had two sons, René and Auguste, whom my father always loved like brothers. You can imagine that they joked with him a lot about the seriousness of his role as uncle and that he made allowances for them if they did not give him the respect his title required. A matter of inheritance had raised some disputes between the people who handled their business affairs, and here is how, today, my cousin René interprets this dispute for me: "The business types found grounds for quibbling, some chance of profit for us, by starting a suit. It was a question of a house and thirty thousand francs left by M. de Rochefort, grandson of Mme. Dupin de Chenonceaux, to our dear Maurice. Maurice, my brother, and I, replied to the business types that we liked each other too much to argue about anything whatsoever, and that if they were intent on quarreling among themselves, we gave them permission. I don't know if they took advantage of the suggestion, but our family disputes were ended in this fashion."

These three young men were kind and unselfish, without a doubt, but it was a better time then than now. Despite the faults of the government of the Directoire, despite the anarchy of ideas, the revolutionary turmoil had left something chivalrous in people's spirit. They had suffered, they had gotten used to losing their fortunes without resorting to baseness, to recovering them without becoming greedy; and surely misfortunes and dangers are salutary tests of character. Humanity is not yet pure enough to avoid contracting the vices of selfishness in the midst of leisure and material pleasure. Nowadays, you would find very few families where relatives, in the case of a disputed inheritance, would put an end to their dispute by embracing each other and laughing in the faces of the attorneys.

In the letter my father wrote from Ivrea to the older of his nephews, he tells once more about the passage over Saint-Bernard and the attack on the fort at Bard. The selections I am going to transcribe show how lighthearted was the behavior, and without the least thought of boasting, at this noble time of our history.

"....I arrive at the foot of a rock, alongside a precipice where my general staff was perched. I present myself to the general, he receives me, I move in, I pay my respects to Bonaparte. The very same night he orders the attack on the fort at Bard. I find myself at the attack along with my general.[52] The cannon-balls, the bombs, the grenades, the shells are rumbling, thundering, exploding on all sides; we're beaten, I'm not hurt at all.

"We go around the fort by climbing across rocky crags and over chasms. Bonaparte climbs with us. Several men tumble into the precipices. We finally get down to the plains, where fighting has been going on. A hussar had just captured a handsome horse. I buy it, and there I am on horseback, a rather necessary thing in time of war. This morning, I'm carrying an order to the outposts; I find the roads strewn with cadavers. Tomorrow or tonight, we're to have a pitched battle. Bonaparte isn't patient; he wants absolutely to advance. We're all for it....

"We're laying waste to a beautiful country. Blood, carnage, desolation follow in our wake. Our leavings are marked by corpses and ruins. We have tried in vain to spare the inhabitants; the stubbornness of the Austrians forces us to fire our cannon at everything. I'm the first one to bemoan the victims, yet the first one to be seized by this accursed passion for conquest and glory that goads my impatient desire to keep fighting and pushing on....

"If you only knew, my friend, how I missed you on the Saint-Bernard Pass! What a good time you would have had! The road—if you can call it a road—was cluttered with avalanches that had fallen during the night. You took one step and fell back three. At every moment you stepped into snow up to your ears. When we arrived at the monastery, the monks made us a lunch. Such noble behavior filled me with enthusiasm for their institution.... They showed me their big dogs; these animals are formed really beautifully and have the

nicest faces. I paid them many courtesies which they seemed to find very satisfying; at any rate, all of us—monks, dogs, and soldiers—parted very good
friends....

"If one could choose one's existence, my choice would be to live with
my dear nephews, to drive them crazy from dawn to dusk, and beyond that, to
bore them to death with lectures and commentary. In spite of war and conquests, I shall live to see this beautiful wish fulfilled, and in the meanwhile,
dear friend, I embrace you and assure you that my keen friendship for you is
equal to the test of time, of absence, of personal concern, of all vulgar considerations, and even of bullets and bombs."

Letter LV (From Maurice to His Mother)   Stradella, 21 Prairial (June 1800).

We're racing along like devils. Yesterday, we crossed the Po and gave the
enemy a drubbing. I am very tired, always on horseback, loaded with sensitive
and difficult missions; I have managed them pretty well, and I'll give you
details when I have a little time. This evening, I have only enough to send you
a kiss and tell you that I love you.

Letter LVI   Headquarters at Torre di Garofolo, 27 Prairial, Year VIII.

Historians, sharpen your pens; poets, climb on Pegasus' back; painters,
prepare your brushes; journalists, lie all you please! Never have you been presented with a more beautiful subject. As for me, my dear mother, I am going to
relate the deed to you just as I saw it and just as it happened.

After the glorious encounter at Montebello, we arrive the 23rd at Voghera.
The next day we leave from there at six in the morning, led by our hero, and at
four in the afternoon we come to the plains of San Giuliano. There we find the
enemy, we attack him, we beat him, and corner him at the Bormida River, under
the walls of Alessandria. Night separates the combatants; the First Consul and
the commanding general take lodgings in a farm at Torre di Garofolo. We
stretch out on the ground, without supper, and go to sleep.

The next morning, the enemy attacks. We go off to the battlefield where
the fighting has started. The front is two leagues long, cannon and musket fire
enough to make you deaf! Never before, according to the most seasoned
among us, had anyone seen the enemy so strong in artillery. By nine o'clock,
the carnage was such that two retrograde columns of wounded and people carrying them had formed on the road from Marengo to Torre di Garofolo. Our
batallions had already been pushed back from Marengo. The right flank had
been turned back by the enemy, whose artillery now formed a cross-fire with
our center. Cannon-balls were raining down on all sides. At the time, the general staff was having a meeting. A cannon-ball passes under the belly of the
horse of Général Dupont's aide-de-camp. Another grazes the rump of my
horse. A shell lands in our midst, explodes, and no one is hurt. They are still
deliberating over what should be done. The commanding general dispatches to
the left flank one of his aides-de-camp, Laborde by name, with whom I am on
rather good terms. He hasn't gone a hundred paces when his mount is killed. I

go to the left flank with the adjutant Général Stabenrath. On the way, we meet a platoon of the first regiment dragoons. The commanding officer comes toward us sadly, shows us the twelve men with him, and tells us that that is what's left of the fifty men who made up his platoon that morning. While he is talking, a cannon-ball passes under the nose of my mount and so stuns him that he falls over on top of me as if dead. I quickly get out from under him. I thought he was killed and was quite surprised when I saw him get up again. He wasn't hurt. I get back on, and the adjutant general and I ride off to the left flank. We find them retreating, and we do our best to rally a batallion. But hardly was that done when we see even farther off to the left a column of deserters taking to their heels. The general sends me to stop them, which is impossible. I find infantry mixed in with cavalry, baggage carts, and pack horses, the wounded abandoned on the road and crushed by the caissons and the artillery. The screaming is dreadful, the dust so thick you can't see two feet in front of you. In this extreme confusion, I hurl myself out of the roadway and gallop ahead, shouting, "Halt up there, at the head of the column!" I gallop on; not one commander, not one officer. I encounter the younger Caulaincourt, wounded in the head and fleeing, carried off by his horse. Finally, I find an aide-de-camp. We set out to try to stop the disorder. We hit some with the flat of our sabres and praise some of the others, for among those poor devils there were still plenty of brave men. I dismount, I have a piece put into position, I form a platoon. I start to form a second. I had hardly begun, when the first one had already bolted. We abandon the enterprise and ride off to rejoin the commanding general. We see Bonaparte beating a retreat.

It was two o'clock; we had already lost—either captured or destroyed —twelve cannon pieces. There was general consternation, horses and men worn down by fatigue. The roads were crowded with wounded. I was already thinking of having to recross the Po, the Ticino, of having to go back through a country whose every inhabitant is our enemy, when in the midst of these sad thoughts a consoling rumor comes to revive our courage. The divisions of Desaix and Kellermann are coming, with thirteen pieces of artillery. We regain our strength; we halt the deserters. The divisions arrive. We sound the charge, and we go back the way we came. We drive into the enemy, they flee in turn, our enthusiasm is at its peak. We are laughing as we charge. We take eight flags, six thousand men, two generals, twenty cannon pieces, and night alone conceals the rest from our fury.

The next morning, the Austrian general, Melas, sends an officer bearing a flag of truce—a general; we receive him in the courtyard of our farm to the music of the consular guard, with the entire guard under arms. He brings some proposals. They are ceding to us Genoa, Milan, Tortona, Alessandria, Acqui, Pizzighitone, altogether a portion of Italy around the region of Milan. They admit to being vanquished. Today, we are going to dine with them in Alessandria. The armistice is concluded. We shall be giving the orders in Melas's palace. The Austrian officers come to ask me to speak to Général Dupont for them. It really is too funny. Today, the French and Austrian armies are as one. The imperial officers are fuming at seeing the law laid down to them this way.

But it is pointless for them to fume: they have been beaten. *Vae victis!* [Woe to the vanquished!]

This evening, Général Stabenrath, named to carry out the articles of the treaty, and with whom I was on the morning of the battle, told me while shaking my hand that he was happy with me, that I had put up a devil of a fight, and that Général Dupont had been informed of it. As a matter of fact, I can tell you, my dear mother, that I was what they call "steady," all day long under fire. We have what seems like an infinite number of wounded, and since they have all been hurt by cannon fire, very few will recover. Yesterday, about a hundred of them were brought to headquarters, and this morning the courtyard was filled with dead men. The plains of Marengo have corpses strewn over an area of two leagues. The air is foul, the heat stifling. We are leaving tomorrow for Tortona; I am glad of it, for besides dying of hunger here, the stench is becoming so strong that in two days, it won't be possible to stand it. God, what a sight! You do not get used to that.

Nevertheless, we are all in a very good mood; that is war! The commanding general has some aides-de-camp who are very friendly to me. No more worrying, my dear mother; peace is here. Sleep soundly. Soon, all we'll have to do is rest on our laurels. Général Dupont is going to make me a lieutenant. I really almost forgot to tell you, so little have I thought about myself for several days. Since his aide-de-camp has been wounded, I'm replacing him temporarily.

Goodbye, my dear mother; I'm dead tired and am going to lie down on the straw. I hug you with all my heart. In Milan, where we're headed for these days, I'll tell you more, and I'll write to my Uncle Beaumont.

Letter LVII   Turin, ——— Messidor, Year VIII (June or July 1800).

(To Citizen Beaumont, Hôtel de Bouillon, Quai Malaquais, Paris.)

Bim, bam, boom, taratata! Forward! Sound the charge! Fall back, make ready to fire! We're lost! Victory! Every man for himself! To the right, to the left, to the middle! Come back, stay where you are, clear out, let's get a move on! Watch out for the shell! On the gallop! Duck, there goes a ricocheting cannon-ball . . . Dead men, wounded, legs missing, arms blown off, prisoners, baggage, horses, mules; cries of rage, cries of victory, cries of pain, dust thick as the devil, hot as hell; poor devils, bastards, shit, a bloody mess, confusion, a fantastic free-for-all: and there you have, my dear, kind uncle, in a few words, a clear and concise view of the battle of Marengo, from which your nephew has returned safe and sound after having been bowled over, together with his mount, by a passing cannon-ball, and after having been treated by the Austrians, for fifteen hours, to the fire of thirty pieces of artillery, twenty mortars, and thirty thousand muskets. However, not everything is so brutal, for the commanding general, pleased with my presence of mind and the way I rallied deserters and brought them back to the fighting, made me a lieutenant on the battlefield at Marengo. I may therefore have one braid on my epaulette, no more. Now, covered with glory and the laurels of victory, after we had dinner at Papa Melas's and gave him our orders in his palace at Alessandria, we have come back to Turin with my general, who has been given the title of envoy extraordinary, minister plenipotentiary of the French government, and we are dictating the laws to Piedmont from our lodgings in the palace of the Duce di Aosta, where we have horses, carriages, entertainment, good food, etc. Général Dupont has wisely dismissed his entire general staff; he has only kept his two aides-de-camp and me, so that here I am an assistant, all by myself, to the minister. Since I do not have a very good head for business, I receive people in the dining room, because in principle, I never speak better than when I am "in my cups." With such maxims one can govern empires wisely.

Unfortunately, the war is now over; too bad, for with three or four more somersaults in the dust of the battlefields, I'd be a general. But I'm not losing heart. One fine morning, things will get messed up again, and we'll make up for lost time by tapping new capital.

Please don't hold it against me, my dear uncle, that I went for so long without writing you. But our running around, our conquests, our victories took up absolutely all my time. From now on, I shall be more regular. It won't be hard for me; I'll only have to follow the impulse of my heart, which always brings me back to my dear uncle, whom I embrace with all my heart.

I beg M. de Bouillon to accept my best regards.

Maurice.

In a third letter on the battle of Marengo, a letter addressed to the Villeneuve boys, and beginning with, "Well now, just listen to this, my dear nephews," my father includes a few details purposely omitted in his other letters. "Your 'respectworthy' uncle, after being grazed by one cannon ball, bowled over with his mount by another, after receiving a blow in the chest from the butt of a musket, which caused him to spit up a bit of blood for an hour, cured himself by chasing about the whole day at full trot and full gallop, etc. Moreover, my friends, it is not my fault if I didn't get myself killed. . . . It would take too long to give you all the gory details, but just imagine what it is like to spend three long days in the broiling plains, without anything to eat. At Torre di Garofolo, the only relief we had was one well for fourteen hundred men."

He finishes by saying, "I send you, my dear friends, twenty-three embraces each, and do present my respects to the eminent ladies."

Letter LVIII   Turin, 10 Messidor, Year VIII (June 1800).

(To Citizeness Dupin, Rue de la Ville-l'Éveque, No. 1305, Faubourg Honoré, Paris.)

Glory and honor to the conquerors! Général Dupont is leaving Milan to assume his duties in Turin as minister extraordinary of the French Republic, and to organize the government of Piedmont. In departing, he is dismissing his general staff, which as I have had to tell you, was not particularly distinguished, and he is only keeping his two aides-de-camp and me. Well, here we are in charge and lounging about like potentates. Upon arriving, I found a lieutenant's commission waiting for me. Général Dupont had requested it from the commanding general, who drew up the terms himself as follows: "I appoint Citizen Dupin lieutenant on the battlefield of Marengo." To be sure, that is a very nice title. I have no more than one step to go before becoming a captain, not ten years to wait, as certain people were telling you. I received my horses in good condition in Milan, and their fine appearance caused quite a stir there.

The person who is going to bear and deliver my letter to you is the best and most agreeable chap imaginable, as brave as a lion and mad as a hare; he was made a squadron leader on the field of battle. He is Laborde, aide-de-camp of Berthier, the one who had his mount shot from under him at Marengo. He is held in high regard by the Consul and all the generals. He has been very kind to me, has done his best to put me forward, and in a word, has been a true friend. I don't need to urge you to give him a splendid reception. Now I am rid of that motley crew of staff assistants, the only one to be retained, and acting as aide-de-camp to the minister plenipotentiary.

The Italians who only yesterday were betraying us are today overwhelming us with their salutations, adulations, protestations, bowings and scrapings. They are the shallowest people you can imagine. They think they are really pleasing us by playing the *Ça ira* whenever we enter a theater. It may pass for the *Marseillaise*, but I'll be damned if they're playing from the heart.

I would like very much for you to stay in Paris a while, for they say Général Dupont is returning there in a few days, and I should be going with him. How wonderful to embrace you so soon, and after a campaign that you didn't have time to worry about, thank God! I cannot tell you anything further, my dear mother, about our grand and glorious life in Turin, which I would gladly exchange for our modest rooms in Paris with you.

Laborde is leaving, so I'll say a quick goodbye. I embrace you.

Letter LIX   Turin, 10 Thermidor, Year VIII.

I already knew, my dear mother, that we were going to be replaced in Turin by Jourdan, and in order to get particulars on this replacement, the general had sent Morin and myself the day before yesterday to Milan to see Général Masséna. We got back this evening with a very satisfactory response. After receiving us very well, Masséna told us to tell Général Dupont that, in the event he should leave Milan, he (Masséna) would always receive him as a close friend and make use of his services in the most suitable manner. Consequently, if war begins again, as Masséna said during dinner, we shall probably be in command of a division. That would suit me fine, for I've never been so eager for battle and glory. Besides, all things considered, ours is a pretty stupid profession when we're not fighting. People always seem to be wondering what we are doing with our sabers and our uniforms when we aren't killing anybody, and we are looked on as the most useless members of society. But if a hundred brass muzzles, a hundred batallions come to threaten our territory, very quickly they will be calling us the avengers, the defenders, the heroes of France. We are like cloaks that people make use of whenever they see rain coming and forget when the weather is fine.

I found Milan very different from the way it was when we were there the first time. It is no longer that terrified city, unsure of its fate, with deserted streets and disheartened inhabitants. It is the picture of plenty, luxury, and pleasures. The *corso*, or main promenade, is brilliant, the way our boulevards once were. Four lines of carriages and whiskies[78] drive back and forth there every evening. The balls are magnificent, and in Milan as in Paris, the émigrés are delighted to come back and breathe the air of their native city. In the big theater, they are giving *Il Barbiere di Siviglia* by Paisiello. I was delighted by it. The piece that Almaviva sings when he is disguised as a music master has a ravishing melody. The quintet in which they send Basilio *al letto* [to bed] is remarkable for its harmonic richness and effect. I can now understand how one puts up with boring recitatives and plots that the singers hardly take the trouble to act out, to get to such beautiful spots.

Upon our return, the general asked me many questions about our trip. People were incredibly happy to see us back again. The rumor had circulated that we had been assassinated along the way. The road is really quite dangerous, and the day before we took it, two carriages had been attacked and pillaged, and a courier killed. Morin and myself had taken strong measures for defending ourselves. First of all, our carriage was an open calèche, from which we could see anyone coming, and quite high-riding, so that we could clearly observe the road and the postilions. Next, each of had a double-barrelled gun loaded with bullets and buck-shot, two pistols, and our sabers. All these precautions were by no means wasted. At Buffalora, the relay master was reluctant to give us fresh horses, saying that we would be attacked. It was eleven in the evening. We put no stock in his fears, and we departed. After an hour's ride, as I was continually watching the high hedges to the right and the left, which bordered the road, I clearly saw some men coming out of them through a narrow pathway. Immediately, I stood up and took aim; Morin did likewise, and our stance scared off the others, who disappeared as quickly as they had appeared. There are several rather well-organized bands of them, but they are not yet seasoned fighters. If you let them, they will attack you in broad daylight. If you're not afraid of them, they'll run off into the shadows. It is hard to believe that, in such a rich country, the inhabitants may be robbers, and yet they are all peasants and even inhabitants of the villages, and they often carry out their raids virtually on their own doorstep.

You scold me for taking so long to write to you. I don't know why. I haven't let twenty-seven days go by without sending you news of myself, and I wrote you two days after the battle. Anyhow, once and for all, never be worried about me. Nothing bad can ever happen to me. It is a rule.

Goodbye, my dear mother, I love and embrace you with all my heart. I embrace with affection my good, my true friend, Deschartres; I don't want him to be angry with me if I don't write to him. I hardly have the time to write to you, and sending news of myself to you is like writing to him too. I embrace my dear old nanny, I haven't forgotten her. Do send me Lefournier's address, I don't know it, and I think I shall never know it, unless you give it to me in capital letters.

Letter LX   Milan, ——— Fructidor, Year VIII (Sept. 1800).

It has been quite some time since I last wrote to you, my dear mother, but the last days of our stay in Turin have been so busy; we have had so much to do in order to put the finishing touches on our administration! We had scarcely arrived in Milan, when we had so many calls to make with Général Dupont, that up to now, I haven't been able to send you any news of myself. The general continues to show much interest in me. Your letters have contributed in no small way to that. I go along on all his trips, on all his outings. He left Deconchy and Merlin behind in Turin, and even though, on the evening of his departure, he had given me the order to accompany the monument for Desaix that he is sending to Paris, one hour after I had gone to bed, he had me awakened in order to leave with him. I was quite content, because it would have been a great big stupid chore to escort twenty carriages and go spend a few days in Paris, when you are no longer there. Dupont has just been appointed lieutenant general. He is now in command of eighteen thousand men, who make up the right flank. Today, Brune passed the division in review with him, and we are leaving tomorrow evening for Bologna. We are going by way of Modena, Reggio, and Piacenza. As you can see, I am a young man who will cover a lot of ground, if not go far. My horses and attendants have stayed in Turin with the general's and will come to meet us in Bologna.

We are spending our time here driving about and attending dinners. We have splendid ones at Pétiet's, the minister of France. Evenings, we go to the *corso* and to the theater, which is magnificent. They have a wonderful soprano and tenor. The ballets are poorly danced, but the décor is superb. In a word, since I am under orders to have a good time, I've decided to enjoy myself thoroughly. Milan is really pleasant, but I am quite happy to be leaving. It may all be fine and lovely, but two months spent in pleasure don't get you any further ahead than if you had slept for two months. And two months spent in the camps can make me a captain. And besides, one should get around and go travelling when one is young—a custom that goes back to Telemachus.

Adieu, my dear mother, I have to go pack my suitcase. I embrace you with all my heart.

                                                                    F.M.S.

Part II

My Early Years
1800 to 1810

I

The mission. —La Tour d'Auvergne. —Parma. —Bologna. —The occupation of Florence. —Georges La Fayette.

Letter I

ARMY OF ITALY, "LIBERTY, EQUALITY" General headquarters at Bologna, 17 Fructidor, Year VIII (Sept. 4, 1800) of the French Republic One and Indivisible.

From Lieutenant Général Dupont to Citizen Dupin, attached to the general staff of the right flank of the Army.

I wish, my dear Dupin, as soon as you receive this letter, that you call at Bercello. There you will gather information about the means of transport that exist along the Po, from Cremona to that point. You will notify the administration at Bercello, as well as that at Guastalla, about the arrival of a corps of troops forming part of the right flank, so that they get busy preparing for the maintenance of these troops, the force of which is not yet determined, but which could increase to two thousand the number of men at each of these two points.

You will descend along the river to the heights of Borgo-Forte, and you will proceed as far as San Benedetto, gathering the most precise information along the way about the number and the position of the ferries and other means of transport.

You will try to discover the strength and position of the Austrian military posts on the left bank of the river. You will ascertain whether they have a pontoon bridge at Borgo-Forte, or elsewhere. You will instruct yourself as to the general position of their army and the strength of the garrison at Mantua.

After having fullfilled these various instructions with all possible speed, you will return to Bologna, or to my general headquarters, if I have left that place.

You will take with you a cavalry soldier as baggage escort, and I authorize you to take such troop escorts as are necessary to you along the way.

It is essential to know if the Austrians are conducting troop movements which indicate hostile intentions. If you can procure some good spies, use them, or direct them to me.

Salutations and friendship.

Dupont.

I presume that this letter will find you in Parma.

Letter II   Bologna, 24 Fructidor.

From Maurice to His Mother

I am sending you this letter from the general, my dear mother, to beg your pardon somewhat—not for my silence, for which I would scarcely pardon myself were it on my account—but to ward off somewhat your reproaches and assumptions. You see that, in short, my behavior is not calculated to lose esteem and confidence, since I was picked out of six assistants to fulfill a delicate mission that could not be entrusted to just anybody. This proof of my activity and conscientiousness in the practice of my profession will give you pleasure, I know, but will it excuse my silence for a month in Milan? Ah! how fine of you, my dear mother, to have guessed without my saying a single word that I had been in that damned Capua, under the influence of a dreadful preoccupation! Don't interrogate me too much, I beg you. There are things one prefers to talk about rather than write. What can I say! I am at an age of intense emotions, and I am not to blame for my feelings. I was carried away, but I also suffered.[1] Therefore, pardon me and remember that I left Milan joyfully, with an ardent will to devote myself to the duties of my post. I will relate everything to you cooly later on, for I have already regained a sense of tranquility here within the turmoil of my profession. I executed the general's commission to the best of my ability. I went through the whole line in three days. I got back yesterday, and the same evening I had the satisfaction of seeing my official report, with which the general was very content, sent with all speed to the commanding general. That is what I call serving not just in a mechanical way, and I love war when I can understand its movements and the thought behind it. For me it is like a beautiful game of chess, whereas for the poor soldier it is a rough game of chance. True, many of the men whom I value in other respects are forced to spend their lives in an obscure weariness which is never embellished with the pleasure of understanding and knowledge. I pity them, and I would share their suffering, if in sharing it I could alleviate it. But that would not be the case; and since education has given me some enlightenment, don't I owe to my country's service, whose defense I have passionately embraced, the limited capacity of my brain as well as the activity of my limbs? M. de La Tour d'Auvergne, that hero whom I lament, was of my opinion when I expressed these ideas to him; he found me as good a patriot as himself, in spite of my grain of ambition and your maternal concerns. His modesty made an impression on me that I will never forget and that will serve as a model all my life. Vanity ruins the merit of the most beautiful actions. Simplicity, a delicate silence about oneself, increases their worth and makes one love those whom one admires. Alas, he is no more! He found a death glorious and worthy of him. Now, you no longer curse him, and you miss him as I do!

Besides, you persist in detesting all heroes. As I am not yet one, I have no fears for the present. But do you forbid me to aspire to heroism? I could renounce this ambition, if you threatened to stop loving me, and go plant cabbages instead of laurels in your garden patch. But I am hopeful that you will grow accustomed to my ambition and that I shall find a way to be pardoned for it.

I traveled through the estates of the Duke of Parma and thought I was back in '88. Fleurs-de-lis, coats of arms, liveries, hats under the arm, courtiers. That does indeed seem quite funny today. They looked at us in the streets as though we were some strange animals. In their glances there was an amusing mixture of fear, shock, and hatred that was totally comic. They have all the prejudices, stupidity, and cowardice of our Parisian royalists. Our commissioner of battles, a completely agreeable young man, spent the evening in one of the great houses of the place, and related to us how the conversation continually revolved around the genealogical tree of each family of the Duke's estates. To amuse himself, he told them that there was in the city a grandson of the Maréchal de Saxe, presently in the service of the Republic. There was a long cry of horror and stupefaction in the assembled group. They dropped the subject, and didn't dare discuss further in front of that young man all they thought of such an abomination. I had a good laugh over it.

In that nice city of Parma I went to see the painting academy and the immense theater, built by the Farnese family, in the style of the ancient circuses. It hasn't been used in two centuries; it is falling into ruins. But it is still admirable. In Bologna I saw the San Pietri gallery, one of the most beautiful collections in Italy. There are the most beautiful works by Raphael, Guide, Gerchin, and Carraci. I also visited the leaning tower, which is nine hundred feet high and leans out nine feet over its base; then the Holy Madonna, a piece of painted board, by Saint Luke, they believe. The Bolognese have such a veneration for her that she gets credit for anything good that happens within a twenty-league radius. They built a superb church in her honor on the beginning heights of the Apennines. It can be reached via a very beautiful corridor a league-and-a-half long, which consists of great symmetrical arcades, financed by wealthy individuals who want to go to heaven. The architects turned it into an object of speculation. Some of the arcades they built were resold at very high prices to the kind of people who, on their last legs and desperate to earn heavenly mercy, feel compelled to accept any and all conditions. It's very edifying!

All these classical and religious beauties in Bologna haven't prevented me from appreciating the excellence of their mortadella cheeses. Not being able to send you any of these, I have chosen a cameo agate for you which struck me as very beautiful, although it may not be an antique, and like M. Jourdain,[2] I can't quite figure out what it's supposed to represent. Goodbye, my dear mother, love me, scold me, provided your letters are long, because I can never get enough of them.

Letter III   Bologna, 9 Vendémiaire, Year IX (October 1800).

To Citizen René de Villeneuve at Chenonceaux near Amboise

To remain a month and a half without having a talk with my dear friends, my dear brothers! Isn't that the most bizarre, ridiculous, and inexcusable thing one could possibly imagine? . . . However, if an unlucky fellow holds some sway over generous hearts, listen, my dear René, to the tale of my misfortunes.

Général Dupont is named commanding lieutenant general of the army's right flank. We leave Milan to go to our headquarters. Halfway there, the general sends me to reconnoiter the Austrian outposts along the Po, from the mouth of the Oglio to the Chiesa and Mincio Rivers. I fulfill this mission as well as I can. I return to Bologna with the most precise details on the positions and strength of the enemy. The general sends my report to the commanding general. They form a plan of attack based on my information. I'm to lead a column on one of the points I've reconnoitered. I envision a brilliant and daring attack. You shall hear them talk of me! The truce is about to expire; I am dying to fall upon the Austrians. We leave Bologna and proceed to Guastalla, a small town on the Po. The day the truce expires, we go to reconnoiter the enemy's outposts; the general announces to all the leaders that we are at war; we are to attack the next day. We await the messenger who is to confirm the order to us. He arrives. My heart goes bumpety bump. Then I say to myself, "It's tomorrow!" Already, I can see my name in the newspaper, and I'm jumping for joy. However, the packet is unsealed, and we read—Nothing doing! It's a damned extension of the truce, may five hundred devils take it![1]

Since that time we have been in suspense, sometimes lulled by rumors of peace, sometimes by rumors of war, and very annoyed by all these delays....

Mama writes me that you are going to return to spend the winter in Paris. If we aren't at war at that time, perhaps I'll get to embrace you there; you run a great risk of being suffocated during that interview. For I love you with a fierce strength, and I'm no little weakling. So if I hug you with all my might and affection, you're as good as dead. Goodbye, my dear René, I embrace you and Auguste. I send my regards to Mme. René and Mme. Auguste, as well as to our dear Mama de Courcelles, and to use her expressions, tell her that the "hussar," as "extravagant" as he is, doesn't stop thinking of the kindnesses she wished to bestow on him. Also hug my "grandniece" Emma. She will surely be as astonished to hear talk of me as she was to see me enter your house so boisterously. Don't be hard on me. Write to me.

Letter IV   Florence, 26 Vendémiaire, Year IX (October 1800).

From Maurice to His Mother

In this attack, we've done a fine job! Nice fellows that we are, we've just broken the truce. In three days, we took possession of Tuscany and the beautiful and delightful city of Florence. Sommariva, his famous troops, his terrible armed peasants, all fled at our approach, and we are the batterers of open doors.

With Général Dupont commanding the expedition, we crossed the Appenines at the head of the advance guard, and now we are delightfully resting beneath the olive, orange, lemon, and palm trees which border the banks of the Arno. However, the insurgent Tuscans have retrenched in Arezzo and are holding at bay Général Monnier, one of the division generals. But we have just sent cannon there, and soon it will be all over.

There was nothing so amusing as our entrance into Florence. Sommariva had sent several bearers of truce flags to meet us, charged with assuring us on his part that he was going to disarm the peasants he had roused and that he begged us to halt, but if we persisted in entering Florence, he would kill himself on the ramparts. A noble speech, but in spite of his promises and threats, we continued our advance. When we were several miles from Florence, Général Dupont sends Général Jablonowski with a squadron of cavalry to find out if the enemy is indeed defending the position. Finding myself rather at loose ends at the time, I follow Général Jablonowski. We arrive by fours, in the military manner, sabers in hand, at a fast trot. Meeting no resistance, we enter the city; no one is there to stop us. At a street corner, we find ourselves nose to nose with a party of Austrian cuirassiers. Our chasseurs want to cut them down. The Austrian officer advances toward us, hat in hand, and tells us, since he and his group form the police guard, they are obliged to withdraw last. We are disarmed by such a good reason, and we politely ask him to go with all possible speed and join the rest of the Austrian and Tuscan army, which has fallen back to Arezzo. We arrive at the main square where the government deputies come to pay us their respects. I establish headquarters in the most beautiful section and in the handsomest palace in the city. I return to Général Dupont. We make a triumphant entrance, and behold, a city taken.

The same evening they light up the grand opera house, they reserve us the best boxes, they send us fine berlins to carry us there, and behold, we are installed as masters. The next day it remained for us to take two forts, each one defended by eighteen cannon and a howitzer. We send word to the two commanders that we're going to furnish them with all the conveyances needed for the evacuation of their garrison. Struck with such a "dreadful" decree, they immediately surrender, and behold, we find ourselves possessors of two forts. The last capitulation made us laugh so hard that we were tempted to imagine the Austrians were on our side. However, it seemed this was not the case.

They have carried away and shipped off to Livorno the famous Venus and the two most beautiful daughters of Niobe. This morning I went to the gallery. It is filled with an immense quantity of antique statues, almost all of them superb. I saw the famous torso, the seashell Venus, the Faun, the Mercury, and a host of Roman emperors and empresses. The city swarms with handsome edifices and is glutted with masterpieces. The bridges, quays, and promenades are laid out a little like in Paris, but this city has the advantage of being situated in a valley famous for its views and its fertility. There are nothing but charming villas, rows of lemon trees, forests of olive trees: you be the judge of how lovely all that seems to us after leaving the Apennines!

This will be fine, provided it lasts, but I believe we will advance from the Ferrara side, if hostilities with the Austrians resume. Then we shall abandon these beautiful regions to return to the arid banks of the Po.

You see, my dear mother, for me things are going along fine. I have no desire at all to leave Général Dupont; he wishes me well. I enjoy the friendship and consideration of those with whom I live here. The general has three aides-de-camp. The third is Merlin, son of the Directeur. He was an aide-de-camp for Bonaparte, and did the Egyptian campaign with him. He is captain of my regiment; his sister had married our colonel a short time before he was killed. Retaining only the aides-de-camp who were brigade leaders, Bonaparte sent him to us when the Army of Reserve returned from its campaign. He is extremely nice. My position is that of correspondence officer attached directly to the general, lodging and living with him. I have definitely become the man entrusted with quick and delicate missions. We have a general staff composed of several officers, but they don't live with us. Our circle consists of Merlin, Morin, Deconchy, Barthelemy (brother of the Directeur), Georges La Fayette, and myself. I am closest to Georges. He is a charming young man, full of wit, frankness, and feeling. He is a second lieutenant in the 11th regiment of hussars and commands thirty hussars in our escort. Together we form what is known as The Joyous Band. Mme. de La Fayette and her daughter are now at Chenonceaux. Our liaison grows in a very natural way from this liaison of our relatives. You would do well to visit them there. Such a trip would distract you, and you have great need of that, my poor mother. The stay at Nohant seems somber to you since I'm no longer there. This thought afflicts me. I would be the happiest man in the world, if you weren't anxious over me. La Fayette and I are making the nicest plans for meeting when peacetime will have come. We see ourselves at Chenonceaux with our dear mothers, having no other cares than to divert them and make up for the worries we gave them. You see that we are preserving our "human" feelings and thoughts, despite war and carnage. I speak quite often of you to Georges, who also speaks to me about his mother. As dear as she may be, you must be still dearer, and beyond all comparison. As for Father Deschartres, in all things he is incomparable, and since we now find him "Mayor of Nohant," I bow down to the ground before him and embrace him with all my heart.

Maurice.

M.E.

II

Rome. —An interview with the Pope. —A simulated attempt at assassination. —Monsignor Consalvi. —Asola. —First passion. —The eve of the battle. —Crossing the Mincio. —Maurice taken prisoner. —Deliverance. —A love letter. —Rivalries and resentments between Brune and Dupont. —Departure for Nohant.

Letter V   Rome, 2 Frimaire, Year IX (November 23, 1800).

Two days after my last letter (which I wrote to you on our second return from Florence), Général Dupont sent me to Rome with dispatches for the Pope and the commander-in-chief of the Neopolitan troops. I left with one of our comrades named Charles His, a man of wit and friend of Général Dupont. We arrived in Rome after thirty-six hours on the road. In spite of all the fear they had tried to instill in us as to the fury of the populace against the French, we found them only extremely astonished to see two Frenchmen arrive alone and in uniform in the middle of a hostile nation. Our entrance into the Eternal City was very amusing. All the people followed us in a crowd, and if we had wanted to display ourselves for money during our stay, we would have made a fortune. Their curiosity was such that they all ran after us in the streets. We are convinced the Romans are the nicest people in the world and only the fees extorted from them by certain corrupt squanderers had drawn their enmity onto us. We have only ourselves to blame for their conduct toward us.

The Holy Father received us with the most sincere signs of friendship and consideration, and this morning we are setting out again for the Army, extremely satisfied with our trip. We have seen all possible things to admire, as much of it ancient as modern. As I have a great penchant for climbing, I amused myself by scaling the outside of the ball on the dome of Saint Peter's. When I was back down, people told me that nearly all the English who come to Rome do the same, which didn't stop me from being convinced of the wisdom of my enterprise.

Goodbye, my dear mother, they are calling me to climb into the carriage. Goodbye to Rome! I embrace you with all my heart.

Letter VI   Bologna, 5 Frimaire, Year IX (November 26, 1800).

You must, my dear mother, have seen through the "prudent" style of my last letter, which I wrote you in the certainty it would be read within the half hour by the secretary of state, Monsignor Consalvi, who despite a somewhat friendly and trusting air, didn't leave off spying on us with all his might. However, we only went to Rome to deliver two letters: one to the Pope, to ask him to release some persons detained for their political opinions, and the other to the commander-in-chief of the Neopolitan forces, to notify his government that we were again demanding the release of Général Dumas[2] and M. Dolomieu, and in case of a refusal, the French bayonets were prepared to perform their function. Although we were definitely only the bearers of despatches, they believed we were sent to stir up an insurrection and to put weapons into the hands of the Jacobins. Firmly convinced of this, they clapped on our back two Neopolitan officers, who under the pretext of guaranteeing our respectful treatment, stuck to us no less than our shadows. They surrounded us with traps and spies; they reinforced the garrison; it was rumored among the people that the French were on their way. It was a devilishly effective rumor. The King of Sardinia, who was in Naples, immediately took off to Sicily. The secretary of state trembled to see us in Rome. He constantly repeated, in order to frighten us, that he feared we would be assassinated and that it would be wise for us not to wear our uniforms. We replied that no species of fear could decide us to change costume, and as for assassins, we were more wicked than they; the first who approached us would be as good as dead. To frighten us more, in the evening, at our door, they had arrested, with great ostentation, some stupid people armed with large poniards. We saw clearly that all this was a comedy, and we continued nevertheless to peacefully wait for an answer from the King of Naples, which M. de Damas, the commanding general, told us ought to arrive any minute. We stayed waiting for it twelve days, and during that time, by our conduct and our manners, we ended by eliciting their general good will. We received and returned visits to all the ambassadors. We made an afternoon visit to the Pope. It was there that my dress uniform and that of my comrade, who is also in the hussars, had their total effect. As soon as we entered, the Pope rose from his seat, pressed our hands, and made us sit to his right and his left. Then we had a very serious and interesting discussion with him about the rain and the nice weather. After fifteen minutes, when he was well informed as to our respective ages, names, and ranks, we presented him our respects: he pressed our hands again while requesting "our friendship," which we had the goodness to offer, and we parted quite content with one another. And not a moment too soon, for I was beginning to explode with laughter at seeing us—my friend and I, two hussar rascals—seated majestically to the right and left of the Pope. It there had been a good thief there, it would have been a veritable Calvary.

The next day, we were introduced at the Duchess Lanti's. There was an enormous crowd. There I met Chevalier de Bernis the elder and Talleyrand the younger, aide-de-camp to General Damas. I renewed my acquaintance with M. de Bernis and began to chat with him about Paris and all of society. My connection with these two personages made a great impression on the minds of the Roman ladies and gentlemen, and only because of that were they willing to acknowledge that we were not brigands who had come to set fire to the four corners of the Eternal City.

The way in which we indulged ourselves also gave them an exaggerated idea of our worth. Général Dupont had given us a great deal of money to represent the French nation properly, and we acquitted ourselves of this task better than anyone. We had carriages, loges, horses, concerts at our lodgings, and fine dinners. They no longer treated us as anything but "Excellencies." It was very entertaining, and we did so well that we are returning without a sou. This time we served our country very comfortably, but we leave to Roman society a great admiration for our magnificence, and to the poor a deep gratitude for our generosity. The latter is also a princely pleasure, and surely it is the sweetest.

The secretary of state extended us the graciousness of sending the most erudite antiquarian of Rome to show us all its marvels. I've seen so many that I'm stupified. All the originals of our beautiful works, and then all the old hovels before which one is supposed to swoon with pleasure. I confess they very much bored me, and despite the enthusiasm for the old Romans, I prefer Saint Peter's of Rome to all those piles of old bricks. However, I was interested in seeing the grotto of the nymph Egeria and the ruins of the bridge on which Horatius Cocles [One-eyed Horatius][3] fought, who was a brave hussar officer in his time. Finally, the news of the resumption of hostilities put an end to our grandeur. We wrote to M. de Damas that the desire to rejoin our colors did not permit us to wait any longer for the reply of the king of Naples, and we left, accompanied by our two surveillants, the two Neopolitan officers, who left us only at our outposts. Bidding us the most amiable farewells, M. de Damas thanked us for the manner in which we behaved.

We have just arrived at Bologna after three days and three nights on the road, and while they are harnessing our horses, I'm conversing with you. Général Dupont is on the other side of the Po. Tomorrow, I will be back with him. Now, I'm hoping we'll go on to Venice. That will depend on our success. I personally am convinced that we'll beat the enemy everywhere. Since the Battle of Marengo, our name brings terror to them.

However, there is vague talk of a new armistice, and the armies have not yet made overtly hostile movements.

My dear mother, how I regret that we didn't see Rome together! You know that in my childhood it was our dream! Whenever I saw anything beautiful, I thought of you, and my pleasure was diminished by the thought that you weren't sharing it. Adieu, I love you and embrace you with all my heart. I'm being called to climb aboard the carriage. I would like to keep on chatting with you, and I will think only of you from Bologna to Casal-Maggiore.

I embrace friend Deschartres. Tell him that I have seen the ruins of the houses of Horace and Virgil, and the bust of Cicero, and I have said to these illustrious shades, "Messieurs, I have explicated you with my friend Deschartres, and I owe to your sublime works more than one "Get to work, you're dreaming!"

An immense botanical garden also made me think of you, my dear tutor, and if, fool that I am, I found nothing interesting in the way of petals, stems, and stamens, at least I found the memory of my ancient and venerable friend. Are you still planting a lot of cabbages? I ruffle my maid's hair-do and embrace her with all my heart.

Letter VII   Asola, 29 Frimaire, Year IX (December 1800).

What a long time it has been, my dear mother, since I have had the pleasure of conversing with you! You're going to ask, "Whose fault is that?" In
truth, it is not too much mine. Since we have been in Asola, we've done nothing but run around to reconnoiter the enemy's posts. Barely returned, we find
a noisy, joyous company whose laughter and revels last well into the night.
We go to bed overwhelmed with fatigue, and the next day we begin again.
You're going to scold me and tell me that I ought to be sensible and go to bed
at an early hour. But if you were of a soldier's stamp, you would know that
fatigue engenders excitement and that our profession induces sang-froid only
when danger is present. In all other circumstances, we are madmen, and we
need to be.

And then I have to tell you a piece of good news of which I have only
just been assured. Morin had proclaimed it to me as imminent, and the general
has just confirmed it by making me a gift of the aide-de-camp's badge, a yellow plume, and a beautiful red shoulder sash with gold fringes.

So now you see me as an aide-de-camp to Lieutenant Général Dupont,
and it is thus you must address me on your letters, so they reach me more
quickly. The new regulation allows him three aides-de-camp. Here I am, finally, in a position of some charm—respected, esteemed, loved—yes! loved by a
very lovable and charming woman, and the only thing lacking for me to be perfectly happy here would be your presence. True, that is a great deal!

You will know then, as the lieutenancy of Dupont and the divisionship of
Watrin are joined here, every evening we form gatherings at which Mme.
Watrin, sparkling with youth and beauty, shines like a star. However, it is not
she! A star of softer fire shines for me.[4]

You know that at Milan I was in love. You guessed it *because* I didn't tell
you. At times, I believed I was loved, and then I saw, or thought I saw, I
wasn't. I tried to forget, I left, not wanting to dream about her anymore.

This charming woman is here. And we talked little; we scarcely glanced
at one another. I felt somewhat resentful, although that is hardly like me. She
was haughty with me, although she has a tender and passionate heart. This
morning, during lunch, we heard cannon firing in the distance. The general
tells me to mount immediately on horseback and go to see what is happening. I
rise and in two leaps hurdle the stairs and run to the stable. As I am mounting
my horse, I turn around and see this woman behind me, flushed, embarrassed,
and casting on me a long look expressing fear, concern, love. I would have
responded to it all by throwing my arms around her neck, but that was impossible in the middle of the courtyard. I confined myself to pressing her hand tenderly as I leapt onto my noble charger, which, full of ardor and audacity, made
three magnificent caracoles as he bounded forward over the road. I was soon at
the outpost where the noise was coming from. There I find the Austrians
repulsed in a skirmish in which they have just engaged us. I return to bring the
news to the general. *She* was still there. Ah, how I was received! And how
pleasant and carefree the dinner was! What delicate attentions she showed me!

This evening, by an unhoped-for chance, I found myself alone with her. Everyone had gone to sleep, fatigued with the excessive demands of the day. I didn't hesitate to tell her how much I loved her, and she, bursting into tears, threw herself into my arms. Then she escaped in spite of me and ran to shut herself up in her room. I wanted to follow her. She begged, conjured, ordered me to leave her alone, and submissive in loving, I obeyed. As we are to mount our horses at daybreak, I have stayed up to talk over the emotions of the day with my dear mother. How lovely it was to get your good big letter of eight pages! What pleasure it has given me! How sweet it is to be loved, to have a good mother, good friends, a beautiful mistress, a bit of glory, splendid horses, and enemies to battle! I have all that, and of all that, what's best is my dear mother.

René has written to me most affectionately to invite me to come to live with him when I return to Paris. He is enchanted with your letters, and who wouldn't be? My God, what a dear you are!

Goodbye, my dear mother, four o'clock has just sounded, the hour at which the general told me to awaken. I leave you to go to his room. Goodbye, I embrace you a thousand times.

I embrace Mayor Deschartres with enough force to suffocate His Mayoralty; my maid as well.

                                                                    Maurice.

There is in certain lives a moment when our faculty for happiness, trust, and intoxication reaches its apogee. Then, as if our spirit could no longer tolerate it, doubt and sadness spread over us a cloud which envelops us forever; or is it really our destiny growing dim, and are we now condemned to slowly descend the slope that we climbed with joy's audacity?

For the first time, the young man had come to feel the effects of a durable passion. The woman of whom he had just spoken with a mixture of enthusiasm and lightness, this graceful little affair that he thought he could perhaps forget as he had forgotten the canoness and several others, would take hold of his entire life and draw him into a struggle with himself which furnished the torment, happiness, despair, and grandeur of his last eight years. From that moment on, this naïve and good heart, open until now to all outer impressions, to an immense benevolence, to a blind faith in the future, to an impersonal ambition which was identified with his country's glory; this heart which a single affection, an almost impassioned filial love, had filled and preserved in its precious wholeness, was divided, that is to say, torn, by two nearly irreconcilable loves. The happy, proud mother, who lived only for that love, was tortured and crushed by a jealousy natural to any woman's heart, but even more disquieting and poignant in her case was that maternal love had been the unique passion of her life. To this inner anguish—which she never confessed, but which was all too certain and which any other woman would have aroused in her—was joined the bitterness of hurt presumptions, respectable assumptions, which I want to explain before going further.

But it must first be said that this charming woman of whom the young man dreamed in Milan and conquered in Asola, this Frenchwoman who had been imprisoned at the English convent at the same time as my grandmother, was none other than my mother, Sophie-Victoire-Antoinette Delaborde. I give her three baptismal names because, in the turbulent course of her life, she bore them successively; and these three names are themselves symbolic of the spirit of the times. In her childhood, they probably preferred to call her Antoinette, the same name as the queen of France. During the conquests of the Empire, the name of Victoire naturally prevailed. From the time of their marriage, my father always called her Sophie. Everything is significant and emblematic (and most naturally so) in those details of human existence which appear most fortuitous.

Doubtless, my grandmother would have preferred a companion of his own rank for my father, but as she herself said and wrote, she was not seriously aggrieved over what was called, in her time and in her world, a *misalliance*. She didn't make more of a case about birth than she had to, and as for money, she knew how to do without it and how to find in her economy and personal privations remedies for the expenses entailed by the posts her son occupied, which were more brilliant than lucrative. But only with great difficulty was she able to accept a daughter-in-law whose youth had been delivered up to frightening hazards, owing to the force of circumstances. This was the delicate point to cut through, and love, which has supreme wisdom and supreme nobility of soul when it is sincere and profound, cut through it resolutely, in my father's soul. A day also came when my grandmother gave in, but we are not up to that yet, and I have many sorrows to recount before getting to that part of my tale.

I know only very imperfectly my mother's story before her marriage. Later I shall talk about how certain people believed they were acting prudently and in my interest by telling me things it would have been better for me not to know, and none of which have been proven to me to be authentic. But even if they had all been true, one fact remains before God: she was loved by my father, and apparently she deserved it, since her mourning for him ended only with her life.

But the principle of aristocracy has so penetrated to the depths of the human heart that, in spite of our revolutions, it still exists underneath all the formal gestures. It will take quite a lot more time before the Christian principle of moral and social equality prevails over the laws and the spirit of society. However, the doctrine of redemption is the very symbol of the principle of expiation and rehabilitation. Our society recognizes this principle in religious theory, but not in fact; it is too grand, too beautiful for it to grasp. And yet this divine something in the depths of our souls brings us to violate the principle of moral aristocracy in our individual lives, while our hearts, which are more fraternal, more egalitarian, more merciful, and consequently more just and more Christian than our spirits, often make us love beings whom society reputes unworthy and degraded.

We sense this condemnation is absurd, that it is abhorrent to God, all the more so because, as practiced by what we call society, it is hypocritical and bears no connection to the fundamental question of good and evil. Jesus, the great revolutionary, told us one day in a sublime speech, that there was more joy in heaven for the recovery of one sinner than for the perseverance of a hundred just souls, and the return of the prodigal son is no frivolous fable, I think. However, there still exists a pretended aristocracy of virtue, which, proud of its privileges, does not allow that the aberrations of youth can be redeemed. A woman born into opulence, carefully brought up in a convent under the eyes of respectable matrons, watched like a plant under glass and established in society under every condition of prudence, comfort, tranquility, respect for self, and apprehension of the power of others, has no great difficulty and perhaps deserves no great credit for leading a sensible, orderly life, for setting a good example, for professing austere principles. And still I deceive myself, for if nature has given her an ardent soul, in a society which does not allow her to manifest her inclinations or her passions, she will still have much difficulty and deserve much credit for not offending that society. Well then, all the more reason why the poor abandoned child who comes into the world with her beauty as her only patrimony is, so to speak, innocent of all the temptations to which her youth will expose her and all the pitfalls to which her inexperience will lead her. It would seem that the prudent matron is placed in this world in order to open her arms to such a child, to console, purify, and reconcile her with herself. What is the purpose of being better and purer than others if not to render goodness fertile and virtue contagious? However, this is not at all the way life is! The world is there to prohibit an esteemed woman from offering her hand to one who is not, or from having her sit beside her—the world, that false arbiter, that lying and impious code of pretended decency and morality! Under pain of losing her good reputation, the pure woman must turn her glance away from the sinner, and if she stretches out her arms to such a person, the world, an areopagus of false virtues and false duties, will close its arms to her.

I say false virtues and false duties because it is not the truly pure women, not the truly respected matrons exclusively who have to rule on the merits of their misguided sisters. It will not be a group of honest folk who make the judgment. All that is a dream. The vast majority of women in the world are lost women. Everyone knows it; everyone admits it; yet no one blames and insults the shameless ones when they blame and insult women less guilty than they.

When my grandmother saw her son marry my mother, she was in despair; she would have wished to dissolve with her tears the contract which cemented this union; however, she did not condemn it dispassionately with her mind; she feared its consequences in her motherly heart. She feared the storms and struggles of such a bold association for her son, as she had feared the fatigues and dangers of war on his behalf. She also feared his censure by a certain segment of society. She suffered in that area of moral pride which a life exempt from censure legitimized in her, but she did not need much time to see that a privileged nature easily flaps its wings and takes flight the moment one gives it space. She was kind and affectionate to her son's wife.

However, the maternal jealousy took hold, and her inner calm rarely overcame it. If that kind of jealousy born of fondness was a crime, God alone has the right to condemn it, for it eludes the severity of men, and especially of women.

Ever since Asola, that is to say, from the end of the year 1800 until the time of my birth in 1804, my father was also to suffer mortally from the division in his soul between a cherished mother and a passionately beloved mistress. It was only in 1804 that he found more peace of mind and strength in the consciousness of a duty accomplished, when he married the woman he had tried to sacrifice for his mother so many times.

While waiting to pursue him in his inner struggles, with both pity and admiration, I rejoin him at Asola, where he wrote the last letter to his mother that I reproduced, dated 29 Frimaire. That date marks one of the great military events of the period, the crossing of the Mincio.

Cobentzel was still in Lunéville, negotiating with Joseph Bonaparte. It was then that the First Consul, wishing to put an end with one bold and decisive blow to the lack of resolution of the Viennese court, ordered the Army of the Rhine, commanded by Moreau, to cross the In River, and ordered the Army of Italy, commanded by Brune, to cross the Mincio. These two lines were brought within a few days' distance of each other. Moreau won the battle of Hohenlinden, and the Army of Italy, which lacked neither good soldiers nor good officers, forced the Austrians to withdraw and thus ended the war by forcing the enemy to evacuate the peninsula. But if the conduct of the army was heroic there as everywhere, if the individual ardor and inspiration of several officers made up for the faults of the commanding general, it is no less certain that this operation was directed by Brune in a deplorable manner. I am not about to give the official story here; for that I refer my reader to the account of M. Thiers, eminent historian of military events, and in that capacity, always clear, precise, compelling, and faithful. He will serve as a witness for the accusations brought by my father against the general who, in that instance, committed more than mistakes. He committed a crime. He left part of his army abandoned, without support, in an unequal struggle against the enemy, and his inertia was the cruel obstinacy of pride. Displeased by the ardor which had inspired Général Dupont to cross the river with ten thousand men, he prevented Suchet from giving him sufficient aid, and if the latter, seeing Dupont's army in the grasp of thirty thousand Austrians and in great danger of being crushed despite a heroic defense, had not gone against Brune's orders and sent the rest of the Gazan division, on his own authority, to the aid of those worthy men, our right flank would have been lost. That barbarous, or inept, act of the commanding general took the lives of several thousand intrepid soldiers and cost my father his freedom. Carried away by his bravery and overly confident in his "star" (which was the prestigious belief of the moment, each man, without imagining he was imitating Bonaparte, believing himself protected by destiny, as Bonaparte did), he was captured by the Austrians, an accident of war more feared than serious wounds and almost more depressing than death for those young men drunk with glory and action.

It was a painful awakening after a morning full of violent emotions that had been preceded by a night of impatience and transport. It was during that vigil, yielding to the most ardent emotions, that he had written to his mother, "How sweet it is to be loved, to have a good mother, worthy friends, a beautiful mistress, a bit of glory, a fine horse, and enemies to battle!" However, he had not told her that the same day, even at that very moment, he was going off to fight those enemies, whose presence contributed to his happiness. He sealed the letter where he had just traced a tender adieu that could well have been his last, and he let her believe he was only going off on his horse to make a reconnaissance. Wholly committed to love and war, although crushed by the fatigue of the day and all the preceding days, it had not even occurred to him to sleep for an hour. Life was so full and so intense at that moment for himself and for everyone! During that same night, he had written to his dear nephew René de Villeneuve, and he had been more explicit. That letter shows a freedom of spirit which charms and would surprise, if it were unique in the history of that period. He talks to him at length about a cameo he had bought him in Rome and which a clumsy apprentice had broken in trying to set; but he announces the sending of other similar objects of art, which Cardinal Consalvi is charged with expediting, "Because you must know," he tells him, "that I am on good terms with His Eminence and on even better terms with the Pope." Then he reveals his own situation and that of the army. "It's two in the morning. In two hours we mount on horseback. We have spent all day placing the troops. We have advanced all our artillery to the front lines, and at daybreak we're going to strike. You will probably hear talk of the 29th, because the attack is a general one throughout the army . . . .

"They're already saddling the general's horses. I hear them in the courtyard, and when I will have written a last word to my mother, I'm going to saddle mine. I leave you now, my dear friend, to go have words with Croatian, Wallachian, Dalmatian, Hungarian and other gentlemen who are waiting for us. It's going to be a fine row. We have eight twelve-pounders in battery. How sorry I am that you're not here to listen to the uproar we're going to make! It would amuse you, I'm sure. I beg you to give my respects to Mme. René and to Mme. de Courcelles.

"How touched I am, my kind friend, by your offers and plans for reunion! I accept them with much eagerness, since in this way I shall see you all day long when I'm in Paris. That happy time will come when we have no other cares than laughing and living together! I love you and embrace you quite tenderly."

The next day he was in the hands of the enemy; he was departing from the theater of war, and leaving behind him the victorious army as well as his friends, who were ready to return to France to embrace their mothers and friends; he was leaving on foot for a long and painful exile.[5] This event also separated him from his beloved mistress, and it plunged my poor grandmother into dreadful despair. It had repercussions for the entire life of this young man, who since '94 had forgotten what suffering, isolation, constraints, and reflection could mean. Perhaps a decisive revolution took place within him. From that time on he was, if not less outwardly gay, at least more defiant and more serious in the depths of his spirit. He had forgotten Victoire in the turmoil and intoxication of war. He rediscovered her image fatally linked to all his thoughts in the harsh intellectual leisure of exile and captivity. Nothing predisposes us to great passion more than great suffering.

Letter VIII   Padua, 15 Nivose, Year IX (January 5, 1801).

Don't be at all upset, my dear mother, I had begged Morin to write to you. Thus surely you already know that I am a prisoner. I am in Padua now and en route to Gratz. I hope to be exchanged soon, Général Dupont having had me redemanded of Bellegarde the same morning I was captured. I can't tell you any more now, but I hope that soon I will announce my return. Adieu, I embrace you with all my soul. I also embrace Father Deschartres and my maid.

These few words were intended to reassure the poor mother. The captivity was longer and harsher than the letter foretold. During the two months that elapsed without receiving any news of him, my grandmother was prey to one of those dismal spells of grief that men rarely know and which they would not be able to survive. In this regard, the constitution of woman is a marvel. Such intensity of suffering with such power to resist it is incomprehensible. The poor mother did not have a minute's sleep and lived only on cold water. The sight of the food they brought her elicited her sobs and near cries of despair. "My son is dying of hunger!" she said. "He is perhaps expiring at this moment, and you want me to eat!" She did not want to lie down. "My son is lying on the ground," she said. "Perhaps they don't even give him a handful of straw to sleep on. Perhaps he's been injured.[3] He hasn't a scrap of linen to cover his wounds." The sight of her room, armchair, fire, the comforts of her life—all stirred within her the most bitter comparisons. Her imagination exaggerated the privations and suffering her beloved child might be enduring. She saw him tied up in a dungeon; she saw him struck by sacrilegious hands, falling from weariness and exhaustion at the roadside, and forced to rise up again and crawl along beneath the cudgel of an Austrian corporal. Poor Deschartres forced himself in vain to distract her. Apart from the fact that he had no understanding of her state of mind and that no one was more of an alarmist by nature than he, he was so sad himself that it was pitiful to see them shift the cards around on the table in the evening, with no awareness of what they were doing or which of them had won the game.

Then, toward the end of Ventôse, Saint-Jean arrived at coursing speed. This was perhaps the only time in his life he forgot to go into the tavern after leaving the post office. It was perhaps also the only time that, with the aid of his lone silver spur, he put that peaceful white horse, who had lived nearly as long as he, to the gallop. At the unaccustomed noise of his triumphant gait, my grandmother gave a start, ran to meet him, and received the following letter:

Letter IX   Conegliano, 6 Ventôse, Year IX (February 25, 1801).

Finally, I'm out of their hands! I breathe. For me this is a day of happiness and freedom! I have the sure hope of seeing you, of embracing you in a little while, and all that I've suffered is forgotten. From this moment on, all my attention, all my advances will lead to rejoining you. It would take too long to tell you my misfortunes in detail. I'll only tell you that after having remained in their hands for two months, constantly marching through the deserted lands of Carinthia and Carriola, we were led up to the borders of Bosnia and Croatia; we were about to enter lower Hungary when, by a most happy turn of events, they made us retrace our steps. One of the last taken, I was one of the first released. I'm now at the second French outpost, where I found a real bed, a piece of furniture I've scarcely used in about three months, because for the month before I was captured I slept in my clothing, and from my capture until today, I've had no other bed than straw. Returning to the army, I hoped to join Général Dupont and my comrades, but I learn that he was recalled because his intrepid crossing of the Mincio excited the jealousy of a man whose incapacity people will soon recognize. In his absence, I was counting on Général Watrin, one of his division generals and friend, who had shown me the greatest kindness under all circumstances. I learn that he also has left for Ancona, from which I find myself more than a hundred leagues away, because I am now behind Treviso. As I presume that Général Dupont has taken my horses and baggage with him, it remains only for me to address myself to Général Monnier, another of his division generals. I don't doubt he will give me the means to return to you, and I'm traveling to Bologna, where he is now. I can no longer serve until my exchange; I was returned on my word of honor.

I feel a joy in being free, able to return to you without anyone being able to reproach me! I am in ecstasy, and yet I have taken on a habit of sadness which still prevents me from comprehending my good fortune.[6] I go to Treviso tomorrow, where I'll obtain new information that will decide my route. Goodbye, my dear mother, no more anxieties, no more grief. I embrace you and live only for the moment of seeing you again. I embrace friend Deschartres and my maid. That poor Deschartres, what a long time since I've seen him!

Letter X   Paris, 25 Germinal, Year IX (April 1801).

After many annoyances and matters which delayed me in Ferrara and Milan, where I located Général Watrin—one of our best friends in the right flank, who, though not without difficulty, made it possible for me to draw my salary in arrears—I began my journey with Georges La Fayette. We overturned four times. However, despite bad roads, bad horses, bad coaches, and brigands,[4] we arrived in Paris safe and sound yesterday morning. I have already seen my nephews, my uncle, my general, and I have been received by everyone with the liveliest effusion. But my joy wasn't complete; you were missing from my happiness. While passing along the Rue Ville-l'Évêque, I gazed sadly at our house, where you no longer were, and I felt my heart sink. I think I was dreaming about returning to duty, to my mother, to my friends; I am sad although happy! Why sad? I don't know! Some emotions cannot be defined. No doubt, it is my impatience to see you.

I went to see Général Dupont the same morning I arrived. He wasn't there. I returned at five o'clock and found him dining with several other generals. Seeing me enter, he rose to embrace me. We clasped each other mutually with the keenest affection and with tears of joy in our eyes. Morin was ecstatic with pleasure. During dinner, the general was pleased to mention several honorable traits of mine and eulogized me. Going back into the salon, we again embraced. After so much danger and toil, this amicable reception was quite sweet for me. I was choked with emotion. There exists a real bond among comrades at arms. They've braved death together a thousand times, they've seen each other's blood run, they're also sure of each other's courage and friendship. We're truly brothers, and glory is our mother. There is a more tender, more sensitive mother whom I love even more. It is toward her that all my wishes are directed. It is of her I think when my general and my friends tell me they're satisfied with me and proud.

I wanted to go and embrace you immediately, but Beaumont tells me that you're going to come here, and Pernon has found you another lodging on Rue Ville-l'Évêque. Pons says that your financial condition permits you to come. So come quickly, dear mother, or I'll run to fetch you. Général Dupont still wishes to detain me in order to present me to all our "highnesses"; I'm not sure what to do. If you were able to come immediately, business and pleasure would join company. So, answer me soon, or I shall leave. What a sweet moment, when one recovers all one holds dear—mother, country, friends! You could not begin to believe how much I love my country. Just as we become aware of the price of liberty once we have lost it, we similarly become aware of our love of country once we have been far away from it. All these Parisians understand nothing of such language. They only know about love of life and money. As for me, because of you I know the value of life. I have already seen so many men fall at my side without hardly noticing, I regard this change from life to death as a very small thing in itself. Anyway, in spite of the little care I have taken of it, I have preserved this life that I wish to consecrate entirely to you when I have given a few more years to the service of France.

I'm going to see the lodging that Pernon found for you, and I'm going to prepare it for your arrival. I think only of that. I embrace you with all my soul.

Letter XI   (No dateline).

To Madame———

Ah, how happy and unhappy I am at the same time! I don't know what to do or say. My beloved Victoire, all I know is that I love you passionately. But I see that you are splendidly prosperous, while I am only a poor little officer that a cannon-ball could carry off before I have made my fortune at war. My mother, ruined by the Revolution, has a great deal of difficulty in maintaining me, and at this moment, on leaving the hands of the enemy, stripped, having scarcely anything with which to clothe myself, I have the look of a man who is dying of hunger rather than the son of a good family. However, you loved me as I was, my beloved and charming friend, and with rare devotion you have put your purse at my disposal. What have you done? What have I done in accepting this help? Despite my certainty that I will acquit myself in a very short time, I suffer dreadfully from this situation in which you have deceptively placed me. This is not a reproach, Victoire, no, it is not, and never will be! But if I had known you were not married and that all that wealth did not belong to you—I am wrong to say what I'm saying, it does belong to you, love has given it to you—but when I think of the ideas that might occur to *him*! He would not have them for long, I would kill him! You see that I'm mad; I love you, and I am in despair. You are free; you can leave him whenever you want, you're not happy with him; it's me you love, and you are willing to follow me, to give up a secure and fortunate position to share the hazards of my slender means. Yes, I know that you are the proudest, most independent, most disinterested being. I know besides that you are an adorable woman and I adore you! But I cannot make up my mind about anything. I cannot accept such a great sacrifice, for which perhaps I would never be able to compensate you. And then there's my mother! My mother calls to me, and I am burning to rejoin her, while the idea of losing you drives me out of my mind! No matter, one must nevertheless take a stand, and this is what I ask of you: do not decide anything yet, do not precipitate matters so that you are no longer able to retract. I am going to spend a certain amount of time with my mother, and I'm going to immediately repay you what you loaned me. Don't be angry, it's the first debt that I want to repay. If you persist in your resolution, we shall see each other again in Paris. But until then, reflect well, and above all, do not consult me. Adieu, I love you desperately, and I am so sad that I almost miss the time when I thought of you hopelessly in the wilds of Croatia.

Letter XII   Paris, 3 Floréal, Year IX (April 1801).

To Madame Dupin, at Nohant

I leave Monday. I shall then finally see you again, my dearly beloved mother, hold you in my arms! I am at the peak of my joy. All these letters, all these responses come unbearably slowly. I repent having waited for them and having put off the sweetest moment of my life. Already Paris wearies me. It is strange, but for some time I haven't found myself at ease anywhere; at Nohant, close to you, I shall ingest the calm I need. My comrades Merlin, Morin, and Deconchy are on their way. We'll be leaving our general all alone. They're not saying anything definite yet about the expeditions; I hope, however, that when they have come to some sort of decision, they won't forget the laurels of the Mincio. On those bleeding laurels, we left our weapons. Must so many brave officers and generous soldiers, who were sacrificed to gain peace, rise from their tombs to cry shame and vengeance against cowardly slanderers? You have no idea what is being said in the commanding general's[5] circle to palliate the horrible indifference with which they let our brave men be assassinated. Someone in his party, either with his permission or by his order, has dared to say, among other things, that I let myself be captured so as to give the plan and movement of our army to the enemy. Général Dupont and my comrades, who happened to be there, happily have taken on these contemptible fellows and put them in their place.

Do not impute all these delays to a cooling of my love for you. Oh, my dear mother, that would be very unjust! But consider that I have complicated matters to settle, debts to pay on all sides. Stripped by the Austrian gentlemen of the twenty-six louis that I possessed, returned without a sou, without an article of clothing, after having traveled three-hundred leagues on foot, do realize that it was necessary for me to borrow from my friends, my comrades, in order to outfit myself and return to France. Thank God, it is all paid for, but I have had some bad luck recently, I for whom everything used to turn out so well. In this campaign there were aides-de-camp who received up to three hundred louis in bonuses, and as for me, who returned after the sharing of the spoils was over, I have had nothing but debts to pay; I have undergone all the misfortunes of war. And yet you will see that I haven't ruined you and that I've spent as little as possible.

Goodbye, my dear mother, I shall pack my bags and arrive—ever too late, considering my impatience. I embrace you with all my heart. How happy I'll be to see Father Deschartres again and my maid!

Maurice.

M.E.

III

Romantic incidents. —Deschartres' unfortunate action. —The Inn of the Black Skull. —Family sorrows. —Trips to Le Blanc, Argenton, Courcelles, Paris. —Continuation of the romantic novel. —Général————. —Uncle Beaumont. —The Year IX in brief.

I hope I may be permitted, in touching upon events quite worthy of a romance, to refer to my parents by their baptismal names. It is, in effect, a chapter in a novel, but true, nevertheless, in every respect.

Maurice arrived at Nohant early in May 1801. After the first exuberant greetings, his mother looked him over with some surprise. The Italian campaign had changed him more than the Swiss one. He was taller, thinner, stronger, paler. He had grown an inch since his enlistment, a rare thing in a twenty-one year old, but probably brought on by the extraordinary exertion of the marches he had been forced to make as an Austrian captive. Despite the transports of pleasure and gaiety that filled the first days of closeness with his mother, it soon became clear that he was given to daydreaming and pursued by a mysterious melancholy. Then, one day, having gone to La Châtre to pay visits, he stayed away for an unreasonably long time. He found a pretext to go back the next day, another to return the day after that, and on the following day confessed to his mother, who was upset and unhappy, that Victoire had come to join him. She had left everything, sacrificed everything, for the sake of an unselfish and unfettered love, of which she had given him irrefutable proof. He was ecstatic with gratitude and tenderness; but he found his mother so hostile to this reunion that he had to keep all his thoughts to himself and conceal the intensity of his affection. Seeing her seriously alarmed at the scandal that such an adventure would cause and already had caused in the small town, he agreed to persuade Victoire to return to Paris without delay. But he could not convince her, nor could he even convince himself, except by promising to follow or join her soon; and therein lay the difficulty. He had to choose between his mother and his mistress, deceive or drive to despair one or the other. The poor mother had expected to keep her beloved son near her until the call came for him to resume his service—a time that could still be rather distant considering all of Europe was working for peace, which had become the unique preoccupation of Bonaparte at that period. Victoire had sacrificed everything, burnt her bridges, and could imagine no other destiny, no other happiness than sharing the life of her adored one, free of all obstacles in the present and without a thought for tomorrow or a regret for the past. But could this devoted son, on returning from a campaign that had made his mother wail, weep, and suffer, bring himself to forsake her after only a few days? Yet was it right, in the face of Victoire's passionate devotion, to speak to her of his mother's suffering and the outrage of straitlaced provincials, and then dismiss her like a vulgar mistress who has just been rash and impertinent? More than a conflict between two different loves, here were two conflicting calls to duty.

He tried at first to reassure his mother by making light of the predicament. Perhaps that was a mistake. With serious reasoning he might have moved her to pity, if not persuaded her. But he dreaded the burden of worry she was prone to create for herself and also her too obvious jealousy that for the very first time would have been justified.

There was no solution to this state of affairs. The faithful Deschartres put an end to the dilemma, making an enormous error in judgment which freed the young man from the scruples weighing on him.

In his devotion to Mme. Dupin, in his contempt for love, which he had never experienced, and in his respect for conventions, the poor pedagogue had the mistaken idea of taking drastic measures, convinced that by creating a stir he could put an end to a situation that threatened to persist. One fine morning he left Nohant before his youthful charge had opened his eyes, and made his way to La Châtre, to the Inn of the Black Skull, where the young woman traveller was still peacefully asleep. He announced himself as a friend of Maurice Dupin. Kept waiting some moments while hurried dressing went on, he was at length allowed to enter. Scarcely noticing the grace and beauty of Victoire, he greeted her in his brusque and awkward way and at once launched into a very formal interrogation. The young woman, amused by his appearance and not knowing with whom she was dealing, replied pleasantly enough at first, then playfully, and finally, taking him for a lunatic, broke into laughter. Thereupon Deschartres, who till then had maintained a dignified tone, got angry and became rude, scolding, and insolent. From reproaches he passes to threats. His sensibility is neither delicate enough, nor his heart kind enough to alert his conscience that he is about to commit a cowardly act by insulting a woman in the absence of her protector. He insults her, he loses his temper, he orders her to take the road back to Paris that very day, and threatens to call in the "proper authorities," if she did not pack up her bags right away.

Victoire was neither timid nor patient. It was her turn to ridicule and enrage the pedagogue. More rapid than circumspect in her repartee, with a gift for vivid speech, in contrast to the stammering that overcame Deschartres in moments of anger, she was a true child of Paris, shrewd and caustic. Boldly she pushes him out the door, closing it in his face, and promising through the keyhole to depart that very day, but in Maurice's company. Deschartres, furious, astonished by such audacity, reflected for a moment and decided on a line of action that added the last touch of madness to his enterprise. He went in search of the mayor and a family friend who held some municipal function or other. He may even have informed the police. The Inn of the Black Skull was rapidly invaded by these respectable representatives of authority. For a moment the townspeople thought a new revolution, or at least the arrest of an important figure, was under way.

These worthies, alarmed by Deschartres' reports, marched bravely to battle, convinced they were at grips with an army of furies. On the way, they discussed the legal means available to force the enemy to withdraw from the town. In the first place, papers would have to be requested and, if none were forthcoming, the culprit would have to depart or be threatened with prison. If papers were produced, an effort would have to be made to find fault with them by resorting to some loophole or other. Deschartres, bloated with wrath, urged them on. He would have had the soldiery called out. However, a display of military power was not judged indispensable; the magistrates crossed the threshold of the Inn, and disregarding the protests of the innkeeper, who was much concerned for his beautiful guest, ascended the stairs with equal amounts of courage and aplomb.

I do not know if they read the riot act at the door, but certainly no barricade of any sort obstructed them, and in the lair of the shrew described by Deschartres they discovered only a tiny woman, pretty as an angel, sitting on the edge of her bed, her hair disheveled and her arms bare, weeping.

The scene immediately reassured the magistrates who, less ferocious than the pedagogue, were rapidly pacified and then moved to pity. I do believe that one of them fell completely in love with the awesome person and that the other understood very well how the youthful Maurice could also have done so wholeheartedly. They began their questioning within the bounds of politeness and even with courtesy. Proudly, she refused to answer until she saw them defend her against Deschartres' abuse, reduce him to silence, and outdo themselves in treating her with paternal kindness. Then, grown calm, she spoke softly to them, with charm, courage, and confidence. Hiding nothing, she told how she had come to know Maurice in Italy and become his lover, renouncing a rich protector for his sake. She said she knew of no law that would make her guilty of the crime of having given up a general for a lieutenant, and riches for love. The magistrates comforted her, pointing out to Deschartres that they had no right to persecute the young woman and insisting that he withdraw. They promised him to induce her, by gentle and persuasive language, to leave the town voluntarily.

Deschartres did, in fact, withdraw, perhaps on hearing the gallop of the horse that carried Maurice to the arms of his beloved. All was peaceably arranged with Maurice's agreement, once he had been mollified, for his indignation with his churlish tutor was such that, God knows, in the first flush of anger he might have run after him and boxed his ears. Deschartres was nevertheless a faithful friend who had saved his mother when her life was in danger, a lifelong friend, and the offense he had just committed had also been fatally inspired by love of his mother and of him. But Deschartres had insulted and outraged the woman he loved. Sweat poured from Maurice's brow and his eyes swam. "For you was Troy lost, O Love!" Luckily, Deschartres was already far away. Crude and inept as always, he was hastening to add to the distress of Maurice's mother by drawing a frightful portrait of the "adventuress" and by predicting a sinister future for the young man, morally blinded by a domineering and dangerous woman.

While Deschartres was putting the finishing touches to his work of anger
and delusion, Maurice and Victoire were gradually being won over by the magistrates, who had become both their friends. They had taken a keen interest in
the young couple, but their first task was to protect the feelings and peace of
mind of the virtuous and respectable mother. Maurice had no need of their
well-intentioned promptings to know what had to be done. He succeeded in
making his friend understand, and she promised to leave that very evening.
However, once the magistrates had withdrawn, they arranged between them
that he would join her in Paris in a few days. It was his right and henceforth
also his duty.

He became even more convinced of it when, returning to his mother, he
found her angry with him and unwilling to admit that Deschartres had been
wrong. The first reaction of the young man was to depart, so as to avoid a violent scene with his tutor, and Mme. Dupin, appalled by the anger between the
two men, did not try to stand in his way. However, not wishing to be defiant or
disobedient to his adored and loving mother, Maurice, even seeming to ask her
opinion on the wisdom of his project, announced a brief trip to Le Blanc, to the
residence of his nephew, Auguste de Villeneuve, and then to Courcelles, where
his other nephew, René, lived. He advanced the pretext of needing to take his
mind off his distress and to avoid a painful and violent break with Deschartres.
"When I come back, in a few days," he told her, "I shall be calm again, and so
will Deschartres, your unhappiness will have vanished, and you will have no
more worries, since Victoire has already left." Seeing her bitter tears, he even
added that Victoire would probably find herself some consolation, and as far as
he was concerned, he would try his best to forget her. The poor child was lying,
and it was not the first time that his mother's slightly timorous affection forced
him to lie. Nor was it the last time, and this necessity to deceive her was one of
the great sorrows of his life, for never was there a more honest, candid, and
confiding character than his. Dissimulation did such violence to his instincts
that he could never maintain it, nor could he at all succeed in evading his
mother's acuity. And so, when she saw him mount his horse the next morning,
she told him sadly that she knew very well where he was going. He gave his
word of honor that he was going to Le Blanc and Courcelles. She did not dare
make him promise that from there he would not go to Paris. She sensed that he
would not promise, or that he would not keep it. She also must have sensed
that in keeping up appearances with regard to her, he was giving her all the
proof of respect and deference that he could, under the circumstances.

My poor grandmother, who had only just gone through mortal suffering
and worry, had to face new griefs and apprehensions. Deschartres had repeated
to her, after his stormy meeting with my mother, that the latter had said, "It
depends entirely on me whether I marry Maurice or not, and if I were self-seek-
ing as you believe, marrying him would be my answer to your insults. I know,
and you do not, just how much he loves me!" From that moment on, Mme.
Dupin was gripped by the fear of such a marriage, which at that time was
groundless; neither Maurice nor Victoire had conceived any such intention. But
to be overly concerned with a danger invariably calls it forth, and my mother's

threat became prophetic. My grandmother and particularly Deschartres hastened its fulfillment by the efforts they made to prevent it.

Accordingly as he had announced and promised, Maurice went to Le
Blanc, and from there he wrote his mother a letter depicting quite well the condition of his soul.

Letter XIII   Le Blanc, Prairial, Year IX (May 1801).

Mother, you are suffering, and so am I. And there is a guilty party
between us who—with good intentions I admit, but without any judgment or
consideration—has done us great harm. This is the first serious sorrow of my
life, since the Terror. It is deep, and perhaps more bitter than that was; then we
were unhappy but not at odds with one another; we thought the same way and
wanted the same things; but today we are divided, not in our feelings, but in
our opinions on several important issues. No greater misfortune could befall
us, and I find hard to accept the deplorable influence our friend Deschartres
exerted on you in this instance. How can it be, my dear mother, that you share
the viewpoint of a man, doubtlessly honest and devoted, but brutal and no
more able to appreciate acts and affections of a certain kind than a blind man
can distinguish colors? It exceeds my comprehension—for having carefully
looked into my heart, I cannot discover the least inclination to do you any
wrong. I feel that my love for you is purer and greater than any other love, and
the thought of making you suffer is as alien and hateful to me as that of committing a crime.

Let us try to think clearly, dear mama. How can my liking for this or that
woman harm you or endanger me in a way to cause you misgivings and endless tears? On all such occasions you have always seen me as a man on the
verge of bringing dishonor on myself, and as far back as the time of
Mlle.——— you let your anxieties run wild, as if this person would lead me to
commit unforgiveable offenses. Would you rather I were a cunning seducer
who caused trouble in families? And when I meet people of free will, must I
act the part of Cato the Stoic? That may be good for Deschartres since he is no
longer young and besides, I might add with all due respect, may never have
been faced with any sinful temptations. But let us come to the point. I am no
longer a child, and I am quite able to judge people who inspire me with affection. Some women are, admittedly, to use Deschartres' vocabulary, mere
wenches and harlots. I do not like them or seek them out. I am neither libertine
enough to waste my powers, nor wealthy enough to keep women of that sort.
But never could these vile words be applied to a woman of feeling. Love purifies everything. It ennobles the most abject beings, and all the more so those
whose only wrong consists in the misfortune of having been cast into the world
without friends, resources or guidance. Why should a woman thus forsaken be
guilty if she seeks help and consolation in the affections of a man of honor,
whereas women of good society, who lack nothing in the way of enjoyment or
consideration, take lovers to relieve the boredom of life with their husbands?
The woman who grieves and troubles you so much gave up, it is true, a man

who loved her and lavished comfort and pleasure on her. But did he love her sufficiently to honor her with his name and to promise her his future? No. Thus when I knew that she was free to leave him, I had no qualms about seeking and winning her affection. Far from being ashamed to inspire and share that love, I am proud of it, no matter what Deschartres and the tongue waggers of La Châtre may say, for among those "ladies" who condemn me with outrage, I know several who have no right to be so prudish with regard to me. I would willingly laugh the matter off, if I could bring myself to laugh, dear mother, while you are so sad for the love of me!

What, after all, do you imagine and are you afraid of? That I am going to marry a woman who would "one day make me blush"? First of all, you must know that I shall do nothing that will ever make me blush, because if I were to marry this woman, I would clearly hold her in esteem, serious love being impossible without such esteem. Furthermore, your fear, or more likely Deschartres' fear, has no foundation whatsoever. Never has the idea of marriage come into my mind; I am much too young to consider it, and the life I lead would hardly permit me to have a wife and children. Victoire no more contemplates it than I do. She was married very young; her husband died, leaving her a little girl whom she looks after carefully, but who is nevertheless a responsibility for her. At this point, she must work in order to live, which is what she is going to do; she has already had a milliner's shop, at which trade she is very skillful. She would have nothing to gain by marrying a poor devil like me, who possesses only his saber and his poorly paid rank and is determined to make no more inroads on your comforts than, excessively to his mind, he already has!

You can see then that not all these predictions of the judicious Deschartres partake of common sense and that his friendship is neither discerning nor enlightened when he chooses to put such fears into your head. On the contrary, his role should be one of consolation and reassurance. He does you positive harm. He resembles the bear in the fable who, to swat a fly on his friend's face, took a paving stone and smashed in his head. Tell him so for me, and let him change his ways, if we are to remain friends. Otherwise it will be difficult. I can forgive him being absurd with me, but not his making you suffer and pretending that my love for you is not steadfast in every way.

Besides, mother dear, don't you know me better than that? Aren't you aware that even if I had made plans to marry, no matter how desirous of it I was (which is not true in this case), your unhappiness and tears would be enough to make me change them? Can I, would I ever make a decision that would go against your intentions and wishes? Remember that it's an impossibility, and sleep peacefully.

Auguste and his wife want me to stay two or three more days. No one could be kinder. Theirs is genuine cordiality and friendship, not mere polite words. The two of them can well afford to be happy. They love one another and have no ambitions or projects . . . but neither do they have any glory! And when you have tasted that wine, you cannot go back to plain water.

Goodbye, my dear mother. I am longing to be with you and comfort you.

Still let me listen two or three days more to the solemn talk and sensible advice of my honorable nephew. I am an easygoing uncle, willing to be instructed. I need more gentle sermons than Deschartres', and I sense that the Nohant air, or that of La Châtre, would not be good for me just yet.

I embrace you with all my heart, and I love you much more than you imagine.

Maurice.

Letter XIV   Argenton.

I stayed at Le Blanc a day longer than I intended, my dear mother, and here I am at Argenton, with our good friend Scévole, who also insists on my staying two days longer and protests loudly when I hesitate to agree. Oh, mother! How my life has changed in three years! It is all so strange. I have not only played music, but good music these past few days. I am going to continue here, since Scévole remains a passionate amateur, and he's as glad to see my violin as he is to see me. Well, previously, I would have forgotten everything else and become absorbed in the music, whereas today it saddens instead of thrilling me. I am afraid of peace, and I wish for a renewal of the fighting with an ardor that I cannot understand or begin to explain. Then I remember that by once again wishing to leave you, I am creating more unhappiness for you. That thought poisons the idea of the enjoyment I would have on the battlefields and the encampments. You would be sad and tormented, and so would I. Is there then no happiness in this world? I begin to think not; madman that I am, I have forgotten it, and this great revelation leaves me stupified. For all that, far from battle I feel unable to find any diversion or self-forgetfulness. Everything seems colorless after such emotions. I had only your love to make me forget them, and now even that happiness has been spoiled because of a few moments!

A frenzy takes me when I see the troops go past, when I hear the warlike sounds of the martial instruments. We of the warrior race are a type of madman whose outbursts redouble like those of other madmen at the sight or sound of whatever brings to mind the causes of their aberration. That's what happened to me this evening on seeing a demi-brigade pass by. I was holding my violin and threw it down then. Goodbye Haydn, goodbye Mozart, when the drum beats and the trumpet calls! I bewailed my inactivity. I almost wept with rage. My God, where is the repose and freedom from care of my early years?

We shall meet again soon, my dear mother. I shall come to find calm and solace in your arms. Goodnight to Deschartres. Tell him that in these parts he enjoys an admirable reputation of being learned in agriculture and, in music, an arrant note-cracker. I embrace you with all my heart. And my poor maid as well; she hasn't cast a stone at me, not her! She can reassure and console you. Heed her, for she has more good sense than all the others.

An affectionate letter from my grandmother brought Maurice back to the fold for a few days. Deschartres received him with a gloomy and slightly arrogant countenance, and on seeing that Maurice did not come to embrace him, turned his back and went to make a scene with the gardener over some lettuce seedlings. A quarter of an hour later, he found himself face to face with his pupil on one of the garden paths. Maurice saw that the eyes of the poor pedagogue were full of tears. He threw his arms around him. Both of them wept without saying a word and returned arm in arm to my grandmother, who sat on a bench waiting for them, delighted by their reconciliation.

But letters arrived from Victoire! At this time she could not have known how to write well enough to do more than make herself understood. Her only education had been some rudimentary lessons in 1788 from an old Capuchin who taught poor children gratis to read and recite the catechism. A few years after her marriage, she wrote letters that my grandmother herself admired for their spontaneity, wit, and grace. But at the time that concerns us here, only a lover's eyes could decipher her unintelligible scrawl and understand the passionate outbursts that had not managed to find the right form in words. He did understand that Victoire had lost hope, that she felt misunderstood, betrayed, forgotten. Then he returned to the subject of his trip to Courcelles. There were fresh fears and more weeping. However, he set out and wrote from Courcelles the 28 Prairial:

Letter XV   Courcelles, 28 Prairial (June 17, 1801).

I arrived here yesterday evening, my dear mother, after a hard, though rapid, journey in the public cart. It was a very sad trip. Your sorrow and tears pursued me like a guilty conscience, and yet within me I knew I had done nothing wrong, for all you ask of me is to love you, and I feel sure I love you. Your tears! How can I be the one to make you shed them, when I wish so to make you happy! But why, after all, are you so distressed? It is inconceivable and completely beyond me. This young woman never thought I would marry her, since I myself never thought so, and whatever she said to Deschartres was the result of an angry outburst, more than justified by the harsh way he ranted at her. I cannot tell you too often that nothing of the sort would have happened if he had only kept silent. I would have seen to it that she left quietly, since her presence at La Châtre (which should not have been your concern) annoyed you so bitterly. But since matters are such, I promise never to flaunt a mistress before you, nor ever to speak of my love affairs. It will make me suffer a bit. I am so accustomed to tell you everything that happens to me and all my feelings that it seems very strange for me to have secrets from you. What a painful obligation is imposed upon me by this lamentable business and Deschartres' inconceivable rashness. Come, let's drop the subject. I don't want a quarrel with him, nor do I want you, for anything in the world, to have a quarrel with him. He can hardly be expected to mend his ways. We ought to cherish his qualities and love one another despite everything.

I roam the waterside and woods here, an earthly paradise. I was welcomed with the warmest friendship. René, along with his wife, was on an island in the park. He came for me in a boat, and we embraced on the water with so much emotion that we almost capsized.

Goodbye, my dear mother, for the time being. Do not grieve any more, love me as always, and understand that I cannot be happy unless you are, for your sorrows are mine. I embrace you with all my heart.

Letter XVI   Paris, 7 Messidor (June 1801).

As you had foreseen, finding myself only a day away from Paris, I couldn't help stopping there briefly. I've seen Beaumont and my general. My fine mare Paméla leaves tomorrow for Nohant; the general leaves tomorrow for the Limousin. He will come back in a fortnight and has promised to stop by Nohant, where I shall help you to receive him. This morning I saw Oudinot, who being somewhat more in favor than we, will, I hope, at the instigation of Charles His, request the rank of captain for me. I am also going to collect my salary, which will allow me to dress up my outfit when I go to see Cardinal Consalvi, who is here to negotiate the important business of the Concordat. It seems that he found it a very difficult decision to make this trip, and on leaving Rome was convinced he was proceeding to the guillotine. Charles His, my companion on the mission to Rome, has already gone to see his Eminence here and been cordially received. Now, now, my dear mother, this little excursion that you already see as a great extravagance will not give a fatal turn to my destiny, will perhaps improve my prospects, and will not cost you a penny. I have not yet heard anything about the twenty-six louis that M. Cobentzel should arrange to have paid back to me; tomorrow I will call on him.

Goodbye, dear mother, I'll soon be back at your side, and with heaven's help, as a captain. Don't grieve, I beg of you, and never doubt the affection of your son.

Maurice's sojourn in Paris continued till the end of Messidor. Various matters served as pretexts. The visit to Monsignor Consalvi, the twenty-six louis from the exchange commission, a series of measures in view of obtaining an advancement he neither expected nor cared about, the mare's injured withers, the Fourteenth of July festivities, such were the more or less serious reasons which covered with a rather transparent veil the days consecrated to love. The poor child did not know how to lie, and from time to time a heartfelt cry escaped him: "You don't wish me to consider the welfare of a woman who abandoned and lost everything for me! It cannot be you who feels this way, my dear mother! You would be more concerned for a servant who lost her place because she chose to follow you. Do you believe that I can be ungrateful to a woman whose heart is noble and loyal? No, this cannot be advice that you would give me! . . .

"Now then, no more grieving, my dear mother, never did I intend to bring unhappiness into your life, and the very thought horrifies me . . . .

"What ideas are you going to have next? That I don't love you any more? How can you imagine such a thing? Filial love is not a transient sentiment, and can only die out in a heartless monster."

But afflictions come in succession, and another blow was about to fall on these three people now joined by a chain of sorrows. The following letter will explain all in a few words.

Letter XVII   Paris, 30 Messidor (July 1801).

M.————[7] is a lunatic and a rascal. I have just had it out with him rather hotly in my uncle's presence, and the letter you are going to receive from him will obliterate, I hope, the painful effect of the other he had the audacity to write you. He is withdrawing every item of the accusation brought against me, so infamous and absurd an accusation that I would laugh, if it weren't the epitome of insolent and cowardly wickedness for him to go to you to blacken my reputation this way. Besides, I foresaw what has happened and expected the full measure of our sorrows to be reached by this latest addition. Anyway, I treated M.———— as was fitting, and you will see by the language he uses today that he retracts from beginning to end his preceding calumnies, that he admits the money Victoire lent mZe was returned after a fortnight by me to Victoire and by her to him, that all the "gifts she carried off in order to eat up the profits" with me, amounted to *one* diamond of little value, which she had retained inadvertently and sent back to him even before hearing of his complaints and slanders. This gentleman admits today that he spoke as he did out of anger and in a fit of jealousy, that he was wrong, and that he has no desire to go through it again. I can well believe him!

Goodbye, my dear mother, I leave tomorrow. Have no fear, I shall show you the proof of all this in writing, but I hope that you won't have to wait for proof to know that your son is not of a mind of disgrace himself. I cannot say if I am Des Grieux, but there is no Manon Lescaut in this case. As for M.————, call him anything you please, but rest assured that he won't begin to insult me again.

My business here is finished. The times do not favor the brave men by whom this peace, so sought after, was won. The status of all the generals is the same, whether they have contributed more competently or less to the cause of peace. Moreau and Masséna are on the shelf, as well as Brune. Important changes and promotions are expected, but it seems to me that more is being done to gratify the enemies of the government than to retain its true friends. Clearly the confirmed traitors and conspirators have the highest hopes and pretensions. Time will tell! No matter, France is my mistress, and I serve no other.

Till we meet again, my dear mother, I love you with all my heart and would prefer death to having really done you wrong.

From M. de Beaumont to Mme. Dupin   Paris, 30 Messidor.

Set your mind at ease, my dear sister, everything went well. Of Maurice's bravery we were all aware, but new to me was his composure, his perfect sense of restraint and decorum. As for his complete self-possession, it befits an older man and is more impressive than any display of anger. I expected there would be a duel, and since such matters are familiar to me, Maurice considered my presence at the explanation as useful as that of any of his merry and dazzling mustachioed comrades. I must confess that my reasons for going were not very Christian, for this Général——— is a poltroon, and I had no fears for our child. Only words were exchanged, though with much warmth, but M.———, to all appearances, seemed satisfied. Moreover, the facts were against him, as he himself admitted. He is still enamored of the young woman, and during Maurice's absence I am going to try to reunite them, for it would be better for her to return to him than to hazard her future with Maurice. Besides, your fear of this love affair is not without grounds. *She* is charming, has much natural wit and true sensibility—all of which present a greater threat. But never fear, I shall keep an eye on them. Your son loves you tenderly, and if you watch over him, you will always be able to manage him. It would be wiser, perhaps, to conceal your fears from him than to reveal them.

All proceeds well here despite the expectation of peace, which distresses our young hero. But the grand hero who presently rules over all things seems determined that we enjoy it. If he can protect himself from plotters, all will go well, but there are so many of them!

Goodbye, my dear sister. I am not very happy with my brother, the duke. Maurice spoke very well on my behalf, but there too plotters have come between us.Greetings to our friend Deschartres, yours now and forever.

Godefroy De. B.

Formerly an abbé and coadjutor to the archbishopric of Bordeaux, Uncle Beaumont, son of Mlle. Verrières and Duc de Bouillon, grandson of Turenne and therefore related to M. de La Tour d'Auvergne, was a witty and sensible man. As a young priest, he had enjoyed a brilliant, if stormy, existence. He was ideally handsome, scintillatingly gay, brave as a hussar lieutenant, a poet in the vein of *L'Almanach des Muses*, and both domineering and lenient; that is to say, soft-hearted and quick-tempered. He also had an artistic streak and would, in other surroundings, have attained the stature of a Gondi,[8] whose early life his had somewhat resembled. Withdrawn from the bustle of public life, he lived quietly after the Revolution, not at all friendly with the turncoat clergy, whom he scorned to some degree, but not narrow-mindedly nor with bitterness. From this time onward a woman ruled his life and brought him happiness. He was always a faithful friend of my grandmother and a fatherly comrade to my father.

But as can be seen from the foregoing letter, this handsome abbé shared the morals of the gracious society of his times, morals which the society of today has not improved, the only difference now being that graciousness has disappeared. My great uncle was a rare combination of insensitivity and effusiveness, at once harsh and kind. It came to him quite naturally to spurn Victoire's noble impulse and place her again under the yoke she had just managed to throw off. "To be rich and lead an amusing life," he thought with his gentle epicurean cynicism, "will be much better for her than to be poor and live with the man she loves. To forget her and her romantic self-sacrifice will be much better for Maurice than to be encumbered with a wife and to upset his mother.

I'll keep an eye on them. I sympathize with this young woman and can give her 'good advice.'" The fact that he was entirely sincere shows the gulf that separates personal interest from any sort of ideal view of society.

Yet he neither favored my father's passionate attachment nor did he ever seriously oppose it, and when Maurice married Victoire, he treated her as his daughter and attempted to reconcile her with my grandmother.

Maurice returned to Nohant in the first days of Thermidor (the last days of July 1801) and remained there until the end of the year. Had he resolved to forget Victoire in order to put an end to the struggle with his mother? It is unlikely, since the young woman waited for him in Paris, where he joined her later, more enamored than ever. But for those four months I have no trace of their correspondence. As the letters ran the risk of being intercepted at Nohant, the recipient probably destroyed each one after he or she had read it.

If we sum up, as we have done for the preceding years, the year 1801 which we have just traversed with my father, we shall see how the life of society at large has an effect on that of the individual.

The year IX is—in fact, if not in name—the last year of the Republic. From the outset of this period, the attempt on his life by an infernal machine gave Bonaparte the most vivid sense of his own importance, a feeling of power much more than of danger, and a singular trust in his personal destiny. It is impossible to know exactly where the superstition of a fiery imagination ends and the charlatanism of a disenchanted and skeptical mind begins in this grandiose manner of entrusting himself to fortune, in this audacity which henceforth forms the foundation of his powerful ambition. Glory has been till now a kind of religion for him and for everyone. As of 18 Brumaire he could still have halted his notions of government and let others do for him what he subsequently did himself for his own all-too-obvious advantage. After the attempt on his life, he no longer has a genuine belief in an alleged destiny which, in his case at any rate, had only been an instinctive faith in the vital forces of France. He, as an individual, comes to personify the human race; he no longer believes in anything but himself; his guiding star is his will-power; his God is his own intelligence. In this respect his words are symbols conveying a hidden meaning that he alone can decipher and of which France is the dupe.

But gradually, under the impact of this lofty reputation, France would lose faith in herself and believe only in Bonaparte; or rather each Frenchman, following the example of Bonaparte, would believe uniquely in himself; the word "country" would take on another meaning: no longer the safeguard of the common good, it would become the guarantee of each individual's interests. The common good, in our societies where inequality still reigns, is yet of a higher order than material possessions. It consists of honor and liberty, and although less than humanity has a right to desire and expect, remains the ultimate foundation of all ideals, the point of departure in the quest for the integrated world humanity longs for. Everyone can take this noble quest to heart, everyone can work for this dawning of fraternal equality. It is still a very abstract idea, but sublime abstractions rule the souls of men and exalt their characters by elevating their thoughts.

Individual interests produce quite a contrary effect. No government constituted on an individualistic principle can satisfy everyone, no one being exactly alike, and the infinite degrees of inequality in fortune and rank create as many adverse interests as there are men engaged in the struggle. It was Napoléon's very great error to believe that, on the strength of handsome presents, of concessions, enticements and an apparent impartiality, he would make all classes happy with his administration and convince them it was in their interest to maintain it. He wore himself out by efforts of incomparable skill, prodigious energy, and exquisite finesse. He won over a great number of pawns whose support he obtained by linking their rise or fall to his own; he formed a majority based on patronage, which helped him govern. He failed to create a new society able to exist independently and survive the loss of its chief. He used his glory as a way to dazzle the masses, to which they submitted with too much infatuation not to reject it soon after with too much ingratitude. By 1815 this man who, like Louis XIV, had taken himself for France, discovered that he was merely a man whom France had abandoned.

It was for want of a social religion, not for lack of genius nor patriotism, that Napoléon failed in his design. It is impossible to know what would have resulted if he had tried to create a new society, but he made no such attempt, and clearly in re-establishing with infinite care the old society, he wasted his magnificent intelligence and erected an ephemeral structure atop whose summit he was unable to remain.

The year 1800 had been glorious and memorable. His faculties had reached their zenith. In 1801 his deterioration became evident in his diplomatic relations. The universal peace he wished to establish was premature. It was demanded by individual interests and the greed of the industrialists; he took the needs of a certain class to be the needs of humanity. Wars fought for principles are not settled by bartering possessions and conceding territory. From this point on, Bonaparte, in presuming to negotiate between the great powers, showed immense conceit. In the absence of principles, France's cause was no longer that of the Revolution but took on the paltry proportions of a transaction. The transaction seemed tremendous and its least detail echoed through the universe, but it was the concern of the European rulers and not of the people, who only took an interest because they were deceived about its consequences and misunderstood where their real advantages lay. So it was that, after much negotiating and many diplomatic encounters, the English industrialists, their profits being endangered, succeeded in frightening the British people and making them long for war the day after the signing of the peace.

Moreover, this peace so shrewdly constructed lasted barely two years, and the letter of the treaties—being concerned only with material interest, which are by nature immoral—promptly corrupted their spirit. The same proved true of all the treaties concluded between the great powers; the nations were drained of their blood for the sake of insincere contracts in which the ulterior motives of the ruling sovereigns and their backers prevailed.

We have only to recapitulate Year IX to recognize the uselessness of all these great deeds, so magnificent in themselves but so wanting in their results.

After methodically playing the charming coquette in the guise of a republican general to the Russian aristocracy, which coquetry singularly diminished the revolutionary pride personified in Bonaparte, it turned out that we had written on sand: Paul I was assassinated by the aristocrats of the North, jealous of our influence. In vain did we cleverly organize the neutral league. England destroyed our alliance at Copenhagen with one savage and forceful stroke. We began, in the first days of April, to negotiate the peace with England; this negotiation lasted six months, during which we lost Egypt, so impetuously acquired under the fatal inspiration of a restless and self-regarding genius. In July our navy covered itself with immortal glory at Algeciras; vain sacrifices, vain glory. Spain, as an ally, lacked energy and would not fight to establish our principles but rather to make sure that a child received a crown in Italy from the hands of the First Consul—another transaction, nothing but a transaction! The 4th of August our sailors engaged in heroic combat off Boulogne against Nelson's flotilla. Blood flowed on both sides, bravery abounded, bodies floated on the water. Our only gains were the maintaining of our conquests and the guarantee of protection for our allies. Our principles gained nothing, since all these agreements could be renounced and their execution deferred; Egypt, where our blood had been shed, and Malta, for which we had found no use, could be retained like weapons forever aimed in our direction; alliances could be formed and plots devised against us.

There was no sign that our ideas had influenced other nations to make changes in the rulers who governed them. We had addressed these nations in our propaganda; momentarily affected by the wonders we were working, they went back to their selfish preoccupations when we ourselves provided the example of a hurried return to the past. The seeds of revolution that these nations possessed were less ready to flower than ours, but had we properly nurtured them, they would have overthrown their despotic governments. They watched France deny her beliefs and crouch beneath the wing of a man stronger and more powerful than all the despots of Europe. How could they believe in the brotherhood of republics? They again adopted the hostility of contending monarchies. The peace had finally been signed, but no one had put down his weapons, and war was being planned everywhere on a scale that would astonish the world. The English came to see Paris; our salons were open to them; Fox conversed with Bonaparte; they were miles apart. Every Englishman understood that in the matter of national cupidity we were children compared to them, and with patience and obstinacy, they would defeat us for sheer wiliness and craft. Poor Frenchmen that we were! Such was not our path, nor our ideal. We were hurled along by false systems, foolish majesty, and deadly prestige.

Our personalities suffered the consequence of the unfortunate impulse Bonaparte had imparted to France. Hearts closed up, ambition became the ruling passion, the intriguers feverishly sought their rewards, the virtuous were sad and seemingly dormant while waiting for some great event which would awake in them the noble vision of a war of principles. Behold my youthful father, already bored with inactivity and wishing to flee from himself into new battles. Condemned to repose, he was no longer happy, because he felt a chill in the life of society around him. We shall soon see him, mocking and indignant, taking part in the intrigues of the new court, and not knowing what to do with his youth, his passion, and his ideals, very soon his life will be prey to an exclusive love. He needed adventure, difficult and worthy deeds to accomplish. He will marry a daughter of the people, which means he will carry on and apply the egalitarian ideas of the Revolution in the intimacy of his own life. He will struggle in the bosom of his own family against aristocratic principles and the world of the past. He will break his heart, but he will have fulfilled his dream of equality.   *P.B.*

IV

Extracts of letters. —Society's swains. —Plans for marriage.
—Musical studies. —Englishmen in Paris. —The return of luxury.
—Celebrating the Concordat. —The ceremony at Notre-Dame.
—What the generals think. —Deschartres in Paris. —Leaving for
Charleville. —Wild animals. —Masonic initiation and acceptance.
—Recurrence of aristocratic prejudices in certain minds. —Reply to
Deschartres. —Life Consulate. —Frustrations of an aide-de-camp in
peacetime. —Disgrace and discontent at headquarters.

1802

Having spent the end of the summer and all of autumn with his mother in
Nohant, Maurice returned to Paris toward the end of 1801. He wrote with the same
regularity as in the past, but his letters are no longer the same. They no longer consist
of the same spontaneous outpourings, or whatever spontaneity they have is somewhat forced. The poor mother evidently has a rival. Her loving jealousy hatched the
very harm she dreaded. In the first letters of the year X, his discussions focus particularly on the inheritance of M. de Rochefort, and he entreats his mother not to take
the advice of business minds but to rely on the Villeneuves' word and settle everything promptly, for the legal proceedings between the counsels and the interested
parties were still going on. At some point he tells her, thanking her for sharing her
feelings on the matter, "Auguste is overwhelmed by your letter. His indecision and
scruples would never have ceased had you not taken it upon yourself to remove
them. He instructs me to tell you, until he replies to your letter himself, that you have
taken a truly noble and grand role in the whole thing and that he feels honored to
have had you treat him this way. He speaks the truth. He and his brother are loyal
friends to us. I told Pons to wrap it up quickly, so that all we'd have left to do is sign.
Can you imagine a more comical situation than ours? For two years our counsels
have been in litigation on our behalf, while we love one another—laughing, dining,
and running around together—and get along in spite of them."

Extracts of Letters

Paris, 14 Frimaire, Year X.

.... Word has it that my general[6] is to make an inspection of Beurnonville's
infantry. Thus we will have no other work than digestion, while receiving our pay

within the confines of Paris. Our campaigns will from now on be waged on the parade grounds and the Champs-Elysées. We are now on very good terms with the *padrone*. Yesterday, my *padrone* took him a detailed plan of the Battle of Marengo. He was welcomed, dined there, and all goes well on that side. . . .

Love to you, kisses to my maid, and a thrashing to Deschartres. . . .

28 Frimaire.

We are leaving for the Ardennes the day after tomorrow, and the most fearsome preparations are taking place at my general's. It is like an arsenal. All you see are cutlasses, bayonets, double-barreled guns, and powder kegs. We are getting ready to wreak great havoc among the wolves and the boars. Reincarnated as Hercules, we're on our way, for lack of anything better to do, to purge the land of savage monsters. Paris and its delights haven't softened our proud hearts, and just when everyone else is establishing their winter quarters at the fireside, we're going out to brave the frost. To hell with peace! Why can't we put our energy to better use? . . . .

Deschartres' old friends would surely like to see him in the mayor's sash.

4 Nivôse.

You thought I was already in the Ardennes, my dear mother, and I did too, but just as I was climbing into the carriage with my general, just as I was shouting to the coachman, "Fire away!" comes a little note from Général Murat, which causes us to go back upstairs and unpack our baggage. We learn that the Consul has designs on us. . . .

Today we celebrated the famous Mincio crossing. Almost the whole right flank was reunited at my general's place. Couplets were the order of the day, and I made up a big parcel of bad verse which was entrusted to his servant to carry in in the middle of dinner. The general hurriedly unsealed it and burst out laughing. It was a mock-heroic narration of the whole incident. He read it aloud, and everyone laughed while also exclaiming over how true it was to the facts. They soon guessed the author and would have had me intone my work, but in order not to repeat what had already been read and reread, I chanted a kyrielle of other couplets on the same subject, a cheap enough way to be showered with glory. Still laughing and singing, we got up from the table and went back into the salon where we embraced one another, Dupont starting with me. If ever equality and fraternity could be seen to reign in earnest among a group of men, it was then and there.

We are taking part in a play at the Rodier's next Sunday. René is forsaking his little suits, which are no longer in style, and I shall leave an impression in my black breeches. Tomorrow we all dine at Vitrolles'. . . .

Paris, 5 January 1802.

. . . . My general is definitely leaving for the Ardennes, and I remain here, immersed in harmony. My music professor, whose name is Gérard, is an excellent teacher. It is a struggle, but I'm hoping to derive great enjoyment from being initiated into the mysteries of composition; I take a two-and-a-half-hour lesson every day and already see myself creating an opera, which I'd like to be able to do at least by a year from now. My head is always full of melodies, and I find quite awesome and off-putting all the work necessary to learn how to bring them into being, but I'm slaving away, and when I get impatient, I swoop down on my piano and practice some cavalry charges. The general laughs like crazy at my plan to write an opera. He says that if they hiss me off the stage, I won't be able to get out of challenging the whole audience to a duel to prove to the public that aides-de-camp should be treated with respect.

We have been inseparable the past few days, my general and I. He spoke to me in all honesty; he is not enamored of the "master"; he says it's hard to know how to take him, that he has fits of temper during which he cannot be approached. It is therefore not the time for me to be asking for a promotion, and I'll keep quiet. However, the general thinks that we'll receive some important mission when the "boss" returns.[7]

I went to the military show; they had us collect in the quarters, and there I saw once again all the aides-de-camp of the Army of the Reserve and the Army of Italy; they received me with open arms, and because, in our joyful mood, we were talking very loudly and all at once, Général Mortier, in charge of the Paris division, came to beg us to be quiet, since only we could be heard. Bruyère, Berthier's aide-de-camp, answering him for the group, said that was the best thing that could happen, considering that we were saying such fascinating things....

All of society's favorites[8]—the G's, the M's, the P's—are the most seasoned young prigs I know. They can talk for an hour without saying anything, they make all their decisions by trial and error, and they have their hearts so set, under the guise of good manners, on imitating each other, that to know one is to know them all. You say that we must live in this world, my dear mother, and it is possible, but nothing could be more stupid than all those people who think they're deserving because of a name whose glory doesn't even belong to them. "Be men, if you want my esteem, and if you are only dolls, don't be so vain and impertinent" is what I'm always on the verge of saying to them, but my morality is outmoded and has never found favor in society. With you, I can afford to think aloud on the subject.

18 January.

.... Yes, Mme. de La Marlière[9] absolutely wants to marry me to a certain Mlle. de Ramière,[10] who has an income of twenty thousand pounds and much talent and wit, according to her. In addition, she is reported to be very pretty. Certainly, my dear mother, a twenty-thousand-pound income could do me no great harm; I would surely like to have it to give to you, but in spite of the vaunted charms of the heiress in question, I swear to you that I don't feel the slightest desire to get married. The least little thing can come along to mar the happy plans one has indulged in! First of all, you must know that this young woman is very pious—devout, in other words. How would you get along, please tell me, with a daughter-in-law who would be scandalized by your opinions? You can surely see that one mustn't rush into these things, and you will surely allow me to give it some thought. I am not absolutely overjoyed to be in such a miserly condition, but I am taking it in my stride, and I have even come to notice that the truest and purest pleasures are not those which may cause us financial ruin. With my music teacher and my rented piano, I have a much better time than in society, and at night, when I forget myself and work on my music until three in the morning, I have the feeling that I'm much calmer and happier than if I had gone to the ball. I am intent on becoming a good harmonist, and I shall succeed. Nor do I neglect my violin. I am so fond of it! My finances are not in very good shape. I was obliged to outfit myself again from head to toe when I went to the military show. But since I pride myself on being one of Apollo's children, if I'm a beggar, it's in the nature of things.

I saw Lejeune[11] at the show. He looked for me all over Paris when he was doing his painting of the Battle of Marengo. He says he's inconsolable at not having "my head at his fingertips" in order to put it into his composition. I shall soon send you your shawl via a very reliable person whom I don't know, but who is leaving for Berry soon.[12]

. . . . I made the acquaintance of several great ladies: Mme. d'Esquelbecq, who deigned to find me "to her liking," according to what I've heard; Mme. de Flahaut, who just published a novel which I was rude enough not to have read; and Mme. d'Andlaw. René is still the best of friends, but he has a great fault: he drinks water like a fish; fortunately it's not contagious. . . .

3 Pluviôse.

. . . . I went to see my house.[9] It is occupied by twenty medical students, and M. Laurent complains that he has only thirty pair of sheets. That's really not very much to keep those fellows in clean linen. But I remonstrated with him that since they didn't hold much store thereby, it was a useless expense. We will see what happens when the artists of the Louvre are lodged, as we are assured, in the Sorbonne. This will bring the "girls" into the neighborhood.

. . . . Yes, certainly, I'm still working at it, but when my father said he had learned how to compose in twenty lessons, I believe he was making fun of us. Nothing is more abstract or more difficult. At the moment, I'm skipping over dissonance to get to modulation. If you knew how hard I work at it! I feel that time is running short, and in the spring I shall have to leave it all behind! The only things in my head are false fifths, minor sixths, tritones, and diminished sevenths. I dream of them all night.

I swear to you by all that's sacred that V——— has a job and costs me nothing. Why do you persist in worrying so? Never will I keep a woman, as long as I'm a poor devil, since I'd be forced to keep her at your expense. Besides, you don't know her and you judge her on the word of Deschartres, who knows her even less. Let's not discuss her, my dear mother, I beg of you, as we wouldn't see eye to eye; only rest assured that I'd rather blow my brains out than deserve a reproach from you and that to cause you grief is the most mortal sorrow that could come to me....

This morning, I rode M. le Daim [Mr. Buck], a horse the general bought for a hundred louis. He is delightful, but he is full of the devil, and he walks the length of the boulevard on his hind legs, like a performing dog. However, I didn't follow the example of the smart set, whose rage is to go riding in the Bois de Boulogne, and who may be seen falling off like flies....

4 Pluviôse.

How kind you are to insist on paying for the teacher and the piano rental! All right, I shall reimburse you at Nohant with correct and beautiful harmony. By next month I hope to be able to write accurately.[13] Général Dupont is coming back from the Ardennes; he sent me some venison and boar, instructing me to have part of it sent to Général Moreau....

.... Tomorrow I'm going with my nephews and their wives to an enormous ball at Lady Higginson's....

Paris, 11 Pluviôse (February 1802).

.... My god, what are you telling me? Whom on earth could I love more than you? You find my letters less loving than in the past. I have no idea why; I find nothing changed in my heart, unless it is that my happiness diminishes as I distress you. Your stay in the country is making you melancholy. It gives me pleasure to contemplate your coming to spend next winter in Paris, so that I'll chase all that away....

I made a "splash" at Mme. d'Esquelbecq's. Thinking to pay me a great compliment, the society ladies found that I had an "English" look. What an idea! Paris is full of serious-looking Englishmen, which look is acknowledged as in the best taste. Apparently, I wore an expression of boredom, and that was taken for a sign of depth. It is true that, by contrast, our small winsome males seem affected and flighty, having found no better way to prove their nationality. If it is because I was in no hurry to take on the manners of this social set that I'm thought to be as serious as an Englishman, all well and good.

To give you an idea of the standards of that society, the two heroes, the two models, the two idols of the eminent ladies are Charles and Juste de Noailles. Their father, who is perfectly absurd, has told it everywhere that Charles resembles the Apollo Belvedere and Juste the Antinoüs.[10] A few prudes repeated it, and as a result, Charles, who believes he is Apollo, is as rigid as a statue and faces his head into the wind. Juste leans his head to the side, like Antinoüs. You may think I'm making jokes, but it's God's truth. I heard it from Laure, who knows all the little family secrets and, far from being mean, is kindness and tolerance personified. I'd never be done, if I wanted to tell you all the foibles of this beautiful set of youth. The Englishmen can see through them, and it makes me furious to see them laugh up their sleeve, without my being able to take them to task for deeply scorning such samples of our nation. There are others of us who awkwardly attempt to ape them and who have their hearts set only on disparaging our country before foreigners; it's revolting, and the foreigners are the first to shrug their shoulders. All those young lords, who are soldiers in their own country, question me avidly about our army, and I answer them with ardor by reciting our immortal exploits, which they too cannot help but admire. I especially recommend that they shouldn't judge the public mind by what they hear in society. I insist that national spirit is as strong among us as it is with them. They might doubt it if we let them lose sight of our victories. But you can understand that I exit from that world sadder and more disillusioned.

Goodnight, my dear mother, I love you more than my life. A thrashing to the mayor, and to my maid I send the thimble for stitching and trimming.

24 Pluviôse.

. . . . Everything is settled with my nephews. In addition to the house, behold the proud owner of forty thousand francs. Damn it, I never imagined myself so rich! You must immediately take out ten thousand francs to pay all your debts—Pernon, Deschartres, my maid.[14] I don't want them to wait; I want you to get rid of all those little afflictions. You have done more for me than I can ever return. Thus, my dear mother, don't quibble over it, or I'll sue to make you accept my money. With the rent from the house and my pay, you see me in possession of an income of seven thousand eight hundred forty pounds. My word, that is quite nice, and I have no reason to brood. With the income from Nohant, we now have between us sixteen thousand pounds[15] a year, which we can enjoy starting next year, and without debts! It is wonderful, and I am really happy to see you spared any more worries. Pay, pay everything you owe, and if only half of the forty thousand is left, I assure you, it will be enough. . . .

Mme. de Bérenger has informed you of the death of the Duc de Bouillon. Beaumont is much affected by it; in spite of their arguments, they really loved each other like brothers. . . .

For my debut, I arranged a quadrille for full orchestra; I hummed it to Julien, who asked for it and played it at Mme. de La Briche's ball with great success. He begs me to have it printed along with his, which pleases me immensely; Mme. de Bérenger wants me to call it "Elisa," after her daughter-in-law. Mme. de La Briche's ball was magnificent. This time my look was found to be "noble," but somewhat "bearlike." That was literally the pronouncement of the eminent ladies. . . .

Paris, 7 Ventôse (February 26).

. . . . So give no more thought to this marriage; Mme. de La Marlière ought to have written you that the young lady was promised to someone else, who probably suited her better than I. I missed the boat by a fortnight, so it seems, and the fact is I don't know if I would have pleased her, because we never met. I couldn't care less; what really distresses me is the loss of one of my friends, Gustave de Knoring, Oudinot's aide-de-camp, whom I sometimes spoke to you about and with whom I used to smoke those big Turkish pipes. At a big dinner given for all the greats by the Ambassador of Denmark, Baron Armfeld, my poor Knoring started a quarrel with a Hanoverian officer. They fought with pistols the next day. They fired six shots at thirty paces. Knoring wanted to lessen the distance to ten. It was his adversary's turn to fire, and he was shot in the chest. If he had taken one of us as his second, this misfortune would not have occurred. Never has it been permitted to fire seven pistol shots. The weapons would have been changed. But he had taken the Prince of Hohenzollern as a second, and princes are known for their stupidity. We buried our poor comrade with all military honors. The procession began with a squadron of dragoons, and a batallion of grenadiers surrounded the coffin. We accompanied it to the Madeleine, where he was buried. The silence was broken only by the wail of the trumpet and the somber roll of the drum. Three discharges over the tomb brought an end to the service. This young man is missed by everyone who knew him. We had done the whole last campaign together.

Général Dupont is finally back. Morin, Deconchy, and I made up our minds to torture him until he went to the court. If he forgets to show up there, they will forget to give him any work and that kind of inaction is not much to our liking. . . . Write me, please, how much I must pay my servant, I forgot. Give Deschartres' ears a tweak for me.

24 Ventôse (March 15).

. . . . My general is suddenly on very good terms with Bonaparte. The latter sent for him, and after a few pleasant reproaches for having stayed away, gave him the command of the second military division, a force of twenty-five thousand men now occupying the Ardennes and the country of Luxembourg. Thus, here we are, fully back in action. Bonaparte added that as soon as Dupont saw a more advantageous job, he should ask him for it.

. . . . The arrival of my mare gave me great pleasure. The Bois de Boulogne is charming; new roads have been cut, and there are daily such a number of calèches and carriages of all kinds, that the guards are forced to direct traffic as at Longchamp. It seems inconceivable, considering we just emerged from a revolution in which all the wealth was seemingly destroyed. Well, there's a hundred times more luxury now than in the old regime. When I remember the solitude of the Bois de Boulogne in '94, while I was exiled in Passy, it seems like a dream nowadays to find myself carried along by the crowd. The crowd consists of Englishmen, foreign ambassadors, Russians, etc., all displaying a magnificence that Parisian society would like to eclipse in its turn. Longchamp will be splendid.

. . . . The princess is marrying M. de La Tremouille, who recently found himself in prison for coming to publish his banns in Paris while he was under surveillance elsewhere. The tearful princess went to see Fouché: she's not afraid of jailors and jails.

. . . . So, my dear mother, don't tell me I no longer like your long letters. I was quite well aware that for a fortnight they've been shorter, and I surely felt something missing in my life. . . .

5 Germinal (March 26).

Our second division includes the departments of Marne, Meuse, and Ardennes. We have twelve forts, eight cavalry regiments, and three demi-brigades. We leave in two weeks. Send me via Frédéric the small bay horse who breaks everyone's legs. We, at this end, will make him tow the mark, and he'll show us a bit more respect than Saint-Jean. Now Beaumont wants to have a hand in getting me married; he's putting all the wigged heads of his acquaintance on the alert. He's as engrossed in this project as Bonaparte was when confronting the fort at Bard. I myself think my dignity would suffer if I appear to be too eager, which I admit, I'm not. . . .

The cannonade is sounding at this very moment for the signature of the peace. Mothers and wives are rejoicing; we, on the other hand, are making somewhat wry faces. . . .

Paris, 23 Germinal (April 13).

Paris is beginning to bore me considerably. It's always the same thing: great affectation, great vanity, and ill-concealed ambition, which will show itself at the slightest provocation. I'm convinced that even the *padrone* won't deny himself, when he dares. The Concordat is not making the slightest impression here. The people are indifferent to it. The rich, even those who pride themselves on being religious, are very much afraid that taxes will be raised to pay the bishops. The military, who can't get a penny out of the war offices, curse when they see the episcopal palace of Paris furnished at the government's expense. You must have read the papal bull written in the style of the Apocalypse, which threatens the transgressors with the wrath of Saint Peter and Saint Paul. My own opinion, for lack of a better one, is that we're heaping ridicule on ourselves. There's going to be a very beautiful ceremony at Notre-Dame, during which they'll enlist the aid of Paesiello's music and every piece of military pomp to help us swallow the mass.

They're preparing a great luncheon at the Porte Maillot . . . All the "lovelies" will be there. They're paying one louis apiece to share two windows among thirty people. Everyone there will be "titled," the Birons, the Delaigles, the Périgords, the Noailles.[16] It will be "chaaaming." Damned if I'll go!

Paris, 30 Germinal, Year X (April 20, 1802).

. . . . The newspapers have undoubtedly given you a very highflown account of the Concordat festival. I was in the cavalry procession with Général Dupont, who had been ordered to participate, along with all the generals now in Paris. Therefore, they all put in an appearance, a little bit like animals under the trainer's whip. We paraded into Paris to the acclamations of a multitude who were more charmed by the military pomp than by what the ceremony stood for. We were all very brilliantly decked out, and I personally was magnificent—Paméla[17] and I, gilded from head to toe.

The legate was in a carriage, and the cross was carried in another carriage preceding him.[18] We didn't dismount until the portal of Notre-Dame, and all those beautiful horses richly caparisoned, prancing and wrangled around the cathedral, were a singular sight to behold. We entered the church to the sound of military music, which suddenly ceased at the approach of the canopy under which the three Consuls were placed and conducted in silence, and even rather awkwardly, to the platform intended for them. The canopy under which the Consuls were received looked like it had come from a bed in a country inn—four mangy plumes and a mean little fringe. The Cardinal's was four times richer and the throne splendidly draped. Not a word of M. de Boisgelin's speech was heard. I was alongside Général Dupont, behind the First Consul, perfectly entranced with the visual beauty and with the Te Deum. Those at the center of the church heard nothing. At the moment of the elevation, the three Consuls knelt. Behind them were at least forty generals, including Augereau, Masséna, Macdonald, Oudinot, Baraguey-d'Hilliers, Lecourbe, etc., none of whom moved from his chair, which caused a strange contrast. Upon leaving, each mounted his horse and went his way, so that only the regiments and the guard remained in the procession. It was five-thirty, and we were dying of boredom, hunger, and impatience. In my own case, I had climbed on my horse at nine in the morning, without lunch, and with the fever that keeps tormenting me. I went to dinner at Scévole's, and today I am writing from my general's. I saw Corvisart, the First Consul's doctor. He assured me that in two or three more days I'll be able to travel and go give you a kiss before leaving for our headquarters. I think my impatience at seeing you again is preventing my recovery.

I send a kiss to the mayor. He would have caused quite a stir at the ceremony, with his sash and his deputies....[19]

Paris, 18 Floréal (May 8, 1802).

I'm leaving Wednesday, my dear mother, and I shall arrive at Nohant on Friday, if you send me some horses at Châteauroux. You see that travel is becoming easier and that Nohant is no longer at the end of the world. I have done everything under the sun to get rid of my fever. I've sent Sir Corvisart on his way; he came to see me every five minutes, had his mind on other things while taking my pulse, and charged six francs for each visit. I consulted an empiricist, who treated me à la Deschartres, with an emetic, a dark medicine the next day, and an herbal tea as bitter as bile the day after that. It seemed as though he was readying me for the next world, so conscientiously did he administer his treatment, but the fact is I'm cured, and I far prefer a jolting cure to a lingering illness. I'm bringing you two dresses instead of the one you asked for. It is not excessive, and I don't want you to wear rags when I am required to be trimmed with gold. The dresses are to my taste, and they've been approved by Apolline and Laure,[20] experts who dress to perfection. I received a fine letter from Deschartres. Tell him that with his pedant's style, his apothecary's logic, and his eunuch's morality, he deserves to treat M. de Pourceaugnac's[11] ailments of body and spirit.

After a month's stay with his mother, Maurice leaves Nohant, spends two or three days in Paris, and meets his general at Charleville, where Victoire was soon to settle, in spite of Deschartres' sermons, which, as we have seen, were not very popular with his pupil. However, that did not discourage the poor pedagogue. He persisted in viewing Victoire as a schemer and Maurice as a young man too easily taken in. He did not realize that the effect of this erroneous judgment would be to make my father more aware each day of his mistress' lack of selfishness, and that the more unfairly she was accused, the more he would try to do her justice and the more attached to her he would become. In this instance, Deschartres used business as a pretext to accompany Maurice to Paris, fearing perhaps that he might remain there rather than take up his duties. At the same time, my grandmother was expressing to her son a desire to see him married, but the worry that the young man's freedom was causing her was getting him accustomed to the idea of giving up his precious freedom. Thus everything they were doing to detach him from his beloved only served to hasten the course of destiny.

During that brief stay in Paris with his pupil, Deschartres felt he should not leave him alone for an instant. The effect was to play the tutor somewhat belatedly to a young soldier who had been liberated through hard and glorious warfare. That my father was kind can be seen from his letters, and deep down he loved his tutor tenderly. He could not really be rude to him and was still enough of a child to derive a certain pleasure in outwitting, like a true schoolboy, the comical surveillance of the grump. One morning, he slipped away from their common lodging and went to meet Victoire in the garden of the Palais-Royal, where they had arranged for lunch at a restaurant. Scarcely had they met, scarcely had Victoire taken my father's arm, when Deschartres confronted them as conclusively as Medusa. Maurice brazened it out, greeted his Argus pleasantly, and invited him to be a third at their luncheon. Deschartres accepted. He was not exactly an epicure, but he loved fine wines, and they were lavished on him. Victoire decided to approach him with witty and gentle humor, and by dessert, he seemed to have become somewhat human, but when it came time to part, my father wishing to take his girlfriend home, Deschartres relapsed into his gloomy mood and set out sadly toward his furnished room.

The stay in Charleville seemed very dull to my father, until his friend came to settle in the home of some decent bourgeois, where she paid a small fee for her board. They imagined she was secretly married to my father, but that was not yet the case. From then on, they almost never were apart and thought of themselves as bound to each other. This irrecusable bond brought about the birth of several children, one of whom lived only for a few years and died, I believe, two years after my birth.[12]

My grandmother was ignorant of all that, as she was also ignorant of the marriage when it took place. From time to time, Deschartres, always on guard from near as well as far, made a worrisome discovery, and did not spare her his findings. Discussions with Maurice resulted, which reassured her for a while but had no visible effect on each of their situations.

Here again are some extracts of letters. If my only wish was to record an ever witty and playful correspondence, I would omit nothing, but since my goal is to show the serious nature of a human existence and the effect of life in general on the emotions of an individual, I shall continue to abridge a great deal.

Charleville, 1 Messidor (June).

. . . . We are dressed to kill, with our great plumes, gold braid, and handsome steeds. They talk about us from here to Soissons and Laon (birthplace of Jean-François Deschartres)! But such glory means little to us, and we would prefer to be less fine than to use up our ardor parading. Besides, people are as curious and prattling here as in La Châtre. The general already had the wish to engage in a love affair, but he no sooner talked to the same woman twice than a huge clamor arose in the three towns of Sedan, Mézières, and Charleville. . . .

He is still the same excellent, brave, capable man, but hesitant, finicky, and expending his energy on doing nothing. The fact is that we have nothing at all to do. Deconchy acts as chief of headquarters and always looks like he's scribbling something. Morin makes envelopes, unmakes them, and remakes them. The general has his horses harnessed and leaves them at his door for three hours before knowing whether he'll go out or stay in. There you have our daily existence. . . .

. . . . I send a kiss to my maid, who can no longer ask me every minute what I did with my cane. . . . My only consolation is that this life of tranquility will permit me to go see you more often. . . .

11 Messidor, from Bellevue near Sedan.

We are still doggedly perched on the heights of Givonne, outside of Sedan. The general, who likes the countryside and the hunting, finds he can more easily satisfy his tastes here, and we are bored to death with riding the woods and fields with him in dreadful weather. I secured a piano, which would serve as my consolation if I could take advantage of it, but scarcely do I sit down than I must be off and running. . . .

Charleville, 16 Messidor (July).

We came back here four days ago to thrust ourselves from country pleasures into the whirlwind of society. The whirlwind consists of silly geese of both sexes around a card table, intent on winning a single crown from one another over a four-hours period. I yawn to the point of dislocating my jaw. Someone here had given me the reputation of being a charming young man, but it had to be revised—I'm now considered a bear. I was less bored at Bellevue; there I had my piano and my violin, with which one could live in a cave. We established a kind of menagerie there that I hasten to rejoin when I need some compensation for the society here. We have a charming wood owl which alights on your fist like a falcon; an eagle-owl caught in the cliffs of the Ardennes, with a seven-foot spread, a terrifying creature, mean as the devil. As for quadrupeds, we have a fox, a young wild boar, a roe deer which follows us like a dog, and a wolf cub, which is my very own. I've taken over his education, and he seems quite inclined not to benefit from it, for he runs away at top speed when I call him. Otherwise he is charming, ferocious, sly, and fights all day long with the fox, who is his personal enemy. In these I hope you recognize the pleasures of a prince, which won't cause you any worry, my dear mother. Hunting, hawking, and animal fights!

.... You amused me very much with the quotation from the Archbishop of Bourges. It is to be expected that we shall see these good princes of the church rear their heads the day after the state has made great sacrifices for them; it is natural that we be thanked by threats and anathemas. You are right, and the general, to whom I read that part of your letter, was very struck by it. The revolutionary tribunes are reproached for their barbaric language, bloodthirsty ideas, constant punishment and threats, and here are the pretended apostles of the religion of peace and forgiveness insulting us and threatening us with celestial wrath. If they could condemn us to something worse than eternal damnation, they would do it. The guillotine is only child's play, an instant of fear and suffering; unfortunately their imaginations cannot create for us anything worse than hell. So don't be surprised at my friendship for wild beasts. They are the essence of gentleness and innocence compared to human beings.

Charleville, 27 Messidor.

For want of real dangers, one may seek imaginary ones, which is what inspired me to become a Freemason. The ceremony took place yesterday, and to give you an idea of all the bad jokes and mystifications aimed at me, suffice it to say that I had provoked these gentlemen to do their worst, formally defying them to intimidate me. To that effect they used all their known methods. I was locked up in every conceivable hole, nose to nose with skeletons; I had to climb into a steeple from which they pretended to throw me, and what I admired most in it all was the appearance of reality they were able to give all these illusions. It was, upon my word, wonderful, and quite entertaining. They had me descend into pits, and after twelve hours of going through all these niceties, they tried to pick a nasty quarrel with me about my good humor and facetious tone; then they decided I should undergo the ultimate torture. Consequently, they nailed me into a coffin, carried me during the night, in the midst of funeral chants, to a church, and I was taken by torchlight down into a vault, put in a grave and covered with dirt, to the sound of the church bells and the De Profundis. After which everyone left.

In a few moments, I felt a hand come to pull off my shoes, and while exhorting it to respect the dead, I gave the biggest kick that could be given. The shoe thief went off to report on my condition and affirm that I was still alive. Then they came to get me to initiate me into the deepest secrets. Prior to the burial, I had been permitted to make my last will and testament; I had bequeathed the vault in which I had been enclosed to the colonel of the 14th, for police use; the rope by which they had lowered me, to the colonel of the 4th

Cavalry, to hang himself; and the bones I was surrounded with, to a certain fearsome fellow mason who had dragged me all day long into cellars and attics while pretending to have saved me from great danger. This proof of my gratitude amused these gentlemen, whom I heard laughing in spite of the gravity of their roles. But what amused me the most, when everything was over, was Morin's anger at an individual who showed great surprise at the way I withstood the tests. Morin was so incensed at all their surprise at his comrade's fortitude, that he would have had everybody draw swords....

Charleville, 1 Thermidor (July).

....I have to tell you of my general's unusual whim. He had heard somewhat vaguely that I was the grandson of Maréchal de Saxe, and he began to question me about it in detail. When he learned that you had been acknowledged by an act of parliament and that the King of Poland was my forebear, you have no idea what effect that produced on him. He speaks of it to me twenty times a day; he overwhelms me with questions. Unfortunately, I was never overly concerned about all that, and it is impossible for me to trace my family tree for him. I don't remember your mother's name, and I have no idea at all if we are related to the Levenhaupts. You must help me indulge this whim of his and give me information on the subject. He wishes to send me to Germany with letters of recommendation of the minister of the interior and the generals, Moreau and Macdonald, so that I will be acknowledged as the only remaining offspring of the great man. I am quite wary of giving in to such an extravagant idea, but I don't want dismiss too abruptly this mania of Dupont's because he pretends that, with my name, I should be a captain, and that he feels confident of obtaining this rank for me momentarily; I feel I deserve it on my own merit, and I shall let him proceed. Do you remember the time when I didn't want sponsorship? That was before I became a soldier; I had beautiful illusions about life, and I thought that to be brave and intelligent was enough to succeed. The Republic had put that mad hope into my head, but barely acquainted with the reality, I recognized that the old system hadn't changed, and that Bonaparte is, I believe, fonder of it than he seems.

The rapid rise of certain men, Caulaincourt among others, is certainly due to favor. Speaking for myself, I shall not dance attendance on favors, but if my friends choose to get me what's due, I'll let them....

I have received a letter from Deschartres. It's entirely friendly and pleasant-sounding. It consists of a short course in morals for the use of egoists and fools. How can a man with so much courage and devotedness in managing his own behavior counsel me with such platitudes? Is it due perhaps to his prejudices? Tell him for me that the canon's life he leads can inspire him with nothing he needs to understand my age, my situation, my character, and my views. All that won't keep me from loving him, but let him know that on certain matters he will never have the least influence over me. In addition, I intend to answer him myself soon, with the frankness obligatory between friends. Let him take care of you; let him keep you loyal company; let him look over your business; let him plan your garden and make you eat its beautiful fruit; let him administer his commune marvelously, and I shall forgive him his outbursts.

Don't worry, my dear mother, my general has no reason to be dissatisfied with me. No, I shall not take steps directly to obtain the rank of captain. The idea of soliciting fills me with disgust; but they will act on my behalf, and I shall always deserve their intervention and justify the zealousness of my friends. *I love you better than life.* That is what I have to say to you, and never doubt it. . . .

To M. Deschartres   Charleville, 8 Thermidor, Year X.

It is very kind of you, my friend, to go to such trouble on my account. Be sure that I am keenly aware of the value of a friend such as you; you put into everything that concerns me a zeal that I cannot acknowledge enough, but let me tell you, without circumlocution, that in certain respects this zeal goes too far; not that I wish to deny you the right to busy yourself with my conduct, as you do with my business affairs and my health, a right owing to affection, and I shall know how to submit to it even when it wounds me; I believe I have already proven that to you under delicate circumstances, but the temper of your zeal makes you see things darkly and to take for tragic things which are not. This is tantamount to seeing things falsely, and the friendship I bear you does not oblige me to join you in error.

When, for instance, you predict that "at thirty" I will be a victim of the "infirmities of old age," and for that reason I will become "incapable of great things," and all that because at twenty-four years of age I have a mistress, you don't frighten me very much. Besides, your logic is most unfortunate when you offer my grandfather, the marshal, as an example, when he was of precisely the "gallantry" that I eschew and who nevertheless won the battle of Fontenoy at age forty-five. Your "Hannibal" was a fool to fall asleep in Capua with his army; we Frenchmen are never more rubust and brave than when we leave the arms of a pretty woman. From my point of view, it is much more wise and chaste to give in to the love of a single woman than to capriciously change women each day, or to go to prostitutes, for whom I admit I have no taste.

It's true that to be consistent with your own logic, it suits you to label as "prostitute" the person to whom I am bound. It is evident that you no more know what a prostitute is than you probably know what a woman is. I take it upon myself to teach you the difference, for I have already known somewhat the life of a hussar, and because I knew it, I hastened to get out of it. We have tilted enough lances over this subject for it to seem useless to me to go back to it, but because you persist in accusing her, I shall persist in defending the one I love.

A prostitute, since you still need it explained, is a being who speculates with her love and sells it. There are many such in the world of society, though they may have famous names and much-frequented salons; I wouldn't stay with one of them for a week. But a woman who meets you when you're down on your luck, who resisted you when your situation seemed glorious, and who gives in to you when you're dressed in rags and dying of hunger (which is how I was when leaving the hands of the Croatians); a woman who keeps strictly faithful from the day she started loving you, and who throws your hundred-louis notes in your face and tramples them in anger, then, in tears, picks them up and burns them, when you wish to provide her with some support upon receiving a small inheritance; no, a hundred times no, such a woman is not a prostitute, and she can be loved faithfully, earnestly, and defended for everything against everyone. Whatever the past of such a woman may be, only a coward could reproach her for it when he profited from her love, when he received her services, and you know very well that without Victoire's help, I would have had a hard time coming back to France. Circumstances force our decisions, often in spite of ourselves, when we are in our youth, without resources or support. Women are weaker than we and, induced by us, who boast of leading them astray through their weakness, can easily be lost. But if you surround the greatest saints in paradise with all manner of seduction, let them struggle with misfortune and abandonment, you'll see whether all of them fare as well as the very women you believe deserve condemnation.

Therefore you are mistaken, my friend, and that is all I have to say to counter the advice you believe to be good, which I consider bad. As far as my mother is concerned, I beg you not to urge me to cherish her. For that I need no encouragement from anyone. Never will I forget what I owe her; my love and veneration for her are inviolable.

Goodbye, my dear Deschartres, I embrace you with all my heart. You know better than anyone how attached I am to you.

Maurice Dupin.

From Maurice to His Mother

Well, yes, my dear mother, I must admit, it is not sadness, as you imagine, that I feel at the turn my life has taken, but discontent. We see great changes taking place in public life, which bode nothing good.[21] Certainly that removes all the difficulties which might have arisen at the First Consul's death, but it is a total return to the old regime, and in view of the need for stability around the most crucial offices of the state, there will hardly be a way anymore to exit from the least crucial offices. You will have to remain where chance cast you, and it will be as before, when a brave soldier remained a private all his life, while a coxcomb became an officer at the master's pleasure. You will see that you won't rejoice long over this kind of monarchical restoration and that, for my sake at least, you will miss the gamble of war and the great republican concept of competition. The post I occupy is not unpleasant in itself, and in time of war, it is brilliant, because it gives us exposure and activates us. But in peacetime, it is rather stupid, and between us, barely honorable. We are, after all, only armed lackeys, dependent on all the whims of a general. If we want to go out, we find we must stay in; if we want to stay in, we find we must go out. But in wartime, it has an attraction; it is not the general we must obey.

He represents our country's standard. He has our will at his command for the good of the public, and it is all right when he orders us, "Go to the right, and if you're not killed on that side, then you'll go to the left, and if you're not killed on the left, then you'll go straight ahead." It is part of military service, and we are only too happy to receive such orders. But at a time of peace, when he tells us, "Get on your horse to accompany me hunting, or come escort me on my round of visits," it is no longer so amusing; it means we are obedient to his personal caprice; our dignity suffers, and mine is, I admit, put to a hard test. Dupont, however, has an excellent disposition; few generals are as benevolent and as generous; but after all he is the general and we are his aides, and if he had not made us his servants, we would be useless, since there is nothing else to do. Deconchy, who is chief of staff, bears it with patience, although day before yesterday he received a small but rather hard-to-take insult. The general was at his mistress's, and made him wait in the yard for three hours. He almost left him then and there, and let all hell break loose. Morin is very carefree and always answers, "It makes no difference to me" to everything that's said to him. As for me, I always tell myself:

> It makes such a difference, that I want no part
> Of any of your meals
> And wouldn't even want a treasure at that price.[13]

So, I have the greatest desire to rejoin my regiment, and because of it, I am going to write to Lacuée, the great doer and reformer. . . .

By virtue of my "high merit and my admirable conduct under stress," I have recently been designated "mate," and I shall soon become "master."[14]

Bellevue, 6 Fructidor.

. . . . We lead an errant, vagabond life, pursuing boars and does across the woods and rocks. Night takes us by surprise and sends us to seek shelter in the first neighboring castle which falls to hand. Scarcely does daylight reappear than we start again on our life of destruction, stopping only to eat our roasted meat at the foot of some pine tree, on the edge of clear brooks where we cool our flasks. The cliffs and precipices do not permit us to hunt on horseback, and the general, who boasts of being a great walker, is soon panting with exhaustion. At first he laughed at us, imagining we would have a hard time following him, but I think he is now somewhat regretful for taking us out. In my particular case, I've recovered the legs I had in Croatia; I leave behind the nimblest guards; I tear down mountainsides, scale ravines, leap over hedges, trying to expend my surplus energy and rediscover the illusion of war. So that the Ardennais hunters compare me to a *brocart*, that is to say a four-year-old roebuck, not so much for his headdress as for his agility.

Today is dedicated to rest, and tomorrow we have a date in Bouillon to attack a boar. Nothing could be more comical than to see the general emaciated, sunburned, unrecognizable, insisting that he is not fatigued and still pretending that he spends his nights reading and writing. It is in style to imitate the great man,[15] but in this case it is for naught.

Charleville, 20 Fructidor (September).

.... We got back only yesterday. To cover the Ardennes deserts, we had formed a sort of caravan made up of three calèches, two cabriolets, a diligence, and a huge baggage wagon filled with food and beds for the ladies, four of whom came along. The party would have been pleasant had it not been for the unruly restlessness of the general, who after having hunted from four in the morning to six in the evening, wanted to leave again during the night, to cover another eight to ten leagues, for other hunting meets. So that instead of relaxing, we spent the night getting lost in the woods and tumbling into the ditches. Four people who were in a calèche turned over and are still disabled.[21a] The general also took a spill out of his buggy and doesn't want to admit he hurt himself. If we were at war, all this would be magnificent, and what we find ridiculous here would be sublime on a battlefield. What is annoying is that because he always wants to get there ahead of everybody, arriving two days before anyone else and attacking two hours too soon, he causes the hunt to fail, and we get hell from all the other hunting parties. We break our backs, and nothing worthwhile comes of it. Perhaps it was somewhat the same at Mincio. We were all as eager and foolhardy as he, but that crossing had no particular value to us.

You consider my desire to go to my regiment a whim. You reproach me for wanting too much freedom. No, my dear mother, I would be more subjugated in the regiment than anywhere else, but I would be a slave to service, to duty, and not to the whim of a man. The general staffs are in total disfavor. Dupont is on the shelf, and I'm at a dead end. The pride of the great man's general staff has reached its peak, and anything that seems to imitate its power will always be kept at arm's length. Every general, under this new system, is necessarily considered a rival if he has any merit, or an enemy if he doesn't. Those in his circle are presumed to share his desires and his opinions. All those men who wielded power before the immortals descended cannot be looked on with favor; their glances and criticism are feared, and even the mocking young aides-de-camp (I tell you this on good authority) who didn't kneel down at Notre-Dame to salute the return of a great show of glitter are feared.

What is even more annoying to me is that I can't return to my regiment without a new order from the Consul. The one just received detaches the aides from their corps, and orders them discharged if their general has just been. It is therefore a massive threat, and exactly like Lacuée. I cannot be reproached however for having joined the staff; the First Consul himself and Lacuée advised me to do so, telling me that it was the most advantageous post wherein to obtain distinction. But now everything is changed! ...

Charleville, First Complementary Day, Year X (September 1802).

.... Monseigneur the Bishop of Metz, whose diocese includes our division, came just in time to moderate our hunting pace to that of a processional. We had to follow the canopy in full dress, up to the see, listen to the great mass and the Te Deum, and in addition, swallow a small pastoral sermon by the great vicar. Today we're giving a big dinner for the Monseigneur, of whom, by the way, I have made a conquest, by my "decent" appearance. It's a jesuitical compliment, because he perhaps noticed that I was among those least charmed by the dull oratory.

Tomorrow, before the sun "has reddened the mountain peaks," we are leaving again for the hunt. Indeed, since it was mandatory, my taste for it returned intact, as "in my younger days" when I was at Nohant. I'm now among the most skillful, and surely the most indefatigable. We'll be back for the first day of Vendémiaire, which we should celebrate by a little war on the plains between Mézières and Sedan. Both parties have already agreed on how many prisoners are to be taken by each side; nothing is yet settled on the question of how many dead and wounded. . . .

Durosnel wrote me to explain in the greatest detail the decree that concerns us. It is the height of ingratitude and injustice. We are no longer attached in any way to our regiments. If we have complaints about our generals, too bad for us; we may leave them, but we cease to be soldiers. They are turning us into an order of servant—even worse, since we cannot change masters. On the other hand, the staff assistants retain all their freedom and all their advantages. It is highly inconsistent, and apparently there are some creatures they wish to reward. Everything is falling into place so as to assure them a court, and there is no lack of courtiers. Their breed has been preserved. *P.A.W.*

V

Summary of the Year X. —The Concordat and M. Thiers.
—Religious sentiment during the Republic. —Napoléon's religious
skepticism. —The cult of the Supreme Being. —The Concordat and
the Restoration. —Vote on the Life Consulate. —My father. —The
religion of love.

I shall proceed no further in my father's life story without casting a brief
glance at the two most important events of Year X, the Concordat and the Life
Consulate. The signing of the peace treaty, which greatly occupied the attention
of the French public at that time, is today only a minor recollection, a passing
event which had no solidity and which was soon considered null and void.

Furthermore, it is obvious that these three political actions of Bonaparte—the peace treaty, the Concordat, and the Life Consulate—are three
aspects of a single concern, of a determined personal purpose. The first two
paved the way for the third. By means of the peace treaty, he came to terms
with the bourgeoisie; by means of the Concordat, he came to terms with the old
nobility and also hoped to gain the respect and trust of the masses. Thus peace,
however beneficial, and religion, however sacred, were no more than the
means he employed to prepare for the seizure of absolute power. Soon he
would be forced to tear up the treaties and again take up arms in order to maintain his dictatorship; soon he would give the Church to understand that, if he
had momentarily feared, he had never respected it, and it would have to bow
before him with the rest.

Neither the legislative branches nor the army wanted the establishment of a
state religion. The bourgeoisie had not the slightest desire for it, and if they had
had the courage of their convictions, they would have spurned it with disdain, for
this was the very class that had toppled the Church, and all of the intelligent men
in its ranks were disciples of Rousseau or Voltaire. But Bonaparte reduced the
bourgeoisie to silence by promising peace with the other nations of Europe, thus
insuring the development of industry and the security of trade. The bourgeoisie
did what it has done ever since: it betrayed its principles and silenced its convictions or preferences, when these conflicted with its financial interests. The army
demonstrated its scorn and anger more openly and for a longer time. But the First
Consul was well aware that, in the case of lasting peace, the interests of the army
could not fail to make common cause shortly with those of the bourgeoisie, and
in the case of a war in the near future, the army would quickly forget its griefs
and would pay scant attention to religious problems.

This oft-praised Concordat was one of the most fatal detours in Napoléon's glorious career, one which laid the groundwork for the hypocritical despotism of the Restoration in a most natural way.

It was a purely political act, since the First Consul did not believe in the Catholic religion and had refused to have his marriage to Josephine consecrated at the very moment he was opening the portals of the cathedral of Paris to the papal legate.

There is no greater profanation of a respected rite than to impose it on others without at the same time accepting it oneself. That is turning religion into a plaything, mocking both the faith that is established by law and the nation that is forced to accept it. It is the age-old lie proclaimed by atheists, that religion is a necessity for women, children, and the masses, but they want none of it for themselves. Bonaparte let himself be convinced or taken in by this lie.

Certainly religion is necessary not only for the masses, women and children, for the simple-hearted and the weak-witted, but for all of mankind—heads of state, nations, republics as well as monarchies.

More than that, public religious rituals are needed, as are laws which enforce respect for whatever the conscience of the people proclaims is the highest expression of their intellectual and moral life.

But that religion must establish itself by faith and not by force, by free choice and not for political reasons. No man has the right to impose a religion on his brother until he has understood and freely accepted it. No lawmaker has the right to re-enact its establishment when the nation has rejected and broken with it.

Any religion which does not acknowledge the law of humanity's spiritual progress, or if you will, continuing revelation; any law claiming divine origin which dictates that, at a given moment in the life of humanity, God has spoken His final word to men, must inevitably be buried under its own ruins, along with any law of human origin which is imposed on mankind as the ultimate enunciation of man's own wisdom.

This truth has become practice in legislative affairs; conservative politics and constitutional governments have drawn from it their fundamental premise, as did the revolutionary movement. Each term and each session of these bodies which create the laws of constitutional societies see laws repealed, amended, unearthed, or created according to the needs or the fears of the moment. This principle is by now indestructible. Its application would be excellent, if all of society were truly represented.

Religions have not followed this doctrine and have, on the contrary, proclaimed the principle of immutability, which entails the practice of intolerance; thus logical and sincere nations have rejected all religion and found themselves temporarily plunged into atheism. Skepticism emerging either from pain or indifference was the next stage in this desperate protestation. Politics then came up with a subtle distinction, albeit irrational and illusory, between spiritual power and temporal power. Politics had been forced to this pass at certain moments in order to prevent its course from being hampered by the fulminations of the Church, and also to prevent the Holy Ark of the past from being shattered too abruptly. For example, at this very moment[22] it would be difficult for the King of France and his ministers, still more difficult for the legislative bodies which are supposed to represent us, to debate among themselves the tenets of our faith and make an arrangement with the head of the Church other than a political and constitutional alliance.

But if ever in our history during the past century there was a moment when it might have been possible to raise this great question with good prospects for success and bring it before the true jury of public opinion, it was precisely at the period when Bonaparte negotiated the Concordat. The Revolution had shattered everything: philosophy had put everything to question. The anarchy and immorality of the Directoire had already made every sane and honest soul feel that if the repudiation of a false religious authority was legitimate, the absence of all religion was a monstrous situation and a state of mortal illness.

And let it not be said that people had fallen into a kind of stupor which prevented them from questioning their opinions and coming to know their own minds. Had this been the case, it would have been yet another reason for law-makers to grant them time to meet and deliberate, instead of dumbfounding them anew by raising before their eyes the specter of the past. But that was not the case. There are historical untruths that everyone repeats without having examined them thoroughly, and I beg pardon of M. Thiers, but he deceives us because he deceives himself when he asserts that the majority of the French accepted the Concordat joyfully and that Bonaparte displayed, in this instance, greater intelligence, relevancy, and ingenuity than anyone else. On that point, M. Thiers (I presume the comparison will not anger him) sees and thinks as Bonaparte did. He believes that a state religion is an indispensable instrument of government, but he does not believe in that religion, and he would not have been able to kneel in all good faith, on that day when, for the first time in a decade, an orthodox prelate raised his hands in blessing over the heads of those in power as they bowed before him in the cathedral of Paris. Suffice it to say it was used as a *means*, in order to prove that they had no respect for religion, which must be an *end* in itself.

No, it is not true that the majority of Frenchmen were indifferent to this great problem—to have a religion or not, "To be or not to be" as Hamlet says, hanging in mortal agony between life and death. It is certainly true that the retinue of Roman Catholic clergy again taking possession of France by decree of the First Consul was greeted by indifference. People were as though bewildered by the surprise move, paralyzed by the unexpected. There had not been sufficient time for them to ask themselves whether they could come to terms within themselves with the horrible idea of nothingness by returning to the religion of the past, by re-examining a great heresy of the past, or by awaiting the light which reflection throws on such serious issues. They saw the ghost rise from its tomb and let it proceed. They were weary of every kind of war, that is true, but not stupefied by fatigue to the point of giving up their personal opinions. And so each individual kept his right to believe, to repudiate belief, or to continue to seek an answer. On this point, things remained absolutely as they had been. Catholicism gained not a single convert and only the sad and empty triumph of our citizens growing still more accustomed to no longer taking the Church seriously.

However, don't those last days which separate the Republic from the Empire show that even if the cause of progress had not triumphed it had at least taken root in the minds of those whose social background ought to have made them hostile to these tentative efforts at peacemaking?

Indeed, this period that has been described to us as one of intellectual apathy and sterility was quite different than it seems today, in view of the triumph of Bonaparte's personal vision. There were still some extraordinarily vigorous elements, as there are in eras of dissolution and renewal. It is not the absence of ideas that makes these periods seem apathetic and undiscerning; on the contrary, it is the multiplicity and diversity of ideas that make them irresolute, slow to act, unsure of themselves. We are in a similar crisis today.

From 1798 to 1802 was a particularly uncertain and troubled period, and as people in times of extreme skepticism—in accord with a law that seems bizarre but reveals something very significant about the functioning of the human mind—were inclined to believe in the supernatural, each individual attempted to resolve his personal perplexities by surrendering responsibility for his destiny to "fortune's favorite," to the "miracle worker," as Napoléon was then called.

Well, the miracle worker, fortune's favorite—despite his intelligence, which was prodigious indeed, and which fortuitously enabled him on more than one occasion to foresee and implement the course of destiny—did not fully comprehend the advantage he could take with regard to moral truth of a society so inclined. He exploited it very successfully in accordance with his theory, which was totally secular, since it was centered on his own conduct. He did not see that a nation so profoundly shaken by new ideas was capable of producing something greater than the unlimited power of one man and that, had that one man always been sensitive to the call of Providence, he would have been able to utilize his remarkable power to accomplish a religious reform which would have been manifest of French progress.

Far from cultivating the generous instincts which at that time were diffuse but actively brewing in the heart of every French citizen, he used his genius only to repress such instincts and utterly destroy them.

His great intelligence was veiled by a cloud the moment he ceased to understand that his mission was not to make us return to pre-Revolutionary days, but to push us forward by every path.

The Revolution had, however, come to a point where, weary of violence, recognizing its mistakes, regretting the past which it had too swiftly destroyed, hoping for higher goals in the future, it might have entered a new phase, under new leaders with uncorrupted ideals, instead of dissolving into anarchy like a vanished dream. Bonaparte wanted order, and he was right; but had he applied his basically administrative genius to the re-establishment of order, he could have accomplished it quite as well without destroying the republican ideal and smothering its fervor. He sensed that a religion represented by ceremony was necessary, and he was right. Religious sentiments are not enough. After the

Revolution had swept away Catholic ritual, these sentiments were more powerful than they had been in France for several centuries. Not for several centuries
past had evangelical doctrine defended itself more heroically against the calumnies heaped upon its noble breast. Certainly men were better in 1800 than in
1750, although they might have been guilty of many errors and even crimes.
They were more enlightened, more enthusiastic, closer to the ideal. But they had
lost sight of their faith. They had yielded to such a wave of reaction that they
had forgotten that the finer part of their hearts and minds came from the Scriptures. At times they believed themselves atheists, or at least genuine deists, disciples of the "religion of nature," when they were actually closest in their feelings and actions to the early Christians. This bizarre situation could not last.
Humanity cannot lie to itself very long with impunity, without destroying its
beliefs; merely a vague instinct for the beautiful, the true, and the good does not
constitute all the morality, all the religion that humanity needs. This instinct is
only a result of principles whose precepts humanity has lost or broken with, and
it is precisely upon these lofty instincts, thrown into turmoil by a social revolution, that a well-defined truth must naturally come to be grafted.

That is what Bonaparte did not understand, or did not want to understand.
Those "ideologues" put everything in question, he thought. They will return to
order only through confidence, and to confidence only through obedience. I
need the assistance of their priests to maintain their respect for the old hierarchy,
which I shall re-establish for them with ceremonies briefly modernized but
which will soon be identical to the old.

It may even be that Bonaparte did not push his reasoning this far and that
he saw in this whitewashing of the papacy only a means to make his usurpation
palatable to the ancient European monarchies and to pious Italy in particular,
which he was transforming into a republic until he could make it his kingdom
and make the city of popes an inheritance for his *dauphin*. He seems particularly to have shown his contempt for French public opinion by imposing the consequences of the Concordat on the nation. What would he have done had that
opinion made itself felt in the form of a popular uprising? Would he have
silenced it with cannon fire?

Is this the way, then, that altars are set up again and a religion restored?
Isn't it rather the way to deal it a death blow, and can one blame the young men
in the army for criticizing the staging of the event?

To criticize is easy, I hear you say, but can I define for you the religion
that Bonaparte ought to have proposed to the people? No, I shall not attempt to
define it, because I am not the French people of 1802. Even if I had in mind
along with my contemporaries a concept eminently suitable for the present time,
it would not have been applicable a half-century ago. Every era harbors the relative truth that suits its needs and that, unchanging in its essential nature, must
adapt its rites, elucidate its symbols, expand its concerns in accordance with
humanity's intellectual and moral progress. Besides, that is not the real problem.
I do not claim that Bonaparte should have, nor do I even imagine that he could
have, made himself the representative of a new faith. But without assuming, as
Mohammed did, the multiple role of religious innovator, warrior, and lawgiver,

couldn't he have said to himself, as all the leading intellectuals of the period did, "Christian doctrine is still the most noble, the most pure expression of the past. No sane mind, no just soul rejects or denies it. Let us keep the Christian faith; let us make participation in its religious services free and accessible to those who do not wish to do away with its ancient ceremonies. *But*, the Catholic Church has lost, in some respects, the concept of true Christianity. The attitude of the clergy has become dangerous; let us put a restraint on the power of the clergy, and since this cannot be simply a material restraint, since what is most necessary is that a moral understanding be reached on the essential doctrinal points the clergy will preach and teach to the people, let us ask the Church to declare its position on fundamental social issues; let us ensure that the Holy See call a council, or renounce being recognized in France. Let that assembly, that solemn and decisive hearing, have all the pomp and publicity that will make the whole world and France in particular witness to the condemnation of Catholic absolutism and to the resurrection of the Scriptures. Let the world finally know where it stands on those esoteric doctrines of the papacy, on the Jesuit society, and other branches. A discussion of this scope is not unworthy of my participation and that of the intellectual elite. It is needed; one day it will be inevitable. May that day come through my influence, my skill, my aspiration, which is broad as heaven itself! If those gifted with powerful intellects do not offer themselves to support and win the cause of Christ; if the priest triumphs over the Messiah; if divine revelation does not emerge, radiant and alive, from the obscure and contradictory interpretations of the Church; if France has no interest in this supreme debate which is to settle her conscience, her morality, and her unity; if this council does not give impetus to life-giving truths, for nations, for kings, for the Church itself, I shall at least have fulfilled my mission and truly attempted the salvation of humanity."

Napoléon saw only the material side of things. He busied himself with the naming of bishops, the salary of the priests, etc. Those were questions of secondary importance. Ill will and evil ambitions should have been rooted out, hidden intentions and political intrigues exposed, had he been impelled only by his personal political aims. He accomplished more difficult things than that, and would have done that, too, if he had been sustained by an inner faith.

I am not raising for discussion here the possibility of the destruction of the Church or its ritual in France. I do not even mean to imply that the liturgy and rites of Catholicism ought to have been subject to any regrettable attacks on their practice. At that time, there could be no question of such an overthrow, and it would undoubtedly still be too soon to try it, but the real duties of man in society had to be settled, and we had to know how the Church would understand them from then on.

Such discussion might have forced concessions from the Church on certain basic issues, concessions it could have freely labeled "elucidations," complementary to their previous explanations. Once officially back on the right track, practicing tolerance, charity, and Christian brotherhood, its clergy would have remained quite rightly silent concerning the sentences passed on those members who had been troublemakers and conspirators. Otherwise, remaining beyond jurisdiction and free of obligation, they carry on, and will always carry on with full justification, that eternal secret society which works in silence against all political authority, whether it be called republic, empire, or monarchy.

By a council, it is true, the Church might have been provoked to suicide at that time. What harm would that have done, if it had proved to the universe that not a single spark of life still flickered in its breast? But it could, by the same token, have revived, rediscovered the noble impulse that many of its members had experienced in the early days of the Revolution. It could have renewed itself, rebaptized in justice and truth for centuries to come. Would Chateaubriand not have risen up to bedeck it with poetic garlands? Weren't there scholars, philosophers, poets, even mystics, throughout the world, great heretics and great saints who would have emerged from the masses, where they remained unheard and unknown, who would have shed light on every facet of the vital questions raised by public conscience?

After all, had a sentence, with justice and foresight, been passed on Catholicism—a religion which was still considered by some people of that time to be absolute revelation and which is today, for many, a series of successive revelations awaiting their realization and continuation? No, it was condemned without due trial, it was swept away in the whirlwind, which still lends great authority to what is true in it, or great influence to what is false. One more reason not to re-establish the Church without submitting it to free and thorough examination—unless Bonaparte's secret plan might have been, as one may still imagine, to expose the Church to new attacks while crowning it with flowers and embalming it for the tomb. An intention as ambiguous as Bonaparte's on this score gives rise to more than one hypothesis, and that is what makes it culpable.

The impulse that led Robespierre to re-establish the kind of religion he had dreamed up—an impulse without sufficient insight, without deep enough self-awareness—was at least a sincere impulse; as fleeting and ineffectual as this bid might have been, it left a more noticeable impression than one might think on the public consciousness. If it was sacrilegious, it was not a premeditated sacrilege, enacted in cold blood. It was as naïve and ignorant as a sacrifice offered by savages to the Great Being. But savages are not skeptics; they adore God as best they can, and the people of Paris were more believing on the Champ-de-Mars in '94 than when they were gathered around Notre-Dame in 1802. This is not to say that any comparison can be made between the religion of the Jacobins and that of the Apostles. But hypocrisy defiles everything it touches, and such are the strange mistakes into which it forces men.

Via the Concordat, Napoléon resurrected and consecrated the ancient divorce between temporal and spiritual power. This was, even from the viewpoint of his own authority, a major error, and I do not understand how he committed it without foreseeing the consequences. Didn't his long and painful negotiations with the Court of Rome, his stinging quarrels with the papal legate, give him to understand in advance that the Holy See at that time was neither more sincere nor a greater believer than he? And when he had finally won the petty victory of getting the Pope to give his blessing to the heresy of constitutional priests, didn't he see clearly that the reconciliation wasn't real and that, in the name of temporal power, he would have to crush the resistance, stifle the protests of spiritual power? The classes at both extremes of the social scale, which the official re-establishment of Catholicism was supposed to win over to his cause—the old nobility and the peasants—would naturally be influenced by clerical discontent and come to consider the harassed Pope a martyr, the Emperor a tyrant and a godless man. With the Concordat, sooner or later the restoration of the monarchy became imminent, inevitable. Bonaparte, who had just applied his keen and mobile intelligence to the study of the canons and laws of the Church, did not understand the essence of the Church. He astonished Monsignor Caprara by his hastily acquired erudition, by his ability to remember ecclesiastic regulations to the letter, but the legate clearly perceived that he had not penetrated to the spirit of the law, and the formidable hair-splitter was made a fool of by the shy and obstinate prelate. It is true that in this conflict the Church emerged the loser of the true meaning and strength of its spiritual power. It thought to recoup these losses by encroaching on temporal power, and thanks to its hidden persistence, thanks to Napoléon's errors, after the fall of this great man, the Church became the true temporal power in France.

Robespierre, in his quick and rough sketch of a new society, had at least avoided that pitfall. He had dreamed for an instant of the concentration of spiritual and temporal power in a single symbol; as the foundation of his system he laid an unpolished rock slab, like the druid stones; but on that rock, with the passing of time and the evolution of ideas, a temple was to rise which would reunite in its embrace religion and society in one indivisible unity. I suppose that had Robespierre and Saint-Just lived a few years longer and had their system triumphed, France would have had a form of worship that each passing year would have purified. Christ would certainly not have been excluded from those honors given the godhead, since the Revolution had already named him their "sansculotte Jesus," a vulgar expression, but nonetheless profound, which revealed a strong feeling for the truth.

But neither Robespierre nor Saint-Just were men capable of carrying so great a project very far. Great themselves, but besmirched by the terrible age that produced them, they might at all events have left some unmistakable signs of their passing. Would that Bonaparte and some of the men around him whom he too quickly absorbed into his radiance had been called to continue the work of the Jacobins, and instead of rejecting and cursing what they had once adored, had they kept faith with the new ideas and understood the law of progress, they might have brought their genius and daring to assist in raising this edifice of our future. And who knows if, a few years later, this great heresy of a new French religion, defended by Napoléon and by the heroism of the nation as a conquest no less precious than our material conquests, would not have been able to negotiate with the Pope? In 1802, wasn't the Pope negotiating with a nation of unbelievers who let their case be argued before him by one clever and imperious man? Wouldn't the Pope's terror have been much greater if that man had been the advocate of an enthusiastic, impassioned, believing nation, defending its philosophical principles as articles of faith, asking equality in the name of Jesus, demanding revision of a doctrine smothered under false interpretations, threatening Europe with real republican and fraternal propaganda, and summoning the head of the Church to call a council where French doctrines might be discussed and brought before the tribune for humanity? Who knows if the preponderant weight of the genius of Napoléon and terror of his weapons might not have wrested from the Holy Father an edict of tolerance for the church of our conscience and our inspiration? Wasn't it a time of miracles and wasn't the Concordat itself also a kind of miracle, albeit from the devil instead of God?

But we need not push our hypotheses so far. More likely the Church would have repudiated and cursed us, but we would at least have defended our cause there—the greatest cause that has ever been argued before humanity —and perhaps we would not have lacked for men to argue it worthily. There are several whose inspiration has been lost in the hushed and remote struggles of religious anarchy, who, given support, enlightenment, and better inspiration by an ever purer, ever growing circle of supporters, might have left a mark on history at which we can only guess.

But that, you will say, would be going back to the time of the Hussites, beginning anew the wars of religion, plunging ourselves once more into the barbarity from which Voltaire had forever saved us. No, humanity does not follow a second time the roads it knows have no exit. The Church would not have been able to fight; it would not have had the temporal power to send our deputies to the stake; it would not have had the spiritual power to combat us victoriously. It would have protested, and prevented nothing; it would have been shaken from pinnacle to base, and our quarrel with the old European monarchies, without ceasing to be ardent and prodigious, would have kept the religious and philosophical character it had in the beginning and which Napoléon hastened to be rid of. That chimera, prejudice, which makes the very words I use, religion and philosophy, into opposing and irreconcilable terms, would have fallen before the clear light of day. And let us even suppose that the spirit of the time would not permit their eternal identification as one and the same; let us suppose that the French might have persisted in believing themselves to be totally philosophical—which is not probable, because in 1794 they had outlined a religion and accepted the wording—that philosophy, which would have matured by being challenged, and that solidarity in the face of danger, which would have been engraved on all hearts as synonymous with homeland, would have imbued us with a strength that would probably not have broken at Waterloo, assuming that a battle so long, so disastrous, and so futile had been needed to maintain a Republic as it was to maintain the Empire.

It is true that, in order for all this to have been possible, it would have been necessary that Napoléon not be a conqueror and a skeptic. It would have required an enlightened man of genius whose intelligence surpassed that of immediate application. Then, making his final adieu at Fontainebleau, he would never have hurled that bitter phrase at us, a curse too justly deserved, addressed to the men of his time, "If I had scorned man, as I have been reproached for doing, the world would recognize today that I had ample reasons for my scorn." Then the unity of man, which includes his rights, duties, and role in life, would not have been shattered as it is today. We would not have a theocracy which the government both defies and endures, a monstrous anomaly where spiritual authority and temporal authority perish alike. This unity of our religion and our society, as simple an idea as the unity of soul and body, would have entered our minds, passed into our laws, customs, arts, into everything, by force of circumstance, by the thirst for glory especially, since to win eternal glory was the passion of the age, and it would have been necessary to defend this religion of equality against foreign armies, as we had to defend the fate of a sovereign without illustrious forebears.

It is permissible to dream when one looks over the past and to regret the errors of a great mind, the weaknesses of a noble character. However, one must take into account, to be fair, the obstacles that made him draw back and the circumstances that deprived him of free judgment. Bonaparte did not consider men worthy of aiding him, and this scorn, so natural to those who see men crawl before them, caused him to narrow the vast bounds of his creative vision. The vision and memory of tumultuous assemblies and useless parliamentary hubbub must have caused him profound disgust. Prey to this disgust, exasperating for so swift and decisive a mind, he dreamed up a system to elect himself consul for life. He understood, then, that the official assent of numerous signatures on a voting ledger kills the sense of political party, but, later, he must have also understood that this system can kill public spirit and create millions of perjurers. The vote of each individual is not the same as the vote of the whole. The true adherence of the masses cannot be won except by bringing them together in assemblies, putting one another to the test, questioning one another, confiding in one another, publicly pledging faith to one another, and thereby being able to escape from restrictive family influences and momentary temptations of personal interest.

When these selfish interests found themselves jeopardized by public misfortunes, each of the coerced signatories thought himself free to betray both his country and the man who, at the end of his career, became once again the true personification of the nation as he had been in the beginning. If Napoléon had wanted or had been able to create a true electoral representation, I firmly believe they would have been more faithful to him, for they would have kept him from being drunk with power without impeding the providential course of his genius. The present head of state[23] understood this clearly and dealt more cleverly with the problem that confronts all usurpations, when faced with the necessity of consulting the nation. However, since whatever is merely a compromise between conscience and necessity is only a decoy, and a decoy cannot last forever, this false constitutional representation in France may well one day be quite as ungrateful towards its creator as was the naïvely acquired representation of the Empire.

May no one attribute to presumption this glance I have cast on past events which are still debated by contemporary public opinion. It is everyone's right, since yesterday's history is already the story of each of us. For me, it is my father's story and consequently mine.

While rereading his letters, written under the hasty, but sincere, impressions of the moment, I cannot help but scrutinize and judge events from my point of view that he judged from his.

My father had no pretensions to being a philosopher, despite the philosophical instruction he had received. He believed himself indifferent to all religion, to every doctrine, and like all men his age, especially those of that era, he gave himself, without reflection, to physical experience. It is clear, nonetheless, that he had, at the bottom of his heart, a total faith in the ideas of progressive Christianity, which have been much discussed since that time by modern schools of philosophy.

My father died when he was thirty: in my vague memories, as in the warm and almost fervid memory of his friends, he remains, therefore, a young man; and I, who grow old, see him, in my memory and imagination, as a child like my son, who is already nearly the age my father was at the end of the Consulate, when I was born. However, when reading his life as written by himself from one day to the next, in his unaffected conversations with his mother, I still receive profound precepts which he would have given me had he lived. And to understand them properly, despite time and the tomb, which separate us, I am forced to consider everything that was fomenting in and around him. I see him summarizing in himself, without being aware of it, during every period of his life, what was happening in public life; and his reaction to it seems to me, despite his apparent optimism, to have had serious consequences not only for me for but everyone.

And so I see him from childhood on, calling aristocracy a "chimera" and poverty a "useful lesson." Suffering because of the Revolution to the depths of his being, knowing that his adored mother was threatened by the guillotine, I never see him curse those ideas which gave birth to the Revolution; on the contrary, I see him approve and give his blessing to the downfall of the the privileged classes. I see him love his country like Tancred,[16] look at war and glory as the proclamation of philosophy's moral conquests, and shout out, "Ah, mother! who could have told your friends the philosophers that one day their ideas would make me, son of a financier, a soldier in the service of a republic, and that those ideas would be at the tips of our sabers?" I see him still more sincere and consistent, still more of a Christian and a philosopher for loving a poor girl enriched overnight, so to speak, for a misfortune greater than poverty, by his recognition that his love had purified her and by his fight against the keenest pangs to restore her reputation despite all obstacles. I see him push respect and love of family to the point of breaking his mother's heart and his own, rather than refuse to legitimize by marriage the children of his love affair. All this is not the behavior of an atheist, and if his words are facetious and disdainful when he speaks of official religion, I see, in the depths of his soul, the tenacious and victorious tenets of the religion of the Scriptures.   *J. J.*

VI

The love story continued. —Meeting with the Turks. —M———'s adventure. —A painful separation. —The general's idiosyncrasies. —Return to Paris. —Caulaincourt, Ordener, Harville. —The eminent ladies. —High society. —The favor. —M. de Vitrolles, M. Cambacérès, M. Lebrun. —M. Hékel. —Eugène Beauharnais and Lady Georgina. —April Fool. —My aunt on my father's side.

Year XI

Letter I   Charleville, 1 Vendémiaire (September 22, 1802).

From Maurice Dupin to His Mother

I just received your letter, my dear mother, and it renders me happy. You preach at me and scold me throughout, but you do so with maternal love—to which I still lay claim, which nothing can *replace* for me, and for which loss I could never be consoled—do you hear?—because *nothing* could *compensate* me for it. Despite your displeasure, you still bear me the same affection. Always, my dear mother, preserve that tenderness for me, for I have never stopped deserving it. I'll admit I did fear that some new false reports or misleading appearances had momentarily chilled the feeling in your heart. That notion haunted me, oppressed my soul, disturbed my sleep. At last, you have just brought me back to life!

And that character, Deschartres, who informed me two days ago that you might not write me for a long time because of the grief I cause you! I proved to him only too well how wrong he was. He takes his revenge by making me suffer, by attacking me in the most sensitive spot. For all his good qualities, he's a bear who claws you when he can't overpower you. He wrote me volumes all last month in order to prove to me, with his usual courtesy, that I was a "dishonored" man, "covered with mud." No more than that! A charming conclusion, and worthy of the exordia he treated me to! But I gladly overlook them because of the motive that sparks his anger and zeal. I haven't yet answered his latest letter, but I'm holding that little satisfaction in abeyance, and shall send him along with it a handsome double-barreled shotgun, so he can supply your table with partridge, if he's not too clumsy.

No, my dear mother, I have never wished to separate my existence from yours. If I have become the "ill-bred drunkard" of the camps and bivouacs—as you claim, but which I do not concede—at least rest assured that in that hectic life I have lost nothing of my love for you. If, without consulting you, I took the "initiative" to write to Lacuée to try to get back into my regiment, it was because time was growing short, because I would have had to wait for your reply and thereby lose the few days I had in which to hope for a positive result. Now it's all over; Lacuée left me not the slightest hope. By virtue of the new orders, I have to stay with Dupont.[24] I'm resigned to it, and the pleasure you take from it reduces my disappointment proportionately.

However, you are wrong, my dear mother, when you speak of the "first" and the "last." In the army, there is no "last," not even the poor soldier. He who does his duty is held in contempt by no one. But there is a place where there are no "firsts," and that is in the generals' antechambers. All are more or less lackeys there, and that hardly suits me. Times have certainly changed in one year. Whether it's the state of peace or something else entirely, this post that once seemed so glorious has become quite distasteful to me. I feel a certain amount of consolation because I don't think anyone is ever trying to humiliate me personally. If that were so, I would prefer to abandon the military and die of sorrow for doing so, rather than lose my sense of dignity.

I shall go neither to India nor to America; it is true that from time to time that idea has crossed my mind with the help of a little rum and a few grievances, but I never confided it to anyone, and those who claim to have heard me on the subject don't know what they're talking about; in other words, they're liars. My mind could not entertain such an idea in light of the dread I have of afflicting you and poisoning your peace of mind.

Now let's get to the subject that tortures you the most. Yes, I did see Victoire again in Paris last winter, during the entire year I was there, and since you want the truth, I'm telling it to you; I only avoided it out of respect to you, for I couldn't blush at this attachment as if it were a crime. Her trip to Brussels is a tale I made up for Mme. de La Marliére's benefit, so that she wouldn't worry you any further with her officious accounts. It is also true that Victoire followed me here and that I found lodgings for her with some decent people on the outskirts of the city; then I gained her access, as she wanted, to a dress shop where she is presently working. I therefore neither betrayed her nor abandoned her to poverty, and in these fears of yours I recognize the kind heart of my beloved mother, who, after so fearing my extravagance toward that person, is now afraid of my ingratitude toward her. The modest conditions in which she's living should finally prove to you that she is very different from what you imagine, since her poverty seems to give you some concern about how I'm treating her. But rest assured, she and I are not at odds with one another, and if I'm "crazy," it's not in the area of duty that I have lost my senses.

Here is another confession that no one has made to you on my behalf and for which I want to take full credit. One fine evening, I gambled at Morin's uncle's and lost twenty-five louis. I think that was the first time I've touched playing cards, and it will be the last. I borrowed money to pay the debt, and I repaid it; that is the secret of my money problems this month. But I'm not complaining; it's my own fault. It's a lesson that I'll profit from. I think it was Sancho who said one must only commit the follies one enjoys. So it is only since I hate gambling, that I've been punished for having gone against my inclination and my instinct. We're leaving tomorrow for a tour within the division. We're going to pass in review all our troops and ready them to appear before the First Consul, who, just between us, is expected to come pay us a visit soon.

Goodbye, my dear mother. Please believe that only your happiness can make me happy and that it will always be the primary motive behind all my deeds and thoughts. I embrace you with all my heart.

My God, how Miémié's idea grieves me! I can't accept it. Speak to her for me, I beg you![24a]

So Auguste has been named tax collector for the city of Paris! I have congratulated him on it.

Letter II   Charleville, 19 Vendémiaire.

In the two weeks we've been on tour, we've seen the whole division, which is superb. In almost all the corps, I rediscovered officers I fought with in Switzerland and Italy. We all took great mutual pleasure in seeing each other again. In Verdun, I met the 1st Cavalry. The colonel left no kind word unsaid about his regret at not having me in the regiment. I expressed to all these men the sorrow I felt at no longer being among them, and I asked them at least to continue holding me in their esteem. They said that to know me was to love me and never to forget me. It seems as if I'm boasting as I report these comments, but it's only with you, my dear mother, that I mention them, because I know you're more affected by these than by any and all "exploits." You must understand, however, that among military men bravery is an integral part of friendship. Hence it is one of my more "subtle" ways of proving to you that I love war and glory.

We dined together, gave a dance, and parted fast friends. We reviewed Durosnel and his regiment at Saint-Mihiel. I was delighted to see him and pleased with the welcome he gave me. You know I've always told you that Durosnel was the best friend I had in Cologne. We made Dupont and the aides-de-camp die laughing with our old stories, and Durosnel had the kindness to intersperse in each of his comic tales some serious reference in my praise. We left him to see the 17th, in Commercy; from there we went to Bar-sur-Ornain, where we had a "run-in" with some Turkish gentlemen. His lordship, the Ambassador of the Sublime Door, had arrived at the outpost with all his Turkish paraphernalia in ten carriages and taken all the horses. But since they'd stopped for three hours to perform their ritual ablutions, our courier arrived right in the middle of their prayers and seized six horses for us, with no heed to the Turks—protests on their part, stubborness on his, intervention of the interpreter, arrival of the general, pandemonium in the house and stables. We want to have lunch, but the Turks are eating everything; they've put up the spit, we take it over. The ambassador and the general have a dialogue worthy of *Le Bourgeois Gentilhomme*, and while they compliment each other and wish each other the "prudence" of lions and the "power" of serpents, our horses are harnessed. We part as much in the dark about each other as ever, and off we go to the races! The stupefied Turks are missing part of their lunch and six horses. The next day, a review of the 16th Cavalry, a dinner given by the officers, with a ball in the evening. The day after, a wolf hunt; we kill two; we call a halt; all was going well up to that point when the day ended with an incident that threatened to be less funny than the one at Bar-sur-Ornain. The halt over, we packed up to get to the theater in Châlons. Dupont climbs into his carriage with the prefect and two or three other local officials, while I climb into a large calèche with the colonel, Malus Jr., deputy inspector for reviews, three captains of the 16th, four hounds, and eight guns. (Take careful note of all the props.) We are harnessed to two new horses. We hand the reins to the colonel, esteeming him the wisest, and I sit up on the box with him. We're rolling along pleasantly enough for fifteen minutes when suddenly we arrive at a long, steep, downhill slope furrowed with deep ruts; we try to rein in the horses; unaccustomed to the reins and especially to the force of the carriage behind them, they start to gallop and then bolt completely. I join forces with the colonel to stop them, we break the reins; then, seeing no more hope of salvation and that we are all going to be dashed into the river, which flows along at the bottom of the slope, I leap to the ground to try to get hold of the horses' heads, but since the ground is very uneven at that spot, I fall. I get up, but just as I'm about to stand, the horses lean in my direction, and the rear wheel passes over my leg between the ankle and the knee. Nothing was broken, and I got away with just a contusion and a deep cut. The colonel jumped a moment after I did and dislocated his wrist. The others were going to make the leap into the river along with the calèche when, fortunately, both horses fell at once, thus ending their terrifying stampede.

But the amusing part, once we were all on our feet again, was to see Malus's face. The fright had so made him lose his head that he no longer knew what he was saying and demanded that we check him over to see if he was hurt. The fact is that the check would have been most unpleasant, for he had *dirtied his trousers*. As you can imagine, we couldn't keep from laughing, which made us forget our troubles. We returned to Châlons, the able-bodied carrying the wounded. We nevertheless left two days later for Charleville, where we arrived without mishap. My leg is a good deal better—the vegeto-mineral water does wonders, and the injury won't amount to anything. In the midst of all these "notable" events, I couldn't find time to write to you because, following our illustrious custom, we do everything so precipitously that we do nothing at all. Dupont is the epitome of misdirected activity.

Letter III   Sillery (no date), Home of M. de Valence.

You wished it, you demanded it, you placed me between your despair and my own, and I have been obedient. Victoire is in Paris. I made the decision. I did the impossible, but sending her off thus, I certainly had to provide for her well-being. I took an advance against my salary from the division paymaster of sixty louis, and I insisted she go to work in Paris; as she was leaving, she sent me back the money. I ran after her, brought her back, and we spent three days together in tears. I spoke to her of you and brought her to hope that someday, when you got to know her better, you would stop fearing her. She resigned herself and left. But exposing oneself to such trials may not be the best way to cure oneself of a passion. In a word, I'll do for you all that human strength allows, but don't speak to me as much of her in the future. I still find it hard to answer you with much composure.

It is simply as false as false can be that she has gotten back together with the Collin fellow. It is entirely possible that this man does have a woman with him in Orléans, but it is not Victoire. A battalion chief friend of mine recently arrived from Paris has been to see her at my behest in order to bring me news of her. He found her making a hat. She is taking good care of herself and working hard; that's the truth.

Goodbye, my dear mother. Troubles always come in pairs. So it's true my maid is leaving you and there's a touch of bitterness in her dealings with you! How sadly do human relationships end! What consoles me is that she tyrannized you a little, and now you're going to be less constrained. She, on the other hand, who loves to boss others, will she order her relatives around? I doubt they'll be as acquiescent as you. Anyway, she's not leaving empty-handed, and if she knows how to be happy, she will be. I embrace you with all my heart.

Letter IV   Charleville, 29 Vendémiaire, Year XI (October 21, 1802).

Don't be alarmed; I haven't needed to use the recipes of "doctor" Deschartres; the open wound has healed. There is only the bruise on the crest of the tibia that's still painful and swollen, but other than that I'm walking very well.

And then, misfortune is always good for something; since I can't get dressed or put on my boots, I'm spared from having to run around like an idiot with Dupont. I'm taking a rest from the hateful role of pleasure server that he considers "military activity" and which is anything but that; I spend my days in my room, in slippers; I read, I write, I scrape away at the violin, I plunge into melancholy, which as you well know is my fundamental character, despite my jovial exterior. The only "soldierly" thing I do is to aim some shots at a target from my window. In the evening, I read some more, write some more, and smoke some more. Deconchy, a very sensible man, comes to keep me company, but as we all have our manias, his is declaiming. He puts everyone to flight with his speeches, and since he knows my legs keep me prisoner, he condemns me to listening to him spout his entire repertoire. My only escape is to drop off to sleep.

During this time, Dupont goes out in society; he bets thirty sous now and then at *bouillotte* [card game], to please the ladies of the area; he slaps his thighs to make himself seem friendly and persuade himself he's having a good time. But since he's bored, he takes it out on his aides-de-camp. He tells us we don't have the "military spirit" because we're not in our boots by eight in the morning. He comes up with escapades worthy of Don Quixote. He thinks himself in war time, orders his horses saddled with the same urgency as if the enemy were at the gates, doesn't wait for the orderlies to saddle theirs, flies off the handle, yells, swears, and takes off at a fast trot. Barely out of the town, he leaves the pathways, saying that to ride like everyone else isn't "military." He cuts across fields, scours the countryside, leaps over ditches, sinks into swamps, exhausts the horses, and comes back as rapidly as if he had the enemy in hot pursuit. He calls that a military excursion and does it all so that the townspeople will say he's full of the devil. From my point of view, such enslavement to the absurd whims of just one person would, if peace were to go on for too long, quickly turn me into a blithering idiot, but everything points to new coming events, thank God!

We expect the First Consul here in a fortnight. For his reception, we're assembling four cavalry regiments and six thousand infantry. By that time I'll be able to get back on a horse, and God only knows what caracoles we're going to perform! What I'm telling you about the coming trip is a state secret and didn't come to us officially at all, but confidentially, through the channel of Berthier. Goodbye, my dear mother, love me forever, despite my sad streak.

Letter V   Charleville, 10 Brumaire, Year XI (November 1).

You truly capture, my dear mother, the pain we feel when we leave those to whom good qualities and long habit have attached us; I understand perfectly the sorrow it caused you, and the weight you nevertheless feel lifted from you. The anticipation of the painful event is even more painful than the event itself. I assure you, for my part, it's very hard to accept that I shall never see my dear Miémié at Nohant again; apart from her moods, she was truly an excellent person, and I would never have believed that she could have decided to leave us. But since this thing has happened in spite of all my regrets, I realize that you'll be freer and better cared for. I congratulate myself daily for the arrangement by which I attached Deschartres to the future of Nohant.[25] He is truly the pearl of honest hearts; no one is more brutal than he, yet more fastidious. I am carried to your side each night, in my imagination, and I observe your long and sad evenings. I assure you that, on my side, I'm not any more joyful here. My leg now serves somewhat as an excuse to shut myself in my room and get out of the eternal dinners and insipid evenings at the prefect's, the commander's, or the war commissioner's. At least when I'm home I can do some music at my leisure, write some bad verse from time to time, and most often, build castles in the air. Dupont is going to Paris in January, whereupon I'll slip off to Nohant, and as I pass through Paris, I shall try to take a few more measures to get out of my post here, which irks me more each day. I'm repeating myself, but I can't tell you often enough how war puts everything in a noble light. In peace time, an aide-de-camp is a pitiful fellow, especially when he's dealing with an unhinged mind. I'd like to move up to captain and go back to the regiment, or at least get into the consular guard, because that is where, in war time, beauty and greatness beckon....

24 Brumaire (November 15).

.... Yesterday, I killed a wolf in the Lannoy forest. They are so numerous that, if not for us, they would do great damage around the countryside. I don't know whether the one I shot down is the same one that had bitten fifteen people in the past few days. I hope so. Moreover, we killed eight of them, and doubtless the villain was among them. They travel in packs, which makes the hunt a little more serious, that is to say, more entertaining. . . .

Apparently Bonaparte's itinerary changed, because my father was free to take leave. It is clear he was unhappy away from Victoire and did everything in the world to get to Paris to see her. For that he had to invent some business, and he needed a letter from his mother to Général Dupont. For Dupont was "more hare-brained and bad-humored than ever. Our man is courting a lady whose husband has been away but had the impertinence to be back in town for a week, and the general, crossed in his love affair, lets it out on us, who can't take it any more." To get his mother to approve his request, Maurice pretends to have acquired ambitions. He says the time is ripe for him to visit his former enemy, Armand Caulaincourt,[26] who he is sure will support him because, after all, this man whose ascent was so rapid has no reason to despise him. "He irritated me a great deal, yet I was never hurtful to him in my replies. I could have given him some cause for worry in his love affairs, but since I loved someone else, I behaved honorably, and he was aware of that. I never believed he was really mean or stupid, far from it, and perhaps now that he's on the right track, he will have given up his airs. At any rate, we'll see."

Maurice also wants to see "old man" Harville again, his first general, and his "big, strapping" Ordener (the father, I believe, of the good Colonel Ordener, himself a big strapper, who behaved in a heroic manner at the gates of Paris in 1814),[27] Eugène Beauharnais, Lacuée, Macdonald, and finally, his friend Laborde, Junot's aide-de-camp. He is acceding to his mother's desire at that time to see him placed in closer proximity to the First Consul, he himself keenly desirous to become part of the consular guard. He made a few attempts, as we shall see, but without success, which was easy to predict, because he was too preoccupied with his love affair to be an effective petitioner and too naïvely proud to be a successful courtier. I often heard his friends express surprise that with so much courage, intelligence, and personal charm, he did not receive more rapid promotion, but I understand why. He was in love, and for several years his only ambition was to be loved. Furthermore, he was not a man of the court, and it was already no longer possible to obtain anything without putting oneself through a great deal of effort. And then some serious matters came along to preoccupy Bonaparte—the business with Pichegru, Moreau, and Georges, that of the Duc d'Enghien,[17] events which explain his decision to restore names from the past to his side, then send them away again, and finally recall them and be reconciled with them.

The letter to Général Dupont was easier for my father to obtain from his mother now that she thought everything was over with Victoire, and she was hoping to see her dear Maurice arrive in Nohant after devoting several days in Paris to making bids for his advancement. I cannot say what resolutions he had formulated in this connection, but he is ordinarily so sincere and even so ingenuous that I deeply believe his intention to go immediately to kiss his mother was real. He planned only to see his girlfriend in Paris, doubtless to console her for the pain of their separation in Charleville and tear himself from her arms to return there soon. But he undoubtedly found her sad, frightened, perhaps even sick—about to become a mother. Then, sacrificing all for a significant love—both the tender demands of his mother and his hopes for military promotion—he spent five months in Paris, continuing to write, appearing to be very caught up in business, promising each week to arrive in Nohant the following week, and in fact unable to extricate himself from his passion and probably not wanting to. Perhaps Général Dupont had also intervened in Charleville to make Victoire leave; there is somewhere in the correspondence a letter from him where, while he does justice to the "young woman's behavior," he expresses to my grandmother his fear that Maurice might "do something foolish," and by that he probably means marry for love.

Here are some excerpts from my father's letters written from Paris between 15 Frimaire and 5 Floréal.

Frimaire, Year XI (December 1802).

. . . . There are many foreigners and liveries in the streets. The doors of people in power are unassailable. It's just like it "used" to be. Whatever the rumor, the people are neither happier nor more content. Yesterday, in a hunting quarrel, Général Lecourbe killed a man. Two hours later, the residents of Corbeil proceeded to his country house and massacred him. This news dismayed all of Paris, especially the palace. Four days ago, during the draft lottery in the Gravilliers section, there was a revolt of the conscripts in which the guard was disarmed; reinforcements arrived, fighting ensued, twelve men were killed. All that isn't awfully hopeful. . . .

I do not know what really happened concerning Général Lecourbe's tragic mishap. None of the works I have been able to consult mentions it. He definitely was not killed there, and maybe what my father recounts is a rumor without basis in fact. Or perhaps it took place as he tells it, except for the grave catastrophe at the end. The memory of a few of my readers will no doubt be richer than mine on the subject. However, the incident has a certain ring of truth. At that time, Général Lecourbe lived in the country bordering on Paris. He was unemployed, and he reappeared on the scene only to defend passionately Général Moreau, accused in 1803. His disgrace seems to have preceded this act of affection toward an unlucky friend, and it then lasted to the end of Bonaparte's rule. Lecourbe was a war hero; one can well believe that the energetic use of his saber[28] to make retreating troops return to their posts was a military virtue which did not much incline him to practice civilian ones, and it must be said that, generally, these glory-covered warriors often retained their barbaric stance in private life. Nor have I anything to confirm the anecdote about the draftees of the Gravilliers section. These are details that one probably would not be able to find in the newspapers of the time, because all of them were strictly subject to the master's direct censorship. We still do not have a complete history of the Empire. The one done by M. Thiers, which I refer to as the most detailed and serious on many points, does not deal with customs and public opinion as much as it should. It scarcely touches on the disaffection of the people, and it never explains the army's complaints in a satisfactory way. M. Thiers flatters the great man too much—although he rightfully places him on the highest rung—by supposing that all the men who had contributed to his illustrious triumphs were blindly ambitious. He does not credit them with any ideas which seem to him worthy of examination and discussion, and yet it would be very important to know what traces of republican sentiment the Revolution had left in the minds of those men, condemned to keep quiet and obey. I am asking that someone write the history of those who fell out of Napoléon's favor, and I would willingly call on the ones who have remained faithful to their original ideas to relate to us themselves, today, their lives and feelings under the Empire. That is what is missing in our understanding of the philosophical history of the Empire. The full significance, the entire truth of a period is not contained in its official account of general events such as war, legislation, diplomacy, and finances.

Excerpts of Letters Continued

Paris, 18 Frimaire, Year XI (December 1802).

 .... I finally got to see Caulaincourt, nor was it easy to accomplish, but I was indeed right to assume he would overlook our little grudges. Scarcely had he recognized old man Harville's former orderly than he cordially embraced me. He asked for news of you with great interest and didn't give me time to ask for his help. I had barely told him that I wanted a position in the guard before he offered his services and agreed to take charge with a very amiable eagerness. He asked me for my service record and promised of his own accord to present it and have the First Consul read it tomorrow at Saint-Cloud. He particularly recommended that I spell out very clearly on my application that I'm the grandson of Maréchal de Saxe, assuring me that this was necessary for success. "But what about Switzerland, what about Marengo?" I asked. "Fine, fine," he replied, "the *present* counts for a good deal, but the *past* holds a great sway nowadays. Talk about the hero of Fontenoy, and don't omit anything in that connection." It was good that I'd gone to dinner with Ordener the evening before, and good that he'd welcomed me with open arms, because Caulaincourt asked me how I got along with him, and at my answer, he assured me that it would all run like clockwork. . . .

Paris, 29 Frimaire.

 .... Yesterday, Auguste[29] donned the sober costume of his office as treasurer of the city of Paris. He put on the black robe, sword, pouch, and we nearly died laughing at him in that get-up. He always cuts a superb figure no matter what he has on, and he wears this outfit very well, but it's so funny to see the clothing of a bygone era reappear! René wants to be palace prefect and his wife, matron of honor. I made her furious by saying that for the moment the eminent ladies would only look at her askance. But the First Consul was so kind and gallant to her that she succumbed to the usual prestige, but finally admitted that all grand seigneurs are proud and insolent. All the more so, in the main, because they too are currying the master's favor.

Mme. de Guibert is still under the influence of the funeral eulogy, and can only speak of her late husband with tears in her eyes. And Barère's presence is everywhere; how edifying it all is![18]

12 Nivôse, Year XI (Januuary 2, 1803).

.... I'm sending you the latest in gray beaver hats. I chose it out of a shipment arriving from London. It's very warm and in the "no strings" style.

René went to Saint-Cloud to see Mme. Bonaparte. Apolline could not have been better received; the memory of M. de Guibert is held in great veneration there. You see how the past is courted.

I saw old man Harville, who welcomed me more warmly that at the Saint-Bernard hospice. He's had time to thaw out.... I send my greetings to the mayor, who's always dear to me and present in my thoughts. (There follows a free-style "illustration" portraying Deschartres' head with donkey's ears.)

18 Nivôse.

You must have received your hat. It's my turn to ask you a favor; send me quickly the set of steel buttons with diamond heads which belonged to my father. René, still dazzled by the brilliance of their shine in '89, has asked me to lend them to him so he can put them on a *lavender* velvet outfit he's readying to go pay court at Saint-Cloud. In truth, it is I who offered him this "brilliant" service.

B————[30] is going to have an appointment that brings in forty thousand pounds a year. That's what the court is all about! It's all because of the names of his fathers, for it's common knowledge that he had more than one. As for Dupont, who is a madman, but who is decent (one has to grant him that), and who certainly behaved admirably in Italy, not only isn't he invited, but he is also given a cold welcome. Twenty times a day I repeat, "It's exactly like it was before," and that the Revolution changed nothing. Alas! Where are our dreams of '89? Where are my extended reveries of Passy? Where are the snows of yesteryear? The opulence resembles that of the old court—rapiers, velvet suits, embroidered jackets, liveries, coaches, etc.....

I don't know the outcome of my request to the First Consul—I haven't been able to get together again with Caulaincourt since our first meeting; I don't like to be a bother, so I'm waiting. Apolline spoke about me in the presence of the First Consul; Ordener happened to be there and sang my praises to Eugène Beauharnais and Clarke.... I finally saw d'Andrezel, and yesterday I dined with Abbé de Pradt at Mme. de La Marlière's....

Paris, ———— Nivôse.

T———— is at the height of favor. Yesterday, Bonaparte sent his aide-de-camp, Le Marois, to ask him outright what position he wants. I am overjoyed for him; he's so good and kind that I'm happy to see him satisfied. But isn't it strange that people can get fine positions, of their own choosing, without leaving their rooms? Do you know what effect that has on me? It gives me an overwhelming desire to drop everything and retire to the country. And that is certainly what I shall do, if the war doesn't begin again soon; for I'm more than willing to serve France, but not as a courtier. I am weary of racing around the world and ruining myself financially only to come to the conclusion that I would have done better for my future to cool my heels in antechambers. The state of the military today is so degraded that I no longer dare put on the uniform I was so proud of a year ago. We can't even take part in the show, nor do they even let us into the court. I haven't tried it myself, and I shall never expose myself to such insults. How far away Marengo seems! I'm rambling, my dear mother, still caught up in my silly ideas of justice and true greatness. Ah, how hard it is to give up the dreams of youth so early! . . .

Paris, 12 Pluviôse (February 1803).

. . . . Don't scold me, I'm doing the best I can. But how can one succeed when one wasn't born a courtier? I saw Caulaincourt again yesterday. He invited me to have lunch with him; he told me that he had put my request in the First Consul's portfolio and had even spoken to him about me, but that he received the reply, "We'll see about it." Very likely that portends a refusal. What would you like me to do about it? Bonaparte himself got me into the general staff, and it was Lacuée who advised me to go ahead. Now Lacuée says it's not worth a damn, and Bonaparte doesn't allow us to get out of it. If it happens, it will be a great favor, but I am not the kind of man who can crawl on his belly to get something so simple and fair. I don't dare give up, though, for my only wish is to remain in Paris, if peace continues; that way, we could spend winters here, and we wouldn't always live separated from each other, which makes my situation as sad for me as it is for you. I go about this business neither "carelessly" nor "idly." But you didn't bring me up to be a courtier, my dear mother, and I don't know how to besiege the doors of those who dispense patronage. Caulaincourt is wonderful to me, and in my presence he told his doorman that I should always be allowed in when I come, whatever the time of day, but he knows that I'm not the sort to abuse this, and if he really wishes to serve me he doesn't need me to bother him.

This evening I'm going to Général Harville's. It is his day to receive guests. I'm going with my hat under my arm, black silk breeches and hose, a green dress-coat! That's what soldiers wear nowadays! . . . Please don't tell me anymore you're going to do your best to think of me as little as possible. I'm already pretty down in the dumps! What do you expect will become of me if you no longer love me? . . .

Paris, 27 Pluviôse.

. . . . I saw Mme. de Tourzel again at ———'s, at a truly beautiful supper he gave, and I was charmed by her. As for the others, both males and females, there are always the same nonentities, the same nonsense. "High society" hasn't changed and won't. I exclude only a few from this judgment, such as Vitrolles, who does have wit and integrity.[31]

In other places, when they aren't aiming for greatness, they're aiming to show how smart they are. Everyone, even Rodier, has become "sensitive" and "thoughtful." At his house, they only speak in moral maxims, which they don't care a fig for deep down. But it's the style. I received the letter from Master Aliboron Deschartres. It is as kind as he is, and that's saying a great deal. . . .

Paris, 7 Ventôse.

Caulaincourt has spoken to the First Consul about me again. He had misplaced my request and asked him for another. Does that mean there's hope? Ah, if the great man only knew how I'd love to send him packing and put an end to inglorious ruin in his service! Let him give us back glory, if he wants to make peace with me. The unfortunate part of it is that it doesn't make the slightest difference to him right now.

. . . . I spent the evening at Cambacérès'. It seemed like the whole of Europe was present. Four hundred carriages were counted on the Carrousel. What's amazing is the eager reception foreigners give to the French military, while the gentlemen of the old court discredit them, and those of the new one disdain them. To get their revenge, both suggest that the foreigners are seeking out bad company. Isn't that funny? So the Duchess of Gordon and the Princess Olgorouky are going "slumming" at Cambacérès'.

. . . . I was overjoyed to see our faithful old friend Hékel again. That made me feel better about the rest. I embrace Jean-Louis-François Deschartres. Oh, my dear mother, don't forget that I love you!

16 Ventôse (March 7).

I assure you that my affairs are on the best possible track, and if no one speaks ill of me to the First Consul at the time my request is presented to him, I can see no reason why he shouldn't grant it. Mme. de Lauriston herself recommended me to her son, who is to show him my petition the next time he gets to work with the First Consul. Caulaincourt, whom I saw again, affirms my certainty that I can't possibly fail. In the meantime, since you criticize my unsociable mood, I am going into society a little. The day before yesterday, Auguste introduced me at Consul Lebrun's. There was a crowd in the salon, and I had to remain behind Auguste as he pronounced the words, "I'm pleased to present to you my uncle, aide-de-camp, etc." At this introducton, Lebrun put on a solemn face to meet the dignified uncle he was looking around for. I was finally able to come forward to make my bow. He was so astonished that he almost forgot to return the bow. At last, after focussing carefully on me, he let out a great burst of laughter in our faces and asked which of us was the uncle and which the nephew. He had a hard time believing I was the older and was very pleasant in his mirth. From there we went on to Cambacérès', where it was my turn to introduce Auguste as my nephew, and the same scene repeated itself. Cambacérès invited me to dinner on Thursday. I shall be sure not to miss it because his dinners are legion among eaters. I saw Georges La Fayette again yesterday, and he introduced me to his wife, Mlle. de Tracy. He's just returned from Italy. I also saw again Mme. de Simiane, sister of M. de Damas, whom I was in contact with in Rome, and I won her over by talking to her about her brother.

When I have finally received that long-awaited reply from the First Consul—and I trust it will be any moment now—I shall be off at top speed to embrace you and tell you that I love you a hundred times more than you think.

28 Ventôse (March 1803).

. . . . I often see my friend Hékel. As he lives quite far away, each of us travels halfway; we meet in the Tuileries, and there we stride through the entire garden, chattering and arguing, till we're out of sight. Really, he's the most educated and eloquent man I've ever met. He holds such lofty views that I always feel myself a better man when I leave him than when we first meet. At present he's trying to obtain a position as headmaster of a lycée; I shall have Dupont give his note to Bonaparte. Will I succeed? I would willingly use "influence" out of affection for this worthy man, but the government is of a mind to give only to those who already have, which is rather the story of all great powers. . . .

Good Friday (April 8, 1803).

. . . . René gave a lovely lunch recently; his guests were Eugéne Beauharnais,[19] Adrien de Mun, Lord Stewart, Mme. Louis Bonaparte, Princess Olgorouky, the Duchess of Gordon, Mme. d'Andlaw, and Lady Georgina, the Duchess of Gordon's niece. It was held for the sake of Eugène, who is in love with and loved by Lady Georgina, considered a stellar beauty by society. The only thing she's missing to merit her reputation is a mouth and some teeth. But she and Eugène have no reason to be jealous of each other on that score. The Duchess would like nothing better for him to marry her, but dear stepfather Bonaparte doesn't see it at all that way. The aunt is going to leave for England, and the lovers are distraught. So much for happiness among the greats! On leaving the meal, we went for a stroll in the Jardin des Plantes, some by carriage or buggy, some in the four-horse calèche of the Duchess. We saw everything down to the least detail. Eugène distributed louis right and left, as others would have given out twelve pence. He conducted us, and he had all he could do to keep from saying "my father's garden" instead of "the king's garden."

After the promenade, the Duchess of Gordon gave a dinner at La Râpée, to which neither Eugène, René, Auguste, nor I were invited. Halfway through the meal, Princess Olgorouky received a note from Mme. de Montesson, inviting her to come to her house that very evening for a concert: the music of Paësiello, with Mlle. Duchesnois reciting. The Princess gulps her food right down, asks for her horses, and leaves. Once at home, she adorns herself with diamonds and arrives completely out of breath at Mme. de Montesson's at nine in the evening. At first the gatekeeper won't let her go up. She tells him she's been invited, gives him her name, goes upstairs, and finds Mme. de Montesson alone, between two candles, in front of the hearth, ready to go to bed. Great astonishment; explanations on both sides. It was an April Fool's prank played by some rascals who weren't invited, and I blush to admit that I know those scoundrels well.

The next day was the day of the grand parade; Auguste and René received a message that they took to be a prank of the same sort, but which didn't end as amusingly. Someone came to tell them that M. de La Villeleroux,[20] while descending the great stairway in the Tuileries, had fallen in the midst of his colleagues and was hurt. They ran laughing to the site, thinking it was an April Fool's joke, but they found him dead in the Ambassador's room, in the hands of Foucroy, councilor of state, who, unable to forgo the chance to experiment, proceeded to administer electric shock, which resulted only in producing dreadful grimaces. He had been stricken with a massive stroke. He was buried at Saint-Roch yesterday, with full senatorial pomp. As for his widow, she screamed loudly the first day. The next day, she spent a great deal of time on her dress and with her cat, who was having kittens. The day of the funeral, she was completely consoled and laughed at the sight of the passersby she observed from her window. The most one can say in her favor is that she's mad, my poor sister.[32]

Bonaparte is going to leave for Brussels in a few days; if I have no answer before he leaves, I'll dash home to embrace you with all my love and strength.

29 Germinal (April 19).

I'm leaving in three days with René for Chenonceaux. Send my horses to Saint-Aignan, and in five days I shall be in your arms. Yes, yes, I should have been there a long time ago. You have suffered, and so have I! You'll walk me around your new gardens and convince me that the frog pond has become Lake Trasimeno, the little pathways royal roads, the meadow a Swiss valley, and the small woods a Hyrcanian forest. Oh, I ask for nothing better! I shall see it all through your eyes, in all its beauty, because you'll be at my side!   *A.M.R.*

VII

The stay in Nohant, return to Paris, and departure for Charleville.
—Bonaparte in Sedan. —Général Dupont's attitude in the presence
of Bonaparte. —The camp at Boulogne. —A squall at sea. —An
exchange of gunfire with the English. —Général Bertrand. —A party
given for Mme. Soult in the camp at Ostrohow. —Général Bisson.
—Outbursts against Deschartres. —A speech in which the army begs
Bonaparte to accept the imperial crown. —My mother in the camp at
Montreuil. —The return to Paris. —My father's marriage. —My
birth.

After having spent three months with his mother, whom he accompanied
to the spa at Vichy, my father returned to Paris, having been recalled by the
Consul's decree ordering all generals to assemble their subordinates, for there
was talk of an expedition to England. However, my father had no desire to join
Dupont in Charleville, and all he could think of was to play truant. From then
on, his life was totally given over to love. In that state of mind, he was scarcely
able to take any productive steps toward his advancement, about which he was
more discouraged than ever, and he spent more time talking about it to his
mother than doing anything practical and serious, in order to justify his stay in
Paris with Victoire. In Messidor, Year XI (July 1803), he wrote to his mother
that his friend Laborde, Junot's first aide-de-camp, had tried to get Junot to
appoint him second aide-de-camp, but Junot's reply was that he wanted his
aides-de-camp to be over forty. Laborde was bowled over by that outrageous
response, and he cried out very angrily, "What the devil, do you want to have
your father as an aide-de-camp? . . . "

On 1 Thermidor, he wrote, "Whatever you say, there are no friends at
court. There aren't even any comrades, and the ones who sought your friendship and help in bad times would look at you askance if you seemed to remember it. . .

" . . . Franceschi, first aide-de-camp of Masséna, wants me to transfer my
talents to that general, who is going to command either the coastal army or the
one in Portugal, and I would prefer that to going to Charleville to carve legs of
lamb for Dupont. . . . "

At this point, Maurice asked his mother to please help him by writing letters to convince Général Dupont that he had tertian fever. It is clear that he

does not want to leave Paris to parade in a peaceful garrison "where you never hear a shell explode," and that he will not tear himself away from his love until "the first gunshot is fired against the enemy."

His mother's fears were re-awakened because she sensed the reason for his reluctance to rejoin the general. She was no longer alarmed by a marriage against her wishes. She no longer believed it would happen, because the passion had persisted without benefit of a marriage contract. But she detected a rival for the heart of her dear child, and she was inconsolable.

". . . . One item in your letter hurt me deeply, my dear mother. You think someone is trying to tear from my heart the filial love I feel for you. That someone would be ill-advised and badly received, I swear it. I hereby give my denial to whoever told you that lie. Mother, I beg you to look with your own eyes. They are so good and true. Never listen to anything but the language of my heart, and only consult your own. In that way we will always understand each other to the detriment of those who would like to disturb and spoil the happiness of our mutual love. As for matters dealing with our money, I don't want you to discuss them with me, or to consult me on anything at all. I consider money as a means, never an end. Anything you do will always be wise, fair, and excellent in my eyes. I know very well that the more you have, the more generous you will be to me; this is a truth you demonstrate every day. But I don't want you to deprive yourself of the least little thing in order for me to have several acres of land more or less. The idea of being your 'heir' gives me the chills, and I can't worry about what will be left after you, for after you, there will only be pain and solitude for me. Heaven preserve me from making plans for a time that I don't want to foresee and that I can't even bear to think about!"

Excerpts of Letters Continued

4 Thermidor.

. . . . Mme. de Bérenger doesn't want to contact Masséna without your permission. She says that if something terrible happened to me in that post, you would reproach her for it all her life. Have no fear; you know that no harm ever comes to me and that I never suffer so much as a scratch. Remember that I can and will only seek out a post which will bring me honor. I won't lift a finger for money or vanity's sake.

10 Thermidor (July 29).

. . . . I'm leaving for Sedan, where Bonaparte is due to pass, and where we have to meet him on the 18th or 20th. In spite of my "fever," I'll be there on time. I don't know if his meeting with Dupont will help me get what I want. I doubt it, because I seem to be having a run of bad luck. I've been a lieutenant for three years now, and all my comrades have been promoted. Evidently, they know how to get ahead better than I, for I've done as much as they, and even more than some. Masséna promised to take me on as his aide-de-camp, and I shall come back to remind him of his promise as soon as I have put in an appearance at Sedan, in full view of "the master."

How kind your letter is! All life's events leave me more or less indifferent, provided you love me and don't doubt me. Therefore, I leave with a happy heart filled more with your kindness than with my plans.

Charleville, 15 Thermidor (August 3, 1803).

. . . . I arrived yesterday; I found Dupont very sarcastic and quite unsympathetic about my "fever." We are expecting Bonaparte any time now. Nothing could be more amusing than the clamor that dominates everything here. There would be less fuss for God Himself. The military are preparing for a full review. The local officials are composing speeches. The young bourgeois are outfitting themselves and forming an honor guard. The workers are putting decorations everywhere, and the people are wide-eyed and open-mouthed. Three of our cavalry regiments and four demi-brigades have met in Sedan. We'll do firearms drills and maneuvers on the plains, which will be the only exciting part, for the rest is being done shabbily and without taste. The lighting for the first day will use up the whole town's supply of grease and candles; luckily there'll be a full moon the next day.

I shall use the occasion to have Dupont ask the First Consul for my appointment as lieutenant in his guard, and since he has never yet had to ask for anything for me, perhaps he'll be willing to do it. But I don't delude myself with the happiness of living in Paris and bringing you there. It is too nice a dream. I am not the type who succeeds in peace time. I am only good for dealing blows and taking them; presenting petitions and receiving favors is not my forte. Dupont is not at all enthusiastic about the idea of a raid on England. Whether out of ill-humor or mistrust, he doesn't want to get mixed up in it. I saw Masséna in Rueil the morning I left for Sedan, and he almost promised me, in case of a raid, that we would sail together. Here is my plan—go to war, or stay in Paris—for life in the garrison is odious.

I fear, my dear mother, the prolonged drought is making you ill. You are so kind as to talk only of me in your letters, and I don't know how you are feeling. . . .

Paris, 8 Fructidor, Year XI (August 26).

. . . . Dupont made me the finest promises, but he didn't keep them. During the week he spent with the First Consul, he didn't find a minute to talk to him about me. Caulaincourt, who accompanied Bonaparte to Sedan and who was very friendly to me, had told me when he arrived, "Well, this is a good chance to have your general nominate you!" When he left, he was stupefied by Dupont's indifference to us all. Then he spoke frankly to me of the First Consul's fluctuations. For example, this winter when he asked him to make me a lieutenant in his guard, referring to me as the grandson of Maréchal de Saxe, Bonaparte answered him, "Absolutely not, I mustn't be associated with people like that." Now it appears that this title would help rather than hurt my case, because the First Consul has already changed his way of thinking. Perhaps in a little while it will be different again. And so you see, my dear mother, what it means to depend on politics, or on the whims of one man. It's as it was of yore. Service and merit don't count. The name one bears is all they care about and nothing else. Thus, Caulaincourt did me a disservice, without knowing or willing it, in singling me out as the marshal's grandson. On that day, Bonaparte's republican sentiments were in the ascendance. But since he probably won't feel the same tomorrow, all these petitions make me very tired and disgusted. An insignificant soldier may in his heart of hearts feel that he's just as worthy as a head of state.

Moreover, he played a mean trick on us at Sedan. Imagine that after having us do maneuvers for four hours, sweating blood and water while we carried out orders, when the time came to file off, Dupont takes the lead in the movement, sword in hand. The orderly indicates our place alongside the general as we defile. Well, instead, Dupont gives us the signal to withdraw, assuring us that it is by order of the First Consul; so, just as we should have been preceding him as a unit, we dispersed. There is no clearer way to tell us that we are not considered part of the army and that it would be more useful to be a drummer or a recruit than an aide-de-camp, since an aide-de-camp is apparently reputed to be the general's footman. You can imagine that I have had my fill of this profession, and I walked away from Dupont without any to-do but with the approval of all my comrades, who really wanted to do the same. Out of spite and against his wishes, we accompanied Dupont on his official visit to the First Consul. He seemed to think that even his own presence was excessive, which impressed me as a form of speechless flattery toward the master, before whom one annihilates oneself and appears without attendants, like a poor beggar in the presence of the sun. At any rate, I don't know what to make of it; Dupont is a brave man in battle, but in peace time he's contemptible, and I'm leaving him. I'm all the more delighted with my decision because I shall get to take you in my arms. The place I hold in your heart is worth more than the one I am giving up. I shall try something else, for I don't want to stop serving my country, but if anyone ever catches me again in the job of aide-de-camp, it will be with a general leading a military expedition.

As we have just seen, Maurice was fed up with his position on the general staff, and at the beginning of Year XII, he began to try in earnest to be transferred to line duty. Dupont felt sorry for having hurt him and requested that he be promoted to captain. Lacuée seconded this request. Caulaincourt, Général Berthier, and M. de Ségur (Auguste de Villeneuve's father-in-law), did all they could to assure the success of this new undertaking, and this time Maurice has a serious reason to remain in Paris. He continues to write to his mother assiduously, but his letters contain so many malicious remarks about certain people who have a special talent for the courtier role, that I cannot transcribe them without offending many individuals, which is not my intent. However, without revealing the identities completely, I will report one of them which is simply amusing:

"Master Philippe is very pleased with himself as usual. Rolland happened to be in the Army of the Grisons with him, and as he was on Macdonald's general staff, he was there all the time. He swore to me that the aforesaid Philippe never heard a gun go off. Nevertheless, he is a captain and a member of the Legion of Honor. So he acts important, considers himself a seasoned fighter, and argues over military questions like an idiot. They think he's wonderful. I teased him a bit the other day. He was saying, in a learned tone, that the dragoons often dismount during battle. I knew it was true but said it wasn't, and I challenged him to cite any time whatsoever "when he'd seen it." It didn't penetrate, and he went right on pursuing his train of thought. Everyone laughed; he was the only one who didn't notice the slur."

At a later date in the same correspondence there is another anecdote I shall include here about the same person:

Vendémiaire, Year XIII.

The Emperor reviewed eleven regiments in Compiègne. Philippe, who had been sent the night before to have the beds made, refused to tell me where he was going when he got into the carriage to leave. He seemed impressed with the importance of his mission and cloaked his words in mystery. One would have concluded that the destiny of the state rested on his actions. "But where are you off to?" "I really can't tell you." "When will you be back?" "I really don't know." One would have thought he was going to run great risks. In fact, he returned the day before yesterday, complaining of excessive fatigue, drained, worn out, covered with dust. "Your horse must be dead tired?" "No, my friend, I didn't get to ride it." "Well then, the Emperor's horses?" "Even less so." "Why then are you so worn out?" "Because I ran up and down the stairs more than a hundred times." To return from a dragoon maneuver having spent his time clattering up and down stairs, that's really very warlike, and this young man will go far. He belongs to the Legion of Honor without having seen any action. I find it very consoling.

My father was not promoted, and his mother wanted him to resign from the service then and there. But the "merciless voice of honor" prevented him from resigning when war, if not imminent, was at least probable. He spent the first months of Year XII (the last months of 1803) with her. As plans for a raid on England were becoming more serious every day, and since we easily believe in what we desire, Maurice hoped to conquer England and march into London as he had marched into Florence.

Thus, he went to join Dupont again in the first days of Frimaire and left Paris, writing to his mother as usual that "there was no danger" and that war would not break out. "I beg of you, don't worry about my trip to the coast; probably my only weapon will be the field glass." This was indeed the way it turned out, but we now know more about how Napoléon had to give up a project that cost a great deal of money, study, and time.

Letter I   Camp at Ostrohow, 30 Frimaire, Year XII (December 22, 1803).

Here I am once again writing to you from a farm, or a sort of fief, which I made into headquarters while steadfastly waiting for Général Dupont. Ostrohow is a charming village located on a hill overlooking Boulogne and the sea. Our camp is set in Roman style, forming a perfect square. This morning I did a rough drawing of it as well as the positions of the other divisions along the sea and sent them all in a letter to the great Dupont. We're in mud up to our ears. We have here neither good beds for sleeping, nor good fires for drying out, nor large armchairs to stretch out in, nor the attentive care of a dear mother, nor delicate fare. Our job is to run around all day long looking for places for the arriving troops, for whom huts haven't yet been put up, getting filthy dirty and soaking wet, going up and down the coast a hundred times a day. It entails the fatigues of war, but war stripped of all its charms, because there is no possibility of moving and no hope of even the least little gunshot to pass the time while waiting for the great expedition, which is no longer talked about here except as something that was never supposed to take place. Therefore don't worry, my dear mother, nothing is ready, and it will probably take a year before we go off to capture English horses.

You can't imagine the shortages that exist here. In our fief of Ostrohow there is only one little bed without curtains, and that is reserved for the general. I had them search all over Boulogne for three mattresses and three camp beds for the three aides-de-camp—everything is taken. We're going to spend our winter in extreme deprivation, and truly I am not complaining when I see the miserable soldiers in camp, living in awful huts, constructed on such marshy terrain that they collapse under their own weight and sink into the ground. The men are literally sleeping in mud, and the number of mattresses will soon really be beyond computation. I'd like to perform the miracle of the five loaves over my bed of straw, but the time of miracles has passed.[33]

I would so like to have Mayor Deschartres here in our camp. I'd make him wield a shovel in style, and we'd see the kind of figure he'd cut in a bivouac with his cotton bonnet, his nightcap, and his rosette!

Letter II   15 Nivôse, Year XII (January 6, 1804).

. . . . The larger the division gets, the less room we have. Morin, De Conchy, and I are going stoically to share the fate of our poor soldiers, for the two miserable hovels where we were living have just been commandeered by a division brigadier. We are going to build ourselves a hut, so as not to bivouac in water. Nor is the political situation any more cheerful; they claim it will be two or three more years before we take action. This is supposedly confidential, yet our soldiers repeat it aloud. The English come daily to harass us with their brigs, cutters, and frigates. We fire many bombs and cannon balls at them from the shore, which are lost in the water. They respond in kind, and it is exactly like a tennis match. I find the Dolland field glass very useful for judging the shots. From time to time we practice rowing our barges and caïques off shore. The English come after us, and we retreat to within range of our guns, which then give them a roaring greeting. The sea doesn't make me the least bit sick, and I always come back with a huge appetite. When we're not on the water, we work on building our hut. This exercise is quite necessary if we're really going to get to sleep on the little bit of straw that we have. Recently we went to lunch with a general friend of ours, on the other side of Cape Gris-Nez. We left on horseback at low tide, following the water mark below the cliffs. We wanted to return at six in the evening by the same route, but as the tide was rising, we found ourselves cut off by the water in many places. Dupont, who always goes off half-cocked, fell into a hole with his horse and thought he was going to drown. Bonaparte had done the same thing in the harbor the day he left Boulogne; he too wanted to cross at high tide; his little Arabian horse got tangled in the moorings of a launch, and Bonaparte fell into water up to his chin. His whole suite jumped in to save him, but he climbed nimbly back on his horse and went to dry out in his hut. This event does not appear in the local newspaper.

.... I wish the mayor a down wind, high tide, and a nice brisk gale. My dear mother, I love you, and I'm very worried about your silence. I hope that you're not being standoffish with me, that you're not going to start accusing me again, not acknowledging the love and respect I have for you. Be sure that I love nothing on earth more than you.

Letter III   Camp at Ostrohow, 7 Pluviôse, Year XII (January 28, 1804).

There are moments of happiness which erase all suffering! I have just received your letter of the 26th. My heart cannot hold all it feels. My eyes fill with tears, which suffocates me; I don't know whether from joy or sadness, but at each expression of your love, I weep as I did at age ten. Oh, my dear mother, my beloved friend, how can I tell you the pain that your sadness and displeasure caused me? Ah! you know very well that I could never willingly hurt you and that the bitterest punishment I could have is to know that I made you cry. Your last letter broke my heart; today's fills me with peace and happiness again. Once again it contains the words and the feelings of my dear mother; she herself recognizes that I'm not a bad son and that I don't deserve to suffer so much. I'm at peace with myself—because when you tell me that I'm guilty, even though my conscience is clear, I'm convinced that you can't be wrong, and I'm ready to take the blame for every crime rather than contradict you.

I don't know who could have told you that I wanted to throw myself into the ocean. I never thought of doing that. It is just that for the moment I felt culpable in the eyes of you who love me so much. If I exposed myself more than once to perish in the waters, it was because I wasn't paying attention to what I was doing. I was truly so unhappy on land that being on the water made me feel easier. The sound of the wind and the violent rocking of the boat corresponded better with what was going on inside me, and being in the middle of that agitation made me feel, as it were, in my own element.

It is true that recently I almost victimized our whole headquarters with my penchant for navigation, but you heard the thing greatly exaggerated. I had been on board a fishing boat, and during lunch I told such an interesting story about fishing for herring that Dupont was tempted to make a similar trip. Although the wind was rather strong, I took him at his word and persuaded him to leave immediately. I went to the admiral to borrow his dinghy, and we staffed it with twenty strong and skillful oarsmen; we had at the helm the best coxswain of the fleet. I went back to get Dupont. Since the wind was freshening, I made him get on board more or less against his will, as was the case for the others as well, and we set sail with a quartering wind at high tide. We unfurled the jigger and the mizzen and were flying, rather than walking, over the water. We were already as far as Cape Gris-Nez, when we noticed porpoises leaping at water-level around our small craft. You know that when those fellows appear on the surface of the water it's a sure sign of terrible weather. Indeed, the wind got quite a bit stronger, and we were going to tack, when suddenly it rose to a fury and propelled us two leagues out to sea. We just had time to bring in and fold our sails. We were surrounded by mountains of water and thrown on top of one another in our puny vessel. The situation was becoming critical—it was superb. Our coxswain cut through the waves with admirable skill. Those who weren't seasick rowed valiantly with me. Finally, after having run a thousand dangers, we succeeded in returning to port at nine in the evening, worn out with fatigue, as you can imagine. The navy was very worried about us, and they sent out two rescue boats that came in with us. That is the whole story. Yes, it was imprudent, but it wasn't a "suicide," and I would have been very annoyed to have missed that tempest, for it was the finest thing I've seen in my life.

The morning of the day before yesterday, the commanding general, Soult, asked Dupont if he wanted to accompany him to Calais, and my general and I went on that errand with him, along with our neighbor and friend, Général Suchet.

I am not telling you about our military operations because an order from the commanding general forbids the transmission of all news from here, not only to journalists, but also to our relatives and friends. However, I can tell you without betraying any state secrets that we never finished our hut. My two comrades found an attic, and I have moved into a summerhouse six feet square, situated at the end of the garden. I had a stove brought in and I'm very comfortable. I have a good view of the sea, for I'm on a bluff, but I run a bit of a risk of being blown away by the wind. At this very moment, we're having such a terrible hurricane that the caisson in our courtyard has just been blown over.

Farewell, my dear mother, keep the pen with which you wrote me your last letter, and take no other in hand when writing to your son, who loves you as much as you are kind, and who kisses you as tenderly as he loves you.

I would like to have our stoic Deschartres here to see the expression on his face when pitching and rolling on the high seas.

Letter IV   General headquarters at Ostrohow, 30 Pluviôse, Year XII.

Division Général Dupont in Command of the First Division of the camp at Montreuil[34] . . . had me running around with him so much these last few days, either on land or on sea, that I couldn't find a minute to write to you. The day before yesterday, when I started a letter to you, a dozen cannon shots came to disturb me. It was the prelude to a cannonade which lasted all day, between our artillery and the English fleet. We rushed over there as one might expect, and for seven hours we enjoyed a view that was as rousing as it was pleasant, for the whole coast was on fire, the whole port covered with ships, and in spite of the two thousand cannon shots that were fired from every direction, we didn't lose a single man. The enemy fire passed over our heads and fell into the fields, without hurting anyone. I noted with pleasure that my beautiful chestnut mare, who is as lively as gunpowder and bolts at a fly, didn't budge at the sound of the cannon. I positioned myself in a battery of four pieces of 36. . . . The mare was so stunned at the initial sound that by the third shot she didn't move at all.

. . . . I saw Général Bertrand here, after having been to see him at his place six times, to no avail. He finally came to dinner at Dupont's, and I found him delightful. His manner is candid, likeable, friendly, unassuming, and unpretentious. We talked about Berry with all the pleasure of two countrymen who meet far from home and go on about everything interesting and dear that they have left behind, especially their mothers.

. . . . Nature is beginning to brighten up here, and I hope you can take a stroll in your garden by now. We have one here which has a wonderful view of the sea, but for me nothing equals the one in Nohant, when I'm there with you.

Is Deschartres still making wonderful discoveries about nothing in particular? Is he preparing some new literary or agronomical treat for the awe-struck department?

Letter V   Ostrohow, 25 Ventôse, Year XII (March 16, 1804).

. . . . A few days ago, all the generals of the camp at Saint-Omer gave a splendid party for Mme. Soult and her husband, the commanding general. As chief engineer, Général Bertrand was in charge of decorations. Général Bisson, who can drink fifteen bottles of wine without getting drunk and is six feet tall and nine feet wide, was in charge of the buffets and the supper (which doesn't prevent him from being a brave soldier. He was at Mincio).[35] I was given the job of conductor, in charge of all the music. I put together an orchestra which didn't play well at all when we first started, but was worthy of Julian by the day of the ball. I composed quadrilles, etc. Truth be told, I put myself out for goslings and buzzards, but my music went well, my musicians outdid themselves, and I don't give a fig for the rest. There were ladies there whose names I withhold and who were out in full force, such as Mme. de La———, who referred to an "epithalamium" as an *épitre à l'âme* [a verse epistle on a romantic subject].

It seems I made a spelling error in my last letter that gave Deschartres something to clamor about. Well, tell him for me in no uncertain terms that he's the one who's mistaken; that *leur* [their] is a demonstrative pronoun which agrees in gender and number with the noun it modifies, that *leur* is used for the masculine and *leure*[21] for the feminine; that since *leurs* is used before words like *horses* and *soldiers*, one should use *leures* before *carriages* and *women*; just as when we speak of the exploits of village mayors, we say "*leure* lumpishness" or "*leure* pedantry." There you have a big noise over a careless error! Well at any rate, I insist that I'm right, if only to make him furious, and if not, I'll cut off his ears.

I'm leaving my musicians, who have acquired through me a taste for Glück, Mozart, Haydn, etc. We are withdrawing to firm ground, returning to our camp at Montreuil, and I'm going to miss being near the sea. You, my dear wicked mother, who aren't fond of my nautical trips, will be delighted.

Letter VI   Fayel, 17 Germinal (April 7, 1804).

We have moved into a manor house which is adorned with the grandiose title of "château." It is really the saddest abode you can imagine, five leagues from Boulogne, four from Montreuil, and one from Étaples; it feels like the end of the world—sea and sand dunes as far as the eye can see. And when the west wind blows, it raises swirls of sand that spread out over the countryside. For the past several years, this sand has been taking over the cultivated land and rendering infertile everything it touches. The château of Fayel is protected from it by several clumps of woods, but outside of that, we're in a desert. Fortunately, we don't contemplate any forty-day fasts, and we don't take umbrage when the devil comes to tempt us. The manor house, they say, belonged to the jealous Fayel, who made his wife eat Coucy's heart.[22] A Monsieur de Fayel and his wife still live here, but as you might imagine, family tradition makes us very circumspect around Mme. de Fayel, who nonetheless is very pretty. Dupont is heartily bored, and the manner he uses when he instructs us—De Conchy and me—becomes quite surly in the end, and even in the beginning.

What? The learned Deschartres does not accept defeat? Is he stupid enough to think I am really defending my pronoun *leure*? You must have died laughing when he withered me with his syntax. It is time to let him know he's right, because he insists, but do tell him that this shouldn't make him assume he has any claim to common sense, for to match the one miserable time that he showed it, I'll prove to him by A + B that he has given me a thousand indisputable proofs of his mental derangement. He has a lot of nerve accusing others of being "illiterate," he who isn't fit to take a place on the rower's bank of a shallop; who doesn't know port from starboard; who can't tell a cutter from a brig, a caïque from a felucca, a praam from a lugger, a lookout from a seamark, a buoy from a pulley block, a jib from a mizzen, between-decks from the hatch, the portholes from the poopdeck, a berth from a hammock, an oar from a boathook, and lastly, the strand from the watermark! And there we have only the basics. What would happen to him if, completely winded, all set to throw up his supper or having already thrown it up, he was put ashore out of pity and tossed onto a horse on the plains? And if I then came to tell him about a front-line shift, a reverse battle formation, an advance by division to form a tight column, a breaking of ranks in the rear by the right to march to the left, a retreat by battalion, by section, by unit, Good Lord, where would he be then? And what would he do if, in the middle of that battle, his restless, recalcitrant horse began to bolt at gunfire, rearing up, buckling, and finally arching his neck because the rider hadn't held his legs close and his hand high enough, tossing him overhead and leaving him prostrate in the plowed field? Well, Sir Grammarian, Sir Purist, how would you get out of that? Would you call on Despautère, Vaugelas, Lhomond, or Bistac[23] for help? In such circumstances, would you consult a Latin primer or a rhetoric? You wouldn't have to look very far to recognize you had lost your center of gravity and that you're a clod. Is that understood, Master Deschartres?

When he confesses that all he is is a Vadius,[24] you shall tweak his ears and tell him for me that I love him dearly. . . .

Letter VII   Fayel, 12 Prairial.

We are very busy here. We were inspected by the minister of war, who set the whole of the Montreuil camp to drilling in formation. Since Dupont is the senior general of the division, he was in command, which afforded me the pleasure of about a twenty-league gallop up and down the line from right to left about forty times. Then for four days we ran around to come "effectively" to an agreement on the text of the speech we are required to make for the First Consul, to beg him "effectively" to accept the imperial crown and the throne of the Caesars. What solemn nonsense! Next we ran around to have it signed by the different units. No one finds such chores annoying; rather they give rise to smiles; he was too "big" to expose himself to those smiles!

We are completely immobile here. The English seem as bored to look at us as we are to face them. They no longer approach us on anything but cutters and brigs, and their fleet stays close to land. The weather was extremely clear yesterday, so that through a field glass I could count one hundred twelve ships on the Dover coast, just off the county of Kent. They seem to be at their moorings. Explain to Deschartres that this means they have dropped anchor near the shore, because now that I've undertaken his instruction, I mustn't miss a single opportunity. Do you mean to tell me that a man with so many projects hasn't tried to persuade the sub-prefecture, of which he is spokesman and guiding light, that the Indre could be make navigable, and that since it flows into the Loire, which in turn flows into the ocean, one could profit from this opportunity to bring us wood from Sainte-Sévère, Saint-Chartier, Culan, Magnier, etc. If the wood was cut and lumbered so as to bring it swiftly to the worksites, we would have a prompt and sure means of reducing the pride of the new Carthage.[25] It is obvious that our young Emperor is waiting only for that before he begins the expedition. Is Deschartres so thoughtless as to refuse to cooperate with him?

Goodbye, my dear mother, I embrace you with all my heart. Alas, it has been five months since I've had the pleasure of doing it in person!

While Maurice was writing thus to his mother, Victoire—henceforth called Sophie, for he had taken to using that name—had come to join him at

Fayel. She was ready to give birth; it could therefore be said that I was already present, albeit unwittingly, at the camp in Boulogne, for in just a few days I would see the light, albeit unasked. It happened that I was born on 16 Messidor, Year XII,[26] in Paris, exactly one month after the day my parents made lasting vows to each other. Knowing she was close to term, my mother wanted to get back to Paris, and my father followed on 12 Prairial. On the 16th, they were secretly married in the town hall of the second arrondissement. The same day, my father wrote this letter to my grandmother:

Paris, 16 Prairial, Year XII.

I took the opportunity to come to Paris, and here I am; Dupont gave his consent because, my four years as lieutenant being up, I am entitled to the rank of captain, and I intend to claim it. I wanted to go to Nohant to surprise you, but I have to stay here several more days because of a letter I received from Dupont this morning, which contains a handwritten request from him for the first available appointment. If I don't succeed this time, I'm going to become a monk. Vitrolles, who wants to buy the land at Ville-Dieu, will leave with me for Berry. M. de Ségur is supporting Dupont's request. At any rate, I hope to see you soon. . . . I received your last letter, which was forwarded from Boulogne. How kind it is! . . . but I won't go into that now. Wednesday, if at all possible, I shall kiss you, which will be a happy day for me! Days like that make up for all the others in a life. My beloved mother, I embrace you!

My poor father had both life and death in his soul that day. He had just carried out his duty to a woman who sincerely loved him and who was going to make him a father once again. I have said that she had already given birth to and lost several children during that union, and on the occasion of the birth of yet another, he had wanted to sanctify his love by a lasting commitment. However, if he was happy to have obeyed that love which had become his very conscience, he suffered from deceiving his mother and disobeying her in secret, as do children who are mistreated. For that alone he was at fault, because far from being mistreated, he would have been able to gain his dear mother's unfailing affection by boldly telling the truth.

He did not have that kind of courage, and it certainly was not for lack of candor, but he would have had to undergo one of those conflicts in which he knew he would be crushed. He would have had to listen to heartrending complaints and witness copius tears, the mere thought of which distressed him. He felt weak in that regard, and who would be harsh enough to blame him? He had already decided to marry my mother and for two years had daily made her swear to give her consent. Two years before, on the verge of sanctifying the promise he had made, he had backed off, terror-stricken when confronted with his mother's ardent affection and despair tinged with jealousy. During those two years, when continual absences had caused his mother constant heartbreak, he had only been able to calm her by hiding the extent of his passion and the future of fidelity he had vowed for himself. How he must have suffered the day when, without letting any of his relatives or best friends know, he conferred his mother's name on a woman who was worthy to bear it because of her love, but with whom his mother would have such difficulty getting used to sharing him. Nevertheless, he did it. He was sad, he was frightened, but he did not waver. At the last moment, Sophie Delaborde, wearing a little dimity dress and only a thin gold band on her finger (for their finances would not allow them to buy a real six-franc wedding ring until several days later), happy and trembling, not unattractive in her advanced pregnancy, and unconcerned about her own future, offered to forego that marriage which would, so she said, neither add nor change anything in their love. He insisted forcefully, and when he returned with her from the town hall, he put his head in his hands and meditated for an hour on the pain of having disobeyed the best of mothers. He tried to write to her; he could only send her the ten preceding lines which, in spite of his efforts, betray his fear and remorse. Then he sealed his letter, asked his wife's pardon for his momentary concession to nature, took into his arms my sister Caroline, the child of another union, swore to love her as much as the one about to be born, and prepared his departure for Nohant, where he wanted to spend a week in the hope of being able to make a full confession and have it fully accepted.

But it was a vain hope. First, he spoke of Sophie's pregnancy, and while caressing my brother Hippolyte, the child of the Little House, he spoke of the unhappiness he had felt in learning of that child's birth, from whose mother he had of necessity become estranged. He spoke of the duty that love for one woman alone imposed on an upright man and the shame of abandoning such a woman after proofs of her great devotion. At his first words, my grandmother collapsed in tears, and without listening to or discussing anything, she used her customary argument, one that showed evidence of loving treachery and a tendency to dramatize herself. "Since you love a woman more than you love me, you don't love me anymore!" she said. "Where are the days of Passy? Where are your exclusive feelings for your mother? How I miss the time when you wrote me these words: 'When they give you back to me, I won't leave you for more than a day, for more than an hour!' I should have died in '93, like so many others! You would have kept me in your heart as I was then, I would never have had a rival!"

What could be said to such vehement love? Maurice wept, answered nothing, and kept his secret.

He returned to Paris without having betrayed it, and lived, quiet and withdrawn, in his modest quarters. My dear Aunt Lucie was about to be married to an officer friend of my father, and they gathered with several friends for some little family parties. One day they had organized some quadrilles; my mother was wearing a pretty pink dress, and my father was playing on his faithful Cremona violin (the old instrument I still have, to whose sound I was born) a dance he had composed. Not feeling very well, my mother left the dancing and went to her room. Since her expression hadn't changed and she had gone out very calmly, the dancing continued. At the last round of chassés, my Aunt Lucie went into my mother's room and immediately cried out, "Maurice, come quickly, you have a daughter." Here is what my father said, as he took me in his arms, "She'll be called 'Aurore,' after my poor mother, who isn't here to bless her, but will bless her one day."

It was July 5, 1804,[27] the last year of the Republic, the first year of the Empire.

My aunt declared, "She was born to music, and in pink; she will be happy." *V.A.S.*

VIII

The date of this work. —My physical description. —My mother's naïve stance on civil and religious marriage. —Mme. Murat's corset. —The general staff in complete disfavor. —Heartbreak. —Maternal diplomacy.

All that precedes was written under the reign of Louis-Philippe.[28] I resume this work on June 1, 1848, reserving what I saw and felt during this writing gap for another stage of my narrative.

I have learned, lived, and grown a great deal during this short interval, and my appreciation now for all the ideas that have filled the course of my life will perhaps be enriched by this belated and swift experience of public life. I shall not be any less honest with myself, but God knows if I shall have the same naïve faith, the same trusting enthusiasm that used to sustain me from within!

Had I finished my book before the recent revolution, it would have been a different book—that of a secluded, I dare say, generous soul—for I had only studied humanity via individuals who were in most cases exceptional and in all cases subjects of my leisurely observations. Since then I have witnessed a campaign in the world of action and am no longer the same as before. I have lost the youthful illusions which my privileged life of reclusive contemplation had allowed me to hold onto longer than one reasonably should.

My book will therefore be a sad one, if the impressions of this recent period remain with me. But who knows? Time passes quickly, and after all, the rest of humanity is no different than I, which is to say that others get discouraged and recover with great ease. God preserve me from thinking, as did Jean-Jacques Rousseau, I'm better than my contemporaries and that I've earned the right to curse them! The desire to separate his own cause from humanity's was a symptom of Jean-Jacques' malady. We have all more or less suffered in this century from Jean-Jacques Rousseau's malady. Let us, with God's help, try to cure it!

I came into the world on July 5, 1804[29]; my father was playing the violin and my mother wore a pretty pink dress. It took but a minute. I at least had that portion of happiness that my Aunt Lucie predicted of not making my mother labor too long. I was born a legitimate daughter, which might very well not have happened if my father had not resolutely trampled on the prejudices of his family; that too was a portion of happiness, for otherwise my grandmother might not have taken such loving care of me as she later did, and I would have been deprived of the small fund of ideas and knowledge which have been my consolation through the troubles of my life.

Physically I was quite strong, and during my childhood, my looks gave promise of great beauty, a promise unkept. This was perhaps my own fault, because at the age when beauty blossoms, I was already spending my nights reading and writing. A daughter of two perfectly beautiful beings ought not have degraded the line, and my poor mother, who valued beauty more than anything, often reproached me in a well-meaning way. But I was never able to devote myself to caring for my looks. As much as I like extreme cleanliness, I have an equally strong dislike for pursuits of a self-indulgent nature.

To deprive yourself of work so as to be bright-eyed; not to run outdoors when God's great sun is so irresistible; not to walk in good thick clogs for fear of deforming your ankles; to wear gloves, which is tantamount to renouncing the dexterity and strength of your hands; to condemn yourself to eternal ineptitude, eternal debility; never to get overtired when everything commands you not to hold back; essentially, to live under a bell jar so as to avoid being weather-beaten, chapped, or faded before your time; these are conditions I always found impossible to abide. My grandmother doubly reinforced my mother's reprimands, and the lessons on hats and gloves were the bane of my childhood. But even though I was not intentionally rebellious, I could not be coerced. I had only one brief moment of youthful bloom, and never any beauty. It was not that my features weren't quite well formed, but rather that I never lent them any expression. My habit of daydreaming, which began almost in the cradle and which I can hardly explain even to myself, early on gave me a "dumb" look. I do not mince words, because throughout my life—during childhood, at the convent, in the intimacy of the family—I was told the same thing, and it must surely have been true.

All in all, with decent hair, eyes, teeth, and no deformities, I was neither an ugly nor a beautiful child, for which I consider myself really lucky, because ugliness carries with it one kind of stigma and beauty another. We expect too much of a striking exterior, and we are too mistrustful of a repulsive one. It is better to have a decent face which neither bedazzles nor frightens anyone; mine did not stop me from getting along well with friends of both sexes.

I have brought up the subject of appearance so as to be finished with it. In a woman's life story, this chapter, which threatens to continue indefinitely, could scare off my reader; I have conformed to custom, which is to give a physical description of the character one puts on stage, and I did it as soon as the subject came up, in order to be completely rid of this triviality for the rest of my narrative. Perhaps I should have skipped over it completely, but when I looked to see what was commonly done, I saw that it had not occurred to some very serious men to leave it out of their life stories. It might therefore have seemed pretentious not to pay this little debt to the curiosity, often a little simpleminded, of the reader.

I hope, however, in the future, one can avoid this demand of curiosity, or if absolutely required, the portrait should be limited to the description on one's passport, drawn up by the local police chief in an unemphatic, uncompromising style. Mine is as follows: dark hair, dark eyes, average forehead, light skin, pronounced nose, receding chin, average mouth, four feet ten inches tall, no particular distinguishing marks.

But while I am on the topic, I must mention a fairly bizarre circumstance: it was only two or three years ago that I learned with certainty who I was. I do not know what motives or musings inspired several people, who claim to have seen me born, to tell me that, at the time, for family reasons easy to surmise in a secret marriage, I was not legally given my true age. According to their version, I would have been born in Madrid in 1802 or 1803, and the birth certificate that bears my name really belonged to another child who was born after me and died shortly thereafter.

Since civil registers had not yet at that period acquired the rigorous exactitude that the new legislation has subsequently given them, since there actually were some odd irregularities in my father's marriage, of which I shall soon speak and which it would be impossible to overlook today, the tale which deluded me was not as unbelievable as it may seem. Besides, when they made me this alleged revelation, they assured me that my relatives would not be truthful to me on this point, so I always refrained from asking them and remained convinced that I had been born in Madrid and was a year or two older than my presumed age. During that period I skimmed my father's correspondence with my grandmother, and an incorrectly dated letter, misfiled in the 1803 collection, confirmed me in my error. When the time came to transcribe this correspondence and I could examine it more attentively, this letter found its correct place and no longer deceived me. So, in the end, a set of letters of no interest to the reader, but very interesting for my elucidation on this point—letters I had never organized and never read—finally assured me as to my identity. I was indeed born in Paris on July 5, 1804[30]; I am indeed *myself*, in a word, which can only leave me feeling pleased, because there is always something disturbing in having doubts about your name, your age, and your nationality. So I endured these doubts for about fifteen years, unaware that in several old, unexplored drawers I had the wherewithal to dissipate them entirely. It's true that this is just one example of the habitually natural laziness which I bring to everything that concerns me personally and that I could have died without knowing whether I had lived as myself or someone else, if I had not decided to write my life story and go into great depth at the beginning.

My father had his banns announced in Boulogne-sur-Mer, and he contracted for marriage in Paris, unknown to his mother; what is not possible today then was, due to the disorder and uncertainty the Revolution had wreaked concerning relationships. The new legal code left ways open to evade reverential acts, and the case of "absence" had been frequently and easily alleged due to the emigration. This was a transitional period between the old and new orders, and the wheels of civil law were not turning smoothly. In order not to bore the reader with extremely dry legal points, I shall not go into the details, although I have all the documents in front of me. There definitely was a lack, or insufficiency, of certain formalities that today would be considered indispensable and were apparently not deemed absolutely necessary at that time.

My mother was typical of this transitional period, from the point of view of morality. All she understood of the civil act of her marriage was that it assured my legitimate birth. She was religious and always had been, without reaching the point of piousness, but the things she believed in in childhood, she believed in for the rest of her life, without worrying about civil law and without imagining that an act sworn before an ordinary citizen in a town hall could replace a sacrament. So she had no qualms about the irregularities that facilitated her civil marriage, but she was so scrupulous regarding the question of a religious marriage, that my grandmother, despite her repugnance, was obliged to attend. This took place later, as I shall explain.

Up to this point, my mother did not see herself as an accomplice in a rebellious act against her husband's mother, and when she was told that Mme. Dupin was very angry at her, she would respond, "Really? That's quite unfair, she doesn't even know me; tell her for me that I'll never marry her son in church, as long as she doesn't approve."

Seeing that he would never overcome her naïve and God-fearing prejudice, which was really her form of belief on a deeper level (for short of denying God, one must desire the intervention of God's thought in a sacred rite such as marriage), my father had the greatest desire to see his own consecrated. Until that happened, he trembled at the thought that Sophie would not consider herself bound by conscience and might call everything into question again. He did not at all doubt her; he couldn't have doubts as far as her devotion and fidelity were concerned. But she had terrible fits of pride when he hinted at his mother's objections. She spoke of nothing less than going far away with her children and supporting them on her own, and thus show that she wanted to receive neither charity nor pardon from that haughty lady, of whom she had a rather false impression and was terrified.

When Maurice tried to persuade her that the marriage contract was not dissoluble and that sooner or later his mother would come to accept it, she said, "I don't agree! Your civil ceremony means nothing, because it permits divorce. The Church doesn't. So we're not married, and your mother has nothing to reproach me for. It's enough for me that our daughter's future (I was already born) is secure. But as far as I'm concerned, I ask for nothing, and I have nothing to be ashamed of."

It is true that society did not sanction this reasoning, powerful and simple though it was. Nor is it any more sanctioned today, now that its basis in civil law is far more established. But at the time these things were going on, people had already witnessed so many upheavals and wonders, they did not quite know on what ground they stood. My mother shared the popular view in all this. She judged neither the causes nor effects of these new bases of revolutionary society. "It'll change again," she said. "I remember a time when religious marriage was the only kind of marriage. Suddenly, they acted like that didn't count anymore and wasn't worth anything. They invented another version which also won't count and can't last."

It did last, but with one essential modification. Divorce was permitted, then abolished, and now there is talk of reinstating it.[36] There has never been a worse time to bring up so serious a question, and although I have some decided opinions on the subject, if I were a member, I would call on the Assembly to proceed to more pressing business. You cannot settle the destiny and ritual practices of the family at a time when society is in a state of complete moral disorder, if not anarchy. Also, when the time does come to discuss it, the religious view and the civil view will again find themselves at odds, instead of seeking the kind of agreement without which the law makes no sense and does not attain its goal. If the possibility of divorce were to be rejected, it would consecrate a condition contrary to actual public morality. If adopted, it would occur in such a way and under such circumstances as to disserve the cause of morality, thus further dissolving the concept of family as a sacred pact. I shall express my opinion at a more appropriate place; now I return to my narrative.

My father was twenty-six and my mother thirty when I was born. My mother had never read Jean-Jacques Rousseau and perhaps had not heard much about him, which did not stop her from nursing me, as she had done and would do for all her other children. But to keep the story of my own life on an orderly course, I must continue to follow that of my father, whose letters serve me as markers, for it is quite obvious that my own memories do not date back to Year XII.

As I said in the last chapter, after his wedding, he stayed at Nohant for a fortnight, and found no way of making a confession to his mother. He returned to Paris under the pretext of pursuing that everlasting captain's commission, which did not come, and he found all his acquaintances and relatives very well treated by the new monarchy: Caulaincourt, master of horse to the emperor; Général Harville, master of horse to Empress Josephine; nephew René, chamberlain to Prince Louis; René's wife, lady's companion to the princess, etc. The last-mentioned presented Mme. Murat with my father's service record, which she put "into her royal corset." This prompted my father to say, on 12 Prairial, Year XII: "Once again, the time has come when ladies dispose of promotions and when the corset of a princess holds more promise than the battlefield. So be it! I hope to wash my hands of that corset when we're at war again, and give proper thanks to my country for what my country forces me to win improperly."

Then, returning to the subject of his personal problems: "I've just been brought, my dear mother, a letter from you in which you give me grief by aggrieving yourself. You claim that I looked worried in your presence and let slip some impatient words. But have I ever, even in thought, directed one of them to you? I'd rather die. You surely know they were intended for Deschartres, in repayment for his hurtful and untimely sermons. Never when I was with you, have I impatiently summoned the day that would take me away. Oh, how painful it all is, and how I suffer over it! I will soon return to demand satisfaction for your letters, wicked mother whom I cherish."

I was born on 12 Messidor.[31] My grandmother had no inkling of it. On the 16th, my father wrote her on quite a different matter.

Letter I   Paris, 16 Messidor, Year XII (July 5, 1804).

From Maurice to His Mother at Nohant

I received your nice letter for Lacuée. I brought it to him myself. He was in Saint-Cloud. I went back there yesterday and saw him. My request is at the war office and should be put before the Emperor next week. My name is on the promotion list. By the same token, other members of our family are rising in the world: M. de Ségur has just been named master dignitary of the Empire and grand master of ceremonies, at a salary of a hundred thousand francs, plus forty as councillor of state. René takes up his functions with a large gold key embroidered on his back. The prince is going to have a guard. Apolline promises me a regiment. The prince will be the high consulate. I rub my eyes to make sure I'm not having an absurd dream, but I might just as well close them again—my ambition won't rise to the occasion, and I always feel torn between going to war and going to live with you. I don't seem able to have a more brilliant future, and the success of others seems to have a strange effect on me. Still, I rejoice in the happiness of those I love, because I am not jealous by nature. But I won't be made happy that way. I would like some activity, some honor, otherwise a bit of comfort and domestic happiness. If I were a captain, you could come here, I would have quite enough to keep a well-sprung cabriolet to take you about, I'd look after you, I'd make you forget all our reasons for sadness. With Deschartres absent, we'd be happy again as in the old days, I'm sure. I love you so much, no matter what you say, that in the end you'll have to believe me. Your last letter was as kind as you are, and in my joy I showed it to everyone.[37] Don't scold me! I embrace you with all my heart.

Beaumont did a melodrama for the Porte-Saint-Martin. It isn't good, but that doesn't mean it won't be a success. And besides, it amuses him so.[38]

I have had to put off my plans until September for a prompt return to your side, due to the Emperor's trip; but then I shall come to harvest the grapes, and if Deschartres is still playing the learned man, I'll camp out in his vats.

Letter II   1 Thermidor, Year XII (July 20, 1804).

The Emperor left yesterday during the night, and you no doubt think I'm on my way to Boulogne. I am doing better than that; I'm preparing to bring you a bouquet for your name day, along with a thousand very tender kisses. De Conchy has taken it on himself to let Dupont know that my business is better managed from here than it would be from there, since Dupont is due to return in a week and I have nothing to gain by seeking the Emperor's attention. The Sedan affair proved to us that, on such occasions, they prefer to hide us rather than show us off. Dupont can't deny it, and he can't think badly of me if I'm not eager to be taken in again. If it was a question of going to get shot at, there would be a place for me, and I'd hasten to get there. But there is no place when it comes to receiving the master's glances, and besides I can't stand it. Whether it means pushing yourself on top of them, flinging yourself at their feet, or killing yourself for them, that trade is hateful to me. If His Majesty wants to know who I am, he'll find my credentials in his valises, because my request is journeying post-haste along with him. Since his particular work goes on as usual, even on the road, my service record and claims are in the portfolios that travel with him, and this will perhaps speed up the promotion I want so badly. M. de Ségur assures me this cannot fail to happen. Berthier said to him yesterday, "I know that officer. He has done good service, he deserves advancement, I myself added a note to his recommendation."

René is definitely certified as chamberlain. His duties consist of presenting the ambassadors to the prince, doing the honors at the palace, and seeing that ceremonial events run smoothly. He shares them with M. d'Arjuzon. Apolline's duties consist of maintaining her elegant toilette and waiting hand and foot on the princess, whom she accompanies like a confidante in a tragedy. I make her mad by calling her Albine or Oenone; I call René Arcas or Arbates.[32] At first they get angry, but eventually they laugh. The eminent ladies have likened the two of them to plague victims, for they no longer set foot in their own house, and they wouldn't have it any other way. Uncle Beaumont's melodrama is in rehearsal. If Deschartres was wise, he would embark on a career in the theater, instead of concerning himself with the land tax revenue and a thousand other nonsensical things. But it would be useless to try to convince him; I'd never get anywhere. I charge you to tell him that, if he doesn't groom his oxen and rake his walk in time for my arrival, he'll have me to contend with....

The Emperor's response with regard to the promotion to captain was that all requests for advancement of general staff members would be postponed for one year. My father shared in the common disfavor and still did not go to wish his mother a happy name day, but this time it wasn't intentional. He had a rather severe case of scarlet fever, during which he seems to have been very affected by the disappearance of young Octave de Ségur, for whom he had a special fondness. The story is mysterious and romantic. Octave was sub-prefect at Soissons; he came to Paris to spend a few days, left one morning, and was not heard from for several years. Later he blew his brains out. An unhappy love affair was the cause of his flight and suicide. My father wrote a ballad on his disappearance, with very remarkable music, and it begins like this:

> Is there no longer any hope
> To find thee once again, Octave?

It is the only piece of his music remaining to me. Every last sheet of his opera, *Elizène*, which he worked on so hard and so passionately, has vanished, but the ballad proves to me that he did have truly musical ideas.

While Maurice was ill, René wrote to my grandmother in order to reassure her, and unwittingly let slip some indiscreet remarks about my having been born, of which he thought she was informed. The question of marriage does not come up at all in these letters; I do not think he had been let in on this secret, but he attributes Maurice's unsuccessful attempts in obtaining a promotion to his persistent attachment to Sophie. This does not seem likely to me, as my father was included in the overall disfavor in which general staffs were viewed. If it is true that by dint of obsessive canvassing he could have had them grace him with exceptional treatment, I do not hold it against him that he was not adept at this kind of success. But my grandmother was frightened and irritated by these insinuations, which were really motivated by the most tender interest on M. de Villeneuve's part, and wrote a rather bitter letter to her son, which gave him a new bout of fever. His reply is full of affection and pain.

Letter III   10 Fructidor (August 28, 1804).

According to you, my dear mother, I'm an ingrate and a madman. An ingrate, never! A madman perhaps I shall become, sick as I am in body and spirit. Your letter hurts me much more than the minister's response, because you accuse me of having engineered my own bad luck, and you would like me to have worked miracles to have averted it. The fact is I don't know the first thing about servility and intrigue. You have only yourself to blame who taught me early on to scorn courtiers. If you hadn't been living far from Paris for several years, withdrawn from the world, you would know that the new regime is worse than the old in that respect, and you would not deem it a crime for me to have remained true to myself. If we had been at war longer, I believe I would have duly won my ranks, but since they have to be won in antechambers, I admit I have no brilliant campaigns to boast of on that score. You reproach me for never telling you what's going on inside me. You are the one who never wished it! How is it possible, when the minute I open my mouth you accuse me of being a bad son? I am forced to keep quiet because you are not satisfied with the only answer I have for you, which is that I love you and I love no one more than you. Weren't you the one who was always against my desire to leave Dupont and return to the lines? Now you realize that I'm at a dead end, but now it's too late. Now, one "has to obtain this as a special favor of His Majesty." Favors and I don't get on well together. You say I have been wronged; that is possible, but I don't know by whom. I am no judge of enemies, and if I have any, it is not my fault. This my conscience can swear to, before God and before you.

In the midst of all this, Octave is nowhere to be found. They are sure now he's been murdered, but not a clue! His father is in despair, and I am dreadfully distressed. That is quite a different kind of family misfortune than disgrace at court! They say that to accept one's own lot, one must always look to those less fortunate. This is a villainous maxim which seems to say that our consolation lies in the desolation of others!

He returned to Nohant and spent another six weeks there without bringing himself to raise the fatal confession from his heart to his lips—but his secret was divined. Toward the end of Brumaire, Year XII (November 1804), on his return to Paris, his mother wrote to the mayor of the fifth arrondissement:

[First Letter of Mme. Dupin to the Mayor of the Fifth Arrondissement]

A mother, Monsieur, probably has no need to justify in your eyes the title with which she introduces herself, in order to solicit your attention.

I have strong reasons to fear that my only son was recently married in

Paris without my consent. I am widowed; he is twenty-six years old, in military service, his name is Maurice-François-Elisabeth Dupin. The person with whom he has contracted marriage is known under several names, the legal one, I believe, is Victoire Delaborde. She should be a little older than my son, both of them living together at number fifteen, Rue Meslay, in the home of a Monsieur Maréchal.[(39)] It is because I think this street is in your district that I take the liberty of addressing my questions and confiding my fears to you. I would hope you would be so kind as to forward my letter to your colleagues in the district where Rue Meslay is located.

This girl, or woman—I do not know which to call her—lived on Rue de la Monnaie until last Nivôse, where she had a hat shop, before moving to Rue Meslay.

Since living on Rue Meslay, my son has had a daughter by her, whom I believe was born in Messidor and registered under the name of Aurore, daughter of M. Dupin and ———. The birth certificate could seemingly shed some light on the marriage, if it took place before her birth, as I believe is the case, considering the child's given name. Several indications make me suspect it could have been contracted last Prairial. I have the honor of writing to a magistrate and, perhaps, a father, which double title makes me vain enough to hope for a reply as promptly as possible and for inviolable discretion, no matter what the results of the inquiry which I take the liberty of requesting from you.

I have the honor, etc.

[Mme.] Dupin.

[Second Letter of Mme. Dupin to the Mayor of the Fifth Arrondissement]

In confirming my fears, Monsieur, you have broken my heart, and it will not be open to the consolation you wish to give it for a long time to come; but it will never be closed to gratitude, and I am fully aware of the value of an intention which does honor to your heart. However, I owe too much to your generous concern not to hope for something more. You seem to believe that "the greatest irregularity committed in this marriage was to have hurt a mother's most respectful and tender feelings." I see you understand such feelings, but you do not know, and I hope you never have to know, to what extent he could have hurt them! I myself still do not know, but my heart tells me that he must feel very guilty, since he thought he had to keep the most important step of his life a secret from me. You alone can help me fathom this secret, because you are up to now its sole depositary, because I do not dare confide to any of my acquaintances in Paris what my son did not dare tell his mother, and because I dare even less to go there myself while he is there and leave an estate which I took pleasure in embellishing for a companion worthy of him and me. And yet I must find out who this unknown daughter-in-law is, whom he seems set on giving me! ...

My present peace of mind and his future well-being both depend on this. For my heart to get used, if it must, to all the consequences of his misdeed, it is essential that my mind grasp every last detail. Your esteemed colleague, the mayor of ———— arrondissment, was kind enough to offer "information from the file which consists of documents produced by the couple." He will not refuse to give you, Monsieur, a valid copy of each and every document, bar none, and I dare expect your kindness—I ought to call it delicacy—in asking him this favor, either in your name or mine....

It is easy to see by this letter—so unhappy, so noble, yet so clever—that my grandmother wanted to look at the evidence first hand, in order to declare, if possible, an annullment of the marriage. She was not as ignorant as she allowed regarding the names and forebears of her daughter-in-law; she pretended to be totally ignorant so as not to give away her plan, and if she was hinting at a sort of pardon (which she was by no means yet inclined to grant), this was in fear of finding that the mayor of the ———— arrondissement (who had performed the marriage) was an accomplice to the irregularities in the contract. So she did not address herself directly to him, but to the mayor of the fifth instead, whose jurisdiction she knew did not extend to Rue Meslay, but on whose integrity she probably had some particulars. Her feminine instinct for delicate ruse was therefore more inspirational to her than clever counsel might have been, and I admit that this little plot against my legitimate birth seems to me of equally incontestable legitimacy.

For his part, my father—probably advised by a professional, because on his own he would have fallen into all the traps of maternal tenderness—must have wanted to keep his marriage a secret until such time as the possibility that his mother could successfully oppose it was over. So they deceived each other—sad fate of their mutual positions—and wrote to each other as if nothing were wrong. I say they deceived one another, and yet they did not tell each other lies. Their only device was, in their letters, to both remain silent about the principal object of their concern.   *S. Bu.*

Letters continued. —The coronation. —An exchange of letters
between my grandmother and a civil official. —Abbé d'Andrezel.
—Letters continued. —Marquis de S————. —A passage from
Marmontel's *Mémoires*. —My first meeting with my grandmother.
—My mother's character. —Her church marriage. —My Aunt Lucie
and my Cousin Clotilde. —My first stay at Chaillot.

Letter IV   End of Brumaire, Year XIII (November 1804).

From Maurice to His Mother

   I was so happy at your side for six weeks, my dear mother, that it is
almost a burden to have to write you now, when I feel like conversing with
you. The calm, the happiness which I enjoyed at Nohant have rendered even
more unbearable to me the tumult, the restlessness, the noise which surround me in Paris.

   My trip was an abridged version of all the hard luck stories of a highway traveller. A delay at Orléans due to lack of space, an accident and new
delay at Étampes. Then at the Berny crossroads, a damned provincial attorney, who was coming to Paris to see the coronation, leaves the coach during
the night to get to Versailles, where he's to be lodged in barracks with members of the other departmental guards, carries off my suitcase, and leaves me
his, wherein, instead of the pretty neckties you gave me, there's a good
chance I'll find only dirty collar bands. The day after my arrival here, I had
to run to Versailles with the attorney's togs and reclaim mine. We crossed
paths; we looked for each other; the damned attorney had me running
around in vain, but finally an exchange took place to both parties' satisfaction, though only after a lot of wasted effort.

   Laure and Auguste, René and Apolline received me with open arms.
I'm hopeful that I won't be forced to return to the rats in my attic at Fayel,
because Général Suchet, who gave me the honor of stopping his carriage
solely to talk to me yesterday, told me that all the division generals were
going to be summoned to take part in the coronation ceremony and that
probably Dupont would not remain in exile. So here I am again for a few
days, and I shall keep you informed of the events in the celebration.

   His Holiness arrives tomorrow. In Rue de Gramont, they no longer
dream of anything but laces, diamonds, and embroideries. These serious
concerns have so made them lose their memory that when I mentioned in

their presence that I was in the fifth year of lieutenancy, René cried out, as if emerging from a dream, "What, Maurice, you're not yet a captain?" This small distraction on the part of a person with whom I have spoken every day for six months about my bad luck, and who, for your benefit, makes himself out to be my "patron," while accusing me of being apathetic and not supporting him in his "zeal," should prove to you once and for all to what extent you can count on the promises of those who mind their own business.

As for Apolline, she takes on airs of sponsoring me which are rather droll coming from someone who is of no service to me at all. She was saying yesterday that if Dupont had only sent her some "good reports" on my behalf, she would have had me make my way in the world, but that I was seeing "too much bad company." The company I see is well worth her circle. Vitrolles, who reported this to me, went into gales of laughter at the impertinence, and dismissed it as coming from a "twit." Let her pass for a twit! But I don't bear her a grudge; everyone is the same. Court airs are a common affliction among those who would never have been admitted there in the past.

I gave your lining to Mme. de La Marlière, so that she could have a quilted wrap, collared in the English style, made for you; it's in vogue, and I myself gave her the design for the collar, so the cut wouldn't be skimpy; for that style can be very pretty or very ugly, depending on how clever the seamstress is. I chose the fabric, and I hope you'll find it pretty. Therefore, don't believe that I can forget anything that concerns you, and forgive me when I fail to mention what concerns only me.

This morning, I am using M. de Ségur's tickets to see the preparations at Notre-Dame. This evening I shall go see the first performance of *Les Désastres de Lisbonne*. All of Paris will be fooled. They expect to see an upheaval, an earthquake. Many of them are afraid of a fire, but I hear from one of the theater's managers that the entire uproar takes place in narrative, which is much more economical.

My lyrical works are enjoying a success here that I didn't envision at Nohant. Everyone always asks to hear the ballad of the divorce again. Saint-Brisson is an enthusiast. In his capacity as principal of a canton, he's here for the coronation, and makes his visits at ten o'clock at night in silk hose and on horseback. He is just as crazy as when you knew him and tells Mme. René some highly questionable stories, which she finds quite acceptable because he always attributes them to some prince or princess.

Goodbye, my dear mother; I miss Nohant. What a good letter you sent! I have so taken to repose, that in spite of the fatigue, the noise, and the confusion, I still feel like I'm in the country. And then you spoiled me so with everything that I have become difficult to please.

I beg D'Andrezel not to forget to work on the words to my opera. Deschartres will help us when it comes to the "machines." I embrace them both, but you above all, and more than anyone.

Maurice.

Letter V   Paris, 7 Frimaire, Year XIII (November 1804).

I was going to leave again for Fayel and miss the coronation ceremony, when our Maréchal Ney finally let me know that he had just despatched a message to Dupont insisting he come and letting him know he's expected the day after tomorrow. I am running to look for my trunk, which was already loaded and which I wrested from the hands of the drivers with great difficulty and at the expense of all my eloquence. I am dropping anchor and hauling in my sails. Dupont is, as a matter of fact, arriving on the eve of the great day. We are on very good terms. He put in for my Cross, and the report will be done after the coronation.

Then I saw the thing. One, two, three, four, five regiments of hussars, cuirassiers, dragoons, carbineers, and mamelukes; one, two, three, four, five, six, seven, eight, nine, ten, eleven, twelve, thirteen, fourteen six-horse carriages filled with people from court; one carriage with ten windows, filled with princesses; the arch-chancellor's carriage, and finally the Emperor's, with eight wonderful cream-colored horses, caparisoned with ornaments one story high, a carriage with ten windows, more stylish and polished than sumptuous, on the roof a kind of centerpiece representing eagles and the crown. Thirty pages in front and behind. The Emperor was in back on the right, the Empress on the left. In front, Princes Joseph and Louis; on horseback around the aforementioned carriage, Maréchals Moncey, Soult, Murat, and Davout. Hand-held horses in blinding gold brocade covers, with double reins of silk and gold, led by mameluke footmen, themselves clothed in the greatest magnificence. The papal carriage, with eight white horses decked with plumes, the Pope seated alone in the back, two cardinals facing him. The golden cross carried in advance of the carriage by an overfed pedant in robes and a square bonnet, seated on a mule.[40] Twenty more carriages, all similar to the first ones, all with the Emperor's arms and livery, transported the rest of the imperial troop of valets.

In Notre-Dame, the throne near the portal in the rear, representing a rather massive triumphal arch whose Greek style harmonized very badly with the Gothic of the church, the Empress seated a little lower than her spouse, the princes two steps below. The tribunes to the right and left in drapery, occupied by the council of state, the legislative body, the canton presidents, the princely houses, and complimentary ticket holders. In the nave, the high-ranking officers of the Legion of Honor.

After the mass, the Emperor descended from the throne with the Empress, followed by the princes and princesses. They crossed the church at a solemn pace on their approach to the altar. The Pope put some oil on the forehead and hands of the Emperor and Empress; then Bonaparte stood up, went to take the crown from the altar, placed it himself upon his head, and pronounced aloud the oath to preserve the rights of his people and their freedom. He returned to his throne, and they sang the Te Deum. Then the return, magnificent illuminations, dances, fireworks, etc. It was very beautiful, very imposing, a play well-staged, the major roles well-played. Goodbye to the Republic! You don't regret it, my dear mother, nor do I, for what it has been, but for what it might have been, for what it was in my childhood dreams!

René is decidedly the chamberlain. Apolline takes her position from the trains six yards long. Auguste is powdered white. Laure is always excellent.

I had the parts to my overture printed, and we performed it at Auguste's with musicians from the Feydeau. I had announced it as the work of one of my friends, and someone very kindly compared it to Haydn's. I hadn't at all expected such a success. Tell this to D'Andrezel to prod his genius; mine is all ready.

(To be read *dolce*.) My Aurore is doing marvellously well, she is wonderfully beautiful, and I am delighted that you asked for news of her.

Your letter overwhelmed me with pleasure. You are truly my dear mother, and all the prideful fantasies of others, which I am witness to, will never furnish those who are nourished on them a quarter of the happiness that I find in the testimonies of your affection. Do preserve this happiness for me! Every day I miss our evening parties and our chats, and our joyful dinners, and the large salon—all of Nohant, when you come right down to it—and my only consolation is the thought of coming back. Goodbye, my dearly beloved mother; speak of me to D'Andrezel and to the engineer Deschartres. Your errands are done.

The preceding letter shows that my existence was accepted by the dear mother and that she could not help showing the interest she took in me; yet she did not accept the marriage, and she and Abbé d'Andrezel were busy looking for the proof of invalidity that her lack of consent could bring to bear. The mayor who had performed this marriage had been deceived by some questionable evidence. Alerted by the claims of my grandmother, who wanted to have a valid copy of the documents, he was not quick to respond, afraid perhaps of the consequences of his error, which could devolve on him or on the justice of the peace. The mayor of the fifth arrondissement, on the other hand, who had no reason not to, and who had had the documents communicated to him, at least responded with a very understandable reserve as to the manner in which the formalities had been conducted, and confined himself to giving some details about my mother's extraction, about Claude Delaborde, bird seller on Quai de la Mégisserie, and about Grandfather Cloquart. The latter was, in that era, still living and wearing (which information is not contained in the stern magistrate's letter) a red greatcoat and three-cornered hat, his wedding attire from the time of Louis XV, the most beautiful no doubt that he had ever possessed, by which he had counted his Sundays for so long and had at last to wear daily for reasons of economy. Apropos of this less-than-brilliant origin of her daughter-in-law, my grandmother wrote to the said mayor on 27 Frimaire, Year XIII, as follows:

. . . . However painful the information that you were kind enough to supply is for my heart, I am no less grateful for your efforts to enlighten my sad curiosity. The lineage afflicts me little, but more so the personal character of the young woman. Your silence in this regard, Monsieur, is for me a confirmation of my misfortune and my son's. It is his first mistake! He is the essence of good sons, and I was cited as the happiest of mothers. My heart is breaking, and I express to you in tears, Monsieur, my appreciation for your courteous behavior and the very particular esteem with which, etc.

To which the mayor of the fifth replied (I have all these letters before me, my grandmother having copied hers and formed a kind of dossier of the whole correspondence):

Madame:

Judging from your response to my last letter, your grief has deluded you on an item which I believe I must rectify, an item most essential to my satisfaction as well as to your peace of mind.

It seems to me, Madame, that the data appropriate to softening the test that a mother's heart is made to undergo in this instance should be based on facts alone. At least it is with this intention and in this spirit that I made some inquiries and transmitted the results to you.

Is unhappiness of spirit perhaps being led too hastily by sentiment to believe in what it fears? In this regard, my letter would seem to contain some inductions contrary to those you have made regarding the personal character of the wife your son has chosen. Willing and able to speak only in certainties, I wanted to judge for myself, and as I told you, I charged an intelligent and capable person with the task of penetrating, under some pretext, the interior of the newlyweds. As I already had the honor of telling you, that person found an extremely modest locale, but well-kept, the two young people having an exterior of decency and even of distinction; the young mother in the midst of her children, herself nursing the last, and appearing absorbed by maternal cares; the young man full of politeness, benevolence, and serenity. As the person sent by me had adopted the pretext of asking for an address, your son descended one flight below to inquire of M. Maréchal, who is married to Mlle. Lucie Delaborde, younger sister of Mlle. Victoire Delaborde; M. Maréchal came up very obligingly with M. Dupin to supply this address. M. Maréchal is a retired officer who presents a very favorable exterior. The final conclusion of my envoy, in whom you can have complete confidence, is that, whatever may have been the antecedents of the young woman (of which I am entirely ignorant), her life is at present most regular and even denotes a habit of order and decency which has nothing affected about it. Furthermore, there was between the two spouses a tone of tender intimacy which supposes good harmony, and I have since had additional information which convinces me that nothing "cries out" for your son's repentance of this contracted union.

I am wrong, of course, for he must sooner or later repent bitterly for having broken the heart of his mother; but you yourself said it, Madame: it is his first, his only mistake! And I have every reason to believe that as grave as it is for you, it is reparable through his affection, and with the grace of yours; it is within your maternal heart to absolve him, and I would be happy to bring you consolation by affirming to you that the "breeding seen in his home" in no way justifies your mournful presentiments.

In this spirit, Madame, I beg you to accept, etc.

However reassuring this kind and honest response was, my grandmother, nevertheless, persisted in arming herself with the evidence that would leave her the hope of destroying the marriage. She again wrote to the mayor who had married her son, in a bitter tone which depicts well the cruel condition of her spirit.

January 30, 1805.

I must, no doubt, congratulate you, Monsieur, on the domestic happiness you enjoy; for if it were otherwise, if some sorrow troubled the peace of your hearth, you would not have neglected for an entire month to respond to an afflicted mother regarding what she holds most dear in the world, and conclude by articulating, as if in passing, that I had not solicited you directly. My observation is directed to you only as a private individual—perhaps a family man known among his fellow citizens; for if I were addressing the public man, I would perhaps have the right to bring to his attention how negligence of this kind may be prejudicial to the interested parties who make claims on his ministry.

I thought I had sufficiently introduced myself to warrant requesting, without indiscretion, some documents which had been offered for communication by a third party. I had thought that public documents by their nature, and whose originals remained in your hands, could be delivered to me, copied, without compromise to you. I suppose, no doubt, I had flattered myself too readily that I would find in you the same respect, interest, and trust that I applauded myself for having inspired in M.———, your esteemed colleague. I hasten to beg your pardon for my mistake and, now, to formalize my request. To this effect, I am remitting to one of my friends, who will present himself to you for this purpose, the enclosed documents, etc.

The friend was Abbé d'Andrezel, who again left for Paris, furnished with all the necessary powers. Abbé d'Andrezel, whose title of Abbé had been dropped since the time of the Revolution, was one of the most witty and amiable men I ever knew. I no longer remember which translations from the Greek he had done, but he was a reputed scholar. He was rector of the University and for some time a censor during the Restoration. However, his royalist sentiments were not extreme, and I often heard him say at the time he exercised that unfortunate office, "What I like about my job is that it allows me to toss into the fire a host of platitudes for which the writers whom I cut up would be grateful, if they could be objective about it. On the other hand, I have the pleasure of rescuing from the scissors of my colleagues a small number of amusing and accurate things which I can forgive because they're witty. The French like to laugh, and provided they're left the freedom to make fun, they'll tolerate the lack of freedom to think. They put greater stock in gaiety than passion, in irony than ideas."

He would add very softly, in the ear of his old friend, my grandmother, "I deal, I admit, with some very stiff-necked pedants who find me too tolerant, and if they succeed in making their silly austerity prevail, the government will become even more ridiculous for the sake of being less ridiculed. I therefore believe I am fulfilling my mandate with greater conscience and wisdom by respecting the French spirit wherever I find it, even in the enemy camp. Besides, it is stronger than I am; when I have laughed, I am disarmed." That way of thinking was not at all relished. He practiced censorship for a short time. Whether he was quietly dismissed or retired in disgust, I'm not sure.

Abbé d'Andrezel had been a very handsome young man, and I think he was still quite a libertine. It was, therefore, rather ungracious of him to take on as serious a commission as the one my grandmother entrusted him with. However, he applied himself to it assiduously, evidenced by the fact that everything in the dossier relative to my father's marriage was either addressed to him or initiated by him. The result of all this activity was that the marriage was indissoluble and that the public official who consecrated it had acted in good faith, all inquiries to the contrary attributable only to personal revenge of no bearing on the contracted marriage.

While Abbé d'Andrezel was doing his part in Paris and my grandmother was writing from Nohant to her son, without revealing her anger and distress, my father, ever mute on the principal subject, talked to her of his affairs and his progress.

Letter VI   18 Frimaire, Year XIII (December 19, 1804).

I bring the cold spell with me from Montreuil. I had to make a quick trip there before the 30th, to present myself before the review inspector in order to be placed on the list of payees. On my return, I found René burning with the greatest zeal on my behalf. He dined at his prince's house with Dupont, and they had a long conversation of which I was the subject. Dupont boasted greatly of "my talent and my valor." The prince was much astonished to learn that I was ranked so low. I am going to be introduced to him, and he claims to have a strong interest in me. Unfortunately, he has very little credit at the moment; if his wife could intervene in my business, the outcome would be a lot more secure.

In order to obey you, I shall again do all I can to enter the guard; I shall again entice the patrons and the courtiers! As for situations in finance, the surety for collectors is one hundred thousand écus ready money. We can't afford to even think about it. . . .

I am working on my opera and sending you a draft of my outline. Tell me what you think.

Dupont is marrying Mlle. Bergon, whose father bears the same name and is inspector of waters and forests. She's a very good musician, we're told. This morning he bought her a piano for four thousand francs and a harp for one hundred fifty louis. I'm delighted; when he has a wife to enrage, maybe he'll leave us alone.

Goodbye, my dear mother, I love you with all my heart. I send a kiss to Andrezel and a thrashing to Deschartres.

Letter VII   January 5, 1805.

Ah, these are so good and those are so tender! How well packed all that was, and how well I recognized in the graciousness of that hamper the cares of my dear mother in everything she sends me! The pâté provides an added bonus in that it prolongs my composition lessons by a solid hour; my master, a true musician, is gluttonous and spoiled, and I put all my questions and observations to him while cramming him full of food. He is, besides, a profoundly learned man, and I work seriously with him.

I did not bring back, as you call them, the "treasures" of Montreuil, and yet I was able to buy a superb piano with four pedals, which is worth at least thirty-five louis and which I bought for eighteen. Imagine that I unearthed this marvel at a M. Grévin's, whose business is supplying caskets to all the parishes in Paris. He had received this piano by way of payment and didn't know what to do with it. God knows by what strange vicissitudes of fate the laws of exchange allowed the transfer to me of an instrument which had formerly been valued in quantities of biers. Where the devil, you'll ask me, did you dig up this undertaker? My master dug him up for me, said master of composition being the organist for Saint-Nicolas, Saint-Laurent, and other places, and furthermore disciple of and collaborator with the famous Couperin. I would love for you to hear him improvise on my piano. "My dazzled genius trembles before his."[33] In addition to his learning, he has the most beautiful feeling for melody, the taste of Mehul, and the grace of Boïeldieu. I confess that, by his side, I forget everything. Apollo and the muses console me, as they did M. Desnazures,[34] for the injustices of destiny....

Letters VIII, IX, and X

At last the coat Duboisdouin had lent me, for which you so scolded me, has turned up! However it wasn't worth all the trouble, because it would have been hard to find one as bad to replace it. My scamp of a lackey, pressured by the necessity of getting a reference from me, came to confess that this coat had for two months been in the hands of M. de Monvillars' cook. I went to see M. de Montvillars, told him my business, he had the coat returned to me at a charge of twenty-eight francs which I paid the cook, and I took back said coat that said cook had considered appropriate to transform into a cloak, which gave it a wholly agreeable, youthful look. I suggest Deschartres use it as a model in creating his own. I have given it to D'Andrezel, who brought me the one you had bought for me, so that I get a new coat out of all this, and Duboisdouin a remodeled one. I made my official visit to Mme. Dupont, who, it seems to me, has all the airs of a newly rich petty bourgeois. Many of her lady relatives were present, in Indian dresses and shaped bonnets. Philippe Ségur and the viscount are working, at shared expense, on the libretto for my opera. The renown of the authors will be a stepping stone for that of the composer.

They're now giving at the Associés a farce of a tragedy, written in all seriousness about twenty years ago by a certain André, wig maker of M. d'Argental, entitled *Le Désastre de Lisbonne*. The first act takes place in Lisbon, the second in Constantinople. There you can see the Grand Turk, in all his magnificence, threatening to have the hero of the play thrown into the lunatic asylum.

They recite lines such as these:

[Hero] To kill myself right here, lend me your scimitar.

[Grand Turk] We shall lend you one more beautiful by far.

Everyone is running to see this tragedy, whose style and plot are enough to make you guffaw.

Mme. Charles de Bérenger was on the verge of death. Another madame, whose name escapes me, went to cast herself at the knees of the Pope so that he might say a mass of intercession for the sick woman. The mass said, the fever ceased, a miracle! He'll be working many more. Four days ago, the Holy Father went to visit the glass works in the Faubourg Saint-Antoine; Mme. Tallien, who is now kept by Ouvrard, was presented to His Holiness, whereupon she begged him to give her his blessing. The Holy Father blessed not only her, but also a rosary she was carrying, and a child as well, from which father I don't know. Beaumont, an eye witness to the event, laughingly remarked, "For all sins, forgiveness; Mme. Tallien will perhaps become a saint." René is ruining himself in clothes and carriages, but all the while he preaches economy to me. He's dazzling. Madame allows herself to be courted by Caulaincourt (Auguste), master of horse to the prince. Her head has been turned by the new court, just as it was before by the Faubourg Saint-Germain, which has turned its back on her completely. A ball, lights, diamonds—no matter where, how, or why—it's always the same frivolity and the same empty-mindedness....

Three days ago, I attended an evening party that Beaumont gave for Prince Ferdinand, first chaplain to the Emperor. We had a regular concert. La Foret, Mme. Armand, Laïs, Guénin, Lancay, etc., and me! The music was excellent. In the midst of all this, a M. de Seulé arrived, a neighbor of Beaumont,[41] a man of about seventy, who has as many thousand pounds a year in income as his age, dressed exactly as thirty years ago, imagining himself young, pleasing, and witty, composing behind a screen some quatrains for everyone, singing them in an awful, cracked counter-tenor, playing the beau with the women. This little old man is a veritable curiosity, and since people look at him with astonishment, he believes they're all infatuated with him. He absolutely insisted that Auguste play a concerto for piano, saying that with his looks he couldn't be anything but a musician. He had already let us have three quatrains to a melody from *Les Folies d'Espagne*, and out of respect for Beaumont, we contained ourselves. But when he came to the fourth, he requested Mlle. Armand, in all seriousness, to accompany him, which she applied herself to with much verve, playing such ridiculous cadences, that Auguste, who was standing behind the piano with that frozen expression of utmost gravity that he's known for, suddenly let out a great peal of laughter. That was the signal. I was opposite him, biting my lips and avoiding looking at Mlle. Armand, who had all she could do to hold in her laughter. But when I saw my dear nephew lose his imperturbable phlegm and laugh with the abandon of a man who does nothing by halves, I lost all control, and I carried along the whole assembly, who obeyed me as to a general order; it was a moment of indescribable, uncontrollable relaxation. The Marquis de Seulé wasn't the least bit put off by it, finished his quatrain with the air of a conqueror, and was applauded furiously by everyone.

Aurore is very aware, my dear mother, of the kiss I gave her on your behalf. If she could speak or write, she would wish you a happy new year, one that turns out to be the best and kindest in the world. She doesn't say anything yet, but I can assure you that she thinks nonetheless. I do adore this child, a love you must allow me; it in no way detracts from my love for you, on the contrary, it makes me understand and appreciate more the one you have for me.

. You no doubt know that Prince Joseph will be "named" King of Lombardy, and Eugène Beauharnais, King of Etruria. There is talk of a declaration of war very shortly....

Letter XI   Paris, 9 Ventôse.

In truth, my dear and beloved mother, if I wanted to take your letter in the tone in which you wrote it, there would be nothing left for me but to throw myself into the river. I'm sure you don't mean one word of what you say; isolation and distance are magnifying your observations. But as clear as my conscience may be, I am nevertheless painfully affected by your language. You always reproach me for my bad luck, as if I could have brought it on myself, as if I hadn't mentioned and proven a hundred times that the general staffs were in complete disfavor.

There are no secret sources or hidden intrigues directed at me behind it. I have no enemies; I am not the object of personal disfavor. I am undergoing a fate common to all those who find themselves in the same position as me, who don't have six years of rank on the general staff, and who haven't been fortunate enough to be deemed an exception, otherwise known as nepotism. The general staff is dead and buried. One thinks no more of Marengo than of going to hell. Bivouacs in the antechamber are the only thing that count. When we want some advancement in our corps positions, Duroc answers us, "You're not part of anything; quit your generals and return to line units." Which is what I tried to do, in spite of you, I admit it; but then we were told in the war offices that people getting back into the line were being taken "out of turn."

You reproach me for not being the object of one of those special favors that are nevertheless pouring down on our family. What do you want me to say? It is very true that René is going to be decorated. Hasn't he earned this better than I? He has been chamberlain for three months, he announces marvelously, he performs peerlessly his service in the salon. I, brute that I am, have only waged war. Is it my fault this no longer counts? Philippe de Ségur, who has never *heard* a cannon fired, is also decorated, and a captain to boot. Is it my fault if I found myself in the middle of bullets and balls? They didn't warn us in advance that this would injure us one day in the future.

We mustn't believe that chance and influence conspire greatly for or against us. The Emperor has his system. I have been well served within his sphere by Clarke and Caulaincourt. Dupont himself did me justice and served me well recently. I complain of no one, and above all, I envy no one. I rejoice in the favors that fall on my relatives and friends. Only I realize that I won't arrive by the same road, because I don't know how to go about it. The emperor alone appoints and makes things happen. The minister of war is no more than a head clerk. The Emperor knows what he's doing and what he wants to do. He wants to bring back to the fold those whose hauteur remained intact, and surround his family and his person with courtiers extracted from the old party. He doesn't need to satisfy some minor officers like us, who have waged war out of enthusiasm and from whom he has nothing to fear. If you were to strike out into the world, launch into intrigue, conspire against him with friends from abroad, all would go better for me; I wouldn't be ignored, abandoned; I wouldn't have had to make bodily payment, to sleep in water and in snow, to expose my life to danger a hundred times, and to sacrifice our small provision to the service of my country. I don't reproach you for your disinterestedness, your wisdom, and your virtue, my dear mother; on the contrary, I love you, and respect you, and venerate you for your character. Forgive me, then, on your side, for being only a brave soldier and a sincere patriot.

We have cause for consolation, however. Comes the war and all this will probably change. We shall be good for something, when it's a question of gunfire, and then they'll remember us.

I don't want to reread the last page of your letter, I burned it. Alas! What are you saying? No, my mother, a gallant man doesn't dishonor himself by loving a woman, and a woman isn't considered loose when she's loved by a gallant man who aims to redress the injustices of destiny toward her. You know that better than I, and my sentiments formed by your lessons, which I have always religiously followed, are only the reflections of your soul. By what unimaginable mishap do you reproach me today for being the man you created morally as well as physically?

In the midst of your reproaches, your tenderness always comes through. I don't know who told you that I had been living in poverty for some time, but you are worrying after the fact. Well, I admit I lived in a "little garret" last summer and that my household of poet and lover made a singular contrast with the golden ornamentation on my military costume. Don't blame anyone for this moment of embarrassment which I didn't mention to you and about which I shall never complain. A debt that I thought I had paid, the money for which had passed through some dishonest hands, was the sole cause of this small disaster, already remedied by my salary. I now have a very pleasant little apartment and lack for nothing.

What is D'Andrezel telling me—that you're perhaps going to come to Paris, perhaps sell Nohant? I don't comprehend any of it. Ah, my dear mother, come, and all our troubles will fly away in tender, sincere explanation. But don't sell Nohant, you would regret it.

Farewell, I embrace you with all my heart, very sad and fearful of your discontent. Nevertheless, God is my witness that I love you and deserve your love.

Maurice.

In a final letter of this correspondence, my father converses at length with his mother about an incident which seemed to trouble her greatly.

Marmontel's *Mémoires posthumes* had just been published. My grandmother had been well acquainted with Marmontel[35] in her childhood, but she never spoke to me about this acquaintance, and the *Mémoires posthumes* explain well enough why. Here is a page from his memoirs:

"The kind of good will that was shown me in this court[42] served me meanwhile to make myself heard and believed regarding an interesting matter. The baptismal certificate of Aurore [GS's grandmother], daughter of Mlle. Verrière, attested that she was the daughter of the Maréchal de Saxe,[43] and after the death of her father, Mme. la Dauphine had the intention to see to her upbringing. This was the mother's ambition. But it took the fancy of M. le Dauphin to say she was my daughter, and this comment left its mark. Mme. de Chalut laughed when she mentioned it to me, but I took M. le Dauphin's joke most seriously. I accused him of levity, and offering to give proof that I had known Mlle. Verrière only since the marshal's voyage to Prussia, more than a year after the birth of that child, I said that it would be equally unfeeling to take her true father away from her as to make me pass for her father. Mme. de Chalut took it upon herself to plead this case before Mme. la Dauphine, and M. le Dauphin conceded. Thus, Aurore was raised at their expense at the convent of the Sisters of Saint-Cloud, and Mme. de Chalut,[44] whose country house was in Saint-Cloud, was willing to assume, for my sake and at my behest, the cares and details of this education."

This passage could not have displeased my grandmother, and Marmontel had a certain right to her gratitude. But in another place, the author of *Les Incas* recounts with less reserve his relationship with Mlle. Verrière. Although he speaks of the conduct, character, and talent of this young actress with esteem and affection, he goes into some intimate details which would necessarily make a daughter suffer. Hence my grandmother wrote to my father about it, to get him to see whether it would not be possible to have the passage suppressed in the new editions. Uncle Beaumont was consulted. He had an equal interest in the matter, since in the same passage Marmontel relates how the beautiful Mlle. Verrière had been compensated by Prince de Turenne—who had been the cause of Maréchal de Saxe withdawing the pension of twelve thousand pounds he had been paying for her and her daughter—once Marmontel promised not to see her any more. You see, Uncle Beaumont was, as I have already said, the son of Mlle. Verrière and that Prince de Turenne, Duc de Bouillon. However, he took the matter less seriously.

"Beaumont assures me," wrote my father to my grandmother, "this doesn't merit the trouble you're giving yourself over it. First of all, we're not rich enough, that I know of, to repurchase the published edition and secure that the next one be corrected; even if we were able to do this, it would add even more spice to the copies sold, and sooner or later we would not be able to prevent new editions from being printed that conformed to the first. Moreover, would Marmontel's heirs give their consent to such an arrangement with the publishers? I doubt it, and we are no longer living in those times when one could prevail either by promises, threats, or by order of the king against the freedom to write. We no longer take the cudgel to those "caddish" authors and printers, and you, my dear mother, who since that time have been on the side of the encyclopedists and philosophers, cannot object that we have altered law and custom. I understand full well that you suffer to hear your mother spoken of so lightly, but how can that affect your life, which has always been so austere, and your reputation, which is so spotless? For my part, it doesn't anger me at all that the present public knows what was already known to an even greater extent about my maternal grandmother by her own society. As I see by the memoirs in question, she was a lovely woman, gentle, without intrigue or ambition, who behaved very well and lived decently, given her position. What was true of her was true of many others. Her errors were circumstantial, and her way of accepting them rendered her loving and kind. That is the impression I am left with from these pages about which you torment yourself so, and you can be sure that the public will not be more severe than I am."

Here end the letters from my father to his mother. No doubt he wrote her many more during the four years he had left to live, which entailed frequent separations once the war began again. But the rest of their correspondence has disappeared, why or how I don't know. So, to continue my father's story, I have his service records to consult, several letters he wrote to his wife, and my own vague memories from childhood.

My grandmother took herself to Paris during Ventôse with the intention of having her son's marriage broken off, hopeful even that he would consent to it, for she had never seen him able to resist her tears. First, she arrived in Paris unknown to him, having specified neither the day of her departure nor alerting him to her arrival, as she usually did. She began by going to see M. Desèze, whom she consulted about the validity of the marriage. He found both the marriage and the legislation behind it crudely executed. He called on two other well-known lawyers, and the result of the consultation was that there was a case to plead, because there is always a case to plead in affairs of this world, but that the marriage would, nine chances out of ten, be upheld by the judges, that my birth certificate attested to my legitimacy, and supposing that the marriage were broken off, the intention as well as the duty of my father would infallibly be to fulfill the desired formalities and contract another marriage with the mother of the child he had intended to legitimize.

It is possible that my grandmother never had the intention of formally taking her son to court. Even if she had conceived of the plan, she certainly would not have had the courage. She was probably relieved of half her grief by renouncing her momentarily hostile intentions, for we double our own pain by holding a grudge against those we love. Yet, she still wished to spend several days without seeing her son, doubtless in order to exhaust the resistance of her own spirit and obtain some new information about her daughter-in-law. But my father discovered that his mother was in Paris; he understood that she knew everything and put me in charge of pleading his case. Taking me in his arms, he climbed into a cab, stopped at the door of the house where my grandmother had gotten off, won in a few words the good graces of the doorkeeper, and confided me to the care of this woman, who carried out the following errand:

She climbed to the apartment of my grandmama and asked to speak to her on whatever pretext came into her mind. Once in her presence, she talked to her about this and that, and chatting all the while, interrupted herself to say, "Take a look, madame, at the pretty little girl of whom I'm the grandmother! Her wet-nurse brought her to me today, and I'm so happy about it that I can't part with her for an instant." "Yes, she looks very healthy and strong," said my grandmother, looking for her box of sweets. And all at once, the good woman, who played her role very well, placed me on grandmama's knee, who offered me some tidbits and began to look at me with a kind of shock and emotion. Suddenly, she pushed me away, exclaiming, "You're deceiving me, this child isn't yours; she doesn't look like you! I know, I know who she is!"

Frightened by the movement that propelled me from the maternal bosom, it seems I began, not to scream, but to cry real tears, which were very effective. "Come, my poor dear love," the porter lady said, taking me back. "They don't want any part of you here, let's go."

My poor grandmother was vanquished. "Give her back to me," she said. "Poor child, all this isn't her fault! And who brought this little one?" "Your own son, madame; he's waiting downstairs, I'll carry back his daughter to him. Excuse me if I offended you; I didn't realize, I'm just an ignoramus! I thought to give you pleasure, to bring you a nice surprise. . . ." "It's all right, my dear, I don't blame you," said my grandmother. "Go find my son, and leave me the child."

My father climbed the stairs four at a time. He found me on the lap, against the bosom of my grandmama, who was crying as she did her utmost to make me laugh. No one told me what transpired between them, and as I was only eight or nine months old, it is probable that I didn't take note of it. It is also probable that they wept together and were loving to each other some more. My mother, who recounted to me this first adventure of my life, told me that when my father brought me back to her, I had in my hands a beautiful ring with a big ruby that my grandmama had removed from her finger, charging me to place it on my mother's finger, which my father made me observe religiously.[45]

Some time had still to pass before my grandmother would consent to see her daughter-in-law, but already rumors were spreading that her son had made a "disproportionate" marriage, and the refusal to receive her necessarily gave rise to some unfortunate inductions against my mother, consequently against my father. My grandmama was alarmed at the damage that her aversion could do her son. She received the trembling Sophie, who disarmed her by her naïve compliance and affectionate kisses. The religious marriage was celebrated under the eyes of my grandmother,[36] after which a family meal officially sealed the adoption of my mother and me.

Later on, when consulting my own memories, which cannot deceive me, I shall tell the impression that these two women so different in behavior and thinking produced on each other. Suffice it for me to say in the meantime that the conduct on both sides was excellent, that the loving names "mother" and "daughter" were exchanged, and that if my father's marriage caused a small scandal among the persons of an intimate and rather restricted circle, the world that my father frequented was not at all concerned about it, and welcomed my mother without asking her for an account of her ancestors or her fortune. But she never liked society and was presented at Murat's court only when she was constrained and forced to, so to speak, by the functions that my father fulfilled later on in the service of that prince.[37]

My mother never felt either humbled or honored to find herself with people who might have considered themselves above her. She artfully mocked the pride of fools, the vanity of upstarts; feeling a connection to the people down to her fingertips, she thought herself more noble than all the patricians and aristocrats on earth. She used to say that those of her race had redder blood and larger veins than the others, which I am tempted to believe, because if moral and physical energy are, in reality, what constitute the excellence of the race, one cannot deny that this energy is condemned to diminish in those who lose the habit of work and the courage of suffering. One can certainly find exceptions to this aphorism, and retort that an excess of work and suffering enervates the human constitution as much as an excess of indolence and sloth. But it is certain, in general, that life's essence begins at the lowest level of society and is lost in proportion to its climb to the summit, like the sap in plants.

My mother was not one of those daring intriguers whose secret passion is to struggle against the prejudices of their time and who believe themselves ennobled by clinging, at the risk of a thousand insults, to the false grandeur of the world. She was a thousand times too proud to expose herself even to indifference. Her attitude was so reserved that she seemed timid, but if one tried to encourage her with patronizing airs, she became more than reserved, she would show her cold and taciturn side. Her bearing was excellent with persons who inspired in her a justified respect; then she was engaging and charming; but her true nature was outgoing, playful, sprightly, and above all the opposite of restrained. Big dinners, long soirées, dull visits, even balls were odious to her. She was a woman who preferred her own fireside, or a brisk and rollicking walk, but whether at home or out running errands, she needed the intimacy, the trust of completely sincere relationships, absolute freedom in her behavior and in the way she spent her time. Therefore, she always lived withdrawn, and more careful to abstain from making bothersome acquaintances than needful of making advantageous ones. This was indeed also my father's basic character, and in this regard, never were spouses better matched. They found themselves happy only in their little household. Everywhere else they suffocated from melancholy yawning, and they left me with this legacy of secret savagery, which has always made society intolerable for me and "the home" a necessity.

All the steps for advancement my father had taken—admittedly without much enthusiasm—came to nothing. He was one hundred percent right in saying that he was not made to earn his spurs in time of peace and that the campaigns of the antechamber would not be his way to success. Only war could make him emerge from the impasse of the general staff.

ing that he was not made to earn his spurs in time of peace and that the campaigns of the antechamber would not be his way to success. Only war could make him emerge from the impasse of the general staff.

He returned to the camp at Montreuil with Dupont. My mother followed him in the spring of 1805 and remained there two or three months at most, during which my Aunt Lucie took care of my sister and me. This sister, of whom I shall speak later and whose existence I have already mentioned, was not my father's daughter. She was five or six years older than I, and was named Caroline. My dear little Aunt Lucie had, as I have said, married M. Maréchal, a retired officer, at the same time that my mother married my father. A daughter was born of their union five or six months after my birth. This was my beloved cousin Clotilde, perhaps the best friend I have ever had. My aunt lived at Chaillot then, where my uncle had bought a small house which was at that time in the middle of the country, but which today would be in the middle of the city. She used to rent the donkey from the neighborhood gardener to take us for rides. We were placed on some hay inside the baskets that were ordinarily used to carry fruit and vegetables to market, Caroline in one and I in the other. It appears that we greatly relished this mode of travel.

Concurrently, the Emperor Napoléon, concerned with other matters and enjoying other kinds of rides, went off to Italy to have the iron crown placed on his head. "*Guai a chi la tocca!*" ["Let him who touches it beware!"] the great man had said. England, Austria, and Russia resolved to touch it, and the Emperor kept his word.

At the moment that the army, gathered on the shores of the Channel, was impatiently awaiting the signal for a raid on England, the Emperor, seeing his his fortunes reversed on the sea, changed all of his plans in one night—one of those nights of inspiration when the fever in his veins cooled, and his discouragement over one enterprise became the overriding impulse in his mind for a new enterprise.   *S.L.F.R.*

X

The campaign of 1805. —Letters from my father to my mother. —The Haslach Affair. —Letter from Nuremberg. —Heroic feats of the Gazan and Dupont divisions on the banks of the Danube. —The honorable conduct of Mortier. —Letter from Vienna. —Général Dupont. —My father passes into the line with the rank of captain and receives the Cross. — The campaign of 1806 and 1807. —Letters from Warsaw and Rosemberg. —Continuation of the 1807 campaign. —The Tilsit raft. —Return to France. —Trip to Italy. —Letters from Venice and Milan. —End of the correspondence with my mother and beginning of my own story.

Admiral Villeneuve was responsible for the failure of the plan to invade England. Instead of leaving El Ferrol and sailing for Brest to join with Ganteaume, he lost his head and capped his astounding errors by allowing himself to be blockaded inside the city of Cadiz. Russia and Austria had concluded a treaty and raised an army of fifty thousand. England provided each allied power with a subsidy of fifteen thousand pounds sterling for each ten thousand men. The alliance of Genoa with France, accomplished two months after the signing of the treaty which represented a third coalition against France, was the obvious pretext to end continental peace. Thus, Napoléon revised all his plans. He decided to stay on the defensive in Italy and take the offensive in Germany.

It took Bernadotte, coming from Hanover, and Marmont, coming from Holland, seventeen days to reach Würzburg, on the right flank of the Austrian army, which, directed by General Mack, was assembled between Ulm and Memmingen, on the right bank of the Danube. It took the army corps, gathered at the camp at Boulogne, twenty-four days to secretly cross France and take up positions on the Rhine.

The Emperor took command of these one hundred eighty thousand men, who received the name Grand Army. The Grand Army was to operate on the Danube, while Masséna, with fifty thousand men, would push Archduke Charles toward the Adige river. Napoléon's plan was to turn General Mack's army around, while moving his own divisions into the lower Danube, thus cutting off Mack's connection with the Russian army, which was advancing by way of Galicia.

The 6th army corps, commanded by Maréchal Ney, including Dupont's division, left its Montreuil quarters, crossed Flanders, Picardy, Champagne,

Lorraine, and arrived at the Rhine on September 23 or 24, 1805. Everyone had marched with unexcelled fervor. They had not fought for five years, and for the first time since becoming emperor, Napoléon appeared at the head of his troops.

"The Dupont division, while crossing the department of Aisne, had left behind some fifty men who were natives of this department," writes M. Thiers (*Histoire du Consulat*). "They had gone off to visit their families, and on the morning of the second day, all had reassembled. After a march of one hundred fifty leagues, in the middle of autumn, without a single day's rest, the army contained neither sick men nor stragglers, a unique phenomenon due to the high morale of the troops and a long encampment."

Letter I   Hagenau, 1 Vendémiaire, Year XIV (September 23, 1805).

From My Father to My Mother

I arrive here with Deconchy to take up quarters for our division, as we usually do. We dine with Maréchal Ney. He warns us that we're going to cover twenty leagues at a stretch, cross the Rhine, and halt only when we come to Durlach, where we'll meet the enemy.

After a march of one hundred fifty leagues, a comparable gallop is likely to finish us all. Never mind, those are our orders. When we cross the Rhine, we'll take command of the 1st hussar regiment and four thousand troops of the Elector of Baden. Thus the division will be twelve thousand men strong. You'll hear talk of us. Ah, my beloved, when I'm far from you, skirmishes and battles are the only distraction I can look forward to, because without you, all pleasures become reasons for sadness, and what the others find worrisome and daunting makes everything seem more bearable to me, because it puts them on my level. I rejoice inwardly to see the troubled expressions on the many people who were very brave and important in peace time. The roads are littered with court vehicles, crowded with pages, chamberlains, and lackeys travelling in white silk stockings. Do watch out for the spattering mud!

Really, if I could find pleasure in anything when not with you, I believe I'd look forward to the approach of the upcoming brawl. Have no fear of infidelity, because for a long time hence I shall only have dealings with the masculine sex. The gentlemen from Austria will have work for us to do, and forced to keep up this pace, I doubt we'll have time left to think about being bad.

I don't plan to go to Strasbourg and see either Borelle, Billette, or Andrieux, who are hardly people to keep company with gunfire. Since I left you, I haven't had a single moment's rest. I haven't slept for six nights and undressed for eight days. Always in the vanguard inquiring for lodgings, I've lost my voice. I ask you whether in this state, when you are all I carry in my heart, I might think of ingratiating myself with the local beauties in the villages we pass through post-haste. I'm the one who'd have more cause for worry, if I didn't believe in your love, if I didn't know all its tenderness. Ah, if once I let myself, I'd even be jealous of your glances, and for a trifle would become the most miserable of men, but away with this insult to our love! I received your letter at Sarrebourg, my dear wife. It is as loving as you are, it has given me back life and courage. How dear is our Aurore! How impatient you make me to come back and take both of you into my arms! I beseech you, my beloved, write to me often. Send your letters to: Monsieur Dupin, aide-de-camp of Général Dupont, in command of the 1st division of the 6th army corps, under orders of Maréchal Ney. That way, no matter where the army goes, I'll receive them. Remember, dear wife, this is the only joy I may taste far from you, amid the strains of this campaign.

Tell me about your love, about our child. Know that you'd destroy my life if you should cease to love me. Know that you're my wife, that I adore you, that I love life only because of you, and that I've dedicated my life to you. Know that nothing in this world, except honor and duty, can keep me far from you, that I'm in the middle of every kind of weariness and deprivation, and they seem nothing to me compared to that caused by your absence. Know that only the hope of seeing you again sustains me and keeps me alive.

Adieu, dear wife, I faint with fatigue. I have a bed for tonight, which I won't have for a long time hence, and I shall make the most of it by dreaming of you. Adieu, then, dear Sophie, I shall write you from Durlach, if I can. I send you a thousand tender kisses; give quite as many of them to Aurore for me. Please don't worry, I know my profession, I'm lucky at war; a commission and the cross await me.

P.S. Where did you get the notion of double pay during war time? The opposite is rather the case, because it's more than just a question of the paymaster's arrival. However, since we don't have a sea to cross, and he'll get here sooner or later, don't be concerned for me and don't hold onto any of the money my mother sends you. Write her to announce your arrival in Paris.

I shall try to help my reader swiftly follow the advance of the Dupont division, which included my father, during the memorable campaign that ended with the battle of Austerlitz.

On September 25th, the 6th corps, to which the division was attached, crossed the Rhine between Lauterbourg and Karlsruhe, and went as far as Stuttgart, having traversed the valleys which descend from the chain of Swabian Alps. By the 6th of October, our six main armies had arrived safely on the other side of the range. On the 7th, they crossed the Danube. But Ney's corps remained on the left bank, covering the road from Württemberg. On the 10th, the army approached Ulm, in order to fully encircle General Mack, who continued to occupy the city. The division remained alone on the left bank of the river; a force of six thousand men, it engaged in an almost unprecedented and victorious battle against a body of twenty-five thousand Austrians. It halted their advance and deprived General Mack's unfortunate army of the last hope of salvation, by closing off the road from Bohemia. On the 14th of October, Général Dupont, who had had to hasten to Albeck in order to conceal from the enemy his small number of isolated soldiers on the left bank, returned to the forested heights of Haslach, which he had made famous by a heroic resistance there three days earlier. Having kept the bulk of the Austrian army in Ulm, it was up to him to prevent the reunion of General Werneck's corps, which had left the city the night before in order to reconnoiter, and could not get back in.

Meanwhile, there was discord at the headquarters of the Austrian general. Mack, faithful to the campaign plan established by the Aulic Council, persisted in waiting in his retrenchments for the arrival of the Russian army of Kutusov. Prince Schwarzenberg and Archduke Ferdinand wanted to reach Bohemia by passing through the Ney and Dupont divisions. But unable to overcome the resistance of the commanding general, the archduke decided, due to his independent position, to carry out his plan. He departed in the night with six or seven thousand cavalry and a corps of infantry to rejoin Werneck.

Murat, heading the courageous Dupont division, the Oudinot grenadiers, and some of his reserve cavalry, set out to pursue them. He followed them for four days without a rest, covering more than ten leagues daily, and came to a halt only beyond Nuremberg, after he had beaten and destroyed that army corps. The French had taken twelve thousand prisoners, one hundred twenty cannon, five hundred vehicles, eleven flags, two hundred officers, seven generals, and the treasury of the Austrian army. Prince Ferdinand avoided being captured and reached the road to Bohemia with two or three thousand cavalry.

Letter II   Nuremberg, 29 Vendémiaire, Year XIV (October 21, 1805).

Here we are, my dear wife, since last night, after relentlessly pursuing the enemy for four days; we took the entire Austrian army captive; barely a few remained to carry the news and the terror into the heart of Germany. Our commander, Prince Murat, is very satisfied with us and should ask the Emperor tomorrow or soon after for the cross for myself and three other officers of the division.

I won't tell you about the risks and exhaustion of the past ten days. Those are the drawbacks of the profession. What are they compared to the worry and sadness your absence causes me! I receive no news from you. Rumor even has it that none of our letters has gotten to France because of the continual enemy disturbance on our left. Imagine my torment, my anguish! How do I know if you aren't terribly anxious over me? If you have received the money I sent you? If my Aurore is all right? To be separated from what is dearest to me in this world without being able to receive a single word! Courage, my darling! Know that our separation cannot alter my love. How happy we'll be when we meet again, never to part! As soon as the campaign is over, how ecstatically I'll fly to your arms, never to tear myself away, and to devote to you as well as Aurore all my care and all my moments! Only this thought sustains me against the stress and worries that assail me when you're far away. In the midst of the horrors of war, I imagine myself back with you, and your dear image makes me forget wind, cold, rain, and all the miseries we're subjected to. On your side, my beloved, think of me. Know that I have pledged you the tenderest love which only death can extinguish in my heart. Know that the least withdrawal on your part would poison the rest of my life and that I was able to leave you only because duty and honor are a sacred law which forced me do so.

We leave Nuremberg tomorrow at five in the morning to get to Regensburg, where we're due in three days. Prince Murat is still in charge of our division.

After the surrender at Ulm, Napoléon headed rapidly toward Vienna, following the Danube valley. The bulk of the army marched on the right river bank. A flotilla carrying artillery and ten thousand men simultaneously sailed downstream, ready to come to the aid of the troops marching on the right bank or of the Gazan and Dupont divisions, which occupied the left bank, under the high command of Général Mortier. A few leagues before Vienna, the corps of the left bank suddenly found itself in the presence of the enemy; it was the Russian army of Kutusov, which had remained behind Mack, at Braunau, and having given up the attempt to protect the Austrian capital, had crossed the Danube at Mautern and gone on to Moravia in advance of the second Russian army. The Gazan division, swept along in Murat's wake, who, along with the advance guard of the main army, had moved too swiftly toward Vienna on the right river bank, had left a day's march between itself and the Dupont division. Mortier, surprised to encounter the Russians, whom he believed were close to Vienna, nevertheless pushed them vigorously back as far as Stein. He soon realized, however, that he was dealing with an entire army, and was forced to pull back to Diernstein. But he found that strategic point occupied by fifteen thousand Russians who had circumvented him. The battle given up that morning was resumed in the darkness. These five thousand heros were surrounded on all sides by masses of men. It occurred to no one to surrender. Several officers advised Mortier to embark alone and cross the river, in order to deprive the enemy of so nice a trophy as a field marshal of France. "No," replied the illustrious marshal, "it's impossible to leave such brave men. We'll either be saved or perish together." There he was, sword in hand, fighting at the head of his grenadiers. Suddenly violent firing was heard from behind Diernstein. It was the indefatigable Dupont division, which had doubled back to get to the firing line when they learned of the marshal's precarious position. The soldiers who had so gloriously fought at Haslach hurled themselves at the Russians, and the columns reunited at Diernstein in a glow of gunfire. The five thousand men of the Gazan division, who had resisted thirty thousand Russians for a whole day, were reduced to two thousand five hundred. Napoléon sent the most outstanding rewards to the Gazan and Dupont divisions. After the campaign they were stationed at Vienna itself to recuperate from their fatigue and wounds.

Letter III   Vienna, 30 Brumaire, Year XIV (November 21, 1805).

My wife, my beloved wife, this day is the happiest of my life. Consumed by anxiety, overcome by fatigue, I arrive in Vienna with the division. I don't know if you love me, if you're in good health, if Aurore is sad or cheerful, if my wife is still my very own Sophie. I run to the post, my heart beats with hope and fear. I find a letter from you; I open it in rapture, I tremble with happiness to read the sweet expressions of your tenderness. Oh, yes, dear wife! I am yours for life, nothing in the world can change the ardent love I feel for you, and for as long as you'll share it, I shall defy destiny, fortune, and absurd inequities. I was in great need of reading a letter from my wife, to help me withstand the trials of my existence.

Having battled like a good soldier, having risked my life a hundred times for the success of our forces, having witnessed my closest friends perish at my side, I had the affliction of seeing our most brilliant exploits ignored, distorted, obscured by the military menials. I'm an old hand, and you must hear me and learn what courtiers are. Having been at the head of the regiments of our divisions since the beginning, I have observed that courage and fearlessness were useless qualities and that the laurels were distributed by favor alone. Think of it! Two months ago we were six thousand, today we're no more than three thousand. For our part, we have taken five enemy flags, two of them Russian; we have taken five thousand prisoners, killed two thousand men, taken four cannon, all in a space of six weeks; and daily we see people cited in the war bulletins *who have done absolutely nothing*, while our names remain obscure. The esteem and affection of our comrades console me. I'll come back a poor devil, but with friends I have made on the battlefield who are more trustworthy than the gentlemen of the court. I annoy you with my dark mood, but to whom can I tell my troubles if not to my Sophie, and who can share and ease them better than she?

Anyway, since our soldiers are worn out from having fought the Russians for eight days *without relief*, we were sent back here from Moravia to get some rest. I lost everything in the Haslach affair.[46] I have since compensated myself for it at the expense of an officer of the Latour dragoons, whom I dismounted.

They are forever promising us wonderful things, but God only knows if they'll come. My mother writes me that you will want for nothing and that I need not worry. By the way, what latest folly do you bring up for my entertainment! I made Debaine laugh tears over it. Mlle. Roumier is my old nursemaid, to whom my mother pays a pension for having taken care of me. She was forty years old when I was born. What a target for jealousy! I am relating your new folly to all our friends.

This morning I saw Billette. Seeing him put me in mind of Rue Meslay, which gave me infinite joy. I hugged him like my best friend, because I could talk to him about you, and he could give me answers. Even though he had no direct news of your health, I questioned him to the point of annoyance.

There is talk of sending us back to France soon, for the war here is over for lack of combatants. The Austrians no longer dare to take us on, they're terrified. The Russians are completely put to flight. People here regard us with stupefaction. The inhabitants of Vienna can hardly believe our presence. By the way, this city is rather insipid. During the twenty-four hours I've been here, I'm as bored as if I were in prison. The rich have fled, the bourgeois tremble and hide, the people are dumbstruck. Rumor has it that we'll depart again within the next three or four days to march on Hungary and force the remains of the Austrian army to put down their arms, and thus hasten the peace.

May you always feel gloomy in my absence. Yes, beloved wife, that is how I love you. Let no one see you, think only of taking care of our daughter, and I'll be as happy as I can be, far from you.

Farewell, dearest friend, I hope soon to hold you in my arms. A thousand kisses to you and my Aurore.

This "rumor" concerning a new march on Hungary ended in the battle of Austerlitz, on December 4, 1805. I do not know if my father was there. Although a number of people have said so, and his obituary notice attests to it, I do not believe it is true, because the Dupont division, exhausted by the feats of Haslach and Diernstein, had to stay in Vienna to recover, and the name Dupont cannot be found in any of the accounts I have read of the Battle of Austerlitz.

In passing, a word on Dupont—the general who was so guilty, or so unfortunate, in Spain at Baylen, and so shamelessly rewarded by the Restoration for having been one of the first to betray the glory of the French army in the person of the Emperor. It is certain that during the campaign just sketched he showed himself to be a great man of war. We saw that my father judged him lightly in peace time, but took him seriously at other times. Did the Emperor mistrust or have a hidden bias against Dupont? Either that was the case, or Dupont liked the role of malcontent. It is also certain that my father's complaints in the letter we just read are manifestations of a collective sentiment. He was not, in his estimation, important enough to merit being the object of special hostility. I do not know who the courtiers, the military menials are whom my father rails against so bitterly. Since he was extremely kind and generous by nature, we must believe that there was some basis for his complaints.

We know, besides, how many enmities, rivalries, and angry feelings the Emperor had to keep in check during this campaign, what audacious and presumptuous mistakes were made by Murat, and what abysmal indignations Ney suffered in this connection. Recourse to history will surely reveal the key to the grievance my father nursed on the battlefields and the noticeable change in disposition of those who had followed the First Consul with such abandon at Marengo. Without doubt, these campaigns of the Empire are magnificent, and our soldiers stand head and shoulders above other heroes. Napoléon is then the greatest general of the universe. But how the court spirit has already spoiled the young enthusiasts of the Republic! From Marengo, my father had written to his mother in a postscript: "My God, I forgot to tell you that I was made lieutenant on the battlefied!" Which proves that he had hardly thought about his personal gain when he fought in the heat of a cause. From Vienna he writes to his wife expressing his scornful doubt that any reward might await him. Under the Empire, it was each man for himself; under the Republic, self-effacement was the rule.

Be that as it may, the apparent disgrace which seemed to have befallen my father's career from the time of the Mincio crossing ceased with the campaign of 1805. He finally got permission to pass into the line, and was named captain of the 1st Hussars on 30 Frimaire, Year XIV (December 20, 1805).[47] He returned to Paris, then took my mother, Caroline, and myself to his regi-

ment; I do not remember where they were stationed. When he left once again
for the 1806 campaign, he wrote to his wife in Tongres, at the depot, where the
quartermaster of the regiment lived. He probably made a trip to Nohant in the
interim, but I can only retrace his history from the several letters which follow.

One might have been tempted to predict that the overwhelming victory of
Austerlitz, which ended the 1805 campaign against the Austrians and Russians,
would have guaranteed Europe a peace valiantly challenged and dearly won,
but that was not the case. Prussia, which had remained in the background since
1792, was to renew hostilities against a victorious France. All of Europe was
surprised at this determination of the Berlin cabinet, as foolhardly as it was
unforeseen, but as M. Thiers writes, cabinets also have their passions, and
"those sudden flare-ups which sometimes consume two men in private life and
induce them to take up the sword, are just as often the reason—more often
even than considered self-interest—which pits two nations against each other."

Napoléon had soon made up his mind in light of this new aggression.
When a Prussian army invaded Saxony, he considered it a declaration of war,
quickly made his preparations, and left Mainz during the last days of September to enter Prussia at the head of the Grand Army. In Mainz the Emperor took
leave of the Empress and his court, and went to Würzburg accompanied only
by his military household.

The Dupont division, always given separate assignments since the Battles
of Haslach and Albeck, and which had occupied the grand duchy of Berg, was
ordered back to Mainz and Frankfurt at the first signs of war. Thus, my father
happened to be in Mainz when Napoléon got there.

From My Father to My Mother   Primlingen, October 2, 1806.

Since Mainz, we have moved about so much that I was unable to find a
moment to send you news. First of all, I love you to the point of idolatry; this is
not news to you, but it's what I'm most eager to tell you. Ah, how weary I am
of being away from you! I really swear, once this campaign is over, come what
may, I won't leave you again.

Our poor colonel is quite sick. The exertion of the march renewed his
nephritic pains, and yesterday he was obliged to return to Frankfurt. His state
of health and his departure under such circumstances deeply affect the regiment, and I miss him even more than anyone else. In the last three days, I did
thirty-six leagues with my company to escort the Emperor. He arrived yesterday evening in Würzburg. We are billeted in the surrounding area. The entire
foot guard has arrived. While we were traveling, the Emperor asked me several
questions about the regiment; at the last one, which the noise of the vehicle
kept me from hearing even though he repeated it three times, I haphazardly
answered, "Yes, Sire." I saw him smile, and I guess I must have committed
some gross stupidity. If he sees fit to retire me for idiocy or deafness, I would
easily be consoled by returning to you!

Now the cold season is upon us, and I very much regret not having
brought my fur pelisse; please be kind enough to send it to Chapotot, who will

get it to me one way or another. Don't use this letter for curling paper because too much heat might be generated between the curling iron and your beautiful hair, while here, far away from you, I'll be freezing in my monkey jacket.

Goodbye, my lovely wife, my dear friend, whom I love, whom I miss, whom I want most in this world. I embrace you with all my heart, I love my Aurore, our children, your sister, everything that belongs to us.

We have postal service at our division, so I hope to receive your news often.

Napoléon's sudden arrival in Würzburg caused the commanders of the Prussian army to change their plans. Stunned by the new tactic which had so powerfully contributed to the swift success of the preceding campaign against the Austrians and Russians, the Prussian commanders, rather than keep the defensive by choosing the most advantageous terrains and letting the French come to them through all the obstacles of a trek over enemy territory, had decided to take the offensive instead, without waiting for the reinforcements which Russia promised them. However, Napoléon's move inspired the Prussians to be more prudently reserved, and they decided to retain the strong positions they held behind the forest of Thuringia.

The French army began its march on October 8th, and the following day, Murat and Bernadotte, who made up the advance guard, defeated the forces of General Tauentzien. On the 10th, Lannes beat Prince Louis at Saalfeld, and the fleeing soldiers informed the Prussian armies of Hohenlohe and Brunswick, positioned behind Jena, of the tragic end of the prince and the dispersal of his army.

The Duke of Brunswick, who was commander in chief, decided to move immediately back to the Elbe by way of Naumburg, leaving Prince Hohenlohe at Jena with fifty thousand men, with Ruchel and eighteen thousand men as a rear guard.

But on October 13th, at the moment when the enemy army began its move, Napoléon arrived in Jena, already occupied by Lannes, and reconnoitered the terrain. The two armies were face to face.

I hardly have to relate here the memorable Battle of Jena, which took place the next morning. The formidable Prussian army was completely beaten. On the French side, only fifty thousand men were engaged.

While Hohenlohe was being defeated at Jena, Bernadotte was marching toward Halle to cross the Saale, reach the Prussian army, and cut off their retreat. As the Duke of Brunswick retreated to the Elbe, he ordered Prince Eugene of Württemberg to guard Halle with eighteen thousand men—the last resource of the Prussian monarchy—and gather up the runaways. On the morning of October 17th, the Dupont division, which followed Bernadotte's corps, arrived within sight of the city. Dupont did not hesitate for a moment. He lined up his infantry, stormed the bridge over the Salle on the run, forced the gates of Halle, crossed the city, and took up battle formation facing the army of the Duke of Württemberg. The fire of twelve thousand well-positioned men greeted the three regiments which made up Dupont's small army. His soldiers scaled the heights under fire and put the enemy to flight. The Duke of Württemberg retreated in disorder to the Elbe. Five thousand men had overcome eighteen thousand. Napoléon rushed to the battlefield and showered Général Dupont's troops with praise.

Ten days later, Napoléon entered Berlin flanked by the imperial guard.

Meanwhile, when King Frederick William refused the proferred armistice in order to join the Russians, who were marching to his rescue, the Emperor decided to enter Poland. Welcomed with enthusiasm by the Poles, to whom he represented the first serious hope of liberation, the French army took up positions around Warsaw during the first days of December.

Napoléon had intended to set up winter quarters on the banks of the Vistula, "but this cannot take place," he wrote to Davout, "until after we have pushed back the Russians." The army did indeed move to encounter the Russians, who were defeated at Pultusk and thrown back beyond the Narew river with great losses.

Toward January 25th, the Russians again took the initiative, and on the 30th, Napoléon took command of the Grand Army. At his approach, the Russian general, Bennigsen, pulled back to Eylau, where a bloody battle was waged which cost more than forty thousand lives and did honor to both the vanquished and the victors. If the enemy were allowed to beat a retreat undisturbed by the victorious army, which was in nearly as bad shape, Napoléon could at least be relieved for some time of the apprehensions which the proximity of the Russian army might cause in the billets.

The Dupont division, reunited with Bernadotte's forces, had remained thirty leagues behind Eylau and had not been able to take part in the battle. After having enclosed the Russians in Königsberg, the Grand Army was ready to take up its quarters on the Passarge river. But Benningsen, elated over not having lost the last of his men at Eylau, and as usual calling himself the victor, wanted to give his bragging a semblance of truth; he emerged from behind the walls where he had taken refuge and had the audacity to position himself opposite Ney. The latter, who was unhappy not to have taken part in the Battle of Eylau, eagerly seized this opportunity for revenge, and vigorously took on the opposing forces. During this time, the Dupont division took possession of Braunsberg on the Passarge river and captured two thousand Prussians. Tired of the continual harassments of the Russians and wanting to assure the peace of his billeting for the entire winter, Napoléon ordered the corps of Bernadotte and Soult, whom he had placed in a sort of ambush until the moment when the campaign would be resumed, to move forward. The Russians, realizing that their retreat via Königsberg might be cut off, pulled back and did not appear again that winter.

From My Father to My Mother   December 7, 1806.

For two weeks, my dear wife, I've been traversing on horseback the wilds of Poland from five in the morning, and after having traveled until nightfall, finding only the smoke-filled hut of some poor devil where I could hardly obtain a bale of hay on which to rest myself. Today I arrive in the Polish capital and may finally post a letter to you. I love you a hundred times more than life; your memory follows me everywhere, both consoling me and driving me to despair. I see you when I fall asleep; I wake up thinking of you; my entire being feels your presence. You are my divinity, my guardian angel whom I invoke, whom I call to in the midst of my fatigues and perils. Since I left you, I haven't enjoyed a single moment of rest, and I don't need to tell you that I haven't tasted a single moment of happiness. Love me, love me—that is the only way to soften the harsh life I lead. Write me. I have only received two letters from you. I've read them a hundred times, I read them yet again. May you always be the same woman who writes me in such a tender and adorable way. Let absence not cool your love. I think it increases mine, if that's possible. Let's not lose hope of being reunited soon. Negotiations are going on in Posen. It's very likely that our success will set the Russians on a peaceful course. I'm going to see Philippe de Ségur shortly and shall give him a parcel for you. He'll know how to get it to you quickly. Tomorrow we cross the Vistula; the Russians are ten leagues from here, seriously disconcerted by our march and our maneuvers. As for me, I'm at the point of wishing for a nice saber stroke which will maim me forever and send me back to you. In this century, a military man can only hope for repose and domestic happiness by losing an arm or a leg. I know no one in the army who wouldn't make the same wish. But there's that damned honor that holds us back. Many complain, but I suffer quietly, for what do I care about the humiliations, deprivations, fatigues? That is not what vexes me about the profession; it is your absence, and I cannot tell that to the others. Those who don't know you wouldn't understand the overflow of my love. Those who do know you would understand it more than I'd like.

Talk to our children about me. I must go in search of forage. Not a moment's peace, not even to enjoy this semi-consolation of writing to you! I love you to distraction. Love me, if you want me to go on living.

After the Passarge affair, my father was made squadron chief, and on April 4, 1807, Murat took him on as aide-de-camp. Deschartres told me that it was on the recommendation of the Emperor, who, having noticed him, said to the prince, "There you have a fine and courageous young man; that's the kind of aide-de-camp you need." My father was so far from expecting such favor that he nearly refused it, seeing that it would bind him even more and create a new obstacle to his dream of total repose in the midst of his family. My mother was quite annoyed over what she called his ambition, and he had to justify himself, as may be gathered from the following letter:

From general headquarters, Grand Duchy of Berg, Rosemberg, May 10, 1807.

After having run around like a rabbit for three weeks and having offered the prince a rather nice sample of my savoir faire concerning military missions, I arrive here and find two letters from you, dated March 23rd and April 8th. The first one devastates me; it seems to me you already no longer love me when you tell me you're going "to force yourself to love me a little less." Fortunately, I unseal the second and quickly see that it's for reasons of love you injure me so. Oh, my dear wife, my Sophie, how could you write such cruel words, send me this mortal poison at a distance of three hundred leagues, expose me to the pain of reading this awful letter for two weeks before I might perhaps have received another to reassure and console me! Thus you see me compelled to thank God I was deprived of your news for so long! Oh, my darling, retract those horrible thoughts, those unjust suspicions. Is it possible that you could doubt me? The most hurtful reproach you could make is to tell me I don't remember Caroline's existence and that you are frightened to think of the child's future. To what do I owe these abusive doubts? Have I for a single moment ceased to think of her as my daughter? Have I made the least distinction in my cares and my affection between her and our other children? From the day I first saw you, have I for one moment stopped adoring you, loving everything that belongs to you, your daughter, your sister, everything you love? You heap reproaches on me as if I left you for nothing but the pleasure of traipsing around. I swear to you by my honor and my love that I didn't ask for a promotion, that the grand duke called me to his side without my having the least suspicion of his intention, and that, finally, I saw with deep sorrow the day which would reunite us move further into the future. Shall I tell you everything? I nearly refused, feeling myself without strength to face the new delay in my return to you. But, dear wife, would I have acted responsibly toward you, toward my mother, who sacrificed her personal comfort to my military career, toward our children, our *three children*,[48] who will soon need the financial resources and considerations of their father, if I'd rejected good fortune which came to me on its own? My ambition, you call it! I, ambitious? If I were less dejected, you would make me laugh with that word. Ah, I've had only one ambition since I met you, namely to make up to you for the injustices of society and destiny, to assure you an honorable life, and to shelter you from unhappiness, if a bullet should hit me on the battlefield. Don't I owe you this, you who for so long put up with my bad luck and who left a palace for an attic out of love for me? Judge me a little better, my Sophie, judge me according to yourself; no, there's not an instant in my life when I don't think of you. Nothing is worth more to me than the modest chamber of my dear wife. That is the sanctuary of my happiness. Nothing is equal in my eyes to her lovely dark hair, her beautiful eyes, her white teeth, her graceful figure, her percale dress, her pretty feet, her little prunella shoes. I am in love with all of it as on the first day, and I desire nothing else in the world. But in order to possess this happiness in complete security, in order not to have to struggle against poverty with children, sacrifices have to be made now. You say that we won't be as happy in a palace as in our little garret, that come peace time the prince will be made king, and we shall be obliged to go live on his estates, where we'll no longer have our privacy, our intimacy, our cherished freedom in Paris. It is quite probable the prince will indeed become king and that he'll take us along with him. But I deny that we couldn't be happy wherever we are together, or that anything could henceforth disturb a love consecrated by marriage. How silly you are, my poor wife, to believe that I'll love you less if I live in "riches and gilding!" And how kind you are, at the same time, to despise all that! But I too despise grandeur and vanity, and the boredom of those pleasures consumes me while I partake of them. You know this well. You know well with what eagerness I steal away to be with you peacefully, in some little corner. It is for my little corner that I work, that I fight, that I accept a reward, and that I aspire to have a regiment, because then you would no longer leave me, and we would have our own home, as quiet, as simple, as intimate as we want it to be. And if I showed some small measure of self-love in wanting sometimes to show you off happy and glittering at my side, to avenge you for the stupid disdain of certain people to whom our little household seemed so pitiful, where would be the harm? I'll be proud, I admit, myself to have been the artisan of our fortune and to owe only to my courage and my love of France what others owe to favor, intrigue, or the chimera of birth. I know some who amounted to something due to the name or the gallantry of their wives. My own wife will have other titles: her faithful love and her husband's esteem.

The beautiful weather is here again. What are you doing, my dearest friend? Ah, how the sight of a beautiful meadow or a forest ready to turn green fills my soul with sad and delightful memories! What sweet moments did I spend with you on the banks of the Rhine last year! Happiness of too short duration, by how many regrets are you followed! At Marienwerder I walked on the banks of the Vistula, alone, prey to my sorrow, my heart devoured by sadness and unrest, I saw everything reborn in nature, and my soul was closed to the feeling of happiness. I was in a spot like the one where you were so afraid, near Coblenz, where we sat on the grass and I drew you close to my heart to reassure you: I felt myself aflame with your memory, I wandered aimlessly like a madman, I searched for you, I called in vain for you. I finally sat down weary and torn by pain, and instead of my Sophie, I found loneliness, restlessness, and jealousy on these desolate shores. Yes, jealousy, I confess; I too, when far way, am obsessed by phantoms, but I don't speak to you of them for fear of offending you. Alas! when the fatigue of marches and the noise of battles are for one moment suspended, I fall prey to a thousand torments, all the furies of passion come to haunt me. I experience all the anguish, all the weaknesses of love. Oh, yes, dear wife! I love you as I did the first day. Ah, may our children talk to you about me constantly! Go out only with them. Let them remind you at all hours of our vows and our union. Also, talk about me to them. I live only for you, for them, and for my mother.

The spring season and the place we're occupying remind me of Fayel. But, alas, Boulogne is very far away, and this sad château leaves me wholly to my sorrows. When I arrived here, I found it completely deserted, everyone had left with the prince for Elbing, where the famous review by the emperor took place. The prince was giving the orders and he dispatched me in a princely manner. Farewell, dear wife. There is much talk of peace, nothing augurs a renewal of hostilities. Ah, when will I be near you! I press you a thousand times into my arms, with all our children; remember your husband, your lover.

Maurice.

How precious is my Aurore to think of me and already to know how to tell you about it!

Having followed the trail of the Dupont division, let us now follow Murat—since this is my father's story—in that short and brilliant campaign. In the month of May 1807, Murat was at the head of eighteen thousand horsemen, mounted on the most beautiful and perfectly trained German steeds. Wishing to see this cavalry corps in its totality, Napoléon passed it in review on the plains at Elbing. "These eighteen thousand cavaliers—an enormous body moved by a single head, Prince Murat—had maneuvered before him for one whole day, and so dazzled him, accustomed even as he was to grand armies, that writing to his ministers an hour later he could not help praising the handsome spectacle that had just struck his sight on the plains at Elbing.[39]"

General Benningsen, who commanded the Russian army and who had not left his billets in Königsberg since the threat posed by the forces of Soult and Bernadotte, decided to take the offensive. On June 5, 1807, the Russian army attacked quite roundly the corps of Maréchal Ney, stationed at the summit of the angle where the Alle and Passarge rivers meet, on which banks the French army was encamped, and forced him to beat a retreat before very superior forces. But the Emperor had foreseen this possibility, and Saalfeld, situated a little behind Ney's corps and at the center of the angle formed by the encampments, had been designated as the first point of concentration in case of attack. At the first sound of the cannon, all the forces had begun marching to take up their positions around Saalfeld.

Benningsen realized the formidable preparations of the French army and suddenly stopped short before Ney's forces, who were retreating in orderly fashion. Giving up ground with each step, he changed from the offensive to the defensive, and retrenched at Heilsberg. The Emperor followed him there; Prince Murat and Soult arrived first in front of the enemy redoubts, and engaged in action before the arrival of Napoléon and the rest of the army. The Carra-Saint-Cyr and Saint-Hilaire divisions, from Maréchal Soult's corps, valiantly resisted the heavy fire of the redoubts and permitted Murat's cavalry, exhausted with fatigue and momentarily unsettled by the shock of General Uvarov's twenty-five squadrons, to regroup and regain the upper hand. These fearless men, supported by the 3rd division of Maréchal Soult and by the infantry of the junior guard, whom Napoléon had ordered to advance under the command of Général Savary, kept up this unequal battle until nightfall, wherein thirty thousand Frenchmen battled in the open against ninety thousand Russians protected by strong retrenchments. General Benningsen did not consider it prudent, after this first attempt, to wait for a general attack by the whole French army; he ordered a retreat.

Napoléon persisted in his plan to follow the enemy army, step by step, looking for an auspicious occasion to attack, and meanwhile had cut off the possibility of retreat by way of Königsberg, the last asylum of the Prussian king, which housed the entire arsenal of the enemy armies.

Murat and a portion of his cavalry were charged with this task. Napoléon gave him support via the forces of Maréchals Soult and Davout, which made up the army's left flank. Soult went as far as the walls of Königsberg; Murat and Davout were to draw closer to Friedland, in order to destroy the Russians with one final effort, in case the battle lasted more than a day, but their assistance was not needed. The Russian army, backed into the angle formed by the Alle river this side of Friedland, was surrounded, cut off, driven into the river, and almost entirely destroyed. It was the last battle of the 1807 campaign.

During the month of June in this same year, my father accompanied Murat, who himself was accompanying Napoléon to the famous conference on the raft at Tilsit. Upon his return to France in July, my father had to leave once again for Italy with Murat and the Emperor, who went there to name some new kings and princes. "His unfortunate dynastic preoccupations would taint the greatness of his plans. He surely was not inclined to change his political thinking. But public opinion must also be taken into account in questions of politics, and the public saw the traffic in crowns as beneficial only for one family.

"The Emperor, who left Paris on November 16th, was in Milan on the 21st. Brilliant festivities were arranged in his honor. The Bavarian court took part in them. Eugène was named Prince of Venice and summoned to succeed to the royal throne of Italy, in the absence of any male imperial descendant.

"After several days spent in Milan, the Emperor traveled to Venice, and his sojourn there was celebrated by festivities which recalled the golden days when Venice was an opulent republic. The regattas, or gondola races, were conducted with royal magnificence. The Grand Canal was covered with boats decorated in the greatest elegance, transformed into floats representing temples, gazebos, peasant huts from different nations, steered by gondoliers dressed in matching costumes. Not one Venetian nobleman was spared the expense of at least a year's income for these celebrations.

"Summoned to Venice, King Joseph spent six days there with Napoléon. During their talks they discussed what the outcomes would be, should those questions dividing the ruling house of Spain be brought up, but nothing was definitively decreed in this regard.

"Having departed from Venice on December 8th, the Emperor was in Mantua on the 11th. There he was reunited with Lucien, who had been separated from his brother since 1804, not, as they say, for political differences, but because he had contracted a marriage which did not fit into Napoléon's dynastic calculations. Retired to the Roman estates, he lived there in wealth and esteem. Joseph had arranged the meeting in Mantua out of his keen desire for a reconciliation. It was very cordial on both sides, but it did necessarily elicit the very question which had caused the break. Napoléon made the most tempting offers, if his brother would obtain a divorce—for Lucien, the throne of Naples or Portugal; marriage for his eldest daughter to the Prince of Asturias; the Duchy of Parma for his wife—nothing could sway Lucien; true to his feelings, he preferred domestic happiness to the glittering deceptions of the throne. Napoléon was inflexible in his politics, Lucien obstinate in his duties. They parted, both touched, but refusing to make concessions.

"The Emperor returned to Milan on the 15th, left there the 24th, and arriving in Alessandria at sunset, he saw the entire plain of Marengo lighted by torches for his passage. After he visited the immense fortification works which made Alessandria the stronghold of Europe, he quickly headed toward Mount

Cenis, which he reached on the 29th, and he was back at the Tuileries by January 1, 1808. All his attention was then turned to Spain."[48a]

I hold in my hands two penultimate letters of my father. They coincide with this episode in the imperial life.

Venice, November 29, 1807.

Having braved the rocky heights of Savoy and Mount Cenis, I overturned into a muddy ditch in Piedmont during the darkest and most detestable of nights, and furthermore in the middle of a forest known for its cutthroats, where the night before, a merchant from Turin had been killed and robbed. Saber in one hand and pistol in the other, we stood guard for three whole hours until help arrived to put us back on our feet. Soon our horses gave out; then the roads became impassable. Arriving at the seashore, a wind arose against us, and we thought we might blow away into the lagoon. Finally, here we are in beautiful Venice, where all I've seen is very ugly water in the streets and all I've had to drink is very bad wine at Duroc's table. For the first time since Paris I shall spend the night in a bed. The Emperor is only staying here a week. I don't have time to tell you more about it. I love you, you are my life, my soul, my God, my everything.

Milan, December 11, 1807.

The dateline, dearest friend, should tell you I am thinking of you doubly, if that's possible, because I'm in a place filled with memories of our love, of my sufferings, of my torments, and my joys. Ah, what emotions went through me when crossing the gardens near the *corso*! Not all of them were pleasant, but what predominates is my love for you, my impatience to be back in your arms. We will quite surely be in Paris by the end of the month. It's impossible to be more bored than I am here; I've had my fill of parties and festivities. All my comrades say somewhat the same thing, albeit they don't have as powerful motives as I to wish for an end to all this show. For me the atmosphere is heavy with greatness, seriousness, formality, and boredom. The prince is sick, and for this reason, I'm hopeful we'll advance the date of the Emperor's return and I'll soon again be with you—my eternal angel, devil, divinity. If I don't find a letter from you in Turin, I'll pull your little ears. Goodbye, and a thousand tender kisses to you, to Aurore, and to my mother. I'll write to you from Turin.

My intention has been to place before my reader's eyes a very quick analysis of the war's events and history, since the lack of more continuous and detailed letters made this the only way I could follow my father. I shall no longer abuse this method of filling the gaps that occur in his life. And furthermore, this so pure and generous life here comes to an end; I shall have little more to tell of him, except for a horrible catastrophe. From now on, I shall be guided by my own memories, and as I do not pretend to write the history of my time apart from my own, I shall tell about the Spanish campaign only what I saw with my own eyes, at a time when exterior objects, strange and incomprehensible to me, began to strike me much like mysterious pictures. The reader will allow me, now, to go back a little in time and take up my life at the moment my awareness began. *E.W.W.*

XI

Earliest memories. —First prayers. —Children's silver egg.
—Father Christmas. —J.-J. Rousseau's theory. —The laurel woods.
—Pulcinella and the street lamp. —Novels-among-four-chairs.
—Military games. —Chaillot. —Clotilde. —The Emperor.
—Butterflies and gossamer. —The King of Rome. —The flute.

It would seem that life is a good thing in itself, because its beginnings are so sweet and childhood such a happy time. There isn't one of us who doesn't remember this golden age as a vanished dream to which nothing can be compared later on. I say a dream, thinking of those early years in which our memories drift uncertainly and can only pick a few isolated impressions out of a vague whole. We would be hard pressed to explain why such a powerful charm is exerted on each of us by those flashes of memory of trifling importance to others.

Memory is a faculty which varies according to the individual, and not being complete in any of us, affords us a thousand inconsistencies. In my own case, as it must be for many others, my memory is extraordinarily developed in certain areas and extraordinarily weak in others. I recall only with effort yesterday's minor events, and most of the details are surely lost to me forever. But when I look a little further behind me, my memories go back to an age where most other people can retrieve nothing from their past. Is this mainly due to the nature of this faculty in me or to a certain precocity in my perception of life?

Are we perhaps all equally gifted in this area, and are our notions of the past clear or confused perhaps only by reason of the greater or lesser emotion they caused us? Certain inner preoccupations make us almost indifferent to things which shake the world around us. It also happens that we remember badly what we have poorly understood. Forgetfulness may be only unintelligence or inattention.

Be that as it may, here is the first memory of my life, and it dates from far back. I was two years old, a servant let me fall out of her arms onto the corner of the fireplace; I was frightened, and I hurt my forehead. All the commotion, the shock to the nervous system opened me to self-awareness, and I saw clearly—I still see—the reddish marble of the mantelpiece, my blood running, the distraught face of my nursemaid. I distinctly remember the doctor who came, the leeches which were put behind my ears, my mother's anxiety, and the servant dismissed for drunkenness. We moved from that house, and I don't know where it was located; I have never been back there since, but if it still exists, it seems to me I would recognize it.

Thus it is not astonishing that I remember perfectly the apartment we lived in a year later on Rue Grange-Batalière. From that time on my memories are precise and nearly without interruption. But from the time of the fireplace accident until the age of three I can only recall an endless series of sleepless hours spent in my little bed and filled with contemplating some fold in the window curtain or some flower on the wallpaper; I also recall that flies and their buzzing interested me very much, and that objects appeared to be doubled, a circumstance impossible for me to explain but which other people have told me they also experienced in their very early childhood. Candle flames especially took on that aspect before my eyes, and I was aware of the illusion but could not overcome it. It even seemed to me that this illusion was one of the pale amusements of my captivity in the cradle, and this cradle-life seemed extraordinarily long to me and immersed in a soft ennui.

From an early age, my mother took on my training, and while my brain did not resist, it did not try to anticipate her in any way; it might have been very backward, left on its own. I walked at ten months; I talked rather late, but once I had begun to say a few words, I learned the rest very quickly, and at four I knew how to read very well, as did my cousin Clotilde, who was taught as I was, by both our mothers in turn. They also taught us some prayers, and I remember I could recite them without a pause from one end to the other, without understanding anything, except those words they made us say when we had put our heads down on the same pillow, "My Lord, I give you my heart." I don't know why I understood this more than the rest, for there is much metaphysics in these few words, but I did understand it, and it was the only place in my prayers where I had an idea of God and myself.

As for the Pater, and the Credo, and the Ave Maria, which I knew very well in French, except for "Give us this day our daily bread," I might just as well have recited them in Latin, like a parrot, they would not have been any more intelligible to me.

They also had us practice La Fontaine's fables by heart, and I knew almost all of them, though their meaning was still a mystery to me. I was so fed up with reciting them that I think I did my best not to understand them until much later, and I was fifteen or sixteen before I perceived their beauty.

People used to have the habit of filling children's memories with a host of riches beyond their grasp. It is not the imposed little labor that I take issue with. Rousseau, by eliminating such labor altogether in *Émile*, risks letting his pupil's brain grow so dense, to the point of not being able to absorb what is reserved for a more advanced age. It is good to get children used, as early as possible, to a moderate but daily exercise of the mind's diverse faculties. But people are too eager to offer them treats. There exists nothing in literature for the usage of little children. All the pretty verse made up in their honor is mannered and stuffed with words that are not in their vocabulary. Hardly anything but nursery songs actually speaks to their imagination. The first verse I ever heard is this one, which doubtless everyone knows, and which my mother sang in the sweetest, freshest voice imaginable:

> Let us go to the henhouse
> To see the white hen.
> A handsome silver egg she'll lay
> For this dear little child today.

The rhyme isn't rich, but that didn't matter to me, and I was keenly impressed by this white hen and by the silver egg which was promised me every evening and which I never dreamed to ask for the next morning. The promise always came back, and the naïve hope came back with it. Reader, my friend, do you remember? You too were promised this marvellous egg at some time in your youth, which did not awaken your greed but rather seemed to you like the most poetic and gracious present on the part of the good hen. And what would you have done with the silver egg if they had given it to you? Your meager hands could not have carried it, and your restless and changeable mood would have soon tired of this insipid toy. What good is an egg—or a toy, for that matter—which never breaks? But the imagination makes something out of nothing, that is its nature, and the story of this silver egg is perhaps the story of all material possessions which arouse our desire. Desire is the great thing, possession very little.

My mother also sang me a song of this kind on Christmas Eve, but because that happened only once a year, I do not remember it. What I have not forgotten is my absolute belief that little Father Christmas would come down the chimney, dear old fellow with a white beard, who at the midnight hour had to come and deposit a present in my little slipper, which I would find on waking up. Midnight, that hour of fantasy beyond the conception of children, which is dangled before them as the impossible conclusion of their vigil! What incredible efforts I made not to fall asleep before the little old man appeared! I had a great desire to see him, and a great fear at the same time, but I could never keep awake until he came, and the next day my first glance was toward my slipper, beside the hearth. What excitement the white paper wrapping caused me, because Father Christmas was very fastidious and never failed to wrap his offering carefully. I would run barefoot to snatch up my treasure. It was never a very elaborate gift, because we were not rich. It was a little cake, an orange, or quite simply a beautiful red apple. But this seemed so precious to me that I hardly dared eat it. Imagination again played its part, which is what a child's life consists of.

I do not at all approve of Rousseau's wanting to suppress the fantastic on the grounds of it being a lie. Reason and disbelief come quite quickly enough on their own. I can remember very well the first year I doubted whether Father Christmas really existed. I was five or six years old, and it seemed to me that it had to be my mother who put the cake into my slipper. Also, it seemed less beautiful and less good than it had before, and I experienced a kind of regret at no longer being able to believe in the little man with a white beard. My son believed in him for a longer time; boys are more naïve than little girls. Like me, he made great efforts to stay awake until midnight. Like me, he did not succeed, and like me, he found in the morning the miraculous cake kneaded in the kitchens of paradise; but also for him, the first year he doubted, the old man visited for the last time. We should serve children the dishes that suit their age, and nothing more advanced. As long as they need a fantasy world, they should have it. When they begin to lose their taste for it, we must certainly keep from prolonging the error and hindering the natural progress of their reason.

To cut short the fantasy life of a child is to go against the very laws of nature. Isn't the childhood of a human being a mysterious state full of unexplained wonders? Where do children come from? Before being formed in their mother's womb, haven't they had some sort of existence in the impenetrable womb of the Divinity? Doesn't the bit of life which animates them come from an unknown world to which it must return? That so rapid development of the human soul in our early years, that strange passage from a state which ressembles chaos to a state of comprehension and sociability, those early notions of language, that incomprehensible work of the mind which learns how to give a name not only to objects outside itself but to action, to thought, to feeling—all that is part of the miracle of life, and I know of no one who can explain it. I have always been astounded at the first verb I heard uttered by small children. I understand how they can be taught substantives, but verbs, and especially those that express feelings! The first time that a child can tell his mother that he loves her, for example, isn't this like a higher revelation he receives and expresses? The outside world, in which this mind-in-work is adrift, cannot yet have given it any distinct notion of the functions of the soul. So far, it only survived through need, and the blossoming forth of the intelligence was achieved only through the senses. It sees, it wants to touch, to taste, and all exterior objects, the use of which it has no inkling, for the most part, and the cause and effect of which it has no comprehension, must at first pass before it like an enigmatic vision. There begins the inner work. The imagination is filled by these objects; children dream in their sleep and doubtless also when they are not asleep. At least for some time they do not know the difference between waking and sleeping. Who can tell why a new object pleases or frightens them? What inspires in them the vague notion of beauty or ugliness? A flower, a small bird never frightens them; a distorted mask, a noisy animal terrifies them. Therefore, when the senses are aroused by such an agreeable or repulsive object, they must reveal to the understanding some idea of trust or terror that could not have been taught; for this attraction or repulsion is already manifest in the child who does not yet understand human language. So there exists within the child something anterior to all the notions which education can give him, and that is the mystery which inheres in the essence of life in mankind.

The child lives quite normally in a milieu which could be called supernatural, where everything in him is a miracle and everything outside of him must seem to him at first sight to be miraculous. We do not help him by trying to hasten, without care and discernment, an appreciation of all the things that vie for his attention. It is good for him to pursue them on his own and explain them to himself during the stage when adult explanations would throw him into even greater confusion than his own simple ones, and perhaps do irreparable damage to his judgment, consequently to the rectitude of his soul.

Thus, even if we spent a lot of time looking for the right idea of Divinity to give children, we would not find a better one than that dear old God in heaven, who sees all that happens on earth. Later will be time enough to make them understand that God is an infinite being, with no idolatrous form, and that heaven is neither the blue sky surrounding us and the earth where we live, nor even the sanctuary of our thought. For what good does it do to expose the symbol to the child, for whom all symbol is reality? This infinite ether, this profundity of creation, this heaven, too, where worlds gravitate, are bigger and more beautiful in the eyes of the child than anything to which our definitions would stretch his thought, and we would render him more foolish than wise if we wanted him to conceive of the mechanics of the universe when his feeling for its beauty is sufficient for him.

Isn't the life of the individual the sum of the collective life? Whoever observes the development of the child, the passage to adolescence, to maturity, and all our metamorphoses until old age, is witnessing an abridged version of the history of the human race, which also has its childhood, its adolescence, its prime, and its maturity. Well then, let us look back to primitive times of humanity, where all human notions appear in supernatural forms, and where history, budding science, philosophy, and religion are written in symbols that our modern logic has to translate or interpret. Even poetry and fable portray the relative truth or reality of those primitive times. Therefore, it is part of the eternal law that each of us go through our veritable childhood, as humanity has done, as certain populations which civilization has hardly touched are still doing. The savage lives in a supernatural world; he is not an idiot, or a fool, or a brute; he is a poet and a child. He proceeds only by poems and songs, as did our forebears, to whom verse seemed more natural than prose, odes than discourse.

Childhood is thus the age of songs, and it can never be given enough of them. The fable, which is only a symbol, is the best form to introduce children to a sense of the beautiful and the poetic, which is the first manifestation of the good and the true.

La Fontaine's fables are too clever and profound for early childhood. They are full of excellent morals, but early childhood does not need moral formulas. The effect would be to involve the child in a labyrinth of ideas where he would lose his way, because all morality implies some notion of society, and a child cannot conceive of society. I think religious ideas, in poetic and sentimental form, are better for him. When I disobeyed my mother and she told me I was making the sainted Virgin and all the angels in heaven cry, my imagination was vividly struck. Those marvellous beings and all those tears provoked fear and infinite tenderness in me. The idea of their existence frightened me, and at the same time the idea of their sorrow filled me with longing and affection.

In sum, I would like children to be given fantasy for as long as they love and expect it and that they be allowed to give it up by themselves, without our systematically prolonging their errors, as soon as they no longer need it as their basic food or they lose their taste for it and alert us by their questions and doubts that they wish to enter the world of reality.

Neither Clotilde nor myself has retained any memory of how much or how little trouble we had in learning to read. Our mothers told us subsequently that they had very little in teaching us; they pointed out only one very ingenuous act of stubbornness on my part. One day, when I was not disposed to receive my reading lesson, I had replied to my mother, "I know how to say 'A,' but I don't know how to say 'B.'" It seemed that my resistance lasted a very long time; I would name all the letters except the second, and when they asked my why I skipped over it in silence, I would reply imperturbably, "It's because I don't know the 'B.'"

The second remembrance that comes back to me on its own—for obviously, given how trivial it is, no one would have thought of reminding me of it—is the white dress and veil which the oldest daughter of the glazier wore the day of her first communion. I was then about three and a half; we lived on the Rue Grange-Batalière, on the fourth floor, and the glazier, who occupied a shop down below, had several daughters who came to play with my sister and me. I no longer know their names and have no special recollection of the oldest, whose white outfit appeared to me the most beautiful thing in the world. I could not stop admiring it, and when my mother abruptly told me that the white was yellowed and that she was very badly dressed, I felt oddly hurt. It seemed to me she was doing me real harm by dissuading me from the object of my admiration.

I remember another time when we were dancing in a circle, this same child sang:

> We'll no more to the woods,
> The laurels are cut down.

I had never been to the woods, as far as I know, and perhaps had never seen laurels. But apparently I knew what they were, for those two short lines set me dreaming. I withdrew from the circle to think about them and fell into deep melancholy. I did not want to share my preoccupation with anyone, but I could easily have cried, I felt so sad and deprived of this charming laurel woods which I had dreamily entered only long enough to have been dispossessed. Let whoever can explain the oddities of childhood, but that affected me so, that its mysterious impression has never left me. Anytime this round was sung I felt the same sadness come over me, and I have never heard it sung by children since without finding myself in the same disposition of regret and melancholy. I always see a vision of the uncut woods before the axe was set to it, and I have never seen a real one as beautiful; I can see it strewn with freshly cut laurels, and I have the feeling that I shall always resent the destroyers who have forever banished me from there. What then did the poet have in mind when he began the simplest of dances that way?

I also remember the pretty round, *Giroflée, girofla*, which all children know, and which again evokes a mysterious woods where you have to go "by your lonesome," and where you meet a King, Queen, Devil, and Love—all equally fantastic beings for children. I do not remember being afraid of the devil; I think I did not believe in him and that they prevented my believing in him because I had a very vivid imagination and was easily frightened.

Someone once made me a present of a superb Pulcinella, all shining gold and scarlet. At first I was fearful, especially for my doll, whom I cherished tenderly and imagined in great danger near this little monster. I would squeeze her carefully into the armoire before agreeing to play with Pulcinella; his enamelled eyes, which turned in their sockets by means of a spring, placed him for me in a kind of middle ground between the mechanical and the living. At my bedtime, they wanted to squeeze him into the armoire next to the doll, but I would never consent, and they went along with my whim, which was to let him sleep on the stove. For there was in our more than modest room a small stove which had painted panels pasted on it and was oblong in shape. A detail which I also recall, even though I have not been back in that apartment since the age of four, was that the sleeping alcove was closeted by doors with brass lattice work on a background of green cloth. Except for an antechamber, which served as a dining room, and a small kitchen, there were no other rooms than this bedroom, which served as a sitting room during the day. My little bed was put outside the alcove in the evening, and when my sister, who was then at boarding school, slept at home, a divan was put out for her next to my bed. It was a green divan in Utrecht velvet. I can still see all that, in spite of the fact that nothing very remarkable ever happened to me in that apartment; but I am convinced that my mind was opening at the time to sustained concentration on itself, for it seems to me that all these objects are filled with my reveries and that I have seen them so much I have worn them out. I had a special way of amusing myself before going to sleep, which was to run my fingers over the brass mesh on the door to the alcove at the side of my bed. The small sound that I drew from it seemed like celestial music to me, and I would hear my mother say, "Listen to Aurore play the lattice."

Coming back to my Pulcinella, who lay on his back on the stove looking at the ceiling with his glassy eyes and wicked smile, I could no longer see him, but I could still visualize him in my imagination, and I would fall asleep very preoccupied by the kind of life this evil creature led, always laughing and able to follow me with his eyes into every corner of the room. At night I had a terrible dream: Pulcinella, now dressed in a red spangled vest, his hump in front, had gotten up, caught fire on the stove, and was running all around, after me, after my doll who fled in a panic, while he reached us with long jets of flame. I woke my mother up with my cries. My sister, who slept next to me, realized what was upsetting me and carried the puppet into the kitchen, saying that it was a nasty doll for a child my age. I never saw him again. But the imaginary impression I had received of burning remained with me for some time, and instead of playing with the fire, as had been my passion until then, just one look at the fire left me in great terror.

We used to go to Chaillot then to see my Aunt Lucie, who had a small house and a garden there. I was too lazy to walk and always wanted to be carried by our friend Pierret, who, from Chaillot to the Boulevard, was rather inconvenienced by my weight. To get me to walk back in the evening, it occurred to my mother to tell me that she would leave me alone in the middle of the street. This was at the corner of Rue de Chaillot and the Champs-Élysées, where there happened to be at the moment a little old lady lighting the streetlamps. Quite convinced that I would not be abandoned, I stopped, determined not to walk any more, and my mother took several steps with Pierret to see how I would take to the idea of remaining alone. But as the street was almost empty, the lamplighter had heard our dispute, and turning toward me, said in a cracking voice, "Watch out for me, I'm the one who collects naughty little girls, and I shut them up in my streetlamp all night long."

It seemed like the devil had whispered to this good woman the idea that could frighten me most. I do not remember ever having felt such terror as that which she inspired in me. The streetlamp with its glittering reflector immediately took on fantastic proportions in my mind, and already I saw myself locked in this crystal prison, consumed by the flame which this pulcinella in petticoats was shooting out at will. I ran screaming after my mother. I heard the old woman laugh, and the creaking of the lamp as she remounted it gave me a nervous tremor, as if I were being raised and suspended above ground with the infernal lantern.

Sometimes we walked along the water to get to Chaillot. The smoke and the noise of the fire pump gave me a fright whose effects I can still feel.

Fear is, I believe, the greatest mental affliction of children; to force them to look at closely or touch the object that frightens them is a cure I don't approve of. It is better to take them away and distract them, because their constitution is dominated by the nervous system, and by the time they recognize their error, they have experienced such violent anguish at having been the object of force, that it is too late for them to lose the feeling of fear. It has done them physical harm that their reason is powerless to combat. The same is true for nervous and faint-hearted women. To encourage them in their weakness is a great mistake, but to be too forceful with them is worse, and coercion often provokes them to real nervous crises, even though their nerves had not seriously been affected at the beginning of the ordeal.

That kind of cruelty was not in my mother's character. When we passed in front of the fire pump, seeing me grow pale and unable to remain upright, she would put me in the arms of the good Pierret. He hid my head against his chest, and I was reassured by the confidence he inspired in me. It is better to treat emotional weakness with consoling remedies than to use force on nature and try to overcome physical symptoms by even more painful physical ordeals.

It was in Rue Grange-Batelière that I first had in my hands an old abridged mythology, which I still own, which is accompanied by large engraved plates, the most comical you can imagine. When I remember the interest and admiration with which I contemplated those grotesque images, I feel like I am still seeing them as they appeared to me then. Without being able to read the text, I learned quite quickly, thanks to the pictures, the basic facts of the ancient myths, which interested me prodigiously. I was sometimes taken to the Chinese shadow plays at the theater run by generations of the Séraphin family and to the fairy plays on the Boulevard. Then too my mother and sister told me the tales of Perrault, and when they ran out of those, they did not mind inventing new ones which were by no means less pretty to me. Along with all that, they spoke to me of paradise and regaled me with what was freshest and prettiest in Catholic allegory, to the extent that the angels and the cupids, the good Virgin and the good fairy, the pulcinellas and the magicians, the little theater devils and the church saints all got mixed up in my brain, producing there the strangest poetic muddle one can imagine.

My mother's religious ideas were never brushed by doubt, seeing that she never examined them. Therefore it did not burden her to present to me as true or emblematic the notions of the supernatural which she would generously douse me with, artist and poet that she herself unknowingly was, believing everything that was beautiful and good in her religion, rejecting everything that was dark and menacing, and talking to me about the three graces or the nine muses as gravely as of the theological virtues or the wise virgins.

Whether education comes about through the efforts of others or we are predisposed to it, it is certain that a love for story took passionate hold of me before I had finished learning to read. This is how it happened:

I could not yet grasp fairy tales by reading them, as the printed words even in their most elementary versions did not make great sense, and it was only by reciting that I came to understand what I had been made to read. I did not read on my own; I was lazy by nature and could not overcome it except with great effort; I looked at books only for their pictures. But everything that I learned by sight and by ear entered my small head in a rush, and I would daydream over it often to the point of losing sight of present reality. As I had for a long while a mania for playing with the fire in the stove, my mother, who had no servant and who I always saw occupied with sewing or looking after the stewpot, could often only rid herself of me by putting me in a prison that she herself had invented—to wit, four chairs, with an unlit footwarmer in the middle for me to sit on when I was tired, for we did not have the luxury of a cushion. These chairs were stuffed with straw, and I did my utmost to unstuff them with my nails; I imagine, now, they had been sacrificed for my use. I remember I was still so little that, in order to dedicate myself to this entertainment, I was obliged to climb up on the chafing dish; in this way I was able to lean my elbows on the seats, and I would claw away with incredible patience. But while thus acceding to the need of keeping my hands busy—a need which has never left me—I was not paying the slightest attention to the straw in the chairs: I was composing aloud interminable stories which my mother referred to as my novels. I have no recollection whatever of those droll compositions which my mother spoke of to me a thousand times, long before I had any thought of writing. She declared them phenomenally boring because of their length and the extent to which I developed the digressions. This is a defect, they say, I still suffer from; I admit I take little notice of present reality, and have today, exactly like when I was four, an insuperable lack of restraint in that genre of creation.

It seemed that my stories were a kind of pastiche of everything with which my little brain had been obsessed. They were always based on a plot in the fairy tale manner, with a good fairy, a kind prince, and a beautiful princess as the main characters. There were seldom wicked characters and never any great misfortunes. Everything turned out for the best, guided by as cheerful and optimistic a conception as childhood allows. What was curious about these stories was their duration and kind of continuity, for I took up the thread wherever I had left off the day before. Perhaps my mother, who listened somewhat automatically and in spite of herself to these long divagations, unwittingly helped me find it again. My aunt also remembers these stories and is amused by the recollection. She recalls having often said to me, "Well, Aurore, hasn't your prince come out of the forest yet? Will your princess soon finish putting on her dress with the train and her golden crown?" "Don't disturb her," my mother would say, "I can only do my work in peace when she starts her novels-among-four-chairs."

I recall more clearly the ardor with which I played those games that were patterned after real behavior. I was disgruntled to begin with, when my sister, or the glazier's oldest daughter tried to get me to play classic children's games, like giant-step or hot-and-cold; I found none of them to my liking, or I quickly tired of them. But with my cousin Clotilde, or other children my age, I could find games that captured my fancy right away. We simulated the battles and flights through the woods which played such a big role in my imagination. And then one of us would be lost and the others would look for her and call her. She would be asleep under a tree, that is to say, under the divan. Someone would go to her aid; one of us would be the mother of the others, or the general, since the military influence inevitably penetrated our nest, and more than once I was the Emperor and commanded the battlefield. We would tear up our dolls—the soldiers and the families—and my father's imagination seemed as youthful as ours, for he could not bear these miniature representations of the scenes of horror he was seeing in the war. He would say to my mother, "Please sweep up the children's battle field. It's odd, but it upsets me to see arms, legs, and all those red rags and tatters on the floor."

We were not aware of our ferocity, as the dolls and soldiers suffered the carnage so patiently. But in galloping on our imaginary chargers and hitting the furniture and toys with our invisible sabers, we were carried to a level of enthusiasm that left us feverish. We were reproached for our boyish games, and no doubt my cousin and I did hunger after virile emotions. I am reminded particularly of one day in autumn when, dinner over, the room had grown dark. This was not in our house, but in Chaillot, at my aunt's, if I remember, for there were bed curtains, and in our house there were none. We were chasing one another through the trees, that is to say, the curtain-folds, Clotilde and I. The apartment had vanished from our sight, and we were truly in a somber landscape where night was falling. They called us to eat, and we heard nothing. My mother came to take me in her arms and carry me to the table, and I shall always remember how amazed I was at seeing the lights, the table, and the objects surrounding me. I was positively emerging from a trance, and the abruptness of coming out took its toll on me. Sometimes, being in Chaillot, I thought I was at home in Paris, and vice versa. I often had to make an effort to be sure where I was, and I saw my daughter undergo this illusion in a very pronounced way as a child.

I do not think I ever saw Chaillot again after 1808, for after the trip to Spain, I did not leave Nohant until just after the time my uncle sold his small property to the state, which was located on the site destined for the palace of the King of Rome. Mistaken or not, I shall put here what I have to say about this house, which was then a real country house, Chaillot not having been built up as it is today.

It was the most modest dwelling in the world, which I understand only now that the actual value of these remembered objects is apparent to me. But at the age I was then, it was paradise. I could draw the plan of the building and the garden, they have remained so fresh in my mind. The garden was the foremost place of delight for me, because it was the only garden I knew. My mother, in spite of what was said about her to my grandmother at that time, lived in hardship bordering on poverty, with thrift and domestic toil worthy of a woman of the people; she did not take me to the Tuileries to show off the outfits we did not have or to give me airs playing with a hoop or jump rope before the gazing passersby. We only left our poor little nook sometimes to go to the theater, for which my mother had developed a taste, as I too already had, but most often to Chaillot, where we were always received with greats shouts of joy. The trip on foot and having to pass the fire pump vexed me at first, but barely had I stepped into the garden when I imagined myself in the enchanted isle of my tales. Clotilde, who was able to frolic about there in the sun all day long, was much more hale and lively than I. She did me the honors of her Eden with the good nature and openhearted cheer that have never forsaken her. She was certainly the better of the two of us, more healthy and less whimsical; I also adored her in spite of a few squabbles, which I was always the one to provoke and to which she responded with a ridicule that very much mortified me. Thus, when she was unhappy with me, she would play on my name Aurore by calling me 'horror,' an insult which left me exasperated. But how could I sulk for long when face to face with a green arbor and a terrace all bordered with pots of flowers? That is where I saw gossamer for the first time, all white and gleaming in the autumn sun; my sister was there that day, for it was she who explained to me in a learned way how the Virgin herself spun these pretty threads on her ivory distaff. I did not dare break them, and I made myself very small in order to pass underneath.

The garden was an oblong, very small in reality, but seemed to me immense even though I went around it two hundred times a day. It was symmetrically laid out in the old-fashioned way; there were flowers and vegetables; not the slightest view, for there were walls on all sides, but it had a sanded terrace at one end which one climbed up to by stone steps, with the usual large, idiotic clay urn on either side. And on this terrace, an idealized place for me, we held our big games of battle, flight, and pursuit.

There, too, I saw for the first time butterflies and big sunflowers, which appeared to me to be a hundred feet tall. One day we were interrupted in our play by a great commotion outside. There were cries of "Long live the Emperor," there was hurried marching that receded in the distance, and the cries continued. The Emperor was indeed passing not far away, and we could hear the trot of horses and the crowd's excitement. We could not see over the wall, but I remember it as being beautiful in my imagination, and carried away by a contagious enthusiasm, we cried with all our might, "Long live the emperor!"

Did we know what an emperor was? I do not remember, but it is likely that he was a constant subject of conversation. I formed a distinct impression of him not long afterward, I cannot say exactly when, but it must have been toward the end of 1807.

He was inspecting the troops on the boulevard, not far from the Madeleine; my mother and Pierret had managed to penetrate right up to the soldiers, whereupon Pierret lifted me in his arms, above the shakos, so that I could see him. That object rising over the line of heads automatically struck the Emperor's eye, and my mother cried, "He looked at you, remember that, it will bring you good luck!" I believe the Emperor heard those naïve words, for he looked at me fully, and I believe I can still see a sort of smile hovering over his pale face, whose cold severity had frightened me at first. I shall therefore never forget his face, and especially the expression in his eyes that no portrait could render. He was at this period quite fat and livid. He wore a frock coat over his uniform, but I could not say whether it was gray; his hat was in his hand when I saw him, and I was magnetized for a moment by that clear gaze, so harsh at first, and suddenly so benevolent and sweet. I saw him again on other occasions, but less clearly, because I was not so close, and he went by more quickly.

I also saw the child King of Rome, in the arms of his nurse. He was at a window in the Tuileries, and he was laughing at the passersby. Seeing me, he began to laugh even more, due to the sympathetic effect that children have on each other. He was holding a large bon-bon in his small hand, and he threw it toward me. My mother wanted to pick it up to give to me, but the sentry who was guarding the window would not allow her to step beyond the sentry line. The governess made a sign in vain that the bon-bon was for me and that he should give it to me. This probably was not on the order sheet for that military function, and he failed to respond. I was very hurt by such behavior and made it a point to ask my mother why the soldier was so dishonest. She explained that his duty was to guard this precious child and stop anyone from coming too close, because some ill-intentioned persons could do him harm. The idea that someone would want to hurt a child seemed to me far-fetched, but at that time I was already nine or ten (for the little king *in partibus* [in name only] was two years old at most), and this anecdote is merely a digression into the future.

A memory which does date from my first four years is that of my earliest musical response. My mother had been to see someone in a village near Paris, I do not know which village. The apartment was very high up, and from the window, as I was too small to see down to the street, I could only distinguish neighboring housetops and a large expanse of sky. We spent part of the day there, but I paid attention to nothing else, so absorbed was I by the sound of a flute which played a flock of tunes that I found wondrous all the time we were there. The sound was coming from one of the highest garrets, quite far away, for my mother could hardly hear it when I asked her what it was. As for me, my hearing was apparently finer and more sensitive at this period, and I did not miss a single modulation of this little instrument—so piercing from nearby, so sweet at a distance—and was charmed by it. It seemed to me I heard it as in a dream. The sky was cloudless and a sparkling blue, and those delicate melodies seemed to soar over the rooftops as far as heaven itself. Who knows if it wasn't an artist of superior inspiration who, for the moment, had no other attentive listener but me? It could just as well have been a cook's helper who was learning the themes from *Monaco* or *Les Folies d'Espagne*. Whoever it was, I experienced indescribable musical pleasure, and I was truly ecstatic in front of that window, where for the first time I vaguely understood the harmony of external things, my soul being ravished alike by the music and the beauty of the sky.   *M.M.M./A.M.F.*

XII

My parent's home life. —Our friend Pierret. —Departure for Spain.
—Dolls. —The Asturias. —The bindweed and the bears. —The
bloodstain. —The pigeons. —The talking magpie.

All my childhood memories are quite infantile, as you will see, but if
each of my readers reflects on his own past while reading mine, if he goes back
with pleasure over the earliest emotions of his life, if he feels himself becoming a child again for an hour, neither he nor I will have wasted his time, for
childhood is good, it is honest, and the best people are those who retain the
most of its innate honesty and sensitivity.

I have very little recollection of my father prior to the Spanish campaign.
He was absent so frequently that I must have lost sight of him for long periods
of time. He was with us, however, for the winter of 1807–1808, because I
vaguely recall quiet dinners by candlelight, and a platter of sweets, albeit very
modest, consisting of vermicelli cooked in sugared milk, which my father pretended he would eat all by himself, so that he could enjoy my disappointed
greed. I remember also that he knotted and rolled his napkin in various ways to
resemble a monk, a rabbit, a puppet, which made me laugh very much. I
believe he would have spoiled me terribly, for my mother was forced to intervene in order to avoid his encouraging all my whims instead of repressing
them. I was told that during the limited time he could spend with his family, he
was so happy that he scarcely let his wife and children out of his sight, that he
played with me for entire days, and that he was not the least bit ashamed to
carry me in his arms on the streets and boulevards when in full dress uniform.

To be sure, I was very happy, for I was well loved; we were poor, but I
was oblivious to it. My father was then receiving a salary which should have
made us comfortable, if the expenses resulting from his duties as Murat's aide-
de-camp had not surpassed his earnings. My grandmother deprived herself in
order to provide him with the rash level of luxury expected of him, and there
still remained debts for his horses, clothing, and equipment. My mother was
often accused of having added to the family difficulties by her disorganization.
I have so clear a memory of our domestic life at this time that I can affirm that
she deserved none of these reproaches. She made her own bed, swept the apartment, mended her old clothes, and did the cooking. She was a woman of
extraordinary energy and heart. All her life she rose at dawn and retired at one
in the morning, and I do not remember a single occasion when she was idle at
home. We received no one except our family and our excellent friend, Pierret,

who treated me with the affection of a father and the concern of a mother.

It is time for the story and portrait of this priceless man, whom I shall miss for the rest of my life. Pierret was the son of a small landowner from Champagne, and from the age of eighteen he was employed at the treasury, where he always held a modest position. He was the ugliest of men, but in this ugliness was embodied such goodness that it inspired trust and friendship. He had a big flat nose, a wide mouth, and tiny eyes; his blond hair curled obstinately, and he had such a pink and white complexion that he always looked young. He was very annoyed at forty when a clerk from the town hall where he served as a witness to my sister's marriage asked him, in all good faith, if he had reached the age of majority. However, he was quite tall and heavy, and his face was constantly furrowed with frightful grimaces due to a nervous tic. Perhaps it was this tic that prevented one from having an accurate idea of what his face was like, but I believe it was above all the honest and innocent facial expression in its rare moments of repose which added to the illusion of youth. He was not the least bit what we call bright, but because he judged everything with his heart and his conscience, you could ask him for advice on the most delicate personal matters. I do not believe that there was ever a man more pure, loyal, generous, or fair; and to the extent that he was unaware of its beauty and rarity, his soul was that much more beautiful. Convinced of the goodness of others, it never occurred to him that he might be exceptional.

He had some very prosaic tastes. He liked wine, beer, a pipe, billiards, and dominoes. Any time he did not spend with us, he spent in a tavern on Rue du Faubourg-Poissonnière, at the sign of the White Horse. He felt at home there, for he frequented it for thirty years, and up to his last day, he took along his unfailing cheerfulness and incomparable goodness. Thus, his life slipped by in an obscure, unvarying circle. He was happy there, and how could he not have been? Whoever knew him loved him, and the notion of evil never touched his honorable and simple soul.

He was, however, very high-strung and, consequently, irritable and sensitive, but his goodness must have been irresistible, because he never succeeded in hurting a soul. No one can imagine the rudeness and tirades I had to endure from him. He would stamp his feet, roll his little eyes, get red in the face, and indulge in the most fantastic grimaces, all the while addressing the most vehement reproaches to you, in not very diplomatic language. My mother had the habit of paying not the least attention. She was content to say, "Aha! There's Pierret in a fury; now we're going to see some lovely faces!" And Pierret would immediately forget his tragic tone and begin to laugh. She teased him a great deal, and it was no surprise that he often lost patience. In his later years, he became even more irascible, and scarcely a day passed that he didn't pick up his hat and leave, declaring he would never set foot in her house again, but he would return in the evening, having forgotten the tone of his morning farewells.

When it came to me, he assumed a paternal right which would have verged on tyranny, if his threats could possibly have been realized. He had witnessed my birth and had weaned me—sufficiently remarkable in itself to give some idea of his character. My mother, being exhausted with fatigue, but unable to reconcile herself to ignore my cries and complaints, and fearing also that I was poorly cared for at night by a maid, had reached the point of no longer sleeping, at a time when she greatly needed sleep. Observing this, Pierret came one evening of his own accord, took me in my cradle and carried me to his home, where he kept me for fifteen or twenty nights, hardly sleeping, so fearful was he for me, and making me drink milk and sugared water with as much solicitude, care, and tidiness as a nanny would have. Every morning he brought me back to my mother, so that he could go to his office, then to the White Horse; and each evening he came to fetch me again, carrying me on foot, in full view of the entire neighborhood, a grown fellow of twenty-two or twenty-three years, hardly caring if he was noticed. When my mother seemed to show resistance or anxiety, he grew red with anger, reproaching her for "imbecilic weakness," for he was reckless with his epithets; he himself would tell her with great pleasure the way he took care of me, and when he brought me back my mother was forced to admire how clean, fresh, and in good humor I was. To care for a ten-month-old so rarely suits the taste and talents of a man, especially a tavern-goer like Pierret, it is a marvel, not that he did it, but that the idea occurred to him. He was the one who finally weaned me and accomplished it honorably, as he said he would.

It is quite true that he always thought of me as a child, and when I was around forty, he was still talking to me as if I were a brat. He was very demanding—not in the matter of gratitude, for he never dreamed of ascribing any value whatsoever to himself—but in that of affection. And when you tested him by asking why he wanted so much to be loved, he would merely reply, "It's just that I love you." And he spoke these tender words with a furious tone and nervous spasm that made him grind his teeth. If, when writing but three lines to my mother, I forgot on a single occasion to send love to Pierret, and I happened to run into him at the time, he would turn his back and refuse to say hello. Explanations and excuses were to no avail. He treated me as a hard-hearted child and swore me eternal hatred and bitterness. He said this in such a comical way, you would have thought he was putting on some sort of show, if you hadn't seen the the big tears brimming in his eyes. My mother, who was familiar with his nervous condition, would say to him, "Be quiet now, Pierret, you're not making any sense." And she would even give him a sharp pinch to get it over with more quickly. Then he would recover and deign to listen to my excuses. A word from the heart and a caress were all it took to appease and render him happy, as soon as you had succeeded in making him listen.

He had become acquainted with my parents during the earliest days of my existence, and in a way that united all of them instantly. A relative of his lived on Rue Meslay, on the same block as my mother. This woman had a child my age whom she neglected and who, deprived of milk, cried all day. My mother entered the room where the unfortunate little one was dying from want, nursed it, and continued to rescue it in this way without saying a word. But Pierret, when coming to see his relative, caught my mother in this act, was duly moved, and pledged himself evermore to her and her kin.

Scarcely had he seen my father than he developed an equally great affection for him. He took care of all his affairs, put them in order, got rid of disreputable creditors, and assisted him with foresight gradually to satisfy the others; finally he delivered him of all material concerns from which my father could hardly have extricated himself without the help of someone trained in the details of business and always concerned for the welfare of others. It was Pierret who chose his domestic help, kept his accounts, paid his bills, and insured that he received his money in whatever unforeseen place the war might take him. My father never left for a campaign without saying to him, "Pierret, I commend to you my wife and children, and if I do not return, consider that it is for the rest of your life." Pierret took his responsibility seriously, for his whole life was dedicated to us after the death of my father. There were those who deemed this domestic situation improper, for what is there sacred in this world, and what soul can be judged pure by those who are not? But to whoever was worthy of understanding Pierret, such a supposition will always be perceived as an outrage to his memory. He was not attractive enough to have rendered my mother unfaithful even in thought. He was too conscientious and too upright not to have kept his distance from her, had he felt himself in danger of betraying, even mentally, the trust of which he was so proud and zealous. Eventually, he married the daughter of a general of no great fortune, and they were very happy together, she being respectable and kind, according to what I always heard said in the presence of my mother, who had an affectionate relationship with her.

When our trip to Spain was decided, it was Pierret who made all our preparations. This was not a very prudent undertaking on the part of my mother, for she was seven or eight months pregnant. She wanted to take me along, and I was still something of an inconvenience. But my father announced a sojourn of some length in Madrid, and my mother had, I believe, some mistrust based on jealousy. Whatever the motive, she was determined to join him, and she let herself be tempted by the opportunity. An army supplier's wife with whom she was acquainted was travelling post and offered her a place in her carriage as far as Madrid.

The only protector this woman had on that occasion was a twelve-year-old groom. Here we were then, on the road together, two women of whom one was pregnant, and two children of whom I was not the more unreasonable or unruly.

I do not recall feeling any chagrin in separating from my sister, who remained at boarding school, or from my cousin Clotilde. Since I did not see them every day, I had no conception of how long, more or less, the separation lasted that used to begin again every week. Nor did I miss the apartment, although this had been my universe, more or less, and I had scarcely existed anywhere else yet, even in thought. What really wrung my heart during the early moments of the trip was the necessity of leaving my doll in the deserted apartment where she would be so lonely.

The attachment that little girls show for their dolls is truly quite bizarre, and I felt it so acutely and for so long that, without venturing to explain it, I can easily describe it. They are really not entirely fooled for a single moment of their childhood as to the kind of existence this inert being has, which is placed in their hands and is supposed to develop a lifelike maternal instinct. At least in my case, I do not ever recall believing that my doll was an animate being; yet I felt for certain ones in my possession a truly maternal affection. I would not exactly call it idolatry, although the custom of making children love these sorts of fetishes is a little barbaric; I was not aware at the time what this affection consisted of, but I think that if I had been able to analyze it, I would have found in it something analagous to what fervent Catholics experience in front of certain images of devotion. They know that the image is not the same as the object of their devotion, and yet they prostrate themselves before the image, adorn it, sprinkle incense on it, make offerings to it. The ancients were no more idolatrous than we, no matter what has been said about them. At no time have enlightened men adored either the statue of Jupiter nor the idol of Mammon; it was Jupiter and Mammon they revered beneath the exterior symbol. But at all times, today as before, uncultivated minds have been quite hindered from making a very clear distinction between the god and the image.

This is true of children in general. They exist between the real and the symbolic. They need to care for or scold, to caress or break this child- or animal-fetish they have been given as a plaything and have wrongly been accused of growing disgusted with too quickly. On the contrary, it is very simply that they grow disgusted with themselves. By breaking it, they are protesting against the lie. For an instant they believed this mute creature was alive, which soon shows them its brass-wire muscles, its undeveloped limbs, its empty skull, its innards of grain or straw. There it was, enduring the examination, submitting to the autopsy, falling awkwardly at the least shove, and collapsing in a ridiculous fashion. How can a child have pity for a being which excites only his scorn. The more he admires it in its freshness and novelty, the more he disdains it when he has discovered its secret inertness and fragility.

I liked to break dolls, imitation cats and dogs, and toy men, just like other children. There were exceptions—certain dolls that I cared for, like real children. When I had undressed the little person, if I saw her arms wobble on the pins which held them to the shoulders, and her wooden hands come apart from her arms, I could have no illusion on her account, and I sacrificed her quickly to impetuous and bellicose games. But if she was solid and well made, if she stood up to the first tests, if she did not break her nose on the first tumble, if her enamel eyes had a special look in my imagination, she became my daughter, I gave her infinite care, and I made the other children respect her with incredible vigilance.

I also had some favorite toys—one among others, which I have never forgotten and, to my great regret, was lost, for I did not break it, and it is possible that it might indeed have been as pretty as it appears in my mind.

It was part of a table centerpiece, quite ancient, for it had served as a toy for my father in his childhood, the entire centerpiece apparently no longer existing even at that time. He had found it again at my grandmother's, while rummaging through a cupboard, and remembering how much this toy had pleased him, brought it home to me. It was a small Venus in Sèvres' porcelain, carrying a dove in each hand. She was mounted on a pedestal which was attached to a small oval tray lined with a mirror and bordered with fretwork of gilded copper. In this embellishment were tulips which served as candleholders, and when the little candles were lit, the mirror, which represented a pool of spring water, reflected the lights, the statue, and the pretty golden ornaments of the border. For me this toy was an enchanted world, and when my mother had told me for the tenth time the charming tale of Gracieuse and Percinet, I set myself to composing imaginary countrysides and magical gardens whose reflection I thought I captured in the lake. Where do children find the vision of things they have never seen?

When our packing for the trip to Spain was completed, I had a cherished doll that they undoubtedly would have let me bring along. But that was not my intent. It seemed to me she might break, or that someone would take her from me unless I left her in my room. After having undressed her and done a very elaborate nighttime toilette for her, I laid her on my little bed and arranged the covers very carefully. At the moment of departure, I ran to look at her one last time, but as Pierret promised he would come to insure that she ate her soup every morning, I began to fall into the state of doubt that children do about the reality of this sort of creature, a state truly peculiar, where budding reason on one side, and the need for illusion on the other, carry on a struggle in a heart already craving to be maternal. I took my doll's hands and joined them on her breast. Pierret commented that this was how a dead person looked. So, I raised her joined hands above her head in an attitude of despair or invocation, to which I very seriously ascribed a superstitious idea. I considered it an appeal to the good fairy and that by remaining in this position throughout my absence, she would be protected. Also, Pierret had to promise not to change her position. There is nothing in the world more true than the extravagant, poetical story of E. T. A. Hoffmann entitled *The Nutcracker*. It captures the intellectual life of the child in its essence. I even like its embroiled ending, where a child loses herself in the world of fancy.[40] The imagination of children is as rich and diverse as these brilliant creations of the German storyteller.

Except for the thought of my doll, which pursued me for some time, I remember nothing about the trip until we reached the Asturian Mountains. But I can still feel the astonishment and terror that those great mountains inspired in me. The abrupt turnings of the road in the midst of this amphitheater, whose peaks enclosed the horizon, brought me a surprise filled with anguish at every instant. It seemed to me we were imprisoned in these mountains, that there was no longer a road, and that we could neither continue nor return. There I saw for the first time, on the sides of the road, bindweed in bloom. These small pink bellflowers, delicately striped with white, impressed me very much. My mother instinctively and very ingenuously opened the world of beauty to me by acquainting me from my very early years with all her impressions. Thus, when there was a beautiful cloud, an extraordinary sunset, a clear flowing stream, she would have me stop by saying to me, "Look how pretty that is." And immediately these objects which I might not have noticed on my own revealed their beauty to me, as if my mother had had a magic key to open my mind to the untutored, but profound, sentiment she had for them herself. I remember that our travelling companion had no understanding at all of the naïve admiration my mother made me party to, and she often said, "Oh, my goodness, Mme. Dupin, how droll you are with your little girl!" However, I do not remember my mother ever using flowery phrases with me. I do not believe she had the means to do it, for if she knew how to write at this time, it was with difficulty, and she did not pride herself on a vain and useless orthography. And yet she spoke purely, as birds sing without having learned to sing. She had a sweet voice and refined pronunciation. Her slightest words charmed or persuaded me.

As she was truly weak with regard to her memory and had never been able to link two ideas in her mind, she endeavored to combat this weakness in me, which in many respects has been inherited. Also, she said to me time and time again, "You must remember what you see there," and each time she took this precaution, I did indeed remember. Thus, seeing the bindweed in flower, she said to me, "Smell them, they smell of honey, and don't forget it!" This is the first revelation of odor that I remember, and by a chain of memories and sensations that everyone knows but cannot explain, I never smell the flowers of the bindweed without seeing the spot in the Spanish mountains and the edge of the path where I picked them for the first time.

But where was this place? God only knows! I would recognize it, if I saw it. I think it was outside Pancorbo.

Another incident that I will never forget and which would have struck any other child was this: we were in quite a flat place not far from habitation. The night was clear, but large trees bordered the road and caused intervals of great darkness. I was on the coachman's box with the young groom. The driver slowed his horses and shouted to the groom, "Tell the ladies not to be afraid; I have good horses." My mother had no need for these words to be relayed to her; she heard them, and being next to the door, she also saw clearly as well as I did, three persons, two to one side of the road, the other opposite, about ten paces from us. They looked small and stood immobile. "Those are robbers," shouted my mother. "Driver, do not go on, turn around, turn around! I see their guns."

The driver, who was French, began to laugh, for this illusion of guns proved to him that my mother scarcely knew what enemies we were dealing with. He judged it more prudent not to undeceive her, whipped his horses, and passed resolutely at a fast trot in front of these three phlegmatic figures, which did not stir in the least and which I saw distinctly but without being able to say what they were. My mother, in her fright, believed she detected pointed hats, and took them for some kind of soldiers. But when the horses, nervous and very afraid on their own account, had run far enough, the driver slowed them, and got down to come to speak to his passengers. "Well, ladies," he said, still laughing, "did you see their guns? They surely had some harm in mind, for they stood their ground all the time they saw us. But I knew my horses would behave. If we had had a spill in that spot, we mightn't have gotten off so lucky."

"But for heaven's sake," said my mother, "what was it then?"

"With all due respect, it was three large mountain bears, my little lady."

My mother was more frightened than ever; she begged the driver to climb up again and take us full speed to the nearest shelter, but this man was apparently accustomed to such encounters, which today would doubtless be very rare at the height of spring on the main highways. He told us that these animals were only dangerous in case the carriage overturned, and he drove us to the relay house without a mishap.

For my part, I was not afraid. I had known several bears in my Nuremburg boxes. I had made them devour certain guilty personages in my improvised novels, but they had never dared to attack my good princess, with whose adventures I surely identified without knowing.

No doubt I am not expected to put into order these memories which date from so far back. They are very disjointed, and my mother could not have helped me organize them after the event, for she remembered less than I. I shall only relate the main events that struck me in the order they come to me.

My mother had even less well-founded fears at an inn which, nevertheless, had a very respectable appearance. I recall this resting place because it was there I noticed for the first time those pretty straw mats shaded with various colors which southerners use instead of rugs. I was very tired, we had been travelling in stifling heat, and my first reaction on entering the room that was opened for us was to throw myself full length on the mat. Probably we had already had some less comfortable shelters in this Spanish territory, disrupted by the insurrection, for my mother exclaimed, "That's better! Here are some nice clean rooms, and I hope we'll be able to sleep." But after a few minutes, having gone out in the corridor, she cried out and came back in a rush. She had seen a large bloodstain on the floor, and this was enough to convince her she was in a den of cutthroats.

Mme. Fontanier (the name of our travelling companion comes back to me now) made fun of her, but nothing could persuade her to go to bed until she had furtively examined the house. My mother's genre of cowardice was quite exceptional. Her lively imagination constantly presented her with visions of extreme danger, but at the same time her energetic nature and remarkable presence of mind inspired her with the courage to examine more closely the objects which terrorized her, in order to escape the danger, which she would have done very adroitly, I have no doubt. At any rate, she was one of those women who, always alarmed at something because they are afraid of dying, never lose their heads because they have a genius for self-preservation.

There she was then, arming herself with a torch and wanting to lead Mme. Fontanier to the discovery; the latter, who was neither as fearful nor as brave, was not terribly concerned. Then I felt myself overcome by a great compulsion to courage, which had little merit since I did not understand why my mother was afraid, but at last, seeing her throw herself all alone into an expedition which made her companion retreat, I attached myself resolutely to her skirt. And the little groom, who was a funny, mischievous fellow, fearing nothing and mocking everything, followed with another torch. We went thus on our voyage of discovery on tiptoe, in order not to rouse the suspicion of the innkeepers whom we heard laughing and chattering in the kitchen. My mother did indeed show us the bloodstain near a door against which she glued her ear, and her imagination was so activated that she thought she heard groans. "I am sure," said she to the groom, "that there is some unfortunate French soldier in there, with his throat cut by these evil Spaniards." And with a trembling, but resolute, hand, she opened the door and found herself in the presence of three enormous cadavers—freshly killed pigs for the provision of the house and consumption by the travellers.

My mother began to laugh and went back to Mme. Fontanier to make fun of her fright. As for me, I became more frightened at the sight of those bleeding and gaping pigs, so basely hung on the wall, with their scorched noses touching the ground, than of anything I could have imagined.

This, however, was not what gave me a clear idea of death; I needed another spectacle to understand what that was. And yet I had killed lots of people in my novels-among-four-chairs and in my military games with Clotilde. I knew the word but not the thing; I had feigned death myself on the field of battle with my Amazonian companions, and lying on the ground and closing my eyes for a few instants I had felt no distress. I learned once and for all what death was in another inn, where someone had given me a live pigeon, out of four or five that were destined to be our dinner; for in Spain, pigeon is, along with pork, the basic food for travellers, and during this time of war and misery, it was a luxury to find it at one's disposal. This live pigeon brought me transports of joy and tenderness; I had never had such a fine plaything, a living toy, what a treasure! But it soon proved to me that a living thing is an impractical toy, for it always wanted to fly away, and as soon as I left it at liberty for an instant, it escaped and I had to pursue it all over the room. It was indifferent to my kisses, and in vain did I call it the sweetest of names, it did not hear me. This tried my patience, and I asked where the other pigeons had been put. The groom told me that they were being killed. "Oh, well," I said, "I want them to kill mine too." My mother tried to make me renounce this cruel plan, but I was adamant to the point of crying and screaming, which caused her great surprise. "It must be," she said to Mme. Fontanier, "that this child has no idea what she's asking. She thinks dying is going to sleep." Then she took me by the hand and led me, with my pigeon, into the kitchen where they were butchering its brothers. I do not remember how they did it, but I saw the violent throes of the dying bird and its final convulsion. I uttered some piercing shrieks, believing that my already well-loved bird had succumbed to the same fate, and I shed torrents of tears. My mother, who had it under her arm, showed me it was still alive, and this was an extreme joy for me. But when they served us the corpses of the other pigeons for dinner and told me that these were the same creatures I had seen so handsome with their shining feathers and gentle gaze, I regarded the food with horror and did not want to touch it.

The further we advanced along our journey, the more terrible became the spectacle of war. We spent the night in a village which had been burned the day before and where all that remained in the inn was one room with a bench and table. There was absolutely nothing to eat but raw onions, with which I contented myself, but which neither my mother nor her companion could resolve themselves to touch. They dared not travel during the night. They spent it without sleeping a wink, and I slept on the table, where they had made me quite a good bed with the cushions from the carriage.

It is impossible for me to say at what precise period of the Spanish war this was. I never bothered to find out at the time my parents would have been able to sort out my memories, and there is no one remaining who can help me. I think we left Paris in the course of April 1808, and that the terrible events of May 2nd[41] broke out in Madrid while we were crossing Spain on our way there. My father had arrived in Bayonne on the 27th of February. He wrote a few lines to my mother from the outskirts of Madrid on March 18, and it was at about this time that I must have seen the Emperor in Paris, on his return from Venice and before his departure for Bayonne, because when I saw him the sun was going down and shone in my eyes, and we were coming home for dinner. When we left Paris, it was not warm, but we had hardly been in Spain when the heat overwhelmed us. If we had been in Madrid during the events of May 2nd, such a catastrophe would undoubtedly have left a keen impression on me, since I remember much less important incidents.

Here is one that is all but fixed in my mind—the meeting that we had near Burgos, or near Vittoria, with a queen, who could only have been the Queen of Etruria.[42] Now we know that the departure of this princess was the prime cause of the uprising of May 2nd at Madrid. We probably met her a few days later, as she was heading toward Bayonne, where the king, Charles IV, was summoning her, in order to reunite his whole family under the claws of the imperial eagle.[43]

As the meeting made a strong impression on me, I can recount it in some detail. I could not say where it took place except that it was in a sort of village where we had stopped for dinner. There was a relay stable at the inn and at the end of the courtyard a large enough garden where I saw sunflowers that reminded me of those at Chaillot. For the first time, I saw them gather the seeds from this plant and was told they were good to eat. There was, in a corner of this same courtyard, a magpie in a cage, and this magpie spoke, which was further cause for astonishment. It said, in Spanish, something that probably meant "death to the French," or "death to Godoy."[44] I only distinctly heard the first word, which it repeated in an affected way, with a really diabolical accent, *Muera, muera!* And Mme. Fontanier's groom explained to me that the bird was mad at me and wished me dead. I was so astonished to hear a bird talk that my fairy tales appeared more serious than I had perhaps believed them until then. It did not occur to me that the words were mechanical and that the poor bird did not understand the meaning. To my mind, because he talked, he had to think and reason, and I was very afraid of this evil genius who tapped his beak on the bars of the cage, repeating, *Muera, muera!*   *M.E.B./C.L.R.*

XIII

The Queen of Etruria. —Madrid. —Godoy's palace. —The white
rabbit. —The toys of the Spanish Infantes. —Prince Fanfarinet.
—I pass muster as Murat's aide-de-camp. —His illness. —The fawn.
—Weber. —Early solitude. —The Mamelukes. —*Orblutes*.
—The echo. —The birth of my brother. —They realize he is blind.
—We leave Madrid.

I was distracted by a new incident. A large carriage, followed by two or
three others, had just entered the courtyard, and they changed horses with
extraordinary speed. The people of the village tried to enter the courtyard,
shouting, *La reina, la reina*! But the host and some others pushed them back,
saying, "No, no, it's not the queen." The horses were changed so quickly that
my mother, who was at the window, did not have time to come down and
ascertain what was going on. Besides, we were not permitted to go near the
carriages, and the innkeepers appeared to be privy to the secret, because they
were assuring the people outside that it was not the queen; yet a woman of the
house carried me right up close to the main carriage and said to me, "Look at
the queen!"

It was a very moving experience for me, because there had always been
kings and queens in my "novels." I visualized them as beings of extraordinary
beauty, sparkle, and richness. Yet the poor queen whom I saw there was
dressed in an outgrown-looking white dress, in the style of the time, very dis-
colored by dust. Her daughter, who seemed about eight or ten years old, was
dressed like her, and they both seemed very brown and quite ugly; at least that
is the impression that has stayed with me. They seemed sad and uneasy. As I
remember, they had neither retinue nor escort. They were fleeing rather than
leaving, and I later heard my mother say in a casual tone, "It's another queen
running for her life." These poor queens were indeed running for their lives,
leaving Spain in foreign hands. They were going to Bayonne to seek protection
from Napoléon, which would not deprive them so much of material security as
it would be the seal of their political deposition. As we know, this Queen of
Etruria[45] was the daughter of Charles IV, hence the Spanish Infanta. She had
married her cousin, the son of the old Duke of Parma. Napoléon, wanting to
secure possession of the duchy, had in return given the young couple Tuscany,
with the title of a kingdom. They had come to Paris in 1801, to render homage
to the First Consul, and they were received with great festivities. As we also
know, the young queen, having abdicated in the name of her son, had returned

to Madrid at the beginning of 1804, in order to take possession of the new kingdom of Lusitania,[46] of which she had been assured by the victory in the north of Portugal. But everything was then again put into question, thanks to the ineffectual politics of Charles IV and to the scant honesty with which the Prince of Peace[47] conducted these politics. We were going to engage in this formidable war against the Spanish nation, which was happening to us as if by a decree of fate and was supposed spontaneously to have imposed on Napoléon the need of securing the fate of all these royal personages at the very moment when they themselves came to implore his support. The Queen of Etruria and her children were following old Charles IV, Queen Maria Louisa, and the Prince of Peace, to Compiègne.

When I saw this queen, she was already under French protection. Strange protection was it that tore her from the bosom of the Spanish people, who were dismayed to see all the members of the royal family thus depart in the midst of a decisive and terrible struggle with foreigners. In Aranjuez, on March 17th, the people, in spite of their hatred for Godoy, had wanted to retain Charles IV. In Madrid, on May 2nd, they had wanted to retain the Infante Don Francis of Paule and the Queen of Etruria. In Vitoria, on April 16th, they had wanted to retain Ferdinand. On all these occasions, they had tried to unharness the horses and keep, in spite of themselves, those cowardly and insensate princes, who did not understand them and fled them out of fear of one another. But compelled by destiny, some had resisted the threats, others the entreaties of the people. And to where were they running? To "asylum" in Compiègne and Valençay.

One would think that at the time I saw the reported scene I understood nothing about the fright of this fugitive queen travelling incognito, but I have always remembered her somber expression, which seemed to betray her fear both of staying or of leaving. It was much the same situation in which her father and mother had found themselves at Aranjuez, in the presence of a people who wanted neither to keep them nor let them go. The Spanish were weary of their imbecilic sovereigns but preferred them, such as they were, to the "man of genius," who was no Spaniard. They seemed to have taken as their national motto the pungent phrase Napoléon had used in a narrower sense: "Dirty linen should be washed at home."

We arrived in Madrid during the month of May; we had suffered such hardship on the way that I remember nothing of the last days of our trip. However, we arrived at our goal without a catastrophe, which was almost miraculous; for Spain was already in revolt at several points, and everywhere the storm was rumbling, ready to erupt. True, we followed the line protected by the French army, but nowhere were the French themselves secure against the new Sicilian Vespers, and my mother, who was carrying one child in her womb and another in her arms, had more than enough reasons to be afraid.

She forgot her terror and suffering on seeing my father, and as for me, the fatigue that overwhelmed me dissipated instantly on seeing the magnificent rooms into which we moved. They were in the palace of the Prince of Peace, and there I truly entered fully into the realization of my fairy tales. Murat occupied the lower story of this same palace, the richest and most comfortable in Madrid, because he had been assigned to protect the queen and her lover; it was more resplendent than the palace of King Charles. Our apartment was located, I believe, on the fourth floor. It was immense, all hung in crimson silk damask. The cornices, beds, arm chairs, sofas—all were gilded and seemed to me solid gold, as in the fairy tales. There were enormous paintings that made me uneasy. Those massive heads that seemed to come out of their frames and follow me with their eyes tormented me to some degree. But I soon became used to them. Another marvel for me was a cheval glass in which I saw myself walking on the rug and at first did not recognize as me, for I had never seen myself thus from head to toe and had no idea of my size, which was actually quite small in relation to my age. However, I found myself so large that it frightened me.

Perhaps this handsome palace and these rich apartments were in very bad taste, in spite of the admiration they aroused in me. In any case, they were terribly neglected and filled with domestic animals, rabbits among others, which ran in and out, without anyone paying attention. Were these peacable hosts—the only ones not dispossessed—accustomed to being received in the apartments, or, profiting from the general confusion, did they pass from the kitchen into the salon? There was one, white as snow, with ruby eyes, which immediately began to act very familiarly with me. It had installed itself in the corner of the bedroom, behind the cheval glass, and our intimacy was soon established there unhampered. However, the animal was rather surly, and several times it scratched the faces of people who wanted to dislodge it; but it was never irritable with me, and it slept on my lap, or on the edge of my dress for hours at a time, while I told it my most beautiful stories.

I soon had at my disposal the handsomest toys in the world—dolls, sheep, households, beds, horses—all trimmed with pure gold, with fringes, in dust covers and straw casings; they were the playthings abandoned by the Spanish Infantes and already partially broken by them. I finished off the task quite briskly, for these toys impressed me as grotesque and disagreeable. Nevertheless, they must have had some real value, because my father saved two or three small figures in painted wood, which he brought to my grandmother as objets d'art. She kept them for some time, and everyone admired them. But after my father's death, they somehow came back into my hands, and I remember a little old man in rags, who must have had a remarkably realistic expression, for he frightened me. Did this skillful reproduction of a poor old beggar, completely emaciated and holding out his hand, slip in among the brilliant baubles of the Spanish Infantes by accident? The personification of misery in the hands of a king's son is surely a strange toy, and would have given him something to think about.

Besides, toys did not concern me in Madrid as they had in Paris. I had changed my setting. Exterior objects absorbed me instead, and with them I even forgot the fairy tales, so much did my actual existence take on an aura of fantasy.

I had already seen Murat in Paris; I had played with his children, but I had no memory of him. I had probably seen him dressed like everyone else. In

Madrid, all golden and plumed, as he appeared to me, he made a great impression. They called him Prince, and since princes always play the leading role in fairy dramas and stories, I believed myself in the presence of the famous Prince Fanfarinet.[48] I called him this quite naturally, without suspecting that I was addressing him epithetically. My mother had a great deal of trouble keeping me from letting him hear this infamous name, which always sprung to my lips when I noticed him in the galleries of the palace. They got me into the habit of calling him My Prince, and he took a great liking to me.

Perhaps Murat had expressed some displeasure on seeing the wife and child of one of his aides-de-camp in the midst of the dreadful events where he happened to be, and perhaps it was considered prudent that we appear to the general as a military necessity. Certainly, every time I was in his presence, I was made to put on a uniform. This uniform was a marvel. For a long time after I was too big to wear it, it remained in our house. Thus I am able to remember it minutely. It consisted of a white cassimere dolman, braided and buttoned in pure gold, a matching pelisse trimmed with black fur and tossed over the shoulder, and trousers of purplish cassimere, with ornaments and gold lace, in the Hungarian style. I also had red moroccan leather boots with golden spurs, a saber, a crimson silk braided belt with loops and aglets in enameled gold, a sabretache with an eagle embroidered in seed pearls. No detail was spared. Seeing me totally equipped like my father, and susceptible to this minor blandishment on the part of my mother, whether he took me for a boy or whether he was just pretending to be fooled, Murat would cheerfully introduce me as his aide-de-camp to the people who came to visit him, and we became part of his inner circle.

It did not hold that much charm for me, because the uniform was very uncomfortable. True, I had learned to wear it well—to let my little saber drag on the palace paving stones and my pelisse hang over my shoulder in the most seemly way—but I felt hot under the fur, I felt smothered under the gold braiding, and I was very happy when we arrived home and my mother again put on my Spanish costume of the time—the black silk dress, edged in wide-mesh silk net starting at the knees and falling in fringes to the ankle, and my flat mantilla in black crepe bordered with a wide band of velvet. My mother was surprisingly beautiful in this costume. Never did a real Spanish woman have such fine tan skin, such velvety black eyes, such small feet, and such an arching waist.

Murat fell ill; they attributed it to his debauchery, but that was not true. His intestines were inflamed, as was the case with a great part of our army in Spain, and he suffered from violent pains, though he was not confined to his bed. He thought he had been poisoned and did not submit to his illness with a great deal of patience, for his cries reverberated through that dismal palace where no one slept soundly in any case. I remember having been awakened by the fright of my father and mother the first time he roared in the middle of the night. They thought he was being assassinated. My father leaped out of bed, took his saber, and ran almost nude to the prince's apartment. I heard the screams of this poor hero, so ferocious in war, so fearful off the battlefield; I too was very afraid and screamed out in turn. It would seem that I finally understood what death was, because I cried out, sobbing, "They're killing my Prince Fanfarinet!" He learned of my distress and loved me more for it. Several days later, he came up to our apartment toward midnight and approached my crib. My father and mother were with him. They were returning from a hunting party and had brought a little fawn which Murat himself placed next to me. I was half awake and saw the head of this pretty little animal which leaned languishingly against my face. I threw my arms around its neck and fell back to sleep again, without thanking the prince. But the following morning, on awakening, I again saw Murat at my bedside. My father had told him what a picture the sleeping child and fawn made, and he had wished to see it. In effect, the poor little creature, who was probably only a few days old and had been chased the night before by the dogs, was so vanquished by fatigue, that it had settled down to sleep in my bed as a small dog might have done. It lay in a curve against my stomach, its head on the pillow, its little legs bent under as if it were afraid of hurting me, and my two arms had remained encircling its neck as I had put them when falling back to sleep. My mother later told me that Murat had expressed regret at not being able to show such a naïve grouping to an artist. His voice awakened me, but at four years old one is not a courtier, and my first caresses were for the fawn, who seemed to want to return them, to such an extent had the warmth of my small bed reassured and tamed it.

I kept it for several days and loved it passionately. But I believe that it died from being deprived of its mother, because one morning I did not see it, and they told me it had run away. They consoled me with assurances that it would find its mother again and be happy in the woods.

Our stay in Madrid lasted at the most two months, and yet it seemed extremely long to me. I had no other child my age to distract me and I was often alone during a large part of the day. My mother was forced to go out with my father and leave me with a servant, Teresa, from Madrid, who had been recommended to her as very reliable but who nevertheless absconded as soon as my parents went out. My father had a servant named Weber, who was really the best fellow in the world and would often come instead of the maidservant to watch me, but this decent German, who hardly knew any French, spoke to me in an unintelligible language, and he stank so, that without realizing the cause of my malaise, I fainted when he carried me in my arms. He did not dare reveal what little care my maid took of me; as for myself, I never thought of complaining; I believed Weber was in charge of keeping an eye on me, and I only had one desire—that he remain in the antechamber and leave me alone in the apartment. So my first greeting to him was, "Weber, I like you, go away!" And Weber, docile as a German, indeed went away. When he saw that I kept very quiet in my solitude, he would often lock me in and go to see his horses, which probably received him better than I. Thus I knew for the first time the pleasure—strange for a child, and acutely felt by me—of finding myself alone, and far from being put out or afraid, I felt something akin to regret on seeing my mother's carriage return. I must have been strongly impressed by my own contemplations, for I recall them with great clarity, while I have forgotten a thousand external events probably much more interesting. In those I have reported, my mother's memories sustained my own; but for what I am going to say now, there is no one who can come to my aid.

As soon as I found myself alone in this large apartment, where I could run about freely, I would stand before the cheval glass and try out theatrical poses. Then I picked up my white rabbit, intending to make him do the same; or I would make a show of offering him to the gods on a footstool that served as an altar. I do not know where I had seen anything comparable, whether in the theater or in an illustraton. I draped myself in my mantilla, to play the priestess, and I would follow all my movements in the mirror. Truthfully, I did not feel the least bit coquettish; my pleasure in seeing my person and the rabbit came when I managed to convince myself, through the intensity of the game, that I was playing a scene for four—two little girls and two rabbits. Thus the rabbit and I, in pantomime, addressed greetings, threats, and prayers to the pair in the cheval glass. We would dance the bolero with them, for after the dances I had seen at the theater, Spanish dancing had intrigued me, and I mimicked the poses and embellishments with the ease children have for imitating what they see. I thus completely forgot the dancing figure in the mirror was mine and was surprised that it stopped when I did.

When I had sufficiently danced and mimed these ballets of my composition, I went out on the balcony to dream. This balcony, which extended the full length of the palace façade, was very large and handsome. The balustrade was white marble, if I am not mistaken, and became so hot in the sun that I could not touch it. I was too short to see above it, but between the balusters I could distinguish all that was happening in the square. In my memory, the square was magnificent. There were other palaces or beautiful large houses all around it, but I never saw a crowd of people there or anywhere else for that matter all the time I spent in Madrid. Probably, after the insurrection of May 2nd, they did not allow the inhabitants to circulate around the palace of the commander in chief. Hence I never saw anything there but French uniforms and—something even more beautiful to my imagination—the Mamelukes of the guard, who were posted at the building facing us. These copper-colored men, in turbans and rich oriental dress, would form into groups that I never tired of looking at. They would bring their horses to drink at a large basin in the middle of the square, and without my realizing the scene was poetic, I keenly responded to what my eyes took in.

On my right, one whole side of the square was occupied by a church of massive architecture—at least that is how it reappears in my memory—surmounted by a cross set on a golden sphere. That cross and that sphere sparkling in the sunset, standing out against a sky more blue than I had ever seen, are a sight I shall never forget. I would contemplate it until my eyes were filled with those red and blue dots, for which we have, in our Berrichon dialect, an excellent word, *orblutes*,[49] derived from Latin [*orbis*: circle; *lux*: light]. This is a word which should pass into our modern vocabulary. It must at some point have become French, although I have never seen it in writing. It has no equivalent, but it expresses perfectly a phenomenon that everyone is familiar with but usually describes only in imprecise circumlocutions.

These *orblutes* amused me no end, and I was not able to account for their wholly natural existence. I took pleasure in seeing float before my eyes those flaming colors that all objects took on and that persisted when I closed my eyes. When the *orblute* is quite complete, it duplicates exactly the form of the object which caused it; it is a kind of after-image. Thus I saw the fiery cross and sphere delineated everywhere I looked, and I am astonished that I was able to so often repeat with impunity this game which could be quite dangerous to a child's eyes. On the balcony I soon discovered another phenomenon which I had been ignorant of until then. The square was often deserted, and even in broad daylight, a gloomy silence reigned in the palace and its surroundings. One day this silence frightened me, and I called to Weber, whom I saw pass in the square. Weber did not hear me, but a voice completely like mine repeated the name Weber at the end of the balcony.

This voice reassured me; I no longer felt alone. But curious to know who was having fun by mimicking me, I went back into the apartment thinking I would find someone there. I was completely alone, as usual. I returned to the balcony and called my mother; the voice repeated the word very softly, but clearly, and that gave me food for thought. I made my voice loud; I called my own name, which immediately came back to me, but less clearly. I repeated it in a fainter tone, and the voice returned faintly but more distinctly, as if someone was speaking in my ear. I did not understand it at all; I was convinced someone was with me on the balcony, but seeing no one, and looking in vain at all the closed windows, I contemplated this miracle with extreme pleasure. It was very strange for me to hear my own name repeated in my own voice. Then a bizarre explanation came to my mind—I was double and there was another "me" nearby, which I could not see but which always saw me since it always answered me. That was immediately settled in my mind as something that had to be and had always been, but that I had not yet noticed; I compared this phenomenon to the *orblutes*, which had at first surprised me as much and which I had become accustomed to without understanding. I concluded that all things and all people had their reflection, their double, their other "me," and I wished keenly to see mine. I called it a hundred times; I forever told it to come to me. It answered, "Come here, come on," and it seemed to me to go farther away or approach when I changed my location. I looked for it and called to it in the apartment, it no longer answered me; I went to the other end of the balcony, it was mute; I came back to the middle, and from this middle to the end on the church side, it spoke to me and replied to my "Come on," with a soft and restless, "Come on." My other me remained at a certain spot in the air or in the wall, but how to reach it and how to see it? My mind was being affected without my realizing.

I was interrupted by the arrival of my mother, and I cannot say why, but rather than question her, I hid what excited me so much. It must be true that children love the mystery of their dreams; certainly I had never wanted an explanation of the *orblutes*. I wanted to mull the problem over all alone. Perhaps I had already been disabused of some other illusion by explanations that I felt had deprived me of its secret charm. I kept silent about this new marvel, and for several days, except for our ballets, I let my poor rabbit sleep in peace and freed the cheval glass to reflect the fixed images of the great persons represented in the paintings. I had the patience to wait until I was alone to begin my experiment again, but finally my mother, having come back without my noticing and hearing me shout myself hoarse, discovered the secret of my passion for the balcony's full sunlight. There was no turning back; I asked her where the someone was who repeated all my words, and she said to me, "It's the echo."

Happily for me, she did not try to explain what an echo was. She perhaps had never tried to explain it to herself; she told me it was "a voice in the air"; so the unknown retained its poetry for me. For another few days I could continue to toss my words to the wind. The voice in the air no longer surprised me, but still it delighted me; I was satisfied at being able to give it a name and to call out to it, "Echo, are you there? Do you hear me? Hello, echo!"

The imaginative life of children being so developed, does that imply that the development of the sentiments[49] lags behind? I do not remember having thought of my sister, of my dear aunt, of Pierret, or of my cherished Clotilde during my stay in Madrid. However, I was already capable of loving, since I already had such warm affection for certain dolls and animals. I believe the indifference with which children part from people whom they are fond of has to do with their inability to calculate the duration of time. When one speaks to them of a year's absence, they do not know if a year is much longer than a day, and it is useless to try to work out the difference for them through numbers. I believe numbers have no meaning at all in their minds. While my mother talked to me about my sister, I had the impression that I had left her the day before, and yet it seemed a long time to me. In the absence of a balance among a child's faculties, a thousand contradictions appear that are difficult for us to resolve once the balance has been established.

I believe my sentimental life did not develop until my mother gave birth in Madrid. I had certainly been told of the coming arrival of a little brother or sister, and for several days I saw my mother stretched out on a chaise longue. One day, I was sent to play on the balcony, and they closed the glass doors to the apartment; I did not hear the least moan. My mother very courageously endured the physical pain and had brought her children into the world expeditiously; this time, however, she suffered for several hours, but I was sent away for only a few minutes, after which my father called me and showed me a little child. I hardly paid any attention. My mother was stretched out on a sofa, her face so pale and her features so drawn that I was reluctant to recognize her. Then a great fear took hold of me, and crying, I ran to embrace her. I wanted her to speak to me, to respond to my caresses, and as they again took me away from her to let her rest, I was in despair for a long while, believing she was going to die and that they wanted to hide her from me. I returned to the balcony to cry, and they could not distract me with the newborn baby. This poor little boy had light blue eyes that were very unusual. Several days later, my mother tormented herself about the pallor of his pupils, and often I heard my father and other people anxiously utter the word "crystalline." Finally, at the end of two weeks, there was no longer any doubt, the child was blind. They did not want to affirm it to my mother. They left her room for doubt. In her presence, they timidly expressed the hope that this crystalline lens would reform by itself in the child's eyes.[50] She let them console her, and the poor invalid was loved and spoiled with as much joy as if his existence had not been a misfortune for him and his family. My mother was nursing him, and he was scarcely two weeks old when we had to start off on our way again to France, through a Spain on fire.   *R.G.-B.*

XIV

My father's last letter. —Recollections of a bombardment and a
battlefield. —Misery and illness. —Supper with candles.
—Embarkation and shipwreck. —Leopardo. —Our arrival at
Nohant. —My grandmother. —Hippolyte. —Deschartres. —The
death of my brother. —The old pear tree. —The death of my father.
—The ghost. —Ursule. —A duel to settle a question of honor.
—Early notions of wealth and poverty. —Portrait of my mother.

[Last] Letter   Madrid, June 12, 1808.

From My Father to His Mother

After long hours of suffering, Sophie gave birth this morning to a big boy
who whistles like a parrot. Mother and child are doing marvelously. Before the
end of the month the Prince leaves for France; the Emperor's doctor, who took
care of Sophie, says she will be able to travel in twelve days with her child.
Aurore is fine. I shall bundle the lot into a carriage which I have just acquired
for this purpose, and we shall take to the road for Nohant, where I certainly
expect to arrive around the 20th of July, in the cool of evening, and stay as
long as possible. This thought, my dear mother, fills me with joy. I keep myself
going with the anticipation of our reunion, of our charming home, without
obligations, without worries, without unpleasant distractions! I've been wanting this complete happiness for so long!

The Prince told me yesterday that he was going to spend some time at
Barèges[51] before going to his destination. For my part, I shall give my horses
leave to go all the way to the waters of Nohant, over which we will have
performed the miracle of the wedding at Cana.[52] I think Deschartres will willingly undertake that feat.

I am saving the baptism of my newborn son for the holidays at Nohant. A
good opportunity for bell-ringing and dancing in the village! The mayor will
be the one to enroll my son into the ranks of Frenchmen, for I don't want him
ever to have any dealings with Castillian notaries or priests.

I can hardly believe that my last two letters got intercepted. They were
such nonsense that they should have been spared by the most rigid of authorities. In one of them, I described to you an African saber which I had acquired.
There were two pages of explanations with citations. You will see this wonder,
as well as the indomitable Leopardo of Andalusia, whom I shall ask
Deschartres to ride a little after having first issued a requisition for all the mat-

tresses in the district to cushion whatever track he selects! Goodbye, my dear mother, I shall inform you of the day of my departure and that of my arrival. I hope it will be even sooner than I have told you. Sophie shares my wild impatience to come and kiss you. Aurore wants to leave this very instant, and were it possible, we would already be on the way.

This joyful letter, so full of happiness and hope, is the last that my grandmother ever received from her son. We shall soon see what a terrible catastrophe was to put an end to all those happy plans and how few days remained to my father to enjoy this costly and long-dreamed-of reunion with the objects of his affection. We shall understand by the nature of this catastrophe what fateful and terrible foreboding there was in his letter's pleasantries on the subject of the indomitable Leopardo of Andalusia.

Ferdinand VII, Prince of Asturias—who was showering attention on Murat and his officers at the time—had given this terrible horse to my father as a consequence of a mission which my father had fulfilled, I think, while in contact with the prince at Aranjuez. It was a sinister present and one which my mother, given her fatalism or intuition, mistrusted and feared. But she was not able to persuade my father to get rid of it in time, even though he admitted it was the only horse he could not mount without a certain degree of apprehension. For him this was all the more reason to want to master the horse, and he took pleasure in vanquishing him. Nevertheless, he did reach the point of saying one day, "I'm not afraid of him, but I don't ride him well because I don't trust him, and he knows it."

My mother maintained that Ferdinand had given Leopardo to him hoping it would kill him. She also maintained that, out of hatred of the French, the surgeon, in Madrid, who had delivered her, had blinded her child. She imagined that in the half-conscious state which followed the climax of her pain, she had seen this surgeon press his thumbs on the eyes of the newborn baby and that he had muttered between his teeth, "This one won't see the sun of Spain."[53]

It is possible this was a hallucination on the part of my poor mother, and yet the way things were at the time, it is equally possible the incident took place just as she thought she had seen it, in the brief moment when the surgeon would have been alone in the room with her, counting on her not being in any condition to see or hear him; but you can be sure I don't want the burden of so terrible an accusation.

We have seen in my father's letter that he had not at first noticed the child's blindness, and I remember hearing Deschartres state that fact when he and my mother were not present. He was still loath then to discourage their faint hope of a cure.

It was in the first half of July that we left. Murat was going to take possession of the throne of Naples. My father was on leave. I do not know if he accompanied Murat to the border and if we travelled with him. I remember we were in the carriage, and I think we were following Murat's retinue, but I have no recollection of my father until we reached Bayonne.

What I remember best was the suffering, thirst, voracious heat, and the fever I experienced during the whole trip. We advanced very slowly through the military columns. It comes back to me now that my father must have been with us, because once, when we were following a rather narrow mountain road, we saw an enormous snake which stretched almost all the way across the road in a black line. My father called for a halt, ran forward, and cut it in two with his saber. My mother had tried in vain to restrain him; as usual she was fearful.

However, another incident makes me think he was only with us for short periods and that he rejoined Murat from time to time. This incident was striking enough to be engraved on my memory, but since the fever kept me in an almost continuous state of drowsiness, the recollection is unconnected with anything that could clarify for me the event to which I was witness. Being at the window one evening with my mother, we saw the sky still illuminated by the setting sun, crosshatched with trails of fire, and my mother said to me, "There, look, it's a battle, and maybe your father is in it."

I had no idea of what a real battle was. What I saw looked to me like an immense display of fireworks, full of gaiety and triumph, a tournament or festival. The sound of the cannon and the great arcs of fire delighted me. I watched it as I would have watched a show, eating a green apple. I do not know to whom my mother then said, "How lucky children are they don't understand anything!" Since I do not know what route these military operations forced us to follow, I cannot say whether this was the Battle of Medina del Rio Seco or a less important engagement in Bessières' brilliant campaign. My father, attached directly to Murat, had no reason to be on the battlefield, and it is not likely that he was. But my mother probably imagined he could have been sent there on a mission.

Whether for the Rio Seco affair or the capture of Torquemada, it is certain that our carriage was requisitioned to carry the wounded, or people more precious than we, and we continued for a fair distance in a farm wagon, with baggage, vivandières, and ailing soldiers. It is also certain that we were traveling alongside the battlefield the next day or the day after, when I saw a vast plain covered with formless debris not unlike the miniature carnage of dolls, horses, and chariots I used to create with Clotilde at Chaillot and in the house on Rue Grange-Batelière. My mother hid her face, and the air was putrid. We were not close enough to these sinister objects for me to realize what they were, and I asked why so many rags had been strewn about. Finally, the wheel hit something which broke with a strange cracking sound. My mother held me down on the floor of the wagon to keep me from looking; it must have been a corpse. I saw several others later on, scattered about on the road, but I was so sick that I do not remember having been very deeply impressed by these horrible spectacles.

Along with the fever, I experienced another kind of suffering which did not do much to alleviate the confusion, but whose anguish was experienced by all the sick soldiers with whom we travelled—hunger, an excessive, sickening, almost bestial hunger. These poor people, who were full of attention and solicitude for us, had passed on to me a disease that explains this phenomenon and that no proper little miss would admit to having suffered even in her childhood.

But life has its vicissitudes, and when my mother sorrowed to see my baby brother and me in that condition, the soldiers and canteen girls said to her, laughing, "Pshaw, my little lady, it's nothing! It's a life-long guarantee of health for your children; it's the true baptism of army kids."

Scabies, since its name must be mentioned, had begun with me, and I gave it to my brother, then to my mother later on, and to others—sad fruit of war and misery, fortunately attenuated in our case by extensive care and purity of blood.

Within several days our lot had greatly changed. We were no longer in a palace in Madrid, with gilded beds, oriental rugs, and silk bed-curtains; we were in filthy wagons, burned-out villages, bombarded cities, roads strewn with the dead, and ditches where we would seek to quench our burning thirst with a drop of water, only to come upon floating clots of blood. The worst was this terrible hunger and more and more menacing lack of food. My mother withstood all this with great courage, but she could not overcome the disgust she felt for raw onions, green lemons, and sunflower seeds, with which I satisfied myself without repugnance. But what nourishment was this for a nursing mother!

We crossed through a French encampment; I do not know where it was; in front of one tent we saw a group of soldiers eating with hearty appetites; my mother pushed me into the middle of the group, asking them to let me eat from their mess pot. Right away these nice people set out to please her, and with compassionate smiles, let me eat my fill. The soup tasted wonderful to me, and when it was half eaten, one of the soldiers said to my mother with some hesitation, "We would urge you to eat some, too, but perhaps you couldn't, because the taste is a bit strong." My mother approached and looked into the pot. There was bread and very greasy broth, but a few blackened wicks were floating in it; it was a soup made of candle ends.

I remember Burgos and another city (or possibly the same one), where the adventures of El Cid were painted in frescoes on the walls. I also remember a superb cathedral, where the working-class men were kneeling on one knee to pray, each with his hat on the other knee and a little round straw mat under the knee that touched the ground. Finally, I remember Vitoria and a servant whose long black hair, crawling with lice, floated down her back. I felt better for one or two days at the Spanish border; the weather had turned cooler, the fever and misery had ceased. My father was most certainly with us. We had recovered our carriage to travel the rest of the way; the inns were clean; there were beds and all sorts of food we had apparently been deprived of for some time, for it seemed entirely new to me, pastry and cheese, among others. My mother washed me up at Fontarabia, and I felt enormous relief at being able to take a bath. She took care of me as she knew how, and after the bath she coated me with sulphur from head to toe and made me swallow little pellets of sulphur ground up in butter and sugar. That taste and odor that I lived with for two months left me with a great repugnance for anything reminiscent of it.

We apparently came across people we knew at the border, because I remember a big banquet and lots of rhetoric which bored me enormously; I had recovered all my senses and regard for things around me. I do not know why my mother got the notion of wanting to return by sea to Bordeaux. Perhaps she was worn out by the fatigue of carriage travel, or perhaps her medical instinct, which she always followed, told her the sea air would cleanse her and her children of the poison of poverty-stricken Spain. Apparently the ocean was calm and the weather fine; otherwise it would have been yet another risk to venture out in a launch along the coast of Gascogne in the Bay of Biscay, which is always so choppy. Whatever the reason, a decked launch was hired, the carriage was loaded onto it, and we set out as if we were on a pleasure trip. I do not know from where we set sail or who it was who came to the dock, lavishing much kind help and attention on us. Somebody gave me a huge bouquet of roses, which I held during the whole trip to keep from smelling the sulphur.

I do not know how long we followed the coast; I had fallen back into my lethargy, and all I remember from this crossing are the departure and the arrival. Just as we were approaching our destination, a gust of wind drove us from the shore, and I saw that the captain and his two mates were extremely anxious. My mother was frightened again, and my father got busy helping the crew, but as we had at last entered the mouth of the Gironde, we struck some sort of reef, and water began to enter the hold. We headed immediately for shore, but the hold was filling rapidly and the launch was clearly sinking. My mother had gotten into the carriage, taking her children with her; my father was reassuring her, telling her we would get to shore before being flooded. However, the deck began to get wet, and he took off his coat and got a shawl ready to tie his two children to his back. "Don't worry," he said to my mother, "I'll take you under one arm, I'll swim with the other, and I'll save all three of you, you can be sure of that!"

We at last reached land, or rather a great wall of fitted stones with a large shed on top of it. There were a few dwellings behind this shed, and immediately several men came to our aid. Not a moment too soon—the carriage was sinking with the launch, and a ladder was thrown to us just in time. I do not know how they saved the boat, but it definitely was saved. It took several hours, during which my mother would not leave the shore, for my father, after having assured our safety, had gone back to the launch to save our things, then our carriage, and finally the launch. I was struck by his courage, his speed, and his strength. Experienced as were the sailors and the local people, they nonetheless admired the skill and resolution of this young officer, who, after having saved his family, would not abandon his captain until the boat was saved, and who directed the whole salvage operation more deftly than they could have done. It is true that he had learned his trade at the camp at Boulogne, but in everything he acted with calm and a rare presence of mind. He used his saber like an axe or a razor, to slice and cut, and for that saber (probably it was the African one he speaks of in his last letter) I know he had an extraordinary affection because, after landing, in the first moment of uncertainty about whether the launch and the carriage would sink immediately or whether we would have time to save anything, my mother wanted to stop him from going back down to the shore, saying, "Oh, let everything we have sink to the bottom, rather than risk drowning"; and he had answered, "I'd rather risk it than abandon my saber." It was in fact the first object he saved. My mother considered herself satisfied with having her daughter safe beside her and her son in her arms. As for me, I had saved my wilted bouquet of roses with as much love as my father had shown in saving us all. I had been very careful not to let go of it while getting out of the half-submerged carriage and climbing the rescue ladder. It was my first concern, just as my father's was his saber.

I do not recall having felt the least fear in all of these encounters. There are two kinds of fear: one relates to temperament and the other to imagination. I have never known the first kind, my constitution having endowed me with a sang-froid just like my father's. (The word "sang-froid" expresses very precisely that composure we get from our physical disposition, for which we can therefore in no way take credit.) As for the fear which results from an overly excitable imagination and is fed only by fantasy, I was tormented by that kind all through my childhood. But when age and reason had chased away the ghosts, I recovered my equilibrium and never suffered any kind of fear.

We arrived at Nohant in the last days of August. I was feverish again and had lost my appetite. The scabies had progressed further; a little Spanish maid, Cecilia, whom we had acquired on the journey, began to have symptoms of it, too, and could hardly bear to touch me. My mother was nearly cured by then, but my poor little brother, whose sores did not show anymore, was sicker and weaker than I. We were two burning, inert masses, and I had no more awareness than he did of anything that had happened to me since the shipwreck in the Gironde.

I came to my senses as we rode into the front yard at Nohant. It was not as beautiful, of course, as the palace in Madrid, but it had the same effect on me, so imposing is a big house to children brought up in small rooms.

It was not the first time I had seen my grandmother, but I have no memory of her before that day. She seemed very tall to me, although her height was only five feet. Her pink and white complexion, her imposing air, her invariable costume consisting of a long-waisted brown silk dress with straight sleeves, which she had refused to modify along the dictates of Empire fashion, her blond wig teased into a tuft on the forehead, her little round bonnet with a cockade of lace in the center—all made her seem to me a being completely apart and different from anything I had seen.

It was the first time my mother and I had been received at Nohant. After my grandmother kissed my father, she went to kiss my mother, too, but the latter stopped her, saying, "Oh, my dear mama, don't touch me or these poor children. You can't imagine what misery we have been through; we are all very ill."

My father, always an optimist, began to laugh, and putting me into my grandmother's arms, said, "Imagine that! These children have a little rash, and Sophie, who has a very vivid imagination, thinks they have scabies."

"Scabies or not," said my grandmother, hugging me to her heart, "I shall take care of this one; I can see that these children are ill; they have very high fevers, both of them. Daughter, go lie down and rest with your son; you have been through a struggle that transcends human strength; I shall look after the little girl. Two children on your hands is too much for you, in your condition."

She took me into her room without any distaste for the horrible state I was in; this excellent woman, though so delicate and so fastidious, laid me on her bed. That bed and that room, still fresh and new at the time, seemed like a paradise to me. The walls were covered with Persian cloth in a bold floral pattern; all the furniture was from the time of Louis XV. The bed, in the form of a chariot with great bouquets of plumes at the four corners, had double curtains, a quantity of scalloped hangings, pillows, and upholstery, whose luxury and elegance astonished me. I did not dare make myself comfortable in such a beautiful place, because I was aware of what a distasteful object I must have been and had already felt the humiliation of it. But the care and caresses I received quickly made me forget all that. The first face I saw after my grandmother's was that of a plump boy of nine, who came in with a big bouquet of flowers and tossed it in my face in a playful and friendly fashion. My grandmother said to me, "This is Hippolyte; give each other a kiss, children." We kissed each other unquestioningly, and I spent many years with him, without knowing he was my brother; this was the child of the Little House.

My father took him by the arm and led him to my mother, who kissed him, thought him splendid, and said to my father, "Well, now he is mine too, just as Caroline is yours." And we were brought up together, sometimes under her care, and sometimes under that of my grandmother.

Deschartres came into my life that day for the first time, too. He wore knee breeches, white stockings, yellow gaiters, a very long and very wide nut-brown coat, and a bellows cap. He came in gravely to look me over, and as he was an excellent doctor, we were obliged to believe him when he declared that I indeed had scabies. But the illness had lost its intensity, and my fever was now only the result of fatigue. He urged my parents to deny that we were carrying scabies, in order not to upset and frighten the whole household. He announced in front of the servants that it was a very innocent little rash; only two other children caught it, and with the proper care given in time, they were quickly cured without knowing what they had been cured of.

As for me, after two hours of rest in my grandmother's bed, in that cool and airy bedroom where I could no longer hear the annoying buzz of Spanish mosquitoes, I felt so much better that I went running in the garden with Hippolyte. I remember that he held me by the hand with extreme solicitude, as though I would fall with every step; I felt just a bit humiliated that he thought me such a little girl, and I soon showed him I was a very resolute boy. That put him at ease, and he introduced me to several very amusing games, among them making what he called dung pies. We would take fine sand or earth, which we would soak in water and then prepare, after having kneaded it well on big slabs of slate, by shaping it into cakes. Then he would sneak them all into the oven, and as he was already very much of a tease, he would enjoy the servants' anger when they came to take their bread and pancakes out of the oven. They would curse and throw out our strange mixtures baked to perfection.

I have never been malicious, because by nature I am not clever. Capricious and domineering, yes, for I was very spoiled by my father, but I had absolutely no talent for premeditation or dissimulation. Hippolyte soon perceived my weak spot, and to punish me for my whims and temper tantrums, he began to tease me cruelly. He stole my dolls and buried them in the garden; then he would mark the graves with a little cross and make me dig them up. He would hang them from branches by their feet and make them endure a thousand agonies, which I was so naïve as to take seriously and which caused me to shed real tears. I have to admit I very often detested him, but I have never been able to bear a grudge, and when he would come looking for me to play, I never could resist him.

The big garden and fresh air of Nohant soon brought me back to health. My mother still stuffed me with sulphur, and I submitted to this treatment, because her influence over me was complete. However, that sulphur was odious, and I would tell her to close my eyes and hold my nose to make me swallow it. To get rid of the aftertaste, I would look for the sourest things to eat. My mother, who had in her head a whole system of medicine based on either instinct or preconception, believed that children could divine what was good for them. Seeing that I was always nibbling at unripe fruit, she offered me lemons, and I craved them so much that I would eat them with their skin and seeds, the way one eats strawberries. My great hunger had passed, and for five or six days my sole nourishment was lemons. My grandmother was horrified by this strange diet, but this time Deschartres, watching me carefully and seeing that I was improving, agreed that nature had indeed taught me to divine the thing that would cure me.

It is certain that I was soon cured and never had any other disease. I do not know if scabies is really, as our soldiers said, a guarantee of health, but all my life I have been able to nurse people with supposedly contagious diseases, as well as poor sufferers of skin ailments whom nobody dared come near, without contracting the merest pimple. It seems to me I could safely nurse victims of the plague, and I think every misfortune has a bright side, morally at least, for I have never seen any physical miseries for which I could not conquer my distaste. This distaste can, nonetheless, be violent, and I have often been very close to fainting when seeing repulsive wounds and operations; but I have always called to mind my scabies and my grandmother's first kiss, and I am convinced that will-power and faith can control the senses, however overwhelmed they may be.

But while I was visibly gaining strength, my poor little brother Louis was rapidly declining. The scabies had disappeared, but fever consumed him. He was livid, and his poor lifeless eyes had an expression of unutterable sadness. It was in seeing him suffer that I began to love him. Until then I had not paid much attention to him, but when he lay outstretched on my mother's lap, so languid and weak that she hardly dared touch him, I grew sad along with her, and I vaguely understood what it means to worry, something which children have the least capacity to feel.

My mother blamed herself for her baby's decline. She feared that her milk was poisoning him, and she struggled to regain her health so that she could pass it along to him. She spent entire days outdoors, with her child lying near her in the shade among carefully arranged cushions and shawls. Deschartres advised her to exercise in order to increase her appetite and, with good nourishment, improve the quality of her milk. Immediately, she started a little garden in a corner of the large courtyard at Nohant, beneath the big pear tree which is still there today. The history of that tree is so bizarre it is practically a novel, although I did not know it until a long time afterward.

On September 8th, a Friday, the poor little blind baby, after having whimpered a long time on my mother's lap, became cold, and nothing could warm him. He lay still. Deschartres came and took him from my mother's arms; he was dead. Such a short, sad existence, of which he himself was unaware, thank God!

The next day we buried him, and my mother hid her tears from me. Hippolyte was responsible for keeping me outside all day. I hardly knew and only faintly understood what was going on in the house. It seems that my father carried on terribly and that this child, in spite of his infirmity, was as dear to him as the others. That night, after midnight, when they had retired to their room, my mother and father cried together, and a strange scene took place between them which my mother related to me in detail twenty years later. I was sleeping in the same room.

In his grief and with my grandmother's remarks impressed on his mind, my father said to my mother, "That trip to Spain was a fatal one for us, my poor Sophie. When you wrote me that you wanted to join me there, and I begged you not to do it, you thought it was a sign of infidelity or cooling of affection on my part, but I was having a premonition of misfortune. What could have been more reckless or more foolish than to run off that way, pregnant to the end of your belt, through so many dangers and deprivations, so much suffering and constant terror? It's a miracle that you came through it; it's a miracle that Aurore is even alive. Our poor boy might not have been blind had he been born in Paris. The doctor in Madrid explained to me that because of the position of the baby in the womb, with his two closed fists pressing on his eyes, the extended pressure that he must have experienced because of your own position in the carriage, often with your daughter on your lap, inevitably impeded the development of the organs of sight."

"You reproach me now, when it's too late," said my mother. "I am in despair. As for the doctor, he's a liar and a scoundrel. I'm certain I was not dreaming when I saw him crush my baby's eyes."

They talked for a long while about their misfortune, and my mother became more and more excitable from lack of sleep and weeping. She would not believe that her son died of debility and fatigue; she insisted that just yesterday he was on his way to getting well and that he had been seized by a sudden spasm. "And now," she said, sobbing, "he is in the ground, the poor child. What a horrible idea to bury what we love like that, to separate ourselves forever from the body of a child we were caressing and caring for an instant before! They take him away from you, they nail him in a coffin, they throw him in a hole, they cover him up with earth, as if they thought he could get out! Oh, it's horrible, and I should not have let them pluck my child from me; I should have held onto him and at least have had him embalmed."

"And when you think that they often bury people who are not dead," added my father. "It's true that the Christian way of burying corpses is the most savage thing in the world."

"Even savages are less savage than we," said my mother. "Didn't you tell me that they lay their dead out on trellises and hang them up all dried out on the branches of trees? I'd rather see my little dead child's cradle hung on one of the trees in the garden than imagine he's going to rot in the ground! And then," she added, struck by the thought that had come to my father, "what if he wasn't really dead? What if they mistook a spasm for death. What if M. Deschartres was wrong? After all, he took him away from me and wouldn't let me stroke and warm him anymore; he said I was hastening his death. He is so harsh, your Deschartres! He frightens me, and I don't dare cross him! But maybe he's ignorant and doesn't know how to tell a coma from death. Look, I'm so tormented that I'm going crazy, and I would give anything in the world to have my child back, dead or alive."

My father resisted this idea at first, but little by little it took hold of him, too, and looking at his watch, he said, "There is no time to lose; I have to get that child. Don't make any noise, don't wake anyone; I swear to you, you'll have him within the hour."

He got up, dressed, quietly opened the doors, fetched a shovel, and ran to the cemetery, which was alongside the house, walled off from the garden; he approached the mound of newly-turned earth and began to dig. It was dark, and my father had not brought a lantern. He could not see well enough to perceive the coffin he was uncovering, and it was only when he had completely laid it bare, surprised by the time it took, that he realized that it was too big to be the child's. It was that of a villager who had died a few days before. He had to dig next to it, and there he did find the little coffin. But while working to pull it out, he leaned his foot heavily on the coffin of the poor peasant, and that coffin, because of the deeper hole he had made beside it, slid down and stood up in front of him, striking him on the shoulder and knocking him into the grave. He said afterward to my mother that he had felt an instant of inexpressible terror and anguish, finding himself pushed by this corpse and thrown into the earth on top of the remains of his son. We know very well how brave a man he was, and he was in no way superstitious. Nonetheless, he reacted with dread, and a cold sweat broke out on his forehead. A week later, he would take his place next to the peasant, in the same earth he had dug up to wrench from it the body of his son.

He quickly recovered his calm and repaired the disorder so well that no one ever noticed. He brought the little coffin back to my mother and opened it hurriedly. The poor child was indeed dead, but my mother consoled herself by bathing him one last time. She had been prevented from doing this by the child's initial crisis. Now, exalted and as if revived by her tears, she rubbed the little body with perfumes, wrapped it up in her most beautiful linen, and placed it back in its cradle to give herself the sorry illusion that she was watching the child sleep once more.

She kept him hidden that way, locked in her room, all the next day, but the following night, all hope gone, my father carefully wrote the name of the child and the dates of birth and death on a piece of paper which he placed between two panes of glass and sealed with sealing wax around the edges.

Strange preparations they were, made with seeming calm, but motivated by frenzied grief. The inscription was placed in the coffin, my mother covered the child with rose leaves, and the coffin was again nailed shut, taken to the garden plot my mother was cultivating, and buried at the foot of the old pear tree.

The very next morning, my mother went back zealously to her gardening, and my father helped her. Everyone was astonished to see them take up this childlike amusement in spite of their grief. They alone knew the secret of their love for this little plot of earth. I remember having seen them cultivate it during the few days between this strange incident and the death of my father. They planted some superb China asters there, which blossomed for more than a month. At the foot of the pear tree, they built a small grassy knoll with a little spiraling path, so that I could climb up there and sit. How many times I did climb up and how often I worked or played there, without suspecting it was a grave! All around were pretty winding paths with grassy borders, flower beds, and benches; it was a child's garden, but complete in all respects, created there as if by magic, with my mother, my father, Hippolyte and I working at it unceasingly for five or six days, the last days of my father's life, perhaps the most peaceful ones he had known, and the most tender in their melancholy. I remember that he kept bringing wheelbarrows full of earth and grassy turf and that when he went to get these loads, he would put Hippolyte and me into the wheelbarrow, enjoying watching us, pretending he was going to dump us out to see us laugh or squeal, depending on our mood at the moment.

Fifteen years later, my husband changed the layout of our yard. My mother's little garden had disappeared a long time before. It had been abandoned while I was in the convent, and there were fig trees planted there. The pear tree had grown large, and he considered removing it because it was beginning to interfere with a pathway whose direction it was difficult to change. I convinced him to spare it. They dug the pathway, and a flower bed became the cover of the child's grave. When the pathway was finished, in fact quite a long time afterward, the gardener said mysteriously one day to my husband and me that we had done right to spare that tree. He seemed talkative and did not have to be coaxed to tell us the secret he had discovered. Several years before, while planting the fig trees, his spade had struck a little coffin. He had unearthed it, examined, and opened it. Inside, he had found the bones of a small child. At first he had thought that some infanticide had been secreted there, but he then found the handwritten card between the two panes of glass, and on it were the names of poor little Louis and the dates of his birth and death, so close together. He had not understood very well, superstitious and devout as he was, what whim would have made someone take this body, which he himself had seen carried to the cemetery, out of consecrated ground, but anyway he had respected the secret; he had confined himself to telling my grandmother, and he was telling us now, so that we could decide what should be done. We decided that there was nothing at all to be done. To have moved the bones to the cemetery would have noised about an incident that not everyone would have understood and that, at the time of the Restoration, would have been exploited by the priests to the detriment of my family. My mother was still living, and her secret had the right to be kept and respected. My mother told me the whole story later, and she was glad the bones had not been disturbed.

So the child remained under the pear tree, and the pear tree is still there. It is even very beautiful, and in the spring it spreads a parasol of pink blossoms over this unmarked grave. I do not see any harm in talking about it now. Those spring flowers give it less sinister shade than would the cypresses in the cemetery. Grass and flowers are the true mausoleums of children, and as for me, I detest monuments and inscriptions; I inherit that from my grandmother, who never wanted one for her cherished son, saying rightly that the greatest griefs cannot be expressed and that trees and flowers are the only ornaments that do not stir up painful thoughts.

I have yet some very sad things to tell, and although they did not affect me beyond the very limited faculties a child can have for experiencing grief, I have always sensed them so present in the memories and thoughts of my family, that I felt their aftereffects all my life.

When the little mortuary garden was nearly completed, two days before his death, my father persuaded my grandmother to have the walls around the big courtyard pulled down, and as soon as she had consented, he set about the task as head workman. I can still see him in a cloud of dust, a pickaxe in his hand, making the old walls crumble, which fell almost of their accord, with a noise that frightened me.

But the workers finished the work without him. On Friday, the 17th of September, he mounted his terrifying horse to go and visit our friends in La Châtre. He had dinner there and spent the evening. They noticed that his normal playfulness seemed a little forced and that now and then he was somber and preoccupied. The recent death of his child kept creeping back into his soul, and he made a generous effort not to let his friends see his sadness. He was dining with those same friends with whom he had played in *Robert, chef de brigands*, under the Directoire—M. and Mme. Duvernet.

My mother had always been jealous, especially of people she did not know, as is typical of that affliction. She was annoyed to see that he was not home early, as he had promised, and she naïvely let my grandmother perceive her irritation. She had already confessed this weakness to her, and my grandmother had already talked her out of it. My grandmother had never known passion, and my mother's suspicions seemed to her very unreasonable. She must have sympathized a little, however, as she had known jealousy in maternal love, but she spoke to her impetuous daughter-in-law in language so weighty that she often frightened her. My grandmother even scolded her, always in a gentle and reasonable way, but with a certain coolness that humiliated and diminished her without relieving her.

That evening she succeeded in subduing her completely, telling her that if she tormented Maurice this way, he would tire of her and would look outside the household for the happiness that she would have chased from it. My mother cried, but after several outbreaks, submitted nonetheless, and promised to go to bed quietly and not wait for her husband out on the road, so as not to make herself sick, as she had been sorely tried by so much fatigue and grief. She still had a lot of milk; she could make herself sick with so much agitation and have a setback which could suddenly take away all her beauty and youthfulness. This last consideration had more effect on her than all my grandmother's philosophy. She gave in to that argument. She wanted to be beautiful to please her husband. She went to bed and to sleep, like a sensible person. Poor woman, what an awakening was in store for her!

Toward midnight, however, my grandmother began to worry, though she said nothing to Deschartres, with whom she was prolonging her game of piquet, as she wanted to kiss her son goodnight before going to bed. At last it struck midnight, and she had retired to her room when she thought she heard unaccustomed movement in the house. Much caution was being observed, however, and Deschartres, who had been notified by Saint-Jean, had gone out with as little noise as possible. But the sound of doors opening and a certain hesitation on the part of her chambermaid, who had seen Deschartres summoned without knowing what it was about, although she had guessed it was something serious by the look on Saint-Jean's face, and, added to that, the worry she had already begun to feel—all precipitated my grandmother's fright. The night was dark and rainy, and as I have already pointed out, my grandmother, though of strong constitution, was never able to walk very far either because of a natural weakness in her legs or because she had been overprotected in her early development. When she had walked once slowly around the garden, she would be exhausted for the whole day. She had really walked only one time in her life—to surprise her son in Passy when she was released from prison. She walked for a second time on September 17th, 1808. This time it was to get his body, at a league's distance from the house, on the outskirts of La Châtre. She set out alone in little prunella slippers, without a shawl, just as she was. Since some time had passed before she had noticed the stirring in the house, which had alerted her, Deschartres arrived before she did. He was already with my poor father; he had already determined that he was dead.

Here is how that fatal accident happened:

At the outskirts of the town, a hundred paces after the bridge which marks the town limits, the road makes a sharp turn. At that place, at the foot of the thirteenth poplar tree, someone had left a pile of stones and debris that day. My father had broken into a gallop as he left the bridge. He was riding the fateful Leopardo. Weber, also on horseback, followed ten paces behind. At the turn in the road, my father's horse hit the pile of stones in the dark. The animal did not fall, but frightened and probably stimulated by the spurs, he reared so violently that his rider was thrown and landed ten paces behind. Weber heard only these words: "Come to me, Weber, I'm dead!" He found his master lying on his back. He had no visible injuries, but he had broken the vertebrae in the neck, and he was no more. I believe he was carried to the inn nearby and that help came promptly from the town, while Weber, seized with inexpressible terror, had come at a gallop to get Deschartres. All was too late; my father had not had time to suffer. He had only had time to recognize the sudden, implacable death that had come to snatch him just at the moment his military career was opening before him, brilliant and without obstacle; just at the moment when, after eight years of conflict, his mother, his wife, and his children were at last accepted by one another and united under one roof, and the terrible conflict of his affections was going to cease and allow him to be happy.

At the fatal spot, the end of her desperate errand, my poor grandmother fell, as if suffocated, on the body of her son. Saint-Jean had hurried to hitch the horses to the berlin and come to carry off Deschartres, the body, and my grandmother, who would not be separated from it. It was Deschartres who recounted to me this night of despair, as my grandmother was never able to speak of it. He told me he had suffered everything the human spirit could bear, short of breaking, during that journey where the poor mother, prostrate over the body of her son, made no other sound than a moan like that of the dying.

I do not know what took place prior to when my mother heard the frightful news. It was six in the morning, and I was already up; my mother was dressing; she had on a skirt and a white camisole, and she was combing her hair. I can still see her as Deschartres came in without knocking, his face so pale and contorted that my mother understood instantly. "Maurice!" she cried, "Where is Maurice?" Deschartres was not crying. His teeth were clenched, and he could only speak in disjointed words: "He fell; no, don't go, stay here, think of your daughter. Yes, it is serious, very serious." And at last, making an effort which might have seemed like brutal cruelty but which was entirely unpremeditated, he said in a tone I shall never in my whole life forget: "He is dead!" Then he let out a kind of convulsive laugh, sat down, and burst into tears.

I can still see what part of the room we were in. It was the room in which I still live and where I am writing this lamentable story. My mother fell onto the chair behind the bed. I can see her livid face, her long black hair spread out on her breast, her bare arms which I was covering with kisses; I can hear her rending cries. She was deaf to mine and did not notice my caresses. Deschartres said to her, "Do look at that child and live for her."

I do not remember what followed. Probably the cries and tears soon overwhelmed me. Children do not have the strength to suffer. The enormous grief and horror annihilated my awareness and removed any realization of what was happening around me. I can only recollect several days later when they dressed me in mourning. The black made a very vivid impression on me. I cried in protest, even though I had worn before the black dress and veil of Spanish women. But probably I had never had black stockings, for these stockings terrified me. I insisted that they were putting the legs of death on me, and my mother had to show me that she too had them. That same day I saw my grandmother, Deschartres, Hippolyte, and the whole household in mourning. They had to explain to me that it was because of the death of my father, and I then said something to my mother which gave her great pain, "You mean my daddy died again today?"

I had to some extent understood the meaning of death, but apparently I did not think it was eternal. I could not grasp the idea of an absolute separation, and little by little I went back to my games and resumed the insouciance of a child. From time to time, seeing my mother crying secretly, I would come up to her and make some naïve remark that nearly broke her heart: "But when my daddy is through being dead, he'll come back to see you, won't he?" The poor woman did not want to undeceive me completely. She told me that we would be waiting a long time for him, and she forbade the servants to explain anything to me. She had a very great respect for childhood, an attitude too often dispensed with in more thorough and learned systems of education.

The house was nonetheless plunged into melancholy, and so was the village, for no one who had known my father had not loved him. His death gave rise to a veritable consternation throughout the countryside, and even those who only knew him by sight were keenly affected by the catastrophe.

Hippolyte was quite shaken by the event, which had not been hidden from him with the same care as it had been from me. He was already nine and did not yet know that my father was also his. He grieved much, but his image of death added a kind of terror to his grief, and at night all he did was cry and scream. The servants, confusing their superstitions with their sorrow, insisted they had seen my father walking about the house after his death. Saint-Jean's old wife swore she had seen him, at midnight, crossing the hall and descending the stairs. He was wearing his dress uniform, she said, and was walking slowly, without seeming to see anyone. He had passed near her without looking at her and without speaking to her. Another had seen him in the antechamber to my mother's apartments. At that time, this was a great empty room intended for billiards, where there was only a table and several chairs. While going through that room one evening, a womanservant had seen him sitting with his elbows on the table and his head in his hands. Some domestic thief must have taken, or tried to take, advantage of the fears of our servants, because for several nights a white phantom did wander about the courtyard. Hippolyte saw it and was ill with fright. Deschartres saw it also and threatened it with gunshot. It did not come back.

Fortunately, I was watched closely enough so that I did not hear these silly stories, and for me death had not yet taken on the hideous aspect that superstitious imaginations have given it. For several days, my grandmother kept me away from Hippolyte, who was losing his head and was in any case a little too impetuous a playmate for me. But she soon worried about seeing me alone too much and about the kind of passive pleasure I took in remaining quietly under her watchful eye, plunged in a reverie that was constitutionally necessary for me, yet something she could find no explanation for. It seems that I would sit for hours at a time on a stool at her feet or my mother's, not saying a word, with a fixed stare, my hands idle, my mouth partly open, and that sometimes I had the look of an idiot. "She's always been like that," my mother would say, "it's her nature. It's not stupidity. You can be sure she's always mulling over something. She used to talk to herself while daydreaming; now she doesn't say anything, but, as her poor father used to say, it doesn't mean she's not thinking." "It is probably true," my grandmother would say, "but it is not good for children to daydream so much. I remember her father as a child, falling into sorts of trances, too, and afterward he would be ill. We must find something to distract the little one and shake her out of it in spite of herself. Our sorrows will kill her if we are not careful; she feels them even if she does not understand them. My daughter, you must also find something to distract you, if only physically. You are naturally healthy, and you need exercise. You must take up gardening again; the child will recover her interest along with you."

My mother obeyed, but probably she was not able to do it very consistently at first. So much weeping had left her with terrible headaches, which kept up for more than twenty years and forced her to stay in bed for one day out of almost every week.

I must say here, so as not to forget it, something that came back to me and that I feel obliged to say because it became a subject for accusation against my mother which has persisted until now in the minds of a number of people. It seems that on the day of my father's death, my mother cried out, "And to think I was jealous! And now I'll never be again." This thought came from the depths of her grief; she was expressing a bitter longing for the time she had indulged in chimerical worries, compared to the real misfortune which had come along to cure her of them in such a horrible way. Either it was Deschartres, who was never able to make his peace with her, or some ill-willed servant, who caused this exclamation to be repeated and distorted. My mother was said to have declared in a tone of monstrous satisfaction, "Anyway, I'll never be jealous again!" It is so absurd for anyone to have taken seriously the remark made on a day of such violent despair, I do not understand how any sensible person could have made this error. Yet not long ago,[50] M. de Vitrolles, an old friend of my father, and the staunchest member of the former legitimist party, told it in that sense to one of my friends. I beg M. de Vitrolles' pardon, but he was dreadfully misled, and such interpretations are an insult to the human conscience. I saw my mother's despair, and those scenes cannot be forgotten.

I return to my own story after this digression. My grandmother, ever worried about my isolation, found me a companion my own age. Mlle. Julie, her chambermaid, offered to bring her niece, who was only six months older than I, and soon little Ursule was dressed in mourning and brought to Nohant. She spent several years there with me, after which she was placed in an apprenticeship. For some time after my marriage, she came back to keep house for me, and then she herself was married and has always lived in La Châtre. Thus we never lost touch with each other, and our friendship, ever stronger with age, is now forty years old, and that is something.

I shall be speaking often of this dear Ursule, and so I shall begin by saying that she was a great help to me mentally and physically following our domestic misfortune. It was certainly a gift from God that the child of the poor who was brought to join in my games was not a servile child. The child of the rich (and compared to Ursule, I was a little princess) instinctively takes advantage of her position, and when her poorer companion submits, the little despot would willingly let her be whipped in her place, as has happened between gentry and peasants. I was very spoiled. My sister, five years older than I, had always given in to me with the compliance which little girls show for their younger sisters, by virtue of their greater maturity. Clotilde alone had stood up to me, but for several months I had not had the opportunity to associate with my peers. I was alone with my mother, who did not spoil me, however, for she had a quick temper and a lively hand, and put into practice the maxim that he who loves well punishes well. But in those days of grief, keeping up the constant struggle against the caprices of a child was quite beyond her strength. She and my grandmother needed to love me and spoil me to console themselves in their sorrow; and naturally I took advantage of it. And then the trip from Spain, the illness and its attendant discomforts had left me in a state of nervous excitation which lasted a fairly long time. I was intensely irritable and not at all in my normal state of mind. I was subject to a thousand fantasies, and I would emerge from mysterious reveries only to demand the impossible. I wanted them to give me the birds which flew in the garden, and I would roll on the ground in rage if they made fun of me; I wanted Weber to put me on his horse (it was not Leopardo; he had been sold immediately), but of course no one was going to let me near any horse. My constantly denied wishes were becoming an agony to me. My grandmother said that the intensity of these fantasies was proof of a vivid imagination, which she hoped to divert. But that would prove a long and difficult process.

When Ursule arrived, after the first moment of joy, for I liked her immediately and sensed without realizing it that she was a very brave and intelligent child, my domineering spirit returned, and I wanted her to submit to all my wishes. Right in the middle of our games, we were supposed to change from one which she liked to one which I liked more, and as soon as she began to prefer that one, I would tire of it. Or else I would insist that she stay quietly with me, saying nothing and "meditating," and if I could have succeeded in giving her the headaches I often had, I would have made her share those too. In any case, I was the most morose, melancholy, and irascible child imaginable.

Thank God, Ursule did not let herself be dominated. Her disposition was cheerful, lively, and so talkative that we gave her the nickname "Cacklebeak," which she has kept for a long time. She always had wit, and her long speeches often made my grandmother laugh through her tears. It was feared at first that she would let herself be tyrannized, but she was too stubborn by nature to need a lesson in it. She could not have done better at opposing me, and when I wanted to play hands and claws, she answered with feet and teeth. She remembers an impressive battle we challenged each other to one day. It seems we had a serious difference of opinion to settle, and as neither of us would give in, we agreed to fight each other as well as we knew how. It was quite a heated battle, and each left her mark on the other. I do not know who was the winner, but the dinner hour coming just at this point, we were going to have to appear at the table, and we were both equally afraid of being scolded. We were alone in my mother's bedroom, and we hastened to wash our faces to remove little traces of blood; we did each other's hair and even showed each other little courtesies in light of the common danger. At last we went downstairs, asking each other if anything showed. The grudge had disappeared, and Ursule suggested that we kiss and make up, which we did, heartily, like two old soldiers after a duel to settle a question of honor. I do not recall if it was our last fight; it is certain that, in peace or war, we lived thenceforth as equals, and we loved each other so much that we could not be separated for an instant. Ursule ate with us at our table, as she has always done since. She slept in our room, and often in the big bed with me. My mother loved her very much, and when she had migraines, she liked to have Ursule's cool, little hands rubbing her forehead gently for a long time. I was a little jealous of her giving these attentions, but whether from the heatedness of our games, or from a lasting tendency to feverishness, my hands were always burning hot, and I made the migraine worse.

We stayed two or three years at Nohant without my grandmother returning to Paris and without my mother being able to decide what was required of her. My grandmother wished to have the entire responsibility for my education and wanted me to stay with her. My mother could not abandon Caroline, who was, it is true, at boarding school, but who would soon need more consistent attention, and she could not make up her mind to give up one or the other of her daughters. My Uncle Beaumont came to spend a summer at Nohant to help my mother make the decision he felt was indispensable to my grandmother's and my happiness; considering everything, and even with my grandmother increasing as much as possible the funds my mother could expect, she still would have a yearly income of only two thousand five hundred pounds, and that was not enough to give a very brilliant education to her two children. My grandmother was becoming daily more attached to me, probably not because of my quirky nature, which was still fairly unpredictable at the time, but because of my striking resemblance to my father. My voice, features, manner, tastes—everything about me reminded her of her son as a child, to the point where sometimes, while watching me play, she would have a kind of hallucination, call me Maurice, and speak of me as her son.

She insisted on developing my intelligence, of which she had a very high opinion. I do not know why I understood everything she said to me and taught me, but she spoke so clearly and well that it was not surprising. I was also showing an inclination for music, which never was sufficiently developed, but which enchanted her because it reminded her of my father's childhood, and she recaptured her young motherhood by giving me lessons.

I often heard my mother raise this question in my presence: "Will my child be happier here than with me? I really don't know, and I won't have the means to have her taught much. Her inheritance from her father *could* be diminished if her grandmother loses interest in her from not seeing her all the time. But do money and accomplishments make someone happy?"

I could already grasp this reasoning, and when she talked about my future to my Uncle Beaumont, who pressed her urgently to give in, I would listen with both ears, without appearing to. I consequently acquired a great scorn for money before I even knew what it was, and also a haunting fear of the wealth with which I was threatened.

This wealth was not inordinate: it was one day supposed to come to around twelve thousand francs net income. But relatively, it was a fair amount, and that frightened me, since it was associated with the idea of being separated from my mother. So, whenever I was alone with her, I would cover her with kisses and beg her not "to give me away to my grandmother for money," though I loved that gentle grandmama who spoke only tender words to me. But this could not compare with the passionate love I was beginning to feel for my mother, which dominated my life until a time when circumstances beyond my control forced me to choose between these two mothers, jealous of each other over me, as they had been over my father.

Yes, I must admit the time came when, placed in an unnatural situation between these two affections which by nature should not have conflicted, I was by turns a victim of the opposing sensitivities of these two women and of my own, too often not spared by them. I shall tell these things in the order that they happened, and I want to try to begin at the beginning. Until the age of four, that is to say until the trip to Spain, I loved my mother instinctively, without knowing it. As I said earlier, I had not been aware of feeling affection, and I had lived as little children and as primitive people live, by my imagination. My sentiments were awakened at the birth of my little blind brother, on seeing my mother suffer. Her despair over my father's death developed me further in this direction, and I began to feel dominated by this love when the idea of a separation caught me unawares, in the middle of "my golden age."

I call it that because it was little Ursule's favorite expression at the time. I do not know where she heard it, but she would repeat it when she reasoned with me, for she was already privy to my sorrows. More because of her disposition than because of her being five or six months older than I, she understood the real world better than I. Seeing me cry at the idea of staying with my grandmother without my mother, she would say to me, "But it's nice to have a big house and a big garden like this to walk in, and carriages, and dresses, and good things to eat every day. And what brings all this? Richness. You mustn't cry, because with your grandmama you'll always have your golden age and you'll always have richness. And when I go to see my mama at La Châtre, she says I have been spoiled at Nohant, and that I am playing the great lady. And I say to her, 'I am in my golden age, and I'm taking my richness while I can.'"

Ursule's reasoning did not console me. Her aunt, Mlle. Julie, my grandmother's chambermaid, who wanted what was best for me and saw things from my grandmother's point of view, said to me one day, "So you want to return to your mother's little garret and eat beans?" This remark was revolting to me; the beans and the garret seemed the ideal of happiness and dignity. But I am getting a little ahead of myself; I was perhaps seven or eight years old when the question about riches was put to me that way. Before telling the result of the battle that my mother was waging single-handedly for me, I must sketch the two or three years we spent at Nohant after the death of my father. I shall not be able to do it in sequence; it will be an overall picture, and a little confused, like my memories.

First, I must tell how my mother and grandmother lived together, these two women as different in their physical being as they were in their upbringing and way of life. They were really the two extreme types of our sex: one fair, blond, serious, calm and dignified in her behavior, a real Saxon of noble race, with grand manners full of ease and benevolent kindness; the other dark, pale, intense, shy and awkward in the presence of high society, and always ready to explode when the storm raged too forcefully within, a Spanish nature, jealous, passionate, angry and weak, mean and good at the same time. It was not without distaste that these two beings so opposite by nature and circumstance had accepted each other; and during my father's lifetime, they had fought too much over him not to hate each other a little. After his death, sorrow brought them together, and the effort they had made to love each other bore fruit. My grandmother could not understand fiery passions and violent instincts, but she was sensitive to intelligence and heartfelt gestures of affection. My mother had all these traits, and my grandmother often watched her with a sort of curiosity, wondering why my father had loved her so much. At Nohant, she soon discovered the attractions of this unschooled nature. My mother was a great artist who had missed her calling for lack of training. I do not know to which art she would have been especially suited, but she had a marvelous aptitude for all of them and for all handiwork. Having had no education, she was ignorant; my grandmother chided her for her barbarous spelling and told her it was up to her to improve it. She began, not to study grammar—that was too late—but to read attentively, and not long thereafter she was able to write nearly correctly and in a style so naïve and pretty that my grandmother, who was a connoisseur of such things, admired her letters. She did not even know the notes, but she had a ravishing voice, light and incomparably pure, and my grandmother enjoyed hearing her sing. Herself a great musician, she appreciated the tastefulness and naturalness of my mother's singing. Then, at Nohant, not knowing how to fill her long days, my mother took up sketching, she who had never touched a pencil. She did it instinctively, as she did everything, and after having very skillfully copied several engravings, she began to do portraits in ink and gouache, which were excellent likenesses, in a charmingly untutored style. Her embroidery was a little lacking in refinement, but she did it so quickly that she made for my grandmother, in only a few days, a percale dress entirely embroidered from top to bottom, like those worn at the time. She made all our dresses and all our hats, which was not surprising as she had been a seamstress for a long time, but it was done with incomparable speed, taste, and novelty. Whatever she began in the morning had to be finished by the next day, even if she had to spend all night on it, and the ardor and power of concentration she brought to the lowliest tasks enthralled my grandmother, who was temperamentally somewhat indolent and awkward with her hands, as were the great ladies of the period. My mother laundered, ironed, and mended all our clothes herself, and more deftly and quickly than the best professional. I never saw her make useless and costly articles like those made by rich ladies. She made no little purses, no little screens, nor any of those little knick-knacks which cost more when you make them yourself than when you buy them ready-made at the shop, but in a household in need of economy, she was worth ten workers. And, too, she was always willing to take on anything. When my grandmother had broken her sewing box, my mother locked herself in her room one whole day, and at dinner she brought her a pasteboard box, cut out, glued, lined, and constructed to perfection by her own hand. And it just happened to be a little masterpiece of taste. Everything was like that. If something was wrong with the harpsichord, without knowing anything about its mechanism or keyboard, she would replace strings, reglue keys, and tune the instrument. She dared anything and succeeded at everything. She would have made shoes, furniture, and locks, if she had had to. My grandmother used to say she was a household fairy, and there was something to it. No undertaking seemed too exotic, mundane, difficult, or fastidious for her; the only things she hated doing were useless tasks, and she would say in an undertone that they were pastimes for "the old contessas."

Thus she was marvelously constituted. She had such native wit that when she was not paralyzed by her timidity, which was extreme with certain people, she was sparkling. I have never heard her equal for mockery and satire, and it was not a good idea to cross her. When she felt really comfortable, she had the incisive, vivid, and comical speech of a true child of Paris, which cannot be compared to that of any other people in the world. And in addition to all that, she had flashes of poetry, when she felt and said things in a way that cannot be said by anyone who is self-conscious or has learned how to say them. She was not vain about her intelligence and did not even suspect she had any. She was sure of her own beauty, without being conceited, and she would naïvely say that she had never been jealous of any one else's, considering she had been fairly endowed in that regard. But what tormented her, in relation to my father, was the superiority of intelligence and education which she attributed to society women. That shows how modest she was by nature, because nineteen out of twenty of the women I have known on every social level were absolute simpletons compared to her. I have seen those who peered at her over their shoulders, and seeing her reserved and shy, imagined she was ashamed of being ignorant or a nobody, but had they gotten on her wrong side, the volcano would have erupted and would have tossed them a goodly distance.

With all this, it must be admitted that she was the most difficult person to deal with in the whole world. I finally managed it during her last years, but it was not without pain and suffering. She was excruciatingly irritable, and to calm her down, you had to feign irritation yourself. Gentleness and patience exasperated her, silence drove her crazy, and for a long time she treated me unjustly because I had paid her too much respect. I was never able to get angry with her, her anger afflicted me without offending me; I saw her as an enfant terrible who was eating her heart out, and I suffered too much from the hurt she was doing to herself to worry about what she was doing to me. But when I undertook to address her with a certain severity, her spirit, which had been so tender toward me in my childhood, let itself be persuaded and won over. I suffered a great deal to achieve this, but it is not yet time to tell about that.

I must, however, paint a complete picture of this woman who has not been understood. And how could one understand the mixture of sympathy and revulsion, of trust and apprehension, which she always inspired in my grandmother (and for a long time in me), if I did not portray all the strengths and weaknesses of her soul? She was full of contrasts; that was why she was loved and hated so much; that was why she herself loved and hated so much. In some ways there is much of her in me, but fewer of the good things and still less of the harshness; I am a copy of her much diluted by nature or much modified by education. I am capable of neither her bitterness nor her brilliance, but when I return to good temper from bad, I deserve less credit, because my resentment was never out of fury and my withdrawal never out of hate. To go thus from one extreme passion to another, to adore what one has just cursed, to caress what one has just broken, requires a rare power. A hundred times I have seen my mother outraged to the point of bloodshed, then suddenly realizing she had gone too far, melt into tears, and then raise up to worship what she had unfairly trampled underfoot.

She was miserly to herself, but generous to others. She scrimped on things of no importance, and then suddenly, afraid she had acted meanly, would give too much. She could be wonderfully naïve. When she spoke ill of her enemies, if Pierret, to hasten the exhaustion of her spleen or merely because he saw the thing as she did, added his malediction to hers, she would change instantly. "Not at all, Pierret," she would say, "you're wrong. You don't see that I'm angry and that I'm saying unreasonable things which I'll very shortly regret having said."

That happened very often on my account; if she thought she had a complaint about me, she would burst out in terrible reproaches, and if I may say so, very undeserved ones. If Pierret or someone else would agree with her, "You lie," she would scream, "my daughter is wonderful, I don't know anyone better, and whatever you do, I'll love her more than you."

She would be sly as a fox, and then suddenly innocent as a child. She would lie without knowing it and in utter good faith. Always carried away by her imagination and her passion, she would accuse you of the most incredible misdeeds, and then suddenly stop and say, "But it isn't true what I just said; no, there isn't a word of truth in it, I dreamed it!" *J.H.C.*

XV

My mother. —A river in a room. —My grandmother. —Deschartres.
—His medical practice. —Hieroglyphic writing. —First readings.
—Fairy tales, mythology. —The Nymph and the Bacchante. —My
great uncle. —The Canon of *Consuelo*. —The difference between
"truth" and "reality" in the arts. —My grandmother's birthday.
—Early musical studies and impressions.

I think I have truthfully sketched my mother's character, and I cannot
proceed further in the recital of my life without taking into account, as much as
it is in me to do, the importance her character had in forming my own.

You can imagine that it took me a long time to appreciate a temperament
so unique and filled with contradictions, especially as we lived together so little after my childhood. In the first period of my life, I felt only her love for me,
an immense love which she later confessed to having fought in herself, in order
to become resigned to our separation, but her love was not of the same nature
as mine. Mine was more tender, hers more passionate; she would scold me
sharply for little misdeeds which, because of her preoccupation, had gone
unpunished for a long time and for which I consequently felt no guilt. I was
always extremely deferential to her, and she always said that there was no one
in the world sweeter or more lovable than I. This was true only with regard to
her. I am no better than anyone else, but I was truly good with her, and I
obeyed her without fearing her, no matter how harsh she might be. An impossible child with others, I was submissive with her, because it gave me pleasure.
She was then, for me, an oracle. She gave me my first notions about life, and
she gave them to me in terms that fit the intellectual needs nature had created
in me. But out of distraction and forgetfulness, children often do things they
have been forbidden to do and which they have not intended to do. She would
scold and hit me, then, as if my disobedience had been intentional, and yet I
loved her so, I was truly in despair at having displeased her. It never occurred
to me during those times that she might have been unjust. I never felt either
rancor or bitterness toward her. Whenever she realized she had gone too far,
she would take me in her arms, weep, and overwhelm me with kisses. She
would even tell me she had been wrong, that she was fearful of having hurt
me; as for me, I was so happy to regain her affection that I would ask her pardon for the smacks she had administered.

How strange we are! If my grandmother had employed a hundredth of
that irrational harshness with me, I would have entered into full revolt. I was

more afraid of her, however; one word from her and I grew pale. But I would never have forgiven her the least injustice, whereas those of my mother passed unnoticed and increased my love.

One day like any other, I was playing in her room with Ursule and Hippolyte while she was drawing. She was so totally absorbed in her work that she was oblivious to our usual din. We had found a game which excited our imaginations. It consisted of crossing a river. The river was drawn on the tiles with chalk and made a thousand turns around that large room. In certain places it was very deep, and we had to find the fordable spot and not miscalculate. Hippolyte had already been drowned several times; we helped pull him out of the large holes into which he was always falling, for he would play the role of either the oaf or the drunkard, and swim on the dry tiles, flapping about and lamenting his plight. For children, these games are an entire drama, a complete scenic fiction, sometimes a whole novel, a poem, a journey, which they mime and invent for hours on end, totally caught up in the illusion. In my case, all it took was five minutes for me to be deeply immersed; then I lost all sense of reality, and I believed I saw the trees, streams, rocks, vast countryside, and the sky at times clear, at times filled with clouds that were about to burst and make the river even more dangerous to cross. What a vast space children believe they are moving about in when they go from the table to the bed and from the hearth to the door!

We had arrived, Ursule and I, on the banks of our river, where the grass was fine and the sand soft. She tried it first, and then she called to me, "You can risk it, it won't be any higher than your knees." She used the formal *vous*, which children use when playing make-believe. They would not feel as if they were playacting if they used the familiar *tu*, which they are accustomed to. They always take on certain roles that express character, and once the type is established, they follow it consistently. They even create very believable dialogue, which professional actors would have difficulty improvising with such truth and inventiveness.

To Ursule's invitation I remarked that, since the water was shallow we could easily cross without getting wet. It was simply a matter of raising our skirts a bit and removing our shoes. "But," she said, "if we run across any shrimp, they will eat our feet." "It doesn't matter," I said, "we mustn't get our shoes wet, we must take proper care of them, for we have a long way yet to go."

Scarcely had I taken my shoes off when the tile felt like real water, and there we were, Ursule and I, wading in the stream. To enhance the illusion, Hippolyte got the idea of emptying the water pot on the floor, thus creating the effect of a torrent and a cascade. We thought this was the height of invention. Our laughter and screams finally drew my mother's attention. She looked and saw all three of us, bare feet and legs, splashing about in what looked like a cesspool, for the color on the tile had run, and our little river was far from clear. Then she became furious, especially with me, since I already had a cold. She took me by the arm, administered corporal punishment with quite an insistent beat, and having put my shoes back on while scolding me, she chased Hippolyte into her bedroom and made me and Ursule do penance, each in her own corner. Such was the unforeseen and dramatic dénouement of our performance, and the curtain fell on very real tears and cries.

Well, I always shall remember that dénouement as one of the most painful shocks I ever received. My mother surprised me at the height of my fantasy, and that sort of awakening has always unsettled me in a traumatic way. On the other hand, being hit never made such an impression on me; it happened often, and I knew perfectly well that my mother's smacks were doing me very little harm. No matter how she shook me and made me into a little package that could be pushed and tossed onto a bed or an armchair, her adept and supple hands could never bruise me, and I was as snidely confident as most children that their parents' anger is tempered with prudence and that parents are more afraid of hurting their children than the children are of being hurt. That time, like all the others, my mother, seeing my despair at her wrath, consoled me with a thousand caresses. This might have been a mistake if I had been a proud, vindictive child, but it was right for me, who had never borne a grudge and who still find that not to forgive those you love is to punish yourself.

To get back to the relations which developed between my mother and my grandmother after my father's death, I must say that the kind of natural antipathy they felt for each other was never more than somewhat overcome, or rather was completely overcome at certain times, followed by quite sharp reversals. Apart, they always detested each other and could not keep from speaking ill of each other. Together, they could not help but enjoy each other, for each was ingratiating in a totally opposite way from the other. Owing to each woman's sense of what was just and right, and to her great intelligence, one never denied the excellent qualities of the other. My grandmother's prejudice did not come so much from her as from her circle of friends. She had a weakness for certain people and tolerated opinions in them which in her heart she didn't share. So, in the company of her old friends, she allowed my mother to be the object of their abomination and appeared to feel the need to justify having taken her into her home and treated her like a daughter. But then again, when she was with my mother, she forgot the ill she had just spoken of her and showed her the affection and trust which I had so often observed and which were not feigned, since my grandmother was the most sincere and upright person I have ever known. But as serious and reserved as she appeared, she was sensitive; she needed to be loved and was grateful for the smallest attentions one paid her.

How many times I heard her say of my mother, "She has nobility in her character. She is charming. She has perfect poise. She is generous and would give you the shirt off her back. She is as grand as a lady and as innocent as a child." But at other times reminiscent of her old maternal jealousy, which had somehow survived the person who had been their object, she would say, "She is a devil, a madwoman. She was never loved by my son, she controlled him, she made him unhappy. She does not miss him." And a thousand other unfounded accusations which seemed to relieve a hidden, incurable bitterness.

My mother behaved in precisely the same way. When it was fair weather between them, she would say, "She is a superior woman. She is still as beautiful as an angel; she is all knowing. She is so gentle and well brought up that you can never get angry with her, and if at times she says something that irritates you, just when you are about to lose your temper, she says something else that makes you want to kiss her. If you could keep her away from her old contessas, she would be adorable."

But when a tempest brewed in my mother's tempestuous soul, it was another story. Then that old mother-in-law was a prude and a hypocrite. She was dried up and heartless. She was encrusted with the values of the old regime, etc. Then pity those poor old friends whose comments and remarks had been the cause of a domestic squabble! Those old contessas were the beasts of the Apocalypse, and she dressed them down from head to toe with such verve and causticity that even my grandmother had to laugh, in spite of herself.

Deschartres, I must admit, was the principal obstacle to their total reconciliation. He could never resign himself to it, and he never let the least opportunity pass to reopen old wounds. This was his fate. He was always rude and disagreeable to those he cherished, why should he have been otherwise to those he hated? He could not forgive my mother for having supplanted him in his pretended influence over the mind and heart of his dear Maurice. He contradicted her and tried to abuse her at every turn; then he would regret it and force himself to make amends by paying her awkward and ridiculous little attentions. At times it even seemed he was in love with her. And who can be sure he wasn't? The human heart is so bizarre, and ascetic men are so inflammable! But he would have eaten alive anyone who dared suggest such a thing. He had the pretensions of a man above any human frailty. Besides, my mother received his advances so badly and retaliated for his bad behavior with such cruel mockery that the old hate always overtook him, intensified by the spleen of each new clash.

When we all appeared to be getting along very well together and Deschartres was making every possible effort to seem less grumpy, he tried to be teasing and nice, and God knows he meant well, poor man! Then my mother made fun of him with such malice and wit that he would lose his head, become brutal, injurious, and my grandmother was obliged to reprimand and silence him.

The three of them played cards in the evening, and Deschartres, who claimed to excel at every game but played them all very badly, always lost. I remember one evening when, exasperated at being persistently beaten by my mother, who had no head for numbers but who by instinct and inspiration was always lucky, he exploded in a frightful fury and, throwing his cards on the table, said, "Someone ought to throw them in your face for having learned to win while playing so badly!" My mother got up angrily and was going to answer him, when my grandmother, with her calm demeanor and gentle voice, said, "Deschartres, if you did such a thing, I assure you I would give you a big slap."

This threat of a slap, made in such a peaceful tone, and of a *big* slap, coming from that half-paralyzed, beautiful hand, so frail it could scarcely hold the cards, was the most comical thing one could imagine. And so my mother broke into uncontrollable laughter and sat down again, incapable of adding a thing to further stupefy and mortify the poor pedagogue.

But this incident took place long after the death of my father. Long years had passed before one heard laughter other than that of children in this house of mourning.

During those years of a calm and ordered life, of a physical well-being I had never known before, of pure air that I had rarely breathed so deeply, my nervous condition disappeared, my temper became more even, and my disposition improved. They began to notice that I was no worse than any other child; it is certain that most often children are obstreperous and capricious only because they are suffering and cannot or will not articulate it.

In my case, I had become so disgusted with medicines—and at that time they were so abused—it had become my habit never to complain about slight indispositions, and I recall more than once having been close to fainting in the middle of playing a game and having fought it with a stoicism that I would probably not today. This was because whenever I was placed in the learned hands of Deschartres, I became, in a real sense, the victim of his system, which was to give an emetic for everything. He was a skillful surgeon, but he knew nothing about medicine, and administered his damned emetic for every illness. It was his universal panacea. I was and always have been bilious by nature, but had I had all the bile of which Deschartres claimed to have relieved me, I would never have survived. If I was pale, if I had a headache, it was bile, and quick the emetic! which produced such convulsions without producing vomit that I was laid low for several days. My mother, on the other hand, believed in worms, yet another medical superstition of the time. All children had worms, and one stuffed them with vermifuges, ghastly black medicines which made them nauseous and took away their appetite. Then, to restore the appetite, one administered rhubarb. Then, if I had a gnat bite, my mother thought it was a recurrence of the scabies, and once again sulphur was mixed in with all my food. In short, it was a perpetual round of drug cures, and children of my generation must have had very strong constitutions to resist all the care that was taken to protect them.

Around the age of five I learned how to write. My mother made me do large pages of upstrokes and downstrokes. But since she herself wrote like a cat, I would have blotted many sheets of paper before learning to sign my name, if I had not made up my mind to find myself a way to express my thoughts by one system of signs or another. I was bored with copying the alphabet every day and tracing the wide and thin strokes of the printed letters. I was impatient to write sentences, and during my recreation hours, which were of course extensive, I practiced writing letters to Ursule, Hippolyte, and my mother. But I never showed them to them, for fear that I would be forbidden to "ruin my hand" with such exercises. I soon achieved the goal of creating an orthography for my personal use. It was simple and loaded with hieroglyphics. My grandmother came upon one of these letters and found it very droll. She claimed it was marvelous to see how I had succeeded in expressing my little ideas with such primitive methods, and she advised my mother to allow me to scribble by myself as much as I wanted. She said, rightly, that one wastes a lot of time trying to teach children beautiful handwriting, instead of thinking about the purpose that writing serves. I was then left to my own pursuits, and when I had finished the pages of exercises, I went back to my natural system. For a long time I wrote in printed characters, like the ones I had seen in books, and I do not recall how I came to write like everyone else, but I do recall that I did as my mother had done, who had learned to spell by studying the way the printed words were composed. I would count the letters, and by some unknown instinct, I learned the fundamentals by myself. When, later, Deschartres taught me grammar, it took only about two or three months, since each lesson only served to confirm what I had already observed and applied.

By the age of seven or eight, I was therefore spelling not very correctly—that I never learned to do—but as well as the majority of Frenchmen who were taught properly.

It was while learning to write by myself that I came to understand what I was reading. Writing forced my awareness of reading, for I had learned how to read before I understood most of the words or could grasp the meaning of sentences. Each day the small frame of this revelation was enlarged until, finally, I could read a fairy tale by myself.

What a pleasure this was for me who loved them so and to whom my mother no longer read since she had been stricken with grief. At Nohant I found the tales of Mme. d'Aulnoy and Perrault in an old edition that I reveled in for five or six years. Oh, the hours I spent with *L'Oiseau bleu, Le Petit Poucet, Peau d'Ane, Belle-Belle ou le Chevalier Fortuné, Serpentin vert, Babiole*, and *La Souris bienfaisante*! I have not reread them since, but I could relate them all from beginning to end; I do not believe there is anything in our adult intellectual life that can compare with these first savorings of the imagination.

I also began to read my *Abrégé de mythologie grecque*, and took great pleasure in doing so, for the myths were like fairy tales in some ways. But in other ways, they pleased me less; all of them had gory symbols amid their poetry, and I preferred the happy endings of the fairy tales. And yet the nymphs, the zephyrs, the echo, all these personifications of nature's pleasant mysteries were turning my mind toward poetry, and I was not enough of a free thinker yet not to hope from time to time to surprise the nymphs and dryads in the woods and meadows.

There was in our bedroom a wallpaper that kept my mind very busy. The background layer was a solid deep green, very thick, varnished, and hung over cloth. This manner of separating the paper from the wall gave the mice free running space, and at night, scenes from another world took place—wild races, furtive scratchings, and very mysterious little cries. But that was not what intrigued me most. It was the border and ornamentation that went around the panels. This border was a foot wide and portrayed a garland of vine leaves that parted at intervals to frame a series of medallions in which you could see Silenuses and Bacchantes laughing and drinking and dancing. Over each doorway was a medallion larger than the others, portraying a figurine, and these figurines seemed incomparable to me. They were not all alike. The one I saw on waking in the morning was a nymph, or a dancing Flora. She was dressed in pale blue, crowned with roses, and was waving a wreath of flowers in her hands. This one gave me enormous pleasure. My first look in the morning was for her. She seemed to laugh and invite me to get up and run and frolic in her company.

The one facing her, which I saw during the day from my work table and in the evening when I said my prayers, had a totally different expression. She neither laughed nor danced. She was a serious bacchante. Her tunic was green, her crown was of vine leaves, and her extended arm rested on a thyrsus. Perhaps these two figures represented Spring and Autumn. Whatever they stood for, the two characters, each about a foot high, made a vivid impression on me. Maybe neither of them had any character or meaning, but in my head they offered a definite contrast between mirth and sadness, benevolence and severity. I held the bacchante in awe, having read the story of Orpheus torn apart by similarly cruel ones; in the evening, when the shimmering light illuminated her extended arm and the thyrsus, I thought I saw the head of the divine poet on the end of a javelin.

My little bed was backed against the wall in such a way that I could not see the figure that plagued me. However, since no one suspected my bias against her, when winter came, my mother changed my bed so that it was closer to the fireplace, and so my back was turned to my beloved nymph and I could only see the formidable maenad. I did not go heralding my weakness, in fact I was beginning to feel ashamed of it, but since it seemed to me that this she-devil persisted in looking at me and threatening me with her motionless arm, I put my head under the covers so as not to see her while I was falling asleep. It was futile; in the middle of the night, she detached herself from the medallion, slid down the door, became as large as a "grown-up," as children say, and crossing to the other door, she tried to tear the pretty nymph from her medallion. The latter emitted heartrending cries, but the bacchante ignored them. She twisted and tore the paper until the nymph detached herself and fled to the middle of the room. The other ran after her, and the poor dishevelled nymph having leaped onto my bed to hide behind the curtains, the furious bacchante moved toward me and pierced the two of us with her thyrsus, which had been transformed into a sharp lance, and each blow inflicted a wound whose pain I felt.

I cried out, I struggled, my mother came to my aid; but although I was awake enough to realize that she was there, I was still asleep enough to see the bacchante. The real and the chimerical were simultaneously before my eyes, and I distinctly saw the bacchante grow dimmer, disappear into the distance, as my mother came closer, becoming as small as she was in the medallion, clambering up the door as a mouse might have, and regaining her place in her vine-covered frame, where she resumed her ordinary pose and serious air.

I fell back to sleep, and again I saw that madwoman up to her old tricks. She would run along the whole border, calling to all the Silenuses and other bacchantes, who were sitting around tables or otherwise amusing themselves in the medallions, and force them to come dance with her and break all the furniture in the room.

Little by little, the dream became hazy, and I derived a certain pleasure from it. The next morning, on waking, I saw the bacchante facing me instead of the nymph, and since I had forgotten about the new arrangement of my bed in the room, I thought for a moment that in returning to their medallions the two figurines had gotten the doors confused and changed places, but this illusion disappeared with the first rays of sunlight, and I did not think about it for the rest of the day.

At night my preoccupation returned, and it went on like this for a long time. As long as it was daytime, I found it impossible to take seriously two colored figures on wallpaper, but when the first shades of night clouded my mind, I no longer dared stay alone in the room. I did not reveal it, for my grandmother made fun of cowardice, and I did not want anyone to tell her how silly I was, but I was almost eight years old and still could not view the bacchante calmly before going to sleep. It is hard to imagine all the pent-up curiosity and emotion children carry around in their brains.

The stay at Nohant of my grand-uncle, Abbé de Beaumont, was a great consolation, a sort of rejuvenation, for my two mothers. He was a cheerful character, a bit carefree, as some bachelors are, a remarkable wit, resourceful and inventive, and disposed to be both egotistical and generous; nature had made him sensitive and warm, celibacy had made him self-centered; but his personality was so lovable, so gracious and attractive, that you had to feel grateful to him for not sharing your troubles unless he knew he had the power to help you forget them. He was the handsomest old man I have ever met. He had my grandmother's fine white skin, gentle eyes, regular and aristocratic features, but his lineaments were even nobler, and his facial expression more animated. At that period, he still wore his hair in powdered pigeon wings and a pigtail *à la prussienne*. He was always dressed in black satin breeches, buckled slippers, and when he put on his violet silk, quilted coat over his habit, he assumed the air of solemnity of a family portrait.

He was fond of comfort, and his quarters were redolent of old-fashioned luxury; his table was as refined as his appetite. He was despotic and imperious in language; gentle, liberal, and lenient in behavior. I often thought of him while sketching the portrait of a certain canon in the novel *Consuelo* [1842].[54] Like him, the bastard son of a high ranking personage, he was fond of sweets, impatient, a joker, an art lover, grand in manner, equally candid and cunning, irascible and agreeable. I exaggerated the likeness to fit the needs of the novel, and it is essential to point out that portraits drawn in this way are no longer portraits; that is why, if they seem injurious to those who think they recognize themselves in them, an injustice is being done to both author and subject. A portrait in a novel, to be worth anything, is always a figure of fantasy. In reality, people are so illogical, so filled with contrasts and incongruities that the portrait of a real individual would be impossible and completely untenable in a work of art. The novel would be forced to bend to the demands of the character and would no longer be a novel. It would have neither exposition, nor plot, nor climax, nor dénouement; it would go completely awry, like life, and would be of interest to no one, because everyone looks for an idealization of life in a novel.[51]

It is therefore nonsense to believe that an author wishes to provoke love or hate for this or that person by endowing fictional creations with traits taken from life; the least difference renders them conventional characters, and I maintain that, in literature, one cannot make a credible portrayal out of a real figure without plunging into enormous difficulties and going far beyond— toward either good or evil—the faults and attributes of the human being who served as the original. It is comparable to acting, which only seems true on the stage if the actor either greatly exaggerates or attentuates reality. Whether caricature or idealization, it is no longer the original model, and this model lacks judgment if he thinks he recognizes himself, if he is either vexed or vain on seeing what art or fantasy has made of him.

Lavater[56] said (these are not his exact words, but his ideas): "Against my system, they pose an argument that I reject. They say that a villain often resembles an honest man, and vice versa. My response is that if anyone is duped by this resemblance, it is because they do not know how to observe; they do not know how to see. There surely may exist between an honest man and a villain a rough resemblance, a superficial one; it is perhaps only a little line, a barely perceptible wrinkle, a 'nothing' that constitutes the difference. But this nothing is everything!"

What Lavater had to say about differences in physical reality is even more applicable to the relativity of truth in the arts. Music is not mimetic harmony; at least mimetic harmony is not music. Color, in painting, is only an approximation; an exact reproduction of real color is not possible. Characters in a novel are, therefore, not living figures. One has to have known a thousand persons in order to depict one. If you had only studied a single one and wanted to make an exact copy, it would resemble no one and would not seem credible.

I made this digression so as not to have to come back to it later.[57] It is not even crucial to the comparison one could make between my Uncle Beaumont and the canon in *Consuelo*, since I portrayed the latter as chaste, and my granduncle took pride in being the opposite. He had had very lovely affairs, and would have been very unhappy not to have had any. There are a thousand other differences that I need not point out, unless it were the one concerning the housekeeper in my novel, who has not the least trait in common with my grand-uncle's housekeeper. The latter was devoted, honest, excellent on all counts. She closed his eyes, and she was his heir, as she deserved to be; yet my uncle sometimes spoke to her as the canon speaks to Dame Brigitte in my novel. Hence, nothing is less real than what seems most true in a work of art.

When it came to women, my grand-uncle had not a grain of prejudice. As long as they were beautiful and kind, he never asked them to give an account of their birth or their past. Thus, he had completely accepted my mother and showed her a paternal affection all his life. He understood her very well and treated her like a well-meaning, but unruly, child, scolding her, consoling her, defending her staunchly when she was treated unjustly, reprimanding her severely when she was unjust toward others. He was always a fair mediator, a persuasive conciliator between her and my grandmother. He saved her from Deschartres' tirades, openly taking sides against him, while Deschartres could never get angry or rise up against grand-uncle's firm and cheerful protection.

The lightheartedness of this lovable old man was therefore a blessing in the midst of our domestic bitterness, and I have often noticed that everything about good people is good, even their apparent defects. At first we imagine these will make us suffer, but little by little we profit from them; and if they are lacking in one area, it acts as a corrective to what we lack in another. They bring balance to our lives, and we come to realize that the defects we reproached them for were very necessary to counteract abusive or excessive tendencies in our own nature.

Grand-uncle's serenity and sprightly temperament then seemed a bit shocking at first. He did sincerely miss his beloved Maurice, but he wanted to distract the two desolate women, and he succeeded.

Soon we came to life a little with his presence. He had such wit, such an active mind, was so gracious in telling stories, in making fun, in amusing others while amusing himself, that he was irresistible. He got the idea to have us put on a play for my grandmother's birthday, and he made the most of this surprise for a long time. The large room which served as an antechamber to my mother's room, and where my grandmother, who almost never came upstairs, was unlikely to catch us in our preparations, was converted into a little theater. We set some planks up over barrels, the actors—Hippolyte, Ursule, and I—still not being tall enough to touch the ceiling in spite of this elevation of the floor. It was a kind of marionette theater, but it was charming. My grand-uncle cut out, glued, and painted the sets himself. He wrote the play and taught us our parts, our couplets, and our gestures. He took on the role of prompter; Deschartres with his flute officiated as the orchestra. We ascertained that I had not forgotten the Spanish bolero, although I had not been made to dance it for almost three years. The ballet part, therefore, was completely left to me, and it was all a marvelous success. The play was neither long nor complicated. It was an occasional piece of the simplest kind, and the dénouement was the presentation of a huge bouquet to "Marie." Hippolyte, being the oldest and most knowledgeable, had the longest declamations. But when the author saw that of the three of us Ursule had the best memory and loved to rattle off her role with aplomb, he lengthened her replies and showed our droll little chatterbox in her true colors. This was the best thing in the play. She kept her own nickname, Cacklebeak, and addressed to grandmama a longwinded compliment and a never-ending series of couplets.

I danced my bolero with no less assurance. Shyness and awkwardness had not yet come to me, and I remember becoming impatient with Deschartres, who either from nerves or incompetence, played out of tune and did not keep time, and so I finished the dance with a flourish of improvised entrechats and pirouettes which made my grandmother break out in laughter. That was all that we wanted, for it had been three years since the poor woman had even smiled. But all of a sudden, as if she had frightened herself, she broke down in tears, and I was hastily dragged from the ramp in the middle of my rapturous choreography and placed on my grandmother's lap, where I received a thousand tear-soaked kisses.

At about the same time, my grandmother began to teach me music. In spite of half-paralyzed fingers and a cracked voice, she still sang wonderfully well, and the two or three chords she could still play to accompany herself were of such fortuitous and expansive harmony, that when she locked herself in her room to reread some old opera scores, in private, and let me stay with her, I was in true ecstasy. I sat on the floor under the old harpsichord, where Brillant, her favorite dog, let me share a corner of the carpet, and I would have spent the rest of my life there, so charmed was I by that quavering voice and the shrill sound of the old spinet. This was because, in spite of the infirmities of the voice and the instrument, the beautiful music was admirably understood and felt. I have heard much singing since then by magnificent voices, but I must say I have never heard better. She had known a great deal of music of the masters, and she had met Glück and Piccini, toward whom she had remained impartial, saying that each had his merits and that one must not compare them but rather appreciate each for his individual qualities; she still knew by heart fragments of Leo, Hasse, and Durante, which I have never heard anyone sing but her, and which I could not even name but would recognize if I heard them again.[58] They were simple and grand in conception, calm and classical in form. She was even able to discern the weaknesses in what was in fashion when she was young, and she never liked what we today call *rococo*. Her taste was pure, rigorous, and serious.

She taught me the principles of harmony, and so clearly that I never felt overwhelmed. Later on, when I had teachers, I no longer understood anything at all and lost my taste for the subject, thinking I had no aptitude for it. But since then I have come to the conclusion it was the teachers' fault, and that if I had been taught only and always by my grandmother, I would have been a musician; for I was temperamentally suited to be one, and I understand the beauty of music, which affects and transports me more than that of any other art form.   *A.C.*

XVI

Mme. de Genlis. —*Les Battuécas*. —Fairy-tale kings and queens. —The green fire screen. —The grotto and the waterfall. —The old château. —First separation from my mother. —Catherine. —The fear my grandmother's age and imposing manner caused me.

My little brain was always filled with poetry, and the books I read kept me breathless in this respect. Berquin, that old companion of children, who I believe is overrated, never excited me. Sometimes my mother read us aloud passages from a story by Mme. de Genlis, that fine lady who has been underrated, and who had real talent. Her prejudices, her often bogus moralizing, her seeming lack of personal resolve between the old and new worlds—what difference do they make today? Considering the limitations that hampered her, she painted as broadly as possible. She must have been a truly excellent person, and certain of her novels take a very liberal view of the future. Her imagination has remained fresh under the ice layers of time, and in her treatment of detail she was a true artist and poet.

There is extant a novel of hers, published under the Restoration, one of the last she wrote, I think, which I have never heard mentioned since that time. I was sixteen or seventeen when I read it, and I cannot say whether it was successful. I do not remember it well, but it made a vivid impression and had a lifelong effect on me. It is an eminently socialist novel entitled *Les Battuécas*. The Battuécas are a small tribe, real or imagined, who live in a Spanish valley encircled by inaccessible mountains. As a result of some devastating event or other, this tribe has withdrawn by choice to a place that offers them all imaginable natural resources, where they perpetuate themselves for several centuries without any contact with outside civilization. They form a small pastoral republic, governed by laws of a naïve idealism, where people are inevitably virtuous. The result is a golden age, in all its happiness and poetry. A young man whose name I have forgotten, and who has lived there in all the simplicity of primitive mores, one day accidentally discovers the forgotten path that leads to the modern world. He ventures forth, leaves the sweet retreat, and there he is, launched into our civilization, with the candor and directness of his native logic. He sees palaces, armies, theaters, works of art, a royal court, worldly women, scholars, famous men; his astonishment, his admiration border on delirium. But he also sees beggars, abandoned orphans, wounds displayed at the doors of churches, starvelings at the doors of the rich. He is even more astounded. One day he takes a loaf of bread from a bakery shelf and gives it to a poor, weeping woman with a pale, dying child in her arms, only to be threatened and treated as a thief. His friends scold him and try to explain what property is. He does not understand. A beautiful lady seduces him. She wears artificial flowers in her hair, flowers which he mistakes for real ones, and he is baffled by their lack of scent. When they explain to him that these are not flowers, he grows fearful of that woman who seemed so beautiful to him, afraid that she too might be artificial.

I no longer remember his many disappointments as he discovers lies and quackery, conventionality and injustice everywhere. What we have here is a Voltaire's Candide or Huron, only more naïvely conceived. It is an innocent work, sincere, without rancor, whose details convey an infinitude of poetry. I believe the young Battuéca returns to his valley and recovers his virtue without recovering his happiness, for he has drunk from the poisoned cup of our century. I would not want to reread this book, for fear of not finding it as charming as I did then.

As far as I recall, Mme. de Genlis draws no bold conclusions; she does not wish to fault society, and in certain respects she is right to accept humanity for what it has become through the very laws of its progress. But it seems to me that, in general, the arguments she puts into the mouth of a kind of mentor whom she has accompany her hero on his inspection of the modern world are rather weak. I used to read them without pleasure or conviction, but it can be assumed that at age sixteen, just out of the convent and still under the sway of Catholic doctrine, I had taken no stand against established society. The naïve reasoning of the Battuécas, on the other hand, delighted me. Bizarre as it seems, I may owe my first socialist and democratic instincts to Mme. de Genlis, tutor and friend of Louis-Philippe.

No, I am wrong. I owe them to my unusual circumstances: to my birth, which straddles, so to speak, two classes; to my love for my mother, a love thwarted and bruised by prejudices which caused me much suffering before I could understand them. I owe them also to my education, which was by turns enlightened and religious, and to all the contrasts my own life proffered me from the tenderest age. I therefore was a democrat not only because my mother's blood flowed in my veins, but also because of the upheavals this blood of the people caused in my heart and in my existence, and if books could affect me, it was only because their leanings confirmed and sanctioned my own.

However, nobility in fairy tales delighted me for a long time. This was because in my childhood dreams princes and princesses embodied civility, goodness, and beauty. I loved their adornments and riches, which were all gifts from the fairies, and those kings had nothing in common with real kings. Besides, the evil spirits treated them most cavalierly if they misbehaved, and in this respect they were subject to a sterner justice than that of nations.

Fairies and spirits! Where were they, those all-powerful beings, who with a stroke of their wands, admitted you into a world of wonder? My mother would never tell me that they did not exist, for which I am now infinitely grateful. My grandmother would not have beaten about the bush, if I had dared ask her such questions. Brimful of Jean-Jacques and Voltaire, she would have destroyed the enchanted edifice of my imaginings without remorse or pity. My mother proceeded differently. She would neither confirm nor deny anything. The way she saw it, reason would prevail soon enough, and I was already beginning to suspect that my daydreams would never materialize; but if the door of hope no longer stood wide open as it had in my earliest days, it was not yet completed closed; I was permitted to ferret around and try to find a little crack to see through. At any rate, I could still dream with my eyes open, and that I did in good measure.

I remember that on winter evenings my mother would sometimes read us some Berquin, sometimes from the *Veillées du château* by Mme. de Genlis, and sometimes passages from other books within our grasp, whose names I no longer recall. At first I would listen attentively. I was seated at my mother's feet, in front of the fire, and between me and the hearth stood an old four-legged screen lined with green taffeta. I could see a little of the fire through the worn taffeta; it produced little stars on the fabric, whose glow I could augment by squinting. Then, little by little, I lost the thread of the sentences my mother was reading; her voice cast me into a state of mental drowsiness that made it impossible to pursue one thought. Images took shape before my eyes and settled on the green fire screen. There were forests, meadows, rivers, cities of strange and gigantic architecture of the kind I still often see in my dreams; enchanted palaces with gardens the likes of which do not exist, with thousands of blue and gold and crimson birds that hovered above the flowers and could be caught as easily as one might pluck a rose. There were green roses, black roses, purple roses, and especially blue roses. It seems that the blue rose was one of Balzac's dreams for a long time. It was mine, too, when I was a child, for children and poets alike are in love with the unreal. I could also see groves bathed in light, spraying fountains, mysterious deeps, Chinese bridges, trees laden with fruit of gold and precious gems. In short, my entire fantastic fairy world was manifest, tangible, and I lost myself in it with relish. Closing my eyes, I continued to see it, but when I reopened them, it was only on the screen that I could recover it. I do not know what trick of my brain had fastened the vision there rather than elsewhere, but I surely contemplated unheard-of wonders on that green fire screen. Once, these apparitions became so real that I was actually frightened, and I asked my mother if she didn't see them too. I insisted there were big blue mountains on the screen, and she shook me on her knees while singing, to bring me back to myself. Perhaps it was to give some healthful sustenance to my overwrought imagination that she invented a childish creation of her own, which I found charming and which enthralled me for a long time. This is what it was.

There is a little woods on our property, where hornbeams, maples, ashes, lindens, and lilacs grow. My mother chose a place where a winding walk led to a sort of impasse. With the help of Hippolyte, Ursule, myself, and my nurse, she cut a small path through the thicket, which in those days was very dense. We edged the path with violets, primroses, and periwinkles, which have since proliferated to the point of invading almost the entire woods. The impasse thus became a little nest, with a bench placed beneath the lilacs and hawthorns, and we would go there to study and practice our lessons when the weather was good. My mother took her needlework along, while Ursule and I brought our games, especially our stones and bricks for building houses, and she and I would give these edifices pompous names. There was the Château of the Fairy, the Palace of Sleeping Beauty, etc. Realizing that these primitive constructions fell far short of what we imagined, my mother one day put aside her work and joined us. "Take that ugly limestone and broken brick out of my sight," she said. "Go find me some stones nicely covered with moss, some pink pebbles and some green ones, some shells, and be sure they're all very pretty, or else I'll go back to minding my own business."

Our imaginations were fired instantly. The point was to bring back nothing but pretty things, and we set out to find all those treasures we had until then blindly been trampling underfoot. How hotly Ursule and I debated if this moss was velvety enough, if that stone was fortuitously shaped, or if these pebbles were sufficiently shiny! At first, everything seemed good to us, but soon we began to compare, were struck by the differences, and little by little, nothing seemed worthy of our new construction. The nurse had to take us to the river to find those beautiful pebbles that sparkled like emerald, lapis, and coral beneath the quick and shallow waters. But once dislodged from their bed, they lost their vivid colors as they dried, leaving us disappointed once again. We would plunge them back into the water hundreds of times to make them shine afresh. There were in our terrain superb quartz, a quantity of ammonite, and antedeluvian stone formations of great beauty and variety. We had never paid attention to all that, but now the smallest object became a surprise, a discovery, a conquest.

There was a donkey that belonged to the house, the best donkey that I ever met; I do not know whether he had been as mean as the rest of his fellows when he was young, but he was old now, very old; he was no longer capricious and resentful. He had a grave and measured gait. Respected because of his old age and good service, he was never punished or reprimanded, and if he was the most blameless of donkeys, it can also be said that he was the happiest and most appreciated. Ursule and I, each placed in one of his hampers, used to travel on his flanks, and it never occurred to him to shake us off. When we returned from the outing, the donkey regained his customary freedom, for he knew neither leash nor rack. Left absolutely on his own, he always roamed about the village, the courtyards, and the grassy parts of the garden, never committing a misdeed, and helping himself to all things with discretion. He often had an urge to enter the house, the dining room, or even the apartment of my grandmother, who found him one day in her dressing room, his nose over a box of iris powder, which he sniffed with a serious and introspective mien. He even had learned to open the doors, which, in former country style, were only latched, and as he knew the ground floor perfectly well, he always went looking for my grandmother, from whom he was sure to receive some dainties. He did not mind being the butt of our laughter; untroubled by taunts, he looked like a philosopher who knew his own mind. His only weakness was the idle boredom that comes with solitude. One night, having found the scullery door open, he climbed the seven or eight steps, crossed the kitchen and the vestibule, unlatched the doors of two or three more rooms, and reached the door of my grandmother's bedroom, but finding it bolted, he started to scrape with his foot to make his presence known. Puzzled by the sound and believing a thief was trying to force the door, my grandmother rang for her chambermaid, who came running in the dark, reached the door, and fell over the donkey, screaming.

But I am digressing. Let me come back to our outings. We took charge of the donkey, and every day, in his baskets, he brought us a load of stones for our building. My mother selected the most beautiful, or the most unusual, and when the materials were gathered, she began to build before our eyes, with her strong, little, diligent hands, not a house, not a château, but a rockwork grotto.

A grotto! We had never heard of such a thing. Our grotto barely reached a height of four or five feet, and two or three in depth. But size means nothing to children, who have the gift of seeing on a grand scale, and as our work went on for several days, during those several days we believed our rockwork would rise to the clouds. By the time it was finished, it had reached, in our mind, the proportions we imagined. To this day I have to remind myself that I could reach the top when I climbed on the stones at the base, and I have to go back and look at the small site it occupied—which is still there—if I am to convince myself that it was not a mountain cavern.

Regardless, it was very pretty; I shall never be able to make myself believe otherwise. It was built of the choicest pebbles in a mixture of bright hues; of stones covered with fine, silky mosses; of superb shells, festooned with ivy on top and with grass all around. But that was not enough. It still needed a spring and a waterfall, for a grotto without quick waters is a body without a soul. To be sure, there was not the slightest trickle of water in the entire thicket. But such a minor detail did not faze my mother. A large washbowl with an enameled green bottom was buried to its rim inside the grotto, edged with plants and flowers to hide the crockery, and filled with limpid water, which we took great care to change every day. "But the waterfall?" we would ardently ask. "Tomorrow you shall have your waterfall," said my mother, "but you mustn't come near the grotto until you are called; for this requires the help of a fairy, and your curiosity might put her off."

We obeyed religiously, and at the appointed hour, my mother came to fetch us. She led us down the path facing the grotto, forbade us to look behind it, and having given me a wand, clapped her hands three times, instructing me simultaneously to strike my wand at the center of the grotto, which now had an orifice sprouting a pipe made out of an elder branch. At the third stroke, water rushing down the pipe spilled forth so profusely that Ursule and I, to our great satisfaction, were drenched and deliriously screaming with joy. For the next two or three minutes, the falls formed a crystal sheet of water as they fell from a height of two feet into the makeshift pool of the washbowl. Then they stopped—after my nurse, hidden behind the grotto, had emptied a jug of water into the pipe, and the "waves" lapping over the rim of the basin had copiously watered the flowers we had planted at its edges. Hence the illusion was short-lived, but it had been perfect and delightful, and I doubt that I experienced greater surprise or admiration when I later saw the great cataracts of the Alps and Pyrenees.

When the grotto had reached its highest degree of perfection, we went to my grandmother, who had not yet seen it. We solemnly asked her to do us the honor of a visit to the thicket, and we prepared everything to surprise her with our waterfall. We fancied she would be enchanted, but whether she found the thing too amateurish, or whether she was ill-disposed to my mother that day, instead of admiring our masterpiece, she ridiculed us; the washbowl simulating a pool (we had even stocked it with little fish, as a welcoming gesture) earned us derision rather than praise. I, for one, was dismayed, for nothing in the world was more beautiful in my eyes than our magic grotto, and I genuinely suffered when someone was bent on ridding me of an illusion.

Our outings on the donkey always put us in a joyous mood. Every Sunday, we would ride to mass on our patriarch of asses, and we took along our lunch, to be eaten after mass in the ancient château of Saint-Chartier, next to the church. The guardian of this château was an old woman who let us into the vast, abandoned halls of the ancient manor, where my mother liked to spend part of the day. What struck me most was the weird appearance of the old woman who, though of ordinary peasant stock, ignored that it was Sunday and went on spinning as busily as on any other day of the week, disregarding the fact that Sunday rest is one of the most rigorously observed customs of our peasants in the Vallée Noire. Maybe the old woman had been in the service of some Voltairian and enlightened village lord, who knows?

I have forgotten her name, but not the imposing aspect of the château, a look it was to preserve for many years to come. It was an awe-inspiring manor house, quite intact and perfectly habitable, although stripped of all furniture. It had immense halls, colossal chimneys, and oubliettes which I remember well. It was a château famous in the country's history. It used to be the mightiest in the province, and for a long time served as residence of the princes of Lower Berry. Philippe-Auguste besieged it in person; it later was occupied by the English, then reconquered during the wars of Charles VII. It formed a large square flanked by four enormous towers. Its owner, tired of having to maintain it, wanted to level it and sell the materials. He succeeded in removing the woodwork and tearing down all the inner partitions and walls. But he could not make a dent in the towers, which were of Roman concrete, and the chimney stacks were impossible to uproot. They are still standing, their long shafts raised forty feet in the air, and never once in thirty years have tempests or frosts loosened as much as a single brick. In short, it is a magnificent ruin, ready to brave weather and mankind alike for many more centuries. Its foundations were built by the Romans; the main body of the structure dated from early feudal times.

It meant quite a trip for us to go to Saint-Chartier. In those days the roads were impassable for nine months of the year. You had to use the meadow paths or take your chances with the poor donkey, who more than once got stuck with his cargo in the loamy ground. Today we can get there in less than fifteen minutes, on a splendid road bordered by beautiful trees. But the château made a much more vivid impression on me when it took greater effort to get there.

The family business got settled at last, and my mother signed the agreement to leave me to my grandmother, who was determined to take charge of my education. I had shown such intense repugnance for this settlement that once it was reached, nobody cared to mention it to me again. The understanding was that I should be detached from my mother gradually, without realizing it, and to begin with, she went to Paris alone, impatient as she was to see Caroline again.

I felt neither too apprehensive nor too distressed, for I was to go to Paris with my grandmother two weeks later; I could even watch the carriage being readied and the luggage packed. I was told that, once in Paris, I would live very close to my dear mama and would see her every day. Nevertheless, I felt a terror of sorts when I found myself without her in this house, which now began to appear as huge as it had in the first days I spent there. I also had to be separated from my nursemaid, whom I loved dearly, but who was about to get married. She was a peasant woman my mother had hired after my father's death to replace the Spanish Cecilia. This excellent woman is still alive and often comes to see me, bringing me some of the fruit from her sorb, a tree that is rare in our terrain but can thrive in hers to reach enormous proportions. Catherine's sorb tree is her pride and joy; she speaks of it like the cicerone of a splendid monument. She has raised a large family and has had the consequent misfortunes. I have often had the chance to do her a favor; it brings happiness to attend the old age of a person who watched over us when we were children. Nobody in the world was gentler to me than Catherine, nor as patient. She tolerated, even innocently admired all my pranks. She spoiled me horribly, but I do not regret it, for my maids would not spoil me for a long time to come, and I had to atone soon enough for the tolerance and tenderness I had received without sensing its worth.

She wept when she left me, even though it was for an excellent husband, a handsome man, very upright, intelligent, and rich to boot—far better company than a whining, moody child; but the lass had a good, uncalculating heart, and her tears gave me a first inkling of what it means to miss someone. "Why are you crying?" I asked her. "Surely we will go on seeing each other!" "Yes," said she, "but I'm going a pretty long half-league away from here, and we won't be seeing each other every day."

This gave me pause, and I began to fret over my mother's absence. Though it was a question of only a fortnight's separation from her then, I remember those two weeks more distinctly than the preceding three years, or perhaps even the three following years, when my mother was still with me. Which goes to show that only pain can teach a child what life is about.

However, nothing remarkable happened in those two weeks. Noticing my melancholy mood, my grandmother undertook to distract me with work. She gave me lessons, proving herself much more indulgent than my mother ever was with regard to my handwriting or to the fables I was to recite. No more reprimands, no more punishments. She had always been sparing of them, and wanting to be loved, she gave me more praise, encouragement, and candies than usual. All of which should have seemed sweet to me, for my mother was rigid and without mercy for my lazy ways and absent-mindedness. But a child's heart is a world unto itself and already quite as strange and inconsistent as that of an adult. I found my grandmother more fearsome and severe in her sweet composure than my mother in her fits of anger. Until then, I had loved my grandmother, showing her my trust and affection. From that moment on, and for quite a long time thereafter, her presence made me cold and reserved. Her caresses embarrassed me or made me want to cry, because they reminded me of the more passionate hugs of my dear little mother. Moreover, I did not share with her all my moments, and there was no continuous, expansive familiarity. She commanded respect, and I found it chilling. If my mother caused me terror at times, it was never more than a painful moment to live through. The next minute I was on her lap, against her bosom, addressing her by the intimate *tu* and *toi*, while with my grandmother the caresses were ceremonial, so to speak. Her solemn embraces were rather like rewards for good behavior. Anxious to teach me manners and rid me of the incorrigible carelessness that was part of my nature and that had never consistently been repressed by my mother, she failed to treat me sufficiently like a child. No longer was I to romp on the floor, laugh noisily, or talk Berrichon. I had to hold myself erect, wear gloves, keep silent, or whisper quietly in a corner with little Ursule. Gently but unfailingly, she repressed every spontaneous impulse of my being. She did not scold, but she addressed me as *vous*, and that said it all. "Dear girl, you sit like a hunchback; dear girl, you walk like a peasant; dear girl, you have lost your gloves again! dear girl, you are too big for such things." Too big! I was seven years old, and no one had every told me I was big. It frightened me terribly that I had grown up so suddenly since my mother's departure. Moreover, I had to learn all sorts of seemingly ridiculous manners. I had to curtsy to people who came to visit. I no longer was to set foot in the kitchen, nor address the servants as *tu* and *toi*, so that they in turn would lose their habitual familiarity with me. Likewise, I was not to use *tu* and *toi* when speaking with my grandmother. I was not even to address her as *vous*. I was to speak to her in the third person: "Will dear grandmama permit me to go into the garden?"

She was certainly right, the excellent woman, to instill in me a healthy respect for her person and for society's code of grand manners she so wished to impose on me. She took possession of me knowing she was dealing with a fretful, intractable child. She had seen how vigorously my mother dealt with me, and she thought that by subjugating rather than correcting me, my mother was only exacerbating my sensibilities, instead of curbing my morbid fits of temper. Which is probably true. A child whose nervous system is sorely off balance returns all the more quickly to her impetuous ways, if she is upset from having been subdued too abruptly. My grandmother was well aware that by being constantly subjected to her calm observations, I would give in so completely, without struggle or tears, to an instinctive obedience, that the very idea of resisting her would become unthinkable. Indeed, she accomplished this goal in a matter of days. I had never dreamed of rebelling against her, but until then, I rarely had refrained from rebelling against others in her presence. From the moment she took me in hand, I felt I would incur her displeasure if I misbehaved in front of her, and her displeasure, expressed so politely but icily, chilled me to the marrow. I did such violence to my instincts that I would tremble convulsively, which worried her without her understanding it.

She had achieved her purpose, which was above all to render me tractable, and she was astonished by her prompt success. "Look at her," she would say, "how sweet and nice she is!" She congratulated herself on having had so little trouble transforming me by methods so completely opposed to those of my poor mother, by turns my tyrant and my slave.

But my dear grandmama had a bigger surprise coming. She wished to be piously respected and, at the same time, fervently loved. She remembered her son's childhood and deluded herself that she could relive it with me. Alas! This was not up to either of us. She misjudged the extent of the enormous distance in age two generations put between us. Nature makes no mistakes, and notwithstanding the infinite kindness and boundless generosity of the way my grandmother raised me, I do not hesitate to say that an aging and invalid forebear can never be a mother; nature is insulted at every turn when an old woman takes absolute charge of a young child. God knows what He is doing when He inhibits the powers of motherhood at a certain age. A little being at the dawn of life needs a young person in full bloom. My grandmother's gravity afflicted my soul. Her somber, scented chamber gave me migraine headaches and spasmodic yawns. She feared the heat and the cold, every draft, every ray of sunlight. I had the impression I was being locked into a box with her when she said, "Have fun quietly." She would give me engravings to look at, and I felt too dizzy to see them. A dog barking outside or a bird singing in the garden made me tremble. I would like to have been the dog or the bird. And when I was in the garden with her, the sense of duty she already had instilled in me chained me to her side without her having to exert any constraint. She walked with difficulty, and I was always near, ready to retrieve the snuffbox or glove which she so often dropped but could not bend to pick up. I have never seen a weaker, less able body, but as she was, at the same time, well fed, well rested, and by no means ill, her difficulty of movement exasperated me inwardly to the utmost. I had seen my mother hundreds of times overcome by violent migraines, prostrate on her bed like a corpse, her cheeks pale, her teeth set; it filled me with despair, but the paralytic languor of my grandmother was beyond me and sometimes seemed intentional. At bottom, there surely was a little bit of self-infliction, which was the fault of her earliest upbringing. She, too, had lived too locked up in a box, and her blood had lost its energy to circulate. When her blood was to be let, it was impossible to draw a drop, so sluggishly did it flow in her veins. I was terribly afraid of becoming like her, and when told not to be loud and boisterous in her presence, it felt like an order to be dead.

In fact, all my instincts rebelled against my grandmother's very different constitution, and I did not truly love her until I was old enough to reason. Until then, I admit to feeling for her lofty admiration coupled with invincible physical dislike. Of course, she noticed my coldness, poor woman, and endeavored to conquer it with reproaches, which only made it worse, for they made me aware of a feeling I had not come to terms with. She really suffered, and I perhaps even more, without knowing what to do about it. Finally, as my mind developed, I had a great change of heart, and she admitted that she had been wrong to think me ungrateful and stubborn.   *U.K.*

Part III

From Childhood to Youth
1810 to 1819

I

Trip to Paris. —The four-wheeled berlin. —The Sologne. —The
Forest of Orléans and the hanged. —My grandmother's apartment in
Paris. —Promenading with my mother. —My Chinese hair-do. —My
sister. —First case of violent upset. —The Negro doll. —Being ill
and hallucinating while delirious.

I believe we left for Paris at the beginning of the winter of 1810–1811,
because it was during my first sojourn at Nohant that Napoléon had conquered
Vienna and married Marie-Louise. I recall the two spots in the garden where I
heard my family discuss both pieces of news. I said goodbye to Ursule; the
poor child was devastated, but I would see her again on my return; besides, I
was so happy at the idea of visiting my mother that I was almost insensitive to
anything else. I had experienced my first separation and was beginning to
develop a concept of time. I had counted the days and hours that had elapsed
far from the object of my love. I also loved Hippolyte, in spite of his mischief.
He, too, cried at the thought of being left alone for the first time in that big
house. I pitied him and would have wished that he be brought along, but all in
all, I had tears for no one. Only my mother was on my mind, and my grandmother, who spent her life studying me, whispered to Deschartres (children
hear everything), "This child is not as sensitive as I would have thought."

At that time it took three whole days, sometimes four, to get to Paris.
Furthermore, my grandmother travelled in stages. But she could not spend the
night in the carriage, and when her big berlin had covered twenty-five leagues
in a day, she was exhausted. This coach was a virtual house on wheels. You
must remember how many little items, packets, and conveniences of all kinds
old people, especially the more refined ones, burdened themselves with while
travelling. The countless pouches of this vehicle were filled with a supply of
food, delicacies, fragrances, playing cards, books, itineraries, money, and Lord
knows what else. You would have thought we were embarking for a month.
My grandmother and her chambermaid, ensconced in coverlets and pillows,
were stretched out in the back. I occupied the front seat, and although I was
quite comfortable there, I had trouble containing my exuberance in such a little
space and not kicking whatever was facing me. Life at Nohant had made me
quite boisterous; also I was beginning to feel perfectly healthy. But soon
enough I would become more peaked and less lively in the Paris air, which has
never agreed with me.

However, the journey did not weary me. For the first time the rolling movement of the carriage did not overwhelm me with drowsiness, which usually happens to young children, and the succession of new objects kept my eyes wide open and my mind alert.

Nonetheless, there is nothing sadder and more gloomy than the route from Châteauroux to Orléans. One must go through all of the Sologne, an arid land without grandeur or poetry. And yet Eugène Sue[1] has praised for us the uncultivated beauty and savage grace of this part of France. Since I have heard him speak of the Sologne in the same way he wrote about it, I am sure his admiration is sincere. But whether the parts of the country one discovers from the road are particularly ugly, or whether an absolutely flat countryside is naturally abhorrent to me, the Sologne—which I have passed through perhaps a hundred times, at all hours of the day and night and in all seasons of the year—has always seemed to me deadly dull and ordinary. What grows wild is as sparse as what is cultivated. The pine forests, which are beginning to grow, are still too young to have any character. They are like splashes of garish green on a colorless ground. The earth is pale; the heather, the bark of the stunted trees, the bushes, the animals, the people especially are pale even to livid—a vast wasteland withering away noxiously in a sort of moral and physical marasmus of man and nature.

The poets and painters usually stand above such considerations, reveling as they do in desolation, which in certain other regions furnishes them with enchanting vistas and retreats. But in isolated places which are also beautiful we need to be reminded of the poverty of those who stagnate there instead of thriving, so that we wish civilization and culture might arrive even at the cost of destroying the poetry. However, the wicked thought of sacrificing the people to their beautiful natural habitat never occurred to me in the Sologne. In the Creuse, I have seen magnificent heathland, vast rolling stretches rich in wild vegetation, strewn with pools of clear water and groves of ancient trees. But the Sologne offers nothing of the kind, at least not in the region my eyes have embraced so many times over an expanse of twenty leagues. Everything there is small and colorless, except for the wide horizon and sky, dependably beautiful and bright.

This difference between the Sologne and the other wastelands I have seen indeed proves something. Nature never gives up when it is fertile, and since the wilderness of the Creuse grows such majestic trees, such lovely heather, and nourishes such healthy livestock, the soil there must be excellent and would produce plentiful crops with little expenditure; whereas the Sologne would require considerable time and cost before it yielded even mediocre returns. Less fertile than the Creuse, the Brenne is still quite superior to the Sologne, and where farmers are not fooled, poets and painters see very clearly. When nature directs their vision to render the colors and outer beauties of a landscape, fecundity and life are sure to abound in the heart of the land. That fecundity is revealed through the growth of parasitic plants—a richness without purpose—just as a character generous in humanity is, when deprived of direction, revealed even in its errant ways. In narrow minds, however, vice itself is neglected, as in the Sologne, where even the ferns and thistle languish.

Let all this be said, however, without prejudice to Eugène Sue, who must know a Sologne other than the one that I have passed through.

Crossing the Forest of Orléans today is no great event, but in my youth it was impressive and fearsome. Large trees still darkened the way for a two-hour stretch, and carriages were often held up there by robbers, a necessary complement for the full emotional experience of a journey. We had to hasten the postilions in order to arrive before nightfall, but no matter how diligent our efforts during this first trip with my grandmother, we landed there in the middle of the night. She did not frighten easily, and when all necessary precautions had been taken, if her efforts were thwarted by some unforeseen circumstance, then she resigned herself admirably to the situation. The chambermaid was not quite as calm, but she was careful not to let it show; and the two of them discussed their apprehensions very philosophically. For some reason, the idea of robbers didn't frighten me in the least, but I was suddenly seized by a violent terror when I overheard my grandmother tell Mlle. Julie this story:

"Now, robberies are uncommon here, and the woods have been pruned along the roadside, not like the way it was before the Revolution. Then, there-was a dense thicket and very few ditches, so that you were attacked without knowing by whom and without having time to put up a defense. I was lucky enough never to have that happen during my trips to Châteauroux. But Monsieur Dupin was always armed to the teeth, as were his servants, when crossing this alley of cutthroats. Robberies and murders were very common, and the authorities had an unusual way of keeping a count and calling attention to them. When the robbers were caught, tried, and found guilty, they were hung from the trees along the way, at the very spot where they had committed the crime; so that from each side of the road, at fairly close intervals, you could see cadavers hung from overhead branches swinging in the breeze. If you frequented the route, you got to know all of the hanged, and each year you could reckon up the new ones, which proves that the reminder was of little use. One winter, I remember having seen a big woman, whose body remained intact for a long time and whose long, black hair fluttered in the wind while the circling crows fought over her flesh. The spectacle was hideous, and the stench followed you all the way to the city gates."

Maybe my grandmother thought I was sleeping during this morbid recital. I was in fact mute with terror, and a cold sweat ran down my limbs. It was the first time that death came to me as a frightening image; that was not instinctive in my case, as the reader may have noticed; I personally have never worried about the shape death might take when it came looking for me. But the hanged, the trees, the crows, the black hair—all those horrible images passing through my mind made my teeth chatter. I never imagined for a moment that we might be attacked, let alone killed, in the woods, but I did see those bodies floating in the branches of the old oak trees, and I pictured them in my mind with the most appalling features. This terror stayed with me for a very long time, and whenever we would cross the forest, up to the age of fifteen or sixteen, it came back to me just as vivid and frightening as the first time—so true is it that feelings based on reality are nothing compared to those the imagination inspires in us.

We arrived in Paris, at a lovely apartment on Rue Neuve-des-Mathurins, overlooking vast gardens across the way, which our windows revealed to us in their entirety. My grandmother's apartment was furnished as it had been before the Revolution, with what she had saved from the wreckage, and it was all still in very good condition and very comfortable. The walls of her room and her furnishings were covered in sky-blue damask; there were rugs everywhere, and a roaring fire in every fireplace.

I had never been so well housed, and all these examples of well-being, which were much less in evidence at Nohant, were a cause for my amazement. I, who had been raised in a poor wooden and tiled room on Rue Grange-Batelière, had no need of all that, and I didn't revel at all in those comforts, which my grandmother would have liked me to appreciate. I only lived, I only smiled when my mother was near me. She would come every day, and my anticipation grew with each visit. I would cover her with kisses, and the poor woman, seeing that it made my grandmother suffer, had to restrain me and herself from too obvious shows of affection. We were, by necessity, allowed to go out together, although that hardly coincided with my grandmother's aim of separating me from her. My grandmother never went anywhere on foot, nor could she do without Mlle. Julie's assistance, who was absentminded, near-sighted, and not very nimble; she would have lost me in the streets or let me get crushed by the carriage traffic. Hence I would never have gotten to walk, if my mother had not taken me with her every day on long outings; and though my legs were quite short, I would have walked to the ends of the earth to have the pleasure of holding her hand, touching her dress, and looking at the things she would tell me to look at. All seemed beautiful to me through her eyes. The boulevards were scenes of enchantment: the Chinese baths, with their tasteless grottos and foolish porcelain figures became a fairy-tale palace; the trained dogs that danced in the street, the little shops with toys, the print merchants, and the bird sellers had the wherewithal to make a child lose her mind; and my mother, who would stop before everything that caught my eye, would partake of my pleasure—child that she herself was—and double my joy in sharing it.

My grandmother had a more enlightened sense of discernment and a great natural detachment. She wished to form my taste and so focused her judicious criticism on all the objects which impressed me. She would point out a badly drawn figure, an assemblage of colors that offended the eye, a composition in language, or music, or clothing that was in bad taste. I could only understand this over time. My mother, less demanding and more naïve, was in more direct contact with my impressions. Almost all the products of art and industry pleased her, provided they had cheerful shapes and bright colors, and what did not please her amused her nonetheless. She had a passion for novelty, and every new style seemed to her the most beautiful she had ever seen. Everything suited her; nothing could make her look ugly or ungainly, despite the criticism of my grandmother, who was sensible enough to remain faithful to the long, fitted waist and full skirt of the Directoire.

In love with the current fashions, my mother was vexed to see my grandmother dress me like a little old lady. My quilted frocks had been cut down from the slightly worn but still new ones of my grandmother, so that I was almost always in dark colors, and on my shapeless torso they came down over the hips. That style seemed awful at a time when the waistline had to be just below the armpits. However, it was much more comfortable. My brown hair was beginning to grow full, and hung down to my shoulders, curling naturally at the slight touch of a damp sponge. My mother pestered my grandmama so much that she had to let her take charge of my poor head to do my hair *à la Chinoise*.

It was the most awful hairstyle you could imagine and was certainly invented for a face that had no forehead. They brushed your hair while combing it against the grain until it stood up perpendicular, and then twisted the tail of hair into a bun at the very top of the skull, making the head look like an elliptical ball crowned by a smaller ball of hair. Thus you would look like a brioche or a drinking gourd. Add to this ugliness the torture of having the hair pulled up in the wrong direction; it took a week of frightful pain and sleepless nights before you would perforce be habituated. To keep it in place, the hair was so tightly pulled by a ribbon, that the skin of the forehead was stretched and the corners of the eyes raised like the faces on a Chinese fan.

I blindly submitted to this torture, even though it did not matter to me whether I looked ugly or pretty, followed the fashion or protested its aberrations. My mother wanted it and liked me that way, so I suffered with stoical courage. My grandmama thought I looked awful and was in despair. But she judged it best not to quarrel over such trivialities, since my mother was helping as best she could to subdue my intense feelings for her.

This was seemingly easy in the beginning. My mother would take me out every day and very often dine or spend the evening with me. I was hardly ever away from her except when I slept. However, an occasion when my dear grandmama was truly wrong in my eyes would soon revive my preference for my mother.

Caroline had not seen me since my departure for Spain, and my grandmother had apparently made it an essential condition for my mother to sever permanently any connection between my sister and me. Why this aversion for an innocent child, strictly brought up, who was a model of austerity all her life? I could not and cannot account for it even today. Why was her daughter scorned and rejected when my mother was admitted and accepted into that society? It was simply a prejudice, an unreasonable injustice on the part of a person who did, nevertheless, know how to rise above the prejudices of her class, when she shed some of the less worthy judgments of her heart and mind.

Caroline had been born long before my father had met my mother; my father had treated and loved her like his daughter; good-natured and rational, she had been my first playmate. She was a sweet and pretty child who never had but one fault in my eyes—she was too absolute in her ideas of neatness and piety. I do not see what could have been feared from her contact with me and why I would ever have been ashamed to acknowledge her to society as my sister, unless it was a sin not to be of noble birth and belong, most probably, to the working class. I never knew what rank Caroline's father held in society, although I presume he was of the same humble and obscure condition as my mother. But wasn't I also the daughter of Sophie Delaborde, granddaughter of a bird seller, and great-granddaughter of old Mother Cloquard? How could they aspire to make me forget I too was of plebeian origin, or convince me that a child carried in the same womb was inferior in nature to me because she could not claim to have the King of Poland and Maréchal de Saxe as her paternal ancestors? What stupidity, or rather what utter childishness! And when a mature person of great intelligence behaves so childishly before a child, how much time, effort, and perfection must it take to erase that impression?

My grandmother did manage to do that, and if that impression was never completely erased from my mind, it was nevertheless overcome through the treasures of tenderness she lavished on me. If there had not been some profound reason why I rejected her laborious efforts to make me love her, I would indeed be a monster. So I am forced to say what her failing was originally, and now that I am familiar with the stubbornness of the nobility, the fault does not seem to be hers at all, but seems to rest entirely with the milieu in which she had always lived and from which she could never completely disengage, in spite of her generosity and intellect.

Thus, she insisted that my sister become a stranger to me, and since I had left her when I was four years old, maybe it would have been easy for me to forget her. This might in fact already have occurred, were it not for my mother, who kept mentioning her to me. My affection for Caroline had not fully blossomed before my journey to Spain, and might not have reawakened without the violent efforts to keep us apart and without a little family scene which made a terrible impression on me.

Caroline was about twelve years old. She was in boarding school, and each time she came to see our mother, the girl implored her to take her to my grandmother's to see me, or to have me come to see her. My mother evaded her plea through some excuse or other, not being able or not wanting to explain her incomprehensible exclusion. Indeed, the poor little girl, being totally unaware of it, no longer able to contain her impatience to hug me, and led only by her heart, took advantage of an evening when my mother was dining at my Uncle Beaumont's. She convinced my mother's porter to bring her and arrived at our place full of joy and anticipation. Still, she was a little afraid of that grandmother whom she had never seen, but maybe she thought that she too was dining at my uncle's home, or perhaps Caroline had decided to risk everything to see me.

It was seven or eight in the evening; I was all alone, playing dejectedly on the carpet of the salon, when I heard a flurry of movement in the next room; my maid opened the door slightly, quietly calling my name. My grandmother seemed to be dozing in her armchair, but she was a light sleeper. By the time I tiptoed over to the door to see what was wanted of me, she turned around and asked me sternly, "Where are you going so mysteriously, my child?" "I'm not sure, mama. My maid is calling me." "Come in, Rose, what do you want? Why are you calling my daughter away as if you have some secret from me?" The maid was embarrassed, hesitated, and ended up saying, "Well, Madame, Mademoiselle Caroline is here."

That name so pure and sweet had an extraordinary effect on my grandmother. She believed that my mother was either openly thwarting or determined to deceive her, and that my sister, or the maid, had been clumsy enough to betray the plan. She spoke harshly and curtly, which certainly happened very rarely in her life. "That child must leave immediately," she said, "and she must never appear here again! She knows very well that she must not see my daughter. My daughter does not know her any more, and I do not know her. As for you, Rose, if you ever try to bring her into this house again, you will be dismissed!"

Rose disappeared in terror. I was upset and frightened, almost sorry and repentant to have angered my grandmother, for I was well aware that this emotion was unnatural to her and must have made her suffer greatly. My surprise at seeing her that way prevented me from thinking of Caroline, whom I could hardly recall. But suddenly, after an exchange of whispers behind the door, I heard a stifled but heartrending sob, a cry from the bottom of the soul, which penetrated to the depths of mine and awakened the sibling instinct. My sister Caroline was crying and going off stricken, shattered, humiliated; her rightful pride in herself was crushed, as was her innocent love for me.

At once my sister's image became clear in my memory. I pictured her as she was in Rue Grange-Batelière and at Chaillot—a tall girl, slender, sweet, modest, and obliging; complying with my whims, singing me lullabies at bedtime, or telling me lovely fairy tales. I broke into tears, rushed toward the door, but it was too late. She was gone. The maid was crying too and took me in her arms, begging me to hide my grief from my grandmother, for she could have been scolded. My grandmother called me back and tried to take me on her lap in order to calm me down and reason with me; I resisted, avoided her caresses, and flung myself in a corner, crying, "I want to go back to my mother, I don't want to stay here!"

Then it was Mlle. Julie's turn to try to make me listen to reason. She talked to me about my grandmother, convinced that I was making her sick and refusing to consider her. "You're hurting your grandmama, who loves you, cherishes you, and only lives for you." But I was deaf to everything; I begged for my mother and sister again, with cries of despair. I was so ill and gasping for breath that it did not even occur to anyone to make me say goodnight to my grandmother. I was put to bed, and all night long (I was told), I moaned and sighed in my sleep.

No doubt, my grandmother spent a bad night, too. I have since become so aware of how good and affectionate she was that now I am quite certain it hurt her to feel compelled to hurt others, but her dignity forbade her to let her pain show, and it was through indirect indulgences and treats that she tried to make the hurt vanish.

When I awoke, I found, on top of my bed, a doll which I had craved the day before. I had seen it in a toy shop when out with my mother and, on returning for dinner, had given an elaborate description to my grandmama. It was a little Negro doll, who seemed filled with laughter and whose white teeth and shining eyes lit up her black face. She was round and shapely; she had on a pink crepe dress trimmed with a silver fringe. She had seemed exotic, fantastic, wonderful, and that morning, before I was awake, poor grandmama had sent for her to satisfy my whim and distract me from my suffering. Actually, my first impulse was of intense pleasure. I took the little creature in my arms, smiled at her pretty smile, and held her like a young mother holds her new-born. But as I gazed at her and rocked her against my heart, the memories of the previous night came back to me. I thought of my mother and my sister, of my grandmother's harshness, and threw the doll away from me. But as the poor thing was still smiling, I picked her up again, held her some more, and soaked her with my tears, abandoning myself to an illusion of maternal love which further vividly intensified my aggrieved feelings of filial love. Then, all of a sudden, I felt dizzy; I let the doll fall to the floor and went into spasms of vomiting hideous bile that greatly terrified my maids.

I do not recall what happened for several days. I had a violent case of the measles, with a high fever. I was probably destined to have had it, but the agi-tation and distress hastened the disease, or made it more intense. I was quite dangerously ill, and one night I had a vision which disturbed me very much. A lamp had been left burning in my room; my two maids were sleeping; I had my eyes open and my head was on fire. Yet it struck me that my ideas were quite clear and that my fixed regard of that lamp made me well aware of what it was. A large mushroom had formed on the wick, and the black smoke that rose from it made a quivering shadow on the ceiling. Suddenly the source of light took on a distinct shape, that of a little man who danced in the middle of the flame. He freed himself little by little and started spinning rapidly; the faster he spun, the taller he became, till he was as tall as a real man; then at last he was a giant whose swift steps hit the ground noisily while his wild head of hair swept the ceiling in circles, with the lightness of a bat.

I let out horrendous shrieks, and someone came to reassure me, but that hallucination returned three or four times in succession and lasted almost until daybreak. It is the only time I recall ever having been delirious.   *E.L.C.*

II

Rose and Julie. —My grandmother's maternal diplomacy. —I
rediscover my true home. —The interior of my great uncle's
apartment. —"The eyes alone own." —My great uncle's gourmet
dinners, his snuffboxes. —Mme. de La Marlière. —Mme. de
Pardaillon. —Mme. de Bérenger and her wig. —Mme. de Ferrières
and her lovely arms. —Mme. de Maleteste and her dog. —The
Abbés. —First signs of a talent for observation. —Five generations
at Rue de Gramont. —The children's ball. —Acquired grace. —The
literary reactionaries of our time.

When my fever had gone down and I was no longer obliged to remain in
bed except as a precaution, I overheard Mlles. Julie and Rose quietly discussing my illness and the reasons for it having been so violent.

I must first say that the happiness of my childhood was influenced by
these two people in whose charge I was later left much too much.

Rose had already been my mother's servant while my father was still
alive. Satisfied with her loyalty and other good qualities, having found her
again in Paris unemployed, and wishing to have me looked after by a suitable,
decent woman, my mother persuaded my grandmother to hire her to watch
over me, take me on outings, and keep me occupied. Rose was a tough, energetic, fearless redhead. She was built like a boy, accustomed to straddling a
horse, galloping like a demon, jumping ditches, sometimes falling, knocking
her skull, and letting nothing deter her. For travelling, she was invaluable to
my grandmother, for she forgot nothing, anticipated everything, kept her clog
on the carriage wheel, relieved the postilion if he dropped off, mended the
traces, and would willingly have donned heavy boots and driven the carriage,
if need be. As one can see, she was powerful by nature—a true charioteer from
Brie, where she had been raised in the country.

She was industrious, courageous, clever, as clean as a Dutch maid, out-
spoken, fair-minded, good-hearted, and devoted. But she had a severe defect
which stemmed from her hot-blooded, impetuous nature, which I was later to
become aware of. She was violent and brutal. Because Rose had loved me
from the time she took care of me as an infant, my mother believed she had
provided me with a friend, and in fact Rose did love me dearly, but she was
subject to fits of anger and tyrannical behavior that were bound to oppress me
later on and make my childhood a sort of martyrdom.

However, I have pardoned her completely, and strangely enough, despite my independent nature and the suffering she heaped on me, I have never hated her. This was because she was sincere and basically generous, but especially because she loved and had always loved my mother. Mlle. Julie was just the opposite. She was gentle and polite, never raised her voice, showed angelic patience in all things, but she lacked openness, a type of person I have never been able to tolerate. She was a young woman with a superior mind; that I say without any hesitation. Coming from her little town of La Châtre, without having been taught anything, hardly knowing how to read and write, she had filled her long leisure hours at Nohant by reading every sort of book. At first these were novels, for which all chambermaids have a passion and which makes me often think of her when I write. Then she read books on history, and finally philosophical works. She knew her Voltaire better than my grandmother, and I even saw her with Rousseau's *Contrat social*, which she understood very well. All the best-known memoirs were absorbed and retained by her cold, practical, sober mind. She was as well versed as a seasoned diplomat in all of the court intrigues of Louis XIV and Louis XV, of Catherine the Great, of Marie-Thérèse, and of Frederick the Great. And if anyone had trouble remembering some relationship among the lords of ancient France to the great families of Europe, he need only ask her; she had it all at her fingertips. I don't know if she retained that degree of aptitude and memory into old age, but I knew her as truly erudite in this discipline, and as knowledgeable in several others, although she couldn't spell a word.

I shall have much more to say about her, for she made me suffer a great deal, and her surveillance reports to my grandmother about my behavior caused me more unhappiness than the well-intentioned screams and blows with which Rose assaulted me, but I shall not complain about either one with bitterness. They worked at my physical and moral education as best they could, each according to a system she believed to be superior.

I admit that I particularly disliked Julie because she hated my mother. In this, she believed she was showing her devotion to her mistress; yet she did her more harm than good. In short, our house was divided into two camps—my mother's, represented by Rose, Ursule, and myself; and my grandmother's, represented by Deschartres and Julie.

To their credit, it must be stated that the differences of opinion which existed between my grandmother's maids did not prevent them from living together in great friendship, and that Rose, without ever abandoning her first mistress's defense, always professed devotion and great respect for the second. They took care of my grandmother with perfect zeal until her very last day, when they closed her eyes. I have therefore pardoned them for all the worries and tears they cost me, one through her savage solicitude for my person, the other through the abuse of her influence on my grandmother.

And so, they were in my room speaking in hushed voices, and how many things I learned from them concerning my family that I would have preferred not to learn at such a tender age! That day, Julie was saying: "Look how stupid the little girl is to adore her mother, while her mother doesn't like her at all. She hasn't come to see her once since she fell ill!"

"Her mother," said Rose, "has come every day to see how she's getting on, but she didn't want to come in because she's angry with Madame over Caroline." "That has nothing to do with it," Julie responded. "She could have come to see her daughter without going into Madame's apartment, but she said to Monsieur de Beaumont that she was afraid of catching the measles. She's worried about her own skin."

"You're wrong, Julie," Rose answered. "That's not the reason. It's because she's afraid of carrying the measles back to Caroline. Why should her two girls be sick at the same time? It's quite enough that one is."

This explanation made me feel better and eased my longing to be in my mother's arms. The next day she came up to the door of my room, through which she shouted her greeting. "Go away, mama dear," I called to her. "Don't come in. I don't want Caroline to catch my measles."

"You see," said my mother to someone who was with her. "She really knows me well! She doesn't blame me. No matter what they do or say, they won't stop her from loving me."

It can be seen from these little domestic incidents that my two mothers were surrounded by people who repeated to them everything they heard and who fed their disagreements. My poor childish heart was beginning to feel buffeted by their rivalry. As I was the object of perpetual jealousy and competition, it was impossible for me not to fall prey to suspicion, just as I myself became the victim of the pain I was causing.

When I was well enough to go out, my grandmother bundled me up carefully and took me by carriage to my mother's, where I had not been since my return to Paris. If I am not mistaken, she was living on Rue Duphot at the time. The low-ceilinged rooms were small and dark, sparsely furnished, and the soup pot was bubbling on the stove in the living room. Everything was very clean, without any sign of wealth or prodigality. My mother had been reproached so much for having brought disorder into my father's life, of having made him go into debt, that I am very happy to remember her as economical, almost miserly, with regard to herself.

It was Caroline who greeted us at the door. She seemed as pretty as an angel, with her little turned-up nose. She was taller than I, even considering our age difference; her complexion was not as dark, her features more delicate, and her knowledgeable expression was a bit cold and mocking. Feeling at home, she responded with aplomb to my grandmother's greeting; she kissed me enthusiastically, gave me a thousand hugs while asking a thousand questions, and proudly and calmly offered my grandmama a chair, saying, "Have a seat, Madame Dupin. I'll have someone call mother. She's at the neighbor's." Then, having notified the porter who ran their errands (they did not have a servant), she returned and sat near the fire. She took me on her knees and began again to question and caress me, without paying further attention to the great lady who had so cruelly affronted her.

My grandmother had certainly prepared some appropriate words to say to this child by way of consolation and reassurance. She must have expected to find her timid and frightened, or sulking, and to go through a scene full of tears or reproaches; however, seeing that none of her expectations was fulfilled, I believe she felt somewhat surprised and discomfited, for I noticed that she was taking pinch after pinch of snuff.

My mother came in after a moment. She kissed me passionately and greeted my grandmother with a fiery, withering look, who understood very well that she was going to have to take the bull by the horns. "My daughter," she said with calm and dignity, "when you sent Caroline to me you no doubt misunderstood my intentions with regard to the relationship which must exist between her and Aurore. I never thought to thwart my granddaughter's affections. I shall never oppose her coming to see you or seeing Caroline in your home. So let us make sure, my dear girl, that there be no further misunderstanding in this regard."

She could not possibily have extricated herself more wisely nor with more tact and fairness. She had not always been so equitable in this regard. It is certainly true that she had not wanted to consent, in principle, to my seeing Caroline even in my mother's home, and that my mother had been obliged to promise not to take me home during our outings—a promise which she had faithfully kept. It is also true that, having seen deeper memories and attachments in me than she had realized, my grandmother gave up a nasty and unenforceable resolution. But having made this concession, she retained her right to close her door to a person whose presence she found distasteful. Her skillful, uncomplicated explanation cut short the possibility of recriminations; my mother sensed it, and her anger was dispelled. "Very well, mother," she said. Then they spoke by mutual agreement of other things. My mother had entered with a stormy soul, and as usual was astonished to find that her mother-in-law's supple, polite firmness obliged her to furl her sails and return to port.

After a few moments, my grandmother rose to continue her round of visits, asking my mother to keep me until she returned to pick me up. This was a further concession and thoughtfulness to show that she did not intend to disturb our effusions by watching over them. Pierret arrived in time to escort her to her carriage. My grandmother favored him because of the great devotion he had shown for my father. She would give him a big welcome. Pierret was not at all among those who provoked my mother against her; on the contrary, he had taken it on himself only to calm and help her remain on good terms with her mother-in-law, but he visited the latter rarely. It was too much of a strain for him to go for half-an-hour without lighting his cigar, without making faces, and without uttering after each sentence his favorite oath, "*Sac à papier.*"

What joy I felt at finding myself once again in the bosom of what seemed like my only, my true family! How kind my mother seemed to me, how lovable my sister, how humorous and obliging my friend Pierret. And the little apartment, so shabby and ugly compared to my grandmother's padded cell (my derisive name for it), became for me, instantly, the promised land of my dreams. I explored its corners; I looked lovingly at its least worthy objects—the little alabaster clock, the vases with paper flowers yellowed under their glass cylinder, the chenille pin cushions that Caroline had embroidered at boarding school, even my mother's footwarmer—that proletarian furnishing now banished from elegant usage, which had served as a stool for my first improvisations on Rue Grange-Batelière. How I loved all of it! I never tired of saying, "Here, I am at home. There, I'm at grandmama's." Pierret would exclaim, "*Sac á papier*! She'd better not go around saying 'at home' in front of Madame Dupin. We'd be reproached for having taught her to speak the way they do at the markets!" And Pierret would burst out laughing, for he was ready to laugh on all accounts, and my mother would tease him, and I would cry out, "At home we really have fun!'"

Caroline would make "pigeons" for me with her fingers; or, using a piece of string that we passed and crossed over each other's fingers, she would teach me all the configurations and combinations of lines that children call "bed," "boat," "scissors," "saw," etc. My grandmother's lovely dolls and handsome picture books seemed as nothing compared to those games which recalled my childhood; for though still a child, I had already had a childhood, a past that had left behind memories and longings, a completed existence which was not to return.

I got hungry; there were neither cakes nor jams at home, only the traditional soup pot for all occasions. My snack passed instantly from the stove to the table. With what pleasure I rediscovered my earthenware dish! I never ate more heartily. I was like a traveller returning home after many tribulations, who savors everything in her little household.

My grandmother returned to pick me up; my heart shrank. But I understood that I was not to take undue advantage of her generosity. I went along with her, laughing to mask my tears.

Neither did my mother wish to take undue advantage of the concession that had been made; she took me home with her only on Sundays. These were Caroline's days at home as well. I believe she was still at boarding school, or perhaps she was beginning to learn the craft of music copyist which she thereafter exercised with a great deal of labor and little profit until the time of her marriage.

Those happy Sundays, so impatiently awaited, passed as in a dream. At five o'clock, Caroline would go to dine at my aunt Maréchal's; mother and I would go to meet my grandmother at my Great-Uncle Beaumont's place.

This weekly dinner which invariably united the same guests was an old, very pleasant family custom. It has practically been lost in the frantic, disorderly life we lead nowadays. For people who did not work but had regular habits, it was the most pleasant and convenient way of seeing one another. My uncle had a blue-ribbon cook who put all his enormous pride into pleasing his usual clientele of highly discerning palates. My uncle's housekeeper, Mme. Bourdieu, and my uncle himself watched over these important doings in an informed way. At exactly five o'clock we would arrive, my mother and I, and would find my grandmother seated in a huge armchair near the fire, facing the equally huge armchair of my great-uncle. Mme. de La Marlière was seated between them, her feet stretched out on the andirons, her skirt a bit raised, with two thin legs showing above very pointed shoes.

Mme. de La Marlière had been an intimate friend of the late Comtesse de

Provence, deceased wife of the man who was to become Louis XVIII. Her husband, Général de La Marlière, had been executed. The reader may remember that my father mentioned her often in his letters. She was a very kind person, extremely cheerful, expansive, talkative, obliging, devoted, noisy, mocking, and a bit bold in her remarks. She was not at all pious, then, and had made fun of the clergy, indeed of almost anything, with complete license. During the Restoration, she became religious and lived thereafter in the odor of sanctity until age ninety, I believe. She was, all things considered, an excellent woman, showing no prejudices during the time I knew her, and I don't think she ever grew bigoted or intolerant. She would hardly have had the right, having made so light of holy things for three quarters of her life. She was very kind to me, and being the only one of my grandmother's friends who was not prejudiced against my mother, she earned my trust and friendship somewhat more than the others. However, I confess that I was not naturally attracted to her. Her shrill voice, Southern accent, odd outfits, pointed chin that jabbed my cheeks when she kissed me, and especially the crudeness of her ludicrous expressions prevented me from taking her seriously or finding pleasure in her little treats.

Mme. Bourdieu would glide back and forth between the kitchen and the salon; she was hardly forty years old at the time. She was a large brunette, full-figured, and of a very definite type. She came from Dax and had a Gascon accent even more pronounced than Mme. de La Marlière's. She used to call my great-uncle, "Papa," and my mother had the same habit. Mme. de La Marlière, who liked to play the child, also called him "Papa," which made my great-uncle seem younger than she.

The apartment that he occupied during all the time I knew him—about fifteen years—was situated on Rue Guénégaud, at the rear of a huge, dreary courtyard, in a house that dated from the time of Louis XIV; the style was homogeneous throughout. The windows were high and long, but there were so many curtains, tapestries, screens, draperies, and rugs for preventing any outside draft from entering the smallest crack that all the rooms were as dark and soundless as caves. The art of protecting yourself from the cold in France, and especially in Paris, was beginning to disappear under the Empire, and it is completely lost now for people of modest means, despite the numerous inventions for economical heating that progress has provided.

The combination of fashion, necessity, and speculation has led us to build houses with more and more windows, so that hardly any plain walls are left in a building; the thinness of the walls and the haste with which these ugly, shaky structures are raised mean that the smaller an apartment is, the colder and more expensive it is to heat. My great-uncle's apartment—situated in a massive building with thick walls, as all buildings should be in a climate as disagreeable and variable as ours—was like a hothouse, thanks to his careful vigilance. It is true that, in days gone by, when you moved into a house, it was for life, and that in building a nest you were digging a grave as well.

The old people whom I knew during that period had retired from active life; they lived only in their bedrooms. They had large, beautiful salons where they entertained guests once or twice a year, but never entered the rest of the time. My great-uncle and my grandmother, who never entertained, would have been able to do without this useless luxury, which doubled their rent. But they would not have considered themselves properly housed without it.

My grandmother had Louis XVI furnishings, but she had no scruples about now and again introducing more modern things, if she thought them pretty or convenient. However, my great-uncle was too artistic to permit anything disparate in his surroundings. Everything in his apartment was in the same Louis XIV style as the door moldings or the ceiling ornamentation. I don't know if he had inherited those luxurious furnishings or if he had collected them himself, but that ensemble of purely antique vintage, complete from fire tongs and bellows to bed and picture frames, would be a real find for the modern-day collector. He had superb paintings in his salon, plus furniture made by Boule, imposing in size and luxuriousness. Because all of that was out of style, my great-uncle's furniture had value only for him; those beautiful pieces—truly objects of art—had given way to a taste for the curule chairs of the Empire and ugly imitations of the Herculaneum style, in veneered mahogany or bronze-painted wood. I was far from being able to appreciate the good taste and artistic value of such a collection, and I even heard my mother say that it was all too old to be beautiful. However, beautiful things are often endowed with a quality which you can feel even without understanding. When I went into my great-uncle's apartment, I felt I was entering a mysterious sanctuary, and as the salon really was a closed sanctuary, I would whisper to Mme. Bourdieu my request to go in. So, while my elders were playing cards after dinner, she would give me a little candle-holder and lead me in mock secret into the huge salon; she left me there for a while, cautioning me not to climb on the furniture and not to drop wax from my candle. I took good care not to disobey; I would set my light down on a table and walk stealthily around the great room, whose ceiling was barely illuminated by my feeble lamp. Consequently, I could only vaguely make out Largillière's large portraits, the lovely Flemish interiors, and the paintings by Italian masters which covered the walls. I took pleasure in the glittering of the gilt surfaces, in the sumptuous folds of the draperies, in the silence and solitude of this venerable room, which it seemed was forbidden to all, while I alone took possession.

This fictive possession satisfied me, for from my earliest years, real possessions have never given me pleasure. I have never coveted palatial estates, carriages, jewelry, or even works of art; yet I like to wander through a lovely mansion, see a swift and elegantly equipped carriage passing, touch and handle jewelry that is well crafted, contemplate products of art or industry in which human intelligence is revealed in some form or another. But I've never experienced the need to tell myself, "This is mine," and I cannot even understand why anyone would ever feel that need. It's a mistake to present me with a rare or precious object, because I find it impossible not to give it away to a friend who admires it and in whom I see the desire of possession. I only hold dear things I have received from people whom I have loved and who are no longer among us. In those cases, I am greedy regardless of their small value. The creditor who would oblige me to sell my old bedroom furniture would wound me sorely, because most of it was given to me by my grandmother, and its pieces bear mute testimony to all the moments of my life. I am never tempted by what belongs to others; I feel I belong to the race of Bohemians about whom Béranger said, "The eyes alone own."

I do not detest luxury; on the contrary, I like it, but I can do without it for myself. I especially love jewelry with a passion. I find no prettier creation than the combining of precious metals and stones, from which the most pleasing and fortuitous forms are wrought in such delicate proportions. I like to study finery, fabrics, colors; I am charmed by tastefulness. I would like to be steadily creative as a designer of jewelry or clothing and, through the miracle of taste, give a kind of life to those rich materials. But I have no particular fondness for using any. A lovely dress is a bother; jewelry leaves marks; and the softening habit in all material things ages and wastes us. I guess I was not born to be rich, and if the indispositions of old age were not beginning to manifest themselves, I would truly like to live in a Berrichon thatched cottage, assuming it were clean,[1] with as much contentment as in an Italian villa.

I say this not at all out of virtue or pretension toward republican austerity. Isn't a cottage—especially for an artist—more beautiful and richer in color, grace, arrangement, and character, than an ugly, up-to-date palace, constructed and decorated in the Constitutional style, the most pitiable one in the history of art? And so I have never understood why contemporary artists, generally speaking, are so mercenary, so ambitious for luxury and wealth. Artists, of all people, are the most able to do without luxury in recreating their dream life for themselves out of very little; for they carry within themselves the gift of poetizing the most insignificant things, of building their cabin to the specifications of poetic taste or instinct. Hence, I see luxury as the resource of stupid people.

However, such was surely not the case of my great-uncle, who had a natural taste for luxury, and I strongly approve of people surrounding themselves with beautiful things when they can be bought serendipitously and for less money than ugly things. This probably applies to my great-uncle, for his means were not enormous, and he was very generous, which is tantamount to saying that he was poor and unable to permit himself impulsive or foolish acquisitions.

He was a gourmand, although he ate very little; his gourmandise was sober and in good taste, like all the rest—not at all sumptuous or ostentatious. He would even pride himself that it was a positive attribute. It was amusing to hear him argue his culinary theories, for sometimes he did it gravely and logically, as though he were making use of all the given data of politics or philosophy, and sometimes with a comic and indignant verve. "Nothing is more stupid," he would say spiritedly, his distinguished accent compensating for the crudeness of his words, "than to go into debt to feed your face. It costs no more to have a delicious omelette than an old, scorched dishrag masquerading as an omelette. It's all in knowing what an omelette is. And when a housekeeper has learned this well, I prefer her in my kitchen to some pretentious chef, who lets his kitchen help call him Sir and baptizes a carcass with the most pompous titles."

All the dinner conversation was in this vein and centered on food. I have given this example to help the reader imagine that canonical type that has practically disappeared in our time. My grandmother, who was extremely fond of delicacies although a small eater, also had scientific theories for making a vanilla custard and an omelette soufflé. My uncle would scold Mme. Bourdieu because she had permitted a few grains more or less of nutmeg in cooking a sauce; my mother used to laugh at their disputes. Only old La Marlière forgot to chatter during dinner, because she ate like an ogre. As for me, I was mortally bored by these long dinners which were served, discussed, analysed, and savored with so much solemnity. I always ate quickly, my mind on other things. A long session at the table always made me sick, and I would ask permission to get up from time to time to play with the old poodle named Babet, who spent her life having puppies and nursing them in a corner of the dining room.

The evening, too, seemed to extend unduly. My mother was not entertained by the card games she was obliged to play to make up a foursome with her old relatives. My uncle was a good loser and did not get angry like Deschartres; La Marlière won constantly because she cheated. My mother herself would say that she was bored by a game in which she couldn't cheat, which is why she refused to play for money.[2]

During this time, the kindly Bourdieu would try to entertain me. She had me build castles of cards or dominoes. My uncle, who was a tease, would turn around to blow on them or nudge the small table with his elbow. He would say to Mme. Bourdieu, whose first name was Victoire, like my mother's, "Victoire, those are stupid games; show the child something interesting. Here, show her my snuffboxes." Then the cabinet would be opened and a dozen snuffboxes would pass in review. They were very beautiful, decorated with charming miniatures of lovely ladies dressed as nymphs, goddesses, or shepherdesses. I understand now why my uncle had so many beautiful ladies on his snuffboxes. But by then he no longer cared for them, and it seemed as though their only function was to beguile the eyes of a small child. So let the clergy have the portraits! I'm glad to say that fashion has passed.

My grandmama would also sometimes take me to visit Mme. de La Marlière, who did not entertain for dinner, as she led a rather impoverished existence. She lived in a small fourth-floor apartment at 6 Rue Villedot. She remained there, I believe, from the time of the Directoire until her death in 1841 or '42. Her interior was less handsome than my great-uncle's, but it was just as intriguing in its homogeneity. I do not believe it had undergone the slightest change from the time of Louis XVI, whose style it mirrored faithfully.

At that time, Mme. de La Marlière was very close to Mme. Junot, Duchesse d'Abrantès, who left some very interesting memoirs and who died quite miserably after a motley life of pleasure and disaster. If I remember correctly, she devoted a page to Mme. de La Marlière, greatly idealized. But friendship allows for that kind of embellishment. All in all, that old friend of Comtesse de Provence, Mme. Junot, and my grandmother had more virtues than faults, which was enough to pardon her for a few shortcomings and absurdities. My grandmother's other friends were, first, Mme. de Pardaillan, the one whom she rightly preferred to all the others. She was a small, kindly old woman who had been very beautiful and who was still neat, dainty, and fresh-faced despite her wrinkles. She was not witty and had no more education than the other women of her time; among those whom I mention, my grandmother was the only one who spoke the language perfectly and wrote it correctly. Mme. de La Marlière, although droll and pungent in her style, wrote worse than our cooks. However, Mme. de Pardaillan, not having a drop of pretentiousness and not aiming to be witty, was never boring. She used a great deal of common sense in her judgments and based her opinions and principles on what she felt, without worrying about the rest of the world. I do not believe she uttered a single mean word in her life, or for that matter, had a single bitter or hostile thought. Hers was an angelic nature, reserved, yet sensitive and loving. She was a faithful soul, motherly toward everyone, pious without being fanatic, and tolerant not through indifference, but through tenderness and modesty. I do not really know if she had any faults, but she is one of the two or three people whom I have met in my lifetime in whom it was impossible for me to discern any at all.

If her mind showed no surface signs of brilliance, I believe there was at least a certain depth to her thoughts. She was in the habit of calling me "poor little one." And one day when I was alone with her, I had the courage to ask her why she called me that. She drew me close and held me as she said in an emotional voice, "Always be good, my poor child, for that will be your only happiness in life." Her tone of prophecy quite impressed me.

"So I can expect to be unhappy?" I asked.

"Yes," she answered, "everyone is condemned to sorrow, but you will have more than others. And remember what I'm saying to you—be good because you will have much to forgive."

"And why will I have to be forgiving?" I pressed her further.

"Because you'll be called upon to forgive the only source of happiness you are destined to know."

Was she suffering from some secret sorrow which led her to make such vague pronouncements? I don't think so; she must have been happy, for her family adored her. I could believe easily enough, however, that she had undergone some heartbreak in her youth, which she had never revealed to anyone. Or rather was it that she understood with her good and noble heart how much I loved my mother, and how much this affection would make me suffer?

Both Mme. de Bérenger and Mme. de Ferrières were so full of their own breeding that it is impossible for me to decide which of the two was more haughty or arrogant. My mother could not have found a better pair of "old contessas" for her entertainment. They used to say of themselves that they had been very beautiful and virtuous, which would further augment their snobbishness. Mme. de Ferrières still had some leftover attractions and took pains to have them noticed. No matter what the weather, from morning on, her arms were always bare in her muff. Her white, very heavy arms astonished me, for I understood nothing about such outdated coquetry. But those lovely sixty-year-old arms were so flaccid that they completely flattened when she leaned them on a table; the sight rather disgusted me. I have never understood why old women feel a need to display themselves; it is especially puzzling in those who have led respectable lives. But perhaps Mme. de Ferrières simply was habituated to that old-fashioned style and did not want to give it up.

Neither Mme. de Bérenger nor Mme. de Ferrières was a favorite of any of the royal females in the old or new regimes.[3] The former felt that such favor was beneath her, and would readily have said, "I should be holding court, not paying court to others." I no longer remember whose daughter she was, but her husband claimed descendance from Bérenger, King of Italy at the time of the Goths. Because of it, he and wife believed themselves to be creation's superior beings, and "looked on all others as though they were dung."[2]

They had been extremely rich and were still quite wealthy, although they claimed to have been ruined by the infamous Revolution. Mme. de Bérenger did not exhibit her arms, but she still had extraordinary pretensions regarding her figure. Her corset was so tight that two chambermaids were required to lace it while holding their knees in the small of her back. If she had been beautiful, as it was said, it was now scarcely evident, especially because of her coiffure. It consisted of a small, flaxen wig curled in the style of Titus, or like a child's, all over her entire head. Nothing is as ugly or ridiculous as the sight of an old woman pretending to be wigless, with short, frizzy, blond hair; all the more so in her case, for Mme. Bérenger was dark-complexioned with large features. In the evening, the blood would rise to her head and the heat of her wig would oppress her; she would take it off to play cards with my grandmother and remain in a fitted black cap, which made her resemble an old priest. But if some visitor was announced, she would hasten to look for her wig, which was often on the floor, or in her pocket, or under her on the armchair in which she was seated. You can imagine what strange bends these little locks of curly hair had taken and how, in her haste, it would often happen that she put her wig on backwards, or even inside out; I had great difficulty in perceiving her former beauty through the series of caricatures she presented.

Mme. de Troussebois, Mme. de Jassaud, and others whose names I cannot recall impressed me in other ways—the former had a chin which reached to her nose, the latter had the face of a mummy; the youngest of the collection was a fair-haired canoness, who had quite a pretty head on a deformed dwarf's body. Although she was unmarried, she had the privilege of calling herself Madame and of wearing a decoration on her hump, because she had the sixteen quarters required for nobility. There was also a Baroness d'Hasfeld, or Hazefeld, who had the manners and bearing of an old Corporal Schlag; finally, a Mme. Dubois, the only one who did not have a "name," and about whom, as a matter of fact, there was nothing ridiculous. I no longer remember which other one had a thick, purple lip, always swollen, split, and chapped; her kisses were odious to me.

There was also a Mme. de Maleteste, still quite young, who had taken a penniless, grumpy old husband just to bear the name of the Malatestas of Italy, a name which is not very attractive, because it simply means "wrong-headed," or rather "evil-minded." Through a remarkable coincidence, this lady spent her life having migraines, and as her name was pronounced "Mal-tête," I really believed it was a nickname they had given her due to her illness and constant complaints. I was so convinced of it that one day I naïvely asked her what her real name was. She was taken aback and answered that I knew it very well.

"Oh, no," I said, "Aching Head, Headache, Bad Head, those aren't names."

"Pardon me, Mademoiselle," she responded proudly, "it is a very fine and distinguished name."

"Well, I don't find it so," I answered. "You should be angry when people call you that."

"I wish you as great a name," she replied emphatically.

"Thank you," I persisted, "I prefer my own."

The other ladies, who did not like her perhaps because she was the youngest, were laughing behind their fans. My grandmother silenced me, and Mme. de Maleteste left a few moments later, highly insulted by my impertinence of which the implications were beyond me.

The men comprised Abbé de Pernon, a kind and good man, thoroughly worldly, always dressed in light grey, whose face was covered with what seemed like large chick-peas; Abbé d'Andrezel, of whom I have already spoken and who always wore a spencer over his frock; Chevalier de Vinci, who had a nervous tic thanks to which his wig was pulled forward by a continual contraction of his eyebrows and frontal muscles, which caused it to depart from the nape of his neck and land on his nose every five minutes. He would catch it just as it was falling off his head and into his plate. He would then replace it far back on his head, so that the distance to travel was greater before the next fall. There were also two or three old men whose names escape me for the moment but which will perhaps come to mind at the proper time and place.

The reader may well imagine the existence of a child who had not imbibed high-born prejudices at her mother's breast, surrounded by these sad personages of glacial playfulness and lugubrious solemnity. I was becoming artistic without being aware of it, artistic with regard to my propensity for observing people and things. Well before knowing that my vocation would be to describe characters well or badly and to portray interiors, the instincts of my destiny overtook me with a certain sorrow and lassitude. It was becoming increasingly difficult to isolate myself in daydreams, and in spite of myself, the world of reality began to weigh on me, tearing me from the fantasies which had nourished the freedom of my early childhood. I could not help observing those faces ravaged by age, which appeared even more frightful for having their praises sung by my grandmother, who still found them handsome out of long habit. I used to analyze the facial expressions, attitudes, manners, the emptiness of idle words, slowness of movement, infirmities, wigs, warts, immoderate stoutness, cadaverous thinness—all the unsightliness, all those misfortunes of old age which are shocking unless borne simply and with good grace. I loved beauty, and in this regard, my grandmother's serene face, youthful and indestructibly beautiful, never offended my sight; on the other hand, most of the others saddened me, and their conversation bored me utterly. I would have preferred not to see, not to hear. My scrutinizing nature forced me to look, listen, miss nothing, forget nothing; and my nascent talent redoubled my boredom by being exercised on such unattractive objects.

In the daytime when I went out with my mother, I would cheer up while telling her about what had bored me the preceding evening. In my own way, I would recreate little burlesque scenes at which I had been the silent, melancholy spectator, and she would roar with laughter, delighted to see me share her disdain and aversion for the "old contessas."

And yet there were certainly among these old women some with real merit, since my grandmama was attached to them. But with the exception of Mme. de Pardaillon, whom I always liked, I was not old enough to appreciate real merit, and I could only see the deformities or absurdities with which these solemn persons were arrayed.

Mme. de Maleteste had a horrible dog named Azor. Nowadays that is a name concierges customarily confer on their dogs, but all novelty has charm, and at that time the name Azor seemed ridiculous only because it designated an old poodle who was remarkably filthy. Not that he wasn't lovingly washed and combed, but his gluttony produced the sorriest results, and his mistress was obsessed with taking him everywhere, saying he was too unhappy when left alone. Mme. de La Marlière, on the other hand, detested animals, and I confess that my usual tenderness for them was not offended when she used her long, pointed shoe vigorously to kick Azor de Maleteste—as he was known. This was the source of a deep hatred between the two women. They would malign each other, and the others were pleased to egg them on. Mme. de Maleteste, who was very sarcastic, would come out with all kinds of mean and cutting remarks. Mme de La Marlière, who was not vindictive, but whose words came quickly and freely, hardly got angry, and exasperated Mme. de Maleteste all the more by the crudeness of her jokes.

A thing that amazed me as much as the name Maleteste was the title of Abbé, which I heard being used for men dressed as everyone else and having nothing religious in their behavior nor grave in their manner. These bachelors, who went to the theater and ate capon on Good Friday, seemed to me a special breed whose existence I was not able to fathom, and I, like one of Gavarni's "Enfants terribles,"[3] would ask them embarrassing questions. I remember one day saying to Abbé d'Andrezel, "Well, if you're not a priest, where's your wife? And if you are a priest, where's your mass?" The question was found to be very witty and very insulting. I hardly suspected it; I had been inadvertently critical, and that was not the only instance of it in my lifetime. I have asked questions or made remarks either absent-mindedly or stupidly that others have found quite probing or caustic.

As I am unable to chronicle my memories exactly, I have perhaps put together people and details which do not date from my first stay in Paris with my grandmother, but insofar as her habits and her circle of friends did not vary, and because each stay in Paris was surrounded by the same circumstances and faces, I shall not have to describe them again in resuming my story.

Here, then, I shall speak of the Villeneuve family, which figured so often in my father's letters.

I have already mentioned that M. Dupin de Francueil, my grandfather, having married twice, had had a daughter from his first wife, who consequently was my father's sister, but much older than he. She had been married to M. Valet de Villeneuve, a financier, and her two sons, René and Auguste, were thus my father's nephews, although uncle and nephews were about the same age.

As for me, I am their cousin, and their children, in Breton style, are my nieces and nephews (or first cousins once removed), although I am the youngest of that generation. People who were not acquainted with my familial situation always found bizarre the reversal of ages that normally apply in such relationships. At present, the few years' difference is no longer noticeable, but when I was a child and the older boys and girls would call me "Auntie," it was always considered a joke. Playfully my cousins, used to calling my father their uncle, would call me their great-aunt, and my name lent itself to their teasing;[4] the whole family, young and old, big and little, would call me "Auntie Aurore."

At the time the Villeneuve family was living, and has since lived for some thirty years, in the same house which they owned on Rue de Gramont. It was a large family, as you will see, whose organization was somewhat patriarchal.[5] On the ground floor lived Mme. de Courcelles, Mme. de Guibert's mother; on the second floor, Mme. de Guibert, Mme. René de Villeneuve's mother; on the third floor lived M. and Mme. René de Villeneuve with their children. Ten years after the period of my life which I am now relating, Mlle. de Villeneuve, having married M. de La Roche-Aymon, was living on the fourth floor; and the old Mme. de Courcelles was still hale and hearty when Mme. de La Roche-Aymon's children were installed with their maids on the fifth floor. All of which meant that, including the ground floor, five generations were living under the same roof, and Mme. de Courcelles could have uttered to Mme. de Guibert the charming proverb, "Daughter, go tell your daughter that her daughter's daughter is crying."

All of these women having married very young, and all being pretty or well-preserved, it was impossible to tell which Mme. de Villeneuve was grandmother and which Mme. de Guibert was great-grandmother. As for the great-great-grandmother, she remained straight, slim, neat, and active. She climbed easily to the fifth floor to visit her daughter's great-grandchildren. It was impossible not to feel great respect and liking for her, seeing her so strong, kind, calm, and gracious. She did not have a single failing, oddity, or conceit. She died without lingering of a sudden ailment which her advanced age was unable to resist. She was still in full charge of all her faculties.

I shall say nothing of Mme. de Guibert, widow of the general; she had talent and merit, but I knew her only slightly. She lived a bit separated from the rest of the family; I never found out why. She was said to have secretly married Barère.[6] She must have been an adventurous person with strange ideas, but a sort of mystery surrounded her; and I have so little curiosity that I never sought to clear it up.

As for M. and Mme. René de Villeneuve, I shall speak of them later, because they figure directly in the story of my life.

Auguste, René's brother and Treasurer of the City of Paris, lived in a lovely residence on Rue d'Anjou, with his three children—Félicie, who was angelically beautiful, sweet, and kind, and who was consumptive like her mother, died young in Italy where she had married Count Balbo (the same one whose moderately progressive writings and opinions have lately caused a stir in Piedmont); Louis, who also died in late adolescence; and Léonce, who was to become Prefect for the Indre and Loiret districts under Louis-Philippe.

Louis was a very witty, mocking, and attractive child. I remember a children's ball which his mother gave; it was the first and last time that I saw the kind and charming Laure de Ségur, for whom my father had so much respect and affection. She was wearing a pink dress trimmed with hyacinths, and she drew me to her on the divan where she was lying, in order to contemplate sadly my resemblance to my father. She was pale and burning with fever. Her children had no idea she was on the verge of death.

Léonce was making fun of all the little girls in their finery. The costumes of those days were quite unusual, and I do not believe the engravings that remain have conveyed them all. At least I have not found a picture in any of them of the layer of red wool net, wide-mesh—a veritable fish net, which Félicie wore and which I considered marvelous. It was worn over a white satin dress, and was finished at the bottom with a fringe of woolen pompons hung at the joinings that formed the mesh. It came from Italy and was highly prized.

I was most impressed by a little girl whose name I never found out and whom Léonce teased a great deal. She was already a coquette, like a woman of the world in miniature, and she was scarcely my age, seven or eight years old. To enrage her, Léonce told her she was ugly; she became so enraged that tears sprang to her eyes from sheer fury. She came over to me and said, "He's not right, is he? Am I not very pretty? I am the prettiest and best dressed girl of all, mama said so." The other children who surrounded us, prompted by Léonce's example, told her that she was wrong and that she was the ugliest. She became so furious that she almost strangled herself with her coral necklace, which she twisted violently around her neck and which fortunately broke.

I was struck by this naïve frustration, by this true, infantile despair, as something far from ordinary. My parents had said a hundred times in my presence that I was a superb little girl, but I did not become vain because of it; I took it to be praise of my good behavior, because every time I behaved badly, they would say I was frightful. As a result, I felt that the concept of beauty, when applied to children, had a purely moral significance. Perhaps I was not inclined by nature to self-admiration; what is certain is that my grandmother, while trying to instill the degree of coquetry she wanted me to have, took away the little which I could have had. She wanted me to be graceful, dress carefully, and be elegant in my ways. Until then, I had had the gracefulness that is natural to all children who are not sick or deformed. But they were beginning to consider me too grown-up to exhibit natural grace, which only appears graceful because it stems from self-assurance and ease. In my grandmama's opinion, gracefulness had to be acquired in one's way of walking, sitting, greeting, picking up one's glove, holding one's fork, presenting an object—in sum, a whole gamut of mimicry that children should learn when very young, so that habit can make it second nature.

My mother thought it ridiculous, and I believe she was right. Gracefulness stems from physical harmony, and if it is not inborn, the work that is put into acquiring it simply makes one clumsier. For me, there is nothing more hideous than a man or a woman who affects certain mannerisms. Such conventionalized grace works only on the stage (precisely for the reason that truth in art is not reality).

Conventional manners were an item of such great importance in the lives of members of the old high society that today's actors mimic them only with much difficulty, despite their studies. I have met some of these old, graceful beings, and I can only say that, regardless of their male and female admirers, I have seen nothing more ridiculous or less pleasing. I would a hundred times sooner see a farmer behind his plow, a woodcutter chopping a tree, a washerwoman lifting her basket over her head, or a child rolling on the ground with his playmates. Animals with beautiful lines are models of grace. Who teaches the horse its swan-like elegance, its proud stance, its wide and supple leaps? And who teaches the bird its indescribable delicacy? And from whom does the young goat learn its dances and inimitable bounding? Away with outmoded grace that consists of artfully sniffing snuff, or showily wearing an embroidered suit, a dress with a train, a sword, or a fan! This last toy, we are told, is handled by beautiful Spanish women with inexpressible grace, that in their hands it is an art. True, but it comes naturally to them. Spanish peasant girls dance the bolero better than our actresses at the Opéra, but their gracefulness comes to them from an inherent physical harmony which is instinctive.

Gracefulness as conceived before the Revolution—acquired grace, in other words—was thus the torture of my early years. I was corrected for everything, and I could not make the slightest movement without being criticized. That tried my patience constantly, and I would often say, "I'd like to be an ox or a donkey; then I'd be allowed to walk my own way and graze where I pleased, instead of their making me a trained dog that walks on its hind legs and offers its paw."

Every cloud has a silver lining, and perhaps my aversion to conventional manners was inspired by this constant petty persecution, to which I owe what remains of naturalness in my ideas and feelings. Falseness, stuffiness, affectation are odious to me, and I sense them even when they are cleverly coated with a façade of false simplicity. I can only see goodness and beauty in what is true and simple, and the older I become, the more I believe I am right for wanting these qualities above all others in human character, artistic works, and social behavior.

Furthermore, I was very aware that acquired grace, even when truly lovely and attractive, was a badge of awkwardness and physical weakness. All of those beautiful ladies and handsome gentlemen who knew how to walk so well on carpeted floors, and how to make reverential bows, would not have been able to take three steps on God's green earth without being overcome by fatigue. They did not even know how to open or close a door, and they did not have the strength to put a log on the fire. They needed servants to advance their chairs. They could not come in or go out alone. What would have become of their gracefulness were it not for servants who took the place of their arms, legs, and hands? I thought of my mother who, with hands and feet more dainty than theirs, would walk two or three leagues on a country morning before lunch, and who used to move large rocks or push a wheelbarrow as easily as she handled a needle or a pencil. I would have far preferred to be a dishwasher than an old marquise like the ones I observed every day, yawning in an atmosphere of old musk!

O, you writers of today, who ceaselessly curse the vulgarity of our times and bemoan the disappearance of those old frills, who have created in these times of constitutional royalty and bourgeois democracy a literature dusted with images of Trianon's nymphs; I congratulate you for not having spent your happy childhood in this rubble of outmoded good taste. You have been less bored than I, you ingrates who renounce the present and future while revering the urn of a charming past which you have only known through paintings.   *P.P.-Y.*

III

The idea of a moral law to regulate one's affections. —Return to
Nohant. —La Brande. —Bivouac in a rattletrap. —The haven. —A
year of happiness. —The Emperor's power at its apex. —First
betrayals. —Gossip and calumny overheard in the salons. —My
brother's first communion. —Our old curé, his housekeeper, his
sermons. —The thief who robbed him, his mare, his death.
—Childhood pranks. —Deschartres' imposter. —My mother's piety.
—I study French and Latin.

I was very dissatisfied, yet I was still not unhappy. I was much
loved—nor has the love of others ever been lacking in my life. Therefore, I do
not regret the life I have led, despite all its sorrows, for the greatest sorrow
must be not to have one's love reciprocated. It was my misfortune and destiny
to be wounded and torn apart by an excess of those affections, whose purveyors sometimes lacked foresight or sensitivity, othertimes appropriateness or
moderation. One of my friends, a man of great intelligence, often voiced a
thought which to me seemed very striking, and he developed it as follows:

"We have established moral rules and laws to correct or develop our
instincts, but we have made none to guide or clarify our affections. We have
religions and philosophies to regulate our appetites and repress our passions.
The duties of the soul are well taught us on an elementary level, but the soul
has all sorts of impulses which give all sorts of special nuances and aspects to
its affections. It has strengths which degenerate into excess, failings which
become chronic. If you consult your friends, if you seek help in books, you'll
get differing opinions and contradictory judgements—proof that there is no
fixed rule for the morality of even the most legitimate affections, and that each
of us, with no guide but himself, judges from his own point of view the moral
state of whoever asks his advice—advice that is useless, moreover, that cures
no suffering and corrects no error. For example, I know of no catechism for
love, and yet love, in all its forms, dominates all our lives—filial love, brotherly love, conjugal love, paternal or maternal love, friendship, benevolence, charity, philanthropy; love is everywhere; it is our very life. However, love eludes
all law, all guidance, all advice, all example, all precept. It obeys only itself,
and it turns into tyranny, jealousy, suspicion, exigence, obsession, inconstancy,
caprice, voluptuousness or brutality, chastity or asceticism, sublime devotion
or ferocious selfishness, the greatest good or the greatest evil, according to the

soul it inhabits or possesses. Shouldn't we create a catechism to correct the excesses of love, for love is excessive by nature, and the purer and more sacred it is, the more excessive it often is.

"Mothers often make their children unhappy by loving them, godless by wanting them to be religious, rash by wanting them to be prudent, ungrateful by wanting them to be tender and full of gratitude. And marital jealousy! What are its permissible bounds, not to be exceeded? Some say there is no love without jealousy; others, that true love knows no suspicion or distrust. What rule of conscience is there which might teach us to observe ourselves, cure ourselves, revive our enthusiasm when it wanes, repress it when it carries us beyond the limits of possibility? This rule has not yet been discovered; that is why I say we live like the blind, and if poets have put a blindfold on Love, philosophers have not found a way to remove it."

Thus spoke my friend, and what he said applied to me, for throughout my life I have been the plaything of other people's passions, consequently their victim. To speak only of my early years, my mother and grandmother, hungry for my love, were tearing my heart to shreds. Even my nursemaid oppressed and abused me only because she loved me too much and wanted me to be perfect by her standards.

With the first days of spring, we packed our belongings to return to the country, which I sorely needed. Whether from too much comfort, or from the Paris air, which has never agreed with me, I was again becoming listless and growing thinner every day. There was no question of separating me from my mother; at that period, I believe, it would have killed me, for I could not yet feel resignation or the desire to obey. My grandmama therefore invited my mother to come back to Nohant with us, and since I showed an anxiety in this connection that made the others anxious, it was decided that my mother would take me with her and that Rose would go with us, while my grandmother would set out with Julie. Since we were somewhat short of funds, we had sold the big berlin and replaced it with a carriage that had only two seats.

I have not yet spoken of my Uncle Maréchal, nor of his wife, my kind Aunt Lucie, nor of their daughter, dear Clotilde. I do not remember anything special about them at this period. I saw them quite often, but I do not remember where they lived. My mother used to take me to their house, and even my grandmother on rare occasions received visits from them and returned their visits. She did not very much like my aunt's easygoing, outspoken ways, but she was too fair-minded not to acknowledge the true friendship they had borne my father, and the soundness and dependability of both husband and wife.

Thus, I had the joy of spending two or three days in continuous intimacy with my mother and Caroline. Then my poor sister tearfully returned to boarding school, where I think Clotilde was also sent for a time to console her, and we took our leave.

We had a classic mishap before arriving at Nohant, which I shall recount in order to show how substantially the condition of the roads and the very face of certain parts of France have changed in the last forty years.

Between Châteauroux and Nohant there is a stretch of country rather like the Sologne, that extends as far as the entrance to the Vallée Noire. It is not nearly as poor or ugly as the Sologne, especially now that all the land along the roadside is cultivated. In places, the terrain has a certain variety of contour, and beyond the wide expanses of heather, one sees in almost every direction the blue horizon of the fertile areas that surround this little wilderness. The proximity of those lands mitigates the unhealthy character of the heath, and if the vegetation and livestock are less flourishing than in our valley, at least they are not dying, as is the case in very extensive barren lands. This desert—for even today it boasts only a few farms and thatched cottages, and in my youth had not even one—is known in the region as La Brande. At its edge, nearer Châteauroux, there is a large village called Ardentes. Is this because at the time of the Romans there were forges there? And were the surrounding moors covered with forests which were gradually cut down and burned to feed these forges? The two names might lead one to believe so—unless a huge conflagration once consumed both woods and village.

Whatever its origin, La Brande was still, at the period of which I speak, an impassable bog, a ground completely abandoned. There was no trace of a road, or rather there were a hundred tracks, as every cart or ramshackle conveyance tried to find an easier and safer crossing than the others, during the heavy rains. One of these was indeed called the road, but not only was it in the worst condition, it was not easy to follow in the midst of all those which crisscrossed it. You would lose your way over and over, and that is what happened to us.

At Châteauroux, beyond which in those days no species of coach ventured, we had lunch at the home of M. Duboisdouin, an old, devoted friend of my grandmother, who had been employed by my grandfather, M. Dupin, in his work as tax collector, and who still had a warm fondness for all of us. He was a pleasant and contented little old man, wiry, strong, and jolly. He lived to a ripe old age without any infirmities. In summer, at the age of eighty-two, he traveled from Châteauroux to Nohant on foot; in other words, he walked nine leagues to pay us a visit, his jacket in a bundle at the end of his cane, on his shoulder, like a young journeyman making his tour of France. He jumped over ditches, he ran, he danced, he dug in the earth, he did all the work in his garden, which yielded the finest flowers and fruit. His hospitality was delightful; he kept us at lunch for hours, then showed us around his property, lingering over every violet and flowering apricot tree, so that it was getting dark when we took our places in a hired rattletrap, driven by a lad of twelve or thirteen, and drawn by a skinny nag.

I do not imagine our little cabby had ever crossed La Brande before, because when he found himself after dark in that labyrinth of twisted tracks, puddles of water, and giant ferns, he became desperate and, abandoning his horse to its own instinct, drove us hither and yon, completely lost in the wilderness for five hours.

I said a moment ago that there was not a single dwelling on the heath. I was wrong; there was one, and that was the landmark you needed to find in order then to drive on to the Vallée Noire with some hope of success. This little cottage was called the Gardener's House because it belonged to a former gardener of Le Magnier, a romantic looking château located a league away, on the border between La Brande and the Vallée Noire, in the opposite direction from Nohant.

But the night was dark, and try as we might to find the Gardener's House, we never came near it. My mother was dreadfully afraid that we had mistakenly stumbled onto the road that led to the Saint-Aoust woods, which terrified her, for in her mind robbers was unshakably associated with woods, even if the woods were only an acre in size.

The danger, however, lay elsewhere. Not only had there never been robbers in our region, but the few travelers who frequented the remote tracks of the heath would not have afforded them much sustenance. The real danger was that we could turn over and get stuck in some hole. Fortunately, the one we encountered toward midnight was dry, but it was deep, and we were so completely grounded in sand that nothing could induce the horse to pull us out. We had to give up that idea, at which point the lad, unhitching the horse, mounting it, and spurring it with his heels, wished us goodnight, and paying no further attention to my mother's remonstrances and Rose's violent threats, vanished and was lost in the shadowy night.

There we were in the middle of the heath, with no roof over our heads, my mother appalled, Rose swearing at the boy, and I weeping because of my mother's anxiety and vexation, which profoundly distressed me.

I, too, was frightened, but not of the night, or the idea of robbers, or the loneliness of the spot. I was terrified by the song of the frogs, myriads of which still live in the swamps of these heathlands. On certain spring and autumn nights, they make such a racket throughout this whole stretch of wilderness, that you cannot hear the sound of your own voice, which adds to the difficulty of calling out to find your traveling companions, if you've become separated from them. This thunderous croaking made me very nervous and filled my soul with inexplicable terrors. It was useless for Rose to make fun of me and explain that it was only the song of the frogs; I didn't believe a word she said; I imagined evil spirits, goblins and gnomes, who were angry at us for violating their solitary domain.

Finally Rose, having thrown stones into all the surrounding puddles and weeds to silence those relentless musicians, managed to talk to my mother and calm her concerning the possible outcome of our mishap. They put me to bed in the back of the vehicle, where I promptly fell asleep; my mother did not try to do the same, but was chatting quite gaily with Rose when at about two o'clock in the morning, something woke me. A ball of fire had appeared on the horizon. At first Rose maintained that the moon was rising, but my mother thought it was a meteor and that she could see it hurtling in our direction.

After a few moments, we realized it was a sort of lamp, which was indeed coming toward us, not without many zigzags and signs of uncertainty in reaching its goal. Finally, we made out the sound of voices and the steps of horses. Again my mother was convinced that robbers were upon us and that we should flee and hide in the thickets, while they looted the carriage, but Rose convinced her that, on the contrary, kindly folk were coming to our rescue, and she ran toward them to confirm it.

It was indeed the good gardener of La Brande, who, like a pilot accustomed to rescuing the shipwrecked, was approaching with his sons, his horses, and a resin candle surrounded by a big piece of oiled paper and tied to the end of a stick, a sort of beacon to alert from afar those stranded on the heath. Our little driver had not been as selfish and incompetent as we thought. He had finally found the haven and come back with its owners to help them find us. They righted the old coach in an instant, hitched two strong farm horses to it—the first ever, perhaps, to sink a ploughshare into the soil of the heath—and brought us to their home, where the housewife was waiting up for us and had prepared a rustic supper, a good fire, and beds. It was like a holiday for us to eat and sleep in this cottage where other children were snoring, not in the least disturbed by our arrival. We were enchanted by the coarse, snowy sheets, the yellow serge canopies, the roosters' song, the dancing fire of dry heather, and above all, by our peasant host's hospitality. The sun was high in the sky when we again set out for Nohant in the old rattletrap, with a spare horse and a guide.

This was not a useless precaution, for the rest of the journey to the entrance of the Vallée Noire (two leagues), took us fully three hours because of the innumerable detours around the quagmires; it was noon when we reached Nohant, and we had left Châteauroux the day before at sunset. Nowadays, with a good horse, we can travel the same distance on a magnificent road in two hours.

The part of the year 1811 that I spent at Nohant was, I think, one of the few times in my life when I was completely happy. I had felt such happiness in Rue Grange-Batelière, although there I had neither large rooms nor large gardens. Madrid had been a disturbing and painful experience for me. The sickly condition it left me in, the catastrophe that befell my family at my father's death, then the struggle between my two mothers, which had early revealed to me the meaning of fear and distress, had been an apprenticeship in unhappiness and suffering. But the spring and summer of 1811 were cloudless, as is proved by the fact that that year left me with no special memories. I know that Ursule spent it with me, that my mother had fewer migraines than before, and that if there were disagreements between her and my grandmama, they were so well hidden that I forgot they could occur and had occurred. Probably, this was the period in their lives when they got along best with one another, for my mother was not a woman who hid her feelings. That was beyond her capacity, and when she was irritated, even her children's presence did not induce her to control herself.

There was a little more gaiety in the house than before. Time does not erase great sorrow, but it dims the memory of it. Nevertheless, almost every day I saw one of my mothers weep when she thought no one was looking, but her very tears proved that she no longer thought of the object of her grief at every hour and every instant. When most intense, sorrows have no single point of crisis; they keep us in a state of continual crisis, so to speak.

Mme. de La Marlière came to spend a month or two with us. She was very entertaining with Deschartres, whom she called "Daddy," and whom she teased from morning to night. She was certainly not as witty as my mother, but there was no ill humor in her jokes. She was fond of Deschartres, and was not hostile to my mother, whose side she always took. That frivolous old lady was kind, easy to live with, and annoying only because of her noisy chatter, flitting about, loud bursts of laughter, repetitious bons mots, and the lack of logic in her remarks as well as in her ideas. Despite her bright, sharp prattle, her ignorance was fantastic. She was the one who had called an epithalamium an *èpître à l'âme* and referred to *Mistouflé* when she meant Mephistopheles. But you could make fun of her without making her angry; she roared with laughter at her own foibles, and with as much good humor she laughed at other people's.

All summer long the little gardens flourished, as did the grottos, the green lawns, the waterfalls. The flower bed under the old pear tree, which unknown to me marked my little brother's grave, was noticeably improved. A barrel of water was placed beside it so that we could keep it well watered. One day, I fell head first into that barrel and would have drowned, if Ursule had not rescued me.

We each had to have our own little garden in my mother's garden, which was itself so small that we should have been satisfied, but a certain sense of ownership is so deeply ingrained in human nature, that a child must have her own square of earth in order really to love that patch cultivated by her own hands and in proportion to her strength. That has always made me think that, even if one is a communist, one must still recognize the right to own property individually. Be it limited or extensive with regard to size, defined in one way or another according to the owner's ability or to the needs of the season, there is no question that the land a man works himself is as much a part of him as his clothing. His room or his house is also a kind of clothing, while his garden or his field is the clothing of his house, and the remarkable aspect of all this is that the same concession to natural instinct that draws a man to own property seems to reject the need for a great deal. The smaller the property, the deeper the attachment of the owner; the more meticulous his care of it, the dearer it is to him. A Venetian aristocrat surely loves his palace less than a Berrichon peasant his cottage, and the capitalist who owns several square leagues gets infinitely less pleasure from them than the artisan who cultivates a mustard plant in his garret. A lawyer friend of mine once said laughingly to a rich client, who was always talking about his land, "Your land? You think you're the only one who has land! I have land, too, there, on my window sill, in my flower pots, and it gives me more pleasure and fewer worries than yours." Since then, my friend has inherited a large estate; he has land, woods, and farms, and with them many worries.

In approaching the idea of communism, which is very impressive because there is much truth in it, we must first distinguish what is essential to the complete existence of the individual from what is essentially collective in his freedom and his work. That is why absolute communism, which is a rudimentary—therefore unrefined and exaggerated—notion of true equality, is chimerical or unjust.

However, I hardly thought of all that thirty-seven years ago![4] Thirty-seven years! What transformations take place in the ideas of humanity during that short space of time, and proportionately how much more striking and rapid those changes are in the masses than in individuals! I do not know if there was such a thing as a communist thirty-seven years ago. That idea, as old as the world itself, had no special name, and it is perhaps a mistake to have given it that name in our time, because the word does not completely express the whole idea.

At that time, such questions were not under discussion. It was the last and most brilliant phase of the reign of individuality. Napoléon was then in the fullness of his glory, power, and influence in the world. The torch of genius would soon grow dim. It threw its brightest ray, its most dazzling light on France intoxicated and prostrate at Napoléon's feet. Grandiose exploits had brought about an opulent, glorious, but insubstantial peace; for the volcano was rumbling throughout Europe, and the Emperor's treaties only gave the old monarchies time to gather their men and their cannon. His grandeur hid his fundamental flaw—the profound aristocratic vanity of the parvenu, which was at the root of all his errors; because of it, the beauty of the genius and character of the man in whom France was personified became ever less helpful for the welfare of his country. Yes, he had an admirable character, for even vanity itself, the pettiest and most contemptible of faults, had not vitiated his natural loyalty, trustfulness, and magnanimity. Hypocritical in small matters, he was sincere in great ones. Arrogant with regard to detail, demanding in petty questions of etiquette, insanely vainglorious of the road on which Fortune had led him, he did not know his own merit, his true greatness. He was modest about his real genius.

All the mistakes which brought about his fall as a leader in war and as a statesman arose from his excessive belief in the talent or honesty of others. It is not true, although it has commonly been said, that he despised the whole human race and respected only himself; that is the sort of remark made by disappointed courtiers or ambitious second-raters, jealous of his superiority. All his life he put his trust in traitors. All his life he counted on the good faith of those with whom he had signed treaties, on the gratitude of those whom he had favored, on the patriotism of his underlings. All his life he was deceived or betrayed.

His marriage to Marie-Louise was a bad maneuver and was bound to bring him misfortune. I remember very well that even the simplest people and those who were most tolerant regarding the divorce law, even those who loved the Emperor most, said under their breath, "This is a political marriage. You can't repudiate a woman you love and who loves you."

Indeed, there will never be a law which can morally sanction a separation deplored by both parties and effected only for material gain. But even if they criticized him for this act, the masses still loved the Emperor. Highly-placed people were beginning to betray him, but they fawned on him as never before.

The upper classes had a hey day. The bourgeoisie, the soldiers, the workers, and the peasants were intoxicated by the birth of the infant King of Rome (for the pride of the soldier of fortune would not have been satisfied by giving him the title of Dauphin of France.). There was not a house, rich or poor, palace or hovel, where the portrait of the imperial baby was not enshrined with false or genuine reverence. But the masses were sincere; they always are. The Emperor walked amid the crowd without an escort. The garrison at Paris numbered only twelve hundred men.

However, Russia was arming, while Bernadotte gave the signal for an enormous and mysterious betrayal. Those who had a little foresight saw the coming storm. The high price of foodstuffs brought about by the continental blockade frightened and disturbed people of small means. Sugar cost six francs a pound, and in the midst of the apparent wealth of the nation, there were shortages of vital necessities. Our factories were not yet sufficiently developed for us to sustain the isolation of our trade. There was a certain degree of general material discomfort, and when people grew tired of blaming England, they blamed the head of state, without bitterness, it is true, but with sadness.

My grandmother had no enthusiasm for the Emperor. My father had not been enthralled with him either, as can be seen from his letters. However, in his last years, he did take a liking to him. He had often said to my mother, "I have a serious grievance against him, and not because he didn't immediately confer the highest rank on me; he had other things on his mind, and there were plenty of men who were luckier, cleverer, and bolder in seeking advancement than I was. But I do hold it against him that he likes to be courted; that is not worthy of a man of his stature. Nonetheless, despite the injury he has done the Revolution and himself, I love him. There is something compelling in him, something indefinable, apart from his genius, that stirs me when our eyes meet. I am not in the least intimidated by him, and that is what convinces me his real worth is much greater than the airs he puts on."

My grandmother did not share this secret warmth which had won my father's heart and which, combined with his honorable soul and ardent patriotism, would have prevented him not only from betraying the Emperor, but from eventually accepting service under the Bourbons. Such a refusal would certainly have been consistent with his character, because after the French campaign, my grandmother, although she had become a royalist, used to sigh and exclaim, "Ah! if my poor Maurice had lived, we would still be mourning him now! He would have been killed at Waterloo, or before the walls of Paris. Or he would have shot himself at the sight of the Cossacks entering the city." My mother said the same thing.

However, my grandmother feared the Emperor more than she liked him. In her eyes, he was insatiably ambitious, a usurper of men's lives, a despot by inclination even more than by necessity. At that time the complaints, criticism, slander, revelations true or false did not yet fill the columns of the newspapers. The press was not only muzzled but servile. It was not only obliged to keep silent, it sought occasions for abjection and adulation of power. That absence of polemics gave the conversations and concerns of individuals an extraordinarily partial and gossipy character. Official praise did Napoléon twenty times more harm than twenty hostile newspapers could have done. People were weary of those inflated dithyrambs and pompous bulletins, of the slavishness of the bureaucrats and the inscrutable hauteur of the courtiers. They revenged themselves by belittling the idol in intimate conversations, and the disaffected salons became dens for denunciations, whispered remarks, petty calumnies, and trifling anecdotes which later brought the press back to life under the Restoration. But what sort of life! Better to have remained dead than revive in that fashion, feeding on the corpse of the vanquished and profaned Empire.

My grandmother's bedroom (as I have said, she did not receive visits in her salon, and her circle had a feeling of solemn intimacy) would have become one of those dens if, with her own wit and good sense, the mistress of the house had not from time to time openly sorted out the true and false elements in the news the women brought there; for it was a society of women, rather than men, and moreover, there was little moral difference between the two sexes, since the men in it acted like garrulous old women. Every day we were served up a malicious witticism of M. Talleyrand against his master, or a bit of scandal overheard in a corridor. One day the Emperor had beaten the Empress; the next day, he had plucked out the Pope's beard. Moreover, they said he was so fearful that he always wore a protective vest. They had to say that, in order to avenge themselves for the fact that no one thought of assassinating him, unless it were some intrepid and fanatical son of Germany, like Stapss or Von Sahla.[8] Another day, word had it he was mad, he had spat in M. Cambacérès' face. Or, his son, torn by forceps from the mother's womb, had died at birth, and the little King of Rome was a Parisian baker's son. Or, since the forceps had squashed his brain, he was obviously a cretin, and at this idea they rubbed their hands, as if by re-establishing the principle of royal succession in favor of a soldier of fortune, France had brought upon herself the punishment of providence for having gotten rid of her legitimate cretins.

But what was astonishing was that in the midst of all those underground rumblings against the Emperor, there was not one regret, recollection, or wish expressed for the exiled Bourbons. I listened with stupefaction to all those remarks; I never heard anyone pronounce the names of the unknown pretenders enthroned somewhere behind closed doors, and when their names struck my ears in 1814, it was for the first time in my life.

This gossip did not follow us to Nohant, except in letters which my grandmother received from her aristocratic friends. She read them aloud to my mother, who shrugged her shoulders, and to Deschartres, who took them for gospel truth; the Emperor was his bête noire, and he quite seriously considered him a cad.

My mother was like the people: at that time she admired and adored the Emperor. As for me, I was like my mother. What must not be forgotten or misunderstood is that those whose hearts were naïvely bound to this man were those whom no personal obligation or material interest linked to his triumph or his fall. With very rare exception, all those whom he had covered with favors turned against him. Those who never thought to ask a favor, considered him responsible for France's greatness.

I think it was that year or the next that Hippolyte made his first communion. Since the elimination of our parish, Nohant's religious observances were carried on at Saint-Chartier. My brother had on all new clothes that day. He wore short trousers, white stockings, and a billiard-green, felt waistcoat. He was still so much of a child that this costume infatuated him, and he managed to obey for several days because he was afraid that if he didn't make his first communion, he would never be allowed to wear the splendid outfit prepared for him.

The old curé of Saint-Chartier was a very fine man, but quite lacking in religious idealism. Although he had a "De" in front of his name, I think he was of peasant origin, or from living with peasants had taken on their manners and speech, so much so that he could preach a whole sermon to them without saying anything that was beyond their understanding. This would have been a good thing, if his sermons had been a little more evangelical, but he spoke to his flock only about parish business, and with good-natured informality would say from the pulpit:

"Dear friends, here's an order from the archbishop to organize still another procession. Monseigneur can afford to talk! He has a fine carriage to carry His Grace, and lots of people to take care of his headaches; but I am an old man, and it is no small piece of work to organize you into a procession. Most of you don't listen when I say 'giddyap' or 'whoa.' You push each other, you step on each other's feet, you shove when you come into church or leave, and it is no use getting angry and swearing at you, you don't listen, and you behave like calves in a stable. I have to take care of everything in my parish and my church. I have to keep order, scold the children, and scare off the dogs. Well, I'm tired of all these processions which are of no use for your salvation or mine. The weather is bad, the roads are a mess, and if Monseigneur had to wallow in the mud like us for two hours, with the rain coming down on his back, he would not have such an appetite for ceremonies. Goodness me, I don't feel like bothering about this one, and if you want my advice, you should stay home. Oh, yes, I can hear old man so-and-so criticizing me, and I'm sure my housekeeper doesn't approve at all. Listen, let those who aren't satisfied go—er—take a walk. You'll do what you like about this, but I'm not marching around the fields. I'll make a procession for you around the church. That's good enough. Well, then, it's settled. Let's be done with mass, which has already lasted too long."

I have heard with my own ears more than two hundred sermons of which the above is a very diluted specimen; his expressions have remained proverbial in the neighboring parishes, especially the final formula, which was like the Amen to all his fatherly preachings and admonitions.

At Saint-Chartier there was a prodigiously stout old lady whose husband was the mayor or deputy mayor of the town. Her life before the Revolution had been stormy—as a novice, she had climbed over the convent walls to follow a

French or Swiss guardsman with the army. I do not know what chain of strange adventures had led her to pass her last good years in our churchwarden's pew, where her manners recalled the regiment much more than the cloister. The mass was constantly interrupted by her ostentatious yawns and her energetic heckling of the curé. "This is the very devil of a mass," she would say aloud. "That rogue will never finish with it!"

"Go to the devil," the curé would answer under his breath, as he turned around to bless the congregation, "Domine, vobiscum."

Dialogues of this sort heard all through the mass, and in so vehement a style that I can hardly reproduce them, had almost no effect on the equanimity of the rustic congregation, and since these were the first masses I heard, it took me some time to understand that they were religious ceremonies. When I came home from the first one, my grandmother asked me what I had seen. "I saw the curé," I answered, "eating his breakfast standing up in front of a big table, and every now and then he turned around to say silly things to us."

The day Hippolyte made his first communion, the curé invited him to lunch after mass. Since this rather big boy was not too at home with his catechism, my grandmother, who wanted his first communion to be, as she put it, an open and shut case, asked the curé to be somewhat indulgent, in view of the boy's poor memory. The curé had indeed been indulgent, and Hippolyte was entrusted with a little gift for him, twelve bottles of muscatel. They sat down to lunch and the first bottle was opened. "Upon my word," said the good curé, "this is a nice little white wine that you can drink your fill of, that doesn't go to your head like the local vintage; it's mild, it's pleasant, it can't do any harm. Drink, my boy, don't be shy. Manette, call the sacristan, and we'll taste the second bottle when we finish the first." The housekeeper and the sacristan took their places and they, too, found the wine very nice indeed. Hippolyte drank without a care, for never before had he drunk at his own discretion. The guests found the wine a bit warming at the second bottle, but after trying it diluted, decided that it did not need water. They went on to the third and fourth pages of the breviary, as the curé put it, that is, to the other bottles in the basket, and little by little, the communicant, the curé, the housekeeper, and the sacristan were so gay, then so solemn, then so self-absorbed, that they parted with very little memory of the circumstances. Hippolyte came home alone through the meadows, for the parishioners who had come to mass had long since gone home. On the way, his head was so heavy that he thought he saw the bushes dancing. He decided to lie down under a tree and take a good nap. After that, his head became somewhat clearer, and he was able to make his way home, where he edified us by his seriousness and sobriety all the rest of the day.

The curé's housekeeper was a tiny little woman, clean, active, devoted, fussy, and shrewish, for this latter defect often appears as the inevitable accompaniment of the good qualities of which it is perhaps the excess. She had saved her master's life and his funds during the Revolution. She had hidden him, and during the persecutions, had denied his presence with great courage and composure. This did not happen in the Vallée Noire where priests and landowners were never seriously threatened nor mistreated in any way. From that time on,

Manette tyrannized her master and made him toe the mark like a little boy. They both died at a very advanced age, one shortly after the other, and despite their quarrels and the lack of ideality in their life, time, which ennobles everything, had imparted a touching quality to their mutual affection. Manette insisted that only she should serve or care for her master, but she no longer had the strength to do it, and when he was ill and she had sat up with him and dosed him devotedly, she fell ill in her turn. For this reason, the curé engaged another servant, so that the old housekeeper could rest and regain her health. But the moment she was up again, she was furious at the sight of a stranger in the house. She could not rest until the other was dismissed.

Then she again became exhausted. She would complain that the work was too heavy and that she had no one to help her. The curé would immediately engage a helper who would also be dismissed a week later. There was incessant shrieking and nagging, and the curé complained to me about it, for he was still alive when I was well past thirty. "Alas!" he said, "She makes me very unhappy. But what can I do? We've been together fifty-seven years, she saved my life, she loves me like a son. Whichever of us survives must close the other's eyes. She scolds me incessantly, she complains as if I were an ingrate; I try to prove to her that she's unfair, but she's so deaf she doesn't hear the church bell!" And saying this, the curé didn't realize that he himself was so deaf that he couldn't have heard a cannon.

He was not very well liked by his parishioners, but I think this was at least as much their fault as his; for no matter what people say about the touching relationship between priests and peasants in the countryside, nothing is so rare, at least since the Revolution, as to see either do justice to the other and show each other a certain indulgence. The peasant demands too much Christian perfection from the curé, while the curé is insufficiently forgiving of this unreasonable requirement and of the shortcomings of the peasant's moral education, which are to some extent the fruits of a Catholicism whose despotism has kept the peasant in fear and ignorance.

In any case, our curé had his good qualities. Such candor and independent character are rarely found in the Church hierarchy today. He never interfered in politics, he did not try to exert influence in order to please some important person or protect himself from another's spite, for he was courageous, even bold, in his fundamental nature. He passionately loved warfare and liked to hear our soldiers tell of their great campaigns, saying that if he hadn't been a priest, he would have wished to be a military man. He certainly had something of both, for he swore like a Dragoon and drank like a Templar. "I'm not a hypocrite," he said, during the Restoration. "I'm not one of those turncoats who have changed their manners since the government protects the clergy. I am the same as I was before and don't expect my parishioners to bow lower or forego drinking and dancing, as if what was permissible yesterday should no longer be so today. I am a rebel, and I don't need new laws to defend myself; if anyone picks a quarrel with me, I know how to deal with him, and I would rather show him my fist than threaten him with the police or the King's prosecutor. I am an old man from the old school, and I don't believe that with their law against sacrilege they've succeeded in making people love religion. I don't bother anyone, and I let hardly anyone bother me. I don't like water in my wine, and I don't force anyone to put water in his. If the archbishop doesn't like what I do, let him say so; he'll get my answer! I'll show him that you don't make a man of my age fall into line like a little seminarian, and if he takes my parish away from me, I won't seek another. I'll retire to my own house. I have put aside eight or ten thousand francs; that's enough for whatever years I have left, and I'll thumb my nose at all the archbishops in the world."

Indeed, when the archbishop came to celebrate confirmation at Saint-Chartier and took lunch at the curé's house with his whole staff, he tried to tease his host, who would not allow it. "You're eighty-two, sir," said the archbishop. "That's a ripe old age!"

"That's right, My Lord," answered the curé, who permitted himself only certain liberties in his speech. "You may have gotten to be archbishop, but you may not get to be my age." The real meaning of the prelate's remark was, "You're so old you're probably in your dotage, it's time you made way for somebody younger." And the answer meant, "I'll keep this place till you force me out of it, and we'll see if you dare insult my white head so grossly."

At this same luncheon, just before the dessert, since the archbishop was supposed to have dinner at my house, the curé, addressing my brother, who was sitting next to him, in what he thought was a very low voice, shouted in his ear as deaf persons do, "Oh, please, take him away and let me be rid of all these grand gentlemen who cost the very devil to entertain and who turn my house upside down. I've had my fill of them, more than I need, to know that they're sneering at me while they eat my partridges and chickens." Those words, spoken aloud in the midst of a silence of which the good curé was unaware, were very embarrassing to Hippolyte; however, seeing that the archbishop and the chief vicar were roaring with laughter, he decided to laugh, too, and everyone left the table, to the great relief of the host and Manette, who, imagining their real feelings were not being heard, expressed them openly in the very teeth of their illustrious guests.

Toward the end of his life, our curé had a shock which must have hastened his demise. He insisted on hiding his money, like many old people who don't dare invest it and thus turn the savings destined to give them security in their old age into a source of torment. He had stowed his hoard in the attic. A neighbor whom he had covered with kindness, they say, succumbed to temptation, climbed onto the roof at night, slipped through an attic window, and carried off the curé's treasure. When the latter discovered the theft, he nearly went mad with anger and grief. He was in bed, almost delirious, when the royal prosecutor came, at his request, to investigate the facts and file the charge. The old fellow's sorrow and indignation were all the more intense because he had guessed the identity of the criminal, but when asked to name the suspect, he felt compassion for this man for whom he had had affection, and perhaps also Christian remorse for the love of money which had possessed him. "Do what you have to do," he said to the magistrate who was questioning him. "True, I've been robbed, but if I have suspicions, I need tell them only to God, and it's not my function to punish the guilty." In vain, the king's officers urged him to speak. "I've nothing to say," he said, turning his back crossly. "I might be mistaken; you magistrates must take this on your conscience, that's your profession, not mine."

The following night, the money was brought back to the attic, and Manette, searching about despairingly, found it in the hiding place from which it had been taken. The thief, full of remorse and touched by the curé's generosity, had immediately made restitution. To bring a halt to the investigation and the gossip of the parishioners, the curé let it be known that he had dreamed he had been robbed, or that his servant, to hide the money better, had put it somewhere else and had forgotten where the next day, because she was so very old that she had lost her memory. Several versions of the story spread, and you can still hear the curé's misadventure recounted with varying details. But he himself told me what I have set down here, and I think it does him honor, and even does the thief honor, for the Christian view that repentance is more pleasing to God than perseverance in good deeds is a fine sentiment of which human justice takes little account.

This old curé was very fond of me. Even when I was thirty-five he still said of me, "Aurore is one child that I've always loved." And he wrote to my husband, thinking apparently that the latter might be offended by his words, "Indeed, sir, take it however you wish, but I dearly love your wife."

Truly, he behaved in a completely paternal fashion to me. For twenty years he dined with me every Sunday after vespers. Sometimes I dropped in on him on my walks. Once I hurt my foot while walking, and I don't know how I would have gotten home—for in those days there were no carriages on the roads of Saint-Chartier—if the curé hadn't offered to take me on the back of his mare; but I should have put the curé behind me, for he was so old by that time that the horse's movement put him to sleep. I was dreamily gazing at the landscape when I realized that the horse, having little by little slowed her pace, had now stopped and was browsing, while the curé snored contentedly. Fortunately, habit had made him a secure horseman, even in his sleep; I used my heels, and the mare, who knew her way, brought us home, even though the reins were loose on her neck.

After dinner, at which he ate and drank copiously, he fell asleep again by the fireside, and his snores made the window panes shake. Then he would wake up and ask me to play him a little piece on the harpsichord or spinet. He could not bring himself to say "piano," the word seemed too new to him. As he grew older, he no longer heard the bass notes. The high notes of the instrument still gave him some sensation in the eardrums. One day he said to me, "I no longer hear anything at all. Goodness, I am really old!" Poor man! He had been old for many long years. Yet he still climbed on his horse at ten o'clock at night and returned to his presbytery in the middle of winter, refusing all offers to send someone with him. A few hours before his death he said to the servant whom I'd sent to inquire how he was, "Tell that Aurore not to send anything else. I no longer need anything, and tell her also that I love her very much, and her children, too."

The greatest proof of devotion one can receive, it seems to me, is to have filled the thoughts of a dying soul. Perhaps too, there is something prophetic in this, which should inspire trust or terror. When the Mother Superior of my convent lay dying, of the sixty girls who had an equal claim on her, she thought only of me, for whom she had never shown special concern. "Poor Dupin," she said several times in her agony, "what a pity that she should lose her grandmother!" She imagined it was my grandmother who was sick and dying, not herself. This left me with great anxiety and a kind of superstitious fear of some impending misfortune.

I was about seven when Deschartres was made my tutor. For quite a while, I accepted his authority, for in the early years he was as calm and patient with me as he was rough and brutal with Hippolyte. That is why I made rapid progress, for he could explain things clearly and concisely when he was calm; but once excited, he became wordy, confused in his explanations, and stuttering with rage, totally incoherent. He mistreated and manhandled Hippolyte horribly, although the boy had ability and an excellent memory. He took no account of the fact that Hippolyte's robust temperament needed phusical activity and that he could not bear excessively long lessons. I must confess, despite my affection for my brother, he was an exasperating child. He liked to break, destroy, tease, and play practical jokes on everyone.

One day, he threw burning sticks into the fireplace, saying that he was "sacrificing to the gods of the underworld," and he set fire to the house. Another time, he put powder into a big log so that it exploded in the fireplace and hurled the soup kettle into the middle of the kitchen. He called that "studying the theory of volcanoes." Then he would fasten pots to the dogs' tails and enjoy their frantic flight through the garden and their howls of terror. He "shoed" the cats, that is, he glued nutshells on each of their four paws and let them loose on ice or the parquet floors, then watched them slip and fall, scramble up and fall again a hundred times, while he shouted fearful oaths. On other occasions, he declared he was Calchas, the Greek high priest, and pretending to sacrifice Iphigenia on the kitchen table, he would seize a knife usually employed on less famous victims, and brandishing it to the right and left, injure others or himself.

On occasion I took some part in his misdeeds, as far as my less impetuous nature allowed. One day, when we had seen a fattened pig slaughtered in the yard, Hippolyte took it into his head to treat the cucumbers in the garden in the same way. He inserted a little wooden plug into one end, which according to him represented the animal's throat; then, pressing the unfortunate plants with his foot, he squeezed out all their juice. Ursule gathered it in an old flower pot to make blood sausage, and I solemnly lit an imaginary fire by her side, to roast the pork, that is, the cucumber, as we had seen the butcher do. This game amused us so much that, going from one cucumber to another, choosing the fattest ones first and finishing with the less fleshy, we soon devastated the entire bed the gardener had been at great pains to grow. You can imagine his chagrin when he saw that scene of carnage. Hippolyte, amid the corpses, was like Ajax, in his madness, immolating the herds of the Greeks. The gardener complained and we were punished, but that did not restore the cucumbers, and we ate none that year.

Another of our naughty pleasures was to make what the children in our village called "dog-traps." These consist of a hole which is filled with loose dirt soaked in water. The trap is then covered with little sticks over which are placed some pieces of slate and a thin layer of earth or dried leaves; when this trap is set in the middle of a road or garden path, one watches for passersby and hides in the bushes to see them sink in the mud, cursing the rascally urchins who "invent themselves such tricks."[5] If the hole is deep, one can break one's legs in it, but ours did not present that danger, since they were rather broad than deep. It was fun to see the gardener's terror when he felt the soil give way under his feet in the finest spots along his raked walks, and we knew it would take him an hour to repair the damage. One fine day, Deschartres fell into a trap. He always wore lovely, pure white ribbed hose, short breeches, and pretty nankeen gaiters, for he was very vain regarding his legs and feet; he was meticulously clean and refined in his footwear. Moreover, like all pedants (it is a characteristic trait by which they can be infallibly recognized even if they are not professional teachers) he always walked with straightened knees and his feet turned outward. We walked behind him, to have a better view of the spectacle. Suddenly the earth collapsed, and there he was sunk to mid-calf in yellowish mud, admirably mixed to dye his hose. Hippolyte acted completely astonished, and all Deschartres' rage burst out against Ursule and me, but we were hardly afraid of him, and had run a good distance before he could recover his shoes.

Since Deschartres would beat my poor brother unmercifully, while limiting himself to ineffectual scoldings for the little girls, we three decided that Ursule and I would take the blame for many of our common pranks. To fool our tutor better, we worked out a little comedy which was quite successful for a while. Hippolyte would take the initiative. "Just see what those silly girls have done now!" he would shout, as soon as he had broken a plate, or made a dog yap too close to Deschartres' ear. "They do nothing but mischief! Stop your nonsense, young ladies!" And he would run off, while Deschartres, peering out the window, would be puzzled at not seeing the girls.

One day when Deschartres had gone to sell some livestock at the fair, for agriculture and the management of our farms were his primary concern, Hippolyte, who was supposed to be studying his lessons in the "great man's" room, decided to be the great man himself. He put on Deschartres' stout hunting coat, which came down to his heels, set the cap with earflaps on his head, and proceeded to march up and down the room with his feet turned outward and his hands behind his back, in the style of our pedagogue. Then he did a scrupulous imitation of his language, went to the blackboard, drew chalk figures, started demonstrating a theorem, got angry, stuttered, and called his pupil a "gross ingoramus" and a "lout." Then, delighted with his own talent as a mimic, he went to the window and took the gardener to task for the way he was pruning the trees; he criticized, reprimanded, insulted, and threatened him—all in Deschartres' style and with the latter's characteristic vocal outbursts. Either because the imitation was so accurate, or the distance between them so great, the gardener, who was a simple, credulous fellow, was taken in, and began to answer back and protest. But imagine his stupefaction when he perceived the real Deschartres, who only a few steps away stood observing this little comedy, noting his double's every word and gesture! The tutor should have laughed at all this, but he could not bear to be made fun of, and Hippolyte unfortunately did not see him, for he was hidden by the trees. Deschartres, who had come back from the fair earlier than expected, crept noiselessly up to his room and suddenly opened the door, just as the mischievous boy was shouting to an imaginary Hippolyte, "You are not working properly, your handwriting is like a cat's tracks, and you spell like a hauler! Biff, bang! Take this box on the ears, you wretched little beast!"

And then there was a double drama—Deschartres' imposter slapped an imaginary Hippolyte while the real Deschartres slapped the real Hippolyte.

Deschartres taught me grammar, and my grandmother taught me music. My mother supervised my reading and writing. I had no religious instruction, although I read Bible stories. I was free to believe or reject the miracles said to have taken place in ancient times. My mother taught me to say my prayers kneeling beside her; she did not fail in that observance, nor has she ever. And her prayers were long, for after I had finished mine and had gone to bed, I could see her still kneeling, her face in her hands, deeply absorbed. However, she never went to confession nor ate meat on Friday, but she went to mass on Sunday, or if forced to miss it, she prayed twice as long. When my grandmother asked her why she practiced her religion in this partial manner, she would answer, "I have my own religion; as for prescribed religion, some of it I take, some of it I leave. I can't abide priests; to me they're humbugs, and I'll never confess to them; they would take all my thoughts the wrong way. I don't think I'm committing a sin, because if I am, it's in spite of myself. I won't overcome my faults; I can't help them; but I love God with a sincere heart; I think He's too good to punish us in another life. We're punished enough for our foolishness in this one; nonetheless, I'm very much afraid of death, but that's because I love life and not because I'm afraid to appear before God, whom I trust and know I have never willingly offended."

"But what do you say to Him in your lengthy prayers?"

"I tell Him that I love Him. He comforts me in my sorrows, and I ask Him to reunite me with my husband in the next world."

"But why do you go to mass? You do not understand what it is about."

"I like to pray in church; I know that God is everywhere, but I see Him better in church, and that prayer said in common seems a better prayer. My attention often wanders, the service lasts too long, but finally there's a good moment when I pray with all my heart, and that relieves me."

"However," my grandmother persisted, "you shun pious people."

"Yes," my mother would answer, "because they're intolerant and hypocritical, and I believe that if God could hate any of His creatures, he would hate religious fanatics the most."

"You condemn your own religion, if you say that those who are the most observant are the most hateful people in the world. By that token, it must be an evil religion, and the further one goes from it, the better one must be as a person. Doesn't that follow logically from your ideas?"

"You ask me too many questions," my mother would reply. "I'm not used to analyzing my feelings; I do what I feel inclined to do, and whatever my heart bids me I do, without asking my mind for a reason."

The reader can see from that conversation and from the religious training given me, or rather the absence of any systematic religious education, that my grandmother was not a Catholic at all. Not only did she hate pious people, as did my mother, she hated piety itself, as well as Catholicism, which she judged with implacable detachment. She was not an atheist, far from it. She believed in that natural religion advocated but not precisely defined by the eighteenth-century philosophers. She called herself a deist and rejected with equal disdain all dogmas, all forms of religion. She declared that she highly esteemed Jesus Christ, and since she admired the Gospels as excellent philosophy, she deplored the fact that the truth had always been entwined with more or less ridiculous fables.

Later I shall make clear which of her ideas I held on to or abandoned. But following the development of my being, step by step, I must say that in childhood my instinct inclined me much more toward my mother's naïve and trusting faith than the critical and rather icy analysis of my grandmama. Without realizing it, my mother imbued her religious feelings with poetry, and I needed poetry—not the stiff and studied poetry that was devised at that period to combat the positivism of the eighteenth century, but the poetry inherent in reality itself, which one absorbs in childhood without knowing what it is or what to call it. To put it simply, I needed poetry as the common people need it, as my mother needed it, as the peasant needs it when he bows down sometimes before God, sometimes before the devil, sometimes confusing one with the other, trying to placate all the mysterious forces of nature.

I passionately loved the supernatural, and my grandmother's explanations of it did not satisfy my imagination. I read with equal pleasure the prodigies of Hebrew and pagan antiquity. I would love to have believed in them; however, since from time to time my grandmother briefly and dryly appealed to my reason, I could not have complete faith. But I revenged myself for the little grief this caused me by refusing to deny anything in my heart of hearts. It was exactly like the feeling I had about the fairy tales I read—I now believed them halfway and only, you might say, in fits and starts.

The guises that religious feeling assumes in various individuals depend on their temperament, and unlike my grandmother, I do not condemn all piety because of the defects of some pious persons. Piety is an intensification of our mental faculties, as drunkenness is an intensification of our physical ones. Any wine can be inebriating if one drinks too much of it; that is not the fault of the wine. There are those who can take a great deal and whom it makes even more lucid. A little dose turns others into idiots or enrages them. But in the last analysis, I think wine only brings out the best or the worst in us, and the best wine in the world is bad for those who have a weak head and are sensitive to it by nature. Religious exaltation, no matter what dogma it rests on, is by analogy a sublime, hateful, or wretched state, depending upon whether the vessel wherein this liquor ferments is secure or fragile. This overstimulation of our being makes us saints or persecutors, martyrs or executioners; and Christianity certainly cannot be blamed because Catholics invented the Inquisition and its tortures.

In general what shocks me in pious people is not the flaws which are the inevitable consequence of their temperament, but the lack of logic in their lives and opinions. No matter how much they deny it, they do what my mother did. They take and leave what they want of their faith, and they do not have the right that my mother was justified in claiming, since she laid no claim to orthodoxy. When I was pious, I scrutinized my every act and never took a step without examining it and asking my timorous conscience whether it was permissible to walk with the right or the left foot. If I were observant today, I would perhaps not have the energy to be intolerant of others, because character never changes, but I would be intolerant of myself, and since maturity brings with it a sort of positive logic, I would consider nothing sufficiently austere for myself. Thus I have never understood society women who go to balls and theaters, show their bare shoulders, take pains to be beautiful, and yet receive all the sacraments, omit none of the obligations of their faith, and feel completely at peace with themselves. I do not refer here to hypocrites: they are not pious; I am speaking of very sincere women whom I have often asked to tell me what secret permits them to sin without scruple against their own convictions. Each of them explained it in her own way, so that I am just ignorant as ever.

Nor do I understand certain men who sincerely believe that all the obligations prescribed by the Christian faith are excellent, who ardently defend their basic principles, and yet carry out none of them. It seems to me that if I believed one act to be better than another, I would not hesitate to do it. What's more, I would not forgive myself if I didn't. This absence of logic in individuals whom I know to be intelligent and sincere is something I have never understood. This will perhaps become clearer to me when I systematically review all my memories—something that will happen for the first time in my life, no doubt, as I set them down, and I shall be able to analyze the soul coming to grips with faith and doubt by recalling how I became pious and how I ceased to be so.

At the age of seven or eight, I had more or less command of my language. That was too soon, for I was immediately made to take up other studies and was not forced to make a closer study of grammar. I was encouraged to do a great deal of scribbling, my style was commented on, but I was only casually made aware of the incorrect usages that crept into it as I became more and more adept in my own facility in expressing myself. At the convent, it was decided that I knew French well enough not to have to go to any French classes, and actually, when put to the test, I did very well on the easy tasks demanded of students my age; but later on, when I began to write, I was often at a loss. In a later chapter I shall tell how, when I left the convent, I relearned French, and how twelve years later, when I wanted to write for publication, I realized that I did not yet know anything; how I set myself to study it all over again, an effort that came too late to be very useful, which is why I am still learning my own language by practicing it and why I am afraid that I shall never know it. Purity and correctness are still what my mind craves today more than ever, and I never make an error out of carelessness or lack of attention, but out of genuine ignorance.

It was my misfortune that Deschartres, who shared the prejudice underlying masculine education, believed that to refine the use of my own language, he should teach me Latin. I was perfectly willing to learn anything I was asked to learn, and I resignedly took my dose of basic Latin. But the French, Latin, and Greek taught to children take too much time, either because they are taught by faulty methods, because they are the most difficult languages in the world, or because the study of any language is the most tedious and sterile activity for children. Unless they have very special aptitudes, children come out of preparatory school knowing neither French nor Latin, and Greek even less. As for me, the time I wasted not learning Latin might have been much better employed studying French, at an age when one learns better than at any other.

Fortunately, I stopped studying Latin quite early, with the result that even if I do not know French very well, I know it better than most men of my generation. I am not referring to men of letters, who I suspect did not acquire their styles and attitudes in school, but to the large number of men who, once they finished their classical studies, never again thought of making language a special object of study. You will notice that they cannot write a three-page letter without making an error in usage or spelling. You will also find that women of twenty to thirty, who have had some education, usually write French better than men, which in my view is the result of their not having wasted eight or ten years of their lives learning dead languages.

All this is by way of saying that I have always found the system used to educate boys deplorable, and I am not alone in this opinion. I have heard all manner of men say that they wasted their time and lost their love of study in school. Those who profited from it are exceptions. Can we not then set up a system in which the intelligence of ordinary children is not sacrificed to the needs of a select few? *S.G.G.*

IV

The tyranny and weakness of Deschartres. —Fischer's minuet.
—The magic book. —We conjure the devil. —The seeker of
affection. —My brother's first loves. —Pauline. —Masters Gogault
and Loubens. —Disinclination for the social graces. —Maréchal
Maison. —The apartment on Rue Thiroux. —Great sadness at age
seven on anticipating marriage. —The army's departure for the
Russian campaign. —Nohant. —Ursule and her sisters. —How
games affected me. —My old friends. —Czar Alexander's war
strategies. —Moscow.

We used to have our lessons in Deschartres' room, a room very neatly
kept, to be sure, but in which the odor of lavender soap reigned so completely as
to finally make me nauseous. My own lessons were not very long, but those of
my poor brother would last all afternoon, because he was condemned to study
his assignment and prepare his homework under the gaze of the pedagogue. It is
true that if he wasn't watched, he would not even open a book. He would make
his way to freedom through the fields and disappear for the entire day.

God had certainly created this impetuous child and put him into the
world to make Deschartres do penance, but Deschartres, a tyrant by nature, did
not take his escapades in the proper spirit of mortification. He would make the
boy horribly unhappy, and the child must have been made of iron not to
explode under the harsh constraints.

It was not Latin that caused his martyrdom; he was not taught it. It was
mathematics, for which he had shown a little aptitude, and in truth he did have
some. It wasn't that he hated study for its own sake, but he preferred movement
and gaiety, for which he had an insatiable need. Deschartres also taught him
music. The recorder being the tutor's favorite instrument, Hippolyte had to learn
it, like it or not; a boxwood recorder was purchased for him, and Deschartres,
armed with his ivory inlaid ebony recorder, would rap the boy's fingers at each
false note. A certain minuet by Fischer must have left callouses on the hands of
the unfortunate pupil. This was all the more blameworthy on Deschartres' part
considering that, no matter how irritated, he was always able to control himself
with the people he liked. He had never brutalized my father as a child, and he
never lost himself with me to the point of physical violence, except for one single time in his life. He probably felt a sort of aversion for Hippolyte due to his
nasty tricks and teasing. And yet he was, because of my father, truly interested

in the boy. Nothing obliged Deschartres to instruct him, but he applied himself to the task with an obstinacy which could not have been motivated by vengeance, for he would have quickly tired of a satisfaction for which his pupil made him pay so dearly. He had imposed this task on himself as a matter of conscience, but the truth is that on occasion his resentment exacted its price.

When I joined Hippolyte for my lessons, he with his elbows on the table and taking aim at invisible targets whenever he was not being watched, Ursule was always present. Deschartres liked this self-assured little girl who spoke up to him and answered his question with precision. Like all violent men, Deschartres happened to like open resistance and became quite easygoing, even lenient, with those who did not fear him. Hippolyte's mistake, and his misfortune, was that he never told him to his face how unjust and cruel he was. If he had threatened but once to complain to my grandmother or leave the house, Deschartres would surely have backed down, but the child feared and hated him, and consoled himself by means of vengeance alone.

He was certainly ingenious at it, and he had a diabolical knack for recognizing and exposing absurdity. Often in the middle of a lesson, Deschartres would be called away to the house or the farmyard regarding some detail related to his agricultural work. These absences would be profitably employed in mocking him. Hippolyte would pick up the ebony recorder and mimic his professor with rare imitative skill. The truth is there was nothing more ridiculous than Deschartres playing the recorder. That pastoral instrument was already ridiculous in the hands of so solemn a personage and in the middle of such a habitually scowling face. Furthermore, he played it extremely pretentiously, arching his fingers gracefully, swaying his large body, and puckering his upper lip so affectedly that it gave him the funniest expression in the world. It was especially during Fischer's minuet that he would display all his techniques, and Hippolyte in fact knew entirely by heart this very piece, which he always failed to read properly when the music and Deschartres' menacing face were before him. But as a result of imitating him, he had learned it in spite of himself, and I believe that he never did any other kind of musical study than that.

Ursule, who was very well behaved during the lesson, would become extremely turbulent during the intermissions. She clambered over everything, thumbed through all the books, shifted all the slippers and soaps from their places, and laughed uproariously at each of Hippolyte's denigrating remarks on the appearance, personal habits, and idiosyncrasies of the pedagogue. He always used to keep on his library shelves little bags of seeds with which he was experimenting in the garden—endlessly dreaming of ways in which to acclimate some new fodder, grain, or legume to conditions in our terrain, and hoping thus to eclipse the glory of some competitor on the agricultural committee. We were careful to mix up for him all those seeds which he had so scrupulously sorted with his own hands. We would mix pastel with colza, buckwheat with millet, so much so that the seeds would all grow helter-skelter, and he would harvest alfalfa where he had sown turnips. He would accumulate manuscript upon manuscript to prove to his colleagues in the agricultural society that M. Cadet de Vaux was an ass, and M. Rougier de la Bergerie was a calf, for it was in those hardly parliamentary terms that he warred against the systems of his competitors in agricultural science. We rearranged the pages of his tracts and added letters to various words to make it look as if he had mispelled them. Once, it happened that he mailed to the printer a manuscript thus embellished and rearranged, and when his proofs were returned to him for correction, he exploded in terrific fury against the cretinous typesetter who committed such egregious errors.

Among his books, there were several which piqued our curiosity, including *Le Grand Albert* and *Le Petit Albert*,[9] and various extremely old manuals of rural and home economics, all filled with quackish notions. There was one whose name I forget, which Deschartres had placed on the highest shelf, and which he valued for the antiquity of the edition. I could not really say just what it was about, or what it was worth; we never did get to peruse it, for the climb to capture and then replace it took up a good portion of the time we snatched unwatched by our tutor. As far as I can recall, there was a bit of everything in it—remedies for healing the human as well as animal diseases, recipes for medicines, foods, liqueurs, and poisons. There was also some magic in it, which interested us the most. Hippolyte had once heard someone tell Deschartres that it contained a formula for conjuring the devil. It was just a question of finding it among all the hodgepodge, and we set ourselves to that task over twenty times. Each time we thought we were getting to the magical page, we would hear Deschartres' heavy step reverberating on the stairs. It would have been much simpler to ask him to show it to us. Probably, in one of his better moods, he would have humorously taught us the procedure for calling up Satan, but it seemed so much more exciting to discover the secret and conduct the experiment on our own.

At long last, Hippolyte came to get us one day when Deschartres was out hunting. He had found, or thought he had found, among various spells, the one that was used for the devil. There were some words to say, some lines to draw on the floor with chalk, and other sundry preparations that escape me which we were unable to fulfill. Whether Hippolyte was making fun of us or whether he in fact believed a little in the power of the formulae, we did what he prescribed—he, book in hand, and we, following in different directions the lines traced on the floor. It was a sort of Pythagorean chart, with squares, diamonds, stars, signs of the zodiac, many numbers and other cabalistic figures, which is now rather hazy in my memory.

What I do recall clearly is the emotion that came over us as we worked. The book said that the first indication of the operation's success would be a burst of blue flame over certain numbers or signs, and we were awaiting this miracle with some degree of anxiety. Not that we really believed in it—Hippolyte being already pretty much of a skeptic, and I having been accustomed by my mother and grandmother (in agreement, on this point) to think of the devil's existence as a hoax, a make-believe bugaboo for little children. But Ursule, though still laughing, grew fearful and left the room, refusing our pleas to come back.

Then my brother and I, finding ourselves alone at work and unsustained by the gaiety of our chum, took up the operation once again with a semblance of courage. Despite ourselves, our imaginations were being fired, and the expectation of a wonder, whatever it might be, was beginning to agitate us a little. Once the flames appeared, we were prepared to forgo the rest of the experiment whereby the two horns of Lucifer would pierce through the floor beneath the center numerals.

"Damn!" Hippolyte commented, "the book says that those persons who don't have the nerve to go to the end may, by quickly erasing certain numerals, make the devil go back underground at the moment his head becomes visible. Except that you mustn't let his eyes come up, for as soon as he's looked at you, you no longer have the power to send him away without speaking to him. I don't know if I'd have the nerve to go that far, but I'd at least like to see the tips of his horns."

"But if he looks at us, and if we have to speak to him," I answered, "what will we tell him?"

"My goodness," he replied, "I'll command him to carry off Deschartres, his recorder, and all his old books."

We certainly took the thing lightly chatting in this way, but we were not any the less affected by it. Children cannot toy with the miraculous without somehow feeling shaken, and by the same token, people of ages past have been children of credulity not so different than we were.

We completed the experiment as well as we could, and not only didn't the devil appear, but there was not even the tiniest little flame. We did put our ears to the ground, however, and Hippolyte insisted that he could hear a little crackling, forerunner of the first sparks, but he was making fun of me, and I was not taken in, although I was also pretending to be listening and hearing something. It was only a game, but a game that made our hearts beat faster. Our jokes reassured us and kept our minds sharp, but I do not know whether we would have dared thus to toy with hell without the other being present. I do not believe Hippolyte tried it again.

We were, nevertheless, a little disappointed to have taken so much trouble for nothing, and we consoled ourselves by recognizing that we did not have half the objects designated by the book for making the spell work. We promised ourselves that we would procure them, and for several days we actually gathered certain herbs and remnants of cloth, but as there were a host of other scientific prescriptions that we did not understand, as well as ingredients that were completely unknown to us, the thing never went any further.

Deschartres' recorder reminds me that there was a crazy man from La Châtre who often used to come around and ask our teacher to play a little tune, and the latter was careful never to refuse him, for he was a very attentive auditor, probably the only one he had ever charmed. His name was M. Demai. He was still young, dressed quite appropriately, with a pleasing expression on his face, except for a big black beard, which was considered to be very shocking at that period when men were all clean shaven and only the military sported mustaches. He was gentle and polite; his madness took the form of a deep melancholy, a sort of solemn preoccupation, never a smile, the calm of unbounded despair or boredom. He would arrive alone at any hour of the day, and we noticed with surprise that the dogs, who were quite vicious, would bark from afar at him, approach with care to sniff his clothing, and withdraw at once, as if they had realized that this was an inoffensive and powerless being. He, on the other hand, paying no attention to the dogs, would enter the house or the garden, and although he had never had anything to do with us before the onset of his madness, he would stop by the first person he met, say a few words to him or her, and remain for a time, without demanding anyone's attention. Sometimes he would enter my grandmother's rooms without knocking, without thinking of having himself announced, and would very politely ask for her news; he would reply to her queries that he was feeling quite well, would take a chair without being asked, and would impassively remain there while my grandmother continued writing or giving me my lesson. If it was my music lesson, he would get up, stand behind the harpsichord, and remain there, immobile, until the end.

When his presence became inconvenient, someone would say to him, "Well, M. Demai, is there anything you wish?"

"Nothing unusual," he would answer. "I'm looking for affection."

"Haven't you found it yet, in all the time you've been looking for it?" "No," he'd say, "and yet I've searched everywhere. I don't know where it could be."

"Have you looked in the garden?"

"No, not yet," he'd say, and struck with a sudden idea, he would go out in the garden, walk along every path and into every nook, sit on the grass beside us watching our games with a solemn air, go upstairs to Deschartres', go into my mother's room, and even into the unused rooms; he went through the entire house, asking nothing of anyone, and responding to whoever might question him that he was searching for affection. The servants, in order to be rid of him, would say, "You won't find it here. Go down toward La Châtre. You'll surely meet up with it there." Sometimes he seemed to understand that he was being treated like a child. He would sigh, and go away. At other times, he would seem to believe what was being said to him, and would hurriedly make his way back to town.

I believe I had heard it said that he had gone mad from lovesickness, but that he would have done so from any other cause, because there were other madmen in his family. Whatever the reason, that poor seeker of affection never fails to move me when I remember him. As children, we loved him with no other motive than our compassion, for he said almost nothing to us; and he paid us so little attention that, despite the fact that he would watch us play together for hours at a time, he could not tell us apart. He called Hippolyte Monsieur Maurice, and often asked Ursule if she was Mademoiselle Dupin, or me if I was Ursule. We had instinctive respect for his misfortune, for we never teased or avoided him. He hardly answered questions and seemed content if no one repulsed or fled from him. He may have been quite curable through a sustained treatment of kindness, distractions, and friendship, but probably his life was devoid of any moral or intellectual caring, for he always came alone and left the same way. He ended up committing suicide. At any rate the unfortunate man was found drowned in a well, where doubtless he was seeking affection, that indefinable object of his painful desire.

My mother left us at the beginning of autumn. She could not abandon Caroline and found herself forced to divide her life between her two children. She lectured me quite a lot to keep me from wishing to follow her; I was sorely distressed, but we were all to leave for Paris at the end of October. It would be two months of separation at the most, and the terror that had taken hold of me the previous year at the idea of an absolute separation had been dispelled by the fact that we had lived side by side practically without interruption since that time. She made me understand that Caroline needed her, that we would soon be reunited in Paris, and that she would come to Nohant again next year, and I gave in.

Those two months passed without problems; I was getting used to the imposing ways of my grandmama, I had become reasonable enough to make obedience easy, and for her part, she had somewhat relaxed her demands regarding my sense of decorum.

In the country, the effects of my sloppiness were less noticeable to her. It was in Paris that she compared me with the little dolls of society and became alarmed at my outspokeness and peasant's manners. Then would begin again the minor persecution which did me dubious good.

We left Nohant as promised, at the first frost. It was decided that Hippolyte would go to boarding school in Paris in order to polish up his rustic behavior. Deschartres offered to take him there, choose the establishment destined to have the good fortune of housing such a considerate pupil, and make him at home there. He was outfitted for the occasion, and as he and Deschartres were to take the coach at Châteauroux, it was agreed that we would cross La Brande together, we in our carriage, driven by Saint-Jean and the two old horses, Hippolyte and Deschartres astride the peaceful mares from the farm. But a few days before leaving, someone realized that Hippolyte would need some boots to make this trip on horseback, for the short pants and white stockings of his first communion had been outgrown.

A pair of boots! For a long time it had been the big boy's dream, his ambition, his ideal. He had tried to make a pair for himself out of some of Deschartres' old scraps and a big piece of leather he had found in the shed, perhaps the hood of some rebuilt buggy. He had worked for four days and nights, cutting, sewing, soaking the leather in the horses' trough to soften it, and had succeeded in constructing for himself a pair of formless shoes worthy of an Eskimo, which came apart at the first wearing. Therefore, his dreams came true when the shoemaker brought him real boots, with iron-tipped heels and straps for spurs.

I think his was the greatest joy experienced by any mortal I have ever witnessed. The trip to Paris, the first move in his life, the ride on horseback, the idea of soon being separated from Deschartres—all that was nothing compared to the joy of having boots. He himself placed that childhood satisfaction, as he remembered it, above all others he has known since, and he often says, "First loves? You bet! Mine was a pair of boots, and I swear I never felt so happy and proud!"

They were hussar's boots, in the style of those days, and they were worn over more or less tight-fitting pants. I can still see them, for my brother made me look at them and praise them so many times, willing or not, that they filled my thoughts to the point of dreaming about them. He put them on the night before our departure and never took them off until we reached Paris, for he slept with them on. But he could not sleep, he was so afraid, not that his boots might rip the bedsheets, but rather that the sheets might dull the shine of his boots. Hence he got up on the stroke of midnight and came into my room in order to examine them by the light of the fire which was still glowing in the hearth. My nursemaid, sleeping in an adjacent alcove, tried to send him away, which was impossible. He awakened me to show me his boots, and then sat down before the fire, not wishing to sleep, for that would have meant losing a few moments of his happiness. Drowsiness did, however, overcome his transports, and when my maid woke me up to leave, we saw Hippolyte, who had slipped down to the floor, asleep on the flagstones in front of the fireplace.

We were leaving before daybreak in order to get to La Brande at sunrise, so that we might be out of there by nightfall. A whole day to travel four or five leagues! Not too much to ask from Saint-Jean, who liked to spare his animals, and never failed to get lost no matter how much of a good start he had had. Whenever his horses found the right path by instinct, he would fall deeply asleep in the saddle—bogs and passengers be damned!

Luckily we did have a guide this time. Deschartres, who knew the road well, cantered along ahead, and Hippolyte, at the flank, aroused the mettle of our horses and kept Saint-Jean alert.

Perhaps I saw my mother a bit less in Paris during the winter of 1811-1812. I was being trained to do without her, and she for her part, sensing that she owed more of herself to Caroline, who had no grandmama to spoil her, went along with the prevailing wish to see me accept what was my due. That season, I was given the diversions and pleasures suitable for someone my age. My grandmother was connected with a Mme. de Fargès, whose daughter, Mme. de Pontcarré, had a charming girl named Pauline.

We got acquainted and remained close until the time of our respective marriages, which distanced us from each other under circumstances which I shall relate when the time comes.

Pauline, who later became a ravishingly beautiful young lady, was blond, slender, slightly pale, lively, agreeable, and a very playful child. She had a magnificently curly head of hair, superb blue eyes, regular features, and was about the same age as I was. As her mother was a woman of intelligence, the child was not at all affected. And yet her deportment was better than mine—she was lighter on her feet and lost her handkerchief and gloves far less often. Hence my grandmother would suggest her as a model at every opportunity, a sure way to make me detest her, had I been as vain as they were trying to make me and had I not had an irresistible need all my life to grow fond of those beings with whom I chanced to live.

Therefore, I dearly loved Pauline, who allowed herself to be loved. That was her nature. She was kind, sincere, amiable, but cold. I do not know whether she has changed. It would surprise me if she has.

We took all our lessons together, and as my grandmother hardly had the time while in Paris to teach me herself, Mme. de Pontcarré was kind enough to include me in Pauline's studies, as Pauline was included in mine. Three times a week, a writing master, a dancing master, and a music teacher came to our house for the two of us. The other days, Mme. de Pontcarré came to get me, and she herself took the trouble to review music theory and teach us piano technique. She was an excellent musician who sang with a great deal of feeling and power. Her beautiful voice and the brilliant ways she found to accompany herself on a more extended keyboard and less shrill instrument than our Nohant harpsichord enlarged my taste for music. After music, she taught us geography and a little history. She used Father Gaultier's method for all these subjects, which was then in vogue, and which I believe was excellent. It was a sort of game, with balls and tokens as in lotto, and we would learn while playing. She was very gentle and encouraging with me, but whether Pauline had poorer concentration or whether in fact her mother was propelled by that desire that mothers have to see their children make rapid progress, she used to brutalize her a little, and even pinched her ears in a completely Napoleonic spirit of instruction. Pauline would cry and scream, but finally the lesson came to a happy conclusion, and immediately afterwards Mme. de Pontcarré would take us out and bring us to her mother's to play. Her mother had a ground-floor apartment with a garden, somewhere on Rue de la Ferme-des-Mathurins or Rue Victoire. I had a very good time there because there were often other children, who, although a few years older, were willing to include us in their games of hide-and-seek and tag. These were the children of Mme. de Brosses, second daughter, I believe, of Mme. de Fargès, consequently Pauline's cousins. The only thing I remember about the boy was his name—Ernest; the girl was already quite grown up compared to us. But she was cheerful, lively, and very witty. Her name was Constance, and she was then at the English Convent, which Pauline and I have since attended. There was also a young man with a pleasant face despite an enormous nose—Fernand de Prunelé. He was the referee of our competitive games, therefore the most obligingly tolerant person insofar as the sulking and whims of the two little girls were concerned. Sometimes we would all dine together, and after dinner, we would be allowed free run of the dining room, where we made a tremendous racket. The servants and even the mothers would come to take part in the games. In a way it was country life transported to Paris, and I had a great need of that.

From time to time, I also saw my dear Clotilde, with whom I quarreled a lot more than with Pauline, because she responded more to my affection and was not inclined to overlook my misdemeanors. She would get angry when I got angry, become obstinate whenever I set the example, and then there would be hugs and kisses and transports of tenderness, as there had been with Ursule—better ones, actually, for we had slept in the same cradle and had been nourished on the same milk, our mothers offering the breast to whichever of us cried first; and although we had never spent much time together since then, there had always been a kind of blood tie between us much stronger than our familial relationship would suggest; we did consider ourselves twin sisters since childhood.

Hippolyte was at boarding school part-time. During the hours he spent at home and during his days off, he took writing and dancing lessons with us. I shall say something about our teachers, about whom I have not forgotten a thing.

M. Gogault, our dancing master, danced at the Opéra. He scraped away on his pocket violin and maneuvered our feet into a turned-out position. Sometimes Deschartres, auditing the lesson, went him one better by reproaching us for walking like bears or dancing like parrots. But we, who hated the pretentious walk of Deschartes, and who thought M. Gogault's way of entering a room singularly ridiculous—like a zephyr poised to perform an entrechat—would hastily turn our feet back inward as soon as he left; and as he had turned them to make them assume the "first position," we would turn them in the opposite direction, for fear they might stay as he had placed them. We called this clandestine work the "sixth position." (Everyone knows that, in principle, ballet has only five positions.)

Hippolyte was as heavy and clumsy as could be, frightfully so, and M. Gogault would declare that never had such a cart horse passed through his hands. His *changements de pied* shook the whole house; his *battements* nearly cracked the walls. When he was told to lift his head without craning his neck, he would take hold of his chin and keep it lifted while dancing. The teacher could hardly help laughing, while Deschartres gave vent to serious and vehement indignation against the pupil, who, nonetheless, thought his willingness to learn had been proved beyond question.

The writing master's name was M. Loubens. He was a most pretentious teacher, capable of ruining the best handwriting with his method. He insisted on arm-and-body position, as if writing were some kind of choreographed mime, but this was all consistent with the kind of education my grandmother wanted to give us. One had to do everything with so-called grace. Hence, M. Loubens had invented various instruments of torture to assure that his pupils would keep their heads straight, their elbows loose, three fingers stretched out on the pen, and the little finger extended onto the paper, so as to support the weight of the hand. As such mechanical movements and muscular tension are contrary to the natural suppleness and skill of a child, he had invented, first, for the head, a sort of crown made of whalebone; second, for the body and shoulders, a belt which was attached to the crown from behind, by means of a strap; third, for the elbow, a wooden bar which could be screwed to the table; fourth, for the right index finger, a lead ring soldered to a smaller ring through which you slipped the pen; fifth, for the hand and little finger position, a sort of boxwood pediment with notches and little wheels. Join to all these indispensable tools for calligraphic study, as taught by M. Loubens, the rulers, paper, pens, and pencils—all worthless unless supplied by the teacher—and you can see that the teacher was engaged in a small business which compensated him a bit for the modest fees generally charged for writing lessons.

At first we found all these inventions hilarious, but after five minutes of trying them out, we acknowledged that it was really agony, that our fingers were being paralyzed, our arms stiffened, and that the headband caused migraines. Our complaints went unheeded, and we were only rid of M. Loubens after he had succeeded in rendering us entirely illegible.

The piano teacher's name was Mme. de Villiers. She was a young woman who always dressed in black; she was intelligent, patient, and distinguished in her manners.

I had in addition, for myself alone, a drawing teacher, Mlle. Greuze, who claimed to be the daughter of the celebrated painter, and who possibly was. She was kind and perhaps talented as well, but she hardly worked at imparting any of it to me; for she would teach me in the stupidest possible way how to do cross-hatching, before learning to draw a line, and how to round off a pair of big, evil eyes with enormous lashes that you had to do one at a time, before having an idea of the composition of a face.

On the whole, all these lessons were more or less a waste of money. They were too superficial to really teach us any art. They had only one beneficial result, and that was to keep us busy and get us into habit of keeping ourselves busy. But it would have been better to test our abilities and then to keep us working at a specialty we were capable of acquiring. Yet, the custom of teaching young ladies a bit of everything is certainly better than not teaching them anything. That is still the way it is done, and it is called giving them the social graces, which, by the way, the unfortunate neighbors, condemned to hear entire days' worth of some exercise for piano or voice, would disavow as neither sociable nor graceful. But it seems to me that each one of us is good at a certain thing and that those who, in their girlhood, show aptitude for everything, show none for anything later. In the latter case, the dominant aptitude should be chosen and developed. Those young girls who have no particular aptitude should not be bombarded with lessons they do not understand, which might make them vain or silly rather than simple and good, which they were to begin with.

However, on the positive side, the type of education I am criticizing does simultaneously develop all the faculties, and in consequence expands the soul, so to speak. Everything adheres to the human intelligence and to the emotions as well. It is a great misfortune to be an absolute stranger to the pleasures of painting if you are a musician, and vice versa. The poet's art is expanded by a sense of all the others; he is at risk to neglect any one of them. The philosophy of antiquity, partially continued during the Middle Ages and the Renaissance, embraced the overall development of mind and body, from gymnastics to music, languages, etc. This was a logically sequential structure, and philosophy was always at the top. All the diverse branches of learning were joined to a single tree of knowledge, and whether you learned rhetoric or the modes of the lyre, it was in order to celebrate the gods, or to spread far and wide the sacred songs of poets. This bears little resemblance to what we do today in learning a sonata or a romance. The arts of our time may have reached a very high level of perfection, but they are at the same time profane in their essence, and we rather accurately depict the lack of dignity in their usage by calling them the social graces.

Education being what it is, I do not regret that my kind grandmother forced me to grapple with these subjects at an early age. If they have not left me with any of the requisite social graces toward others, they have at least been a source of pure and unalterable pleasure for me, and as they were inculcated at an age when the mind is fresh and receptive, they caused me neither hardship nor distaste.

However, I do exclude the dance, which M. Gogault made so ridiculous for me, and the great art of calligraphy, which M. Loubens made me hate. When Abbé d'Andrezel came to see my grandmother, he would sometimes come into the room where we were having our lessons; on sighting M. Loubens, he would exclaim, "Hail to the Professor of Belles-Lettres," a title M. Loubens, whether or not he understood the pun, gravely acknowledged. "Good God!" the Abbé would later declare, "if we really taught belles-lettres with the aid of collars, straight-jackets, and iron rings—in the Loubens' style—how many fewer men of letters we would have, and how many more pedants!"

At that time we occupied a very pretty apartment at 8 Rue de Thiroux. It was between the ground and second floors, with rather high ceilings for a mezzanine, and very roomy compared to most Paris apartments.

As in Rue des Mathurins, it contained a handsome salon that no one ever entered. The dining room faced the street. My piano was between the two windows. But I was so disturbed by the noise of the traffic, the street cries of Paris—more frequent and varied then than they are today, the organ grinders, the coming and going of visitors, that I practiced without any joy, simply to relieve my conscience.

The bedroom, where my grandmother received visitors, faced a courtyard that ended in a garden; there, I believe, in a large, detached pavilion in the Empire style, lived a former purveyor to the army. He allowed us to play in his garden, which was only a sanded backyard with some plants, but we made it go a long way. Above us lived Mme. Périer, very pretty and chic, sister-in-law of Casimir Périer. On the third floor lived Général Maison, a soldier of fortune, whose fortune was certainly considerable, but who was one of the first to abandon the Emperor in 1814. His retinue, provisions, baggage-laden mules (I think he was either leaving for Spain at that time, or returning) filled the yard and house with noise and movement, but what impressed me most was his mother, an old peasant who had not changed one iota of her dress, language, or rustic parsimoniousness. As shaking and bent as she was, she would be there in the courtyard during the coldest weather, when the logs were being chopped and the coal parcelled out to the householders. She had preposterous arguments with the concierge, from whose hands she wrenched the so-called porter's portion of fuel whenever he had chosen a slightly oversized log. That had its nice as well as nasty side, but I defy anyone to affirm that, in the foreseeable future, the peasant will be brought from poverty to riches without carrying his avarice to the limit. The poor old lady's existence was a continual round of fatigue, concern, and fury.

We lived in that apartment on Rue Thiroux until 1816. In 1832 or '33, while I was looking for lodgings, I noticed a sign on the front door and I entered, hoping it was my grandmother's old apartment that happened to be vacant. But it was the pavilion at the back, and I believe they were asking 1,800 francs for it, which was much too high a price, given my resources at the time. However, I gave myself the pleasure of looking at it, in order to walk around the planted courtyard, where nothing had changed, and to see the casement windows of my grandmama's apartment across the way, from which she used to signal me to come in when I had lost all sense of time in the garden. While chatting with the porter, I learned that the house had not changed owners, that the owner was still alive and was living in precisely the mezzanine apartment I coveted. I wanted at least to have the satisfaction of revisiting the apartment, and under the pretext of making an offer for the pavilion, I had myself announced to M. Bucquet. He did not recognize me, and I would not have recognized him either. I had last seen him still youthful and sprightly. I found an old man who no longer left his house and who, apparently under doctor's order to do a little exercise, had a billiard table installed next to his bed in what had been my grandmother's bedroom. As for the rest, apart from my room, which had been joined to another apartment, nothing was changed in the layout of the other rooms: the Empire-style ornamentation, ceilings, doors, panelling, even the wallpaper in the antechamber, I believe, were the same as in my time. But it was all dark, dirty, smoky, and odorous of tobacco instead of the exquisite scents of my grandmother. I was especially struck by the smallness of the house, the courtyard, the garden, and the rooms, which had once seemed so vast to me, and which had remained so in my memory. My heart sank at finding this house of memories so ugly and gloomy.

At least I still have some of the furnishings which recall my childhood to me, even the large carpet which Pauline and I found so amusing. It is a Louis XV carpet, with figures that all had names and meanings for us. This circle was an island, that back section an ocean channel to be crossed. A certain rosette with purple flames was Hell, certain garlands were Paradise, and a wide border depicting pineapples was the Hercynian Woods.[10] How many fantastic, perilous, or delightful voyages our small feet embarked on, on that old carpet! The life of children is a magic mirror where real objects become the happy images of their dreams, but a day comes when the talisman loses its power, or else the mirror breaks and its shards are dispersed, never to become whole again.

Thus were dispersed all the people and almost all the things which filled my Paris life until the age of seventeen or eighteen. My grandmother and all her old friends of both sexes died one by one; my relationships changed. I was forgotten by, and I myself forgot, a majority of the people whom I had seen daily for such a long time; I entered a new phase of my life; may I therefore be forgiven for dallying in the phase which had almost disappeared entirely.

From time to time, I used to see my father's nephews and the numerous family members who were attached especially to the eldest, René, the one who lived in the lovely little townhouse on Rue de Gramont. So far, I have said nothing about his children, so as not to embroil the reader in this complication of generations; I have, moreover, nothing to say about his son Septime, whom I did not know well and did not find at all to my liking. My grandmother's dream was to marry me to him or his cousin Léonce, Auguste's son, but I was not a rich enough match for them, and I think that neither they nor their parents ever considered it. The comments of my maids alerted me very early on, in spite of myself, to this dream of my grandmother, and such marriage plans become a torment for a child. I was preoccupied by them long before the appropriate age, which produced great anxiety in me. Léonce did appeal to me as one child can find another appealing; he was cheerful, lively, and obliging. Septime was cold and taciturn, or at least it seemed so to me because I believed myself destined more particularly for him, my grandmother being more friendly with his father than with Léonce's. But whether Léonce or Septime, either match terrified me, because since my father's death, their parents did not see my mother at all and greatly mistreated her in their talk.

I therefore believed that my marriage would mean a forced break with my mother, sister, and Clothilde, and I was at that time so submissive to my grandmother that the idea of resisting her had not even entered my mind. Hence I was always quite ill at ease with all the Villeneuves, although in fact I liked them very much; and sometimes, while playing with their children at their house, in the midst of our laughter, a great desire to cry would overtake me—groundless apprehensions, gratuitous suffering! No one was thinking of separating me from my mother then, and those children, happier than I, hardly dreamed of curbs to their freedom or mine in the future.

Septime's sister, Emma de Villeneuve, today Mme. de la Roche-Aymon, was a gracious, charming person, sensitive and gentle, for whom I felt, from childhood on, a particular liking. I was at ease with her, and had she but divined my tormented ideas, I would, with the slightest encouragement, have opened my heart to her. But it did not enter her mind that, after having laughed on her lap and skipped all around her, I went away filled with melancholy, reproaching myself to some degree for the friendship I felt for my father's family—those who had been introduced to me as enemies of my mother.

Emma and Septime's mother, Mme René de Villeneuve, was one of the prettiest women of the Imperial Court. She was, at the time, Queen Hortense's lady-in-waiting.[11] I sometimes saw her in the evening, with her long trailing gowns and antique diadems, which impressed me greatly, but for some reason I was afraid of her.

René was King Louis' chamberlain. He was one of the most lovable men I have ever known, and I loved him like a father until the time when everything fell apart around me.[12] Later, in his old age, he called me to him, and I eagerly responded. Had I not, I would have begrudged myself.

Hippolyte did not last long in the boarding school where Deschartres had placed him. He found boys there who were as wild as he and even more wicked, and who brought out so well all of his happy predispositions for uproar and unruliness that my grandmother, seeing that he was working even less than at Nohant, took him back when we left.

It was during the winter of which I have just spoken that the immense preparations for the Russian campaign took place. In all the homes to which we were invited, we found officers leaving for duty and coming to make their farewells to their families. Although no one was confident of gaining access to the very heart of Russia, our country was so used to winning that everyone was certain that satisfaction would be obtained by means of some glorious treaty as soon as we had crossed the border and surrendered in a few battles on the nearest Russian steppes. So little thought was given to the climate that I remember one old lady who wished to give all her furs to a nephew of hers, a cavalry lieutenant, and how he laughed at her maternal precautions. Young and proud in his narrow, tailored little military jacket, he took out his sabre and answered that it was thus one warmed oneself in war. The good lady responded that he was going into a country which was always covered with snow. But it was April, the gardens were blooming, and the air was balmy. Young men, especially Frenchmen, readily believe that December will never come. That proud young man must have more than once missed his old aunt's furs during the fatal retreat.

The experts—and God knows they are never lacking after the fact—have affirmed that they had all foreseen the poor chances of this gigantic enterprise, that they had considered Napoléon a reckless conqueror, and finally, that they had had a premonition of some immense disaster. I do not believe a word of it, or at least I had never heard anyone express such fears, even at the homes of those who were enemies, out of principle or out of jealousy, of the grandeurs of the Empire. Mothers who were watching their children depart complained of the Emperor's indefatigable activity, but yielded themselves up to the worries and personal regrets inevitable in such cases. They would curse the Conqueror, the Ambitious One, but never did they have the slightest doubt as to his success, and by that time I heard and understood everything. The thought that Napoléon might be defeated never came into the minds of anyone except those who were betraying him. They knew very well it was the only way to defeat him. The openly biased people, all the while they were cursing him, had absolute confidence in him, and I heard one of my grandmother's friends say, "Well, and once we have taken Russia, what are we going to do with it?"

Others were saying that he was planning the conquest of Asia and that the Russian campaign was but a first step toward China. "He wants to be master of the world," they would cry, "and he has no respect for the rights of any nation. Where will he stop? When will he be satisfied? It is intolerable; he succeeds in everything."

And no one said he might suffer reversals and make France pay dearly for the glory with which he had intoxicated her.

With the spring of 1812 we returned to Nohant; my mother came to spend part of the summer with us, and Ursule, who went back to her parents every winter, returned to me, to my great delight and hers as well. Aside from the affection Ursule felt for me, she adored Nohant. She was more sensitive to creature comforts than I; she also delighted in more freedom than I did, since she was allowed complete liberty except for a few sewing and arithmetic lessons her Aunt Julie gave her. I must say she never abused the privilege and that she was a worker by nature. My mother taught her reading and writing, and while I was taking my other lessons from Deschartres or my grandmama, rather than running around, she stayed in my mother's vicinity, whom she adored and rendered the most thoughtful services. She knew how to make herself useful, and my mother was sorry she did not have the means to take her back to Paris during the winters.

The accursed winter was always the despair of poor Ursule. Completely different from me in this regard, she felt exiled when she went back to her family. It was not that her parents were abjectly poor. Her father was a milliner and earned enough money especially at the country fairs where he would go and sell wagon-loads of hats to the peasants. His wife, to promote his sales, kept a refreshment booth at these fairs, but they had many children, consequently money problems.

Ursule could not adjust to the annual change in habits and diet without complaining. They thought "richness" was going to her head, they had regrets about having let her eat "white bread" too soon, and they began to speak of taking her back and putting her in some apprenticeship, so as to give her a profession. I would not hear of it, and my grandmother hesitated for some time. Part of her wanted to keep Ursule, thinking one day she could run my household and be both useful and happy; but there was quite a long time between then and now; one never knew what might happen, and Ursule was not simply born to be a maid. She was too proud, frank, and independent to make one think she would willingly be subservient for money. She would need a "position," not a place in domestic service. Therefore, we had to guarantee her some position with a family she would like and who would like her. If, for some unforeseen reason, our family failed her, what would happen to her without an acquired profession, given her taste for good living? Mlle. Julie judiciously opined that the poor child would be horribly unhappy, and she insisted that we ought not let her accustom herself any longer to the household whose memory tormented her so during our absences. My grandmother gave in, and it was resolved that Ursule would leave permanently at our next departure for Paris, but that until then neither she nor I would be informed of this decision, so as not to upset our present happiness. In fact, the end of my happiness was approaching; along with the loss of Ursule, I would also have to sustain the loss of my mother, and I was to fall under the yoke and into the company of the housemaids.

However, that summer of 1812 was still cloudless. Every Sunday, Ursule's three sisters came to spend the day with us. The eldest, whom we called by her feminized last name [Godignonne], as was the regional custom, was a lovely person, angelic in her kindness, to whom my heart still strongly warms; she sang us rounds, taught us *cob, marelle, évalines, traîne-balin*, and *aveuglat*.[6] All these are games of the Berry region, whose names are in fact as old as the games themselves—names which would not even be found in the immense nomenclature of children's games in *Gargantua*.

We loved those little pastimes with a passion. The house, the garden, and the small woods echoed with our games and laughter. But toward the end of the day, I had had enough, and if we would have had to spend two days like that in a row, I would not have been able to stand it. I had already become accustomed to working, and I suffered from a kind of indefinable boredom in the midst of my amusements. Not for anything in the world would I have admitted that I missed my music or history lessons, and yet in spite of myself I did miss them. My brain, left to drift among childish pleasures and pointless games, reached satiety. If it had not been for the pleasure of seeing my dear Godignonne again, by Sunday evening I would have been ready to forego having Ursule's sisters return the following Sunday; but by the following Sunday, my gaiety and passion for play would return early in the morning and last through at least part of the day.

That year we had another visit from Uncle Beaumont, and my grandmama's nameday was once again prepared with "surprises." We were already no longer so naïve or self-confident as to wish to put on a show. My uncle contented himself with inventing some couplets to the tune of *"Pipe de tabac,"* which I had to sing at lunch while offering my bouquet. Ursule had to declaim a long prose compliment, half-serious, half-comic. Hippolyte had to play Fischer's minuet on the recorder, without a single error, and he even had the honor, that day, of blowing and spitting into Deschartres' ebony one.

The visits we made and received put me in touch with young children who have remained my friends for life. Capitaine Fleury, who is mentioned in my father's early letters, had a son and daughter. The daughter, a charming and fine person, died a few years after her marriage; her brother, Alphonse, has remained like a brother to me. M. and Mme. Duvernet, my father's friends who shared in his joyous theatrical forays in 1797, had a son with whom I have hardly lost touch since he was born, and whom I today call my old friend, although he is younger than I am. Finally, our closest neighbor lived, and still lives, in a lovely Renaissance château, formerly the property of Diane de Poitiers. This neighbor, M. Papet, would bring his wife and children over to spend the day with us, and his son, Gustave, was still in baby gowns when we made his acquaintance. These are three fathers of their own familiies whom I knew in petticoats and diapers, whom I lifted in my already strong arms to help them pick cherries from the trees in my garden, who tyrannized me for entire days (for from childhood on, I loved little children with maternal passion), and who, nevertheless, have often since believed themselves more reasonable than I. The two eldest are already balding, and I am getting gray. I have some trouble these days convincing them that they are children, and they no longer recall the innumerable peccadilloes for which I can reproach them. It is true that forty years of friendship have somewhat made up for many a piece of abuse—torn dresses, broken toys, furious tantrums—I shall let these pass, and even worse! It was partly my fault; I could never keep from laughing, along with my brother and Ursule, at their turpitudes. It had not been that long since we had committed such shameful tricks.

In the middle of our games and golden dreams, the news from Russia arrived, toward autumn, sounding lugubrious tones and parading frightening and painful visions before our starry eyes. We were beginning to hear reports from the newspapers, and the Moscow fire struck me as a great act of patriotism.[13] Today I have my doubts as to how that catastrophe should be judged. The way in which the Russians waged war against us was surely wild and inhuman, which can have no analogy among free nations. To devastate one's own fields, burn down one's houses, starve out vast regions in order to deliver an invading army into cold and hunger would be heroic on the part of a population that acted out of its own accord; but the Czar who dared, like Louis XIV, to claim, "I am the state, the state is me" did not consult the serf populations of Russia. He ripped them from their homes, wasted their land, chased them before his armies like so many miserable herds—without consulting them or worrying about their protection; those wretched people might have been infinitely less oppressed, ruined, and despairing under our victorious army than they were under their own, which was operating under the savage orders of an authority without compassion or any notion of human rights.

Supposing that before burning Moscow, Rostopchin had taken the advice of several rich and powerful families, the population of that vast city would nonetheless have been obliged to submit to the sacrifice of house and home; and one may well doubt that they would unanimously have consented to that, had they been consulted, had they any claims to make and rights to uphold. The Russian war was the ship tossed by the storm, which threw its cargo overboard to lighten the ballast. The Czar was the captain; the sunken cargo, the people; the ship to be saved, the sovereign's policy. If ever authority has profoundly despised and discounted the lives and property of men, the ideal version of such a system is to be found in absolute monarchy. However, from the moment our disasters in Russia had started, Napoléon's authority began once more to represent French individualism, dignity, and independence. Those who claimed otherwise during our armies' battle against the Coalition fell into a fatal error. Some of them (the ones who were preparing to betray) brazenly put forth this lie contrary to their public conscience. Others (the fathers of that "liberalism" which was just being born) probably believed it sincerely. But history is beginning to do justice to their role in this affair. To bring up, at that moment, the encroachments of the Emperor on our political liberties was tantamount to making Russia's Alexander the first agent of French liberalism.

I was only eight years old when I heard for the first time the debate over the formidable problem of the future of France. Until then, I had regarded my country as invincible and the imperial throne as that of God Himself. At that time, we sucked the pride of victory along with mother's milk. The vision of nobility had spread, had been communicated to all classes. To be French was illustrious in itself. The eagle was the coat of arms of the entire nation. *S.A.D.*

V

Army and Emperor lost for fifteen days. —A vision. —A word from
the Emperor on my father. —The German prisoners. —The
Tyroleans. —Separation from Ursule. —Familiar address. —The big
yellow bed. —My father's tomb. —Talleyrand's bon mot. —The
politics of the old contessas. —A patriotic child. —Another vision.
—Mme. de Bérenger and my mother. —Starving soldiers in the
Sologne. —The Jacobin innkeeper. —My grandmother's illness.
—Mme. de Bérenger destroys our garden. —The corset. —"Lorette
de Bérenger." —The Allies enter Paris. —My grandmother's opinion
of the Bourbons. —The cannon-ball. —Lovely ladies and the
Cossacks.

    Children are impressed in their own fashion by general events and public
calamities. All around us, no one spoke of anything but the Russian campaign,
and for us it was something immense and fabulous, like the expeditions of
Alexander the Great into India.
    What struck us most forcefully, if I am not mistaken, is that there was no
news of the Emperor or the army for fifteen days. The possibility that a body
of three hundred thousand men and Napoléon, the man who filled the world
with his name and Europe with his presence, had vanished this way, like a pilgrim sunk in snow, whose corpse is never recovered, was incomprehensible to
me. I had strange dreams, wild imaginings that made me feverish and filled
my sleep with apparitions. Then a singular fantasy, which stayed with me for a
long time afterward, began to invade my brain, stimulated as it was by the
tales and comments that came within my hearing. At a certain point in my
dream, I would imagine I had wings, that I was crossing the distance, and that
as I plumbed the horizon's depths with my eyes, I was discovering the endless
snow, the vast steppes of white Russia; I was gliding, getting my bearings in
the air, and finally locating the wandering columns of our unfortunate legions.
I guided them in the direction of France; I showed them the way, for what
troubled me most was the idea that they did not know where they were and
that they were heading for Asia, plunging deeper and deeper into the wastelands, with their backs turned to the West. When I regained awareness, I was
tired and in pain from the long flight; my eyes were blinded by the snow, and
I was cold and hungry, but I felt great joy at having saved the French army
and its Emperor.

Finally, toward the 25th of December we learned that Napoléon was in Paris. But his army had stayed behind, still engaged for two more months in a disastrous, horrible retreat. We had no official word about the suffering and misfortunes of that retreat until quite some time later. The Emperor being in Paris, we believed all was saved, all back to normal. The reports from the Grand Army and the newspapers told only part of the truth. It was from personal letters and from the stories of those who escaped the disaster that people managed to reconstruct what had happened.

Among the families my grandmother knew, there was a young officer who had left for this terrible campaign at the age of sixteen. He grew a head taller during the course of the forced marches and unheard-of exhaustions. No longer receiving any news of him, his mother went into mourning. One day, a species of thug colossal in size and bizarrely decked out burst into her bedroom, fell at her knees, and grabbed her in his arms. Her first cries of fear soon turned to joy. Her son had grown six feet tall. He had a long black beard and skirts instead of pants, the dress of a poor vivandière who had frozen to death along the way.

I believe this is the same young man who, a short time later, had a fate similar to my father's. Having escaped safe and sound from the extreme peril of war, he was killed on an outing; his runaway horse, with him on it, smashed into a wagon shaft. Having learned of the accident, the Emperor commented brusquely, "The mothers claim I get all their children killed in the war. Yet here is one whose death I am not responsible for, as was the case with Monsieur Dupin. If someone is killed on a wicked horse, is it still my fault?"

This linking of M. de ——— with my father shows what a fabulous memory the Emperor had. But what point was he making by complaining about being hated by mothers? I have never been able to figure it out. I do not recall the precise period of M. de ———'s catastrophe. It must have been at a time when aristocratic France was abandoning the Emperor's cause, and he was reflecting bitterly on his destiny.

It is impossible for me to recall whether we went to Paris in the winter of 1812–1813. That part of my existence has gone completely from my memory. Nor could I say whether my mother came to Nohant in the summer of 1813. She probably did, for otherwise I would have been upset, and I would remember it.

In the matter of politics, tranquility had reestablished itself in my mind. The Emperor had left Paris again; the war recommenced in April. The condition of war going on around us seemed normal then, and people got worried only when Napoléon acted covertly. They had found him downcast and discouraged after his return from Moscow. The discouragement of a single man was still the only public misfortune they were willing to admit and dared foresee. Starting in May, the victories of Lutzen, Dresden, and Bautzen lifted people's spirits. The armistice they talked about seemed to me the sanction of victory. I no longer had visions of having wings and flying to the rescue of our legions. I went back to my life of games, outings, and easy study.

In the course of the summer, an assortment of prisoners passed through our area. The first one we saw was an officer who had sat down by the side of the road on the step of a little summerhouse that closed off our garden on the road side. He had on a suit of fine cloth, very handsome linen, wretched shoes, and a woman's picture attached to a black ribbon on his chest. My brother and I looked at him with great curiosity, while he gazed at the picture sadly, but we did not dare speak to him. His servant came up to him. He got up and started off again without paying attention to us. An hour later, a rather large group of prisoners passed. They were headed in the direction of Châteauroux. No one was leading or guarding them. The peasants barely looked at them.

The next day, as my brother and I were playing in front of the summer-house, one of those poor devils happened by. The heat was overwhelming. He stopped and sat on the step, which offered a little shade and coolness to passers-by. He looked like a typical German peasant—heavy-set, blond, with a naïve expression. That made us bold enough to speak to him, but he replied, "No understand." That was all he could say in our language. So I asked him with gestures if he was thirsty. He answered by pointing with a questioning look at the ditch water. We made it clear that it was not drinkable and that he should wait for us to return. We ran to get him a bottle of wine and an enormous piece of bread, which he rushed at with cries of joy and thanks, and when he felt restored, he held out his hand to us several times. We thought he wanted money, and we didn't have any. I was about to go and ask my grandmother for some, when he guessed my intention. He stopped me and made us understand that all he wanted was a handshake. His eyes were full of tears, and after carefully look-ing for the right expression, he finally managed to say, "Children very good."

Deeply moved, we returned home to tell grandmama about our adven-ture. She burst into tears, thinking about the time her son had had a similar fate among the Croatians. Then, as new columns of prisoners appeared along the road, she had a cask of the local wine and a supply of bread brought to the little building. We took possession of it, my brother and I, and played the whole day, until evening, at the job of canteen keepers. Those poor people behaved with the utmost discretion and gentility, and showed us the keenest gratitude for the small morsel of bread and glass of wine informally offered on their way. They seemed particularly touched to see two children do the honors, and by way of thanking us, they arranged themselves as a choir and sang us Tyrolean songs that enchanted me. I had never heard anything like it. The strange words, the well-pitched voices harmonizing, and the traditional yodeling vocalization that marks the refrain of their national songs were very new in France at the time. I was not the only one who was impressed by them. All the German prisoners interned in our part of the country were treated with the kindness and hospitali-ty once natural to the natives of Berry, but the prisoners owed the greater sym-pathy and better treatment than pity alone would have assured them to their songs and their talent for waltzing. They became friends and companions of all the families where they were billeted; some even married into those families.

I do believe this was the first year I spent at Nohant without Ursule. We probably had been to Paris during the winter, and on my return the projected separation became an accomplished fact, for I do not recall that it occasioned any surprise or tears. I know that that year, or the next, Ursule came to see me every Sunday and we had remained so close that not a single Saturday went by without my writing her a letter urging her to come the next day and enclosing a little gift, some little trifle of my own creation: a beaded work, a paper cut-out, a bit of embroidery. Ursule would find them all magnificent and deem them sacred tokens of our friendship.

I was surprised and very hurt when she suddenly stopped using the familiar form of address with me. I thought she no longer cared for me, and when she protested that she did, I then thought she was teasing, or being stubborn, or whatever. But that seemed to me like a gratuitous insult, and to console me she had to reveal that her Aunt Julie had forbidden her, on solemn oath, to continue on inappropriately familiar footing. I ran for redress to my grandmother, who confirmed the decree, telling me that I would understand later how necessary it was. I confess I have never come to understand it.

I insisted that Ursule address me familiarly when we were alone. But since that would have hindered the habit that was being imposed on her, and since she had been scolded when speaking to me in the presence of her aunt for having let *tu* escape several times instead of the more polite *vous*, I was forced to accept this loss of her natural and easy familiarity with me. I suffered long over this, and I even tried addressing her as *vous*, to reestablish the equality between us. This upset her very much. "Since no one is forbidding you to call me *tu*," she said to me, "don't take that pleasure from me, for that would give me two regrets instead of one." So, as we were smart enough to amuse ourselves with words we had used in early childhood, I said familiarly to her, "Now you see what happens with this 'richness' business that you tried to make me accept and that I never shall. It just keeps you from loving me."

"Don't you believe that about me," Ursule said, addressing me in polite form. "Rich or poor, I'll always love you best in the world."

This outstanding girl, who truly kept her word to me, was learning to be a seamstress, and became very skilled at it. Far from being lazy and wasteful as they feared she might, she is one of the most hard-working and sensible women I know.

I now recall positively that my mother spent that summer with me and that I felt distressed, because until that time I had slept in her room when she was at Nohant; but for the first time I was denied that indulgence. My grandmother said I was too big to sleep on a sofa, and in fact the little day-bed I had used was getting too short. But the big yellow bed that my father had been born in and that was my mother's at Nohant (the very one that I still use) was six feet wide, and it was a holiday for me when she let me sleep there with her. In it I was like a baby bird in its mother's bosom; it seemed as though I slept better there and had lovelier dreams.

Despite grandmama's orders, for two or three evenings I had the patience to wait up until eleven o'clock, when my mother retired to her bedroom. Then I would silently get up, tip toe barefooted out of my bedroom, and go to snuggle in the arms of my dear mother, who did not have the courage to send me away and who was happy herself to fall asleep with my head on her shoulder.

But my grandmother became suspicious, or was alerted by her informer, Mlle. Julie. She came upstairs and caught me by surprise at the moment when I was sneaking out of my room; Rose was scolded for closing her eyes to my escapades. My mother heard the noise and came out into the hallway. There were some rather lively words exchanged; my grandmother claimed it was neither healthy nor chaste for a girl of nine to sleep next to her mother. The truth was she was angry and did not know what she was saying, for on the contrary, nothing is more chaste or more healthy. As for me, I was so chaste that I did not even really understand the meaning of the word "chastity." Anything to the contrary was unknown to me. I heard my mother reply, "If someone is lacking in chastity, it's you for having such ideas! It's by talking about it too soon that you deprive children's minds of their innocence, and I assure you if that's how you're planning to raise my daughter, you'd have done better to leave her to me. My caresses are more virtuous than your thoughts."

I cried all night. I felt myself physically and morally attached to my mother by a chain of diamond hardness that my grandmother sought in vain to break but that only kept tightening around my chest, to the point of suffocation.

For the next few days, there was much coldness and gloom in the relations with my grandmother. The poor woman saw clearly that the more she tried to separate me from my mother, the more she herself was losing my affection, and she had no recourse but to make up with her in order to make up with me. She took me in her arms and on her lap to embrace me, and for the first time I hurt her deeply by shaking myself free and saying, "I don't want to kiss, since it isn't chaste." She said nothing, set me down, stood up, and left the room with more speed than she had seemed capable of.

That shocked and troubled me even after a moment of reflection, and I wasted no time joining her in the garden; I saw her take the path which goes along the cemetery wall and stop before my father's tomb. I do not know if I have already mentioned that my father had been laid to rest in a small vault dug out beneath the cemetery wall, so that his head lay in the garden and his feet in consecrated ground. Two cypresses and a bank of rose bushes and white laurel mark this burial place, which today is that of my grandmother as well.

She had stopped before that tomb, a place she rarely had the courage to go to, and was weeping bitterly. I was overcome, I threw myself at her, I pressed her weak knees tightly to my chest, and I made her a promise that she very often recalled to me afterward, "Grandmother, it is I who shall console you." She covered me with tears and kisses, and went with me at once to find my mother. They embraced without any other explanations, and peace returned for a little while.

My role, it would seem, was to reconcile these two women and lead them to embrace, at each new quarrel, by invoking my father's name. The day came when I understood this and dared do it. But at the period that I am discussing I was too much of a child to remain impartial between the two of them; I maintain it would have taken a great deal of detachment or arrogance for me to judge calmly which one was right or wrong in their disagreements, and I confess it has taken me thirty years to see things clearly and cherish almost equally the memory of both.

I believe the foregoing incident dates from the summer of 1813. However, I won't swear to it, because there is a sort of lacuna in my memory. Even if I am mistaken about the date, it does not matter. I do know it did not happen any later.

We had a brief stay in Paris the following winter. Beginning in January 1814, my grandmother, frightened by the rapid progress of the invasion, sought refuge at Nohant, which is, so to speak, the mid-section of France, consequently the most protected from political events.

I believe we left there at the beginning of December, and that in making preparations for an absence of three to four months, as in other years, my grandmother in no way foresaw the fall of the Emperor and the invasion of Paris by foreigners. He had been back there since the 7th of November, after the retreat from Leipzig. Fortune was abandoning him. He was being betrayed, he was being deceived on all sides. When we arrived in Paris, Talleyrand's latest bon mot was making the rounds in the salons, "It's the beginning of the end." This remark which I heard repeated ten times a day, that is, during all the visits which followed in succession at my grandmother's, at first seemed silly to me, then sad, and then hateful. I asked just who this Talleyrand was. I found out that he owed his success to the Emperor, and I asked if his remark were a regret or a jest. I was told that it was ironical and a threat, that the Emperor indeed deserved it, that he was an opportunist, a monster. "In that case," I asked, "why did this Talleyrand accept anything from him?"

I was in for many other surprises. Every single day I heard praised acts of treason and ingratitude. The politics of the old contessas made my head ache. My studies and recreations were disturbed by it, and saddened.

Pauline had not come to Paris that year; she had remained in Burgundy with her mother, who, clever woman that she was, had become rabidly reactionary, and awaited the Allies as the Messiah. Starting on New Year's Day, there was talk of the Cossacks having crossed the Rhine, and for an instant, fear silenced hatred. We went to visit one of my grandmother's friends near Château-d'eau—Mme. Dubois, I believe. Several people were there, including her grandsons or nephews. Among these young men, I was struck by the speech of a lad of thirteen or fourteen, who, all by himself, was standing up to his entire family and all the visitors. "Do you mean," he said, "that the Russians, Prussians, and Cossacks are in France, coming to take over Paris, and people are going to let them do it?"

"Yes, my child," the others said, "everyone in his right mind will let them do it. Too bad for the tyrant. The foreigners are coming to punish him for his ambition and to rid us of him." "But they're foreigners," said the brave child, "therefore our enemies. If we don't want the Emperor any more, it is up to us to send him away; but we mustn't let our enemies rule us, that's a disgrace. We must fight them." Everyone laughed at him. The other big boys, his brothers or cousins, advised him to take a great sword and set off to meet the Cossacks. They all made fun of this child's admirable impulses that nobody appreciated except myself, who dared not say a word before this audience of almost total strangers, but whose heart responded with sudden feeling at the idea, at last clearly expressed in my presence, of France's dishonor. "Go ahead, make fun," said the young lad, "say whatever you like. But just let those foreigners come , and if I find a sword, even if it's twice my size I'll use it, you'll see; and all those who don't do as I do will be cowards."

He was made to hold his tongue and taken from the room. But he had made at least one convert. He alone, a child whom I have never seen again and whose name I never learned, had formulated my thoughts. They were all cowards, these people who shouted in advance, "Long live the Allies!" It was not so much the Emperor I cared about any longer, for amid the reckless profusion of foolish chatter of which he was the object, from time to time an intelligent person—my grandmother, Uncle Beaumont, Abbé d'Andrezel, or my mother herself—would utter a well-deserved judgment, a criticism based on the vanity which had brought him down. But what about *France*? That word had been so important at the time of my birth, it had made a deeper impression on me than if I had been born during the Restoration. From childhood on, providing you had all your faculties, you had felt a sense of your country's honor.

So I returned home quite sad and upset, and my fantasy about the Russian campaign came back. This fantasy preoccupied me and made me deaf to the declamations that were wearing me down. It was a vision of combat and slaughter. I again found my wings, I had a flaming sword, like the one I had seen at the Opéra in some play I no longer remember, where the exterminating angel appeared in the clouds,[7] and I swooped down on the enemy battalions, scattered them in disarray, and hurled them into the Rhine. This fantasy soothed me somewhat.

However, in spite of the joy people believed would accrue once the tyrant fell, they were frightened of those fine fellows the Cossacks, and many of the wealthy fled. Mme. de Bérenger was the most fearful; my grandmother offered to take her back to Nohant, and she accepted. I wished her ill with all my heart, for this prevented my grandmama from bringing my mother along. She would not put two such incompatible natures together. I was outraged at this preference for an outsider. If there really was any danger in staying in Paris, it was my mother, above all, whom we had to shield. I was getting ready to embark on a project of revolt—to stay with her and die with her, if need be.

I talked it over with my mother, who calmed me. "Even if your grandmama wanted to take me along," she told me, "I myself wouldn't consent. I want to stay near Caroline, and the more risks they talk about, the more I have to and want to. But rest assured, it hasn't come to that yet. Never will the Emperor, never will our troops allow the enemy to reach Paris. This is the old contessas' wishful thinking. The Emperor will beat the Cossacks at the border, and we'll never see a single one of them. When they're all exterminated, old Bérenger will come back to Paris to bemoan her Cossacks, and I'll come to see you at Nohant."

My mother's confidence dissolved my fears. We set out on the 12th or 13th of January. The Emperor had not yet left Paris. As long as people saw him there, they felt reassured that they would never see other rulers, unless they were there as guests and to pay him homage.

We were in a large travelling calèche, which my grandmother had acquired, and Mme. de Bérenger, along with her maid and little dog, followed us in a big berlin drawn by four horses. Our carriage, though quite heavy, moved briskly compared to hers. Travelling was quite difficult. The weather was dreadful. The road was crowded with troops, supply wagons, campaign provisions of all sorts. Columns of conscripts, soldiers, and volunteers passed in both directions, mingled noisily, and went their separate ways, shouting "Long live the Emperor!" "Long live France!" Mme de Bérenger was frightened by these frequent encounters which prevented our vehicles from advancing. The volunteers often shouted, "Long live the nation!" and she thought herself back in 1793. She claimed they had a hangdog expression and gave her insolent looks. My grandmother mocked her a little behind her back, but she was very much under her sway, and never contradicted her openly.

In the Sologne, we came across soldiers who seemed to be returning from afar, judging by their tattered clothing and starved look. Were they detachments recalled from Germany or driven back at the border? They told us, but I no longer remember what they said. They were not begging at all, but as we proceeded at a walking pace through the sand marshes of the Sologne, they crowded around our carriages with pleading eyes. "What on earth do they want?" asked my grandmother. These poor men were dying of hunger and had too much pride to say so. We had a loaf of bread in the coach; I held it out to the nearest one within my reach. He let out a frightening cry and pounced on it so violently, not with his hands but with his teeth, that I only had time to pull my fingers away or he would have devoured them. His companions surrounded him and bit straight into the loaf that he was gnawing like an animal. They did not fight among themselves, they did not think of sharing, they made room for each other to bite into the common prey, and they cried their eyes out. It was a heart-rending spectacle, and I could not help crying as well.

How was it possible, in the heart of France—a poor country, it is true, but one which had not been devastated by war and in which scarcity had not been widespread that year—for our soldiers to die of hunger along a highway? That is what I saw and still cannot explain. We emptied our storage box of food supplies; we gave them everything there was in both carriages. I believe they told us that their orders had been issued in error and that they had not had any rations for several days, but the details escape me.

Horses were often in short supply at the relay stations, and we were obliged to spend the night in some very poor lodgings. In one of these, the innkeeper joined us for conversation after dinner. He was outraged at Napoléon for having allowed France to be invaded. He said that partisan warfare must be waged, all the foreigners butchered, the Emperor sent packing, and a republic proclaimed—but the right one, the true one, he said, "one nation undivided and imperishable." That conclusion was not to Mme. de Bérenger's liking; she charged him with being a Jacobin, for which she in turn was charged on her bill.

We finally arrived in Nohant and had been there only three days when a most distressing event gave my thoughts another direction.

My grandmother, who had never been sick in her life, came down with a serious illness. As she had quite a unique constitution, the turns her illness took were of a unique character. First she fell into a deep sleep for two days, from which it was impossible to wake her. Then, when all the alarming symptoms had disappeared, we noticed she had a large, gangrenous sore on her body, as a result of the minor abrasion left by the saline poultices. This sore was horribly painful and slow to heal. She had to stay in bed for two months, and her convalescence was just as long.

Deschartres, Rose, and Julie took care of her with great devotion. As for me, I felt that I loved her more than I had been aware of before that time. Her suffering, the danger of death, which threatened more than once, made her dear to me, and her illness, for me, had the quality of a mortal sorrow.

Mme. de Bérenger stayed with us for six weeks, I believe, and left only when my grandmother was completely out of danger. But if this lady felt any distress or concern it did not show much, and I doubt that her heart was really touched. I honestly do not know why my grandmama, who had such a great need for affection, had become so particularly attached to this haughty, imperious woman, in whom I have never been able to discover the least charm of mind or character.

She was very active and unable to stay still. She considered herself an expert at planning or improving the design of a garden or park, and no sooner had she seen our formal garden than she got it into her head to transform it into an English landscape—a preposterous idea—for on a flat terrain, without much of a view, and where trees are slow to grow, the best thing to do is conserve at all possible cost those which happen to be there; to plant for the future, not create clearings which show you the poverty of the surrounding lines of vision; and above all, especially when the road is right out front and very close to the house, to screen yourself as much as possible behind walls or hedges, to preserve your privacy. But our hedges horrified Mme. de Bérenger, our square beds of flowers and vegetables, which seemed so beautiful and bright to me, she called a cabbage patch. Emerging from the first crisis of her illness, hardly had my grandmother regained her voice and hearing than her friend asked for permission to set the axe to the little woods and the pick and shovel to the paths. My grandmother was not fond of change, but her will was so weak at that moment (and besides, Mme. de Bérenger exerted such influence on her) that she gave her free rein.

So there we have that fine lady in action—she summons a score of workmen, and from her window directs the clearing operation, pruning here, destroying there, and always seeking a view which is nowhere to be found, for good reason: nothing can change the fact that, while the countryside is pretty enough from the second-story window, when you are in the garden—on a level with the countryside—you see it flat and without panorama. To fulfill her desire, it would have been necessary to raise the earth in the garden by fifty feet. Each opening cut in the beds and tree clumps resulted only in our being able to enjoy the view of a vast, cultivated plain. The breach was growing larger; fine old trees that had no say in the matter were being cut down; Mme. de Bérenger drew patterns on paper, passed them from her window along a line of string to the workers, shouted after them, went upstairs, came downstairs, went back upstairs, lost her patience, and destroyed the little shade we had, without any profit in the exchange. At last she gave it up, thank God, for she could have made a clean sweep, but Deschartres pointed out to her that my grandmother, once she was well enough to go out and see for herself, might perhaps miss her old hedges a great deal.

I was struck by the manner in which that lady spoke to the workmen. She was far too eminent to condescend to find out their names and deal with them as individuals. However, from her window she had dealings with each one in turn, and nothing in the world would have made her say "sir," or "my friend," or "old man," as they say in Berry, regardless of the age of the male you are addressing. She shouted to them at the top of her lungs, "Man Number Two!" "Listen, Man Number Four!" This caused gales of laughter among our quizzical peasants, but not one budged or turned his head in her direction. "By gum," they said to each other shrugging their shoulders, "we're all of us men, and we can't guess which one she's after—that woman."

It took some thirty years to undo the havoc wrought on our property by Mme. de Bérenger and to close off the openings for her "vistas."

She had another mania which vexed me even more than the one for English gardens. She was laced into her corsets so tightly that by evening she was as red as a beet, and her eyes were popping out of her head. She declared that I had the posture of a hunchback, that I was cut from a piece of wood, and that I needed some shape. Consequently, on rather short notice she had a corset made for me—who was unfamiliar with that instrument of torture—and she did so fine a job of lacing me into it herself that I nearly took ill the first time.

I was hardly out of her presence when I deftly cut the lace, as a result of which I was able to endure the steel and whalebone ribs, but she soon became aware of the deceit and laced me in even more tightly. I instituted a rebellion and took refuge in the cellar. Not content with cutting the lace, I threw the corset into an old hogshead of wine lees, where no one thought of looking for it. They searched, to be sure, but whether it came to light six months later, at harvest time, is something I never inquired about.

Little "Lorette de Bérenger" (we had learned from Mme. de La Marlière to call those pampered dogs by the surnames of their mistresses) was a cranky beast who used to jump into the faces of the most dignified big dogs and force them to act out of character. In these encounters, Mme. de Bérenger would shriek and take ill; so that our friends Brillant and Moustache could no longer set foot in the salon. Every evening, Hippolyte was given the task of taking Lorette for a walk, because his saintly look inspired Mme. de Bérenger's confidence, but Lorette spent a difficult fifteen minutes at his hands. "Poor little dear; darling little creature!" he would say on the doorstep, where the mistress could hear it, but hardly out the door, he would toss Lorette into the air with all his might, in the middle of the courtyard, not caring very much how or where she'd come down. I do believe that Lorette also imagined herself as having sixteen quarterings of nobility, for her impertinence showed her to be a stupid, detestable animal.

Mme. de Bérenger and Lorette finally left. We missed only her maid, who was a worthwhile person.

Grandmama's illness had not allowed for much laughter at the expense of that old contessa. The news from the outside world was not very good either, and one day in the spring, my convalescing grandmother received a letter from Mme. de Pardaillan, which said, "The Allies have entered Paris. They have done no damage. There was no pillaging at all. They say that Czar Alexander is going to give us the brother of Louis XVI for a king, the one who was in England and whose name I don't recall."

My grandmother stirred her memory. "That must be," she said, "the one they called Monsieur. He was a rather wicked man. The other, Comte d'Artois, was a despicable good-for-nothing. Well, my girl, there you have our cousins[14] on the throne, but they are nothing to brag about."

Such was her first impression. Then, following the tendencies of her peers, she was the dupe for a while of the promises made to France, and underwent an initial infatuation, not for the people restored, but for the goods. That did not last long. When piety became the order of the day, she regained her disgust for hypocrites, which I shall tell about later.

I was anxiously awaiting a letter from my mother; it arrived at last. My poor darling mother had been sick with fright. By sheer chance, one of the five or six cannon-balls launched over Paris and aimed at the statue on top of the column at Place Vendôme happened to land on the house where my mother was living at the time, in Rue Basse-du-Rempart. The cannon-ball had penetrated the roof, gone through two stories, and come to rest on the floor above the room where she happened to be. She had fled with Caroline, believing that Paris was going to be a heap of debris in a few hours. She was able to return home for a peaceful night's sleep, but only after she had seen, along with other members of the dismayed and dumbfounded crowd, the entry of the barbarian Cossacks, whom lovely ladies rushed to embrace and crown with flowers.   *M.D.*

VI

The domestic struggle is embittered. —I come to know real grief.
—A discussion with my mother. —My entreaties, her promises, her
departure. —First night of sleeplessness and despair. —The deserted
room. —First deception. —Liset. —An adventurous plan. —My
treasure. —My grandmother is stricken. —I abandon my plan.
—Thoughts on the relationship one should have with servants in
order to make equality habitual. —My grandmother is forced to
neglect me. —Lessons by Deschartres. —Botany. —My contempt
for what is taught me.

My mother came to spend a month with us, then had to return home to
take Caroline out of boarding school. I began to understand that from now on I
would see less and less of her at Nohant. My grandmother was talking about
spending the winter there, and I fell into the greatest distress I had ever felt in
my life. My mother did her best to give me courage, but she could not fool me
anymore; I was old enough to realize the demands of the situation which had
been forced on both of us. Bringing Caroline into the family would have settled everything, but about that my grandmother was inflexible.

My mother was not at all happy at Nohant. She suffered there; she felt
constrained and emotionally suffocated, and had to curb her irritation at every
moment. My persistence in openly preferring her to my grandmother (I could
not pretend, even though it would have been in all our interests) increasingly
embittered my grandmother toward her. It should also be made clear that my
grandmother's illness had changed her personality very much. There were
some days when she was in such a mood as I had never seen before. Her sensitivity became excessive. At certain times she spoke to me so curtly that I was
shattered. Mlle. Julie assumed an extraordinary and deplorable influence over
her, receiving all her confidences and exacerbating all her displeasures, acting
undoubtedly with good intentions but without discernment or fairness.

Yet my mother would have put up with all that for me, if she had not
been constantly concerned about her other daughter. I understood this and did
not want Caroline sacrificed on my behalf; however, Caroline, for her part,
began to be jealous of me, poor child, to complain about the yearly absences of
her mother and sobbingly reproach her for preferring me.

Thus we were all unhappy, and I, the innocent cause of all this domestic
bitterness, felt the repercussions even more painfully than the others.

When I saw my mother packing her bags, I was seized with fright. Since she had been very annoyed that day by some of Julie's remarks, saying that there was no longer any way of putting up with the authority of a maid who was more of a mistress in the house than the mistress herself, I thought my mother was leaving for good. I guessed, at any rate, that her visits would be further and further apart, and I threw myself into her arms and at her feet. I rolled on the ground, begging her to take me and telling her that, if she didn't, I would run away from Nohant to Paris, alone and on foot, to be with her.

She sat me on her lap and tried to make me understand her position. "Your grandmother," she told me, "can reduce my income to fifteen hundred francs if I take you with me."

"Fifteen hundred francs!" I exclaimed, "but that's a lot! It's surely enough for all three of us."

"No," she replied, "it wouldn't even be enough for Caroline and me, because your sister's board and expenses cost me half that amount, and I have plenty of difficulty trying to live and dress myself for the rest. You'd understand that, if you had the least idea of what money is. So if I take you along, and my income is reduced by a thousand francs a year, we'll be so poor, so poor that you won't be able to stand it, and you'll ask me to give you back your Nohant and your fifteen thousand pounds a year."

"Never! never!" I exclaimed. "We'll be poor, but we'll be together; we'll never leave each other; we'll work, we'll live in a tiny garret and eat beans, as Mlle. Julie says. What's wrong with it? We'll be happy, and nobody will keep us from loving each other any more!"

I was so convinced, so eager, so desperate, that my mother began to waver. "Maybe what you're saying is true," she answered, with the simplicity of a child—generous child that she was. "I've known for a long time that money doesn't make people happy, and certainly if I had you with me in Paris, I'd be much happier being poor than I am here, where I want for nothing and have my fill of dislikes. But I'm not thinking of myself, it's you; and I'm afraid you may reproach me some day for having deprived you of a good education, a good marriage, and a good inheritance."

"Yes, sure!" I exclaimed. "A good education, where they're trying to make a wooden doll out of me! A good marriage, with a gentleman who'll be ashamed of my mother and show her the door in my own house! A good inheritance, which will have cost me all my happiness and force me to be a bad daughter! No! I'd rather die than have all those fine things. I'm perfectly willing to love my grandmother, I'm willing to come and take care of her and be her partner at *grabuge* or lotto, when she's bored, but I don't want to live with her. I don't want any part of her château or her money. I don't need them. Let her give them to Hippolyte, or Ursule, or to Julie, since she loves Julie so much. As for me, I want to be poor with you; a person can't be happy without her mother."

I don't remember all the other things I added, but I was eloquent in my own way, for my mother was actually influenced. "Listen," she said, "you don't know what poverty means for young girls! I do happen to know, and I don't want Caroline and you to travel the same road as I when I found myself orphaned and without bread at the age of fourteen. God forbid I should die and leave you like that! Your grandmother might take you back, but she would never take your sister, and what would become of her? But there is a solution. One can always earn enough money by working, and I don't see why I should continue to do nothing and live off my income like a grand lady, especially since I know how to work. Listen closely to me! I'm going to try to open a hat shop. You know that I've been a milliner and that I can create hats and hairstyles better than the chatterboxes who comb your grandmama's hair every which way and make her pay through the teeth for their ugly head scarves. I won't set up shop in Paris, it would cost too much; but by economizing for a few months and borrowing a small amount that my sister or Pierret will surely be able to find for me, I'll open a boutique at Orléans, where I've already worked. Your sister is clever with her hands, you are too; and you'll learn that trade much faster than Monsieur Deschartres' Greek or Latin. There'll be enough work for the three of us. I know that business is good in Orléans, and it's not expensive to live there. We're not princesses and we'll live frugally, as we did on Rue Grange-Batelière. Later on, we'll take Ursule in with us. Then we'll save some money, and if I can give each of you eight or ten thousand francs in a few years, it will be enough for you to marry some honest worker, who'll make you happier than any marquis or count. The truth is, you'll never be comfortable in their world. They'll never forgive you for being my daughter and for having a bird seller as a grandfather. They'll make you ashamed every chance they get; and if you were unfortunate enough to adopt their grand airs, you'd no longer forgive yourself for being only partly noble. So it's decided. Be sure to keep it a secret. I'm going to leave, and I'll stop at Orléans for a day or two to find out what shops are for rent and look at them. Then I'll make all my preparations in Paris, and when it's all arranged, I'll write you secretly via Ursule or Catherine, and I'll come here and take you. I'll make my intentions clear to my mother-in-law; I am your mother, and no one can take away my rights over you. She'll be angry, and she'll take back the surplus income that she gives me, but I won't care a fig; we'll leave here to become the proud owners of our little boutique, and when she rides by the main street of Orléans in her coach, she'll see in nice big letters, 'Widow Dupin, Milliner.'"

This marvelous plan went to my head. It almost made me hysterical. I jumped around the room, bursting into shrieks of laughter, crying at the same time. It was as if I were drunk. My poor mother certainly was sincere and believed in her solution; otherwise she never, without due consideration, would have spoiled the carefree submissiveness of my early years by a misleading dream; for I was surely carried away by this dream which lasted for a long time and made me more restless and troubled than was natural for my age.

I then put as much enthusiasm into having my mother leave as I had into stopping her. I helped her pack her bags, I was gay, I was happy; I had the feeling she would come back to get me by the end of a week. My playfulness and high spirits surprised my grandmama throughout dinner, even more so since I had cried so much that my eyelids were almost bleeding, and the contrast was inexplicable. My mother whispered a few words in my ear to make me aware of my conduct, so as not to arouse any suspicions. I was so careful and so discreet that no one ever got wind of my design, although I had to keep it hidden in my heart for four years, along with all the emotions that fear and hope inspire. I never disclosed it to anyone, not even Ursule.

Nevertheless, as night began to fall (my mother was to leave in the early dawn), I was uneasy and frightened. It seemed to me my mother had not given me that look of understanding and security I would have needed to console me. She became sad and preoccupied. Why was she sad if she was to return so soon and if she was going to work toward our being reunited, toward our happiness? Children do not come to doubt by themselves and are not aware of obstacles unless they see doubt in those they have faith in; then they fall into deep anguish, which makes them bend and tremble like helpless blades of grass.

I was sent to bed as usual at nine o'clock. My mother promised not to go to bed herself without coming to my room to say good-bye again and renew her pledges to me. But I was afraid she would not want to wake me if she thought I was asleep, so I did not go to bed; that is to say, I got up again as soon as Rose was gone, for after she had put me to bed, she went down to wait with Julie until my grandmother retired. This process was a very long one. My grandmother ate a little and very slowly; then, while they arranged a dozen little caps and shawls of linen, silk, wool, and cotton wadding on her head and shoulders, she listened to Julie report on the intimate matters of the family, and to Rose on the details of running the household. This lasted until two o'clock in the morning, and only then did Rose go to bed in the alcove adjoining my small bedroom.

This little bedroom looked out on a long hallway and was almost opposite the door to my mother's dressing room, through which she usually passed to return to her room; I could not miss intercepting her as she went by, and talking to her again, before Rose came to interrupt us. But it was possible that we were being watched exceptionally closely that night, and in my fear of no longer being able to unburden myself to the object of my love, I intended to write her a long letter. I exercised extreme skill and patience to rekindle my candle without matches, using my nearly extinguished fire; I succeeded and wrote on pieces of paper torn from my notebook of Latin verbs.

I can still see my letter and the rounded, childish handwriting I had at the time. But what did I say? I don't remember any more. I know I wrote in the heat of enthusiasm, that my heart overflowed the paper, so to speak, and that my mother revered it for a long time. But I have not found it again among the papers she left me. My impression is that never was a deeper and purer passion more naïvely expressed, for my tears literally watered the page, forcing me at every instant to retrace the letters they washed away.

How would I give this letter to my mother if Deschartres were to accompany her upstairs? Since I still had some time to plan, I thought of going into my mother's room on tiptoe. I would have to open and close some doors right over Mlle. Julie's room. The house was awfully resonant owing to the huge stairwell, where the slightest breath vibrated. I did manage it, however, and put my letter behind a small portrait of my grandfather, which was almost hidden behind a door. This was a pencil drawing, which did not show him young, slim, and stylish as did the large pastel in the salon, where he was wearing a lounging jacket of russet taffeta with diamond buttons, his hair gathered up with a comb, a palette in his hand, and facing a landscape sketched in pink and turquoise blue. In the drawing, he seemed old and worn, wearing a wide, square-cut jacket, his hair in pouch and pigeon wings, his face fat and jowly, and bending over a worktable—as he must have looked shortly before his death. By way of an address, I had written, "Put your answer behind this same portrait of Dupin Senior. I shall look for it tomorrow, when you are gone." All I had to do now was find a way of telling my mother to look behind this portrait; I hung her nightcap on it, and in the cap I pencilled a note, "Move the portrait."

Every precaution taken, I returned to bed without making the slightest noise. But I remained sitting on my bed, for fear that fatigue would overcome my resolution. I was exhausted from the tears and emotions of the day, and at each moment I dozed off, but my quickening heartbeats awoke me with a start, for I thought I heard footsteps in the hall. Midnight finally chimed on Deschartres' clock, whose bedroom was separated from mine by only a wall. Deschartres came up first; I heard his heavy, steady footsteps and his doors closing with majestic slowness. My mother came a quarter hour later, but Rose was with her. She had come to help her close her trunks. It wasn't Rose's intention to hinder us, but she had often been reprimanded for her weakness on similar occasions, and I could no longer rely on her. Besides, I needed to see my mother in private. So I slid back under my covers, still half dressed, and did not move. My mother passed; Rose stayed with her a half-hour and then went to bed. I waited another half-hour until she was asleep, then, braving everything, I gently opened my door and went to find my mother.

She was reading my letter, she was crying, she clasped me to her heart; but she had come down from the heights of our romantic plan to a feeling of hopeless indecision. She was counting on my getting used to my grandmother, she reproached herself for having gotten my hopes up, and she urged me to forget her. Her words were daggerthrusts, cold as death, into my poor heart. I lovingly admonished her, and I was so vehement that she again committed herself to come back and get me in three months at the latest, if grandmama did not take me to Paris in the winter and if I persisted in my resolve. But this was not enough reassurance for me; I wanted her to answer the ardent pleas of my letter, in writing. I wanted to find a letter from her after she had left, behind the portrait, a letter which I could reread in secret every day to keep up my courage and hopes. This was the price she had to pay to send me back to bed; then I went to try to warm my poor frozen body in my even colder bed. I was feeling sick; I would have wished to sleep, as she wanted me to, in order to forget my anxiety for a moment. It was impossible. My being was filled with doubt or rather despair; for children, one is the same as the other, since they live only by dreams and by trust in their dreams. I cried so bitterly that my brain felt split, and when daybreak came, pale and sad, it was the first time I had ever seen the dawn after a night of suffering and sleeplessness. How many others like it I have seen since, I wouldn't want to count!

I heard the doors re-opening and the bags being taken down; Rose got up, but I did not dare reveal that I was not asleep. She would have been touched, but my love, by virtue of its intensity, cloaked itself in an aura of secrecy as in a romantic novel. Nevertheless, when the carriage rolled into the courtyard, when I heard my mother's steps in the hall, I could not hold back; I leaped barefoot over the tiles, threw myself into her arms, and losing my head, I begged her to take me along. She reproached me for hurting her when she was already suffering so much by leaving me. I gave in, I returned to my bed, but when I heard the last sounds of the coach carrying her away, I could not restrain my cries of despair, and even Rose, in spite of the severity with which she was beginning to arm herself, couldn't restrain her tears on finding me in this pitiful state, which was too stressful for someone my age and would have driven me mad, if God, who had destined me to suffer, had not endowed me with extraordinary strength.

I did rest, however, for a few hours, but I was hardly awake when my grief found me again, and my heart broke at the idea that my mother had left perhaps forever. As soon as I was dressed, I ran to her room, threw myself on her unmade bed, furiously kissing the pillow which still bore the imprint of her head. Then I went up to the portrait where I was to find a letter, but Rose came in and I had to conceal my pain; not that the kind-hearted girl would have made a crime of it, but I was feeling a sort of bitter-sweetness in hiding my suffering. She proceeded to straighten the room, remove the sheets, air out the mattress, and close the shutters.

Seated in a corner, I watched her work; I was as if stupefied. It seemed like my mother was dead and that silence and darkness would claim this room to which she would no longer return.

It was only later in the day that I could find a way of going back in without being seen, and I ran to the portrait, my heart beating in expectation. But I moved Old Francueil's picture and turned it over in vain, nothing had been entrusted to him for me; not wanting to further an illusion which she surely was already regretting having fostered in me, my mother had deemed it better not to answer me. For me this was the final blow. For the whole of my recreation time, I remained motionless and stunned in the now cold, mysterious, mournful room. I did not cry any more; I had no tears left, and I was beginning to suffer from a pain much deeper and more excruciating than that caused by her absence. I told myself that my mother did not love me as much as I loved her. I was unfair in this instance, but actually it was the revelation of a truth which would be reconfirmed every day. My mother felt more passion than affection for me, as she did for everyone she loved. It was as if great lacunae were forming in her soul, unknown to her. Along with transports of love, she would have stretches of forgetfulness or lassitude. She had suffered too much; she often needed not to suffer any more; and I, I was almost craving suffering, so much strength did I still have to spend in that pursuit.

I had as a playmate a little peasant boy two years younger than I, to whom my mother taught reading and writing. He was by then nicely behaved and intelligent. I made it not only my pleasure but something like a religious duty to continue the education begun by my mother, and I got my grandmother to agree that he could come to take his lesson every morning at eight o'clock. I would find him settled in the dining room having already splattered a large page with letters. Obviously, I was not subjecting him to M. Loubens' method, hence he had a most legible and pretty handwriting. I corrected his mistakes, I had him do spelling, and I made him explain the meanings of words. For I remembered knowing how to read a long time before understanding what I was reading. That led to many questions on his part and many explanations on mine. Thus I gave him some notion of history, geography, etc., or rather some ways of thinking about these subjects which were still so fresh in my mind that they passed easily into his.

On the day of my mother's departure, I found Liset, (the Berrichon diminutive for Louis) weeping profusely. He did not want to tell me in front of Rose why he was upset, but when we were alone, he told me he was crying over "Madame Maurice." I began to cry along with him, and from that moment we became fast friends. He would go to the fields when his lesson was over and return when my play time started. He was neither gay nor boisterous. He liked to chat, but he kept quiet when I was sad, walking behind me like a confidant in a tragedy. Hippolyte, the mocker, who also missed my mother very much, but was not able to sustain sadness over any length of time, called him my "faithful Achates."[15] However, I confided nothing to him; I sensed the gravity of the secret my mother had confided to me in a moment of impulsiveness, and I did not want to risk discovering just yet that the secret was only a ploy.

However, days and weeks passed in succession and still my mother sent me no special message; she did not give the slightest hint in her letters that she was thinking of our plan. My grandmother settled in for the winter at Nohant. I had to resign myself but not without great inner strife. I had a fantasy related to my predominating concern, which consoled me from time to time. It was to imagine that, when my suffering became too much, I could put into action the little threat I had made to my mother about leaving Nohant alone, on foot, to find her in Paris. Sometimes this plan seemed perfectly feasible to me, and I promised myself to tell Liset about it when I had definitely decided to set out. I was counting on him to come with me.

Neither the length of route, nor the threat of cold, nor any danger whatsoever made me hesitate; but I could not resign myself to begging along the way, and I did need a little money. Here is how I figured on getting some in case of need. My mother had given me a very beautiful unpolished yellow amber necklace, which my father had brought her from Italy and which had only sentimental value. I had heard someone tell my mother how expensive it had been, two louis! It seemed to me a very considerable sum. In addition, I had a small coral comb, a ring with a diamond as large as a pinhead, a blond tortoise shell candy box adorned with a small gold disk worth a good three francs, and several worthless fragments of jewels given to me by my mother and grandmother to serve as ornaments for my doll. I assembled all those riches in a little corner cupboard in my mother's room, where no one went but me, unseen, on certain days; I called this "my treasure." At first I thought of entrusting it to Liset or

Ursule, so they could sell it in La Châtre. But they might have been suspected of having stolen these jewels, which I felt were worth a lot of money; so I thought of a better solution, entirely in keeping with the method used by the wandering princesses in my fairy tales—to take my treasure along in my pocket, and every time I would be hungry en route, I would use a stone from my necklace as payment, or break a small piece from my golden heirlooms. On the way, I would surely find a goldsmith to whom I could sell my candy box, my comb, or my ring, and I imagined I would have something left to give my mother on arriving, to compensate for the expense I was going to cause her.

Thus assured of the possibility of my flight, I felt a little calmer, and in my moments of grief I would slip into the gloomy, deserted room, open the corner cabinet, and console myself by looking at my treasure, my means to freedom. Having exceeded the bounds of imagination, my unhappiness began to be so real that I would certainly have taken the key to the pasture gate, even if only to be caught again and brought back at the end of an hour (a possibility I did not dwell on, I was so sure of my speed and skill in hiding myself in the hedges along the way), if my grandmother had not had a new accident.

One day, in the middle of her dinner, she suffered a dizzy spell, closed her eyes, became pale, and remained lifeless, as if petrified, for an hour. She did not faint, but fell rather into a kind of cataleptic state. She had persisted in leading an indolent life, without physical exertion, thus planting the seeds of the paralysis which would later take her life and was presaged from then on by a succession of similar kinds of accidents. Deschartres felt this symptom was very serious, and the way he told me about it changed all my ideas. My heartfelt affection for my grandmama revived when I saw her sick; I then felt a need to stay beside her, caring for her, as well as a great fear of hurting her further by making trouble. This kind of catalepsy returned five or six times a year for two years and reappeared again at the onset of her last illness.

I then began to reproach myself for having had such wild plans. My mother was not encouraging them; on the contrary, she seemed to want to make me forget them by having me forget her, since she wrote me so rarely that I had to send her two or three letters to receive one from her. She realized, undoubtedly a little late but accurately, that she had overfed my fancy, and she wrote me, "Run, play, walk, grow, get your nice rosy cheeks back, think only happy thoughts, feel well and become strong, if you want me to be at ease and a little consoled during my separation from you."

I found she had become quite patient in withstanding our separation, but I loved her all the same; then my grandmother became so feeble that the least annoyance might have killed her. I solemnly renounced (still always to myself) putting my flight into action. So as no longer to think about it and because my accursed "treasure" filled me with temptation or longing, I removed it from the room in which the sight of it as well as its aura of secrecy doubly affected me. I gave it to my maid for safekeeping, after having sent Ursule everything she would be able to accept without being accused of any indiscretion by her parents, who were very strict and touchy about such matters.

I could not conceal from myself the fact that my grandmama's illness and the repeated attacks had damaged her inner stability and serene nature. In her case, her so-called mental faculties, as society understands them—that is, the art of conversation and writing—had not suffered in the least, but her judgment and sound appreciation of people and things had been impaired. Up to that time, she had kept a certain distance between her servants (and even her friends) and her innermost thoughts. She had resisted succumbing to first impressions and prejudice. This was no longer entirely true, even though it still seemed to be. The servants had too much of a say in family decisions, which prompts me to say something I know about from experience—that servants should never be informed, however esteemed and worthy of respect they may be, about sensitive details regarding money or feelings. I do not think my character can be suspected of aristocratic prejudice or arrogance because I make this restriction. But the reader will permit me here to explain my thoughts fully on this important aspect of private life.

To my way of thinking, in an enlightened and orderly household, there exists neither master nor servant, and I should like to bar these nasty words from the language, which are no longer useful for anything but prejudice. No one is master of a free man, who can quit your service as soon as he is dissatisfied with you. No one is a servant, unless he wants to be one, that is to say, wants to be exploited. The more appropriate term is the word "domestic," and it should be understood in its literal meaning, as "someone employed to work in a house (*domus*)." In effect, a domestic is an employee, and nothing else. You give him a job in your home, for a definite period of time, according to his abilities, by virtue of an agreement which binds neither of you. If you both agree and if the contract is not a burden to either of you, then there are few reasons to deceive or hate each other; there are even many reasons for staying together, if each party is honest and reasonable, but there is no reason to feel condemned to living under the same roof if your personalities are incompatible.

I do not like it when employers exaggerate the "good master" role with their servants under the pretext that their status is an unfortunate or humiliating one. If people feel humiliated by serving, then a lack of dignity on their part is to blame, for I see no reason why they have to debase themselves. To be responsible for the care of a household, for the health and cleanliness of a house, for the preparation of meals taken together, for the upkeep of a garden or stable, is to work, to fulfill a function, not to serve. To climb up behind a carriage, to put the master's shoes on and do for him all the little things he can do for himself is different. But I am happy to see that the practice of "servitude" is decreasing every day, that fewer healthy young men are being dressed by "their attendants," that new carriages have seats in front and back so that the servants are also seated comfortably, and that they even make carriages lower nowadays, where you only have to push the spring by yourself to raise and lower the steps, enabling you to do without the vain embarrassment of having a mannequin trailing behind, who catches cold in the winter and roasts in the summer, without benefit to anyone. These are some of the indications that progress has been invincibly made toward achieving equality in people's attitudes, even among the least disposed to recognize it in principle.

Thus, personal services are decreasing every day and will finally be limited to the help a domestic is engaged to perform for a sick or debilitated individual, in which case it is a form of assistance. His function is modified; he becomes a kind of nurse, and if the patient is sullen and irritable, the person assisting him will not be humiliated in having to patiently put up with him, as long as no abuse is involved.

So, there is nothing debasing about domestic functions, if the employee's feelings are clear about his duties and his rights, if he does not let his employer take advantage of him or forget his due, and if he is not subjected to any demands outside those within the terms of their agreement.

Bursts of temper on both sides, altercations, even temporary injustices —all of which inevitably occur in daily relationships—would be much less serious in the kind of relationship I have described if each party formed a sound idea about equality. One can say to an overly sensitive domestic, "Why do you get upset over a single instance of my moodiness when I have put up with so many of yours at other times? Don't I ever have similar disagreements with my friends and relatives? So why are you more humiliated about it than they? Have I forbidden you to explain yourself, if your infraction of the rules is involuntary? As for your repeated, intentional violations, I am within my rights to caution you and complain to you about them, just as you have the right to complain and point it out to me if I exact something from you not included or foreseen in our agreement. But nothing in these explanations destroys the pact of equality between us. If I were so violent or so crazy as to raise my hand against you, you would have the right to do the same to me, and our equality would not be violated on account of this, for it happens that among the masses, people do fight among friends and among brothers and sisters. It may be irrational, but as long as nothing requires you to patiently endure it, I don't see how you can feel debased by the expressions of my irrationality."

It can thus be seen that, by painting everything in the worst possible light concerning relationships with domestic help and even by going to the extreme of an exceptional, violent case, a servant is a servant only when he wants to be one. He is despicable when he lets himself be lowered in order to profit from the repentance or weakness of the master. Past practice of this absurd and revolting tactic has, unfortunately, created a breed of men who were deservedly branded with the names "lackey" and "valet"; but their vices were originally the work of their masters, and when the latter come to understand the concept of equality, and practice it, this breed will disappear. It is almost unheard of in the country, where the small tenant farmers, the share-croppers, and the well-off growers also have "domestics" whom they treat no differently from their own family members. It is there that we see the true relationship being understood and carried out. If a farmer occasionally beats his pig-keeper, it is as if he were beating his child. In addition, masters and servants eat together, as was the practice in noblemen's homes in the past; it is too bad (as well as inconvenient and expensive) that this practice has disappeared, and I am hopeful of its return when time and progress will have given the breed of lackeys its due, so that what remains are only employees, who will sometimes be our friends and always our equals.

That is the ideal, and there, as with everything else, you have to have it in you to conduct yourself equitably amid the pitfalls that exist in relationships where, in reality, understanding and insight are still lacking on both sides. But in that reality, we have to admit, sadly and painfully, that there are still many domestics who want to be lackeys in spite of us, and that among the better ones, there still remain preconceived notions of inequality which are very difficult, if not impossible, to eradicate. That is why the ones we call our "retainers," the old and faithful friends of the family, who have preserved the traditions and practices of the past, seem most of the time bad-tempered, tyrannical, and unbearable to those who feel on a level with their servants, not enslaved by them. Those good people knew the manners of submission—a great zealousness, furious pride in doing their duty, loyalty, sometimes a wonderful impartiality. This was fine in its own time, but be aware that it is hardly possible or advantageous now.

Man never really yields himself. A person cannot submit and thus sacrifice himself as the servant, except on condition, one day or another, of becoming the master in reality, which is what always did happen. They had exploited that human being's life, used it up, exhausted it; they had taken advantage of his patience and devotion; and in return, he became indispensable. He took privileges beyond the original agreement; he had given up his youth, strength, and dignity. You owed him some compensation, and you could not give him too much, for no sacrifice could be comparable to the one from which you had profited. So, by virtue of an unspoken right, he became the master in your house, the jealous manager of your habits or needs, the inevitable confidant of your innermost concerns, the advocate for one son as opposed to another; one of your friends had his favor, another his antipathy. At first it seemed amusing, but little by little you gave in, and as the lives of the old master and servant were prolonged, their utter intimacy became, most of the time, a torment for both—the master feeling oppressed for having been too well served, the servant no longer knowing any boundaries, and getting no more satisfaction out of his demands, for having been exploited and dominated for so long.

I have seen so many cases like this, I have put up with so much of it on my own account as a result of having unsuspectingly and trustfully accepted devotedness in return for which I was then supposed to pay by giving up my entire life's independence, that I would like to give a taste of my ideas to the good-natured people who run the same risks, if they fail to understand exactly how and why all this must be changed concerning present and future practices.

In perhaps the very near future, we are destined to have no more lackeys, even no more servants, but rather employees, associates of a kind, in our domestic life. We are in a time of transition, where these employees are ill-equipped to exercise their rights and duties. Our own duty is slowly to lead them to this outcome, which will assure the security and dignity of our households. To achieve this, we have to establish a new relationship with our servants, completely different from that of the past. Thus, two pitfalls have to be avoided with equal care: offensive arrogance and degrading familiarity. What has to be done away with as completely as possible is the useless personal attention we receive, for when this attention becomes useless, it is no longer assistance which a man gives his fellow man, but a kind of homage given to a master by his slave. What is also necessary is the absolute discontinuance of the forms of language which sanction the practice of servitude. I detest it when a servant speaks to me in the third person, if he says "Madame is served" when he can just as well inform me that dinner is on the table. People here in Berry have no idea of the jargon of high-society lackeys, but they have a polite way about them which I find very touching, although it might seem laughable to those who don't understand it. When you ask them to do something, they answer "Gladly!" Mme. de Bérenger found that revolting. "I should hope so!" she would disdainfully reply. This was a gratuitously harsh way to reward the simple and kindly people who only wanted to show her their zeal.

I think one should be scrupulously polite to servants and never tell them, "Do this!" but rather ask, "Would you please do this?"; never forget to thank them when they do you a small favor on their own, even if it was only to hand you something; never needlessly call them to have them do something you can do yourself—open or close a window, put a log on the fire, etc. Such nonsense has always repelled me, as has being dressed or having one's hair done by chambermaids.

A chambermaid is an employee who has to sew, store, maintain and preserve linens, clothing, and other items. She is far from a slave whose job includes coming into contact with your body and cleaning your person. Only chronic invalids, sick people, and the debilitated elderly are entitled to that kind of attention.

But along with absolutely discontinuing everything that makes domestic chores degrading, it is also necessary to discontinue sharing close familiarity, confidences, outpourings of the heart, even purposeless conversations and casual chats. I do not mean that for the future; I limit its necessity to our present period of transition; but here and now its necessity is urgent, and I believe I can affirm that servants do not yet exist who are capable of not abusing our heart's intimacy with them, which is to their detriment as well as ours. They would have to come to know themselves better and feel themselves our equals. But as they are now, they have to be our slaves or our masters from the moment we ask them to do something besides fulfilling their regular functions for us.

Now, the function of consoling, distracting, serving us in our passions, keeping our secrets, or intervening in our family disputes—that function, to my mind, can never be bought for money and never will. It can only be miserably perverted and corrupted between two beings, one of whom feels inferior to the other. There is a fair exchange between a function and its remuneration. There is none between an outpouring of the heart and the willingness to listen, unless, by reciprocal exchange, you take a turn at being your servant's confidant, willing to oblige him, serve him in his love affairs, listen to his tales of woe, intervene in his family problems, etc. If this is the case, if you do all this, I have no quarrel; however, be alert to such questions as these: Will the exchange be absolutely equal, and do you want to be for him exactly what he is for you?

When he is worried, will you try to distract him by telling him all the little items of gossip that you encourage him to tell you to relieve your worries? Will you take the side of the persons he loves and be against those he detests, as it pleases you to have him do? Will you intrigue, or be diplomatic, with his friends or enemies as his interests or passions dictate, as you like to see him do on your behalf? If you have made up your mind, go to it, but I would be wary, and I maintain that if you tip the scale the least bit, you are taking advantage of your chosen friend. You are an ingrate, an egotist. He will sense it sooner or later, if he does not yet; he will take advantage of it; he will avenge himself through aversion or betrayal, if he has not already, unless you compensate him for his devotion by paying him extra, by some kind of improvement in his material well-being. You are free to do so, but then never hope to satisfy him, and prepare to sacrifice your own well-being for his, suffer his dependency, become his slave, make him your heir or be robbed by him. For moral and intellectual services are not paid for with money, and he will be right in finding that what you possess is not at all enough to repay your obligations to him. Having never obtained from you a moral devotion equal to his own, he will place no limits on his material demands, and the injustice, ingratitude, or deceit you complain about will be of your own doing.

Wait then until the future permits you to make an intimate friend of your servant, and until then do not give him the slightest access to the sanctuary of your heart; for if he does not enter there as your equal, he will profane it or feel degraded. You must do everything you can to drag him out of this so-called inequality, in which he still believes, to elevate his function as an employee, but you must limit yourself to this domain.

This was a really long digression, but I think everyone will find it useful, for I am not exaggerating when I say that everyone veers to one extreme or the other in this kind of relationship and that no one has found the perfectly work-able balance, not even I who preach and have often given in to the bad habits and temptations of a morbid impatience, or of an unmeditated leniency with the old servants, the loving and unbearable tyrants whom my grandmother bequeathed to me. Precisely because I regret not having always been rational in this respect and having thereby been destined to spawn ingrates, I believe I have a right to warn others while accusing myself.

And whether or not my discourse is useful to others, it has at least served my need to begin the recital of a period in my life where I was much too much handed over and very often sacrificed to the exaggerated influence of servants.

I have mentioned that my grandmother's illness had perceptibly damaged not the lucidity of her mind, but the stability and serenity of her nature. Her emotional health was weakened along with her physical health, and yet she was only sixty-six years old, an age which is not necessarily marked by infir-mities of the body or spirit, an age which I saw my mother reach and surpass without it bringing the least decline in her emotional and physical energy.

My grandmother could no longer stand the noise of children, and I volun-tarily made myself more and more silent and motionless at her side, but not without effort and suffering. She sensed that this could be injurious to my health, and she hardly kept me near her any longer. She was plagued by frequent drowsiness, and as she slept so lightly that the slightest breath was a painful awakening, to escape from this continuous discomfort she wanted to regulate her daytime sleeping. She therefore closed herself in her room at noon to take a nap in her big easy chair, which lasted until three o'clock. Then came footbaths, rub-downs, and a thousand special cares that required her confinement with Mlle. Julie, so much so that I hardly saw her any more, except at mealtimes and during the evening, to be her partner or hold her cards while she played out a hand of patience or solitaire. This was a mediocre amusement for me, as you can imagine, but I have never had to reproach myself at all for showing one moment of ill-humor or weariness.

I was thus left to myself more and more each day, and the short lessons she gave me consisted of a look at my commonplace book every two or three days and a harpsichord lesson that lasted barely a half-hour. Deschartres gave me a Latin lesson to which I was more and more ill-disposed, for that dead language had no meaning for me, and a lesson in writing French verse, which made me nauseous, for I had no aptitude at all in that genre, which I love and admire anyway and which came to me no more naturally than arithmetic, at which I have always been notoriously inept. Nevertheless, I did study arithmetic, versification, and Latin, and even a little Greek and a little botany for good measure, and none of it appealed to me. To understand botany (which is not at all a science considered to be within the purview of young ladies) it is necessary to know about the mystery of procreation and the role of the sexes; indeed, that is about all that merits curiosity or interest in the way plants are structured. As you can well imagine, Deschartres made me skip over that issue, and I was much too innocent for the slightest observation in this area to occur to me on my own. Botany was thus reduced for me to purely arbitrary classifications, since I did not grasp its unspoken laws, and to its Greek and Latin nomenclature, which was but arid work for the memory. What use was it for me to know the scientific names of all those pretty meadow plants to which the peasants and herdsmen have given names that are often more poetic and always more meaningful—wild thyme, shepherd's-purse, sorrel, cat's foot, balsam, ragwort, wild succory, lamb's lettuce, five fingers, forget-me-not, daisy, bellwort, etc. The barbarous-sounding botanical names seemed to me the fantasy of pedants, just as for Latin and French versification, I wondered, in my superb ignorance, of what use were these dessicated categories and rules which inhibit the flow of thought and nip it in the bud. I quietly repeated to myself what I had often heard my candid mother say, "What good is all that rubbish?" She had the common sense of a Nicole,[16] and I, without knowing it, had the instinctive rebelliousness of a very logical mind—as pragmatic as it was romantic. This may seem paradoxical, but I shall be coming back to this point so often that the reader will permit me to bypass it for the time being. *G.M.S.*

VII

My relationship with my brother. —Similarities and incompatibilities
in our characters. —My maid's violence toward me. —Moral
tendencies developed in me by her tyranny. —My grandmother
becomes a royalist of sorts. —The portrait of Czar Alexander.
—Return from the Isle of Elba. —More fantasies. —My mother
comes back to Nohant. —I forgive my maid. —The Army of the
Loire passes through. —Général Subervie's cockade. —Général
Colbert. —How Nohant almost provided the fuel and setting for a
patriotic Vendée. —The army is disbanded. —Colonel Sourd.
—Brigands of the Loire. —Deschartres' peaches. —My father's
regiment. —Our cousin visits us. —Mme. de La Marlière's piety.
—My mother leaves Nohant. —My brother leaves Nohant. —Alone.

Later on I shall go into a more detailed explanation of what I liked and
disliked about my various studies. What I want to recall here is the emotional
state I was in, abandoned, so to speak, to my own thoughts, with no one to
guide me, no one to talk to, or confide in. Yet I needed to exist, and it is no existence to be alone. Hippolyte was becoming more and more rowdy, and the only
point of our games was to run about and make noise. I soon had more than my
fill of this kind of play, which always ended in my feeling hurt and his feeling
rebuffed. Still, we loved each other, we have always loved each other. There
were certain similarities of character and intellect between us, despite enormous
differences. He was as matter-of-fact as I was romantic, and yet he had in his
disposition a certain sense of artistry and, in his gaiety, a penchant for satirical
observation which appealed to my sense of humor. No visitor came to the house
but Hippolyte would judge him, see through his character, mimic, and analyse
him with great penetration but excessive causticity. I was considerably amused
by all that, and together we were terribly irreverent. I needed some merriment,
and no one has ever made me laugh as he did. But one cannot always laugh, and
I needed to share serious thoughts even more than foolish ones at that time.

So, my gaiety with him, if not exactly forced, at any rate often had a nervous and feverish quality. At the slightest provocation it turned into sulking and
then tears. My brother claimed I was mean, which I was not, as he himself admitted later in life; it was only that I felt a secret melancholy, a deep dissatisfaction
which I could not disclose to him, which he might have made fun of as he made
fun of everything including the brutal and tyrannical ways of Deschartres.

I had come to the conclusion that everything I was learning would be of no use to me since, despite my mother's silence on this matter, I was still determined to join her and work by her side as soon as she deemed it feasible. Consequently, studying bored me, especially since I did not imitate Hippolyte, who resolutely avoided it as much as he could. I studied out of obedience, but without any desire or enthusiasm; it was merely a tedious task I performed for a certain number of dull, slow-moving hours. My grandmama knew it and reproached me for my laziness, my coldness toward her, and my perpetual absent-mindedness, which often made me seem stupid and for which Hippolyte was the first to tease me without mercy. The reproaches and mockery hurt my feelings, whereupon I was accused of being too vain. Whether I was indeed too vain, I don't know, but I am sure my resentment came, not from hurt pride, but from a deeper source—a heartache that went unassuaged.

Until then, Rose had exerted control over me rather gently, considering her impetuous temperament. She had been restrained by the frequent presence of my mother at Nohant, or more likely she had obeyed an instinct which was beginning to change, for there was no duplicity in her—I am glad to do her justice on that point. I think she was one of those good mother-hens that care for their young most tenderly as long as the chicks can sleep under their wings, but who peck at them freely the moment they begin to fly and run about on their own. As I grew older, she stopped petting me, and indeed I had no more need of that, but she also started to mistreat me, which I could very well have dispensed with. Eager to please my grandmother, she took over, as her understudy, the care and responsibility for my physical upbringing, and made it a misery. If I ventured out without taking all the minutely prescribed precautions against catching cold, I was immediately not just scolded, but deafened; the term is no exaggeration to describe the storm of her voice and the flood of insulting epithets that shook my nervous system. If I tore my dress, or broke my wooden clog, or if playing in the bushes I got a scratch that might suggest to my grandmother that I had not been well looked after, Rose would beat me, rather mildly to begin with, as a way to intimidate me; then little by little more seriously, as a systematic repression; and finally, just because she needed to demonstrate her authority and had acquired the habit of violence. If I cried, I was beaten harder; if I had let a scream escape my lips, I think she would have killed me, for in her paroxysm of rage she had no control over herself. Day by day, impunity made her more brutal and more cruel, and in so becoming, she took advantage, oddly enough, of my good nature; for if I did not have her dismissed (my grandmother would never have forgiven her for so much as laying a finger on me), it was only because I loved her in spite of her abominable temper. It is my nature to endure the unendurable for a long time, a very long time. But it is true, once my patience is thoroughly tried, it snaps all at once and forever.

Why was I attached to that girl to the point of letting her oppress and rule me so constantly? The answer is simple—she loved my mother; she was the only person in the household who still talked to me about her sometimes, and always with admiration and affection. Her intelligence was not acute enough to penetrate the depths of my soul and see the sorrow which consumed me, or to understand that my absent-mindedness, carelessness, and bad moods had no other cause; but when I was ill, she would nurse me with infinite tenderness. To amuse me, she would humor me in a thousand ways as no one else did; if I was exposed to the slightest danger, she extricated me from it with a presence of mind, courage, and energy which somehow reminded me of my mother. She would have thrown herself into a fire or into the sea in order to save my life. Above all, she never exposed me to the thing I feared more than anything else—a scolding from my grandmother—but always protected me from it. She would have told a lie to spare me from my grandmother's disapproval, and when some slight misdeed placed me in a position of choosing between being beaten by my maid or scolded by my grandmother, I far preferred to be beaten.

Yet these beatings offended me deeply. When my mother hit me, I had never felt any grief other than the pain of knowing she was angry with me. Besides, she had long ago given up that sort of punishment which she thought appropriate only for small children. Rose, acting on the contrary belief, adopted this system at a time in my life when it could humiliate and debase me. If it did not make a coward of me, it was only because God had given me a very accurate instinct for true human dignity. From that point of view, I thank Him with all my heart for all I have suffered and endured. I learned at an early age how to rise above undeserved insult or injury. In my relationship with Rose, I had a profound sense of my innocence and her injustice, for I never had any vice nor any character flaw which could have warranted her violent outbursts. My faults were involuntary, and so slight that I cannot even now understand her rages, if I do not call to mind that she was a redhead, and so hot-blooded that, in the depths of winter, she wore a cotton dress and slept with the window open.

So I became used to the humiliation of being in a state of subjection, and found that it nurtured a sort of natural stoicism which may have been useful in helping me survive despite my excessively sensitive feelings. I learned to harden myself against misfortune, and in that regard, I was encouraged by my brother, who in the midst of our escapades, would say with a laugh, "Tonight, we'll be beaten." Mercilessly beaten by Deschartres, he accepted his fate with a mixture of hatred and unconcern. He found his revenge in satire; I found mine in my heroism and in the forgiveness I bestowed on my maid. This contest between moral and physical strength even exalted me in my own estimation, and when a punch in the head shook my nerves and brought tears to my eyes, I would wipe them away in secret. I would have blushed to let them be seen.

Yet I would have done better to scream and to sob. Rose was not unkind; she would have felt remorse had she realized she was hurting me. But it may be that she was not entirely conscious of her brutalities, rash and impetuous as she was. One day, when she was teaching me to embroider my initials on a pair of stockings and I took three stitches instead of two, she gave me a furious slap on the face. "You should have removed your thimble before hitting me," I said coldly. "One of these days you're going to break my teeth." She stared at me in sincere astonishment, looked at her thimble and at the mark it had left on my cheek. She could not believe it was she who, only a moment ago, had put that mark on me. There were times when she threatened me with a hard slap immediately after administering it, which she had apparently done unconsciously.

I will not pursue this dull topic any further; suffice it to say that, for three or four years, hardly a day passed without my receiving some unexpected blow which did not always hurt me physically, but which, each time, was a cruel shock that, trusting and affectionate though I was, made my whole soul turn rigid. Since I was loved nonetheless, perhaps I had no reason to convince myself I was unhappy, particularly since I could have brought this state of affairs to an end, but never chose to do so. But whether or not I was justified in bemoaning my fate, I felt unhappy, I believed myself to be unhappy, and therefore I really was unhappy. I even got into the habit of deriving a sort of bitter satisfaction from constantly protesting inwardly against my fate, from insisting on loving no one but the person who was absent and who seemed to have abandoned me to my misery, from refusing to show any affection for my grandmama or share my thoughts with her, from criticizing the education she gave me while deliberately keeping her in ignorance of its shortcomings, and lastly, by looking upon myself as an unfortunate creature singled out for subjection, injustice, ennui, and eternal regrets.

Hence, let no one ask me anymore why it is that, while I can claim a kind of nobility of birth and am able to enjoy a certain level of comfort, my solicitude, my natural inclinations, my innermost heart—if I may so put it— have always gone out to the oppressed. This tendency was developed in me of necessity, through the pressure of outside circumstances, long before the search for truth and the reasonings of a moral conscience made it a duty. I can therefore take no credit for it, and those who think as I do are no more justified in praising me for it than those who think differently are in blaming me.

What is sure, what cannot be disputed in good faith after one has read the story of my childhood, is that I did not choose my opinions out of caprice, or because as an artist I took a fancy to them, as people have said; they were the inevitable outcome of my early sorrows, my most sacred affections, the very circumstances of my life.

My grandmother, after briefly resisting the bias of her class, had become not so much a royalist, but a "partisan of the old regime," as the saying went. It had always cost her something to accept, not the fortunate usurpation of the man of genius, Napoléon, but the insolence of the parvenus who shared his good fortune without having earned it in the same way. New upstarts were now appearing on the scene, but she was less shocked by their arrogance, as she had seen this trait before; besides, my father, with his republican leanings, was no longer with us to point out to her how ridiculous these people were.

It must also be said that after the long tension of the Emperor's glorious and absolute rule, the kind of anarchy which followed on the heels of the Restoration was something new, something that in the provinces took on an aura of freedom. The liberals spoke up, envisioning a sort of political and moral nation as yet unknown in France, a "consitutional" nation, which no one visualized very clearly and which existed only in words; a monarchy without absolute power, a liberality of opinion and speech regarding all aspects of political institutions that had been badly shaken, but patched on the surface. There was much tolerance in these matters in certain bourgeois circles which my grandmother would gladly have listened to in preference to her old coterie. But "the eminent ladies" (as my father used to call them) did not give her much chance to think for herself. They had the intolerance that goes with passionate belief; anyone who dared regret the Corsican was condemned to the most tenacious and blind hatred; they forgot that, only yesterday, they had not hesitated to consort with his followers. Never has there been so much pettiness, gossip, and hatred, so many accusations and denunciations.

Fortunately, we lived far removed from the centers of intrigue. The letters which my grandmother received brought only an echo of it, and Deschartres indulged in supremely absurd declamations against the "tyrant," whom he credited with less than average intelligence. As for me, I heard so many different things that I no longer knew what to think. Czar Alexander was the great law-giver, the modern-day philosopher, the new Frederick the Great, the man of genius par excellence. Someone sent a portrait of him to my grandmother and she gave it to me to frame. His features—which I examined attentively, since people said that Bonaparte was only a child compared to him—left me unmoved. He had an ungainly head, a flabby face, an insincere expression, a foolish smile. I have never seen him in person, but among so many pictures that were profusely circulating in France at the time, there must have been some good resemblances. None of them inspired my liking, and in spite of myself, I still remembered the fine clear gaze of "my Emperor" which had once met mine, in an era when I was told it would bring me luck.

Then all of a sudden, in early March, we heard he had landed, he was marching toward Paris. Whether the news came from Paris or the South, I do not know, but my grandmother did not share the confidence of the ladies who wrote, "Let us rejoice! This time he will be hanged, or at the very least, locked in an iron cage." My grandmama thought quite differently and told us, "The Bourbons are inept, and Bonaparte is going to drive them out forever. They are fated to be dupes. How can they believe that those generals who have betrayed their master will not now betray them and go back to him? God forbid that all this should lead to terrible reprisals, and that Bonaparte should treat them as he did the Duc d'Enghien!"

For my part, I have only a faint recollection of what went on at Nohant during the Hundred Days. I was lost in endless daydreams that are hazy in my recollection. I was bored with the incessant talk of politics, and all these abrupt reversals of opinion were incomprehensible to my logical young mind. I saw everyone transformed from one day to the next. In our province, bourgeois and peasants had suddenly turned royalist, and I could not understand why. Where were all the benefits the Bourbon Restoration was supposed to bring, which had been heralded with so much fanfare?

Each day brought some vague news of Napoléon's triumphal entry into every city along his way, and at once, many who had shouted "Death to the tyrant!" and dragged the tricolor in the mud suddenly became Bonapartists again. I did not understand it all well enough to become indignant, but I did feel involuntary disgust and a kind of disenchantment with life. It seemed to me the world had gone mad, and I returned to the fantasy I used to have when the Emperor was campaigning in Russia and France. I found my wings again, and I flew to meet him and ask him to account for all the bad things people said about him, and for all the good.

Once, I imagined that I carried the Emperor through space and set him down on the dome of the Tuileries. There, I had a long conversation with him; I asked him a thousand questions. I told him, "If you prove to me by your answers that you are an ambitious, bloodthirsty monster, as people say, I shall hurl you down and dash you to pieces on the steps of your palace, but if you can vindicate yourself, if you are what I have believed you to be—a kind, great, just Emperor, a father to his people—I shall restore you to your throne and defend you against your enemies with my flaming sword." Then he opened his heart to me and confessed he had often done wrong because of his immoderate yearning for fame, but he swore to me that he loved France and that henceforth his only thought would be to ensure the happiness of its people; whereupon I touched him with the flaming sword that would make him invulnerable.

It is very strange that I should have had these waking dreams often while memorizing some verses of Corneille or Racine, which I was to recite for my tutor. It was a kind of hallucination, and I have noticed that many young girls, as they approach a certain crisis in their biological development, are prone to ecstasies or visions that are even more bizarre. I would probably not remember mine were it not for the fact that they obstinately assumed the same form for several consecutive years and that they became fixed, I cannot tell why, on the Emperor and the Grand Army. To be sure, I often had preoccupations that were more personal and acute; my imagination ought only to have conjured up fantasies of my mother in that Garden of Eden which she had once envisaged for me, to which I constantly aspired. Yet that was not the case; I thought of her all the time but never saw her in my mind's eye; while the pale face of the Emperor, of which I had barely had a glimpse, rose constantly before me and became animated with life and speech the moment I heard his name spoken.

To close this subject, I shall say that when the *Bellerophon* carried him to St. Helena, I sank the boat with a stroke of my flaming sword; I drowned all the Englishmen on board, and once more carried the Emperor to the Tuileries, after making him solemnly promise that he would never go to war again to gratify himself. What was peculiar about these fantasies was that I did not appear in them as myself, but as a sort of all-powerful genie, an angel of the Lord, Destiny, the good fairy of France, what you will, but not the eleven-year-old girl who was studying her lesson or watering her small garden while an imaginary self wandered about in the air.

I have tried to limit this description to its physiological facts. It was not the result of spiritual exaltation or political infatuation, for it took hold of me during my worst spells of languor, indifference, and boredom, and often when I had been listening without interest and almost in spite of myself to the political gossip of the day. I did not believe in my fantasy, saw no superstitious meaning in it, never took it seriously, and never spoke of it to anyone. It wearied me, and I did not deliberately evoke it. It took hold of me through some cerebral process that was quite unpredictable and independent of my own will.

The presence of enemy troops in Paris made life there hateful and unbearable to those in whom a fanatic devotion to royalty had not stifled love and respect for their country. My mother left Caroline with my aunt and came to spend the summer at Nohant. It had been some seven or eight months since I had last seen her, so my joy can easily be imagined. Besides, with her arrival, my whole life was transformed. Rose lost her authority over me and gladly took a rest from her fits of rage. More than once I had been tempted to complain to my mother, as soon as she arrived, of the ill treatment I suffered at the hands of that woman, but since Rose did not suspect, in the sincerity of her heart, how much she wronged me; since far from dreading my mother's arrival she rejoiced with all her heart at the prospect of seeing "Madame Maurice" again; since she prepared her room with solicitude and counted the days and hours with me; since, in short, she loved my mother, I forgave her everything, and not only did I not reveal how violent she was with me, but I even had the courage to deny it when my mother began to suspect the truth. I remember one day when her suspicions became serious, and it was rather to my credit that I dissipated them.

My brother had devised a scheme for making glue to catch birds. I don't know whether it was in the *Grand* or the *Petit Albert*, or in our old manual of witchcraft that he found the recipe. It was a simple matter of grinding mistletoe from an oak tree. We did not succeed in making glue, but we did manage to smear our faces, hands, and clothing with a paste of an ambiguous greenish hue. My mother was busy gardening nearby, absorbed in her work as usual, and not even noticing that we were splashing her with our bucket. Suddenly I saw Rose approaching at the end of the path, and my first impulse was to flee. "What's the matter with her?" my mother asked Hippolyte, as she awoke from her reverie and saw me run away. My brother, who never liked making enemies, answered that he had no idea, but my mother's suspicions were aroused; she called me back, and questioning Rose in my presence said, "This isn't the first time I've noticed how afraid the child is of you. I believe you're abusing her."

"But just look at her!" replied the redhead, disgusted to see me so dirty and stained. "Wouldn't it try anyone's patience to have to spend one's life washing and mending her clothes?"

"Well," said my mother in a harsh tone, "do you imagine, by any chance, that I had you taken into service here for anything else than to wash and mend her clothes? Did you think you were hired to receive a pension and read Voltaire, like Mlle. Julie? You'd better get that notion out of your head. Wash, mend, and let my child run, play, and grow; that's the way I mean it to be, and not otherwise."

As soon as my mother was alone with me, she plied me with questions. "I see you tremble and turn pale when she gives you a stern look. Does she scold you hard?"

"Yes," said I, "too hard."

"Still," rejoined my mother, "I hope she has never forgotten herself so far as to lay a finger on you, for I'd have her dismissed this very evening!" The thought of being responsible for the discharge of this poor woman who loved me so much, despite her fits of temper, stifled the confession I was about to make. I remained silent. My mother would not let it drop. I realized that, for the first time in my life, I had to lie, and to my mother! My heart silenced my conscience. I lied, and my mother, still unconvinced, attributing my discretion to fear, put my generosity to a severe test by making me repeat several times that I was telling her the truth. I confess I felt no remorse. This falsehood could harm no one but myself.

In the end she believed me. Rose never knew what I had done for her. Restrained by my mother's presence, she softened her manner, but later, when we were alone together again, she made me pay dearly for the foolish softness of my heart. I was too proud to admit it to her, and as usual, I suffered oppression and insult in silence.

An imposing and moving spectacle roused me from absorption in my own existence during part of the summer of 1815 that my mother spent with me. It was the passage and disbanding of the Army of the Loire. It is common knowledge that after having used Davout to deceive this noble army, after having promised it complete amnesty, on July 24th the King issued an ordinance summoning Ney, Labédoyère, and nineteen others whose names were dear to the military and to France, before a court-martial. Thirty-eight more were sentenced to banishment. The Prince d'Echmühl had resigned, since his position as commander-in-chief of the Army of the Loire was no longer tenable. The Restoration was planning to reward him for his submission; as his successor, it appointed Macdonald, who was entrusted with the task of disbanding the army "quietly." He transferred headquarters to Bourges.

According to Achille de Vaulabelle's *Histoire des deux Restaurations*: "Two orders, dated August 1st and 2nd, announced these two changes to the troops. In the text of the orders, Macdonald did not use the term 'disbanding'; he merely said that in order to lighten the population's burden of lodging the military, the forces would be 'dispersed.' This measure was the beginning of the Army's dissolution; brigades and divisions were dismantled; regiments of the same corps, or the same branch, were dispersed over great distances; certain regiments were scattered, down to their battalions and squadrons. Once all these ties were broken, the ordinance stipulating a reorganization of the Army was made public (August 12th) and the actual disbanding was carried out, but one detachment, one regiment at a time, so as to minimize the effect of complaints, to isolate protest and resistance."

And so it was we witnessed fragmented scenes that gradually enabled me to understand at last what was happening in France. I must say that until then it had been difficult for me to distinguish genuine patriotism from party loyalty. I was almost frightened by the Bonapartist instinct that awoke in me when I heard people curse, decry, and slander everything that had so recently been respected or feared. My mother, quite as innocent as I was in these matters, had not waited for the old contessas to return before she derided and detested the old regime, but she had no fixed opinion on anything. She had nothing to say when my grandmama, indicting ambitious men and conquerors as "great destroyers of mankind," told her that a monarchy tempered by liberal institutions, a system for lasting peace, and a return to comfort, individual freedom, industry, arts and letters, would be better for France than the reign of the saber. "Didn't we curse war enough, you and I, when our poor Maurice was with us?" she would ask her. "Now we are paying the price for all that imperial glory. But let this first angry reaction against us in Europe subside, and you will see if we do not enter an era of calm and happy security under these Bourbons, whom I do not like much more than you do, but who guarantee us a better future. Without them, our national identity would have perished. Bonaparte had seriously compromised it by trying to overextend it. If a royalist party had not emerged to hasten his downfall, where would we be now after this military disaster? France would be dismembered, and we would be Prussian, English, or German."

That is the way my grandmother reasoned, rejecting the possibility of something that I nevertheless regard as certain: If a royalist party had not emerged to sell out our country and betray it, the whole universe united against us could not have defeated the French army. My mother, who willingly admitted the superiority of her mother-in-law, quietly let herself be persuaded, and consequently I did too. I was therefore disillusioned, as it were, with the Empire and resigned to the Restoration when, one day under a burning sun, we saw the glorious arms that had shone at Waterloo glittering on all the slopes of the Vallée Noire. It was a regiment of lancers, decimated by that unprecedented disaster, which first arrived to occupy our region. Général Colbert set up headquarters at Nohant. Général Subervie installed himself in the château at Ars, half a league away. Every day the generals, their aides-de-camp, and a dozen staff officers dined or lunched with us. Général Subervie was a handsome fellow, very gallant with the ladies, jovial and even teasing with the children. Since, through his encouragement, I had become a little too fresh with him and he had pulled my ears a little too hard while we were playing together, I took my revenge one day with a piece of mischief whose import I hardly understood. I cut a pretty cockade out of white paper and pinned it on top of the tricolor cockade on his hat, without his noticing. The whole Army was still wearing the imperial colors, and the order to discard them came only a few days later. So, off he went to La Châtre with his white cockade and was surprised to see the officers and men he met staring at him in astonishment. At last, some officer—I forget who—asked him to explain his white cockade, a request the general could not understand until, removing his hat, he sent the cockade to the devil, and me along with it for good measure.

I saw that pleasant Général Subervie again, the first time since those days long ago, in 1848, at the Hôtel de Ville, a few days after the revolution, when he had just accepted the post of Minister of War. He had forgotten none of the circumstances of his stay at Nohant in 1815; he scolded me for the white cockade, and I upbraided him for pulling my ears.

A few days later, in 1815, I would surely not have played such a trick on him, because in my heart I had abjured my brief attempt at royalism, and this is how it came about.

From the first word my grandmother spoke, indeed just from her dignified air and her old-fashioned style of dress, one could tell she belonged to the royalist party. People even assumed she was more attached to that party than she really was. But she was the daughter of Maréchal Maurice de Saxe, she had had a brave son in the service, she was full of gracious hospitality and delicate attentions for the so-called Brigands of the Loire, whom she perceived only as valiant, generous men, brothers-in-arms of her late son (some of them, including Général Colbert, I believe, had actually known him). Moreover, my grandmother inspired respect—tender respect—in anyone with a noble heart. Those officers whom she entertained so well accordingly refrained from saying a word in her presence that might have offended her, given the opinions she was supposed to have; just as she, for her part, refrained from saying a word or recalling an event that might have made more bitter their misfortune, with which she sympathized. That is why I was able to be in the society of these officers for several days before any new emotion stirred my heart and changed the disposition of my mind. But one day, when, as a rare occurrence, we were only a small party at dinner, Deschartres, who could not hold his tongue, ruffled the feelings of Général Colbert. Alphonse Colbert, a descendant of the great Colbert,[17] was a stout and ruddy-faced man of about forty. He had fine manners and was agreeably gifted; he sang pastoral romances, accompanying himself on the piano; he was full of attentions for my grandmother, who thought him charming, while my mother uttered quietly that for a military man she found him rather tame.

I tend to think it was on this very day that the order to disband the army had arrived from Bourges. Whether for this reason, or because of Deschartres' inappropriate remarks, the general became heated. His round, dark eyes snapped, the color rose in his cheeks, his long-pent indignation and grief exploded, and he spoke with great energy, "No!" he cried, "we have not been defeated, we have been betrayed, and we still are. If we hadn't been, if we could trust every one of our officers, I assure you our brave men would show those Prussian gentlemen and those Cossack gentlemen that France is not a prey to be devoured with impunity." Fired with French honor, he spoke of the shame of accepting a king imposed by foreigners, and he depicted the shame with such heartfelt conviction that my soul was stirred, just as it had been on the day in 1814 when I heard a boy of thirteen or fourteen declare he was going to take a big saber and defend his country.

Seeing that the general was growing more and more excited, my grandmother tried to calm him by saying that the soldiers were exhausted, and the people only wanted peace. "The people!" he cried. "Oh, you don't know them, the people! They don't reveal their wishes, their real thoughts in your châteaus. They're careful what they say in front of their former lords who have returned and whom they distrust. But we soldiers know their sympathies and their longings, and believe me, the game is not over yet! The government wants to disband us because we're the last remaining force, the last hope this country has;

but it is only up to us to reject the order as an act of treason and an insult. Good Lord! this region is ideal for partisan warfare, and I don't know what stops us from organizing here the nucleus of a patriotic Vendée.[18] Ah, the people! the peasants!" he said, rising from his chair and brandishing his table-knife. "You'll see them join us! You'll see them come, bringing their scythes and their pitchforks, and their rusty old firelocks! We could hold out for six months in your sunken roads and behind your tall hedges. Meanwhile, the whole of France will rise; moreover, if we have to fight alone, it's better to die with glory fighting than offer our throats to the enemy. There are still many of us who are only waiting for a word to raise the banner of the nation again, and perhaps I am the one who should set an example."

Deschartres was now quiet. My grandmother took the general by the arm, removed the knife from his hand, and made him sit down, all in such a tender, motherly fashion that he was moved. He seized the old lady's hands and covered them with kisses, begging her forgiveness for having frightened her. Grief overcame his anger, and he burst into tears, unburdening his heavy heart for the first time perhaps since Waterloo.

We were all weeping, except Deschartres, but even he refrained from further argument, silenced at last by a kind of respect for misfortune. My grandmother led the general to the salon. "My dear general," she said, "in the name of God, give yourself the relief of tears, but never before a living soul say such things as have just escaped you. I am as sure as one can be of my family, my guests, and my servants, but you see that, in these times and when some of your comrades are forced to flee to escape a possible death sentence, you risk your life by giving way to your despair in this manner."

"You recommend prudence, dear Madame," he replied, "yet it is not prudence but daring that you should recommend. You think I am not speaking seriously, you think I am prepared to accept the ignominious disbanding of the army which our enemies are foisting on us! It is another Waterloo, minus the honor, that they are imposing on us. A little boldness would save us."

"Civil war!" cried my grandmother. "You want to rekindle civil war in France, you worshippers of Napoléon! He, at least, shrank from leaving such a stain upon his name, and sacrificed his pride rather than face such a horrible expedient! I want you to know that I never liked him, but once in my life I admired him. And that was the day he chose to abdicate rather than arm Frenchmen against one another. He himself would disavow your attempt today. So be faithful to his memory by following the noble example he has set for you."

Whether these arguments made an impression on the general, or whether his own thoughts were, in substance, consonant with my grandmother's, he calmed down, and in subsequent years he resumed his service under the Bourbons. For all those who, like him, had carried their loyalty and grief beyond the Loire, it has been only legitimate to pursue their military careers under a different regime, when they could do so without stooping too low.

In the excerpt quoted from M. de Vaulabelle's history, we have seen that the order to disband the army came disguised in the form of various decrees of partial dispersion. One evening, the village green of Nohant and all the roads leading to it were filled with a dense crowd of horsemen still resplendent in their uniforms, who had come to receive Général Colbert's orders. It took only a moment. Then, silent and somber, they broke into groups and rode off in different directions

The general and his staff appeared resigned. M. de Colbert was not the only one who had conceived the idea of a patriotic Vendée. The same thought had run through the disquieted ranks of the Army of the Loire, but we know now that this had been a plot of the Orleanist party[19] and that the officers were well advised not to be taken in by it.

One morning, as we were having lunch with several officers of the lancers, the conversation turned to the colonel of the regiment, who had fallen on the battlefield at Waterloo. "Good old Colonel Sourd," they were saying, "what a loss to his friends; how sad for all the men under his command! He was a hero in battle, and an excellent man in private life."

"And you don't know what became of him?" asked my grandmother.

"He was riddled with wounds, one arm smashed by a cannon-ball," answered the general. "They managed to carry him to the ambulance; he survived the event, and there was some hope he might be saved, but there hasn't been any news of him since, so everything leads us to believe that he is no more. Another man took command of the regiment. Poor Sourd! I shall miss him as long as I live!"

As he spoke these words, the door opened. An officer, with one empty sleeve folded and pinned to his buttonhole, his face plastered with bandages that concealed horrible scars, appeared and rushed toward his companions. The whole company rose, and a shout burst from every throat; they ran to him, hugged him, pressed him with questions, and wept. And Colonel Sourd joined us to finish the lunch that had begun with his funeral eulogy.

Lieutenant-colonel Ferroussat, who had assumed command in his stead, was glad to relinquish his authority, and when the time came for the troops to be discharged, Sourd insisted on taking his place at the head of his regiment, which had welcomed him back with transports of joy impossible to describe.

Here I must mention M. Pétiet, Général Colbert's aide-de-camp, who was really as kind as a father to me. He was always ready to play with me, like the merry fellow he still was, notwithstanding his rank and years of service, which were already adding up. He was no more than thirty, but he had been a page to the Empress and had joined the army at a very early age. He had not lost the gaiety and mischievousness of a page; my brother and I adored him, and never left him a moment's peace. He is now a general.[8]

At the end of a fortnight, Général Colbert, M. Pétiet, Général Subervie, and the other officers under them left Nohant for Saint-Amand, if I am not mistaken. My grandmother had already become so fond of Général Colbert that she wept at his departure. He had been an excellent guest indeed, as were the many senior ranking officers we successively had to lodge in the course of that summer. We missed them all. Yet, as the dispersion of the army went on, my interest diminished, at least with regard to the officers, who grew resigned to the events and began to be more concerned about the future than the past. Several of them were by now quite reconciled to the Restoration and had new commissions in their pockets. My grandmother was pleased and congratulated them warmly. But this sudden new acceptance of the monarchy was still repugnant to my mother, consequently to me, for I continued to be guided in my impressions by what I read in her eyes, and in my opinions by what came from her lips.

More than one officer courted her, for she still had much charm, and I think she could easily have made a new and honorable marriage at the time, but she would not hear of it; though she was surrounded by attentive gentlemen, I have never seen less coquettishness or greater reserve than she displayed.

It was an impressive spectacle, the steady passage through the Vallée Noire of an army that still retained all its proud appearance. The weather was clear and warm. All the roads were covered with those noble phalanxes marching in good order and in solemn silence. We were seeing for the last time those fine uniforms so gallantly worn, "worn out by victory," as has been so aptly said; those tanned, handsome faces, those proud soldiers who had been so fierce in battle, now so gentle, so human, so disciplined in peace. There was not a single act of looting or violence to reproach them for. I never saw one of them drunk, although wine is cheap in these parts and the peasants gave it freely to the soldiers. My mother and I could stroll at any hour on the roads, as in normal times, without fear of insult. Never were misfortune, banishment, ingratitude, and calumny borne with so much patience and dignity, but that did not prevent people from calling those men the Brigands of the Loire.

Deschartres even complained loudly that a volume of his *Thousand and One Nights* was missing and that four beautiful peaches had disappeared from the espalier where he had been watching them ripen—two misdeeds for which Hippolyte may well have been responsible. But Deschartres still blamed the Brigands and only calmed down when my grandmama said to him very gravely, "Well, Deschartres, when you write the history of this period, you will not omit such a capital event. You will say, 'A whole army marched through Nohant, ravaging and destroying an espalier on which four peaches had been counted before this tragic time.'"

Regiments from every branch of service passed before us—chasseurs, carabineers, dragoons, cuirassiers, artillery units, and the colorful mamelukes with their superb horses and uniforms like stage costumes, that I had seen in Madrid. My father's regiment also filed past, and the officers, several of whom had known him, came into our courtyard and asked to pay their respects to my grandmother and mother. The two women—choked with emotion, on the verge of fainting—welcomed them. On seeing me, an officer whose name I do not recall exclaimed, "And this is his daughter. There is no mistaking the resemblance." He took me up in his arms and hugged me, saying, "I saw you when you were very little, in Spain. Your father was a gallant officer and as kind as an angel."

Many years later, when I was more than twenty, one of these officers, discharged on half-pay, came up to me on the boulevard, wanting to know if I wasn't the daughter of "poor Dupin"; and in a restaurant, some officers who were dining at a table came up to my companions to ask the same question. They were noble remnants of our glorious army, but I have such a poor memory for names that I would not venture to mention any, for fear of making a mistake. Whenever such encounters occurred, I always heard my father praised in the warmest and most affectionate terms.

I have already said that my brother was a keen observer and judicious critic for his age. He shared his observations with me, and we noticed that the reconciliation between the new government and the military always began in the highest ranks. Thus, by the time most of the army had passed through, some senior officers were displaying with satisfaction banners bearing the fleur-de-lis, which had been embroidered, people said, by the Duchesse d'Angoulême and sent to them as tokens of good will. The junior officers appeared more hesitant and uncommitted. The non-commissioned officers and the men were all openly and courageously Bonapartists, as they were called then; when the final order came to change the flag and cockades, we saw imperial eagles burnt to ashes amidst floods of tears. Some of the men spat on their "spotless" cockades before pinning them to their shakos. The officers who had rallied to the monarchy were in haste to part company with those faithful soldiers and take their places in the army now reorganized on a new basis and with new personnel. It is my opinion that many of them were disappointed in their hopes and that the fine promises with which they had been lured into carrying out the dispersion without protest resulted only, in later years, in meager pensions.

When the last uniforms had disappeared in the dust of our country roads, we all felt great sadness and fatigue; having watched so many men march by, we felt as if we had been marching ourselves. We had witnessed the funeral procession of glory, the interment of our national identity. For my grandmother it had meant reawakened memories, deep and poignant emotions. For my mother, the sight of all those young and dashing officers had brought a keener sense that she would never love again, and that although she was still young and active, the years before her would be spent in solitude and regret. For Deschartres, it had been a real headache to have to assign and wrangle over hundreds of lodgings every day. All our servants were exhausted from having attended to more than forty people and their horses, day and night, for two months. My grandmother's limited finances and her wine cellar showed the strain, but she delighted in entertaining on a grand scale and had spent a year's income on it without complaint.

From running about with the soldiery, my brother had taken it into his head to join the army, and he would hardly hear of studying any more. As for me, who, like him, had been on a forced holiday all this time, I was overwhelmed and exhausted by idleness, for from my earliest years, doing nothing has always tired me more than anything else.

Yet I found it very hard to get back to work. The brain is a tool that gets rusty without constant, albeit moderate, exercise. Politics made me sick; Nohant was no longer the haven of peace and privacy it had been. The authorities of the neighboring town had been replaced mostly by ardent royalists who paid official calls on my grandmother and talked of nothing but the altar and the throne, the latest moves of the "Jacobin" faction, and the latest repressive measures of the kind, paternal government which was sending Ney, Labé-doyère, and other "rascals" to the scaffold. These visitors made a great show of enthusiasm for the monarchy when talking to my grandmother, as they believed she had connections and influence in the right circles. The fact is she had none, nor did she pretend to. She had spent the second half of her life in a sort of seclusion which had given her but few opportunities of being useful to others, and she was not so delighted with the old regime as people imagined.

As far as I was concerned, I was no longer tempted to fall into the trap of monarchism. I was ashamed to have people assume I was a royalist out of family solidarity. I thought my mother was too indifferent to these matters, and privately Hippolyte and I blasphemed against the "Petticoat King,"[20] whom the soldiers had taught us to mock and sing satirical songs about, in secret. But we had to be very careful to let none of this slip out, for Deschartres would have thrown a fit on the subject, and Mlle. Julie was not in the habit of keeping anything she heard to herself.

My cousin René de Villeneuve came to stay with us in the fall. He was perfectly amiable and cheerful, knew how to amuse himself in the country, and was not at all a royalist, although he was careful to keep up appearances. My grandmother talked to him about the future of my brother, who was going on sixteen and was ready to jump out of his skin, so eager was he to be rid of Deschartres and start life on his own. He had been taught mathematics with the view that he might join the navy, but M. de Villeneuve, who had just concluded a marriage between his daughter and Comte de La Roche-Aymon, and who was counting on this new connection to open many new doors for him, urged my grandmother to get the boy into a cavalry regiment, where he hoped to procure sponsorship and advancement for him. M. de Villeneuve promised to take the matter in hand at once, and my brother was ecstatic at the prospect of owning a horse and wearing boots all the days of his life.

After M. de Villeneuve, came Mme. de La Marlière, who had suddenly turned religious and attended both mass and vespers on Sundays. I found it most amazing. Finally, there arrived good Mme. de Pardaillan, and then, all these having left, my mother left in her turn. Not long after, Hippolyte packed his things and joined his regiment of hussars at Saint-Omer; so that, by the beginning of 1816, I found myself quite alone at Nohant with my grandmother, Deschartres, Julie, and Rose.

Then passed the two most wearisome, dream-filled, melancholy years I had yet known.   *A.D.*

VIII

How history is taught. —I study it like a novel. —A tutor
"unteaches" me music. —First literary attempts. —Art and feeling.
—My mother makes fun of me, and I give up the life of letters.
—My great unpublished novel. —Corambé. —Marie and Solange.
—Plaisir the swineherd. —The hidden ditch. —Demogorgon. —The
secret temple.

I cannot always pursue my life as a sequential narrative, because my
memory of the order in which the small events occurred often fails me. I know
I spent the years of 1814, '15, '16, and '17 with my grandmother at Nohant,
without going to Paris. I shall therefore summarize in a general way my mental
development during those four years.

The only subjects I really liked were history, geography (history's obligatory appendix), music, and literature. I could reduce these preferences even
further by saying that I really loved, then and forever, only literature and
music, because what then excited me about history was not the philosophy of
progress that all the modern theorists have since taught us to deduce from the
flow of events. At that time, no one had popularized that clear and precise
notion, which is truly, if not the great discovery, at least the great philosophical
certainty of modern times, and of which Pierre Leroux, Jean Raynaud, and
their school of 1830–1840 have set down the best exposition and deductions in
their work, *Encyclopédie nouvelle*.

At the time I was being taught history, there was generally no idea of the
way order and unity figured in the evaluation of facts. Today, the study of history coincides with the theory of progress; it can trace a line of such magnitude
that all lines heretofore broken off and scattered are drawn back to it. It allows
us to witness humanity in its infancy, development, efforts, trials, successive
conquests. Even its deviations, inevitably leading to a turning that puts it right
back on the road to the future, only serve to confirm the law that drives and
sweeps it along.

According to the theory of progess, God and humanity are a single unit.
There is but one religion, one truth anterior to man, co-eternal with God,
whose varied manifestations in man are the relative and progressive truth of
the varying phases of history. Nothing could be simpler, grander, or more logical. With this notion—on one hand the conducting rod of an eternally progressive humanity, on the other the torch of an eternally revealing and reveal-
able God—it is no longer possible to float aimlessly in the study of man's

history, since it is the history of God Himself in His relationship to us.

In my time, we proceeded simultaneously, separating history into parts which had no relation to each other. For example, sacred and profane history being contemporary to one another had to be studied vis à vis one another, without admitting that there could be a link between them. Which one was true, which one fictitious? Both were laden with miracles and fables equally inadmissible to reason, but why was the God of the Jews the only true God? No one told us, and in my particular case, I was free to reject the God of Moses as well as Jesus, of Homer as well as Virgil. "Read," I was told, "take notes, copy out extracts, retain it all. These are things one must know and can't afford to be ignorant of."[9]

Knowledge for the sake of knowledge, that was the maxim upon which my education was founded. It was not a question of learning to make yourself a better, happier, or wiser person. You learned in order to chat with educated people, to be up to reading the books on your shelves, and to kill time in the country, or elsewhere. And since my kind of nature does not easily grasp how useful it is to have rejoinders for the learned talkers, instead of listening to them silently or not at all, and since children do not generally worry about being bored, for they readily enjoy anything but studying, another motive, another inducement had to be provided. So we were told of the pleasure of pleasing our parents, an appeal was made to our feelings of obedience, to our dutiful conscience. Still, it was the best and most successful appeal for some-one of my nature, whose ideas were independent but whose outward behavior was compliant.

I have never acted rebelliously toward those I loved and whose natural domination I was bound to accept, for there is such a thing as natural domina-tion, be it only the one of age, not to mention the one of blood. I have never understood how not to yield to persons with whom one cannot or will not break, even if convinced they are wrong, nor how one could hesitate between sacrificing oneself and gratifying them. That is the reason why my grandmoth-er, my mother, and the nuns at the convent have always found me inexplicably docile while at the same time unshakably stubborn. I emphasize the word "docile," because I was struck by the meeting of their minds on this expression which was used to describe my character as a child. The expression may not have been accurate. I was not docile, because inwardly I did not yield. But not yielding outwardly would have required me to hate, and on the contrary, I loved. This only proves that affection was more precious to me than reason, and that in my actions I more readily followed my heart than my head.

It was thus solely due to my affection for my grandmother that I did my best to study things that bored me, that I learned by heart thousands of verses whose beauty was beyond my understanding; Latin, which seemed insipid to me; versification, which was a straight jacket for my poetic inclinations; arith-metic, which was so contrary to my constitution that I literally felt dizzy and faint when doing addition. I also submerged myself in history to please her, but in this case I was finally rewarded for my obedience: I found history prodi-giously entertaining.

However, for the reason mentioned—the absence of moral theory—history did not satisfy my appetite for logic, which was just beginning to awaken; but it lured me for different reasons: I sensed its purely literary and romantic aspects. Great personalities, beautiful deeds, strange adventures, poetic details —details, in a word, were fascinating to me—and I found an inexpressible pleasure in telling all that, in giving it form in my extracts.

Little by little, I realized that I was hardly supervised; that, because she found my extracts well-written and interesting for my age, my grandmother no longer consulted the book to see if my version was really faithful. This served my purposes more than you can imagine. I no longer brought to the lesson the books I had used for summaries, and as no one asked for them anymore, I let myself go more boldly into what I personally deemed worthy. I was more philosophical than my profane historians, more enthusiastic than my sacred ones. Giving in to my emotions and not worrying whether I concurred with authors' opinions, I colored my writing according to my ideas, and I even remember that I was not too timid to embroider a bit the bareness of certain backgrounds. I did not alter the essential facts, but when an insignificant or unexplained character fell into my hands, obeying an invincible need for "art," I gave him whatever personality I could logically deduce from his role or from the nature of his behavior in the general drama. Unable to submit blindly to the author's judgment, if I did not always rehabilitate what he was condemning, I at least tried to explain and excuse it; and if I found him too cold to the objects of my enthusiasm, I delivered myself of my own fiery feelings and scattered them through my notebook in expressions which often made my grandmother laugh because of their naïve exaggeration.

In short, when I found an occasion to pad a small description in the middle of my narrative, I did not resist. For that to happen, all I needed was a brief phrase from the text, a bare indication. My imagination took hold of it and began to embellish; I brought about various interventions through sunshine and storms, flowers, ruins, monuments, choirs, the sounds of the sacred flute or Ionia's lyre, the clash of arms, the whinnying of steeds, and whatever else occurred to me. I was classical to a fault, but if I did not have the artistry to discover a new form, I did have the pleasure of keen feelings and of seeing in my mind's eye all that past reviving before me.

It is also true that, because I was not poetically disposed every day and could indulge in it with impunity, I sometimes found myself copying word for word whole pages of the book, when my assignment was to render the meaning. But those were my days of languor and distraction. I gladly compensated for them when I felt my ambition rekindled.

I did somewhat the same with music. As a matter of duty, I studied the dry exercises I had to play for my grandmother, but when I was sure I could manage them passably, I rearranged them to my fancy, adding phrases, changing the forms, improvising haphazardly, singing, playing, and composing both music and words, when I was sure no one was listening. God knows to what foolish musical aberrations I thus abandoned myself! It gave me extreme pleasure.

The music I was being taught was beginning to bore me. I was no longer my grandmother's pupil. She took it into her head that she could not teach me music herself, or that her health no longer allowed her to sustain the role; she no longer demonstrated anything and limited herself to making me keep time when I played the boring music my tutor had brought me.

That tutor was the organist at La Châtre. He knew music, surely, but he did not feel it at all, and he did not make a conscious effort to teach it to me. His name was M. Gayard, and he had a ridiculous face and figure. His hair was always in a pigtail tied with string, and pigeon wings, and he wore the wide, square-cut jacket of the old regime, although he was barely fifty. For a while during the Restoration you saw some individuals resume those old styles of hairdressing and clothing, to show how attached they were to the principles of the "good old days." Others, such as M. Gayard, had never given up those ways; it was doubtless the habit of seriousness that had made him keep wearing powder and short breeches.

He was, however, just middling serious when no longer under the eyes of the curé at La Châtre, or of my grandmother at Nohant. He arrived on Sunday at noon, had himself served a copious lunch, tuned the piano and the harpsichord, gave me a two-hour lesson, and went off to romp with the maids until dinner. Then he ate for four, spoke hardly a word, made me play a piece for my grandmother that he had drummed into me instead of explaining, and left, his pockets full of delicious tidbits that he wangled from the chambermaids.

I appeared to make progress with this teacher, but in reality I was learning nothing at all and was losing my admiration and love for music. He brought me music that was stupid and easy, but sounded brilliant. Fortunately, some little gems sometimes slipped into this medley, unknown to him—some sonatinas by Steibelt, a few pages from Glück and Mozart, and some pretty Pleyel and Clementi études. The proof of my aptitude for music is that I would quickly discern by myself what was worth studying, and I brought to it a certain simplicity of feeling which pleased my grandmother, but for which M. Gayard gave me no credit. He banged the keys and played methodically, without nuances, color, or heart. His playing was clipped, correct, loud, without charm and without inspiration. I sensed it, and I hated his approach. On top of that, he had huge, ugly, hairy paws, fat and dirty, which revolted me, and the odor of powder mixed with the smell of dirt made my lesson unbearable. My grandmother must have known he was a worthless, soulless tutor, but she thought I needed to keep my fingers limber, and as hers became more and more paralyzed, she gave me M. Gayard for technique.

Indeed, M. Gayard showed me how to move my fingers, and he gave me a lot of music to read, but he taught me nothing. Never did he require me to inform myself of the key the piece he was having me play was written in, nor of the timing, and still less of the feelings and musical ideas. I had to divine all that myself, because I had forgotten all the rules my grandmother had taught me so clearly, which it would have been good to review over and over while applying them. I applied them automatically, no longer with awareness. When I made a mistake, M. Gayard delivered some puns and parodies by way of criticism. "It was thus I went through my paces," he would say, "the last time I was shown the door." Or else he had some sayings in prep school Latin:

> *Sic* hangs Pierret on his harp
> *Quod* he didn't play F-sharp.

And the whole lesson went that way, unless he preferred to fall asleep near the stove, or stroll around the room eating prunes or hazelnuts, because he ate constantly and was hardly concerned with anything else.

Singing was no longer even mentioned, although that was where my instincts and vocation lay. I felt a great release when I improvised bits of lyrical melody or recitative in prose or in blank verse, and it seemed to me that singing could have been the true way for me to express my sentiments and my emotions. When I was alone in the garden, I accompanied all my actions with singing. For example, "Roll, my wheelbarrow, roll! Grow, grow, little lawns that I sprinkle! Pretty butterflies, come land on my flowers!" etc., and when I thought about my dear absent mother, I sang interminable laments in a minor key, which little by little soothed my melancholy, or else induced tears which relieved me—"Mother, do you hear me? I cry and I sigh," etc.

At about age twelve I tried to write, but that was fleeting; I did several "descriptions," one of the Vallée Noire seen from a certain spot where I often went when walking, and the other of a moonlit summer night. Those are all I remember, and my grandmother had the kindness to declare to whoever wanted ed to believe her that they were masterpieces. Judging by the phrases which have remained in my memory,[10] these masterpieces were good for the water-closet. But what I recall with more pleasure is that, in spite of the imprudent eulogies of my grandmama, I was in no way ecstatic about my small accomplishments. Ever since, I have had a conviction: that is, that no art form can render the charm and freshness of the impression produced by the beauty of nature, just as no artistic expression can equal the force and spontaneity of our intimate feelings. In the soul is something more than in the form. Enthusiasm, passion, revery, pain do not find adequate expression in the domain of the arts, whatever the art, whoever the artist. I beg the masters to forgive me; I venerate and cherish them, but they have never rendered to me what nature has given me; what I myself have felt, a thousand times, to render for others was impossible. Art seems to me an eternally impotent and imperfect aspiration—along with all other human manifestations. Unfortunately for us, we have a yen for the infinite, and all our expressions quickly reach their boundaries; that yen itself is vague, so that the satisfaction it gives us is a species of torment.

Modern art has indeed experienced that torment of impotence, and it has attempted to expand its scope in literature, music, and painting. In the new forms of Romanticism, art believes it has found a new power of expansion. Art may have gained thereby, but the powers of the human soul are only relatively lifted, and the thirst for perfection, the longing for the infinite, remains the same—eternally avid, eternally unfulfilled. This, for me, is an irrefutable proof of the existence of God. We have a desire for the ideal, which never dies;

therefore, that desire has a cause. That cause exists nowhere within our reach, that cause is the infinite, that cause is God.

Hence art is a more- or less-achieved attempt to manifest emotions which can never be completely expressed and which in themselves surpass all expression. Romanticism, while adding to art's scope, did not alter the fact that human powers are limited. A hailstorm of epithets, a deluge of notes, a conflagration of colors attest to or express nothing more than elementary and simplistic conceptions. No matter how I try, my words and sounds will unhappily contain nothing of the essence of a ray of sun or the murmur of a breeze.

And yet there are sublime expressions in art, and I would not want to live without having recourse to them constantly. But the greater these expressions, the more they stimulate my thirst for a better one, a higher one, that no one can give me, and that I cannot provide either, because to express this idea of "better," we would need a cipher that does not exist in our vocabulary and that we shall probably never discover.

This leads me to state more clearly and positively that I have never been satisfied with anything I have ever written in my life; no more so with my first attempts at the age of twelve than with the literary works of my mature years, and there is no modesty on my part in this statement. Each time I saw or felt a subject worthy of art, I hoped, I naïvely believed I could render it as it had come to me. I ardently threw myself into it; sometimes I completed my task with keen pleasure, and sometimes, when penning the last page, I said to myself, "This time I've done it!" But, alas! I have never been able to reread the proofs without saying to myself, "That's not it at all. I imagined and felt and conceived it totally otherwise. It is cold, it is beside the point, it is overstated, and it is not enough." And if the work had not belonged to a publisher every time, I would have put it away in a corner intending to redo it, although I would have forgotten it there to attempt another.

Accordingly, I felt, from my very first literary attempts, that I was not up to my subject, and that my words and phrases spoiled it even for me. One of my descriptions was sent to my mother, to show her how clever I had become; she replied, "Your beautiful phrases really made me laugh; I hope you're not going to start to talk that way." I was not at all put out by the way she received my poetic lucubration. I thought she was perfectly right, and I replied, "Don't worry, mother dear, I won't become a pedant, and when I want to tell you that I love you and adore you, I shall say it plainly, as I just did."

I therefore stopped writing, but the need to invent and compose harried me nonetheless. I needed a world of fiction and never ceased to create one for myself, one which I carried with me on my walks and sitting still, in the garden and the fields, in my bed, before falling asleep, and on waking, before getting up. I had a novel going on in my head all the time to which I added a chapter more or less as soon as I found myself alone, and for which I was forever collecting material. But can I possibly give an idea of this way of composing? I lost it and shall always miss it, because it was the only one which might have realized my fantasy.

I would not go into a recital of the way my imagination worked if I thought such an eccentricity was limited to me personally. For I hope my reader has noticed that I am much more concerned with making him review and criticize his own existence—existences we have in common—than to entertain him with my own. But I have reason to believe that my intellectual history belongs to my generation not one of whom who has not written a poem or novel at a young age.

I was well into my twenty-fifth year when, observing my brother scribbling away, I asked him what he was doing. "I am trying to write a novel," he said, "moral in content and comic in form, but I don't know how to write, and it seems to me that you could edit my rough draft." He told me the plot, which I found too unlikely, and I was shocked by the details. But as concerns this discussion, I asked him how long he had had the fantasy of creating a novel. "I've always had it," he answered. "When I envision it, it sometimes fascinates and amuses me so, that I laugh out loud. But when I want to put it into some kind of order, I don't know where to begin or leave off. It all becomes confused under my pen. I can't find the right expression, I become impatient, I get disgusted, I burn what I just wrote, and I'm through with it for a few days. But soon the impetus returns, like a fever. I think about it in the daytime, I think about it at night, and once again I must put down my scribblings, always at the risk of burning them."

"How wrong you are," I told him, "to try to put your fantasies into a form, a logical outline! Don't you realize that you're declaring war on them, and that if you stopped projecting them outside you, they'd always be active and buoyant inside you, and fruitful? Why not do as I do, who have never spoiled the conception of my creations by trying to formulate them?"

"So," he said, "it's a sickness that runs in the family? You too dig away in the void? You too have idle daydreams, like me? You never told me."

I was already angry at having given myself away, but it was too late to take back what I had said. By confiding his secret to me, Hippolyte had a right to mine, and I told him what I am going to tell the reader now.

From early childhood, I needed to fashion my own inner world, a poetic and fantastic world. Little by little I needed also to make it religious or philosophical, that is to say, moral or sentimental. Around the age of eleven, I read *The Iliad* and *Jerusalem Delivered*. Ah! how quickly I devoured them, how frustrated when I came to the last page! I grew sad and as if stricken with grief to see them end so soon. I did not know what to do next; I could not read anything else; I could not tell which of the two poems was my favorite; I understood that Homer's was the more beautiful, the greater, the more direct one; but Tasso's intrigued and provoked me more. It was more romantic, more apt to appeal to my time and my sex. There were situations in which I wanted always to dwell—Erminia with the shepherds, for example, or Clorinda delivering Olindo and Sophronia from the burning stake. What enchanted scenes I saw spread out before me! I took possession of those situations; I established residence, so to speak; the characters became mine; I made them act or speak, and I changed the sequence of their adventures to my liking; not that I thought I could do better than Tasso, but because the amorous preoccupations of the characters irked me, and because I wanted them to be as I felt them—passionate only through religion, war, or friendship. I preferred martial Clorinda to timid Erminia; her death and her baptism made her divine in my eyes. I hated Armida, I despised Rinaldo. I vaguely felt about the woman-warrior and the woman-sorcerer what Montaigne had said about Bradamanta and Angelica, apropos of Ariosto's poem [*Orlando furioso*]: "The former, unaware of her beauty, energetic, generous, not mannish but virile; the latter, of a languid beauty, mannered, delicate, artful; the former, disguised as a boy, crowned with a shining helmet; the latter, dressed for seduction, coifed with a beaded veil."[21]

But beyond the characters of Tasso's work soared Jerusalem, the Christian Olympus, as did the pagan gods over Homer's; and through the poetry of these symbols, the need for religious sentiment, if not a definitive faith, took ardent hold of my heart. Since no one was instructing me in religion, it occurred to me I needed one, and I made one for myself.

I contrived it very secretly in myself; religion and novel grew side by side in my soul. I have said that the most romantic souls are the most positivistic, and though it seems paradoxical, I maintain its validity. The romantic appetite inclines toward the ideal. Everything in the world of ordinary reality that impedes the impulse toward the ideal is easily put aside and counted as worthless from the point of view of romantic logic. Primitive Christians, followers of all the sects engendered by a Christianity taken literally, are romantic spirits, and their logic is rigorous and perfect; I defy anyone to prove the contrary.

So there I was, an imaginative child, innocent, isolated, abandoned to myself, engaged in a quest for an ideal, and unable to imagine a world, an idealized humanity, without placing at its zenith a god, the ideal itself. That great creator Jehovah, that great causality Jupiter did not speak to me directly enough. I could well see the relation of that supreme power to nature, but I did not feel it sufficiently specific for humanity. I did what humanity had done before me. I searched for a mediator, an intermediary, a man-god, a divine friend for our unhappy race.

Homer and Tasso, crowning my first readings of Christian and pagan poetry, showed me so many divinities, sublime or terrible, that my only problem was choosing—but it was a great problem. I was being prepared for my first communion, and I understood absolutely no catechism. The gospel and the divine drama of the life and death of Jesus secretly wrung torrential tears from me. I hid them, fearing my grandmother's mockery. Today I am sure she would not have mocked, but the seeming rule she had made for herself not to interfere in my faith threw me into doubt; it is also possible that the eternal lure of mystery in my most intimate emotions was itself inflicting on me the mental injury of being deprived of a direction.[11] If, in seeing me read and learn the dogma by heart without giving it the slightest thought, my grandmother imagined she would find me a *tabula rasa* when it came time to teach me her point of view, she was wrong. The child is never a *tabula rasa*. It responds, wonders, doubts, seeks, and if we do not give it the wherewithal to build a house, it makes a nest with whatever straw it can gather.

That is what happened to me. As my grandmother had taken only one precaution, that of fighting my penchant for superstition, I could not believe in miracles, nor could I believe in Jesus' divinity. But I loved the figure, nevertheless, and said to myself, "Since all religion is fiction, let me create a novel which might be a religion, or a religion which might be a novel. I don't believe in my novels, but they give me as much happiness as if I did. Anyhow, if I happen to believe in them once in a while, no one will know. No one will foil my illusion by proving that I'm dreaming."

And behold, while dreaming one night, there came to me a shape and a name. The name had no meaning that I know of; it was the kind of fortuitous collection of syllables that is sometimes formed in dreams. My phantom was called Corambé, and it kept that name. It became the title of my novel and the god of my religion.

When I begin to speak of Corambé, I begin to speak not only of my poetic life, because that model character has so long in secret filled my dreams, but also of my moral life, which was one with my poetic life. Corambé was not, in truth, simply a character from a novel; it was the form that my religious ideal had taken and was to retain for a long time to come.

Of all the religions I was made to study, without being encouraged to adopt any of them, under the pure and simple guise of history, not one truly satisfied me, yet each had something that drew me. Jesus Christ was certainly the model of perfection for me, superior to all the others, but the religion which forbade me, in the name of Jesus, to love other philosophers, other gods, other saints from antiquity, was restrictive and stifling. I needed *The Iliad* and *Jerusalem* in my fictions. Corambé was created by itself in my mind. It was as pure and as charitable as Jesus, as shining and handsome as Gabriel; but it needed a little of nymphic grace and Orpheus's poetry. Consequently it took on less austere forms than the Christian God and more spiritual aspects than the gods of Homer. And then, I also had to complement it at times with a woman's garb, because what I had loved best and understood best until then was a woman—my mother. Hence it often appeared to me with female features. In sum, it had no sex and put on many different guises.

There were some pagan goddesses whom I cherished—wise Athena, chaste Diana, Iris, Hebe, Flora, the Muses—and the nymphs, all charming creatures whom I did not want to be deprived of by Christianity. Corambé had to possess all the attributes of physical and moral beauty, the gift of eloquence, the almighty charm of the arts, and above all the magic of musical improvisation; I wanted to love it as a friend, as a sister, all the while giving it the reverence due to a god. I did not want to fear it, and for that reason, I wished it to have a few of our failings and weaknesses.

I looked for a failing which would fit its perfection, and I chose excessive kindness or leniency. This in particular pleased me, and as Corambé's existence unfolded in my imagination (I hesitate to say by means of my will, to such an extent did these dreams seem rather to take form by themselves), it greeted me with a series of trials, sufferings, persecutions, and martyrdoms. I used the term "book" or "song" for each of these stages of its humanity—for it did become a man or woman on touching the earth—and sometimes the omnipotent and superior God, of which it was, after all, merely a celestial minister assigned to the moral government of our planet, prolonged its exile among us to punish it for having too much love and pity for us.

In each of these songs (I believe my poem contained at least a thousand, although I never attempted to write down one line), a world of new characters grouped themselves around Corambé. All of them were good. There were some evil ones who were never seen (I did not wish them to appear), but whose malice and madness were revealed through images of disaster and scenes of desolation. Corambé consoled and made reparation ceaselessly. I saw it in delightful country settings, surrounded by forlorn and tender beings, whom it charmed with its talk and song, listening to the tales of their trials and leading them back to happiness through virtue.

At first I was quite conscious of this new labor of mine, but after a very short time, perhaps a few days (for a child a day seems like three), I felt possessed by my subject much more than it was possessed by me. The daydream came to be a sort of sweet hallucination, but so frequent and sometimes so perfect, that it left me as if transported out of this world.

At any rate, the real world soon shaped itself to my fantasies. It adapted itself to my needs. My brother, Liset, and I had several friends, girls and boys, with whom we took turns meeting in the fields to play, run, pilfer, clamber. My own most frequent preference was to go with the daughters of one of our tenant farmers, Marie and Solange, who were in fact somewhat younger and more childish than I, by nature. Almost daily—from noon until two o'clock, my allotted play time—I would run to the farm and find my young friends busy caring for their lambs, looking for their hens' eggs scattered in the bushes, picking fruit in the orchard, looking after the "ovines," as we say in Berry, or "stripping" leaves to provide the animals with provisions for the winter, depending on the season. They were always at work, and I helped them with zest, for the pleasure of being with them. Marie was a most uncomplicated and obedient child. The younger, Solange, was rather headstrong, and we gave in to all her fancies. My grandmother was very glad that I was getting exercise, but she said she could not conceive why I was so happy with these muddy little peasant girls, with their turkeys and their goats, I who wrote such beautiful descriptions and who had the moon sitting on a silver skiff.

I knew very well the secret of my pleasure and kept it to myself. The orchard where I spent a part of my day was enchanting (it still is), and it was where my novel, in all its fullness, came to me. Although this orchard was quite pretty as it was, I did not view it exactly as it was. My imagination transformed a three-foot high mound into a mountain, a few trees into a forest; a footpath which went from the house to the meadow into the road that leads to the end of the world; the pond bordered with ancient willows into a whirlpool or a lake, according to my whim. And I saw my fictional characters moving, running off together, dreamily walking alone, sleeping in the shade, or singing and dancing in this paradise of my idle dreams. The chatter of Marie and Solange did not disturb me at all. Their simplicity, their pastoral chores in no way jarred the harmony of my tableaux, and I saw in them two small nymphs transformed into country girls, preparing everything for the arrival of Coram-bé, who would pass by this place one of these days and return them to their true form and destiny.

Besides, if they did succeed in distracting me and making my phantoms disappear, I did not hold it against them, because there came a time of day when I also took pleasure in playing with them. When I was there, their parents were tolerant about wasted time, and we often left the distaffs, sheep, and baskets to abandon ourselves to wild gymnastics, climbing trees, or rolling down from the top of the mountain of sheaves piled high in the barn—a delirious game, I confess, one I would still love, if I dared try it.

These fits of intoxicating movement and gaiety only served to enhance the pleasure I felt when I fell back into my contemplations, and my brain, profiting from the physical stimulation, was richer in images and fantasies. I was aware of it and did not deprive myself of it.

Another friendship, one I cultivated less assiduously, but into which my brother sometimes drew me, involved a swineherd by the name of Plaisir. I have always been deathly afraid of pigs, and yet perhaps precisely because of that, by the great authority he exerted over those mean and stupid animals, Plaisir inspired me with a sort of respect and awe. Everyone knows that a herd of pigs can be dangerous company. Those animals have a strange instinct for solidarity among themselves. If one isolated pig is offended, it emits a cry of alarm which instantly brings all the others. They then form a sort of battalion which closes in on the common enemy, forcing it to escape into a tree; for it is useless to think of running, the lean pig being, like the wild boar, one of the fastest and most tireless runners that exist.

So it was not without terror that I would find myself in the fields, in the midst of these animals; and being there time and again never mitigated the terror. However, Plaisir had so little fear and such control over those he tended—he could pull up from under their noses the sweet tubers and field beans they found in our ground—that I worked at making myself tough in his presence. The most fearsome animal in the herd is the bull hog, the one our herders call Cadi, which, being reserved to reproduce the species, often grows to extraordinary size and strength. Plaisir had so well tamed him the Cadi that he could ride astride him with a sort of wild and comic mastery.

Walter Scott did not disdain to introduce a swineherd in *Ivanhoe*, one of his most beautiful novels. Plaisir could have served as the model. He was a completely primitive creature, endowed with the talents of his uncivilized state. He felled birds by aiming stones with remarkable accuracy, and he practiced mainly on the magpies and crows, who come in winter to keep the swineherds company. You can see them hanging around the animals, looking for worms or grain in the mounds of earth the pigs turn over with their snouts. This gives way to major altercations among these quarrelsome birds; the one who has seized the prey jumps on the pig's back to devour it at leisure, the others follow it there to jostle it, and the impassive, indifferent head or back of the quadruped becomes a theater for embittered struggles. Sometimes these birds also perch on the hog only to keep warm or to better observe the work from which they may profit. I often saw an old ash-colored crow standing thus on one leg, looking melancholy and pensive, while the hog labored deeply in the ground, his efforts causing her to shake; annoyed and losing patience, she decided to reprimand him by pecking at him.

Plaisir spent his life in this wild company, wearing in all seasons a shirt and pants of hemp cloth which, like his bare hands and feet, had taken on the color and hardness of the earth. Like his herd, he fed on roots that crept along under the soil, armed with the triangular iron instrument that is the scepter of swineherds and which they use to dig and chop under the furrows, always buried in some hole or crawling under the bushes in pursuit of snakes and weasels. When a pale winter sun made the frost sparkle on the broad terrain upturned by the incessant labors of his herd, Plaisir seemed to me like a gnome of the glebe, a sort of devil between man and werewolf, animal and plant.[12]

On the edge of the field where we saw Plaisir during an entire season, the ditch was hidden by beautiful vegetation. Under the low-hanging branches of the old elms and intersecting brambles, we children could walk around in shelter, and there were dry and sandy hollows with linings of moss and dried grass where we could stay protected from the cold and the rain. I found those retreats uncommonly pleasant especially when I was alone and the redbreasts and wrens, emboldened by my stillness, came up close to observe me inquiringly. I loved to slip unseen into the natural cradles formed beneath the hedge, feeling as if I had entered the kingdom of earthly spirits. There my novel received much of its inspiration. Corambé came there in the guise of a swineherd to find me, as Apollo did with Admeta. He was as poor and dusty as Plaisir, but his face was different and would sometimes emit a ray by which I recognized the exiled god, condemned to lowly and sorrowful labors. The Cadi was an evil spirit dogging his footsteps but subdued, despite his malice, by the irresistible influence of the spirit of patience and goodness. The small birds in the bushes were sylphs who came to pity and console him in their pretty language, and the poor, willing penitent would still smile, despite his tattered rags. He would tell me how he was expiating someone's pain and how his abjection was destined to redeem the soul of one of my characters who had been guilty of ostentation or indolence.

In the hidden ditch I also saw the apparition of a mythical character who had greatly impressed me in my early childhood. It was the Demogorgon of old, the genius from the earth's core, that "dirty, little old man, covered with moss, pale and deformed, who inhabited the bowels of the planet." This is how my old mythology treatise described him, the one that further affirmed how very bored Demogorgon was alone in that sad place. The idea had indeed occurred to me at times of making a large hole to try to free him, but when I started dreaming of Corambé, I no longer gave credence to the pagan fables, and Demogorgon was reduced to a mere fanciful character in my novel. I conjured him only so that he could come and talk to Corambé, who told him of the woes of men and thus consoled him for living in neglect, among the litter of ancient creation.

Little by little, the fiction that absorbed me took on such convincing proportions that I felt the need to create a sort of ritual for myself.

For a period of about a month, I succeeded in escaping all supervision and in making myself so invisible during my recreation hours that no one could have said what was happening to me, not even Rose, even though she never left me in peace, and not even Liset, who followed me everywhere like a little dog.

Here was my invention: I wanted to raise an altar to Corambé. I had at first thought of the rock grotto, which still existed although abandoned and in shambles, but the path was too well known and frequented. In those days, certain parts of the little woods around the house afforded an impenetrable thicket. The trees were still young and had not yet stifled the growth of hawthorne and privet at their foot, as dense as meadow grass. In those clumps of trees which hugged the row of hedges on each side, I had thus noticed there were some where no one ever went and where even the eye could not penetrate during the leafy season. I chose the densest, I cleared a passage for myself, and looked for a suitable site in the middle. It was there as if waiting for me. In the center of the thicket, three lovely maples rose from a common root, and the growth of the shrubbery, inhibited by their shade, was rounded out in a circle, as if to form a small chamber of greenery. The ground was overgrown with magnificent moss, and no matter which way you looked, you could not distinguish anything in the interstices of brushwood two feet away. So I was as alone there as if hidden in the depths of a virgin forest, while thirty or forty feet away were winding paths where people could go back and forth without suspecting a thing.

It was next a matter of decorating to my taste the temple I had just discovered, and for that I proceeded in the way my mother had taught me. I went in search of the most beautiful pebbles, a variety of shells, and the freshest moss. I erected a sort of altar at the foot of the main tree, and above it I hung a wreath of flowers, suspended by string laced with pink and white shells that descended from the branches of the maple like a chandelier. I trimmed some of the brush to better define the shape of the little rotunda, and I intertwined ivy and moss, so as to form a sort of colonnade of greenery, with arcades, from which hung other small wreaths, birds' nests, large cockles in the guise of lamps, etc. The result was a creation so pretty it made my head spin, and I dreamed about it at night.

It was all accomplished with the greatest precaution. They could see me ferreting in the woods, tracking down nests and shells, but it looked as if it were only out of idleness that I was gathering these little treasures; and when my apron was filled, I would wait till I was totally alone to penetrate the thicket; this did not happen without hardship and scratches, for I did not want to clear a trail that would give me away, and each time I would enter from a different side to avoid the traces of trampled ground or broken shrubs that would have been left by repeated attempts.

When everything was ready, I took possession of my empire in sheer delight, and sitting down on the moss, took to dreaming of the sacrifices I would offer up to the divinity I had invented. To kill birds or even insects to please it seemed barbaric and unworthy of its perfect sweetness. I took it upon myself to do the opposite, that is, on its altar to render unto life and liberty all the creatures I could find. I then went in search of butterflies, lizards, little green frogs, and birds; I was never short of the last, for I always had a host of snares set on all sides, in which I often caught them. Liset caught some in the fields and brought them to me; the outcome was that for the duration of my secret ritual, I was able every day to deliver up, in honor of Corambé, a swallow, a redbreast, a goldfinch, even a house sparrow. The lesser offerings—butterflies and beetles—hardly counted. I put them in a box that I laid on the altar and opened after having invoked the good spirit of freedom and protection. I think I had begun to resemble a little that poor crazy man who was looking for affection. I asked for it from the woods, the plants, the sunshine, the animals, and heaven knows what invisible beings, which only existed in my dreams.

I was no longer childish enough to hope that this spirit would appear; however, to the extent that I materialized, so to speak, my poem, my imagination became singularly exalted. I was as close to idolatry as I was to devotion, because my ideal was as pagan as it was Christian. And there came a time when, running to visit my temple in the morning, I would begin, in spite of myself, to endow the least disarrangement with a superstitious meaning. If a blackbird had scratched at my altar, if a woodpecker had nicked my tree, if some shell was detached from its festoon, or some flower from its wreath, I would have it that nymphs or angels had come to dance and frolic during the night, by the light of the moon, in honor of my good spirit. Each day I replaced all the flowers and made a pile from the old wreaths which littered the altar. When, by chance, the warbler or the finch I had sent flying to freedom landed on a tree and rested there a moment instead of fleeing in fright into the undergrowth, I was enchanted; it seemed that my offering had been more pleasing than usual. I dreamed deliciously there, and while seeking the marvels that attracted me so, began to find, vague in thought but sharp in feeling, a religion suited to the needs of my heart.

Unfortunately—fortunately perhaps for my youthful brain, which was not yet strong enough to resolve the problem—my shelter was discovered. By searching high and low, Liset found me, and flabbergasted at the sight of my temple, cried out, "Ah! mam'selle, what a pretty little shrine for the Corpus Christi!"

He found my mysteriousness appealing and wished to help me make the place more beautiful. But the spell was broken. From the moment other feet than mine had tread the sanctuary, Corambé no longer lived there. The dryads and cherubs abandoned it, and my rituals and sacrifices seemed to me no more than a puerility that even I myself had not taken seriously. I destroyed the temple with as much care as I had taken to erect it. I dug a hole at the foot of the tree and buried the garlands, shells, and all the rustic ornaments under the debris of the altar.   *P.D.*

IX

Liset's ambition. —The energy and listlessness of adolescence.
—The gleaners. —Deschartres turns me into a communist. —He
spoils Latin for me. —A storm during haying. —The Beast. —Story
of the altar boy. —-The hempworkers' evenings. —The sacristan's
stories. —My brother's visions. —Beauties of winter in the country.
—The Brotherhood of Lark Trappers. —The Corambé novel gets
along without the essential ingredient. —First communion. —The
traveling players. —The mass and the opera. —Brigitte and Charles.
—For some people childhood is never over.

My brother was so happy to be leaving, that I could not feel unhappy to
see him go. However, the house seemed very big to me, and the garden very
melancholy, and life very sad when I found myself alone. Since he was laughing when he left, I would have been embarrassed to cry, but I cried the next
morning when I woke up and told myself I would not be seeing him anymore.
Seeing me with red eyes at play time, Liset felt it his duty to cry, although he
had been more tortured and thrashed by Hippolyte than cherished by him. He
was a very sensitive child, whose parents did not care to make him happy and
who had turned all his affection to me. His dream of ultimate happiness was one
day to be the groom for my horses and have a cap with gold braid. I did not
have any sympathy for this kind of ambition, and I swore to him that never in
my life would I dress my servants in gold braid. I have kept my word; I cannot
bear such costuming, but that was Liset's fantasy, his poetry, and I was never
able to make him understand that it was all foolish vanity. The poor child died
while I was at the convent, and I was soon to leave him, never to see him again.

In the midst of my endless daydreams and sorrowing about my life, I was
growing extraordinarily fast. I gave every sign of being tall and robust;
between the ages of twelve and thirteen, I grew three inches, and I acquired a
strength which was quite exceptional for my age and sex. But there my development stopped, right at the point where most other people's begins. I did not
grow any taller than my mother, but I was always very strong, and capable of
sustaining the kind of walking and exhausting activity that is almost always
thought of as manly.

Having at last understood that I was never sick except when deprived of
exercise and fresh air, my grandmother had resolved to let me run loose, and as
long as I did not come back with any damage to my clothes or my person, Rose

relinquished me little by little to physical freedom. Nature inspired me with an invincible need to assist her in the work she was performing in me, and those two years, even though they were the ones during which I cried and day-dreamed the most, I did the most racing about and was the most active. My body and my mind alternately summoned up a kind of fretfulness of activity and a feverishness of contemplation. I would devour the books that were put in my hands and then suddenly leap through an open ground floor window, if it were nearer to me than the door, and go frisking about in the garden or the countryside like a runaway colt. I loved solitude with a passion, and I loved the company of other children with an equal passion; I had friends and compan-ions everywhere. I always knew in what field I would find Fanchon, Liline, Rosette, or Sylvain. We tore about the roadside ditches, the trees, and the streams. We tended the flocks, that is, we did not tend them at all, and while the sheep and the goats were regaling themselves in the new-grown wheat, we created wild dances, or else we picnicked on the grass with our cakes and cheese and dark bread. We helped ourselves to milk from the goats and ewes, even the cows and mares, if they weren't too recalcitrant. We cooked birds or potatoes under hot coals. Pears and crabapples, wild plums, bushberries, and tubers were all feasts for us. But it was best not to be caught at it by Rose, for I was forbidden to eat between meals, and if she appeared armed with a green switch, she would let the blows fall impartially on me and my accomplices.

Each season brought its pleasures. At haying time what joy it was to role in the hay on top of the wagon, or in the small haystacks in the fields! All my friends, all my little rustic companions would come to glean in our fields after the haymakers, and I would quickly go and do the work of each of them, that is, I would take their rakes and with one swipe, chop out of our hay crop as much as each one could carry. Our farmers did not look kindly on this, and I could not understand why they didn't enjoy giving as much as I did. Deschartres would get angry; he said I was making thieves out of all these chil-dren, who would one day make me repent the freedom with which I gave and allowed others to take.

It was the same thing at harvest time; it was no longer handfuls that the village children would carry away, but sheaves. The poor women from La Châtre would come in bands of forty and fifty. Each would call me to follow in her row with her, for they had their own set of rules and would beat anyone who gleaned outside her row. When I had spent five minutes with one gleaner, she would have her day's worth of gleanings, since I did not hesitate to reach into our sheaves with both hands; and when Deschartres scolded me, I remind-ed him of the story of Ruth and Boaz.[23]

Deschartres' elaborate and painstaking teaching, directed toward instill-ing in me an appreciation of the pleasures and advantages of ownership, dated from this period in particular. I do not know if I was predisposed to the oppo-site doctrine, or if he was an inadequate teacher, but I surely reacted by throw-ing myself blindly into the most absolute communism. Of course, I did not give my utopia that name; I do not believe the word had been invented yet. But I decreed within myself that equality of fortune and circumstance was God's law and that everything which destiny gave to one was stolen from another. With all apologies to present society, that idea came into my head at the age of twelve and remained intact except for slight modifications needed to adapt it to the moral demands of given situations. My ideal remained enveloped in a dream of paradisiacal brotherhood, and when I became a Catholic later on, this dream found its support in the teachings of the Gospel. I shall come back to this again.

Innocently I explained my utopia to Deschartres. Poor man! if he were alive today, given the reactionary leanings formed by his own set of circumstances, some of the new ideas would have made him end his days in a state of fury! But in 1816 this utopia did not seem dangerous to him, and he took pains to debate it methodically. "You will change your mind," he would say to me, "and you will come to despise humanity too much to want to sacrifice yourself for it. But you must begin right now to combat this tendency to openhandedness that you inherit from your poor father. You do not have any idea of the value of money; you think you are rich because you see around you land which is yours, harvests which ripen for you, livestock which is cared for and fattened to bring you bags full of money every year. But with all of that, you are not rich, and your grandmama had a good deal of trouble maintaining her household at a respectable level."

"But wait a minute," I would say. "What is prompting my grandmama keep up those expenses, which are mainly a good wine cellar and an excellent table for her friends? Because, if it were only for herself, she eats like a bird, and a bottle of muscat would last her a good two months. Could it be that people come to see her just to drink her wine and eat her delicacies?"

"But one must have this, one must have that," Deschartres would argue. I would deny everything; I conceded that my grandmama needed all the comforts I saw her enjoy, but I insisted that Deschartres and I could well put ourselves on the dark gruel diet of the Spartans. He did not find that idea amusing. He mocked the fervor of my unschooled stoicism, and he would take me to see our fields and meadows, urging me to get acquainted with my legacy and insisting that it was never too early to learn to keep track of my expenses and income. He would say to me, "Here is a piece of land which belongs to you. It cost so-and-so much, it's worth so-and-so much, and it brings in so-and-so much." I would listen to him as if I understood, and a moment later, when he wanted me to recite my lesson in landowning back to him, it would be clear that I had not heard it or had already forgotten it. His figures meant nothing to me; I knew very well which stands of wheat had the prettiest corn cockles and the loveliest wild sweet peas, and in which hedgerows grew snapdragons and saxifrages, where to find the whitecapped mushrooms or the morels, and on which flowers at the water's edge the green dragonflies or the tiny metallic blue beetles would land; but it was quite impossible for me to tell whether we were on our own or the neighbor's land, or the extent of the field, or how many rods, acres, or hectares it covered, whether the land was of best or poorest quality, etc. I drove him to despair; I would smother spasmodic yawns, and I would end up by uttering some absurdity, which would make him laugh and scold at the same time. "Ah, poor little head, poor little brain," he would sigh. "She's just like her father; he was very intelligent about certain brilliant and useless things, but was totally impractical. No logic, not a grain of logic!" What would he say today if he knew that thanks to his explanations, I have such an aversion to owning land that I am no better at forty-five than I was at twelve! I confess, to my shame, that I cannot tell my land from my neighbor's, and that when I walk three steps from my house, I have absolutely no idea on whose land I am.

It would seem that this good man did his best to turn me away forever from everything he called agriculture. I already loved and have always loved the poetry of country scenery, but he did not want it to mean any of those things to me. If I admired the imposing forms of the large oxen ruminating in the grass, I had to listen to the story of the whole transaction in which the price of that ox had been argued, and the higher bid of farmer So-and-So, and all the important reasons Deschartres, encouraged by a certain intelligent M. Marchois of his acquaintance, had thought worth mentioning in order to lower the price by thirty francs. Then this or that bull had an ailment that he insisted I go and look at. The bull had sore feet, or a blunted horn, or a skin disease, or Heaven knows what. Goodbye poetry and the idealized serenity of my Apis,[24] king of the meadows. Those nice sheep which smothered me as they pressed their weight against me, trying to eat from my pockets, I had to observe their brain operations, if they had cerebral infections; it was horrible. He mercilessly scolded my gentle companions, the shepherdesses, who would tremble in his presence and go away in tears, while I, planted there at his side as both judge and plaintiff, would loathe my role of master and landowner, which must sooner or later make me the object of hate. I would either be hated for my stinginess or mocked for my carelessness—that was the inevitable pitfall, and I have indeed fallen into it. The farmers here despise my negligence, and I have for many years had the reputation of being some kind of imbecile.

When I wanted to go in one direction, Deschartres would take me in the other. We would start out toward the river, which throughout its whole course, under the branches of willows and along the locks in the little ravine, offers a succession of lovely settings, cool shade, and little constructions in the most picturesque rustic style. But on the way, Deschartres, armed with his spyglass, would see geese in one of our fields. We would have to climb back up the arid hillside and, in the torrid summer heat, go and give the geese a dressing-down, or the goat which might be eating the bark off the young elms, already stripped so bare I could not see what harm it did. And then we would catch a boy in the bushy foliage of a tree, stripping the leaves. Or the neighbor's donkey, having broken through the hedge, would be cutting a swathe "the width of his tongue"[25] through our hayfield. There were always misdeeds to reprimand, punishments to mete out, threats and continual disputes, which sometimes involved my best friends. That would distress me greatly, and when I would tell my grandmother about it, she would give me money so that I could, unknown to Deschartres, go and repay a delinquent's fine or take a message of amnesty on her behalf.

But I did not like that role either; it fell far short of fulfilling my idea of fraternal equality. By pardoning these villagers, it seemed that I was lowering them in my own esteem. Their thanks wounded me, and I couldn't help telling them I was only performing an act of justice. They did not understand me. They acknowledged that they were guilty, very guilty, through their children; they had not properly shepherded their little flock. They wanted to beat them in front of me, to please me; that was odious to me, and truly feeling myself becoming each day more of an artist, with instincts for poetry and tenderness, I cursed the destiny which caused me to be born a lady and mistress of a great house against my will. I envied the life of the shepherds. My sweetest dream would have been to wake up one fine morning under a thatched roof, to be named Naniche or Pierrot, and lead my sheep along the roadsides, without having to worry about M. Lhomond and his colleagues,[26] without having to side with the rich, without apprehensions about a future that was made to seem so complicated by those who explained it to me, difficult to manage, and so foreign to my character. In that small fortune which I was being constantly asked to count and re-count, I could see nothing but an encumbrance which I would never be able to shed, and as it turns out, I was not in the least mistaken.

My taste for the vagabond's life notwithstanding, a sense of destiny urged me to cultivate my intelligence in spite of my conviction that all learning was but vanity and illusion. Even in the midst of my most intense rural pleasures, I would be seized with the need for solitude, for reflection, or with a compulsion to read. And going from one extreme to another, after a period of feverish activity, I would be absorbed in my books for several days, and could not be coaxed out of my room or out of my grandmother's little boudoir. Those around me were at a loss to define my character, sometimes scatter-brained to the point of folly, sometimes serious and sad to the point of melancholy.

Deschartres had softened a good deal since my brother was no longer there to drive him to distraction. He often took pleasure in the lessons I understood well, but the unevenness of my mood occasionally brought back his outbursts, and he accused me of not trying, when I was really only going through a growth crisis. Sometimes he threatened to strike me, and since this sort of warning seemed already a half-accomplished fact, I was always on guard, determined not to tolerate from him what I would no longer accept from Rose. Usually he was lenient with me and appreciated the alacrity with which I understood his teaching, when it was clearly presented. But on certain days my mind was so far away that finally one day he threw a big Latin dictionary at me. I think the missile would have killed me if I had not agilely avoided it by ducking. I did not say anything; I gathered up my notebooks and my texts, put them in the closet, and went for a walk. The next day he asked me if I had done my translation, and I answered, "No, I know quite enough Latin as it is; I don't want anymore." He never brought it up again, and the Latin was dropped. I do not know how he worked that out with my grandmother; she did not mention it to me either. Probably Deschartres was ashamed of losing his temper and was grateful to me for keeping it a secret, and at the same time he understood I was irrevocably determined never to subject myself to Latin again. This incident did not keep me from loving him, even though he was the sworn enemy of my mother, and I had never been able to resign myself to the awful way he had treated Hippolyte. One day after he had beaten him cruelly, I said to him, "I'm going to tell Grandmama," and I proceeded to do so. He was severely reprimanded, at least as far as I know, but he never held it against me. As we were very open with each other, a quarrel was impossible.

He had much the same temper as Rose, which is why they could not stand each other. One day, when she was sweeping my room and he was passing in the corridor, she tossed some dust on his beautiful, shiny shoes. He called her an idiot, and she called him a brute; the battle was on, and Rose, aiming her broom between the pedagogue's legs as he descended the stairs, nearly caused him to break his neck. From that time on they cordially hated each other; every day brought new quarrels, which even degenerated into fisticuffs. Later on his disputes with Julie, though less energetic, were even more bitter. The cook was also at knife-points with Rose, and they used to throw plates at each other. Then again the same cook would also fight with her aged husband, Saint-Jean. We changed valets at least ten times because they could not get along with Rose or Deschartres. No household was ever more upset with battles and shouting. Such was the sad result of my grandmother's excessive lenience. She did not want to be parted from her servants nor set herself up as judge in their disputes. Deschartres, while trying to establish peace, added instead the turbulence of his anger. All of this disgusted me enormously and served to augment my love of the fields and the society of shepherds, who were so gentle and lived in such harmony.

However, when Deschartres took me with him, my boundaries expanded, and I had a certain amount of freedom. Rose would forget about me, and I could be as wild as I liked. One evening the haying went on quite late into the night. The last wagonload was being gathered from a field. The moonlight was bright, and they wanted to finish because a storm was threatening. In spite of their haste, the sky clouded over, and the thunder and lightning began as we started for the farm. We were on the river bank, a quarter of a league away from home. The wagon, which had been hurriedly loaded, was poorly balanced. Two or three times on the way, it toppled and had to be righted. We had very young draft oxen who were afraid of the thunder and moved only with repeated prodding, panting in fear like skittish horses. The band of gleaners, men and women, had waited for us in order to help with the loading and hold up, with their rakes, the unsteady load, which was threatened by each rut in the road. Armed with a prod that he used unskillfully, Deschartres "sputtered, sweated, and swore."[27] The farmers and their workers dramatized their lamentations, as if they were taking part in the Russian retreat, which is typical of how the Berrichon farmer vents his impatience. The rolling thunder made a terrifying din, and the wind blew furiously. They could no longer see to drive, except by lantern light. The children were frightened and crying. One of my little friends was so undone that she could not carry her small armload and would have left it in the middle of the road if I had not taken it. What's more, she herself had to be dragged along by the hand, because she had covered her head with her apron so as not to see the "fire in the sky," and she was falling into all the holes. It was very late when we at last reached home in a real downpour. At the house they were worried about us; at the farm they were worried about the oxen and the hay. For my part, this bit of rural life had delighted me, and the next day I tried to write a description of it, but the result did not satisfy me, and I tore it up without showing it to my grandmother. Each new attempt to express my feelings would discourage me for a long time from trying again.

Autumn and winter were the times we enjoyed ourselves most. Country children have the most freedom and the fewest chores then. Before the March wheat, there are wide open spaces where the flocks can wander without doing any harm. The sheep, in fact, take care of themselves while the shepherds, gathered around their campfire, talk, play, dance, and tell stories. It is hard to imagine all the fantasies there are in the minds of these children who live in the midst of natural surroundings without understanding anything about them and who have the strange ability to see with their own eyes what their imaginations invent. I have heard several whom I knew to be very truthful, and too innocent besides to have made it up, so often tell about apparitions they had witnessed, that I am certain they did not think they saw, but actually did see the objects of their fear, as a result of a perception which is peculiar to rustic natures. Their parents, who were less simple than they and sometimes even quite skeptical, were also subject to these visions.

I have therefore always thought that such visions should be studied more closely and analysed in the cold light of reason more conscientiously than they have been thus far. Such a study would be useful to the understanding of history and to the knowledge of human nature, about which scholars generalize too much, in my opinion. The human race had, in its infancy, certain faculties, or infirmities if you will, which were inherent to its state of ignorance, but to say that superstition and fear are always the cause of phantoms is not absolutely true. I have seen peasants who were neither gullible nor easily frightened be seized when they least expected it with a hallucination peculiar to country folk. We know that this hallucination nearly always takes the form of an imaginary animal. In several articles published in *Illustration*,[28] I have collected various beliefs prevalent in our Vallée Noire and also told of the apparitions of the Great Beast.

I shall not go into it again, but I must confess here that for a long time I believed in the existence of this beast. In my childish explanations of it, I believed that there was some nearly extinct animal species of which only a few rare examples remained hidden away in our part of the country where the *pastural*[(13)] gave them a more secure hiding place than could be found elsewhere, because the Beast appears mostly in those places between one and two in the morning, the hour when the cattle are rounded up and tied for the night. I supposed that the Beast was nocturnal, perhaps even amphibious, and that it could remain hidden under water during the day; that scientists and worldly people could very well be unaware of its existence, and that fear kept the peasants from observing it closely enough to get a more precise idea of it. Anyway, I enjoyed supposing the ancient creature still had a few remaining descendants living and wandering over the earth, isolated and lonely beings, destined soon to disappear, perhaps unable to bear the light of day, and so tired of their miserable circumstances that they hovered in the footsteps of man as if to ask for refuge and servitude. But man had refused to tame or use them. He had feared and tried to kill them, but as everyone knows, the Beast is impervious to bullets and buckshot. "Which is proof," I would say to Deschartres, "that it is an antediluvian animal whose skin or scales are different in nature from that of any animal we know of. Maybe this Beast lives for several centuries, maybe there is even only one in the universe, and that is why we cannot find any remains we can study and compare with the living example." In any case, I invented for this Beast a whole zoological history which caused the scholarly Deschartres much amusement.

"There is a much simpler explanation," he would say to me, "which solves the whole problem. The Beast does not exist, no one ever saw it, but everybody believes in it out of stupidity; it is characteristic of those who are easily taken in by lies to want others to be similarly taken in. When a peasant is convinced that his father saw the beast, he must then convince his son that he saw it too, and they lie to each other from generation to generation."

Deschartres' explanation was not any better than mine; I had trouble persuading myself the Beast did not exist, but indeed—and I believe I am sure of it finally—it does not. However, the peasant doesn't keep the lie alive from father to son just for the pleasure of transmitting an error and of bequeathing the fear he inherited. The primitive animal I mused on is in the peasant himself. He is not constituted the same way as the more rational, more civilized, but less poetic and less sincere being, who has been modified by a different education and the customs of a different milieu. The peasant knows no other history than tradition and legend. His brain is other than that of the city dweller. He has the capacity to transmit to his senses the actual perception of the objects of his beliefs, of his reveries, of his meditations. It was in this way that Joan of Arc really did hear celestial voices that spoke to her. To accuse her of imposture is to devaluate humanity. She had hallucinations, but she was not insane. All those peasants who have recounted their visions to me and whom I have known all my life are neither crazy nor cowardly; several are very matter-of-fact and brave men, some of them even skeptics in many other areas. There are former soldiers among them, who fought in campaigns at the time of the Empire, whose intelligence was developed during their military service, who know how to read, write, and figure, but none of that alters the fact that they have seen the Beast and might see it again.

I was once witness to one of these incidents. I was returning from Saint-Chartier; the priest had given me a pair of pigeons which he had put in a basket and entrusted to his altar boy, telling him to go with me. He was a boy of fourteen or fifteen, tall, strong, in excellent health, and of a very calm and lucid turn of mind. The curé was educating him, and he has since become a schoolteacher. At the time he perhaps knew less French than I, but certainly more Latin. This, then, was quite a polished and intelligent peasant.

It was around three o'clock when we came out of vespers; it was in the middle of summer, and the weather was perfect; we took the shortcuts through the fields and meadows, and we talked at complete ease. I was asking him about his studies. His mind was perfectly free and open; he stopped near a bush to tie up his broken clog with a piece of reed. "Keep walking," he said, "I'll catch up with you." So I continued walking, but I had not gone thirty paces when I saw him running toward me, pale, with his hair standing on end. He had left his wooden shoes, basket, and pigeons right where he had stopped. He had seen, just as he was stepping into the ditch, a horrible man who had threatened him with his stick.

At first I believed him, and I went back to see if the man was following us or if he had gone off with our pigeons, but I distinctly saw the basket and the clogs of my companion and no human being on the path, in the field, or anywhere near or far.

I was seventeen or eighteen at the time and no longer easily frightened. I said to the child, "It was a poor vagabond who was starving and was tempted by our pigeons. He must have been hiding in the ditch. Let's go and see." "No," he answered, "not even if you cut me in pieces."

"What?" I replied. "A big, strong boy like you afraid of a man all alone? Come on, cut off a stick and come with me to get our pigeons. I'm certainly not going to leave them there."

"No, no, mam'selle, I won't go," he cried, "because I would see him again, and I don't want to see him anymore. My sticks and my courage won't do any good, because he's not a human man. He's more like an animal."

I was beginning to understand, and I was all the more insistent that he return with me to the basket and his shoes. Nothing could convince him to do it. I went alone, telling him at least to watch me go, to prove to himself that he had been dreaming. He promised me he would, but when I came back with the clogs and the basket, my little rascal had taken to his heels and was perfectly happy to let me carry the things all the way to the outlying houses of the village, which he reached ahead of me. I tried to shame him. It was useless. He, in fact, mocked my disbelief and thought I was crazy to brave a werewolf to recuperate two miserable pigeons.

The fine courage I had on that encounter I probably would not have had three years earlier, for at that time, when I was spending a good half of my life with the shepherds, I confess their terror had pervaded me and that, without exactly believing in fairies, ghosts, or in Georgeon, the devil of the Vallée Noire, my imagination had been deeply influenced by these phantoms. But I was not of country stock, and never had the least hallucination. I had many visions of objects and forms in my daydreaming, but they were almost never frightening, and even if they were, I never deceived myself. The skeptical tendency of the child of Paris still struggled within me against the credulity of children in general.

The fireside tales of the people who came to flail the hemp put the finishing touch to my mental confusion. To keep the dust and noise of their work away from the house, and because half the village wanted to hear their stories, they were set up at the entrance to the courtyard, facing the square, alongside the cemetery, where the crosses could be seen, by moonlight, over a very low wall. The old women took turns with the storytellers. I have described these rustic scenes in my novels.²⁹ But I shall never be able to recount that flow of marvelous and preposterous stories which we listened to so intensely and which all bore the stamp of their locality or of the various occupations of those who told them. Even the sacristan had his own brand of poetry, which threw a veil of wonderment over the things of his experience—the sepulchers, the bells, the screech-owls, the steeple, the rats in the steeple, etc. The mysterious actions he attributed to these rats could fill a book. He knew all the rats, and for forty years he had named them after important people of the village who had died. After each death, a new rat would follow him about at his heels and torment him with his grimaces. To pacify these strange spirits, he would take food to them in the steeple; but when he went back the next day, he would find the most bizarre designs outlined by these suspect rats with the very food he had brought them. One day he would find all the white beans arranged in a circle, with a cross of red beans in the center. The next day, it was the opposite combination. Another time, the red and the white would alternate systematically, forming a chain of several circles, or unfamiliar letters, but so well drawn that one would have sworn it was the work of a "human person." No animal is too insignificant, no object too inanimate to be included in the peasant's world of fantasy; and the Christianity of the Middle Ages, which is still his religion, is every bit as rich in mythological personifications as the older religions.

I was an avid listener to all these recitals; I would have listened all night, but they were not good for me: they gave me sleepless nights. My brother, who was five years older, was even more affected by them, and his example confirmed my belief that those of peasant stock have the capacity for hallucination. He belonged to that stock through his mother, and he did have visions; while I, in spite of the consuming fear and sinister dreams of my sleep, did not. Twenty years later, he swore to me he had heard the crack of a goblin's whip in the stable and the paddles of the washerwomen at night on the banks of the stream. It was of him I spoke in the articles entitled *Les Visions de la nuit dans les campagnes*, and his narratives were completely sincere. In the case of real danger, he was more than brave: he was fearless. In adulthood as in childhood, he always made it a kind of practice to hold fear in contempt. At least he risked his life at any moment and for the most insignificant reason. But what can I tell you? He kept to his native ground, he had hallucinations, and he believed in the supernatural.

I have said that autumn and winter were the most carefree seasons for us; I have always passionately loved winter in the country, and I have never understood the preference of the rich, who have made Paris the place to spend the holidays during the season of the year most alien to dances, pretty clothes, and frivolity. Nature summons us to family life at the hearthside in winter, and besides, it is in the country that the few lovely days of that season can be felt and appreciated. In the large cities, in our climate, that awful, stinking, frozen mud almost never dries up. In the fields, a ray of sunlight or several hours of wind make the air healthy and the earth clean. The poor proletarians in the city know this well, and it is not for their pleasure that they remain in that cesspool. The absurd and artificial life of the rich in our society exhausts itself in the struggle against nature. The rich in England have better sense; they spend the winter in their country castles.

In Paris it is assumed that nature dies for six months, and yet the wheat is already growing in autumn, and the "pale winter sun" (we are all supposed to call it that) is then at its most vivid and brilliant of the whole year. When it dispels the mists, when it sets in sparkling purple on evenings of freezing cold, one can hardly bear the brightness of its rays. Even in our colder regions, badly misnamed "temperate zones," nature is never divested of its aspect of life and ornament. The vast grainfields become covered with those short, fresh carpets over which the sun, low on the horizon, shoots broad flames of emerald. The meadows are clad in splendid mosses—luxurious bounty of winter. The ivy, that useless, but sumptuous, vine, is marbled with scarlet and gold. Even the gardens are not without riches. The primrose, the violet, and the Bengal rose are blooming just beneath the snow. A few other flowers—thanks to a fortuitous location, a dip in the terrain—survive the frost and provide a delightful surprise at any moment. The nightingale may be absent, but how many other migrating birds, noisy and splendid guests, come to land or rest on the tops of the tall trees or at the water's edge! And what is more beautiful than the snow when the sun turns it into a cloth of diamonds, or when the frost suspends it from the trees in marvelous archways and indescribable festoons of ice and crystal? And isn't it a pleasure to feel oneself surrounded by family at the fireside during those long evenings in the country, where we belong so intimately to each other, where even time seems to belong to us, and where life, turning inward, becomes purely intellectual and moral?

In winter, my grandmother allowed me to have my "club" in the big dining room, with an old stove that gave off the best heat. My club consisted of twenty or so village youngsters who brought their *saulnées*. A *saulnée* is an almost endless string, the length of it looped with slipknots made out of horsehair, for catching larks and other small birds in the snow-covered fields. A good *saulnée* stretches around a whole field. It is wound on a spool made for the purpose and is laid before daylight in just the right places. The snow is swept away all along the furrow, and grain is thrown into it; two hours later, hundreds of larks are trapped. We would go to harvest them with big sacks which the donkey carried back full. As there would be serious disputes about the shares, I had set up a cooperative system, and it worked very well. The *saulnées* cannot be used for more than two or three days without putting new horsehair on them (because many break in the stubble of the fields), or without re-looping them, that is, replacing the slipknot in each untied horsehair. We agreed, then, that this long and painstaking job should be shared, as well as the laying of the traps, which is also an exhausting task requiring rapid sweeping of the snow. We divided up, without counting or measuring, the string and the horsehair; the horsehair was the especially precious commodity, and it was also as a group that we acquired our plunder by going into the meadows and stables to pull out of the horses' tails and manes everything those animals were willing to let us take without rising in revolt. Indeed, we had become very adept at this occupation, and we managed to thin out the hair of the untethered colts without getting in the way of their fantastically flying hoofs. The task done by all of us together was completed with surprising speed, and we had on occasion re-looped two or three hundred spans in one evening. After the hunt came the triage. In one pile we put the larks and in the other the birds of lesser value. We would retain a certain selection for our own Sunday feasting, and one of the children would go and sell the rest in town, after which I would divide the money among them all. They were very happy with this arrangement, and there was not any more quarreling and mistrust among them. Every day our Brotherhood gained new recruits, who preferred this kind of agreement to battles and disputes. No longer did anyone think of getting up before all the others to go and empty the traps of his companions, and Sunday was a real feast-day. We did our own cooking of the winged creatures. Rose was in a good mood on those days, for she was cheerful and good when she was not in a fury. The cook was quite open-minded on the subject of our cooking, and only old Saint-Jean frowned on us and maintained that the tail of his white horse was dwindling away daily. We knew it was true.

Throughout all these games, the novel of Corambé continued to unfold in my mind. It was a permanent dream, as disconnected, as incoherent as the dreams of sleep, and which I could keep track of only because the same sentiment always ruled it.

That sentiment was not romantic love. I knew from books that love existed in life and that it was the basis and core of most novels and poems. But feeling nothing myself which could explain why, in this arrangement of unfathomable affections—these hieroglyphs, so to speak—one being would devote himself exclusively to the pursuit of another, I carefully avoided guiding my novel over that terrain which, for my imagination, was a frozen wasteland. It seemed to me that, if I were to include male and female lovers in it, it would become banal and tiresome, and that out of the charming characters with whom I was spending my dream-life, I would be making conventional beings like those I often found in books, or at least strangers preoccupied with a secret that could not interest me, since it did not correspond with any emotion I could experience on my own. On the other hand, friendship, filial or fraternal love, understanding, the purest of attractions reigned in my enchanted world; my heart, as well as my imagination, was entirely wrapped up in that fantasy, and when I was unhappy about something or someone in real life, I would think of Corambé with almost as much faith and consolation as of a demonstrated truth.

I was at this stage when I was told that in three weeks I would be making my first communion.

This was a more embarrassing situation for my grandmama than for me. She did not want to give me an unreservedly philosophical education; everything that smacked of extremism repelled her; but at the same time as she submitted to the dictates of custom (and at the beginning of the Restoration she could not have avoided it without a certain amount of scandal), she feared that my passionate nature might fall prey to superstition, which she really loathed.

She thus chose the solution of telling me that I had to go through this ceremony with decency and for appearances' sake, but to be careful not to offend divine wisdom and human reason to the point of believing that I was going to "eat my Creator."

My natural docility took care of the rest. I learned my catechism like a parrot, without trying to understand it and without even thinking of mocking its miracles, but very determined not to retain a word of it as soon as the thing was "under lock and key," as we used to say. Confession was extremely repugnant to me. My grandmother, who knew that the good curé of Saint-Chartier spoke and thought with a certain crudeness, put me in the hands of another good and elderly curé, the one from La Châtre, who had more education, and who, I must say, respected the ignorance of my age and did not put to me any of those infamous questions by which a priest often manages to soil, intentionally or not, the purity of childhood. No sets of questions or examinations of conscience were placed in my hands, and I was told simply to confront the errors I felt guilty of.

That made me quite uncomfortable. I could indeed identify several, but it seemed to me they were not significant enough to satisfy the curé. First of all, I had once lied to my mother to protect Rose, and often to Deschartres to protect Hippolyte. But I was not a liar by nature—I had no need to be—and Rose herself, since she always hit me before asking questions, did not make lying a condition of my victimization. I had had something of a sweet tooth, but that was such a long time ago I could hardly remember it. I had always lived among people who were so chaste that any idea of what might have been the opposite of chastity had never formed. I had been irritable and violent-tempered in the past, but I had no further reason to be since I was back in good health. Of what, then, could I accuse myself, unless it was to have at times preferred playing to studying, to have torn my dresses and lost my handkerchiefs—misdeeds for which my maid thought I deserved to be labeled an enfant terrible.

In truth, I do not know what crimes a child of twelve can accuse herself of, unless the poor thing has already been corrupted by bad examples and hideous influences, and in those cases, it is the crimes of others she has to confess.

It seemed it was not worth bothering a priest with the little I had to tell; my curé made do with it and told me, as a penance, to recite the Lord's Prayer when emerging from the confessional. That seemed a very mild punishment to me, for it is a very beautiful prayer, sublime, and simple, and I directed it to God with all my heart, but I did not feel any less humiliated to have kneeled in front of a priest for so little.

In any case, never was a first communion so unceremoniously expedited. I went to La Châtre once a week. The curé gave me five minutes worth of instruction; I had my catechism at my fingertips by the first week. On the eve of the appointed day, I was sent to spend the evening and night with a kind and charming lady who was a friend of ours. She had two children younger than I. Her daughter, Laure, a beautiful and remarkable person in every way, has since married my friend Fleury, son of the Fleury who was a friend of my father's.

There were still other children in the house; I enjoyed myself enormously as we played all kinds of games under the gaze of the good parents, who took part in our innocent joy; I went to bed so tired from having laughed and frolicked that I had forgotten all about the solemn occasion of the next day.

Mme. Decerfz, that charming and excellent woman who had agreed to accompany me to church for my lesson, has often reminded me since how wild and noisy I was when I returned to her house that afternoon. Her mother, also a very excellent woman, said to her at the time, "Well, there's a child who isn't very reverent. That wasn't how we prepared for the sacraments in my day."

"I don't see that she's doing any harm," answered Mme. Decerfz. "She's happy, so she has a clear conscience, and children's laughter is music for our dear Lord."

The next morning, my grandmother arrived. She had decided to attend my first communion, not without difficulty, I think, because she had not set foot in a church since my father's marriage. Mme. Decerfz told me to ask for her blessing and forgiveness for any displeasure I might have caused her, which I did more willingly than for the priest. My grandmama kissed me and took me to the church.

Once there, I began to wonder what was expected of me; I had not yet given it a thought, I was so astonished to see my grandmother in a church! The curé had told me I had to believe, or I would be committing a sacrilege; I did not have the least desire to be sacreligious, not the least inclination toward revolt or impiety, but I did not believe. My grandmama had prevented me from believing, and yet she had ordered me to take communion. I wondered if both she and I were not committing an act of hypocrisy, and even though I seemed as calm and serious as I had appeared carefree and unconcerned the night before, I felt very ill at ease; two or three times I had the urge to get up and say to my grandmother, "That's enough, let's go!"

But suddenly a thought came to mind which calmed me. I was going back over the Last Supper in my mind, and the words, "This is my body and my blood" seemed no longer anything but a metaphor; Jesus was too holy and too great to have wanted to deceive his disciples. He had summoned them to a meal in the spirit of brotherhood, he had invited them to break bread together in his memory. I no longer felt anything ridiculous in the tradition of the Last Supper, and finding myself at the communion rail near an old poverty-stricken woman who received the wafer before me with great devotion, I had my first notion of the significance of these communions of equality, whose symbols, in my opinion, the church has misunderstood or falsified.

I returned quite reassured, then, from the communion table; and the contentment of having found a solution to my minor anxiety gave my face a new expression, I was later told. My grandmother, touched and frightened, torn perhaps between the fears of having made me a believer or having made me lie to myself, hugged me gently to her heart when I came back to her, and shed some tears which fell on my veil.

All that was a puzzle to me; I expected that that evening she would give me a serious explanation of the act she had made me perform and of the emo-

tion she had shown. Not so. It was arranged for me to take a second communion a week later, and then nobody spoke to me about religion anymore; it had
no more importance than if nothing had happened.

On the religious holidays, I was still sent to La Châtre to see the processions and attend the services. I took advantage of those occasions because I
spent the time in the Decerfz household, where I cavorted with the children,
and where they spoiled me so that I turned everything upside down, leaving it
all damaged—furniture, dolls, even the children, to some extent, as they were
too delicate to withstand my peasant ways.

When I returned home, tired of all the exertion, I would fall back into my
fits of melancholy. I would again bury myself in reading, and my grandmother
had a good deal of difficulty getting me back to a regular schedule of studies.
Nothing resembles the artist more than the child. He has his moods of labor
and indolence, his ardent thirst for production, and languor full of disaffection.
My grandmother had never had the artist's temperament, even though she had
certain talents; I am not convinced she ever had a childhood. She had a nature
so placid, so steady, so seamless that she could not understand the heights and
depths of mine. She gave me so few tasks (and there lay the problem) that she
was astonished to see me overcome by them sometimes; and since at other
times I accomplished four times as much, she accused me of caprice and calculated resistance. She was mistaken; I simply did not have control over myself.
She always scolded me affectionately, but with a certain bitterness, and there
she was wrong; she wanted me to conquer my moodiness, to get used to disci-
plining myself, and there she was right.

Since on top of everything she spoiled me, she allowed me a kind of dissipation which went to my head throughout the whole summer following my
first communion. A company of itinerant actors came to La Châtre—a rather
good troupe, by the way—which performed melodrama, comedy, vaudeville,
and especially comic opera. There were some good voices, a fairly good
ensemble, a lead male singer and two women singers who were not without
talent. The troupe was really too distinguished for that quite miserable per-
forming-space—the same room in which my father had done amateur theatricals with his friends, the Duvernets—a former convent church, where you
could still see the outlines of the ogives inexpertly covered by plaster more
recent than that on the walls, the whole thing topped by a ceiling of rough
beams which had been installed after the fact; and it was furnished with hard
wooden benches placed in tiers. Nonetheless, the ladies of the town came to sit
there in their finery, and when there were flowers and ribbons everywhere, the
unclean bareness of the room was no longer noticeable. The amateur players of
the community, whose leader was still M. Duvernet, made up a very satisfactory orchestra. People in the provinces were still artistic at that time. There was
no village so poor or small that one could not put together a good quartet; and
every week its members would meet, sometimes at one house and sometimes
at another, to play what the Italians call *musica di camera* [chamber music], a
noble and honorable form of relaxation that has disappeared along with the
old-time virtuosos, the last guardians of that sacred fire, from our provinces.

I always loved music, even though my grandmama neglected me in that area and M. Gayard filled me with more and more distaste for studying it his way. It was rare that my grandmother placed her stiff white fingers on the old harpsichord or that she warbled those majestic pieces from the old masters, but her warbling was better than anyone else's singing. I had nearly forgotten that I, too, was a born musician and could feel and interpret what others created or produced. The first time I was sent to attend the plays at La Châtre, our travelling singers were giving *Aline, reine de Golconde*. I returned from this performance absolutely enchanted, and I knew almost the whole opera by heart, melodies, words, accompaniments, recitatives. Another time it was *Montano et Stéphanie*; then *Le Diable à quatre*, *Adolphe et Clara*, *Gulistan*, *Ma tante Aurore*, *Jeannot et Colin*, and, goodness knows, all the pretty, easy, tuneful, and gracious operettas of that time. I regained a passion for music, and I would sing away all day and continue all night in my dreams. The music had totally poeticized for me these performances to which Mme. Duvernet very kindly took me every week. The memory of the handsome theaters and first-rate actors I had seen in Paris had faded. That had been so long ago that the comparison did not occur to me at all. I did not notice the shabbiness of the scenery or the inappropriateness of the costumes; my imagination and the power of the music filled in anything that was lacking, and I thought I was attending the most beautiful, splendid, finished performances in the world; those country players singing and declaiming in a barn gave me as much pleasure and well-being as the great artists of Europe in the noblest theaters of the world have done since.

Mme. Duvernet had a niece named Brigitte, a good child, kind and full of fun, with whom I soon formed an intimate friendship. With the youngest son of the house, Charles (my old friend of today), and two or three other persons of equal standing (I think the eldest of the group was not yet fifteen), we spent those happy days preceding each play in some very absorbing games. Since to us everything was a spectacle, even the morning religious service, we alternately acted out mass and comedy, procession and melodrama. We dressed up in their mother's cast-offs, which we plundered mercilessly; with flowers, mirrors, lace, and ribbons, we made what was sometimes theater, sometimes church decor; and we would sing together at the top of our lungs, sometimes choruses of comic-opera and sometimes those of mass and vespers. All this was accompanied by bells ringing at full peal almost at the top of the house, by makeshift instruments down below, which imitated the overtures and accompaniments that were to be played that evening, and by the howling of the neighborhood dogs, whose nerves could not take it. It was the wierdest, and yet the most joyous, cacophony. At last it was dinnertime; we would quickly shed the improvised costumes. Charles would hurriedly remove his mother's embroidered petticoat, which he had made into a surplice. Brigitte's long black hair had to be combed again. I would run and pick the evening's bouquets from the small garden. We would sit down at the table with great appetites. But Brigitte and I could not eat anything, our stomachs were so knotted with the anticipation of going to the theater.

O happy times—when one can be so amused, absorbed, and impassioned over so little—are you past and gone for all my friends and for all those who are no longer young? Here I am, getting old, and yet in so many ways the good Lord has granted that I remain a child. Theater still amuses me sometimes as if I were twelve years old, and I confess it is the most naïve kind—pantomime, fairy plays—which entertains me the most. It still happens sometimes when I have spent a year away from Paris, that I dine hastily with my children and friends and feel my heart pulsing as the curtain rises. I hardly give the others time to eat, and I get impatient with the slowness of the cab; I don't want to miss anything; I want to grasp the play, however silly it may be. I don't want anybody talking to me, I'm so busy listening and looking. The others make fun of me, but I am unaware of it, because this fictitious world displayed before me finds me such an avid and willing spectator. Well, now, I think that in the audience there are a good many people who have been just as unhappy as I have been, just as soured in their views about life and in their human experience, who are, without daring to admit it, just as absorbed, just as entertained, just as childlike as I. We are an unfortunate race, and that is why we have an imperious need to be taken out of the real world by the deceptions of art; the more it deceives, the more we enjoy it. *J.H.C.*

X

Recital of a profound unhappiness that everyone will understand.
—An act of spite. —Mlle. Julie's denunciation. —Penitence and
solitude. —Autumn evening in the doorway of a thatched cottage.
—My heart is broken. —I harden myself to my affliction and
become, once and for all, an enfant terrible. —I rejoin my mother.
—Disappointment. —I enter the convent of English sisters. —The
origin and appearance of this monastery. —The Mother Superior.
—New heartbreak. —Mother Alippe.—I begin to assess my situation
and resign myself. —Total seclusion.

Despite all the distractions and giddiness, at the bottom of my heart I still
nursed an ill-fated desire for my absent mother. There was no hope at all for
our cherished plan; although it was always on my mind, she had forgotten it
completely. I always protested in my innermost thoughts the future my grandmama put so much stock in providing for me. Education, accomplishment,
wealth—I persisted in despising all of it. I longed to see my mother again, talk
to her again about our plan, tell her I was resolved to share her lot—to be uneducated, hard-working, and poor with her. And I must admit, on the days when
this resolution dominated me, I completely neglected my lessons. I was scolded, and my resolution became even more steadfast. One day, when I had been
reprimanded more than usual, as I left my grandmama's room I threw my text
and notebooks to the ground, took my head in both hands and, believing I was
alone, cried to myself, "Yes, indeed, it's true. I don't study because I don't
want to. I have my reasons. One day everyone will know what they are."

Julie was behind me. "You're a bad child," she told me, "and your
thoughts are even worse than your deeds. One might forgive your dissipation
and laziness, but your grandmama is so unhappy with your stubbornness and ill
will, you would deserve it if she sent you back to your mother."

"My mother!" I cried. "Send me back to my mother! That's all I want,
the only thing I ask."

"Nonsense, you don't think that," Julie replied. "You say that because
you're angry. You're beside yourself right now. I'll take care not to repeat what
you've said, because you'd be sorry later on if you were taken at your word."

I retorted with vehemence, "Julie, I understand you very well, and I know
you. I know that when you promise to keep silent, it's because you have really
decided to talk. I know that when you question me sweetly and winningly it's

to root out of me what I'm thinking, which you use to poison me in the eyes of my grandmama. I know that right now you're provoking me on purpose and that you're taking advantage of my anger and distress to make me say even more. Well, you needn't give yourself such a chore. What's in my heart, you shall know, and I give you permission to make it known. I don't wish to remain here; I wish to return to my mother, and I don't wish anyone to separate me from her any longer. She is the one I love and will always love no matter what anyone does. Her alone I am willing to obey. Go, hurry, submit your report; I am ready to put my name to it."

Had the poor girl really taken on the role of agent provocateur against me? On the face of it, yes; but in her heart, certainly not. She only wished me well. She took no wicked pleasure in having me scolded; she suffered along with my grandmother because of what they called my ingratitude. How could she have understood I was not an ingrate toward their affection but a rebel against my circumstances? My grandmother was certainly mistaken about it, so Julie might well have been. But still, it is undeniable that this girl had in her expression, voice, and whole bearing the sort of self-righteous cunning that smacked of trickery and duplicity, which was supremely antipathetic to me.

For whatever reason, this was the first time I had pushed her to the limit and struck a blow to her pride. She was mortified, and she was surely swept by a wave of revenge, because she immediately went to report my outburst in the worst possible light. And it was wrong of her, because she wounded my grandmama to the core, who scarcely had the strength to withstand any new blows to a mother's heart. The least pain quickened in her the memory of her son, as well as eternal regret and devouring jealousy of the woman who had contended for that love and was now contending for mine. She was, I am sure, suffering mortal sorrow, and if she had let me see it, I would have fallen at her feet; I would have given up all my rebellious ways, for I have always been excessively weak-willed in the face of pain I have caused, and my reconciliations have always brought me closer than my resistances have distanced me. But they were very careful to hide my grandmama's feelings from me, and Julie, personally irritated with me, did not come to say, "She's suffering, go and console her."

They adopted an ill-advised system: they resolved to arm themselves with severity, thinking they would frighten me by taking me at my word, and Mlle. Julie announced that I was to retire to my room and not come out. "You won't see your grandmother anymore," she told me, "since you detest her. She is giving you up; in three days, you will leave for Paris."

"You lied," I answered her, "viciously lied; I don't detest my grandmother, I love her. But I love my mother more, and if I'm sent back to her, I'll thank the good Lord, and my grandmother, and even you."

With these words, I turned my back on her and climbed the stairs to my room with a resolute heart. There I found Rose, who knew nothing of what had just happened and said nothing to me. I had neither soiled nor torn my clothes that day, and nothing else mattered much to her. I spent three long days without seeing my grandmama. I was allowed to go down for meals only after she had finished hers. I was told to go into the garden for fresh air when she had retired, and she would closet herself, or someone would closet her, quite literally; for when I passed the door to her room I heard the iron bar being put in place with a kind of affectation, as if to tell me that any repentance would be useless.

The servants seemed dismayed, but I conducted myself with such obvious aloofness that not one of them dared speak to me, not even Rose, who perhaps guessed correctly that the approach they were taking was wrong and would arouse my love for my mother rather than cool it. Deschartres, either by design or as a consequence of an understanding comparable to Rose's, did not speak to me either. Nor was there any question of my having lessons or studying during this term of penance.

Did they want to make me feel bored with having nothing to do? They should have forbidden me books, but I was not restricted that way, and having the library at my disposal as usual, I did not have the least desire to distract myself by reading, as children often desire only what they cannot have.

Thus I spent three days in an assiduous tête-à-tête with Corambé. I related my sorrows to him, and he consoled me by agreeing that I was right. I was suffering for the love of my mother, for love of humility and poverty. I believed I was fulfilling a great role, accomplishing some holy mission, and like all romantic children, I wore my calm and perseverance as something of a banner. They had wished to humiliate me by isolating me like a leper in this house where everything usually was handed to me; this only raised me in my self-esteem. I made some pretty reflections on the moral servitude of those lackeys who no longer dared speak a word to me, who only the evening before would have flung themselves at my feet because I was favored. I compared my disgrace to all the famous disgraces I had read about in history, and I compared myself to those great citizens who, for their virtues, had been banished by their ungrateful states.

But pride is an insipid companion, and I gave it up after a day. "All this is extremely stupid," I told myself. "Let me observe the others as well as myself and see what I can conclude. No one is making any preparations for my departure; no one really wants to send me home to my mother. They want to test me; they think I'll ask to remain here. They have no idea how much I want to live with her, and so I must show them. Let me remain impassive. Whether my confinement lasts a week, a fortnight, a month, it doesn't matter. When they're completely convinced that my mind is made up, they'll let me leave, and then I'll come to terms with my grandmama; I shall tell her that I love her, and I shall say it so well that she'll pardon me and give me back her affection. Why must she condemn me because I prefer the one who brought me into the world and whom God himself commands me to prefer above all others? Why should she think me ungrateful if I don't want to be brought up her way and share her life. What use am I to her here? I see less and less of her. The company of her women servants seems more important to her or more agreeable than mine, since she spends most of her time with them. If she keeps me here, it is certainly not for her sake, it is for mine. Well, am I not a free being, free to choose a suitable life and future? Let's face it, there's nothing tragic about what's happening to me. My grandmother wanted in all good will to make me well-bred and rich: I am very grateful to her for it, but I cannot get used to doing without my mother. My heart would gladly sacrifice all these seeming benefits for her. She'll be grateful to me for it, and God will take it into account. There is no reason for anyone to be upset with me, and my grandmama will acknowledge it, if I can succeed in reaching her and defending myself against the false accusations that have crept between us."

Thereupon, I tried to gain admission to her room, but I found the door still barricaded, and I went into the garden. There I encountered a poor old woman who had been given permission to gather dead wood. "You aren't making much headway, Mother," I said to her. "Why don't your children help you?" "They're in the fields," she said, "and I can no longer stoop down to pick up what's on the ground; my back is too old."

I began at once to do her work, and because she dared pick up only the dead wood that was on the ground, I went to find a bush hook to knock down the dried shrubs and pull off the branches within my reach. I was as strong as a peasant and soon had a splendid pile. Nothing inspires like physical labor, when a purpose or sentiment is behind it. Night came and I was still at work cutting, making bundles, tying them, providing the old woman with a week's supply instead of the day's supply that she would have had trouble collecting. I had forgotten to eat, and since no one notified me any longer of anything, I did not dream of stopping. Finally, hunger seized me; the old woman had left a long time before. I hefted onto my shoulders a load that weighed more than I did and carried it to her thatched cottage, which was at the edge of the hamlet. I was dripping with sweat and bleeding because the bush hook had more than once split open my hands, and the thorns had left a deep cut in my face.

But the autumn evening was superb, and the blackbirds were singing in the thickets. I have always been especially fond of the song of the blackbird; less brilliant, less original, less varied than that of the nightingale, it can more easily be likened to our musical forms, and it has certain phrases of rustic simplicity which might almost be written down and sung by incorporating just a few of our musical conventions. That evening the song of the blackbird seemed to be Corambé's own voice that sustained and encouraged me. I was sagging beneath my burden; I felt my strength increase, to such an extent does imagination govern our abilities; I even felt a freshness pass through my bruised limbs. I arrived at the cottage of old Mother Blin as the first stars sparkled in the still rosy sky. "Ah! my poor little darling," she said, "just see how tired you are! you'll be sick!" "No, " I told her, "but I've worked really hard for you, and that ought to be worth a piece of your bread, for I am famished." She cut me a huge slice from her moldy, black loaf, which I ate seated on a stone outside her doorway while she put her little children to bed and said her prayers. Her emaciated dog (all peasants, no matter how poor, have a dog, or rather the shadow of a dog, that lives by snatching what it can, but nonetheless loyally guards the miserable hovel that does not even shelter it), having growled a great deal, grew tamer at the sight of my bread and came closer to share this modest supper.

Never had any meal tasted so good, never was any hour so sweet nor nature more serene. My heart was free and light, my body hale, as happens after hard work. I was eating peasant bread after doing peasant work. "And this isn't a 'good deed,' as they say in the prideful vocabulary of the chateau," I thought. "It is simply a first act in the life of poverty that I hereby embrace and commence. Here I am free at last: no more tedious lessons, no more sickening sweets that one must find good or be considered ungrateful; no more fixed hours for eating, sleeping, or playing without desire or need. The end of my labor has marked the end of my day. Hunger alone has signaled the hour for my meal; no more lackeys to hand me my plate or remove it at their whim. See how the stars are coming out now; it is clear; it is cool; I'm weary and I rest, with no one standing by to tell me, 'Put on your shawl,' or 'Go indoors, you might catch cold.' No one is thinking about me; no one knows where I am; if I want to spend the night on this stone, it concerns no one but me. This is indeed supreme happiness, and I can't understand how it can be called a punishment."

Then I thought that I would soon be with my mother, and I said a tender but joyous good-bye to the countryside, the blackbirds, the bushes, the stars, the tall trees. I loved the country, but I did not yet know I would never be able to live anywhere else; I believed that paradise would be anywhere my mother was. I rejoiced at the idea that I would be helpful to her, that my physical strength would save her from fatigue. "I'm the one who'll carry her wood, make her fire, her bed," I said to myself. "We shall have no servants, no tyrannical slaves; we shall belong only to each other; we shall at last be as free as the poor."

I was in a truly euphoric state of mind, but Rose had not forgotten me as completely as I thought. She was searching for me and was upset when I returned to the house. But seeing the enormous gash on my face and having seen me work for old Mother Blin, Rose, who had a kind heart, did not dream of scolding me. Besides, ever since I was in disgrace, she was very sweet and even sad.

The next day she woke me up early. "Come," she said, "it cannot go on like this. Your grandmama is hurt; go give her a hug and beg her forgiveness." "I should have been allowed to do that three days ago," I answered her, "but will Julie let me into her room?" "Yes, yes," she replied, "I'll see to it!" And she took me through the back passageways to my grandmama's room. I went gladly, although without great remorse, because I did not really feel guilty or in any way intend, when showing her my affection, to give up the separation that I considered an accomplished fact. But in the arms of my dear grandmother the cruelest, sharpest, and least deserved of punishments awaited me.

Until that time, no one in the world—my grandmother least of all—had made any serious criticism of my mother. It was easy enough to see that Deschartres hated her, that Julie would denigrate her to curry favor, and that my grandmother had great bouts of bitterness and coldness toward her. But these were only remarks of no substance, unfounded hints, postures of disdain. In my naïve partiality to my mother, I attributed the profound regret my father's marriage had caused his family to her lack of wealth and breeding. My grandmama seemed to have made it her duty to respect in me the respect I had for my mother.

During those three days that had caused her so much pain, my grandmama had apparently sought the quickest, surest way of binding me to her and her favors that I cared so little about by shattering in my young heart the trust and love which drew me to another. She thought, she pondered, and she settled on the most baleful means of all.

As I knelt beside her bed and had taken her hands to kiss them, she told me in a trembling, bitter voice that I did not recognize, "Stay on your knees and listen to me carefully, because what I am going to say to you, you have never heard before and shall never hear again from my lips. These are things that are said only once in a lifetime, because they are never forgotten, but unless they are known—for, unhappily, they exist—a life may be ruined, a soul may be lost."

After this chilling preamble, she began to tell me the story of her own life and that of my father, such things as I already knew, then that of my mother, such as she believed she knew, at least as she understood them. In doing so, she was without pity and without intelligence; I dare say it because there are in the lives of poor people pressures, misfortunes, and fatal decrees that the rich can never understand and so judge only as poorly as the blind judge colors.

Everything she said was factually true and rested on circumstances which did not allow the least doubt. But I could have been told this terrible story in a way not calculated to destroy my respect and love for my mother, and told thus, the story would have been a great deal more credible and truthful. It would have meant telling everything—the causes of her misfortunes; her isola-tion and misery from the age of fourteen; her corruption by the rich, who exist to lie in wait for hunger and cast a slur on innocence; and the unpitying rigor of public opinion, which allows no going back and accepts no expiation.[14] I should also have been told how my mother had redeemed her past, how she had loved my father faithfully, and how, since his death, she had lived humbly, grieving and retired from the world. I knew this last point very well, or at least I believed I knew it. But they wanted me to understand that, if they were telling me all about the past, they were sparing me the present, and that there was in my mother's current life some new secret they did not want to tell me and that would make me fearful for my own future if I went to live with her. Finally, my poor grandmama, exhausted by this long recital, beside herself, her voice hoarse, eyes watery and red, loosed the final and most frightful word—my mother was a lost woman, and I was a blind child who wished to fling herself into an abyss.

For me it was like a nightmare; my throat was tight; each word spelled my death; I felt the sweat pour down my brow; I wanted to interrupt, get up and run away, repulse this frightful confidence with horror; I was not able, I was rooted to the spot where I knelt, my head was battered and bowed by this voice that swept over me and withered me like a wind storm. My icy hands no longer held my grandmother's burning ones; I think I unconsciously shoved them from my lips in terror.

Finally, I rose without saying a word, without begging for a kiss, without bothering to ask for forgiveness; I went up to my room. Rose was on the stairs. "Well," she said, "is it all over?" "Yes," I said, "it's all over, forever." And remembering that this girl had never said anything bad about my mother, certain she knew everything that I had just been told and that she was no less attached to her first mistress, Rose, although she was ugly, seemed beautiful to me; although she was my judge and almost my executioner, she seemed to be my best, almost my only, friend. I embraced her without restraint, and running to hide, I fell to the floor, prey to convulsions of despair.

The tears that erupted did not relieve me. I have always heard it said that weeping alleviates sorrow; I have ever proved the exception: I do not know how to cry. From the moment tears spring to my eyes, sobbing takes me by the throat, I choke, I breathe out cries and groans; and because I am afraid of the sounds of my pain, because I hold back from crying, it often happens that I faint dead away, which is probably how I shall die someday, if I happen to be alone, overtaken by some new unhappiness. That hardly worries me; everyone must die of something, and we each have in us the seeds of our own destruction. Probably the worst of deaths, the saddest and least desirable, is the one that cowards choose—to die of old age, that is to say, after everything that one has loved, after everything that one has believed in on earth.

At that time, I was not stoical enough to hold back my sobs, and Rose, hearing my gasps, came to comfort me. When I had regained a little control of myself, I did not wish to malinger; I went downstairs at the first call for lunch and forced myself to eat. My exercise books were given back to me, I pretended to work, but my tears had been so acrid and burning that my eyelids were raw; I had a terrible migraine; I was not thinking anymore, I was not living, I was indifferent to everything. I no longer knew if I loved or hated anyone, I no longer felt impassioned over anyone or resentful toward anyone. I had what seemed an enormous burn inside me and a searing emptiness where my heart should have been. I was aware only of a kind of contempt for the whole universe and a bitter disdain for life as it would henceforth be for me; I no longer loved myself. If my mother was detestable and hateful, then I, the fruit of her womb, was, too. I do not know how to explain why I did not become twisted by misanthropy from that moment. Terrible harm had been done me that could have been irreparable; they had tried to dry up the source of my moral, religious, and emotional life.

Happily for me, God had made me able to love and to forget. I have often been reproached for being forgetful of harm. Since I have had so much to take, it is a merciful way to be.

At the end of several days of unspeakable suffering and overwhelming exhaustion, I realized with astonishment that I still loved my mother more than ever and that I did not love my grandmother any less than before. I had appeared so unhappy, and Rose had depicted me in such a painful state, that they believed a grand repentance had come about. My grandmama knew very well she had done me great harm, but she imagined that she had been cruel in order to be kind and that she had acted for my benefit. There was nothing new to discuss; I was not questioned; it would certainly have been useless. My lips were sealed on the subject. Life began to flow once more like a peaceful stream, but for me the stream was muddied, and I no longer looked into it.

In effect, I no longer made any plans, I gave up my sweet reveries. No more novel, no more daydreams. Corambé was silent. I lived like a machine. The harm was deeper than anyone thought. Being loving, I still loved others. Still a child, I took pleasure in life. But as I have said, I did not like myself anymore, I no longer cared about myself at all. I had systematically resisted the advantages of education; I had disdained to enhance my intellectual being, believing that my spiritual being would gain thereby. But my ideal was obscured, and I could no longer make out the future I had created and tailored to my fancy for so long. From then on I glimpsed only future struggles against public opinion of which I had never dreamed, and some unimaginably sad enigma to which no one had given me the answer. I had been told about awful dangers whose nature they assumed I would guess, but being simple and incurious by nature, I guessed nothing at all. Besides, just as I am active in pursuing what appeals to my instincts, so am I lazy in confronting what is hostile to them, and I did not seek to solve the enigma of the sphinx; but something terrible seemed to be in store for me if I persisted in leaving my grandmother, and that something, without making me afraid, did take away the charm of utter confidence I had had in building my castles in Spain.

"It will be worse than poverty," they told me, "it will be shame!" "Shame for what?" I asked myself. "Will I blush to be my mother's daughter? Oh, if it were only that! they know quite well that I'll have no part of such cowardly shame." I then imagined, without blaming anything in particular, some mysterious connection between my mother and someone else who might exercise unjust or illegitimate power over me. And then I intentionally abstained from thinking about it. "We'll see soon enough," I thought. "They want me seek answers; I shall not."

In order for me to live I have always had to have a fixed resolve to live for someone or something, people or ideas. This need had come to me naturally as it were, from childhood on, by force of circumstance, out of frustrated affection. It remained with me though my aim may have been obscured and my impulse wavered. They wished to tie me to another aim that they had shown me, from which I had obstinately turned away. I asked myself if it was possible, and sensed it was not. Wealth and education, pretty manners, wit, what they called "society," appeared to me in tangible forms, such as I was able to conceive them. "It all boils down," I thought, "to becoming a pretty young lady—spruced, starched, versed—tinkling on a piano in front of people who nod approval without hearing or understanding, caring for no one, wanting only to shine, aspiring to a rich marriage, selling her liberty and individuality for a carriage, a crest, a few scraps of silk, and some écus. That does not appeal to me and never will. If I must be forced to inherit this chateau, those sheaves of corn that Deschartres tallies up again and again, this library where nothing amuses me, and that wine cellar where nothing tempts me, it is no great happiness or lovely fortune! I have often dreamed of distant voyages. Voyages would have tempted me if I hadn't had the dream of living for my mother. Well then, fine! If my mother doesn't want anything from me, some day I'll leave; I'll go to the end of the world. I'll see Mount Etna and Mount Gibel, I'll go to

America, I'll go to India. They say it's far, that it's difficult, so much the better! They say you can die there, what does it matter? While I wait, let me live from day to day, let me live by chance. Since nothing I know tempts me or gives me comfort, let come what may."

Thereupon I tried to live without dreaming of anything, without fearing anything, and without wanting anything. That was difficult for me at first; I had formed such a habit of dreaming and hoping for a fine future that, in spite of myself, I began to dream about it again. But then the sadness would become so great and the memory of the scene of which I had been part so stifling, that I needed to escape from myself, and I would run to the fields to numb myself with the lively peasant boys and girls who loved me and snatched me from my lonely rumination.

Several months then passed which produced nothing and which I remember only vaguely because they were empty. I behaved very badly, working only enough to prevent my being scolded; hastening, so to speak, quickly to forget what I had just learned; no longer meditating on my work as I had done until then through a need for logic and poetry that had had its secret charm; running more than ever through the paths, bushes, and pastures with my noisy acolytes; turning the household upside-down with wild games; assuming a cheerful manner, sometimes forced, when my inner sadness threatened to reveal itself; finally turning completely into an enfant terrible, as my maid called me. And she was beginning to be right, who no longer beat me, however, seeing I had grown large enough to return as good as I got and that I was in no mood to suffer it any longer.

My grandmother saw all this as well and said to me, "My child, you no longer have any common sense. You used to have a mind, and you are doing your utmost to become or to appear stupid. You could have been attractive, and you are making yourself ugly on purpose. Your complexion is swarthy, your hands rough, your feet are getting deformed in those clogs. Your mind is becoming as warped and ungainly as your body. Sometimes you respond hardly at all and have the air of a free-thinker who disdains everything. At other times you speak without rhyme or reason, like a magpie that babbles for the sake of babbling. You have been a charming little girl, you must not become a preposterous young woman. You have no manners, no grace, no sense at all of what is fitting. You have a kind heart and a pitiful head. All that must be changed. Besides, you need tutoring in the social graces, and I cannot provide it for you here. I have therefore resolved to put you into a convent, and we shall go to Paris for that purpose."

"And am I going to see my mother?" I cried.

"Yes, certainly, you shall see her," my grandmama replied coldly. "And afterward, you shall leave her and me for as long a time as necessary to complete your education."

"Well," I thought, "a convent; I don't know what that is, but it will be new, and after all, since I'm not happy with the life I'm living, I shall be able to profit from the change."

Thus it was done. I saw my mother again, with my usual rapture. I had one last hope: that she would find the idea of the convent useless and ridiculous and that she would take me back with her when she saw how I had persisted in my resolution. On the contrary, she preached the advantages of riches and accomplishments, and did it in a way that astonished and wounded me, because I did not find her as frank and straightforward as usual in her remarks. She mocked the convent; she strongly criticized my grandmother on that score, who, although detesting and scorning religious devotion, was placing me in the care of nuns; but all the time she condemned her, my mother acted just as my grandmother did. She told me the convent would do me good and that I had to enter it. I have never had a strong will on my own behalf; I entered the convent without dread, regret, or repugnance. I took no account of the consequences. I was not aware that perhaps I would ironically be entering "society" when I crossed the threshold of the cloister; that I could form relationships there, habits of mind, even ideas that would incorporate me, so to speak, in the class with which I had wanted to break. On the contrary, I believed this convent was a neutral land and the years I would spend there a sort of way station in the midst of the struggle I was undergoing.

Once again in Paris, I saw Pauline de Pontcarré and her mother. Pauline was prettier than ever; her character had remained cheerful, easygoing, lovable. Nor had her heart changed. It remained perfectly cold, but that did not prevent my loving and admiring this apathetic beauty as I had in the past.

My grandmother had questioned Mme. de Pontcarré about the convent of the English sisters, the same convent where she had been a prisoner during the Revolution. A niece of Mme. de Pontcarré had been educated there and was on the point of leaving it. My grandmama, who had a rather clear memory of the convent and the nuns she had known there, was delighted to learn that Mlle. Debrosses had been well cared for and received a distinguished education, that sudents were well taught, that the tutors of the social graces were renowned; in short the English convent merited the reputation it enjoyed in the world of society, comparable to that of the convents of the Sacré-Coeur and Abbaye-aux-Bois. Mme. de Pontcarré had decided to place her daughter there, which, in fact, she did the next year. My grandmother therefore decided on the English convent, and one winter day, I was made to don the uniform of purplish serge, my outfits were put into a trunk, a hack drove us to the Rue de Fossés-Saint-Victor, and after we had waited a few minutes in the parlor, a door connecting to the convent was opened and then closed behind us. I was cloistered.

This convent was one of three or four British communities established at Paris during the time that Cromwell was in power. After having been the persecutors, the English Catholics were cruelly persecuted, and gathered in exile to pray and make a special plea to God for the conversion of the Protestants. The religious communities remained in France, although the Catholic kings regained the scepter in England and took revenge on their enemies in a manner that was scarcely Christian.

The community of English Augustines was the only one that had survived in Paris and whose housing had come through the revolutions without much disturbance. Tradition of the convent had it that the English queen, Henriette de France, daughter of our Henry IV and wife of the unfortunate Charles I, had often come to the convent with her son James II, to pray in the chapel and cure the scrofulous poor who crowded wherever they went. A dividing wall separated the convent from the Scottish school. The Irish Seminary was four doors away. All our nuns were English, Scottish, or Irish. Two-thirds of the pensioners and lodgers, as well as half the priests who came to officiate, were also from those nations. There were hours during the day when all classes were directed not to speak a word of French, the best possible method for learning English quickly. Our nuns, reasonably enough, rarely ever spoke to us in any other language. They maintained the customs of their region, taking tea three times a day, and permitting those of us who were well behaved to take tea with them.

The cloister and the church were paved with long funerary flagstones under which rested the venerated earthly remains of Catholics of early England, dead in exile and entombed by special grace in this inviolable sanctuary. Everywhere on the tombs and walls were epitaphs and religious maxims in English. In the chamber of the Mother Superior and in her special parlor were large old portraits of English princes or prelates. The beautiful and gallant Mary Stuart, considered a saint by our chaste nuns, shone there like a star. In a word, everything in that house was English, past and present, and once having passed through the grille, it seemed as if you had crossed the Channel.

For a peasant girl from Berry like me, this was too astonishing to be gotten over in a week. We were first received by the Mother Superior, Madame Canning, a very fat woman between fifty and sixty years old, beautiful despite her physical bulk, which contrasted sharply with her nimble wit. She prided herself, with reason, on being a woman of the world; she had elegant manners and fluency in conversation notwithstanding her strong accent; there was more mocking obstinacy in her gaze than self-contained sanctity. Her reputation was for kindness. And as her knowledge of the world enabled the convent to prosper, and as she was skilled in the ways of forgiveness—by virtue of the power of pardon that reserved for her the useful and helpful capacity, without appeal, of reconciling everyone—she was loved and respected by nuns and pensioners alike. But from the first, her look did not please me, and I had reason subsequently to believe that she was hard and shrewd. She died in the odor of sanctity, but I believe I am not wrong in thinking that she owed the veneration which surrounded her to her habit and her air of superiority.

When presenting me, my grandmother could not deny herself a little pride by saying that I had been very well educated for my age and that I would lose valuable time if I were put in the class with the younger children. Classes were divided into two sections: lower and upper. According to my age, I really belonged in the lower class, which was made up of thirty or so pensioners from six to thirteen or fourteen years of age. As a result of the reading I had been made to do and the ideas that the reading had developed in me, I really belonged to a third class that it would have been necessary to create for me and two or three others; but I had not been trained to work methodically, and I did not know a word of English. I understood a good deal of both history and philosophy, but I was very ignorant, or at least uncertain, about the sequence of periods and events. I would have been able to chat about anything with the professional teachers, and perhaps even have understood more clearly or been a little ahead of those who conducted our classes, but the first scholar who came along would have been able to embarrass me greatly on points of fact, and I would not have been able to pass a regular examination on any subject whatsoever.

I was well aware of this, and I was very relieved to hear the Mother Superior say that, not having received the sacrament of confirmation yet, I would perforce have to enter the lower class.

It was the recreation period. The Mother Superior called over one of the best-behaved girls of the lower class, entrusted me to her, and sent us out into the garden. I began immediately to go everywhere, look at everything, poke about in every corner of the garden, like a bird seeking a place to build its nest. I did not feel intimidated at all, although everyone was staring at me. It was apparent to me that everyone had more elegant manners than I; I watched the "big" girls passing back and forth, who did not play but chattered as they walked arm in arm. The young girl in charge of me told me the names of several; they were great names and very aristocratic, but that did not have the expected effect on me. I learned the names of the walkways, chapels, and arbors that adorned the garden. I was overjoyed to learn that we each were permitted to stake out a little corner of the beds and cultivate it as we wanted. Because this sort of amusement appealed only to the youngest girls, I felt that I would lack for neither earth nor labor.

A game of prisoner's base had started and I was chosen for one side. I did not know the rules of the game, but I did know how to run. My grandmother came out for a walk with the Mother Superior and the bursar, and she appeared to take pleasure in seeing me already so lively and at home. Then, she decided to take her leave and led me to the cloister to say good-bye. It was a solemn moment for her, and the excellent woman dissolved in tears when she embraced me. I was somewhat moved, but I thought it was my duty to accept my lot with a stout heart, and I did not cry. Then, looking fully into my face, my grandmother pushed me from her and cried, "Ah, you insensitive creature! you can leave me with no regret, that is obvious to me." And she left, her face hidden in her hands.

I was struck dumb. It seemed to me I had behaved well in not showing her any weakness, and from my point of view, my courage or resolution should have pleased her. I turned around and saw the bursar near me; she was named Mother Alippe, a little old woman as round as she was kind, a woman with an excellent disposition. "Well," she said to me, "what is it? Have you said something to your grandmother that displeased her?"

"I didn't say anything at all," I replied, "and I thought that I shouldn't say anything."

"Look here," she said, taking my hand, "are you unhappy at being here?" Because she spoke with a tone of frankness that could not be mistaken, I responded to her without hesitation, "Yes, Madame, in spite of myself, I feel sad and alone in the midst of people whom I don't know. I feel that there is no one here yet who can love me and that I'm no longer with my relatives who do love me a great deal. That's why I didn't want to cry in front of my grandmother, because it is her wish that I stay where she puts me. Was I wrong?"

"No, my child," Mother Alippe answered, "perhaps your grandmother didn't understand. Go and play, be good, and everyone here shall love you as much as at your relatives. Only remember, when you see your grandmama again, tell her that you didn't show sorrow in parting from her in order not to increase her own."

I returned to the game, but my heart was heavy. It seemed to me, and still seems to me, that my grandmother's reaction was very unjust. She was to blame if I considered the convent a penance she had imposed on me, because she had never failed to tell me, in her moments of scolding, that when I was at the convent, I would miss Nohant and the little comforts of my paternal home. It seemed as though she had been hurt by seeing me endure my punishment without rebellion or fear. "If it's for my own good that I'm here," I thought, "then I would be an ingrate to resent being here. If it's for my chastisement, well then, behold me chastised. What more do they want? That I suffer from being here? It's as though I'm to be beaten more severely because I refuse to cry at the first blow."

My grandmother went that same day to dine with my Great-Uncle Beaumont and recounted to him in tears how I had not wept. "Oh well, so much the better," he said with his philosophical cheeriness. "It is rather sad to be in a convent; don't wish that understanding on her. What wrong has she done that you impose reclusion on her and tears in the bargain? Dear sister, I have already told you that maternal love is often very egotistical, and we would have been very unhappy if our mother had loved her children as you love yours."

My grandmother was rather irritated by this lecture; she left early. Nor did she come back to see me for a week, although she had promised to return the day after I entered the convent. My mother, who came to see me in the interim, told me what had happened, and as usual, took my side. This augmented my inner bitterness. "Grandmama was wrong," I thought, "but my mother is wrong as well to aggravate things; I was wrong to do what I did, even though I thought I was right. I didn't mean to show any spite, but she thought I meant to show pride. My grandmama blames me for that, my mother approves of it; neither one understands me, and I see very well that this aversion they have for each other will surely render me unjust also, and very unhappy, if I ally myself blindly to either one."

From that time on I was happy in the convent; I experienced a powerful need to be rid of all those inner torments; I was weary of being the apple of discord between the two people I cherished. I almost wished to be forgotten.

That is how I accepted the convent, and accepted it so well that I came to be happier than I had ever been in my life. I believe that among all the children I knew there I was the only satisfied one. Everyone else missed her family, not only out of affection for her relatives, but also because she missed her freedom and comfort. Although I was from a less wealthy family and had never known great luxury, and although we were quite well treated at the convent, there was certainly a great difference as regarded material existence between Nohant and the cloister. In addition, the seclusion, the Paris air, and the unfailing sequence of the same routine—all of which I now regard as deadly to the progressive development or continual modification of the human system—soon made me somewhat ill and listless. In spite of all that, I spent three years there without longing for the past or dreaming of the future, and realized my happiness in the present—a situation understandable to all those who have suffered and know that, for them, the sole human happiness is the absence of excessive hurt, and yet an exceptional situation for children of wealth and one that my classmates did not understand when I told them that I had no wish for an end of my captivity.

We were cloistered in every sense of the word. We were able to leave the convent only twice a month and allowed to sleep outside only once a year. There were vacations, but I did not have any; my grandmother said that she preferred not to interrupt my studies so that my tenure in the convent might be shorter. She left Paris a few weeks after our separation, did not return for a year, and then left again for yet another year. She had also exacted a promise from my mother that she would not ask to take me out. My Villeneuve cousins offered to have me with them on the days we were allowed to leave the convent, and they wrote to my grandmother to ask permission. But I, too, wrote to her, to beg that she not give permission, and I had the courage to tell her that, if I couldn't go out with my mother, I didn't want to go out with anyone else, nor should I have to. I trembled to think that she might not listen to me, and although I did feel a slight urge for outings, I had decided that I would make myself sick if my cousins came for me armed with permission from my grandmother. This time, however, my grandmother approved, and instead of reproaching me, she praised my sentiments in a way that I found even a little exaggerated. I had done nothing but my duty.

And so I spent over two years behind the cloister grille. We had mass in our chapel, we received visits in the parlor, we took our private lessons there, the teacher on one side of the barrier, we on the other. All the casements of the convent that opened on the street were not only barred, but were also hung with canvas screens. It was quite truly a prison, but a prison with a big garden and numerous companions. I confess that not for a moment did I experience any of the rigors of captivity, and the meticulous precautions that were taken to keep us under lock and key and prevent our having even a glimpse of the outside world only struck me as funny. These precautions were the sole stimulus of a desire for liberty, because the Rue des Fossés-Saint-Victor and Rue Clopin were tempting neither as places to walk nor even for the view. Not one of us would ever have dreamed of crossing her mother's threshold alone; still we all peeped through the crack in the cloister door, or stole furtive glances through the slits in the window screens. To thwart the surveillance, to descend two or three steps into the courtyard, to catch sight of a passing hack, this was the ambition and dream of forty or fifty playful and prankish girls, who would, before long, be touring all Paris with their parents without taking the least pleasure in it, mixing with the crowds in the streets, and regarding the passing scene no longer as forbidden fruit beyond the confines of the convent.

During those years, my moral being underwent changes that I could never have foreseen and that my grandmother viewed with a great deal of pain, as if in putting me there she ought not to have foreseen them herself. The first year, I was more than ever the enfant terrible I had begun to be, because a sort of despair, or at least a desperation in my affections pushed me to lose myself and revel in my own mischievousness. Thereafter, I passed almost immediately into a sort of ardent and nervous piety. And by the end, I had achieved a state of calm observance, firm and joyful. The first year, my grandmother scolded me a great deal in her letters. The second, she was more frightened of my devotion than she had been of my rebellion. And finally, she appeared almost satisfied and let me know she was content, although her contentment was always mixed with uneasiness.

This is a résumé of my life in the convent, but the details contain certain particularities of which more than one person of my sex will recognize the effects—sometimes good, sometimes bad—of a religious education. I shall report them without the least prejudice and, I hope, with perfect sincerity of heart and mind.   *R.I.H.*

XI

Description of the convent. —The lower class. —The pain and sadness of children. —Miss D., Class Mistress. —Mary Eyre. —Mother Alippe. —Limbo. —The sign of the cross. —The "devils," the "sages," and the "beasts." —Mary Gillibrand. —Escapades. —Isabelle Clifford. —Her strange creations. —Sophie Cary. —The convent's mystery. —Searches and expeditions for liberating the "victim." —The underground passageways. —The mysterious impasse. —A walk on the rooftops. —A comical accident. —Whiskey and the lay sisters. —The cold. —I become a devil. —My relations with the sages and the beasts. —My leave days. —Great uproar against me. —My correspondence is intercepted. —I move to the upper class.

Before recounting my life in the convent, I must first describe the convent a little. Where we live has such a great influence on our thoughts it is hard to separate the memories from the places.

It was a collection of buildings, courtyards, and gardens, which made it more of a village than a house. There was nothing outstanding for the architect, nothing of particular interest to the antiquary. Since its construction, which went back no more than two hundred years, there had been so many successive changes, additions, or renovations, that the original character was to be found only in very few sections. But this heterogeneous whole had its own character, something of labyrinthine mystery and complexity, and a certain poetic charm with which cloistered nuns know how to endow the most ordinary things. I spent a whole month learning how to find my way around by myself, and even then, after a thousand furtive explorations, I never got to know all the round-about ways and hidden corners.

The façade, lower than street level, gave no hint of anything unusual. It was a large structure, ugly and bare, with a small arched doorway that led to a flight of stone steps—wide, straight, and steep. At the top of seventeen steps (if I remember correctly), you found yourself in a small courtyard paved with flagstones and surrounded by low buildings with blank walls—on one side, the church; on the other, the cloister.

A porter who lived in the courtyard and whose lodge abutted the cloister door gave access to people outside to a corridor through which they had contact with those inside by means of a turning box for leaving parcels and four grilled parlors for visiting. The first parlor was set aside especially for nuns' visitors; the second was intended for private lessons; the third, which was the largest, was where the resident students saw their relatives; the fourth was where the Mother Superior received members of society, which did not preclude her from having a salon in another part of the main building and a large grilled parlor where she conversed with ecclesiastics or members of her family, when she had important private business to conduct.

That was all that men, and even women who did not have special permission to enter, might see of the convent. We shall penetrate this well-guarded interior.

The courtyard door is armed with a grating and opens noisily on the echoing cloister. This cloister is a quadrangular gallery, paved with sepulchral stones on which are inscribed innumerable skulls, crossbones, and *requiescant in paces*. The cloisters are vaulted, lighted by wide, arched windows opening on the inner courtyard, with its traditional well and flower bed. One end of the cloister opens on the church and garden, another on the new building, where are located, on the ground floor, the upper class; on the mezzanine, the workroom of the nuns; on the first and second floors, the cells; and on the third, the dormitory of the boarders of the lower class.

The third angle of the cloister leads to the kitchens, the cellars, and then to the building of the lower class, which is joined to several other very old ones that no longer exist,[15] for even in my time they were threatening to cave in. It was a maze of dark corridors, winding stairways, small apartments detached or connected by uneven landings or passageways with warped planks. This was probably what remained of the original construction, and the efforts that had been made to join the old buildings to the new attested either a great period of economy during the times of revolution or a great ineptitude on the part of the architects. There were galleries that led nowhere, openings like those seen in dreams, through which you could hardly pass and in which you are running through strange buildings that are closing in and suffocating you in their suddenly converging corners. This part of the convent defies all description. I shall give a better idea of it when I recount the mad explorations our wild, schoolgirls' imaginations made us undertake. At present, suffice it to say that the functions of these structures were as incongruous as their assembly. Here were the quarters of a tenant; next door, those of a pupil; farther down, a room for piano practice; elsewhere, a linen closet; then rooms vacant or temporarily occupied by friends from overseas; and then there were anonymous corners such as those where old maids, especially nuns, collect, for no apparent reason, a host of objects which must be quite surprised to find themselves together: remnants of church ornaments with onions, broken chairs with empty bottles, cracked bells with torn, old clothes, and so on.

The garden was vast and planted with superb chestnut trees. On one side it abutted that of the Scottish school, from which it was separated by a very high wall; on the other side it was bordered by small houses, all tenanted by pious ladies who had retired from the world. In addition to this garden there was also, in front of the new building, a double courtyard planted as a vegetable garden and bordered by other houses likewise rented to elderly matrons or boarders who roomed privately. This part of the convent ended in a laundry room and a door that opened on Rue des Boulangers. This door was opened only for tenants, who had a visiting parlor on that side. After the large garden I mentioned, there was another even larger one, which we were never permitted to enter and which served for the consumption of the convent. It was a huge vegetable garden which extended as far as that of Sisters of Mercy and was filled with magnificent flowers, vegetables, and fruits. We observed through a vast fence the golden grapes, majestic melons, and beautiful, variegated garden pinks, but the fence was virtually unassailable, and you risked your bones to scale it, which did not prevent some of us from making two or three impromptu penetrations.

I have not spoken of the church and the cemetery, the only really remarkable places in the convent; I shall speak of them at the right time and place. I find my general description is already much too long.

Let me say, by way of summary, that, including nuns and lay sisters, boarders, tenants, lay teachers, and servants, we were about a hundred twenty or thirty persons lodged in the most bizarre and inconvenient manner, some too crowded into designated areas, others too scattered over a space where ten families might have lived very comfortably, even while cultivating a little land for their enjoyment. Everything was so spread out that people wasted a quarter of their day just in coming and going. Nor have I spoken of a vast laborabory where mint cordial was distilled, or of the "cloister chamber" where certain lessons were given and which had served as a prison for my mother and my aunt; of the poultry yard that polluted the lower class; of the rear classroom where we had lunch; of the cellars and sub-cellars, of which I shall have a great deal to say; or, finally, of the front classroom, the refectory, and the chapter-house, for I would never be done convincing you, by all these dispersions, how little the nuns believe in logical layout and true ease of habitation.

On the other hand, the cells of the nuns were charmingly clean and filled with all those knick-knacks that fastidious devotion patiently cuts out, frames, illuminates, and beribbons. On all corners, grapevines and jasmine hid the decay of the walls. The cocks crowed at midnight, as if in the countryside; the bell had a pretty, silvery sound like a feminine voice; in all the passageways, a niche cut gracefully into the wall opened to show you a plump and mannered madonna, in the seventeenth-century style; in the workroom, fine English engravings presented to you the chivalrous figure of Charles I, at all ages of his life, and all the members of the papist royal family. In short, everything—from the small lamp that flickered all night in the cloister to the heavy doors at the entrance to the corridors which were closed each evening with a solemn noise and a gloomy grinding of bolts—had a certain charm of mystical poetry which, sooner or later, would make an impression on me.

Now I shall tell my story. My first reaction on entering the lower class was painful. About thirty of us were crammed into a small, low-ceilinged room. The walls were covered with a vile yellow paper the color of egg yolks; the ceiling dirty and pealing; filthy benches, tables, and stools; a wretched stove which smoked; the stench of henhouse mixed with that of coal; an ugly plaster crucifix. This was where we were to spend two-thirds of the day, three-quarters in winter, and we were just then in the winter season.

Nothing makes me more depressed than the custom that educational institutions seem to have of rendering the classroom the saddest and most punitive place; under the pretext that children would ruin the furniture and damage the accessories, we remove from their sight everything that would stimulate their thoughts or charm their imaginations. We claim that pictures and ornaments, even designs on wallpaper, are distracting for them. Why then adorn churches and chapels with paintings and statues, if not to elevate the soul and rekindle it in its languor through the view of sacred objects? Children, it is said, are habitually dirty or clumsy. They throw ink around, they like to break things. However, these tastes and habits do not originate in their parents' house, where they are taught to respect the beautiful or the useful, and where, as soon as they reach an age of reason, it does not occur to them to commit all that havoc. It has so much attraction for them in boarding and preparatory schools only as a sort of revenge against the negligence or stinginess with which they are treated. The better you lodged them, the more careful they would be. They would think twice before soiling a carpet or cracking a frame. Those ugly, bare walls which confine them soon become an object of horror, and they would tear them down if they could. You want them to work like machines; you want their minds—devoid of all distraction—to function by the hour and be inaccessible to all that makes for intellectual life and its renewal. It is a wrong and impossible wish. The studying child already has all the needs of the creating artist. He must breathe pure air, he must have at least some comfort for his body, he must be impressed by images from outside, and he must refresh at will the quality of his thoughts through the appreciation of color and form. Nature is a continuous spectacle for him. By shutting him up in a barren, unwholesome, and dismal room, you stifle his heart and mind as well as his body. I would like for everything to be cheerful around the urban child, from the time he is in his cradle. The child of the country has the sky and trees, plants and sunshine. The urban child too often wilts, mentally and physically, in squalor in the home of the poor, in bad taste in the home of the rich, or in the absence of taste in the home of the middle class.

Why are Italians born with some sort of feeling for beauty? Why do a mason from Verona, a shopkeeper of Venice, a peasant of the Roman countryside like to contemplate beautiful monuments? Why do they understand beautiful paintings, good music, while our proletarians, more intelligent in other respects, and our middle classes, reared with greater care, love the false, the vulgar, even the ugly in the arts, unless some special form of education comes along to improve their instincts? Because we live with the ugly and the vulgar, because our parents have no taste, and because we pass on the traditional bad taste to our children.

To surround childhood with pleasant, lofty objects, which are at the same time instructive, would be only a token. Above all, it would be necessary to entrust childhood only to persons distinguished either in feeling or intellect.

Hence, I do not understand why our nuns—so lovely, so kind, and endowed with such noble or gracious manners—had placed at the head of the lower class a person of repulsive appearance, expression, and bearing, with language and character to match. Fat, dirty, stooped, bigoted, limited, irascible, strict to the point of being cruel, sly, vindictive, she was, from the first look, an object for my moral and physical disgust, as she already was for all my classmates.

There are unsympathetic types who sense the dislike they inspire, who can never overcome it even if they want to, because they drive others from the proper course merely by preaching to them, and because they are reduced to "seeking their own salvation," which is the most sterile and least pious thing in the world. Miss D. was one of those. I would be unjust toward her if I did not state the pro as well as the contra. She was sincere in her devotion and a rigid practitioner; she brought to her religion a stubborn exaltation which made her intolerant and hateful, but which would have had a kind of grandeur had she dwelt in the desert like the anchorites whose faith she professed. In her dealings with us, her austerity became fierce; she took joy in punishing, revelled in scolding, and in her mouth, scolding was meant as insult and outrage. She mingled deception with her strictness and would pretend to leave the room (which she should never have done as long as she was in charge of the class) in order to overhear us speaking ill of her, delighted to catch us red-handed in the act of being honest. Then she would punish us in the most stupid and humiliating way. She would make us, among other obsequies, kiss the ground for what she called our wicked words. That was part of convent discipline, but the nuns were satisfied with a simulation and would pretend not to see we were kissing our hand while bowing toward the floor; Miss D., on the other hand, pushed our faces into the dust, and might have crushed them if we had resisted.

It was easy to see that her personality demanded her severity, and that she experienced a sort of rage to be hated. There was in the class a poor little English girl about five or six years old, pale, delicate, sickly, a real *chacrot*, as we say in Berry, to designate the skinniest and weakest chick in the brood. Her name was Mary Eyre, and Miss D. did try her best to take an interest in her and perhaps even love her like a mother. But that accorded so little with her mannish and brutal nature that she could never see it through. If she reprimanded her, the child was struck with such terror or so provoked that the teacher was at length forced, so as not to lose face, to confine or beat her. If the teacher became human enough to tease and want to play with her, it was like a bear with a grasshopper. The little girl would always get furious and scream, either for the sake of rebellious mischief, or out of anger and despair. From morning till night the irritating struggle between this big, nasty woman and this glum and miserable little child was unbearable to see and hear, to say nothing of the flare-ups and rigors of which we were all in turn the object.

I had wanted to go into the lower class out of a feeling of modesty, which is rather common among children whose relatives are overly vain, but I soon felt humiliated and heartsick to be under the iron rule of this old flogger in soiled petticoats. She got up in a bad mood, she went to bed the same way. I was scarcely three days in her sight before she took an aversion to me and made it clear that I was going to have to deal with a nature as violent as Rose's, minus the latter's frankness, affection, and generosity. From the first attentive glance with which she honored me—"You appear to me a very dissipated person," she said—from that moment on, I was ranked among her chief dislikes, for gaiety pained her; the laughter of childhood made her grit her teeth; health, humor, youth, in short, were crimes in her eyes.

Our times of relief and relaxation were those when a nun led the class in her place, but that lasted an hour or two at most during the whole day.

It was an error on the part of our nuns to concern themselves so little with us directly. We loved them; they all had some distinction, charm, or solemnity, something sweet or serious, even if only in appearance and dress, which soothed us like magic. Their reclusion, their renunciation of world and family had this unique advantage to society, namely, that they could devote themselves to forming our hearts and our minds, and this task would have been easy for them if they had concerned themselves with it exclusively. But they claimed not to have the time for it, and they indeed did not, because of the long hours they gave to church services and prayers. That is the disadvantage of convent schools for girls. They employ what they call "lay teachers," types of female "proctors," who play the hypocrite in front of the nuns, and, unsupervised, brutalize or exasperate the children. Our nuns would have been more deserving of the gratitude of God, our parents, and ourselves, if they had sacrificed to our happiness and salvation (to use their own expression), a portion of the time they selfishly consecrated to seeking their own.

The nun who took over from these ladies from time to time was Mother Alippe. She was small and as round and rosy as an overly ripe lady-apple that is starting to wrinkle. She was not at all affectionate, but she was fair, and although she was not particularly gracious toward me, I liked her, as did the others.

Responsible for our religious instruction, she asked me, on the first day, about the place where "languished" the souls of the children who had died without baptism. I knew nothing at all on that score; I did not suspect that there was a place of exile or punishment for those poor little creatures, and I answered boldly that they went to rest in the bosom of God. "What are you thinking of and what are you saying, unhappy child?" cried Mother Alippe. "You did not hear me. I am asking you where the souls of the children go who have died without baptism."

I was at a loss. One of my classmates, taking pity on my ignorance, whispered to me, "In limbo!" Since she was English, her accent confused me, and I thought she was playing a bad joke on me. "In Olympia?" I said aloud, turning around and bursting into laughter. "For shame!" cried Mother Alippe, "you are laughing during catechism?" "Excuse me, Mother Alippe," I answered, "I didn't do it on purpose."

As I was sincere, she was appeased. "Well," she said, "since it was in spite of yourself, you will not have to kiss the ground, but make the sign of the cross in order to collect and compose youself."

Unfortunately I did not know how to make a proper sign of the cross. It was Rose's fault; she had taught me to touch the right shoulder before the left, and my old curé had never noticed it. At the sight of this enormity, Mother Alippe knitted her brow. "Are you doing that on purpose, *Miss*?" "Alas! no, Madame. Why?"

"Begin that sign of the cross again."

"All right, Reverend Mother!"

"Again!"

"Gladly, and again?"

"And that is how you always do it?"

"My God, yes."

"*My God*! You said '*my God*'! You are swearing!"

"I don't think so."

"Ah! unfortunate girl, where do you come from? She is a pagan, a real pagan, indeed! She says that souls go to Olympia, she makes the sign of the cross from right to left, and she says 'my God' ouside of prayer! Well, you shall learn your catechism with Mary Eyre. Even she knows more than you do!"

I was not very humbled, I confess; I bit my lips and pinched my nose to keep from laughing, but the religion of the convent appeared to me to be such a stupid and ridiculous affair that I resolved not to let it bother me, and above all never to take it seriously.

I was mistaken. My day would come, but it did not come as long as I was in the lower class. For me that was a milieu totally unfit for reflection, and I would surely never have become devout if I had stayed under the odious yoke of Miss D. and under the iron, pedantic rule of good Mother Alippe.

I had not taken any stand on entering the convent. I was more inclined to docility than revolt. It was obvious to all that I arrived there without ill humor and without grief; I wished nothing more than to submit to the general discipline. But when I saw that this discipline was so stupid in a thousand ways and so nastily administered, I cocked my hat and resolutely enlisted on the side of the "devils."

This name was given to the girls who were not and did not wish to be devout. The devout ones were called "sages." There was an intermediate variety whom we called "beasts," and who sided with no one, roaring with laughter at the mischievousness of the devils, lowering their eyes and falling silent as soon as the teachers or the sages appeared, and never failing to say as soon as there was any danger, "I didn't do it!"

And to that selfish refrain of "I didn't do it," certain beasts who were complete cowards soon took up the habit of adding, "It was Dupin or Gillibrand."

Dupin was me; Gillibrand was something else—the most striking figure in the lower class and the most eccentric in the whole convent.

She was an eleven-year-old Irish girl, much bigger and stronger than I was at thirteen. Her resonant voice, her frank, bold face, her independent and indomitable character had caused her to be given the nickname "Boy"; and although she was indeed a woman, who later became beautiful, she was not characteristically female. She was the personification of pride and sincerity, had a truly beautiful nature, physical strength that was completely manly, courage that was more than manly, rare intelligence, a complete absence of coquettishness, an exuberant personality, and a profound disdain for all that was false and lax about society. She had many brothers and sisters, of whom two were at the convent; one (Marcella), an outstanding person, never married, and the other (Henriette), then a friendly child, became Mme. Vivien.

Mary Gillibrand, or Boy, was absent because of some indisposition when I entered the convent. They painted me a frightful picture of her. She was the bane of the beasts, who naturally had approached me to begin with. The sages had felt me out, and since they feared Mary's noise and irrepressibility, they tried to put me on guard against her. I admit that I, too, was fearful, given their depiction. There were some inventive girls who would tell, in an aura of mystery, and firmly believed, how she was really a boy whose parents had absolutely insisted on making into a girl. She broke everything, she harassed everyone, she was stronger than the gardener; she impeded the hired women in their work; she was a scourge, a plague. Woe to the one who would dare stand up to her! "We'll soon see," said I. "I'm strong too, I'm not a coward, and I indeed like to be left to speak and think as I wish." Nevertheless, I waited for her with anxiety. I would not have wanted to feel I had an enemy, or even someone unfriendly, among my classmates. To have to contend with the D., our common enemy, was quite enough.

Mary arrived, and from the very first look, her sincere face appealed to me. "That's good," I told myself, "we'll get along after all." But it was up to her, having been at the convent longer, to approach me. I awaited her peacefully.

She began the banter. "Mademoiselle is named *du pain*? some bread? she's called Aurore? dawn? rising-sun? What pretty names! and what a lovely face! She has the head of a horse on the neck of a chicken. Sunrise, I prostrate myself before you; I wish to be the sunflower which will greet your first rays. It seems that we take limbo for Olympia; a fine education, faith, and one which promises to entertain us!"

The entire class broke out into a huge peal of laughter. The beasts especially laughed hard enough to dislocate their jaws. The sages were glad to see two devils, whose association they feared, in combat.

I began to laugh as good-naturedly as the others. Mary saw right away that I had no vanity, hence no resentment. She continued to make fun of me, but without meanness, and an hour later, she gave me a thump on the shoulder that could have killed an ox, which I gave back to her, smiling and without batting an eye. "That's good!" she said, rubbing her shoulder. "Let's go for a walk."

"Where?"

"Anywhere, except to the classroom."

"How do we do that?"

"It's quite tricky! Watch me, and do the same."

We were getting up to change tables; Mother Alippe was coming in with her texts and notebooks. Mary took advantage of the stir, and without the least precaution, without even being noticed by anyone, crossed the threshold and went to sit in the deserted cloister, where three minutes later I joined her without further ado.

"Is that you?" she asked me. "What did you think up to get out?"

"Absolutely nothing, I did what I saw you doing."

"That's very good! she said. "Some of them invent stories, they ask to go practice the piano, or they have a nosebleed, or they claim they're going to offer up a salutary prayer in church; these are worn out excuses and useless lies. As for me, I've rejected lying, because lying is cowardly. I go out, I go back in, they question me, I give no answer. They punish me, I couldn't care less, and I do everything I want."

"That suits me too."

"So you're a devil?"

"I want to be one."

"As much as I?"

"Neither more nor less."

"That's the spirit!" she said, giving me a handshake. "Let's go back in now and behave in front of Mother Alippe. She's a good woman, let's save ourselves for the D. Every evening, outside of class, do you understand?"

"What do you mean, 'outside of class'?"

"The evening recreation periods in the classroom, under the eyes of the D., are very boring. We disappear on leaving the refectory, and we don't go back until it's time for prayers. Sometimes the D. pays no attention; most often, she's delighted, because then she has the pleasure of insulting and punishing us. The punishment is to wear one's nightcap all the next day, even at church. In this weather, it's very comfortable and good for one's health. The nuns whom you meet thus make the sign of the cross and shout, 'Shame! shame!' which doesn't hurt a soul. When you've had to wear the nightcap many times in a fortnight, the Superior threatens to deprive you of going out. She lets your parents prevail on her, or she forgets. When the nightcap becomes a chronic condition, she decides to keep you in, but what difference does that make? Isn't it better to give up one day of pleasure than to bore yourself voluntarily all the days of your life?"

"That's good thinking, but what does the D. do to you when her hatred goes to extremes?

"She insults you like the fishwife that she is. You don't answer her, she rages all the more."

"Does she strike you?"

"She is dying to, but she has no pretext for going that far, because the sages and beasts tremble before her, and the others, like us, despise her and keep silent."

"How many of us devils are there in the class?"

"Not many, at the present moment, and it was time for you to come along to reinforce us a bit. There are Isabelle, Sophie, and the two of us. All the others are beasts or sages. Among the sages, there are Louise de La Rochejaquelin and Valentine de Gouy, who have as much spirit as the devils and are good, but not bold enough to desert the class. But rest assured, there are those of the upper class who go out in the same way and who will come to join us tonight. My sister Marcella is sometimes among them."

"And what do you do then?"

"You'll see, you'll be initiated this evening."

I awaited nightfall and the supper hour with great impatience. On leaving the refectory we began our recreation period. In summer the two classes mingled in the garden. In winter (and it was winter), each class returned to its own area, the older girls to their handsome, spacious study hall, and we to our sad quarters, where we did not have enough space to play, and where the D. forced us to "play quietly," that is to say, have no fun at all. The departure from the refectory brought about a moment of confusion, and I marveled at how much the devils of the two classes fostered this little disorder, thanks to which we could escape easily. The cloister was illuminated only by a small lamp which left the other three galleries in semi-darkness. Instead of walking straight ahead to reach the lower class, we would rush into the gallery on the left, let the herd file past, and we were free.

I then found myself in the darkness with my friend Gillibrand and the other devils whom she had named to me. Of those who were with us that evening, I remember only Sophie and Isabelle; they were the oldest of the lower class. They were two or three years older than I, two charming girls. Isabelle, blond, tall, hale, pleasant rather than pretty, the most vivacious of characters, teasing though kind, noteworthy and noted above all for the talent, ease, and busyness of her pencil. She was clearly gifted with a genius for drawing. I do not know what became of this natural gift, but it could have made her name and fortune, had it been developed. She had what none of us had, what women usually do not have, what they did not teach us at all, although we had a drawing teacher—she really knew how to draw. She was capable of successfully composing a complicated subject; she created in the wink of an eye, and without seeming to give it much thought, groups of characters who were all realistic in their movements, all comic while possessing a certain grace, all grouped with a sort of *maestria*. She was not lacking in spoken wit, but drawing, caricature, and obsessive composition served as the main expression of it, which was simultaneously thoughtful and spontaneous, fabulous, whimsical, satirical, and impassioned. She would take a piece of paper, and with her spattering pen, or a poor stub of charcoal which the eye could scarcely follow, she dashed off hundreds of figures, all well-grouped, boldly drawn, and pertinent to the drawing's theme, which was always original and often bizarre. There were processions of nuns who were crossing a Gothic cloister, or a cemetery, in the moonlight. The gravestones lifted at their approach, the dead in their shrouds began to move. They were emerging, starting to sing, play various instruments, take the nuns by the hand, make them dance. The nuns were afraid, some of them ran away shrieking, others became bolder, began to dance, dropped their veils, their mantles, and went off into the distance, twirling and capering with the ghosts in the misty night.

In others there were false nuns, who had goats' feet or Louis XIII boots, with enormous spurs, which were revealed from beneath their trailing robes by an unexpected positioning. Romanticism had not yet been discovered, and here she was deeply into it without being aware of what she was doing. Her lively imagination had furnished her with a hundred subjects for *danses macabres*, although she had never heard of them and did not know the term. Death and the Devil played all the roles, all the possible characters in her terrible and burlesque compositions. And then there would be interior scenes, striking caricatures of all the nuns, the resident students, the servants, the tutors of social graces, the teachers, the visitors, the priests, etc. She was the faithful and eternally fertile chronicler of all the little events, the mystifications, panics, battles, amusements, nuisances of our monastic life. The constant drama of Miss D. with Mary Eyre daily provided her with twenty pages, each more faithful, more pitiful, more humorous than the one before. All told, we could no more grow weary of seeing her create than she herself could grow weary of creating. Since she would create in this way on the sly, at all hours, during lessons, under the very eyes of our Arguses, she often had only the time to tear out the page, crumple it up in her hands, and throw it out the window or into the fire, in order to escape discovery, which would have brought sharp reprimands or severe punishments. How many of her unknown masterpieces did the stove of the lower class devour! Perhaps retrospective imagination makes me exaggerate their worth, but it seems to me that all those creations, sacrificed as soon as they were produced, are very much to be regretted, and that they would have surprised and interested a true master.

Sophie was the bosom friend of Isabelle. She was one of the prettiest and the most gracious person in the convent. Her supple waist, slender and shapely at the same time, affected a British languor, instead of the awkwardness common to those islanders. She had a round, strong, elongated neck, with a small head whose swaying movements were full of charm, and the most beautiful eyes in the world; a straight forehead, short and stubborn, crowned with a forest of shiny brown hair; her nose, though ugly, did not manage to spoil her ravishing face. She had a mouth—rare among Englishwomen—pink, quite literally filled with small pearls; a wonderful glow and velvety skin, very fair for a brunette. In short, they called her "the jewel." She was kind and sentimental, passionate in her friendships, implacable in her aversions, but manifesting the latter only by means of a silent, unconquerable disdain. Adored by many, she deigned to love a chosen few. I was taken with great affection for her and Isabelle, and this was returned with more protectiveness than enthusiasm. It was in the order of things. For them I was a child.

When we had gathered in the cloister, I saw that all of them were armed, some with a log, some with a pair of fire tongs. I had nothing, but I was bold enough to go back into the classroom, seize an iron rod that was used to stir the stove, and get back to my accomplices without being noticed.

Thereupon, I was initiated into the great mystery, and we set out on our expedition.

This great mystery was the traditional legend of the convent, a fantasy which had been handed down from generation to generation, and from devil to devil, for perhaps two centuries; a romantic fiction which could well have had some basis in reality in the beginning, but which now certainly rested only on the needs of our imaginations. It was a question of "liberating the victim."

There was a female prisoner somewhere—some even said several prisoners—shut up in an impenetrable hole, either a cell hidden and immured in the thick walls, or else a dungeon located under the vaults of the immense subterranean passageways which extended under the convent and beneath a large part of the Saint-Victor district. There were, in fact, magnificent cellars, a veritable underground city whose end we never saw, and which offered several mysterious exits to different points of the vast site of the convent. We were convinced that these caverns went for a great distance to join the excavations which stretch out under more than half of Paris and beneath the surrounding countryside as far as Vincennes. Rumor had it that by following the fine cellars of our convent, one could connect with the catacombs, the quarries, the palace of the Thermae of Julian, and who knows where else. These underground passageways were the keys to a world of darkness, terror, and mystery—an immense chasm carved out under our feet, closed off with iron doors, whose exploration was as perilous as the descent into hell of Aeneas or Dante. For that reason it was absolutely necessary to penetrate that region, in spite of the insurmountable difficulties of the undertaking and the terrible punishments which the discovery of our secret would have provoked.

To reach the subterranean passages was one of those unhoped-for pieces of good luck which happened once or twice at the most in the life of a devil, after years of perseverance and intense application of mind. Entering through the main door was completely out of the question. That door was situated at the base of a broad staircase next to the kitchens, which were also cellars, and where the lay sisters always stayed.

But we were convinced that we could gain entry underground through a thousand other places, even through the roofs. According to our way of thinking, every blocked-up door, every dark nook behind a staircase, every wall that sounded hollow could be a secret link with the subterranean passages, and we looked for this link in good faith as high up as the eaves.

I had read with delight and terror, at Nohant, the *Château des Pyrénées* of Mrs. Radcliffe. My companions had their brains full of other Scottish and Irish legends, sufficient to make one's hair stand on end. The convent, too, had an abundance of stories of lamentable events, ghosts, hiding places, unexplained apparitions, mysterious noises. All that, plus the idea of finally solving the formidable mystery of the victim, so kindled our wild imaginations that we convinced ourselves that we heard sighs and moans coming from under the paving stones or issuing from the cracks in the doors and walls.

There we were, launched—my classmates for the hundredth time, I for the first—in search of that elusive captive who was languishing we knew not where, but somewhere certainly, and whom we were perhaps being called on to discover. She must have been quite ancient considering the great number of years she had been sought in vain! She could well be two hundred years old, but we did not pay attention to such details. We searched, we called to her, we thought of her incessantly, we would never give up.

That evening I was led into a part of the buildings which I have already sketched, the oldest, the most ramshackle, the most exciting for our explo-

rations. We fastened on a little corridor, edged by a wooden handrail and leading to an empty stairwell, without any known exit. A staircase, likewise edged
by a railing, went down to this unknown region, but an oak door blocked the
entrance to the staircase. To get around the obstacle, we had to cross from one
railing to the other by walking on the outer edge of the worm-eaten balusters.
Below was a dark void whose depth we could not fathom. We had but a small
taper which shed light only on the nearest steps of the mysterious staircase.
This was a game which could have broken our necks. Isabelle went first, with
the resolve of a heroine, Mary with the ease of a gymnast, the others with
greater or lesser agility, but all with happiness.

Here we are at last on this strictly forbidden staircase. In an instant we
are at the bottom of the steps, and with more joy than disappointment, we find
ourselves in a square space situated under the gallery, a true impasse. No door,
no window, no visible purpose to this species of vestibule that leads nowhere.
Why then a staircase to go down into an impasse? Why a solid, padlocked door
to seal off the staircase?

We divide the little candle into several stubs, and each girl examines her
vicinity. The staircase is made of wood. There must be a secret step that opens
to a passage, a new staircase, or a trapdoor. While some of us explore the staircase and try our skill at separating the old planks, others tap the wall and look
for a knob, a chink, a ring, one of those myriad devices which, in the novels of
Radcliffe and in the chronicles of the old manor houses, move a stone, turn a
portion of the woodwork, open some sort of entrance to unknown regions.

But, alas, nothing! the wall is smooth and built of plaster. The flagstone
renders a flat sound, all the paving stones are level, the staircase conceals no
secret. Isabelle is not discouraged. At the apex of the angle which goes back
under the staircase, she declares that the wall sounds hollow; we knock, we
verify the fact. "It's there!" someone exclaims. "There's a walled-up passageway, and it's the one to the famous hiding place. It's the way down into the
sepulcher that imprisons living victims." We put our ears to this wall, we hear
nothing, but Isabelle is sure she hears vague moans, chains creaking. What to
do? "It's quite simple," says Mary, "we must demolish the wall. With all of us
helping, we shall certainly be able to make a hole in it."

Nothing seemed easier to us; there we were, working on that wall, some
trying to break it open with their logs, others scraping it with their shovels and
tongs, without thinking that in applying ourselves thus to those poor trembling
walls we risked causing the building to come crashing down on our heads. Fortunately we could not do it much harm, because we could not strike a resounding blow with a log without calling someone's attention to the noise. We had to
be satisfied with pushing and scratching. However, we had succeeded in chopping rather noticeably into the plaster, lime, and stones, when the bell rang for
prayers. We barely had time to begin our perilous climb, put out our lights,
separate, and get back to the classrooms in the dark. We put off to the next day
the pursuit of our undertaking, and arrangements were made to meet at the
same place. Those who arrived first need not wait for those who might be
delayed by a punishment or unusual surveillance. We would work at hollowing

out the wall, each girl doing her best. The same would be done the next day. There was no risk that anyone would notice it, since no one ever went down into that impasse abandoned to spiders and mice.

We helped each other brush off the dust and plaster with which we were covered, we went back to the cloister and returned to our respective classes as they were kneeling for prayer. I no longer remember if we were noticed and punished that evening. So often we were that no punishment is associated with a particular date. But quite often, too, we could pursue our task with impunity. In the evening Miss D. would knit, while prattling and wrangling with Mary Eyre. The classroom was dark, and I believe her eyesight was poor. Nor did her rage for spying endow her in any way with second-sight, and it was always easy for us to escape. Once out of class, where could they catch us in this village of a convent? Miss D. had nothing to gain by creating a scandal and pointing out to the community our frequent escapades. She would have been reproached for not knowing how to prevent what she was complaining about. We were perfectly indifferent to the nightcap punishment and to the furious rantings of that unamiable person. The Mother Superior, who was prudently indulgent, was not easily persuaded to deprive us of going-out privileges. She alone had the right to pronounce this supreme decree. The discipline was therefore not very rigorous, in spite of the nasty disposition of the monitor.

The pursuit of the great mystery, the search for the hiding place lasted the whole winter that I spent in the lower class. The wall of the impasse was noticeably defaced, but we got only as far as the crossbeams, before which we had to stop. We searched elsewhere, we hunted in twenty different places, always without achieving the least success, always without losing hope.

One day we got the idea of looking under the roofs for some attic window which might serve as the upper access to the subterranean world that we dreamed of so much. There were many of these windows whose purpose we were not aware of. In the eaves was a small room where we could practice on one of some thirty pianos scattered throughout the establishment. Each day we had one hour for this practice, though very few of us cared much about it. However, I really did want to practice; I had always loved music. I had an excellent tutor, M. Pradher. But I was becoming much more artistic along the lines of fiction rather than music, for what was more beautiful than the novel we were actively pursuing with our shared expense of imagination, courage, and excitement?

Hence the piano hour was, every day, an hour for adventure, in addition to those in the evening. We would meet in one of the scattered rooms, and from there we would set out for the wherever and however of fantasy.

From the garret where I was supposed to be doing scales, I could observe a labyrinth of roofs, overhangs, penthouses, lofts—the ensemble covered with mossy tiles and garnished with weathered chimneys that offered a vast field for new exploration. There we were, on the roofs; I no longer know whom I was with, but I know that Fannelly (whom I shall speak about later) was leading the march. To jump through the window was not very difficult. Six feet below us there stretched a gutter that formed a seam between two gables. To clamber over these gables, to come up against others, to jump from slope to slope, to travel like cats was more imprudent than difficult, and the danger, far from restraining us, egged us on.

There was in this mania for seeking the victim something profoundly stupid and also heroic; stupid, because we had to suppose that these nuns, whose sweetness and goodness we adored, practiced some frightful torture on someone; heroic, because we were risking our lives every day to liberate an imaginary being, object of our most generous concern and chivalrous enterprise.

We had been there for an hour, looking out over the garden, surveying a whole section of the buildings and courtyards, and being very careful to huddle behind a chimney whenever we noticed the black veil of a nun who could have raised her head and seen us against the clouds, when we wondered how we would retrace our steps. The arrangement of the roofs had allowed us to go down and jump from a higher to a lower level. Going back up was not so easy. I even believe that without a ladder it would have been completely impossible. We scarcely knew anymore where we were. Finally, we recognized the bedroom window of a private student, Sidonie Macdonald, daughter of the famous general. We could reach it by making a final jump. This one was more dangerous than the others. I went about it too abruptly, and kicked my heel into a transom window which illuminated a gallery and through which I would have fallen from a height of thirty feet into the area of the lower class, if by chance my awkwardness had not caused me to swerve a little. I escaped with two knees badly scraped on the tiles, but that was not at all the object of my concern. My heel had broken part of the frame of that damned window and had shattered half a dozen panes, which fell inward with a dreadful noise, quite close to the entrance to the kitchens. Immediately a great hum arose from among the lay sisters, and through the opening which I had just made, we heard the resounding voice of Sister Thérèse shouting at the cats and accusing Whiskey, the bold tomcat of Mother Alippe, of quarreling with all his colleagues and breaking all the windows in the house. But Sister Marie defended the cat's manners, while Sister Hélène believed that a chimney had just collapsed on the roofs. This debate caused that crazy, nervous laughter which, among little girls, nothing can stop. We heard people climbing the stairs, we were going to be caught in the act of walking on rooftops, but we could not take one step toward safety. Fannelly was completely stretched out in the gutter; another girl was looking for her comb. As for me, I had yet another handicap. I had just discovered that one my shoes had fallen off my foot, dropped through a broken pane, and landed at the entrance of the kitchens. My knees were bleeding, my mad laughter was so convulsive that I could not utter a word, and pointing to my shoeless foot, I spelled out the hazard with signs. A new round of laughter exploded, no matter that the alarm had been given and the lay sisters were approaching.

Soon we were reassured. We were sheltered and hidden by overhanging roofs from which it was hardly possible to find us without climbing up to the broken window by ladder, or without following the same route we had taken. Because of this, we could afford to defy the nuns. Thus, when we had recognized the advantage of our position, we began to let out Homeric meows, so that Whiskey and his family might be caught and convicted in our place. Then we reached Sidonie's window, who received us very ungraciously. The poor child was practicing her piano unconcerned about the feline howlings which vaguely struck her ear. She was sickly and nervous, very gentle, and incapable of understanding the pleasure we could derive from running across the rooftops. When she heard us, chased from ambush, coming en masse through her window, to which she had her back turned while playing the piano, she uttered piercing cries. We hardly took time to reassure her. Her shrieks were going to attract the nuns; we dashed into her bedroom, reaching the door precipitously, while she stood up trembling, aghast to see this strange procession race by, without a clue as to what was happening and unable to recognize any of us, so great was her fright.

In an instant we were scattered; one girl went back up to the high room from which we had set out, and raced over the piano keys with all her might; another made a big detour to get back to the classroom. As for me, I had to go in search of my shoe and retrieve this piece of evidence, if there was still time. I succeeded in not meeting the lay sisters and in finding vacant the entrance to the kitchens. *Audaces fortuna juvat* [fortune favors the bold], I told myself, thinking back to an aphorism Deschartres had taught me. And in fact I did retrieve the lucky shoe, which had chanced to fall into a dark place and attracted no one's attention. Whiskey alone was accused. My knees were very sore for a few days, but I did not call attention to them, and the explorations were not diminished.

I really needed all this romantic excitement to counter the routine of the convent, which was very distasteful to me. We were fed well enough, the thing which has anyway always concerned me the least, but we suffered cruelly from the cold, and the winter was very rigorous that year. The habits of getting up and going to bed were as harmful to me as they were unpleasant. I have always liked to stay up late and not wake early. My circulation is slow, and the expression "sang-froid" describes my physical and emotional constitution. A devil among the convent's devils, I never lost my composure, and I engaged in the biggest follies in the world with a seriousness which delighted my cohorts immensely, but I was quite literally paralyzed by the cold, especially during the first half of the day. The dormitory, located under the attic roof, was so glacial I could not fall asleep, and to my sorrow I heard all the hours of the night striking. At six o'clock, two servants, Marie-Josèphe and Marie-Anne, mercilessly came to wake us. To get up and dressed by candlelight has always seemed sorrowful to me. To wash we had to crack the ice in water which had little cleansing effect. We had chilblains, our swollen feet would bleed in our too narrow shoes. We would go to mass by candlelight, we would shiver on our benches or fall asleep on our knees, in a posture of meditation. At seven o'clock, we would breakfast on a piece of bread and a cup of tea. At last we would see, on entering the classroom, a little brightness in the sky and a little fire in the stove. I did not thaw out until noon; I had dreadful colds, sharp pains in every limb; I suffered from them afterwards for fifteen years.

But Mary could not bear complaints; as strong as a boy, she pitilessly mocked whoever was not stoic. She did me the favor of making me pitiless toward myself. I did deserve some credit, for I suffered more than anyone else, and the Parisian air was already stifling me.

Yellow, apathetic, silent, I appeared in class as the calmest and the most submissive person. I had but one altercation with the ferocious D., which I shall recount later. I was not given to "back talk" or acquainted with anger; I do not recall showing the slightest inclination for it during the more than two years I spent at the convent. Thanks to this character trait, I never had but one enemy, and consequently I was only once the object of antipathy, which is why I bore a sort of grudge against D., who caused me to experience the feeling that was most opposed to my being. I was always liked, even in my time of worst deviltry, by my most sullen classmates and by the most demanding teachers or nuns. The Mother Superior used to say to my grandmother that I was "still waters." Though Paris had chilled the fever of activity I had undergone in Nohant, nothing prevented me from running on the roofs in December and from spending entire evenings bareheaded in the garden in the dead of winter; for in the garden, too, we were seeking the great mystery, and we would go down there through the windows when the doors were locked. The fact is that at those hours we were living in the mind, and I no longer noticed I was carrying along a sick body.

With all that—my pale face and my air of being chilled to the bone, of which Isabelle made the most amusing caricatures—I was inwardly cheerful. I laughed very little, but the laughter of others cheered my ears and my heart. An instance of folly did not make me react with joy, but I would unsmilingly top it by a greater one, and I had more success than anyone with the beasts, who did not hate me and who especially trusted my generosity.

For example, it often happened that the whole class was punished for the misdeed of a devil or for the blunder of a beast. The beasts did not want to give each other away, but they had no scruples about betraying the devils, only they did not dare. Everyone trembled before Gillibrand, and yet Gillibrand was kind and never used her strength to mistreat the weak ones. But she had wit enough for twelve devils, and her mockery exasperated those who did not know how to respond to it. Isabelle made herself feared by her caricatures, Lavinia by her lofty airs of disdain. I alone did not inspire fear; I was a devil with the devils, a beast with the beasts, solely because I was nonchalant by nature or physically listless. I conquered the beasts completely by sparing them collective punishments. As soon as the teacher would say, "The whole class will be punished if I do not discover the culprit," I would stand up and say, "It is I." Mary, who set me a good example in all things, followed mine in this, and the others were grateful to us.

My grandmama was going to leave Paris and got permission to take me out two or three Thursdays in a row. The Mother Superior did not dare tell her I had been marked by all the mistresses and teachers as doing absolutely nothing and that the nightcap was my constant headdress. My grandmother would then perhaps have thought I was wasting my time and that it would be better to take me back with her. For this reason my dissipation and my escapades were passed over lightly.

I looked forward joyously to those outings, but joy was not the result. I had already become used to communal life, a very sweet habit to melancholy characters, and my character was at the same time the saddest and the gayest in the whole convent; sad through reflection, when I relapsed into myself, or my sickly, painful body, or the memory of family sorrows; gay, when the laughter of my companions, the sudden interruption of dear Mary, or the unusual humor of romantic Isabelle came along to tear me away from pitying my own existence and communicate to me the life that was in the others.

At my grandmama's, all my bitter past, tormented present, uncertain future came back. There was too much concern over me, they questioned me, they found me changed, heavier, preoccupied. When night fell, I was taken back to the convent. That transition from the small, warm, perfumed, illuminated salon of my grandmother, to the dark, empty, and icy cloister; from the tender embraces of grandmama, of my dear mother, of my great-uncle, to the cold and sour "good evening" of the porters and the nuns at the turning box made my heart sink for a moment. I shivered when crossing by myself those galleries paved with tombs, but at the end of the cloister the sweetness of the retreat was already making itself felt. The Vanloo Madonna seemed to be smiling for me. I did not feel devout toward her, but already her little bluish lamp threw me into a vague and sweet reverie. I was leaving behind a world of emotions too strong for my age, and of demands for feeling that should have been spared me. I heard Mary's voice calling to me impatiently. The smaller beasts came to inquire with curiosity about what I had seen during the day. "How sad you must feel to come back!" I did not answer. I could not explain why I had that peculiarity of being more comfortable in the convent than with my own family.

On the eve of my grandmother's departure, a great storm rose up against me in the chambers of the Mother Superior. I enjoyed writing as much as I disliked speaking, and I amused myself by making of our pranks and of the rigors of the D. a sort of satirical diary which I sent to my grandmama, who found it highly entertaining and who in no way preached submission or wheedling and, still less, piety. It was standard practice for us to put, in the evening, on the sideboard of the Mother Superior's antechamber, the letters we wished to send. Those not addressed to relatives had to be left open. Those for relatives were sealed; their secrecy was supposed to be respected.

It would have been easy for me to send my manuscripts to my grandmother by a surer means, since her servants often came to bring me various objects and inquire about my health, but I had supreme confidence in the Superior's honesty. She had said in front of me to my grandmother that she never opened letters addressed to relatives. I believed her, I was fair-minded, I was not suspicious. But the volume and the frequency of my missives worried the "reverend mother."[16] She broke the seals without ceremony, read my satires, and suppressed the letters. She even played this trick on me three days in a row without mentioning it, to get to know the style of my mocking chronicles and the way in which the D. governed us. A person of heart and intelligence would have benefited thereby. She would perhaps have scolded me, but she would have dismissed the D. Surely a person of sincerity would not have set a trap for a child's innocence and would not have abused a secrecy she had authorized. The Mother Superior preferred to question Miss D., who understandably did not recognize herself in the portrait, more lifelike than flattering, that I had traced of her. Her hatred, already inflamed by my calm appearance and the very real gentleness of my manners, obviously was exacerbated. She called me an abominable liar, an *esprit fort* (that is to say, impious), an informer, a serpent, and who knows what else! The Superior summoned me and created a frightful scene. I remained impassive. Next she promised benignly not to make my "calumny" known to my grandmother and to keep my secret about these abominable letters. I did not see it that way. I sensed the duplicity in that promise. I answered that I had rough copies of my letters, that my grandmother would receive them, that I would insist on the truth of my assertions before her and before the Mother Superior herself, and that, since there was no security in the relations I had trusted, I would ask to change to another convent.

The Superior was not a wicked woman, but believe it or not, I never felt that she was a very good one. She ordered me to leave her presence while heaping threats and insults on me. She was a person of high society, and she knew how to behave royally when need be, but she became very vulgar when she was angry. Perhaps she did not thoroughly understand the connotations of her expressions in French, and I did not yet know enough English for her to speak to me in her language. Miss D. had lowered her head, closed her eyes, in the beatific attitude of a saint who hears the voice of God Himself. She put on airs of pity for me and of merciful silence. An hour later, in the refectory, the Mother Superior entered, followed by a few nuns who formed a cortège for her; she moved along the tables as if making an inspection; then, stopping before me and rolling her big black eyes, which were very beautiful, she told me in a solemn voice, "Ponder the truth!" The sages turned pale and made the sign of the cross. The beasts whispered to each other while looking at me. I was soon overwhelmed with questions. "All that means," I answered, "is that in three days I shall no longer be here."

I was furious, but I was also sorely distressed. In no way did I wish to change to another convent. I had already formed attachments which I suffered to see broken so soon. Meanwhile, my grandmother arrived. The Superior closeted herself with her, and foreseeing that I would tell her everything, decided to hand over my letters and present them as a tissue of lies. I believe that she got the worst of it and that my grandmother vigorously criticized the abuse of confidence which the Superior had to reveal to her. I believe that she took up my defense and spoke about taking me home at once. I do not know what transpired between them, but when I was called up to the Superior's parlor, both women were trying to look solemn, and both were very animated. My grandmother embraced me as usual, and not one word of reproach was addressed to me, except as concerned my inattention and the time wasted on childish activities. Then the Superior announced that I was to leave the lower class, where my intimacy with Mary brought disorder, and that I would immediately join the older girls. This good news, which finally brought to an end all obstacles to a noticeable improvement in my life, was however, communicated to me in a severe tone. It was hoped that, having no further relations with Miss D., I would give up my habit of satirizing her, that I would break my habit of deviltry with the terrible Mary, and that this separation would be as beneficial to one as to the other.

I answered that I would willingly consent never to concern myself with Miss D., but I was not willing to promise that I would no longer love Mary. The force of circumstances was deemed sufficient to separate us, since we would only have the recreation hour in the garden in which to see each other anymore. Satisfied with the result of this affair, my grandmother left for Nohant. I went into the upper class, where Isabelle and Sophie had preceded me. I swore to Mary that I would remain her friend for life and to the death, but I had not yet finished with the terrible D., as will soon be seen.   *R. S.*

XII

Louise and Valentine. —The Marquise de La Rochejaquelein. —Her
memoirs. —Her salon. —Pierre Riallo. —My classmates in the
lower class. —Héléna. —Convent wit and humor. —The Countess
and Jacquot. —Sister Françoise. —Madame Eugénie. —Single
combat with Miss D. —The storage closet. —Solitary confinement.
—Poulette. —The nuns. —Madame Monique. —Miss Fairbairns.
—Madame Anne-Augustine and her silver stomach. —Madame
Marie-Xavier. —Miss Hurst. —Madame Marie-Agnes. —Madame
Anne-Joseph. —On intellectual incapacity. —Madame Alicia. —My
adoption. —Conversations at a quarter to nine. —Sister Teresa.
—The distillery. —The ladies of the choir and the lay sisters.

I shall not leave the lower class without talking about two student boarders whom I liked very much although they were not considered devils in any way. Neither were they among the sages, and even less among the beasts, for they were remarkably intelligent. I have already mentioned their names —Valentine de Gouy and Louise de La Rochejaquelein.

Valentine was a child of barely nine or ten, if I remember correctly, and since she was small and delicate, she hardly seemed older than Mary Eyre or Helen Kelly, the two tots of the lower class, at the time. But Valentine was far ahead of most children her age, and one could have as much fun with her as with Isabelle or Sophie. She learned everything with marvelous facility. She was already as advanced in all her studies as the older girls. She had a charming wit, was very open and kind. My bed was next to hers in the dormitory, and I liked to take care of her as if she were my daughter. On the other side I had a little girl named Suzanne, Sophie's sister, whom I had to take care of even more, for she was always ill.

The other object of affection I left in the lower class, but who joined me before long in the upper class, Louise, was the daughter of the Marquise de La Rochejaquelein, widow of M. de Lescure,[30] the same woman who left interesting memoirs about the first Vendéan uprising. I believe that the political personage who presently[17] represents a faction of the Royalist party in the National Assembly, whose ideas are more chivalrous than reassuring, is the brother of this same Louise. Their mother certainly was a heroine out of a historical novel. The truthful story she told contains narrative which is very dramatic, sincerely felt, and moving. Although the situation of France and the rest of

Europe seem to me completely misconstrued, given the royalist view, no one could have more fairly judged her party or better depicted the strong and weak, the good and bad sides of the various elements in the struggle. This book was written by a courageous and spirited woman. It will remain one of the most colorful and useful documents of the revolutionary period. History has already corrected some of the factual errors and naïve exaggerations of partisanship which are understandably found in it, but history will also profit from the curious revelations of the author, whose strict judgment and truthful intelligence signal the causes of the monarchy's demise at the same time as she dedicates herself heroically to this expiring monarchy.

Louise had the warmth and spirit of her mother, the courage and a little of the political intolerance of the old Chouans,[31] and much of the grandeur and poetry of the bellicose peasants in the midst of whom she had been raised. I had already read the Marquise's book, which had been recently published. I did not share her opinions, but I never argued about them, for I felt that I owed respect to her family's beliefs. Besides her lively stories, her charming portraits of the customs and landscape of the Bocage held a vital interest for me. Once, several years later, I went to Louise's home and met her mother. As that household left a deep impression on me, I shall tell about this visit, which I might forget if I left it to be reported in its place.

I no longer remember exactly where the house was. It was a large town house in the suburb of Saint-Germain. I arrived modestly by hired cab, according to my means and my custom, and I had the driver stop in front of the door, which did not open for such humble vehicles. The doorman, an old liveried servant of a good house, tried to stop me at the entrance. "Excuse me," I said to him, "I'm going to visit Mme. de La Rochejaquelein."

"You," he said, eyeing me scornfully from head to foot apparently because I was wearing a cloak and hat without any flowers or lace, "well, go in!" And he shrugged his shoulders as if to say, "Those people open their doors to everybody!"

I tried to close the door behind me. It was so heavy I could not push it all the way with my fingers. I did not want to soil my gloves, so I did not persist, but I had already climbed the first few steps of the stairway when that old Cerberus came running after me. "And what about your door?" he shouted at me.

"What door?"

"The one to the street."

"Oh, pardon me," I said laughing, "that's your door, not mine." Grumbling, he went off to close it, and I wondered if I would have an equally poor reception from the illustrious lackeys of my childhood friend. Finding many of those gentlemen in the antechamber, I realized there were guests, and I asked for Louise. I was only going to be in Paris for two or three days, and I wanted to grant her request to see me and chat with her only a few minutes. She came for me and led me to the salon with the same gaiety and cordiality as ever. On the side of the room where she seated me beside her, there were only young people, her sisters or her friends. On the other side, there was a circle of older people surrounding her mother's chair, set forward and a little apart from the others.

I was very disappointed to see that the heroine of the Vendée was a fat woman, very red-faced and rather coarse looking. On her right stood a peasant from the Vendée. He had come from his village to see her, or to see Paris, and had dined with the family. Undoubtedly he was a "right-minded" man, and perhaps a hero of the last Vendéan uprising. He did not seem old enough to have been in the first one, and Louise, whom I asked, answered simply, "He's a good chap from back home."

He was dressed in heavy trousers and a round-cut jacket. He wore a sort of white sash on his arm, and an old rapier knocked against his legs. He looked like a country policeman on a procession day. He was a far cry from the half-shepherd, half-bandit partisans I had imagined, and the fellow had a way of saying "Madame la Marquise" that nauseated me. However, the marquise, who was almost blind by that time, pleased me by her impressively kind and simple manner. She was surrounded by beautiful ladies dressed for a ball, who showed her great respect, but who certainly did not venerate her white hair and unseeing blue eyes as much as my naïve heart was disposed to. Mine was a silent homage, even more sincere since by that time I was neither religious nor royalist.

Hearing her talk, I felt she was more natural than witty, at least on that occasion. The peasant, saying goodbye, shook hands with her, and put his hat on before leaving the salon, which did not make anyone laugh. Louise and her sisters were as simply dressed as they were simple in their manners—manners that bordered on brusqueness. They did not do embroidery; instead they had distaffs and affected spinning flax in the fashion of peasant women. I was content to find all that charming, and it could well have been.

On Louise's part, certainly, it was all natural and spontaneous, but the surroundings in which I saw her playing the chatelaine of the Vendée did not harmonize with those country-girl manners. A beautifully illuminated salon, a gallery of elegant and formally-dressed patrician ladies, an anteroom crammed with lackeys, a doorman who verged on being rude to people who came by cab, were not quite harmonious; all these details made me only too aware of the impossibility of a public, legitimate marriage between the people and the nobility.

The thought of marriage reminds me of one of the strangest and most significant adventures in the life of Mme. de La Rochejaquelein. She was then the widow of M. de Lescure and was still pregnant with the twins, whom she was to lose a few days after their birth. A refugee in Brittany, in the hamlet of La Minaye, at the home of poor peasants who were faithful during misfortune, pursued by the Bleus, constantly on her guard, watching over the flocks under the name of Jeannette, often sleeping in the woods with her mother (also a heroic woman whom one adores when reading these memoirs), fleeing in wind and rain to hide in some furrow or trench while the patriots searched the houses where she had been hidden, Mme. de La Rochejaquelein had almost had to marry a Breton peasant. Here is how she herself relates the episode:

"My mother wanted, for the sake of greater safety, to use a most unusual stratagem. Two Vendéan peasant women had married Bretons, since which time they were no longer harassed. My mother, trying to assure me of complete rest during my confinement, could not find a better means. She cast her eye on Pierre Riallo. He was an old widower who had five children. But birth certificates were required. La Ferret had a sister who had betimes gone to settle on the other side of the Loire with her daughter. We sent Riallo to La Ferret's village to get the birth certificates. Everything was about to work out: the municipal officer was alerted and had promised us to tear out the page from the register when we wanted him to. We were supposed to invite the Bleus to the wedding supper, but execution of the plan was suspended because of the serious warnings we were given. They told us we had been betrayed and were being pursued with special vigor. We changed lodgings, and we even separated. . . . "

A few weeks later, Mme. de Lescure and her mother, changing hiding places, separated from Pierro Riallo, who had them conducted to their new refuge:

"That excellent man," she says, "wept as he left us. He took from his finger a silver ring like those that Breton peasant women wear, and gave it to me. I have worn it ever since."

Thus the widow of M. de Lescure, later to become Marquise de La Rochejaqualein, had been in a way engaged to Pierre Riallo. Nothing was more austere certainly than that engagement in the very presence of death, nothing more chaste than the affection of the old peasant and the gratitude of the young marquise. But what would have happened if the marriage had taken place and if Pierre Riallo had refused the fraudulent suppression of the civil marriage certificate? Surely, noble Jeannette would have sooner died than consent to ratify this monstrous misalliance. At that time, the Breton peasant was indeed her equal, or even above her. She was a poor outlaw quite happy to receive his generous hospitality and magnanimous protection. Under the Restoration, it had doubtless not been forgotten. Any peasant who showed up in her salon was received, as long as he had on the white arm band over his elbow. They would spin flax like the shepherdesses, they had touching and affectionate memories, but she was, nonetheless, Madame la Marquise, and false equality could not have fooled the peasant. If the son of Pierre Riallo had appeared to ask for the hand of Louise or Laurence[32] de La Rochejaquelein, they would have considered him crazy. M. de La Rochejaquelein,[33] today a political spokesman but formerly the "son of refugees," would not willingly be the brother-in-law of some Breton laborer. And so, Pierre Riallo is really a symbol of the relationship between the common people and the nobility. The latter trust him, accept his sublime devotion, his supreme sacrifices, and offer him their hand. They would willingly be his betrothed during times of danger, but in the name of the monarchy and the Catholic religion, they refuse him the right to make his living, the right to education, the right to be everyone's equal; in a word, when it comes to a true union of the classes, they tremble at the very idea.

I was already thinking about all that as I left Mme. de La Rochejaquelein's salon. Yet, quite sure that all I had seen there was not a show, knowing well that Louise and her family had heartfelt memories, I told myself that, owing to the force of circumstance, what I had seen was only a charming little salon entertainment.

Before ending this digression, permit me to point out a kind of parallel that exists between the adventure of the Marquise at Pierre Riallo's cottage and the ideas about civil marriage my mother still entertained in 1804. In 1804, my mother did not believe she was really married to my father, because she had been married only in a civil ceremony. In '93, Mme. de La Rochejaquelein would not have believed herself married to Pierro Riallo, because the municipal officer promised to tear up the certificate. This lack of respect for a purely civil formality marks the transition from one set of laws to another and the transformation of a society.

I now leave my premature anecdote, which dates from 1824 or 1825, or perhaps 1826, and retrace my steps. I return to the convent, where Louise, with her lively intelligence, noble heart, and lovable character, did not inspire in me any of the thoughts I would later have without ceasing to love her. I have lost sight of her now for a long time. I do not know whom she married; I do not even know whether she is still alive, so withdrawn am I from "society," so many things have I gone through that separate me from the past and have made me lose even the slightest trace of my early relationships. If she exists, if she remembers me, if she knows that George Sand is the same person as Aurore Dupin, she must sigh, lower her eyes, and deny she ever loved me. I know the effect of public opinion and prejudice on even the most generous souls, and I am neither astonished nor shocked by it. As at peace with my conscience today as I was with my deviltry thirty years ago, I love her still, that Louise. I still love the royalists, the devout, and even the nuns whom I then loved, who, I am sure, now say my name only while making the sign of the cross. I do not wish to see them again; I know they would preach to me what they call the return to the truth. I know I would be forced to cause them the pain of failure in their pious projects. So it is better not to see one another again rather than to see each other with our hearts defended, but that does not mean my feelings are dead. They are still tender toward my first loves. My own religion does not condemn to eternal damnation those who oppose my beliefs. That is why I shall speak of my convent friends without worrying about what the spirit of social class or political party has done to them since. I shall speak with the same enthusiasm, the same effusion, of those who have probably rejected me as of those who have kept an unalterable memory of me. I can still see them as they were, and I do not want to know what they have become. I see them as pure and as mild as the morning of life when we first knew each other. The tall chestnut trees of the convent seem to me like those Elysian fields where souls from every corner of the universe meet to exchange warm and peaceful greetings without having to be wary of the worldly fluctuations or childish differences here below.

The reader will pardon me for briefly listing the classmates I left behind in the lower class; I do not remember them all, but it pleases me to find some of their names in my memory. There were, besides those I have already mentioned, the three Kellys—Mary, Helen, and Henriette; the two O'Mullan sisters—sweet, tawny Creoles; the two Carys—Fanny and Suzanne, Sophie's sisters; Lucy Masterson, Catherine and Maria Dormer; Maria Gordon, a delicate and sickly child, sweet and intelligent, who married a Frenchman and became an excellent wife and mother—a distinguished woman in every respect; Louise Rollet, the daughter of a master smith from Berry; Lavinia Anster; Camille de Le Josne-Contay, as stiff and serious as an old-time Huguenot but nevertheless very Catholic; Eugénie de Castella, a partial devil and an excellent person besides, with whom I was quite close; one of the three De Fargues, daughters of a mayor of Lyon; Henriette Manoury, who came, I believe, from Le Havre; finally Héléna de Narbonne, a rather persecuted, oppressed child, through her own fault perhaps, but who inspired me with pity, for she was often a victim of deviltry.

Sometimes Héléna was too fond of me. Hers was a troubled and troubling nature. We had to do all her schoolwork, take over all of her tasks, even write her confessions, which was not always done very seriously, I admit. I would protect her against Mary, who could not stand her. I spared her many punishments, saved her from many tempests, yet I doubt that she remembers. She was very proud of her name, and we held that against her, even those who had more illustrious ones, for to be fair to most of us, we practiced Christian equality from every point of view and did not dream of considering ourselves greater or lesser than the others.

This same Héléna de Narbonne distinguished me with a nickname that described me best, for like all of my classmates, I had several. She had named me *Calepin*, because I had a mania for pocket notebooks; Sister Teresa had nicknamed me Madcap and Mischievous; in the upper class, I became Auntie and Marquis de Saint-Lucie.

I was amused to find my elementary books from the lower class, the *Spelling Book*, the *Garden of the Soul (Le Jardin de l'âme)*, etc. They are filled with sayings, riddles, and what gives me the most joy, conversations in dialogue which we wrote to one another during the hours of silence, for general silence was a punishment in very common usage. The cover of anyone's book passing from hand to hand under the table became our way of having a group conversation. We also had cardboard letters that we passed on a long string from one end of the class to the other. We quickly formed words, and if a girl was isolated in a corner, separated from the others for special punishment, she was kept abreast of all that we were plotting. As for written confessions, examinations of conscience that we did for the little ones, I found a scribbled example; I do not know who wrote it nor for whom it was done.

Confession of ———

Alas, my dear Father Villèle:[18] It has often happened that I smudged my face with ink, snuffed the candle with my fingers, and given myself indigestion "from beans," as the grown-ups say where I come from; I have scandalized the young ladies in the class by my sloppiness; I have acted stupid, and I have forgotten whatever it was we were supposed to think about, more than two hundred times each day. I have slept through catechism and snored at mass; I have said that you were not handsome; I have dripped my taper on Mother Alippe's veil, and I did it on purpose. I have made at least fifteen blunders in French and thirty in English this week, and I have burned my shoes at the stove and polluted the classroom. I'm at fault, I'm at fault, I'm very much at fault. . . .

You can see how innocent our malice and impiety were. However, we were severely scolded and punished when Miss D. got her hands on these writings, which she called licentious and dangerous. Mother Alippe pretended to be angry, punished a bit, confiscated, and I'm sure, entertained the workroom with our nonsense.

Everyone remembers the wholehearted laughter of childhood at things which in themselves were perhaps not at all funny. Laughter comes easily to little girls. For us everything was a subject for uncontrollable hilarity—a mispronounced name, a ridiculous face in the parlor, any unusual incident in church, the meowing of a cat, and who knows what else. Panic was as contagious as joy. A little one would scream when she saw a spider, and soon the whole class was screaming without knowing why. One evening at vespers, something happened that no one was ever able to explain. One of us screamed, her neighbor stood up, a third ran out, and soon it became a general stampede; everyone left the classroom at the same time, turning over chairs, benches, lights, and fled into the cloister, falling over each other, dragging along the teachers, who shouted and ran no less than the pupils. It took an hour to reassemble the scattered flock, and nothing comprehensible could be gained from the explanations.

In spite of all this feverish gaiety in the lower class, I suffered there so much, both morally and physically, that I still remember the day I entered the upper class as one of the happiest of my life.

I have always been sensitive to a deprivation of bright light. It seems to be a source of my physical well-being. I inevitably become depressed in a gloomy atmosphere. The upper classroom was very large; there were five or six windows, several of which overlooked the gardens. It was heated by a good fireplace and a good stove. Besides, it was early spring. The chestnut trees were about to bloom, their rosy clusters raised up like candelabras. I thought I was entering paradise.

The class mistress, whom we often ridiculed and who was certainly rather odd in her manners, was at heart a very good person and even more absent-minded than Miss D. We called her the Countess, because she put on airs, and I reserve this nickname for her. She had an apartment in the garden on the ground floor, separated from us by a vegetable garden; from her window, when she was not in class, she could see part of our escapades. But she was much more interested in seeing what was going on in her apartment from the classroom. For there, at her window, or in front of her door, lived, scratched, and squawked at the sun the sole object of her affection—an old, gray, threadbare parrot, a surly beast on whom we heaped our insults and disdain.

Grave error on our part, for Jacquot probably deserved all our gratitude,

since we owed our liberty to him. Thanks to the constant distraction he provided, the Countess left us to our follies. Perched on his stick within full view,
Jacquot would let out piercing shrieks when he was annoyed. Immediately, the
Countess would run to the window, and if a cat was lurking near the perch, or
if Jacquot had broken his chain with impatience and undertaken a pleasure trip
to the neighboring lilacs, she would forget everything, rush out of the classroom, dashing through cloister and garden, and hurry to scold or caress the
adored creature. During that time, we danced on the tables or left the class to
do as Jacquot, taking little pleasure trips to the cellar or attic.

The Countess was a youthful woman somewhere between forty and fifty
years old, unmarried, very well-born—one could not ignore it, for she said it
every time she could—in straitened circumstances, and, I believe, rather uneducated, for she did not give us any type of lessons and only served to watch the
class as a chaperone. She was boring and ridiculous, but kind and accommo-
dating. Some of us had come down with the flu, and treated her so badly that
we forced her to lose her temper. I personally have never had anything but
praise for her, and I even reproach myself for having laughed with the others at
the magisterial manner, the pretentious phrases, the ever-present, wide-
brimmed black hat, the ceremoniously draped green shawl, even the verbal
slips which we mercilessly noted and then injected into our conversation very
prominently without her ever realizing it. I should rather have taken her side,
for she often took mine with the nuns. But children are ingrates (that age is
pitiless!) and mockery seems to them an inalienable right.

The second chaperone was a very severe nun, Madame Anne-Françoise.
This thin, pale old woman had an enormous hooked nose. She scolded often,
insulted too much, and was roundly disliked. I felt nothing for her, neither
reserve nor attraction. She treated me neither well nor poorly. I never saw her
show a preference for anyone, and she was suspected of being a free-thinker
because she was interested in astronomy. Indeed her manner was very different from that of the other nuns. Instead of taking communion with them every
day, she only went near the sacraments on the important feast days of the year.
Her sermons were devoid of consolation. They were always filled with
threats, and in such bad French that we could not take them seriously. She
punished a great deal, and when by chance she wanted to joke, she was hurtful and inappropriate. Her strong face was not lacking in character. She
looked like an old Dominican monk, and yet she was not fanatic nor even
very religious for a nun.

The principal mistress of the upper class was Madame Eugénie (Maria-
Eugenia Stonor). She was a tall woman, well-proportioned, of noble bearing,
graceful even in her solemnity. Her face, pink and wrinkled like that of almost
all the nuns who were getting along in years, might have been pretty, but she
had a disdainful, mocking expression which at first put us off. She was more
than severe, she had a terrible temper, and indulged her personal antipathies,
which made her many irreconcilable enemies. She was not affectionate to anyone, and I know only one boarder who loved her—me.

This affection I could not help but show for the Ferocious Eyeshade (we called her that because she had weak eyes and wore a green taffeta visor) astonished the whole upper class. This is how it came into being.

Three days after entering the upper class, I met Miss D. at the garden gate. She glared at me; I looked straight at her with my habitual calm. My admission to the upper class had been a defeat for her, and she was furious. "You are quite proud of yourself," she said to me, "you don't even greet me."

"Good day, Madame, how are you feeling?"

"You seem to be making fun of me."

"If it pleases you to think so."

"Ah! don't take on those impudent airs, I can still let you know who I am."

"I hope not, Madame; I have no more quarrel with you."

"We shall see!"

And she went on her way with a threatening gesture.

We were at recess, and everyone was free in the garden. I took advantage of it to pick up a few notebooks I had left in a closet adjoining the lower class study room. That closet, where they stored inkwells, desks, and large buckets of water for washing the classrooms, was also used as a *cabinet noir*, a prison for the little ones, Mary Eyre and others.

I was there a few minutes looking for my notebooks when Miss D. appeared to me like Tisiphone.[34] "I am very glad to find you here," she said. "You shall apologize to me for your impertinent manner of looking at me a while ago."

"No, Madame, I was not impertinent, and I will not apologize to you."

"In that case, you shall be punished in the same way as the little girls; you shall be shut in here until you come down a peg."

"You haven't the right, you're no longer in charge of me."

"Just you try to leave!"

"I will."

And taking her by surprise, I cleared the closet door and went straight toward her. Beside herself with rage, she just as quickly ran at me, caught me in her arms, and pushed me back toward the closet. I have never seen anything as ugly as that fat nun in a fury. Half-smiling, half-resisting, I pushed her away, I backed her against the wall, until she tried to strike me; then I raised my fist at her, I saw her go pale, I felt her weaken, and I remained with my arm raised, certain that I was stronger and that it would be very easy to get her out of my way. But in order to do that, I would have to strike her or let her fall, or at least give her a hard shove and risk hurting her. I was no more angry at her then than I am now, and I have never been able to hurt anyone. I smiled and let her go, and I was just about to go away, satisfied with having pardoned her and having made her feel the superiority of my reflexes over hers, when she treacherously took advantage of my generosity by coming back at me and pushing me with all her might. My foot struck a large bucket of water which rolled with me into the closet; the D. shut me in, double-locked the door, and fled, vomiting a torrent of insults.

My situation was critical. I was literally in a cold bath; the closet was very small and the bucket enormous; when I stood up I still had water up to my ankles. Nevertheless, I could not help laughing when I heard the D. shout, "Ah! that perverse, wretched girl. She has made me so angry that I am going to have to go back to confession. I have lost my absolution." I kept my head, climbed onto the closet shelves to get my feet dry, tore a blank page from a notebook, found pens and ink, and I wrote to Madame Eugénie more or less as follows: "Madame, I now do not recognize any other authority over me than your own. Miss D. has just committed an act of violence upon my person and locked me up. Kindly come to set me free...."

I waited for someone to show up. Maria Gordon, I believe, also came to look for a notebook in the closet, and seeing my head appear at the dormer window, was very frightened and tried to run away. But I made her recognize me and take my note to Madame Eugénie, who would have been in the garden. A minute later, Madame Eugénie appeared, followed by Miss D. She took me by the hand and led me away in silence. The D. was silent also. When I was alone with Madame Eugénie in the cloister, I kissed her impulsively, out of gratitude. The gesture pleased her. Madame Eugénie never kissed anyone, and no one dreamed of kissing her. I saw she was touched, as a woman would be who has never known affection but who, nevertheless, is not insensitive to it. She questioned me. She was very adept at questioning; she seemed not to hear the answers, yet neither words nor facial expressions were lost on her. I told her everything, and she saw I was telling the truth. She smiled, shook my hand, and made a sign that I should return to the garden.

The Archbishop of Paris was coming to confirm us in a few days. Pupils who had made their first communion and not yet received the other sacrament were being chosen. They would be sent on a retreat to a communal room where Miss D. would be supervisor and reader. She was the one who made the religious exhortations. They came for me that very day, but Miss D. refused to see me and ordered me to make my retreat all alone in whatever room the nuns wished to assign me. Then Madame Eugénie openly took my side. "Is she contagious?" she asked mockingly. "Then let her come into my cell." She took me there, in fact, and Madame Alippe came to join us. They remained in the corridor while I got settled in the cell, and I heard their conversation in English. I do not know whether they knew that I understood almost everything.

"Tell me," said Madame Eugénie, "has this child been hateful since you know her?"

"She is not at all hateful," answered Mother Alippe, "just the reverse; she's good, and that D. is not. But the child is a devil, as they say. Oh, that makes you laugh? You like devils, we all know it." (*That* is good to know, I thought.)

And Madame Eugénie replied, "Since she's still quite wild, it may not be the right moment to confirm her. She wouldn't bring the necessary reverence to it. Let's give her time to become more serious, and especially not put her into contact with anyone who holds a grudge against her. Will you let me take charge of the child and release her from your claims?"

"All but the claim of Christian friendship," answered Mother Alippe, "and Miss D. is in the wrong. Don't worry, she'll not start in on her again."

Madame Eugénie went to find the Mother Superior, as far as I recall, to come to terms with her, and perhaps have her speak with Mother Alippe and Miss D. about what had just transpired and what was to be done about it. While I was in the cell of my protectress, Poulette came to find me there; Poulette was the name the younger girls had given to Madame Mary Austin (Marie-Augustine), Mother Alippe's sister, and the trustee of the convent. She was the idol of the boarding students. She would grumble in a certain maternally affectionate way. Since she had no duties toward us, she made it her job to spoil and scold us merrily for our foolishness. She had a store of treats that she sold to us, and she often gave them to those who were out of money, or at least she opened accounts for them that they both forgot to settle. That dependably cheerful, good woman, with no arrogance in her piety, who could be unceremoniously hugged and kissed on both cheeks, whom we even teased without ever seriously angering, came to console me for my misadventures and took my side to such an extent that I could have abused it had I not been eager to reach a peace with everyone.

After an hour of babbling to Poulette, I received the visit of Miss D. The Mother Superior, or her confessor, had reprimanded her. She was sweet as honey, and I was most amazed by her affectionate manner. She announced to me that my sacrament had been postponed until the next year, that they did not believe me sufficiently disposed to receive grace, that Madame Eugénie would come to tell me, but that she herself, before going to the neophytes' retreat, had wanted to make her peace with me. "Tell me," she said, "do you want to admit that you were wrong and give me your hand?"

"With all my heart," I told her. "All that you suggest to me with sweetness and kindness, I shall willingly do."

She kissed me, which did not please me greatly, but everything was settled, and never again did we have a misunderstanding.

The following year, having become very devout, I was confirmed and I made a retreat under the sponsorship of the same Miss D. She had much consideration for me and praised my conversion highly. She gave us long readings which she then developed and commented on with a certain crude and sometimes touching eloquence. She would begin very emphatically, which grew on us little by little, and which finally moved us. That retreat is all I remember about her since the time I was formally installed in the upper class. I pardoned her with all my heart, and I do not retract my pardon, but I do persist in saying that we would have been infinitely better off and happier if the nuns solely had been in charge of our education.

Before returning to the account of my life in the convent, I wish to speak about some of our nuns in some detail. I do not believe I have forgotten any of their names.

After Madame Canning (the Superior), of whom I have already spoken, after Madame Eugénie, Mother Alippe, the good Poulette (Marie-Augustine), one of the elders was Madame Monique (Maria Monica) a very grave and austere person, whom I never saw smile and with whom no one ever became familiar. She was the Superior after Madame Eugénie, who had succeeded

Madame Canning during the time I was there. The authority of the Superior was not permanent. There was an election every five years, I believe. Madame Canning was the Mother Superior for thirty or forty years, until she died. Madame Eugénie requested that she be relieved of that position after five years' service, since her vision was failing. She had become almost blind. I do not know if she is still alive. Neither do I know if Madame Monique is still living. I know, a few years ago, Madame Marie-Françoise had succeeded her.

In my day, Madame Marie-Françoise was a novice who used her family name, Miss Fairbairns. She was a very beautiful person, fair skin with dark eyes, fresh coloring, a very firm expression, very decisive, frank, but cold. This coldness, a very British characteristic, heightened by cloistral reserve and Christian retirement, was to be sensed in most of our nuns. Often our affectionate advances toward them were coldly rejected. That is the only collective reproach I can make them. They did not have enough desire to make us love them. Another elder was Madame Anne-Augustine, if I recall her name correctly. She was so old that when we followed her upstairs, we had time to learn our lessons. She could never say one word in French. She, too, had a very solemn and austere expression. I do not believe she ever uttered a word to any of us. The rumor was that she had had a very serious illness and that she was only able to digest because she had a silver stomach. Madame Anne-Augustine's silver stomach was one of the legends of the convent, and we were silly enough to believe it.

We even imagined that we heard the clicking of that stomach when she walked, so of course she was for us a very mysterious and somewhat frightening being—that ancient piety, who was half metal statue, who never spoke, who sometimes looked at us dumbfounded, and who did not even know a single one of our names. We trembled as we greeted her; she would bow her head slightly and pass like a specter. We pretended she had been dead for two hundred years and that she moved around the cloisters out of habit.

Madame Marie-Xavier was the most beautiful person in the convent, tall, well-built, with regular and delicate features; she was always pale as her wimple, sad as a tomb. She claimed to be very ill, and awaited death impatiently. She is the only nun I have seen in despair for having taken her vows. She scarcely hid it and spent her life sighing and weeping. However, she did not dare break those eternal vows, which civil law did not recognize. She had sworn on the Holy Sacrament; she was not enlightened enough to go back on her word or pious enough to resign herself. Hers was a weak, tormented, miserable soul, more passionate than tender, for she never expressed herself except in fits of anger, as though she were exasperated by boredom. She inspired much comment among us. Some of us thought she had taken the veil out of despair in love and that she was still in love; others, that she hated and lived on rage and resentment; still others accused her of having a bitter and unsociable character, and of not being able to submit to the authority of the elders.

Although it was all hidden as well as possible, it was very easy for us to see that she lived apart, that the other nuns blamed her, and that she spent her life rejecting or being rejected. She did, however, take communion with the others, and she spent, I believe, about ten years under the veil. But I found out shortly after I left the convent that she had broken her vows and left, and no one knew what had transpired in the secret recesses of the community. What was the outcome of the sad tale of her life? Did she find the object of her passion, free and repentant? Did or didn't she have a lover at all? Did she go back into society? Did she overcome the scruples and remorse of the religious life that had kept her captive so long, in spite of her lack of vocation? Did she go back into another convent to end her days in mourning and penitence? None of us, I believe, ever found out. Or else someone told me and I have forgotten. Did she die after that long illness of the soul that was devouring her? Our nuns gave as a pretext a doctor's diagnosis that had condemned her to die if she did not change her climate and regimen. But it was easy to see by their rather bitter smiles that not without struggles and blame had it all taken place.

Another novice, by the name of Miss Croft, who was also very pretty and whom I had seen enter as a postulant, has followed in the footsteps of Madame Maria-Xavier; she left the convent and gave up her vocation before taking the black veil.

Miss Hurst, a novice whom I saw take the veil of eternal sorrow very deliberately and without repenting, was the niece of Madame Monique. She was my English tutor. Every day, I spent an hour in her cell. She taught with clarity and patience. I liked her very much, she was perfect for me, even when I was still a devil. Her religious name was Maria Winifred. I have never read Shakespeare or Byron in English without thinking of her and thanking her with all my heart.

There were two other novices when I went into the convent, who were reaching the end of their novitiate and who took the veil before Miss Hurst and Miss Fairbairns. I have forgotten their family names, I only remember their religious names. They were Sister Mary-Agnes and Sister Anne-Joseph. Both were small and slight, and they looked like two children. Mary-Agnes especially was a most unusual little creature. Her tastes and habits were in perfect harmony with the dainty smallness of her person. She loved little books, little flowers, little birds, little girls, little chairs; all the objects she chose and used were as tiny and neat as she. She carried off this genre of preference with a certain childlike grace and more poetry than idiosyncrasy.

The other little nun, larger, however, and also less intelligent, was the sweetest and most affectionate creature in the world. She did not have even a tinge of English reserve or Catholic mistrust. She never met us without kissing us, and in a tone which was sentimental and playful at the same time, called us by the most affectionate names.

Children tend to abuse familiarity, so the student boarders had little respect for that good little nun. The English girls especially considered her easily affectionate manner a defect. I must say that in the convent and elsewhere I have always found that breed to be haughty and stiff on the surface. The character of Englishwomen is more turbulent than ours. Their instincts are more animalistic in every respect. They are less in charge than we of their feelings and passions. But they are more in charge of their actions, and from childhood it seems that they practice hiding them and make a habit of impassive composure. You would think that at birth they were put into the kind of stiffening from which those famous starched ruffs were made, that have become symbols for pride and prudishness.

To get back to Sister Anne-Joseph, I liked her as she was, and when she came to me with open arms and a moist eye (she always looked like a child who has just been scolded and asks for protection or consolation from the first passerby), it never occurred to me to pass judgment on the banality of her caresses; I returned them with the sincerity of a completely instinctive friendship; for with her it was impossible to maintain a measured affection. She was not able to put two sentences together, because she could not connect two ideas. Was it stupidity, timidity, or frivolity? I thought rather that it was intellectual ineptness, a clumsiness of mind, so to speak. She jabbered away without saying anything, but she wanted to say a great deal and could not, even in her own language. There was not a lack, but a confusion, of ideas. Distracted from what was on her mind, she said words other than those she meant to say, or she stopped her sentence right in the middle, and we had to guess the rest while she began another. Her actions were similar. She did a hundred things at once and did none of them well; her devotion, her sweetness, her need to love and be affectionate seemed to make her the ideal nurse, which was the task she had been given. Unfortunately, in the same way that she confused her right hand with her left, she confused patients, treatments, and illnesses; she would make you swallow your enema and put the cough syrup in the syringe. And then she would run to look for some drug at the pharmacy, and thinking she was going up, went downstairs, and vice versa. She spent her life getting lost and found. One always met her hectic and doleful over a scratch that one of her "dearest sisters" or one of her "dearest children" had suffered. Good as an angel, stupid as a goose, they said. And the other nuns would often scold her or tease her unmercifully about her mistakes. She complained about having rats in her cell. They replied that, if there were any, they had come from her brain. Desperate when she had committed an act of folly, she wept, lost her wits, and was completely unable to recover again for the moment.

What name can we give to these affectionate creatures, harmless, full of good will, but indeed incapable and ineffectual? There are many characters like that, who do not know how to and cannot do anything, and left to themselves, would not find a function in the world to suit them. We crudely refer to them as idiots and imbeciles. It strikes me that the judgment of those who consider such people sacred is preferable. God acts mysteriously in them, and we must respect God in beings whom He seems to overwhelm with too many thoughts, or burden by concealing the key to their intellectual labyrinth.

Will our society ever be rich and Christian enough so that we no longer have to say to the misfits, "You're on your own; too bad for you."? Will humanity ever understand that those who are capable only of loving are good for something and that even the love of a fool is a treasure?

Poor little Sister Anne-Joseph, you did the right thing in turning to God, who alone does not reject advances from a simple heart; as for me, I thank Him for making me love you for that holy simplicity that could only give tenderness and devotion. Let those who have found too much love in this world demand more complexity!

I have saved for last the nun I loved most. She was beyond doubt the pearl of the convent. Madame Mary-Alicia Spiring was the best, the most intelligent, and the most lovable of the hundred and some women, young and old, who lived for a while or a lifetime in the English convent. She was not yet thirty when I met her. She was still very beautiful, although she had too much nose and too little mouth. But her large blue eyes bordered with black lashes were the most beautiful, the most frank, the most gentle eyes I have ever seen in my life. All her generous, maternal, and sincere soul, all her devoted, chaste, and worthy existence showed in those eyes. One could have called them, in Catholic fashion, mirrors of purity. For a long time I had the habit, that I have not entirely lost, of thinking about those eyes when I felt oppressed by the kind of frightening night visions that pursue you after waking. I would imagine myself meeting Madame Alicia's gaze, and that pure beam put the ghosts to flight.

There was something of the ideal in that charming person. I am not exaggerating, and whoever saw her for an instant at the parlor grille, whoever knew her for a few days at the convent felt for her one of those sudden attractions mixed with profound respect that special souls inspire. Religion had been able to render her humble, but nature had already made her modest. She was born with the gift of all the virtues, all the charms, all the powers that the Christian ideal only as understood well by a noble intelligence could develop and preserve. One could sense there was no conflict in her and that she lived in beauty and goodness as in her necessary element. Everything about her was harmonious. Her bearing was magnificent and graceful under the sackcloth and wimple. Her rounded, tapered hands were charming despite a rigidity of the little fingers, which was not usually visible. Her voice was pleasant, her pronunciation was exquisitely distinct in both languages, which she spoke equally well. Born in France of a French mother, raised in France, she was more French than English, and the mixture of the best of the two races made her a perfect being. She had British dignity without its stiffness, religious austerity without its harshness. She sometimes scolded, but in few words, and they were such just and well-motivated reprimands, such direct, clean reproaches—yet accompanied by such encouraging hope—that one felt chastened, ashamed, convinced by her, without being hurt, humiliated, or vexed. The more sincere she was, the more we valued her; the less worthy we felt of the friendship she held for us, the more we loved her; but we always remained hopeful of deserving it, and so desirable and salutary was that affection, we never failed to obtain it.

Several nuns had "daughters," some more than one, among the student boarders; that is to say, on the recommendation of her parents, or on the request of the child and with the consent of the Mother Superior, there was a sort of special maternal adoption. The mothering consisted of particular little attentions, gentle or severe reprimands, according to the offense. A daughter had permission to enter her mother's cell, to ask for her advice or protection, sometimes to go have tea with her in the nun's workroom, to give her a bit of needlework on her feast day, in short to love her and tell her so. Everyone wanted to be Poulette's or Mother Alippe's daughter. Madame Marie-Xavier had daughters. We wished fervently to be Madame Alicia's, but she was stingy with that favor. As she was secretary for the community, she was charged with all the Superior's office work, and thus had little leisure and much fatigue. She had had a beloved daughter, Louise de Courteilles (who later became Mme. d'Aure). Louise had left the convent, and no one dared hope to replace her.

That ambition came to me as to gullible folk who believe anything is possible. The girls around me were all smitten with filial passion for Madame Alicia, but no one dared reveal it. I went to tell it to her bluntly, without worrying about the sermon that awaited me. "You," she said, "you, the biggest devil in the convent? So you really want to make me do penance? What have I ever done to you to make you want to impose on me the guidance of such a bad girl as you? You want to replace my good Louise, my sweet, well-behaved child, you terror? I think that you're crazy, or you want me to be."

"Just try," I said to her, without being disconcerted, "Who knows? Maybe I'll reform. Maybe I'll become charming to please you!"

"That will be the day," she said. "If it's in the hope of mending your ways that I take you on, I will perhaps resign myself, but you are giving me a rough road to salvation, and I would have preferred another."

"An angel like Louise Courteilles doesn't count toward your salvation," I replied. "You didn't deserve any reward for her; you would deserve a great deal for me."

"But what if, after having gone to great trouble, I don't succeed in making you well-behaved and pious? Can you promise to help me at least?"

"Not too much," I answered. "I don't know yet what I am and what I can be. I feel that I love you very much, and I think, however I turn out, you will be forced to love me, too."

"I see that you aren't lacking in pride."

"Oh! you'll see that it isn't that—but I do need a mother. Actually, I have two of them who love me too much, whom I love too much, and we only manage to hurt one another. I can hardly explain that to you, and yet you who have your Mother in the convent should understand it. But be a mother to me in your fashion. I think I shall be satisfied. It's in my own interest that I ask you, and I am not overestimating myself at all. Go on, dear mother, say yes, for I warn you that I have already spoken to my grandmama and to the Mother Superior, and they will also ask you."

Madame Alicia resigned herself, and my classmates, astonished by that adoption, said to me, "You're pretty lucky, aren't you! You, a devil incarnate, always mixed up in ridiculous pranks, you have Madame Eugénie to protect you and Madame Alicia to love you. You were born with a silver spoon in your mouth."

"Maybe!" I replied, with the conceit of a brat.

My affection for that admirable person was, however, more serious than anyone thought, and certainly more serious than she herself believed. I had never felt but one passion in my small being, that of filial love; that passion persevered in me. My real mother at times responded too much to it, and at other times not enough, and since I had been at the convent she seemed to have made a vow to repulse my bursts of affection and render me unto myself, so to speak. My grandmother was sulking because I had accepted the test she had imposed on me. Neither of them was more reasonable than I. I needed a wise mother, and I began to understand that maternal love, to be a refuge, must not be a jealous passion. Despite the wasteful conduct into which my moral being seemed to have absorbed itself and evaporated, I always had my hours of sad reverie and gloomy reflection which I did not share with anyone. I was sometimes so sad while committing my follies that I was forced to pretend I was ill to keep from admitting them. My English classmates made fun of me and said,[35] "You are low-spirited today? What is the matter with you?" Isabelle was in the habit of repeating, whenever I was liverish and dispirited, "She is in her low spirits, in her spiritual absences." She would do my tasks, I would laugh and keep my secret.

I was a devil less by inclination than through passivity. I would have turned good if my devils had wanted to. I liked them, they made me laugh, they drew me out of myself. But five minutes of Madame Alicia's severity did me more good, because in that severity—whether due to special feelings of friendship or to Christian charity—I felt a more serious and durable interest than in the exchange of gaiety between my classmates and me. Had I been able to live in the workroom or the cell of my dear mother, after three days I would no longer have thought one could have a good time playing on the rooftops or in the cellars.

I needed someone to cherish and place in my thoughts above all other beings; to imagine perfection, tranquility, power, and fairness through that being; to venerate an object superior to me, and to give heartfelt, assiduous worship to something like God or Corambé. This something took on the grave and serene features of Marie-Alicia. She was my ideal, my holy love, my chosen mother.

After I had played devil all day, I slid into her cell in the evening after prayers. That was one of the prerogatives of my adoption. Prayers were over by eight-thirty. We went up the stairway to our dormitory, and in the long corridors (that were also called dormitories, because all of the cell doors faced out onto them) we would find the nuns lined up in two rows, returning to their cells while chanting aloud their prayers in Latin. They would stop before a madonna on the last landing, and there they separated after several verses and responses. Each one would enter her own cell without speaking, for between prayers and sleep, silence was their rule.

But those who had a duty to perform for the sick or for their daughters were dispensed from holding to that rule. Thus, I had the right to enter my mother's cell between a quarter to nine and nine o'clock. When the great clock struck nine, her light had to be out and I had to be back in the dormitory. So, sometimes she could only give me five or six minutes, and those even with reservation, her ears attentive to the quarters, demi-quarters, and warning strokes that the old clock rang, for Madame Alicia was scrupulously faithful to the observance of the slightest rules, and she would not have wanted to be even a second late.

"Well," she would say to me as she opened the door on which I scratched in a certain way to gain admittance, "here is my torment again." That was her habitual greeting, and the tone in which she said it was so good, so welcoming, her smile so tender and her look so gentle, that I was quite encouraged to go in. "Let's see," she would say, "what news did you come to tell me? Would you by chance have been good today?"

"No."

"You aren't in your nightcap, however?" (As we know, that was the mark of penance which had almost become a permanent part of my head.)

"I only had to wear it for two hours this evening," I said.

"Ah! very good! And this morning?"

"This morning I had it on at church. I hid behind the others so you wouldn't see me."

"Ah, fear not! I look at you as little as possible, so as not to see that ugly cap. And so, you will have it on again tomorrow?"

"Oh, probably!"

"Then you don't want to reform?"

"I can't yet."

"Then what are you doing here with me?"

"I came to have you scold me."

"Oh, that amuses you?"

"That does me good."

"I don't see it at all, and it certainly does me no good, you wicked child."

"So much the better," I said to her; "that proves you love me."

"And that you don't love me," she admonished.

Then she would scold me, and I took great pleasure in her scolding. "At least," I said to myself, "here is a mother who loves me for myself and who argues with me." I would listen to her with the introspection of a person determined to change her ways, yet I did not in any way dream of doing so. "Well," she would say, "you will change, I hope. Your foolishness will bore you, and God will speak to your soul."

"Do you often pray that that will be so?"

"Yes, often."

"Every day?"

"Every day."

"So, you see, if I were good, you would love me less and wouldn't think about me so often."

She could not keep from laughing, for she had that fund of gaiety that is the stamp of good souls and clear consciences. She would take me by the shoulders and shake me, as if to shake out the devil that possessed me. Then the hour would strike, and she would laughingly throw me out. And I would go back up to the dormitory, bearing, as if by magnetic influence, some of the serenity and candor of that beautiful soul.

I have only told these details to complete the portrait of my dear Marie-Alicia, for I shall frequently have occasion to refer back to my relations with her. I shall now finish my list by saying that we had four lay sisters, only two of whom I remember well, Sister Teresa and Sister Hélène.

Sister Teresa was a tall old woman of the handsome type. She was cheerful, brusque, teasing, and winningly good. She is another of my cherished memories—the one who baptised me Madcap. She did not know a word of French and could not say three words correctly in any language. She was a Scotswoman, skinny, strong, very active, always putting us off in a way that attracted us, pleased at the tricks we played on her, and capable of swatting us with a broom while laughing louder than anyone. She too loved the devils and was not afraid of them.

Her job was to distill mint water, a perfected industry at our convent. The plant was grown in the nuns' garden, in special, large plots. They cut it down three or four times a year, like alfalfa, and took it to a vast cellar room that was Sister Teresa's laboratory. That cellar was located right under the room of the upper class and was accessible by going down a wide stairway. So, naturally, it was one of our first stops when we left for our escapades. But when the distiller was absent, everything was locked up tight, and when she was present, it was unthinkable to frolic among her stills and retorts. We would stop before the open door and tease her, which she took very well. However, since I knew how to carry out my mischief quite coolly, I soon succeeded in penetrating the sanctuary. At first and for some time, I limited myself to observation; I liked to watch her. Alone in that huge cave, lighted by a shaft of daylight that fell from the vent onto her violet gown, her greyish black veil, and her lined face as lusterless as baked clay, she looked like a witch from *Macbeth*, making her incantations around the cauldrons. Sometimes she was as immobile as a statue seated by the still where the precious liqueur flowed out drop by drop; she would read the Bible in silence, or murmur her prayers in a hoarse, monotonous voice. She was as beautiful in her rugged old age as a Rembrandt portrait.

One day, when she was preoccupied or dozing, I tiptoed right up to her, and when she saw me in the midst of her flasks and all the fragile paraphernalia which a playful battle would have put in jeopardy, she was forced to capitulate and tolerate my curiosity. She was so kind that she took me under her wing, God knows why, and from then on I could often slip in by her side. When she saw that I was not clumsy and did not break anything, she let herself be entertained by my hanging around, and while scolding me for not being in class, she never pushed me out, as she did the others. The odor of the mint made her eyes hurt and gave her migraines. I helped her spread and stir her fragrant mash, and on summer days, when we were suffocating in class, I found a great sense of well-being by taking refuge in that cellar where the aroma enchanted me.

The other lay sister, Sister Hélène, was the head servant of the convent. She made the beds in the dormitory, swept the church, etc. Since, after Madame Alicia, she was the nun dearest to me, I shall have much more to say about her in the right time and place, but at this stage of my narration I have nothing to say about her. For a long time I did not notice her at all.

The other two lay sisters did the cooking. Thus, at the convent as elsewhere, there was an aristocracy and a democracy. The "choir ladies" lived like patricians. They wore white, and had fine linen. The lay sisters worked like proletarians, and their dark habits were of coarser cloth. They were true women of the people, without any education, and much less absorbed by the church and the services than by running the large household. There were not enough of them for that task, so we had, in addition, two lay servants, Marie-Anne and Marie-Josèphe, her niece, two excellent creatures who compensated me well for the loss of Rose and Julie.

In general, everyone was as good as God in that large family of women. I never had a single wicked classmate, and among the nuns and mistresses, except for Miss D., I never found anything but affection or tolerance. How could I not cherish the memory of those days, the most tranquil, the happiest of my life? I suffered there physically and morally through my own doing, but nowhere have I ever suffered less at the hands of others.   *S.B./F.K.*

XIII

Isabelle's departure for Switzerland. —Sophie's protective friendship for me. —Fannelly. —The friendship roll. —Anna. —Isabelle leaves the convent. —Fannelly consoles me. —A look backward. —Misunderstood measures of the nuns. —I write verse. —I write my first novel. —My grandmother comes back to Paris. —M. Abraham. —Serious preparation for presentation at court. —I relapse into family grievances. —I am presented to suitors. —Visits to the old contessas. —I am given a cell. —Description of my cell. —I begin to tire of deviltry. —*The Lives of the Saints.* —Saint Simeon Stylites, Saint Augustine, Saint Paul. —Christ in the Garden of Gesthemane. —The Gospel. —I enter the church one evening.

My first sorrow in the upper class was caused by Isabelle's departure. Her parents were taking her to Switzerland with her older sister, who was not at the convent. Isabelle left, overjoyed at the prospect of such a wonderful trip, saddened only because she would miss Sophie, and paying little attention to my tears. That hurt me. I loved Sophie, and I was doubly jealous, because she preferred Isabelle to me and because Isabelle preferred her to me. I suffered a few days of intense grief. But jealousy in friendships is not one of my failings; I despise and overcome it fairly easily. When Sophie wept over her friend and rejected my consolation, I did not act proud. I begged her to share her longings, to be sorrowful with me without restraint, and to talk to me about Isabelle without ever worrying that she would try my patience and affection for her. "In fact," Sophie said as she threw herself into my arms, "I don't know why Isabelle and I treated you like a child. You have more feeling than we imagined, and I swear to be your true friend. You will permit me to love Isabelle most of all. It is her right by seniority, but after Isabelle, I realize it is you I love more than anyone else here."

I joyfully accepted the part I had been assigned and became Sophie's inseparable companion. She was dependably kind and charming, but I must admit that, where heartfelt feeling and complete devotion were concerned, I always put myself at her disposal. Sophie's feelings were exclusive in spite of herself; she was unable to share her soul with more than one person. I would sometimes accuse her of ingratitude; then I would realize I was wrong, and without forsaking her presence, I opened my heart to other friendships.

Mary left on a trip to England. She was to return shortly, and I was not overly distressed, because my promotion to the upper class had kept us very much apart and because, on her return, she was to join me there. But she was away longer than expected. She did not return for a year, and then she went back to the lower class. The affection that now possessed me made up for all these losses, and I found in Fannelly de Brisac the most loving of all my friends.

She was small, blond, as fresh as a rose, and with an expression so lively, so open, so kind, that it was a pleasure to look at her. She had magnificent ash-blond hair which hung in long ringlets above her blue eyes and rounded cheeks. As she was always in motion—unable to walk without running or run without bouncing like a ball—the continual movement of her hair was the merriest thing in the world. Her ruby lips knew only how to smile, and being from Nérac, she had a little Gascon accent that charmed the ear. Her eyebrows met above her little nose, her eyes sparkled. She was always on the move and venturing, never lost in daydreams. She would babble on without a break. She was all fire, all heart, all sunshine, a true Southern type, the most lovable, the liveliest, the most considerate companion I have ever had.

She liked me first and told me so, without knowing how I would react. I responded immediately and with all my heart, without knowing where it would lead me. But my lucky star presided over this inspired pact of friendship. I found in her a wealth of goodness; the sweetness of an angel in the restlessness of an imp; a soul radiating moral well-being; an inexhaustible abundance of courage; an eager, clever kindness; an instinctve uprightness and generosity which were unfailing; a character of such integrity and equanimity as is rarely encountered. Since that time, she has always lived far from me; we have almost never written to each other. She was not a "penwoman," as we used to say in the convent. We have not seen each other again. She married a very respected man, M. Le Franc de Pompignan, but one whose political and social tenets must be completely opposed to mine.[19] But in spite of that, there is one thing I am as sure of as I am of my own existence, and that is that Fannelly still loves me warmly and tenderly, that no cloud has obscured the irresistible and total understanding we felt for each other thirty years ago, that she never thinks of me without knowing she loves me and that I love her in return. Who wouldn't have loved her? She had not a single defect, not a single failing. Seeing her laugh—so breathless, so airy—you would have thought she hadn't a care in the world, and yet her mind was always on pleasing others; she thrived, in a sense, on the affection she bore you and the pleasure she wished to give you. I always see her coming into the classroom ten times a day (for she knew how to leave the room better than anyone), turning her pretty little blond head right and left as she looked for me. She was near-sighted, despite her beautiful eyes. "Auntie," she would say, "where is my Auntie? What have you done with my Auntie? Girls, girls, who has seen my Auntie?" "Here I am," I would call to her, "come here to me."

"Ah! it's indeed my Auntie! You saved me a place next to you. Good, good, we're going to laugh. But what's the matter, Auntie? You look worried, tell me what's wrong!"

"Nothing."

"In that case, laugh! Are you bored? Oh, yes, I'll bet you are. You've been quiet for at least an hour. Come on, let's pack up; I've found something enchanting."

And she would lead me off to comb the garden or tramp the cloister, having always prepared some outlandish surprise to amuse me. There was no way to be sad or even dreamy around her, and what was remarkable about this natural charmer was that her constant motion never wore you out. She wrested you from yourself and never made you regret that you allowed it to happen. For me she was sanity—health for body and soul. Heaven sent her to me who always needed precisely someone else's initiative to exist.

I found it very comforting to be so loved, and I should add that this child was the only person in my life who I felt loved me at any time with unchanging intensity and placidity.

How did she manage, during two years of close friendship, not to tire of me for one instant? Because she was exceptionally generous. Also because she had a most unusual spirit. She had found a way to transform me, turn me into an amusing person, lift me so completely out of my bouts of listlessness and depression, that she had decided I was as lively as she. She did not suspect it was she who made me buoyant.

In the convent, we had the childish and droll tradition of drawing up lists and adhering to the order of affections thus established. We all demanded this of one another, which proves that women are born jealous and insist on their rights in the domain of friendship as they lack other means to command respect in society. Thus we would make up a roll of our more or less intimate friends; they were listed in order of preference, and the initials of our four or five favorites formed an emblem that could be seen on notebooks, walls, desk tops, as in olden times certain figures and colors were put on one's coat of arms and palfrey. Once we had given a girl first place, we did not have the right to take it away in order to give it to someone else. The rule of seniority was law. And so, in the upper class, Isabelle Clifford was invariably at the top of my list, followed by Sophie Cary. When Fannelly came into my life, she could only have third place, and although Fannelly had no better friends than me, although she never had other friends than mine, she accepted third place without jealousy or chagrin. After her came Anna Vié, who was fourth; and for nearly a year I formed no other friendships. The name of Madame Alicia still crowned the list; she shone alone, above them all, as though she were my sun. The initials of my four classmates formed the word *Isfa*, which I wrote on all the objects I had for my use in the classroom, as though it were a cabalistic formula. Sometimes, I would surround it with a halo of little *a*'s to signify that Alicia filled all the rest of my heart. How many times Madame Eugénie, who with her weak eyes managed somehow to see everything, and stuck her curious little nose into all our papers, must have wracked her brain to discover what this mysterious word meant! Each of us, having some logograph of the same sort, let her assume that we had a special language and that, with the aid of this language, we conspired to undo her authority. But she questioned in vain. We told her they were letters written haphazardly to test the quills. A mystery is an especially nice thing when there is no real secret behind it!

Anna Vié, my fourth, was very intelligent, gay, mocking, mischievous, the wittiest talker in the convent. It was impossible not to be pleased in her company. She was plain and poor, and these two forms of disgrace that she laughed about all the time were the source of her greatest charm; she was an orphan whose only means of support was an old Greek uncle, M. de Cesarini, whom she barely knew and feared greatly. A devil of the first order, especially hot-tempered, dreaded for her sarcasm, she nevertheless had a noble and generous heart. Her sparkling gaiety hid a great reservoir of bitterness. Her future, which appeared to her in the darkest light; her wit, which caused her to be feared more than loved; her poor little faded black dresses; her small form, which was not developing at all; her yellow, bilious complexion, her strange little eyes—all were subjects for her surface jests and secret suffering. Because of this, everyone believed her to be envious of her classmates' advantages. That was not the case. She had great surety of judgment, lofty ideas, and when she loved you enough to put aside her laughter, her noble tears drew your sympathy. For a long time we cherished the shared dream that she would come to live at Nohant when I returned there. My grandmother seemed to approve of the plan, but Anna's uncle, to whom she spoke of it first, was not in favor of it.

I have seen her once or twice since our parting. She married a M. Desparbès de Lussan, of the family of Mme. de Lussan who had been a close friend of my grandmother. Once married, Anna was not the same person. She had grown, her complexion had become whiter; though still not pretty, she had become attractive. She lived in the country near Ivry. Her husband was neither young, nor rich, nor handsome, but she was pleased to have him. And either to humor him or to reconcile herself to her lot, which did not appear too exciting, she transformed herself from the very determined skeptic I had known into a devoutly religious woman.

Another change which surprised me even more, and which hurt me, was her constrained and cold behavior toward me. I was not yet George Sand, and I hardly dreamed of becoming her. I was still a Catholic, and so unknown to the world that no one thought of saying anything bad about me. The reserve of my former friend would perhaps not have prevented me from seeing her again, because I thought I understood that she was no happier in society than in the convent, and that she would feel the need to open up to me were we ever alone together. But I did not live in Paris, and the twelve or thirteen years I spent at Nohant after my marriage perforce cut me off from my friends from the convent. I learned that Anna had lost her husband after a few years of marriage, and I do not know what has become of her. Would that she could be happy! She always despaired of that ability, and yet she richly deserved it.

For almost a year, Sophie, Fannelly, Anna, and I were inseparable. I was the link among them, for before Sophie had accepted me as her second, and the two others had taken me for their first, they had not been close. Our friendship was unclouded. I did suffer a little from Sophie's frequent expressions of indifference, the result of her belief that she should love the absent Isabelle more than she did me, while I felt obliged to love the absent Isabelle and the indifferent Sophie more than Fannelly and Anna, who adored me totally. But that was the rule, the law. We would have thought we deserved the odious epithet "fickle" if we had changed the order of the names on the roll. I must say in my own defense that, despite the list, despite the rule of seniority, despite exchanged promises, I could not keep myself from feeling that I loved Fannelly more than all the others, and I often presented her with this rationalization: "By my will you are only my third, but against my will you are my first, and perhaps my only, friend." She would laugh. "What does it matter to me," she would say, "if you count me as your third, if you love me as I love you? Go on, Auntie, I don't ask more than that of you. I am not proud, and I love those you love." Isabelle returned from Switzerland after a few months, but she came to say goodbye; she was leaving the convent for good. She was going to England. I fell into a state of total despair, more especially as, completely absorbed in Sophie, Isabelle was barely aware of my existence and would turn around and say, "What does the little one have to cry about?" I felt that was very cruel, but when Sophie told her that I had been the one to console her and that she had accepted me as a friend, Isabelle made an effort to console me and insisted that I accompany them on their walks. She returned to visit us one other time, and left shortly after. She married very well. I have never seen her since.

That separation left Sophie inconsolable. I, whose friendship with Isabelle had been of shorter duration and less fulfilled, allowed myself to be consoled by dear Fannelly, and I was right to do so, as Isabelle had never considered me anything but a child. Moreover, she was perhaps more sentimental than loving.

My year, or more nearly eighteen months, of deviltry went by like one day, without my really being aware of it. Sophie and Anna claimed to be bored to death in the convent, and whether it was just an affectation or the truth, all my classmates said the same thing. Only the devout refused to complain, but they seemed no happier for that. Apparently all these children had been happy with their families. Those who, like Anna, had no family, and whose leave days were not happy, dreamed of a host of pleasures, balls, delights, travel, and heaven knows what other signs of liberation from the discipline of duties. Confinement and rules are apparently what is most antipathetic to adolescence.

As for me, if I suffered physically from being cloistered, I was not aware of any mental torment; my imagination did not anticipate the years to come, and the future inspired me more with fear than longing. I have never liked to look ahead. The unknown terrifies me; I prefer the past, though it saddens me. The present is always a kind of compromise between what we have wanted and what we have gotten. Such as it is, we accept or tolerate it, as we have tolerated and accepted many things. But who knows what we shall be able to accept or tolerate tomorrow? I have never allowed anyone to tell my fortune; I certainly do not believe in clairvoyance, but the earthly future always seems to me to be something so serious that I do not like people to talk to me about it even in riddles or conundrums. On my own account I have never asked God for anything in my prayers except to have the strength to withstand what happens to me.

With this turn of mind—which has never changed—I was happier in the convent than anywhere else, for there, as no one really knew the details of anyone else's past, no one could speak to anyone else about what would probably become of them. Parents always speak of the future to their children. This future of their offspring is their continual worry, their loving and anxious pre-occupation. They would like to arrange it, make it secure; they spend their lives thinking about it, and yet, all their careful planning is undone by fate. Children never profit from the counsel they are given. A certain instinct for independence or curiosity most often impels them in the opposite direction. Nuns do not have that kind of concern for the children they raise. For them, there is no earthly future. They know only heaven or hell, and the future, in their language, is called salvation. Even before becoming devout, this kind of future did not frighten me as much as the other. Since, according to Catholics, one is free to choose between salvation and damnation, since grace is never withheld and the least bit of good will puts you on the path where the angels themselves deign to tread before you, I told myself with haughty confidence that I ran no risk and that I would think about all that when I felt like it. And I did not hurry to think about it. I was not wary of questions of personal interest. Such consideratons have never affected me even in matters of religion. I want-ed to love God simply for the joy of loving Him, I did not wish to fear Him. That is what I would say when someone would try to frighten me.

Without reflecting or caring about this life or the one to come, I thought only about amusing myself, or more exactly, I did not even think about that; I did not think about anything. I have spent three quarters of my life this way, in a dormant state, as it were. I do believe I shall die without having really thought about living, and yet, I shall have lived in my fashion, as dreaming and meditating are imperceptible actions that fill the hours beautifully and engage one's intellectual energies without asking too much of them.

And so I lived at the convent, not noticing how, and always ready to enjoy myself as my friends saw fit. Anna loved to chatter, so I would listen. Sophie was a melancholy dreamer, so I would follow her around in silence, not disturbing her musings, not being sulky with her when she emerged from them. Fannelly loved to run, laugh, poke about, plan some kind of deviltry, so I would be impetuous, joyful, and active with her. Fortunately for me, it was she who predominated; Anna followed us out of friendship, and Sophie did so for want of anything better to do. And so began a period of escapades and vagabondage which lasted entire days. We would meet in some corner or other. Fannelly, whose little purse was always the fullest and who managed to buy secretly from the porter anything she wanted, always surprised us with deli-cious things to eat. A magnificent melon, cakes, baskets of cherries or grapes, fritters, pâtés, and goodness knows what else! She would wrack her brain to regale us with something unexpected and wonderful. For one whole summer we lived on contraband food of the craziest kind! You had to be fifteen not to get sick from it. For my part, I would contribute the tidbits that Madame Alicia and Sister Teresa gave me; the latter, turning out her own delicious dumplings and puddings, would call me into her laboratory to fill my pockets with them.

To pool our delicacies and eat them in secret during the times we were not allowed to eat was a feast, a fine picnic, replete with uncontrollable laughter and infernal pranks, such as throwing the crust of a jam tart up to the ceiling and watching it artfully stick there, hiding chicken bones in the works of a piano, scattering fruit peels in a dark stairway so unsuspecting persons would slip and fall. All this seemed enormously witty and would make us drunk on our own laughter, for all we ever had to drink was water or lemonade.

Our search for the victim was carried out with ardor, and I could tell of many disappointments this caused us. But I have already told of too many childish pranks and, I fear, with too much complacence.

I would not want, however, to forget that my point in retracing my life is to awaken my readers' interests in their own lives. Should I destroy as childish and useless the preceding pages? No! The gaiety, even the mischievousness, of adolescence, always mixed with a certain poetry or a great flurry of imagination, represents a phase of our existence that we never remember without feeling ourselves better for it when we are older. Adolescence is an age of candor, courage, and often unreasonable, but always sincere and spontaneous, devotion; if age gives us experience and judgement, it takes away this early artlessness, which would make us perfect beings if we could retain it as we acquire wisdom. For want of reason, these treasures of our first youth are lost or fruitless, but by taking ourselves back to that time of moral prodigality, we regain possession of our real wealth, and not one of us would be capable of an evil act if the image of our early innocence were always in our mind's eye. That is why these memories may be as beneficial to everyone else as they are to me.

Nevertheless, I must abridge, since if I were to set down everything I remember with pleasure and with a clarity that surprises even me, I would fill an entire volume. Suffice it to say that I spent a long time in this state of deviltry, doing nothing whatever except learning a little Italian, a bit of music, something of drawing—as little as possible, to tell the truth. I only worked hard at English, which I hastened to learn because, if you did not understand that language, you missed half of what went on in the convent. I also began to feel the urge to write. We all had a mania for writing, and those girls who lacked imagination spent their time writing letters to each other—letters often full of tender, naïve charm, the kind of letters we were strictly forbidden to write, as if they had been love letters, but which prohibition served only to make more ardent and more frequent.

Let me say in passing that the great fault of monastic education is the attempt to exaggerate chastity. We were forbidden to walk about in two's; there had to be at least three of us together at a time; we were forbidden to kiss; there was concern over our innocent letter-writing, and all this would have given us something to think about if we had had so much as an inkling of the evil instincts that were apparently attributed to us. I know I would have been deeply hurt if I had understood the reason for these strange restrictions. But most of us, raised simply and chastely in the bosom of our families, attributed this system to piety, which inhibits the expression of human sentiments in order to foster an all-consuming love for the Creator.

So I began to write, and my first attempt, like those of all young minds, took the form of the alexandrine. I knew the rules of versification, and I had always, in reaction to Deschartres, maintained an absolute opposition to them; I was totally misguided; there is no middle ground between prose and regular verse. But I attempted to do something between the two—to versify the prose and conserve a kind of rhythm, without worrying about the rhyme and the caesura. This meant that I took total liberty, claiming that the rule was too rigid, that it hindered the outpouring of my thoughts. Thus, I wrote many so-called poems, all of which were crowned with success in the convent, where no one, I admit, was too rigorous. Next, I was taken with the idea of writing a novel, and although I was not yet in the least devout, I wrote a novel about Christian piety.

The would-be novel was really a long story, for it contained only about a hundred pages. The hero and heroine met one evening, in the country, at the foot of a madonna, where they were saying their prayers. They admired and inspired each other. But even though convention required them to fall in love, they did not. I had resolved, on Sophie's advice, to lead them to the point of love, but when I arrived at that point, after I had described them both as beautiful and perfect, and in an enchanting place (at the entrance to a Gothic chapel, shaded by giant oaks, at sunset), I was unable to portray the awakening of their love for each other. I did not have it in me; not a single word would come forth. I gave up the attempt. I made them ardently pious, even though piety was no more part of me than was love, but I understood it because I had the spectacle of it before my eyes, and perhaps, too, the germ of that kind of love was beginning to blossom in me without my realizing. The fact remains that my two young creations, after several chapters devoted to voyages and adventures which have completely slipped my mind, gave themselves to God—the young lady took the veil, and the hero became a priest.

Sophie and Anna thought my novel "nicely written," and the details pleased them. But they declared that Fitz Gerald (that was the name of the hero) was a very boring character and that the heroine was hardly more interesting. There was a mother, who pleased them more, but all in all, my prose had less success than my verses, and did not engage even me. I wrote another novel, a pastoral one, which I judged worse than my first and with which I lit the stove one winter's day. Then I gave up writing, having come to the conclusion that it could never amuse me, and finding that in comparison with the infinite sweetness I had tasted in my imagination, writing would be a cold, lifeless pastime.

I still continued, without confiding the fact to anyone, my endless poem of Corambé. But I worked by fits and starts because, as I have said, life in the convent was the real novel, and the subject was the victim in the cellar, a much more interesting subject than any imagined one, since we took it seriously.

My grandmother arrived in the middle of the second winter I spent in the convent. She left two months later, and I went out five or six times in all. My boarding school manners pleased her no more than my country ways had. I was completely unpolished. I was as distracted as ever. The dancing lessons given me by M. Abraham, former teacher of Marie-Antoinette, had not rendered me at all graceful. Yet M. Abraham did his utmost to imbue us with courtly bearing. He would arrive wearing a square-cut jacket, a mousseline jabot, a white cravat with trailing ends, breeches and black silk stockings, buckled shoes, a powdered wig and purse, a diamond on his finger, and a fancy handkerchief in his hand. He was about eighty years old, still slender, gracious, and elegant; he had an attractive, wrinkled face, veined with red and blue on a yellow background, like an old leaf colored by autumn, but still fine and distinguished. He was the best of men, the politest, the most serious, the most proper. He gave lessons to groups of fifteen or twenty, in the Mother Superior's large parlor, whose grille we would cross on that occasion. There, M. Abraham demonstrated proper deportment with mathematical precision, and after the routine steps he would sit in an armchair and say to us, "Young ladies, I am the king, or the queen, and as you are all destined to be presented at court, we shall practice how you enter, curtsy, and leave—all of which is part of the ceremony."

At other times we would learn about more ordinary ceremonies. We played at being a roomful of important personages. Our teacher had some of us sit while others practiced entering and leaving; he would show how to greet our hostess, then a princess, a duchess, a marquise, a countess, a vicountess, a baroness, or the wife of a judge, each with the degree of respect or alacrity her rank entitled her to. We did the same for a prince, duke, marquis, count, viscount, baron, knight, judge, vidame, and abbot. M. Abraham played all these roles and would greet each one of us, to teach us how to respond to all the bows, how to retrieve a glove or receive a proffered fan, how to smile, how to cross the room, how to sit down, how to change seats, and who remembers what else! Every move was anticipated, even the right way of sneezing, in this French code of manners. We would burst out laughing and were purposely awkward in all sorts of ways to discourage him. Then, at the end of the lesson, to send the good man off happy (for it was barbarous to laugh at such kindness and patience), we affected all the graces and expressions he asked of us. For us it was a comedy we could hardly play without laughing to his face, but he taught us how to play the parts more or less well. The deportment of Father Abraham's time must surely have been very different from that of today; since the more purposely ridiculous and affected we were, the happier he was, and the more he would thank us for being so eager to learn.

In spite of so much attention and instruction, I still slouched, moved too abruptly, walked too naturally, and could not bear the thought of gloves or deep curtsies. My grandmama would scold me excessively for these vices, but in her own way, that is, sweetly and with tender words. It took great self-control for me to hide the annoyance and irritation these eternal little critiques caused me. I would so like to have pleased her! I was never able to. She adored me, lived only for me, and yet it seemed that, in my simple ways and in my unfortunate lack of coquetry, there was something she could not abide, an aversion she could not overcome, perhaps a kind of original sin which smacked of my lowly ancestry in spite of all her efforts. But still, I was not a total clod; my calm and naturally confident character did not call forth inappropriate or vulgar behavior. I was preoccupied most of the time, God knows by what, probably by nothing. I had nothing to chat about with my grandmother. What was there to talk about? Our escapades, the cellars, our laziness, the convent friendships? They were always the same, and I did not have my sights on society and the future she would have liked to see me absorbed in. I was already being presented with prospective husbands without being aware of it. When they had left, I was asked how I had liked them, and it turned out that I had not looked at them. I was scolded for thinking of other things during their visits—a game of prisoner's base or the purchase of some rubber balls might be running through my brain. I was not precocious; I had been a late talker in my early childhood, and so it had been with everything else. Physically I had developed rapidly, and I had the appearance of a young lady, but my mind, sluggish and wrapped up in itself, was still that of a child. Far from allowing me to remain in that state of innocence, they wanted to hasten my growing up.

That great solicitude of my grandmama arose from a depth of tenderness. She felt herself growing old and slowly dying. She wanted to see me married, establish me in society, be certain I would not fall under the influence of my mother. Fearing she would not have enough time, she attempted to instill in me the rituals of society and a distrust of my mother's family. She wished to distance me from that lower-class environment she feared I would fall into again when she left me. My character, my sentiments, and my ideas all refused to go along with her. Respect and love made me hold my tongue. Sometimes she took me for a fool, other times she thought me sly. I was neither. I loved her, and I suffered in silence.

My mother seemed to have given up trying to come to my aid in this mute and painful struggle. She always made fun of high society, was always hugging me and admiring me as though I were something prodigious, and showed little concern for my future. It seemed as though she was ready to accept for herself a future in which I was no longer an essential party. I was desolate over her apparent abandonment of me after the passion she had showered on me in my childhood. She no longer took me to her apartment. I saw my sister once or twice in two or three years. My outings were filled with visits to the old contessas my grandmother made me call on with her. She apparently wanted them to take an interest in my youth, to create relationships and support for me among those who would survive her. These ladies continued to be repugnant to me, the only exception being Mme. de Pardaillon. In the evening, we would dine either in the home of my Villeneuve cousins or with my Uncle Beaumont. I had to return to the convent just when I was beginning to feel at ease with my family. Thus, my leave days were dismal. In the morning, joyful and eager, I would arrive *chez nous*, my heart full of happiness and impatience. Three hours later, I would be getting sad. I would be even more so when saying goodbye. Only back in the convent would I feel calm and cheerful.

The happiest occasion within its walls was when I finally got my own cell. All the young ladies of the upper class had one; only I had remained for a long while in the dormitory, and this because everyone feared the noise I made at night. We suffered horribly in that dormitory under the eaves, from winter's cold and summer's heat. We slept badly because there was always one little girl who cried in the night out of fear or from a stomach-ache. Also, not having one's own place, not being by oneself for one hour a day or night, goes against anyone who loves to dream and muse. A communal life is the ideal of happiness among people who love one another; I experienced that in the convent and have never forgotten it. But all thinking beings need their hours of solitude and composure. Only by having these can they truly enjoy the delights of communality.

The cell I was finally given was the worst one in the convent. It was an attic room in the wing alongside the church. It was next to a similar one occupied by Coralie Le Marrois, an austere, pious, fearful, and simple person whose proximity might, they thought, keep me in line. I got along well with her despite the differences in our tastes; I was careful not to disturb her prayers or her sleep, and to decamp noiselessly when going to join Fannelly and any other chatterboxes on the landing, with whom we would wander part of the night among the onions in the storage room or in the tribunes of the organ. We had to pass the convent maid Marie-Josèphe's room, but she was a sound sleeper.

My cell was about ten feet long by six feet wide. From my bed, I could touch the sloping ceiling with my head. The door, when opened, scraped the chest of drawers facing it, next to the window; then to close the door, you had to get into the window's embrasure. The window had four small, square panes and looked out on a covered drainpipe that obstructed my view down to the courtyard. But my view of the horizon was magnificent. From over the tops of the great chestnut trees in the garden I could see part of Paris. Large tracts of nurseries and vegetable gardens extended around the grounds. If not for the blue line of monuments and houses that formed the horizon, I could have fancied myself not quite in the country, but in a large village. The convent belltower and the low buildings of the cloister served to set off the foreground. At night, under the light of the moon, it was a ravishing sight. I would hear the churchbell sounding close by, and I had some trouble getting used enough to it to be able to sleep, but gradually it became a pleasure to be awakened gently by its melancholy timbre, and to hear in the distance the nightingales take up again their interrupted song.

My furniture consisted of a bed of painted wood, an old dresser, a wicker chair, a threadbare rug, and an extremely pretty little Louis XV harp that had formerly shone in my grandmother's beautiful arms, and that I would play a little when singing. I had permission to practice the harp in my room; it gave me an excuse to spend a free hour there every day, and although I did not practice at all, this hour of solitude and reverie became precious to me. The sparrows, attracted by my bread, entered fearlessly and ventured as far as my bed to feed. Although this miserable cell was like a furnace in summer and literally an icebox in winter (the moisture on the roof froze into icicles that hung from my leaky ceiling), I loved it passionately, and I remember kissing the walls fervently when I left, I was so attached to it. It would be hard for me to say what a world of dreams seemed connected to that dusty, wretched little niche. Only there did I regain my bearings and my self-possession. By day, I would think of nothing; I would watch the clouds, look at the branches, follow the flight of the swallows. At night, I would listen to the distant, muffled sounds of the great city that came like a slowly diminishing rattle to mix with the rustic sounds of the suburb. At daybreak, the noises of the convent would come awake boldly drowning out those dying sounds. Our roosters would start crowing; our bells would ring matins; the blackbirds in the garden would repeat over and over their morning song; then the monotonous voices of the nuns chanting the service would float up to me through the halls and the thousand cracks in this resonant pile. In contrast to the nuns' voices, those of the house purveyors, rough and raucous, would rise up from the deep well of the courtyard directly below me; and finally, the strident call of Marie-Josèphe, in charge of waking us, hurrying from room to room, grinding the bolts as she unlocked the corridor doors, brought an end to my aural contemplation.

I slept little. I have never been a sound sleeper. I have never felt impelled to sleep until just when it was time to think about waking up. I would dream of Nohant; in my dreams it had become a paradise, and yet I felt no rush at all to return there; and when my grandmother announced that I would have no vacation because I had to make the most of my studying time so as not to remain in the convent for years, I accepted it without bitterness, so much did I fear to encounter anew in Nohant the problems that had made me not regret having left it.

Those studies for which my grandmama sacrificed the pleasure of seeing me were more or less worthless. She really cared only about my deportment, and since becoming a devil, I no longer cared to bother with those lessons. Sometimes this errant idleness bored me, but how to break the habit after letting myself sink into it for so long!

The moment came at last for a great change to take place in me. I became religious. It happened suddenly, like a passion that ignites in a soul unaware of its own powers. I had used up, so to speak, my laziness and complacency toward my fellow devils and my reaction of silent, systematic rebellion to discipline. The only forceful love I had experienced—filial love—had left me worn out and crushed. I worshipped Madame Alicia, but that was a tranquil kind of love; I needed a burning passion. I was fifteen years old. All my needs stemmed from my heart, and my heart was bored, if I may put it that way. The cult of personality had not awakened in me. I did not have that immoderate concern for myself that I have since seen develop at that age in almost all the young girls I have known. I needed to love outside of myself, and I knew of nothing on this earth that I could have loved with all my might.

Still, I did not look to God. The religious ideal—what Christians call grace—came over me and took possession of me by surprise. The sermons of the nuns and mistresses had absolutely no effect on me. Even Madame Alicia had no appreciable influence on me. This is how it happened; I shall recount it without explaining it, because in these sudden transformations of the spirit, there is something mysterious which we should not try to plumb.

Every morning at seven we heard mass; we would go back to the chapel at four o'clock and spend half-an-hour there. The pious girls would use the time for meditation, prayer, or some inspirational reading. The others would yawn, doze, or whisper when the mistress did not have her eye on them. For want of anything else to do, I picked up a book I had been handed and which I had not yet deigned to open. The pages were still stuck together by their gilt edges; it was an abridged version of *The Lives of the Saints*. I opened it at random. I happened on the odd legend of Saint Simeon Stylites, in which Voltaire had found much to ridicule and that seemed more like the story of an Indian fakir than a Christian philosopher. The legend made me smile at first, then its very strangeness struck me, held me; I reread it more attentively, and I found in it more poetry than absurdity. The next day I read another story, and the day after that I devoured several with keen interest. I did not believe the miracles, but the faith, courage, stoicism of the confessors and martyrs seemed wondrous to me and plucked some secret string that was beginning to vibrate in me.

At the back of the choir was a superb painting by Titian, which I never could see very clearly. Hung too far away and in a dark corner, and itself very dark, in it you could only make out some masses of a warm color on a somber background. It pictured Jesus in the Garden of Gesthemane at the moment when he falls fainting into the angel's arms. The Saviour has sunk to his knees, one of his arms extended on those of the angel, who has lifted to his chest the fine head of the desperate and dying Christ. The painting was hung directly facing me, and by dint of looking at it, I had guessed more than realized its contents. There was just one moment of the day when I could somewhat grasp the details; that was in winter, when the setting sun cast a ray of light on the angel's red drapery and on the bare, white arm of the Christ. The sparkle of the glass made that fleeting moment blinding, and at that very moment I would always experience an indescribable emotion, even at a time when I was not and did not imagine I would ever become devout.

While leafing through *The Lives of the Saints*, my eyes returned more often to the painting; as it was summer, the setting sun no longer illuminated it at the prayer hour, but I no longer needed to see the object of my contemplation as much as to meditate on it. By unconsciously searching those indistinct and impressive masses, I attempted to understand the meaning of Christ's death, the secret of his chosen, yet so bitter, suffering, and I began to have a presentiment of something grander and more profound than what I had been told; I would become deeply sad myself, as though afflicted with untold pity and suffering. A few tears welled up in my eyes, I wiped them away furtively, ashamed of being moved without knowing why. I could not have said it was the beauty of the painting, since only enough could be made out to say that it seemed to be something beautiful.

Another painting, more visible but less deserving of visibility, depicted Saint Augustine under the fig tree, with the miraculous ray of light within which was written the famous *Tolle, lege* [Take it, read it], the mysterious words that the son of Monica believed he heard coming from the foliage and that impelled him to open the Gospel. I looked up the life of Saint Augustine, which had been alluded to in the convent since, as patron saint of the order, he was especially venerated there. I took extraordinary pleasure in that story, which evoked a great character of sincerity and enthusiasm. From it, I turned to that of Saint Paul, and the *cur me persequeris?* [why do you pursue me?] made a powerful impression on me. The smattering of Latin Deschartres had taught me allowed me to understand part of the service, and I started to listen to it and began to find in the psalms recited by the nuns wonderful poetry and simplicity. By that time a week had flown by, during which I found the Catholic religion worthy of study.

The *Tolle, lege,* finally convinced me to open the Gospel and read it attentively. On first reading it did not impress me greatly. It did not have the attraction of novelty. I had already enjoyed the simple and wonderful side of it, but my grandmother had so successfully managed to convince me the miracles were ridiculous, she had so often repeated Voltaire's jokes about the evil spirit's being transported from a person possessed by it to a herd of pigs, she had so well warned me against being carried away, that I resisted out of habit and was unmoved when rereading the Passion.

The evening of that same day, I sadly tramped the stones of the cloister at dusk. Everyone was in the garden; I was out of sight of the chaperones, fraudulently as usual, but I had no thoughts of mischief and no desire to be with my classmates. I was at loose ends. There was nothing more to accomplish by way of deviltry. I saw several nuns pass and some student boarders on their way to pray and meditate in the church by themselves, as was the custom of the most devout girls during their free time. I thought about pouring ink into the fount, but that had been done before; about hanging Whiskey by his paw from the bell cord of the cloister, but that, too, was an old trick. I realized my disorderly existence was nearing an end, that I must enter a new phase, but which one? To become a sage or a beast? The sages were too reserved, the beasts too cowardly. But were the devout, the fervent girls happy? No, their devotion was too gloomy, as though it were an illness. The devils dreamed up thousands of annoyances, indignations, ways of making them furious—a fury they could not easily repress. Their lives were torture, a struggle between ridicule, on one hand, and a slackening of devotion, on the other. Moreover, faith is like love: searching does not reveal it; we find it when we least expect to. I did not know that, but what made me resist a devout life was the fear of finding it in a spirit of calculation or through a desire for personal gain.

"Besides, not everyone who wants faith finds it," I told myself. "I don't have it, I never will. I made my last attempt today: I read the very book, the life and doctrine of the Saviour, and I wasn't touched. My heart will remain empty."

While communing thus with myself, I watched the zealous ones pass like phantoms in the coming dark, stealing off to pour out their souls at the feet of that God of love and contrition. A curiosity came over me to know in what attitude and with what composure they prayed so in solitude; by chance, an old hunchbacked tenant went by, so little and deformed that, in the shadows, she seemed more like a witch hurrying off to her sabbath than a wise virgin. "Let's see," I said to myself, "how the little monster writhes on her bench! I shall make the devils laugh when I describe it."

I followed her, crossed the chapter house behind her, and entered the church. No one went there at this hour without permission, which is what made me decide to go. By entering illegally, I was retaining my devil's prerogative. It seems rather curious that the first time I chose to enter a church on my own, I did so to show my disobedience and derision.   *S.B./F.K.*

XIV

Tolle, lege. —The sanctuary lamp. —Religious fervor takes me unawares.

No sooner had I stepped into the church than I forgot all about the old hunchback. She scampered off and disappeared like a rat in some crack in the woodwork. My eyes did not pursue her. The look of the church at night had captured and charmed me. This church, or rather chapel, had nothing remarkable about it except its exquisite cleanliness. It was a large rectangle, bare of ornament, newly whitewashed, and seemed more Anglican than Catholic. There were, as I have said, a few paintings hung at the back of the choir; the very simple altar was adorned with beautiful candles, the freshest flowers, and lovely cloths. The nave was divided into three sections: the choir, reserved for the priests and special guests[20] who were given permission to be there on feast days; the space before the choir was where the student boarders, the servants, and tenants heard mass; the section to the rear of the choir was reserved for the nuns. This last sanctum had a parquet floor that was waxed every morning, as were the nuns' stalls, which formed a semicircle against the low back wall and which were made of a beautiful walnut that shone like a mirror. An intricately wrought iron grille with a matching door separated the two naves. The door, however, was never closed. On either side, heavy wooden pillars fluted in the rococo style supported the organ and the exposed tribune, which formed a kind of raised jube between the two parts of the church. Thus, contrary to common practice, the organ stood alone, almost at the center of the nave. This seemed to increase its resonance and heighten the sonority of the choir when we sang chorales or motets on the major feast days. The space before the choir was paved with tombstones, and on these great stones you could read the epitaphs of former elders of the convent who had died before the Revolution. Several ecclesiastical personages, and even some important laity from the time of James Stuart—some Throckmortons among them—lay there at our feet. It was said that, when you went in the church at midnight, all those souls would lift their tombstones by their skulls and, looking at you with blazing eyes, beseech you to pray for them.

Nevertheless, in spite of the darkness that filled the church, it did not seem at all gloomy to me. It was lighted by one small silver sanctuary lamp whose white flame was reflected in the polished marble of the floor, like a star in still water. Its light evinced a few pale gleams on the corners of the gilded frames, the chased candlesticks of the altar, and the gold leaf of the tabernacle.

The door at the back of the rear choir section was open because of the heat, as was one of the large casements which faced the cemetery. The scent of honeysuckle and jasmine floated in on a cool breeze. A star lost in the immensity was framed by the window and seemed to look down on me attentively. Birds were singing; everything was in a calm state of enchantment, composure, and mystery the likes of which I had hardly ever conceived.

I remained in contemplation, thinking of nothing. Little by little, the few people here and there in the church quietly left. At last only a nun kneeling behind the choir remained; then having meditated enough and wanting to read, she crossed in front of the altar and came forward to light a small candle from the sanctuary lamp. When the nuns came to the altar, they did not just genuflect; they actually prostrated themselves before it and stayed that way for a moment, as though crushed, as though annihilated before the Holy of Holies. The nun who came now was tall and stately. It must have been Madame Eugénie, Madame Xavier, or Madame Monique. We could hardly tell these ladies apart in the church because they always came in with veil lowered and body completely hidden under a cloak of black bunting which trailed behind them.

The severe mode of dress, the slow and silent gait, the simple but gracious way of pulling the lamp toward her by lifting her arm to reach its ring, the light projecting on her great black shape when she raised the lamp back up, her long and deep prostration on the stone before setting out again in the same silence and with the same slow pace on the path she took to her stall—everything, even the anonymity of this phantom-like nun who seemed ready to pass through the tombstones and re-enter her bed of marble, caused me to feel both terror and ecstasy. The poetry of the holy place filled my imagination, and I stayed on even after the nun had done her reading and left.

It was getting late, prayers had been sounded, the church would soon be closed. I was oblivious to everything. I did not know what was happening to me. I was absorbing an atmosphere of indescribable sweetness more through my soul than my senses. Suddenly my whole being was mysteriously shaken, a whirling whiteness passed before my eyes on the way to surrounding me. I thought I heard a voice murmuring in my ear, "*Tolle, lege.*" I turned around thinking it was Marie-Alicia speaking to me. I was alone.

I did not let myself be deluded by pride, I did not believe in miracles. I was well aware of the kind of hallucination I had fallen into. It neither intoxicated nor frightened me. I attempted neither to heighten nor escape it. I felt simply that faith had filled my being and that it had come to me, as I had hoped, through my heart. I was so grateful, so ecstatic, that tears streamed down my face. I again felt that I loved God, that my thought embraced and accepted fully this idea of justice, tenderness, holiness that I had never doubted, but which had never touched me directly; finally, I felt a direct bond, as if the insuperable obstacle that had stood between the hearth of infinite warmth and the dormant flame in my soul had been swept away. A vast, immense, limitless path was opening before me; I burned to set out on it. I was no longer held back by a whit of doubt or reserve. The idea of having to regain control, of having to scoff at myself for the ardor of this attraction, did not even enter my thoughts. I was like those who advance without looking back, who hesitate a long while before crossing the Rubicon, but who, when they have finally touched the other side, no longer see the one they have left behind.

"Yes, yes, the veil is rent," I said to myself, "I see the light of Heaven, I shall go forth! But, first let me give thanks!"

"To whom? How? What is Thy name?" I repeated to the unknown God who was calling me to Him. "How shall I pray to Thee? What words worthy of Thee and able to show Thee my love will my soul be able to utter? I do not know, but it does not matter. Thou readest in my heart; Thou knowest that I love Thee." And my tears fell like rain, sobs wracked my chest. I had slipped behind my bench. I literally wet the pavement with my weeping.

The sister who was coming to close up the church heard the moaning and sobbing; she looked around her, not without fright, and came on me without recognizing me, or me her, because of her veil and the darkness. I got up quickly and left without dreaming of looking at her or speaking to her. I felt my way back to my cell; it was a journey. The building was so partitioned into corridors and stairways that to get from the church to my cell, which were actually adjoining, took at least five minutes of quick climbing, what with detours and roundabouts. The last spiral staircase, although rather wide and not too steep, was so warped that it was impossible to mount unless you were careful and held onto the rope that served as a railing; going down, you were thrust forward no matter what you did.

They had said prayers in class without me, but I had prayed better than anyone else that evening. I fell asleep, exhausted, but in a state of unspeakable bliss. The following day, the Countess, who had happened to notice my absence at prayer, asked me where I had spent the evening. Not one to lie, I answered her unhesitatingly, "At church." She looked at me doubtfully, saw that I was telling the truth, and said nothing more. I was not punished; I have no idea what she thought of this oddity in my behavior.

I did not seek out Madame Alicia to open my heart to her. I made no declaration to my friends, the devils. I did not feel moved to reveal the secret of my happiness. I was not in the least ashamed of it. I did not have to do battle for one moment with the desire for what the devout call "respect from human beings," but I was rather protective of my inner joy. I awaited the hour of meditation in the church with impatience. I could still hear the *Tolle, lege* from my ecstacy of the night before. I could not wait to read the divine book again, yet I did not open it. I dreamed about it, I knew it almost by heart, I beheld it, in a sense, in myself. The miraculous side of the experience, which had shocked me, was no longer a factor. I not only felt no urge to examine it, I felt a kind of contempt for the idea of such an examination; after the powerful emotion I had imbibed in all its fullness, I told myself I would have had to be insane or foolishly self-destructive to try to analyze, criticize, or question the source of such intense pleasure.

From that day, all struggle ceased; my piety took on the character of a passion. Once my heart was won over, I resolutely rejected reason with a kind of fanatical joy. I accepted everything, I believed everything, without struggle, without suffering, without regret, without false shame. To be ashamed of what I adored? How ridiculous! To need someone else's approval to abandon myself to what I felt to be perfect and beloved in every way? It was not that my character was superior to anyone else's, but I was not a coward, and I could not have been if I had tried.   *S.B./F.K.*

Part IV

From Mysticism to Independence
1819 to 1832

I

The reactions of Anna, Fannelly, and Louise. —Mary's return and her jibes. —General confession. —Abbé de Prémord. —Jesuitism and mysticism. —Communion and rapture. —The last nightcap. —Sister Hélène. —Enthusiasm and calling. —The reaction of Marie-Alicia. —Élisa Anster. —The pharisee and the publican. —Feelings and instincts run parallel.

After four or five days, Anna, noticing that I was silent and absorbed, and that I was going to church every evening, said to me in stupefaction, "Really my dear Calepin, what does this mean? One would swear you were becoming religious!"

"I already have, my child," I answered tranquilly. "Not possible? I give you my word of honor."

"Well then," she continued after a moment's reflection, "I will not say anything to dissuade you. I think it would be futile. I have always thought of you as an impassioned person. I won't be able to follow you on that path. My nature is colder; I reason. I envy your happiness, I approve of your submission, but I don't believe I could ever experience blind faith. If that miracle did happen, though, I would do as you and accept it sincerely."

"Will you still love me?" I asked her.

"At present, you would be easily consoled," she answered. "Devotion is all consuming and rewarding. But since I hold your sincerity in the highest esteem, I shall remain your friend no matter what happens." She added still more kind words and always showed herself to be full of good sense, affection, and indulgence toward me.

Sophie did not pay much attention to my transformation. Deviltry was going out of style. My conversion gave it the last blow. Perhaps we had all been equally bored by our inactivity, without letting each other know. Besides, Sophie was a melancholy devil, and at times she had brief fits of devotion accompanied by bouts of profound sadness which she wished neither to explain nor admit.

The one I feared distressing the most was Fannelly. She spared me the pain of having to refuse to run around with her anymore by speaking first. "Well, Auntie," she said, "so you've settled down? So be it! If you feel good about it, I shall be happy, and if you like, I shall settle down too. It is not beyond me to become religious in order to do as you do and always be with you."

She would have done as she said, that generous and abundant soul, if it had depended on an act of the heart. But her ideas were not as steadfast and exclusive as mine. Anyway, among the devils there were only two, Anna and myself, who were susceptible to what was known as a conversion. The others had never been rebellious: distraction stood in the way of their piety, but they nonetheless believed, and from the day the mischief stopped they were more regular in their pious practices, although they did not become exaltedly devout.

Anna was a free-thinker. That was just the word to describe her good mind and independent will. I, too, was considered a free-thinker but had neither mind nor willpower. My only strength was passion, and when the passion of religion exploded, it devoured everything in my heart; nothing in my brain stood in the way.

I have mentioned that Anna, too, plunged into piety after her marriage, but as long as she remained in the convent, she kept her disbelief. My fervor probably made me less agreeable to her, and although she had the generosity never to make me aware of it, I was naturally drawn toward other friendships, as I shall explain shortly.

I had remained close to Louise de La Rochejaquelein. She was still in the lower class because she was younger than we, but she had always been much more reasonable and knowledgeable than I was. I met her in the cloister a few days after my conversion, and hers was the first reaction I was curious to get. Since she was neither a devil, nor a beast, nor devout, her opinion was special.

"So," she said to me, "are you still as idle, as rowdy as ever?"

"What would you think of me," I asked her, "if I told you that I am consumed by religion?"

"I would say," she answered, "that you are doing the right thing, and I would love you even more than I do." She hugged me with great effusion and added no other encouragement, seeing, no doubt, from my look that I would go further than her advice.

Mary came back from England or Ireland around that time. She was a full head taller, her features had become even more masculine, and her manners were more than ever those of a good-hearted, impetuous, carefree boy. She returned to the lower class and revived deviltry to such an extent that her parents took her back after a few months. She mocked my devotion mercilessly, and whenever we met, hounded me with the most comic sarcasm. She never angered me though, for she had a pure wit, that is, without a drop of bitterness, and a way of teasing which amused too much to injure. Further on in my memoirs I shall tell how we met again around the age of forty, still feeling love for each other and reminiscing joyously about our youth.

But I have reached a point where I must speak only of myself for a while, since my religious fervor claimed me for a solitary life, seemingly without expansiveness, for several months.

My sudden conversion gave me no time to breathe. Totally given to my new love, I wanted to savor all its joys. I went to my confessor to beseech him to reconcile me officially with heaven. He was an old priest, the most paternal, simple, sincere, chaste of men, and yet he was a Jesuit, a "father of the faith," as they say since the Revolution. But he was all righteousness and charity. He was called Abbé de Prémord, and was confessor to a minority of parishioners, since Abbé de Villèle, the official director of the community and student boarders, could not attend to everyone.

We were sent, willing or not, to confess each month, a detestable practice which debased the conscience and condemned to hypocrisy those who lacked the strength to resist.

"Father," I said to the Abbé, "you know very well how I have confessed up to now; that is, you know I haven't confessed at all. I would come to you and recite a formula for the examination of conscience that makes the rounds of the class and that is the same for everyone who is constrained and forced to make confession. Thus, you never gave me absolution, nor did I ask you to. Today, I do ask it of you, and I wish to repent and confess my sins seriously. But I must admit that I don't know how to go about it, because I cannot remember any voluntary sins; I have lived, thought, believed as I was taught. If it was a crime to have turned away from religion, my conscience, which was silent, did not give me any warning. Nonetheless, I must repent. Help me to know myself and to see what is reprehensible in me and what isn't."

"Wait, my child," he told me, "I see that this is a so-called general confession, and that we will have much to talk about. Sit down." We were in the sacristy. I went to get a chair and asked him if he wanted to question me. "No," he said, "I never ask any questions; the only one I shall put to you is: Are you really in the habit of using formulas to examine your conscience?"

"Yes, but there are many sins which I don't realize I have committed, because I am entirely ignorant in that area."

"All right then, I forbid you ever to consult a formula or to look for the secrets of your conscience anywhere but within yourself. Now, let us talk. Tell me, simply and calmly, of your entire existence as you remember it, as you conceive and judge it. Don't reconstruct anything, don't pick out either the good or evil actions and thoughts, don't see in me either a judge or a confessor, speak to me as a friend. I shall tell you afterward what I feel I should encourage or correct in you in the interest of your salvation, that is, of your happiness in this life and the next."

This plan put me quite at ease. I poured out the story of my life, not as extensively as I am doing at present, but nonetheless with enough detail and precision to make the account last three hours. The good man listened with sustained interest and the affection of a father; several times I saw him wipe away tears, especially when I came to the end and simply revealed how grace had touched me at a moment when I least expected it.

Abbé de Prémord was a true Jesuit and at the same time an honorable man, with a sensitive and gentle heart. His moral code was pure, humane, lived by, so to speak. He did not lean toward mysticism, he preached in a down-to-earth way with eloquence and bonhomie. He did not favor our absorption in the dream of a better world to come to the point of forgetting the art of behaving well in this one, which is why I say he was really a Jesuit, in spite of his candor and virtue.

When I had finished talking, I asked him to judge me and pick out the counts on which I was guilty, so that, kneeling before him, I might confess and repent them, to be worthy of general absolution. But he answered, "Your confession is made. If grace did not enlighten you earlier, it is not your fault. It is now that you could become guilty if you were to lose the fruit of the salutary feelings you have experienced. Kneel to receive absolution, which I shall give you with all my heart."

After he had pronounced the sacramental formula, he told me, "Go in peace, you may receive communion tomorrow. Be calm and joyous, do not burden your mind with vain remorse, give thanks to God for having touched your heart; give yourself completely to the ecstasy of a holy bond between your soul and the Saviour."

He spoke to me as he should have, but we shall soon see that this saintly quietude was not enough for my zeal and that I was a hundred times more devout than my confessor, which I say in praise of that fine man; he had, I believe, attained a state of perfection and was no longer given to bouts of ardent proselytism. Without him, I truly believe I would be either mad or a cloistered nun at this moment. He cured me of a raving passion for the Christian ideal. But in doing so, had he acted as a simple Christian or a clever Jesuit?

I received communion the next day, Assumption Day, August 15th. I was fifteen years old and had not approached the sacrament since my first communion at La Châtre. It was during the evening of August 4th that I had felt those emotions, those unfamiliar pangs that I called my conversion. As you can see, I wasted no time; I was eager to make an act of faith and give testimony, as they called it, before the Lord.

That day of true first communion seemed to me the most beautiful of my life, so full did I feel of effusion and, at the same time, strength in my certitude. I do not know how I went about praying. The sacred formulas were not enough for me. I read them in order to observe the Catholic ritual, but then I spent whole hours alone in church praying profusely, pouring out my soul at the feet of the Eternal, and with my soul went my tears, my memories of the past, my flights into the future, my affections, my devotions—all the treasures of fiery youth that dedicates itself unequivocally to an ideal, an elusive good, a dream of infinite love.

The form this orthodoxy took into which I threw myself was childish and narrow, but I lent it a sense of the eternal. And what a flame that feeling lights in a pure heart! Anyone who has experienced it knows that no earthly affection can comparably satisfy the intellect. The Jesus that the mystics interpreted and recreated for their use is a friend, a brother, or a father, whose eternal presence, untiring solicitude, tenderness, and infinite indulgence cannot be compared to anything actual and possible; I do not like the fact that the nuns have taken him for a husband. There is something in that which surely nurtures hysterical mysticism, the most repugnant form mysticism can take. Only at an age when human passions are still silent does such a love of Christ pose no danger. Later on, it gives rise to aberrations of feeling and disturbing fantasies. Our English nuns were not mystical at all, luckily for them.

I spent the summer in the most complete beatitude. I received commu-

nion every Sunday and, at times, two days in a row. I again found the materialized idea of eating the flesh and drinking the blood of God to be fabulous and
incredible, but then what difference did it make to me? I gave it no thought. I
was possessed by a fever which did not reason, and I found joy in not reasoning. I was told, "God is within you, He is beating in your heart, He fills your
entire being with His divinity; grace is circulating in you with the blood of
your veins!" This complete identification with the Divinity made itself felt in
me like a miracle. I literally burned like Saint Theresa, I no longer slept or ate,
I walked without perceiving my body's movements; I condemned myself to
worthless austerities, since I no longer had anything left to sacrifice, alter, or
destroy in me. I did not notice the fatigue of my fast. Around my neck I wore a
filigree rosary which scratched me and which I thought of as my hair shirt. I
felt the drops of my blood as coolness, a pleasant rather than painful sensation.
All in all I was living in a trance, my body was numb, it no longer existed. My
thoughts took strange and unexpected turns. Were they even thoughts? No,
mystics do not think. They dream endlessly, they contemplate, they aspire, they
burn, they consume themselves like lamps, and they would be incapable of
giving an account of their way of life, which is so special that it cannot be
compared to anything else.

Therefore, I am afraid of making little sense to those who have not gone
through this sacred malady, for I well remember the state I lived in for several
months without being able to clearly define it for myself.

It goes without saying that I had become well-behaved, obedient, and
industrious. That took no effort on my part. From the moment my heart was
captured, it was easy to make my actions correspond to my beliefs. The nuns
treated me with great affection, but I must say, without flattery and without trying to augment my fervor by any of the seductive means that religious communities are accused of exerting on their pupils. Theirs was a calm devotion, a trifle cold perhaps, stately, and even proud. Except for a single sister, they had
neither the gift nor desire for enticing converts, this reserve stemming perhaps
as much from the nature of their Order as from the British character, from
which they did not deviate in the slightest.

Besides, what admonitions, what exhortations could anyone possibly
have directed at me? I was so entirely caught up in my faith, so logical in my
enthusiasm! No half-heartedness, neglect, or laxity was possible in an impassioned spirit such as mine. The cord was too taut to slacken on its own; it
would sooner have snapped.

Marie-Alicia continued to be angelically good to me. She did not show
me more love after my conversion than before, and this was reason enough for
me to increase my affection for her. Experiencing the sweetness of this maternal friendship, so pure and constant, I savored the perfection of that most perfect of souls who cherished me for myself, having loved the sinner—the
impossible and unruly child—as much as she loved the convert—the submissive and well-behaved one.

Madame Eugénie, who had always treated me with an indulgence that
was considered partiality, became more strict as I became more tractable. I no

longer sinned now except by oversight, and she scolded me rather harshly for that, even though my transgressions were involuntary. One day, lost in my pious reveries, I had not heard an order she was giving me, and she mercilessly imposed the punishment of the nightcap on me. The nightcap for "Saint Aurore!" (The devils enjoyed calling me that.) There was a cry of surprise and a murmur of amazement in the class: "Look how much," they said, "that strange and contradictory woman loves devils: ever since this one fell into the holy water fount, she can no longer stand her!" The nightcap did not bother me, I was aware of my innocence, and I was even grateful to Madame Eugénie for not sparing me more than she would have anyone else in a similar situation. I did not think she loved me less, for she was proving her preference for me as if in secret. If I was ill or unhappy, she came to my cell at night and questioned me coldly, even mockingly, but that teasing solicitude, that way of visiting me which she had never done for anyone else whom I knew of, meant much more coming from her than it would have from another. I did not feel the need to open my heart to her as I did with Marie-Alicia, but I was susceptible to the portion of affection she could give me, and I kissed her long, white, cold hand in gratitude.

In the midst of my initial fervor, I entered into a friendship that was considered even stranger than the one with Madame Eugénie, but which has left me the sweetest, dearest memories.

In the list of our nuns, I mentioned a lay sister, Sister Hélène, about whom I intended to speak at length when I reached the part of my story where her life and mine joined; I have arrived at that point.

One day, as I was crossing the cloister, I saw a lay sister sitting on the bottom step of the stairway, deathly pale, bathed in a cold sweat. She was sitting between two slop pails which she was bringing down from the dormitory to empty. Their weight and stench had overwhelmed her courage and her strength. She was pale, thin, on the way to becoming consumptive. This was Hélène, the youngest of the lay sisters, assigned to the most arduous, revolting duties of the convent. Because of that, she was an object of disgust for the meticulous student boarders. They would have shuddered to sit next to her; they even avoided brushing up against her clothing.

She was ugly, of a common physical type, marked by freckles on a dull, ashen complexion. And yet, there was something touching about that ugliness. Such apparent calm in the face of suffering smacked of a disposition and unconcern for misfortune that was hard to fathom at first, and which could have been taken for plain indifference, but which revealed itself once you had read into her soul, every hint of which bore witness to the obscure and primitive poem of her poor life. Her teeth were the most beautiful I have ever seen—white, small, healthy, and set like a string of pearls. When we dreamed of perfect beauty for ourselves, we spoke of Eugenia Yzquierdo's eyes, Maria Dormer's nose, Sophie's hair, and Sister Hélène's teeth.

When I saw her in such a weakened state, of course I ran to her; I supported her in my arms; I did not know what to do to revive her. I wanted to go to the workroom to call someone. She regained her strength in time to stop me, and getting up, she tried to resume her burden and continue her work, but she dragged herself along in such a pitiful way that it did not take much virtue for me to grab her buckets and carry them for her. I met her later, broom in hand, going toward the church. "Sister," I said to her, "you're killing yourself. You're too ill to work today. Let me go tell Poulette to send someone to clean the church, and you go to bed."

"No, no!" she said curtly, obstinately shaking her head. "I don't need help; one can always do what one wants to do, and I want to die working."

"But that is suicide, and God forbids you to seek out death, even by working."

"You don't understand," she replied. "I am anxious to die because I have to die. The doctors have condemned me. So, I would rather be reunited with God in two months than in six."

I did not dare ask her if she spoke thus out of fervent belief or desperation, I asked only if she would consent to my helping her clean the church, since it was my recreation period. She consented, saying, "I don't really need it, but one mustn't keep a good soul from a good deed."

She showed me how to go about waxing the floor of the rear choir, how to dust and polish the nun's stalls. It was not very difficult, and I did one side of the semicircle while she did the other, but young and strong as I was, the work wore me out, while she, inured to fatigue and already recovered from her fainting spell, with the air of a dying woman and the seeming slowness of a turtle, was able to finish her task quicker and better than I.

The following was a feast day; there were none for her since the same domestic chores were required daily. By chance I met her again as she was going to make the beds in the dormitory. There were thirty or so of them. She asked me herself if I wanted to help her, not because she wanted her work lightened, but because she had begun to enjoy my company. I followed her on an impulse of kindness which seemed quite natural, even though I would not have been prompted by her kind of religious devotion that inspires a love for pain. When the work was finished, shortened by half because of my help, we had left a few moments of leisure, and Sister Hélène said to me as she sat down on a chest, "Kind as you are, you really should teach me a bit of French, for I can't speak a word, and that hinders me with the French servants that I oversee."

"Your request delights me," I told her. "It proves to me that you're no longer thinking of dying in two months, but rather of living as long as possible."

"All I want is what God wants," she replied. "I don't seek death, nor do I shun it. I can't keep from the desire, but I don't ask for it. My ordeal will last as long as it pleases the Lord."

"My good Sister," I said to her, "then you are indeed seriously ill?"

"The doctors claim that I am," she answered, "and there are times when I suffer so much that I believe they are right. But after all, I feel so strong that they just might be wrong. Anyway, let God's will be done!"

She rose, adding, "Would you like to come to my cell this evening to give me my first lesson?"

I consented with misgivings, but without hesitation. That poor nun repelled me in spite of myself—not she as much as her foul clothing, the odor of which made me nauseous. Besides, I much preferred my hour of ecstasy at night in church to the boredom of giving a French lesson to a person of very little intelligence, whose English was quite poor.

However, I resigned myself, and came evening, I entered Sister Hélène's cell for the first time. I was pleasantly surprised to find that it was immaculately clean and perfumed with the scent of jasmine, which rose up to her window from the courtyard. The poor sister was clean as well; she was wearing her new purple serge dress; her little toilet articles arranged on a table showed that she took care of her person. She saw in my eyes what was on my mind. "You're surprised to find someone who willingly performs the vilest tasks to be clean and even fastidious," she told me. "It's because I abhor filth and stench that I gladly accepted those duties. When I arrived in France, I was revolted by the tarnished andirons and rusty locks. At home we could see our reflections in the wood furniture and the humblest metal utensils. I thought I'd never get used to living in a country where people were so neglectful. But to make things clean, you must touch unclean things. As you see, my desire to seek salvation suggested to me a condition that was to my taste."

She laughed as she said all that, for she had the good cheer of truly courageous people. I asked her what she had been before becoming a nun, and she began to tell me her story, in poor English, using a simple, rustic language whose grandeur and naïveté it would be impossible for me to convey. I shall not attempt it, but here is the gist of her tale:

"I'm a Scottish mountain girl. My father[1] is a prosperous farmer burdened by a large family. He is a good, fair man, but he is as obstinate in his will as he is energetic in his labor. I tended his flocks, I did not spare myself in household chores or watching over my little brothers and sisters, who loved me dearly. I loved them as much. I was happy, I loved the country, the meadows, the animals. It did not seem to me that I could live cooped up, ever, in a city; I did not give much thought to my salvation. Then, a sermon I heard completely changed my way of thinking and inspired me with such a great desire to please God that I no longer got pleasure or peace with my family. That sermon preached renunciation, mortification. I wondered what I could do that would be most pleasing to God and most cruel for myself, and I thought that leaving the countryside, losing my freedom, separating myself from my family forever, would be a true martyrdom for me. I resolved to do so at once. I went to find the priest who had given the sermon, and I told him that I had a calling. He did not believe me and took me to the bishop, to have that wise religious man test if my calling was real. The bishop asked me if I was unhappy staying with my parents, if I was disgusted with my land or my condition, and finally, if I had some motive of spite or anger for leaving everything that held me there. I answered him that, if that were the case, my calling would not be great, and that I only believed in it because it imposed the greatest sacrifices on me that I could imagine. After the bishop had thoroughly questioned me without finding fault, he said to me, 'Yes, you have a great calling, but you must get your parents' permission.'

"I returned home and spoke to my father first; he told me that if I even returned to see the priests he would kill me. 'Fine,' I told him, 'I shall go back, you will kill me, and I shall go to heaven sooner. That is all I want.' My mother and aunts were in tears, and seeing that I was not, they accused me of not loving them. That was very painful, as you can imagine, but it was the beginning of my martyrdom, and since I could not have myself cut to pieces or burned alive for the love of God, I had to be content with a broken heart and rejoice in this test. I could only smile at the tears of my relatives, because I knew I would suffer still more than they, and was content to suffer.

"I returned to see the priest and the bishop; my father mistreated me, locked me in my room, and when the day came when I wished to leave to begin my calling, he tied me to the foot of a bed. The more suffering and pain inflicted on me, the more I desired it. Finally, my mother and one of my aunts, seeing that my father was furious and fearing he would cause my death, tried to make him consent to my departure. 'All right,' he said, 'let her leave at once, but let her take my curse with her.'

"He came to untie me, and when I tried to kneel before him and embrace him, he shunned me, refused to bid me farewell, and left. He was truly distressed, my poor father! He got his shotgun; it seemed as though he was going to kill himself. My older brothers followed him, and when I was alone with the women and children, they all fell to their knees around me to make me renounce my sacrifice. And I laughed and said, 'More, more! You will never make me suffer as much as I want to.'

"There was a small child, my older sister's child, an absolute cherub whom I especially had raised and who always trailed at my skirts in the fields and around the house. Everyone knew I adored that child. They put him on my lap, he cried and hugged me. I rose to put him down. I took my bundle and walked toward the door. The child ran ahead of me and lying down on the threshold, said, 'Since you want to leave me, you'll have to walk over my body.' I thanked God for sparing me nothing, and I walked over the child. For a long time after, I heard his cries and the sobs of my mother, my aunts, sisters, and all the children who had been kept from running after me. I turned around and pointed to heaven by raising an arm above my head. My family was not irreligious. There was a great silence. Then I went on walking and did not turn around again until I was far enough away not to be seen. I looked at the roof of the house and the smoke. I was forced to sit down for a moment, but I did not cry, and I reached the bishop as tranquil as I am now. He entrusted me to some pious ladies who sent me here, because they feared my father might come to take me back by force if I were left in my country. That is my story. It is not very long or well told, but I cannot express myself better."

That simple and awesome story was all it took to excite my piety and inspire within me instantly an enthusiastic predilection for Sister Hélène. I saw in her a saint of old, rough-hewn, ignorant of life's refinements and the compromises between heart and conscience, an ardent and calm fanatic, like Joan of Arc or Saint Geneviève. She was indeed a mystic, the only one, I believe, in the community; indeed, she was not thoroughly English.

Struck as if by electricity, I took her hands and cried, "You are more powerful in your simplicity than all the sages in the world, and I believe that, without realizing, you're showing me the road I'm to take. I shall become a nun!"

"Very well," she told me, with the trust and directness of a child, "you'll be a lay sister with me, we'll work together."

I felt as if heaven was speaking to me through the mouth of that inspired woman. At last I had met a true saint like the ones I had dreamed of. The other nuns were like earthly angels who savored the calm of paradise through anticipation, without struggle or suffering. This one was a more human and, at the same time, more divine creature. More human, because she suffered; more divine, because she loved to suffer. The cloister was not a place where she sought happiness, rest, an absence of worldly temptations, or freedom for meditation. Poor country girl, brought up on hard labor, she had not encountered the seductions of the century! All she had dreamed of and accomplished was an everyday martyrdom; she had imagined it with the wild and grandiose logic of primitive faith. She was exalted to a state of delirium beneath a cold and stoic facade. What a strong character! Her story made me shiver and burn. I saw her in the fields, listening to the mysterious voices in the branches of oak trees and in the murmuring grass, like our great shepherdess. I saw her walking over the body of that beautiful child, whose tears fell on my heart and welled up in my eyes. I saw her standing alone in the road, cold as a statue but with a heart pierced by the seven swords of sorrow, lifting her sunburnt hand to the sky, and by the energy of her will, reducing to silence that entire wailing family, stunned with respect.

"Oh, Sainte-Hélène," I said to myself as I left her, "you're right, you know the way! You are one with yourself. Yes! when we love God with all our might, when we prefer Him over everything, we do not tarry; we don't wait for His orders, we anticipate them and prepare our sacrifices. Yes! you have engulfed me in the fire of your love, and you have shown me the way. I shall be a nun; it will be the despair of my relatives, consequently of me. Only that despair will earn me the right to say to God, 'I love Thee!' I shall live as a nun and not as a lady of the choir, in affected simplicity and idle bliss. I shall be a lay sister, a servant crushed by fatigue, a sweeper of tombs, a porter of filth—anything they wish, provided that I be forgotten after having been cursed by my loved ones; provided that, devouring the bitterness of sacrifice, I have only God as a witness to my suffering, and His love as my reward."

I wasted no time in confiding to Marie-Alicia my plans to become a nun. She was not at all elated. The worthy and reasonable woman said to me, smiling, "If that idea appeals to you, nurture it, but don't take it too seriously. One must be stronger than you think to accomplish a difficult thing. Your mother will not readily consent to it, your grandmother even less. They will say we encouraged you, and that is not at all our intention or our way of doing things. We do not cherish callings at the onset, we wait until they have fully developed. You don't know yourself yet. You think that a person matures overnight. Come now, dear 'sister,' more water must flow under the bridge before you sign that document." And she showed me her vows, written in Latin, in a little black wooden frame above her prie-dieu. Those words, contrary to French law,[1] were a permanent commitment; one signed it at a little table in the middle of the church, on which the holy sacrament was placed.

I suffered quite a bit over Madame Alicia's doubts, but I denied myself this suffering as if it were a revolt of my pride. However, I continued to believe, without saying so, that Sister Hélène had a greater calling. Marie-Alicia was happy. She said so without affectation or pomposity, and one could see she was sincere. At times she said, "The greatest happiness is to be at peace with God. I would not have been so in the world. I am not a heroine; I fear, and perhaps sense, my weakness. The cloister serves me as a refuge, and monastic rule as moral hygiene; given these powerful aids, I go my way without much effort or merit."

Thus reasoned that profoundly humble soul, or if you prefer, that perfectly modest mind. She was all the stronger for believing she was not.

When I tried to reason with her the way Sister Hélène would have, she shook her head gently, "My child," she told me, "if you are looking for merit through suffering, you will find plenty in the world. Believe me, a mother of a family merely by bringing her children into the world has more pain and work than we do. I do not regard monastic life as a sacrifice comparable to those that a good wife and mother must impose upon herself every day. Therefore, do not torment yourself, and wait for what God will inspire in you when you are at an age to choose. He knows what is best for you better than you or I. If you wish to suffer, be patient, life will grant your wish, and perhaps if your zeal for sacrifice persists, you will find that you must seek your martyrdom in the world, not in the convent."

Her wisdom filled me with respect, and it was she who kept me from uttering those imprudent vows which young girls sometimes make prematurely in the secrecy of their effusion before God—terrible oaths, which sometimes weigh on over-scrupulous consciences for an entire lifetime and which, admissible or not in the eyes of God, are never broken without severe damage to the dignity and sanity of the soul.

Nonetheless, I did not deny myself Sister Hélène's zeal; I saw her every day and watched for opportunities and ways to help her in her arduous tasks, giving up my daily recreation periods to share them and those in the evening to give her French lessons in her cell. As I have said, she had little intelligence and could hardly write. I taught her more English than French, for I soon realized that we would have to begin with English. Our lessons lasted barely half an hour. She tired quickly. Her strong mind had more will than brain power.

Thus we had half an hour to chat, and I enjoyed her conversation, which was, however, that of a child. She knew nothing, she wished to know nothing outside the limited circle in which her life had enclosed itself. She had a profound mistrust, which characterizes the peasant, of any knowledge foreign to practical living. When uninspired, she spoke poorly, could not find the right words or marshal her thoughts, but when she regained her religious enthusiasm, she had flights of sublime spontaneity, and words would come to her that were strangely profound in their childish concision.

She did not doubt my calling; she did not try to hold me back and make me hesitate in my preparation; she believed in the strength of others as in her own. She did not burden her mind with any obstacles and was certain it would be quite easy to obtain a dispensation that would allow me to enter the community, in spite of the statute which only admitted English, Irish, and Scottish women to the convent. I admit that I shuddered at the thought of becoming a nun elsewhere than in the English convent—proof that I did not have a true calling—and since I admitted to her the doubts which this preference for our convent raised in me, she reassured me with charming indulgence. She wanted to find my legitimate preference, and this lack of courage did not, to her mind, alter the excellence of my calling. I have already said, somewhere in this work, concerning La Tour d'Auvergne I think, that the mark of true grandeur is never to demand of others the great tasks one imposes upon oneself. Sister Hélène, that creature full of sublime instincts, behaved thus with me. She had left her family and her country, she had joyously come to bury herself in the first convent that had been assigned to her, and she consented to let me choose my retreat and contrive my own sacrifice. In her eyes, it was enough that a person like me, whom she regarded as a great mind because I knew my language better than she knew hers, would deliberately accept the idea of being a lay sister instead of preferring to hold to my class.

So, together, we built castles in Spain. She found a name for me, Marie-Augustine, the one I had chosen at confirmation and which had already been assumed by Poulette. She assigned me a cell next to hers. She authorized me, in the meantime, to pursue gardening and grow flowers in the courtyard. I had retained the taste for puttering in the soil, and since I was too old to have a small garden to myself, I spent part of my recreation periods wheelbarrowing grass and making paths in the plots assigned to the little girls. The adoration those children had for me was something rare. I was teased a bit in the upper class. Anna sighed at my mindlessness but remained kind and affectionate. Pauline de Pontcarré, my childhood friend who had entered the convent six months earlier, told her mother, in front of me, that I had become an imbecile, seeing as I could no longer live with anyone but Sister Hélène or seven-year-old children.

Nevertheless, I had entered into yet another friendship which should have raised me in the eyes of the smartest girls, since it was with the most intelligent girl in the convent. I have not yet spoken of Élisa Anster, even though she was one of the most remarkable individuals in this series of portraits through which my story takes me. I was saving her as the principal jewel in this precious crown.

An Englishman, Mr. Anster, the nephew of our Mother Superior, Madame Canning, had married a beautiful Indian woman in Calcutta, with whom he had had many children—twelve, perhaps fourteen. The climate had claimed all their lives in early childhood except a son, who became a priest, and two daughters—Lavinia, who had been my classmate in the lower class, and Élisa, her older sister, my friend in the upper class, who today is Mother Superior of a convent in Cork in Ireland.

Mr. and Mrs. Anster, seeing all their children perish as if their splendid constitutions had suddenly dried up in an adverse environment, and being unable to leave their business, resolved to suffer the pain of separating from their three remaining children. They sent them to England to Mrs. Blount, Madame Canning's sister. At least that is the story which was told at the convent. Later, I heard otherwise, but what is the difference? What is certain is that Élisa and Lavinia had vague recollections of their mother writhing in despair on the Indian shore as the boat moved away at full sail. Placed in the convent at Cork, Élisa and Lavinia came to France when Mrs. Blount decided to come and live in the English convent with her daughter and two nieces. Was the family wealthy? I have no idea; such things were of little concern among the religious. I believe the father was still in India when I knew his daughters. The mother certainly was, and had not seen her children in a dozen years.

Lavinia was a charming child—timid, impressionable, blushing at the slightest thing, perfectly sweet—which did not stop her from being a little devilish and hardly devout. Her aunts and her sister scolded her often. She was not overly impressed by it.

Élisa was of incomparable beauty and superior intelligence, the most admirable result possible of a union between the English and Indian races. She had a Grecian profile of an exquisite purity of line, a complexion of—no exaggeration—lilies and roses, superb chestnut hair, blue eyes of remarkable kindness and penetration, and a touch of haughtiness in her facial expression; her look and smile proclaimed the tenderness of an angel; her straight forehead, strongly angular face, the suggestion of squareness in her lavishly proportioned shape revealed great will-power, strength, and pride.

From her earliest childhood, all the forces in this vigorous soul had been turned toward piety. She came to us a saint, as I always knew her, firm in her resolve to become a nun, and cultivating one exclusive friendship in her heart, the memory of a nun from her convent in Ireland, Sister Maria Borgia de Chantal, who had always encouraged her vocation, and whom she eventually rejoined when taking the veil. The greatest token of friendship she could have given me was a little reliquary, which I still keep on my mantel, that had been given to her by that nun. I can still read on the inside cover, "M. de Chantal to E. 1816." It meant so much to her that she made me promise never to part with it, and I have kept my word. It has followed me everywhere. The glass broke while I was travelling, and the relic was lost, but the medallion is intact, and the reliquary itself has become a relic for me.

Lovely Élisa was first in all subjects, the best pianist in the convent, the one who did everything better than the others, because she had natural talent and unflagging will, in equal proportion. She accomplished all that in view of preparing herself to direct the education of the young Irish girls of Cork who would one day be entrusted to her, for she felt about her convent in Cork the way I felt about my English convent. Maria Borgia was her Alicia and her Hélène. She did not comprehend how she could be a nun elsewhere, and her calling was all the more assured since she persisted in it with joy.

She was certainly wiser than I in wanting to make herself useful in the cloister. As for me, I did my studies submissively, with as much attention as possible, but in reality I had progressed in my schoolwork no more since becoming religious than I had done previously. My only goal was to submit to the rule, and since my mysticism commanded me to foresake all the vanities of the world, I did not see why a lay sister should wish to know how to play the piano, draw, or be acquainted with history. Therefore, after three years in the convent, I came out much more ignorant than I was when I went in. I had even lost those attacks of love for studying that would take hold of me from time to time at Nohant. Devotion preoccupied me quite differently than deviltry had. It sapped my intelligence for the benefit of my heart. After weeping in adoration for an hour in church, I was exhausted for the rest of the day. This passion, abundantly released in the sanctuary, could not be rekindled for anything terrestrial. There remained in me no strength, enthusiasm, or perception for anything else. I was deadening my mind—Pauline was right to say so—but nevertheless, I feel I was growing in a certain sense. I was learning to love something other than myself; exalted devotion has a great effect on the mind it possesses: at the very least, it radically destroys self-love, and if the mind is in some ways dulled, it is also purged of many petty and mean preoccupations.

Even though we human beings are a mass of inconsistencies when it comes to conducting our lives, a certain fatal logic always brings us back to situations similar to those to which instinct had led us in the past. If you recall, my grandmother's concerns and the lessons she gave me at Nohant provoked in me, on occasion, the same mood of inert submissiveness and secret disgust as the one in which I found myself in the face of studies imposed on me in the convent. At Nohant, aspiring only to become a worker with my mother, I had despised study as being too aristocratic. In the convent, thinking only of becoming a servant with Sister Hélène, I despised study as being too worldly.

I no longer remember how it happened that I became friends with Élisa. She had been cold and even harsh to me during my stage of deviltry. She had an instinct for authority that she could not control, and when a devil disturbed her meditation in church or knocked over her notebooks in class, she turned purple; her beautiful cheeks rapidly took on a violet color, her closely-set eyebrows came together in a nervous frown; she muttered words of indignation; her smile became loathesome, almost terrible; her haughty and imperious nature betrayed itself. Then we would say that her Asian blood was in the ascendance. But the storm quickly passed. Will-power, stronger than instinct, won out over anger. She exerted an effort, became pale, smiled, and that smile, passing over her features like a ray of sunlight, brought sweetness, bloom, and beauty back to them.

Nonetheless, one really had to know her well to love her, and in general, she was more admired than pursued.

When she introduced herself to me, it was not at all half-heartedly. She revealed her own faults with much eloquence, and unreservedly opened her austere and tormented soul to me.

"We're walking toward the same goal on different roads," she would say to me. "I envy yours, because you follow it effortlessly, and you have no struggle to bear. You do not care for the world, you sense only troubles and weariness there. You have an aversion to praise. One might say you're letting yourself slip from the world into the cloister on an easy slope, and that your being has no rough spots to hold you back. As for me," she said (and speaking thus, her face beamed like an archangel's), "I have the pride of Satan! I stay within the temple, like the rich pharisee, and I must pay dearly to go through the door, where I find you asleep with a smile, in the publican's humble spot. I sense a certain affectation in the choice of my future in religion. I want to obey, but I also feel the need to command. I love approval; criticism irritates me, mockery exasperates me. I have neither instinctive indulgence nor native patience. To overcome all that, to keep myself from lapsing into evil a hundred times a day, a sustained effort of will is necessary. In short, if I am to surface from the depths of my passions, I shall do so with much difficulty, and I shall need a great deal of help from heaven."

With that, she cried and struck her breast. I was forced to console her—I, who felt like an atom next to her. "It's possible," I told her, "that I don't have the same faults as you, but I have others, and I don't have your qualities. The Lord tempers the wind to the shorn lamb. As I don't have your strength, I am spared intense sensations. I deserve no credit for humility since, by nature, by social position perhaps, I despise many things that are valued in the world. I don't know the pleasure that can be derived from praise; neither my person nor my mind is remarkable. Perhaps I would be vain if I had your beauty and your gifts. If I have no taste for commanding, it's because I wouldn't have the perseverance to govern anything. After all, remember that the greatest saints are those who have suffered the most to become what they are."

"How true!" she cried. "There is glory in suffering, and the rewards are proportionate to the merits." Then, suddenly letting her charming head fall into her beautiful hands, "Ah!" she said, sighing, "What I'm thinking is still prideful! It seeps into my every pore and takes on any form to conquer me. Why do I wish to find glory at the end of my combats and a higher place in heaven than you and Sister Hélène? Truly, I'm a most unhappy soul. I can't forget or neglect myself for a single instant."

In internal struggles such as these this valiant and austere girl consumed her most brilliant years, but it seemed as though nature had created her for that, because the more agitated she became, the more resplendent she was with plumpness, color, and health.

It was not the same for me. Without struggle and storm, I was exhausting myself in pious effusion. I began to feel ill, and soon the physical discomfort changed the nature of my devotion. I was entering the second phase of this strange life.   *C.M.*

II

The cemetery. —A mysterious outrage against Sister Hélène. —My first instinctive doubts. —Mother Alippe's death. —Élisa's fears. —My second bout with discontent. —Listlessness and fatigue. —The sickness of scruples. —My confessor orders me to have fun by way of penance. —Perfect happiness. —Devotions of a cheerful kind. —Molière at the convent. —I become author and director of theatricals. —Unprecedented success for *Le Malade imaginaire* performed for the whole community. —Jane. —Rebellion. —The death of the Duc de Berry. —My departure from the convent. —The death of Madame Canning. —Her administration. —The election of Madame Eugénie. —The decline of the convent.

I had spent several months of bliss; my days would slip by like hours. I enjoyed total freedom since I was no longer of a mind to abuse it. The nuns took me with them through the whole convent: into the workroom, where I had tea with them; into the sacristy, where I helped them store and fold up the altar adornments; into the organ loft, where we rehearsed our choruses and motets; into the novice chamber, which served as a classroom for plain song; and finally into the cemetery, the place most forbidden to all the student boarders. Located between the church and the garden wall of the Scottish school, the cemetery was nothing but a bed of flowers, with neither tombstones nor epitaphs. Swellings in the grass were the only signs of burial places. It was an enchanting place, everything shaded by beautiful trees, shrubs, and luxuriant bushes. On summer evenings, you were almost overcome by the smell of roses and jasmine; in winter, when it snowed, the border violets and the Bengal roses still showed from under their spotless shroud. A pretty, rustic chapel—rather more a shelter for a statue of the Virgin Mary and all festooned with vines and honeysuckle—separated that sacred corner from our garden, and the shade of the tall chestnuts spread over the little chapel roof. I spent delightful hours there in reverie, not thinking about anything in particular. In my days of deviltry, whenever I could slip into the cemetery, it would be to collect the fine rubber balls that the Scots would lose over the walls. But now my mind was not on rubber balls. I was absorbed in the dream of a coming death, an existence of intellectual slumber, a forgetfulness of all things, a hypnotic contemplation. I chose my spot in the cemetery. I would imagine myself stretched out in sleep, as if it were the only place in the world where my body and soul could rest in peace.

Sister Hélène sustained me in my dreams of happiness, yet she, poor girl, was not happy. She was suffering greatly, even though her physical strength had rallied and she was on the way to recovery, but I do believe her sickness was in her mind. I believe she was scolded—even persecuted to some extent—for her mysticism. There were nights when I found her weeping in her room. I hardly dared question her, for the minute I opened my mouth, she shook her stubborn head disdainfully, as if to tell me, "I've put up with much more than this; you can do nothing for me." At the same time, she would throw herself into my arms and weep on my shoulder, but never did a complaint, a murmur, an admission escape her sealed lips.

One evening while passing through the garden, I heard the sounds of a heated argument just beneath the Mother Superior's window. I could not, nor did I want to, catch the dialogue, but I recognized the sound of the voices. The Mother Superior's was grating and angry, Sister Hélène's agonizing and interspersed with groans. In the days when I still sought to solve the mystery of the victim, such material would have provided me with rich fantasies; I would have slipped into the stairwell, then into the antechamber, and surprised the secret I had so avidly pursued. But my piety forbade me from spying, and I passed as quickly as I could. However, the heartrending voice of dear Hélène followed me in spite of myself. She did not seem to be pleading; I do not think her strong character could have stooped to that; she seemed to be emphatically protesting and complaining of a false accusation. Other voices, unrecognizable to me, seemed to blame and reprove her. Finally, when I was too far away to hear anything clearly, it seemed that the muffled cries came after me through the nocturnal breeze and laughter of the student boarders at recreation.

This was the first blow to reach my soul's serenity. What did go on in the secrecy of the chapter-house? Were they unjustly suspicious? Had they no mercy for an error, these nuns who appeared so docile, with such calm demeanor? And what kind of error could a saint like Sister Hélène have committed? Wasn't it her overzealous faith and devotion they were reproaching her for? Was I somehow involved in the matter? Were they making a crime of our sacred friendship? I had distinctly heard the Mother Superior pronounce in an angry voice, "Shame! shame!" That accusing word, applied to a soul as pure and innocent as that of an infant, a veritable angel, wounded me as much as a gratuitous insult. A line from Boileau sprung unbidden to my lips, "Does such bitterness enter the souls of the faithful?"[2]

Surely Madame Canning was not a female Tartuffe. Her virtues were real, but she was harsh and rather devious. I had been witness to this myself. From where in her sanctimonious soul could she have tapped this flood of bitter reproaches and humiliating threats that the tone of her voice betrayed to my ear? I wondered how it was possible, barring profound stupidity, not to cherish and admire Sister Hélène; how it was possible, if one had esteem and affection for someone, to humiliate and make her suffer to such a point, even for her own good, even to help her find her salvation. I asked myself whether it could be a quarrel or a test; if a quarrel, it was a disgraceful way to resolve anything; if a test, it was cruel and hateful.

All of a sudden I heard cries (perhaps only my troubled imagination made me hear them), a dizziness passed before my eyes, and my trembling body broke out in a cold sweat, "They're beating her, they're martyrizing her!" I cried to myself.

May God forgive me for this thought, for it was probably mad and unfair, but it took hold of me like an obsession. I was on the main path at the far end of the garden, tortured by those muffled sounds that seemed to be following my every step. It seemed but a leap to the cell of Sister Hélène, so willingly did I believe that my feet were not carrying me, that I could fly at the speed of my thoughts. If I hadn't found her in her cell, I probably would have sought her in the Mother Superior's room.

Hélène had just come back; she was distraught, her face streaming with tears. My first reaction was to look for traces of violence, see if her veil had been torn or her hands bloodied. I had suddenly become suspicious, like those who unexpectedly shift from blind trust to severe doubt. Only her dress was dusty, as if she had been thrown to the ground, or as if she had rolled on the floor. She pushed me away, saying, "It's nothing! I am very sick, I must go to bed; leave me alone!"

I left so that she could go to sleep, but I remained in the corridor, hidden by the darkness, my ear glued to the door. Her moans tore my heart. Some commotion came from the direction of the Mother Superior's chamber. Doors were opening and closing; I could hear the rustle of clothing not far from me. The suspense was eerie, dreadful. When all was quiet again, I returned to Sister Hélène's side.

"I know I shouldn't question you," I said to her, "and that you don't want to answer me. But let me help you and take care of you." She had a fever, she said, but her hands were icy, and she was shaking uncontrollably. She asked me only for something to drink; there was nothing but water in her cell. In spite of her protests, I ran to find Madame Marie-Augustine (Poulette), who I thought lodged off the same dormitory.[2] Poulette was the head nurse, the one who supervised and kept the keys to the pharmacy. I told her that Sister Hélène was very sick. And what did she do? Cheerful, kind, and motherly Poulette shrugged her shoulders unconcernedly and answered, "Sister Hélène? She's not sick, she doesn't need a thing!"

Shocked by this inhumane attitude, I went to find Sister Teresa, the elderly lay sister in charge of the stills—the large Irishwoman in the cellar where the mint was stored. She also worked in the kitchen; she would have been able to heat up some water, to prepare an herbal tea. She greeted me with no more concern than Poulette. "Sister Helen!" said she, laughing, "she is in her bad spirits."[3] However, she added that she would brew her some lime-blossom tea, and went about it leisurely, snickering the whole time. She handed me the tea and a little mint liqueur, saying, "You drink some too, it's very good for stomach aches and for madness."

As I could do no better, I returned to my patient who lay utterly abandoned. She was shivering with cold; I went to get a blanket from my bed, and the hot tea seemed to warm her a bit. In class they were saying prayers, about to retire for the evening. I went to the Countess, who truly could never refuse me a thing, and asked her if I could watch over Sister Hélène, for she was ill. "What!" she said with astonishment, "Sister Hélène is sick and you are the only one to care for her?"

"That is indeed the case, Madame. Do I have your permission?"

"Go ahead, my dearest," she answered, "for whatever you do can only please God." And that is how I was treated by that ridiculous and excellent person, of whom I had made so much fun, a person who found nothing in the world to worry or quarrel about, unless it concerned her parrot and Mother Alippe's cat.

I stayed close to Sister Hélène until they came to lock up the corridor doors. By then she was sleeping, and seemed quiet when I left her. She had suffered agonizingly during several hours, to the point of saying while writhing on her bed, "Why can't I die?" But not one complaint against anyone escaped her lips, and the next day I found her at work, smiling and almost cheerful. The good-natured flexibility of a child was united, in her, with the resignation and courage of a saint.

This mysterious adventure had affected me more than it did her; I could see from the way the sisters treated me and from the freedom they gave me to see her any hour of the day that I had had nothing to do with the storm she had passed through. But I was nonetheless pensive and crushed, not shaken in my religious faith as much as disturbed in my happiness and trust.

Around that same time, I think, Mother Alippe died of an endemic pulmonary catarrh, which also endangered the lives of the Mother Superior and several other nuns. I had never been particularly close to Mother Alippe; however, I did like her and had been able to appreciate, in the lower class, her sense of fairness and justice. She was sorely missed, and her sudden death only a few days after she was stricken was accompanied by ravaging circumstances. Her sister, Poulette, who took care of her, and who, as nurse, also had to take care of the Mother Superior and the others, showed wonderful courage in her grief until she herself fell into a deathlike faint in the infirmary, right in the middle of her duties, on the day Mother Alippe was buried.

That burial was full of sad, poetic beauty—the chants, the tears, the flowers, the service in the cemetery, the pansies we quickly planted on her tomb and then hastened to pick and share among us, the profound and resigned sorrow of the nuns—everything seemed to lend a saintly air and somewhat secret charm to this peaceful death, this separation of but a day, as the kind and courageous Poulette said.

But I had been terribly shaken by something else beyond my comprehension. We had learned of Mother Alippe's death that morning when coming out of our cells. We greeted each other sorrowfully, crying; we were sad, but calm, knowing from the evening before that the poor woman was doomed and in her death throes. They had shielded us from this supreme struggle, but had not given us any hope. Out of respect for the slumber of childhood, these sad hours passed in almost complete silence. We had not heard the sound of a bell nor prayers for the dying. The lugubrious apparatus of death had been hidden from us. We immersed ourselves in prayer on that cold and foggy dawn. A lifeless day was rising over our bowed heads. Suddenly, in the middle of the Ave Maria, a horrible shriek pierced our midst; everyone stood up, shocked, except for Élisa; she had fallen to the ground, stricken by terrible convulsions.

Through an effort of will she pulled herself together to hear Mass, but soon again she was taken by the same nervous attack and obliged to leave. That whole day she seemed more dead than alive; in the days that followed, she would suddenly emit a shrill cry in the middle of her meditations or her studies; she walked around with a haggard expression, as if tracked by a specter.

As she was offering no explanation, at first we attributed these physical traumas to her grief. But why such violent grief, when she was no closer to Mother Alippe than most of us? As soon as we were alone she explained to me what was making her suffer: only a thin partition separated her room from the alcove in the small infirmary where Mother Alippe had died. That whole night she attended, so to speak, Mother Alippe's agony. She had heard every word, every groan of the dying woman, and the final gasp for life had affected her sensitive nerves sympathetically. She had to force herself not to relive it while telling me about that night of anguish and terror. I did my utmost to calm her; we said a prayer to the Virgin that she liked to have me say with her in time of spiritual distress. It was an English prayer that had come from her dear Madame Borgia, and in accord with the communal thinking of early Christianity, was not meant to be said alone. These were the words: "Verily, I say, where three of you are joined in my name, I shall be among you." Lacking a third classmate as assiduous as we in the service of a particular ritual, just the two of us said it together. Élisa had a prie-dieu in her cell, arranged like that of a nun. We lit a small, pure-white taper, and at the foot of it we placed a bouquet of the prettiest flowers we could find. Such flowers and virgin wax were uniquely sacred offerings for this prayer. Élisa loved these external practices of devotion; she felt they were very important and attributed to them secret powers for curing the anxieties to which she was prone. She cherished ritual.

I did think she was materializing her faith somewhat, which I considered a harmless and loving pasttime, but I shared it rather out of affection for her than inclination. I always found that the only true prayer was internal, a wordless effusion of the heart, without pretentious language or even ideas. Élisa loved all aspects of devotion—the content as well as the form. She had a taste for "paternostering." Truly, she knew how to make manifest the poetry that was inside her.

Nevertheless, Madame Borgia's prayer calmed Élisa only for an instant, and she admitted to me that she felt assailed by involuntary and inexplicable fears. The phantom of death had risen before her in all its horror; that rich and vibrant constitution trembled in terror at the idea of destruction. At every hour of the day, Élisa would have offered up her life to God, and she was certainly not the type to recoil in the face of martyrdom. But when suffering and death materialized before her eyes, the shock to her imagination was extreme; that strong-willed soul had the nerves of a weakling. She reproached herself, but could do nothing about it.

I do not know why this bothered me so. I was in a disenchanted mood; I found it strange and irritating that my dear, saintly Élisa, such a strong and valiant figure, was so upset over so solemn and majestic a thing as the death of a sinless human being. I had never been afraid of death in the abstract. My grandmother had made me consider it with a philosophical calm that enabled me to react to Christian death less coldly than a stoic, though just as serenely. For the first time, death, as seen through Élisa's morbid vision, appeared as something dark. While blaming her to myself for not seeing it as I did, I felt her terror becoming contagious, and that night, as I was passing through the hall where the body had been laid out, I experienced a sort of hallucination: I saw passing before me the shade of Mother Alippe in a white robe that was waving and tossing over the flagstones. I could hardly stifle a shriek much like Élisa's. I stopped myself, but I was ashamed. I blamed myself as much for this vain terror as I would have for blasphemy, and I felt almost as discontent with Élisa as I did with myself.

In the middle of these disillusionments which I did my best to ignore, a mood of sadness overtook me. One evening I went into the church and could not pray. My efforts to revive my flagging soul only served to abuse it further. I had been feeling ill for a while, I had unbearable stomach cramps, and could neither sleep nor eat. A fifteen-year-old cannot bear with impunity the deprivation I was subjecting myself to. Élisa was nineteen, Sister Hélène twenty-eight. I was visibly weakening under the strain of my exaltation. The day following that evening, which was a painful counterpart to my euphoric vigil of August 4th, I arose with much difficulty; my head felt heavy and distracted at prayers. Mass left me unenthused. The evening was the same. The next day, I exerted my will to such an extent that I recaptured my zeal and my ecstasy. But the following day was worse. The period of fervor was spent; an unsurmountable weariness was overcoming me. For the first time since I had become pious, I felt something akin to doubt, not about religion, but about myself. I was convinced that grace was abandoning me. I recalled the ominous saying, "Many are called, but few are chosen." Finally, I began to believe that God did not love me anymore because I did not love him enough. I fell into bleak despair.

I confided my trouble to Madame Alicia. She smiled and tried to show me that a poor state of health was the cause, the effects of which must not be taken so seriously.

"Everyone is subject to these lapses of the soul," she told me. "The more you torment yourself, the worse they will become. Accept them in a spirit of humility, and pray for this test to be over; if you have not committed a serious offense that warrants this fatigue as a punishment, then just abide patiently, be hopeful, and pray!"

What she was telling me was the fruit of her great philosophical experience and enlightened reason. But my distraught mind could not profit from it. I had tasted too much joy in the ardors of devotion to calmly sit back and await their return. Madame Alicia had said, " . . . if you have not committed a serious offense. . . . " So I began looking for what I had done wrong; for to suppose that God would be as whimsical and cruel as to remove me from His grace without any other motive than to test me, I could not allow. "I concede that He test me in my external life," I told myself. "One accepts, indeed one seeks martyrdom. But for that, God's grace is needed, and if He takes it from me, then what does He want me to do? I can do nothing without Him; if He abandons me, is it my fault?"

Thus I complained against the object of my adoration, and like a jealous and angry lover, I would willingly have leveled bitter reproaches at Him. But I trembled before these rebellious instincts, and pounding my chest, told myself, "Yes, it must be my fault. I must have committed a crime, and my embittered or bewildered soul must have refused to make it known to me."

And there I was, scrutinizing my conscience, searching for my sin with unbelievable severity toward myself, as if not being able to find the sin was what made one guilty! At last I convinced myself that a number of venial sins must be equal to a mortal sin, and I continued searching for the numerous venial sins that I must have committed, that I was probably committing at any given moment without realizing it, for it is written that if the just sin at least "seven times a day," the ordinary Christian must acknowledge that he sins at least "seventy times seven."

There had perhaps been much pride in my elation. Surely there was excessive humility in my reaction. I could not do anything halfway. I took on the fatal habit of examining every little detail. I say "fatal," because one cannot treat oneself this way without developing a disproportionate sensitivity and without endowing the slightest change in feeling and thought with childish importance. That is only one step away from the morbid disposition that exerts itself over others and alters loving relationships through irritability and silent demands, and if a virtuous Jesuit had not at the time been my soul's physician, I would have become as intolerable of others as I was of myself.

For about a month or two I lived under constant subjection to this torture, without recovering grace, by which I mean the perfect confidence that makes one feel truly aided by the divine spirit. And so all my arduous efforts to find grace served only to deprive me of it even more. I had become what the faithful would call "scrupulous."

The devout young girl, tormented by scruples of conscience, only became more miserable. She could not even receive communion without distress, for between absolution and the next sacrament, she could not escape the fear of having committed a sin. Venial sins do not make one lose absolution; a fervent act of contrition erases the stain and allows one to approach the sacred altar. But for a mortal sin, one must abstain from communion or risk committing a sacrilege. The remedy is to go quickly to your confessor—or in his absence, to the first priest you can find—in order to obtain new absolution. A stupid remedy, a true abuse of an institution whose basic principles were great and saintly and which for the faithful becomes a bit of gossip, a childish pleading, an obsession with the Lord reduced to the level of a jealous, fickle creature. If a mortal sin had been committed the very moment or the evening before receiving communion, shouldn't one have to abstain and wait for a longer atonement, a more difficult reconciliation than that which occurs in the five minutes of confession between the priest and the sinner? Ah! the earliest Christians—those who made public confessions at the door of the temple before believing themselves cleansed of their sins, those who subjected themselves to terrible trials and years of penance—they had not intended it thus. Their intention was that confession transform a being and truly make a new person emerge from the spoils of the old one. The vain simulation that is secret confession, the short and banal admonishment by a priest, the silly penance which consists of repeating some prayer—were these born of the pure, effective, and solemn institution of early times?

Confession has no more than a very limited social use, because the secrecy that has insinuated itself into the act has opened the door to more drawbacks than benefits to domestic security and dignity. Having become a vain formality that allows one to take the sacraments, it does not leave the believer with a feeling of profound respect or durable repentance. Its effect is almost nonexistent for casual or luke-warm Christians. For fervent believers, on the other hand, it is of great importance, but it is as a director of conscience, not as a confessor, that the priest really acts on those people. The proof is that one often sees the two functions separated and performed by two different people. In that case, the confessor is wiped out, since the director decides what must be revealed to him. The former is like the nurse to whom the doctor in charge hands over and prescribes the menial chores. Absolution is good from either one, but the director alone knows the secret of the sickness and its cure.

The confessor's influence is therefore real only when he is also the director of conscience. For that, he must know the individual, and cultivate and guide him assiduously; at that point, the priest becomes the true head of the family, and it is usually through the woman that he rules, as M. Michelet demonstrated so well in his fine, appallingly true book.[4] In any case, when priest and penitent are sincere, confession still has a helpful function. However, human weakness and the clergy's will to control and intrigue, as well as loss of faith in the very heart of the church rather than in the heart of the woman, have sufficiently proven that the benefits of this institution, diverted from its path and perverted by centuries of mismanagement, have become rare, while its dangers and the evil it often produces are immense.

I speak here in a spirit of justice and examination; my personal experience would lead me to other conclusions, if I resorted to personal opinion to judge the rest of the world. I had the good fortune to meet a worthy priest who was for a long time my serene friend and wise counselor. If I had run into a fanatic, I would be dead or insane, as I have said before; if I had met an imposter, I would perhaps be an atheist, at least I might have become one by reaction over a length of time.

Abbé de Prémord was the generous dupe of my confessions for some of that time. I accused myself of unresponsiveness, of indiscipline, of disgust, of irreverent thoughts, halfhearted efforts to pray, laziness in class, distraction at church and consequent disobedience, and I said I was like that all the time, without real contrition, without progress in my conversion, without the force to triumph over these feelings. He scolded me very gently, preached perseverance to me, and sent me away, saying, "Go now and hope; do not become discouraged; you are sorry for your sins, therefore you shall triumph."

And so, one day when I was accusing myself vehemently and weeping bitterly, he interrupted me right in the middle of my confession with the abruptness of a kind man annoyed at his time being wasted. "Wait a minute," he said to me, "I no longer understand you, and I'm afraid that your moral health is in jeopardy. Would you kindly permit me to find out about your behavior from the Mother Superior, or anyone else whom you designate?"

"What would you learn from that?" I asked him. "The indulgent people who care about me will tell you that I seem virtuous, but if the heart is evil and the soul misguided, only I can be the judge, and the good testimony those people give you on my behalf will only make me feel more guilty."

"You would then be a hypocrite?" he replied. And he continued, "Oh, no, that is impossible. Let me find out about you, I insist. Come back at four o'clock and we will discuss it further."

I believe he saw the Mother Superior and Madame Alicia. When I went back he said, with a smile, "I knew that you were raving mad, and that is why you deserve a scolding. Your teachers are delighted with your excellent conduct, you are a model of sweetness, punctuality, and sincere piety, but you are sick, and that is affecting your imagination. You go around sad, somber, as if in a trance. Your classmates do not know you anymore, they are so amazed and sorry for you. Be careful! If you continue this, you will make piety hated and feared, and the example of your suffering and restlessness will prevent more conversions than it will encourage. Your relatives are upset over your exalted state. Your mother thinks the convent schedule is killing you; your grandmother thinks we are fanaticizing you and that your letters reveal serious emotional distress. You know very well, on the contrary, we are trying to calm you. For my part, now that I know the truth, I insist that you drop this exaggeration. The more sincere it is, the more dangerous. I want you to live fully and freely in body as well as soul, and because in this sickness of scruples there is, unknown to you, a great deal of pride disguised as humility, as penance I order you to go back to the games and innocent pleasures of your peers. From this evening on, you will run about in the garden like the others instead of lying prone in the church for recreation. You will skip rope, you will play tag. Your appetite and sleep will come back quickly, and when you are no longer physically ill, your brain will better assess these so-called offenses you feel you must accuse yourself of."

"Oh my God," I cried, "you are imposing a harsher penance on me than you think. I have lost my taste for games and my cheerful disposition. But my mind is so flighty that, if I don't constantly watch myself, I will forget God and my salvation."

"Do not believe that," he replied. "Besides, if you go too far, your conscience, which will have recovered its health, will surely warn you, and you will heed its reproaches. Remember that you are ill, and that God does not appreciate the feverish outbursts of a soul in delirium. He prefers pure and unremitting homage. Now, obey your doctor. In a week I want them to tell me about the big change in your looks and behavior. I want you to be loved and listened to by all your classmates, not only by the good ones, but most of all by those who are not. Teach them that love of duty is a sweet thing and that faith is a sanctuary from which one emerges with a serene face and a benign soul. Remember that Jesus wanted his disciples to have their hands washed and their hair scented. This meant, do not imitate those fanatics and hypocrites who cover themselves with ashes and whose hearts are as unclean as their faces; be pleasant to others, so that the doctrine you preach is pleasant to them. And so, my child, it means not burying your heart in the ashes of misunderstood penance. Perfume your heart with great graciousness and your spirit with loving playfulness. As that was your nature, people must not think that piety makes your mood grim. God must be lovable in His servants. Go now, do your act of contrition, and I shall absolve you."

"What! my father," I said, "I am to seek diversions and distractions this evening and, tomorrow, go to communion?"

"Yes, that is really what I want," he replied, "and since I order you to enjoy yourself as penance, you will have fulfilled your duty."

"I will submit to anything, if you promise that God will be glad, that He will return to me those sweet raptures, those spiritual bursts that make me feel and savor His love."

"I cannot promise for Him," he said with a smile, "but I shall be accountable, you will see."

And the good man dismissed me amazed, upset, and terrified by his order. However, I obeyed—passive obedience being the foremost duty of a Christian—and I quickly realized how at fifteen it is not really difficult to regain the taste for jump ropes and rubber balls. Gradually I resumed playing, first with satisfaction, then with enthusiasm, and then with passion, because physical activity was a necessity for children my age, of my constitution, and I had been deprived of it for too long not to be drawn to its novelty.

My classmates responded with true kindness, first dear Fannelly, then Pauline, Anna, and then all the rest, devils as well as sages. Seeing me so cheerful, they briefly thought I might become wicked again. Élisa reproached me a bit, but I told her the story, as I did all those who sought and deserved my trust, about what had happened between Abbé de Prémord and me, and my gaiety was accepted as legitimate and even meritorious.

All that my good director had predicted came true. I promptly regained my physical and mental health. My thoughts grew calm; questioning my heart, I found it so sincere and pure that confession became a short formality destined to give me the pleasure of communion. It was then I tasted the ineffable state of well-being that the jesuitical spirit affords each person according to his bent and scope: a spirit of conduct admirable in its understanding of the human heart and in the results it could obtain for the good if, as with Abbé de Prémord, every man who professed and preached it had a love of good and a horror of evil. But cures become poisons in certain hands, and the force of this Jesuit tool has reaped death and life in equal measure in society and in the church.

Then about six months passed which have remained in my mind like a dream and which I ask only to recover in eternity for my share of paradise. My spirit was at peace. All my thoughts were happy. Only flowers sprouted in the soil of my brain, which but lately had been bristling with rocks and prickles. At any hour of the day I saw the sky open before me, the Virgin Mary and her angels smiling and calling me: life and death were immaterial. The empyrean beckoned in all its splendor, and I no longer sensed in me a speck of dust to retard the soaring of my wings. The earth was a waiting place where everything was aiding and inviting me to find my salvation. The angels bore me aloft like the prophet, for fear that, in the night, "my foot might tread on a stone."[5] I did not pray as much as I had in the past; I was forbidden to do that; but now everytime I prayed, I felt once again those surges of love, perhaps a little less impulsive, but a thousand times sweeter. My guilty and sinister thoughts of the Heavenly Father's wrath and Jesus' indifference no longer came to me. I went to communion every Sunday and feast day with an incredible serenity in my heart and soul. I felt as free as the air in this pleasant and vast confine of the convent. If I had asked for the key to the cellars, they would have given it to me. The sisters spoiled me as their beloved child, my good Alicia, my dear Hélène, Madame Eugénie, Poulette, Sister Teresa, Madame Anne-Joseph, the Mother Superior, Élisa, the old student boarders and the new, the upper and lower classes. "I was drawing all hearts in my wake."[6] So easy is it to be perfectly good when one feels perfectly happy.

My return to merriment was like a resurrection for the upper class. Since my conversion, deviltry had hardly had a wing to flap. It revived in a new and totally unexpected form: we became harmless, rose-water devils; that is to say, simply mischievous, without a trace of rebellion, without a break in our duties. We worked during our work period, we laughed and played during our recreation period, as we had never done before. There were no more coteries, no more taking sides among devils, sages, and beasts. The devils calmed down, the sages cheered up, the beasts gained wisdom and confidence, because we learned how to use and amuse them.

This great progress in convent behavior came about by means of shared entertainment. Five or six of us from the upper class got the idea to improvise some charades, actually little comedy skits, arranged in advance by scenarios and then delivered extempore. As I had, thanks to my grandmother, a little more background in literature than my classmates, and a kind of facility for putting characters on stage, I was named author for our little troupe. I chose my actors, I ordered the costumes; I was very well supported and I had very remarkable subjects. The back of the classroom, which overlooked the garden, became a theater at the alloted times. Our early attempts were like the first steps of art in its infancy; at the beginning, the Countess tolerated them; then she began to enjoy them and invited Madame Eugénie and Madame Françoise to come and see if they found nothing objectionable in this diversion. The ladies laughed and approved.

Our presentations quickly made great progress. They lent us some old folding screens for the wings. We acquired accessories from everywhere.

Everyone brought material from home for costumes. The problem was how to dress up as men. Modesty and the nuns would not have allowed it. I made up a Louis XIII costume which reconciled decency with artifice. We gathered our skirts from below, up to mid-calf, to make breeches; we put on our blouses backwards, shifted and fanned them out over crumpled handkerchiefs that we tucked into the front and sleeves, to make doublets. Two aprons sewn together made our cloaks. Ribbons, hats, wigs, and trinkets were not hard to find. When we were short of feathers, we made them out of paper, cut out and ruffled. Boarding students are skillful, inventive, and know how to make do with what they have. We were allowed to use boots, swords, and felt slippers. Our relatives furnished those things. In brief, our costumes were acceptable, and the audience was tolerant regarding our stage sets. They willingly took a long table for a bridge and a wooden stool covered with a green rug for a grassy bank.

They allowed the lower class to come and see our performances, and we signed up whoever wanted to participate. One fine day, the Mother Superior, who liked to have a good time, told us she had heard marvelous things about our theater and that she wanted to attend with the rest of the community. The Countess and Madame Eugénie had extended our recreation period until ten o'clock, and until eleven on performance days. The Mother Superior extended it that day until midnight, which meant she really wanted to enjoy a whole evening out. Her request and subsequent permission were greeted with rapture. They all rushed at me, saying, "Let's go, author! Let's get to work, Live-wire! (This was the latest nickname they had given me.) We must put on an outstanding show; we need six acts, in two or three sets. We have to hold the audience with bated breath from eight till midnight. That's your job. We'll help with everything else, but for that, we rely on you."

I took seriously the responsibility they placed on me. I had to make the Mother Superior laugh, to put even the most somber people in our community into good spirits, and yet not go too far; the least frivolity could make them cry Scandal!, and close the theater, which would be a great disappointment for my classmates. If I merely bored them, they could as well close the theater under the pretext of disorderliness in our evening recreation and a slackening of our daytime studies; and the pretext was plausible, for these entertainments surely went to their young heads, especially to those in the lower class.

Fortunately, I was very well read in Molière and, by omitting the love scenes, could still find enough comic material to fill an entire evening. *Le Malade Imaginaire* gave me a perfect scenario. I could not remember exactly the dialogue and the sequence of events. Molière was forbidden at the convent, as one would expect, and being stage director had made me no less virtuous. However, I was able to recall enough of the plot in my script to veer just far enough from the original; I prompted my actresses in the major parts of the dialogue, and was able to communicate to them the flavor of the whole play. Not one of them had read Molière, not one of our nuns knew even a line. So I was very sure my play would attract them all by its novelty. I no longer recall who played what part, but they all acted with great intelligence and gaiety. Partly because I forgot, partly on purpose, I cut out a lot of medical crudeness, for I played the part of M. Purgon. But hardly had I set my actresses in motion, hardly had I delivered a few lines, when I saw the Mother Superior burst out laughing, Madame Eugénie wipe her eyes, and the whole audience brighten up.

Every year, on the Mother Superior's birthday, a play would be put on with much more care and pomp than we were using now. Then a real theater was built. There was an ad hoc store of decorations, footlights, a thunder machine; roles were learned by heart and very well played. But those presentations were hardly joyous; they were always tearful little dramas by Madame de Genlis.[7] With my folding screens and candle ends, my actresses confidently recruited among those whose instinct strained to express itself, my scenario based only on memory, our improvised dialogue, and one rehearsal as sole preparation—I could have ended up with a complete fiasco. That was not the case. The liveliness, the verve, the true humor of Molière, though recited piecemeal and presented in fragments, brought the audience to its feet. Never in nuns' memory had they laughed so heartily.

The success of the first few scenes gave us courage. For the intermission I had prepared a spoof with a parade of clowns, borrowed from *Monsieur de Pourceaugnac*. I had only told my actresses to stay in the wings, which meant behind the folding screens, and not to display their weapons until I came out on the stage to set the example. When I saw that everyone was receptive, I quickly changed costume, and playing the apothecary, I began the intermission, brandishing the classic instrument above my head. I was greeted with Homeric laughter. Everyone knows that this kind of humor has never scandalized the religious. Immediately, my black regiment in white aprons arrived on the scene, and this burlesque exhibition (Poulette had lent us the infirmary's entire arsenal) put the community into such a good mood that I thought we were going to bring down the house.

The play ended with the reception ceremony, and as I knew all the lines by heart, they were all able to learn them. Our success was complete, their enthusiasm reached its limit. Because they recited their services in Latin, these ladies could appreciate the humor of Molière's Latin parody. The Mother Superior declared herself thoroughly entertained, and I was overwhelmed with praise for the wit and humor of my inventions. I tried desperately to whisper to my classmates, "It was Molière, all I did was remember." They did not hear me; they didn't want to believe it. One of them who had read Molière over vacation told me very softly, "Be quiet! It's useless to tell these ladies where it all came from. They might even close the theater if they knew we were performing Molière for them. Since they weren't shocked, there's no harm in not telling them if they don't question you."

As a result, no one dreamed it was the wit of Molière channeled through my brain. For an instant I felt a pang of guilt in accepting these compliments. I took stock to see whether my vanity was not profiting; I realized that just the opposite was the case and that, unless one were mad, one could only feel badly in receiving homage for another's work. I accepted this mortification out of respect for my classmates, and the theater continued to prosper and attract the Mother Superior and the other nuns on Sundays.

What followed was a succession of pastiches drawn from my memory and arranged according to the means and possibilities of our theater. The wonderful result of our recreation was that we enlarged the circle of relations and friendships among us. Camaraderie and the need to help one another in creating a diversion in common generated a benevolence, a condescension, a mutual indulgence, and the absence of any rivalry. Finally, the need to love, so natural in young hearts, formed around me a group that grew daily and which soon included the whole convent—nuns and student boarders, lower and upper classes. I can recall without vanity the time when I was the object of an adoration unprecedented in the annals of the convent, since it was the work of my confessor and the result of the tender, expansive, and joyful devotion to which he had trained me.

They were deeply grateful that I was devout, agreeable, and amusing. The gaiety spread to those whose characters were the most solemn and whose devotions were the most melancholy. It was at this time that I began a close friendship with Jane Bazouin, a pale little person, reserved, sweet, and sickly looking, though she had yet suffered no illness, whose beautiful large black eyes, kind and enduring tact, and childlike little smile took the place of beauty. Jane was, and always will be, an adorable creature. Combined in her were Fannelly's kindness, devotedness, and untiring good will with Élisa's stern and firm piety, and the whole was crowned with a calm and modest grace that had no peer but in Jane herself.

She had two sisters who were prettier and brighter than she: Chérie, who was the prettiest and most lively, the most sought after of the three, because of her ingratiating manner—the poor charming girl died two years later; and Aimée, who was beautiful by distinction and intelligence, and who went through a sickly childhood and then married M. d'Héliand at the age of twenty-seven. Aimée was in all respects a superior person. She had a cold way about her, but her heart was loving, and her intelligence rendered her gifted in all the arts, in which she excelled without effort and without any visible passion.

These three sisters were in private rooms, with a governess to take care of them, but they had the same classes and prayer times as we. We vied for Chérie's and Aimée's friendship. Jane's only friends were her sisters. She was too shy and reserved to look for any others. This modesty moved me, and I soon saw that it was not coldness or stupidity that caused her isolation. She was just as intelligent, as well-educated, and much more loving than her sisters. I found a treasure of good will in her, and peaceful, durable affection. We remained very close until 1831. I shall explain later why, though I did not stop loving her as she deserved, I did stop seeing her without telling her why.

My little Jane showed, in our pastimes, that she was just as capable of graciousness and joy as the most sparkling among us. Once, she was even punished with the nightcap by the Countess, who did not always take kindly to our pranks, for our high spirits escalated a notch every day, and the most staid let themselves be drawn in. I recall that it had become, for me as everyone else, as irresistible as an electrical impulse. Certainly, I refrained from subjecting the Countess to ridicule, and I did my best to spare her when the others took her on. But when, for the hundredth time, she let herself be fooled by the apple candle that Anna or Pauline had placed in her lantern, and when she spoke one word for another with the assurance of a totally absent-minded person, seeing the whole class break out in a single peal of laughter, I had to do the same. Then she would turn to me with a hurt look, and as Julius Caesar had said to Brutus, would say to me, draping herself in her large green shawl, "And you too, Aurore!" I would really want to apologize, but she had a way of pronouncing the silent "e" that made it sound like an "o." Anna imitated her very well, and turning toward me she would call, "Auroro, Auroro!" I could not contain it, the laughter became a reflex. I would have laughed at the stake, as they used to say.

The merriment went so far that several impetuous girls turned it into a rebellion. This was at the time of the Restoration, when there had been an epidemic of revolt in all secondary schools and boarding schools, even the female establishments. As this news was transmitted to us blow by blow, with the relation of events which were sometimes serious, sometimes comic, the most enterprising among us would say, "Can't we too have our little revolution? Will we be the only ones not to follow the trend? Can't we have our own little notice in the newspapers?"

When she was upset, the Countess became stricter, for she was fearful. Our good nuns, at least some of them, wore long faces, and for three or four days (I think our neighbors, the Scots, had also had their own revolution), there was a pervasive mistrust and terror that really entertained us. So, a feigned rebellion was plotted to see how these ladies would react, especially the Countess. I was not involved; the girls were good enough to spare me the pangs of my rigid conscience, but they surely expected me to share in the general laughter when the plot climaxed.

It happened thus: one evening in class, as we were all seated around a long table, the Countess at the head, mending her rags by candlelight, I heard the girl sitting next to me say to her neighbor, "Let us raise!" The words were passed around the table, which was immediately lifted by thirty pairs of small hands, and rose, in effect, to just above the level of the Countess' head. In another world as usual, she was surprised at the diminishing light, but the moment she looked up, the table and light were lowered to normal. We did this quite a few times before she realized what was going on. It was a little like the scene of the simpleton at the witch's house in *Les Pilules du Diable*.[8] I found the thing so amusing that it did not even bother me to go along with everyone else when the command, "Let us raise!" was given. But finally the Countess noticed our game and stood up, furious. They had agreed to make mean, ugly faces to scare her at that point. Each one took on a conspirator's pose, arms folded, scowling brow, and whispers of the terrible word "revolt" resounded around her. The Countess was unable to face up to the storm. Convinced that the fatal moment had come, she fled, with her shawl streaming, like a seagull spreading its wings and taking flight through the tempest.

She had lost her wits; she headed across the garden to hide and barricade herself in her room. To add to her terror, we threw torches, candles, and footstools out the window as she passed. We really did not try to, nor could we reach her, but the din, accompanied by screams of "Revolt! revolt!" nearly made her die of fright. For an hour we were left to ourselves and our irrepressible laughter, without anyone daring to try to restore order. Finally, from afar we heard the booming voice of the Mother Superior, who arrived with a batallion of elder nuns. It was our turn to be afraid, because we liked the Mother Superior, and as our rebellion was only a sham, it pained us to be scolded and punished as if for a real one. We immediately ran to bolt the doors of the inner and outer classrooms; we hastily rearranged everything, rescued the stools and the torches, straightened and relit the candles; then, when all was in order, everyone fell to her knees and loudly began the evening prayers, while one of us reopened the doors, after some faltering, at the moment the Mother Superior arrived.

The Countess was deemed a madwoman and a visionary, and Marie-Josèphe, the servant who tidied up the classroom in the morning, and who was most cooperative, did not report the few broken candles and pieces of furniture. She kept our secret, and that was the end of our revolution.

Everything was going along just fine; carnival time had arrived, and we prepared an evening of theater that was like nothing else we had ever hoped to produce. I no longer recall what play of Molière or Regnard I had put on the boards. The costumes were ready, the parts given out, the violinist engaged. For that occasion we were to have a violin, a ball, a dinner, and the whole night to enjoy ourselves as we pleased.

But a political event which was predictably due to reverberate in the convent as a public disaster forced us to send our costumes back to storage and closet our gaiety in our hearts.

The Duc de Berry had been assassinated by Louvel at the entrance to the Opéra. An isolated crime, impulsive, as are all blood-crazed acts, it served as a pretext for persecution and also for a sudden change in the policy of Louis XVIII.

The news was brought to us the morning after and commented on by our nuns in a very dramatic and gripping way. For a week, we talked of nothing else. The slightest details of the prince's Christian burial, the despair of his wife, who, they said, had cut off her blond hair at his tomb—all the circumstances surrounding this royal, domestic tragedy reported to us embellished, amplified, and poeticized in the royalist newspapers and special circulars were defrayed by the tears and sighs of our recreation time. Almost all of us belonged to noble families, royalist or bonapartist, who had rallied to the throne. The English girls, who were in the majority, took part in the royal mourning on principle; besides, the tale of a tragic death and the tears of an illustrious family were as thrilling for our young imaginations as a play by Corneille or Racine. They did not tell us that the Duc de Berry had been somewhat brutal and debauched; they painted him as a hero, a second Henri IV, his wife as a saint, and the rest followed from that.

Perhaps I alone struggled against the current. I had remained a bonapartist and did not hide it, although I never debated with anyone.

During that time, anyone who supported Bonaparte was taken for a liberal. I did not know what liberalism was: I was told it was as bad as Jacobinism, which I knew even less about. I therefore became upset when everyone repeated to me, with varying tonal emphasis, "What kind of party preaches, commits, and approves of assassination?"

"If that's the case," I answered, "I'm anything you please but not liberal," and I let them fasten around my neck some little medal stamped in honor of the Duc de Berry, which had become a badge for the whole convent.

A week of mourning is very long for girls in a convent. One evening, someone made a funny face, someone else smiled, a third made a clever remark, and there it was, general laughter broke out in the class, becoming so violent and contagious that it turned into tears.

Gradually they let us return to our amusements. My grandmother was in Paris. As they were giving her good reports on my conduct, she no longer had any reason to scold me seriously, and she also realized that my innocence and lack of coquettishness were not inappropriate for a sixteen-year-old; hence she treated me with all her maternal good will. But a new worry had taken hold of her concerning me—my faith and the secret desire I cherished, which she had probably learned from Mme. de Pontcarré (who would have heard it from Pauline), of becoming a nun. She had found out the summer before, through various letters from people who had seen me in the parlor, that I seemed distressed, sad, and "entirely steeped in God." Such melancholy piety had not really worried her. She reasoned to herself that at my age it could not last. But when she saw me in good health, refreshed, happy, getting on no one's nerves, and nevertheless returning to my cloister each time with more pleasure than I had left it, she became fearful and resolved to take me with her as soon as she left for Nohant.

That news hit me like a thunderbolt right in the midst of the most perfect happiness I had ever felt in my life. The convent had become my earthly paradise. I was neither a student nor a nun, but something in between, with absolute freedom, in a space that I cherished and left with many regrets, even for a day. Nobody was then as happy as I. I was a friend to everyone, the mentor and master of all revels, idol of the youngsters. Seeing me so happy and persistent in my wish to take the veil, the nuns began to believe it, and though not encouraging me, they no longer said No. Élisa, who alone had not been taken in and cheered by my liveliness, firmly believed it; Sister Hélène, more than ever. I believed it then myself and for a long time after I left the convent. Madame Alicia and Abbé de Prémord were the only two people who had doubts, probably knowing me better than the others, and both told me almost the same thing, "Hold on to this idea, if it does you good! But no careless vows, no secret promises to God, and above all, no avowals to your relatives before you are absolutely certain that what you want today is what you will always want. Your grandmother intends for you to marry. If in two or three years you are not married and have no desire to be, we will talk again of your plans."

The kind Abbé had made it very easy for me to become likable. In the beginning, I had been a little frightened by the idea that, as soon as I had some influence on my classmates, my duty would be to preach to and convert them. I had admitted to him that I did not feel suited to this role. "You want me to be loved by everyone here," I had said to him. "Well, I know myself well enough to tell you that I won't be able to make myself loved without myself loving, and I shall never be able to say to anyone I love, 'Your piety is the price of my friendship.' No, I'd be lying. I don't know how to importune, to persecute, or even to insist. I'm too weak."

"I am asking for nothing of the kind," my indulgent director had answered. "Preaching and importuning would be in poor taste at your age. Be yourself pious and happy is all I ask of you, and your example will preach better than all the talks you can give."

He had been right in one way, my fine old friend. It is true that my classmates had grown better in my company, but religion preached thus, through gaiety, had stimulated their high spirits, and I do not know if that was such a sure way to adhere to Catholicism.

I did adhere to it with confidence, and I think I would have continued, if I had not left the convent. But I had to leave. I had to hide from my grandmother, who would have been dreadfully hurt, the kind of mortal regret I experienced in tearing myself away from the numerous and engaging people who were so dear to me. My heart was broken; however, I did not cry, for I had a month to prepare myself for the separation, and when it came, I had so strongly resolved to accept it without a sigh, that I appeared calm and complacent in front of my poor grandmama. But I was sick at heart and felt that way for quite a long time.

I must not conclude my last chapter on the convent without mentioning that, at the time I left, everyone was saddened or dismayed by the death of Madame Canning. I had managed, considering her character, to show her the respect my piety owed her, but I had never been drawn to her instinctively. Yet I was one of the last people she affectionately named in her dying hours.

This powerfully-constituted woman no doubt had possessed the right qualities for her role in monastic life, having maintained absolute control over her community since the Revolution. She left the mother house in flourishing condition, with a considerable number of students and good connections to society, which should have assured a lasting and brilliant clientele in the future.

Nevertheless, this prosperous situation vanished along with her. I had witnessed the election of Madame Eugénie, who still liked me and might have spoiled me even more if I had stayed at the convent. But Madame Eugénie found herself unequipped to exert absolute authority. I do not know if she abused it, if her management was poor, or if people disagreed with her decisions, but she asked at the end of a few years to relinquish her power, and I was told that her request was readily accepted. She had let business matters decline, or rather, I think, she could not prevent them from going that way. Everything is based on fashion in this society, even convents. Under the Empire and Louis XVIII, the English convent was very much in vogue. The great names of France and England had played a role. The Mortemars and Montmorencys had their heiresses there. The daughters of the Empire's generals, who had rallied to the Restoration, were sent there, no doubt in order to establish relations favorable to the aristocratic ambitions of their parents, but the reign of the bourgeoisie was coming, and although I had heard the old contessas accuse Madame Eugénie of having let the convent "go to the dogs," I remember when I left, just a few days after Madame Canning's death, the third estate had already made lucrative inroads into the convent, with her help. So, one could have called that rising class the bouquet of her flourishing administration.

Hence I had seen our personnel rapidly increase by a number of charming daughters of businessmen or industrialists, who were already as well bred and for the most part as intelligent—a thing which was considered remarkable and worth remarking—as the little ones from the great houses.

But this prosperity had to be, and was, shortlived. The "upper crust," as they are referred to today by ordinary folks, then found the milieu too common, and for the titled, the vogue shifted to Sacré-Coeur or Abbaye aux Bois. Several of my old classmates were transferred to those monasteries, and little by little the patrician Catholic element broke with the age-old retreat of the Stuarts. Then, no doubt, the bourgeois, who had flattered themselves with the hope of seeing their heiresses rub elbows with nobility, felt frustrated and humiliated. Or else, the Voltairian spirit of the reign of Louis-Philippe, which had been hatching since the early days of his predecessor, began its proscription of religious education. The fact remains that at the end of a few years I found the convent almost empty, with seven or eight student boarders instead of the seventy or eighty of us that had been there, the vast house as filled with silence as it had been with noise, and Poulette desolate and complaining bitterly about the recent Superiors and the ruin of our former glory.

I found out the latest details about the establishment in 1847. The situation had improved but never returned to its former level—a great injustice of changing fashion, for by and large, the English nuns were always, in every respect, a flock of wise virgins, and their reasonable, gentle, and kind ways could not have vanished in twenty-five years.   *M.L.*

III

Paris, 1820. —Marriage plans postponed. —A daughter's saddened love. —Mme. Catalani. —Arrival at Nohant. —Spring morning. —An attempt at working. —Pauline and her mother. —Plays at Nohant. —New inner strife. —My brother. —Colette and Général Pépé. —Winter at Nohant. —A February evening. —Misfortune and sorrow.

I hardly remember the surprises and impressions which met or must have met me in those first few days I spent in Paris, promenaded and deliberately distracted by my dear grandmother. I was dazed, I think, by the grief of leaving the convent and tormented by the dread of some marriage proposal. My grandmama, who was painfully changed and weakened, spoke of her death, imminent, according to her, with great philosophical calm, but she would add, becoming more tender and pressing me to her bosom, "My daughter, I must marry you off quickly, because I am going away. You are still very young, I know that, but no matter how little desire you have for entering society, you should make an effort to accept the idea. Believe me, I would die terrified and in despair, if I left you without direction and support in life."

In the face of this threat of her despair and terror at the supreme moment, I too was terrified and desperate. "Will someone want to marry me?" I asked myself. "Will it be an arranged marriage? Have they made me leave the convent just for that? Who, then, is this husband, this master, this enemy of my wishes and hopes? Where is he hiding? When will she introduce him to me, saying, 'My daughter, you must say Yes, or deal me a mortal blow!'"

I soon saw, however, that she was only vaguely and preliminarily concerned with these important plans. Mme. de Pontcarré proposed someone; my mother proposed, through my Uncle Beaumont, someone else. I saw Mme. de Pontcarré's match, and she asked my opinion. I told her the man had seemed very ugly to me. On the contrary, it turned out he was handsome but that I had not looked at him, and Mme. de Pontcarré told me I was a little goose.

I was completely reassured when I saw that they were packing for Nohant without deciding anything, and I even heard my grandmama say that she thought I was still very young and that I needed to be given yet another six months', maybe a year's respite.

Relieved of one awful anxiety, I soon lapsed into another. I had hoped my dear mother would come to Nohant with us. I did not know what new storm had just erupted during those last days in Paris. My mother answered my questions abruptly, "Certainly not! I will only return to Nohant when my mother-in-law is dead!"

I felt that all was shattered yet again in my sad domestic existence. I did not dare ask any questions. I had a poignant fear of hearing, from one side or the other, the bitter recriminations of the past. My piety as much as my filial affection forbade me from listening to the slightest criticism of one or the other. I tried silently to bring them together; in my presence, they embraced, tears in their eyes, but these were tears of repressed suffering and mutual reproach. I saw it clearly, and I hid mine.

Yet again I told my mother I would declare myself, so as to be able to stay with her, or at least convince my grandmama to take her along with me.

My mother strongly rejected this idea. "No, no!" she said, "I detest the country, especially Nohant, which only brings back excruciating pain. Your sister is a grown girl now, who needs my supervision. Be off, and don't be so upset, we'll see each other again, and maybe sooner than you think!"

This persistent allusion to the death of my grandmother was heart-rending for me. I tried to tell her how deeply it hurt me. "Do as you like!" my mother said, irritated. "If you love her more than me, so much the better for you, since you belong to her now, body and soul."

"I belong to her with all my heart, out of gratitude and devotion," I answered, "but not body and soul against you. One thing is sure: if she demands that I marry, it will never be, I swear, to a man who would refuse to see or respect my mother."

This resolution was so strong in me that my poor mother should indeed have held it in some esteem. Subdued as I now was by Christian submission and no longer having any energy to resist the tears of my grandmama, to the extent that gradually my favorite dream of monastic life was disappearing before the fear of distressing her, I would, nevertheless, have found in my filial instincts the strength that Sister Hélène had had when she resisted her father to go to God. Less holy and more humane, I believe I would have stepped over the body of my grandmother to extend my arms to my humiliated and outraged mother.

But my mother no longer understood my feelings. They had become too sensitive and tender for her bluff, unsubtle nature. She had only a smile of distinct unconcern in response to my effusive comment. "Hold on, hold on! I know that well enough!" she said, "I'm not worried about that. Do you know that no one can marry you without my consent? Would I ever give it to a man who would put on airs with me? Come, come! I don't care about all the threats. You belong to me, and even though people may succeed in making you rebel against your mother, your mother will know how to reclaim her rights!"

Thus my mother, exasperated, seemed inclined to doubt me and, in order to vent her own bitterness, lay the blame on my poor, distressed soul. I began to foresee something strange in this noble, but untamed, character, and there surely was something fearsome in her beautiful, black eyes which for the first time struck me with terror.

In contrast, I found my grandmother immersed in a deep and pathetic sadness which profoundly touched me. "What can I say, my child?" she asked me, when I tried to mend the rift. "Your mother cannot or will not acknowledge the great efforts that I have made, and always make, to render her happy. It is neither her fault nor mine if we are not fond of each other. But I have behaved well toward her in all things, and she is so difficult that I can no longer bear it. Can she not let me end my life in peace? She has so little time to wait!"

As I opened my mouth to divert her from this thought, "Let's not discuss it!" she continued, "I know what you want to say. I am wrong to make a sixteen-year-old sad with my gloomy ideas. We shall not think about it. Get dressed. Tonight, I want to take you to the *Italiens!*"

I really did need to be entertained, but precisely because I was desperately sad, I had neither the desire nor the strength for it. I believe that was the night I first heard Mme. Catalani in *Il fanatico per la musica.*[9] I also think that it was Galli who played the role of the burlesque dilettante, but I saw and heard little, preoccupied as I was. I had the feeling the singer was misusing her talents and that her fancy for singing the variations written for the violin was unmusical. I was just emerging from the choruses and motets of our convent chapel, and in a number of pieces used for effect—like those sung during the benediction to the holy sacrament—there were some antiphons vocalized in the rococo style of sacred music from the last century, but we were not taken in by these breaches and, for the most part, had been put on our way to good taste. The opera bouffe of the Italians, so artistically embellished by the fashionable singer, caused me only astonishment. I had more pleasure listening to Chevalier de Lacoux, an old emigré friend of my grandmother, play a few Spanish tunes on the harp or guitar, some of which had lullabied me in Madrid and that reawakened in me like a dream of the past asleep in my memory.

Rose had married and was to leave us to go live in La Châtre as soon as we returned to Nohant. Impatient to rejoin her husband, to whom she had been married on the eve of her trip to Paris, she could hardly conceal her joy and would repeat to me with a redhead's fervor what left me quaking with fear, "Don't worry, your turn will come soon!"

I went one last time to embrace all my dear convent friends. I was truly down-hearted.

We arrived at Nohant during the first few days of spring 1820, in my grandmother's large, blue calash. Again I found my little room in the hands of workmen who were replacing the wallpaper and paint, because my grandmama was beginning to find the large floral print on orange linen too old-fashioned for my youthful eyes and wanted to delight them with a fresh lilac color. However, my four-poster bed, shaped like a hearse, was spared, and the four worm-eaten plumes again escaped the vandalism of modern taste.

I was temporarily moved into my mother's large suite. There, nothing had changed, and I slept deliciously in the huge bed with gilded pomegranates that brought back all the affection and dreams of my childhood.

Finally, for the first time since our definitive separation, I saw the sun come into this empty room where I had cried so much. The trees were in bloom, the nightingales were singing, and I heard at a distance the traditional and solemn cantilena of the laborers, which summed up and characterized all the clear and tranquil poetry of the Berry region. My awakening was, however, an indescribable mixture of joy and pain. It was already nine in the morning. For the first time in three years, I had overslept, without the sound of the angelus and Marie-Josèphe's shrill voice to snatch me from the sweetness of my last dream. I could idle away yet another hour without incurring any penance. To escape from the rules, to be at liberty, is an incomparable state in which only souls steeped in reverie and retreat can fully indulge.

I went to open my window and returned to bed. The fragrance of plants, youth, life, independence came to me in gusts, but the sense of the unknown future that loomed up before me also overwhelmed me with deep restlessness and sadness. I did not know how to explain this morbid turn of mind so little in keeping with the fresh ideas and physical health of adolescence. I felt it so acutely that a very distinct memory has remained after so many years without my being able clearly to discover by what chain of ideas, what memories of yesterday, what apprehensions of tomorrow, I came to shed bitter tears at a time when I should have regained, amid transports of happiness, possession of the paternal home and of myself.

What simple pleasures, nonetheless, for a boarding school student released from the cage! Instead of the sober uniform of purplish serge, a pretty chambermaid brought me a fresh dress of pink gingham. I was free to arrange my hair in my own style, without Madame Eugénie coming to tell me it was indecent to reveal my temples. Lunch was enhanced by all the delicacies that my grandmother loved and lavished on me. The garden was an immense bouquet. All the servants, all the country people came to welcome me. I hugged all the good women of the neighborhood, who found my looks much improved because I had "filled out," or, in their parlance, "put on weight in the right places." The Berrichon patois rang in my ears like beloved music, and I was struck by the absence of the hissing nasality typical of British speech. The big dogs, my old friends, who had growled at me the night before, recognized me and covered me with affection in their intelligent and candid way that seems to ask forgiveness for having had a brief lapse of memory.

Toward evening, Deschartres, who had been at some distant fair, finally arrived in his short jacket, wide gaiters, and cap with ear flaps. The dear man had not yet gotten it through his head that I had changed and grown up over the last three years, and when I jumped on him to kiss him, he asked where Aurore was. He called me "mademoiselle"; finally, like the dogs, he recognized me, but only after fifteen minutes.

All my former childhood friends were as changed as I was. Liset had been "hired out," as we say. I did not see him again, for he died a short while afterward. Cadet had become our valet. He waited at table and innocently said to Mlle. Julie, who accused him of breaking all the carafes, "I only broke seven of them last week." Fanchon was our shepherdess, Marie Aucante had become the village beauty. Marie and Solange Croux were charming young girls. For three days, my room was filled with visitors. Nor was Ursule among the last.

But, like Deschartres, everyone called me "mademoiselle." A few were in awe of me. That made me aware of my separateness. The gap in social hierarchy among children who had, until then, considered themselves equals had widened. I could not do anything about it; it would not have been tolerated. It made me miss my convent friends all the more.

Then for several days I devoted myself entirely to the physical pleasures of again running through the fields and taking in the river, the wild greenery, the flowering meadows. I had lost the habit of waking in the country, and the spring air intoxicated me, so that I was no longer pensive and would sleep long nights with pleasure, but soon my mind's idleness weighed on me, and I thought about how to fill up this endless leisure which had been given to me through my grandmother's indulgence.

I even experienced the need to go back to a structured life, and I outlined for myself a schedule from which I did not deviate as long as I was free to manage my own time. I was ingenuous enough to make myself a time frame for my working day. I would devote one hour to history, one to sketching, one to music, one to English, one to Italian, etc. But the time for really learning on my own had not yet come. By the end of a month I had only reviewed, in ad hoc notebooks, my minimal studies from the convent when guests of my grandmama arrived—Mme. de Pontcarré and her charming daughter, Pauline, my lively, blond classmate.

Pauline, at sixteen as at six, was still the indifferent beauty who let herself be loved without dreaming of reciprocating. Her personality was as charming as her face, her figure, her hands, her amber-colored hair, her cheeks of lilies and roses. But as her feelings never showed, I never knew if they existed, and I could not say if this pleasant companion was indeed my friend.

Her mother was quite different. Her passionate soul matched a dazzling mind. Too full-blooded and stout still to be beautiful (nor do I know if she ever was), she had such magnificent black eyes and such a lively expression, a beautiful voice with such soul for singing, conversation so heartening, so many ideas, so much activity, and so much affection in her manners that she exerted irresistible charm. She was the same age as my father, and they had played together as children. My grandmother loved to talk to her about her dear son, and had recently formed a friendship with her although they had always been acquainted; but the affection soon gave way, on my grandmother's side, to aversion, which I did not notice soon enough to prevent her suffering.

At the beginning, all went so well between them that I in no way resisted the lure of the friendship for my own benefit. Very naturally, I spent a lot more time with Pauline and her mother, both of whom were sprightly and active, than at the armchair where my grandmother would write or doze for almost the whole day. She herself insisted that mornings and evenings I go for long walks and practice music with these ladies during the day. Mme. de Pontcarré was an excellent teacher. She launched Pauline and me into reading scores, accompanying us with gusto and supporting our voices with the sympathetic power of her own. Together, we sightread *Armide, Iphigénie, Oedipe*,[10] etc. When we were a bit more sure of ourselves in a piece, we opened the doors so that grandmama could hear, and her judgment was not the least useful lesson. But more often than not her door was bolted shut. My grandmother had preserved the habit of being alone, or with Mlle. Julie, who read to her. We were too young and energetic for our steady company to please her. The poor woman was quietly fading, but it was not yet obvious. She would appear at meals with a little rouge on her cheeks, diamonds in her ears, her posture straight and graceful in her quilted housecoat; chatting easily and answering to the point, a slave to the considerate breeding that made her hide or conquer her frequent lapses, she seemed to be enjoying a beautiful aging exempt from infirmities. For a long time, she concealed an increasing deafness and, until her last moments, made her age a mystery apparently for the sake of etiquette, for she had never been vain even in the full bloom of youth and beauty. Yet, she was going away, as she often said in a low voice to Deschartres, who, having always considered her overly sensitive and easily disheartened, did not believe it and flattered himself that he would die before her. She feared the least bit of noise, the bustle of the day was unbearable to her, and having made the effort to run a salon for an hour or two, she felt the need to confine herself in her bedroom, begging us to go busy ourselves or take a short walk away from where she was sleeping, as she slept so lightly.

Therefore, I was quite shocked and somewhat frightened the day she told me that I was inseparable from Mme. de Pontcarré and her daughter, that I was neglecting her, that I was throwing myself headlong into new friendships, that I was too fanciful, that I did not love her—all expressed with grief and inexplicable tears.

I felt these reproaches to be so undeserved that they appalled me. Their injustice left me speechless, but in a heart so good and righteous, such injustice seemed rather like the approach of sad and gentle madness. All I could do was cry with my poor grandmama, stroking and consoling her as best I could. Since she reproached me for whispering frequently to these ladies and seeming mysterious in their presence, I was happy to reveal a secret concerning herself, and confessed to her that for a week we had been building a set and rehearsing a play for her birthday, but that I much preferred giving away the surprise than letting her suffer one more day with her imaginings. "Oh, my goodness!" she said to me, also laughing through her tears, "I know very well that you are preparing me a big celebration and surprise! How could you imagine that Julie hadn't told me?"

"She certainly did the right thing, since she saw you were worried about our secret. Then why, dear grandmama, were you still so pained?"

She confessed to me that she did not know why she had turned it into a cause for grief, and as I proposed to forget the play and not be involved, in order to spend all my time close to her, she cried out, "Definitely not! I do not want that! Mme. de Pontcarré will do quite enough to show off her daughter; I do not want, as usual, that you be put aside and eclipsed by her!"

I no longer found any of it comprehensible. Never had the idea of a rivalry surfaced in Pauline's mind or mine. Probably Mme. de Pontcarré had thought about it no more than we, but my poor jealous grandmama could not forgive Pauline for being more beautiful than I, and at the same time as she assumed that the mother was inclined to denigrate me, she was also jealous of the affection that this same mother showed me.

As jealousy is fraught with inconsistencies, so these little scenes had to be replayed before me, and I believe they were exacerbated by Mlle. Julie, who definitely did not like me at all. I had never hurt nor caused her any harm; on the contrary, quick as I was to forgive, I valued the intelligence of that cold person and liked to consult her marvelous memory for historical facts, but my mother had hurt her too much for Julie to forgive me for being my mother's daughter and for loving her.

Hence it was that, wiping away a few secret tears and in between a few thunderheads of those storms that good breeding stifles, I disguised myself as Colin to act in a play and make my grandmother laugh. The theater, decorated with natural foliage, formed a charming bower. M. de Trémauville, an officer friend of Mme. de Pontcarré, finding himself in cavalry detail in the area, had come to spend a fortnight with us and had taken over with great tact and good taste. He played himself in the role of Captain, for Colin had enlisted in despair at the caprices of his beloved Colette. I no longer recall which Carmontelle[11] proverb had been adapted for our purpose. Pauline, in the rustic style of opéra-comique, was as beautiful as an angel. Deschartres also played a role, and badly at that. Nevertheless, all went very well, despite the apprehensions of Pauline, who cried with fear when going on stage. Never having been subject to this type of timidity, I played very determinedly, which consoled my grand-mama a bit for seeing me dressed as boy while Pauline radiated all the loveliness of her beauty in the finery of her sex.

Some time afterward, Mme. de Pontcarré left with her daughter and M. de Trémauville, whom I remember as the best man in the world; a wonderful family man, he treated Pauline and me as his own children, and we took such advantage of his easy and likeable nature that my grandmother herself, in her happier moments, had nicknamed him "Nursemaid to the Demoiselles."

But some deep resentment remained in my grandmother's heart against Mme. de Pontcarré and Pauline. Pained over their departure, I was nevertheless relieved to see an end to the odd and incomprehensible quarrels they had caused me. Hippolyte came home on leave, and at first we were uncomfortable with each other. He had become a handsome hussar sergeant, rolling his r's, breaking horses which could not be broken, and having man-to-man talks with Deschartres, who permitted him to tease him as my father had about equitation and other subjects. After a few days, our old friendship revived, and we began to run and frolic together. It seemed as though we had never parted.

It was he who gave me a taste for riding, and the physical exercise must have considerably influenced my character and way of thinking.

The course in horsemanship he gave me was neither long nor boring. "You see," he said to me one morning when I asked him to give me a first lesson, "I could play the pedant and have you cram your head with the instruction manual that I teach at Saumur to recruits who retain nothing from it and who, in short, only learn by constant doing and daring. But to begin with, it all boils down to two things—to fall or not to fall; the rest will come later. Well then, as one must expect to fall, we will go look for a good spot, so that you don't get too badly hurt." And he took me to a vast meadow where the grass was thick. He mounted Général Pépé,[12] leading Colette by hand.

Pépé was a healthy looking colt, grandson of the terrible Léopardo, on whom, in my budding enthusiasm for the Italian revolution, I had bestowed the name of a heroic man who became my friend later on in life. Colette, originally called Mlle. Deschartres, was raised by our tutor and had never been mounted. She was four years old and had been out to pasture. She seemed so gentle that my brother, after having made her circle the meadow several times, judged that she would behave well and heaved me onto her.

God watches over children and lunatics. Colette and I, both novices, had every possible chance to rub each other wrong and come to a violent parting. Nothing of the kind happened. From that day forward, we were to live and gallop together for fourteen years. She would earn her retirement and calmly end her days in my service, without the shadow of a cloud in our good understanding.

I do not know if I would have been afraid, given a chance for reflection, but my brother did not give me a chance. He vigorously whipped Colette, who made her debut with a frantic gallop, accompanied by bucking and kicking in a most crazy fashion, but not at all viciously. "Hold on tight," my brother said. "Grab on to the mane, if you want, but don't let go of the reins and don't fall off! That's the key, to fall or not to fall!"

It was Hamlet's "to be or not to be." I concentrated all my attention and will-power on not vacating the saddle. Five or six times, partly unseated, I saved myself by the grace of God, and after an hour, exhausted, dishevelled, and above all else intoxicated, I had acquired the degree of confidence and presence of mind necessary to continue my equestrian education.

Colette was a superior being of her species. She was thin, ugly, large, and awkward while at rest, but she had an untamed look, and her eyes were of a beauty which redeemed her structural flaws. In motion, she had majestic mettle, grace, and suppleness. I have mounted some magnificent horses, admirably trained, but I have never since found the intelligence and adroitness of my rustic mare. She never missed her footing, shied, or threw me to the ground, unless it was due to my own carelessness or imprudence.

As she divined all that one required, I hardly needed more than a week to learn how to handle her. Her instinct and mine tallied. A tease and temperamental with others, she surely yielded of her own free will to my domination. At the end of a week, we were jumping over hedges and ditches, climbing steep slopes, crossing deep waters, and I, the "still waters" of the convent, had become something bolder than a hussar and more robust than a peasant; for children do not know what danger is, and women are sustained by the force of their instincts which exceed manly power.

My grandmother did not seem surprised by a metamorphosis which nevertheless astonished me; from one day to the next, I no longer recognized myself, whereas it was her observation that I bore the same contrasts of languor and elation which had marked the adolescence of my father.

It is odd that, loving me in such an absolute and tender way, she had not been alarmed in seeing me take a liking to this sort of danger. My mother could never see me on a horse without hiding her face in her hands and crying out that I would end up like my father. My grandmama would respond with a sad smile to those who asked her the reason for her tolerance on this subject, and told a well-worn but amusing anecdote about the sailor and the city man:

"Well, Monsieur, your father and your grandfather perished at sea in storms, and you are a sailor? If I were in your place, I would never have wanted to board a ship!"

"And you, Monsieur, how did your parents die?"

"In their beds, thank heavens!"

"In that case, if I were in your place, I would never want to go to bed!"

Nonetheless, I happened one day to fall exactly in the same spot where my father was killed, and to hurt myself quite badly. It was not Colette but Général Pépé who played me that nasty trick. My grandmother knew nothing about it. I kept quiet and rode harder than ever.

My brother returned to his regiment. Old Chevalier de Lacoux, who had come to visit and made me practice the harp, also left. I stayed alone at Nohant for the entire winter, with my grandmother and Deschartres.

Until that moment, despite the pleasant company of those diverse guests, I had struggled in vain against a deep melancholy. I could not always disguise it, but never did I want to reveal what the cause of it was, not even to Pauline or my brother, who were surprised by my moods of despondency and inattention. I let them ascribe it to a sickly disposition or some vague annoyance, but the reason was quite clear to me—I missed the convent. I was sick for it in much the same way as one gets homesick. I could not feel bored having such a full life, but I felt displeased when I compared even my best moments to the placid and regular days of the cloister, to the cloudless friendships, the steady happiness I had forever left behind. My soul, already weary since childhood, had craved repose, and only in the convent had I tasted, after the first flush of religious enthusiasm, almost a year of absolute tranquility. There I had forgotten all of the past; there I had dreamed of a future that mirrored the present. Also, my heart had formed a habit of loving many people at the same time and conveying to them or receiving from them a continual nourishment of kindness and pleasure.

I have said it, but I shall say it yet again at the moment of burying this dream of monastic life in my distant but always tender memories: communal living with gently lovable beings who are gently loved is the ideal happiness. Affection thrives on preference, but in this type of fraternal society where some sort of faith serves as a bond, the preferences are so pure and so wholesome that they augment the heart's resources instead of depleting them. It allows us to be so much better and more easily generous with our secondary friends, to feel we must lavish on them kindness and courtesy, in compensation for the enthusiastic admiration we reserve for those beings more directly sympathetic. It has often been said that a beautiful passion expands the soul. What passion more beautiful than that of evangelical brotherhood? I had felt myself fully alive in that enchanting milieu, but wasting away ever since, day by day, hour by hour, and never taking stock of what was lacking, sometimes trying to forget and divert myself, as befitted the innocence of my age. I felt a terrible void in my thoughts, a disgust, a weariness with everything and everybody around me.

My grandmother was the sole exception; my affection for her grew immensely. I managed to understand her, to grasp the secret of her sweet, maternal weaknesses, no longer to see in her the strong, cold spirit that my mother had exaggerated for me, but rather the sensitive and delicately susceptible woman who made others suffer only because she herself suffered through sheer love. I saw the peculiar inconsistencies which had more or less always existed between her resolute mind and her weak nature. Forced to study her, and realizing that it had to be done so as to spare her all the little griefs I had caused her, I finally solved this enigma of a rational mind at grips with a foolish heart. Superior woman that she was through her upbringing, judgment, honesty, and courage in the important things, she became weak and petty in the thousand little trials of everyday life. At first I felt disappointed to have thus to judge a person whom I had become accustomed to seeing as grand in her severity as in her goodness. But reflection brought me around, and I began to love the weak sides of this complex nature, whose flaws were only the excesses of her finest virtues. The day came when we exchanged roles and when the tenderness I felt for her deep within me resembled a mother's anxiety.

It was like an inner portent or warning from above, for the moment was approaching when she would no longer be for me anything but a poor child to care for and look after.

Alas! the time was short enough, snatched as it was from the rigors of our common destiny, in which, myself emerging from the shadows of childhood, I could finally profit from her moral influence and the intellectual gift of her intimacy. No longer having any reason for being jealous about me (Hippolyte had also been the cause of some final outbursts), she became wholly lovable in our tête-à-têtes. She knew so much and was so wise, she expressed herself with such elegant simplicity, she had so much taste and breeding, that her conversation was the best of books.

We spent the last evenings of February together, reading a portion of Chateaubriand's *Génie du Christianisme*. She did not like the form, and the substance seemed false to her, but the numerous citations within the work prompted some admirable opinions from her regarding the masterpiece from which I was reading her excerpts. I was surprised she had hardly ever permitted me to read with her; I mentioned it, expressing to her the pleasure I derived from such lessons, when she said to me one evening, "Stop, my child. What you are reading to me is so strange that I am afraid I have taken ill and am hearing something other than what I am listening to. Why do you speak to me of corpses, shrouds, bells, and tombs? If you are making all that up, you are wrong to put such gloomy ideas into my mind."

I stopped, terrified; I had just read her a refreshing and cheerful page, a description of the savannahs, in which there was nothing like what she thought she had heard. She quickly pulled herself together and smiled, saying, "Oh, my! I think I dozed off and had a dream while you were reading. I feel very weak. I cannot read or listen any longer. But I am afraid of feeling idle or bored either. Give me the cards, and let us have a hand of *grabuge*. That will distract me."

I eagerly took part in the game, and I succeeded in cheering her up. She played with her usual care and lucidity. Then, daydreaming for a moment, she organized her ideas as if for a supremely important speech, for surely she felt her soul escaping. "That marriage was not at all suitable for you," she said, "and I am happy to have broken it off."

"What marriage?" I asked her.

"Haven't I spoken to you about it? Well then, I shall tell you. It was with an incredibly rich man, but he is fifty years old and has a big scar from where a saber struck him across the face. He is a general of the Empire. I don't know where he saw you, maybe it was at the visiting room in the convent. Do you recall that?"

"Not at all."

"Well, he apparently knows you, and he asks for your hand in marriage with or without a dowry, but is it conceivable that Bonaparte's men are as prejudiced as the rest of us? He requested as a foremost priority that you would never see your mother again."

"And you refused, didn't you, grandmama?"

"Yes," she answered, "here is the proof."

She handed me a letter that I again have before me, for I kept it as a souvenir of that sad evening. It was from my cousin René de Villeneuve and read as follows:

"I am disconsolate, dear grandmother, not to have been at your side to insist on the proposal arranged for Aurore. His age offends you, but really this person of fifty looks almost as young as I. He has plenty of wit, schooling, and all that it really takes for assuring the happiness of such a union; for though one can certainly find younger men, one cannot be sure of their character, and a future with them may be quite uncertain; in its stead you have here a higher social standing, money, reputation—everything. I will cite you a few examples that I base my reasoning on. The Duc de Caylus, who is sixty-five, married Mlle. de La Grange two years ago, who was then sixteen. She is the happiest of women, behaving wonderfully well, although she was taken into society and overwhelmed with compliments, for she is as beautiful as an angel.[3] She acquired an excellent education and good principles. That makes all the difference. Come then without fail to Paris at the beginning of March. I bid you make this trip in the interest of our dear child, etc."

"Well then, grandmama," I cried out, frightened, "are we going to Paris?"

"Yes, my child, we shall leave in a week. But set your mind at ease, I do not want to hear anything about this marriage. It is not so much the age that bothers me as the condition which I mentioned to you. I was so happy with my old husband that I am not too afraid for you to marry a fifty-year-old man, but I know you would not subscribe to.... You needn't reply. I know how you feel now, and I am sorry for not having always genuinely understood your situation as I do at this moment. You love your mother out of duty and religion, as you loved her through habit and instinct in your childhood. I did believe that I had to put you on guard against over-involvement and trust. Perhaps I was wrong to do it in a moment of pain and anger. I certainly saw I was hurting you. It seemed to me, at that time, that you should learn the truth from me, and that it would have been more unbearable from anyone else. If you think I have exaggerated or judged your mother too harshly, forget what I said and know that despite all the wrong she has done me I give her credit for her good qualities and her conduct since the death of your poor father. Besides, even if she was, as I sometimes thought, the worst of women, I believe you owe her some respect and loyalty. She is your mother! Nothing can change that! Yes, I realize it. I was frightened to see you so blinded: then I was frightened to see you become so pious. I am reassured about you now. I see you as devout, tolerant, and mindful of the tastes of intelligence. I almost regret that I do not believe in all that you practice, for I see that you draw from it a strength which is not in your nature and which has sometimes struck me as beyond your years. So while you were at the convent, confined throughout the year, without vacations, deprived from going out during the nine or ten months I spent here, you wrote to me many a time pleading for permission not to go out with the Villeneuves or Madame de Pontcarré. At first, I was distressed and jealous, but I was also touched by it, and now I feel that asking you to break with your mother to enter into a favorable marriage would revolt your heart and conscience. So be at peace, and go to bed. There will never be a question of anything like that."

I passionately hugged my dear grandmother, and confident that she was perfectly calm and lucid, I retired to my bedroom, leaving her in the experienced hands of her two serving women, who put her to bed at midnight, after the two-hour toilette and peaceful dallying to which she was accustomed.

As I have already said, bedtime for my grandmother was a very strange little ritual: camisoles of quilted satin, lace bonnets, ribbon rosettes, perfumes, special rings for nighttime wear, a particular snuff-box, and finally, a whole pile of splendid pillows, for she slept sitting up, and it was necessary to arrange her so that she could wake up without having moved. It was as if each night she prepared herself for a state occasion and delighted in the strangeness and solemnity of it.

I should have realized that the sort of auditory hallucination she had had while listening to me read and the sudden clarity of her ideas, even the retraction she had intended when speaking of my mother, indicated a highly unusual mental and physical condition. Going back on her own decrees, taking the blame on herself, asking to be pardoned, so to speak, for an error in judgment, all this was certainly unlike her. Her actions would continually contradict her words, but she would not admit it, and would readily uphold her opinions. Thinking back on it, I had a twinge of uneasiness and went down to her room around midnight on the pretext of retrieving a forgotten book. She was already in bed and tucked in, having felt drowsy a little earlier than usual. Her maids had not noticed anything out of the ordinary about her, and I went back up quite at peace.

For three or four months I had slept very little. It had taken me one week in true privacy with my grandmother to realize how little instruction I had acquired at the convent and to recognize, along with the truthful Deschartres, that I was, according to his favorite expression, "crassly ignorant." The desire not to provoke grandmama, who sometimes rebuked me a little sharply for having made her pay for three years at the convent without learning a thing, impelled me, more than curiosity or vanity, to want to learn a little on my own. It hurt me to hear her say that religious education was stupefying, and I had been studying in secret to allow her to give credit to my nuns.

In this I was undertaking an impossible task. Whoever is missing a good memory can never be truly educated, and of that I was totally bereft. I went to great pains to put my few notions of history in order. I did not even have a memory for language, and already I was forgetting English, which a short time ago had been as familiar to me as my own tongue. Therefore, I racked my brain with reading and writing from ten at night until two or three in the morning. I would get four or five hours of sleep. I would go riding before my grandmother awoke. I ate breakfast with her, practiced my music for her, and hardly ever left her for the remainder of the day, for she had imperceptibly become accustomed to spending less time with Julie, and I had taken it upon myself to read her the newspapers or to remain in her bedroom sketching while Deschartres read them to her. That I found particularly odious. I have no idea why that daily chronicle of the real world saddened me so profoundly. It took me out of my dreams, and I believe that youth lives only on the contemplation of the past or the anticipation of the unknown.

I remember that night being extremely beautiful and calm. The moonlight was shadowed by those small white clouds that Chateaubriand compared to tufts of cotton. I did not study at all, I left my window open, and sightread Paesiello's *Nina* at the harp. Then I felt cold and went to sleep dreaming of how sweetly effusive my grandmother had been toward me. By finally allowing me to feel secure in my daughterly feelings, and by averting the fear of a struggle which had burdened my entire life, she let me breathe easier for the first time. I could finally reunite and blend my two rival mothers in the same love. At that moment I felt I loved each of them equally and believed I could make them accept the idea. Then I thought about marriage, the fifty-year-old man, the next trip to Paris, the threat of being introduced into society. None of it phased me. For the first time I was optimistic. I had just gained a victory which seemed to me decisive over the future's most serious obstacle. I convinced myself that I had acquired an ascendancy of tenderness and persuasion over my grandmother which would allow me to escape her concern for my future security, that little by little she would see through my eyes, would let me live happily and freely at her side, and that after having devoted my youth to her, I could close her eyes without her exacting my promise to renounce the cloister. "All is well as it is," I thought. "It is quite needless to torment her with my hidden intentions. God will protect them." I knew that Élisa had left the convent, that she was being taken into society, resigning herself to go to balls, but that nothing shook her resolution. She wrote to me that she accepted the trial which her parents had wanted her to undergo, that each day she felt stronger in her vocation, and that maybe we would meet again in County Cork as nuns, if my being French excluded me from the English community in Paris.

Then I dropped off to sleep in a frame of mind that I had not known for a long time, but at seven in the morning Deschartres entered my room, and when I opened my eyes I saw misfortune on his face. "I'm afraid your grandmother is lost," he told me. "She tried to get up during the night. She was stricken with apoplexy and paralysis. She fell and could not get up. Julie just found her on the floor, cold, unable to move, and unconscious. She is in bed, warming up, and a little revived, but she is not reacting to anything and cannot move. I have sent for Dr. Decerfz. I am going to bleed her. Come quickly to help me."

We spent the day caring for her. She recovered her faculties, remembered that she had fallen, complained only of the bruises she had suffered, noticed that one side of her body was "dead" from the shoulder to the heel of her foot, but attributed this numbness to exhaustion from the fall. However, the bleeding gave her a little ease in the movements she made with our help, and toward evening there was such a perceptible improvement that I was reassured, and the doctor left, setting my mind at ease. But Deschartres was not deceived. She asked me to read her the newspaper after dinner and appeared to hear it. Then she asked for a deck of cards but could not hold them in her hand. Then she began to ramble and complain that we would not relieve her by applying the queen of spades to her arm. Frightened, I quietly asked Deschartres, "Is it delirium?"

"Alas, no!" he answered. "She doesn't have a fever, it's her 'second childhood!'"

This pronouncement affected me worse than a death notice. I was so upset that I left the room and fled to the garden, where I fell to my knees in a corner, wanting to pray but not being able to. The weather seemed insolent in its beauty and tranquility. I believe that I myself was in a second childhood at that moment, for I was amazed in a mechanical way that everything seemed so lovely around me while I felt death in my soul. I returned quickly. "Take heart!" Deschartres told me, for he tended to become kind and affectionate in times of affliction. "You must not become ill; she needs us!"

She spent the night mildly rambling. At daybreak she fell soundly asleep until evening. This apoplectic slumber was a new danger to contend with. The doctor and Deschartres drew her out of it successfully, but when she awoke she was blind. The following day, she was able to see, but objects to her right seemed to be on her left. Another day she stuttered and lost her memory for words. Finally, after a series of strange phenomena and unforseen crises, she became convalescent. Her life was temporarily saved. She was lucid for hours at a time. She suffered little, but she was a paralytic, and her feeble and shattered mind actually entered the childish phase Deschartres had predicted. She no longer had any will of her own except for continual velleities impossible to satisfy. She had no more capacity for reflection or courage. Her eyesight was poor and she could hardly hear anymore. Finally, her beautiful intelligence, her beautiful soul were dead.

There were many different phases in the illness of my poor grandmother. In the spring she was better. During the summer, for a short while we believed there had been a radical improvement, for she had recovered some spirit, gaiety, and a portion of her memory. She would spend part of the day in her armchair. She would drag herself along, leaning on our arms, to the dining room, where she heartily ate her meals. She would sit in the sunlit garden; sometimes she still listened to her newspaper and even concerned herself with business matters and her will, showing solicitude for all her staff. But with the coming of fall, she relapsed into a constant lethargy and died without suffering or consciousness of her end, in a coma, on the 25th of December 1821.

I lived, thought, and changed a great deal in those ten months during which my grandmother had recovered, at best, only a partial existence. Without wanting to sadden my readers too much with painful details of a slow and inevitable deterioration, I shall recount how my life revolved around the bedside of the poor dying woman.   *B.A.B.*

IV

Sorrows, strolls, and dreams. —Fighting sleep. —My first serious reading. —*Le Génie du Christianisme* and *L'Imitation de Jésus-Christ*. —Absolute truth and relative truth. —Scruples of conscience. —Wavering between mental development and regression. —The solution. —Abbé de Prémord. —My opinion of Jesuit thought. —Readings in metaphysics. —The war in Greece. —Deschartres sides with the Grand Turk. —Leibnitz. —My brain's great impotence, my heart's victory. —Relaxation of devotional practices, with an increase in faith. —Country and provincial churches. —Jean-Jacques Rousseau, *Le Contrat social*.

If destiny had made me pass immediately from my grandmother's control to that of a husband or the convent, it is possible that, always subject to accepted influences, I would never have become myself. There is no initiative at all in a sleepy nature such as mine, and the unquestioning devotion so in keeping with my languid mind would have forbidden me from asking my reason to sanction my faith. My grandmother's barely perceptible, but continuous, efforts to open my eyes resulted only in a kind of inner reaction. A husband as Voltairian as she would have done even worse. It was not through the mind that I could be changed; not being at all clever, I was insensitive to teasing, which in addition, I did not always understand.

But fate had decreed that on my seventeenth birthday there would be a lull in external influences and that for almost a whole year I would belong entirely to myself, in order to become—for better or worse—what I would be more or less for the rest of my life.

It is unusual that a child of good family, especially a child of my sex, is left to take care of herself at such a young age. Even in her most lucid moments, my paralyzed grandmother no longer gave the least thought to my moral or intellectual development. Always kind and loving, she still would worry about my health sometimes, but all other concerns, including my marriage, which she could no longer arrange by correspondence, seemed removed from her memory.

My mother did not come, in spite of my pleas, saying that my grandmother's condition could be prolonged indefinitely and that she could not leave Caroline. I had to resign myself to that simple explanation and accept the loneliness.

Deschartres—crushed at first, then resigned—seemed to change completely toward me. He surrendered, more or less willingly, all his authority to me, demanded that I take responsibility for the house, that all the orders come from me, and treated me as a mature person, capable of assuming command over others and myself.

It was a great deal to expect of my capabilities, and yet it was lucky that he did, as you will shortly see.

It was not very hard for me to maintain the established order in the house. All the servants were loyal. As overseer, Deschartres still directed the work in the fields, about which it had been impossible for me to understand the first thing, in spite of all his former efforts to make me acquire a taste for it. I was a born dabbler, nothing more.

Poor Deschartres—seeing that by depriving me of my only and dearest intellectual companion my grandmother's condition threw me into deep ennui and despair, that I was visibly losing weight, and that my health was obviously suffering—he did all he could to distract me and make me snap out of it. He granted me full ownership of Colette, and to awaken my interest in riding, which was failing along with my taste for activity, he brought over all the colts and fillies from his land, begging me to try them and use them to suit my pleasure. These efforts cost him more than one fall in the meadow, and he was forced to agree that, for all my ignorance I was more secure in the saddle than he, who prided himself on equitation theory. He was so rigid and stiff on horseback that he quickly tired, and furthermore I rode too fast for him. Therefore, he gave me a squire, or rather a page—little André, who was as steady as a monkey planted on a pony, and begging me not to let a day go by without riding, he gave us free access to the country fields.

Always coming back to Colette, whose skill and disposition were beyond compare, I became accustomed every morning to riding eight or ten leagues in four hours, stopping at a farm sometimes for a bowl of milk on my way to adventure, exploring the countryside at random, going everywhere—even socalled impossible places—and indulging in endless daydreams, which André, coached very well by Deschartres, would not have considered interrupting with the slightest remark. He would only revert to his natural self when I stopped to eat at a peasant's house, because then, as ever, I would ask that he sit with me at the table, and there, summing up his impressions of the ride, he would cheer me up with his candid comments and Berrichon speech. Barely back in the saddle, he would become silent again, a burden that I would never have thought of imposing on him but which I found extremely pleasant, because that dreamy galloping, or that total forgetfulness the spectacle of nature affords us while the horse, left to walk at a slow pace, stops to graze at the bushes without our noticing; the slow or fast succession of landscapes, some gloomy, some delightful; the absence of purpose; the yielding to time taking flight; the picturesque gatherings of flocks or migratory birds; the soft noise of the water splashing under the horses' hooves—all that is rest or movement, spectacle for the eye or sleep for the soul on a solitary ride, would surround me and suspend my train of thought and the memory of my sorrows.

Thus I turned into a thorough poet solely by inclination and character, without realizing or knowing it. Where I was looking for mere physical relaxation, I found an inexhaustible source of spiritual pleasure which I would indeed have been at a loss to define but which cheered me up and revived me more and more every day.

If anxiety had not led me back to the side of my poor invalid, I think I would have become oblivious, riding for days at a time, but since I went out very early—almost always at daybreak, as soon as the sun shone overhead I would gallop back home. Then I often noticed that poor André was dead-tired; I was always surprised by that, since I have never run out of strength on horseback, where I think that women, because of their seat and the flexibility of their limbs, can, in effect, last much longer than men.

Nevertheless, I would sometimes surrender Colette to my young page, so that he could rest in the smoothness of her gait, and I would ride either the old Normandy mare that had saved my father's life in battle more than once because of her intelligence and surefootedness, or the terrible Général Pépé, whose back muscles rippled powerfully. But by time we were on the way back I was no longer weary, and I returned much more awake and active than when I had left.

Thanks to this healthful activity, I suddenly felt my resolve to educate myself cease to be a painful duty and become an all-powerful attraction for its own sake. At first, downcast by worry and grief, I had tried to wile away the long hours I spent at my patient's side reading novels by Florian, Mme. de Genlis, and Van der Velde.[13] They seemed to me charming, but interrupted as this reading was by the cares and anxieties of my duties as sick-nurse, it left hardly any impression; then, to the extent that the fear of death had temporarily vanished and been replaced by a sad, tender, almost maternal habit of concern, I returned to more serious reading, which soon became a passionate attachment.

I had had, at first, to fight sleep, and I would constantly dip into my grandmother's snuff-box to keep from being overcome by the gloomy and tepid atmosphere in the room. I also drank a lot of black coffee without sugar, and sometimes even brandy, to keep from falling asleep when she wanted to chat all night; for from time to time, she would take the night for day, and would be angry at the darkness and silence in which, she said, we wanted to keep her. Julie and Deschartres sometimes tried opening the windows, to show her that it really was nighttime. Then she was deeply aggrieved, saying that she was quite certain it was broad daylight and that she was going blind, since she could not see the sun.

We thought it better to concede on every issue and, above all, drive away her distress. So we would light many candles behind her bed to make her believe she was seeing daylight. We would stay awake around her, ready to answer when she emerged at any moment from her slumber to talk to us.

The beginnings of this bizarre existence were very painful for me. I had a desperate need for the little sleep I had previously been granted. I was still growing. Hindered by this kind of life, my development was turning into an indescribable, nervous anguish. Stimulants, which I despised as being incompatible with my calm nature, caused me stomach problems and did not serve to keep me awake.

But since the resumption of horseback riding prescribed by Deschartres had renewed my health and strength in just a few days, I was able to keep watch and work without stimulants, as without fatigue, and only then, feeling my physical constitution change, did I find an unknown pleasure and ease in study.

It was my confessor, the parish priest of La Châtre, who had lent me a copy of *Le Génie du christianisme*.[14] For the six·weeks after the onset of my grandmother's illness, I could not bring myself to re-open the book, having closed it on a page which marked such deep grief in my life. The priest had asked me to return it. I begged him to wait a little longer, and I resolved to go back to the beginning in order to read it completely and thoughtfully, as he had suggested.

Ironically the one reading intended by my confessor to rivet my soul to Catholicism, produced just the opposite effect—detaching me from it forever. I devoured the book, loved it passionately, form and substance, faults and virtues. I closed it convinced that my soul had grown one hundred cubits, that the reading had been for me a reverberation of Saint Augustine's *Tolle, lege*, that from then on I had acquired a foolproof power of persuasion, and that not only could I read anything, but also that I could study all the philosophers —secular ones and heretics—with the pleasant certainty of finding in their mistakes the confirmation and pledge of my faith.

Once renewed in my religious fervor, which isolation and the sadness of my situation had cooled considerably, I felt my devotion mirrored in the magical glow of romantic poetry. Faith no longer made its presence felt as blind passion, but as blazing light. For a long time Jean Gerson[15] had held me under the sweet dominion of humility of spirit, annihilation of thought, absorption in God, and scorn for human knowledge, with a healthy admixture of fear of my own weakness. *L'Imitation de Jésus-Christ* would be my guide no longer. Gerson, whom I admired as a saint of bygone days, was losing his influence; Chateaubriand, the man of feeling and enthusiasm, was becoming my priest and initiator. I did not yet see the skeptical poet, the man of worldly glory, beneath Chateaubriand's modern vision of a degenerating Catholicism.

This was not my fault at all, and I had no intention of confessing it. The confessor himself had put the poison in my hands. I had served myself trustingly from it. The abyss of doubt was open, and I had to descend into it, not as Dante, toward the end of his years, but in the flower of my youth and in all the brightness of my first awakening.

Alas! only you are logical, only you are truly Catholic, converted sinner, Jan Huss's murderer, guilty and repentant Gerson! It is you who said:

"My child, do not allow yourself to be touched by the beauty and refinement of men's speeches. Never read my words to become more clever or wise. You will gain more by destroying the evil in yourself than by digging into difficult questions. . . . After much reading and learning, you must always come back to a single principle: It is I who give men knowledge, and I grant to the young ones a clearer understanding than men can ever convey. . . . A time will come when Jesus Christ, Master of masters, Lord of angels, will appear in order to listen to the lessons of all men; that is to say, to examine the conscience of each. Then, lamp in hand, he will visit the recesses of Jerusalem, and that which was hidden in the darkness will be brought to the light of day, and the reasoning of men will have no place at all. . . . I am the one who elevates a humble spirit to the point where it penetrates more secrets of eternal life in a moment than another can learn in ten years of schooling. I teach without the noise of words, the clash of opinions, displays of honor, and the flurry of proofs. . . . My child, don't be so curious, and don't burden yourself with useless cares. . . . And as for all of you, how does this or that concern you? Follow me! . . . What does it really matter if this one is in such and such a mood, or that one speaks in such and such a tone? . . . You have no obligation whatsoever to answer for others. You will account for yourself. Why then are you embarrassed? . . . I know all men; I see everything that happens under the sun, and I know the particular state of everyone, what he thinks, what he desires, what his intentions are. . . . Do not trouble yourself with things that distract and greatly tarnish the heart. . . . Learn to obey, dust that you are! learn, earth and clay, to lower yourself beneath everyone's feet. . . . Remain firm and hope in me, for words are only words. They strike the air, but do not move the stone. . . . Man's enemies are in his own mansion, and he must not give credence to those who proclaim, Christ is here! or He is there! . . . Do not rejoice in anything but your own self-contempt and the fulfillment of my will alone. . . . Leave yourself behind, and you shall find me. Live without choice and without possessions, and thus you shall earn much. . . . Thus you shall renounce yourself always, at all hours, in small as well as large things. I exclude nothing. I want to find you detached from everything. . . . Leave yourself, resign yourself. Give all for all. Look for nothing, take nothing back, and you shall possess me. You shall have a free heart, and darkness will not blind you any more. . . . May the aim of your efforts, prayers, and wishes be to strip yourself of all property and, naked, follow a naked Jesus Christ, to die in yourself and to live eternally in me. . . . 'Blush, Sidon,' says the sea! . . . Blush then, idle and grumbling servants, upon seeing that the people of the world are more ardent for their loss than you are for your salvation!"

There you have not the true spirit of the Gospel, but the true law of the priest, the true prescription of the orthodox Church: Forget, bury, despise yourself; destroy your reason, confound your judgment; shun the sound of human words. Crawl, and turn into dust under the law of the divine mystery; do not love anything; do not study anything; do not know anything, do not possess anything—neither in your hands nor in your soul. Become an abstraction dissolved and prostrate before the divine abstraction; scorn humanity, destroy nature; turn yourself into a handful of ashes, and you shall be happy. To have everything, you must give up everything. That is the essence of that book, sublime and stupid in equal measure, which may create saints, but will never create a human being.

I have told without bitterness and scorn, I hope, of the delights of contemplative devotion. I have not fought the loving and grateful memory of monastic education. I have judged my heart's past with my heart. I still cherish and bless those who enraptured me with the gentle magnetism of their angelic simplicity. Consequently, regardless of your beliefs, reader, you must forgive me for judging myself and analyzing the essence of what I had been fed.

Forgiven or not, I would not be any less sincere. This book is not a systematic rebuttal. God prevents me from altering, in premeditated fashion, the charm of my own memories; this book is the story of my life, and I wish to be truthful in everything I tell about it.

Therefore—I won't hesitate to say it—Jean Gerson's Catholicism is anti-evangelical and, taken literally, is a doctrine of abominable selfishness. I realized it the day I compared it, not to *Le Génie du christianisme*, which is a work of art and not of doctrine, but to all the thoughts that work of art suggested to me. I sensed a full and open struggle in me between the intent and effect of the two readings: the one, the absolute annihilation of the intellect and heart with a view toward personal salvation; the other, the development of mind and feeling with a view toward a communal religion.

Then I reread the copy of *L'Imitation* that Marie-Alicia[(4)]had given me, which I still see before me, her name written in that dear, venerated hand. I knew by heart that masterpiece of form and eloquent concision. It had captivated and persuaded me in every respect; logic is a powerful force in children; they are not acquainted with sophism or capitulations of conscience. *L'Imitation* is pre-eminently the book of monastic life, the code of the cleric; it can be fatal to the soul of anyone who has not broken with human society and its duties, and at that time I had broken, in soul and will, with my duties to those outside the convent; I had devoted myself to eternal seclusion by drinking from that fountain of personal bliss.

On rereading it after *Le Génie du christianisme*, it seemed completely new to me, and I saw all the terrible consequences of its application to the business of life. It commanded me to forget all earthly affection, banish all pity from my breast, break all family ties, have only myself in view, and leave all others to God's judgment. I began to be afraid and seriously repent having stepped between family and cloister without taking a definite stand. Too sensitive to the problems or needs of my relatives, I had been indecisive, fearful. I had allowed my ardor to cool, my determination to waver and turn into vague desire mixed with pointless regrets. I had made numerous concessions to my grandmother, who wanted to see me educated and literate. I was the idle and grumbling servant who did not want to give up all earthy attachments or personal considerations. I had, therefore, repudiated the doctrine from the day when, yielding to my mentor's orders, I had become cheerful, affectionate, obliging with my classmates, obedient and devoted toward my relatives. Everything in me was sinful, even my admiration for Sister Hélène, my friendship for Marie-Alicia, my concern for my invalid grandmother. Everything in me—conscience as well as behavior—was criminal, or else *L'Imitation* had lied.

Why then did the erudite and learned Abbé de Prémord, who wanted me to be loving and caring, and my kind Mother Alicia, who rejected the thought of my religious vocation—why then did they give and recommend that book to me? There was a great inconsistency there; for although it had not led me actually to be callous toward others, the book had done me harm. It had held me to some golden mean between heavenly inspiration and earthly cares. It had pre-

vented me from wholeheartedly accepting a taste for domestic life and inclinations toward family. It had led me to an inner revolt, of which my passive submission was the cruel symptom—too cruel, had it been understood. I had
deceived my grandmother with silence, when she thought I had been convinced. And who knows if, unknown to her, her worry, irritability, unfairness
had not encountered a secret reason in me that justified them. She had often
found my caresses cold and my promises evasive. Maybe without quite realizing it, she had felt me opposed to the security of her affection.

Frightened more and more by my thoughts, I was deeply grieved by the
weakness of my character and by the dimming of my spirit, which had not
allowed me to follow a straight path. I was all the more distressed since, by the
time I perceived all this, it was already too late to make amends—the day after
that unhappy day when my grandmother had lost the ability to understand my
reversion to her ideas about my present and my future.

Everything had been worked out for now: whether she lived physically
and spiritually disabled for one or ten years, my rightful place was conspicuous
at her side, but for the rest of my life I would have to choose between heaven
and earth. Either the manna of asceticism which had half-nourished me was a
pernicious food which I should purge myself of forever, or else the book was
right—I had to reject art, science, poetry, reasoning, friendship, and family;
spend day and night in ecstasy and prayer beside my moribund grandmama,
and from there, break with all things and fly off toward holy places, never to
redescend to human attachments.

Here is what Chateaubriand replied to my exalted logic: "Defenders of
Christianity (in the eighteenth century) lapsed into an error that had already
lost them the argument. They did not realize that it was no longer a question of
disputing such and such a dogma, since the foundations were being completely
rejected. Starting with the mission of Jesus Christ and ascending from event to
event, they undoubtedly established the truths of the faith very solidly; but that
type of reasoning, adequate in the seventeenth century, when the substance was
not being questioned, was no longer valid for our time. It was necessary to take
the opposite direction, to go from effect to cause, to prove not that Christianity
is excellent because it comes from God, but that it comes from God because it
is excellent. . . . It was necessary to prove that, of all the religions that had ever
existed, the Christian religion is the most poetic, the most human, the most
favorable to liberty, the arts, and letters. . . . They had to show that there is nothing more divine than its ethics; nothing kinder, more solemn than its dogmas,
doctrines, and services. They had to say that it promotes talent, purifies taste,
develops virtuous passions, gives vigor to the mind. . . . that there is absolutely
no shame in believing in Newton and Bossuet, Pascal and Racine: finally, it
was necessary to call forth all the magic of the imagination and all the desires
of the heart to succor this same religion they had been armed against. . . . But
wasn't there some danger in examining religion in a completely human light?
And why? Does our religion fear enlightenment? The fact that it can withstand
the severest and minutest test of reason is high proof of its celestial origin. Are
we to be eternally reproached for hiding our dogmas in a holy night, for fear

that their falsehood will be discovered? Will Christianity be less true because it seems more beautiful? Let us banish a pusillanimous fear. Let us not allow our religion to perish from too much religion. We are no longer in an age when it was adequate to say, 'Believe, do not question.' We shall be questioned in spite of ourselves, and our timid silence will decrease the number of faithful while augmenting the growing ranks of disbelievers."

You can see that the issue had been very neatly posed before me—on one hand, to stifle in myself everything but the immediate and exclusive contemplation of God; on the other, to look around me and absorb all that can give to the soul the elements of force and life it needs to render glory to God. The alpha and omega of the doctrine: let us be clay and dust, or let us be flame and light; question nothing if we wish to believe, or to believe everything we must question everything. Which one should I listen to?

Was one of these books completely heretical? Which one? Both had been given to me by my spiritual mentors. Were there then two contradictory truths in the bosom of the Church? Chateaubriand proclaimed truth to be relative. Gerson declared it absolute.

I was immersed in a sea of perplexity. Galloping on Colette, I was all for Chateaubriand. By the light of my lamp, I was all for Gerson. And at night I would blame myself for my morning thoughts.

An external consideration gave victory to the neo-Christian. My grandmother had again been, for several days, in danger of dying. I had tormented myself with the thought that she would never reconcile herself with religion and would die without the sacraments, but even though she was now and then able to understand me, I had not dared say a word to her which might make her aware of her condition and yield to my wishes. Though my faith imperiously demanded this alternative, my heart forbade it still more vigorously.

I was in frightful anguish over this, and all my scruples of conscience from convent days came back to me. After nights of terror and days of distress, I wrote to Abbé de Prémord to ask him to take charge of my conduct and allow me to confess to him all the debilities in my filial love. Far from condemning them, the excellent man sanctioned them. "You have done well a thousand times, my child, to keep silent," he wrote me in a long letter full of indulgence and kindness. "To tell your grandmother that she was in danger would have killed her. To take the initiative in the delicate matter of her conversion would have been contrary to the respect that you owe her. Such an impropriety would have been sharply felt by her, and would have perhaps driven her away from the sacraments forever. You were well advised to remain silent and to pray to God to help her directly. Don't ever be afraid when you are advised by your heart—the heart cannot deceive. Pray always, hope, and whatever your poor grandmother's end may be, count on infinite wisdom and grace. Your duty toward her is to go on lavishing the most loving attention on her. When she sees your love, your modesty, the humility and, if I may say so, the discretion of your faith, she will want, perhaps, to reward you by granting your secret wish, and committing an act of faith herself. Believe in what I have always told you: see to it that you love divine grace. It is the best encouragement that we can offer."

The kind and virtuous old man thus also came to terms with human affection. He was acknowledging hope of my grandmother's salvation even if she were to die without official reconciliation with the Church or even without having considered it. The man was a saint, a true Christian, should I say despite, or because, he was a Jesuit?

Let us be fair. From a political point of view, as republicans, we hate or dread that sect obsessed by power and anxious for control. I say "sect" in speaking of Loyola's disciples, for it is a sect, I affirm it. It is an important modification of Roman orthodoxy. It is a very palatable heresy. It has simply never declared itself as such. It has undermined and conquered the papacy without an open declaration of war, but it has mocked papal infallibility while proclaiming it to be sovereign, and has been much more clever in that than all the other heretical factions, consequently more powerful and durable.

Yes, indeed, Abbé de Prémord was more Christian than the intolerant Church, and he was also heretical because he was a Jesuit. Loyola's doctrine is a Pandora's box. It contains all evil and all good. It is a seat of progress and a pit of destruction, a code of life and of death. As official doctrine, it kills; as *sub rosa* doctrine, it revives what it has killed.

I called it "doctrine," but to avoid argument I would call it "*esprit de corps*," or "institutional tendency," if you prefer. Its dominant force consists especially of opening to each of us our own path. That is why its truth is supremely relative, and once that truth is admitted in the recesses of conscience, the Catholic church is turned upside down.

Disputed, discredited, and singled out for horror by men of progress, that doctrine is still the last keystone of Christian faith in the Church. Beyond it is but the blind absolutism of the papacy. It is the only practicable religion for those who do not want to break with Jesus Christ as God. The Roman church is a big cloister where the duties of man in society are irreconcilable with the law of salvation. If you suppress love and marriage, inheritance and family, the concept of Catholic renunciation is perfect. But its code is the work of the genius of destruction: once it recognizes a society other than the monastic community, it becomes a labyrinth of contradictions and inconsistencies. It is forced to lie to itself and permit to each what it forbids to all.

Therefore, for anyone who thinks, his faith is shaken. But here comes the Jesuit who says to the troubled and confused soul, "Go as you can and according to your strength. The word of Jesus is forever accessible to the interpretation of the enlightened conscience. He has sent us to bind or release the tie between the Church and you. Believe in us, give yourself to us, we are a new church within the Church, a tolerated and tolerant church, a safeguard between concept and deed. We have discovered the only way to set the diffuseness and uncertainty of human beliefs on some sort of base. Having completely accepted the practical impossibility of an absolute truth, we have discovered the truth that suits every circumstance and every believer. This truth, this base, is intention. Intention is everything, deed is nothing. What is evil may be good, and vice versa, according to the aim one has in mind."

Jesus had therefore spoken to his disciples in the sincerity of his divine heart when he said to them, "The spirit revives, the letter kills. Don't do as those hypocrites and fools who would have religion consist only of the observance of the fast and outward repentance. Wash your hands, and repent in your hearts."

But Jesus had had at his command only a greatly expanded range of words we all use. The day the papacy and the councils declared themselves infallible in the interpretation of those words, they killed Him; they put themselves in Christ's place. They conferred divinity on themselves. Likewise, led perforce to condemn to the stake—in this world and the next—all who would deviate from their interpretation and its resulting precepts, they broke with true Christianity, shattered God's pact of infinite grace, of fraternal affection among all mankind, and replaced the evangelical feeling, so human and universal, with the fierce and despotic outlook of the Middle Ages.

In principle, the Jesuits' doctrine was then, as its name suggests, a return to the true spirit of Jesus, hence a heresy in disguise, since the Church had so baptized all protests—secret or overt—against its sovereign decisions. This insinuating and penetrating doctrine had side-stepped the issue of reconciling the decisions of orthodoxy with the spirit of the Gospel. It had rejuvenated the forces of proselytism by touching the heart and reassuring the spirit, and while the Church said to all, "Without me there is no salvation," the Jesuit would say to each, "He who does his best according to his conscience shall be saved."

Shall I now say why Pascal[16] was right in discrediting Escobar and his cohorts? It would be entirely useless; besides, everyone knows and feels it—how a doctrine that could have been so generous and beneficent became, in the hands of certain men, one of atheism and betrayal; that is the true story and comes under the sad fatality of human events. The fathers of the Spanish Jesuit Church had the advantage at least over some Roman popes in not having been declared infallible by the monarchical powers nor recognized as such by a considerable portion of the human race. One must never judge the ideas of institutions by historical results. By that account, it would have been necessary to outlaw the Gospel itself, since so many monsters have triumphed in its name, so many victims have been sacrificed, so many generations have passed bent under the yoke of slavery. The same juice, extracted in varying doses from the meat of a plant, gives life or death. Thus with the doctrine of the Jesuits; thus with the doctrine of Jesus Himself.

The "institute" of the Jesuits—for that was the modest title of that powerful sect—comprised then in principle, explicitly or implicitly, a doctrine of progress and freedom. It would be easy to demonstrate it by proofs, but this would take me far afield and serves no purpose. I am recapitulating personal opinions and feelings, borne in on me through an ensemble of lessons, counsels, and events that I should not entirely reveal (for if the confessor owes discretion to the penitent, the penitent owes the confessor the silence of loyalty, even from beyond the grave, regarding certain decisions which could be misinterpreted); but this ensemble of personal experiences persuades me to judge the pure idea of this sect with neither too much subjective feeling nor too much moral severity. If one judges it in the present, I know just like everybody else that it contains political dangers and possible obstacles to progress, but if one judges it as having substantially served the total idea of progress, one cannot deny that it was responsible for great strides in the human spirit and that its apostles of philosophical liberty suffered greatly in the last century for the cause of intellectual and moral freedom. But so goes the world condemned as it is to perpetual misunderstanding. Too many needs for liberation crowd and obstruct the way to the future at given moments in the history of mankind, and he who sees his goal without seeing that of the worker alongside him often thinks he sees obstacles where he might have seen help.

The Jesuits prided themselves on envisioning three aspects of perfection: religious, political, social. They were mistaken; their very institute, through its essentially theocratic laws and esoteric bias, could only liberate the intellect by binding body, conduct, and actions (*perinde ac cadaver*). But has any doctrine until now unravelled the great mystery of that triple quest?

I apologize for this rather long digression. To acknowledge a predilection for the Jesuits is, in the times in which we live, a delicate matter. You strongly risk being suspected of spiritual duplicity when you show such courage. I confess that I am not at all embarrassed by falling suspect.

Caught between *L'Imitation de Jésus-Christ* and *Le Génie du christianisme*, I again found myself in the middle of great perplexities concerning my spiritual conduct in relation to my enlightened grandmother. I requested the Jesuit's intervention to solve the new problem. I felt drawn toward study by an unfamiliar thirst, toward poetry by a passionate instinct, toward examination by a proud faith.

"I fear that pride may seize me," I wrote to Abbé de Prémord. "There is still time for me to retrace my steps, to forget all these mental displays which my grandmother relished, but which she will no longer enjoy or dream of asking from me. My mother will be rather indifferent to the whole thing. Therefore, no immediate duty pushes me toward the abyss, if it is indeed an abyss, as the ghost of Thomas à Kempis[5] cries in my ear. My soul is tired and somewhat dulled. I ask you for the truth. If it is mere gratification that I am to renounce, nothing would be easier than to give up my studies; but what if it is a duty toward God or toward my brethren . . . ? I fear, now as always, that I am dwelling on some stupidity."

Abbé de Prémord had the effervescence of strength and serenity. I have never known a soul so pure and self-assured. He answered me, that time, with the obliging irony which he was wont to use against the terrors of my conscience.

"My dear casuist," he wrote to me. "If you fear pride, then don't you already have some self-esteem? Anyway, it is an improvement over your usual fears. But really, you are in too much of a hurry. In your place, I would wait until I knew enough to give rise to temptation before I examined my conscience on the subject of pride, for perhaps up to now you really have no cause to fear that temptation too much. But, look, I have quite a good notion of your common sense, and I am convinced that as soon as you have learned something, you will understand all the more what you are lacking in order to know a great deal. So, leave fear of pride to the imbeciles. What is vanity for faithful hearts? They know not what it is. Study, learn, read all that your grandmother would have allowed you to read. You wrote to me that she had indicated to you everything in the library that a chaste young lady should leave alone and never open. On saying this, she entrusted you with the keys. I do likewise. I have complete confidence in you, mine still better founded, who know the essence of your heart and thoughts. Do not render all those free-thinkers and children-eating intellectuals so great and terrible. One can easily upset the weakminded by slandering the clergy, but can one slander Jesus and His doctrine? Overlook all invectives against us. They prove no more against Him than our faults would, if the criticism were deserved. Read the poets. They are all religious. Do not fear the philosophers, they are all powerless against faith. And if any doubt, any fear arises in your mind, close those poor books, reread one or two verses from the Gospel, and you will feel like a teacher to all those teachers."

Thus spoke that exalted, simple old man, with charming wit, to a poor seventeen-year-old girl who confessed the weakness of her character and ignorance of mind. Was this really prudent for a man who considered himself completely orthodox? Most certainly not; it was good, kind, and generous. He was nudging me forward, as one does a fearful child, to whom one says, "What frightens you is nothing. Look and touch. It is a shadow, an empty illusion, a ridiculous scarecrow." And indeed the best way to strengthen the heart and reassure the mind is to teach contempt for danger by setting an example.

But can a method so useful in reality be applicable to abstract things? Can the faith of a neophyte be thus subjected to great trials at the outset?

My old friend practiced the method of his institution with me; he practiced it with candor, for there is nothing more candid than a Jesuit who is innately candid. It can be developed for good, or exploited for evil, according to whether the Jesuit's thinking is politically motivated toward good or evil.

He viewed me as capable of intellectual expansion, but hindered by a very strict conscience which could return me to the narrow path of the old Catholicism. Now then, in the hands of a Jesuit, any thinking being is an instrument that must be made to vibrate in the concert he conducts. The group spirit suggests to its better members a great fund for proselytism, but in the worse ones becomes ardent pride, collective nonetheless. A Jesuit who, meeting a soul endowed with some vitality, would let it waste away or destroy itself in barren quietude, would have failed in his duty and his principle. Thus, Chateaubriand—perhaps by intention, perhaps unwittingly—suited the purpose of the Jesuits by calling on the lures of the mind and appeals of the heart to rescue Christianity. Like them, or by their example, he was heretical, he was innovative, he was worldly, he was confident and bold.

After having read *Le Génie* as a captive, I then savored it with delight, finally reassured by my good priest and encouraging my restless soul, "Onward, onward!" Then, without further ado, I sat down with Mably, Locke, Condillac, Montesquieu, Bacon, Bossuet, Aristotle, Leibnitz, Pascal, Montaigne, in all of which my grandmother herself had marked the chapter or pages to omit. Then came the poets or the moralists—La Bruyère, Pope, Milton, Dante, Virgil, Shakespeare, and many others—all without order and method, as they fell to my hand, and read with intuitive ease that I have never regained since and that was even beyond my normally slow ability to comprehend. My brain was immature and my memory as unreliable as ever, but my senses were susceptible and my will determined. For me it was a matter of life and death—to find out if, after having understood everything that I could possibly conceive of understanding, I would choose life in the world or the voluntary "death" of the convent.

The solution surely is, I thought, to test my vocation all dressed up at balls, as Élisa is forced to do, I, who essentially hate those things. But the more I will have seen of those silly amusements and stood the strain of society, the less sure I will be that my zeal and not my laziness is driving me to the peace of the convent. My test, therefore, will not be there. (In this respect, I was indeed correct, and was not mistaken about myself.) It lies in the examination of religious and moral truth. If I withstand all the objections of the age, in the guise of philosophical reasoning or poetic imagination, I shall know that I am worthy of devoting myself to God alone.

Were I to render an account of each reading's impression on me and talk about its effects, that would entail a book of criticism that could well turn into volumes, but who would read it nowadays? And wouldn't I be dead before I had finished?

Besides, my recollection of all of it is no longer clear enough in my mind, and I would run the risk of putting my present impressions into my account of the past. I shall spare those for whom I write the personal details of this unusual education and summarize its results chronologically.

In the early stages, I read with the audacity of conviction that my good Abbé had advised. Armed to the teeth, I defended myself as valiantly as my ignorance allowed. And then, having no plan, intermingling in my readings believers and non-believers, I would find in the former the means of answering the latter. Metaphysics did not trouble me at all; I understood very little, in the sense that it never proved anything to me. Once I had trained my youthfully flexible understanding to follow its abstractions, I found only emptiness or uncertainty in its conclusions. My mind was and always has been too ordinary and too little inclined to scientific probing to need to ask God to initiate my soul into the big mysteries. I was a creature of feeling, and only feeling, as far as I was concerned, would form the questions as I should ask them, which, once the experiment was completed, soon became the only questions within my reach.

I therefore bowed respectfully to the metaphysicians, and all I can say to my credit in relation to them is that I refrained from regarding as vain or ridiculous a science which overtaxed my faculties. I do not blame myself for having then said, "What good is metaphysics?" Later on I was a bit more arrogant when I reconsidered it further. Much later on, I became reconciled to it by understanding it a little better still. And, in short, I now say that metaphysics is the search for truth suited to great minds and that, not being of that race, I have no great need for it. What I need I find in religion and philosophy, which are its daughters—its incarnations, if you will.

Then, as now, by getting a better grip on philosophy, especially of the easy-going eighteenth-century philosophy that was still that of my time, I did not feel shaken by anything or anyone. But Rousseau came along. Rousseau, man of passion and feeling par excellence, and I was finally shaken.

Was I still Catholic the moment when, having saved the best (Jean-Jacques) for last, as if by instinct, I was finally to fall under the spell of his touching reason and fervent logic? I do not think so. While still practicing the religion, still refusing to break from its formulas interpreted in my fashion, I had left, without my least suspecting it, the confines of its orthodoxy. Unknown to myself, I had broken irrevocably with all its social and political conclusions. The spirit of the Church was no longer in me; perhaps it never had been.

There was a great fermentation of ideas at the time. Italy and Greece were fighting for national independence. The Church and the French monarchy declared themselves against those noble attempts. My grandmother's royalist newspapers thundered against insurrection, and the religious element, which should have embraced the cause of the Eastern Christians, strove to prove the rights of the Turkish Empire. That monstrous inconsistency, that sacrifice of religion to political interests had a strangely rousing effect on me. Liberality of mind and religious feeling were becoming synonymous for me. I shall never forget—can I ever forget?—how Christian enthusiasm pushed me boldly, for the first time, into the camp of progress, which I would never leave.

Already, and from childhood, the religious ideal and the practical one had articulated from deep inside me and then out through my lips into the startled ears of the good Deschartres the sacred word "equality." Of liberty I cared little then, not knowing what it was and not being ready even later to grant it to myself. At least what was called "civil liberty" did not mean much to me. Without absolute equality and Christian brotherhood, it made no sense. It seemed to me, and I confess still does, that this word "liberty," placed ahead of the two others in the republican motto, should have been at the end, and could even have been omitted as a pleonasm.

But national independence, without which there was no hope for fraternity or equality, I understood very well, and disputing it, to my mind, was equivalent to the theory of piracy, or to the impious and savage proclamation that might makes right.

You did not have to be a wonderfully bright child or a particularly intelligent young lady to realize that. So I was confused and disgusted to hear my friend Deschartres, who was by no means devout or religious, combat at one and the same time the question of Greek independence, as the Church did, and the question of progress put forth by the philosophers. The pedagogue had but a single idea, a single law, need, instinct: absolute authority and blind submission. To demand obedience, at any price, from those who should obey, was his dream. But why should some command others? That is what he, who had knowledge and practical skill, would never answer, except with hollow maxims and pitifully trite remarks.

We would have ludicrous debates, since I could not possibly take seriously a mind so baroque and obstinate in certain matters. My convictions were too powerful to be shaken or consequently for me even to feel vexed for one moment by his contradictions. I remember how, one day, expounding hotly on the divine right of the sultan (I do believe, God forgive me, that he would not have denied the Holy Grail to the Grand Turk himself, so wrapped up was he in the victory of the master over his rebellious pupils), his foot got caught in his slipper and he fell down full length on the lawn. That did not keep him from finishing his sentence, after which he very gravely added, while dusting off his knees, "I think I really fell." To which I answered, laughing at his concerned expression, "So shall the Ottoman Empire." He, too, began to laugh, but not without a remnant of anger, while calling me Jacobin, Regicide, Hellenizer, Bonapartist—all rendered synonomous insults through his horror of being contradicted.

However, he was as kind as a father to me and extremely proud of my studies, which he imagined he still directed because he was arguing with the outcome.

Whenever I was puzzled by the mathematical proofs mixed in with the theology or philosophy of Leibnitz or Descartes, a total mystery to me, I would go find and compel him to make me understand by analogies those intangible matters. In that he showed great skill and clarity, truly professorial intellect. Afterward, wanting to decide for or against a book, he would return to the beaten track and relapse into his old refrains.

Therefore, in politics, I was completely outside the bosom of the Church and did not intend to worry about it at all, for our nuns had no opinion on French affairs and had never told me that religion demanded taking sides for or against anything whatsoever. Nothing along those lines that I had seen, read, or understood in the religious teachings obligated me to ask the spiritual to defend the temporal. Mme. de Pontcarré, an impassioned legitimist, bitter enemy of the doctrinaires of the time, whom she also called Jacobins, had surprised me by her need to equate religion with absolute monarchy. Chateaubriand, in his pamphlets which I eagerly read, also identified the throne with the altar, but that had not greatly impressed me. Chateaubriand affected me as a man of letters and did not instruct me as a Christian. His oeuvre, in which I had intentionally skipped *René* as a masterpiece to be read later, no longer pleased me except as an initiation into the poetry of the works of God and great men.

Mably[17] had strongly displeased me. For me those open and liberal outbursts, increasingly hindered by despondency in the face of practical application, were a perpetual disappointment. "What's the use of those noble principles," I asked myself, "if they must be suppressed by a sense of moderation? What is true, what is right ought to be observed and applied without limitations."

I was ardently intolerant, as befitted my age. I would throw the book across the room, or into Deschartres's face, telling him that it was biased on his side, and he would send it back the same way, saying that he could not accede to such a muddle-head, such a dangerous revolutionary.

Leibnitz[18] seemed to me the greatest of all, but how hard he was to swallow when he addressed me from such heights! I would say to myself, as Fontenelle[19] did, but change the starting point of his skeptical sentence: If I had been able to understand it well, ". . . I would have foreseen the logical conclusion, or that there was no conclusion at all."

"And what do I care, after all," I, too, would say, "about monads, unities, pre-established harmony, and *sacro-sancta Trinitas per nova inventa logica defense*; or minds that are able to say ME, the square of the velocities, dynamics, the relation between the sine of incidence and of refraction, and so many other subtleties which you have to be both a great theologian and savant even to misunderstand!"[6]

I would burst out laughing in private at my wishful thinking that I could profit from what I did not understand. But that captivating preface to the *Théodicée*, which summed up so well Chateaubriand's ideas and the sentiments of Abbé de Prémord on the utility, and even necessity, of knowledge, would keep coming back to me.

"True piety, and even true godliness," Leibnitz said, "consists of God's love, but an illuminated love, whose fervor is accompanied by enlightenment. Such love produces that delight in good deeds which—by referring everything back to God, as if to a central core—transforms the human into the divine. Perfections of understanding must fulfill those of will. The practice of virtue, as well as that of vice, can be the result simply of habit; you can acquire a taste for it, but you would not know how to love God without realizing his perfections. Would you believe that there are Christians who have fancied themselves devout without loving their neighbors or pious without understanding God? Several centuries have passed without the public having really perceived that error, and there are still considerable traces of the reign of darkness. . . . The old fallacies of those who reproached the Deity or who have made Him into an evil principle have been revived nowadays. They have had recourse to His irresistible power when His supreme goodness would have been more appropriate, and they have resorted to despotic authority when they should have conceived a power ruled by the most perfect wisdom."

When I read that over, I said to myself, "Well, you can still take heart! How beautiful to see that lofty mind devoted to worship! Shouldn't I be conscientious enough to wish to understand what it has conceived and taken care to explain? But I lack some rudiments of science, and Deschartres is after me to abandon these great summaries in order to study the details. He wants to teach me physics, geometry, mathematics. Why not, if that is necessary to believing in God and loving others? Leibnitz really puts his finger on my problem when he says that you can be fervent out of habit. My soul's laziness could lead me to piety, but wouldn't God reject such piety?

I took one or two lessons. "Continue," Deschartres said to me, "you are grasping it!"

"Do you think so?" I replied.

"Certainly, and that is the crux."

"But will I retain it?"

"That will come."

And after we had worked several hours, "Great man," I said (I always addressed him that way), "believe it or not, it's killing me. It's too far—the goal is too far. You have lightened my load in vain. Do believe that my head is not made like yours. I cannot wait to love God, and if I have to grind away like this all my life so that I can finally tell myself, in my old age, why and how I should love Him, I shall waste away while waiting, and I shall have perhaps devoured my heart at the expense of my brains."

"It is very good to love God!" said the naïve pedagogue. "Love Him as much as you want, but He doesn't belong in the discussion."

"Ah, that is because you don't understand why I want to learn."

"Nonsense! You learn—for the sake of learning!" he answered, shrugging his shoulders.

"That is exactly what I do not want to do. Well, good night, I'm going to listen to the nightingales."

And I went off, not weary of brain—Deschartres was too good at demonstrating his proofs not to stimulate the intellect—but heavy-hearted, into the cool night air and the delights of reverie, to look for the life that would be right for me and that I resisted in vain. My eager heart rebelled against the unmoved state in which the dry work of attention and memorization left it. It wished to learn only through emotion; I would find in the poetic expressions of books based on imagination as well as those on nature, which renewed and complemented each other, an inexhaustible conductor to that inner emotion, to that continual divine ecstasy which I had tasted at the convent and had then called grace.

Therefore, I must say that the poets and eloquent moralists had more effect on me than the metaphysicians and philosophers, in preserving my religious faith.

Shall I be ungrateful toward Leibnitz, however, by saying that he did me no good because I did not understand and retain everything of his? No, I would be lying. Surely we profit from things whose appearance we forget, if their essence has become part of us even to a small degree. We remember nothing of last night's dinner, yet it nourishes our bodies. If my reason takes in little even now of systems contrary to my sentiment; if the strong objections raised against Providence, in my own eyes, by the sight of what is terrible in nature and what is evil in humanity are defeated by a moment of sweet daydreaming; if, finally, I feel that my heart is stronger than my reason in supporting my faith in God's wisdom and supreme goodness, perhaps it is solely to the innate need to love and believe that I owe this serenity and solace. I have understood enough of Leibnitz without being able to argue for his science to know that there are more good reasons still to preserve faith than to abandon it.

Thus, through that quick and confused glance that I perilously gave toward the realm of arduous wonders, I had apparently almost fulfilled my goal. That poor scrap of learning which Deschartres considered amazing on my part fulfilled perfectly the Abbé's prediction by teaching me that I still had everything to learn, and the demon of pride which the Church always presents to those who wish to learn had indeed really left me alone. Since I have not heard much more from it, I can say that I am still waiting for its visit; as for all the mistaken compliments on my knowledge and ability, I always laugh inwardly, recalling the pleasantry of my Jesuit: "Perhaps up to now you really have no cause to fear that temptation too much."

But the little that I had extracted from the my spiritual darkness had forfified my faith in religion in general and in Christianity in particular. As for Catholicism, had I even thought about it?

Not in the least. I had scarcely suspected that Leibnitz was a Protestant and Mably a philosopher. That had not been a factor in my inner debate. By elevating myself above the forms of religion, I had sought to embrace the pure idea. I went to mass, but did not as yet examine the service.

However—recalling it well, I must say it—the service was becoming heavy and pernicious for me. I felt that my piety was cooling. There were no more charming displays—flowers, paintings, cleanliness, soft songs of the chapel, profound evening silence, edifying spectacle of beautiful nuns bowed in their stalls. No more contemplation, no more compassion, no more heartfelt prayers were possible for me in public churches where the service is stripped of its poetry and mystery.

At times I would go to my parish at Saint-Chartrier, at other times to the one at La Châtre. In the village, it was the prospect of the blessed saints and ladies of traditional devotion, horrible fetishes one would have thought destined to frighten some savage horde; the absurd bellowing of inexperienced cantors, who in all sincerity would make the most grotesque puns in Latin; the decent women who fell asleep over their rosaries while snoring out loud, and the old parish priest who swore right in the middle of the sermon at the impropriety of dogs allowed in church. In the town, it was the provincial toilette of the ladies, their whispering, their backbiting and gossip set out before the whole church as if it were a place meant for inspecting and slandering each other; it was also the ugliness of the statues and the atrocious yapping of the schoolboys allowed to sing the mass, who played tricks on each other the whole time. And then all that handling of consecrated bread and filthy lucre that went on during the services, the quarrels of the sacristans and the choirboys over a dripping candle or a poorly aimed censor. I hated all that disorder, the burlesque incidents, the lack of attention of each which hindered that of everyone at prayer. I did not dream of breaking with compulsory observance, but I was delighted when a rainy day would force me to read the mass in my room and pray alone, safe from that crude convergence of sham Christians.

And furthermore, those formulas for daily prayers, which had never been to my liking, were becoming more and more insipid. M. de Prémord had allowed me to replace them with the outpourings of my soul when I would feel so inclined, and gradually I forgot them so well that I would no longer pray except by inspiration and free improvisation. It was not very Catholic, but I had been allowed to "compose" prayers at the convent. I had circulated some in English and French which were found so "flowery" that they had been thoroughly relished. I had immediately scorned them myself, my conscience and heart decreeing that words are only words and that an outpouring as passionate as that of a soul to God cannot be expressed by any form of human speech. Hence, every prescribed prayer was a ritual I adopted in a penitent spirit, but ended by becoming a drudgery that deadened my fervor.

That was my predicament when I came to read Rousseau's *Émile, La*

Profession de foi du vicaire savoyard, Les Lettres de la montagne, Le Contrat social and his *Discours.*

The language of Jean-Jacques and his manner of inference took hold of me like glorious music lighted by a huge sun. I compared him to Mozart; I understood everything! What pleasure for an awkward and obstinate pupil finally to happen to open her eyes fully and see no more clouds before her! I became, politically, the ardent disciple of that master, and so I remained unreservedly for a rather long time. As for religion, he seemed to me the most Christian of all writers of his time, and making allowances for the century of philosophical crusading in which he lived, I forgave him more easily for having renounced Catholicism because the sacraments and title had been conferred on him in an irreligious manner well-designed to disgust him with it. Born Protestant, he became Protestant again *ipso facto* due to justifiable, perhaps unavoidable, circumstances; his heretical nationality did not bother me any more than Leibnitz's had. What's more, I liked the Protestants very much, because, not being forced to admit them into the discussion of Catholic dogma, and remembering that Abbé de Prémord damned no one and allowed me my heresy in the silence of my heart, I saw in them sincere people who differed from me only in forms absolutely unimportant before God.

Jean-Jacques was the halting point in my intellectual endeavors. From that intoxicating reading on, I indulged in the poets and eloquent moralists with no more worries about transcendent philosophy. I did not read Voltaire. My grandmother had made me promise not to read him until age thirty. I kept my word. Since he was for her what Jean-Jacques has so long been for me—the apogee of her admiration—she thought that my judgment should be fully mature to savor his conclusions. When I did read him, I savored it very much indeed, without being changed in any way whatsoever. There are temperaments which never take hold of certain other temperaments, however superior they may be. And that does not depend, as one might imagine, on natural aversions, no more than the captivating influence of certain geniuses depends on similarities of constitution among those who are captivated. I did not like Jean-Jacques's personal character; I forgave his injustice, his ingratitude, his sickly conceit, and a thousand other bizarre things only through the compassion his sufferings aroused in me. My grandmother had not liked Voltaire's grudges and cruel wit, but had made allowances for aberrations in his personal dignity.

Besides, I do not particularly hold with knowing the author through the work, especially authors of the past. In my youth, I pursued them still less under the sainted arches of their writing. I had great enthusiasm for Chateaubriand, the only living one of my masters at that time. Yet I had no desire at all to meet him, and only reluctantly did I eventually set eyes on him.

To keep my memories in order, I should perhaps continue the chapter of my readings, but one runs the great risk of boring by talking too much about oneself, so I prefer to mix this retrospective self-examination with some of the outside circumstances that were attached to it.   *T.A.-D.*

V

The son of Mme. d'Épinay and my grandfather. —A strange system
of proselytism. —My grandmother's commendable attitude. —She
orders me to hear her confession. —She receives the sacraments.
—My thoughts and the Archbishop's sermons. —A serious quarrel
with my confessor. —The old parish priest and his servant. —The
unreasonable behavior of a skeleton. —Claudius. —Deschartres'
goodness and simplicity. —The spirit of charity among the people of
La Châtre. —The village festival. —Discussions with my tutor,
thoughts on scandal. —The definition of public opinion.

During that summer's most beautiful days, my grandmother improved
quite noticeably and even took an interest in letter-writing again and in seeing
family and friends. The letters I wrote under her dictation were just as charming and judicious as any she had ever composed. She received friends who
could not believe she had suffered a weakening of her faculties as had distressed and was still distressing Deschartres and me so much. There were hours
when she conversed so well that she seemed to be herself again, and even more
sparkling and gracious than in the past.

But when night fell, little by little the light from this dimmed lamp grew
weaker. One could sense great confusion in her ideas or an apathy more frightening still, and the nights were not all without delirium—a restless, melancholy,
childlike delirium. I no longer thought of asking her to perform a religious act,
even though my good Alicia advised me to take advantage of a moment of sanity to bring her to my point of view without dread. Alicia's letters unnerved me
and gave me qualms of conscience, but they were never urgent enough for me to
bring myself to discuss with my grandmother her spiritual conduct.

However, the ice was broken in a totally unexpected way. The Archbiship
of Arles wrote to my grandmother about just this matter, announced his arrival,
and came to visit her.

M. Leblanc de Beaulieu, recently appointed after a long bishopric at
Soissons as Archbishop *in partibus* [titular] of Arles, which was equivalent
to a perfect sinecure of retirement, was my bastard uncle. He was born of
the very passionate and publicized love affair between my grandfather Francueil and the famous Mme. d'Épinay.[20] The whole story had been revealed
by the quite indiscreet and unseemly publication of the charming, but thinly
veiled, correspondence between the two lovers.

The illegitimate child, born at Leblanc, nursed and brought up at Beaulieu, received both names and was put in the monastery at an early age. My grandmother met him when he was still quite young, when she married M. de Francueil, and looked after him like a mother. He was nothing less that devout by that time, but he had become so as a result of a serious illness in which the terrors of hell had overwhelmed his weakened mind.

It was strange that the son of two remarkably clever human beings was rather an oaf. Such was this excellent man, who was compensated by not having a grain of malice in his oafishness. As there are very many wicked oafs, one must take goodness into account whether or not it is accompanied by cleverness.

This good Archbishop was the striking image of his mother, who, as Jean-Jacques made sure to tell us (and as she herself declared coquettishly) was absolutely ugly, but had quite a nice figure. I still have one of the portraits she gave to my grandfather. My grandmama gave another to my cousin Villeneuve, in which she was depicted in a naïad's costume—in other words, in as little as possible.

But her face had a lot of character, it was said, and she made all the conquests she could have hoped for. The Archbishop had her ugliness, unmitigated by character and no more expressive than a complacent frog. On top of that, he was ridiculously fat, more a gorger even than a glutton, for gluttony requires a certain sense of discrimination that he lacked. He was very lively, very loose in his manners, unbearably jovial no matter how sorrowful one might be in his presence; verbally intolerant, but accepting in actuality; a great spouter of puns and monkish jokes; as vain as a woman about his priestly garb, rank, and privileges; shameless in his need for comfort; noisy, irascible, scatterbrained, meek; always eating, drinking, sleeping, or laughing out of boredom; in short, surely the most sincere Christian, but the least likely to proselytize that one could ever imagine.

He was, in fact, the only priest who could have brought my grandmother to fulfill her Catholic duties, because he was incapable of sustaining any argument against her and did not even try.

"Dear Mama," he said to her, summing up his letter without preamble, from the first hour he spent at her side, "You know why I've come. I haven't taken you by surprise and shan't go roundabout to get to the point. I want to save your soul. I know very well that that makes you laugh; you don't think you'll be damned because you won't have done what I ask you. I, however, believe you will; and as you are now cured, thank God, you can well afford to do me this favor without it costing you the least little mental twinge. Thus I beg of you—you who have always treated me as your son—to be very nice and very cooperative to your overgrown child. You know that I'm too afraid to debate with you and your volumes of great books. You know too much for me, but that is not the point. The point is to show me a great sign of friendship, and here I am, quite ready to ask you for it on bended knee, except that my belly would get in the way. So, your granddaughter, here, will take my place."

I was flabbergasted at such a speech, and my grandmother began to laugh. The Archbishop pushed me toward her feet. "Go on, then," he told me. "Do you need to be begged to come to my aid?"

Then, my grandmother, seeing me on my knees, passed from laughter to sudden emotion. Her eyes filled with tears, and she hugged me, saying, "So then, do you believe I shall be damned if I refuse you?"

"No," I exclaimed impetuously, carried away by a burst of inner truth stronger than any religious prejudice. "No, no! I am on my knees to bless you, not to preach to you."

"There's a silly little girl for you!" exclaimed the Archbishop. And, taking me by the arm, he tried to put me out of the room, but my grandmother held me to her bosom. "Let her stay, my dear Jean Leblanc," she said to him. "She preaches better than you do. I thank you, my child. I am pleased with you, and to prove it to you, because I know that at the bottom of your heart you want me to say Yes, I do say Yes. Are you happy, Monseigneur?"

Monseigneur kissed her hand, weeping copiously. He was truly moved by such sweetness and affection. Then, he rubbed his hands together, smacked his paunch, and said, "Well, that's what I call uplifting! We must strike while the iron is hot. Tomorrow morning, your old parish priest will come to hear your confession and give you communion. I took the liberty of inviting him to lunch with us. We shall thus have it out of the way, and by tomorrow evening you won't have to think about it any more."

"And I shan't," said my grandmother with sarcasm. She was cheerful for the rest of the day. The Archbishop was even more so—laughing, cavorting with words, romping with the big dogs, repeating ad nauseum the proverb that a dog could indeed look at a bishop; scolding me for having helped him so poorly, nearly bungling everything and putting us in a fix by my simplemindedness; criticizing me for not having two cents' worth of nerve, and saying that, left to me, we'd be out in the cold.

I was heartbroken to see things happen this way. I felt that to force the sacraments on someone in that fashion, who did not believe in them and who saw their acceptance only as condescending toward me, was to burden ourselves with a sacrilege. I convinced myself to say as much to my grandmother, for reasoning with Monseigneur was hopeless.

But everything rapidly took on a different cast, thanks to the generous mind and tender heart of the poor invalid, who, though on her deathbed physically the next day, had spiritually revived.

She had had a very bad night during which it was impossible for me to think about anything but looking after her. The following morning her mind was clear and her will certain. "Let me do it," she said, as soon as I greeted her. "I believe, in fact, that I am going to die. And so, I can guess your scruples. I know that if I die without making my peace with those people either you will reproach yourself, or they will reproach you for it. I do not want to put your heart at odds with your conscience or with your friends. I feel sure of being neither a coward nor a liar by conforming to customs which, when it is time to leave those you love, do not set a bad example. Put your mind at ease; I know what I am doing."

For the first time since her illness, I felt she had become my grandmother again, the head of the household, capable of directing others and consequently herself. I withdrew submissively.

Deschartres found her quite feverish, and became furious with the Archbishop. He wanted to throw him out of the house, blaming him, probably with reason, for a new setback in her tottering existence.

My grandmother pacified him and even told him, "I want you to remain calm, Deschartres."

The parish priest came, still the same old man whom I have spoken about and whom she had considered too rustic to be my confessor. She wanted no other, knowing just how she would dictate to him.

I wanted to go out with everyone else to leave them alone. She ordered me to stay; then, turning toward the priest, "Sit there, my old friend," she said to him. "You see that I am too ill to get out of bed, and I want my daughter to hear my confession."

"Very well, very well, my good lady," replied the priest, thoroughly confused and trembling.

"Get on your knees for me, my dear," my grandmother continued, "and pray for me, with your hands in mine. I am going to make my confession. This is not a joke. I have been thinking about it. It is not a bad idea to sum up one's life when leaving this world, and if I had not been afraid of showing disrespect for tradition, I would have liked all my friends and servants to be present for this recapitulation of my conscience. But after all, my daughter's presence is enough for me. Tell me the words, father; I do not know them, or I have forgotten them. When I have finished, I shall pray for forgiveness of my sins."

She repeated the words and then said, "I have never done nor wished any harm to anyone. I have done all the good I could. I have neither lies, nor harshness, nor impiety of any sort to confess. I have always believed in God, but—hear this, my daughter—I did not love Him enough. I lacked the courage; that was my mistake. And since the day I lost my son, I have not been able to take it on myself to bless or invoke Him for the slightest thing. To have struck me a blow beyond my strength seemed too cruel. Now that He is calling me, I thank Him and implore Him to forgive my weakness. He gave me my child, and He took him from me; may He reunite us, and I shall love Him and pray to Him with all my soul."

She spoke in such a soft voice and such a loving and resigned tone, that I wept copiously, and all the fervor of happier days came back to my prayers with her.

The old priest, deeply touched, got up and said to her with great unction and in his country parlance, which was accreting with age, "My dear sister, we'll all be forgiven, because the good Lord loves us and knows real well that when we all repent, it's for Him we love. I mourned him a lot too, you know, your dear child, and I answer you true that he's at God's right side, and that you'll be there along with him. Say your act of contrition with me, and I'll be giving you absolution."

When he had pronounced absolution, she ordered him to have everyone come in, and in the interval she said to me, "I do not believe that kind man has the power to forgive me for anything whatsoever, but I do admit God has that power, and I hope He has heard the good intentions of all three of us."

The Archbishop, Deschartres, all the house servants and the farm workers attended the viaticum. She conducted the service herself, had me stand at her side, and arranged the others as she wished, according to the friendship she felt toward them. She interrupted the priest several times to say, for she understood Latin very well, "I believe in that," or, "That is meaningless." She was attentive to everything and, maintaining her admirable lucidity of mind and uprightness of character, did not want to buy her official reconciliation at the price of the least hypocrisy. This aspect was not grasped by the majority of those present. The Archbishop pretended not to pay any notice, and the priest paid none at all. He was there with his heart and had had the foresight to leave his priestly judgment outside. Deschartres was very disturbed, afraid the patient might suffer a relapse under this great emotional effort. I alone was just as observant of everything as my grandmother, and not missing one of her words, not one of her facial expressions, I admiringly watched her resolve her submission to the religion of her time and country without for an instant giving up her own private convictions and without compromising in any way her personal dignity.

Before receiving the host, she again began to speak, saying very loudly, "I want to die here in peace with everyone. If I have harmed anyone, let him speak, so that I may make amends. If I have caused anyone pain, may he forgive me, for I am sorry."

She was answered by affectionate sobs of benediction on all sides. She was given communion; then she asked for rest and remained alone with me.

She was exhausted and slept until the evening. Several days of feverish prostration followed this excitement. Then signs of health returned, and we had another few weeks of security.

This familial event left a strong impression on me. Even though my grandmother's faculties had fallen back into a semi-torpor, to my way of thinking she had clearly regained her role vis-à-vis me through that day of courage and total reason, and I no longer accorded myself the right to judge her conscience and her behavior. I was struck with great respect and at the same time loving gratitude for her effort to accommodate me; it was impossible for me not to accept every aspect of her way of repenting and reconciling herself with heaven as being worthy, deserving, and pleasing to God. I went over that whole phase of her life of which I had been witness and a part; I found, with respect to my mother, my sister, and myself, some unintentional injustice, always rectified by great efforts on her part and by real sacrifices. For the rest, I found wise forbearance, unselfish kindness, perfect righteousness, lack of prejudice, disdain for lying, abhorrence of evil, and charity and thoughtfulness toward all—in truly inexhaustible measure; in sum, the best qualities—the most completely Christian virtues.

And what crowned this noble life was precisely that lack of courage she had chosen to accuse herself of during her confession. It was that immense inconsolable pain which she had not been able to offer up to God in the form of submission but which had not prevented her from being large and generous with her peers. Oh, how those outbursts of bitterness, those words of injustice, those tears of jealousy that had caused me such suffering in my younger years seemed venial to me now! How petty and selfish I felt for not having forgiven her at the time! Greedy for happiness, indignant at suffering, cowardly in my silent childish resentment, I had not understood what this despairing mother was suffering, and I had considered myself the cause when I should have guessed at the deep source of her wound and consoled her by giving of myself without reserve.

My heart gained greatly from this repenting. I drowned the pride of my resistance in abundant tears, and all my religious intolerance was dissipated forever. My heart that had only as yet known passion in filial and divine love opened into unknown tenderness, and making just as much of an about-face as at the time of my conversion at the convent, I felt all the powers of emotion and reason ordering me to be humble, no longer merely for the sake of Christian virtue, but as a consequence brought on by natural equity.

All this made me feel even more strongly that absolute truth no more resided in the Church than in any other religious medium; that there might exist more relative truth in it was all I was prepared to concede, which was why I did not yet consider breaking with it.

The sacraments my grandmother had taken had been but a compromise on the Archbishop's part, since, without them he would have had to damn her—albeit with tears—without recourse. Note must be taken that this good prelate was not a hypocrite. His desire was not to have the Church triumph in the eyes of the gaping provincials. Politics was foreign to him, and his faith in the infallibility of popes and in conciliar letters was "strong as iron," as he put it. He truly loved my grandmother: having known no other mother, he considered her his own. He left, saying, "Let her die now, it's all the same to me. I'm not young, and I shall join her soon. Life's not such a great thing! But I would never have gotten over losing her if she had persisted in her last wrongs."

I took the liberty of disagreeing with him. "I swear to you, Monseigneur," I said, "she doesn't believe in infallibility any more today than she did yesterday. What she has done is very Christian—with or without it she would've been saved—but it is not Catholic. Or else the Church recognizes two Catholicisms, one that gives in to all its prescriptions, the other that has reservations and makes protest against the letter of the law.

"Indeed, you are quibbling quite a bit!" exclaimed the Archbishop, striding, or rather spinning, through the garden like a top. "Do you also, by chance, dabble in Voltaire? Our dear mama is capable of having infected you with those long-winded writers. Let's take a look at how you spend your time here! What are you reading?"

"At present, Monseigneur, I am reading the Church Fathers, and I am finding many contradictory points of view."

"There aren't any!"

"I beg your pardon, Monseigneur! Have you read them?"

"How stupid she is! Indeed! Why are you reading the Church Fathers?

There are many things that a young person may read, but I'm sure that you are becoming a free-thinker and that you have taken it upon yourself to pass judgment. That is ridiculous at your age!"

"It is only for myself, as I don't share my thoughts with anyone."

"Yes, but that will come. Take care. You were on the right path when you left the convent; at the moment, you're sounding the dismiss. You ride horses, you sing in Italian, you go shooting—so I've been told! I must hear your confession. Examine your conscience for tomorrow. I bet I'll have to rebuke you."

"I'm sorry, Monseigneur, but I will not make my confession to you."

"And why not?"

"Because we would not understand one another. You would overlook all that I do not, and scold me for what I deem innocent. Either I am no longer a Catholic, or else I am in a different way than you."

"What does that mean, you little bridled goose?"

"I know I am, but you won't be the one to improve me."

"Come, come, I must scold you. Therefore, take heed, miserable child. . . . but I see it's dinner time. I shall continue this later. I'm as hungry as a horse. Let's hurry back."

And after dinner he forgot to lecture me. He forgot it down to the last minute, and went away leaving me very grateful for that kindness but very little edified as to his type of piety, which could not be mine.

The night before he left, he did one of the stupidest things. He went into the library and proceeded to set fire to some books and mutilate several others. Deschartres found him burning, cutting, chopping and quite relishing his work. He stopped him before the loss was considerable, threatened to inform my grandmother of the damage, and could only wrench the taper and blade from his hands by pointing out that this library was under his custody, that he was responsible for it, and as mayor of the town, moreover, he had been authorized to bring charges against vandals, archbishops or not. I arrived to make peace. The scene was lively and most grotesque.

A few days later, I went to confess to my priest at La Châtre, who was a man of good manners, adequately educated, and apparently intelligent. He asked me questions which in no way offended my chastity, but which, to my way of thinking, were a breach of decorum and delicacy. I do not know to which village gossip he had lent an ear. He thought I was in the early stages of love for someone and wanted to hear from me if this was true.

"Not at all," I answered. "I haven't even given it a thought."

"However, I have it from a reliable source. . . . "

I rose from the confessional without listening to any more and, seized with uncontrollable indignation, replied, "Monsieur, since no one forces me to come to confession every month, not even the Church, which prescribes only yearly sacraments, I cannot understand your doubting my sincerity. I told you I had not even entertained the idea of the emotion you ascribe to me. That was already answering too much. I should have told you it was none of your concern."

"Excuse me," he replied in a haughty tone of voice. "The confessor must interrogate, for there are obscure thoughts that may go undetected, which can lead us astray."

"No, Monsieur. Thoughts that one is not aware of do not exist. Those which are obscure may already exist, but can, however, be so innocent as not to need confession. You ought to believe that either I have no obscure thoughts, or else that they cause my conscience no unrest, since before your interrogation, I had recited the words which end confession."

"I am quite pleased this is so," he responded. "I have always found your confessions edifying, but you have just shown an outburst of temper that stems from pride, and I urge you to repent and confess it here and now, if you want me to give you absolution."

"No, Sir!" I answered him. "You are in the wrong, and have given rise to my response, which I am not, I must say, in a state to repent right now."

He rose also and spoke to me very curtly and angrily. I answered nothing. I bowed and never saw him again. I no longer even went to mass in his parish.

Even now, I am still not certain if I was right or wrong to break in that way with such a righteous man and good priest. Since I was a Christian and believed in the practice of Catholicism, I should perhaps have accepted in a spirit of humility the suspicion he expressed to me. I was incapable of that, and I felt no remorse for my pride. All the conviction in my being revolted against this question that was indiscreet, imprudent, and in my opinion, outside the bounds of religion. I would have, at best, responded to questions about friendship outside the confessional, in the informality of a private setting, but such informality did not exist between him and me. I hardly knew him, he was not very old, and besides, I did not find him sympathetic. If I had had some innocent secret to tell, I would have seen no reason to go to him, who was neither my director nor my spiritual mentor. He seemed thus to want to usurp a moral authority I had not given him, and this awkward interruption of a sacrament to which I accorded such spiritual severity disgusted me as if it had been a sacrilege. I felt that he had confused human curiosity with the priest's role. Furthermore, Abbé de Prémord, that scrupulous guardian of the sacred ignorance of girls, had told me, "One must not ask questions; I never ask any." I could not and was never again able to have faith in any other priest but him.

It was impossible to think of making confession to my old parish priest at Saint-Chartier. I was too intimate, too familiar, with him. I had played with him too often during my childhood. I had played too many tricks on him, and considered him just as incapable of directing me as I did myself of confessing to him seriously. I would go to his mass and afterward have lunch with him. He would wipe my muddy shoes himself as best he could. I had to hold back his arm to keep him from drinking, because he would be taking me home on his mare. He would recount his household problems to me, his housekeeper's temper; I would scold both of them in turn for their mistakes. There was no way to change such relations, short of going before the penitential court for an hour each month. I knew through my brother and my peasant girlfriends how he listened to confession. He heard not a word, and as these mischievous children would mockingly confess to the greatest outrages, he responded to everything,

"Very good, very good. All right, is it nearly done?"

I could not have rid myself of these thoughts, and as I really felt my devotion to the Catholic faith diminishing day by day, I did not want to leave myself open to seeing it depart suddenly, in spite of myself, without feeling justified by some truly serious reason for renouncing it.

I had never avoided meat on Fridays and Saturdays at my grandmother's. She did not wish to. Abbé de Prémord had advised me early on to submit to this breaking of the rules. Thus, little by little, I came to the point where I practiced only prayer, and even that was almost always improvised.

Oddly—or understandably—I was never more religious, more enthusiastic, more absorbed in God than in the midst of this diminishing of my passion for the ritual. New horizons were opening to me. What Leibnitz had announced to me—that divine love would be redoubled and reanimated by a more illuminated faith—Jean-Jacques had made me understand, and my freedom of spirit, reinforced by breaking with the priest, made me feel it. I felt very secure, and from that day the fundamental principles of faith were stamped on my soul. My political leanings, or rather my hopes for humankind, caused me to feel, without hesitation or scruple, that the spirit of the Church had strayed from the straight path and that I should not follow it on the crooked one. I finally reached this conclusion: no Christian church had the right to say, "Outside me there is no salvation."

Since then I have heard Catholics uphold what I, at that time, still wanted to convince myself of—that such a conclusion did not absolutely come from the decrees of the Papal Church. I think they were deceiving themselves, as I had tried to do. But supposing they were right, one would have to conclude that there was not, had never been, and never would be any orthodoxy here or anywhere else. As soon as God does not reject the faithful from any church whatsoever, Catholicism no longer exists. I do not deny or object to the fact that it still serves excellently a rather large number of religious minds and that it is the declared faith of the majority of French people, but once it admits of its own accord that dissidents are not damned, it must also admit debate, and no human power can legitimately curtail the debate, as long as it is serious, tolerant, and sincere, for all curtailments are a persecution, all lies an insult against which the laws of every nation owe each and every one of us impartial protection.

The young man I was supposedly fond of was a member of the ———— family.[21] I shall call him Claudius, the first name that comes to mind and does not belong to anyone else I know. His family was one of the most noble in the area and had been quite wealthy. Educating ten children had completely ruined Claudius' parents. Several had sullied the family name by reckless behavior which ended tragically. Three sons remained. About the two eldest, I have nothing to say that pertains to this phase of my philosophic and religious existence. The only one who was indirectly involved was the youngest.

He was handsome and not lacking in learning, intelligence, or wit. He was planning a career in science, where he has since gained some reputation. Poor at that time even more through his mother's sordid greed than the force of circumstance, he was preparing to be a doctor. Great sacrifices and much hard work had affected his health. He was thought to be consumptive. He recovered somewhat but died of disease in his prime.

Deschartres, who had been close to his father and inclined to take an interest in a gentleman student, introduced me to him and had even engaged him to give me some lessons in physics. I was also busy with osteology, hoping to learn a bit of surgery, consequently some anatomy, so as to assist Deschartres, if need be, in those operations where I could assist, or even replace him in cases of lesser injury. Deschartres had cut off arms, amputated fingers, set wrists, and patched up cracked skulls in my presence and with my help. He found me very skillful, quick, and capable of overcoming my own revulsion when necessary. Quite early on, he had gotten me used to holding back tears and overcoming faintness. That was a very great service he had done me—to teach me to help others.

This Claudius brought over the heads, arms, and legs which Deschartres needed in order to show me where to begin. He would have me draw them from the real model; lack of time kept us from getting any further than the bony structure. A doctor in La Châtre even lent us a complete skeleton of a small girl which remained stretched out on my dresser for some time and which reminds me that I should mention an incident of susceptibility to imaginative power which proves that every weak female can take herself in hand.

One night I dreamed that my skeleton got up and came to draw the curtains from around my bed. I woke and, seeing it quite at peace on the spot where I had left it, went peacefully back to sleep.

But the dream persisted, and the little girl's bones engaged in such outlandishness that she became unbearable to me. I got up and put her outside, after which I slept quite well. The following night she started her foolish pranks again, but this time I paid her no mind, and she decided to behave herself for the remainder of the winter, on my dresser.

Coming back to Claudius, he was less mischievous than my skeleton, and I never had, at that time, anything but conversations with him about my lessons. He went back to Paris, and as I had asked him to send me about a hundred books, he wrote to me several times giving me information and asking my preference regarding editions. I wanted to own several works which had been lent to me, a host of poets whom I had not read, and various simple treatises whose names escape me now, of which Deschartres had given him a list.

I do not know if he looked for a pretext to write to me more often than necessary. It did not seem so, until a very serious letter, slightly pedantic but nonetheless rather beautiful, that I recall began like this: "You truly philosophic soul, you are quite right, but you are the truth that kills."

I do not remember the rest, but I do know it surprised me and that I showed it to Deschartres, asking him, in all innocence, why these great eulogies to my logic were mingled with a sort of despairing reproach.

Deschartres was not much more experienced in these matters than I. He was also surprised; he read, reread, and told me ingenuously, "I do believe this might be a declaration of love. What on earth did you write to this boy?"

"I have already forgotten," I told him. "Perhaps a few lines about La

Bruyère,[22] with whom I'm obsessed at the moment. He is using this as a pretext, as you can see, to come back to the conversation the three of us had when he was last here."

"Yes, I see," said Deschartres. "You uttered, in one of your moralistic spells, such beautiful condemnations of society that I said to you, 'When one sees things so black, there is only one thing to do, and that is to become a nun! Now do you see to what stupid consequences that would lead as inflexible a mind as yours?' And Claudius had cried out in indignation. You then talked about life in retreat and about abnegation in a rather specious way, and presently this young man tells you that you love only abstract things and that he will die of grief because of it."

"Let's hope not," I replied. "I believe you're mistaken. He's telling me rather that my detachment from worldly things is contagious, and that he himself is turning to skepticism at this point."

Rereading the letter, we convinced ourselves that it was not a declaration, but on the contrary, an overly solemn adoption of my point of view, in the tone of a man who takes himself for a philosopher victorious over life's illusions.

In fact, Claudius wrote me other letters clearly explaining the resolution that he had come to since he had known me. I was, in his eyes, a superior being who had settled her doubts in one fell swoop. There was no goal but science; medicine was but a secondary branch; he wanted to raise himself to transcendent ideas, to have no other passion, and to delve into the exact sciences in order to discover the reason for the Creation.

No longer searching for a pretext to write, he wrote often. His letters were worth reading for their cold and trenchant sincerity. Deschartres found that this exchange of ideas was not useless to me, and nothing seemed more natural to him than a serious correspondence between two young people who could quite possibly be smitten with each other all the while talking of Malebranche[23] and Company.

There was, however, no such relationship. Claudius was too pedantic not to derive a kind of satisfaction out of not being in love, in spite of the opportunity. Coquettish feelings were too foreign to me, and even the slightest notion of love still too far removed for me to see anything in him but a teacher.

But this and several other aspects of my life were being resolved in a direction away from all the accepted customs of polite society; Deschartres, far from holding me back, was pushing me toward what we call "eccentricity" without either of us suspecting. One day he said to me, "I've just come from visiting Count V——, and have had quite a surprise. He was hunting with a young boy whom I was going to treat with little ceremony, as befit his smock and cap, until the Count said to me, 'This is my daughter. I have her dress in this boy's outfit so that she can run, climb, and leap along with me, without hindrance from clothing that encumbers women at an age when they most need to develop their strength.'"

This Count was interested in medical matters, I believe, and to his way of thinking that mode of dress was an appropriate health measure. Deschartres allowed himself to be convinced. Having taught only boys, I think he was eager to see me as male and convince himself I was one. My skirts disturbed the seriousness of his teaching, and it is true that when I took his advice and donned the masculine smock, cap, and gaiters, he became ten times more pedantic and crushed me under his Latin, presuming that I could understand it much better.

As far as I was concerned, I found my new costume far more pleasant for running than my embroidered petticoats, torn bits of which remained caught on the underbrush as I passed. I had become thin and agile, and had not so long ago given up the aide-de-camp's uniform of Murat that I could not still remember it.

It also must not be forgotten that at that time the unpleated skirts were so narrow that a woman was literally in a sheath and could not decently cross a stream without leaving a shoe behind.

Deschartres was mad about hunting and would take me along compulsively. That discomfited me precisely because of the problem of crossing through the thickets which had grown up in profusion around our countryside and were covered with murderous thorns. My preference was hunting quail, with a trammel net and birdcall, in the green wheat fields. He would make me get up before dawn. Lying in a furrow, I would give the call while, at the other end of the field, he flushed out the game. Every morning we would bring back eight or ten live quail to my grandmother, who would admire and pity them a bit but, because she only ate small game, would not allow me to feel too sorry for these poor creatures which were so pretty and subdued.

Deschartres, normally very affectionate toward me and concerned with my health, could think of nothing else when he heard a quail clucking near his net. I, too, got carried away by this savage entertainment of lying in wait to capture the prey. Thus, my role as caller, consisting of being stretched out in wheat fields flooded by the morning dew, revived all the acute pain in my extremities that I had felt while at the convent. Deschartres noticed one day that I could not mount my horse and had to be hoisted up. The first movements of riding caused me to scream, and it was only after a good bit of vigorous galloping in the early heat of the day that the pain subsided. He was surprised and finally figured out that I was suffering from rheumatism. This was just one more excuse to prescribe strenuous exercise and the masculine attire that allowed me to accomplish it.

My grandmother saw me like that and wept. "You look too much like your father," she told me. "Dress like that for running, but change into girl's clothing when you come back, so that I am spared the illusion, because it makes me terribly ill; there are times when I mix up past and present to such an extent that I am no longer sure what period of my life I am in."

My way of living evolved so naturally from my unusual situation that it seemed quite normal not to behave like most other girls. I was considered very strange, yet I was infinitely less so than I could have been, if I had inclined to being affected or odd. Left on my own in all matters, no longer controlled by my grandmother, almost forgotten by my mother, urged to total independence by Deschartres, feeling little moral or emotional confusion within me, and despite the change I had undergone in religious ideas, planning always to retire to a convent with or without taking vows, I had no concern for what the people around me called "public opinion": it had no value and appeared to me to be of no use.

Deschartres had never looked at the world from a practical point of view. In his desire to dominate others, he brooked no objection to his judgments, referring everything back to his wisdom, to his "omnicompetence," which was to his mind infallible, and "looked on all others as though they were dung"[24]—except for my grandmother, himself, and me. However, he did not laugh at criticism, as I did. It made him angry. He was indignant to the point of furious abuse against "ridiculous" people who took it upon themselves to censure my lack of respect for their customs.

I must also say that he was bored. He had led an unusually active life which he had had to curtail quite a bit since my grandmother's illness. With his savings he had bought a small tract of land ten or twelve leagues away from us, where he had formerly spent entire weeks. He no longer dared spend a night away from us for fear of finding his patient in a worsened state; so, his flesh was beginning to crawl with rage, especially so since he was deprived of the company of his woman friend, who had taken the place of all he had not known in life. He needed to be attached to someone in particular, to whom he could show the admiration and infatuation that he granted to no one else. Hence I had become his god, perhaps even more than my grandmother had ever been, since he considered me his work and believed he could love himself in me, as in a reflection of his intellectual ideals.

Even though he often overwhelmed me, I agreed to satisfy his need for discussion and discourse by sacrificing hours to him that I would have rather spent in my own pursuits. He thought he knew everything, and he was wrong. But as he knew a lot and had an awesome memory, he did not stifle one's intelligence; only his exuberant vanity was a strain. Notwithstanding his scowling expression and absolute language, he craved a few moments of light-hearted abandon. He was clumsy at teasing, but he laughed good-naturedly when I teased him. In sum, he could bear anything from me, and while he had a violent aversion to whoever did not admire him, he could not do without my arguing and provocations. This was a faithful cur, and biting everyone else, would let his ears be pulled by the child of the house.

Here are some of the quite normal circumstances by which I managed to frightfully scandalize the male and female gossips in the town of La Châtre. At that time, no woman of the area was permitted to go riding, unless it was on the crupper, behind her hired man. My costume—not only the boy's running outfit, but even the long riding skirt and round hat—was considered an abomination; the study of skeletons, a profanation; hunting, destructive; study, an aberration; and my relationships with young men—all sons of my father's friends, whom I had continued to treat as childhood chums and whom I saw quite rarely at any rate, but whose hands I shook without blushing or trembling like a lovesick hen—were deemed effrontery, depravity, what have you. Even my religion was subject to commentary and slander. Could one be considered pious while partaking in such shocking activities? Impossible! There was devil's work behind it. I was dabbling in the occult. Once I had pretended to take communion but had carried the host away in my handkerchief—someone had seen it! I had had a rendez-vous with Claudius and his brothers, and we had made a target out of the wafer—shot it full of holes. Another time, I had entered the church on horseback, and the priest had chased me out just when I was prancing around the main altar; and since that day, I had not been seen at mass nor taken any sacrament. André, my poor country page, was not totally guiltless in all this: he was either my lover or a sort of apprentice whom I used in my conjurings. He could not be made to admit anything concerning my activities, but I would go into the graveyard at night with Deschartres to dig up corpses. I never slept, and I had not been to bed for a year. The loaded pistols that André always carried in his holsters when he accompanied me on horseback and the two big dogs that followed us were not normal either. We had shot at some peasants, and my dog Velléda had throttled some children. Why not? My savagery was well known. I took pleasure in seeing arms broken and skulls cracked; and each time there was some bleeding to be done, Deschartres called me in to be entertained.

My report of all this may seem exaggerated. I would not have believed it myself, if I had not subsequently seen it in writing. There is nothing more stupidly malicious than a small-town inhabitant. The situation has its amusing side; when these ravings got back to me, I had a good laugh, hardly suspecting they would cause me great pain later on.

I had already suffered a small dose of persecution from those imbeciles, from which I emerged victorious. In midsummer, just when my grandmother was feeling her best, I had danced a bourrée without incident at the village festival, despite the threats made against me, though unknown to me. Here is what happened.

I frequently visited a spinsterish person who lived in the country a quarter of a league from my house. Once again it was Deschartres who had taken me there and who deemed her the most decent person in the world. I still think he was right, for I have always seen this fine old girl either busy with her aged uncle, who was dying from a lingering disease and whom she cared for out of a true sense of filial piety, or else tending to farm and household chores with touching activity and simplicity. I liked her quaint, half-rustic interior kept with Dutch cleanliness, her chickens, her orchard, her cakes that she took from the oven herself to serve me hot. I especially liked her directness, common sense, devotion to her uncle, and her realistic attitude toward domestic chores, which brought me back down to earth and presented me with a charmingly pure and salutary example.

A sister of hers came, who also seemed to me a good woman, but whom the town moralizers chose to think and talk of maliciously; I have never known why, and I still believe there was no other reason than the fancy for defamation which devours provincial minds.

This sister had been in the area for a fortnight, and I had seen her several times. She told me she would come to our village festival; she came, and I spoke to her as to someone with whom I was on good terms.

There was general indignation, and it was decreed that I was trampling ostentatiously on convention. It was an insult to the right-minded ladies and gentlemen of the town. I suspected nothing. Some kind soul came to warn me, and as I had heard nothing bad about this woman that actually made any sense, I found it despicable to turn my back on her; so, I continued to speak to her each time I found myself near her, in the course of the festivities.

Several bourgeois workmen who thought they were smart pretended I had done it on purpose to flaunt "public opinion," and agreed to offer me what they called an "affront," that is to say, they would not ask me to dance. I did not notice this in the least, because all the peasant boys from our estate asked me, and as usual, I could not decide whose invitation to accept.

But it seems that I did run the risk of not being honored by the village boys' invitations to dance, had they all been equally stupid. It so happened that I had some anonymous friends who agreed to stem the tide; among others, there was a tanner to whom I have always been grateful for having acted as my champion in this whole affair, even though I had never spoken to him before. Around him thus gathered in ever-growing numbers a group of protectors, and I danced with them, while Deschartres paraded at my side, wearing a fearsome expression.

He explained to me afterward what had happened. I reproached him for not having warned me. I would have left the dance rather than serve as a possible pretext for some brawl. But that was not how Deschartres saw things. "I would have loved that," he exclaimed, sick at not having had the chance to let loose, "I would have loved one of those asses to utter a word that would have given me the excuse to break his arms and legs!"

"Tut," I said to him. "You would have had to set them, and you're already burdened enough without that." Practicing free of charge, Deschartres had a large clientele.

This little incident did not bother either of us much at all, but it gave us the opportunity to talk about public opinion, and it occurred to me for the first time to wonder what importance should be attached to it.

Deschartres, who was always in open contradiction with himself, was never concerned about public opinion regarding his own behavior, but he thought he should respect it on principle. As for me, the Holy Scripture was still ringing in my ears, including these words among others, "Beware, he who is the cause of scandal!"

But scandal had to be defined. "Let's start with that," I told my tutor. "Then we shall see how to define public opinion.

"'Public opinion' is a very vague term," Deschartres said. "There are all sorts. There is the opinion of the sages of antiquity, which is not that of modern man; that of the theologians, which is but eternal controversy; that of the peoples of the world, which varies further depending on the culture. There is the opinion of the uneducated, which we must call prejudice; finally, there is that of the idiots, which we must utterly scorn. 'Scandal,' on the other hand, is quite definable. It means brazenness in evil, in vice, in all wrongdoing."

"You say 'brazenness' in evil. Can there thus be modesty in evil, in vice, in wrongdoing?"

"No, that is just a manner of speaking. But, nevertheless, a certain shame for the errors into which we may fall still derives from a respect for public morality."

"Yes and no, great man! He who does evil out of negligence, out of blind devotion, out of passion, without being aware of it at any rate, does not dream of hiding it from himself. If he can forget God's judgment, it is not surprising that he can forget man's. I pity his folly. But the one who hides from himself adeptly, and knows how to preserve himself from blame, seems to me much more odious. The latter sins quite knowingly against God, since he gives it enough thought to avoid the judgment of men. Him I despise!"

"That is very accurate. Thus, one must not have anything evil to hide."

"Do you believe that you and I, for example, have any vice to blush about, any proclivity for evil?"

"Certainly not."

"Then why are they crying 'scandal' all around us?"

"Such idiocy doesn't prove anything. However, you must not push the spirit of independence, which I share with you in this matter, to extremes. You have been called to live in society; if ever this or that notion happened to offend the ideas of your circle, no matter how innocent or advantageous I judge it, you would indeed have to consider giving it up."

"That depends, great man! Notions that are indifferent in themselves must be sacrificed to 'manners,' as my poor grandmama used to say when she was teaching me, and by 'manners' she meant affection, kindness, the spirit of family or charity. But can or must we abandon notions that are essentially good, though they are poorly understood or misinterpreted? To save the honor of a relative or friend, we may be forced to leave our own open to suspicion. To save his life, we may be condemned to lying. For our having helped an unfortunate person wrongly or rightly crushed by public censure, society's intolerance may end up making us share the disapproval that he bears. In the exercise of Christian charity, which is the first of all virtues, I see thousands of tasks which must scandalize or offend almost everyone. Thus, when Jesus said, 'And whosoever shall offend one of these children who believe in me, it is better for him that a millstone were hanged about his neck, and he were cast into the sea,' he was talking about what evil is, and he meant it in an absolute way, quite in keeping with his doctrine; he said in talking about a sinner, 'He that is without sin among you, let him first cast a stone at her'; and his teachings to the disciples can be summed up thus, 'Bear up under insult, blame, slander, all sorts of persecution from those who do not believe in my word.'[25] Therefore, what society calls 'scandal' is not always scandal, and what it calls 'public opinion' is only an arbitrary convention which changes according to the times, the places, and the people."

"Doubtless, doubtless," said Deschartres. "Truth on this side, error on the other. But the good citizen respects the beliefs of the milieu in which he lives. This milieu consists of wise men and fools, capable people and incompetents. The distinction is not difficult to make!"

"Thus, there are two public opinions?"

"Yes, the true and the false, the roots of all other variations."

"If there are two, there aren't any."

"Witness the paradox!"

"It's just like the Orthodox Church, great man! There is only one, or there isn't any. You tell me that I will have to respect the milieu into which destiny has cast me. That's the paradox! If that milieu is bad, I will not respect it, I warn you."

"There you go again with your false logic. I taught you logic, but you go to extremes and, by abusing the consequences, make wrong what was right to begin with. Society is not infallible, but it has authority. In cases of doubt, we must rely on authority. Any act, no matter how good in itself, may scandalize."

"Must one give it up?"

"No! One must perform it, but sometimes with prudence. Sometimes one has to hide his good deed, despite the proverb, 'He who hides has something to hide.'"

"Good for you, great man! You uttered the word 'prudence.' That's quite another matter. It is no longer a question of defining good or evil, scandal or public opinion. All that is vague in the scheme of things human. One must have prudence! Well, I tell you that prudence is a personal amenity, a personal privilege, but private conscience being the only judge, due to a lack of absolutely competent judges in society, I believe I am completely free to lack prudence, if it pleases me to bear all the blame and persecution that go along with demanding and perilous duties."

"That presumes too much upon your strength. You won't find that as easy as you believe, or else you'll be opening yourself up to much unhappiness."

"I don't presume to possess great strength. I know that I'll be tackling a very rough task; I will thus take care beforehand to make it as light as possible. There is a very simple way to do that."

"Let's hear what you propose!"

"From now on, starting with that first day when my eyes were opened to the inconsistency of things human, I shall break with the business of what we call society, living in retreat while doing good, either in a convent or here, asking no one's approval, having no need of the lowly society of insensible people, worrying about God, a few friends, and myself—that's all. What could be simpler? Didn't my grandmother arrange the entire second half of her life that way?"

Whenever I abandoned myself to the thought of putting off for as long as possible the choice of a position in life; whenever I would talk about waiting till the age of twenty-five or thirty to decide between marriage or a religious vocation, and, until then, delving into science with Deschartres in the calm solitude of Nohant, he had no arguments to fight with, as this dream appealed so much to him, too. In spite of his limited imagination, he helped me fabricate dreams and ended up believing that, by instilling wisdom in me, he had made me superior to himself.

During our conversations, then, I almost always brought him around to my conclusions, even in matters of feeling, where he was certainly not inferior to me. All the while mocking his self-esteem and his contradictions, I felt quite strongly that he was at the very least my equal in matters of the heart. However, mine being younger and more excitable, it could sustain longer surges; his being numbed by age and the habit of material comfort, it needed to be awakened from time to time. He pretended to prefer wisdom to truth and reason to enthusiasm, but deep down his soul really had some virtues for which I had as yet only an ambition, and a sense of duty that allowed him continually to crush his personal interests underfoot.

The summary I have just made of our talks over one or two weeks has not since needed revision. I have changed my point of view several times concerning life's practicalities and details, in view of further enlightenment and progress, but everything that resulted in my basic philosophy for daily use was decided once and for all the first time my mind was led squarely to face the question of duty through actual experience, whether frivolous or serious. When I had scruples of devotion at the convent, that is to say uncertainties of judgment, I think I was more logical than Abbé de Prémord and Sister Alicia. I did not want to be Catholic half way, and I thought I had not reached my goal as long as one grain of sand might make me trip, as it were. I undertook the impossible because nothing seems impossible to children. I believed in something absolute that does not exist for humanity and the path to which has been hidden from us by a supreme wisdom. As soon as I thought myself justified in reasoning my beliefs and refining them by seeking the support and approval of my best instincts, I had no more doubts and did not have to rescind my decisions. That was not strength of character. The doubts simply did not reappear.

Many matters were solved for me like that from then on, with or without Deschartres; with or without Abbé de Prémord. Many others were still closed books, among them everything that related to love or marriage. The time had not come for me to think about that, as none of those strings had yet been plucked.

When I remember those mental exertions and the sudden joy my certainties gave me, it indeed seems I was as silly as those scholars who believe they have uncovered the wisdom of the centuries by themselves. But when I ask myself today, quite calmly and after a lifetime of experience, if I was right so heartily to scorn false ideas and vain duties that destroy faith in serious duties, I find I was not wrong, and I sense that if I had it to do again, I would do the same.   *D.A.P.*

VI

My grandmother's illness worsens. —Extreme fatigue. —René,
Byron, Hamlet. —A morbid state of mind. —Suicidal thoughts.
—The river. —Deschartres' lecture. —The classics.
—Correspondence. —Excerpts from a young girl's letters. —My
grandmother's last days. —Her death. —Christmas night. —The
cemetery. —The next night's vigil.

We have seen how a very minor, personal incident had led me to raise
serious questions about society. Isn't this always the case for everyone? And
though it may suit us to say we must not take it personally, it will never be otherwise when it comes to worldly matters. Anyone whose intention it is to commit an evil act, if he were rebelling against the opinion of a virtuous and
enlightened public surrounding and guiding him, is necessarily brought to consider that opinion as law, if he has a feeling for right and wrong; but anyone
who has to deal solely with unfair idiots is obliged to interrogate himself
before giving in to them and go on from there to recognize that nowhere,
between God and himself, is there any legitimately absolute control over the
actions of his personal life. The broad implication of this indisputable truth is
that freedom of conscience is inalienable. In evaluating the action in terms of
its intention, the Jesuits had already proclaimed this principle though probably
without envisioning its implications beyond their order.

The little adventure of the village festival had thus been the prelude to a
monstrously ridiculous slander which was concocted on my account soon
afterward to a most brilliant crescendo. It seemed that the disdain with which I
treated it was the cause for a furor on the part of the good folk of La Châtre,
and that my independent spirit (obviously presumed, since they knew me only
by sight) was an outrage to the code of honor of their parish.

I have already mentioned that the little hamlet of La Châtre was remarkable for its proportionately large population of thinking people. This is still true,
but everywhere good minds are the exception, even in large cities, and in small
towns we know that the majority rules. It is like a flock of sheep where each
animal, pushed by all the others, follows wherever the general movement leads.
Hence there is an instinctive aversion for the one who stands apart; independence of judgment is the predatory wolf which unsettles the wits in that pen.

My good relations with family friends did not suffer from all this, and I
have kept them intact and friendly throughout my life. But you can well imagine that my determination not to see through the eyes of just anybody only

became greater and more acute when I learned of this public outcry. I found such great comfort in this position that I was almost grateful to the idiots who had suggested it to me.

As autumn approached, my poor grandmother lost the small bit of strength she had recovered. She could no longer remember immediate things; she no longer had a sense of time, nor any desire for serious occupation. She dozed constantly and never slept. Two women stayed with her night and day. Deschartres, Julie, and I took turns spending either the day or night watching over her or helping the women with their ministrations. In those tiring duties, Julie, even though very ill herself, was extremely courageous and patient. My poor grandmother scarcely allowed her any rest. More demanding with her than with the other servants, she had a need to scold and contradict her, and Julie was often obliged to have us intervene so that her patient would give up whims which were impossible to satisfy without endangering her.

Wanting to manage three areas at once—the care of my grandmother, the walks necessary for my health, and my education—I had decided, seeing that four hours of sleep were not enough for me, to go to bed only every other night. I do not know if I made the right choice, but I quickly became used to it and felt much less tired doing that than sleeping in snatches. Sometimes, it is true, the patient would ask for me at two in the morning, when I was deep in the pleasures of sleep. She wanted to know if it was really two in the morning as the others were telling her. She did not settle down until she saw me, and when finally reassured it was true, she was still able to send me back to bed with tender words. But one would never know for sure whether she would get upset all over again a quarter of an hour later, so I would choose to read by her side and give up my night's sleep.

This taxing schedule no longer affected my health appreciably—youth adapts quickly to changes in habit—but my state of mind was profoundly affected. My thoughts became gloomy, and I sank little by little into a melancholy which I no longer had the desire to fight.

Since Deschartres would fuss over it, I tried to hide my morbid disposition from him. Not talking about it made it twice as bad. I had not read *René*, that brilliant hors d'oeuvre to *La Génie du Christianisme*;[26] in a hurry to return the book to my confessor, I had put it off until I had my own copy. I finally did get to read it, and I was singularly affected by it. It seemed to me that René was myself. Even though I had known no dread like his in my own life and although I inspired no passion which might be a cause of horror and dejection, I felt crushed by a disgust for life which seemed to me amply justified by the emptiness of all things human. Ailing already, what happened to me was what happens to people who look up their illness in medical books. I suffered in my imagination from all the symptoms described in that desolate poem.

Byron, about whom I knew nothing at all, dealt me an even more crushing blow; the enthusiasm aroused in me by melancholy poets of an order less exalted or somber—Gilbert, Millevoie, Young,[27] Petrarch, etc.—found itself eclipsed. Shakespeare's Hamlet and Jacques were the end of me.[28] All those great cries of eternal human suffering simply crowned the oeuvre of disillusionment which the moralists had begun. Being acquainted with only a few facets of life, I trembled at the thought of approaching others. The memory of what I had already suffered made me fear and even despise the future. Too much of a believer in God to damn humanity, I made do with Rousseau's paradox proclaiming man's innate goodness, at the same time decrying society's influence, and attributing to collective behavior what individual behavior would never have considered.

Given that the conclusion to this sophistry was isolation in the form of a contemplative, sequestered life as the only means to keep one's peace of mind, did it not then mean that I was reverting once again, via freedom, to Gerson's Catholic stoicism, and that horrified at the emptiness of life, I had been going around in a vicious circle?

Only Gerson promised and gave bliss to the cenobite, and my moralists as well as my poets left me nothing but despair. Gerson, always logical in his narrow point of view, had advised me to love my neighbor solely with an eye to my own salvation; that is, not to love him at all. I had learned from others how better to understand Jesus and love my neighbor literally better than myself; from this had come an infinite pain at seeing my peers do harm which to me seemed so easy to avoid, and a bitter regret at not being able to carry away into solitude the hope of their conversion.

I resolved to live in isolation: my convent dream had been replaced by a dream of chosen confinement in country seclusion. It seemed to me that my heart, like René's, had died without having lived. Having so clearly discovered through the eyes of Rousseau, La Bruyère, even Molière (whose *Misanthrope* had become my Bible)—actually through the eyes of all those who had lived, felt, thought, and written—the perversity and stupidity of mankind, I would never be able to love a single person with enthusiasm, unless he were, like me, a kind of savage, at odds with this dissembling society and misleading world.

If Claudius, along with his intellect, knowledge, and skepticism regarding things human, had had, like me, a religious ideal, he might perhaps have served. I did consider him, at least to the extent of questioning myself on the subject; but unlike me, he rapidly came to deny God, saying that, indeed, that was his starting point. This caused a rift between us, and our epistolary friendship cooled. I could forgive him only by thinking that with further study he would see the light.

That did not happen. Even though we were later to be linked rather intimately, the inner suffering his atheism caused me was never dispelled, even when I no longer had my mind habitually focused on these rather serious topics. In his mature years, his atheism produced in him theories of surprising perversity, and I sometimes wondered if he believed in them or if he were making fun of me. There even came a time when he was seized by such transports of evil and frightened me to such an extent that I stopped seeing him and refused to renew our old friendship. But why should I recount that phase of his existence? There is nothing to be gained by stirring the ashes of the dead unless they have left a remarkable impression.

Thus, at the age of seventeen, I secluded myself, by an act of will, from the world. Laws of property and inheritance, brutal repression, legal battles, privileges of wealth and education, class prejudice and moral intolerance, the puerile gossip of people in society, the degrading effects of material interest—everything that stems from pagan institutions or customs and has been perpetuated by a so-called Christian society revolted me so completely that in my soul I was led to rail against the work of centuries. I had no notion of progress, which was not popular then and which I had not come across in my reading. Thus, I saw no way out of my agony, and the idea of working to hasten the promises of the future—even in my obscure and narrow milieu—did not enter my mind.

My melancholy thus came from sadness, and my sadness from suffering. From there to disgust with life and desire for death was but a small step. My domestic existence was so gloomy, my body so overwrought by a continuous struggle against overwhelming pressure, my brain so tired from thoughts too precociously serious and by reading too absorbing for my age that I ended up with that grave moral disease—attraction to suicide.

God forbid, however, that I attribute this serious consequence to the writings of the masters and desire for truth. In a happier family situation and in a better state of health, either I would not have construed the books as I did, or they would not have impressed me so much. Like almost everyone my age, perhaps I would only have been moved by the ideation and not delved so much for meaning. Neither philosophers nor poets are responsible for the harm they may do to us when we drink inappropriately or immoderately from the wells they have dug. I certainly felt that I had to protect myself—not from them, but from myself—and I turned to faith to sustain me.

I still believe in what Christians call grace. No matter what we call those transformations which occur in us when we cry out to the divine principle of the infinite for help in our weakness; whether this blessing be called succor or acceptance of our plight; whether our aspiration be called prayer or emotional relief, it is certain that the soul is replenished through religious élan. I have always felt grace so clearly in myself that it would have been crass of me to have given expression to it with my pen. To pray to heaven, like some believers, for rain or sunshine, for what to eat or money to buy it, to conjure up hail or lightning, sickness or death, is idolatry; but to ask for courage, wisdom, love is not to seek to alter natural law, but to draw from a hearth which would not ceaselessly attract us if, by its very nature, it were not capable of giving us warmth.

Thus, I prayed for and received the strength to resist suicide. The temptation was sometimes so alive, so sudden, so strange that I could certainly attest the fact that I had fallen prey to a kind of madness. It took the form of an obsession and from time to time bordered on monomania. Water especially attracted me as if by some mysterious charm. I no longer walked anywhere except along the river bank, and no longer thinking about finding pleasant spots, I followed it mechanically until I came to a deep place. Then, motionless on the edge, as if held by a magnet, I felt a feverish gaiety in my head as I said to myself, "How easy it would be. I'd only have to take one step."

At first, feeling very sure of myself, I did not fight the strange charm of this temptation, but then it took on an intensity which frightened me. I could no longer tear myself away from the river bank at will and began to question myself, Yes or No, often enough and for a long enough time to risk being thrown by a Yes to the bottom of the clear water which attracted me.

My religion, however, forced me to regard suicide as a crime, and thus I overcame the temptation. I refrained from going near water, for the nervous reaction—I do not know what else to call it—was so pronounced that I could not even touch the edge of a well without a reflex that was almost painful to resist.

I had thought myself cured of it, however, until going to see a patient with Deschartres. We found ourselves riding together on the banks of the Indre. "Watch out," he said to me, not suspecting my monomania. "Ride behind me; the ford is very dangerous. Right next to us, on the right, it's twenty feet deep."

"I'd prefer not to ride here at all," I answered, suddenly losing confidence. "You go on. I'll make a detour and meet you by the mill bridge."

Deschartres made fun of me. "Since when have you been afraid?" he said to me. "This is absurd. We've been in worse spots a hundred times and you used to think nothing of it. Come on! We have to hurry. We have to be back by five o'clock to give your grandmama dinner."

As a matter of fact, I, too, thought my reaction somewhat ridiculous, so I followed him. But right in the middle of the ford, a dizziness seized me, my heart leaped, my vision blurred, I heard the fatal Yes roaring in my ears. I reined my horse abruptly to the right and found myself in deep water, wracked by hysterical laughter and joy.

If Colette had not been the best animal in the world, I would have perished, and really innocently this time, since no forethought at all was involved on my part; but Colette, instead of drowning, began to swim, carrying me toward the river bank. Deschartres returned me to reality with his frantic yelling. He had already ridden after me. I realized he might drown since he was clumsy and badly mounted. I shouted to him to stay where he was and from then on concerned myself only with holding on. It is difficult not to be separated from a swimming horse. The water lifts you up, and your own body weight constantly submerges the animal, but I was very light, and Colette had uncommon courage and strength. The greatest difficulty was getting ashore. The bank was too steep. There was a moment of terrible anxiety for poor Deschartres, but he did not lose his head, and he yelled to me to grab hold of the tip of a willow branch which was within my reach and let the animal drown. I managed to get free of her and to safety, but when I saw poor Colette's desperate efforts to climb the embankment, I completely lost sight of my own situation, and, though drawn a moment before toward my own demise, I was now in anguish over her possible death, which I had not envisioned. I was going to throw myself back into the water to try, uselessly no doubt, to save her, when Deschartres arrived to pull me out, and Colette had the presence of mind to recross the ford to where the other mare had remained.

Fortunately, Deschartres did not follow the example of the schoolmaster in the fable, who delivers his lecture before saving the child, but even though the lecture came after the rescue, it was not any the less harsh. Distress and worry sometimes made him furious. He called me an animal, a dumb beast, drawing on the full range of his vocabulary. Since he was livid and since copius tears accompanied his insults, I embraced him without contradicting him, but as the harangue continued on the way home, I decided to tell him the truth, as if talking to a doctor, and consult him about this inexplicable attraction that still haunted me.

I thought he would have trouble understanding, so little did I myself understand what I was confessing to him, but he did not seem surprised. "Oh, my God!" he cried. "That, too? Well, it's hereditary." He told me then that my father had been subject to these kinds of dizzy spells, and he made me promise to fight them by a proper diet and by religion—a word which I heard him use, I think, for the first time.

There seemed no point in his rebuking me for my sickness since it was involuntary and something I struggled against, but this did lead us to a general discussion of suicide.

To begin with I allowed him that reasoned and willful suicide was faithless and cowardly. So it would have been for me. That seemed as absolute as any other moral law. In the area of religion, however, all martyrs were suicides: if God wanted man, in an absolute and incontrovertible way, to keep the life imposed upon him, faithless and sullied as it might be, Christian saints and heroes might well give allegiance to idols rather than let themselves be tortured and devoured by animals. There have been martyrs so eager for this so-called sacred death that it was said of several of them that they flung themselves singing into the flames without waiting to be pushed. Thus does the religious ideal condone suicide and the Church canonize it. It has done more than canonize martyrs: it has canonized saints who voluntarily killed themselves through excessive mortification.

In the area of society, apart from acts of patriotic and military heroism which may be considered glorious suicides like those of Christian martyrdom, weren't cases conceivable where death was a duty tacitly demanded by our fellow men? To sacrifice your life to save another's, even the most unspeakable of men, is condoned by society; and to sacrifice your life to appease your own sense of shame—does society, though not demanding it, entirely disapprove of it? Don't we all have in our hearts and on our lips that instinctive cry of conscience in the face of infamous behavior, "How can you, how dare you go on living after that?" Isn't the man who commits a crime, and then kills himself, halfway absolved? Someone who has done a grave wrong to another and who, unable to make amends, condemns himself to atone for it through suicide, isn't he to be pitied and to some extent redeemed? The bankrupt who survives the ruin of his trustees is sullied with a permanent stain; only his voluntary death can demonstrate the probity of his conduct or the reality of the disaster. This may sometimes be an exaggerated point of honor, but it is a point of honor. When suicide is the product of well-founded remorse, is it just another scandal for the world? The world—rather the attitude of established societies—does not consistently see it that way, since by the pardon it grants, the world considers suicide a reparation for a bad example and a tribute rendered to public morality.

Deschartres granted me all that, but he was put off when I pushed further. "Now, it can happen," I said, "as a consequence of what we have accepted, that a soul enamored of goodness and truth senses, nevertheless, within itself some evil instinct; and such a soul, subject to evil, might not be able to promise, in spite of its remorse and resolutions, not to have recourse to evil for the rest of its life. Then, it may consider itself with disgust and disdain, and not only desire death but seek it as the only method to avoid the evil."

"Oh, be careful," said Deschartres. "Right now you're getting really fatalistic. And what do you say to free will, you who are Christian?"

"I admit that, today," I answered, "I feel doubts more distressing than I can say, and I ask no better than that you address them. Doesn't what happened to me a while ago prove that you can be led toward bodily death by a phenomenon in which conscience and will have no part at all and where God's help seems not to intervene?"

"Do you conclude from that that if physical instinct can cause us to seek physical death, moral instinct can push us in the same way toward moral death? The conclusion is false. Moral instinct is more important than physical instinct, which is unthinking. Reason is all-powerful, not only always over physical evil, which numbs and paralyzes it, but over moral evil, which has no strength against it. Those who do evil are people deprived of reason. Strengthen the reason within yourself, and you'll be safe from all dangers which conspire against it, and you'll even overcome your blood and nerve disorders; you'll prevent them, at the very least, by this moral and physical practice."

This time I acknowledged that Deschartres was completely right; later, however, I had many soul-searching doubts. I believed that free will existed in healthy minds but that its exercise could be hampered by circumstances entirely beyond our control, which our wills might fight against in vain. It was not my fault if I was tempted by death. It could be that I had helped this evil exist through a regimen overly stimulating to both mind and body, but the fact was I had been deprived of counsel and rest. My sickness was the inevitable consequence of my grandmother's illness.

Since my immersion in the river, my obsession with drowning had faded, but in spite of Deschartres' medical and intellectual care, the attraction to suicide persisted in other forms. Sometimes I had a strange feeling when handling firearms or loading pistols; sometimes the vials of laudanum which I was in contact with while preparing endless washes for my grandmother brought on new vertigo.

I do not remember too well how I got rid of my obsession. It happened by itself, with a little more rest which I afforded my mind and with Deschartres managing to provide me more sleep by sitting up with my grandmother more than once in my place. I thus succeeded in forgetting my fixed idea, and perhaps reading the Greek and Latin classics that Deschartres assigned me helped. History takes us out of ourselves, especially history of times long past and lost civilizations. I often cleared my mind with Plutarch,

Titus Livy, Herodotus, etc. I also passionately loved Virgil in French and Tacitus in Latin. Horace and Cicero were Deschartres' gods. He explicated them for me, since I persisted in not wanting to study Latin over again. Thus he read for me his favorite passages with a decisiveness, clarity, and color which I have never heard since.

I also found it a pleasant distraction to write lots of letters—to my brother, Madame Alicia, Élisa, Mme. de Pontcarré, and several of my friends who were still at the convent or, like myself, had left for good. Earlier, I had not been up to the numerous convent correspondents who provoked and vied for my attention, and it had not taken too long before the majority of them forgot me. Thus, only a few choice friends remained. I have kept almost all their letters, which are sweet souvenirs for me, even from people of whom I have completely lost track. Those from Madame Alicia are simple and always affectionate. They date from 1820 to 1830. Imbued with the sweet tranquility of religious life, they have for the most part a tone of cheerfulness which attests the constant serenity of that good soul. She always calls me "my dear child," or "my dear torment," just like the times when I used to get scolded in her cell.[7]

There is a great deal of wit, gaiety, or charm in the girls' letters I have saved. To brighten the melancholy fabric of my story, I shall quote some sections showing the mischievous and gracious manner of one of these amiable classmates.[29]

Angers, April 5, 1821.

I really envy you, dear Aurore, the pleasure of riding horseback through the fields. I torment my sweet papa so that he will get me a horse, because I dream of myself in a cocked cap. I have wrung a promise from him. Meanwhile, I stride through our immense town gardens on foot. 'Would you believe, my dear,' as we used to say in class, that there are broad expanses, straight avenues, incredibly long terraces, and towers which overlook a kind of promenade where lots of people pass and where I often go to watch? Since the town hall was once an abbey, there are still—in a walled-in part of the gardens, which is like a big garden separated from the rest—old ivy-clad church ruins, yew trees sculpted to points, and long dark paths bordered by tall lime trees. Everything reminds you of monks in this place where nothing has been changed, and I picture them reading their services in these shadows where I love to daydream or recite Tasso's verses. . . . Those of Dante, which you sent me, seemed magnificent to me, and I never get tired of rereading them. No, really, I no longer sing

> Già riede la primavera,
> Col suo fiorito aspetto.
> [The flowery face of spring
> Is already laughing.]

But I still like Metastasio. . . . Goodnight, my little Aurore. I am going to bed, even though it is only nine-thirty, as I do not feel at all disposed, like you, to spend my nights working. I have no consuming interest except my pleasure. . . .

June 17.

A few days ago I went to what one calls here a *tantarare*. It is made up of a company of older people who play Boston in a very badly-lit room. Some young people, who've accompanied their mothers, yawn or are dying to. As for me, my lot was bearable. By chance I found myself next to a friendly young woman my own age. We chatted a lot. You would have been astonished to hear us arguing about French history! Since it is not my best subject, I turned the conversation to the period which I like best, the Age of Chivalry. Then we searched for men among those whom we know worthy of the handsome title of knight, and we were not able to find more than two or three. Then we had to give them ladies—the task appeared too difficult for us, although deep down each of us thought she was one.... You ask if I'm still writing verse. Not really. I left the taste for that in the convent, where the only romances for me to sing were those I composed myself. Now it is a great pleasure to be able to sing all the ones I want.... What? You're shooting pistols at a target with your friend Hippolyte? And to think that I used to brag to you about gunpowder burns! You are certainly much more spoiled than I, and I am going to complain to my papa, who says I cannot have bullets. He thinks the noise and the heat will do permanent damage!... For example, I still detest needlework. I realize, however, that it is certainly necessary for a woman, but I have found a kind of work which I do like—spinning. I have a charming little spinning wheel with a pretty ebony distaff, which is certainly the equal of Amélie's rosewood distaff in *Gaston de Foix*[30].... But are you ever lucky to have a horse of your own! As far as animals go, I have only a turtle dove who takes care of waking me in the morning by flying over my bed.... I scarcely share your singular desire to go back to the convent. As far as nuns go, I only liked Poulette, but the new Mother Superior, not at all. It always amazes me that you can bear to remember her, as I could not become attached to her but for the love of God.... I have heard from Mary Gillibrand. She's at Sacré Coeur and still as nasty as she was with us. That is another person you used to like whom I cannot abide. It seems that she is very happy in her new pension telling all the horrid tricks she used to play on our old boarders on Rue des Boulangers.

December 27.

... I only get our convent news from you, and you are the only one with whom I can indulge in idle chatter, since Madame Eugénie's letter inspection prevents me from writing further to the friends we left behind. I would have to use too much restraint in my letters. For instance, I would not dare, for anything in the world, talk to them about M. de La Morandaye, who is now (in the absence of M. de Lauzun) the only handsome dancer in the Calvados regiment. ... You will easily picture him when I tell you that he and I are like two peas in a pod, especially at a dance, where both of us have very high color. We are the same height. Like me, he is a little plump. He has blondish hair and little half-closed blue eyes. Lastly, when we dance together people take him for my brother. Mama says that if she had married two or three years earlier, she could have had an equally charming son. . . . At the last ball I attended, there were three officers, one of whom was M. Gilbert des Voisins. He was wearing wide red pants and little green laced boots, which made me want him to ask me to dance, but this was a wish he did not share . . . one does not dance during Advent. Mama gave some concerts where we shone, as you can imagine. I was very nervous, but the audience here is scarcely expert. My harp is very good, although no bigger than yours at the convent. It has a charming tone. It is made of gray satinwood and all gilded. I still sing a little, and people say my small voice is due to my shyness.

January 18, 1821.

It is past three o'clock. I have left the ball, and while the maid undresses mama, I have time to begin a letter to my little Aurore. Since opposites attract, I like to chat with you, and I want to tell you about this evening's pleasures while they are still warm and vibrant. Alas! Despite all I may say to work you up, the pleasures were not unmixed. Again I danced with everyone except those little green boots, which had been my temptation. And as obstacles heighten one's fantasies, I want him more than ever. I really need to rest after three balls in a row. It is a chaotic life, and perhaps you are right not to want one like it. But spending the winter alone in the country—the thought of it is terrifying! I don't think I would have the courage. Life is all rosy around me, and I imagine that reflection would make me sad.

The person who wrote me thus was extremely pretty, despite her self-mockery. True, she was a bit fat and mildly cross-eyed, but this did not keep her from being light on her feet and having the sweetest expression and the loveliest eyes. Her voice was small, but she sang marvelously. She had a quizzical nature, filled with good will, and saw the amusing side of everything. She was highly original, loving pleasure without being a coquette, and speaking her mind quite forcefully at times without losing an exquisite reserve in her manners and behavior.

These charming girlish missives would sometimes arrive at the same time as an argumentation in materialist philosophy from Claudius and an exhortation filled with sweet unction from Abbé de Prémord. My intellectual life was thus certainly varied, and if I was sometimes sad, I was never in the least bit bored. On the contrary, even in the midst of my greatest disgust with existence, I used to complain about the rapidity of passing time, which was never long enough to hold everything with which I wanted to fill it.

I always loved music. In my room I had a piano, a harp, and a guitar. I no longer had the time to practice, but I read through many scores. Though my situation made it impossible for me to pursue my talent in any way, at least I assured myself a source of great pleasure by getting used to reading and interpreting music.

I also wanted to learn geology and mineralogy. Deschartres used to fill my room with quarry stones. I learned only to see and observe the natural details he pointed out to me, for there was never enough time. That would have required the recovery of our dear invalid.

Toward the end of autumn she became very calm, and though I still deluded myself with hope, Deschartres regarded this improvement as a new step in her deterioration. My grandmother was not, however, at an age where recovery would have been impossible. She was seventy-five and had only been sick once in her life. The depletion of her strength and her faculties was thus rather mysterious. Deschartres attributed this absence of recuperative power to poor blood circulation in a system of too-narrow vessels. One ought rather to have attributed it to an absence of will and to a gradual wearing away of her spirit since the unbearable sorrow of losing her son.

The whole month of December was gloomy. She no longer got up and rarely spoke. Yet since we were used to being sad, we were not afraid. Deschartres thought she might live like this for a long time—in a limbo between life and death. On December 22nd, she awakened me in order to give me a knife with a mother-of-pearl handle, without being able to explain why she had thought of it or why she had wanted to see me have it. She no longer had any clear thoughts. Yet she roused herself once more in order to tell me, "You are losing your best friend."

Those were her last words. A leaden sleep fell over her calm face, which was still fresh and pretty. She never woke again, and died at daybreak without any suffering, at the sound of the Christmas bells.

Neither Deschartres nor I cried. When her heart stopped beating and her breath stopped clouding the mirror, it had been three days since we had last cried for her, but in this supreme moment we felt nothing but the satisfaction of thinking she had passed over the threshold to a better life, without physical suffering or anguish. I had dreaded the horror of a death agony—Providence spared her that. There had been no struggle between the flesh and the spirit. Perhaps her soul had already flown off to God on the wings of a dream that reunited her with her son while we were watching over her unfeeling corpse.

Julie made her last toilette with the same care as in happier days. She put on her lace bonnet, her ribbons, and her rings. The custom where we lived was to bury the dead with a crucifix and prayer book. I brought those I had favored at the convent. When she was adorned for the grave, she was still beautiful. No rictus had altered her noble features. Her expression was one of sublime tranquillity.

During the night Deschartres called to me; he was very excited and said to me in a strained voice, "Are you brave? Don't you think the dead deserve a service even more tender than prayers and tears? Don't you believe the dead can see us from on high and that they are touched by the faithfulness of our sorrows? If you believe this, come with me."

It was about one in the morning. It was a clear cold night. The frost on top of the snow made walking so difficult that, crossing the courtyard and entering the cemetery that bordered it, we fell several times.

"Be calm," Deschartres said to me, still excited beneath a strange appearance of sang-froid. "You are going to see the one who was your father." We approached the grave, opened to receive my grandmother. Under a small vault made of rough stones was a coffin which the second one would join in a few hours.

"I wanted to see it," said Deschartres, "and monitor the workers who dug this grave today. Your father's coffin is still intact; only the nails have fallen out. When I was alone, I had the urge to lift the lid. I saw the skeleton. The head had come away by itself. I lifted it up and kissed it. I took such great comfort from that—I, who had not been able to receive a last kiss from him—I said to myself that perhaps you had not received one either. Tomorrow this grave will be closed. They will probably never open it again except when you die. You have to go down there, you have to kiss that relic. It will be a lifetime memory. Someday, you will have to write your father's life story, even if it is only for your children, who will not have known him. Show a sign of love and respect now to one whom you scarcely knew yourself and who loved you so much. I tell you, from where he is now he will see you and bless you."

I was sufficiently moved and excited myself to find perfectly reasonable what my poor tutor was saying to me. I felt no repugnance at all; I found nothing bizarre in it. I would have been remorseful and angry with him had he not acted on his impulse. We climbed down into the open grave, and I followed his example and religiously performed the act of devotion.

"Do not speak of this to anyone," he said to me, still outwardly calm after having closed the coffin and as we were leaving the cemetery. "They would think us crazy, and yet we were not, were we?"

"No, certainly not," I answered with conviction.

From that moment on, I observed that Deschartres' beliefs had changed completely. He had always been a materialist, which he had not succeeded in hiding from me, although he had taken pains to find neutral terms in his vocabulary to avoid explaining his position on the Divinity and the immateriality of the human soul. My grandmother was a deist, as they said in her time, and had not allowed him to turn me into an atheist. He had had great difficulty not doing so, and had I once been drawn toward negation, he might have confirmed it in spite of himself.

But within him a sudden and characteristically radical turnabout took place, for soon afterward I heard him forcefully uphold the authority of the Church. His conversion had been a change of heart, like mine. In the presence of the cold bones of a loved one, he had not been able to accept the horror of the void. With the death of my grandmother reviving the memory of my father's death, he found himself before a double grave, crushed by the two greatest griefs of his life, and his soul had ardently protested, in spite of his cold reason, against the sentence of eternal separation.

During the day that followed the night of strange solemnity, together we escorted the remains of the mother to those of the son. All the friends came and all the villagers attended. But the noise, the vacant faces, the battling of beggars who, anxious to receive the usual distribution, pushed us almost into the grave, in order to be the first to receive alms; the greetings of condolence, the true or false airs of compassion, the loud weeping, and the banal exclamations of some well-meaning servants—in short, everything which was formal and made a show of regret—pained me and seemed disrespectful. I was impatient for everyone to leave. I felt infinitely indebted to Deschartres for having taken me there during the night to pay my solemn and profound respects to that tomb.

In the evening, the whole household, overcome by fatigue, went to bed early. Deschartres himself was spent by an emotion which had taken a completely new form in his life. I did not feel overwhelmed. I had been deeply moved by death's majesty; my emotions, at one with my beliefs, had been sad but peaceful. I wanted to see my grandmother's room again and to devote this last night of vigil to her memory, as I had devoted so many others to her presence.

As soon as all sounds in the house had ceased, and when I was certain I was the only one still up, I went downstairs and shut myself in her room. No one had yet thought of putting it in order. The bed was unmade, and the first detail I noted was the clear imprint that showed on the mattress and sheet from the inert weight of her dead body. There I saw the hollowed outline of her shape. Pressing my lips to it, it seemed to me I could still feel death's chill.

Half-empty vials were still on her bedside table. The odor of the incense they had burned around the corpse filled the air. It smelled like benjamin, always her favorite, which had been brought back to her from India in a coconut shell by M. Dupleix. There was still some left; I burned it. I arranged the vials as they were the last time she had asked for them, and I drew the curtains half way, as she was wont to request. I lit the night-light, which still contained some oil. I stoked the fire, which had not yet gone out. I stretched out in the large armchair, and I pretended she was still there and that by trying to doze off perhaps I would once again hear her feeble voice calling to me.

I did not sleep, but two or three times I seemed to hear her breathing and the kind of waking moan which my ears knew so well. But nothing distinct materialized in my imagination, which was too greedy for some sweet vision to attain the exaltation which might, in itself, have produced it.

In my childhood, I had had bouts of terror over ghosts, and at the convent some apprehensions had come back. Since my return to Nohant, all that had so completely vanished that I missed it, fearing that my imagination would henceforth become insensitive to poetry. The religious and romantic act which Deschartres had helped me perform the night before could easily have brought back my childhood fears, but far from that, it had filled me with total despair at ever being able to communicate directly with the beloved dead. I never thought that my grandmother would actually appear, but I may have deluded myself into thinking that my tired head might feel a kind of vertigo which would cause me to see her face again, shining with an aura of eternal life.

But nothing came. The north wind whistled outside, the foot-warmer sang on the hearth, and so did the cricket which my grandmother had never allowed Deschartres to harass even though it often awakened her. The pendulum sounded the hours. The repeater watch fastened to the invalid's night table, which she often consulted with her finger, remained silent. I finally felt a fatigue which sent me off into a deep sleep.

But when I woke up several hours later, the reality of her death had left me, and I roused myself to see whether she was sleeping peacefully. Then the memory came back to me along with soothing tears with which I covered the pillow still bearing the imprint of the shape of her head. Then I left the room where seals were affixed the following day and which seemed to me profaned by these materialistic formalities.   *L.K.P.*

VII

My guardian. —The arrival of my mother and my aunt. —A strange
change in relationships. —The reading of the will. —An illegal
clause. —My mother's resistance. —I leave Nohant. —Paris,
Clotilde. —1823. —Deschartres in Paris. —My vow. —A break
with my father's family. —My cousin Auguste. —A divorce from
nobility. —Domestic trials.

My cousin René de Villeneuve, then my mother, with my aunt and uncle
Maréchal, arrived a few days later. They came to be present at the reading of
the will and the removal of the seals. My new existence was going to depend
on the contents of this will. I am not speaking in terms of money—that was not
on my mind, and besides my grandmother had provided for that—but rather in
terms of who was going to replace her as my guardian.

She had wanted above all that I not be entrusted to my mother, and the
manner in which she had explained it during the period of full lucidity when
she had drafted her last will had greatly upset me. "Your mother," she had said,
"is stranger than you think, and you do not know her at all. She is so uncivilized that she loves her children the way birds do, with great care and ardor
during early infancy, but when they have wings, when it is a matter of reasoning and using instinctive tenderness, she flies to another tree and pecks at them,
chasing them away. You could not live with her now for three days without
feeling terribly unhappy. Her disposition, her education, her tastes, her habits,
her ideas will shock you completely when she is no longer held in check by my
authority standing between the two of you. Do not expose yourself to such
grief; do consent to live with your father's family. They want to care for you
after my death. Your mother will very willingly agree to this, as you may
already suspect, and you will maintain a cordial and lasting relationship with
her, which you would not have at all if the two of you become too close. They
tell me that by a clause in my will I can entrust the remainder of your education and the responsibility for settling you to René de Villeneuve, whom I am
naming your guardian, but I want you to agree in advance to this arrangement,
because Mme. de Villeneuve, especially, would never be willing to take on the
care of a young person who would only reluctantly go to live with her."

During these moments of brief, but lucent, wisdom, I was completely
under my grandmother's influence. What also gave great weight to her words
was my mother's singular and even hurtful attitude, her refusal to comfort me
in my suffering, the lack of pity my grandmother's state inspired in her, and the

kind of mocking, sometimes threatening, bitterness of her rare and exceptionally irritated letters. Not having merited this suppressed anger that seemed to
smolder within her, I was upset over it, and I was forced to admit that she was
either unfair or peculiar. I knew that my sister Caroline was not at all happy
with her, and my mother had written, "Caroline is going to be married. She is
tired of living with me. I think, after all, that I'll be freer and happier when I
am living alone."

My cousin had come soon after to spend a fortnight with us. I think that
in order to make up his mind, or at least to convince his wife to take charge of
me, he had wanted to get to know me better. For my part, I also wanted to get
to know this adoptive father whom I had not seen very much since my childhood. I had always found his kindness and gracious manners appealing, but I
needed to know if behind this pleasant exterior there was not a store of beliefs,
of whatever kind, which might be irreconcilable with those that had developed
within me.

He was cheerful, had a charmingly balanced disposition, a pleasant and
cultivated wit, and such exquisite politeness that people of all ranks were grati-
fied or moved by him. He was very well read and had such a reliable memory
that he had retained, I believe, all the verse he had ever read. He asked me
about my reading, and as soon as I mentioned a poet, he would effortlessly
recite—with a charming voice and diction, and no hint of declamation—some
of the most beautiful passages. He had no intolerance at all in matters of taste
and enjoyed Ossian as much as Gresset.[31] His conversation was always an open
book which offered you a chosen page.

He liked walking in the countryside. At that time he was only forty-five,
but since he did not look more than thirty, they never failed to say at La
Châtre, seeing us ride together, that he was my intended and that this was yet
another impertinence on my part, to ride alone with him, thumbing my nose at
the world.

In him I found no provincial narrow-minded prejudice nor petty judgments. He had always lived in the world at large, and my eccentricities did not
offend him in the least. He did pistol-shooting with me, he allowed himself to
read and chat until two or three in the morning, he challenged me to jump
ditches on horseback, he did not make fun of my philsophical essays, and he
even encouraged me to write—assuring me that writing was my vocation and
that I would acquit myself admirably in it.

Following his advice, I again tried to write a novel, but this one did not
fare any better than those I had written at the convent. There was no love in it.
It was always a fiction apart from me, one which I felt unable to depict. The
writing held me for a while, and I gave it up when it started to turn into a treatise. I felt as pedantic as a book, and not wishing to be so, preferred to keep
silent and carry on inwardly the eternal poem of Corambé, where I felt myself
true to my emotions.

Finding my guardian so conciliatory and such agreeable company, I never
dreamed that a battle of ideas could begin between us. At that time, my philosophical ideas were entirely speculative. I did not believe in the possibility of

their general application. They elicited neither alarm nor personal antipathy in those who did not pay them serious attention. My cousin laughed at my liberalism and was scarcely angry about it. He recognized the new court[32] but remained attached to memories of the Empire, and since, at that time, bonapartism and liberalism were both often based in the same instinct for opposition, he confessed to me that the believers and obscurantists of the new court made him nauseous and that he could hardly bear the religious and monarchical intolerance of some salons.

He made me certain recommendations about respect and deference toward Mme. de Villeneuve, which made me think he was not the absolute master in his own house, but my cousin, his wife, was not a believer at that time, and especially valued good manners and breeding. Since I worried about my country ways, he assured me that they did not show when I did not want them to and that it was only a question of persisting in not wanting them to show. "As for the rest," he said, "if you sometimes find your cousin a bit severe, you should sacrifice your schoolgirl's vanity to her momentary demands, and as soon as she's seen you give in gracefully, she'll reward you with fairness and generosity. Chenonceaux will seem an earthly paradise to you who've never seen anything; and if you have a few bad moments, I shall manage to make you forget them. I feel you'll be charming company for me—we'll read, discuss, gad about, and laugh together as well—for I see that you, too, tend to be cheerful when you don't have too many things to be anxious about."

I entrusted my future to him with great confidence. He assured me, too, that his daughter Emma (Mme. de La Roche-Aymon) shared the same special feeling I had always had for her, and we three would forget the pressures of society, which pleased the two of them as little as it did me.

He had also spoken to me about my mother, without bitterness and in very fitting terms, confirming all my grandmother had said to me about her lack of desire to have me with her. Far from recommending a complete break, he encouraged me to carry on with my deference toward her. "Only," he told me, "since the link between you seems to be weakening by itself, don't strengthen it again unwittingly, don't write to her more than she appears to want you to, and don't complain about the coldness she shows you. That is the best thing that could happen."

This advice was painful to me. In spite of all I could find in it which was wise and perhaps necessary for my mother's own happiness, my heart always felt a passionate impulse toward her, followed by dismal sadness. It was not that I thought she didn't love me; I sensed that the grudge she held against me for loving my grandmother meant that she, too, was jealous in her way, but her way frightened me; I did not understand it. Until recently, my preference for her had been only too well demonstrated.

Several months later and the day after my grandmother's death, when my cousin René returned to take me away, I had indeed made up my mind to go with him. However, my mother's arrival overwhelmed me. Her first embraces were so warm and sincere—and I was also so happy to see my little

Aunt Lucie again, with her working class speech, her good cheer and high spirits, her frankness and motherly pampering—that I flattered myself into thinking I had rediscovered my childhood dream of happiness in the bosom of the maternal family.

But scarcely had a quarter of an hour elapsed when my mother, very irritated by the fatigue of the trip, by M. de Villeneuve's presence, by Deschartres' scowl, and especially by her unhappy memories of Nohant, vented all her heart's stored-up bitterness against my grandmother. She was incapable of containing herself, in spite of my aunt's efforts to calm her and laugh off the effect of what she called "Sophie's excesses." My mother made me see that a rift had opened, unknown to me, between us, and that the ghost of the poor dead woman would remain there a long time and drive us to despair.

Her tirade against my grandmother left me aghast. I had heard it all before, but I had not really understood. All that my mother's accusations had signified to me was that my grandmother had some blameworthy harshness along with tolerable foibles. Now that poor sainted woman was accused of being vicious! My mother—I, too, must say it—my poor mother would say the most appalling things in anger.

My firm resistance to this torrent of injustice only provoked her. Certainly, I was very emotional inside, but seeing her so overwrought, I thought I should contain myself and show her, from the first outburst, an unshakable will to respect the memory of my benefactress. Since my revolt against my mother's feelings was offensive enough to her spleen, I believed that no amount of apparent civility, calm, or control over my secret indignation could be excessive.

This effort of reason, this sacrifice of my own inner anger to a feeling of duty, was precisely the worst tactic I could have imagined with respect to a nature like my mother's. It would have been better to be like her, to scream, rage, smash things—in short, to frighten her—to make her believe I was as violent as she and that she could not get the better of me.

"You're going about it all wrong," my aunt said to me when we were alone together. "You're too calm and proud. That's not the way to behave with my sister. I'm on to her! She's my big sister, and she would have made me very unhappy during my childhood and youth if I'd acted like you. Whenever I used to see her in a bad mood, spoiling for a fight, I used to tease and make fun of her, until she'd practically explode. That speeded things up. Then, when I felt her really worked up, I'd get angry too. And suddenly, I'd say to her, 'That's enough. Want to hug and make up? Hurry up, or I'm leaving.' She would come around right away, and the fear of seeing me start again would prevent her from starting too often herself."

I was not able to profit from this advice. I was not the sister, hence the equal, of this ardent, unlucky woman. I was her daughter. I could not forget filial sentiment and respect. When she returned to her senses, so did all the signs of my affection, but it was impossible for me to precipitate this return by kissing lips still warm with insults against someone I adored.

The reading of the will brought on new outbursts. Forewarned by a betrayer of all my grandmother's confidences (I have never found out who it

was), my mother had known for a long time about the clause which would separate me from her. She also knew about my compliance with this clause—
hence her anger in advance.

She feigned total ignorance until the last moment, and my cousin and I
were still deluding ourselves that the sort of aversion she was showing toward
me would make her readily accept the testamentary disposition, but she had
fully armed herself to hear the reading. No doubt someone had prejudiced her
in advance and persuaded her to see in the clause an insult which she must not
accept. She thus stated in no uncertain terms that she would not allow herself
to be declared unfit to keep her daughter, that she knew the clause to be a nullity since she was my natural and legitimate guardian, that she would go to
court, and that neither entreaties nor threats would make her renounce her right
over me, which was, in effect, complete and absolute.

Who could have told me five years earlier that this much desired reunion
would be a grief and unhappiness for me? She now reminded me about my old
passion for her and bitterly reproached me for having allowed my heart to be
corrupted by my grandmother and Deschartres. "Oh, my poor mother!" I cried.
"Why didn't you take me at my word then? Then I wouldn't have regretted a
thing. I would have left everything for you. Why did you deceive my hopes
and desert me so utterly? I confess I doubted your affection. And now see what
you are doing—you're breaking, you're mortally wounding the very heart you
claim to want to heal and restore! You know that it took four years for me to
forget my grandmother's momentary injustice toward you, and now every day,
all day, you shower me with your injustices toward her!"

However, as I actually submitted to her desire to keep me with her, she
appeared to calm down. My cousin's extraordinary politeness now and again
disarmed her. She did not completely close her mind to the idea of allowing me
to return to the convent as a boarder, and I wrote to Madame Alicia and to the
Mother Superior about it, in order to have a retreat ready to take me in as soon
as I had received permission to go.

There was no vacant lodging available at the English sisters. They would
gladly have taken me in as a student boarder, but my mother did not want that,
saying she was counting on my coming and going without being encumbered
by rules and regulations, that she wanted to marry me off in her own way, and
consequently did not want her relations with me impeded by a convent grille
and gatekeeper.

My cousin left me, telling me to be brave and persist sweetly and deftly
in my desire to go to the convent. He promised me he would see about getting
me lodged at Sacré Coeur or Abbaye-aux-Boix.

My mother would not hear of staying with me at Nohant, even less of
leaving me there with Deschartres, who was to stay on as a farmer, still having
a year's lease remaining, and Julie, who was keeping her lodging there according to the wish expressed by my grandmother. My mother only knew how to
live in Paris; and though she had a true feeling for the poetry of the fields, a
love and talent for gardening, and great simplicity in her tastes, she was at an
age when habits are ingrained. She needed the noise of the street and the bustle

of the boulevard. My sister had just recently gotten married; my mother and I were to live in my grandmother's apartment on Rue Neuve-des-Mathurins.

I left Nohant with pangs of regret like those I had felt when I left the English sisters. I was leaving behind all my studious habits, all my heart's memories, and my poor Deschartres, alone and numb with sorrow.

My mother let me take only a few of my favorite books. She had a deep distrust for what she called my "originality." However, she did allow me to keep my chambermaid, Sophie, to whom I was attached, and to bring along my dog.

I do not know what circumstance prevented us from moving right away to Rue Neuve-des-Mathurins. Perhaps there was a removal of seals in order. We went to my aunt's on Rue de Bourgogne and spent two weeks there before moving into my grandmother's apartment.

It was a great consolation for me to see my cousin Clotilde again—beautiful and kind soul, firm, courageous, tactful, faithful to her affections, endowed with a charming disposition, sustained cheerfulness, talent, and a knowledge of the human heart preferable to the one found in books. No matter how caught up in domestic storms we were at that time, there was never then nor since any cloud between us. She, too, found me somewhat original, but she deemed that very nice, very amusing, and loved me as I was.

Her sweet gaiety was balm for me. However miserable or prematurely serious you are, at seventeen you need to laugh and frolic in order to exist. Ah! If I had had this adorable companion at Nohant, I would perhaps never have read such beautiful things, but I would have loved life and been more accepting of it.

We played a lot of music together, teaching each other what we knew. I taught her how to read, and she taught me how to say the words. Her voice, a bit husky, was extremely supple, and she had an easy and pleasant diction. When I sat with her at the piano, I forgot everything.

At this time an event occurred which impressed me a great deal, not that it was really important, but because it brought me face to face, at the start of my adult life, with a preview of certain probabilities. Deschartres was called upon to render an account of his administration at a family meeting. This happened at my aunt's home. My uncle, who did things bluntly and was my mother's advisor, found a deficiency in the farm's payments, a three-year lapse, consequently eighteen thousand francs owed by Deschartres. A lawyer had been called in to this meeting for reasons I no longer remember.

In brief, Deschartres had not paid for three years. I do not know whether, out of tolerance, or fear of letting him be ruined, my grandmother had ever given him receipts for portions of the debt. But such receipts could not be found. I myself had never taken any payment from him and thus had never given him any receipt.

As I have mentioned, the poor man had purchased a small property on the heathland not far from us. Since he had more imagination than luck in his undertakings, he had wrongly imagined his fortune to be there. It was not that he loved money, but rather that all his knowledge and self-esteem were tied up in the prospect of transforming a sparse, uncultivated terrain into rich luxuriant land. He had thrown himself hastily into this farming venture with faith that it could not fail. Things had gone wrong, his steward had stolen from him. And then, thinking to do right by both of us, he had wanted to exchange our live-stock with his. He brought us lean cattle which did not fatten up with us, or which died of overeating in a few days. He sent to his place our greedy and spoiled beasts which could not get used to his gorse and broom, and rapidly wasted away. It was the same with grain and everything else. All in all, his land had brought him little, and Nohant even less, relatively speaking. Consid-erable and repeated losses had made it necessary for him to sell his small prop-erty, but he could not find a buyer and make good his arrears.

I knew all that, even though he had never spoken to me about it. My grandmother had warned me about it, and I knew that we lived at Nohant only because of the revenue from the house on Rue de la Harpe and from some gov-ernment pensions.

Those resources had not been sufficient for my grandmother's habits; besides, her illness had occasioned rather large expenditures. There was gen-uine financial need in the house, and not having the wherewithal to replenish my wardrobe, I arrived in Paris with as many belongings as could fit in a pock-et handkerchief, plus a single dress for all occasions.

Deschartres, unable to furnish his wretched receipts, to which no one had previously given a second thought, arrived to explain or try to explain his situ-ation, or obtain a reprieve. He seemed extremely worried. I wished I could have spent a minute alone with him to reassure him; my mother saw to it we didn't, and the interrogation began around a table piled high with ledgers and papers.

My mother, strongly biased against the poor tutor and eager to give back to him in full measure everything he had made her suffer in the past, felt a hor-rible kind of joy in witnessing his embarrassment. Above all, she wanted to make him look dishonest in my eyes. Her major complaint to me was that I did not share her aversion.

I saw that the situation was desperate. My mother had let slip the words "debtor's prison"; I hoped she would not carry out such a dire threat, for the proud Deschartres, his honor attacked, was capable of blowing his brains out. His pale, tense face was that of a man who had made such a decision.

I did not let him answer. I declared that he had paid me and that in the troubled state that my grandmother's health had put us, neither of us had ever thought about the formalities of receipts.

My mother rose, her eyes blazing and her voice choked, "So, you received eighteen thousand francs," she said. "Where is the money?"

"Apparently, I spent it, since I no longer have it."

"You must show it or prove how it was spent."

I consulted the lawyer and asked him if, as sole beneficiary, I had to ren-der accounts to myself and if my guardian had the right to demand accounts of my management of my grandmother's revenues.

"Certainly not," replied the lawyer. "There are no questions to ask of you in that regard. I ask only about the existence of your receipts. You are a minor and haven't the right to forgive a debt. Your guardian has the right to insist that the debt be paid to you."

This response gave me back the strength I had almost lost. To fall back on a series of lies and fabricated explanations would perhaps not have been possible for me. But from the minute that it was a question of persisting with a Yes to save Deschartres, I believed I ought not to hesitate. I do not know if he was in as great danger as I imagined. No doubt they would have given him time to sell his property in order to pay off the debt, and even if he had sold it for a low price, he still had the allowance left to him in my grandmother's will to live on.[8] But the idea of dishonor and debtor's prison shocked me.

My mother said, as the lawyer had suggested, "If Monsieur Deschartres paid you eighteen thousand francs, we'll certainly know about it. You wouldn't swear to it, would you?"

I shivered, and I saw Deschartres ready to confess everything.

"I would swear to it!" I exclaimed.

"Swear to it then," my aunt said to me, who thought me sincere and wanted to see an end to the interrogation.

"No, don't," responded the lawyer.

"I want her to swear to it!" exclaimed my mother, whom I later had great difficulty forgiving for having inflicted this torture on me.

"I swear to it," I answered her, very emotionally, "and God is on my side against you this time!"

"She lied! She's lying!" cried my mother. "Pious prig! Philosophist! She's lying and stealing from herself!"

"Oh, as far as that goes," said the lawyer, with a smile, "she certainly has the right and is only defrauding her dowry."

"I'll take her and her Deschartres, too, to a justice of the peace," said my mother. "I'll make her take an oath in the name of Christ, on the Bible!"

"No, Madame," said the lawyer, calm as a businessman. "Leave it for now."

"And as for you, Mademoiselle," he said to me with a kind of benevolence due either to approval or pity for my lack of self-interest, "I am sorry for having tormented you. Since I am responsible for upholding your interests, I felt myself obliged to. But no one here has the right to put your word in doubt, and I think we should let the whole matter drop."

I really do not know what he thought about all this. I had not been concerned with that and had no experience in reading the face of a lawyer. Deschartres' debt was crossed off the ledger, we took care of other things, and we parted.

I managed to get a moment alone on the stairs with my poor tutor. "Aurore," he said to me with tears in his eyes, "I shall pay you back; you know that, don't you?"

"Certainly, I'm sure of it," I answered, seeing that he was feeling slightly humiliated. "A fine affair! In two or three years, your property will be at full yield."

"Of course! Absolutely!" he cried, giving himself over to the joys of his illusions. "In three years, either it will bring in three thousand francs in revenue, or I shall sell it for fifty thousand francs. But I confess that for the time being I can only get twelve thousand, and if they had withheld your grandmother's pension for six years, I would have had to beg for some kind of living. You saved me, you suffered. I thank you."

As long as I could stay at my aunt's, near Clotilde, my existence, despite frequent shocks, was tolerable. But when I moved to Rue Neuve-des-Mathurins, it was no longer so.

My mother, who was irritated by everything I loved, declared that I would not be going to the convent. She let me go there once, to greet the nuns and my classmates, but forbade me to go back. She abruptly dismissed my maid, whom she didn't like, and even got rid of my dog. Him I mourned, for that was the last straw.

M. de Villeneuve came to ask her if I could go to his home for dinner. She answered that Mme. de Villeneuve had only to come herself to make such a request. She was doubtless within her rights, but she spoke so curtly that my cousin lost his temper, told her that his wife would not set foot in her house, and left never to return. I only saw him again more than twenty years later.

Just as my good cousin forgave and still forgives me for not sharing all his ideas, so do I forgive him for having thus abandoned me to my sad fate. Could he have avoided it? I do not know. It would have required a patience on his part which I myself would not have had on my own account, if I had had to deal with my mother. And even if he had silently swallowed her first storm of abuse, wouldn't she have begun again the next day?

However, it took me years, I confess, to forget the way he left me, without even a word of farewell or consolation, without a glance, without offering me any hope, without writing to me the next day to say that I would always find his support when I could call on him. I imagined he was weary of the problems that his powerless guardianship created for him and that he was happy to find an opportunity to be rid of them. I wondered if Mme. de Villeneuve, who was already mature in age, could not have convinced my mother through some semblance of politeness which would have flattered her, to allow me to continue my visits to them; or whether, at the very least, they could not have tried a little more, short of just leaving me there, to inspire some common interest, through trust, to which to have recourse later without fear of seeming importunate. I expected something like that, but it did not happen. My father's family remained silent. The fear of finding their door shut against me kept me from ever knocking at it. Perhaps I had too much pride, but it was impossible for me to concede to making overtures. I was a child, it is true, and although I was not at fault, it was still up to me to make the first step. But you will see what held me back.

My other cousin, Auguste de Villeneuve, René's brother, also came to see me one last time. Although we were not as close, our relationship was for some reason less formal. He, too, was very kind, but a little lacking in tact. I complained to him about René's desertion. "I should say so!" he said to me from his fund of nonchalant composure. "You didn't act the way you were told. They wanted to see you enter the convent; you didn't do it. You go out with your mother, her daughter, her daughter's husband, with Monsieur Pierret. You've been seen on the street with all those people. It's an impossible society. I don't speak for myself—it wouldn't matter to me—but for my sister-in-law, and for women from those honorable families to which we could have gotten you entry via a good marriage."

His frankness clarified for me an important question for my future. I asked how it was possible for me, dealing with a person like my mother, whom the most polite and humble resistance exasperated, to enter a convent against her will, refuse to go out with her, or visit her circle. Since he could not give me a satisfactory answer, I asked him, in addition, if refusing to see my sister, her husband, and Pierret—in case that were possible for me—seemed to him reconcilable with the ties of blood, friendship, and duty.

He did not pursue it. He only said, "I see that you side with your mother's family and that you've made up your mind never to break with those nice people. I thought otherwise! I was wrong."

"At moments of distress and inner rage," I said to him, "I've come to the point of wanting to leave my mother, who makes me very unhappy. And since I don't see that she is happy about our reunion, I would prefer the convent even more, or perhaps I could arrange a marriage for myself which would remove me from her absolute authority. But however wrong she might be, I have resolved always to see her and not become party to any affront made to her."

"Well," he continued, still just as composed, and making nervous grimaces which were habitual with him and seemed to help him gather his ideas and words, "in moral terms, you're right. But the world doesn't work that way. What we call a good match for you is a man of wealth and good breeding. I can assure you that no men like that will come here to find you, and that even when you've waited three years, until you've reached your majority, it will not be any easier for you to marry well than it is today. I certainly would not take on the task—they would fling remarks at me about how you had lived three years with your mother and all kinds of nice people around whom they wouldn't be terribly comfortable. Thus, I advise you to marry yourself off as best you can. What difference does it make to me if you marry a commoner? If he's a good man, I shall certainly see him, and I surely will not love you any less for it. Well, goodbye until then! I see your mother circling around us. She's going to throw me out." Whereupon, he took his hat and left, saying, "Farewell, Aunt!"

I did not hold a grudge against him. He had never been responsible for me. His frankness put me at ease, and his promise of eternal friendship amply consoled me for the loss of a good match. I found him to be as amiably uncaring and calmly good-natured a few years after my marriage.

But this rupture, temporary with him but definitive with the rest of the family, gave me food for thought.

Perhaps I had for some years forgotten who I was and how my royal blood had been diluted in my veins by mingling, in my mother's womb, with plebian blood. I do not believe, I am even certain I did not then believe it was above my station to consider inevitable and natural the idea of entering a noble family, just as I did not believe myself demeaned for no longer having such pretensions. On the contrary, I felt delivered of a great weight. I have always felt repugnance—first through instinct, and later through reason—at becoming part of a caste which exists solely by the negation of equality. Supposing that I had decided on marriage, which was not yet the case, I would, as much as possible, have kept my promise to my grandmother, but without being convinced that one's birth had any serious value, and only in case I had met a nobleman who was free of arrogance and prejudices.

What my cousin Auguste clearly intimated to me was that, by society's standards, things are not like that and cannot be. While admitting that my point of view was, for me, religious and honorable, he declared that it dishonored me in the eyes of society, that no one would forgive me for having done my duty, and that even he himself would not take on the task of finding someone who would sanction me.

Thus, what was I to do according to him and his world? Flee from my mother's house? Let it be known, by some outcry, that she was not making me happy? Or worse still, let it be assumed that my reputation was in danger if I remained near her? That was not so. And had it been, would proclaiming the repercussions of my situation have made me more marriageable in the eyes of my cousins?

If I did not run away, was I to rebel openly against my mother, insult her, threaten her? What did they want me to do? Anything I could have done would have been so impossible and hateful that I still cannot fathom it.

To say I did my duty is doubtless too much of a defense; but if I am emphasizing my personal situation, it is just that I have my heart set on proving what society's good opinion, what the justice of its decisions and the importance of its protection mean.

People always depict those who shake off society's shackles as perverse, or at the very least so proud and blundering that they disturb the established order and ruling custom for the sole pleasure of doing evil. I am, however, one minor example among a thousand important and conclusive ones of the injustice and thoughtlessness of that more or less elite coterie which modestly calls itself society. By using the words "thoughtlessness" and "injustice," I am greatly understating the case; I ought to say "impiety," because, as far as I am concerned, I could not otherwise consider the reprobation that was mine for having performed the most sacred of family duties.

Let it be known that I never laid the blame on my paternal relatives. They belonged to that society; they could not rewrite the code for their use and mine. My grandmother, unable to bring herself to imagine a future for me that was contrary to her wishes, had extracted a promise from them to reinstate me into the caste where, through their wives,[9] the Villeneuves, who were not of old stock, had themselves been reinstated. They found it natural to impose on me the sacrifices they had had to make in order to remain there. But they forgot that, to carry these sacrifices to the point of trampling on filial respect (which they certainly would not have done themselves), I would have needed, over and above a wicked heart and failed conscience, to believe in the principle of inequality.

Well, I did not accept such a principle. I had never understood, never assumed it. From the least beggar to the greatest king, I knew by instinct, by conscience, and especially by the law of Christ, that God had neither placed a seal of nobility nor vassalage on anyone's forehead. Even the gifts of intelligence were nothing before Him without the will to do good, and He allowed innate intelligence to sprout from the brain of a thief as freely as from a prince's.

I wept over my relatives' desertion. I loved them. They were the sons of my father's sister, my father had adored them, my grandmother had blessed them, they had smiled on my childhood. I liked some of their children—Mme. de La Roche-Aymon, René's daughter; Félicie, Auguste's daughter, an adorable creature, who died in the prime of life; her brother, Léonce, who had a charming turn of mind. But I quickly made up my mind about what had to be severed between us—certainly not affectionate family ties, but rather those of shared beliefs and status.

As for the fine marriage they were to arrange for me, I confess it was a great relief to me to be rid of the prospect. I had given my consent to one of Mme. de Pontcarré's proposals, which my mother had rejected. I saw that, on one hand, my mother would never want anything to do with the nobility, and on the other, the nobility wanted no more of me. I finally felt free, by dint of circumstance, to break my promise to my grandmother and follow my own heart when it came to marriage (as my father had done), the day I would feel so inclined.

I was still so far from it that I did not renounce the idea of becoming a nun. My short visit to the convent had revived my ideal of happiness in that direction. I certainly knew I was no longer devout in the way my dear recluses were, but one of them, Madame Françoise, was not either, and passed for a student of science. She lived there as peacefully as a Dominican father of old. The idea of rising, through study and contemplation of the highest truths, above family storms and worldly pettiness, beckoned to me one last time.

It is certainly possible that I would have made that decision at my majority (that is, after a three-year wait) if my life had been tolerable until then. But it became less and less so. My mother would not let herself be moved or persuaded by my submission. She persisted in seeing me as a secretly irreconcilable enemy. At first she gloried in having rid herself of my guardian's control, and mocked me for the despair she attributed to me. She was surprised to see me so completely detached from worldly grandeur, but she suspected it and swore she would "break down my guile."

Suspicious in the extreme and given, in a totally sick and disordered way, to accuse what she did not understand, she provoked incredible quarrels on any pretext. She would rip my books out of my hands, saying that she had tried to read them but had not understood a word, and that they must be bad books. Did she really believe I was an evil or lost soul, or did she simply need to find some pretext for her accusations in order to be able to denigrate the "fine education" I had received? Every day there were new revelations she had discovered about my "perversity."

When I asked her insistently where she had gotten such strange notions about me, she said she had had correspondence with La Châtre and that she had known, daily and hourly, all the disorders of my conduct. I did not believe it; the idea that my poor mother was insane frightened me. One day, she guessed it by the increase of silence and attention, which were my usual responses to her abuse. "I see," she said, "you're pretending to think I'm out of my mind. I'm going to prove to you that I can grasp things clearly and that I'm in full control."

Then she held up a sheaf of correspondence, without letting me see the handwriting, but reading whole pages to me that she certainly was not making up. They were the fabrications of monstrous lies and idiotic delusions that I have already mentioned and that I had derided so at Nohant. The little town's bits of garbage had taken hold of my mother's impressionable imagination; they had become so ingrained there as to destroy the simplest kind of reasoning; they never entirely dissolved until some years later, when she finally saw me without bias, and when all causes for bitterness had disappeared.

She said that she had been thus informed by one of the closest friends of the family. I did not say anything in response; I could not say anything. I felt sick and disgusted. She went to bed, victorious over having crushed me. I went to my room; I stayed there on a chair until daylight, dazed, not thinking of anything, feeling drained altogether in body and soul. *L. K. P.*

VIII

My mother's peculiarity, magnanimity, and turbulence. —A night of revelations. —Parallels. —Le Plessis. —My father James and my mother Angèle. —Country happiness. —Return to health, youth, and high spirits. —The children of the household. —Opinions of the time. —Loïsa Puget. —M. Stanislas and his mysterious quarters. —I meet my future husband. —His prophecy. —Our friendship. —His father. —More bizarre behavior. —My brother's return. —Baroness Dudevant. —The dotal system. —My marriage. —Return to Nohant. —Autumn 1823.

To endure such a trying existence, I would have to have been a saint. I was not, despite my ambition to become one. I had no sense of physical strength behind my efforts of will. My whole being was terribly shaken. My mother's behavior put the finishing touch to all my upsets and pain, and dealt such a rude shock to my nervous system, that I was not sleeping at all anymore and felt as though I were starving to death, unable to overcome the nausea provoked by the mere sight of food. I was constantly wracked by bouts of fever, and my heart felt as sick as my body. I could no longer pray. I tried to recite my devotions at Easter. My mother refused to allow me to go to see Abbé de Prémord, which would have strengthened and consoled me. I made my confession to an old churl who, having no understanding at all of the inner turmoil I suffered by accusing myself of filial disobedience, questioned me on the why's and wherefore's, and on whether or not these spiritual revolts were fully justified.

"That is not the issue," I replied. "According to my religion, they don't need to be justified to be wrestled with. I blame myself for being too weak in this struggle."

He persisted in asking me to make my confession to him about my mother. I did not answer, hoping to be granted absolution without having to relive the scene at La Châtre.

"Besides, if I questioned you," he said, struck by my silence, "it was to put you to the test. I wanted to see if you would accuse your mother, and since you did not, I see that your repentance is sincere and that I can grant you absolution."

I found such a test inappropriate, as well as a threat to the security of family life. I resolved never to confess to just anyone, and began to feel a great distaste for the mishandling of a sacramental practice. I received communion the following day, but without any enthusiasm no matter how hard I tried, and I was even more shocked and distressed by the noise pervading the church than I had been in the country.

The people in my mother's circle treated me very well, but they could not or did not know how to protect me. My kindly aunt claimed that one had to laugh at her sister's fusses, and believed I could do just that. Pierret—usually more just and intelligent than my mother, but at times as touchy and capricious—mistook my sadness for coldness, and berated me in that frenetically comic manner of his that could no longer distract me. Good Clothilde could do nothing for me. My sister was cool and reacted to my first effusiveness with distrust, as if she were waiting for some wicked behavior on my part. Her husband was a fine man who had no influence on the family. My Great-Uncle Beaumont was not at all affectionate. He had always been prone to an egotism that would no longer permit him to tolerate a pale, sad face at the table without teasing it to the point of cruelty. He was also aging rapidly, suffering from gout, and frequently stormed around his house and even at his guests, when they did not make an effort to distract him or succeed in amusing him. He was beginning to savor gossip, and I do not know to what extent my mother had filled him with the talk about me at La Châtre.

My mother was not always tense and irritable. She had her better moments of candor and affection, by which she drew me back. That was the worst of it. Had I been able to be cold and indifferent, I would perhaps have become stoical, but I found that impossible. She had only to shed a tear, indicate the slightest concern for me, and once again I would begin to love and hope. But that was the road to despair; the next day everything was destroyed and again in doubt.

She was unwell. She was going through a crisis, exceptionally long and painful in her case, but which never diminished her energy, courage, or irritability. This active being could not cross the threshold of old age without a terrible struggle. Still pretty and vivacious, she was not typically jealous of other women's youth and beauty. She was chaste, no matter what people may have said and thought about her, and her morals were beyond reproach. She needed violent emotion, and as much as it had saturated her life, it was never enough for that strange and almost certainly fatal hatred she had of peace of mind and body. She had to constantly recharge the restless atmosphere with new turbulence—changing her lodgings, picking a fight or making up with someone or other, spending a few hours in the country and then suddenly hurrying away, dining in one restaurant and then in another, even redoing her wardrobe from top to bottom each week.

She had little habits that quite typified this anxious mobility. She would buy a hat she thought charming. The same evening, she would find it hideous. First she would remove the bow, then the flowers, and finally the ruffles. She would move them all around with great skill and taste. Then she would be pleased with it all the next day. But on the following day, there would be another radical change. And so it went for a week, until the wretched hat, for all its transformations, lost its charm for her. Then she would wear it with great disdain, saying she could not care less about her appearance, until the fancy for a new hat took her.

Her hair was still dark and very beautiful. She tired of being a brunette and put on a blond wig that did not quite succeed in ruining her looks. She liked herself as a blonde for a while, then, declaring herself a "towhead," she adopted a light brown color. She soon reverted to an ash blond, then to a soft black, and was so adept that I envisioned her with different hair color for each day of the week.

This childlike frivolousness did not preclude her doing laborious tasks and very exacting household chores. She also basked in her imagination, and would read M. d'Arlincourt[33] with passion, late into the night, which nonetheless did not prevent her from getting up at six the next morning and starting all over again her round of toilette, errands, needlework, laughter, despair, and carryings on.

When she was in good spirits, she was truly charming, and it was impossible not to be swept up in her bouyant gaiety and vivid witticisms. Unfortunately, it would never last an entire day; lightning would strike from some remote corner of heaven.

Yet she loved me, or at least she loved in me the memory of my father and my childhood, but she also hated in me the memory of my grandmother and Deschartres. She had harbored too much resentment and endured too many humiliations not to feel the need for a lengthy, dreadful, and thorough volcanic eruption. Reality was not an adequate source for her accusations and curses; imagination had to play a part as well. If she had indigestion, she would believe herself poisoned, and would not be far from accusing me.

One day, or rather night, I thought that all the bitterness between us would be wiped away and that we would henceforth understand and love each other without suffering.

During that day she had been extremely violent, and as usual, she was kind and reasonable in her appeasement. She went to bed and asked me to stay near her until she fell asleep, as she was feeling sad. I do not know how I got her to open her heart to me, but it was then I learned of all the unhappiness in her life. She told me more than I wanted to know, but I must say she did it with simplicity and remarkable dignity. She became animated recalling her feelings—laughed, wept, accused, even debated—with much wit, sensitivity, and power. She wished to initiate me into the secrets of all her misfortunes, and as if carried away by the idea that she had been destined for such pain, she sought in me the excuse for her suffering as well as the renewal of her soul.

"After all," she recapitulated, sitting up in her bed, so beautiful with her red madras scarf tied around her pale face illuminated by those big black eyes, "I don't feel guilty for anything. It doesn't seem to me that I have ever knowingly committed a malicious act; I was pulled, pushed, often forced to know and to act. My only crime is to have loved. Ah! If I hadn't loved your father, I'd be rich, carefree, and beyond reproach. Before that day, I had never given a thought to anything. Had anyone taught me to think? Me? I didn't know A from B. I was no more guilty than a lark. I said my prayers morning and night, and God never made me feel they weren't well received.

"No sooner had I bound myself to your father than misfortune and torment followed me. I was told—I was taught—that I was unworthy of love. I didn't comprehend and scarcely believed it. I felt my heart was more loving and true than those of the fine ladies who despised me and to whom I returned the favor. I was loved. Your father used to say to me, 'Scorn them, as I do.' I was happy, and I saw that he was happy. How could I have convinced myself I was disgracing him?

"And yet, that's what people told me, using every conceivable innuendoe, when he was no longer there to defend me. Then I had to think, to wonder, to question myself, finally feeling humiliated and hating myself, or else showing up others in their hypocrisy and despising them with all my might.

"It was then that I—so jaunty, sure of myself, outgoing—realized I had enemies. I, who had never hated, began hating almost everyone. I had never given a thought to the nature of your fine society, with its morality, manners, pretensions. What I had glimpsed of it had always made me laugh, as if it were something very droll. Then I saw that it was evil and false. Oh, I can tell you plainly that if, since my widowhood, I have conducted myself properly, it was not to please those who demand of others what they don't practice themselves. It was because I could no longer do otherwise. I have loved only one man in my life, and after I lost him, I no longer cared about anyone or anything."

She wept torrential tears at the memory of my father, crying out, "Oh, how good I would have become had we been able to grow old together! But God snatched him away from me right in the middle of my happiness. I don't curse God—He's the Master—but I loathe and curse humanity!" And she added ingenuously, as if weary of this outpouring, "When I think of it . . . ! Fortunately, I don't think of it all the time."

This was the counterpart to the confession that I had heard and accepted from my grandmother. The grief had had totally opposite effects on mother and wife. One, no longer knowing what to do with her passion and unable to bestow it on anyone, accepted heaven's decree, yet felt her energy converted into a hatred of mankind; the other, no longer knowing what to do with her compassion, had blamed God, but had bestowed treasures of charity on her fellow human beings.

I remained wrapped in the thoughts evoked by this poignant contrast. My mother abruptly said to me, "Oh well, I've told you too much, I can see that, and now you condemn and despise me, knowing all the facts! I would do better to tear you from my heart and have nothing left to love after your father, not even you!"

"As for my despising you," I replied, taking her all trembling and rigid in my arms, "you are quite mistaken. What I despise is society's contempt. Today I stand with you against it much more than I did at the time you always reproach me for having forgotten. Then you only had my heart, but now my reason and conscience are with you. That is the result of the fine education you are always scoffing at, of the religion and philosophy you hate so much. For me your past is sacred, not only because you're my mother, but because reason has proven to me that you were never guilty."

"Oh, truly? My God!" my mother cried out, listening to me avidly. "Then what do you condemn me for?"

"Your aversion and rancor for the world, for the entire human race, on which you're bent on revenging yourself for your suffering. Love made you happy and generous; hate makes you unhappy and unfair.

"It's true, it's true," she said. "Only too true! But what can I do? One must love or hate. I can't be indifferent and forgive out of apathy."

"At least forgive out of charity."

"Charity? Yes, as much as you want for the poor wretches forgotten or despised because they're powerless! For the poor lost women who die in the gutter because they could never be loved! Charity for those who suffer without having deserved it? I'd give them the shirt off my back, you know that! But charity for the contessas, for Madam So-and-So, who disgraced a husband as good as mine at least a hundred times with her love affairs? For Monsieur So-and-So, who only condemned your father's love for me the day I refused to become his mistress? All such people, don't you see, are vile; they do evil, they love evil; yet words of religion and virtue flow from their lips."

"But you must see, in addition to divine law, there is an inescapable law that commands us to forgive those who injure us and to forget personal hurts, for that law strikes and punishes us when we have ignored it too often."

"What do you mean? Explain it to me clearly."

"By bracing the mind and arming the heart against the wicked and guilty, we get in the habit of disowning the innocent and overwhelming those we respect and cherish with our suspicions and harshness."

"Oh! You're speaking for yourself," she exclaimed.

"Yes, I'm speaking for myself, but I could just as well be speaking for my sister, for your sister, for Pierret. Isn't that what you also believe, don't you say so yourself when you're at peace?"

"It's true, I infuriate everyone when I get going," she replied, "but I don't know how to act otherwise. The more I dwell on it, the more I start up again, and what seemed most unjust on my part when I went to sleep is the very thing that seems fairest when I wake up. My head works too much. Sometimes I feel that it's bursting. I'm only healthy and reasonable when there's nothing on my mind. But it is altogether out of my control. The more I don't want to think, the more I do think. Oblivion must come to me on its own, from exhaustion. Can that be learned in your books, the power not to think at all?"

You can see from this conversation how impossible it was for me to bring reason to bear on my mother's passionate nature. She mistook the emotions of her tumultuous thoughts for thinking, and looked for relief in a fit of exhaustion which numbed any sustained awareness of her unjust behavior. At heart, she was admirably upright, but this was obscured in each instance by the feverish imaginings she no longer was young enough to overcome, having moreover spent her life completely ignorant of the necessary intellectual weapons she might have used.

She was, nonetheless, a very spiritual soul and loved God fervently as a refuge against the injustices of others as well as her own. Only in Him did she find clemency and impartiality, and though counting on His boundless compassion, it did not occur to her to rekindle and foster the spark of such perfection in herself. There were no words with which I could make her understand the idea of that connection of the will to Him who gave it to us. "God," she would say, "knows very well we are weak, since it pleased Him to make us so."

My sister's piety was often a source of irritation to her. She abhorred priests, and spoke to Caroline of "your clerics" as she spoke to me of "your old contessas." She frequently opened the Gospel to read a few passages. This was either good or bad for her, depending on whether she was in a good or bad mood. Calm, she would be moved by the tears and balm of Magdalene; irritable, she treated whoever was nearby as Jesus treated the money lenders in the temple.

She fell asleep blessing and thanking me for the good I had done her, declaring that from now on, she would always be fair with me. "You needn't worry any longer," she told me. "I see very clearly now that you don't deserve all the grief I've caused you. You see things in their true light, your judgments are sound. Love me, and be quite certain that, deep down, I love you."

That lasted three days—rather a long time for my poor mother. Spring had come. My grandmother had always observed that at that time of year my mother's character became more embittered and, at moments, bordered on insanity. I saw that she had not been mistaken.

I think my mother sensed her malady, and wanted to be alone in order to hide it from me. She took me to the country, to the home of some people she had met three days before at a dinner party given by an old friend of my Uncle Beaumont. She left me there the day after our arrival, telling me, "You don't look well—the country air will do you good. I'll come for you next week." She did not come back for four or five months.

I landed among new faces, in a new milieu where I was thrust by chance, and where Providence led me to find some excellent people, generous friends, for a time of respite from my sufferings and a new perspective on humanity.

Mme. Roëttiers du Plessis was the most frank and generous creature in the world. A rich heiress, she had been in love with her uncle, James Roëttiers, a captain in the cavalry, from the time she was a little girl. He was a thoroughgoing soldier whose exuberant youth had caused the family some anxiety. But her heart's instincts had not misled young Angèle. James was the best of husbands and fathers. When I met them, they had five children and had been married ten years. They were as much in love as when they first met, and have always loved each other thus.

Although gray at age twenty-seven, Mme. Angèle was attractive. She lacked grace, having always been as impetuous and forthright as a boy, and was complete devoid of coquetry, but her face was delicate and pretty; her freshness, contrasted with that silvery head of hair, gave her a unique beauty.

James was in his forties and balding, but his round blue eyes twinkled with wit and merriment, and his entire face expressed the goodness and sincerity of his soul.

The five children were all girls, one of whom had been raised by James's older brother. The other four, dressed as boys, rushed and swarmed through the most cheerful and clamorous house I had ever been in.

The château was a large villa from the time of Louis XVI, set right in the heart of Brie, two leagues from Melun. No vistas, no poetry whatsoever in the surroundings, but to compensate, an enormous park with beautiful vegetation—flowers, immense lawns—all the comforts of a dwelling for every season, and a large farm nearby that furnished the adjacent meadows with magnificent livestock.

Mme. Angèle and I liked each other instantly. She looked like a boy without behaving like one, while I had been brought up somewhat like a boy though I didn't look like one. But we had between us that rapport that knew nothing of feminine wiles or vanity, where we both felt on meeting that we could never become rivals about anyone or anything, and as a result we could love each other without suspicion or fear of ever quarreling.

She was the one who induced my mother to leave me at her house. She had counted on our spending a week with them. By the next day my mother was bored, and as I sighed at already having to leave the beautiful park, so cheerful in its spring finery, and those open, friendly faces that looked so inquiringly at mine, Mme. Angèle, with her decisiveness and assured good will, solved the problem. She was so irreproachable as a family mother, that my own mother could not worry about what "people" would say. Since this household was a neutral ground in relation to her antipathies and resentments, she agreed without my begging.

When there was no sign of my mother by the end of the week, I became upset, not at being left with a family that I felt was so respectable and perfect, but from fear of being a burden, and so I confessed my predicament.

James took me aside, saying, "We are well acquainted with your family history. I knew your father slightly in the army, and I caught up with what has happened since his death the day I saw you in Paris—how you were raised by your grandmother, and how you once again fell under your mother's authority. I was curious to find out why you weren't getting along with her. They told me. Within five minutes I understood that she could not keep from speaking ill of her mother-in-law in front of you, that this hurt you deeply, and that she would torment you all the more when you hung your head in silence. Your unhappy appearance aroused my interest. I told myself that my wife would love you as I already loved you, that you would be steady company for her, and an agreeable friend. You spoke longingly of the happiness of living in the country. I decided that I'd give myself the pleasure of giving you that joy. I spoke quite openly to your mother that evening, and she told me just as openly that she was weary of your melancholy face and wanted to see you married; I told her that there was nothing easier than to marry off a young woman with a dowry, but that her way of life didn't give you much choice, because it was obvious to me that you're the kind of person who would want to choose for herself, and you're right. So, I persuaded her to spend a few weeks here, where you can see that we entertain many of my friends or comrades whom I know quite thoroughly, and about whom I would not let her be misled. She trusted me, she came, but she got bored, and she left. I'm certain that she'll agree to let you stay with us as long as you wish. Would you agree to that yourself? It would make us happy; we already love you. I look upon you as a daughter, and my wife is exceedingly fond of you. We won't torment you on the subject of marriage. We shall never bring it up, for it would seem as if we were trying to get rid of you, and that would not suit Angèle at all. But if among the good people in our circle of visitors there is someone you like, tell us, and we'll tell you honestly if he's suitable for you or not."

Mme. Angèle seconded her husband's invitation. There could be no mistaking their sincerity, their empathy. They wanted to be mother and father to me, and I assumed the habit of calling them that, a habit I have always kept. The entire household soon also took on the habit, right down to the servants, who would say to me, "Mademoiselle, your father is looking for you," or " . . . your mother is asking for you." These phrases say more than a detailed account of the care and attention, the delicate and sustained affection these two wonderful human beings showed me. Mme. Angèle dressed me in new clothes and shoes, for the ones I had were worn out. I had at my disposal a library, a piano, and an excellent horse. I was in my glory.

At the beginning, I was bothered by the assiduous attentions of a nice, retired officer who courted me. He had absolutely no income beyond his pension and was the son of a peasant. Discouraging him made me very uncomfortable. He was not at all to my liking, though he was such a decent fellow that I could not believe he was only interested in my dowry. I discussed it with my father James, explaining that he annoyed me, but that I was terribly afraid of humiliating him and letting him think I looked down on him because of his poverty, yet I did not know how to go about getting rid of him. James took charge of the matter, and the good fellow went off without any ill will toward me.

Several other offers of marriage were received by my Uncle Maréchal, my Uncle Beaumont, Pierret, and others. Despite my cousin Auguste's predictions, there were some very "satisfactory" ones, in the parlance of society, with respect to money and even family. I refused them all, not discourteously—my mother would have persisted all the more—but with sufficient tact so that I would be left in peace. I could not accept the idea of being asked for in marriage by men who did not know me, had never seen me, and whose only aim, consequently, was to conclude a business transaction.

My good parents Du Plessis, aware that I was not in any hurry, genuinely demonstrated that they, too, were in no hurry for me to come to a decision. My life with them was at last in harmony with my desires and soothed my sick heart.

I have not mentioned everything I had suffered at the hands of my mother. There is no need to describe all the details of her violence and its causes; they were so outrageous that they would appear untrue to life. Besides, what good would it do? My heart has forgiven her actions a thousand times, and as I do not believe myself better than God, I am quite certain He, too, has pardoned

her. Why then should I offer those details for judgment by a great many readers
who perhaps are ordinarily no more patient, no more just in practice than my
poor mother during her nervous attacks. I painted a faithful portrait of her character; I showed its strong and weak sides. Her situation should be seen simply
as an example of a destiny created far less by a person's physical and mental
being than by the influence of society; the despair and indignation of a generous soul, reduced to doubting everything and no longer able to control herself,
because she was refused acceptance when she proved herself worthy.

That alone was useful to mention. The rest is my own affair. I shall only
say that I lacked the strength to endure the inevitable effects of her grief. My
father's death had been a catastrophe that my young age had prevented me
from comprehending, but I was to suffer and be aware of its consequences
throughout all the days of my youth.

I understood those consequences at last, but that realization did not yet
allow me the necessary strength to accept them. I would have to have known a
wife's passion and a mother's tenderness to reach the complete tolerance I
needed. I had the pride of my innocence, inexperience, and instinctive equanimity. My mother was right in often telling me, "When you have suffered as
much as I have, you'll no longer be Saint Tranquility."

I had succeeded in controlling myself, that was all, but I had had several
attacks of mute anger that caused me terrible harm, after which I had again felt
attracted to suicide. This strange malady took different forms in my imagination. This time I had felt the desire to die of hunger and narrowly missed gratifying this wish in spite of myself, because eating took such an effort of my will
that my stomach rejected all food; my throat tightened, nothing would go
down, and I could not repress a secret pleasure in telling myself that death by
starvation would occur without my having had a hand in it. Thus I was very
sick when I went to the Du Plessis family, and my melancholy had turned into
a kind of stupor. The succession of emotions had perhaps been too much for
me at my age.

The country air, a well-regulated life, varied and plentiful food from
which I could, from the first, choose what was least repugnant to the rebelliousness of my ruined appetite, the absence of harassments and worries, and
above all, the friendship—the blessed friendship that I needed more than all the
rest—soon cured me. Until then, I had not known how much I loved the country and how essential it was for me. I thought it was only Nohant that I loved.
Le Plessis took hold of me like some Garden of Eden. In that hideously flat
countryside, the park itself was the only natural thing that merited more than a
glance. How charming were those immense grounds where deer bounded in
the thickets, in hidden glades, around the still waters of those mysterious pools
that one discovers under old willows and tall wild grass. Certain places had the
poetry of a virgin forest. A forest in full, vigorous growth is at all times and at
every season a wonderful thing.

There were beautiful flowers and fragrant orange groves around the
house as well, and a luxuriant kitchen garden. I have always loved kitchen gardens. Everything was less rustic, better maintained, better planned, and thus

less picturesque and romantic than at Nohant. But what long archways of branches, what views of greenery, what lovely weather for galloping along the sandy paths! And then there were the young hosts, their faces always bright, those wonderful enfants terribles! The shouting, the laughter, the unruly games of tag, a swing you could break your neck on! I felt I was still a child myself. I had forgotten it. My schoolgirl's tastes returned—wild races, laughter for no reason, moving for the love of moving, noise for the sake of noise. Gone were those frantic walks or morbid daydreams of Nohant, those activities into which you throw yourself with frenzy to shake off your grief, that exhaustion in which you would like to lose yourself forever. It was a true pleasure party, shared by many—the family life I was so meant for without realizing it that I have never been able to put up with any other kind without falling into a depression.

It was there that I renounced, once and for all, the dream of the convent. During the past several months, I had instinctively kept coming back to that, through all the crises in my existence. At Le Plessis, I finally understood that I would never be able to live comfortably anywhere but in the fresh air, the open spaces—always the same, if need be, but without constraints on my use of time and without being forced to relinquish the spectacle of the peaceful and poetic outdoors.

And on seeing Angèle's happiness, I finally understood, not the raptures of love, but the complete sweetness of married life and true friendship—that ultimate trust, that absolute and calm devotion, that inner security which had reigned between her and her husband from the very first days of their youth. For whoever might receive only a promise of ten years of such happiness, those ten years would be worth a lifetime.

I had always adored children, was always seeking out at Nohant and the convent the company of children younger than I. I had so loved and looked after my dolls that I had developed a pronounced maternal instinct. My mother Angèle's four daughters put her through plenty of torment, but it was that sweet torment which Madame Alicia had so complained of with me, and it was even more than that. They were the children of her womb, the pride of her marriage, her total preoccupation, the dream of her future.

James had only one regret, which was not to have had at least one son. To give himself this illusion, he chose to see his daughters dressed as boys for as long as possible. They wore trousers and red jackets trimmed with silver buttons, and looked like impish, brave soldiers. Often joining the group were the three daughters of his sister, Mme. Gondoüin Saint Agnan, the oldest of whom was very dear to me, and also Loïsa Puget, whose father had been associated with James in running a factory, and finally, a few sons of relatives and close friends—Norbert Saint Martin, son of the youngest of the Roëttiers, Eugène Sandré, and the nephews of an old friend. When all the youngsters were gathered, I was the oldest of the flock, and I led the games, which I enjoyed as much as the fledglings for quite a while, even after I was married.

So, once again I became young; at Le Plessis, I rediscovered my real age. I was free to read, spend the evening in company, meditate; I could read what I wanted and had unlimited access to books. It did not occur to me to take advantage of that. After a day of horseback riding and games, I would drop off to sleep immediately and wake up to begin all over again. The only thought I had then was the fear of having to think. I had had too much of that at one time; I needed to forget the world of ideas and give in to the world of peaceful feelings and youthful activity.

It seems that my mother had heralded me there as a "pedant," a "free-thinker," an "original." This description had somewhat frightened my mother Angèle, and so it was all the more to her credit that she took an interest in my misfortunes. But she waited in vain for my great mind and vanity to appear. Deschartres was the only human being with whom I had allowed myself to be pedantic. Since he was pedantic himself and quite dogmatic about everything, it was hardly possible to engage otherwise in discussions with him. What would I have accomplished at Le Plessis with my meager store of knowledge? No one would have been impressed, and I found it much more pleasant to forget it than to have others and myself celebrate it. Since my ideas did not meet with any sort of contradiction from those around me, I did not feel the need for debate. In this old bourgeois family, illusions about one's lineage would only have been a subject for good-natured joking, and as no one professed such notions, there were no opponents. They did not think about it; they never worried about it.

In that era, the bourgeoisie did not have the arrogance it has since acquired, and love of money had not yet become a principle of public morality. Even had it been so elsewhere, it would not have been at Le Plessis. James was witty, honorable, and sensible. His wife, who was warm and loving, had brought him wealth when he had nothing. Pure love and total unselfishness were the religion and ethic of this noble woman. How could I ever have found myself at odds with her or her family about anything whatsoever? It never happened.

Their political views were based on unreasoned bonapartism, to the point of passion against the restoration of the monarchy, which they viewed as the work of the Cossack lance and the betrayal by the great generals of the Empire. They did not see in the bourgeoisie, of which they were a part, a more widespread betrayal, a more critical invasion. This was not yet visible then, and no one really had quite understood the Emperor's downfall. The remnants of the Grand Army never dreamed of attributing it to doctrinal liberalism, which nonetheless played a large role. In times of oppression, all the opposing forces quickly arrive at consensus. At that time, Carnot[34] personified the republican ideal, and the true bonapartists reconciled themselves to that ideal because the man had been a hero with Napoléon through the country's misfortunes and dangers.

As I was not yet conversant with the history of my times, and not enough given, at that moment, to reflection or to the study of causes whereby to extricate myself when facts diverged, I could continue being a republican along with Jean-Jacques Rousseau, and a bonapartist with my Du Plessis friends. Like most of the French of the period, my friends were no more clearsighted than I.

Yet there were opinions around us that should have given me pause for thought. James's older brother and some of his oldest friends had rallied to the monarchy and hated the memory of the Empire's ruinous wars. Was it out of self-interest, money considerations, or a love for security? James fought against them like a true knight of France, aware only of his country's honor, abhorrence of things foreign, shame in defeat, and the pain of betrayal. After seven years of the Restoration, he still wept for the heroes of the past, and as he was neither stupid, ridiculous, nor blindly militaristic, we always listened eagerly to his long, oft-repeated war stories that were always picturesque and gripping. I knew them by heart, and yet I listened, discovering in them a historical novelist's penchant that enticed me, although I was far from imagining myself becoming a novelist. Several passages in my novel *Jacques* [1834] were suggested to me by vague memories of my father James's tales.

Since I have mentioned Loïsa Puget, of whom I lost track after two or three years, I owe a few words to that remarkable child whom I hardly knew as a young lady. She was a few years younger than I, which made a great difference at the time, such that I can only recall with some amazement the nature of our relationship. There is no doubt she was almost the only person at Le Plessis with whom I sometimes discussed art and literature. So, she was quite precocious intellectually and showed great talent while being unusually lazy in all her studies. She was, I believe, a victim of her own facility. She understood everything at the first try, and quickly absorbed all musical and literary ideas. Her mother had been a professional singer in the provinces, and although her voice was cracked, she still sang quite well when she agreed to be heard at small gatherings. She was a fine musician as well and hounded Loïsa to study seriously rather than improvise haphazardly. Loïsa, who was happy at her improvising, scarcely heeded her mother. She was an enfant terrible, more so than any of the others at Le Plessis. Pretty as an angel, full of funny retorts, she knew how to get everyone to spoil her. I believe she also spoiled herself, her facile mind being content with superficial ideas. With utter spontaneity, she produced things that were consistently gay, joyously rhythmical, clear in tonality, and perfectly natural. These qualities transported them well beyond the vulgarity of the genre. But I, who remember her more than she might imagine (because I was already at the age of reason, while she was still at the age of intuition), knew that she had much more in her than she had produced. If someone had told me that, secluded and somewhat forgotten in the provinces, she had created a more serious and sincere oeuvre than her former tunes—albeit still using the same form (for form and size have nothing to do with quality)—I would not have been the least surprised at an enormous advance on her part.

Living in the house was a quite incredible character by the name of Stanislas Hue. He was an old bachelor, crowned with a yellowing mane, whose harsh features were reminiscent of Deschartres', but there was not a trace of that special beauty which, in spite of weather, age, and a comically surly expression, revealed the beauty of my tutor's soul. Good Father Stanislas, as we so readily call those old men without families who pass into grumbling monkhood, was neither good nor priestly. We often found him amusing, as he was not devoid of knowledge or wit, but he gladly thought and spoke ill of everyone. He took a dim view of everything, and perhaps did not have the right to be a misanthrope, not being better or kinder than the next one.

His quirks amused the family, although no one dared laugh at them in front of him. I did dare, however, being accustomed to making Deschartres laugh in spite of himself, and believing that making fun of someone directly was better than circuitous mockery. I made him furious, and then he recovered. And then he blew up and calmed down, heaven knows how many times. At times he showed a weakness for my teasing and invited it. Other times, it irritated him in a comical way. In general, he was very obliging with me. The handsome horse I rode was his. It was a black Andalusian named Figaro, twenty-five years old, but which still had the suppleness, spirit, and stability of a young horse. Several times, when I had put the master in a bad mood, he refused to let me ride his horse; Figaro would suddenly develop a limp. My father James would go to fetch him for me when Stanislas' back was turned. We galloped off and came back two hours later to tell him that Figaro was feeling much better, the air having done him good. He would take his revenge, according to James, with a thoroughly nasty comment in his journal, for he did keep a journal, day by day, hour by hour, of everything said and done around him. Thus, he had recorded twenty-five years of his life, down to the most insignificant details, in a mountain of notebooks that needed an entire wagon whenever he moved, and its own private room in his lodgings. I do not believe there existed a man more weighed down by his memories or more inconvenienced by his past.

Another one of Stanislas' manias was to let nothing go astray that was left lying around. He would gather forgotten or abandoned objects from everywhere in the house and garden—a broken spade, a pocket handkerchief, an old shoe, an old andiron, a pair of scissors. His apartment at Le Plessis was a museum crammed to the ceiling with rags and old scraps of metal. It was neither greed nor a penchant for larceny that drove him, as all these things were of no use to him, and once in his Capernaum, an object was not destined to leave until his death. One could only presume the cause of this craze to be a basic meanness and tendency to find fault that led him to make less meticulous people go looking for their mislaid objects. It was his secret joy to make the servants, the children, and the hosts of the household all go through a great deal of trouble and searching. We could not put a book on the piano or living room table, hang a hat on a tree, leave a rake against a wall or a candlestick on the stairs, without the object disappearing within five minutes, never to show up again. All the while, he would be spying on us, laughing up his sleeve, and stroking his chin. "Don't bother looking," Mme. Angèle would say, "or step into Father Stanislas' store, if you can." Now that was an impossibility. He locked himself in when he went into his own quarters and took the key with him when he left. No living soul had ever swept or dusted his curiosity shop. He went off to die at another château—M. Rochambeau's, I believe—where he had all his acquisitions sent on ahead in vans. When all of these treasures emerged from the dust to be inventoried, I was told they decided to value the lot at eighteen francs rather than run up the considerable expense of taking stock.

That old fox had, so they said, a pension of twelve thousand francs. If my memory serves me well, he had been an administrator in the war offices. Not wanting to spend his small fortune, he took rooms with friends at the cheapest possible rate, and accumulated his interest. In the long run, he was an impossible boarder, grumbling in his own way, which consisted of making caustic jokes about the muddy coffee or ruined sauce, tearing the cook or housekeeper to pieces. He was the godfather of James's youngest daughter; he appeared to love her very much and shrewdly let it be known that he would be responsible for her future dowry, but he did nothing of the kind. Pleased to have infuriated his world, he died without a thought for a soul.

My mother, sister, and Pierret occasionally came to spend a day or two at Le Plessis, to see if I was getting along well and wanted to remain. That was just what I did want, and everything went well between my mother and me until the end of spring.

At that time, M. and Mme. du Plessis went to Paris for a few days. Although I stayed with my mother, they came to fetch me every morning to gad about with them, dining at a "cabaret," as they would say, and "strolling" the boulevards in the evening. The cabaret was always the Café de Paris or the Frères Provençaux; the strolls were to the Opéra, Porte Saint-Martin, or some mime drama at the Cirque that might awaken James's wartime memories. My mother was invited to all these outings, but although she enjoyed this kind of entertainment, more frequently she let me go without her. It seemed as though she wanted to abdicate all her rights and maternal functions to Mme. du Plessis.

On one of those evenings, after a performance, while we were having ice cream at Tortoni's, my mother Angèle said to her husband, "Look, there's Casimir!" A slender young man, rather elegant, with a cheerful face and military bearing, came to greet them and responded to their eager questions about his father, Colonel Dudevant, much loved and respected by the family. He sat down near Mme. Angèle and asked her, in a whisper, who I was. She replied out loud, "She's my daughter." "Then," he continued in a whisper, "is she my wife? You know, you promised me the hand of your oldest daughter. I thought it would be Wilfrid, but this one's age seems more suitable. I accept, if you wish to give her to me." Mme. Angèle began to laugh, but the joke was prophetic.

A few days later, Casimir Dudevant came to Le Plessis and joined our children's games with an enthusiasm and gaiety of his own that could only be taken as a good augur of his character. He did not court me, which would have endangered our familiarity; it did not even occur to him. An easy camaraderie developed between us, and he would tell Mme. Angèle, who had long been in the habit of calling him her son-in-law, "Your daughter is a nice fellow," while I would retort, "Your son-in-law is a good child."

I do not know what prompted the joke to spread. Old Stanislas, hard-pressed to find mischief, would shout to me in the garden where we were playing tag, "Hurry up and catch your husband!" Casimir, swept along by the game, would shout back, "Set my wife free!" We began to think of each other as husband and wife, with just as little embarrassment and passion as young Justine and Norbert would have.

One day, in the park, after Father Stanislas had made some malicious remark to me on the subject, I linked my arm in his and asked the curmudgeon why he had to give a wicked twist to the most innocent things.

"Because you're crazy if you think you're going to marry that boy," he answered. "He'll have sixty or eighty thousand francs in income, and he certainly doesn't want you for a wife."

"I give you my word of honor," I told him, "that it never for a moment occurred to me to take him for a husband. This little joke might have been in bad taste if it hadn't begun among people as innocent as we all are here. But because it can be misinterpreted by afflicted brains like yours, I'm going to ask my mother and father to put an end to it quickly."

My father James, the first one I ran into when I returned to the house, responded to my protest by saying that Stanislas was just rambling. "If you're going to pay attention to the epithets of that old Chinaman, you'll never be able to lift a finger without him finding something to carp on. That's not the issue. Let's talk seriously. Colonel Dudevant indeed has a fine fortune and a good income: half is the result of his wife's inheritance, and half is his own, but in his half one has to include his retirement pensions as Officer of the Legion of Honor, as Baron of the Empire, etc. In his own title, he has only a rather nice property in Gascony, and his son—who is his natural son and not his wife's—has only the right to half of this inheritance. He'll probably have all of it, because his father loves him and has no other children, but when it is all added up, his fortune will never be greater than yours, and at the beginning, it will be even less. Therefore, that is no reason why you should not be man and wife, as we were saying in jest, and this marriage would be even more advantageous for him than for you. So, have a clear conscience, and do as you please. Fling back the joke if it offends you; otherwise, ignore it.

"I can ignore it," I replied. "I fear I would look ridiculous, and give it substance, if I were to dwell on it."

Things remained as they were. Casimir left and came back. On his return, he was more serious with me and asked me for my hand in marriage, with much frankness and brevity. "This may not be the way it's done," he said to me, "but I wanted the consent to come first from you alone, of your own free will. If I am not repugnant to you—and you cannot in any case make a decision so quickly—look me over more carefully, and you can tell me in a few days, or in a while—whenever you wish—whether you authorize me to have my father contact your mother."

This put me greatly at ease. M. and Mme. du Plessis had spoken so highly of Casimir and his family that I had no reason not to grant him more serious attention than I had up to now. I found him to be sincere in his words as well as in his entire manner. He never spoke to me of love, he admitted to being little disposed to sudden passion, or enthusiasm, and in any case, incapable of expressing these sentiments in a seductive manner. He spoke of an unfailing friendship and compared the peaceful domestic happiness of our hosts to that which he hoped he could vow to provide for me. "To prove to you that I'm sure of myself," he said, "I want to confess that I was impressed at first sight by your good and sensible manner. I found you neither beautiful nor pretty; I didn't know who you were; I had never heard talk of you, and yet when I jokingly said to Mme. Angèle that you would be my wife, I immediately felt that, should it come about, I would be quite happy. Each day this hazy notion became clearer, and when I started laughing with you and joining in your games, it seemed to me that I'd known you for a long time and that we were two old friends."

I think that at that time in my life, just as I was emerging from such great indecision between convent and family life, a suitor's sudden passion would have terrified me. I would not have understood it; it would have seemed feigned or ridiculous, as had that of the first suitor who had made an offer at Le Plessis. My heart had never outstripped my naïveté; no stirrings within my being could have clouded my reasoning or lulled my mistrust.

So I found Casimir's reasoning to my liking, and after having talked to my hosts, we remained on terms of that pleasant camaraderie that had become our accepted way of relating to each other.

I had never been the object of exclusive attention—that willing and happy submission which astonishes and touches a young heart. Soon it was impossible for me not to consider Casimir my best and most reliable friend.

We arranged with Mme. Angèle for an interview between the Colonel and my mother, and made no plans at all until then, since the future depended on my mother's whims, and she could ruin everything. In case she refused, we were no longer to think about it and to retain our good opinions of each other.

My mother came to Le Plessis and was struck, as I was, with loving respect for the old Colonel's handsome face, silver hair, and air of distinction and kindness. They talked together and with our hosts. Later, my mother told me, "I said Yes, but not in such a way that I can't take it back. I don't know yet if I care for the son. He's not handsome. I would have liked a handsome son-in-law to offer me his arm." The colonel took my arm to go to see an artificial meadow behind the house, all the while discussing agriculture with James. He walked with difficulty, having already had violent attacks of gout. When the three of us were separated from the other walkers, the Colonel spoke to me with great affection, said that he was extraordinarily taken with me, and would consider it a great happiness in his life to have me as his daughter.

My mother stayed for a few days, was pleasant and gay, teased her future son-in-law as a test, found him to be a good boy, and left giving us permission to stay together under the eye of Mme. Angèle. It had been agreed that, to set the date of the marriage, we would await the return to Paris of Mme. Dudevant, who had been spending some time with her family at Le Mans. Until then, we were to become acquainted as relatives whose futures are destined to affect each other, and the colonel was to decide, in the event of his death, what he wanted to leave his son.

At the end of two weeks, my mother burst in at Le Plessis like a bomb-

shell. She had "discovered" that Casimir, in the midst of some dissolute existence, had for a short time been a waiter. I do not know where she had hatched
that nonsense. I think it was a dream she had had the night before, and, on
waking, believed. Her grievance was greeted with laughter, which made her
angry. It was useless for James to answer her seriously, telling her that he had
almost never lost sight of the Dudevant family, and that Casimir had never fall-
en into any dissolution; Casimir himself protested in vain that there was no
shame in being a waiter, but that he had left military school only to embark on
a campaign as second lieutenant; then had left upon the demobilization of the
army, taken a law degree in Paris while living with his father, enjoying his hospitality, or following him to the country, where he was treated like the son of a
respectable family, and had never had, not even for a week or a day, the leisure
to work in a café. My mother obstinately persisted and claimed she was being
deceived and mocked by them. Taking me aside, she spewed forth a frenzied
stream of abuse against Mme. Angèle, her morals, the atmosphere in her home,
and the intrigues of Du Plessis, who made a business of arranging marriages
between heiresses and adventurers in order to line his pockets, and so forth.

She was having such a violent fit that I feared for her sanity and strove to
distract her by saying I would pack my bags and leave with her right away; that
while in Paris, she could gather all the information she could possibly want;
that until she was satisfied, we would not see Casimir. She calmed down right
away. "Yes, yes," she said. "Go pack our bags!" But I had scarcely begun when
she said, "On second thought, I'll leave; I don't like it here. You do, so you
stay. I'll collect some information and let you know what I find out."

She left that very night, came back again to create similar scenes, and in
short, without needing much urging, left me at Le Plessis until Mme. Dudevant arrived in Paris. Seeing then that my mother was again reconciled to the
marriage and that she was calling me back to her with what appeared to be
serious intentions, I joined her at Rue St. Lazare at a new, rather ugly and
small apartment she had rented behind the old Tivoli. From the windows of
my dressing room, I saw a large garden where, for a very small fee, I could
walk during the day with my brother, who had just arrived and settled into an
attic room above us.

Hippolyte had completed his military service, and even though he was on
the verge of being appointed an officer, he did not want to renew his tour of
duty. He had developed an aversion to military life, into which he had thrown
himself with such passion. He had expected more rapid advancement, but he
was convinced that the abandonment by the Villeneuves had filtered down to
him, too, and he found garrison life, without the hope of war or honor, stultifying to his intelligence and unprofitable for his future. He could live without
hardship on his small pension, and I offered to let him stay with us, uncontra-
dicted by my mother, who was very fond of him, until he had seen to arranging
a new profession for himself, which was his plan.

His intervention between my mother and me was very helpful. He was
much better able than I to deal with her temperament. He laughed at her
tantrums, flattered her, or teased her. He even scolded her, and from him she

accepted everything. His hussar's hide was not so easy to penetrate as my thin skin, and the insouciance with which he responded to her tirades made them so ineffectual that she would immediately abandon them. He did his best to comfort me, telling me I was crazy to be so affected by her moods, which seemed to him quite minor compared to the guardhouse and regimental beatings.

Mme. Dudevant came to pay her official visit. Her affection and intelligence certainly did not measure up to my mother's, but she did have the manners of a great lady and was sweetness itself on the outside. I blindly gave in to the sympathy that her suffering little airs, her weak voice, and her pretty, refined features aroused in me from the first, and would arouse in me longer than was good for me. My mother was flattered by her overtures, which soothed the very spot in her pride that was bruised. The marriage was settled; then everything was discussed again; then it was broken off; then renegotiated. This went on until autumn, and once again I was often very unhappy and ill. Try as I might to agree with my brother that basically my mother did love me and did not herself believe a word of those insults that poured out of her mouth, I could not get used to the swings from wild gaiety to gloomy anger, from effusive affection to seeming indifference or sudden aversion.

She never changed her mind about Casimir. She had taken a dislike to him because, she said, his nose didn't please her. She accepted his attentions but enjoyed putting his patience to the test—a patience that was limited but which held up with the help of Hippolyte and the intervention of Pierret. But she told me more stories than were needed to hang him, and her accusations fell so short of the truth that it was impossible for them not to produce the opposite reaction of indulgence or blind faith in the hearts of those she had wished to harden or disillusion.

She finally made up her mind, after several financial parleys that were quite cutting. She wanted to marry me off under the dotal system, and the older M. Dudevant raised some objection due to the charges of distrust she had so incautiously expressed about his son. I had urged Casimir to resist with all his might this conservative property measure which almost always results in the sacrifice of an individual's peace of mind to the tyrannical immobility of real estate. For nothing in the world would I have sold the house and garden at Nohant, but certainly a part of the land, enough to give me an income proportionate to the expenses involved in maintaining a relatively large residence. I knew that my grandmother always had been embarrassed by not having ready cash. But my husband had to concede in the face of my mother's obstinacy, as she relished the pleasure of committing a final act of authority.

We were married in September 1822, and after the wedding guests had come and gone, and we had stayed a few days with our friends the Du Plessis, we left with my brother for Nohant, where we were welcomed with delight by Deschartres. *E.R.G./I.I.*

IX

Retreat to Nohant[10] —Needlework and its moral usefulness to
women. —The desirable balance between effort and leisure. —My
robin. —Deschartres leaves Nohant. —The birth of my son.
—Deschartres in Paris. —Winter of 1824 at Nohant. —Changes and
improvements which plunge me into melancholy. —Summer at Le
Plessis. —The children. —The ideal in their society. —Aversion for
the positivist view of life. —Ormesson. —The funeral of Louis
XVIII at Saint-Denis. —The deserted garden. —Montaigne's
Essaies. —We return to Paris. —Abbé de Prémord. —Retreat to the
convent. —Aspiration to monastic life. —Maurice at the convent.
—Sister Hélène hastens our departure.

I spent the winter of 1822–1823 at Nohant, somewhat ill, but absorbed
in the sentiment of maternal love which came to me through the sweetest
dreams and the most vivid aspirations. The transformation which takes place
at such a time in the life and thoughts of a woman is usually sudden and complete; thus it was for me. The cravings of the mind, the turmoil of thinking,
the thirst for study as well as observation—all vanished as soon as the precious burden had made itself known, and even before those first tremors had
revealed its existence to me. In this phase of waiting and hope, Providence
wants physical and sentimental life to predominate. Thus the late night hours,
the reading, the reveries—intellectual life, in other words, was quite naturally
eliminated without my willing it or my least regret. The winter was long and
hard; for a long time a thick blanket of snow covered the ground already hardened by severe frosts. My husband loved the country, too, although differently
than I, and as he had a passion for hunting, he left me with long hours of
leisure which I took up by preparing the layette. I had never done any sewing
in my life. Even though she maintained that it was necessary to know how to
do it, my grandmother had never imposed it on me, and I believed myself
thoroughly unhandy. But when there was the incentive of dressing the little
person whom I saw in all my dreams, I threw myself into it with a kind of
passion. My good Ursule came to give me my first inkling of whipstitching
and turning down seams. I was astonished to see how easy it was, but at the
same time I could see that there, as everywhere, one could be creative; one
could be a maestro with the scissors.

Since then I have always liked needlework, and I find it a pastime to which I can sometimes devote myself with an almost feverish passion. I even tried to embroider the little bonnets, but I had to limit myself to two or three, or I would have gone blind. I was far-sighted, and my vision was excellent, but also what we used to call "gross." I do not distinguish details, and counting the threads in fine muslin, reading a fine diagram, looking at things up close are, in short, so painful as to make my head spin and drive a thousand pinpoints into the base of my skull.

I have often heard accomplished women say that domestic tasks, particularly needlework, are stultifying and insipid, and that they are a part of the slavery to which our sex is condemned. I have little taste for slavery, and I deny that these tasks are a product of it. It has always seemed to me that they have a natural and irresistible attraction for us, since at all periods of my life I have felt it, and that they have sometimes calmed my greatest agitations. Their influence is stultifying only for those who scorn them and do not know how to exact that quality of craft which is possible in everything. The man who spades the earth, does he not perform a harder and more monotonous task than the woman who sews? Yet, a good workman who spades quickly and well does not get bored with digging, and he tells you with a smile that he likes hard work.

To like hard work is the farmer's simple and profound maxim which every man and woman can utter without risking the inference of bondage. On the contrary, it is through hard work that our destiny escapes that rigorous law whereby man is exploited by man.

Hard work is a natural law from which none of us can be exempt without falling into evil. In socialist conjectures and aspirations of recent times, certain thinkers have believed they could resolve the problem of work by inventing a system of machines which would entirely eliminate physical effort and weariness. If that should happen, the preponderance of intellectual life would be as deplorable as is today the lack of balance between these two modes of existence. To find a balance is the problem which needs to be resolved—to see that the hard-working man has a sufficient ration of leisure and that the man of leisure has a sufficient ration of hard work. The physical and moral life of every man requires this absolutely, and if we cannot achieve it, we cannot hope to arrest our slide into decadence, which leads to the end of all happiness, dignity, wisdom, of all bodily health and mental lucidity. We are racing in that direction—no use denying it.

The cause, in my view, is none other than this: the minds of one part of humanity are too free, the minds of the other part too much in bondage. We shall seek in vain new political and social reforms; we need first and foremost a new breed of men. The present generation is sick to the marrow of its bones. After an attempt at a republic where the true aim from the outset was to try to establish as nearly as possible an equality in their conditions, we had to admit that making citizens equal before the law was not enough. I even venture to think that making them equal in the eyes of fortune would not have been enough. We would have to have had the power to make them equal in the true sense.

Too much ambition, leisure, and power on one side, and, on the other, too much indifference to sharing power and noble pastimes—that is what we found at the heart of this nation from which true men had disappeared, if indeed they ever existed. Men of the people, suddenly enlightened by knowledge and spurred on by great aspirations, have arisen and found themselves to be without prestige or influence over their brothers. Those men were wise as well, and devoted themselves to finding the solution to labor. The masses answered them, "No more work, or let us go back to work under the old laws. Make us a new world, or don't entice us away from our toil with fanciful dreams. Secure us the bare necessities, or unlimited abundance—we see no possible middle ground; we don't believe in it, we don't want to try it, and we can't wait for it."

There will, however, be no choice. Machines will never replace men absolutely, thank heaven, for that would be the end of the world. Man is not made to do nothing but think. When he thinks too much, he goes crazy, just as he becomes dull when he does not think enough. As Pascal said, "We are neither angels nor beasts."

And as for women, who need an intellectual life no more or no less than men, they also need manual labor appropriate to their strength. Too bad for those who cannot bring to such labor good taste, perseverance, skill, or desire, which are all the pleasure of hard work! For they are not men or women.

Winter is beautiful in the country, no matter what one says. It was not exactly my first winter, and it passed as quickly as a day, except for the six weeks I was obliged to spend in bed completely motionless. This order from Deschartres seemed severe to me, but what wouldn't I have done to preserve the hope of being a mother? It was the first time I had ever been imprisoned for reasons of health. But there was an unexpected compensation. The snow was so thick and stayed on the ground for so long that the birds were dying of hunger, and allowed themselves to be taken in the hand. All kinds were brought to me. My bed was covered with a green cloth, fir branches were tied to the bedposts, and I lived in this bower, surrounded by chaffinches, robins, greenfinches, and sparrows who, suddenly tamed by warmth and food, would come to eat out of my hands and warm themselves at my knees. When they recovered from their apathy, they would fly about the room, gaily at first, then anxiously, and then I would have the windows opened for them. Others would be brought to me and revived in the same manner, and after several hours or days of intimacy with me (that would vary according to the species of bird and the amount of suffering each had undergone), they would demand their liberty. It sometimes happened that some of those I had already marked and let go would be brought back to me. They seemed actually to recognize me and settle into their familiar nursing home as after a relapse.

One robin seemed determined to stay. The window was opened twenty times, and twenty times he went to the sill, looked at the snow, tried his wings in the open air, performed an elaborate pirouette, and returned in the manner of a sensible person who remains where he is well off. He stayed until halfway through the spring, even when the windows were open all day. This little bird was the most amusing and cheerful of guests. He was astonishingly impudent, bold, and gay. Perched on an andiron when the weather was cold, or on the tip of my foot extended toward the fire, he would go into a veritable frenzy at the sight of the bright flames. He would fly right into the middle of them, penetrate them in rapid flight, and return to his place without having singed a feather. At first this mad act terrified me, for I was very fond of him, but I got used to it, seeing that he did it with impunity.

He had an appetite as strange as his actions, and since he was very curious, he ingested everything from candle wax to almond paste. In short, his self-imposed domestication transformed him to the point where he had a good deal of difficulty becoming re-accustomed to rustic life when, toward the middle of April, after having succumbed to the magnetism of the sun, he found himself outside in the garden. For a long time we saw him flitting from branch to branch, and I never went out walking without seeing him come chirping and swooping around me.

My husband was getting along with Deschartres, who was coming to the end of his lease at Nohant. I had forewarned M. Dudevant about Deschartres' irritable and uncompromising character, and he had promised to handle him carefully. He kept his word, but he was naturally impatient to come into his own authority in our affairs, and Deschartres, for his part, wished to be in charge solely of his own. I persuaded my husband to offer Deschartres the opportunity of spending the rest of his life with us, and I eagerly pressed him to accept. It did not seem to me that Deschartres could live anywhere else, and I was not wrong. But he expressly refused, and candidly told me the reason. "For twenty-five years, I have been the sole and absolute master of this house," he said, "governing everything, supervising everyone, and having only women to direct me, for your father never interfered with anything. Your husband has not displeased me, as he has not interfered with my management. Now that that is at an end, it is I who would anger him, in spite of myself, by my criticisms and contradictions. I would be bored with having nothing to do, and I would be irritated when my advice was not taken. Anyway, I want to work for myself and manage my own affairs. You know how I have always intended to make my own fortune, and I feel the time has come."

This tenacious illusion on the part of my poor tutor was even harder to combat than his appetite for authority. It was decided he would leave Nohant on the day of Saint-Jean, the 24th of June, which was the last day of his lease. We left for Paris ahead of him, and there—after several days spent with our good friends at Le Plessis—I rented a little furnished apartment on Rue Neuve-des-Mathurins, at the Hôtel de Florence, the home of one of the Emperor's former chefs. This man, whose name was Gallyot, and who was a kind and decent man, had in the course of his serving impromptu snacks, contracted a singular habit—that of never going to bed. As we know, the Emperor's idea of a snack was always a chicken roasted to perfection, whatever the time of day or night. A man's existence had to be dedicated to the continued presence of that chicken on the spit, and Gallyot, charged with this responsibility, had slept on a chair for ten years, always fully dressed, always ready to jump to his feet. This demanding regimen had not saved him from obesity. He continued his work habits, as he was no longer able to lie down on a bed without suffocating, and claimed that the only way he could really sleep was with one eye open. He died of a liver ailment when he was in his fifties. His wife had been a chambermaid to the Empress Joséphine.

It was in their buildings, at the back of a second courtyard arranged as a garden, that I found a little pavilion where my son Maurice came into the world on the 30th of June, 1823, without mishap and very healthy. It was the most beautiful moment of my life, when after an hour of deep sleep which followed the terrible pains of that ordeal, I saw, on waking, the little being asleep on my pillow. I had dreamed about him so much before his arrival, and I was so weak, that I wasn't sure I wasn't still dreaming. I was afraid to move lest the vision vanish as it always had before.

I was kept in bed much longer than I should have been. It is usual in Paris to take many more precautions with women in this condition than it is in the country. When I became a mother for the second time, I got up the second day and was fine.

I nursed my son as I later nursed his sister. My mother was his godmother, and my father-in-law was his godfather.

Deschartres arrived from Nohant, full of plans for making a fortune and very stiff and formal in his bright-blue antique suit with gold buttons. He looked so provincial in his outdated attire that people turned to look at him in the street. But it didn't bother him, and he passed by majestically. He examined Maurice closely, unwrapped him, and looked him over on all sides, to make sure that there was nothing to criticize or correct. He didn't kiss him—I don't remember ever having seen Deschartres caress or kiss anyone—but he held him asleep on his lap and contemplated him a long time. Then, satisfied with having seen the child, he returned to his theme that it was time for him to live for himself.

I spent the following autumn and winter at Nohant, completely preoccupied with Maurice. In the spring of 1824, I was seized with a deep depression whose cause I could not explain. It was everything and nothing. Nohant had been improved, but turned inside out; the house and garden had changed. There was more order and less abuse among the servants; the rooms were better kept, the paths straighter, the courtyard more spacious; the dead trees had been burned, the lame and unhealthy old dogs had been killed, the old horses no longer in service had been sold—in short, everything was renovated. It was undoubtedly better. Furthermore, all this kept my husband busy and satisfied. I approved of everything and had no reasonable cause for sorrow, but the mind has its oddnesses. When this transformation had been achieved, when I no longer saw old Phanor take possession of the hearth and put his muddy paws on the rug, when I learned that the old peacock who used to eat out of my grandmother's hand would no longer eat the strawberries in the garden, when I could no longer repair to the dark and neglected spots where I had played my childhood games or had my adolescent reveries, when practically a whole new interior foretold a future where nothing of my past joys and sorrows would fit, I was troubled; and without reflection, without consciousness of anything really being wrong, I felt overwhelmed by a new distaste for living which once again took the form of illness.

One morning at breakfast, without any obvious reason for distress, I suddenly burst into tears. My husband was astonished. I could not give him any explanation except that I had experienced similar attacks of despair and probably was suffering some sort of derangement or breakdown. He agreed, and also attributed his own anxiety to our stay at Nohant, to the recent loss of my grandmother (of whom everyone spoke to him in a most melancholy fashion), to the country air—exterior causes, in short—which he felt in spite of the hunting and riding and his life as a landowner. He confessed to me that he was not at all happy in Berry and that he would rather live somewhere, anywhere, else. We agreed to try, and we left for Le Plessis.

Thanks to a financial arrangement which our friends agreed to make with us for the purpose of putting me at ease, we spent the summer with them, and I recaptured the carefree abandon so necessary to youth. Life at Le Plessis was charming; the lovable character of our hosts was reflected in the varied natures of their numerous guests. We put on plays, we hunted on the grounds, we took long walks, and we entertained so many people that it was easy for everyone to find the right group for company. Mine was formed from everyone the château had to offer in the way of children. From the toddlers to the young girls and boys, cousins, nephews, and friends of the family, we found ourselves in a group of a dozen or so, which was augmented further by the children and adolescents from the farm. I was not the oldest member, but being the only married one, I was the natural governor of this considerable personnel. Loïsa Puget, who had become a charming young lady; Félicie Saint Agnan, who was still just a grown-up girl, but whose lovable nature evoked in me a preference for her which in time became a serious friendship; Tonine du Plessis, the second daughter of my mother Angèle, who was still a child and who, like Félicie, was to die in the flower of youth—these were my favorite companions. We organized games of all kinds, from badminton to prisoner's base, and we invented rules which allowed even those who, like Maurice, were still crawling on all fours, to play a pretended part in the general activity. Then there were the excursions—real expeditions, considering the short legs of those who followed us through the grounds and immense gardens. When necessary, the bigger carried the smaller ones, and the gaiety and movement were unceasing. In the evening, when the adults gathered, it often happened that many of them took part in our rumpus, but when they tired of it, which happened very quickly, we would say mischievously to one another that those ladies and gentlemen didn't know how to play, and that we would have to exhaust them with racing the next day to make them sick of it.

My husband, like many of the others, was a little astonished to see me return suddenly to being so lively and wild in these activities, which seemed so different from my usual melancholy pursuits. Only I and my carefree band were not surprised. Children do not question their pleasure and readily grasp that one can dream of nothing better; as for me, I was aware once again, in conditions of primitive innocence, of showing one of the two sides of my character, just as I had at Nohant from the ages of eight to twelve, and at the convent from thirteen to sixteen, alternating repeatedly between withdrawn solitude and and utter giddiness.

At fifty years of age, I am exactly as I was then. I love reverie, contemplation, and work; but beyond a certain point, sadness takes over, because contemplation turns to melancholy, and if perforce reality appears in a sinister form, either my soul is obliged to succumb, or gaiety must come to my rescue.

Thus, I have an absolute need for true and wholesome gaiety. The lewd kind disgusts me and the intellectual kind bores me. Brilliant conversation entertains me when I feel like putting forth the effort required to listen to it, but I cannot endure a conversation of any substance for long without feeling very tired. If it is serious, it seems like a political gathering or business meeting; if it is slight, it is no longer a pleasure for me. When one has something to say or hear, the subject is thoroughly exhausted in an hour, and thereafter one is just floundering. I myself do not have a sufficiently tenacious mind to discuss a number of serious matters in succession, and it is perhaps to console myself for this deficiency that I tell myself, when listening to very talkative people, that nobody is any good at talk for more than an hour a day.

What can be done then to liven up the hours of a group living in the closeness of everyday life? Usually talking about politics occupies the men, and talking about fashions takes care of the women. I am neither a man nor a woman in that regard; I am a child. While doing some handiwork, which occupies my eyes, or while walking, which occupies my legs, I need to hear around me a vital exchange which does not remind me of the emptiness and horror of human existence. Accusations, blame, suspicions, meanness, mockery, condemnations—these are what wait at the end of all political or literary discussions, because understanding, confidence, and admiration are unfortunately more concisely expressed than are aversion, criticism, and gossip. Saintliness is not my natural condition in life, but poetry is my reason for being, and everything that extinguishes the dream of the good, the simple, and the true—a dream which alone sustains me against the terrors of the century—is torture I avoid as much as possible.

That is why, having met few exceptions to my frightfully positivist contemporaries, I have nearly always lived, by instinct and by choice, with people to whom I could have been a mother, give or take a few years. Furthermore, in all situations where I have been able to choose my style of living, I have looked for ways to idealize the reality around me and transform it into an illusionary oasis, where the wicked or idle would not be tempted to enter or remain. A dream of a golden age, a mirage of pastoral innocence, artistic and poetical, took possession of me in childhood and has followed me into maturity. Thus, a host of simple, but active, amusements has been heartily shared by those around me, and all the more innocently and warmly by those with the purest hearts. It is those pure hearts who, on becoming acquainted with me, are no longer astonished by the contrasts of a mind so inclined to melancholy and so eager for gaiety; or perhaps I should say, of a soul so unsatisfied with what interests most people and so easily charmed by whatever they judge to be childish or visionary. I cannot better explain myself; I don't know myself very well from the theoretical point of view; I hold mainly to the experience of what defeats or revives me in everyday life.

But because of these contrasts, certain people have gotten the impression that I am very peculiar. My husband, who was more indulgent, considered me an idiot. Perhaps he was right, and little by little he managed to make me feel so strongly the superiority of his reason and intelligence, that for a long time I was overwhelmed by it and intimidated in front of others. I did not complain. Deschartres had taught me not to forcefully contradict the infallibility of others, and my own natural laziness adapted itself very well to a regime of silence and self-effacement.

With the approach of winter, as Mme. du Plessis was going to Paris, my husband and I went into consultation about our next residence. We did not have the means to live in Paris, and furthermore neither of us liked Paris. We loved the country, but we were afraid of Nohant; probably we were afraid of finding ourselves alone face to face again, with totally different inclinations and characters which could not interrelate. We did not want to hide anything from each other, but neither did we know how to clarify anything; we never argued—I had too great a horror of argument to challenge someone else; on the contrary, I made enormous efforts to see things through my husband's eyes and think and do as he wished. But the minute I had come to agree with him, I would fall into dreadful sadness, because I no longer felt in agreement with my own instincts.

He was probably experiencing something similar without realizing it, and he aligned himself eagerly with me when I talked to him about surrounding ourselves with friends or doing new things. If I had had the knack of moving us into a more outward and animated existence, if I had been a little lighter in spirit, if I had been interested in the activity of varied social relationships, he would have been jostled and sustained by daily interaction with others. But I was not at all the kind of companion he needed. I was too exclusive, too introverted, too unconventional. If I had known what was wrong, if the cause of his ennui and mine had been clear to my inexperienced and unpenetrating mind, I might have found the remedy; perhaps I would have succeeded in transforming myself. But I did not understand a thing about myself or him.

We looked for a small house to rent in the Paris region, and since we were not very well off, we had great difficulty finding a little comfort without spending a lot of money. The house we rented was a rather poor dwelling. But it was at Ormesson, in a beautiful park, surrounded by very pleasant companions.

The area was then rather ugly and mournful, terrible roads, vineyard hillocks which obstructed the view, and a dirty village. But not far from there, the pond of Enghien and the beautiful gardens of Saint-Gratien provided pleasant walks. Our housing was attached to the residence of a very distinguished lady, Mme. Richardot, who had lovely children. An adjoining residence, belonging to M. Hédé, Baker to the King, was rented and occupied by the Malus family, and each evening, our three families would gather at Mme. Richardot's to play charades in the most comically improvised costumes. Also, my Aunt Lucy and dear Clotilde, her daughter, came to spend several days with us. That autumn was a very peaceful season in my life's history.

My husband went out a great deal; he was often called to Paris for some business or other, and would return in the evening to take part in the diversions of the gathering. This style of life was considered quite normal—the men occupied elsewhere during the day, the women at home with their children, and in the evening, recreation with several families together.

A strange and magnificent ceremony, the last of its kind that France has seen and that it will probably never see again, at least in the same form, summoned us all as if to a theatrical event. It was the funeral at Saint-Denis of Louis XVIII.

Louis XVIII had died without even rippling the surface of the Bourbon restoration. Charles X succeeded him without disturbance. The liberal party even welcomed him with real or feigned benevolence. The entire nation wore official mourning. It was a singular thing that this mourning was taken up spontaneously, like a change of fashion, and after having struggled for some time against what appeared to me to be hypocrisy or gratuitous adulation, I, too, went along in order not to stand out like a spot of color among all those other women dressed in black from head to toe. Those around me were all members of the bonapartist or liberal opposition, and wore their black crepe with a smile, saying that black was becoming and that one would look like a person from the provinces or a grocer's wife if one didn't wear it. I had to wear it in order not to be considered a "free-thinker."

None of us had thought to get tickets for the ceremony. None of us wanted to brave the waiting, the crowd, the fatigue which are an inevitable part of these state occasions. The evening before the funeral, Mme. Richardot was taken with the fancy of wanting to go. Energetic and decisive, she persuaded us all to come, and although getting into the church seemed an impossibility, we were off at seven in the morning to try our luck. It happened as she had predicted—thousands of people who had procured tickets well in advance had to return to Paris without getting in, and we, who did not have any, were immediately placed in one of the best sections of benches. "On these occasions," said Mme. Richardot, "you always have to count on two things—the confusion you find and the will-power you bring."

She presented herself with determination to the officials in charge and requested a little space for herself and her party. "In a little while," was the answer after some negotiating, "—if there aren't too many of you."

"Oh, goodness," she replied with aplomb, "there are only sixteen of us." The official began to laugh and seated all sixteen of us so well that we did not miss a single detail of the spectacle.

It was awesome to behold—banks of votive candles against the black hangings, and at the front of the nave a huge flaming cross that hurt my eyes with its glare, and promptly gave me a headache. The beautiful structure of the basilica was completely hidden under draperies; the profusion of light was dazzling, yet did not dispel the darkness of this monument in mourning. It took two hours or more for my eyes to get used to that sharp flickering against the opaque velvet. Nearby, I heard Mme. Pasta[35] say to those who admired the decor, "It's not beautiful at all, it's ugly. It resembles Hell, or a witches' sanctum."

The music, although wonderful, was muffled, as if buried in a cellar. The ceremony was endless. Those ancient forms of royal and religious protocol would have been of historic interest to me, stripped of the mass of silly and incomprehensible details which burdened them. A funeral oration delivered by a frail voice in a completely dead spot was heard by perhaps twenty persons. Some sort of anthem, sung around a seated prelate whom two priests crowned and uncrowned with his pointed mitre at each verse and response, went on for two hours and seemed to me the worst joke that any man could pretend to be serious about. Then came all the princes of the royal family in the violet mourning of the court and in costumes which recalled those of the last Valois kings. They left their places, returned to them, executed deep bows, kneeled on a cushion, made obeisance to the departed king and to the new king. But all this was done in such enigmatic pantomime that each spectator would have had to have a handbook or guide to explain the meaning and reason for each movement. This was the first time I saw Louis-Philippe, then Duc d'Orléans. He still looked young and seemed even more so compared to all the other princes, who were old, bent, and acted embarrassed or were uncomfortable in their costumes. He wore his with ease and seemed to have rehearsed his part, for he performed it strutting, with head held high and a kind of smiling expression. I heard some of those around me saying how well he looked, while others muttered about his audacious, mocking air. Someone passed along a bad political pun, which had just made the rounds in the auditory and was already traveling from one gallery to another—"They should have given the Duc d'Orléans a different cushion than the one on which the other princes kneeled, a cushion without tassels [*sans glands* : *sanglant* : bloody]."

The joke itself was not very *sanglant* [incisive], though it pretended to be an allusion to the part Philip-Egalité, father of Louis-Philippe, was supposed to have played in the dramatic death of Louis XVI.[36]

Finally, the really dramatic moment came when the huge lead casket was lowered into the open vault. The ropes broke, and the pallbearers who were carrying it narrowly escaped being dragged down and crushed. The expression which the effort and danger of this operation lent their faces, the funeral sounds of drums and cymbals, and the shock which swept through the audience broke the monotony of the performance, and many of the women whose nerves were at the breaking point, exacerbated by hunger, fatigue, and boredom, burst into tears and were unable to restrain their sobbing.

Finally, at four o'clock in the afternoon, we were at last permitted to leave the church which we had entered at eight in the morning. Never did daylight and fresh air seem so welcome to me.

When winter came, the Richardot and the Malus families returned to

Paris. We remained alone at Ormesson. I still enjoyed being there. I spent long hours in the solitude of the spacious English gardens, a melancholy landscape of huge trees and lawns. There was a very pretty fountain and a tomb heavily shaded with cypress trees, which was purely ornamental but nevertheless had a good deal of character. I thought of this tomb again later, when writing certain pages of *Lélia* [1833].

Maurice was growing remarkably and would run around me as I walked along reading. It was in this park that I read the *Essaies* of Montaigne in their entirety. I have never tired of those engaging treatises and that cheerfully good mind whose skepticism never appeared as dangerous or depressing to me as it has to others. Montaigne does not seem like a skeptic to me, but a stoic. Though he seldom arrives at a conclusion, he teaches constantly; without preaching, he engenders a love of wisdom, reason, tolerance for others, observation of oneself. His boldness inspires a taste for restraint, and his doubts lead one to the need for faith. In any case, his is like all work that springs from a great intelligence—it makes one reflect sanely and calmly.

One day, when I was letting Maurice jump up and down on a little patch of grass no bigger than his two feet, the gardener of the house, who was a sort of steward whenever the masters were absent, admonished me roundly about the "damage" which my "young man" was doing. I answered perfectly pleasantly that I could see no damage, and I took my child away, but each time I met this surly man, he looked at me so ferociously and answered my greeting with so much disdain that he made me frightened for my little boy and threatened the serenity of my walks.

My husband sometimes spent the night in Paris; my manservant slept in a building some distance away, and I was alone with my womanservant in a house isolated from the other inhabited dwellings. I was imagining some terrible things ever since I had heard, on one of those foggy nights when sounds are weirdly ominous, the screams for help of a man being beaten. It sounded as if he were being butchered. I have since learned the facts of this strange incident, but I cannot or shall not relate them.

I was gradually reassured, seeing that the gardener who frightened me was not personally aggrieved with me, but only very put out by our presence, which perhaps frustrated some plan of his for occupying the extension or for misappropriating household goods. I remembered Jean-Jacques Rousseau being turned out of one estate after another, and one retreat after another, by scheming and ill-will of this kind, and I began to regret not being in my own home.

Yet I felt sorry to leave this place when, one day, my husband, having quarrelled violently with this same gardener, decided to move our household to Paris. We took a furnished apartment, small but pleasing due to its seclusion and view of the gardens, on Rue du Faubourg Saint-Honoré. There I often saw old and new friends, and our surroundings were quite cheerful.

However, my sadness returned—a vague and nameless sadness, perhaps even pathological. I was worn out from having nursed my son; I had not got back my strength since that time. I blamed myself for this depression, and I thought that it might be caused by the almost imperceptible cooling of my religious faith. I went to see my Jesuit, Abbé de Prémord. He had aged much in three years. His voice was so feeble and his lungs so spent that one could hardly hear him. We talked a long time, nevertheless, and on several occasions he recaptured some of his gentle eloquence to comfort me, but he did not succeed finally; there was too much tolerance in his doctrine for a soul so hungry for absolute faith as mine was. This faith was escaping me; I do not know who could have given it back to me, but certainly he could not. He was too sympathetic about the agonies of doubt. Perhaps he understood them all too well. He was too intelligent, or too human. He advised me to go and spend some time in the convent. He asked permission for it from the Mother Superior, Madame Eugénie. I asked the same permission of my husband, and I went into retreat at the English convent.

My husband was in no way religious but found it perfectly agreeable that I was. I did not discuss with him my inner struggles in the area of faith; he would have understood nothing about an anguish he had never experienced.

I was welcomed into the convent with infinite tenderness, and as I was really unwell, I was immersed in maternal care. It was perhaps not the place to help me adapt to my new life. All that gentle goodness, that delicate solicitude brought back memories of a happiness whose absence had been unbearable to me for a long time and made the present seem empty and the future frightening. I wandered about in the cloisters with a desolate and trembling heart. I wondered if I had not turned my back on my calling, my instincts, my destiny, by leaving this silent refuge from profane knowledge, where I would have laid to rest the agitations of my timorous spirit and chained to an indisputable law my rebellious will, which I did not myself know how to deal with. I entered that little chapel where I had felt so much saintly ardor and divine joy; I found there only the longing for the days when I believed I had the strength to make eternal vows. I had not had that strength, and now I felt I did not even have enough to live in the outside world.

I tried to see, too, the dark and slavish side of monastic life, in order to become attached again to the sweetness of the liberty I could regain at any moment. In the evening, hearing the rounds of the sister who locked the many doors of the hallways, I would have liked to shiver at the sound of the creaking bolts and the sonorous echos rebounding from the vaulted ceilings, but I did not feel anything of the sort. The cloister held no terrors for me. It seemed to me that I cherished and longed for everything about that communal life where you can truly belong, for by depending on everyone, you are in reality dependent on no one. On the contrary, I saw much ease and freedom in that captivity which protects, in that discipline which guarantees hours for devotion, in that monotony of duties which preserves you from the unexpected!

I would go and sit in the classroom, on those cold benches, among those smoke-blackened desks, and I would watch the students laughing during their recess. Some of my former classmates were still there, but they had grown up and changed so much that they had to be introduced to me. They were curious about my life; they were envious of my "liberation," while I was trying to do nothing but recapture the thousands of memories brought back to me by every little nook and cranny of the classroom, every little mark on the wall, every nick in the stove or the desktops.

My good mother Alicia did not encourage me any more than she had in the past to live on frivolous dreams. "You have a charming child," she would say, "that is all you need for happiness in this world. Life is short."

Yes, a peaceful life is short. Fifty years are like a day when the soul is at rest, but one day of stirring emotions can add up to centuries of fatigue and malaise.

However, the things she said to me about the joys of motherhood—a joy which she did not allow herself to feel deprived of, but one which she clearly would have eagerly savored—responded to my most intimate instincts. I did not know how I would have been able to give up Maurice; all the while I was longing to remain in the convent, in spite of myself I would look for him around me at every step I took. I asked to have him join me. "Oh, yes, indeed," Poulette said, laughing. "A boy among nuns! Is he at least quite small, that little man? Let's have a look at him. If he can fit in the turning box, we'll let him in."

The box was a hollow cylinder which turned on a pivot in the wall. It had an opening on only one end, where parcels from outside were placed; it was then turned toward the inside and emptied. Maurice fit quite comfortably into this box and bounced smiling into the midst of the nuns who had run up to receive him. All those black veils and white dresses surprised him a little, and he began to call out one of the three or four words he knew, "Rabbits! Rabbits!" He was made so welcome and was stuffed with so many sweets that he quickly became accustomed to the pleasures of the convent, and could run about in the garden without any scowling gardener coming to scold him, as had happened at Ormesson when he jumped on the grass.

I was permitted to have him every day. He was spoiled, and my good mother Alicia proudly called him her grandson. I would have spent all Lent there, but a remark from Sister Hélène caused me to leave.

I had found this dear and saintly person cured and strengthened both physically and spiritually. This had surely been mandatory physically, because when I had left, she had again been at death's door. But spiritually the cure had gone too far. She had become rude and almost savage in her proselytism. She was not profuse in her welcome, brusquely reproaching me for my "earthly happiness," and since I showed her my child as an answer to her reproach, she looked at him disdainfully and said to me in English, in her biblical style: "All is deception and vanity outside the love of the Lord. This precious infant is only a puff of air. To give him your heart is to write on sand."

I showed her that the child was pink and plump, and since she did not want to have belied a speech made with so much conviction, looking at him again, she said to me, "Bah! he's too pink; he's probably consumptive!"

It so happened that the child was coughing a little. I immediately thought he was ill, and I allowed my mind to be influenced by Hélène's self-styled prediction. For this completely self-absorbed, fierce nature, which I had once so admired and envied, I felt a sudden revulsion. She affected me like an oracle of misfortune. I left in a cab, and I spent the night fretting over the sleep of my little boy, listening to his breathing, becoming panicky over the pretty, high color in his cheeks.

The doctor came to see him first thing in the morning. There was nothing at all wrong with him, and I was ordered to take much less care of him than I had been doing. But the scare I had had removed all desire to return to the convent. I could not keep Maurice there at night, and besides it was dreadfully cold there during the day. I returned to say my good-byes and thank-you's.   *J.H.C.*

X

Émilie de Wismes. —Sidonie Macdonald. —M. de Sémonville.
—The Demoiselles Bazouin. —The mysterious death of Deschartres,
perhaps a suicide. —My brother gets a head start toward a disastrous
habit. —Aimée and Jane at Nohant. —Trip to the Pyrenees.
—Fragments of a journal written in 1825. —Cauterets, Argelès, Luz,
Saint-Sauveur, the Marboré, etc. —The shepherds come down from
the mountains. —The passage of the flocks. —A dream of pastoral
life takes possession of me. —Bagnères-de-Bigorre. —Spelunking at
Lourdes. —Retrospective fear. —Departure for Nérac.

Before finding a suitable apartment, we had spent a couple of weeks with my aunt. Her daughter, Clotilde, was still a wonderful friend to me. We played a lot of music together. Once settled in their neighborhood, I saw them often during the winter.

During that time I again saw several of my friends from the convent who had returned to life outside or were married. Émilie de Wismes, still something of a joker, was to marry a M. de Cornulier, whom it pleased her to describe as old and ugly. I was surprised to see her accept her lot so gaily. One evening I met her with her parents, coming out of the Opéra. "Oh, come look!" she said to me. "I want to point him out to you—the one going by, over there." She indicated the first ridiculous-looking person who happened by in the corridor—a threadbare coat, a bewigged head. I was shocked, at which point she burst out laughing. "Don't worry," she finally said, "it isn't that gentleman; I don't know him at all. My intended is twenty-two, and he's better-looking."

I saw Sidonie Macdonald again, living near the Luxembourg park, in the same apartment where, twenty years later, I dined with Louis Blanc, member of the provisional government of the Republic. Sidonie was married to the grandson of M. de Sémonville, chief referendary to the Chamber of Peers. It was not until 1839 that I met M. de Sémonville, a kind and charming old man who, at the age of eighty, had the mind and heart of a young man, and having been seized with an exalted affection for me at first sight, would talk to me about his love with the timidity and naïveté of a school boy. I was told he had been very much the libertine; he seemed so little inclined to that in his speech that I thought he must have been no more than an ardent romantic. He died not long after I met him.

The friends whom I saw the most of were the Demoiselles Bazouin. The eldest, Chérie, had died; the second one, Aimée, was quite seriously ill; Jane, the youngest, my favorite, was gentle and serious. Chérie's death had devastated Aimée. Jane, the weakest and most delicate of the three, found superhuman strength by selflessly caring for her sister with angelic tenderness. I have never known a more beautiful soul than Jane's. She still typifies for me the true saint. Her self-imposed austerity could add nothing to the candor or the exquisite purity of her instincts. Even aside from her piety, she was one of those rare natures to whom thoughts of evil are unknown, to whom evil would be impossible. She had the mind of a mature person and the indestructible innocence of a small child. A nearly divine peace reigned within her, along with an exquisite sensitivity and Christian humility which were complemented by a taste for modesty and the never-ending need to sacrifice her own personality for that of others. All that beauty of character was to be seen in her large dark eyes, usually timid but at times searching and penetrating, deep as a quiet night and gentle as a warming sun.

Happy was the man who married her even if he did not comprehend his good fortune.

Their father was rich and lived grandly, but in an almost total withdrawal from the world. I never understood what kind of a man he was or why he waited so long to give his daughters in marriage. He spared nothing to make their existence enchanting. Their furnishings were splendid; gardens, horses, travel, the best teachers of the arts, exotic flowers, rare birds, superb country houses—everything that could foster and gratify their charming tastes was lavished on them. Their smallest desires were anticipated and provided for delicately and sumptuously. And yet they were not happy; at least Aimée languished under the burden of a deep-rooted malady and dissatisfaction which she tried vainly to shed for fear of causing her sister pain; and Jane, who would have been happy anywhere with birds and flowers, suffered constantly from the suffering of Aimée.

They planned a trip to the Pyrenees for the following June, and my husband was to take me to his father's near Nérac. It was arranged that they would come via Nohant and that we would rejoin them at Cauterets before going to Guillery.

Colonel Dudevant was in Paris with his wife, whom I did my best to like, although she was not at all pleasant. My father-in-law was the best of men. We often dined at their home along with Deschartres, whom the old colonel loved to tease and whom he called a Jesuit, while Deschartres called him a Jacobin, names equally unmerited on both sides.

Deschartres was settled at the Place Royale. He had a very pretty and inexpensive apartment there. He had furnished it and appeared to enjoy a certain ease of circumstance. He would tell us of small business dealings which had been unsuccessful, but which were destined to lead to a larger and inevitably successful transaction. What was this great transaction? I understood little about it; I could not manage to pay much attention to the complicated explanations of my poor pedagogue. It had something to do with rape oil and colza. Deschartres was tired of applied agriculture. He did not want to sow and reap anymore, he wanted to buy and sell. He had, alas, made connections among people with "ideas," like himself. He made plans and calculations on paper, and what was most surprising for him who was so disagreeable and so unwilling to value any judgment but his own, he bestowed his trust on strangers and lent them his money.

My father-in-law often said to him, "Monsieur Deschartres, you're a dreamer, and you're going to get cheated." He would shrug his shoulders and pay no attention.

Maurice was very dear to Deschartres and was also extravagantly spoiled by the colonel. As for Mme. Dudevant, she could not abide toddlers, and mine having had several mishaps on her floor, she was so disgusted by these improprieties that she urged me to bring him to her house again only on assurance that all necessary precautions had been taken. That was very difficult, as Maurice had not yet grasped the solemnity of sworn oaths. He was eighteen months old.

In the spring of 1825, we returned to Nohant, and three months went by without any news from Deschartres. As I was surprised not to get answers to my letters, and since I could not ask my father-in-law about it as he had left Paris, I sent to Place Royale for information.

Poor Deschartres was dead. He had risked all of his small fortune and lost it in ill-fated enterprises. He had said nothing about it even up to his last hours. No one had known anything, and no one had seen him for a long time. He had bequeathed his furniture and possessions to a laundress who had cared for him devotedly. Otherwise, there had been no remembrances, no complaints, no requests, and no good-byes. He had disappeared from the face of the earth, taking with him the secret of his blighted ambition or betrayed confidence; he was probably resigned, for in everything concerning himself alone—physical suffering as well as misfortune—he was a true stoic.

His death affected me more deeply than I cared to admit. Even though I had at first felt a kind of involuntary relief at being freed from his tiresome dogmatism, I already sensed that, in him, I had lost the presence of a devoted heart and the contact with a mind remarkable in many ways. My brother, who had hated him for his tyranny, mourned his loss but did not wish him back. My mother did not spare him just because he had passed on, and she wrote, "At last Deschartres is gone!" For many who had known him, he did not figure among their best memories. The recognition of him as an honest man was the only credit they could grudgingly bestow on such an anti-social being. In short, with the exception of two or three farmers whose lives he had saved, characteristically refusing any payment, there was hardly anyone but me who shed a tear for "the great man," and I had to hide even that, in order not to be mocked or hurt those whom he had too cruelly hurt. But in truth he did take with him into the oblivion of things past a significant part of my life—all my childhood memories, happy and sad, and all the sometimes unfortunate, sometimes beneficial stimulation to my intellectual development. I felt myself an orphan a little more than before. Poor Deschartres! He had gainsaid his nature and his destiny by ceasing to live for the sake of friendship. He had believed himself an egoist, but he was wrong; he was unable to live for and by himself.

It occurred to me that he could have committed suicide. I could not obtain any precise details of his last moments. He had been ill for several weeks, ill with sorrow probably, but I could not believe that so hearty a constitution could be so quickly broken by the prospect of financial ruin. Besides, he must have received a last letter from me in which I was still asking him to come to Nohant. With his enterprising mind and belief in the inexhaustible resources of his genius, wouldn't he have regained hope and confidence if he had given himself time for reflection? Hadn't he instead succumbed to a moment of discouragement and hastened the catastrophe with some strong remedy intended to take away the illness and the sorrow along with the life? He had reprimanded me so often on this subject that I would hardly have believed such a dire inconsistency on his part if I had not remembered that my poor tutor was inconsistency personified. At other times he had said to me, "The day your father died, I was ready to blow my brains out." Another time, I had heard him say to someone, "If I were hopelessly incapacitated, I would not want to be anyone's burden. I'd take a dose of opium and end it all, without telling a soul." And lastly, he habitually spoke of death with the disdain of the ancients and applauded the "sages" who, by means of suicide, had willfully escaped the tyranny of external control.

It is time I spoke of my brother, who had already caused me much pain and was living sometimes with me, sometimes at La Châtre, and sometimes in Paris.

He had married, shortly after I, Mlle. Émilie de Villeneuve,[37] an excellent person and relatively rich, who had a house in Paris and was soon to inherit property bordering our own. From the start he did not manage her small fortune very well. He was, by turns, feverishly involved in taking care of his financial interests and absorbed by an unfortunate passion for the local wine, which was so widespread among the country dwellers of Berry that permanent abstention from it was almost unheard of; he depleted more than he increased the resources of his family, thus finding himself plagued by debts, and drowned his worries in drink.

This absurd and fatal infirmity, for I cannot consider drunkenness anything but a slow and persistent illness, was the death of one of the most charming minds, best hearts, pleasantest tempers I have ever known. My brother had much of our father's wit and soulfulness, just as in his youth he had his looks and demeanor. But after the age of thirty, a moral and physical coarsening erased the resemblance, and he single-mindedly entered on a suicidal course by which his nature was abused, his abilities extinguished, and his very heart embittered; his body survived his soul for a number of years.

From that came the real suffering and misfortune that surrounded him, but alas, in that excruciatingly equitable, final summing up which the dead not only permit but command us to make of their lives, I realized how many of his errors were unintentional and how that soul, which is now delivered from its fatal brutalization, was by nature inoffensive, intelligent, and good. Calm and reasonable conversation had become impossible for him in his last years, but subtracting the time out for periodic alienation from drunkenness, one could yet reconstruct a valuable life and blessed memories by recollecting all the hours of lucidity, when he was himself.

His savage passion for wine and strong spirits hurled a huge stone into the pond of my domestic tranquility. Others around me have been infected by it, others have also died of it, and still others have been cured—not exactly in time to save their family's happiness, but in time to save their own existences.

My brother and his wife had a pretty little girl about the age of Maurice. They often brought her to me and sometimes even left her with me for an entire season, so that she could grow strong in the country whenever the running of the house in Paris forced them to be away for any length of time. Léontine was therefore partly brought up with Maurice, under my care.

Hippolyte was with us, I remember, when M. Bazouin came with his daughters and a kindly old magistrate friend of his named M. Gaillard. We took drives together. Aimée would ride my homely, amenable Colette, accompanied by my brother, who gave up drinking for a few days.

On the 30th of June, our servants and workers celebrated Maurice's birthday. They brought him to me in a framework of flowers, built by the village carpenter, decorated by the gardener, rather like those in which relics or figures of saints are carried in the Corpus Christi procession.[38] They placed the child and the frame in the middle of a table, fired a round of pistol salutes, and danced a bourée.

The following 5th of July was my birthday. I was twenty-one. On that day we left for the south of France. I kept an account of that trip in the form of a diary which serves as a guide to my recollections. Several pages, which I shall quote, portray my emotional state. I was quite unhappy, as you will see. Besides, I was ill, though perhaps less so than I appeared. I had a persistent cough, frequent palpitations, and some symptoms of consumption. But I have often had a recurrence of this problem, which has always taken care of itself and which I have been obliged to attribute to nerves. At the time of my story I did not think I was nervous, I thought I was consumptive.

Trip to the Pyrenees (July 5, 1825)

In ten minutes I shall have left Nohant. There is nothing I am really sorry to leave behind unless it is my brother. But how this old friendship of times past has cooled! He laughs, he is cheerful at the hour of my departure, he is indeed! So then, good-bye Nohant; perhaps I shall never see you again.

Chalus

My servants were weeping. I could not restrain myself—I did likewise. In the carriage I read several pages of Ossian. Daylight deserted me there, right in the midst of shadows and errant stars; so I resorted to reflection, not a small problem for me who would rather go through life without thinking at all. I made some beautiful resolutions about the trip—I would not worry about Maurice's every whimper, I would not get impatient with the long rides, I would not get upset at the fits of temper of "my friend."

Périgueux

I have traveled through some charming countryside; I have seen some beautiful horses. The town seems pleasant, but I am deathly sad. I cried a lot while out walking, but what good is it to cry? I have to get used to smiling though my soul feels dead.

Tarbes

A beautiful sky, rushing streams, strange formations of boulders carried by the torrent, varied costumes, a village fair, the lively folk of this whole southern part of France. Tarbes is very pretty; but my husband is still very ill-humored. The traveling bores him; he wants to be there already. I can understand that, but it isn't my fault if the trip is two hundred leagues. . . .

Gradually this amphitheater of white mountains comes closer and takes on color. In spite of the excessive heat, I climbed up on the driver's seat of the carriage with my husband to get a better view. At last we entered the Pyrenees. Surprise and admiration nearly overwhelmed me. I have always dreamed of high mountains. Of these I had only a vague memory which is now reawakening and being filled in; but neither the memory nor my imagination prepared me for the emotions I feel. I had no idea of the height of these masses which reach the clouds or of the variety of venerable detail they display. Some are fertile and cultivated right up to the summit; others are devoid of vegetation but bristle with imposing rocks strewn about as if in the aftermath of a cataclysm.

The road follows the rushing waters upstream to Cauterets. Leaving Pierrefitte, climbing an incline which was incredibly steep for harnessed horses, hearing the roaring fury of the torrent, the soul seems to shrivel, and cold fear envelops the heart. There the daylight has a bluish tinge, and the sky is shrunk by black mountains of marble and slate to which cling the dark heather and a few dwarf trees. The road snakes along the flanks of a gorge, along the rocky walls of a chasm. Outcrops of stone protrude and hang over. The precipice deepens; the torrent thunders and plunges deeper, sometimes completely disappearing under a mass of wild and splendid vegetation, sometimes foaming white as snow between the bare rock walls which press in on it, or among the boulders crowding its course. In some places, the flow comes nearer and becomes peaceful, limpid, and blue as the sky. Small-leaved linden trees, covered with blossoms, grow on its banks and reach up to the level of the road, presenting their fragrant tops to the travelers.

All that seemed both terrible and delightful. An incredible and irrational fear gripped me, a fear of heights, which was not without its charm. I was intoxicated, and I wanted to shout. Our servant Vincent, whose place I had taken on the driver's seat and who was in the carriage with Maurice and Fanchon, poked his head out of the window from time to time and said, "It's very nice, I must say it is really very nice."

Finally, I saw Jane and Aimée at a crossroads. An instant later we were frantically embracing. At the hotel there was a room for us right beside theirs. . . .

The accommodations are primitively simple and exorbitantly expensive. The little town, or rather hamlet, is built entirely of unpolished marble. The streams are crystal-clear; everything is clean, repaired after each thaw; and the town is full of rather unpleasant society people. We are in a huge hotel of furnished apartments.

This morning, hardly awake, I ran to the window. Well! It seems we are in the plains! Where did last night's mountains go? Where did they hide the waterfalls whose noise I hear? The fog had come in so thick and white we could not even see the foot of the Pyrenees. It cleared gradually in remarkable shreddings. It was not like the fog of our flatlands, a delicate curtain which gently rolls up. It was a thick veil slashed with narrow openings or pierced with holes. Cauterets is built in a crater whose upper edges locate the horizon, not below eye level but overhead. Through the shreds of fog I was astonished to see a little piece of scenery, a chalet, a tree, a flock of sheep arranged on a vertical plane like a painting suspended in air, like a dream tossed out into space. The shifting mist shrouded it quickly and let another scene be discovered—a path, a rock, a mountainside. It was impossible to comprehend visually. Finally, it all became clear. What I had thought was sky was actually clouds, and what had looked like empty space was solid earth. . . .

Monsieur hunts with a passion. He kills antelopes and eagles. He gets up at two in the morning and comes back at nightfall. His wife complains of his absence. He does not appear to foresee that a time may come when she will welcome it.

Cauterets

In the dream of love in which I indulge, the husband would not willingly create reasons for his frequent absence. When unavoidable duties or serious business necessitated it, the tenderness he felt and which he inspired in his wife would, on his return, be all the more intense and well-founded. It seems to me that absence endured with sorrow stimulates affection, but the kind of absence which is passionately sought by one of the two provides a great philosophical lesson in humility for the other. No doubt an excellent lesson, but a most chilling one!

Marriage is beautiful for lovers and useful for saints.

Outside of saints and lovers, there are a great many ordinary souls and peaceable hearts who are unfamiliar with love and who have no wish for sainthood.

Marriage is the ultimate goal of love. If love is no longer, or never was, a part of it, what remains is sacrifice. All well and good for those who understand the terms of sacrifice. It requires a measure of courage and degree of intelligence that do not grow on trees.

There are compensations for sacrifice which the ordinary mind can appreciate: the world's approbation, the sweet security of routine, a tranquil and sensible little devotion which does not require excitement, possibly even money; that is to say, playthings—silks, luxuries, trinkets—a thousand little items which allow you to forget that you're deprived of happiness.

So all is well, apparently, since the majority are ordinary. Not to be content with a taste for the ordinary is to demonstrate an inferiority of judgment and lack of good sense.

There is perhaps no middle ground between the power of great souls who attain sainthood and the comfortable stupor of small minds who attain insensibility.

Ah, but there is a middle ground—it is despair! . . .

But there is also the return to childhood, a thing good and sweet to cling to, whatever they may say! Running, riding, laughing at nothing, never worrying about health or about life! Aimée scolds me a lot. She does not understand why one would throw oneself into a whirlwind of activity, why one would need to forget. "Forget what?" she asks me. "I don't know. Everything. Especially that one exists. . . . "

Now Maurice is sick, and I am becoming ill again also. I hardly live at all anymore, or do I live too much? I can no longer get absorbed in anything. . . .

Maurice is better. I am going crazy again. My husband is arranging a party to go to Gavarnie with the Leroy family. Sometimes I want to go, too; then I don't, then I do. . . .

Yes, indeed. There is a good deal of temperament here. I am forming a great friendship with Zoé, although Aimée wants to discourage me from it. She claims Zoé is too gay, but she does not see her clearly. Zoé is gay—as I am. Aimée wants me to enjoy the society of Mme.————, whom she has begun to dote on, and who to me is nothing but a shrew. They want me to sing *Ebben'*, *per mia memoria* [Well then, from what I can remember] this evening. *Ebbene*, I do not want to sing. Am I a singer? I did not come to Cauterets to go to parties and find Paris in this countryside full of antelopes and eagles. No, I am going off to see the snows, waterfalls, and bears, God willing. There was one the other day no more than a league from here, a hundred paces from the road. He watched us pass with a look of great contempt. . . .

I left in rather a sad mood; Aimée said some harsh things to me. A certain Mme.————, who told everybody she came to take the waters in the hope of conceiving a child (which seems to me a very intimate thing to tell people), told her I was wrong to go on excursions without my husband. I do not see how that can be, since he makes the arrangements, and I go where he wants to go.

I can see that the people Aimée likes do not particularly like me. I must say I return the compliment. We must not quarrel over that; we must get our minds off those little irritations and not get involved in petty jealousy and gossip. Jane is still an angel. Her sister, too, after all. There are only small differences in our points of view about other people. That will pass, as my aunt always says.

My aunt!—I think of you. How good you are! How cheerful! How funny you are when you say, "All this, all this—it isn't worth a tinker's damn." You say it about everything. Oh, I only hope you're right! . . .

From Cauterets to Luz the trip is even more beautiful than all the rest. It is the same kind of beauty we found from Pierrefitte to Cauterets, but still more somber, more crevassed, more frightening. The chasm of Pont d'Enfer makes one want to jump into it. It is a fearful torrent that plunges and tumbles over itself with a frenzied gaiety....

Luz

We saw the ball at Luz-Saint-Sauveur from the open windows on the ground floor. It was as silly as the one at Cauterets, although a little fancier. Always that barbarous music with the dulcimer in the background. It would perhaps be very typical of the region if it used some of the local melodies, but nobody bothers with them. These goodly minstrels play contradances which set your teeth on edge. The lovely ladies and fine gentlemen show off their finery and strike their poses, while discussing their intestinal ills and rheumatism....

Indeed, I had not yet seen anything. From Luz to Gavarnie is the primeval chaos, the descent into Hell. The torrential river is the *rauco suon della tartare tromba*[39] [raucous sound of the horns of Hades].The grotto of the Gèdre garden is like the grotto of Apollo at Versailles created by nature and in cyclopean proportions, only there is no Apollo, and it is much better. The Marboré is indescribable. Surrounded by a wall of ice, snow, and limitless rock, one stands at the center, showered by drops from cascades of twelve hundred feet straight down. Bridges of snow, over which pass processions of shepherds and flocks of sheep! How can I describe it? You cannot see enough; you cannot take it all in with your eyes. It is too astonishing. You do not even think of danger. My husband is the most intrepid of men. He goes everywhere, and I follow him. He looks around at me and scolds me. He says I am trying to be "different" from the others. Damned if it had even occurred to me! I turn and see Zoé, who is following me. I tell her that she is trying to be "different" from the others. My husband gets angry because Zoé laughs. But the spray from the falls brings great tranquility, and anger soon vanishes.

Some are fearful, others are cold. One man, a salesman, compares the valley, which is divided into little cultivated fields, to a "card of samples." A very pretty, very elegant lady from Bordeaux all of a sudden cries out in a flute-like voice, with her strong accent, "Oh, my stomach's growling." That means she's hungry. Her husband, on the other hand, complains of colic and its consequences. Mlle.———— is feeling unwell in her sedan chair. Her carriers, who have gone seven leagues at a fast pace, are not feeling any better, even though they have not been foolish enough to start out with a stomach full of three glasses of that treacherous, purgative spring water. That particular combination of diet, waters, and walking makes every outing a medical emergency.

I remain behind to take care of Mlle.————, who is beautiful and kind, and this keeps me from being "different" from the others enough to admire the Marboré at leisure. Zoé said to me with a sigh, "It's awful not to be alone, or with intelligent people, or at least healthy people. We make the supreme effort to come and see something of unbelievable magnificence, something unique in all the universe, and we have to hold this one's head, reassure that one, and listen to everyone's nonsense!"

The worst of it is that almost the minute we arrive, we have to leave. There is no shelter, and we must make our way back over seven leagues of steep road only two or three feet wide, where the horses do not like to be at night. Then, too, as soon as the sun goes down, you're pursued by a deathly cold. Your teeth chatter as soon as you're not drenched with sweat from the effort of the climb.

As for me, I wanted to return to Cauterets the same evening. I did not think Maurice was well enough to leave him two nights in a row with his maid and Vincent. That morning I had hired a spare horse at Luz, a frightening but excellent horse. We start ahead, Zoé and I. We quickly leave behind the guides and the procession. We take at a gallop the most incredible places in the road. Zoé is wildly courageous. It intoxicates me; I keep right up with her. We arrive at a place called Chaos a half-hour ahead of everybody. We can stop and contemplate our surroundings. "My goodness," says Zoé. "Here we are alone; how wonderful! We can be different all we want! Let's enjoy the view!"

Zoé is beside herself, and for good reason. I like her enthusiastic nature, her generous spirit, her intelligent heart. We start off again at a gallop as we hear the group arriving, and slow down only when we are far enough away to resume our conversation freely. What do we talk about? Ah, such beautiful theories wasted on just the two of us. Love, marriage, religion, friendship, whatever. She concludes, "We have a little more intelligence and reasoning power than many others who never think about anything, and that is our problem!"

I said good night to Saint-Sauveur and good-bye to the excellent horse who had not caused me to break my neck, though I had certainly done my best to bring it about. I got back to my other mount and returned to Cauterets in the dark, after having ridden thirty-six leagues. I am certainly none the worse for it, especially since I found Maurice sleeping like an angel and all the little annoyances forgotten. However, Aimée still pouts at me sometimes. She prefers elegant society. Yet she is not part of it, and I am no longer, thank God! . . .

We visit back and forth. It is absurd, since we won't see each other again, and it is tiresome. We were visited by Princesse de Condé, widow of the Duc d'Enghien. She is neither young nor beautiful, and she does not look particularly distinguished. She has a great air of patronizing geniality, which her admirers take for interest in them and which makes them very proud. There is no reason to be.

Général Foy is here. He is very ill. I met him alone, very pale, a gentle face, sad, defeated. He is dying, they say.

Mme. de Rumford, widow of a scientist well-known to imbeciles like me for his soups and chimneys, just arrived with a very pretty young niece.

Another scientist, Magendie, has just explored the mountain pass via the Mallet tower. He almost perished from the cold on the way. His porters became demoralized and nearly abandoned him in the ice and snow.

We live on bear and antelope, but we hardly see any of them. The other day, though, on the way to the lake at Gaube, we saw a wild goat pursued by hunters. The goat made fools of them.

Cauterets (continuation of the diary)

The bridge of Espagne, the falls at Cerizey, the lake at Gaube, the glacier of Vignemale, what wonders! But we see them all too fast. We should be able to live a month at each place, and live in our own way, with friends of our choice. It is all so beautiful, so gripping, so awe-inspiring that we are as if crazed or intoxicated the first time we see it. And then—hurry, hurry—we have to go on because we have to get somewhere. And when we get there, we have to leave again, because we have to get back. I lose my sense of direction, and even I am always in a hurry to get back to my little one, so my thirst for nature's marvels is never quenched.

Would we tire of them if we had them all the time? No, it is impossible, unless this invigorating air and stimulation of mind is fatal to those of us who live in the flatlands. I do not know, but as for me, so far, the more I tire myself out, the more I want to do. Activity has taken hold of me like a fever. I cough and choke all the time, but I hardly know I am suffering. Yes, actually, I do suffer, I realize it when I am alone. The other day I was walking among the boulders behind the Labatte gardens. I was seized with stomach cramps so severe that I had to lie down on the grass. A native woman who was going to the washhouse had seen me among the rocks; she followed me to tell me there were snakes and that it was dangerous to go there. I did not care, I was suffering so much and feeling so much pain; but I made an effort to leave in order not to burden this woman, who seemed sympathetic. I followed her to the washhouse and watched her beat and wring the clothes. She could make herself fairly well understood in French, and she felt very unfortunate to live in this beautiful countryside where I would like to spend my life but where she saw only trouble and hardship. All these mountain people speak of the winter with terror. Their summer is so short that they do not have time to relax with it.

My friends the Bazouins are not enjoying themselves here. They have turned into meticulous bathers and drinkers of the waters. I do not know what Aimée's illness is. She certainly is ill, but she does not seem half as ill as I, and I think that if she did not drink anything at all and wore herself out with walking, she would regain her strength. But her father is old and heavy, and they are prisoners here, not enjoying anything, not seeing anything, going on little "health walks" which maintain the illness to perfection; and they think I am killing myself because I refuse to let myself be killed by doctors. The doctor here is furious with me because I won't listen to him.

I wrote a good deal about the Pyrenees during and after that trip. My first notes, scribbled hurriedly in a pocket diary from which I have just quoted, are written with a certain sponaneity, as you can see. But what happened to me after the fact is what must happen to many inexperienced writers. Dissatisfied with the carelessness of its primitive form, I composed in notebooks a trip which I am re-reading now and which turns out to be heavy and very pretentious in style. And yet this pretentiousness was naïvely pursued, I remember well. As the Pyrenees receded in the distance, I was afraid I would lose those vivid impressions I had had there, and I sought words and phrases to retain them, without finding any which were worthy of my subject. My retrospective admiration knew no limits, so I became dedicated to overwriting.

In any case, it was clear that I was not going to be satisfied with my own efforts, for I finished nothing, and I had not yet acquired a taste for writing.

This diary recalls to me a situation which I had nearly forgotten: there was a little disagreement between the elder of the Bazouin sisters and myself on the subject of choosing company, on which our opinions differed as much as our daily habits. Aimée was a person of talent and exquisite distinction. She liked everything in society that was elegant and in any way ornamental—names, manners, accomplishments, titles. Scatterbrained as I most surely was, I inwardly regarded all that as vanity and went looking for intimacy and simplicity, along with poetry. Thank God, I found them in Zoé, who was a really good person as well as someone with a heart as eager for affection as mine was. She was as romantic as Aimée was practical, as outgoing as Jane was reserved and pensive. I loved all these diverse natures, but they, unfortunately, did not take kindly to one another.

I was most certainly right about not wanting to submit to the mineral waters' cure. When, after a crushing showerbath, I found myself wrapped in blankets like a mummy, packed into a sedan chair, and brought back to my room with the express order to remain in bed for the rest of the morning, I thought I would go crazy, and I staged an open revolt. With a program like that, with all the visits to make and receive, I would not have seen my child all day, and I would not have had a glimpse of the Pyrenees. I hastened to terminate the treatment and confine myself to the people whose company I enjoyed. Zoé and her family lived in the house just opposite ours. The street was not very wide, and we could talk to each other from our windows and come and go to each other's houses ten times a day.

We left Cauterets at the end of August, I think, fleeing the thickening fogs which were already cooling the air. The bathers were leaving; a few remaining hikers were as offended as I to see nature disappear in the mists just at the moment when our solitude offered the chance to enjoy it. I say "solitude" only in relation to the tourists, because at that season the local inhabitants, in their turn, became very animated. The entire population of shepherds came down from the mountains where they had been secluded for the three summer months with their livestock, and returned to the plains. There was a continuous procession of men and partly wild animals, and this migration was a beautiful sight. The rugged shepherds, suntanned and looking more like Arabs than Frenchmen, walked in groups, in their picturesque costumes, accompanied by small horses or mules carrying their household goods, which consisted of a few blankets, some ropes and chains, and those great vessels of dazzling copper in which they collect and process the milk. Behind them followed their combined flocks—cows, sheep, goats, calves, and colts. Many of these, born during the season in the mountains, had never seen people other than their guardians, and seized with indefinable terror while passing through the villages, they would plunge into the narrow side streets, sweating and desperate; and it was not a good idea to get in their way. Alongside these caravans were running those Great White Pyrenees dogs, believed to be the original breed of the canine race—superb animals who, like purebred bulls, have heads, necks, and shoulders disproportionately large compared to their hindquarters, which seem as though trimmed for racing. The voices of these guard dogs sound a deep bass note, and in the night, as the procession passed under my window, there was something strange and wild in their sonorous barking and in the hurried and heavy sound of hooves on the granite street.

In my imagination I pictured the life of the shepherds on the mountains to be a perfect dream, and I recalled the *O fortunatos!*[40] passage that Deschartres had translated for me: "Oh, happy would be the pastoral dwellers, if only they knew how fortunate they were!"

To live thus in the solitude of sublime mountains during the loveliest season of the year, above the storms, emotionally and actually; to be alone or with several compatible friends, in the presence of God; to be so immersed in physical existence, along with the wolves and the bears, the perils of isolation, and the fury of tempests, that you, too, feel as inventive, agile, courageous, and strong as the animals; to have long hours of reflection to yourself for contemplation of the starry sky and the magic sounds of the wilderness; to possess all that is most beautiful in creation joined to possession of yourself—that was the ideal which came to replace, in my young head, that of monastic life, and which reigned there for many years.

I remembered Isabella Clifford, a friend in the convent, telling me about Switzerland and her dream of being a shepherdess in a lovely little chalet in the Bernese Oberland. I would have liked to become a shepherd, to have the broad chest and strong legs of that wild species I watched descend, grave, pensive, as if they had become unused to seeing and hearing other men. I would have liked to put my child on a mule, along with my blanket and several books—my entire happiness and fortune—and go off to spend three months of each year in a poetic Thebaid.[41]

But I would have wanted to take along my heart and mind. Those shepherds, several of whom resembled elder priests, studying their missals and together singing their ancient hymns, certainly represented, to my eyes and perhaps also in reality, great grandeur and poetry. But they felt only vaguely the mysteries and joy of their existence, and their sacred books were for them, they said, a bulwark against the fears and tedium of exile in the wilderness. For me, biblical thoughts would have been, on the contrary, a supplement to this contemplative life, and it seemed to me that my prayer would not have been a trembling supplication but a perpetual hymn.

These thoughts are very clear in my mind, since, besides finding traces of them in all my recollections, what I am saying about them is actually a summary of the long and naïve outpouring in my diary.

We had wanted to see Bagnères-de-Bigorre before leaving the mountains. Coming out of the mountain gorges and central ridge of the Pyrenee chain, we met the scorching summer of the slopes and valleys. The heat was unbearable at Bagnères, and nature, though still beautiful, no longer had that aura of grandeur and mystery that had held me in its spell. And besides, it was a plea-sure spot containing many English people, opulent lodgings, exhibitions of luxury carriages and teams, parties, shows, crowds, and noise. This was no longer for me. We spent only a few days there, even though Maurice positively blossomed in that gorgeous sunlight and took a liking to all those splendidly outfitted "horseys."

Before setting out for Nérac—and we were delaying as long as possible because of the even more intense heat we would encounter there and because of my fear that the trip would be hard on the child—my husband and I took a very interesting excursion with one of our friends[42] from Cauterets whom we had come across again at Bagnères. This friend had heard about the cave explorations at Lourdes, a strenuous outing which tempted few travelers. It tempted us. We made the trip on horseback, and having lunched at Lourdes, we engaged a guide and set out on the road to the caves.

The entry was not enticing. We had to crawl on our bellies, one by one, under the rocks, and even though there was enough room, this momentary entombment in darkness was vaguely terrifying.

But several hours' exploration of this subterranean world was like an enchantment. The tunnels were sometimes suffocatingly narrow, sometimes so vast that their limits were beyond the range of our torches; there were invisible torrents roaring deep in the bowels of the earth, chambers strangely juxtaposed on one another, bottomless wells—that is, caverns plunging to impenetrable depths, their powerful waters pounding furiously against their resounding sides; there were swooping bats, and porticos, arches, intersecting pathways, a whole fantastic city carved and built by what we naïvely call the caprice of nature—in other words by awesome convulsions of geological formation; a pretty trip for the imagination, exhausting for the body, but we did not concern ourselves with that. We wanted to go in every direction, explore everything. We were a little crazy; the guide threatened to abandon us. We walked over cornices above chasms which reminded us of Dante's Inferno; there was even one we decided to climb down into. The men started resolutely down, stepping into the crevices as a chimney sweep would do, and I followed them, tied to a rope which we made with all our scarves knotted end to end. Soon we had to call a halt, as we ran out of everything—footholds and safety scarves.

It was late at night when we returned on horseback through a light rain in misty moonlight. We reached Bagnères at two in the morning. I was much more excited than tired, and during my sleep I experienced the phenomenon of retrospective fear. While spelunking I had thought only of daring and laughing. In my dreaming, the subterranean city appeared before me with all its terror. It collapsed and tumbled on me; I hung from thousand-foot ropes which would suddenly break, and I would find myself in yet another city on a lower level than the first, constantly descending and getting lost in a thousand tunnels and Piranesan grottos down to the center of the earth. I woke bathed in a cold sweat, and when I went back to sleep, I set out on other travels toward still more feverish visions.

I have no recollection of the trip from Bagnères to Nérac. It has been thus with many landscapes I have traveled through while in the grips of an internal preoccupation; I have simply not seen them. The Pyrenees had exalted and intoxicated me like a vision that would stay with me and enchant me for years. I carried it with me so that I could wander there at any time of the day or night and put my own oases of fantasy into those magical and grandiose vistas I had traveled through so quickly, but which nevertheless remained so complete and clear in my memory that I could still see them in every minute detail. *J.H.C.*

XI

Guillery, my father-in-law's "château." —Fox-hunting.
—Peyrounine and Tant-belle. —The Gascons, fine folk, though
much maligned. —Peasants, bourgeois, and nobles: hearty eaters,
magnificent idlers, good neighbors and friends. —Trip to La Brède.
—A few words about premonitions. —Return by way of Castel-
Jaloux at night, on horseback, in the thick of the woods, escorted by
wolves. —Pigon devoured by wolves. —They come to our very
windows. —A wolf eats away at my bedroom door. —My father-in-
law attacked by fourteen wolves. —The Spaniards, nomadic
shepherds and bandits in the Landes. —The growing and collecting
of cork. —The charm of winter in this region. —The death of my
father-in-law. —A portrait and character study of his widow,
Baroness Dudevant. —Her woeful situation. —Return to Nohant.
—Comparison of Gascony and Berry. —Blois. —Mont-d'Or.
—Ursule. —Duris-Dufresne, the deputy from Indre. —A song.
—A memorable scandal in La Châtre. —A rapid summary of
various short trips and the reasons for them, up to 1831.

Guillery, my father-in-law's "château," was a maisonnette with five
casement windows in a row, not unlike one of those country inns to be found
on the outskirts of Paris, and furnished like all farm houses in the South, that is
to say, with strict simplicity. Living in it was, nonetheless, a pleasant and easy
enough affair. The region had at first struck me as being quite unprepossessing,
but I soon got used to it. With the onset of winter, which is the most agreeable
season in this land of scorching sands, the woods of pine and cork oak took on
a druidical look beneath their lichen, while the ground, cooled and compacted
by the rains, put forth a vernal cover that was to disappear by the time spring
came to Northern France. The spiny furze blossomed, lush moss strewn with
violets spread beneath the copses, the wolves howled, the hares bounded,
Colette arrived from Nohant, and the woods echoed with hunting.

I really took a fancy to it. It was plain hunting, without the flashy showing off of hounds and gear, technical jargon, red coats, and those pretensions
and rivalries normally associated with sport. It was my kind of hunting, hunting for hunting's sake. Friends and neighbors used to come the night before,
and we would quickly have as many burrows stopped as possible. We then set

off at dawn, mounted as well as could be on horses of which we required only soundness of leg. Nor did we make fun of falls, which were sometimes unavoidable, the paths being criss-crossed by roots which were completedly hidden in the sand and against which precaution of any sort was useless. You simply landed on the fine sand, picked yourself up, and that was that. As it turned out, I never fell once; whether from good luck or Colette's superior instincts, I have no idea.

We went hunting in any weather. Some peasants who were very familiar with the area and were expert poachers would bring over their small pack of hounds. The animals did not look like much, but they were actually much more experienced than those of connoisseurs. I shall never forget the unassuming gravity of Peyrounine bringing his three-and-a-half pair, which quietly took up the scent, to the rendezvous, and uttering in his clear and gentle voice, with a faint smile of satisfaction, "*Aneim, ma tan belo!*"

Aneim, that is to say, Take heart, corresponds to the Italian *animo. Tan belo* stands for the name, Tant-Belle, beauteous queen of crooked-leg bassets, true detective—supremely stubborn, shrewd, and unwearying—always first to sniff out the game and last to respond to the retreat.

We were a fairly large party, but the woods were vast, and riding no longer resembled, as in the Pyrenees, a forced march within the confines of a narrow ledge, with no room to spread out. It was possible for me to go off hunting on my own, without fear of getting lost, as long as I kept within range of the little fanfare Peyrounine whistled for his hounds. Now and then I could hear him in the woods, admiring to himself the feats of his favorite hound and murmuring proudly though discreetly, "Oh, my beauty! Oh, my bonny!"

My father-in-law was kind and lively, irascible but affectionate, sensitive and fair-minded. I would have gladly spent the rest of my days with this amiable old man, and I am sure we would never have known such a thing as a family row. But I was doomed to lose all my natural protectors, and he was one whom I was not to have for long.

The Gascons are fine folk, no more boastful or mendacious than their fellow provincials, who are all somewhat so. They are witty, quite uncultured, very lazy, kind, generous, compassionate, and stouthearted. The bourgeois, at the time I am writing about, were, as regards upbringing and intellectual development, considerably inferior to those from my province. On the other hand, their cheerfulness was more sincere, they were quicker to make friends, and their souls were more receptive. There was just as much petty gossip, but it was infinitely less malicious than back home, and if memory serves me, it was not even malicious at all.

The peasants, with whom I was not on very intimate terms since it was only toward the end of my stay that I became somewhat familiar with their dialect, appeared happier and more self-reliant than the ones at home. All those living within the radius, though at some distance from the isolated dwelling of Guillery, were very well off, and I never saw one of them come to ask for help. On the contrary, they seemed to treat "m'sieu le baron" as an equal; although courteous to the point of ceremony, they almost seemed to conspire at providing him with some sort of protection, as if he were some honorable neighbor whom they were bound to reward. They showered him with gifts, and all winter long he lived on the live poultry and game which they brought him for New Year's. All the fare, it should be noted, was of Pantagruelian[43] proportions, for we were in the land of the goddess Manduce. Hams, stuffed pullets, fattened geese, overfed ducks, truffles, and millet and corn cakes abounded there as in the isle where Panurge felt so happy. The maisonnette called Guillery, which looked so destitute on the outside, was—with respect to food—an Abbey of Thélème from which no one emerged, whether of high or low birth, without noticing an appreciable increase in weight.

This regimen did not suit me at all. The fatty sauces were like poison for me, and I often refrained from eating, although I was famished on returning from a hunt. My health suffered in consequence, and I was visibly wasting away in the midst of the countless cages filled with ortolans and woodpigeons busily eating themselves to death.

By autumn, my husband and I had taken a ride to Bordeaux and continued on to La Brède, where Zoé's family had a country house. There I had a violently upsetting experience from which my dear friend's moving words of courage and affection saved me.[44] The effect which her keen intelligence and unequivocal remarks had on me in this moment of utter despair lasted for several years, and lent my conscience the composure it had been vainly seeking until then. After strolling beneath the huge oaks planted by Montesquieu, steeped in fervent thought and pleasant meditations which, I confess, had nothing to do with remembrance of the philosopher, I returned to Guillery tired but serene. And yet I might have punned that the title of his work, *L'Ésprit des lois,*[45] had, in a manner of speaking, infused my new way of accepting life.

To get to Bordeaux we had gone down the Garonne; to have come back to Nérac the same way would have been too time-consuming. Moreover, it took no more than three days' absence for me to be sick with anxiety about Maurice. Sister Hélène's words at the convent as well as those uttered by Aimée at Cauterets had filled me with uneasiness to the point that maternal love had become, and would for a long time remain a real torture for me. I would fall victim to idiotic fears and false presentiments. I remember one evening while dining with friends at La Châtre suddenly imagining that Nohant was on fire and that I saw Maurice in the midst of the flames. I was ashamed of my foolishness and said nothing. All the same, I asked for my horse, left in breathless haste, and arrived at full speed, so possessed by the image that, on beholding the place still standing, I could not believe my eyes.

So I came back from Bordeaux by land, in order to arrive sooner. In those days there were few roads, or they were badly kept up. We reached Castel-Jaloux at midnight, and on stepping down from a ramshackle cart, I was delighted to find my servant, who had brought our horses. We had only four more leagues to go, but those were leagues in the countryside, along an execrable road, in the dea d of night, and through a huge pine forest completely uninhabited. It was real cutthroat country, where bands of Spaniards—whom it would have been unpleasant enough to encounter in broad daylight—were on the prowl. Yet the only living creatures we encountered were wolves. As we were riding perforce at footpace in the dark, these fellows were tranquilly trailing us. My husband noticed them from the restlessness of his horse, and he told me to go in front and rein in Colette to allay her fears. At that moment, I saw two eyes shining to my right. Then I saw them move over to the left. "How many of them are there?" I asked. "I believe there are only two," my husband replied. "But others may come along. Don't go to sleep. That's all you have to do."

I was so weary that the warning was to the point. I remained alert, and we reached home safely at four in the morning.

In those days, people were quite accustomed to encounters of this sort in the forests of pine and cork oak. Not a day went by without one hearing the shepherds crying out from copse to copse to warn one another of the enemy's presence. These shepherds were admittedly of a less romantic nature than their Pyrenean counterparts, but they were far from lacking character, with their slashed mantles and rifles in lieu of crooks. Their skinny black hounds looked anything but imposing, though they were as fearless as any mountain dog.

For some time, Guillery also had its trusty guardian. Pigon was a cross between a prairie and a mountain dog, and not merely courageous but heroic where wolves were concerned. He would go off on his own at night and taunt them in the woods, and come back in the morning with shreds of their flesh and skin clinging to his fearsome spiked collar. But, alas, one evening someone forgot to put on his armor; the intrepid creature set out on his nocturnal hunt never to return.

The winter turned out to be more severe than usual in this region. Not only the Garonne but its tributaries overflowed their banks. For a few days we were cut off; the hungry wolves became very brazen—they devoured all our pups. The house stood in the open, having neither fence nor courtyard, so these wild animals were able to come and howl right beneath our windows. One of them wiled the whole night away gnawing at the door of our quarters which were on ground level. I could hear it very clearly. I was reading in one bedroom, my husband was asleep in the other. I opened the glass door and called Pigon, thinking it was he who had come back home and was wanting to come in. I was on the point of opening the shutter when my husband awoke and called out to me, "No, don't! It's a wolf!" So soothing is the force of habit that he turned over and went back to sleep, and I picked up my book, while the wolf continued eating away at the door. It could not do much damage, since the door was sturdy, but it did gnaw in such a way as to leave marks. I do not think it had evil intentions. Perhaps it was a young one wanting to cut its teeth on some object or other, as pups do.

One day, toward sunset, as my father-in-law was on his way to visit a friend of his half-a-league away, he came across one wolf, then two, then three, and in a flash he counted fourteen of them. He did not pay too much attention—wolves don't often attack, they shadow their prey. They wait until the horse bolts and throws its rider, or until it stumbles and comes down with him, in which case, you must get to your feet quickly, otherwise they go for your throat. Since his horse was used to this kind of encounter, my father-in-law journeyed on unruffled. When he stopped at his neighbor's gate to ring, however, one of his fourteen fellow travelers leaped at the horse's flank and bit into the hem of his cloak. His only means of defense was his whip, which he flourished, but without scaring the enemy. It then occurred to him to dismount and furiously wave his cloak in the very teeth of his assailants, who ran for their lives. All the same, he admitted that the gate certainly seemed slow to open and that he was more than pleased when he finally saw that it was.

This adventure in the old colonel's repertoire was already ancient history. At the time I am writing about he was so gouty that it took two men to put him on his horse and help him off. Yet, when he was astride his dappled bay nag with its flaxen mane, he still had a martial air about him, in spite of his ample greatcoat, long cloth gaiters in olive-green, and his white hair flowing in the breeze. He unobtrusively handled his mount better than any of us.

I have mentioned the bands of Spaniards roaming the countryside. They were mostly Catalan, nomadic inhabitants from the other side of the Pyrenees. Some came seeking work as day-laborers and did inspire confidence despite their unprepossessing appearance. Others arrived in groups with their herds of goats, which they put to graze on the vast wastes of the surrounding heath. It often happened that these groups ventured up to the edge of the woods, where their flocks were a definite nuisance. The ensuing discussions were highly unpleasant. The groups would withdraw without saying a word, stand aloof, then fingering their slings or tossing their staffs with remarkable precision, would serve notice that, in the future, they were not to be pushed too far. People were really afraid of them, and I do not know whether an end has been put to their pasturing, but I do know that a few years back this vexatious practice still existed and landowners had been wounded and even killed in these conflicts.

Yet these were men of the same stock as those austere mountaineers whose poetic lives I had envied in the Pyrenees. They were extremely devout. Who knows if they thought they were exercising some religious prerogative in turning our barren stretches over to their herds? Maybe they looked on this vast and virtually empty land as some sort of virgin territory which had been entrusted to them by God and which they were to defend in His name against the encroachments of private property.

Guillery, then, was a place of wolves and brigands, yet we were happy there and at ease. There was considerable socializing. Since large and small landowners in the neighborhood had absolutely nothing to do, and, what's more, cultivated a penchant for doing nothing, they devoted their waking hours to going on outings, hunting, and meeting and dining at one another's houses.

Cork is an exceedingly lucrative product in these parts. This is the only region in France where it grows plentifully, and since it continues to be of much finer quality than Spanish cork, it brings a very high price. I was astonished when my father-in-law, pointing to a small stack of bark in a shed, commented, "There's the crop for the year—four hundred francs in expenses, twenty-five thousand francs net profit."

The cork oak is a huge, ungainly tree in summer. Its foliage is coarse and dull, its dense shade stifles any vegetation around it, and removing its bark, that is to say, the cork, right up to the main branches leaves it bare and misshapen. The most recently stripped trunks are blood-red, while the others, darkened soon by the onset of new bark, look burnt or smoked black, as though a conflagration had passed and engulfed the giants right up to the waist. But in winter this evergreen is resplendent. The only thing that really frightened me in the woods were the countless herds of black-spotted swine roaming about, shrilly and fiercely squabbling over the acorns.

The *quercus suber*, or cork oak, requires no attention. You neither have to prune nor train it. It adapts to its place, and prospers on seemingly parched sand as if by magic. When it is twenty or thirty years old, it is ready to be barked. As it ages, not only the quality of its bark improves but the bark itself is renewed more readily, the reason being that, every ten years from then on, they begin the tree's dressing by means of two long vertical incisions made at the right time. Then, after letting nature do its preliminary work, the worker inserts a small, special tool between the two top layers, and easily takes hold of the cork, which comes off in two large, neatly-cut strips. I do not know why this operation always struck me as distasteful, as though there were something cruel about it. These curious trees did not seem to suffer in the least, however, and while subjected to periodic decortication, grew to be centenarians twice over.[11]

The pine forests were just about as cheerless as the ones of cork oak. All those identical smooth trunks, like so many towering columns, topped with clumps of unrelieved greenery; then those impenetrable shadows, and those gashes exuding resin—all were enough to provoke a fit of depression, in the event one had to travel some distance with nothing else to do "but count the orange trees of the marsh," as my father-in-law used to say. On the other hand, other aspects combined with the delightful climate to make for a natural setting which was, all in all, not without interest: stands of saplings with sandy, undulating paths winding through them; rivulets babbling beneath the massive ferns; the wild peatbogs opening on a heath as vast, unending, flat, and blue as the sea; picturesque old manorhouses, gigantic relics of another age, that appeared all the more grand as the recent constructions nearby were, characteristically, diminutive; finally, the Pyrenees, lying thirty leagues away as the crow flies, and yet, given certain atmospheric conditions, suddenly looming on the horizon like a silvery pink wall notched with rubies.

Half a league away, we paid a weekly visit to Marquise de Lusignan, the fair and amiable lady of the very romantic and stately manor of Xaintrailles. Lahire was slightly farther away. At Buzet, on the magnificent plains of the Garonne, the Beaumonts enticed us with their many parties and charades held at their splendid château. Making his way through the woods, good-hearted August Berretté would come every day from nearby Laugareil. From elsewhere came Gramont, Trenquelléon, and that nice little doctor called Larnaude. From Nérac came Lespinasse, D'Ast, and so many others whom I remember fondly, all of them friendly people, extremely kind and responsive to me, both men and women—good-natured folk, youthful and sprightly, even the older ones, getting along well together, without class distinctions or differences of opinion. I have nothing but sweet and endearing memories of that part of the country.

I had counted on seeing my dear Fannelly in Nérac, who had become Mme. Le Franc de Pompignan. She was away either in Toulouse or Paris, I do not remember which. I did manage to see her sister, Aména, also a delightful woman, with whom I enjoyed talking about the convent.

We went to spend the final days of winter in Bordeaux, where we renewed acquaintance with the pleasant circle we had found at the thermal springs in Cauterets and where I met my husband's aunts, uncles, and cousins—all worthy individuals who displayed affection for me.

Every day, I saw my beloved Zoé, her sisters and brothers. One day when I happened to be at her place without Maurice, my husband suddenly appeared, looking very pale, and announced, "He's dead!" I thought he was talking about Maurice, and fell to my knees. But Zoé, who had understood and heard the rest of my husband's words, quickly shouted to me, "No, no, your father-in-law!" The bonds of maternal love are fierce—I felt a sudden pang of joy, but it lasted only an instant. I really did love my old papa, and I burst into tears.

We left that very day for Guillery and spent a fortnight with Mme. Dudevant. We found her in the same room where, within a period of two days, her husband had succumbed to an attack of gout in the stomach. She had not yet stepped outside this room that she had shared with him for nearly twenty years, where the beds still stood side by side. I found that touching and decorous. This was suffering as I understood it, bereft of any fear or loathing that the decease of a loved one might have occasioned. I embraced Mme. Dudevant with real affection, and cried so hard all day by her side that it never occurred to me to wonder at her dry eyes and serene countenance. Moreover, I was under the impression that excessive grief was making her hold back her tears and that she must have been suffering frightfully at not being able to shed them, but this repressed sensitivity was purely a product of my imagination. Mme. Dudevant was not only cold, but a chilling individual. Undoubtedly, she had loved her excellent mate and was missing him as much as it was possible for her to do, but she was like the cork oaks—she had a very thick coating which shielded her from contact with the outside world; however, in her case the coating was very tenacious and never came off.

Not that she was disagreeable, but her graciousness was only skin-deep. In lieu of genuine grace, she possessed abundant savoir-vivre. She loved no one in the real sense of the word, and was interested in nothing but herself. She had a sweet and pretty face on a flat, bony, angular, broad-shouldered frame. Her face inspired confidence, but the face alone does not express the whole being. By looking at her rough, dried-out hands, her gnarled fingers and big feet, one could presume that here was a personality lacking charm and the finer shadings, equally incapable of showing affection and responding to it. She was a sickly person, who perpetuated her illness by resorting to inadequate treatment, the outcome of which was that she wasted away. In winter, she wore fourteen petticoats, which failed to round out her figure. She tried countless quack remedies, and whenever she found the weather to her liking, say once a month, she ventured to take a step or two, at the most, outside the house. She spoke little and ever so faintly that one would lean forward in that attitude of respect instinctively prompted by debility. In her conventional smile there was a suggestion of bitterness and treachery which startled me at times and that I could not fathom. Hidden like so many fine little needles in her compliments was an attempt to be epigrammatic. If she had had any wit, she would have been nasty.

I do not believe, however, that she was fundamentally bad. Poor health and lack of courage had embittered her inwardly, and having been constantly on guard against the extremes of heat and cold, or any other external factors which might bring on some bodily upset, she had come to show similar wariness and aloofness with respect to social issues, attachments, and ideas. As a result, she was all the more tense and nervous, and when anger unexpectedly came over her, one would marvel at seeing a sort of feverish vigor suffuse this exhausted body and at hearing this languid voice and honeyed tongue assume an acrimonious tone and utter very forceful language.

She was, in my opinion, quite unfit for managing her own affairs, and when she suddenly found herself in charge of house and fortune, she was struck with dread and self-centered anxiety, which naturally turned to greed, ingratitude, and a kind of duplicity. Bored with her idle detachment, she lured into her presence a succession of friends and relatives, her husband's as well as her own. She made the most of their successive tributes, was unable to get along with any of the individuals concerned, and took pleasure in tricking each and all by dividing her fortune among several heirs whom she hardly knew and by cheating out of a just reward even the old servants, those who had shown her thirty years' solicitude and loyalty.

She was rich in her own right, and having no children, not even adopted ones, it seemed that she ought to have surrendered to her stepson at least a part of his father's inheritance. Nothing of the sort! She had long ago written into the will that she was to enjoy the interest accruing to this small fortune, and she had even attempted to seize outright possession of it through the drafting of a clause which, fortunately for my husband's future, ran counter to the rights guaranteed him by law.

Forewarned of the dispositions of his father's will, my husband was not surprised to see his situation remain unchanged. He continued to be very deferential and displayed as much affection as possible toward his stepmother, in the hope that, later on, she might improve his lot. To no avail. She never did love him. She chased him from her deathbed and left him with only what she had been unable to take away from him.

As far as I am concerned, this miserable woman did me—but in other connections—all the harm she could. Yet I have always pitied her. No existence I know of is more deserving of compassion than that of a wealthy, childless individual who has reason to believe that the endless marks of respect surrounding him or her are motivated by self-interest, and who must treat all who draw near as candidates for generosity. When that individual happens to be instinctively egocentric besides, then the scales have been tipped toward the consummation of a sterile, bitter existence.

We went back to Bordeaux, then once again to Guillery in the month of May, but this time the region did not appeal to me. The fine sand becomes so light when it is dry that a mere step raises clouds of scorching dust which you cannot help swallowing. We spent the summer at Nohant, and henceforth until 1831, I was away only very briefly at a time.

Here then was something like a settling down, which I looked on as definitive and which determined the future course of my marriage. Living modestly at home, in an unvarying, restricted milieu seemed, at first glance, to be the wisest course to follow. Yet, it would have been better to have led a nomadic life and to have cultivated a host of acquaintances. Nohant is an austere retreat in itself. Compared to Guillery, it looks elegant and cheerful. However, it is more secluded and, as it were, suffused with melancholy. Even when people gather there, filling it with noise and laughter, there is part of one's soul that remains forever gloomy and is even overcome with a kind of listlessness which stems from the climate and the nature of the population and its surroundings. The native of Berry is dull. When by some miracle he happens to be nimble of mind or sanguine, he leaves his province, in annoyance at not being able to stir things up around him. On the other hand, if he has no choice but to stay at home, he takes to drink and loose living, but with little or no relish, in the manner of the English, whose blood has been mixed with his more than is commonly believed. When a Gascon is tipsy, the man from Berry is already drunk, and when the former is slightly drunk—at which point he usually stops imbibing—our native is completely *besotted*, and will continue on his merry way until he collapses. One cannot help using that ugly word, the only one which really describes the effect drink has on Berrichon folk. The poor quality of the wine is largely to blame, but the want of temperance does appear to be rooted in a melancholic, phlegmatic nature that cannot tolerate excitement and attempts to drown it in stupefaction.

Apart from drunkards, who are many and whose disorderly ways reduce their families to poverty and despair, the population is honorable and soberminded, but cold and seldom friendly. There is very little social intercourse. Farming is quite backward, a consuming task for the landowner, requiring patience and hard labor. The cost of living is high compared to the South. Hospitality is, accordingly, a rare commodity; when extended, it smacks of ostentation. Above all, there is a pervasive laziness, a phobia about locomotion, explained by the protracted winters, by the problems involved in traveling about, and particularly by the sluggishness of people's minds.

Twenty-five years ago this way of life was even more pronounced—there were fewer roads, and people stayed closer to home. In spite of the fact that it was fairly well-populated and extensively cultivated, this handsome region was utterly bleak, and my husband seemed taken aback and frightened by the solemn silence that settles over our fields once the setting sun hushes the few restrained sounds of labor. There are no howling wolves here, but by the same token, there are no singing and laughter, no shepherds' cries or hunters' calls. Everything is quiet to the point of voicelessness; all is at rest to the point of seeming dead.

I have always loved this countryside, its particular type of nature, and its stillness. I not only cherish its charm but submit to its gravity, and am loath to shake off this presence even when I perceive its dangers. But my husband had not been cut out for study and reflection. His Gascon blood notwithstanding, he was not naturally lively either. His mother was Spanish; his father descended from the Scotsman Law.[46] The reflective atmosphere did not make him moody as it did me. Rather, it got on his nerves. He would have fared all right in the South, whereas Berry weighed on him. For quite some time he detested it, but once he had learned its ways and acquired a taste for the pastimes it offered, he took to it as if it were a second home.

I soon realized that a serious effort should be made to enlarge the circle of my acquaintances. The illness and advanced age of my grandmother had curtailed the number of friendships I had been able to build, and these had lapsed through my years of absence. I looked up childhood playmates, but they were not, as a rule, to M. Dudevant's liking. He made other friends. I readily accepted those in whom I sensed a measure of congeniality, and went farther afield to find the companions who were to suit both him and me.

Kind-hearted James and his excellent wife, my dear mother Angèle, came to spend two or three months with us. They were followed by their sister, Mme. Saint-Agnan, and her daughters. The eldest, Félicie, was an angel.

The Malus family also visited us. The youngest of them, Adolphe, who had a heart of gold, fell ill during his stay, and both of us, along with my brother, escorted him as far as Blois. We saw the ancient château, which by then had been converted into barracks and a powder magazine, and left to be defaced by the soldiers, whose rowdiness and bustle did not prevent certain parts of the structure from housing myriad birds of prey. The guano of different species of owls was so thick that it was impossible to set foot in the wing built by Gaston d'Orléans.

I had never beheld a more beautiful example of Renaissance art than this vast edifice, forsaken and ravaged as it was. I have seen it since restored, panelled, admirably rejuvenated, and, so to speak, retrieved from the ravages of time and neglect. But what I have never recaptured is the strange and deep impression which gripped me that first time when, at sunrise, I gathered yellow wallflowers that grew in the cracks between the fateful stones of Catherine de Medici's observatory.

In 1827, we spent a fortnight at the waters in Mont-d'Or. I had had a fall, and for a long time was bothered by a sprain. We took Maurice with us. He was becoming a little boy and, right in the middle of his babyish clamor, would start to observe the world around him with large, inquisitive eyes.

Auvergne struck me as a delightful region. Less expansive and spectacular than the Pyrenees, it had all of that region's coolness, scenic waters, and charmingly hidden nooks. The forests of fir are even more pleasant than the spruce trees in the lofty mountains. The waterfalls, less awesome, have gentler harmonies, and the ground, less tortured by storms and landslides, brings forth a profusion of flowers.

Ursule had come to live with me as housekeeper. The arrangement did not last for long, however, owing to the incompatibility of temperament between her and my husband. She was somewhat put out with me for not having taken her side. Close to anger when she left, she soon realized that I could not have behaved otherwise, and we renewed our friendship that has never failed me since. She got married at La Châtre to a fine man who has made her happy, and she is now the only person with whom I can review my whole life without any major gap, from infancy to a full half-century.

The 1827 elections signaled a very pronounced and widespread opposition movement in France. Hatred of Villèle's[47] government brought about a solid merger of liberals and bonapartists, whether members of the nobility or bourgeoisie. In general the population in our province remained aloof from the debate. Only the functionaries championed the government, and even then not unanimously. My cousin, Auguste de Villeneuve, came from Le Blanc to vote at La Châtre, and although he was an eminent public official (he was still treasurer for the city of Paris), he agreed with my husband and his friends to nominate Duris-Dufresne.[48] Auguste spent a few days with us, displaying a great deal of affection both for me and Maurice, whom he called his great-uncle. Seeing how oblivious he was of bygone days and how paternally he behaved toward me, I effaced from my memory the fact that he had deeply hurt me in the past.

Duris-Dufresne, brother-in-law of Général Bertrand, was a republican of the old school, a model of old-fashioned rectitude, unpretentiousness, and affability. I was taken with this exemplum of a former era, still marked with the elegance of the Directoire, but with more Spartan ideas and morals. His small, closely cropped wig and his earrings lent a touch of originality to his delicate, animated features. His manners were extremely refined. He was a socially acceptable Jacobin.

Heavily involved at the time with everything related to the opposition, my husband was nearly always in town. It was his desire to set up a central place for meetings and to rent a house in La Châtre for balls and gatherings which might continue even after the nomination of Duris-Dufresne.

Our receptions were to give rise to a highly comical scandal. In those days—and the same may even be said today in La Châtre—there were two or three "societies" that, within living memory, had never danced with one another. The points of difference between the first, second, and third were quite arbitrary, and it was impossible to distinguish one from the other unless you had studied the whole matter thoroughly.

Although politically "warring" with the Sub-Prefecture, I was strongly attached to M. and Mme. de Périgny, a likeable young couple, with whom I existed on the best neighborly terms. They too wanted to hold receptions; their social standing more or less obliged them to do so. We agreed to simplify the question of whom to invite by using a common list.

I passed on my list, which was rather general. Naturally, I had included the names of all those whom I knew ever so slightly. But, horror of horrors, it turned out that several of the families whom I liked and respected with good reason had been pronounced second- and third-rate according to the ways and customs established by the bourgeois aristocracy of La Châtre. As a result, when these worthy personages found themselves face to face with their "inferiors," there were outbursts of anger and indignation. A curse was called down on the presumptuous Sub-Prefect, who had behaved like that, they claimed, only to show his contempt for all local folk by putting them "like eggs, in one and the same basket."

The following verse from a song Duteil[49] and I had composed on the evening in question provides a succinct but true account of the momentous event.

> Seven days go by.
> They fill the punchbowl high.
> They wax the ballroom floor.
> The host is at the door.
> Three new guests arrive, whose colors are suspect—
> In the town they all were asking
> Whether everyone was masking
> At the sub-prefect's.

Reading it over, I feel that the song as a whole, without being particularly droll, does portray local manners, and deserves to be preserved among La Châtrian traditions recorded in the archives. It is entitled "An Administrative Social, or, The Sub-Prefect Turned Philosopher." Here are the first two verses, which summarize the affair. The tune is that of "Les Bourgeois de Chartres":

> Oh hear, La Châtriens,
> Peasant, bourgeois, and noble,
> Of a would-be gentleman,
> Who caused a lot of trouble.
> This young man, distracted by philosophy,
> And forgetful as a stone
> Regarding proper form and tone,
> Annoyed the bourgeoisie.
>
> Observing in advance
> That more than one original
> Put on a knowing glance
> And called himself a liberal,
> He thought he'd treat our wives, who find the nobles crass,
> To a democratic ball,
> To which he'd welcome one and all,
> As if they were going to mass.

We have already seen the outcome of this affair. Thanks to the song, however, the dénouement almost took a tragic turn. The verses had been composed at Périgny's fireside and were supposed to remain confidential, but Duteil could not refrain from singing them. People remembered them and copied them down. They went the rounds of the town and caused an uproar. I had already completely forgotten the song when I noticed the glaring eyes around me and heard the cries of rage. All this had the positive effect of deflecting people's wrath from the target of my friends, the Pérignys, and concentrating it on me. The local bigwigs swore they would no longer favor me with their presence. Annoyed at so much silliness, Périgny closed his drawing room doors. I left mine open, and even increased the number of invitations I extended to the second social circle. There was no better way of teaching the first circle a lesson; not being a functionary, I was free to ignore them. As it turned out, the resentment they harbored against me did not last for more than two or three suppers. Moreover, I made excellent friends in this first circle, friends who would have nothing to do with the conspiracy and who openly betrayed the "cause." Consequently, my drawing room was so crowded that one could hardly breathe, and the confusion was such that the ladies belonging to the first and second circles got carried away to the point of touching each other's fingertips when executing the figure in a country dance known as the *moulinet*. A few of the truly orthodox called it a "mob scene." I enjoyed thanking them very humbly for having done me the honor of coming even though I was a member of the third circle. They hawked their anathemas, which did not keep them from eating the pâtés or toasting the insurrection with champagne. Such was the onset of pervasive decadence in the hierarchical makeup of this little oligarchy.

My daughter Solange was born at Nohant in the month of September 1828. When the doctor arrived, I was already asleep and the infant was dressed and adorned with pink ribbons. I had been longing for a girl, and yet I did not experience the same joy as when I had had Maurice. I was afraid my daughter might not live, since she was born prematurely as the result of a fright. The evening before, Léontine, my small niece, had had a bad dream. She had run to the head of the stairs to call her mother, and had started screaming so piercingly that I imagined she had tumbled down the steps and broken her bones. I immediately began to feel pains, and on getting up the next day, I just had time to get the little shirts and bonnets ready. Fortunately, I had finished making them.

I remember the astonishment of one of our friends from Bordeaux,[50] who had come to see us. Finding me alone in the drawing room at the crack of dawn, where I was busy unfolding and arranging the layette, part of which was still in my sewing box, he asked, "What ever are you doing?" "Well, as you can see," I replied, "I'm hurrying up for someone who's coming sooner than I expected."

My brother, who had seen how frightened I had been the night before in connection with his daughter, and who really cared for me when he had his wits about him, rode at breakneck speed to get a doctor. It was all over when he got back, and he was so overjoyed to see that the baby was alive that he was practically beside himself. He hugged me and uttered reassurances to the effect that my daughter was handsome, sturdy, and that she would survive. But only a few days later, after seeing that she was coming along fine, did I feel totally relieved.

The dash on horseback had famished my brother. Food was served, and two hours later he came into my room in such a state of inebriation that, attempting to sit down at the foot of my bed, he landed on his backside in the middle of the floor. My nerves being still very much on edge, I was overcome with hysterical laughter. He came to his senses and did his best to collect his thoughts. "Well, I'm tipsy," he said. "What of it? What do you expect? This morning I was very excited, very apprehensive. Then I was very glad, very happy. It's joy that's gone to my head, not the wine. I swear, it's rather my affection for you that keeps me from standing on my two legs." How could I refuse to forgive him in the face of such persuasive reasoning?

I spent the following winter at Nohant. In the spring of 1829, I went to Bordeaux with my husband and the two children. Solange had been weaned and had become the sturdier of the two.

In the fall, I went to Périgueux to spend a few days with Félicie Molliet, one of my friends from Berry. I pushed on as far as Bordeaux to embrace Zoé. I caught cold on the way and was very unwell on my return.

Finally, in 1830, the month of May, I believe, I made another quick trip from Nohant to Paris, with Maurice. I am leaving out or mixing up the dates of three or four brief stays in Paris, with or without my husband. The purpose of one of these was to get some medical advice concerning my health, which had considerably deteriorated. Broussais informed me that I had an aneurism in the heart; Landré-Beauvais, that I was consumptive; Rostan, that nothing whatsoever was wrong with me.

These brief absences notwithstanding, I can say that from 1826 to 1831 I lived continuously at Nohant. Up to that time, in spite of vexations and serious problems, it was there that conditions had undoubtedly been best for my mental health. After 1831,[51] however, the balance between satisfaction and discomfort shifted. I felt that I had to make a decision. I made it unhesitatingly, and my husband agreed to it. I went to live in Paris with my daughter, on condition that I would be able to return to Nohant every three months and remain for three months; and until the time Maurice went into preparatory school in Paris, I scrupulously respected the plan I had drawn up. I left him in the hands of a tutor who had already been with us for two years and who has remained, since that time, one of my most trusted and worthy friends. He was not only a teacher for my son, he was a companion, an older brother, almost a mother. However, it was impossible for me to part company with Maurice for long and not to watch over him for six months of the year.

I have had to skim over these days of retreat and apparent inactivity. Not that they hold no memories for me, but the exertions of my will were so inwardly directed at the time, and my personality was so subdued, that I would have nothing to tell but the story of others around me. And my right to do so has, I feel, its limitations, especially with respect to certain individuals.

Without going back over what has been said, and yet at the same time wanting to summarize the effect that these particular years had on my subsequent life, I shall describe the sort of person I was on arriving in Paris in the winter of 1831, with the intention of writing. *D.A.G.*

XII

A retrospective glance over the several years sketched in the preceding chapter. —Troubled home. —Vanished dreams. —My religion. —Does freedom of worship include the freedom to abstain from worship? —The quiet death of a fixed idea. —The death of Cricri. —Vague, but persistent, plans for a future to my liking. —Why these plans? —Managing a year of my income. —I resign. —In fact, I am suspended. —My brother and his troublesome addiction. —Salty winds, salty faces. —Trying out a modest profession. —The museum of painting. —Art makes revelations without assuring me any speciality. —No aptitude for the natural sciences, despite a love of nature. —I am granted an income and freedom. —I leave Nohant for three months.

I had done a tremendous amount of living in those few years. It even seemed to me that I had lived a hundred years under the dominion of the same idea, so tired did I feel of a brittle gaiety, a home life without intimacy, and of a loneliness that boisterous drunkenness rendered more than absolute around me. Yet I had no cause seriously to complain of any directly harmful conduct, and even if that had been the case, I would not have consented to act on it. My poor brother's disorder, and that of those who allowed themselves to be led astray by him, had not become so advanced; I still felt I inspired a fear in them which was not really condescension but rather instinctive respect. For my part, I had given his drinking all possible tolerance. I would try to laugh as long as they restricted themselves to being incoherent, tiresome, rowdy, even sick and disgusting; and I even got used to putting up with a jovial tone which, in principle, revolted me. But when they began to get on each other's nerves, when they became obscene and vulgar, when my poor brother himself—so subdued and repentant in the face of my upbraidings—became brutal and nasty, I turned a deaf ear, and as soon as I could, returned to my little room without a comment.

There, I was quite able to keep busy and distract myself from the noise outside, which often lasted until six or seven in the morning. I had become accustomed to working all night at my sick grandmother's bedside; now I had other patients, not whom I had to care for but whose ravings I had to hear.

But my loneliness was profound and complete; it would have been fatal for a tender soul and youth still in its prime, had it not been imbued with a dream which had assumed the importance of a passion—not in my life, since I had sacrificed my life to duty—but in my mind. An absent being, with whom I would have endless conversations, to whom I related all my reflections, all my reveries, all my humble virtues, all my platonic ecstasy; a being who was in reality excellent, but whom I adorned with all manner of perfection uncomprised by human nature; in sum, a man who, in the course of a year, made an appearance for a few days, sometimes only a few hours; as romantic with respect to me as I myself was; who in no way threatened my religion or my conscience—it was he who sustained and consoled my exile in the world of reality.[52]

My religion had remained the same, its foundation never wavering. The rituals of the past vanished for me, as for my whole century, in the light of study and reflection, but the eternal doctrine of believers—that God is good, that the soul is immortal, and that hope lies in the life to come—had resisted all examination, all disputation, even at times of desperate doubt. Some sanctimonious characters have judged me otherwise and declared me to be without principles, from the beginning of my literary career, because I allowed myself to challenge purely human institutions which it pleased them to look on as God-given. Some political characters have also decreed me an atheist regarding their rigid or changeable dogmas. Evidently bigots and hypocrites find principles only where blindness and cowardice exist. Should it bother me?

I am not writing to defend myself from those who are prejudiced against me. I write for those whose natural sympathy, based on a conformity of instincts, allows them to open their hearts to me and assures me of their trust. Those are the only ones for whom I can do some good. The harm that others may do to me, personally, I have never given much consideration.

Besides, it is not indispensable to the salvation of the human race that I may have lost or found the truth. Others will find it again, however much it may go astray in the world during this century. All I myself can and must do is profess my faith simply, though it might seem insufficient to some and excessive to others.

To enter into a discussion of religious ritual is to be concerned with the external aspects of worship that go beyond the scope of this work. Therefore, I do not need to say why and how I extricated myself from them day by day, how I tried to entertain them again in order to satisfy my inner logic, and how I abandoned them frankly and definitively the moment I recognized that logic itself ordered me to disengage from them. That is not the important religious point in my life. There, my memories reveal no anguish and no uncertainty. The truly religious question I had formulated more loftily in my earlier years. God, His eternal existence, His infinite perfection were scarcely called into doubt unless I was sick with depression. (Intellectual questioning is an exception and should not count in summing up the life of the soul.) What absorbed me at Nohant as at the convent was the ardent or sober, but assiduous, search for the rapport that can and must exist between the individual soul and the universal soul we call God. As I belonged neither to the world of action nor intention; as my contemplative nature absolutely shunned its influences; as, in short, I could not and would not act unless by virtue of a law superior to custom or public opinion, it was very important for me to seek in God the key to the enigma of my life, the notion of my true duties, the sanction for my most intimate feelings.

For those who see only a law of fate in the Divinity, blind and deaf to the tears and prayers of intelligent creatures, such continuous concern of a mind with an insoluble problem falls into what has been called mysticism. If I am a mystic, so be it! Apparently, there is not a very great variety of intellectual types in the human species, and I may belong to that one. It was not incumbent on me to conduct myself in the light of pure reason, by the calculations of personal interest, by the strength of my own judgment, or by submission to that of others. I had to find—not outside of, but above, the fleeting notions of humanity, and above myself—an ideal of strength, of truth, a type of immutable perfection to embrace, to contemplate, to consult, and to implore endlessly. For a long time I was bothered by the habit of prayer I had contracted, rather regarding the spirit than the letter; for as you have seen, I had never been able to adhere to it literally. When my idea of God came to fruition at the same time as my soul; when I thought I understood what I had to say to God, what to thank Him for, what to ask Him for, I again found my old effusions, tears, enthusiasm, and confidence.

Then, I enclosed belief within me like a mystery, and not wanting to dispute it, I let others argue and make fun without my listening or hearing, without feeling challenged or troubled for a single instant. I shall tell how this serene faith was again shaken later by my own restlessness, without the actions of others having any bearing.

I was never pedantic about these preoccupations—no one ever suspected them—and when, a few years afterward, I had written *Lélia* [1833] and *Spiridion* [1838], two works which for me encompass much emotional turmoil, my closest friends wondered on which days and during which hours of my life I had passed along those harsh roads between the summits of faith and the chasms of terror.

Here are a few words that "the Malgache"[53] wrote to me after *Lélia*: "What the devil is this? Where did you get all that? Why did you write this book? Where does it come from, where is it going? I knew you were very dreamy, I believed you were a believer at the core, but I would never have suspected that you could attach so much importance to penetrating the secrets of that very large 'maybe' and to examining from every direction that immense 'question mark' which you would do better not to worry about any more than I do.

"People laugh at me here because I like the book. Perhaps I am wrong to like it, but it has gripped me and keeps me from sleeping. May the good Lord bless you for shaking and stirring me like this. But who then is the author of *Lélia*? Is it you? No, this character is a fantasy. It does not resemble the you who is jolly, who dances the bourrée, who appreciates species of butterflies, who does not despise a pun, who sews fairly well, and who makes very good jam! It may very well be that, after all, we did not know you, and that you were slyly hiding your daydreams from us. But is it possible you can have thought of so many things, mulled over so many questions, and devoured so many psychological marvels without anyone ever having suspected it?"

So, I reached Paris; that is to say, the start of a new phase of my existence, with very definite ideas about my personal response to abstract things, but with great indifference and considerable ignorance regarding matters of reality. I had no inclination to know them; I had no preconceived ideas about anything whatsoever in this society to which I wanted less and less to belong. I did not expect to reform it; I was not sufficiently interested in it to have that ambition. Such detachment and laziness were probably the culpable, but inevitable, result of a life of isolation and apathy.

One last word, however, about orthodox Catholicism. By passing lightly over my abandonment of ritual worship, I did not mean that I held worship in general in as little account as I perhaps seemed to. To tell and to judge, simultaneously, is not a very easy job when one does not want to halt the telling too often and try the patience of the reader.

Let us therefore say very quickly here and now that the need for organized religion is still not a completely settled thing for me and that, today, I see as many good reasons to accept as to reject it. However, if we recognize, along with all the schools of modern philosophy, that governments are bound to the principle of absolute religious tolerance, I find I am perfectly within my rights to refuse to follow rituals which do not satisfy me, not one of which can replace or even liberate the impulse of my thoughts and the inspiration of my prayers. In such a case, we must also recognize that, if some minds need to perform accepted rituals to hold on to their faith, there are also others who need to be left completely alone for the same purpose.

However, there lies a serious moral question for the legislator. Will man be better by adoring God in his own way or by accepting established rules? I see in prayer or in communal thanksgiving, in honors paid to the dead, in the consecration of birth and the other principal stages of life, wondrous and holy things that purely civil contracts and acts do not replace. Furthermore, the spirit of these practices seems to me so lost and so warped that, in many cases, observance makes a sacrilege of them. I cannot declare myself for practices adopted out of moral caution or calculation, which is as much as to say out of cowardice or hypocrisy. The habit of ritual seems a lesser profanation, but a profanation nevertheless, and I do not see any way of keeping any kind of ritual worship from being abused.

My whole century has been on a quest and still is. I am no wiser than my century.[12]

Why this solitude which had bridged the most vital years of my life no longer suited me, that is what I have not yet told and what I can very well.

The absent being, whom I could almost call "the invisible man," and whom I had made the third term in the premise of my existence—God, myself and him—was tired of my superhuman aspiration to sublime love. Being kind and sensitive, he did not say so, but his letters became increasingly rare, his expressions keener or colder, according to my interpretation. His passions needed a different kind of food than rapturous friendship and a life through letters. He had made a vow that he had kept for me religiously and without which I would have broken with him, but he had not made me a vow restrictive with respect to the joys and pleasures he might find elsewhere. I felt I was becoming a terrible burden to him, or that I was no more than an intellectual amusement. In all modesty I leaned toward the latter but found out later I had made a mistake. This only made me happier that I had put an end to his heart's constraint and the hindrance of his destiny. For a long time I went on loving him in silence and dejection. Then I began to think of him with calm, with gratitude, and now I never think of him except with genuine affection and justifiable respect.

Once my mind was made up, neither explanation nor reproach were needed. What would I have complained about? What could I expect? Why would I have tormented that good and beautiful soul or spoiled his promising future? Besides, there is a point in detachment when the one who has taken the first step must no longer be questioned or persecuted, on pain of being forced to become cruel or miserable. I did not want it to be like that. He did not deserve to suffer, and I did not wish to diminish in his respect by risking his irritation. I do not know if I am right to consider pride as one of woman's first duties, but I cannot help but scorn a persistently desperate passion. That, it seems to me, is a crime against heaven, which alone gives and takes back true affection. You can no more dispute the possession of a soul than that of a slave. You must render to man his liberty, to the soul its impulse to soar, and to God the flame emanating from Him.

When this quiet, but irreversible, divorce was over, I tried to continue the existence which, on the surface, had not been ruffled or modified, but that was impossible. My little room no longer needed me.

At that time I used what had formerly been my grandmother's boudoir, because it had only one door and could not be used as a passageway by anyone, under any pretext. My two children occupied the larger, adjoining bedroom. I could hear them breathe, and I could keep watch without disturbing their sleep. My boudoir was so small that, with my books, my herbarium, my butterflies, and my pebbles (I kept right on amusing myself with natural history without learning a thing), there was no place for a bed. I made do with a hammock. My desk was in an armoire that opened like a secretary, and that a cricket I called Cricri, whom my presence had tamed, occupied for a long time as well. He lived there on my sealing wafers, which I took care to choose in white, for fear he might poison himself. He came to nibble on my paper while I was writing, after which he would go sing in a favorite drawer. Sometimes he walked over my handwriting, and I was obliged to drive him off so that he would not take it into his head to taste the fresh ink. One evening, not hearing or seeing him around, I searched for him everywhere. I found only the two hind legs of my friend, between the casement window and the frame. He had not informed me that he liked going out; the serving woman had crushed him when closing the window.

I enshrouded his sad remains in a datura flower, which I kept for a long time as a relic, but it is hard for me to explain the impression this childish event made on me, coinciding as it did with the end of my poetic love affair. I tried hard to put it into verse; I had heard it said that wit consoles us for everything, but while writing "La Vie et la mort d'un esprit familier," ["The Life and

Death of a Familiar"] a work unpublished and fit to remain so forever, I caught myself in tears more than once. I imagined in spite of myself that the cricket's little cry, which is, so to speak, the very voice of the domestic hearth, could have sung my real happiness, that it had at least soothed the last disclosures of a sweet illusion and flown off forever with it.

The death of the cricket therefore marked, in a symbolic manner, the end of my sojourn at Nohant. I drew my inspiration from other thoughts; I changed my way of life; I went out; I walked a lot during the autumn. I drafted a kind of novel that has never seen the light of day;[55] then, having read it, I concluded it was worthless, but that I could write one less bad and that, all in all, it was no worse than many others that allowed their authors to live after a fashion. I realized that I wrote quickly, easily, for a long time without fatigue; that my ideas, sleeping sluggishly in my brain, awoke and became coherent, through deduction, as the pen ran over the pages; that in my life of recollection I had often observed and understood rather well the personalities that chance had paraded before me, and that, consequently, I knew human nature well enough to depict it; in short, that of all the small tasks of which I was capable, literature, properly speaking, was the one that offered me the most chance of success as a profession and—let us not mince words—a way to earn my bread.

A few people with whom I talked it over at the beginning were skeptical. Could poetry exist, they asked, along with a monetary preoccupation? Was it to find a material profession, then, that I had lived so long in the ideal?

The subject had actually given me food for thought for a long time. Even before my marriage, I had felt that my station in life, my small fortune, my freedom to do nothing, my so-called right to give orders to a certain number of human beings—peasants and domestics; in short, my role as heiress and chatelaine, in spite of its modest proportions and imperceptible significance, was contrary to my taste, my logic, and my abilities. Let it be remembered how my mother's poverty, which had separated her from me, had influenced my child's brain and heart; how I had, in the depths of my being, spurned inheritance and planned over time to flee life's comforts for work.

These romantic ideas were followed, in the early stages of my marriage, by the will to please my husband and be the woman of the house that he wanted me to be. Domestic cares have never annoyed me, and I am not one of those lofty beings who cannot come down from the clouds. I live in the clouds a lot, certainly, which is one more reason I often feel the need to descend. Often tired and obsessed by my own agitations, I would have gladly said, like Panurge on the stormy sea, "Happy is he who plants cabbages! He has one foot on land, and the other is only a spit away!"[56]

But that "spit," that something or other between the land and my second foot, was exactly what I needed and could not find. I would have liked a reason, a motive as simple as planting cabbages, but logical as well, in order to explain to myself the purpose of my activity. I saw perfectly well that in taking great care to economize on all levels, as I had been told to do, I succeeded only in realizing how impossible it was to be economical without also, in certain cases, being selfish; the closer I came to the land, digging deeply into the little problem of making it yield as much as possible, the more I saw that it yielded little, and that those who had little or no land to dig could not exist even by using both arms. The income was too low, the work too unsteady, and exhaustion and illness all too inevitable. My husband was not inhuman and did not check up on the details of my expenditures, but when, at the end of the month, he saw my accounts, he tore his hair out and made me do the same, by telling me that my income was too low by half for my free-spending ways, and that there was no possibility whatever of living at and maintaining Nohant on that footing. It was true, but I could not take it on myself to reduce to the barest necessities the comforts of those whom I was in charge of and to refuse the needs of those whom I was not. I was open to everything that was prescribed or suggested to me, but I did not know how to go about it myself. I would grow impatient, I would become careless. People knew it and often took advantage.

My management lasted only one year. Ten thousand francs had been set as my limit; I spent fourteen, for which I was as ashamed as a child caught red-handed. I proffered my resignation, and it was accepted. I handed over my accounts and even renounced an allowance of fifteen hundred francs for clothing and personal needs guaranteed to me by the marriage contract. I did not need much, and I preferred to live at the disposal of those in charge, rather than make demands. From that period until 1831, I did not own an obol. I did not take a hundred sous from the communal purse without asking my husband first, and when I requested him to pay my personal debts at the end of nine years of marriage, they amounted to five hundred francs.

I am not reporting these little things by way of complaint against having suffered coercion or stinginess. My husband was not a miser, and he refused me nothing, but I had no needs; I desired nothing beyond the current expenses he established for the household, and pleased not to have responsibility any more, I granted him unlimited and unchecked authority. He had therefore quite naturally gotten into the habit of thinking of me as a child under his jurisdiction, and he had no cause to get irritated with such a submissive child.

If I have gone into such detail, it is because I have to tell how, in the midst of this very real nun's life I was leading at Nohant—which lacked neither cell, vows of obedience, silence, nor poverty—the need to exist by myself finally made itself felt. I suffered to see myself useless; not being able to help the poor in any other way, I became a country doctor, and my gratis clientele had grown to the point of overwhelming me with fatigue. To economize, I had also to become a bit of a pharmacist, and when I returned from my rounds, I would exhaust myself in preparing ointments and syrups. The job did not weary me—what did it matter to me whether I daydreamed there or elsewhere? But it did occur to me that with a little bit of my own money, my patients would be better cared for and my practice could make use of several specialists.

Then, too, slavery is something inhuman that we can only tolerate while dreaming perpetually of freedom. I was not my husband's slave; he very gladly left me to my reading and my concoctions, but I was in the servitude of a given situation, from which it was not up to him to free me. If I had asked him for the moon, he would have laughingly told me, "Find the means to pay for it, and

I'll buy it for you." And if I had let myself go so far as to say that I would like to see China, he would have answered, "Find the money! Make Nohant yield, and go to China!"

I had therefore mulled over more than once the problem of finding resources, however modest, which I might dispose of, without remorse and without permission, for an artistic treat, for a well-deserved charity, for a fine book, for a week-long trip, for a small gift to a not very well-to-do friend, for God knows what little trifles one can do without, yet without which one is not a man or a woman, but more likely an angel or an animal. In our wholly facti-tious society, the total absence of currency constitutes an impossible living condition—terrifying poverty or absolute powerlessness. Not having responsi-bility is a state of bondage something like the shame of being declared legally incompetent.

I had also told myself that the moment would come when I could no longer stay at Nohant. That resulted from causes which were still transitory then, but that I sometimes noticed were getting worse in a most threatening way. I would have had to drive out my brother, who, hampered by the bad management of his own fortune, had come to live with us as an economy, and also another friend of the house[57] for whom I had, in spite of his bacchic fever, a very real friendship—a man who, like my brother, had heart and wit to spare one day out of every three, four, or five, depending on "how the wind blew," as they would say. Well, there were salty winds which made them commit many a folly, salty faces whom they could not greet without feeling the need to drink, and when they had gotten drunk, it turned out that, of all these things, the wine was yet the saltiest: there is nothing worse than witty and good-natured drunk-ards—you cannot get angry with them. My brother was susceptible to wine, and I would be forced to lock myself in my cell, so that he would not come to me and weep all night. This was if he had not exceeded a certain dosage; if he had, then he would have the strong desire to strangle his best friends. Poor Hippolyte! How charming he was on his good days, how unbearable on the bad ones. Such as he was, and in spite of some indirect consequences more serious than his ramblings, tears, and rages, I preferred to think in terms of exiling myself rather than sending him away. Besides, his wife lived with us, his poor, excellent wife, who had only one recompense in the world—being in such frail health that she spent more time in her bed than on her feet, and that she slept soundly enough not to notice too much, yet, what was happening around us.

With a view to freeing myself and getting my children away from possi-ble sorry influences; certain as I was that I would be allowed to go away on the condition of not asking for a share, much less half, of my income, I was trying to create some modest profession for myself. I had attempted translation—it took too long, I was too scrupulous and conscientious; pencil or watercolor portraits done at a sitting—I caught the likenesses very well, my little heads were not drawn badly, but the métier lacked distinction; sewing—I was quick at it, but I could not see well enough close up, and I learned that it would only bring in ten sous a day at the most; designing—I thought of my mother, who had not been able to get back into it for lack of a little capital. For four years, I went along groping, or slaving at nothing worthwhile, in order to discover within me any capability whatsoever. Once, I thought I had found it. I had painted some ornamental birds and flowers in diminutive compositions on snuff boxes and cigar cases of chestnut. There were some very pretty ones among them that the varnisher admired when, on one of my trips to Paris, I took them to him. He asked me if this was my profession; I answered Yes, just to see what he would say. He told me he would put these little objects on display, to see what they would bring. After a few days, he informed me that he had refused eighty francs for the cigar case—I had made up a price of a hundred francs out of thin air, thinking I would be offered a hundred sous.

I contacted some people at Maison Giroux and showed them my samples. They advised me to try a lot of different objects—fans, tea chests, work boxes—and assured me I would have an outlet for them in their establishment. I therefore brought back from Paris a supply of materials, but I wasted my eyesight, time, and effort trying out different techniques. Certain woods came out beautifully, as if by a miracle; others split or were ruined at the varnishing stage. I had accidents that slowed me down, and all told, the raw materials cost so much that, counting time wasted and objects ruined, I foresaw—given a steady outlet—only enough income to put very dry bread on the table. Nevertheless, I stuck to it, but the fashion for these objects died out in time to prevent me from pursuing failure.

And then, in spite of myself, I felt that I was an artist, without ever having dreamed I could be one. During one of my short trips to Paris, I had one day gone into the art museum. Of course it was not the first time, but I had always looked without seeing, persuaded that I was no judge and not being aware at all that one can feel without verbal understanding. I began to be singularly moved. I went back the next day, then the day after; on my next trip, wanting to get to know, one by one, all the masterpieces and understand the differences among schools that went beyond the recognition of different styles and subjects, I would go off mysteriously, all alone, as soon as the museum was open, and stay there until it closed. I was transfixed before the Titians, the Tintorettos, the Rubenses. First, the Flemish school took hold of me by how it made reality poetic; then, little by little, I came to feel the reasons why the Italian school was so appreciated. As I had no one to tell me in what ways it was beautiful, my increasing admiration had all the attraction of a discovery, and I was completely surprised and thrilled to find in paintings pleasures equal to those I had savored in music. I was far from having any great discernment; I had never had the slightest serious notion regarding this art form, which is not necessarily revealed to the senses any more than the others, except with the aid of a special gift and training. I knew very well that to stand before a picture and say, "I can judge because I can see, and I can see because I have two eyes" was the impertinent utterance of a philistine. I therefore said nothing; I did not even question myself to find out what obstacles or affinities there were between me and the creations of a particular genius. I would contemplate, I would submit, I would be transported into a new world. At night I saw parading before me all those great faces which, at the hands of the masters, took on the seal of spiritual authority, even those that expressed only physical strength or health. It is in beautiful painting that one senses what life is, as in a splendid summation of the shape and expression of beings and things too often obscured or blurred by the movement of reality and by the judgment of the one who contemplates them. It is to see the spectacle of nature and humanity through the feelings of the genius who created it. How fortunate a naïve mind is, which brings to such works neither a critic's prejudices nor any pretension to personal ability! The universe was being revealed to me. I saw into the present and past at the same time; I was becoming a classicist and a romantic, simultaneously, with no knowledge of what that artistic feud signified. The world of truth surged forth through all my own fantasies and all the ignorance of my own viewing. I felt like I had acquired an unnamable and infinite treasure of whose existence I had been uninformed. I could not have said what treasure—I did not know what to call the surge I felt in my heated and, as it were, expanded mind—but I had caught the fever and had come away from the museum, straying from one street to another, not knowing where I was going, forgetting to eat, and suddenly realizing it was time to go hear *Die Freischutz* or *Guillaume Tell*.[58] I would then enter a pastry shop and eat a brioche for dinner, telling myself with satisfaction that, in view of the small amount of cash I had, skipping any meal gave me the right and means to go to a performance.

You can see that, involved in my projects and my emotional state, I had acquired little learning. I had read some history and some novels; I could sightread music; I had cast an absent-minded glance at the newspapers and purposely closed my ears a bit to the politics of the moment. My friend Néraud, a true scholar, an artist to his very fingertips in the field of science, had tried to teach me botany; but while dashing through the countryside—he loaded down with his tin box, I carrying Maurice on my shoulders—I had only been dabbling, or as the good folks say, "only gotten as far as the mustard." Furthermore, I had not even studied the mustard carefully, and all I knew was that that plant belonged to the family *cruciferae*. I would let myself be distracted from species and specimens by the sun gilding the fog, by the butterfies pursuing the flowers, and by Maurice pursuing the butterflies.

And then I would have liked to have seen and known everything at once. I got my professor to chat, and on all things he was brilliant and interesting, but I only let myself be initiated into the beauty of specifics; my recalcitrant memory made the exact side of the science seem arid to me. This was a big mistake; Malgache, which is what I called Néraud, was an admirable initiator, and I was still at an age to learn. All he wanted me to do was inform myself in a general way, which would have allowed me afterward to lend myself to thorough studies on my own. I confined myself to understanding selected matters that he outlined in delightful letters about natural history and in tales of his distant voyages, which opened up for me just a bit the world of the tropics. I recaptured the vision he had given me of the Ile-de-France, when writing the novel *Indiana*, and all I could do was spoil his descriptions when adapting them to the scenes of my book, for I could not simply copy his notebooks, which he had collected for me.

Very simply stated, since I brought to my literary projects neither a tested talent, nor special studies, nor the consciousness of anything more than a vaguely troubled life, nor a deep knowledge of the world of facts, I had no real ambition at all. Ambition rests on self-confidence, and I was not silly enough to rely on my small gift. This, I felt, resided in very limited resources—the analysis of feelings, the portrayal of a certain number of characters, the love of nature, the familiarity, if I may say so, with the scenes and mores of the country—but that was enough to begin with. "As I go along in life," I said to myself, "I shall see more people and things, I shall expand my circle of personalities, I shall enlarge my cadre of scenes, and if, in addition, I need to embark on the novel of induction, as the historical novel is called, I shall study history in detail, and I shall divine through my own thought the thought of men who no longer exist."

When the resolution was ripe to go and seek my fortune—a thousand écus was all I had ever dreamed of—to declare it and follow it through was a matter of three days' time. My husband owed me an allowance of fifteen hundred francs. I asked him for my daughter, and for permission to spend three months twice a year in Paris, with two hundred fifty francs for each month I was absent. That presented no difficulty. He thought it was a whim of which I would soon be weary.

My brother, who thought likewise, said to me, "You imagine you can live in Paris, with a child, on two hundred fifty francs a month? It is really laughable—you, who don't know the price of a chicken! You're going to come back in two weeks, emptyhanded, for your husband has definitely decided to ignore any requests for a new subsidy."

"That's fine," I answered. "I'll try. Let me borrow the apartment you occupy in your Paris house for one week, and keep Solange for me until I have lodgings. I shall come back soon indeed."

My brother was the only one who tried to combat my resolution. He felt a little guilty about the disgust my house inspired in me. He would not admit it to himself, and only unwittingly admitted it to me. His wife understood better and showed me her approval. She had confidence in my courage and destiny. She felt I was taking the only means at my disposal of avoiding or postponing a more painful decision.

My daughter, so far, had little understanding; Maurice would also have realized nothing, if my brother had not taken care to tell him I was going away for a long time and perhaps would not come back. He took that line, hoping my poor child's grief would hold me back. My heart was broken over his tears, but I succeeded in calming him and giving him confidence in my promise to return.

I got to Paris shortly after the scenes at the Luxembourg and the trial of the ministers.[59]   *J.L.P.*

XIII

By way of a preface to a new phase of my narration. —Why I do not
mention everyone who influenced my life either through persuasion
or persecution. —A few lines by J.-J. Rousseau on the same subject.
—My feeling is completely the opposite of his. —I do not know how
to assail the lives of others, and due to inveterate Christianity, I have
not been able to throw myself into the politics of personalities.
—I resume my story. —The garret on Quai Saint-Michel and the
eccentric life I led for a few months before settling down.
—A disguise that was extraordinarily successful. —Singular errors.
—M. Pinson. —Émile Paultre. —Mlle. Leverd's bouquet.
—M. Rollinat, Sr. —His family. —François Rollinat. —A rather
long digression. —My chapter on friendship, less beautiful but as
heartfelt as Montaigne's.

Let us establish one fact before going further. As I do not intend to
deceive the reader in any way while narrating what concerns me, I must begin
by saying outright that I *do* wish to hold back, so as not to distort or disguise,
several circumstances in my life. I never imagined I had any secrets to keep
from my friends. In this regard the frankness of my relations and the respect
which has always surrounded me in my private life are witnesses to my sincerity. But with regard to the public, I do not see myself as having the right to lay
bare the past of every person whose existence has touched mine. My silence
may stand for indulgence or respect, oversight or deference—I am not obliged
to explain its cause. It will probably stem from a combination of causes, and I
urge the reader not to be prejudiced in favor of or against the persons about
whom I speak little or not at all.

All my affections have been genuine, and yet I have broken off several of
them knowingly and voluntarily. In the eyes of my circle, I acted too soon or
too late, I was right or wrong, according to how much they knew about the reasons behind my decisions. Aside from the fact that these private debates would
hold very little interest for the reader, just presenting them for appraisal would
be contrary to decorum, for I would sometimes be forced to reveal myself at
someone else's expense.

Can I, however, push decorum so far as to say that I have been unfair, on
certain occasions, just for the pleasure of being unfair? There the lie would
begin, but who would be taken in? Furthermore, everyone knows that in any

quarrel, whether over family or public opinion, over self-interest or generosity, over sentiment or principles, over love or friendship, the mistakes are reciprocal, and one can only understand and ascribe motives to some at the expense of others. Some people in my life I have viewed with illusions born of ardor, and later made the great mistake of recovering my lucid vision. *All* they had to ask of me was one speck of civility; I defy anyone to say I have ever been remiss in this! However, their irritation was keen, and I understand this very well. We are disposed, in the first moments of a break-up, to be outraged by disillusionment. When calm sets in, people become more just. Whatever the case may be with these persons, I do not want to have to depict them; I do not have the right to reveal their traits to the curiosity or indifference of passersby. If they are living in obscurity, let us allow them that sweet privilege. If they are famous, let us permit them to depict themselves, if they deem it appropriate, and let us not practice the sad profession of biographer to the living.

The living! We do indeed owe it to them, I think, to let them live. A long time ago someone said that ridicule was a lethal weapon. If that is true, how much more so is blame for some action, or merely exposure of some weakness! In circumstances more serious than those I am alluding to here, I have seen perverseness born and grow by the hour; I am familiar with it, I have watched it, and I have not even characterized it, generally speaking, in my novels. I have been criticised for my imagination's lack of malice. If this is a shortcoming of my mind, be sure it exists in my heart as well, and that it goes against me to bear witness to ugliness in real life. That is why I shall not display it in a true story. Were it proved to me useful to display, I would not be any less convinced that the pillory is a bad pulpit, and that he who has lost hope of rehabilitation in the eyes of mankind will not make an effort to be reconciled with himself.

Besides, I am inclined to forgive, and if some souls who have been culpable with respect to me can be rehabilitated by others, I am ready to give them my blessing. The public does not act thus; it condemns and throws stones. Therefore, I do not want to turn over my enemies—if I may use a word that does not have much meaning for me—to judges without heart or wisdom, or to the decrees of a public opinion that is not guided by the least notion of religion, or enlightened by the slightest principle of charity.

I am not a saint. I must have made—correction! I certainly have made—my share of mistakes, serious ones at that, in conflicts between me and several individuals. I must have been unjust or impulsive, as are those beings who are slow to make up their minds and reluctant to submit to the cruel punishments created for them by the imaginings of overstimulated sensibilities. The conciliatory spirit I bring to this text has not always dominated my emotions the moment they first occurred. I may have grumbled about my sufferings and complained about certain actions in the privacy of a relationship, but never have I, in cold blood, with premeditation, and under the dominion of cowardly rancor, prosecuted anyone in the court of public opinion. I have refused to do it even where the purest and most serious people claim the right to do so—in politics. I was not born for the job of executioner, and if I have steadfastly refused to take part in this act of social warfare, through scruples of conscience, generosity, or an easy-going character, all the more reason not to contradict myself when it is a question of my own isolated cause.

And let it not be said that it is easy to write about your life when you cut out of the account certain essential areas where your will was operant. No, it is not easy, for you must readily make the decision to let absurd tales and outrageous lies run their course, and I made that decision in undertaking this work. I have not entitled it "my memoirs"; it is by design that I chose the words, "Story of My Life," in order to convey that I did not mean to tell others' stories without restrictions. So, in every situation where the life of one of my fellows may have caused mine to deviate from its natural path, I have nothing to say, not wishing to make a public trial of the influences I may have undergone or withstood, or of the persons who, through persuasion or persecution, may have brought me to act one way or another. If I have drifted or strayed, I have at least the great consolation of being certain today, after reflection, that I never acted except with the conviction of fulfilling a duty or exercising a legitimate right, which at bottom is the same thing.[13]

Just lately I received a small volume, recently published,[14] of Jean-Jacques Rousseau's unedited fragments, and I was sharply struck by this passage, which had been part of a projected preface or introduction to *Les Confessions*: "The ties I have had to several persons force me to speak of them as freely as of myself. I cannot make myself known well unless I make them known also; and so, one must not expect that, by holding back on the occasion of these writings whatever cannot be kept silent without hindrance to the truths that I must tell, I shall have a consideration for others that I do not have for myself."

I have my doubts whether, even if you are Jean-Jacques Rousseau, you have the right to prosecute your contemporaries before their contemporaries, for a wholly personal reason. There is something in that which revolts the public conscience. We would prefer if Rousseau had let himself be accused of flightiness or ingratitude toward Mme. de Warens, rather than learn through him the details that spoil the image of his benefactress. We could have surmised that there were motives for his inconstancy, excuses for his forgetfulness, and judged him all the more generously because he would have seemed worthy of it through his own generosity.

Seven years ago, I wrote at the beginning of this account, "As we are all dependent on one another, there is no isolated fault. There is no error to which someone is not the cause or accomplice, and it is impossible to accuse ourselves without accusing the next one, not only the enemy who denounces us, but sometimes even the friend who defends us. That is what happened to Rousseau, and that is bad."

Yes, that is bad. After seven years on a work interrupted a hundred times by general and particular preoccupations that have given my mind all the leisure for fresh reflection and all the benefit of a fresh examination, I again find myself of the same conviction and certitude regarding myself and my work. Under the scrutiny of the literary public, certain personal confidences, whether confessions or justifications, become an assault on the conscience or reputation of another; or else they are incomplete, and for that reason, untrue.

Having established all this, I continue. I am excising from my memories a portion of the interest they may hold, but there will still be enough that is useful in them, in more than one respect, for me to take the trouble to write them down.

At this point my life becomes more active, more filled with details and incidents. It would be impossible for me to recover them in the order of their exact dates. I prefer to classify them by their progressive order of importance.

I looked for lodgings and was soon settled on Quai Saint-Michel, in one of the garrets of the big house on the corner of the block, at the end of the bridge, opposite the Morgue. There I had three small, very clean rooms leading to a balcony from which I had an extensive view of the Seine, and where I could contemplate, face to face, the gigantic monuments of Notre-Dame, Saint-Jacques-la-Boucherie, Sainte-Chapelle, and others. I had sky, water, air, swallows, rooftop greenery; I did not feel too much part of modern Paris, which would not have suited my taste nor my resources, but more so in the picturesque and poetic Paris of Victor Hugo, the Paris of the past.[60]

I paid, I believe, three hundred francs a year rent. The five flights pained me greatly—I have never been able to climb stairs, but I indeed had to, and often with my big daughter in my arms. I had no servant; the woman caretaker, who was very dependable, very clean, and very kind, helped me do my housework for fifteen francs a month. I had my evening meal brought in from a cheap restaurant, whose cook was also very clean and honest, for about two francs a day. I myself scrubbed and ironed the linen underwear. Thus, I succeeded in financing my existence within the limits of my allowance.

The most difficult thing was buying furniture. Obviously, I was not in a position to be extravagant. I was given credit, and I managed to pay, but getting furnished, however modestly, could not be accomplished all at once; several months passed, as much in Paris as in Nohant, before I could move Solange to these poor surroundings from her Nohant palace, relatively speaking, without her suffering from it or noticing the difference. Little by little, everything fell into place, and as soon as I had her near me, with board and service assured, I could settle down, not go out during the day except to take her for a walk in the Luxembourg, and spend all my evenings next to her, writing. Providence came to my aid. While growing a pot of reseda on my balcony, I met my neighbor, who, better off than I, was growing an orange tree on hers. This was Mme. Badoureau, who lived with her husband, a primary school teacher, and a charming daughter of fifteen, a sweet and modest blonde, eyes always lowered, who was smitten with Solange. This excellent family offered to have Solange play with the other children who came to take private lessons, whenever she grew weary of the small amount of space in my garret, and of the monotony of the same playthings. That made the child's existence no longer merely bearable, but pleasant, and these fine people were unsparing in their care and affection for her, without ever wanting to let me pay them for it, although their profession would have made payment seem completely normal and remuneration well deserved.

Until then—that is to say, until my daughter was with me in Paris—I lived in a less complacent and even very unusual manner, but one that nevertheless was leading directly to my goal.

I did not want to exceed my budget; I did not want to borrow a cent; my debt of five hundred francs, the only one in my life, had tormented me so much! What if M. Dudevant had refused to pay it? He paid it readily, but I had not dared reveal it to him until I was very ill and afraid I would die "insolvent." I went looking for work and did not find any. (I shall tell in a moment where I stood with my literary possibilities.) I had a small portrait on display in the café at Quai Saint-Michel, in the same house, but no customers came. I had failed to catch the likeness of my lady caretaker, and ran the risk of damaging my reputation in the quarter.

I would have liked to read; I had no supply of books. And then it was winter, and it is not economical to stay in your room when you have to count the logs. I tried to settle in at the Mazarine library, but it was so cold there I think I would have been better off working in the towers of Notre-Dame. I, who have always been the chilliest person I have ever known, could not bear it. There were some old hoboes there who would settle in at a table—motionless, peaceful, mummified—seemingly unaware that their blue noses were turning to crystal. I envied their state of petrification; I watched them sit down and get up as if moved by a spring, to assure myself they were not made of wood.

Then, too, I was eager to get rid of my provincialism and get into the swim of things, to be *au courant* with ideas and customs. I had an urge to do this; I was curious. Except for the most salient books, I knew nothing of the modern arts; I was especially thirsty for theater.

I was well aware that for a woman without money to fulfill these fantasies was impossible. Balzac used to say, "You can't be a woman in Paris without an income of twenty-five thousand francs." And this paradox on the price of elegance became a truism for the woman who wanted to be an artist.

Yet I saw my young friends from Berry, my childhood companions, live in Paris with as little as I, and keep abreast of everything that interested intelligent young people. Literary and political events, the excitement of the theaters and the museums, the clubs and the streets—they saw everything, they went everywhere. My legs were as strong as theirs, and so were my good little Berrichon feet, which had learned to walk on bad roads, balancing on thick wooden clogs. But on the pavements of Paris I was like a boat on ice. Delicate footwear cracked in two days; overshoes made me clumsy; I wasn't used to lifting my skirts. I was muddy, tired, runny-nosed, and I saw my shoes and clothing—not to mention the little velvet hats—spattered in the gutters, falling into ruin with frightening rapidity.

I had already observed and experienced these things before I dreamed of settling in Paris, and had brought up the problem with my mother, who lived there in elegance and comfort on three thousand five hundred francs a year: how to make do with the cheapest mode of dress in this frightful climate, short of living confined to one's room seven days a week. She had replied to me, "At my age and with my habits, it's not hard; but when I was young and your father

was short of money, he got the idea to dress me like a boy. My sister did likewise, and we went everywhere on foot with our husbands—the theater, all sorts
of places. Our cost of living was reduced by half."

At first this idea seemed amusing to me, and then very ingenious. Having
been dressed like a boy during my childhood, then having hunted in smock and
gaiters with Deschartres, I did not find it at all shocking again to put on a costume which was not new to me. At that period, the fashion was singularly helpful to the disguise. Men were wearing long, square redingotes called "proprietor's coats," which went down to the heel and showed so little of the shape that
my brother, when donning his at Nohant, had laughingly said to me, "Pretty,
isn't it? It's the fashion, and it's very comfortable. The tailor takes his measure-
ments on a sentry box, and out comes an item that would fit a whole regiment."

So, I had a "sentry box redingote" made for myself, out of thick gray
cloth, with matching trousers and vest. With a gray hat and a wide wool tie, I
was the perfect little first-year student. I cannot tell you the pleasure I derived
from my boots—I would gladly have slept in them, as my brother did in his
youth, when he put on his first pair. With those little iron heels, I felt secure on
the sidewalks. I flew from one end of Paris to the other. It seemed to me that I
could have made a trip around the world. Also, my clothing made me fearless.
I was on the go in all kinds of weather, I came in at all hours, I sat in the pit in
every theater. No one paid attention to me, no one suspected my disguise.
Aside from the fact that I wore it with ease, the absence of coquettishness in
costume and facial expression warded off any suspicion. I was too poorly
dressed and looked too simple—my usual vacant, verging on dumb, look—to
attract or compel attention. Women understand very little about wearing a disguise, even on the stage. They do not want to give up the slenderness of their
figure, the smallness of their feet, the gracefulness of their movements, the
sparkle in their eyes; and yet all these things—especially their way of glanc-
ing—make it easy to guess who they are. There is a way of stealing about,
everywhere, without turning a head, and of speaking in a low and muted pitch
which does not resound like a flute in the ears of those who may hear you. Furthermore, to avoid being noticed as a man, you must already have not been
noticed as a woman.

I never went to the pit alone, not because the people I saw there were any
more or less uncouth than elsewhere, but because of the paid and unpaid
claques who wrangled a great deal at that time. They did a lot of pushing and
shoving at first performances, and I was not strong enough to fight against the
crowd. I always placed myself in the center of the small batallion of my friends
from Berry, who protected me as best they could. One day, however, when
seated under the gaslight, I happened to yawn, in all innocence and frankness,
with no ulterior motive. The clappers seemed intent on roughing me up. They
called me names that impugned my masculinity. I found myself getting very
angry and rebellious when they tried to provoke me, and if my friends had not
been numerous enough to impress the claque, I really think I would have gotten myself beaten up.

I have been telling about a very brief and incidental time in my life, although rumor had it that it went on for several years; ten years later, my as-yet-beardless son was often taken for me. He was amused by these cases of mistaken identity. Since I am on the subject, I remember several that are apt and that date from 1831.

At the time, I used to have dinner at Pinson's, a restaurant on Rue de l'Ancienne-Comédie. As one of my friends called me Madame, in front of M. Pinson, he thought he should do likewise. "Oh, no!" I said to him. "Since you are in on the secret, call me Monsieur." The next day, I was not in my disguise, and he called me Monsieur. I reproached him for it, but he could never keep pace with my frequent change of costume. He would no sooner get used to saying Monsieur, when I would reappear dressed as a woman, and he would succeed in saying Madame only by the day I again became Monsieur. That fine and decent Father Pinson! He was a friend to his clients, and when they did not have the means to pay, he not only waited, but opened his wallet to them. For my part, although I very seldom imposed on his kindness, I have always been as grateful for his trust as for a favor rendered.

Planet[61] had formed a small club of people from Berry, at which, for a very modest monthly fee, one could read the papers and work in a passably well-heated place. One day, when I had gone up there to talk to him, Émile Paultre, one of our friends from Nevers to whom I had not yet been introduced, came in and joined the conversation. The next day, I was dining with Planet at Pinson's. I was not in my disguise. Paultre came in, and I told Planet to call him over to see if he would recognize me. As he did not appear to, Planet, wanting to see if this was through discretion, asked him if he knew the name of the boy he had met the evening before. "Indeed no," he answered. "Who was he?"

"So-and-So from La Châtre."

"All the same," he resumed, "he was an unbearable little pedant."

"Why?" I asked in my turn. "Did he say something foolish?"

"No, but he was too smart for his age. If I were fifteen, it might occur to me that Planet was sometimes mistaken, but I wouldn't take the liberty to tell him so."

I could not help laughing. He looked at me in astonishment, then, utter shame. "Oh, Madame," he exclaimed, "I beg your pardon! The young man was your brother; there is an extraordinary resemblance. Well, after all, what did I say? The boy was quite nice—just a little too self-assured, but that will pass."

"Like it or not," he said to Planet as he left, "I made a blunder. The lady will hold it against me." Planet tried to placate him by telling him that brother and sister were one and the same. He refused to believe it, and almost got angry at what he took for a hoax.

Afterward, we struck up a friendship. He has a pure and worthy character, a serious mind, and a highly-developed intelligence.

But it was at the first performance of *La Reine d'Espagne* by Delatouche[62] that I had a comedy of my very own. I had free tickets from the author, and this time I could sit in state in the balcony, in my gray redingote, beneath the loge in which Mlle. Leverd—an actress of great talent, who had once been pretty, but whom small pox had disfigured—displayed a superb bouquet, which she dropped on my shoulder. I was not sufficiently absorbed by my role to pick it up. "Young man," she said to me in a majestic tone, "my bouquet! Come, now!" I was oblivious. "You are hardly gallant," the old gentleman beside me said, as he reached to pick up the bouquet. "At your age, I would not have been so preoccupied." He presented the bouquet to Mlle. Leverd, who exclaimed, rolling her r's heavily, "Ah, really, is it you, Monsieur Rollinat?" And they went on to chat about the new play. "Good," I thought to myself. "Here I am right next to a compatriot who may recognize me, even though I don't recall ever having met him." M. Rollinat, Sr. was the attorney general for our district.

While he was chatting with Mlle. Leverd, Duris-Dufresne,[63] who was in the orchestra, came up to the balcony to greet me. He had already seen me in my disguise, and sitting down for an instant in M. Rollinat's empty seat, he spoke to me, I remember, about La Fayette,[64] whom he wanted me to meet. M. Rollinat returned to his seat, and they spoke to each other in low tones; then the deputy withdrew, bowing to me with a little too much deference for the costume I was wearing. Fortunately, the attorney paid no attention and said to me as he sat back down, "Well, now, it seems we are compatriots? Our deputy has just told me you were a very distinguished young man. Pardon me, but I would have said 'child.' How old are you, then? Fifteen? Sixteen?"

"And you, Monsieur," I said to him, "who are a very distinguished attorney, how old are you then?"

"Oh, me," he replied, laughing, "I am past seventy."

"Well then, like me, you don't seem as old as you are."

The response pleased him, and conversation ensued. Although I have never been very witty, however little wit a woman may have, she always has more than a schoolboy. Good old Rollinat was so taken with my high degree of intelligence that on several occasions he exclaimed, "Remarkable, remarkable!" The play was an utter failure, in spite of its barrage of wit, charming plot, and dialogue in the Molière spirit, but, admittedly, the main subject and its crude details were dated. Besides, the young audience was romantic. Delatouche had mortally wounded what people then called La Pléiade, by publishing an article entitled "La Camaraderie." I alone, perhaps, in the whole theater, liked both Delatouche and the romantics.

During the intermissions, I chatted till curtain time with the old attorney, who judged the strengths and weaknesses of the play competently and soundly. He was fond of talking, and listened to himself more readily than to others. Happy at being understood, he took a liking to me, asked my name, and invited me to come see him. I invented a name, which he was surprised not to recognize, and I promised to look him up in Berry. He concluded by saying, "M. Dufresne did not deceive me—you are a remarkable child. But I find you weak in the classics. You tell me your parents educated you at home and that you haven't gone to classes and don't intend to. I see perfectly well that that kind of education has its good side; you're artistic, and about everything regarding ideas and feelings, you know more than your age would suggest. You have an ease and aptitude in language that make me think you will one day be a successful writer. But, believe me, study the classics! Nothing replaces that foundation. I have twelve children. I put all my boys in a preparatory school. Not one of them has your precociousness when it comes to judgment, but they are all able to get along in the various professions that a young man might choose; whereas you—you're compelled to be an artist, and nothing else. Now, if you fail at art, you will very much regret not having received a general education."

I was convinced that this good man was not fooled by my disguise and that he was wittily amusing himself by provoking me to play my role. The effect on me was that of a conversation at a masked ball, and I took so little trouble to sustain the fiction that I was very astonished to learn later that he had taken part in it with the best faith in the world.

The following year, M. Dudevant introduced me to François Rollinat,[65] whom he had invited to come and spend a few days at Nohant, and whom I told to ask his father about a little fellow with whom he had chatted so kindly at the first and last performances of *La Reine d'Espagne*.

"Just so," answered Rollinat. "My father was talking to us the other day about that encounter, while we were having a general chat about education. He said he had been struck by the flow of wit and the manners of the young people today, and of one in particular, who had spoken to him about all sorts of things, like a little savant, and yet confessed to him that he knew neither Latin nor Greek and was studying neither law nor medicine."

"And it never occurred to your father to think that that little savant might be a woman?"

"You perhaps?" exclaimed Rollinat.

"Exactly!"

"Well! of all the conjectures my father entertained, including vain inquiries as to which family you might be a son of, that is the only one that never occurred to him, or us. He was captivated and intrigued; he is still trying to find out, and I shall be careful not to undeceive him. I ask your permission to introduce him to you, without revealing anything."

"All right. But he won't recognize me, for in all probability, he didn't look at me."

I was mistaken. M. Rollinat had paid such careful attention to my face that, on seeing me, he leaped up on his slender, still nimble legs, exclaiming, "Oh, how stupid of me!"

From then on, we were like friends of twenty years' standing. And since I am on the subject, I shall speak here of this person and his family, although it will push my story a little ahead. But I shall resume it shortly.

M. Rollinat, Sr., in spite of his theory on classical education, was an artist from head to toe, as indeed are all somewhat eminent attorneys. He was a man of feeling and imagination, mad about poetry, very much a poet and quite mad himself; angelically kind, enthusiastic, lavish; eagerly amassing a fortune for his twelve children, but unwittingly spending it as he went along; idolizing, spoiling, and forgetting them when at the gaming tables, where, winning and losing by turn, he staked everything he had, including his life.

You could not have found a more youthful or lively old man, taking his drinks straight and never getting drunk, singing and frolicking with young people without ever becoming ridiculous, because he had a pure mind and innocent heart; enthusiastic about everything to do with art, endowed with a prodigious memory and exquisite taste, he was very surely one of the finest specimens Berry has produced.

He spared nothing for the education of his numerous children. The eldest was a lawyer, another a missionary, a third a scholar, another in military service, the others, artists and teachers, the girls as well as the boys. The ones I have known particularly well are François, Charles, and Marie-Louise. The last was my daughter's governess for a year. Charles, who was wonderfully gifted, had a magnificent voice, a wit as delightful as his character, but his proud and contemplative soul always refused to give itself over to the crowd, and he went to live in Russia, where he successively taught several children in the homes of some of the greats.

François had completed his studies early. At twenty-two, having received his law degree, he came to practice at Chateauroux. His father turned his office over to him, figuring he was giving him a fortune and never doubting his son could easily meet all the needs of the family, with his fine talent and a clientele. Consequently, the father never worried about another thing, and died gambling and smiling, leaving more debts than money, and the whole family to raise or establish.

François bore this dreadful responsibility with the patience of a Berrichon ox. Also a man of imagination and feeling, and an artist like his father, but a more serious philosopher, from the age of twenty-two, he plunged his life, will-power, and strength, into the arid work of procedural law, in order to honor all commitments and give his mother and eleven brothers and sisters a good life. No one suspected what he suffered from this self-denial; from this distaste for a profession he had never liked and from which any success due to his talent never managed to exhilarate him; from that narrow, frustrated, submissive way of life; from the worries of the present, the anxieties of the future, the gnawing worm of those damnable debts—although care and fatigue wrote the suffering on his somber, preoccupied face. Habitually dull and preoccupied, Rollinat revealed himself only in flashes, but then he would show the clearest mind, the surest tact, the most subtle penetration. When he was in private, or well-protected among intimates, when his relieved heart permitted his spirit to cheer up, he became most originally whimsical. And I know of nothing as hilarious as his sudden shift from an almost lugubrious gravity to a mirth that bordered on delirious.

But all I have said here does not and cannot begin to tell the treasure of exquisite goodness, generous candor, and deep wisdom that this elite soul contained, unknown to itself. I was able to appreciate it from the first time I saw him, and consequently I have deserved a friendship that I count among the most precious blessings of my life. Beyond the feelings of esteem and respect that I had for this person's character, so tried by the need for abnegation and modesty in his domestic heroism, a peculiar likeness of feeling, a sweet agreement in our ideas, a conformity or, better said, an extraordinary similarity in our appreciation of all things, revealed to each of us what we had dreamed of as the perfect friendship, a feeling set apart from all other feelings by its sanctity and serenity.

It is very rare that between a man and a woman some livelier thought than befits the fraternal bond does not come along to trouble the relationship, and often the faithful friendship of a mature man is only the generosity of a passion conquered in the past. A woman of integrity, however, can escape the sexual trap, and the man who does not forgive her for not having shared his secret agitations is not worth the benefit of friendship. I must say that, in general, I have been fortunate in this respect and that, for the most part, in spite of my romantic trust, which people have often teased me about, I have had the instinct to discover beautiful souls and preserve their affection. I must also say that, not being at all a coquette and even having a sort of horror of that strange habit of provocation which not all honest women deny themselves, I have rarely had to struggle against love in friendship. Also, when it was there to be discovered, I never found it offensive, because it was serious and respectful.

As for Rollinat, he was not the only one of my friends who had, from the very first day, done me the honor of loving me only platonically. But I have always confessed to all of them that I had a sort of unexplainable preference for him. Others have respected and served me as much as he—others whom the link of childhood memories should moreover make more precious to me. They are no less so to me. But because I do not have such links with Rollinat, because our friendship dates from only twenty-five years ago, I must consider it as built more on choice than on habit. This is the friendship about which I have most often been pleased to agree with Montaigne:

"If pushed to say why I loved him, I feel it can only be expressed by answering, 'Because it was him, because it was me.' There is beyond all my discoursing, and beyond what I can say in particular about it, some inexplicable and fateful force which mediated this union. We sought each other out before we met, because of the stories that we had heard about each other, which made a greater impression on our feelings than such stories usually do.... And at our first meeting we were both so taken with each other, so familiar, so grateful to each other, that nothing, from then on, was as close as we were to each other... having started so late... [our knowledge of each other] had no time to lose, and had no need to conform to the pattern of dull and ordinary friendships, which require so many precautions by way of long and preliminary conversations."[66]

From my youth on, indeed from childhood, I had dreamed of the ideal friendship, and I admired enormously those great examples from antiquity, in which I suspected no sexual element. Later on I would learn that they were accompanied by that extravagant or morbid tendency about which Cicero asked: *"Quis est enim iste amor amicitiae?"* ["So what is this so-called love between friends?"][67] This gave me a sort of fright, as did anything that bore the stamp of possible aberration or depravity. I had envisioned heroes so pure, and then I had to imagine them so corrupt and barbaric. Thus, I was overcome with disgust and even great sadness when, at the age when one is permitted to read everything, I understood the story of Achilles and Patroclus, of Harmodius and

Aristogiton. It was, in fact, Montaigne's chapter on friendship which brought about my disillusionment, but thereafter that same chapter, so platonic and so ardent, that virile and saintly expression of a sentiment raised to the level of a virtue, became a sort of sacred law that guided my soul.

I was, however, deeply wounded by the scorn that my dear Montaigne had for my sex when he said, "To tell the truth, the ordinary capacity of women is not sufficient to respond to this exchange, or to the nurturing communion of this sacred bond; nor do their souls seem steady enough to sustain the strain of such a close and lasting knot."[68]

While meditating on Montaigne in the gardens at Ormesson, I had often felt humiliated as a woman, and I confess that in every reading of philosophical teachings, even in religious books, this moral inferiority attributed to women set my youthful pride in revolt. "But that is false," I would protest to myself. "This ineptitude and frivolity that you throw up to us is the result of the bad education to which you have condemned us, and you compound the evil by putting it in writing. Improve our lot; allow men to share it; make them virtuous, mature, and strong-willed, and you will see very well that our souls emerged equal from the hands of the Creator."

Then, questioning myself and taking stock of the alternations between languor and energy, that is to say the irregularity of my essentially feminine constitution, I saw clearly that an education somewhat different from that of other women, due to fortuitous circumstances, had modified me; that my small bones had been hardened by fatigue, or else that my will, developed by the Stoic theories of Deschartres on one hand, and Christian mortification on the other, had grown accustomed to compensate for limits set by nature. I also felt that the stupid vanity of adornment, as well as the suspect desire to please all men, had no hold on my mind, schooled to scorn them by the lessons and example of my grandmother. Therefore, I was not a woman completely like those whom some moralists censure and mock; I had in my soul an enthusiasm for the beautiful, a thirst for the true; and yet I was a woman like others—dependent, nervous, prey to my imagination, childishly susceptible to the emotionalism and anxieties of motherhood. But did these traits have to relegate me to secondary standing in artistic and family life? That being society's rule, it was still within my power to submit patiently or cheerfully. What man could have set me an example for a secret heroism to which God was the only confidant, hearing my protests against a slighted dignity?

That woman may differ from man, that the heart and mind answer to a sex, I do not doubt. Equality will always be an exception. But even supposing that woman's education should make the necessary progress (I would not want it exactly like that of man), woman will always be more artistic and poetic in her life; man will always be more so in his work. But must this difference, essential for the harmony of things and the noblest enticements of love, consitute a moral inferiority? I am not talking socialism here; at the time when this fundamental question began to preoccupy me, I did not know what socialism was. I shall tell later how and why my mind refused to follow that path for liberating women—a deviant path, in my opinion, which theorists of woman's nature and destiny have been forced to take in reaction to public opinion. But I would speculate privately, and I did not see why Philosophy was too great a lady to grant us equality in her esteem, just as God grants us equality in His promises of heaven.

Thus, I was going along nourishing a dream of male virtue to which women could aspire, and was constantly examining my soul with a naïve curiosity in order to find out whether it had the power of such aspirations, and whether uprightness, unselfishness, discretion, perseverance in work—all the strengths, in short, that man attributes exclusively to himself—were actually unavailable to a heart which accepted the concept of them so ardently. I did not sense myself to be perfidious, or vain, or talkative, or lazy, and I wondered why Montaigne would not have liked and respected me as much as a brother, as much as La Boétie.

While meditating also on that passage concerning the absorption of the whole being in an *"amor amicitiae"* ["love between friends"], which he thought ideal, but declared to be impossible between a man and a woman, I believed along with him, for a long time, that the transports and jealousies of love were irreconcilable with the divine serenity of friendship. And at the time I met Rollinat, I was seeking friendship without love, as a refuge and a sanctuary in which I might forget the existence of any stormy and heart-breaking affection. Gentle and fraternal friendship provided me already with concern and devotion, whose value I did not underestimate, but by a combination of circumstances that was probably fortuitous, not one of my former friends —man or woman—was exactly the right age to know and understand me well, some because they were too young, others because too old. Rollinat, younger than I by several years, did not consider himself different from me on that account. An extreme weariness of life had already given him a point of view of hopelessness, while an invincible enthusiasm for ideas kept him keen and alive under the weight of absolute resignation to external matters. The contrast in that intense life—the embers beneath the ice, or rather beneath his own ashes—corresponded to my own situation. We were astonished to have only to look each within himself to recognize the other's state of mind. Our habits of life were different on the surface, but there was a similarity in our make-up which made our mutual dealings as easy from the beginning as if they had been founded on habit: the same mania for analysis; the same scrupulous judgments that went as far as indecision; the same need for a notion of sovereign good; the same absence of many of the passions and appetites that govern or influence the lives of most people, consequently the same incessant reverie; the same deep despondency, the same sudden bursts of gaiety; the same innocence of heart; the same incapacity of ambition; the same princely indulgence in fantasy at times when others profit to bring about their glory and fortune; the same triumphant satisfaction at refusing to entertain anything reputed to be serious that seemed frivolous to us and beyond the pale of duties we ourselves considered to be serious; and finally, the same good qualities or the same faults, the same slumberings and the same awakenings of the will.

Duty, however, binding us hand and foot, plunged us completely into our work, and we stuck to it with invincible persistence, feeling nailed down by these duties which we accepted without dispute. Other persons, outwardly more brilliant and active, often preached courage to me. Rollinat never preached to me except by example, without even suspecting the worth and effect of that example. With him and for him I formed a code of true and sound friendship, a friendship not unlike Montaigne's conception, wholly by choice, wholly selective and perfect. At first, this bore resemblance to a romantic convention, but it lasted for twenty-five years, without the "sacred bond" of our souls being ruptured for a single instant, without a single doubt having grazed the absolute faith that we had in each other, without some demand or personal preoccupation having reminded one that he was a separate being from the other, a separate existence from the single soul containing two beings.

Each of us has, during his long span, formed other attachments entailing a more complete affection, in view of the laws of life, but they have taken nothing from the entirely spiritual union of our hearts. Nothing in this peaceful and, so to speak, paradisiacal union could cause the other persons associated with us on a more intimate level to be jealous. The person whom one of us preferred to all others immediately became dear and hallowed to the other, and his chosen company. In short, this friendship has remained worthy of the most beautiful novels of chivalry. Although it has never declared itself but platonically, it has had and will always have the grandeur of a declaration to ourselves, and this pact between two enthusiasts has taken on all the firmness of a religious conviction. Founded on esteem in the beginning, by now it has become so engrained as no longer to need that esteem; and if one of us were possibly to stray into some vice or crime, he would still be able to tell himself that there existed on earth one pure, sane soul who would not be cut off from him.

I remember, at this moment, a circumstance in which another one of my friends accused him hotly, in my presence, of a serious wrongdoing. It had no foundation at all, and all I could do was shrug my shoulders; but when I saw that the prejudice against him persisted, I could not help saying impatiently, "Well, what if it were the case? The mere fact that it's he, makes it all right. I couldn't care less."

More often accused than he, because my existence has been more visible, I am certain he has had to answer for me more than once, as I did for him. There is not a single other of my friends who has not argued with me about some opinion or some personal act and who, consequently, has not sometimes had to dispute my character with him. Such arguments are a right that must be alleged to friendship under life's ordinary circumstances, and which friendship often considers a duty. But where this right has not been reserved and not even expected because of unlimited trust, where this right disappears in the plenitude of ardent faith, there only is the great, the ideal friendship. I, for one, need an ideal. Let those who don't need it do without it.

But you who still float between the boundaries of poetry and reality that wisdom does allow, you for whom I write and to whom I have promised to say some useful things as the occasion arose, you will forgive me this long digression in favor of its conclusion, which is this:

Yes, you must poeticize the beautiful feelings in your soul, and not fear placing them too high in your esteem. You must not bring together all the needs of the soul into one and the same appetite for happiness, which would be apt to make us selfish. Ideal love—I have not yet spoken about that, it is not time—ideal love would epitomize all the most divine feelings we can conceive of, and yet it would take nothing away from ideal friendship. Love will always require two egotists, because it bears with it infinite satisfaction. Friendship has less at stake: it shares all the sorrow, but not all the pleasures. It is less rooted in reality, in gain, in the intoxications of life. Thus, it is rarer, even in a very imperfect state, than love in whatever state you find it. It *seems* widespread, however, and the label of friend has become so common that one can say "my friends" when speaking about two hundred persons. This is not a profanation, in the sense that you can and must love, even individually, all those whom you know to be good and deserving. Yes, believe me, the heart is large enough to lodge many affections, and the more you accord it sincere and devoted ones, the more you will feel your heart grow in strength and warmth. Its nature is divine, and the more you sometimes feel it burdened to death beneath the weight of disappointment, the more the pressure of its suffering attests its immortal life. So, do not be afraid to be fully affected by surges of benevolence and sympathy, nor to give in to the sweet or painful of the many concerns that make demands on generous spirits. But be no less attentive to the cultivation of special friendship, and do not believe yourself absolved from having a real friend, a perfect friend; that is to say, a person whom you may love enough to want to be perfect for, a person who may be sacred to you and for whom you may be equally sacred. The great goal we must all pursue is to kill the great evil that gnaws at us—the cultivation of self-love. You will soon see that when you have succeeded in becoming excellent for someone, you are not long in becoming better for everyone; and if you go on to seek ideal love, you will see that ideal friendship has admirably prepared your heart to receive its benefits.   *J.L.P.*

XIV

A last visit to the convent. —My eccentric life. —Deburau. —Jane
and Aimée. —Baroness Dudevant forbids me to compromise her
name in the arts. —My pseudonym. —Jules Sand and George Sand.
—Karl Sand. —Cholera. —Saint-Merry's cloister. —I change
garrets.

There was perhaps not as much of a contrast as you might think when I
descended from the heights of sentiment to the life of the literary student that I
am in the process of narrating. In those days, I crudely called it my life as a
street Arab, and there was indeed a residue of aristocratic mockery in the way I
pictured it; for actually my character was taking shape and real life was opening before me, dressed as I was in men's clothing, which allowed me to be
enough of a man to see a milieu that otherwise would have remained forever
closed to the bumpkin I had been until then. At that period, I looked on the arts
and politics no longer only inductively and deductively, as I would have done
given some historical fact, but as both history and novel of living beings in
society. I contemplated the spectacle from every point of view I could—the
wings and the stage, the loge and the pit. I climbed to every floor—from clubroom to studio, from café to attic. Only the salons were out of my purview; I
was familiar with the society between artisan and artist; however, I had only
rarely attended its meetings, and had always escaped as often as possible from
its parties, which bored me to distraction. But I was familiar with its private
life, which had nothing more to reveal to me.

Some hardly charitable people, whose evil minds were always ready to
vilify an artist's mission, have said that, during and after this period, I showed
a curiosity about vice. They were cowardly liars, is all I have to say. Any poet
knows that a poet does not voluntarily defile his being, his thoughts, or even
his outlook, especially when he is doubly a poet by virtue of being a woman.

Even though there was nothing in this bizarre existence that I would later
have wanted to hide, I knew when adopting it the immediate effects it might
have vis-à-vis propriety and the way I arranged my life. My husband was
aware of it, and offered neither blame nor obstacle. The same was true of my
mother and my aunt. I was thus squared away with the duly constituted authorities in my life. But in the rest of the milieu where I had grown up, I expected
to encounter more than a little severe criticism. I did not want to expose myself
to it. I went about making my choices and finding out which friends would
stand by me and which would be scandalized. At first glance, it seemed I had

attracted a lot of acquaintances about whose opinion I cared nothing and whom I could ignore. As for the people I really liked and expected some reprimand from, I decided to break with them without a word. "If they love me," I thought, "they will pursue me, and if they don't, I shall forget they exist; but I shall always be able to cherish them as in the past. There won't have been any wounding words between us; nothing will have spoiled the memory of our affection."

Why indeed would I have wanted to see them? What could they know of my purpose, my future, my desire. Did they know, did I myself know—while burning my bridges—whether I had any talent, any perseverance? I had never given anyone a clue to the enigma in my mind; I had not yet found it for certain. And when I talked about writing, I did it lightly, making fun of it and myself.

However, a kind of destiny was pulling me. I felt it to be invincible, and I threw myself resolutely into it. Not a grand destiny—my creative imagination was as yet too unreliable for me to harbor any kind of ambition—but the destiny to be morally and artistically free, in a world where I asked only to go unnoticed and to be allowed, unenslaved, to earn my daily bread.

Nevertheless, I wanted to see my closest friends in Paris one last time. I went to the convent to spend several hours. Everyone there was so preoccupied by the effects of the July Revolution, the absence of students, the general upheaval from which they were suffering the real effects, that I had no trouble not talking about myself. I saw my good mother Alicia for only an instant. She was busy and in a hurry. Sister Hélène was in retreat. Poulette walked me around the cloisters, through the empty classrooms and dormitories, into the quiet garden, saying at each step, "Things are bad! Things are indeed bad!"

There was no longer anyone left from my time, except the nuns and the maid, Marie-Josèphe, that brusque and merry servant who seemed to me the most cordial and only responsive creature among those anxious souls. I understood that nuns cannot and must not love with their hearts. They live for an ideal, and attach real importance only to the exterior conditions which are the setting for that ideal. Anything that interferes with the kind of regulated meditation that needs immutable order and absolute serenity is considered a tragic event, or at least a crisis. Outside friendships avail them nothing. Worldly things, in their eyes, are of value only to the extent that they support the exceptional conditions of their existence. I stopped longing for the convent when I saw that, there, the ideal had been subordinated to such conditions. The life of a religious community can be immobilized like any other, and the cannons of July had not worried that they would disturb the peace in the sanctuaries.[15]

My own ideal was lodged in a corner of my brain, and I needed only a few days of complete freedom to have it blossom. I carried it with me into the street, my feet on the icy patches, my shoulders covered with snow, my hands in my pockets, my stomach a little empty sometimes, but my head all the more filled with dreams, melodies, colors, shapes, lights, and phantom figures. I was no longer a lady, nor was I a "gentleman." I was jostled on the sidewalk like a thing that got in the way of busy passers-by. I didn't care; I wasn't busy. No one knew me, no one looked at me, no one gave me a second thought; I was an atom lost in the immense crowd. No one said, as they had at La Châtre, "There's Madame Aurore, wearing the same hat and dress she always wears"; or as they did at Nohant, "There goes our lady on her big horse. She must be out of her mind to gallop like that." In Paris, no one thought anything at all about me; they didn't see me. I had no need to hurry in order to avoid banalities; I could create a whole novel going from one end of town to another without meeting anyone who would ask me, "What the devil has you so engrossed?" That was worth more than a convent cell. And I could have said with satisfaction what René said with sadness—I am walking in a "desert of men."

After I had well surveyed and, so to speak, chewed and savored one last time all the nooks and crannies of the convent and my cherished memories there, I left, telling myself I would no longer pass through this gate behind which I was leaving affections preserved at a stage when the gods have no wrath and the stars are not obscured. A second visit might have entailed questions about my domestic life, my plans, my religious convictions. I had no desire to argue. There are those human beings whom we respect too much to contradict, and from whom we only want to carry away a blessing.

When I came home, I put my beloved boots back on and went to see the pantomimist Deburau. His ideal—an exquisitely distinguished performance, served up twice a day to the gamins of the city and suburbs—delighted them. Gustave Papet, the "rich m'lord" of our Berry clan, distributed barley sugar to the whole pit, and then as we were leaving, famished, he would take three or four of us to eat at the Vendanges de Bourgogne. Out of the clear blue sky, he took it into his head to invite Deburau, whom he didn't know at all. He went back into the theater, found him taking off his Pierrot costume in a basement room which he used for changing, took him by the arm, and brought him along. Deburau had charming manners. He did not allow himself to be tempted by the least bit of champagne, fearing, as he said, for his nerves, and needing the most complete state of calm for his act. I have never seen an artist more serious, conscientious, or devout about his art. He loved it passionately and spoke of it with reverence, while speaking of himself with extreme modesty. He studied constantly and did not take his talent at all for granted, in spite of continual and even excessive practice. He did not worry whether the wonderful subtlety of his physiognomy and the originality of his improvisation were appreciated by other artists or grasped by the uninitiated. He worked to satisfy himself, to try out and realize his fantasies; and these products of his fancy, which seemed so spontaneous, were worked out in advance with extraordinary care. He merited my full attention; he was not at all affected, and I saw in him, in spite of the antics of the genre, one of those great artists who deserve the title of master. Jules Janin had, at that time, just published a little treatise on the artist, which though witty, had not given me any idea at all of Deburau's talent. I asked him if he was pleased with this appreciation. "I am grateful for it," he said to me. "It is well intended on my behalf, and my reputation has profited. But it is not a work of art. It is not what I thought it would be. It is not serious enough. Janin's Deburau is not me; he hasn't understood me."

I have seen Debureau several times again since and have always felt a great deference for the street clown as well as the respect due to the man of conviction and discipline.

Twelve or fifteen years later, I attended a benefit performance for him. At the end of it, he accidentally fell through a trap door. I sent for news of him the next day, and he himself wrote to tell me that nothing was wrong, a charming letter which ended thus, "Pardon me for not having a better way to thank you. My pen is like the voice of the mute that I play, but my heart is like my face; it expresses the truth."

A few days later, this excellent man, this artist of the highest caliber, died as a result of his fall.

After the convent, I still had something left to sever—not in my heart, but in my life. I went to see my friends Jane and Aimée. Aimée had not been a friend by choice. There was something cold and brittle about her at the time, which had never appealed to me. But aside from the fact that she was the adored sister of Jane, she had so many impressive qualities—was so high-minded and upright, and, failing spontaneous kindness, so generously fairminded—that I was truly attached to her. As for Jane—that sweet, strong, humble, angelic nature—I retain an affection for her today as when in the convent that I can only compare to the deepest maternal feelings.

Both were married. Jane was the mother of a good-sized baby whom she gazed at in silent ecstasy with her big black eyes. I was happy to see her happy; I embraced mother and child most tenderly, and I left promising to come back soon, but resolved never to return.

I kept my word and congratulate myself for it. Those two young heiresses, become countesses, and more conservative than ever in every way, belonged henceforth to a world which would only have scorned my bizarre way of life and considered my independent spirit an anathema. A day came when it was necessary for me either to justify myself in the face of false accusations or to take sides against principles of faith and ideas of respectability that I did not wish to slight or challenge in other people. I knew Jane had willingly passed the test of heroism in friendship, but she had been reproached for it, and I loved her too much to want to cause any chagrin, any trouble whatsoever in her life. The kind of jealous egotism that must assert itself is not part of my character, and my ability to assess a situation which is clearly exposed before me is unfailing. The one I had made for myself was very clear. I was openly flaunting the rules of society. I was cutting myself off from it in full consciousness; I therefore had to expect that it would cut itself off from me once it was aware of my eccentric life. It wasn't yet. I was too obscure to need to be mysterious. Paris is a sea where thousands of little boats pass unnoticed among the great vessels. But the day might come when some chance event might posit me between lies I did not wish to tell and reproaches I did not wish to receive. Unheeded reproaches are always followed by coolness, and coolness is only a step away from a break. That was the idea I could not stand. Truly proud people do not expose themselves to breaks, and when they are loving, they do not provoke them, they anticipate them, thereby averting them completely.

I returned without sadness to my garret and my utopian existence, certain that I was leaving behind regrets and good memories, satisfied at having nothing left to dispatch.

Baroness Dudevant was, as we say in the Latin Quarter, quite briskly worked up over my life. She asked me why I was staying in Paris so long without my husband. I told her that my husband was satisfied. "But is it true that you intend to publish books?"

"Yes, Madame."

"Tut!" she cried (a Gascon expression she habitually used, which meant, "You don't say!") "What a droll idea!"

"Yes, Madame."

"That's all very well and good, but I hope you won't put my name on the leather bindings?"

"Oh, certainly not, Madame. There's no danger of that."

There was no other discussion. She left soon after for the South, and I never saw her again.

I had scarcely thought about the name I was supposed to put on the "leather bindings." In any case, I had resolved to remain anonymous. I sketched out a first work that Jules Sandeau[69] then entirely revised, and Delatouche put the name "Jules Sand" on it. This work attracted another publisher, who asked for another novel under the same pseudonym. I had written *Indiana*[70] while at Nohant. I wanted to give it to the publisher under the pseudonym requested, but Jules Sandeau, out of modesty, did not wish to take credit for fathering a book which he knew nothing about. That did not please the publisher. A name is a selling point, and as the little pseudonym had created a good demand, he really wanted to keep it. Delatouche was consulted and settled the question by a compromise: Sand would remain intact, and I would find another first name which would be uniquely mine. Without looking further, I quickly chose George, which seemed to me appropriate for someone from rural Berry. Jules and George, unknown to the public, would pass for brothers or cousins.

Thus I acquired the name, whereas Jules Sandeau, who retained the legal rights to *Rose et Blanche*, wanted to resume using his own name for all his writing, so as not to, he said, "bedeck himself with my feathers." At that period he was very young, and it was gracious of him to exhibit such modesty. Since then, he has proven to be very talented in his own right, and he has made a name with his own name. I myself kept the name of Kotzebue's assassin,[71] which had passed through Delatouche's mind, and which began my reputation in Germany to the extent that I received letters from there begging me to identify myself as a relative of Karl Sand, as if it meant an additional chance for success. Despite the veneration of German youth for the young fanatic whose martyr's death they thought so beautiful, I confess I had not dreamed of choosing for a pseudonym the name of the symbolic dagger of illuminism. Secret societies do suit my imagination regarding the past, but they do not only and exclusively exist by the dagger; and those who thought they saw a sort of protest in favor of the political assassin in my persistence in signing my name Sand, and in everyone's habit of calling me by that name, were absolutely mistaken. That is not part of my religious code nor revolutionary instinct. The mode of a secret society has never even seemed to me properly applicable to our time and country; I have never imagined that, here and now, it could foster anything but tyranny, and I have never accepted the dictatorial principle within myself.

Therefore, I probably would have changed this pseudonym if I had believed I was destined to achieve some fame, but until the moment the critics erupted against me apropos the novel *Lélia* [1833], I flattered myself that I could move about unnoticed in the most humble literary crowd. On seeing that, in spite of myself, this was no longer possible and that all my work—including my pen name—was being attacked viciously, I retained the name and pursued the work. To do otherwise would have been cowardly.

And by now I am bound to this name, even though it is, as someone said, half the name of another writer. So be it. That writer, I repeat, has enough talent so that those four letters do not spoil any of his leather bindings, nor do they hurt my ears when spoken by friends. It was a whim of Delatouche which gave it to me. Again, so be it. I am honored to have had this poet, this friend, as my mentor. A family whose name I had found good enough for me found the name Dudevant (that the aforementioned Baroness used to write with an apostrophe [D'Udevant or du D'evant])[16] too illustrious and fine to compromise in the republic of the arts. Thus, I was baptized, unknown and unconcerned, between the sale of *Indiana*, which was then my whole future, and a thousand-franc note, which was then my whole fortune. It was a contract, a new marriage, between the poor apprentice poet who I was and the humble muse who had consoled me in my hardships. God keep me from disturbing what I had left to destiny. What is a name, in our revolutionized and revolutionary society? A cipher for those who do nothing; a sign or an emblem for those who work or fight. The one I was given, I earned myself, after the event, by my own toil. I have never exploited someone else's work; I have never taken, bought, or borrowed a line, a page, from anyone whatsoever. I have nothing left of the seven or eight hundred thousand francs that I earned over twenty years, and today, as twenty years ago, I live from day to day by this name which protects my work, and by this work from which I did not save a penny for myself. I do not think anyone has anything to reproach me for, and without meaning to brag—I did only what I was supposed to—my conscience sees no reason to change the name which designates and personifies it.

But before going on to literary things, I still have to give a brief account of various events which preceded them.

My husband came to see me in Paris. We did not live together, but he came to dinner at my place and he took me to the theater. He seemed satisfied with the arrangement which, without any quarrels or questions, was making us independent of each other. It did not seem to me that my return to our house was as pleasant. However, I knew how to make my presence bearable by not criticizing or interfering with any of the changes made during my absence. In effect, for me it meant no longer being at home. I no longer considered Nohant something that belonged to me. My children's room and my little cell next to it were neutral territory where I could camp for the time being, and if many other things displeased me, I had nothing to say, and said nothing. I could not blame anyone for the resignation I had freely handed in. Several friends thought I should not have done it, but that I should have confronted the motives behind that decision. In theory they were right, but the practice does not always conform so easily to the theory. I do not know how to mount a battle for purely personal reasons. All my faculties and strength can go to work in the cause of a sentiment or an idea, but when it is only a question of myself, I give up the game in apparent weakness, which is, after all, only the result of very simple reasoning: Can I replace what I am asking the person to give up? If the answer is Yes, I shall be found within my rights; if the answer is No, my rights will always appear unjust to him, and will never really seem legitimate to myself.

To challenge someone and persecute him for enjoying his preferences, you must have a more serious reason than the enjoyment of your own. At that time, nothing apparent was happening in my house that would cause my children to suffer. Solange was going to come with me; Maurice was living with his gentle tutor, Jules Boucoiran, during my absence. There was nothing to make me believe this state of things wouldn't last, and it was not my fault that it didn't.

At the time I set up housekeeping, with Solange, on Quai Saint-Michel, notwithstanding my need to re-establish my natural sedentary habits, living conditions in general soon became so tragic and depressing that I was made to feel their repercussions. Cholera struck some first floor apartments in our surrounding neighborhoods. It spread rapidly, climbing from one landing to the next, in our building. It carried off six people, and stopped at the door of our garret, as if it disdained such puny prey.

Among the group of friends from home who had clustered around me, not one was attacked by this deadly terror, which seemed to summon evil and usually delivered it irremediably. We were worried for one another, but hardly for ourselves. So, in order to avoid useless anxiety, we all agreed to meet every day, in the Luxembourg garden, even if only for an instant, and if one of us did not show up for roll call, we would run to his house. None of us was stricken even slightly; yet none of us did anything to change his routine, nor did we take precautions against contagion.

The ceaseless procession passing below my window and crossing the Saint-Michel bridge was horrible. On certain days, big covered wagons used for moving households, which became hearses for the poor, followed one another without interruption, and what was more frightening was not the dead piled pell-mell like parcels, but the absence of relatives and friends behind the funeral carriages; also, the drivers quickening their pace, swearing and whipping the horses; the passers-by retreating in fright from the hideous cortège; the fury of the workers, who believed there was some fantastic plot to poison them, who raised their fists against the sky; and the defeat, or indifference, which rendered all facial expressions irritable, or unresponsive, after those threatening parties had passed.

I had thought about leaving Paris for my daughter's sake, but everyone said that moving to a new place and journeying there were more dangerous than salutary, and I also told myself that, if we had already been infected by the disease without knowing it at the time of our departure, it was better not to go to Nohant, which it had not reached, and did not.

Besides, in the face of a public calamity which spares no one, you quickly learn to do your share. My friends and I decided that, since cholera attacked the poor more readily than the rich, we were among the most threatened; consequently, we should accept the risk without letting the general disaster affect us, since we were each responsible for ourselves, just like the workers, furious or desperate, who believed themselves the object of a special malediction.

In the middle of this sinister crisis came the poignant drama of Saint-Merry's cloister.[72] I was at the Luxembourg garden with Solange, toward the end of the day. She was playing in the sand; I was watching her from behind the wide pedestal of a statue, where I was seated. I was aware that some great disturbance was supposed to be brewing in Paris, but I did not believe it would reach my quarter so quickly; absorbed, I didn't see that all the strollers had suddenly disappeared. I heard the drum roll for the attack, and picking up my daughter, saw that we were the only females left in this immense garden. A file of soldiers ran through the park from one gate to the other. I started back to my garret in the midst of all this confusion, seeking out side streets so as not to be trampled by the waves of curious people who, after gathering and pressing at one spot, were surging forward and crushing one another, carried away by sudden panic. Every step of the way, we ran into frightened people who shouted at us, "Don't go on, go back, go back! The troops are coming, they're shooting at everyone." What was even more alarming was that just then all the market stalls were being dismantled in such a rush that passers-by risked having their heads knocked in. Solange lost courage and began to cry desperately. When we got to the Quai, everyone was fleeing in a different direction. I forged on, realizing that the worst thing was to remain outdoors, and quickly went into our place without pausing to see what was happening, without even feeling afraid, having never yet seen street warfare and imagining nothing of what I later saw; that is to say, the intoxication which first of all seizes the soldier, who, taken by surprise and fear, turns into the most dangerous enemy that ordinary people could encounter in a brawl.

And it should not surprise anyone. In almost all those deplorable, or magnificent, events for which a city serves as a theater, the mass of spectators, and often the actors as well, are ignorant of what is going on two steps away; they run the risk of slaughtering one another, each one subject to the fear of being killed. The idea which set off the raging fury is often still more elusive than the deed, and whatever that idea may have been, it is transformed, in the minds of the uneducated, into a thousand outlandish fictions. A soldier is no different. Discipline has not helped clarify his sense of reason; in fact, if he claimed to use it, his discipline would require him to renounce it. His leaders push him into the massacre through fear, in the same way that agitators often push the people to provocation. From one side to the other, before the fuse has been lit, horrible tales, atrocious lies are circulated, and the phantom carnage has already performed its function in some sick imaginations.

I shall not relate the major event in the midst of which I found myself. I am only writing my own history. I began by simply trying to calm my poor child, who was sick with fear. It occurred to me to tell her they were only hunting for bats on the Quai, just as she had seen her father and Uncle Hippolyte do on the terrace at Nohant, and I succeeded in pacifying her and putting her to sleep to the noise of the fusillade. I put the mattress from my bed in the window of her little room, to deflect any stray bullets that might come that way, and I spent part of the night on the balcony, trying to make sense of what was happening in the darkness.

We all know what happened. Seventeen insurgents had seized the post of the little bridge at the Hôtel-Dieu. A national guard regiment surprised them in the middle of the night. "Fifteen of these poor wretches," said Louis Blanc, in *Histoire de dix ans*, "were cut to pieces and thrown into the Seine; two were caught in the nearby streets and murdered."

I did not see that atrocious scene, shrouded in the shadows of the night, but I heard the furious clamor and the incredible shrieks; then a deadly silence spread over the city, now asleep, worn out from such terror.

Noises more distant and vague attested, however, more resistance at some unknown point. In the morning, we went out and looked for the day's food, aware that the authorities threatened to blockade people in their houses. To see the display of troops assembled by the government, one would hardly suspect it was a question of eliminating a handful of men who were fighting to the death.

It is true that a new revolution could have grown out of this desperate act of heroism—an empire for the Duc de Reichstadt, a monarchy for the Duc de Bordeaux, as well as a republic for the people.[73] All of these factions had, as usual, prepared the event and dreamed of the reward. But when they discovered that their reward was death on the barricades, the factions made themselves scarce, and the heroic martyrdom was carried out in full view of Paris, dismayed by such a victory.

The 6th of June was terrifyingly solemn as seen from my high vantage point. Traffic was prohibited; troops guarded all the bridges and entrances to all the adjacent streets. From ten in the morning until the end of the enforcement, the long vista of deserted Quais took on, in broad daylight, the appearance of a dead city, as if cholera had killed off the last inhabitants. The soldiers who were guarding the side streets looked like ghosts struck dumb. Immobile, as if petrified along the parapets, they broke the mournful face of solitude by neither word nor movement. At certain times of the day, no living beings but the swallows could be seen grazing the water with nervous swiftness, as if the unusual calm had frightened them. There were hours of grim silence, jarred only by the sharp cries of the martins around the towers of Notre-Dame. Then suddenly the distracted birds flew back into the depths of the old towers, the soldiers again took up their guns, which were gleaming in stacks on the bridges. They received their orders in hushed voices. They parted to let bands of cavalry cross, some of whom were pale with anger, others wounded and bloody. The captive population reappeared at their windows and on the rooftops, eager to peer at the scenes of horror that were going to take place beyond the old city. The sinister noise had begun. The shots of the firing squad sounded the death knell at more and more regular intervals. Seated at the balcony door, and keeping Solange busy in her room to prevent her looking out, I could count each assault and retort. Then the cannon thundered. Seeing the bridge congested with litters returning via the old city and leaving a trail of blood, I thought the insurrection, for being so murderous, was still raging; but its blows were getting weaker, you could almost have counted the number of dead from each volley the assailants fired. Then silence reigned again, the populace came down from the roof tops into the streets; the house porters, expressive symbols of property's call to arms, shouted to each other in triumph, "It's over!" And the conquerors who had done nothing but look on withdrew in disarray. The King walked about the Quais. The bourgeoisie, from city and suburbs, fraternized on all the street corners. The troops were dignified and serious. They had believed, for an instant, that a second July revolution was in the offing.

For several days, the approaches to the square and to Quai Saint-Michel revealed large stains of blood, and the Morgue, cluttered with cadavers, whose piled up heads in front of the windows formed what seemed to be a solid mass of hideous masonry, exuded a stream of red that trickled away slowly under the arches, without mingling in the river's waters. The smell was so fetid and I had been so disconsolate—as much, I admit, for the poor dying soldiers as for the proud prisoners—that I could not eat anything for two weeks. For a long time afterward, I could not even stand the sight of meat; it always seemed to smell of that odor of butchery that had mounted, acrid and hot, at my wakings on the 6th and 7th of June, in the midst of the belated gusts of springtime.

I spent the autumn at Nohant. It was there that I wrote *Valentine*,[74] my nose in my small armoire, which I used as a desk, and where I had earlier written *Indiana*.

Winter in my attic was so cold that I realized it would be impossible to write there without burning more wood than my finances would allow. Delatouche moved out of his garret, which was also on the quais, but on the fourth floor, and facing south to the gardens. It was also more spacious and comfortably equipped—I had yearned for a Prussian stove for a long time. He turned over his lease to me, and I moved to Quai Malaquais, where I soon welcomed Maurice, whom his father had brought in order to start him in school.

Here I am, already at the period of my first steps into the world of letters, and having felt pressed to provide a framework for my outer life, I have as yet said nothing about the little forays I had made to arrive there. Now is the time to talk about the ties I had established and the hopes that had sustained me.

A.F.M.

XV

Four men of letters from Berry. —Delatouche and Duris-Dufresne.
—My visit to M. de Kératry. —My dream of an income of fifteen
hundred francs. —*Le Figaro*. —A walk in the Latin Quarter.
—Balzac. —Emmanuel Arago. —Balzac's first luxury. —His
contrarieties. —Delatouche's aversion for him. —Dinner and a
whimsical evening at Balzac's. —Jules Janin. —Delatouche
encourages and inhibits me. —*Indiana*. —Those who said it was
about me and my own story were wrong. —Theory of Beauty.
—Theory of Truth. —What Balzac thought. —What the critics and
public thought. —Corambé. —The apparitions fly away. —Work
saddens me. —Alleged manias of artists.

At that time, there were three of us from the Berry province in
Paris—Félix Pyat, Jules Sandeau, and I—all literary apprentices under the
direction of a fourth Berrichon, Delatouche. This teacher should have been,
and undoubtedly wanted to be, the tie among us, and we counted on being one
family under Apollo, of which he would be the father. But his bitter, touchy,
and miserable disposition was traitor to the intentions and needs of his heart,
which was kind and generous. He quarreled in turn with all three of us, after
having made us quarrel a little with one another.

In a rather detailed obituary article on Delatouche, I stated all that was
good and bad about him. I was able to state the bad side without feeling I had
in any way betrayed the gratitude I owed him or the keen regard I had paid him
for several years before his death. To show how inevitable and involuntary was
this bad side—that is to say, his unhappy restlessness, his morbid sensitivity, in
short, his misanthropy—I only had to quote a few fragments from his letters, in
which he is depicted in his grandeur and suffering by several graceful, powerful phrases. I had already written about him during his lifetime with respect
and affection. I never had anything to reproach myself for concerning him, not
even the trace of an offense, and I would never have known how or why I
could have displeased him, had I not seen with my own eyes, during his rapid
decline, how deeply possessed he was by an irremediable hypochondria. He
dealt fairly with me when he saw that I was fair to him; that is to say, prompt to
run to him as soon as he opened his fatherly arms, willing to forget his rages
and injustices, made up for many times over, to my way of thinking, by a surge
of affection, an apology, or a heartfelt tear.

I would not be able, here, to sum up his entire character or his personal relationship with me, as I did in a special little opus, without straying from the order of my narrative—a fault I have already indulged in too much and which has often seemed inevitable to me, since people and things need to appear full blown in the memory of the speaker before they can be well appreciated and, in the final analysis, equitably judged.[17]

But to avoid constant interruptions in my narrative, I shall simply state here what kind of relationship we had when I published *Indiana* and *Valentine*.

My kind old friend Duris-Dufresne, who was among the first to whom I had confided my writing project, had wanted to put me in touch with La Fayette.[75] The deputy assured me the general would take a liking to me, find me very congenial, and launch me with care into the world of the arts, where he had many contacts. I denied myself that interview, although I also felt drawn to La Fayette, whom I went to hear speak from time to time in the Chamber of Deputies, conducted there by my "papa." (This was how the ushers in the Chamber referred to the old deputy when we looked for each other in the corridor after a session.) But I felt so insignificant that I could not take it upon myself to bother the patriarch of liberalism.

Then again, if I needed a literary patron, it was much more for advice than support. I wanted, above all, to know if I had any talent; I did not want a penchant to be mistaken for a gift. Duris-Dufresne naïvely considered me a great intellect after I had read him several pages—at Nohant, in strictest confidence—about the emigration of the nobility in '89. I found his partiality and gallantry highly suspect. Besides, he was interested only in politics, to which I was hardly attracted.

I pointed out to him that friends are too easily dazzled and that I would need an impartial judge. "But let's not look for him in such high places," I would say to him. "Such famous people don't have the time to linger over unimportant things."

He suggested one of his colleagues in the Chamber, M. de Kératry, who wrote novels and whom he recommended as a sharp and severe judge. I had read *Le Dernier des Beaumanoir*, an extremely badly written work, based on an outrageous subject, in which the spicy flavor of the romanticism was redeemed only by its audacity. However, some pages were rather beautiful and moving. It was a bizarre mixture of Breton patriotism and romantic aberration; the conception was youthful and the plot details antiquated. "Your illustrious colleague is out of his mind," I told my papa. "And as for his book, one day I'll be able to write some that are just as bad. However, he may still be a good judge, though a bad practitioner. His work isn't that of a total imbecile, far from it. Let me see M. de Kératry. But since I live under the roof, and you tell me he is old and married, ask him when he is free, and I'll go to his place."

I had an appointment with M. de Kératry by eight the next morning. It was very early. My eyelids were swollen, and I was still not awake.

M. de Kératry seemed to me older than he was. His face, framed by white hair, was very dignified. He led me into a pretty bedroom, where I saw reclining under an elegant pink silk comforter a charming little woman who cast a glance of languishing pity on my thin woolen dress and crusted shoes, but to whom it did not occur to invite me to sit down.

I did so without her permission, and asked my new patron, as I huddled closer to the fireplace, if his daughter was sick. My first remark was singularly obtuse. The old man answered me, bursting with Breton pride, that the woman was his wife, Mme. de Kératry. "Very well," I said, "I congratulate you. But she's ill and I'm disturbing her. So, I'll warm up a bit and be on my way."

"Just a minute," replied my patron. "Monsieur Duris-Dufresne told me that you want to write, and I promised him to talk to you about this plan of yours. I shall be very brief, and I shall tell you frankly—a woman shouldn't write."

"If that's what you think, we have nothing to talk about," I replied. "There was no point in waking Madame de Kératry and me so early just to hear that cliché."

I got up and left without a fuss, prone more to laughter than anger. M. de Kératry followed me to the foyer and kept me there a few minutes as he developed, for my benefit, his theory on the inferiority of women, on the impossibility of the most intelligent among them to write a good book (such as *Le Dernier des Beaumanoir*, I suppose). And since I continued on my way without arguing and without a cutting retort, he ended his harangue with a Napoleonic stroke that was intended to crush me: "Take my word for it," he said gravely, as I was opening the outer door of his sanctum, "don't make books, make babies!"

"Honestly, sir," I answered, trying to control my laughter and shutting the door in his face, "take your own advice, if you think it so good."

Delatouche revised my answer, in relating that lovely interview. He had me say, "Make them yourself, if you can." I was neither so mean nor so witty, especially considering that his little wife had the look of an innocent angel. I returned home highly amused at the originality of this romantic Chrysale,[76] and certain I would never rise to the heights of his literary inventiveness. As everyone knows, the plot of *Le Dernier des Beaumanoir* consists of the rape of a woman believed to be dead, by the priest who is in charge of preparing her for burial. To be fair, however, let us add that the book has some very beautiful passages.

I made Duris-Dufresne laugh till he cried, telling him of my adventure. At the same time, he was furious and wanted to take an axe to that chauvinistic Breton. I calmed him by saying that I would not give up another morning, even for a publisher!

From then on, he no longer opposed my plan of going to see Delatouche, against whom he had strongly warned me up to that time. I had only to write a word—my name would have been sufficient—to assure me a warm welcome from my fellow countryman. I was very close to some of his family. He was a cousin of the Duvernets, and his father and mine had been friends.

He called on me and received me in a fatherly way. Since he had already learned about my talk with M. de Kératry from Félix Pyat, he marshaled all his wit, which was exquisitely tempered and remarkably polished, to uphold the opposite point of view. "But, nevertheless, don't delude yourself," he told me.

"Literature is an illusory resource, and I myself, despite the superiority of my beard, don't even earn fifteen hundred francs a year, from one year to the next."

"Fifteen hundred francs!" I exclaimed. "If I had fifteen hundred francs to add to my small income, I would consider myself very rich, and I wouldn't ask another thing from heaven or mankind—not even a beard!"

"Oh," he answered, laughing, "if you don't have any more ambition than that, the problem is simplified. Earning fifteen hundred francs a year won't be the easiest thing in the world, but it is possible, if you don't get discouraged at the beginning."

He read a novel of mine whose title and subject I cannot even recall, for I burned it shortly afterward. He quite rightly found it detestable. However, he told me I should be able to write a better one. "But you must live in order to know life," he added. "The novel is life, told with art. You have an artist's nature, but you don't know reality. You're too much of a dreamer. Wait patiently for time and experience; rest assured, those two sad counselors will come soon enough. Let life be your teacher, and try to remain a poet. You need do nothing else."

Moreover, as he saw I was somewhat embarrassed to make ends meet, he offered me the opportunity to earn forty or fifty francs a month, if I would help edit his little newspaper. Pyat and Sandeau were already employed at that job. I became part of the staff as if for good measure.

Delatouche had bought *Le Figaro*, which he more or less put together himself in his own living room, while chatting at times with his editors, at times with the numerous visitors he received.[18] Those visitors, who ranged from fascinating to comical, unwittingly provided a show for the staff, who, tucked away in the corners of the apartment, had no qualms about eavesdropping and making remarks.

I had my little table and carpet next to the fireplace, but I was not very assiduous at this work, about which I understood nothing. Delatouche took me a little in tow to get me started. He would give me a topic and a scrap of paper on which it had to fit. I scribbled ten pages that I threw into the fire, not a word of which was on the assigned subject. The others wrote with wit, ease, and daring. We talked and we laughed. Delatouche dazzled us with caustic remarks. I kept my ears open and enjoyed myself very much, but I was not doing anything productive. At the end of the month, I received twelve francs, fifty centimes, or fifteen francs at the most, for my part in the collaboration. Even so, it was far too much.

We doted on Delatouche's fatherly kindness, and with us he became young again, to the point of childishness. I remember a dinner we gave for him at Pinson's and a wonderful walk in the moonlight we made him take through the Latin Quarter. We were followed by a cab which he had hired by the hour to take him somewhere or other, but which he kept until midnight, without being able to extricate himself from our lunatic company. He climbed into it some twenty times and, persuaded by our arguments, always climbed out again. Our walk had no destination, and we wanted to prove to him that this was the most agreeable way to take a stroll. Obviously it suited him, for he gave in to us without too much resistance. The driver of the cab, victim of our teasing, had accepted his fate with patience. I remember that we had arrived, not knowing how or why, at the Sainte-Geneviève hill. As the driver was very slowly going along the deserted street, we spent our time climbing in one door and out the other, in single file, leaving the doors open and the steps down, and singing some unmemorable ditty in a lugubrious tone. I no longer remember why that seemed funny to us, or why Delatouche laughed so heartily. I think it was the joy of feeling foolish for once in his life. Pyat pretended we did have a goal—to serenade all the grocers in the neighborhood; he went from shop to shop singing at the top of his voice, "A grocery man is a rose."

That was the only time I saw Delatouche truly light-hearted, for his habitually satirical mind had a fund of melancholy which often rendered his lively moods mortally sad. "Aren't they happy?" he would say to me, giving me his arm as we brought up the rear, while the others ran on ahead, making a racket. "They drink only watered-down wine, and they're drunk! What good wine youth is! How good it is to laugh for no reason! Oh, if only we could enjoy life like this two days in a row, but as soon as we know who we're laughing at and why, it's no longer funny, and we feel like crying."

Growing old was Delatouche's great sorrow. He could not come to terms with it, and it was he who said, "We're never fifty, only twice twenty-five." In spite of this rebelliousness of spirit, he felt older than his age. Already ill, and aggravating his illness by the impatience with which he dealt with it, in the morning he was often in an irascible mood, and I would quietly withdraw. Then, he would call me back, or come and get me, never saying he was sorry, but effacing with a thousand niceties and fatherly indulgences the upset he had caused.

When I later looked for the reason for his sudden aversion, I was told he had been in love with me, jealous without admitting it, and wounded never to have been found out. That was not the case. I mistrusted him at the beginning, since Duris-Dufresne had put me on guard due to his own misgivings. Hence I would have had the discernment, in his case, that I have often lacked in other circumstances, being insufficiently versed in coquettishness. But in that situation, I had a good chance to see whether my trust would light on a disinterested heart, and I soon realized that the jealousy of our "boss," as we called him, was thoroughly intellectual and exerted itself on everyone who approached him, without regard to age or sex.

He was a friend, and above all a teacher, who was jealous by nature, like old Porpora,[77] whom I depicted in one of my novels. When he had nurtured an intelligence, or developed a talent, he could not stand it if any other aid or inspiration than his own dared approach.

A friend who knew Balzac[78] slightly introduced me to him, not as the local muse, but as a good provincial who was in awe of his talent. It was true. Even though Balzac had not yet produced his masterpieces, I was strongly impressed by his original style, and I considered him already a master worth studying. Though he was less ingratiating than Delatouche, I found Balzac to be an excellent teacher—more open and even-tempered. It is common knowledge that his self-satisfaction knew no limits and that it was so well founded that you had to forgive him for it. How he used to enjoy talking about his creations, telling them to us in advance, making them up as he talked, reading them as drafts or proofs! Naïve and as joyous as a child, he asked advice as if we were all children, not listening to the answers, or using them to fight against it, with his obstinate superiority. He would never lecture; he spoke about and for himself alone. Only once did he forget himself and talk about Rabelais, with whom I was not familiar at the time. He was so marvelous, so dazzling, so lucid, that we said to ourselves, on our way out, "Oh yes, he really will have the future he dreams of. He understands too well what he is not, not to make a great personality of himself."

He lived at that time on Rue de Cassini, in a small, cheerful mezzanine, between the ground and second floors, next door to the Observatory. It was through Balzac, or at his house, that I met Emmanuel Arago, a man who was to become like a brother to me, and who was then a child. We quickly became friends. I could act like a grandmother with him, since he was still so young that, during the course of a year, his arms had outgrown the length of his shirt-sleeves. Nevertheless, he had already published a volume of verse and a very witty stage play.

One fine morning, having sold *La Peau de Chagrin* at a good price, Balzac took a dislike to his mezzanine and talked about moving; on second thought, however, he settled for transforming his small poet's-rooms into a series of boudoirs fit for a marquise, and one fine day, he invited us to come and have ices within his silk-lined walls bordered with lace. This occasioned much laughter in me; I did not realize he took this need for luxury seriously or that it was anything more that a passing whim. I was wrong. Those fanciful needs became the tyrants of his life, and to satisfy them he often sacrificed more basic comforts. From then on he lived a little in this manner—short of necessities in the midst of his vanities, depriving himself of soup and coffee rather than doing without silver tableware and porcelain from China.

He was soon reduced to unheard-of expediencies so as not to be parted from his revivifying knick-knacks; being an artist of whimsy, a child of golden dreams, he lived in a fairy palace of his imaginings; but also being a strong-minded man, he readily accepted all the worries and deprivation, rather than force some semblance of reality on his dream.

Childlike and great; always envious of trifles and never jealous of true glory; sincere to the point of modesty, proud to the point of braggadocio; trusting himself and others; very generous, very kind, and very crazy, with an inner reserve of reason which controlled all aspects of his work; brazen yet celibate; drunk on water; intemperate regarding work, but sober in the other passions; materialistic and romantic to equal excess; credulous and skeptical; filled with inconsistencies and mysteries—that was Balzac when still young, already inexplicable to those who wore themselves out by the perpetual study of himself to which he condemned his friends, and which did not yet seem to any of us as interesting as it really was going to be.

In fact, at that time, many competent judges denied Balzac's genius, or at least did not believe he was destined for such an influential and expansive career. Delatouche was among the most recalcitrant. He talked about him with a frightening aversion. Balzac had been his disciple, and their rupture, for which Balzac never knew the motive, was still fresh and bleeding. Delatouche would give no good reasons for his resentment, and Balzac often said to me, "Watch out! One fine day you'll see—without your suspecting, without even knowing why—he'll turn into your mortal enemy."

In my opinion, Delatouche was obviously wrong in denigrating Balzac, who spoke of him only with regret and tenderness, but Balzac was wrong in thinking the animosity was irreparable. Over a time, he could have won him back.

It was still too soon, then. Several times I tried to tell Delatouche what could reconcile them, in vain. The first time, he leaped almost to the ceiling. "So, you've seen him?" he yelled. "You're really seeing him? That's the last straw!" I thought he was going to throw me out the window. He calmed down, sulked, came back. In the end, he let me have "my" Balzac, when he saw that this friendship took nothing away from the one he laid claim to. But at each new literary relationship I decided to establish or accept, Delatouche was bound to go into the same fits of anger, and even those people I was indifferent to seemed to him to be enemies, unless he himself had introduced me to them.

I spoke very little of my literary projects to Balzac. He hardly gave them any credence, or never dreamed to consider whether they were in line with my ability. I did not ask him for advice; he would have told me, as much out of modesty as out of egotism, that he kept his opinions to himself. That his way of being modest was hidden under the guise of presumption, I have discovered since, and it was a nice surprise; as for his egotism, it too had its reactive side, in the form of devotion and generosity.

Dealing with him was extremely pleasant, though a little wearying for me whose supply of ways to change the subject of the conversation was limited. But his soul was very serene, and at no time did I see him moody. With his big belly, he would clamber up all the flights of steps of the building at Quai Saint-Michel, and would arrive puffing, laughing, and talking, before even catching his breath. He would pick up the paperwork on my table, meaning to learn a little of what it might be about; but immediately reminded of his own work in progress, he would begin to tell me about that, and all in all, I would find it more instructive to my fantasy than all the impediments posed by the exasperating questions of Delatouche.

One evening, when we had dined on a strange assortment of food at Balzac's—I believe we had boiled beef, a melon, and whipped champagne—he tried on a brand new dressing gown, showing it off to us with girlish joy, and wanted, thus appareled, to accompany us, candle in hand, up to the Luxembourg gate. It was late, the place was deserted, and I pointed out to him that he would get murdered going back home. "Not at all," he told me. "If I meet some thieves, they'll take me for a madman and will be afraid of me. Either that, or they'll take me for a prince, and pay me homage." It was a calm, beautiful night. He accompanied us thus, carrying his lighted candle in its pretty holder of chased vermeil, speaking of the four Arabian horses he did not yet have, that he should have soon, that he never did get, and yet firmly believing he sooner or later would have. He would have walked us to the other end of Paris, if we had let him.

I did not know any other celebrities, and had no wish to. I found such an opposition of ideas, feelings, and theories between Balzac and Delatouche that I feared my poor mind would be lost in a chaos of contradictions if I listened to yet a third master. Once during that period, I saw Jules Janin, to ask him for a favor. That is the only approach I ever made to a critic, and since the favor was not for myself, I had no hesitation asking for it. I found him to be a good fellow, devoid of affectation or any display of vanity, having the good taste not to show his wit unnecessarily, and talking about his dogs with more affection than he talked about his writing. Since I also like dogs, I found myself very much at ease; a literary conversation with someone I did not know would ordinarily have intimidated me badly.

I have said that Delatouche exasperated *me*. That was so for himself as well, and he worked to the point of self-disgust in everything he undertook. From time to time, he indulged himself by talking about his novels before they were written. He did so with more discretion and more intimacy than Balzac, and even more readily, when he had an attentive audience. For example, you had better not take it into your head to rattle a piece of furniture, or poke the fire, or sneeze while he was speaking; he would immediately stop talking and ask, with polite concern, if you had a cold or a leg cramp, and feigning forgetfulness, he would make you beg him to go on by pretending to forget where he had left off. He had a thousand times less talent for writing than Balzac, but since he had a thousand times more talent for reciting his ideas through the spoken word, what he told so wonderfully seemed wonderful. By the same token, whatever Balzac would tell in an often imperfect manner would often suggest only an imperfect literary work. But when Delatouche's work was in print, we would look in vain for the charm and beauty of what we had heard, and we would have the opposite surprise in reading Balzac. Balzac knew that he expressed himself poorly when he spoke—not without warmth and spirit, but without clarity and order. He also preferred to read, when he had his manuscript at hand, while Delatouche, who invented a hundred novels without writing them down, almost never had any to read, or else he read a few pages which did not convey his idea and which visibly depressed him. He did not write easily, so he loathed prolific writers—except Walter Scott, whom he adored—and he would aim the most absurd invectives and acerbic comparisons against Balzac's abundance.

I always thought that Delatouche expressed too much of his real talent in talk. Balzac expressed only his nonsense. He threw his surplus conceptions into talking and kept his deeper wisdom for his writing. Delatouche exhausted himself in fine performances, and although his source was rich, it was not rich enough to be spent so generously.

And then his terrible health cut short his flight at the very moment when he spread his wings. He wrote beautiful lines of verse, free-flowing and full, mixed with over-worked and slightly empty ones; he wrote some very remark-

able and original novels, and others that were weak and uncontrolled; he produced some very sharp and ingenious articles, and others so personal they were
incomprehensible, hence of no interest to the public. The highs and lows of his
superior intellect might be explained by the cruel ups and downs of his illness.

Delatouche also had the misfortune of getting too involved in what other
people did. At that period, he read everything. As a journalist, he received
everything that appeared in print, pretended not to glance at it, and passed on
the copy to the first one of his editors who came in, saying, "Swallow your
medicine. You're young, and it won't kill you. Say whatever you want about it;
I don't want to know what it is." But when we brought him the finished
account, he would criticize the critique with a lucidity which proved that he
himself had swallowed the medicine, and had even savored its bitter taste.

I would have been a fool not to listen to all that Delatouche told me, but
that perpetual analysis of everything, that dissection of others as well as himself; all that brilliant and, more often than not, fair criticism, which would end
up negating himself and others, was inordinately depressing to my spirit; so
many guidelines began to cramp me. I was learning about everything that must
not be done, nothing about what must be, and I was losing my self-confidence.

I recognized then, and still do, that Delatouche helped me enormously by
directing me to hold back. In that era, they were doing the oddest things in literature. The eccentricities of young Victor Hugo's genius had intoxicated the
youth, who were bored by the old refrains of the Restoration. They no longer
found Chateaubriand sufficiently romantic; the new master was just barely
romantic enough for the ferocious appetites he had unleashed. The little rebels
in his own school, who surely realized that he would never have accepted them
as disciples, wished to outdo him. They searched for outlandish titles and revolting subjects; in the steeplechase of startling exhibitions, even many gifted people gave in to fashion, and sporting bizarre rags, rushed headlong into the fray.

I was very tempted to do as the others, since my masters seemed to be setting a bad example, and I sought out oddities I would never have been able to
execute. Among contemporary critics who resisted the tide of eccentricity,
Delatouche discerned what was good and beautiful in both old and new schools.
He held me back, on that slippery incline, by his comical mockery and serious
advice. But then he would immediately throw me into inextricable difficulties.
"Avoid pastiche," he would say. "Use your own fund of knowledge; read in
your own life, in your own feelings; render your impressions." When we had
chatted about one thing or another, he would say to me, "You're too absolute in
your feelings; your character is too far out of the mainstream; you know neither
society nor individuals. You haven't lived and thought like everyone else. Your
brain is empty." I would agree with him, and I would return to Nohant, ready to
go back to making lacquered tea chests and snuff boxes out of chestnut.

I finally began *Indiana* without a purpose, without a hope, and without
any outline, resolutely putting out of my mind all that had been proposed to me
as precept or example, foraging neither in the ways of others nor in my own
preconceptions for the subject and characters. No one has failed to point out
that *Indiana* was about me and my life. That is absolutely untrue. I have creat-

ed many female characters, and I think that when people have read the present account of the impressions and reflections of my life, they will clearly see that I never portrayed myself in feminine guise. I am too romantic ever to have seen the heroine of a novel in my mirror. I never found myself beautiful or pleasing enough, nor consistent enough in the interplay of character and behavior to be of poetic or even general interest. I would have tried to embellish my person and dramatize my life, in vain; I would never have come to the end of it. My own self, coming to haunt me face to face, would have given me chills.

I am far from saying an artist does not have the right to depict and recount what is inside' him; the more metaphorical flowers he heaps on his own head before the public, the better he will do, as long as he is clever enough to conceal his identity beneath the embellishments, or as long as he is dashing enough not to become ridiculous thereby. But as far as I am concerned, I was cut from too mottled a cloth ever to lend myself to any type of idealization. If I had wanted to show myself in serious depth, I would have told a life story which, up to that point, bore more resemblance to that of the monk Alexis (in the not very entertaining novel *Spiridion* [1839]) than to the passionate young Creole, Indiana. On the other hand, if I had taken the other aspect of my life as a subject—my need for childishness, merriment, utter silliness—I would have created a character so unbelievable that I would not have been able to find anything for it to say or do that would have made any sense.

I did not have the slightest theory when I began to write, nor, I believe, when the urge to write a novel put a pen in my hand. That does not prevent my instinct from having, albeit unaware, given rise to the theory that I am about to set forth, that I have generally followed without realizing it, and that is still being discussed in literary circles as I now write about it.

According to this theory, the novel should be a poetic, as well as an analytical work. It must have characters and situations that are true to life—even based on real life—that form a grouping around a type whose function is to embody the sentiment or main idea of the book. This character-type generally embodies in some way the passion of love, given that almost all novels are love stories. According to the aforementioned theory (and this is where it takes effect), that passion, consequently that character-type, must be idealized; the author must not be afraid to endow it with all the triumph he aspires to, or all the sorrow he has seen or felt. But in either case, it must not be cheapened by chance events; it must perish or succeed, and one must not be afraid to endow it with exceptional importance, powers beyond the ordinary, or subject it to delight or suffering that completely surpass the habitual, human ones, and that even surpass what most intelligent people think is believable.

In sum, the idealization of a sentiment yields the subject, leaving to the art of the storyteller the care of placing that subject within a situation and a realistic framework that is drawn sensitively enough to make the subject stand out; that is, if he really wants to create a novel.

Is this theory valid? I think so, but it is not, and should not be, considered absolute. Over time, Balzac made me understand, through the variety and power of his conceptions, that one could sacrifice the idealized subject for the truth of the portrayal, or for the critique of society or humanity itself.

Balzac summed this up completely when he said to me later on, "You are looking for man as he should be; I take him as he is. Believe me, we are both right. Both paths lead to the same end. I also like exceptional human beings; I am one myself. I need them to make my ordinary characters stand out, and I never sacrifice them unnecessarily. But the ordinary human beings interest me more than they do you. I make them larger than life; I idealize them in the opposite sense, in their ugliness or in their stupidity. I give their deformities frightful or grotesque proportions. You could not do that; you are smart not to want to look at people and things that would give you nightmares. Idealize what is pretty and what is beautiful; that is a woman's job."

Balzac's speech had no disdain or causticity behind it. His brotherly feeling for me was sincere; he has idealized woman too often for anyone to ever accuse him of holding the Kératry theory that women are inferior.

Balzac, all-embracing spirit, not infinite or without fault, but the most expansive and the most gifted in the various qualities which were displayed in the novel in our time; Balzac, master unequalled in the art of painting humanity as it exists in modern society, was a thousand times right in not insisting on an absolute system. He revealed none of this to me while I was searching, and I do not hold it against him. He did not know it himself; he too was searching and groping for his own means. He tried everything. He saw and proved that all means were good and all subjects fertile for a mind as pliant as his. He further developed what he felt were his strongest assets, and made fun of wrongheaded criticism that seeks to impose on artists a framework, a subject, and methods. This is an error to which the public still subscribes, not realizing that this or that arbitrary theory is always the expression of a single individual, hence would be the first to declare its independence by contradicting the point of view of an adjacent or opposing theory. We are struck by these contradictions when we read half-a-dozen critical articles on the same work of art; we then see that each critic has his own criteria, his own passion, his own particular taste, and that if two or three of them agree to advocate any particular principle in the arts, the judgments they make of it show, by way of some very diverse appraisals and biases, that no fixed principle really governs.

Besides, it is just as well that this is the case. If there were but one school and one doctrine, art would quickly perish, lacking boldness and experimentation. Man always goes painfully in search of absolute truth, of which he only has intimations, and which he will never find in himself. Truth is the object of a search for which all the collective forces of our species are not excessive. And yet, strange and fatal error, as soon as a man of some ability approaches this quest, he would like to forbid it to others and give as his unique discovery the truth he believes he has acquired. Even the quest for freedom's true principle is used to feed the despotism and intolerance of human pride. What sad folly! If the various societies have not yet been able to avoid this, let the arts at least free themselves and find life in the absolute independence of inspiration.

Inspiration—that is something very hard to define and very important to recognize as a superhuman factor, as an almost divine intervention. Inspiration is for artists what grace is for Christians, and no one has yet dreamed of forbidding believers to receive grace when it descends into their souls. However, there are self-styled critics who would flatly forbid artists to receive inspiration and obey it.

And I am not talking here about some professional critics; I am not restricting my plea to one or several coteries. I am fighting a public and universal prejudice. People want art to follow the beaten path, and when one style has been well received, an entire century cries out, "Give us more of the same! That is the only thing we like!" Then, pity the poor innovators who must succumb or sustain a terrific battle until their protest, a cry of revolt at the beginning, becomes, at the last, a tyranny that crushes other equally legitimate and desirable innovations.

I have always found the word "inspiration" very ambitious, and applicable only to first-class geniuses. I would never dare apply it to myself without recognizing the folly of a term which implies incontestable success. Yet, there must be a word which does not make modest people blush and which expresses that sort of grace that descends more or less vividly, more or less richly on all those who love their art. The humblest worker may have his moment of inspiration; the heavenly fluid may be as precious in a vase of clay as in a vase of gold. The only difference is that one preserves it pure, and the other may alter it, or may crack. Christian grace does not act alone, or in an inevitable way. The soul has to receive it, as the good earth receives the sacred seed. Inspiration is no different. So let us see it for what it is, and let it not imply anything presumptuous under my pen.

When I began writing *Indiana*, I felt a very vivid and distinct emotion that resembled nothing I had experienced in my previous attempts. But that emotion was more painful than pleasurable. I wrote the book all in one spurt, without any outline, as I have already said, and literally without knowing where I was going, without even realizing the social problem I was approaching. I was not a Saint-Simonian[79] and never had been, although I had real sympathy for several ideas and people of that sect; but I did not know them at that time, and I was not influenced by them.

The only thing I had in me was a very clear and ardent feeling of horror at brutal and beastly enslavement. I hadn't been victim of it, nor was I then; that can be seen by the freedom I enjoyed, which no one contested. Therefore, *Indiana* was not, as everybody said, my story in disguise. It was not a complaint formulated against a particular master. It was a protest against tyranny in general; and if I personified this tyranny in a man, if I placed the conflict in the framework of a domestic situation, it was because I had no ambition other than to write a novel of manners. That is why, in a preface written after the book, I defended myself from the charge of wanting to attack social institutions. I was very sincere, and I did not claim to know more than I was saying. The critics taught me more about it and made me examine the questions more closely.

I wrote the book under the power of an emotion and not a system. This emotion, which had slowly accumulated during the course of a lifetime of reflection, overflowed as soon as the vessel of a given situation opened to receive it. But it found itself very constricted, and a kind of combat between the emotion and the execution kept me for six weeks in a state of exertion that was new to me.

Meanwhile, my poor Corambé vanished as soon as I started to feel in a mood to persevere with a certain subject. He was of too tenuous an essence to bend to the demands of form. I had hardly finished my book when I wanted to regenerate my usual flow of reveries. Impossible! The characters of my manuscript, shut in a drawer, were happy to remain quiet. I hoped in vain to see Corambé reappear, and with him those thousands of beings who lulled me every day as pleasant day dreams, those vague figures, those half-distinct voices that floated around me like paintings brought to life behind transparent veils. Those dear visions were but the precursors of inspiration. They cruelly hid from me at the bottom of the inkwell, no longer to emerge, except when I plucked up my courage to pursue them.

I would have much to relate about that phenomenon of semi-hallucination that had occurred to me all my life and that completely and suddenly disappeared. But I would be afraid of resuming a previous chapter of this work which is perhaps already too long and detailed;[80] I shall limit myself to recalling that I had started—at so early an age, I could not say exactly when—an unwritten novel made up of thousands of stories linked together through a main fantastic character called Corambé (a name without any significance, whose syllables put themselves together by chance in a dream). This character was, during a few years in my childhood, a kind of god I had invented, whom I had at certain times been ready to believe in and turn into an object of worship.

The ardent Catholicism which possessed me in the convent made me forget Corambé, but I did not repulse him in fear, as an idolatrous belief. For that creation of my dreams had only prepared me, through angelic fantasies, to be carried away by the divine character of Jesus. I have kept my enthusiasm for the latter; as for Corambé, I do not doubt that he was for me, in childhood, a more human and more plausible interpretation of the divine master than the one the Church in our time claims to give us. Had Corambé been involved in politics, he would not have let a gasping Poland be devoured by bloodthirsty Russia; had he gotten involved in socialism, he would not have abandoned the cause of the weak for that of the strong, or the moral and physical life of the poor to the caprices of the rich. He would have been more Christian than the papacy.

When I reached the age when one laughs at one's own naïveté, I returned Corambé to his proper place; that is, I reintegrated him into my imagination, among my dreams; but he continued to occupy a central position, and all the fictions that continued to form around him always emanated from that principal fiction.

The fragmented plan I followed when I created for myself, under that hallucinatory spell, a host of novels, which fell into oblivion without ever being written, had its own peculiar logic. One mysterious character—not omnipotent, but endowed with supernatural powers—would mediate in all situations, and interrupt or resume them at will. As anyone can see, it was very convenient. It was an idea that I found sublime for my personal use, but I knew it was unsuitable for anyone but me, hence unsuitable for the public. Once I realized that, I had no choice when recounting whatever human stories I had in mind but to leave the action and solution to chance or to the logic of human ideas. Well, I lived through all this, but so sorrowfully that for several years I felt a profound bitterness toward my celebrity, a bitterness that I naïvely dared reveal to a few people in the midst of my success. But I should have kept it to myself, seeing that people took this ingenuous pain for an affectation.

Today, as I relate this in the most detached manner possible, who will believe me and understand me if I say that true poems remain in the soul's sanctuary, never to emerge? Surely some soulmates, but that will be all; and so as not to bore the others, I speak here of Corambé and the considerable image-content of my dreams only as a psychic phenomenon which I did not deny myself because it had an ineffable charm, an otherworldly purity, and never posed a threat to my sanity.

In fact, except perhaps during my childhood, I never had any desire to convince myself those apparitions existed outside my mind. I understood perfectly that I was under the power of a kind of vision, evoked by me, but not so much a caprice of my will as a capricious reflection of my inner concerns. Therefore, now, I did not consider myself as having been cured of a mental aberration, but rather deprived of a faculty. I have no idea if that so-called faculty would ever have become pernicious. Perhaps only a small disturbance in my physical equilibrium was needed to turn those happy visions of landscapes and paradisiacal gardens inhabited by imaginary beings into somber and terrifying ones, and in that case, it is possible I would have ended by believing they were real. I don't think so, but who knows? The fatigue of such an experience may, in the long run, wear down the resistance of one's reason.

That is what I told myself, as a consolation, when the effort of will I had to make to evoke creatures whose inner logic would persist for the length of a book paralyzed my faculty for seeing unexpected creatures come before me by themselves. I could no longer leave those I had evoked to move on to a new group, nor the place to which I had brought them for another site in my ceaseless imaginings. Nonetheless, I could not refrain from making Ralph and Indiana travel from one end of the globe to the other, and perhaps from committing some errors in the geography of their final refuge. I hardly paid it any mind, I was so ill at ease with the reality I was approaching.

Yet later on, once I had completely accepted it, the necessity of appearing minimally reasonable (a necessity I recognized without understanding it very well) gave me pleasure of a different sort. My characters took on another way of manifesting themselves. I no longer saw them floating in a corner of my room, or passing through my garden, but when closing my eyes, I would see them more clearly drawn, and their words engraved themselves more distinctly in my mind, rather than reaching my ears in mysterious murmurs. When they came during my sleep, they only annoyed me, but when I was at my small desk in the armoire, in my little room, they spoke to me and acted, for better or worse, on my white piece of paper. Their abrupt and imperious manner also had its charm—less sweet and less lasting, since almost everything vanished as soon as I put down my pen—but the characters had more energy and were more appreciable to my judgment.

Still another phenomenon occurred which I cannot explain to any degree. As soon as I had finished my first manuscript, it erased itself from my memory, perhaps not as absolutely as the numerous novels I had never written, but to the extent that I only remembered it vaguely. I would have thought that the habit I had developed of writing down specific characters, passions, and situations would have fixed them, bit by bit, in my memory. Nothing like that happened, and that forgetfulness through which my brain has immediately buried the product of its work has done nothing but flourish. If I did not have my works on a shelf, I would even forget their titles. Someone could read me half a volume of certain of my novels which I have not had to proofread within recent weeks, and barring two or three important names, I would not guess they were mine. I have a better recollection of the insignificant circumstances that existed while I was writing than of the things I was writing about, and according to my remembrance of the situation I found myself in at the time, I can say whether a book was more or less a success or failure. But if someone unexpectedly put me before my own works in the guise of critic, I could answer in all good faith that I did not know them and would have to reread them attentively to have any opinion at all about them.

I hope, then, that no one expects me to talk much about my books. I would have to read too much and too attentively to form a judgment. For the last fifteen years, from the time I saw they were being read and discussed, I have invested the greatest care in delivering them in as finished a form as I was capable of. But with the exception of one or two, I never could rework any part of them. Once the energy is spent, I remain without the least bit of certainty about the value of what it produced; and I would change everything if I had to change anything. When I take up a novel again to adapt it for the theater, I cannot retain one word of the dialogue, and I transform or modify the characters, as much out of the impossibility of grasping them again as for the demands of the stage.

I do not know if all this is worth talking about. It is not my style to talk about myself regarding purely individual matters that lack solidarity with other individuals. The number of artists is considerable enough for it to be worthwhile for them to see another artistic nature try to account for itself, but I sometimes fear that I have said exceptionable things, as if I were a member of a different species. I felt less embarrassed in recounting the dreams of my childhood, because all children are artists, and even the most practical people remember having been poets for a long time in their lives before getting down to the business of practical living. I was a child for so long—I developed my individual faculties so late, or rather I sought my own reasoning for so long—that finally I was left, in spite of time and experience, with a need to appreciate everything secretly through an ideal that was probably too naïve, so much so that I feel embarrassed and somewhat intimidated when I try to analyze the contents of whatever intelligence I used.

Worldly people—by which I mean those who are not artists by profession—are usually rather curious to know under what external influences and in what particular conditions artists produce their works. Their curiosity is a little infantile, and I personally have never been able to completely gratify them, no matter how much good will I exerted in answering their questions without discourtesy or dishonesty. I must confess that the questions were sometimes so complicated or strangely phrased that I was astounded, and my first reaction was to answer honestly, "I don't know." For example, an Englishwoman, who claimed to be very fond of my novels, asked me one day, as she looked at me with eyes as big as an owl's, "What do you think about when you write a novel?"

"Goodness," I answered, "I try to think about my novel."

"Oh, does that mean that you can't always think while you're writing? That must be a very great hardship!"

In addition, what we call inspiration in the arts is something whose operation varies so much that the more we inquire into its particular manifestations, the less likely we are to understand what is going on in the mind. Many famous artists have had bizarre working habits. Balzac claimed to have more than he really had, and still more were attributed to him. I caught him by surprise more than once, in broad daylight, working like everyone else, without drugs, without a special costume, without any pangs of "childbirth," wreathed in smiles, his eye limpid, and his face glowing.

It is said that some artists abuse their need for coffee, alcohol, or opium. I do not really believe that, and if it sometimes amuses them to create under the influence of substances other than their own intoxicating thoughts, I doubt that they kept up such lucubrations or showed them off. The work of the imagination is exciting enough, and I confess I have only been able to enhance it with a dash of milk or lemonade, which would hardly qualify me as Byronic. Honestly, I do not believe in a drunk Byron writing beautiful verses. Inspiration can pass through the soul just as easily in the midst of an orgy as in the silence of the woods, but when it is a question of giving form to your thoughts, whether you are secluded in your study or performing on the planks of a stage, you must be in total possession of yourself.   *C.D.P./H.M.D.*

Part V

Literary and Private Life
1832 to 1850

I

Delatouche changes abruptly from critical to enthusiastic.
—*Valentine* is published. —The impossibility of planned
collaboration. —*Le Revue des Deux Mondes*. —Buloz. —Gustave
Planche. —Delatouche is displeased and breaks with me.
—Summary of our relationship afterwards. —Maurice goes to
school. —His unhappiness and mine. —The sadness and harshness
of the school routine. —An "execution" at Henri IV. —Love knows
no reason. —Maurice makes his first communion.

I was still living at Quai Saint-Michel with my daughter when *Indiana* was published.[1] In the interval between its commission and publication, I had written *Valentine* and begun *Lélia*. *Valentine* thus appeared two or three months after *Indiana*, and this book was also written at Nohant where I still regularly went to spend three months out of six.

Delatouche climbed up to my attic and found the first copy of *Indiana*, which the publisher, Ernest Dupuy, had just sent me, and on the cover of which I had at that precise moment inscribed Delatouche's name. He took it, sniffed it, turned it this way and that, curious, anxious, and more than usually scornful that day. I was on the balcony; I wanted to draw him out there, to talk of something else. There was no way. He wanted to read, he read, and at every page he cried out: "Well! it's a pastiche, school of Balzac. A pastiche, what can I say? Balzac, what can I say?"

He came out on the balcony, volume in hand, criticizing me word by word and demonstrating point by point that I had copied Balzac's style and that, by doing so, I had succeeded in being neither Balzac nor myself.

I had neither sought nor avoided imitating Balzac's style, and it did not seem to me the reproach was justified. Before condemning myself, I was waiting until my judge, who carried off my book, went through the whole thing. On waking the next morning I received this note: "George, I am writing to beg your pardon; I am at your knees. Forget my harsh words last night, forget all the harsh things I said to you during the past six months. I spent the night reading your book. Oh, my child, how pleased I am with you!"

I believed that my success would be limited to this paternal note, and I in no way anticipated the prompt return of my publisher, who asked me for *Valentine*. The newspapers all praised this "Monsieur G. Sand," insinuating that a woman's hand must have slipped in here and there to reveal to the author certain refinements of the heart and mind, but declaring that the style and judgments were too virile not to be those of a man. They were all a little "Kératry."

That did not bother me at all, but it did make Jules Sandeau suffer, who modestly wished no credit where none was due. I have already said that this success made him determined to assume his own name again and to renounce our collaborative efforts, which we had already judged to be unworkable. Collaboration is an art requiring not only, as one would expect, mutual confidence and a good relationship, but a particular skill and an ability to proceed *ad hoc*. Moreover, we were too inexperienced, both of us, to share the work. When we tried, each of us entirely revised the other's work, and this successive reworking made our labor like that of Penelope's shroud.

The four volumes of *Indiana* and *Valentine* sold, I found myself in charge of three thousand francs, which enabled me to leave my little back room, have a servant, and permitted me a little more ease. *Le Revue des Deux Mondes* had just been bought by Buloz,[1] who asked me for some short stories. I wrote *Métella* [1835] for this review and other things besides.

Le Revue des Deux Mondes published the elite writers of the time. With two or three exceptions, perhaps everyone who has retained a name as a journalist, poet, novelist, historian, philosopher, critic, traveller, etc. has passed through the hands of Buloz, an intelligent man who did not know how to express himself, but who was quite sensitive beneath his rough exterior. It was very easy, a little too easy in fact, to make fun of this stubborn, blunt Genevese. When he was not in too bad a mood, he would good-naturedly submit to teasing, but it was not easy not to let oneself be influenced and managed by him. He held my purse strings for ten years, and in the lives of artists, these strings which open only to give us a few hours of liberty, in exchange for so many hours of slavery, are our very lifelines. During our long association, I sent Buloz to the devil a thousand times, but I, in turn, so enraged him that we are even. Besides, in spite of his demands, harshness, craftiness, Buloz, like all bullies, had moments of sincerity and real sensitivity. In certain small ways, he resembled poor Deschartres. That is why I tolerated for so long the peevishness that infiltrated his attempts at a candid friendship. We quarreled; we went to court. I regained my liberty without damages, a result we could have achieved without a trial, if he had not been so stubborn. Shortly afterward, I saw him weeping for the loss of his eldest son, who had just died in his arms. His wife, Mlle. Blaze, a distinguished woman in her own right, had just called me to her side in this moment of extreme anguish. I held my hands out to them with no thought of our recent quarrel, nor have I recalled it since. All friendships, no matter how stormy and imperfect, contain bonds stronger and more durable than the battles over material interests and fleeting angers. We believe we detest people we still love in spite of everything. A mountain of arguments separates us from them, but a single word is sometimes sufficient to make us leap over this mountain. Buloz' words, "Ah, George, how unhappy I am!" made me forget all questions of numbers and procedure. And he too, at other times, had seen me weep and had not mocked me. Since then, although often solicited to join crusades against him, I have flatly refused; nor have I bragged to him of having done so, in spite of the fact that criticism in *Le Revue des Deux Mondes* continued to declare that I had had a great deal of talent as long as I worked for them, but since the break, alas! Naïve Buloz! What do I care!

What I did care about was the sudden angry reaction of Delatouche. The crisis forecast by Balzac erupted one morning without any apparent cause. Delatouche especially hated Gustave Planche, who had paid me a visit, bringing a long article of praise that had recently appeared in *Le Revue des Deux Mondes*. As I was not yet working for the *Revue*, the praise was disinterested, and I could not help but gratefully accept it. Is that what wounded Delatouche? He gave no sign of it. He was then living full-time at Aulnay and did not often come to Paris; therefore, I was not immediately privy to his nasty mood. I was preparing to pay him a visit when M. de la Rochefoucauld, to whom he had introduced me and who was his neighbor in the country, informed me that he only spoke of me now with execration, that he accused me of being intoxicated by fame, of having sacrificed my true friends, of despising them, of only associating with men of letters, of scorning his advice, etc. Since there was no truth in these reproaches, I imagined him in one of his usual sulks, and to take him out of it more subtly than through a letter, I dedicated *Lélia*, which was about to be published, to him. He "took it wrong," as we say in Berry, and declared that I had done it in revenge. In revenge for what? Then it occurred to me he could not forgive me for seeing Gustave Planche, and I begged Planche to apologize for a very cruel article he had written in which Delatouche had been very harshly criticized. I think it was in answer to a violent attack against the group of romantics whom Planche had sometimes championed. Whatever it was, Gustave Planche, moved by the good things I told him about Delatouche, wrote a very kind, even respectful letter, as was fitting between a young and an old man, to which Delatouche, increasingly irritated, did not deign to reply. He continued to inveigh and incite against me people with whom I was linked. He succeeded in taking from me two friends out of the five or six of which our intimate circle was composed. One of them later came to beg my pardon. The other I later had to defend against the abuses of Delatouche himself. But then, I knew my Delatouche; I knew what one had to accept and reject in his indignations, which were too violent and bitter not to be partly unjust.

Less than two years after this rage against me, Delatouche came to Berry to his cousin's house, Mme. Duvernet, and made to realize his error by her and by her son, my friend Charles, expressed a great urge to come to see me; yet he could not make up his mind to do so. He addressed gracious words to me in one of his novels, forgetting that his words had been too sharp for me now to succumb to such literary advances. Not by compliments would this wound to our friendship be healed. I did not place much stock in compliments; I never needed them. I have never asked of friendship that I be considered a great mind, but rather that I be treated as a loyal friend. Finally, I gave in to direct approaches, to a request for service in 1844. Such treatment is the most honorable apology one can exact, and then I did not hesitate a moment. I threw my arms around my old friend, dreadful but dear, who from that moment went out of his way to make me forget the past.

Another, more profound problem for me was the entrance of my son into *collège*.[2] I had looked forward impatiently to the time when he would be nearby;

and neither he nor I knew what *collège* really was. I do not wish to say anything against communal education, but there are children whose character is antipathetic to the regimentation of the schools, to that constant discipline, that absence of maternal care, poetic surroundings, tranquility and freedom of thought. Poor Maurice was born an artist; he had all the tastes; he had, along with me, absorbed all the habits; and although he did not know it yet, he had all the independence of the artist. For him, entering school seemed almost a celebration, and like all children, he eagerly looked forward to a change of place and routine. I took him then, gay as a little finch, to Henri IV, happy myself to see him so well disposed. Sainte-Beuve,[3] a friend of the headmaster, assured me that Maurice would be the object of particular concern. The assistant was a family man, an excellent man, who received him like one of his own children.

His father and I made the tour of the building with him. Those great tree-less courtyards; those uniform cloisters with their cold modern architecture; that sad clamor of recreation—the discordant and almost furious voices of children prisoners; those mournful faces of the subject masters—young, classless people who are there, for the most part, as slaves to poverty, and necessarily victims or tyrants; everything, right down to the drum—a most effective instrument in stirring the nerves of men going into battle, but stupidly brutish in calling children to the contemplation required by study—tightened my heart and evoked in me a sort of terror. I stole a glance at Maurice's expression and saw him divided between astonishment and a feeling somewhat analogous to my own. He stood firm just the same; he was afraid his father would ridicule him. But when the moment came to part, he embraced me with a heavy heart and eyes full of tears. The assistant took him in his arms very paternally, seeing very well the storm that was about to break. It did break, in fact, at the moment I hurried away to hide my malaise. The child slipped out of the arms that were holding him, ran to glue himself to me, crying out in desperate sobs that he did not wish to remain there.

I thought I would die. It was the first time I had seen Maurice unhappy, and I wanted to take him away. My husband was more firm, and certainly had all the right reasons on his side. But obliged to flee the caresses and the supplications of my poor child, his cries following me to the bottom of the stairs, I returned home sobbing and weeping almost as much as he, in the carriage which brought me back.

I went to see him two days later. I found him decked-out in the frightfully heavy, unsanitary, square-cut uniform. I do not know if the custom still exists of having those who enter the school wear the uniforms of those who leave. It was a truly despicable way of making money, because parents were required to pay for a uniform at the outset. I vainly fought it, claiming it was unhealthy and could cause skin infections among the children. Another barbarous custom consisted of the absence of chamber pots in the dormitories, coupled with the prohibition of going out to relieve oneself. On the other hand, greed permitted the sale of unhealthy sweets that made the children sick.

Yet, the headmaster was among the most honest and humane, and well-disposed to fight the abuses, which were not of his doing. He had a gentle and

agreeable successor. But then came M.———, who posed as a moral man in
the manner of a police sergeant, and who knew how to make the children as
miserable as the rules would allow him. A fierce partisan of absolute authority,
it was he who authorized a so-called intelligent father to have his son beaten by
his Negro in front of the whole class, which, through some Muscovite or
Creole taste, was militarily convoked to witness the event and was threatened
with severe punishment at the least sign of disinclination. I have forgotten the
name of that headmaster and of the father of the child; I do not want to ask my
son to remind me of their names, but everyone who was a student at Henri IV
at that time will be able to attest the fact.

My second visit to Maurice ended like the first; my friends accused me of
weakness. I admit I felt neither Roman nor Spartan in the face of the despair of
a poor child condemned to submit to a brutal and mercenary regime, without
having done anything to merit such cruel punishment. They dragged me along
to the Music Conservatory that day, thinking that Beethoven would do me
some good. I had wept so hard coming back from the school that my eyes were
all bloodshot. That hardly seemed reasonable, and it wasn't. But reason never
weeps; that is not its business; nor do our hearts reason; they have not been
given to us for that.

The *Pastoral Symphony* did not comfort me at all. I still remember my
efforts to weep silently as one of the most excruciating tortures of my life.

Maurice could not visit without the fear of increasing my pain, which I
could not hide from him; he was only partially resigned. His free days brought
about new crises. He arrived in the morning—gay, noisy, drunk with his liberty.
I spent a good hour washing him, combing his hair, because the filth he brought
from the school was quite unbelievable. He did not want to go out at all; all he
wanted was to remain with his sister and me in my small apartment, sketch figures on paper, look at pictures, or cut them out. Never has a child, or later a man,
been better able to amuse himself with sedentary work. But at every instant he
looked at the clock, saying he had only so many more hours to spend with us.
His face grew longer as the time ran out. When it was time for dinner, instead of
eating, he began to weep, and when the hour to return had rung, the deluge was
such that often I was forced to send word he was ill; and it was true. Childhood
does not know how to combat grief; Maurice was suffering true homesickness.

When they prepared him for his first communion, a customary procedure
at the school, I saw that he accepted religious teaching with great naïveté. Not
for anything in the world would I have had him begin his spiritual life with an
act of hypocrisy or atheism, and if I had found him disposed to mock religion, as
so many others do, I would have given him the serious reasons which had come
to me in my childhood and made me decide not to protest against an institution
whose spirit rather than letter I accepted. But recognizing that he challenged
nothing, I carefully refrained from raising any doubts in him. Such a discussion
would not have befit his age, and his mind was not in advance of his years. He
therefore made his first communion with great innocence and fervor.

I had just spent one of the unhappiest years of my life, that of 1833, and
it remains for me to summarize it.   *H.L.*

II

What I gained by becoming an artist. —Organized begging.
—Swindlers of Paris. —Begging for employment and for fame.
—Anonymous letters and those which should have been. —The
visits. —The English, the curious, the loafers, the advice-givers.
—The millstone. —Reflections on charity and on the use of one's
goods. —Religious and social duty in flagrant opposition. —Future
problems and present law. —Material and intellectual inheritance.
—The obligations of family, justice, and probity, in actual society,
versus renunciation according to the Gospel. —Inevitable conflict
within oneself. —What I had to conclude for my own conduct.
—Doubt and pain. —Reflections on human destiny and the workings
of Providence. —*Lélia*. —Criticism. —Troubles that pass and those
that last. —The malady at large. —Balzac. —Departure for Italy.

The year 1833 inaugurated a number of my deep and real concerns which
I thought I had put behind me but which were only beginning. I had wanted to
be an artist; at last I was one. I imagined that I had reached my long sought
goal—independence and mastery of my own life. I had just shackled a ball and
chain about my ankle that I had not foreseen.

To be an artist! Yes, I had wanted to be one, not only to escape from the
material prison where property, large or small, closes one in a circle of odious,
trivial occupation, but also to escape the control of public opinon insofar as it
was narrow, stupid, egotistical, weak, provincial; to live outside the world's
prejudices insofar as they were false, outdated, arrogant, cruel, impious or dull,
but moreover and above all, to reconcile myself with myself. I could not bear
to be idle and useless, leaning, in my position as master, on the shoulders of the
workers. If I could have dug the earth, I would have joined them rather than
ever hear the words which, from my childhood, I had heard muttered around
me whenever Deschartres' back was turned, "He wants us to work up a
sweat—him with his full belly and his hands behind his back!" I saw clearly
that those in my employ were often more lazy than tired, but their apathy did
not justify my idleness. I did not think I had the right to ask the least work of
them as long as I myself did nothing, because to occupy yourself only with
your own pleasure is to do nothing.

I would not, by preference, have chosen the literary profession, and
celebrity still less. I would have preferred to live by the labor of my hands,

earning enough so that my small, clear profit guaranteed my right to work —my inheritance being too small to permit me to live anywhere except under the conjugal roof, where unacceptable conditions prevailed. Since I was told that the only obstacle to my freedom was lack of a little money, I had to earn that money. At last I did earn it. There were no more reproaches or dissatisfactions in that regard.

I would have wished to live obscurely, and as I had succeeded in remaining incognito during the interval between the publication of *Indiana* and *Valentine*—to the extent that the newspapers always referred to me as *monsieur*—I flattered myself that this little success would not affect my sedentary habits or my small circle of intimates, composed of people as unknown as myself. From the time I moved to Quai Saint Michel with my little girl, I had lived so retired and peacefully that I desired no other improvement in my fate than a few less stairs to climb and a few more logs for the fire.

In settling in at Quai Malaquais, I thought myself in a palace, so comfortable was Delatouche's garret in comparison with the one I was leaving. It was a little somber even in broad daylight; there were not yet buildings as far as the eye could see, and the big trees in the surrounding gardens made a thick curtain of green, where blackbirds sang and sparrows twittered with the same freedom as in the heart of the countryside. I felt I possessed a retreat and a life conforming to my tastes and needs. Alas! soon I was to sigh, there as everywhere, for peace, and to seek in vain, as Jean-Jacques Rousseau did, solitude.

I did not know how to preserve my liberty, protect my door from the curious, the unemployed, beggars of every description, and soon I perceived that neither my time nor my year's earnings would suffice for a day of this mad influx. I locked myself in, then, but it was an unceasing, terrible battle between the bell, the discussions with the servant, and the multiple interruptions.

Surrounding artists in Paris, there is an organized ring of beggars of which one is a dupe for a long time, and of which one continues to be a victim, owing to scruples of conscience. These are people feigning to be former artists living in misery, who go from door to door carrying subscriptions covered with false signatures, or out-of-work artisans, or mothers who have just pawned their last rags in order to give their children their daily bread. There are sick actors, poets without publishers, false sisters of charity. There are even fake missionaries, self-proclaimed parish priests. It all forms a huge assemblage of infamous vagabonds, who have escaped from prison, or are worthy of being thrown there. The best are old fools whom vanity, lack of talent, and finally, drunkenness have reduced to real poverty.

When one has been simple enough to let oneself be taken in by the first story, the first face, the band marks you as prey; it surrounds you, surveys you, knows your hours of coming and going, even knows the days you receive your funds. It approaches discreetly at first; then there are new faces and new stories, more frequent visits, letters in which you are warned that in two hours, if the help asked of you does not arrive, there will be found only a cadaver in the designated lodging. The fate of Elisa Mercoeur and Hegesippe Moreau[4] henceforth serves as theme and threat for every poet who does not blush to beg, and thinks himself too great to do anything else but dream of the stars.

I am not so simple as to be taken in by all these interesting tales of woe, but there are so many real and undeservedly unfortunate among those who ask for help, that to distinguish the true from the false can drive one crazy. As a general rule you can say that, ninety times out of a hundred, those who beg are the false, or infamous, poor. Those who really suffer in spite of their courage and uprightness prefer to die than beg. You must seek them out, discover them, often even deceive them, in order to make them accept assistance. The others besiege you, pursue you, threaten you.

But there are also unfortunate individuals, having neither great virtues nor great vices, who are deprived of the heroism of silence (a really cruel heroism to ask of the poor human species)—those whose courage is exhausted, whose will is worn out by lack of success or given up through lack of power. There are also women who, through a heroism which is not resignation, drink the cup of humility and reach out their palms to save their husbands, their lovers, above all, their children. It is enough to bear the risk of abandoning to hunger, despair, or suicide, even one of these innocent victims among the ninety-nine swindlers, to render your sleep uneasy: that is the weight that clamped on my life as soon as my small allotment for the day had gone beyond the bare essential.

Not having time to get at the truth, because I was riveted to my work, for a long while I leaned toward the very simple judgment that it was better to give a hundred sous to a criminal than risk turning away an honest man. But the exploitative network grew larger with such rapidity and in such proportion that I was forced to regret giving to some, because I had to refuse others. Then I noticed contradictions and lies in the pathetic stories they were telling. There was a time when, not in the least embarrassed, all of these hangdog faces came the same day of the week. I tried to refuse the first; the second came and insisted. I held my ground; the third did not come. I saw then that it was an organized band. I should have notified the police; I was reluctant to do so, not convinced of the facts.

But other beggars arrived, perhaps from another band, perhaps a rear guard of the first. I gathered the courage which I had not been able to do before, for fear of humiliating someone in despair, and asked for proof. A few unskilled beggars suddenly disappeared in the face of my suspicion, naïvely letting me see that it was founded. Others pretended to be insulted; others furnished me with the apparent means of verifying their impoverishment. They gave their names and addresses; they were false names, false addresses. I went to hideous hovels. I saw children wasted away by hunger, covered with sores, and when I brought help, I discovered, one fine day, that these hovels and these children had been rented, that these ragged, sick beggars did not belong to the woman so bitterly weeping before me, who sent them packing with great swipes of her broom as soon as I had gone.

Once, I sent a note to an unhappy poet who was to have been found asphyxiated, like Escousse, if by such and such an hour he did not have my answer. They knocked in vain; he pretended to be dead. They broke down the door; they found him eating sausages.

Nevertheless, since, in the midst of all this vermin which cling to people of conscience, I did from time to time happen to reach some truly needy individuals, I could never resolve entirely to reject the beggars. For several years I paid a small fee to several people to have them make inquiries for me for several hours each morning. They were deceived a little less often than I was, that is all; and since I no longer live in Paris, the ruinous correspondence of hundreds of beggars continues to reach me from all parts of France.

Among these are a number of poets and authors who desire patronage, as if a patron can supply what is lacking not only in their talent, but in the most simple notion of the language they pretend to write. There are a number of misunderstood women who wish to become actresses. They have never tried to act, true, but they feel they have the vocation to play leading roles; a number of unemployed young people ask for the first available job in the arts, or in agriculture, or in accounting—they are apparently good at everything—and even though you do not know them, you must recommend and answer for them as for yourself. The more modest avow they have no education, they are suited for nothing, but that, under penalty of being inhumane, you must find them something to do. There are also a number of democratic workers who have resolved the "social problem" and who will make poverty disappear in our society, if you give them the funds to publish their system. These are infallible. Whoever doubts them has sold out to pride, greed, or egotism. There are, in addition, a number of bankrupt small-businessmen who need five or six thousand to start up again in a little boutique. "A mere pittance!" they say. "You're good, you will not refuse me." Finally, there are painters, musicians, who have had no success because they have too much genius, and jealous teachers have rejected them; there are soldiers who have enlisted and who wish to buy back their freedom; Jews who ask for autographs in order to sell them; young ladies who wish to come to my house as servants, in order to become my students in literature. I have at home a chest full of absurd letters, of social theories to save all the inhabitants of the planet—all with a postscript asking for a little help in the meantime, and in duplicate and triplicate, adding an insult at the second request and a threat at the third.

Nonetheless, I have the patience to read all these letters, if they are not impossible to decipher, or when they do not contain sixteen pages of microscopic characters. My conscience is such that I begin each of the philosophical, musical, or literary lucubrations, and continue to read unless I am revolted at the start by errors that are too gross, or aberrations that are too revolting.

When I see a shadow of a talent, I set the letter aside and answer it. When I see a great deal, I give myself to it entirely. The latter do not require any great effort from me. But honest mediocrity is still abundant enough to absorb a good deal of my time and cause me a good deal of fatigue. Real talent never asks anything; it offers and gives a pure proof of sympathy. Honest mediocrity does not ask for money, preferring compliments in the form of encouragement. Downright mediocrity, a degree lower, begins by asking for publishers or newspaper assignments. Stupidity asks—nay imperiously demands —money and fame.

Add to such persecution anonymous letters full of vile insults; the efforts, often just as brazen, of saints—male and female—who wish to have me return to the bosom of the church; priests who offer to buy back my soul, if I send them the wherewithal to restore a chapel, or raise a statue to the Virgin. Strange visitors: the Trappists; the teachers discharged in 1848; the willing stool pigeons, a species of imbecilic instigator who comes to declaim against all governments and gets confused, pretending to favor legitimism in republican houses and vice versa; the bohemian artists; the Spanish refugee colonels and captains, from every faction successively quelled, in that country of vicissitudes; superior officers by the dozens, bedecked with ribbons, who ask for twenty francs and retreat with twenty sous: in a word, poverty either false or true, humble or arrogant; vanity of the confident or spiteful variety; the sputtering rage of fanatics; indiscretion, folly, vulgarity or stupidity in all its forms—that is the canker that sets upon all celebrity, that upsets, troubles, fatigues, ruins, and finally, kills, unless you adopt this fierce principle: "Every misery is merited," unless you write on your door: "I give nothing," and unless you sleep soundly, telling yourself, "I have been exploited by rogues; so much the worse, from now on, for the hungry ones who are honest."

And I still have not mentioned the merely curious, a very mixed group among which you risk turning your back on some truly sympathetic individuals in order to be rid of the crowd of idlers who importune you. In this latter category there are traveling Englishmen who simply want to be able to jot down in their notebooks that they have seen you; and as I have forgotten too much of my English to make the effort to speak with them, those who do not know three words of French speak to me in their language, and I answer them in mine. They don't understand; they say "Oh!" and leave satisfied. As I know that some of them have a pencil all sharpened to write down my answers even before having climbed back into their carriages, for fear of forgetting them, I sometimes amuse myself by answering with an "Oh!" in return, or when their faces bore me, by telling them such unintelligible things that I defy them to retain any of it. It is true that there also exist the too-intelligent busybodies, who speak for you, putting their words in your mouth.

The malevolent busybodies are another kind, who come intending to shrive you, and leave as your enemy when they have not been able to pry out anything more than a few trivial remarks about the weather. There are also the poseurs, who come to let you know that they think you're worthy and that you've no time to lose to put your feeble talents into their more experienced hands and greater minds. They give you subjects for novels, characters, theatrical plots. In brief, they are the prodigiously rich who feel benevolence for you, and charitably come to give you ideas.

You cannot imagine the eccentricity, impropriety, ridiculousness, vanity, madness, and stupidity of all the types who pass in review before the unfortunate artist afflicted with some little renown. These frenzied demands have only one good result, which is to inspire a lively interest and joyous concern for the modest and authentic talent that does reveal itself to you. You are in a hurry, then, to give to it the good will which so many false and pretentious suitors have forced you to suppress.

So, hardly had I arrived at the goal I had sought than a double deception appeared. The independence I thought I had found in two forms—use of time and use of resources—was transformed into irritating and continual bondage. Seeing how far my labor was from being able to take care of the needs of the poverty around me, I doubled, I tripled, I quadrupled the dosage of work. There were moments when it was excessive, when I reproached myself for my needed hours of repose and distraction as a weakness of character, an egotistical satisfaction. By nature an extremist in my convictions, I was governed for a long time by this law of enforced labor and limitless charity, as I had once been by the idea of Catholicism, when I forbade myself the games and pleasures of adolescence to devote myself to prayer and contemplation.

It was only by opening my mind to the dream of great social reform that I eventually consoled myself for the narrowness and powerlessness of my devotion. As so many others, I had told myself that certain social bases were indestructible, and that the only cure for the abuses of inequality was in individual, voluntary sacrifice. But this theory of private charity opens the door to selfishness as well as devotion. You can walk through wholeheartedly, or just pretend to. No one is there to say whether you are in or out. There is certainly a religious law which prescribes that you give, not only your superfluity, but even to the point of need yourself. There is surely a viewpoint which counsels charity, but there is no power constituted to constrain you to give, or to control the extent and affirm the reality of your gifts.[2] You are therefore free to cheat, to be an atheist before God, a hypocrite before man. Poverty is at the mercy of the conscience of each individual; and while some courageous, sincere individuals make excessive sacrifices, other cold, calculating individuals abstain from supporting them, and let them carry an impossible burden.

Yes, impossible! because if it were otherwise, if a handful of good people could save the world and suffice, by their work and limitless abnegation, to destroy poverty and all the vices it engenders, those should consider themselves lucky and proud of their mission, and the hope of success would draw a greater number to the glory and joy of sacrifice. But this abyss of poverty is not among those the gods consent to close after swallowing some sacrifice. It is bottomless, and it would be necessary for all of society to hurl their offerings into it, in order to fill it for an instant. In the present state of affairs, it even seems that partial help only digs it deeper and wider, because charity degrades, condemning those who count on it to abandon themselves.

We have taken away from the clergy, from religious communities, the immense wealth they possessed; we tried by a great social revolution to create a caste of active, hard-working owners of small properties in place of a caste of inert and dangerous beggars. Thus, charity did not save society even when widely practiced by a sizable and constituted body; thus, the wealth dedicated to charity was far from sufficient, since this wealth—mobilized and distributed under another form—has left the abyss gaping and misery multiplying. And you see that in using this example, I am assuming that everything was for the best—that the clergy and the convents only used their wealth for the purpose of giving charity, and that the sale of the nationalized properties only enriched the poor. We know that was not strictly true.

Yes, yes, alas! charity is powerless, alms useless. It has happened, it will happen again, that violent crises will force dictatorial action, whether popular or monarchical, to cut into the heart of the problem and compel considerable sacrifice from the wealthy classes. Equality will be momentarily right in the minds of men, never absolutely, unless a new principle develops to permanently consecrate it in the free belief of every man.

Governments, whatever they are, can hardly do more. Do not be too harsh on them. Suppose they wished, at any price, to inaugurate the principle of universal well-being, under one form or another. They would wish it in vain. The resistance of the masses would always break the will of individuals, however ardent, however miraculous it might be. Every government by decree is a dream, unless it be that of time.

Meanwhile, what should we of good intention do? Sacrifice ourselves or refrain?

I have gone over this problem a thousand times and not resolved it. The law of Christ—sell everything, give your money to the poor, and follow me —is prohibited, today, by human laws. I do not have the right to sell my goods and give them to the poor. Even if specific property laws did not constrain me, the moral law of inheritance—which includes that of education, dignity and independence—places an absolute constraint on us, under penalty of an infraction of duty towards our family. We are not free to impose a baptism of poverty on the children to whom we have given life. They are no more our property morally than serfs were the legal property of a lord. Poverty is degrading, there is no denying it, because where it is total, you can only suffer humiliation, and because, in such a case, you can only escape it by dying. No one can thus legitimately throw her children into the abyss in order to pull out others. If we are all children in the eyes of God, we are especially obliged to those He gave us. Therefore, everything that binds the future liberty of a child is an act of tyranny, even if also an act of godliness and virtue.

If some day in the future, society demands of us the sacrifice of our inheritance, without a doubt it will provide for the existence of our children; it will make them honest and free in the bosom of a world where work will constitute the right to life. Society can only legitimately take from each by giving to all. While waiting for the reign of this idea, which is still a utopia; compelled to flounder between the bonds of family, which are still sacred, and the terrible difficulties of earning a living; forced to abide by constituted laws, that is to say, to respect the property of others and to make our own respected, or else end up in prison or in the hospital— what is then the duty of those who perceive, in good faith, the abyss of suffering and despair?

This is an insoluble problem, if one is not resigned to living at the heart of a flagrant contradiction, between the principles of the future and the necessities of the present. Those who cry out to us that we must preach by example, must possess nothing, and must live as did the primitive Christians seem to be right. However, in ironically prescribing that we give everything, and live on alms, they are not logical either, because they engage us to consecrate, by our example, the principle of poverty which we reject in our social theories.

Some socialists approach the question more frankly; indeed I know some who have told me, "Don't give alms. By giving to those who beg, you consecrate the principle of their servitude."

Well, those very individuals who spoke to me thus in a moment of passionate conviction, a moment later gave alms themselves, overwhelmed by the pity that surges up from our innards, and which surpasses reason. And as by giving alms we are still more humane and useful than by reducing ourselves to the necessity of requiring them, I think they are right to violate their own logic and resign themselves, as I do, to not being at peace with themselves.

The truth remains nonetheless absolute, in the sense that we cannot, or must not, acknowledge as just the laws which today govern property. I do not think they can be wiped out in any durable or useful way by a sudden and violent overthrow. We have seen well enough that the redistribution of wealth would entail a terrible struggle, with no solution, unless it be the establishment of a new class of large property owners devouring the small ones, or a stalemate among those utterly selfish barbarians.

My reason can only admit to a series of successive changes leading men, without constraint and through a demonstration of their own best interests, to a general solidarity whose absolute form is as yet difficult to define. During the course of these progressive transformations, there will still be contradictions between the goal to be pursued and the needs of the moment. All the socialist schools of recent times have glimpsed the truth and have even seized on some essential facet, but none has been able wisely to trace the code of laws which must result from this collective effort at some point in history. It is very simple: man can only propose; history disposes. Someone who thinks himself the most advanced wise man of his century will suddenly be thwarted by events and situations wrapped mysteriously in the designs of Providence, just as certain obstacles which seem minor to the most prudent will resist human efforts for a long time.

For my part, I did not have entire freedom of choice in my personal conduct as regards the use of the wealth which fell to me. Placed by contract under the dotal system, which is a sort of substitute for ownership, I had to consider Nohant as a small entailed property of which I was only the trustee, and I could not have eluded this law except by being a faithless trustee to my children. I made it a matter of conscience to transmit intact to them this small inheritance which I had received for them, and I believe I reconciled, as far as possible, the ethic of the family and the ethic of humanity in giving to the poor only the revenue from my work. I do not know if I was wrong. I thought I was right. I am sure I have abstained many years from every personal satisfaction, that I spent nothing on vanity, luxury, indolence, greed—passions which I did not have and thus could not satisfy. Slender merit certainly! The only sacrifice that may have cost me a little was to renounce travel, which I would passionately have loved and which might have developed me as an artist, but from which I had to abstain, at least to meet the needs of others. To renounce staying in Paris was also personally harmful to me in many respects; but I believed I ought not hesitate to make this sacrifice, which brought its reward, because my love for the country and life among intimates compensated me for my social isolation.

Thus, I did nothing heroic, and in reality I saw that nothing heroic could be done without at some point dishonoring my conscience. To thrust my children, in spite of themselves, into the fanaticism of ardent convictions seemed to me an affront to their moral liberty. I thought I had to tell them my beliefs and allow them to decide whether to share or reject them. I thought that, foreseeing future crises, I had to work to lessen in them a blind and dangerous confidence which inheritance inspires in the young, and to preach the necessity of work. I thought I had to make my son an artist, not raise him to be only a landlord, and yet not force him to be only an artist by depriving him of his property. I thought I had to fulfill with scrupulous fidelity all the obligations which, under penalty of dishonor and breaking one's word, contracts involving money impose on us all. As for money, I did not know how to make it at any cost, or how to make a lot of it even while working with sustained industry. I knew how to part with it, consequently having to refuse some who asked, rather than strictly exacting it from those who owed me, and whom I might have reduced to penury. Monetary relations are constituted in such a way that assistance to some can mean, if one is not careful, a cruel denial to others. How can one do better? I do not know. If I knew, I would have done it, because my intention was very sincere. But I do not see how. I have never found the means to render my social dedication beneficial to my fellows to any great degree, and I cannot attribute this inability to insufficient resources. Even if they were considerably larger, the number of unfortunates in my charge would only have increased, and millions of louis from my hands would have drawn millions of poor about me. Where would have been the limit? If the Rothschilds gave their fortune to the poor, would they wipe out poverty? We know very well they would not. So, individual charity is not the remedy. It is not even a palliative. It is nothing other than a need our conscience imposes, an emotion which is manifested and never satisfied.

Therefore, I have reasons drawn from experience, reasons forged in my very entrails, not to accept the social condition as being good and durable, and to protest against this condition until my last hour. It has been said that I have adopted this spirit of revolt through pride. What does my pride have to do with all this? At first, I accepted the established order without thought and without battle. I practiced charity, and I practiced it for a long time with a good deal of discretion, innocently believing that it was a virtue one should keep hidden. I followed the Gospel to the letter: "Let not the left hand know what the right hand gives." Alas, seeing the extent and the horror of poverty, I recognized that pity was so pressing an obligation there was no particular merit in feeling its pangs and that, moreover, in a society so opposed to Christ's laws, to maintain silence about such afflictions could only be weakness and hypocrisy.

Those are the certainties to which the beginning of my life as an artist led me, and it was only the beginning. But hardly had I confronted this problem of general poverty in our society than fear to the point of dizziness took hold of me. I had done a good deal of thinking; I had felt a good deal of sorrow in my solitude in Nohant, but I had been absorbed and somewhat numbed by my personal preoccupations. I had probably given in to the taste of the century, which was then to bury oneself in egotistical suffering, imagine oneself a René or an Obermann,[5] and attribute to oneself extrordinary sensitivity, consequently suffering in ways unknown to the common herd. The milieu in which I had isolated myself was made to persuade me that not everyone thought or suffered as I did, since I saw about me only those preoccupied with material interests, sunk forthwith in satisfying these interests.

When my horizon was enlarged, when all the sadness, all the need, the despair, the vice of the great social scene appeared to me; when my reflections did not anymore have as their object my own destiny, but that of the whole world, of which I was only an atom, my personal despair reached out to all beings, and the law of fate rose up before me so terrifyingly that my reason was disturbed.

Picture a person having attained the age of thirty without having opened her eyes to reality, gifted, nonetheless, with very good eyes to see everything —an austere and serious person to the depths of her soul, who let herself be rocked to sleep for such a long time by poetical dreams, by an enthusiastic faith in divine things, by the illusion of an absolute rejection of all interest in the collective life—who, suddenly struck by the strange spectacle of this collective life, embraces and penetrates it with all the lucidity that the strength of pure youth and clear conscience can give.

And I opened my eyes at a solemn moment in history. The republic dreamed of in July had ended in the massacres of Varsovie and the holocaust of Saint- Merry's cloister. Cholera had just decimated the world. Saint Simonism, which had captured my imagination for a moment, was felled by persecution, and aborted without having once and for all settled the great question of love and, in my opinion, having even sullied it a little. Art too had, by deplorable aberrations, soiled the cradle of its romantic reform. The times were prone to fear and irony, dismay and impudence—some lamenting the ruin of their unstinted illusions, others laughing on the first rungs of a tainted victory; no one believed in anything anymore—some through discouragement, others through atheism.

Nothing in my former beliefs regarding the social order was so neatly formulated as to help me struggle against this cataclysm with which the materialistic era began, and I did not find in republican or socialist ideas of the moment sufficient light to fight the darkness to which Mammon was giving vent over the world. Thus I remained alone with my dream of an all- powerful, but no longer loving, Divinity, because He was abandoning the human race to its own perversity or madness.

Afflicted by this profound despondency, I wrote *Lélia* in fits and starts and without any aim of making it a book or publishing it. However, when I had tied a large number of separate fragments haphazardly together in the form of a novel, I read them to Sainte-Beuve, who encouraged me to continue and who advised Buloz to ask me for a chapter for publication in *Le Revue des Deux Mondes*. In spite of the foregoing, I still had not decided to turn this fantasy into a book for public consumption. It was too dreamlike, too much of the "school of Corambé" to be enjoyed by many readers. I was, therefore, in no rush, and I deliberately refrained from any consideration of the public, feeling a kind of sad relief in abandoning myself to the randomness of my reveries, even isolating myself from the real world, to trace the synthesis of doubt and suffering as it presented itself to me in one form or another.

This manuscript dragged along for a year, often abandoned with scorn and picked up again with ardor. It is, I believe, a book less usual from the artistic point of view, hence more esteemed by artists as a particular example of spontaneous inspiration. I wrote two prefaces to the book, where I said everything I had to say about it. Therefore, there is no need to repeat myself. The form of narration was a great success. The substance was extremely bitterly criticized. Readers insisted on seeing real people in all the characters, personal revelations in all the situations; they went so far as to viciously and obscenely interpret passages written with the greatest candor, and I remember that, in order to understand what they accused me of having said, I was forced to have things explained to me of which I was ignorant.

I was somewhat impervious to this barrage of criticism and the wretched slurs that followed. What one knows to be entirely false is hardly troublesome. One has the feeling that eventually it will work out as it should among well-disposed people, allowing for disagreement about the intention and tendencies of a book.

I was only astonished, and still am, at how ideas can arouse personal enmity. I have never understood how artists who think and create in opposing ways could be enemies. That one may debate and combat the aims of a work I concede, but to deliberately misinterpret its thoughts in order to render it blameworthy; to distort the text by false citations or unfaithful accounts; to slander the life of an author in order to do him harm; to hate the person through the book—such behavior is one of life's enigmas which I have not resolved and probably never will. I recognize the phenomenon; I perceive it in every age and as regards every idea, but I am astonished that the horror of the inquisition, widely experienced today, has not sufficed to cure mankind of this rage for mutual persecution, where it sometimes seems that the critic is sorry not to have at his disposal the hangman on his right and the butcher on his left, while proceeding with his judgments.

I viewed these outbursts of rage with sadness, yet with a certain tranquility. Not for nothing had my solitude bestowed on me a great disdain for all that was not truthful. If I had loved and sought society, I would probably have been tormented by the slanders that could momentarily make it inaccessible to me; but seeking only serious friendship, and knowing that nothing could influence those close to me, I never really felt the effects of the malice, and my task in this regard was so easy that I never included that persecution among the misfortunes of my life.

Moreover and in any case, those troubles that only affected my own personal existence, today, I count for nothing. Not that I have borne them courageously. No, I was and perhaps still am excessively sensitive, and one in whom, in moments of crisis, reason does not govern at all. But I value moral agonies as I believe reason must value them, once it has regained the ascendancy. I see in my past, as I see in the pasts of all those loving beings whom I have known, terrible heartbreaks, overwhelming disappointments, hours of real anguish; but I attribute it to personality, the nature of which is to be violent in youth. To youth belongs the wish to seize and fix the dream of happiness. If it easily renounced that; if it did not eagerly pursue it; if, the day after a catastrophe, it did not rise up from despair with a new assurance; if it did not live with dreams, ardent beliefs, enthusiastic devotions, bitter disdain, hot indignation—in a word, with all the defeats and renewals of the will—it would not be youth, and this drive to discover the world of its imagination and the ideal of its heart, through the imminence of disaster, is almost a right youth exercises, as well as a law to which it submits.

But all that, seen from a distance, recedes into the world of vanished dreams. None of us ever regrets being delivered from those torments, just as none of us regrets having felt them. All of us know we must live when we have the strength of our emotions, because we must have lived when we are in the age of reflection. We should only regret those trials in life that have wreaked a real and permanent damage.

What sort of damage? I shall tell you. Every pain, be it slow or rapid, that saps our strength and leaves us diminished is a true misfortune for which it is not easy for us ever to console ourselves. A vice, a moral crime, a meanness —these are among the misfortunes that make us suddenly old, and that merit the pity we may have toward ourselves and ask of others. There are, in the moral order, sicknesses analogous to those in the physical order, in that they leave us infirm and forever broken.

Is your body free from infirmities contracted before old age? However full of suffering you may be, do not complain; you are as well off as a human being can hope to be. So it is with your soul. Do you feel in possession of your faculties for the exercise of the true and the just? Whatever the passing crises of discouragement or passion, do not fault your destiny for having tried you too rudely; you, too, are as happy as mankind may hope to be.

This philosophy seems very easy to me, now. To let oneself suffer because suffering is inevitable, and not to curse it when it has gone, because it has not rendered us worse—all honest souls can practice this humble wisdom to their benefit.

But there is a pain which is more difficult to bear than all those that strike us individually. It has taken such a large place in my thoughts, it has held such sway over my life—to the point of poisoning my phases of purely personal happiness—that I must relate it, too.

This pain is the malady at large—the suffering of the entire race; it is the sight, the knowledge, the contemplation of human destiny here below. One tires very quickly of contemplating oneself. We small beings are quickly exhausted, and each of our personal stories is quickly reviewed in our own memory. Unless you believe yourself sublime, can you only examine and contemplate yourself? Besides, who really in good faith thinks himself sublime?

The poor madman who thinks he is the sun, and who from his gloomy cell cries out to passers-by, "Beware the brightness of my beams!"

We only succeed in understanding ourselves and in feeling truly ourselves when we forget ourselves, so to speak, and lose ourselves in the great consciousness of humanity. It is then that, along with certain joys and honors whose reflection enlarges and transfigures us, we are suddenly seized with unshakable dread and stinging remorse at the evil, crime, madness, injustice, stupidity, and shame of this nation which covers the globe and calls itself human. No pride, no egotism can console when that idea absorbs us.

In vain you will say to yourself, "I'm a reasonable person among these millions who aren't. I don't suffer from the ills toward which their stupidity draws them." Alas! you will not be any the prouder, because you cannot make your brothers as brotherly as yourself. Your isolation will frighten you the more you believe yourself better and feel yourself happier than the others.

Even your innocence, the knowledge of your sweetness and your probity, the serenity of your own heart will not be a refuge from the profound sadness which envelops you, if you feel that you live in an impure milieu, on a sullied earth, among beings without faith or law, who devour one another and for whom vice is far more contagious than virtue.

You have a happy family, I suppose, excellent friends, an entourage of souls as good as your own. You have succeeded in escaping the contact of sick humanity. Alas, poor man, you are all the more alone!

You are sweet, generous, sensitive; you cannot read history without shivering at every page, and the destiny of innumerable victims whom time devours wrings sainted tears from your eyes: alas, poor heart, what good are these piteous tears! They dampen the page you are reading and will not bring back a single soul sacrificed.

You are devoted, active, ardent; you speak, write, act with all your strength on minds who are willing to listen. They throw stones and mud on you. So what! you're courageous, you persevere. Alas, martyr! you will die a painful death, and your last prayer will still be for those whom others cause to suffer.

Very well, it is not necessary to be a saint to sympathize, thus, with the lives of others and feel that the malady at large can poison and destroy your happiness. Everyone, yes, everyone feels this pain in common, and those who seem the least preoccupied with it are still preoccupied enough to fear the repercussions on the fragile edifice of their security. This preoccupation grows day by day, hour by hour as the world is enlightened, communicates its life, and feels itself vibrate from one end to the other like a chain. Let two people meet, three men gather together, and from an initial discussion of individual interests, they quickly move to larger interests over which to question, answer, and impassion themselves. Even the peasant, supposedly disinterested and disdainful of everything beyond his acre, today wants to know if, on the other side of the hill, human beings aren't more tranquil and satisfied than he is.

It is a law of life. But of all life's laws, it is the cruelest, and when it becomes a law of conscience, it is the tormenting duty of all who confront the powerlessness of each.

This is not a political recrimination. Politics of the moment, however interesting it may be, is never anything more than a horizon. The cloud of pain that hangs over the world and the cry of suffering which is exhaled from it issue from the innermost convulsions of its very being, and no possible revolution would be able to stifle or destroy the deepest causes of those convulsions. When one is fully sunk in this pursuit, one eventually succeeds in confirming the operation of good and evil in humanity, of grasping the mechanics of its actions and reactions, of knowing finally how this eternal battle works. Nothing more. Why it works, only God would be able to tell us—He who has made human beings so slowly progressive, who could have made them more intelligent and powerful in behalf of good rather than evil.

Before this question that the soul may address to His supreme wisdom, I admit that the terrible silence of the Divinity confounds understanding. There, we feel our will break against the iron door of impenetrable mysteries, because we cannot admit of the Sovereign Good, all light and perfection, answering a supplicating, groaning humanity by a blatant rule of His own convenience.

To become an atheist and suppose an unintelligent law ruling the fortunes of the universe is to admit something far more extraordinary and unbelievable than to avow oneself of limited reason surpassed by the motives of infinite reason. Faith thus triumphs over its own doubts, but the wounded soul feels the limits of its power shrink narrowly back on itself, and secure its devotion in such a little space that pride forever flees and sorrow remains.

Those were the preoccupations under whose aegis I had written *Lélia*. I did not speak to anyone about them, knowing that no one in my circle could answer me, and in a certain way, too, perhaps I cherished the secrecy of my reverie. I had and have always been thus, liking to feed alone on an idea slowly digested, however gnawing and devouring it might be. The only egotism I permit is that of silent discouragement, which—perhaps through an inner grace—ends by yielding to the necessity of living, finally exhausted in contemplating its own causes.

It is true that, by keeping so silent with my friends, the lament I gave out in publishing my book must have had greater reverberations. I did not think of that at first. Not considering myself and my own pain of much account, I told myself that my book would be read by few and would be likely to cause laughter at my expense, as a collection of fantasies; that it would not cause anyone to ponder the hard problems of doubt and belief. When I saw that it caused other troubled souls to sigh, I persuaded myself, and I still persuade myself that the effect of this kind of book is more beneficial than harmful, and that in this materialistic century such books are more valuable than *Contes drolatiques*, even though they are much less entertaining to most readers.

Apropos of *Contes drolatiques*, which Balzac published about this time, I had a fairly lively argument with him, and as he wished to read me several passages against my will, I practically threw the book in his face. I recall that, while I treated him like a vulgar lout, he treated me like a prude, and he left, hurling from the stairs: "You're a damn fool!" But all that only made us better friends. Balzac was thoroughly innocent and kind.

After several days spent in the forest of Fontainebleau, I had a longing to see Italy, which I hungered for as every artist does, but which pleased me in a way contrary to what I expected.[6] I quickly tired of seeing pictures and monuments. The cold made me feverish, then the heat prostrated me, and the beautiful sky ended by boring me. But I found solitude in a corner of Venice, that would have held me there a long time had I had my children with me. I shall not repeat here, rest assured, any of the descriptions which I published either in *Lettres d'un Voyageur* or in any of the novels I set in Italy and particularly in Venice. I shall only give a few details that have their natural place in this recital. *H.L.*

III

Monsieur Beyle (Stendhal). —The cathedral at Avignon. —Trip to Genoa, Pisa, and Florence. —Arrival in Venice by way of the Apennines, Bologna, and Ferrara. —Alfred de Musset, Géraldy, Léopold Robert in Venice. —Financial distress. —Pretty picture of an Austrian officer. —Catullus the Elder. —Dilemma. —Punchinello. —A strange encounter. —Departure for France. —Carlone. —Bandits. —Antonino. —Meeting with three Englishmen. —Theater in Venice. —La Pasta, Mercadante, Zacometto. —Standards of equality in Venice. —Arrival in Paris. —Return to Nohant. —Julie. —My friends from Berry. —The ones from the garret. —Prosper Bressant. —*Le Prince*.

On the steamship that was taking me from Lyon to Avignon, I encountered one of the most remarkable writers of the age, Beyle, whose pen name was Stendhal.[7] He was the consul at Civitavecchia, returning to his post after a short stay in Paris. He had a brilliant wit, and his conversation recalled that if Delatouche, though less delicate and graceful, but more profound. At first glance, he also looked somewhat like the same man: fat, with a very fine physiognomy under a mask of flesh. But on occasion, a sudden melancholy would beautify Delatouche, while Beyle remained mocking and satirical no matter when you looked at him. I chatted with him for part of the day and found him very likable. He made fun of my illusions about Italy, assuring me that I would soon be sick of it and that artists in search of beauty in that country were yokels. I could scarcely believe him, seeing that he was tired of his exile, and returning to it only unwillingly. He made great fun of the typical Italian, whom he could not bear and to whom he was most unjust. He especially warned me of a deprivation I was never to experience, the lack of satisfying talk and everything else that he thought comprised intellectual life—books, newspapers, matters of current interest. I indeed understood what such a charming, original, and mannered wit must miss so far from relationships that could appreciate and stimulate him. He struck, above all, a pose of disdain for all vanity, and sought out in every interlocutor some sort of pretentiousness to tear down, under the rapid fire of his ridicule. But I do not believe he was bad; he took too much trouble to appear that way.

All his warnings about boredom and the intellectual vacuum in Italy tempted rather than alarmed me, since I was going there, as everywhere, to escape the wittiness he believed I craved.

We ate dinner with a few other choice travelers,[8] in a bad village inn, the ship's pilot not daring to clear the Saint-Esprit bridge before daybreak. Stendhal was madly gay, got rather drunk, and dancing around the table with his huge furry boots, became somewhat grotesque—not a very pretty sight.

At Avignon, he took us to see the grand, beautifully situated church where, in a corner, an old Christ figure painted on wood, large as life and truly hideous, provided a topic for his most unbelievable ranting. He detested those repulsive images whose—for him—barbarous ugliness and brazen nudity the Mediterraneans cherished. He had the urge to attack the figure with his fist.

I, for one, was not altogether sad to see Beyle take the longer land route to Genoa. He was afraid of the sea, and my intention was to arrive quickly in Rome. We thus took leave of each other after a few days of a lively attachment, but as the nature of his wit betrayed a habitual taste or fancy for the obscene, I must admit I had had enough of him, and if he had taken the sea route, I would probably have gone via the mountains. He was, moreover, an eminent man, whose wisdom showed more wit than justice in all that was to his liking; a true and original talent; an awkward writer whose story-telling, neverthless, captured his readers and held them fast.

I came down with a fever in Genoa that I attributed to the sharp cold of the Rhône trip, but that really had nothing to do with it; later on, I came down with it again in Genoa during good weather, with no other cause than the Italian air, which was hard for me to get used to.

I continued my trip anyway, not exactly ill, but gradually so worn out by tremors, weakness, and drowsiness that I saw Pisa and Camposanto with great apathy. I even became indifferent to choosing one direction or another: Rome or Venice were determined by heads or tails. Venice came up heads ten times. I decided to call this fate, and left for Venice via Florence. A new attack of fever in Florence. I saw all the fine things one had to see, but I saw them through a kind of dream that made them seem slightly strange. The weather was perfect, but I felt icy, and while looking at Cellini's *Perseus* and Michelangelo's square chapel, it seemed, at times, I was a statue myself. At night, I would dream I was turning into a mosaic, and I carefully counted my little squares of lapis lazuli and jasper.

I crossed the Apennines during a cold and clear January night in a rather comfortable open carriage that, accompanied by mounted police in canary-yellow uniforms, served as a postal vehicle. I have never seen a more deserted route and less useful police, for they were always one full league ahead of or behind us, and scarcely seemed to care about serving as a target for bandits. But despite the concerns of the courier, we had no other encounter except that with a small volcano, which I took for a roadside lantern and which the driver grandiloquently referred to as *il monte fuoco* [the fire mountain].

I could not see anything in Ferrara or Bologna, I was so debilitated. I revived a bit during the crossing of the Po, whose course through vast and sandy plains is characterized by sadness and desolation. Then, I fell back to sleep until Venice, hardly surprised to feel myself gliding in a gondola and watching, as though a mirage, the lights of San Marco square reflected in the water, and the great cut-out forms of Byzantine architecture silhouetted against the immense moon, itself more fantastic at this moment of rising than at any other.

Venice was indeed the city of my dreams; all I had imagined was still less than how it actually appeared to me, mornings as well as evenings, in calm, sunny days as well as in the somber reflected light of storms. I loved this city for itself—the only one in the world I could have loved this way, since a city has always had the effect on me of a prison, tolerable only because of my companions in captivity. In Venice, one could be alone for long periods, and one came to understand how, in the time of its splendor and freedom, its children had virtually personified and cherished it, not as a thing, but as a living being.

A great malaise and terrible headaches of a kind I had never known followed my fever and, from that time on, have settled in my skull in the form of frequent, unbearable migraines. I was planning to stay in this city only a few days, and in Italy only a few weeks, but unexpected events kept me longer.

Alfred de Musset suffered worse than I from the effects of the Venetian air, which strikes many foreigners, something that people should be made more aware of.[3] He caught a very grave illness—typhoid fever—that nearly killed him. Though also very ill, I gained unexpected strength to care for him, not only from my feeling of respect for his great genius, but also from the appeal his character held for me in the endless moral sufferings induced in his poetic nature by the conflict between his feelings and his imagination. I spent seventeen days at his bedside, with no more than one hour of rest each day.[9] His convalescence lasted almost as long again, and when he left, I remember the fatigue produced a strange effect on me. I had accompanied him in the late morning to Mestre by gondola, and I was returning to my place via the small canals in the interior of the city. All those narrow canals, which serve as streets, are crossed by small single-arch bridges for pedestrians. My vision had been so weakened by the vigils, I saw everything upside down and, in particular, those strings of bridges, which rose before me like inverted arches.

But spring was coming, the springtime of northern Italy, perhaps the most beautiful in the world. Long walks in the Tyrolian Alps and then in the Venetian archipelago, strewn with charming islets, soon restored me to writing condition, and not a moment too soon, since my finances were depleted and I lacked the wherewithal to return to Paris. I took a tiny lodging in a more than modest location in the interior of the city. There, alone all afternoon, going out only in the evening for some air, working again at night to the singing of some tame nightingales, which live in all the balconies of Venice, I wrote *André* [1835], *Jacques* [1834], *Mattéa* [1835] and the first of the *Lettres d'un Voyageur* [1834].

I sent various parcels to Buloz, which ought quickly to have let me pay my expenses up to date (for I had been living on credit), and return to my children, whose absence tugged more sharply at my heart each passing day. But especially bad luck plagued me in Venice; the money did not come. Weeks passed, and each day my existence became more problematic. It is true you can really live cheaply in this city, if you are willing to restrict yourself to eating sardines and shellfish—sound nourishment, in any case, that the extreme heat renders more than sufficient for the weakened appetite. But you cannot do without coffee. Foreigners get sick mainly because they are afraid of a diet that requires drinking black coffee at least six times a day. Harmless to the nerves and indispensable as a tonic as long as you live in the debilitating atmosphere of the lagoons, this stimulant is again too strong as soon as you set foot on firm ground.

Thus, coffee was a costly commodity my consumption of which had to be regulated. Lamp oil for the long night's work was used up very quickly. I still kept a rented gondola, from seven to ten at night, that averaged fifteen francs a month, but it came with a gondolier so old and crippled that I did not dare dismiss him, for fear he would die of hunger. However, it did occur to me that I was dining for six sous in order to have enough to pay him, but that he could afford to get drunk each night.

This poor old Catullus, whom I mentioned in *Lettres d'un Voyageur*, brings to mind an anecdote characteristic of the Austrian occupation of Venice.

One evening on the gondola, which was tied up in a corner of the landing, while waiting for my old barcarolle to run whatever errand I had sent him on, I heard the housing of the gondola getting sprinkled by some passer-by whom I imagined drunk or distracted. The jalousies being closed, I had nothing to fear from this indecent watering, when I heard Catullus' hoarse voice cry, "German pig! Do you think you can befoul my gondola? Do you think it's a milepost?"

"Be advised," the other answered in broken Italian, "that I am an officer in the service of Her Austrian Majesty, and I have the right to piss on your gondola or anywhere I damn please."

"But there's a lady in my gondola!" the gondolier yelled back.

Then the Austrian officer, who was not drunk at all, came to open the door of the cabin and, looking at me, said, "The signora has had the courtesy and wisdom to keep quiet. She has been discreet. Her servant, however, will go to prison tomorrow, and he is damn lucky that I do not run through his body with my sword."

And poor Catullus would have actually been taken to prison had I not defended him by saying he was drunk, and by pretending that the Austrian had showered my gondola with honor.

Such vile harassment could occur on any day, at any time. At the slightest smell of suspect tobacco, the customs employees would enter apartments and rummage in closets and drawers. You were fortunate if they did not pocket a scarf or a pair of stockings at an opportune moment, as I had seen them casually do to my own luggage at customs in Genoa and elsewhere.

Punchinello was then the only revenge of the oppressed population. Under the favored shelter of the Venetian dialect, which the newly-arrived Germans did not understand, he spouted against them the most pleasant abuse; whenever a suspicious foreign face would join the audience, the urchins of the quarter would warn Punchinello with a certain cry to watch his tongue. I saw two Hungarian spies ridiculed for a quarter of an hour without knowing it, accepting clever backhanded compliments, until a third Hungarian arrived, whose smile revealed he understood Venetian.

Moreover, in all the marionnette shows, there was always a stupid character in the role of Tedesco [the German]. His function was to come for an Italian lesson to Punchinello, who was disguised as a language teacher and passed himself off as an academician *della Crusca* [from the Academy of Chaff=the Academy of Discards]. Tedesco would do his utmost to pronounce some words, and murder them, each time receiving a volley of blows from Punchinello's stick, to the laughter and stamping of feet that expressed the frenzied delight of the audience.

This complicity of hatred against the foreigners served, at the very least, to unite the population in a fraternal way, and nowhere else but in Venice did I see such good behavior in public. You could always count on quickly calming down two dockhands ready to do battle by telling them that they were acting like Germans.

Thus, I would have loved all people and things in Venice, were it not for the odious and revolting Austrian occupation. The Venetians are good, likable, witty, and barring their rapport with the Slavs and Jews, who have taken over parts of their commerce, they are as honest as the Turks, who are as loved and esteemed there as they deserve.

But, despite my compassion for this beautiful city and its inhabitants; despite the pleasures of a life geared toward work by the sheer ease of its customs; despite the astonishing discoveries that each random step revealed in the most picturesque assortment of enchanting decoration, splendid retreats, and charming nooks, I was growing impatient and fearful of the all-too-real poverty in which I was going to find myself, as well as the impossibility of leaving, which did not seem near solution. I would write in vain to Paris and would go in vain to the post office; nothing arrived. I had sent volumes; I did not even know whether anyone had received them. It was possible that no one in Venice had ever heard of *Le Revue des Deux Mondes*.

One day, when I had nothing left, literally nothing, and having eaten for less than nothing, I was lounging in my gondola, enjoying the last of my resources since the two weeks were already paid for in advance, thoroughly engrossed in my situation and wondering with real distaste whether I should dare confide it to even a single one of the few people I knew in Venice, the most ridiculous, but clear and persistent, idea struck me that I would find someone that very day, a person from my own country who, knowing my nature and position, would rescue me without my being embarrassed to ask for a loan. With this irrational, but strong, conviction, I opened the jalousie and began to look carefully at all the faces in the gondolas which passed me on the San Marco canal. I saw no one whom I knew, but the idea persisted. I went to the public gardens, looking for groups of strollers, and contrary to my usual custom, paying attention to each face and every voice.

Suddenly, my eyes caught those of a rather fine, respectable-looking man whom I had previously met at the waters of Mont Dore, and who, being associated with my husband, had come to see us often at Nohant. He knew me right away. He ran up to me, very surprised to see me there. I told him my story, and on the spot he readily opened his wallet, assuring me that at the very moment he noticed me he had been caught up in thoughts of Nohant and Berry, puzzled as to why this memory appeared to him so vividly in the midst of other matters unrelated to me or my family.

Whether this was a result of chance or of his fantasy after the fact, on hearing me amusedly tell of my presentiment, I really don't know. I am just stating the facts as they occurred.

I refused to take more than two hundred francs from him. He was going to Russia, and as he was to spend a few days in Vienna, I had good reason to expect to pay him back, with money received from Paris, before he continued his trip, and with which I could also depart for France.

My hopes were fulfilled. Scarcely had he left Venice when a postal employee, who had been ordered to investigate, discovered in an abandoned rack the letters and bank notes from Buloz, forgotten there for about two months either by accident or design, despite all inquiries and entreaties.

I put all my affairs in order at once, packed, and left at the end of August, during a stifling heat wave.

I have always had a horror of public coaches. I preferred to hire a carriage which, traveling for short stages, would enable me to go through the lovely countryside on foot and serve as protection during my stops. My driver was a worthy man who was not afraid of bandits, and for that I hired him at face value; for at that time, one of the chief problems was still to confront the real or imagined terror of the drivers and innkeepers. It was arranged in advance between Carlone and me that our day's distance was fixed, even if we should find—as had already happened to me—bands of frightened peasants shouting at us to turn back. The Austrian police were well-trained, and these panics seemed clearly to be hoaxes. I did not want them to serve as an excuse for extra days on the road. Carlone promised me, grinning, always to forge ahead and thrash any bandits he might encounter.

The nickname Carlone was fitting. That is what the colossal statue of San Carlo Borromeo, standing at the edge of Lake Maggiore, is called. The suffix *one*, we know, expresses size and bulk. Being a Milanese whose height was in proportion to his girth, my guide had acquired his nickname legitimately.

I had always kept in the bottom of my trunk, should the need arise, a pair of linen pants, cap, and blue shirt, in anticipation of a climb through the mountains. I could thus compensate my legs for their disuse during the days and nights of scribbling and the trips by gondola, and I went a long portion of the trip on foot. I saw all the great lakes, of which in my opinion, Lake Garda is the most beautiful; I crossed the Simplon, going in a single day from the torrid heat of the Italian slopes to the glacial cold of the Alpine crests, by evening recovering a spring freshness and coolness in the Valley of the Rhône. I am not writing a travelogue; therefore, I shall only say that this scenery kept me in constant rapture. I had wonderful weather until the crossing of the Tête Noire, between Martigny and Chamonix. There, a superb thunderstorm proffered me the most beautiful spectacle in the world. But as the mule with which they had persuaded me to burden myself wished neither to advance nor retreat, I threw the bridle over his neck and, running easily over grassy hillsides, arrived at

Chamonix before the rain, whose thick clouds came up heavily behind me, reverberating sublimely through the mountains.

I had only two chance meetings during the entire trip. The first was with Antonino, a little hairdresser I had had as a servant in Venice, an excellent fellow whose loyalty and intelligence had inspired me to ask him to accompany Alfred de Musset to Paris. It had been agreed that, if he chose not to keep him, I would keep him on my return. But Antonino had been overcome with homesickness and was returning across the Alps on foot. Meeting thus face to face—I dressed less elegantly than he, but more appropriately—he recognized me in my outfit and stopped short, crying out like a native of his country: "Ah! by the blood of Diana!"

Then, he came up to kiss my hand, a custom of every servant in Italy—even waiters at the inns—and it occurred to me that, for an onlooker, it would have been very strange to see this patched and threadbare gentleman, wearing remnants of gloves and a piece of gold chain, gallantly kissing the hand of a street urchin in overalls, both white with dust from head to foot.

Poor Antonino was in dire straits. Having wanted to leave Paris without being dismissed, he had not the right to claim trip fare, and was returning without a cent to his name, treading on worn-out soles. But ever the hairdresser in his habits, he reeked of pommade for a mile, and ever the Venetian, he preferred to beg rather than not see his beloved city again.

I was amused by his tales of woe, for he spoke real Italian quite purely, in a manner both haughty and diverting, never failing to mention Venice the Beautiful in his patriotic exclamations, and complaining about the ultra-sophisticated race of Parisians.

I gave him something to soften the hardships of his trip and had a great deal of difficulty getting him to accept it, since he did not understand that my costume and my going on foot were only whims, and said to me, "I can see that misfortune has also befallen the signora."

Finally, he accepted, with tears and sensitive gestures that were mannered and spontaneous at the same time.

My second encounter came in two parts. During the crossing of the Simplon, three Englishmen climbed the steep route ahead of me. The first watched me pass without too much puffing and, coming to a halt, called to me with admiration, "This is really a rough one!"

On Mont Blanc, the same three Englishmen were going down a precipitous path as I was climbing up. I recognized the first one who passed, greeting me as though I were an acquaintance, but the one walking behind him merely heaved a sigh and said in a mournful tone, "This is really a rough one!"

Undoubtedly, had I seen the trio a third time, the one who had not yet spoken to me would have said the same thing.

Before turning my back completely on Italy, I would like to say a few words about the theater in Venice, although my shaky finances allowed me to see only a few productions. Mme. Pasta was then singing at the Fenice, with Donzelli—a lesser talent than Rubini, but attractive and charming—who had been duly appreciated in Paris. There was a first performance of *La Fausta*, an

opera by Mercadante, in which Mme. Pasta, playing a role in the genre of Phèdre, was still extremely brilliant. Betrayed by her voice, she would frequently
sing off-key from one end of her role to the other, but the Italian public, more
generous than our own, taking into account the moments when she had truly
excelled as a tragedian and singer, applauded her and called her back with
great emotion. As for the composer's ovation, it was unprecedented, and
Parisian custom cannot give you even the slightest idea of what it was like.
Called back for encores between each act, the maestro was condemned to cross
the stage between curtain and footlights fifteen or twenty times in succession.
Modest, awkward, and childlike, old Mercadante submitted to this sentence
half-laughing, half-trembling, and dragging La Pasta along with him as if to
save face, who, in turn, was smiling for all she was worth.

La Pasta was still beautiful and young on stage. Small, fat, and short-
legged, as are many Italians, her magnificent bust seemed to have been made at
the expense of the rest of her. Nonetheless, she had the means to appear tall
and to move with ease, so much nobility was there in her bearing and so much
skill in her gestures. I was quite disappointed the next day to find her standing
in her gondola, dressed in accordance with the strict economy which had
become her chief concern. That beautiful cameo face which I had seen up close
at Louis XVIII's funeral, fine and soft as velvet, was only a shadow of its former self. Under her old hat and coat you could take her for an usherette. Still,
when she motioned to her gondolier the place where she wanted to land, with
that gesture, the great queen, if not the divinity herself, reappeared.

I also saw at the Fenice a ballet of unbelievable splendor in its decor and
costumes, but of such stupidity as art that even in our most remote provincial
towns, where they advertise on posters that the backdrop is made of gold, no
one would have stood for it. In fact, the gold was dripping from the palaces and
costumes; the result was so extremly foolish and ugly that it seemed clear to
me that, for the present, the Venetians, always so impassioned and enlightened
in their appreciation of art of the past, had deteriorated into barbarism.

However, dramatic art seemed still to have its national expression in burlesque, in a theater where parodies, classical farces, and comedies by Gozzi,
were performed in Venetian. The actor who played Zacometto (the Venetian
version of the Fool) seemed, by his precision and seriouness, to be every bit the
equal of Deburau—indeed even more perfect, as he often played speaking parts
and recited marvelously. I have forgotten his name. The charm of Gozzi's plays,
depicting local popular customs, lay in their gaiety and simplicity. But the theater, although clean and large, was primarily for plebians, and there was no single artist whose talent was worth mentioning among those who took the stage.

I also saw in the public gardens an open-air theater, built like any other
performance hall except that the roof was non-existent, and its absence allowed
the sun to inundate the public and the stage. In broad daylight those painted
sets and made-up actors were the most horrible sight you could imagine. They
played some dramas of Kotzebue, translated into Italian, and here as everywhere a few poor wretches were feelingful and quite eloquent. I think that, in
comedy, there were relatively more who excelled than in our own miserable

traveling shows in the provinces. Italians have, or at least had at that time, a more serious, hence finer and purer, sense of comedy than we do. This is perceptible in the nature of the people, and would pervade its art, if art could be revived in a people under foreign domination.

The principal charm of Venice, as I see it, which I have not found anywhere else, are its egalitarian ways. Though an oligarchy, it had had the wisdom to simulate equality through its sumptuary laws; then, the misfortunes of defeat turned this appearance into reality. Moreover, the setting lends itself perfectly to the dissolution of the classes, in their work and leisure as in their feelings and interests. The lack of carriages and scarceness of land have made for a homogeneous population, who, though jostling one another on the sidewalk or crowding one another in the canals, show concern for the safety of each. All the walking and boating make for heads on a level, where all eyes meet, where all mouths converse; this exchange of idleness and playfulness that forms the basis of life became a sympathetically vibrating line of communication before the cruel insolence of the foreign army. Finally, the beauty of the place, the cheapness and convenience of life, the absence of formality, the proximity of the mountains and of the sea, the wonderful climate (barring one month of winter and two of summer), the cordiality of relationships that my style of living allowed me to limit to a select two or three friends—all this would have kept me in Venice, if my children had been with me. I thought a lot about some day buying one of those old deserted palaces that were selling for ten or twelve thousand francs, in order to return with them to settle in a habitable corner and live on labor and poetry among splendid ruins. I thought about it again when good old Pépé[10] tried to stir up this great city-state to take arms against Austria. But despite his sublime efforts, it again fell under the yoke, and republics are no more.

From Geneva I came straight to Paris, starved to see my children again. I found Maurice grown and almost adjusted to school. He had excellent grades, but my return, which was so great a joy for both of us, was soon bound to bring back his aversion for everything that did not concern the two of us. I returned too soon for the good of his classical education.

His vacation was beginning. We left together for Nohant to rejoin Solange, who had spent my absence there, entrusted to a maid in whose care and watchfulness I had complete confidence, and for whose character I thought I could vouch. This woman seemed to me devoted, and conscientiously performed her duties. I found my big baby clean, blooming, energetic, but so submissive in regard to the maid that it bothered me, considering the child's nature as an enfant terrible. It put me in mind of my own childhood and of Rose who, adoring me, tried to break my spirit. I observed without comment and noticed that switches played a role in this model education. I burned the switches and moved the child into my room. Julie's pride was sorely wounded by this action. (Her name was Julie, like my grandmother's old chambermaid.) She became bitter and insolent, and I saw that under her essential qualities as a housekeeper she hid a dreadful baseness as a woman. She turned to my husband, whom she fawned on and who had the weakness to listen to the stupid, hateful slander she liked to spread about me. I dismissed her, hoping to avoid an argument and paying her generously for the services she had rendered. But she left with hate and vengeance in her heart, and M. Dudevant kept up a correspondence with her that later enabled him to locate her again.

I did not brood over it, and had I been on guard against her cowardly hatred, it would have mattered neither more nor less. I do not know how to hide what I dislike; moreover, I did not foresee that my peaceable relationship with my husband would finally erupt in a storm. Arguments had been rare, and no longer existed since we had become independent of each other. The entire time I had spent in Venice, M. Dudevant had written amicably to me, giving me news about the children and encouraging me to travel for my education and my health. These letters were later produced and read by the public prosecutor, after my husband's attorney complained of the suffering his client had endured due to loneliness.

Not foreseeing anything dark in my future, I had a moment of true happiness when I found myself at home in Nohant with my children and friends. Fleury was married to Laure Decerfz, my charming childhood friend, younger than I, but already settled when I was still a hellion. Duvernet had married Eugénie, whom I knew only casually, but who came to me like a frank child, asking me to address her as *tu* right away, since I already used *tu* with her husband. Mme. Duteil, also younger that I, was already an old friend; Jules Néraud, my beloved Malgache; Gustave Papet, a playmate from childhood, then a friend; the excellent Planet, friend only since 1830, but whose innocent nature and tender affection made themselves known from the very beginning; finally, Duteil, one of the most charming men in existence when only slightly drunk, and my dear Rollinat—these were my true, completely devoted friends. Death has taken two of them.[4] The others still keep faith with me.

Fleury, Planet—and Duvernet, in his frequent trips to Paris—had been friends since my days at Quai Saint-Michel, and then at Quai Malaquais. Among the eight or ten people who comprised this fraternal intimacy, almost all dreamed of a future of freedom for France, without suspecting they would one day play a more or less active role in coming events, whether political or literary. There was even a child, a pretty child of twelve or thirteen, involved with us by chance, and practically adopted by us. Intelligent, gracious, appealing, and most entertaining, this urchin, who would become one of the best-loved actors, and whom I would meet again when casting my plays, was named Prosper Bressant.

I lost track of that fellow when I left for Italy, and of the others later and gradually, but the Berry nucleus, which—circumstances being favorable—I would always be able to find, I found again in Nohant in 1834, with renewed pleasure after an absence of about a year.

I took a walk with several of them to Valençay, and after my return I wrote, under the influence of a lively chat with Rollinat, a short article entitled *Le Prince*, which—so they told me—upset Talleyrand.[11] Having refrained from angering him previously, I was truly sorry to have published this little tirade. Never having met the man, I had felt no personal animosity toward him. He had merely served as an example and pretext for a complete outburst against the ideas and methods of the school of false politics and shameful diplomacy of which he was the chief minister. But although that old duffer was hardly sacred; although he had one foot in the grave and already belonged to history, I felt sorry—justifiably or not—for not having better hidden his personality in my critique. My friends told me, in vain, that I had used the historian's prerogative, so to speak; in my heart of hearts I knew I was not a historian, especially for things present. I knew my vocation did not oblige me to attack the living, first of all because I did not have enough talent in this field to produce a useful work of destruction, and, finally, because I was a woman, and battles between the sexes are not equal; the man who insults a woman commits a wanton act of cowardice, while a woman who wounds a man first, without provocation, abuses her impunity.

I did not destroy my little work, because what was done was done, and we should never take back a publicly expressed thought, pleasing or not. But I promised myself never to write about people unless I had more good than evil to say, or unless forced by a slanderous personal attack.

At times, I could well have used a certain zest for controversy. I did feel the heat of my indignation when it came to lies, and was asked a hundred times to involve myself in daily political conflicts. I obstinately refused, even when certain friends pushed me as though to a duty. If they had wanted me as partner in a newspaper, one which would comment generally on conflicts from party to party, from idea to idea, I would have applied myself to it with courage, and dared much more than many others have. But to limit the size of the warfare to a daily duel between two, to put individuals on trial, to summon them for factual details to the court of public opinion was antipathetic to my nature and, probably, to my constitution. I would not have been able to last twenty-four hours under such conditions of anger and resentment, without which even just severities cannot be carried out. It has been painful for me to be a part of the editorial staff of a daily newspaper or even a review, where my name appears to be in sympathy with political or literary executions. Some have told me I lacked character and that my feelings were luke-warm. The first point may be true, but since the second is false, I do not think one is necessarily the result of the other. I recall a large number who, in 1847, reproached me strongly for my political apathy and preached the course of action in very fine terms, but were, in 1848, much more calm and easygoing than I had ever been.[12]

Before beginning the year 1835, when for the first time in my life I felt won over by a strong interest in current events, I shall speak about a few people with whom I was beginning or would soon begin to be connected. As these people still remain outside the political world, it would be difficult for me to return to them when I do get involved in it; thus, in order not to interrupt my principal topic, I shall complete here and now, in some measure, the story of my relations with them, as I have already done for Delatouche.   *M.G.P.*

IV

Mme. Dorval.

I had been linked with Mme. Dorval[13] for a year, against the objections of some of my friends, who had judged her unfairly. I would have sacrificed a great deal to the opinions of my sincerest friends, and I often did, even when I was not entirely convinced, but for that woman, whose heart and mind were on a par, I stood my ground, and I was right.

Born on the provincial stage, raised in suffering and poverty, Marie Dorval grew up sickly and strong, pretty and faded, as cheerful as a child, but also as sad and good as an angel condemned to tread the most difficult roads in life. Her mother was one of those excitable types who arouse the sensitivity of their children at too young an age. At the least mistake, she would tell Marie, "You're killing me, you're worrying me to death!" And the poor child took these exaggerated reproaches seriously, spent entire nights in tears, praying fervently and asking God, with heart-rending repentance and remorse, to give back her mother, whom she accused herself of having murdered—all because of a torn dress or a lost handkerchief.

Thus in turmoil from childhood, an intense, inexhaustible, and to some extent, necessary, life of emotions developed within her. Like those delicate and charming plants that can be seen growing, flowering, dying, and being reborn ceaselessly, attached firmly to a rock under a crashing waterfall, this exquisite soul always bent under the weight of violent anguish, opened at the slightest sunbeam, and avidly sought the breath of life around her, no matter how fleeting or poisoned it sometimes might be. Dead set against looking ahead, she found in the force of her imagination and in the ardor of her soul the joys of a day and the illusions of an hour, which were bound to be followed by naïve astonishment or bitter regret. Generous, she always forgot or forgave. Endlessly colliding with regenerated sorrows and new disappointments, she lived, she loved, she always suffered.

All was passion with her—motherhood, art, friendship, devotion, indignation, religious aspiration—and because she neither knew how nor wanted to moderate or repress anything, her existence had a terrifying fullness, an excitement beyond human endurance.

It is strange that I should be attached for so long, indeed permanently, to that poignant nature which reacted on me not at all in a morbid way—Marie Dorval loved what was great and beautiful too much not to communicate it to everyone, even in her hours of despair—but I was susceptible to her depressions, without being able to participate in her sudden and truly marvelous recoveries. I have always sought out serene souls, needing their patience and wanting the support of their wisdom. With Marie Dorval I played the completely opposite role, that of calming and persuading her; and this role was very difficult for me, especially at a time when I was troubled and frightened of life to the point of despair, and found nothing consoling to tell her that was not belied within myself by a suffering less expansive, but equally profound as hers.

However, it was not just out of a sense of duty that I listened untiringly to her passionate and incessant complaints against God and man. It was not just devotion and friendship that chained me to the spectacle of her torments. I found a strange charm in them, and in my pity there was a profound respect for that store of pain that was spent only to be renewed.

With very few exceptions, I cannot stand the company of women for long, not because I feel they are inferior to me in intelligence—I have imbibed so little of it in my day-to-day life, everyone I know has more female company around than I—but woman is, in general, a nervous, anxious being who communicates to me her eternal confusion about everything, in spite of myself. I begin by listening reluctantly, then I let myself take a natural interest, and, finally, I discover that all the infantile disturbances narrated to me do not amount to a row of beans.

Some women turn vain as soon as they become serious, and those who are not artists by profession often arrive at an immoderate pride once they leave the realm of gossip and exaggerated preoccupation with little things. This is the result of an unfinished education, but were this education non-existent, there would still reside in woman a sort of morbid excitation which is hers by nature and which causes intense suffering, except when, in rare cases, the excitation becomes a source of attraction.

I therefore prefer men to women, and I say this without malice, seriously convinced that the goals of nature are logical and complete; that satisfaction of passion is only one restricted and coincidental side of that attraction of one sex for the other, and that outside of all physical relations, souls seek in each other a sort of intellectual and moral alliance in which one sex complements the other. If it were otherwise, men would flee women, and vice versa, when the reign of passion was over; whereas, on the contrary, the principal element of civilization is in their calm and subtle rapport.

Despite my preference, which I have never tried to deny, assuming that to deny it would be unintended hypocrisy and utterly irrational; despite my antipathy to hearing women's confidences, which are rarely true and often insipid; despite my preference for the more honest and fuller chord that men strike in my spirit, I know and have known several women who, through their truly womanly candor and grace, more aptly called angelic than manly, have put my heart and head completely at ease.

Mme. Dorval, however, was not one of those. She was the epitome of feminine anxiety at its height. But she was also the most interesting and sincerest expression of it. Concealing nothing about herself, she contrived nothing. She had an openness of rare eloquence—eloquence sometimes savage, never trivial, always innocent in its directness and always betraying her quest for an unreachable ideal, a dream of pure happiness, of heaven on earth. This superior mind, extraordinary in psychological insight and rich in fine and profound observations, passed from the harsh to the pleasing with astounding rapidity. When she discussed her life—that is to say, her disappointment in the day before and her belief in tomorrow—it was in the midst of bitter tears or infectious laughter, which dramatized or lit up her face, her gestures, her whole being with flashes alternately terrifying or brilliant. The world knew only one side of that impetuous woman, for anyone who saw her in the grip of artistic expression could, up to a point, represent her to himself as she was in reality, but that was only part of her. No one has ever created nor, I believe, could ever create a role in which she was completely revealed in all her animation without sting, immense tenderness, infantile tantrums, splendid audacity, artless delivery, roars, sobs, and sympathetic laughter—the last a momentary respite she seemed eager to give her overwhelmed listener.

Sometimes the gaiety was desperate; however, real laughter would soon take hold and give her new power. She was like a rubber ball that hit the ground to bounce back endlessly. Those who heard her for an hour were dazzled. Those who heard her for whole days were left shattered but drawn to that fatal existence by an invincible attraction, that which draws suffering to suffering and softheartedness to the edge of heartbreak.

When I became acquainted with her, she was at the height of her talent and fame. She was playing in *Antony* and *Marion Delorme*.[14]

Before acquiring the reputation she deserved, she had passed through all the vicissitudes of itinerant life. She had belonged to those travelling companies whose directors would, to liven up the intermission, propose a game of dominoes on stage to the best player in the audience. She had sung in the choir of *Joseph*,[15] in torrential rain, clinging to a ladder and covered by an umbrella for four. The wings of the theater (it was an old church) had fallen into ruin, and the choristers had to remain aloft on a breach in the wall hidden by the curtains. The choir had been interrupted by an exclamation of one of the coryphées crying to the one on the rung above him: "Animal, you're poking my eye out with your umbrella. Down with the umbrella!"

At fourteen she played Fanchette in *Le Mariage de Figaro*[16] and some other role the name of which escapes me, in another play. She had only one dress in the world, a little white one, which served for both roles. But in order to give Fanchette a Spanish look, she basted a band of red calico to the hem of her skirt, and removed it quickly after the play, to look as if she were wearing another costume when the two plays were played the same evening. During the day, dressed in an outgrown child's wool sweater, she washed and ironed her precious white dress.

One day, when she was thus dressed and occupied, a rich old man from the provinces came to offer her his heart and his money. She threw her iron in his face and then went to relate the insult to a boy of fifteen, whom she regarded as her lover, who wanted to kill the seducer.

Having married young, it was when she was singing comic opera at Nancy, I believe, that her little girl broke her leg in the wings when a piece of the set fell. She felt compelled to run from her child to the stage and from the stage to her child, without interrupting the performance.

As mother of three children, with the added responsibility of her old, sick mother, she worked with untiring courage to lavish them with care. She came to Paris to try her fortune. To her this simply meant an ambition to escape poverty. But having a horror of any other resource than her work, she stagnated for several years, in fatigue and privation. It was not until her role as the miller's wife in the melodrama *Deux Forçats*[17] that her eminent dramatic qualities began to be noticed.

From that point on, her successes were brilliant and rapid. She created the woman of the new drama, the romantic heroine of the theater, and if she owed her fame to the masters of that art, they also owed her something: the conquest of a public that wanted to see, and did see, this art personified in three great artists—Frédérick Lemaître, Mme. Dorval, and Bocage.

Mme. Dorval created, in addition, an exceptional character-type in the leading role of *Jeanne Vaubernier*,[18] as Mme. du Barri. You would have to have seen her in this role, in which, exquisitely graceful and charming in her triviality, she resolved a difficulty which seemed insurmountable; but you would have to have seen her in *Marion Delorme, Angelo, Chatterton, Antony*, and, later, in the drama *Marie-Jeanne*,[19] in order to find out what jealous passion, chastity, and maternal heart dwelled in her, all equally intense.

Nevertheless, she had to struggle against her inborn shortcomings. Her voice was husky, and she rolled her r's excessively. Her entry into the part was without nobility or even grace. Her conventional delivery was clumsy and constrained, and since she was too intelligent for many of the roles she had to play, she often said, "I don't know of any true way to say false things. There are conventional stage expressions that can only come out of my mouth the wrong way, because they don't exist in reality. I've never said, in a moment of surprise, 'What do I see?' and in a moment of hesitation, 'Where have I wandered?' I often have entire speeches in which not a single word strikes me as possible, and which I would like to improvise from one end to the other, if they would only let me."

During the warm-up scenes of her roles, no matter how true and well-written they were, her faults came out more than her fine points. Those who were used to her were not concerned, knowing that the first spark that radiated from her would ignite the public. Her enemies (all great artists have many, who are quite relentless) would rub their hands together in the beginning, and people who saw her for the first time, without having been forewarned, were astonished that she had been so highly praised. But as soon as she was immersed in the role, a supple and unstudied grace animated her person; as soon as the situation called for conflict, the actress's emotions burrowed into it almost to the point of horror; and when passion, terror, or despair burst forth, the coolest were carried away, the most hostile were reduced to silence.

I believe only *Indiana* had been published when I wrote to Mme. Dorval, drawn by a deep sympathy, to ask if she would receive me. I was not at all well-known, and I did not know if she had even heard of my book. But my letter must have struck her by its sincerity. The very day she received it, while I was talking about that same letter to Jules Sandeau, the door to my garret opened and a woman effusively flung her arms around my neck, out of breath, crying, "Here I am!"

I had never seen her except on stage, but my ear recognized her voice immediately. She was better than pretty—she was charming—and so charming was she that her prettiness was of no consequence. It was not a face, it was a countenance, a soul. She was still slim, and her waist was a supple reed which always seemed to sway to a mysterious breeze she alone felt. Jules Sandeau compared her that day to the broken feather which adorned her hat. "I'm sure," he said, "one could search the whole universe for a feather as light and soft as the one she found. Such a singularly marvelous feather flew toward her by the law of affinities, or else it fell from the wing of some fairy in passage."

I asked Mme. Dorval how my letter had convinced her to come so quickly. She told me that its declaration of friendship and sympathy had recalled to her what she had written to Mlle. Mars,[20] after having seen her perform for the first time. "I was so naïve and sincere," she added, "I was convinced that a person was worth nothing and only became something through the enthusiasm her talent inspired in others. I remembered while reading your letter that, when I wrote mine, I felt like a true artist for the very first time, and that my enthusiasm was a revelation. I said to myself you also are, or will be, an artist. And then I remembered further that Mlle. Mars was cold and proud with me, instead of understanding and beckoning me. I didn't want to be like Mlle. Mars."

She asked us to come to dinner the following Sunday, for she performed every evening during the week, and spent the day of rest in the midst of her family. She was married to M. Merle, a distinguished author who had written some charming vaudeville plays, the *Ci-devant Jeune Homme* among others, and who, almost until his last days, wrote the theater column for the *Quotidienne* with spirit, taste, and almost always with impartiality. M. Merle had a son, and the three daughters of Mme. Dorval, and several old friends made up the familiar gathering; the games and laughter of the children naturally dominated.

People really do not know how touching the lives of theatrical artists are when they have families and take them seriously. I believe, today, the majority are in a state of domestic happiness, or are at least duty-bound; it is high time we give up for good our prejudices toward them. Actors have a better reputation than actresses, the reason being the seductions to which female youth and beauty are subjected, seductions gratifying for the men involved, but whose consequences are almost always fatal for the women. But even though actresses have a questionable status according to civil law, even though—I shall go further—they are abandoned to their basest passions, they are almost always mothers of ineffable tenderness and heroic courage. Their children are usually even more happy than those of society women; the latter, who neither can nor wish to admit their mistakes, hide and distance the fruits of their love, and when they do introduce them into the family by means of a marriage, the least suspicion of wrongdoing brings down strictness and disapproval on the heads of these unhappy children.

Among actresses, a fault confessed is a fault redressed. Public opinion in that world only stigmatizes those who abandon or ignore their offspring. Let the official world condemn these mothers as it sees fit, the poor little ones will have no complaint of the more tolerant welcome they receive at home. There, young and old parents, and even legitimate spouses who came after the fact, adopt children without vain discussion, and surround them with care and caresses. Bastards or not, they are all family offspring, and when their mother has talent, they are consequently ennobled and treated, in their small world, like little princes.

Nowhere are the ties of blood more tightly drawn than among performing artists. When the mother is forced to work at rehearsal five hours a day, and at performance five hours every evening; when she hardly has time to eat and dress, the brief moments when she can caress her children are moments of passionate ecstasy, and days of rest are truly holidays. How joyfully she then takes them to the country! She becomes a child with them, and in spite of the mistakes she might have made in the past, she again becomes pure of spirit and instantly sanctified by contact with innocent souls.

Also, those who dwell in virtue (and there are more than you think) are worthy of particular veneration, for they generally have troublesome burdens to bear: fathers, mothers, old aunts, sisters either too young or also mothers—all lacking courage or talent. This entourage is often needed to take care of the artist's children, whom she cannot raise herself with any consistency, and who are an eternal source of worry. But this entourage often also uses and abuses, or it quarrels, and the artist must emerge from the rapture of make-believe to become a peacemaker in this troubled reality.

Far from repudiating her family, the artist summons and draws it closely about her. She tolerates, pardons, sustains; she nourishes some and raises others. No matter how prudent she is, her salary suffices only by virtue of very hard labor, for the artist cannot live with the parsimony that the small businessman and humble bourgeois employ. The artist needs elegance and a wholesome outlook, of which the greedy townsman does not shrink from depriving himself and his children. The artist has a feeling for beauty and, consequently, a true thirst for life. She needs a ray of sunshine, a breath of fresh air, which—modest as it may be—becomes more costly every day in populous cities.

Futhermore, the artist keenly feels the needs of intelligence. She does not live, does not grow, except by it. Her goal is not to amass a little annuity to leave to her children; her children are raised to become artists in their turn. We want our children to have what we ourselves possess, and sometimes we want it all the more if we have been deprived of it and have miraculously formed our intellectual life by sheer will-power. We know what we have suffered and how we risked failure. We wish to spare our children those dangers and tests. They will, therefore, be raised and instructed like children of the rich; however, the artist is poor: the median salary in Paris for artists who are somewhat distinguished is five thousand francs per year. In order to earn eight or ten thousand, a very substantial talent is necessary, or rarer and harder to attain (for there are hundreds of unknown or little-known talents), a notable success is necessary.

Therefore, artists arrive at solutions to these difficult problems only through endless hardships, and all the instances of narcissism and childish jealousy that one can accuse them of taking too seriously often conceal depths of dread or sorrow, questions of life and death.

This latter point was very real for Mme. Dorval. She earned at most fifteen thousand francs by never resting, by living in the simplest manner, and having the taste and cleverness to make her residence and style of living as elegant as possible, without luxury. But great and generous as she was, often paying debts which were not hers, unable to resist the parasites who had no rights over her except by their persistence, she was always at the end of her resources. In order to dress her daughters, or to save cowardly friends, I saw her sell everything short of the little jewels she cherished as souvenirs and kissed like relics.

Often repaid by the blackest ingratitude, by reproaches which were surely blasphemies in certain mouths, she consoled herself in the hope of her daughters' happiness. But one of them broke her heart. Gabrielle was sixteen years old. She was a classic beauty. I had not seen her more than three times before I realized she was jealous of her mother and dreamed only of casting off her authority. Mme. Dorval would not hear of the theater for her daughters. "I know too well what it is," she would say. And in this protest were all the terrors and tenderness of a mother.

Gabrielle did not hesitate to tell me that her mother dreaded the rivalry of her youth and beauty on the stage. I reproved her, and she very naïvely displayed her anger and dislike for anyone who sided with her mother. I was surprised to see so much bitterness hidden beneath that angelic face, against which I now felt myself forewarned; for by confiding in me, she had apparently imagined I was entirely on her side.

Not long after, Gabrielle fell in love with a man of letters of some talent, Fontaney, who wrote little articles in *Le Revue des Deux Mondes* under the name Lord Feeling. But his talent was of small scope and, commercially speaking, practically useless. Fontaney owned nothing, and furthermore he was consumptive.

Mme. Dorval wanted him out of the picture. Gabrielle angrily accused her of wanting to take him away from her. "Ah," cried the mother, wounded and dismayed, "here comes that loathesome refrain of jealous daughters. You want to stop them from running to their doom, you break your heart by being forced to break theirs, and to console you, they accuse you of being vicious, nothing less!"

Mme. Dorval deemed it necessary to put Gabrielle in a convent. One fine morning, Gabrielle disappeared, carried off by Fontaney.

Fontaney was a decent man, but his soul, like his mortally stricken body, was devoid of energy, and his spirit, like his purse, was devoid of resources. Since Mme. Dorval could not have refused him the hand of Gabrielle after the scandal of the elopement, he had no other course but to ask for a double pardon. The courageous mother might have given asylum to this sick man who wanted to become a husband on the brink of his grave and to this so-called abused daughter who posed as a victim because someone had tried to prevent her from becoming one.

But Fontaney did completely the opposite of what reason and justice would have required. He took Gabrielle to Spain, as if he were afraid that her mother would send the police after her, and they tried to get married without consent, but they did not succeed and were forced in no uncertain terms to ask for it. After the marriage was consented to and concluded, they asked for money. Mme. Dorval gave all she could. Naturally, they found she had hardly any, and that was pronounced a crime. Instead of looking for work in Paris, the young couple left for England, thus consuming at once, in travel and moving expenses, the little they possessed. Did they hope to create occupations for themselves in London? This hope did not materialize. Gabrielle was not an artist, although she had been raised as an heiress to art might have been, with teachers of art and the advice of true artists. But beauty does not go far without courage and intelligence.

Fontaney was not much better endowed. He was a nice young man, with an interesting face, capable of kind and gentle feelings, but very limited in ideas, yet too fastidious not to have understood, if he had thought about it, that to carry off a young girl, without the means or strength to create a life for her, is a mistake one should be reluctant to flaunt. He became discouraged, and his consumption made horrifying progress. This disease can be contagious between husband and wife. Gabrielle caught it and succumbed in several weeks, prey of poverty and despair.

The unfortunate Fontaney came back to die in Paris. He was given hospitality for several days at Saint-Gratien, at the home of the Marquis de Custine, and there he had the indecency to complain bitterly of Mme. Dorval. Creating illusions about himself, as consumptives are prone to do, he claimed to have been robust and well before the stay in London, where his wife's privations and anxieties about the future had killed her. He deceived himself completely. The first words that Mme. Dorval had said to me about him were these: "He has a small talent, very little courage, and hopeless health." Indeed, seeing him was enough to notice his dry cough, his extreme thinness, and the despondency of his countenance. Poor Gabrielle attributed these frightening symptoms to the pangs of passion and, innocent as she was, did not suspect that the satisfaction of that passion would be the death of both of them.

As for the aid Mme. Dorval should have sent them, in the difficult and frightening penury in which she herself lived, harassed, as I witnessed, by creditors who seized her salary and threatened to seize her funiture, this aid would have been a weak palliative. Besides, Fontaney himself confessed he had been ashamed to let it be known to what extremes he had been reduced, and such shame would have made more sense from a man who had no expectations from his wife's mother, and who was used to being a pillar of security. Fontaney showed himself to be especially irritated not to have inspired that security in Mme. Dorval.

In spite of inner remorse, Fontaney was so crushed by the fate of his wife, embittered by his own suffering, and desperate at the onset of death, that he vented his rage in bitter confidences. May God pardon him, but they were blameworthy, those complaints. Guilty, too, were the fair number of people who listened and sympathized, for not having the good sense to dispel them by seeking out the facts and reflecting on the frailty of the complainer.

Mme. Dorval's enemies joyfully seized on the most odious and absurd reproach that could be invented against her as a mother, she who had torn herself inside out every hour of her life for her children. She, a bad mother, when her maternal feeling was passionate to the point of ecstasy! When she herself died of its pains! You will hear the whole story, and you will see soon enough that she knew how to love.

One day, when the complaints of Fontaney and her daughter were reported to her, clearly with malicious intent, and among them the complaint that Gabrielle had been mistreated and beaten by her, she became melancholy and preoccupied; then, ignoring the tactless and cruel questions being addressed to her, she exclaimed: "Ah yes! my God, I should have beaten her! I ask your pardon, God, that I didn't have the courage to do so!"

Steeped in sorrow, the poor woman picked herself up again from this new blow, through her work, through the affection of those close to her, and through concern for her youngest daughter, Caroline, a beautiful child, fair and peaceful, whose precarious health had long caused Marie mortal anguish. Instead of lending support and treating the sickly child as one who had a need and right to be spoiled, her two older sisters entertained themselves by being jealous.

But Caroline was good; she loved her mother. She deserved to be happy, and she was. After her sister Louise got married, she in turn got married, to René Luguet, a young actor in whom Mme. Dorval sensed real talent, a generous soul, and a reliable character.

Nevertheless, I saw Mme. Dorval dejected during the first months of that new family forming around her. She often felt ill. One day, I found her in the rear of her apartment on Rue du Bac, bent, as if broken, over a tapestry loom. "Yet, I'm happy," she told me, crying copiously. "Well—I'm troubled, and I don't know why. My emotions have used me up before my time. I feel old and tired. I need to rest, I try to rest and here's what happens to me—I don't know how to rest." Then she went into detail about her private life. "I have broken violently with violent sorrows," she told me. "I want to live in others' happiness, and do what you told me—forget myself. I also would have wished to feel at one with my art—to love it—but that is impossible. It's a stimulant that makes me need more stimulation; so, only half-stimulated, all I have left are feelings of pain, frightening memories, and for every diversion in the past, a thousand pinpricks of present reality, too weak to take away the hurt, but strong enough to compound it with impatience and anxiety. Ah! if I had an income, or if my children no longer needed me, I would take a real rest!"

And as I observed that she had just complained of not knowing how to rest, "It's true," she told me, "boredom has been devouring me since I no longer have anything to worry me. Louise has married the man of her choice; Caroline has a charming husband she adores. M. Merle is today still as cheerful and satisfied as always, provided that nothing or no one disturbs his comfort; calm personified, lovable, easygoing, charming in his egoism. Nothing is going badly, except this apartment, which you find so pretty, but is so dark it reminds me of a tomb."

And she started crying again. "Are you hiding something from me?" I said to her. "Not at all!" she exclaimed. "You know very well I have the opposite fault, that of piling all my troubles on you, and that it's always you whom I ask for courage. But don't you understand boredom? Boredom without apparent cause, because if one knew the cause, one might find the cure. When I tell myself that perhaps it's the absence of passion, I feel such fear at the idea of beginning again that I prefer a thousand times the dullness into which I have fallen. But in the kind of sleep I'm sleeping, I dream too much, and I have bad dreams. I would like to see heaven or hell, to believe in the God and the Devil of my childhood, to feel myself victorious in some sort of battle, and discover a paradise, a reward. Well, I see nothing but a cloud, a doubt. I occasionally force myself to feel devout. I need God. But I don't understand Him in the shape religion renders Him. It seems to me the Church is also a theater, and men there, too, play a role.

"Here," she added, showing me a pretty reproduction in white marble of Canova's *Magdalene*. "I have spent hours looking at this weeping woman, and I wonder why she weeps—whether it's repentance for having lived, or regret for not living any longer. For a long time I studied her only as a model of form; now she sets off my thoughts. Sometimes she annoys me; I'd like to push her to make her get to her feet again. Sometimes she terrifies me, and I, too, am afraid of being irrevocably shattered.

"I would like to be you," she resumed, in response to the reflections which hers had suggested to me.

"I love you too much to wish that on you," I said to her. "I've been bored, in the sense you mean, not since today or yesterday, but since the hour I came into the world."

"Yes, yes, I know that," she exclaimed, "but it's a grand boredom, or a powerful boredom, if you prefer. Mine is feeble; it's disheartening. You unearth the reason for your sadness, and when you grasp it, your course is set. You take yourself in hand by saying: 'That's the way it is, it can't be otherwise.' That is what I'd like to be able to say. And then, you believe that there is a truth, justice, and happiness somewhere; you don't know where; it doesn't matter to you. You believe one has only to die to enter something better than life. I feel all that in a vague way, but I desire it more than expect it."

Then, interrupting herself suddenly, she asked, "What is an abstraction? I read this word in all kinds of books, and the more it's explained to me, the less I understand it."

I had not said two words before I saw that she understood better than I did—for she imagined I was perceptive, but it was she who was.

"Well," she continued ardently, "an abstract idea means nothing to me. I cannot put my heart and my insides into my head. If God has common sense, He intends, in us as well as outside, that everything should be in its place and fulfill its function. I can understand God abstractly and can contemplate, for a moment, the idea of perfection, through a kind of veil, but that doesn't last long enough to convince me. I feel the need to love, and devil take me if I can love an abstraction!

"And then what? This God that your philosophers and priests show us—the former as an idea, the latter in the form of Christ—who can say He is anywhere but in your imaginations? Let Him be shown to me, I want to see Him. If He loves me a little, let Him tell me so and console me. This Magdalene, she saw Him, she touched Him—her wonderful dream! She cried at His feet, she wiped them with her hair. Where can I meet the divine Jesus once again? If anyone knows, let him tell me and I will run there. What a magnificent reward, to adore a perfect being who really exists! Can you believe if I'd known Him I would've been a sinner? Do our senses lead us astray? No, it's the thirst for something entirely opposite. It's the rage to find true love, which always beckons and recedes. Let saintly men be sent to us, and we women will quickly become saints. Let me be given a memory like the one that weeping woman carried into the desert, and I will live in the desert like her. I will cry over my beloved, and I won't be bored, I promise you."

Such was that ever-impassioned, troubled soul whose effusions I am probably spoiling by trying to paraphrase them. For who can render the fire of her words and the animation of her thoughts? Those who have heard and understood will never forget them.

This depression was only temporary. Soon Caroline had a son whom her mother named Georges, and that child became Marie's joy and supreme love. Her devoted heart had to have a being to whom she could give herself completely, day and night, without rest or restriction. "My children," she said, "claim I loved them less and less as they grew up. That isn't true, but it is true I loved them differently. As they gradually had less need of me, I worried less about them, and it's worry that arouses passion. My daughter is happy. I would trouble her happiness, if I seemed to doubt it. Now her husband is her mother: it is he who watches over her and worries if she sleeps badly. I need to forget my slumber, my rest, and my life, for someone. Only little children are worth being brooded over every hour that way. When you fall in love, you become the mother of a man who either offers no resistance without being grateful to you, or else does resist for fear of feeling ridiculous. But children, those innocent dears we cradle, who warm themselves at our hearts, are neither proud nor ungrateful. They need us; they exercise their right, which is to make us slaves. We belong to them as they belong to us, completely. We suffer everything from them and for them, and as we ask nothing of them but to live and be happy, we find it sufficient when they deign to smile at us.

"Here!" she said, showing me little Georges. "I asked for a saint, an angel, a god I could see, and God sent him to me. Here is embodied innocence, perfection, and beauty of soul. Here is what I love, what I serve, what I pray to. I sense divine love in one of his caresses and see heaven in his blue eyes."

That immense tenderness, which awakened in her more vitally than ever, gave new vigor to her genius. She created the lead in *Marie-Jeanne*, and found in it those cries which tear the soul, those accents of grief and passion that are no longer heard in the theater, because they could not come out of anything but that heart and that constitution; because those cries and accents would be savage and grotesque coming from anyone else but her, and would need a personality like hers to render them terrifying and sublime.

But this fatal role and profound love dealt the death-blow to Mme. Dorval. She got horribly sick after her great success, escaping a perforated lung by a miracle. She was terrified at the idea of dying. Georges lived, so she wanted to live.

She played *Agnes de Méranie*, and then tried something very curious, which was to play classical tragedy at the Odéon. This was neither in her manner nor in her voice. Nevertheless, she had spoken Ponsard's verses with such great intelligence, and she had been so sober and chaste in *Lucrèce*, that the public was curious to hear her speak the verses of Racine. She studied *Phèdre* with infinite care, consciously seeking a new interpretation.

In the midst of these studies, she talked to me about herself with the naïve modesty belonging only to genius. "I don't claim to improve on Rachel's[21] portrayal, but I can do something different. The public does not expect to see me imitate her; it would be nothing more than parody. But I want to capture the audience, not for the actress, but for Racine. It is not a matter of discovering the original intention of the poet; there is nothing so childish as all this research into the true tradition, as they call it. It is a matter of setting off the beauty of the conception and the charm of the language by showing that they lend themselves to all natures and can be expressed by the most variant types."

In fact, she performed marvels of intelligence and passion in that role. For whoever had not seen Rachel, Marie was written in the annals of the theater for that portrayal. Besides, Rachel had not yet grasped it, then, with as much perfection as today. She was too young, and youth cannot muster the restraint and fear that Phèdre's plight requires. The role is searing, and Mme. Dorval was searing. Rachel is searing in it, now, and Rachel is perfect, because she still has the youth, beauty, and ideal grace that, by then, Mme. Dorval lacked. Rachel inspires love; she inspired it then, although not yet at the height of her talent. Mme. Dorval no longer inspired love, but considering that there are more lovers than artists in any audience whatsoever, all the artists who saw her in this role appreciated her profoundly, and felt the full impact of the smallest detail, which no one, perhaps not even the great performers of the Empire, had ever revealed.

In 1848, I saw Mme. Dorval struck with terror and dismay by the revolution that had just taken place. M. Merle, although moderate in character and tolerant in his opinions, belonged to the legitimist party, and Mme. Dorval imagined she would be persecuted. She even dreamed of scaffolds and proscriptions, her active imagination not knowing how to take things halfway.

Only one cause of her alarm was founded. The disturbance was bound to strike those who lived by work that had adapted itself to the political principles then being questioned. Artisans and artists, all those who live from day to day, find themselves momentarily paralyzed in such crises; and Mme. Dorval, having to struggle against age, weariness, and her own fear, could resist this passing disaster only with difficulty. I was in no less precarious a position; the crisis overtook me when I was in debt after the marriage of my daughter. On one side, I was being threatened with the seizure of my furniture; on the other, the pay I earned from my work was reduced by three-quarters, and further publishing was suspended for several months.

But I was pretty nearly oblivious to the dangers of that situation. The privations of the moment are nothing; I am not talking of those. The only real pain of such moments is not to be able to acquit yourself immediately to those who reclaim their credit, and not to be able to help those suffering around you. But when you are sustained by a social faith, an impersonal hope, personal anxieties, no matter how serious, are lessened.

Mme. Dorval might very well have understood and had a feeling for prevailing political ideas, but she sharply spurned such examination and concern on the grounds that she had enough of her own troubles. Thus, she saw only chaos and dreamed only of bloody catastrophes in the February Revolution. Poor woman! This was prophetic of the awful pain that was to strike her family.

In the month of June 1848, after those abominably long days which had just killed the republic by arming its children against each other, and by creating a deep breach between the two forces of the revolution—the people and the bourgeoisie—that twenty years will perhaps not suffice to mend, I was at Nohant, threatened by the cowardly hatred and imbecilic terrors of my province. I no longer cared about anything, except what had touched me personally in the events. My soul was dead, my hope crushed under the barricades. In the middle of that despondency, I received the following letter from Marie Dorval:

"My poor, dear, good friend, I didn't dare to write you because I thought you were too busy; besides, I couldn't. In my despair I would have written you too insane a letter. But today I know you are at Nohant, far from our horrible Paris, and alone with your good heart which has given me so much love. I read, through my tears, your letter to ———. I find you there ever and wholly present, as in the novel about the foundling.[22] Poor foundling! Then I absolutely needed to write to you to obtain a few words of consolation for my poor devastated soul. I have lost my grandson—my Georges—did you know? But you don't know the deep, irreparable sorrow I feel. I don't understand why God should take such dear creatures away from us. I want to pray to God, but I feel only anger and rebellion in my heart. I spend my life over his little tomb. Does he see me? Do you think so? I no longer know what to do with my life; I no longer know my duty. I would like to love my other children, but I no longer can. I have looked for consolation in prayer books. I have found nothing there that speaks to me of my situation, or of the children we lose. Must we thank God for such terrible misfortune? No, I cannot! Did Jesus himself not cry, 'My God, why have you forsaken me?' If that great soul doubted, what will become of us other poor creatures? Ah, my dear, how unhappy I am! He was all my happiness. I thought he was my reward for having been a good daughter and always very devoted to a family whose weight was very dear, but also very heavy on my shoulders. I was so happy. I envied no one. I courageously struggled in a despicable profession, which I filled with my best—when illness didn't stop me—and with the idea of making my whole world happier around me. Revolutions, time lost for art—we were still happy. Our poor little ones made barricades, sang La Marseillaise, and the sounds from the street redoubled their gaiety. Well, several days afterwards, these same sounds redoubled my poor Georges' convulsions. He had fourteen days of agony. We were on the cross for fourteen days. He fell at our feet on the 3rd of May. He yielded up his little soul on May 16th, at 3:30 in the afternoon.

"Excuse me for making you sad, my dear, but I appeal to you whom I love so much, who have always been so good to me, you who were the wherewithal—without you it couldn't have been—of that lovely trip to the South of France with my son. That trip which restored my health (too well, alas!), made that child so joyful, filled his poor little existence, so soon to end, with pleasures, walks, and sunshine.

"I appeal to you so that you'll write me a letter to give my soul a little strength. I ask your help once more. The beautiful words coming from your noble heart and elevated reason—I know very well where to find them, but I find much greater comfort if they come directly from your heart to mine.

"Good-bye, my dear George, my friend and cherished name! June 12th, 1848, 2 Rue de Varennes, Marie Dorval."

I have chosen not to change a word or suppress a line of that letter. Although I do not usually publish praises addressed to me, this one is sacred. It was the last blessing of that soul who loved and believed, in spite of everything. And that tender veneration for the objects of her friendship shows the treasure of moral piety which was still in her. Consolations addressed to her were never wasted. She made a new effort to lose herself in work and take up her task of self-sacrifice. But alas! her strength was depleted. I was fated never to see her again.

I spent the winter at Nohant, and the last letter that came from her trembling hand she wrote in 1849, to her beloved Caroline, on the 16th of May, anniversary of that fatal day which had taken away her Georges. Caroline sent me that crumpled letter from a feverish hand, whose tortured script was something tragic:

Caen, May 15th, 1849.

Dear Caroline, your poor mother has suffered all the torments of hell. Dear daughter, here we are on that sorrowful anniversary. I am asking you to close my poor Georges' room and forbid entrance to everyone. Do not let Marie play there. You will pull the bed into the middle of the room. You will place his open portrait on it, and you will cover it with flowers, also in all the vases. You will send to the market for these flowers. Make him all the springtime he can no longer see. Then, you will pray the whole day long in your own name and in the name of his poor grandmother.

I kiss you tenderly,

Your mother.

To this heart-rending letter was attached another one, from Caroline to me:

My mother died on May 20th, a year and four days after Georges. She fell ill in the stage coach on the way to Caen to perform. She went to bed on arriving and never got up again, except to return to Paris, where she died in our arms two days later. She suffered much, but her last moments were calm. She thought about the poor little angel she was going to join; you know how she loved him. This love killed her. She suffered for a year. She suffered in every way. People were so unjust, so cruel to her! Ah, Madame, tell me that now she is happy! I kiss you as she would have done herself, with all my soul.

Caroline Luguet.

The last book she read was your *Petite Fadette* [1849].

May 23rd, 1849.

Dear Madame Sand, she is dead, that admirable, poor woman! She leaves us inconsolable. Pity us!

René Luguet.

Now here are the details of that cruel death after such a cruel life. It was René Luguet who gave them to me in an exceptional letter, half of which I am forced to suppress. You will see why.

Dear Madame Sand, oh! you are right, it is a great misfortune for us, so great, you see, that it has destroyed all our joy on earth. On my side, I have lost everything—friend, companion in misfortune, mother. My intellectual mother, the mother of my soul, the one who gave vigor to my heart, the one who made me an artist, who made me a man and who taught me my duties; the one who made me loyal and courageous, who taught me to appreciate the beautiful, the true, and the great. And more—she cherished my dear Caroline and she adored our children. She is dead. You can imagine how I weep for her.

Dear Madame, you whom she loved so much, you whom she venerated, let me tell you part of her suffering, and you will have the measure of mine. She died of grief, of discouragement. Disdain, yes, disdain killed her. . . . When the poor woman went calling to ask for employment of her talent and her genius, people opened their eyes wide at the name of Dorval on her card.

"Genius! That's what we need. No question!" But she was missing one or two teeth, her dress was black, her glance sad. "Sorry! Events have brought disaster to the theaters, which has in turn brought. . . . " It was precisely at the height of that crisis that our first great misfortune occurred; my Georges died. Marie, stricken to the heart, remained standing at first without letting us see the depth of her wound, then stretched out her hand to anchor herself to something. We quickly sought some great diversion for this grief: a great creation! ———— came with a fine part. She read it, learned it, and was sublime in it. It was the anchor of salvation. It was necessary, no matter what she did, that several hours a day would be stolen from her sorrow. . . . Without motive, without excuse, without a word of explanation, the part was taken away from her. . . . Her fate was sealed. She took the blow right in the heart. Now they say they are sorry. It's about time!

This poor mother's life was escaping through three deep wounds: the death of an adored being; oblivion and injustice everywhere; and, at home, the fear of poverty. This is where we were last April 10th. I was going to Caen. She was supposed to come and join me there, but first she wanted to make a last effort, a last attempt at having a corner at the Français and five hundred francs a month. She was told that, soon, thanks to some clever calculations, three hundred francs would be saved on lighting, and if the board's reluctance could be overcome, they would think about giving her a small allowance. This was the final blow, for at that moment I saw her angelic glance turned toward me, and death was in it.

She left for Caen, and then and there, in two hours, the sickness became so grave I had to call for a consultation. Her condition was very serious: she had a pernicious fever and an ulcerated liver. I thought I heard my own death sentence being pronounced. I couldn't believe my eyes when I looked at that angel of suffering and resignation, who didn't complain, and who, smiling at me sadly, seemed to be saying, "You're here, you won't let me die!"

From that moment I spent forty nights at her bedside, on my feet. She had no other watch, no other nurse, no other friend but me. I wanted to accomplish that task alone. For forty days I was there, keeping death at bay, like a faithful dog protecting his master when he's in danger.

Then I saw the coming of weakness and profound melancholy. She began to speak endlessly of her childhood, her younger days; she summed up her whole life. I felt crushed by despair, by fatigue. Several times I fainted. I had to do something. Although the doctors warned that travel could be fatal, since I saw death approaching rapidly and she was calling for Paris, for her daughter and her little Marie in a tone that still makes me shiver . . . I asked God to send a miracle, and ordered a stage coach. I picked up this adored creature and began to dress her myself. She let me do it, as if I were her mother. I carried her down in my arms, and an hour later we left for Paris, both of us dying, she of her illness, I of despair.

Two hours later, during a terrible storm, we overturned, but we hardly noticed. Nothing mattered to us!

Finally, the next day she was in her own room, with all of us. Thank God, she was still alive, but the illness, which had been dulled by the trip, regained the upper hand, and on May 20th, at one o'clock, she told us, "I'm dying, but I am resigned! My daughter, my good daughter, goodbye . . . Luguet . . . sublime. . . ." Those were her last words. Then she exhaled her last breath through a smile. Oh! that smile still blazes before my eyes, and I have to look quickly at my children and dear Caroline in order to accept life!

Dear Madame Sand, my heart is broken. Your letter revived all my torments. That adorable Marie! You were her last poet. I read her *La Petite Fadette* at her bedside. Then, we talked for a long time about all those fine books whose touching scenes she retold in tears. Then, she spoke to me of you, of your heart. Ah, dear Madame Sand, how you loved Marie! How well you understood her soul! How she loved you, and how I love you! And how unhappy I am! It seems to me my life is pointless and that I can no longer bear it except through duty.

I am looking forward to the day I can speak to you of her and tell you everything extraordinary in grandeur and beauty that angel said to me during her days of melancholy and sorrow.

Your affectionate and disconsolate Luguet.

I shall quote still one more letter from that good, great heart who was worthy of such a mother. I ask his pardon in advance. These outpourings hardly expected publicity, but here it is not a matter of respecting the modesty of the living; it is a matter of raising a monument to her who is dead. She was one of the greatest artists and best women of this century. She was misjudged, slandered, scoffed at, defamed, and abandoned by many who should have defended her, as well as by some who should have blessed her. At least some voices must be raised over her tomb, and these voices will tilt the balance on the scale where public opinion weighs good and evil with a careless hand. These voices are the voices of friends who knew her for a long time and received and appreciated all the secrets of her intimacy: the voices of her family. They will prevail against those who see her from afar and judge her by happenstance.

Paris, December '49.

Dear Madame Sand, I saw your play *Champi* yesterday. Never have I felt such emotion at the theater. Ah, that devoted boy, faithful guardian of the existence of the poor persecuted woman! Happy son who saved his Madeleine! Not everyone has his happiness. How I wept! Curled up in the depths of my box, my handkerchief in my teeth, I thought I would suffocate.

Ah, that is because for me it was no longer François and Madeleine; it was she and I. It was not a man and a woman who could or should finally have married; it was not even a son and a mother; it was two souls who needed each other. Ah, I saw the ten most beautiful years of my life pass—my devotion, my hope, my goal, my sustenance, everything! Oh! I was too happy for ten years; it had to be paid for.

Dear Madame Sand, excuse all these tears on the subject of a success that gladdens all those who know you, but to whom can I tell what I suffer, if not to you? Won't you come to Paris to see your play? And us! Don't look for us at the Rue de Varennes any more. Oh no! We have fled that cursed house. We would all have died there. The doors, the halls, the sounds on the stairs made us shudder at every hour. The cries from the street came every morning at the same time to remind us of the moment she had said this or that. In the end it is these nothings that kill! We have dragged our sorrow elsewhere. . . . Caroline kisses you tenderly—poor child, she, too, is grief-stricken. My tenderness for her increases daily. She so deserves to be happy.

René Luguet.

Thus, she was loved; thus, she was mourned—Marie Dorval! Her husband, M. Merle, had already fallen into a state of decline followed by paralysis. Lovable and good, and yet profoundly selfish, he found it very simple to remain, with his terrible infirmities and inexhaustible debts, in the charge of Luguet and Caroline, to whom he was nothing except a duty bequeathed by Mme. Dorval. But they fulfilled this duty until the end, despite the vicissitudes of an artist's life and the bad times they had to go through, so dear and sacred was the idea of continuing the task of devotion she left to them.

Yes, if she was betrayed and spat upon, this victim of art and destiny, she was also cherished and missed. And I am not speaking only of myself, who am not yet used to the idea that she no longer exists, and that I shall no longer be able to help console her; of myself, who have the conviction that I shall find her again in a better world, as saintly as the day her soul left the bosom of God to come and wander in our insane world and fall from weariness on our cursed paths.	*K.A.*

V

Eugène Delacroix. —David Richard and Gaubert. —Phrenology and magnetism. —Saints and angels.

Eugène Delacroix[23] was one of the first friends I made in the art world, and I pride myself on still being able to count him among my old friends. Obviously, "old" here refers to the longevity of the relationship and not to the person himself. Delacroix does not age, and never will. He and his genius are young. Notwithstanding the uniquely piquant contradiction whereby his intellect is constantly criticizing the present and mocking the future, while his delight is in knowing, savoring, interpreting, and cherishing exclusively the works and often also the ideas of the past, in his art he is an unparalleled innovator and risk taker. For me he is the foremost artist of our time, and in relation to those of the past, he is bound to remain one of the foremost in the history of painting. Considering that this art form has not generally made much progress since the Renaissance, and that it appears to be relatively less appreciated and less understood by the masses, it is only natural that an artistic type like Delacroix—who for so long was either stifled or threatened by artistic decadence and general perversion in taste—should have reacted with all his instinctive might against the modern world. In all the obstacles that surrounded him, he sought monsters to overthrow, and believed he had found them most often in the idea of social progress, whose partial or excessive side he chose solely to notice. His is too much of an opinionated, passionate temperament to adapt itself to abstractions. His attitude toward social issues parallels that of Marie Dorval in matters of religion. Such powerful imaginations require solid ground on which to erect the edifice of their thoughts. One must not ask them to wait for the light to go on. They abhor vagueness; they require broad daylight. It is quite simple—they are both day and light unto themselves.

One must not expect to soothe them by saying that certainty is, and will always be, beyond what we do here and now, and that hope for the future need not be diminished by the spectacle of current affairs. Those penetrating eyes of theirs often see forward-looking men forced to take backward steps, and from that moment on, they conclude that the philosophy of the century is going in reverse.

This is the right place to say that the philosophy of those of us who pride ourselves in being progressive should itself demonstrate a certain growth in tolerance. We want only one truth to exist in art, in politics, and, generally, in every area that is not an exact science, and that, too, is a truth. But as soon as we have formulated that truth for our own benefit, we fancy we have found the true formula, we persuade ourselves that there is but one, and henceforth we mistake the formula for the thing itself. That is where the error, struggle, injustice, and chaos of futile arguments begin.

There is but one truth in art, and that is beauty; there is but one moral truth, and that is goodness; there is but one truth in the political arena, and that is justice. But as soon as you set out individually to establish the framework from whence you claim to be excluding all, in your opinion, that is not just, good, and beautiful, you succeed only in so narrowing or deforming your concept of the ideal, that you are fated—mercifully so—to find yourself alone in your opinion. The framework of truth is vaster, vaster by far, than anything we as individuals can imagine.

Only the notion of infinity can expand a bit this finite nature of ours, yet it is the one concept we find most difficult to grasp. Disputation and denigration, nitpicking and muckraking have, especially these days, taken on such epidemic proportions that many young artists have died in the name of art, having forgotten—such was their quickness of tongue—that it was ultimately a question of proving themselves by their works and not by their theories. The infinite cannot be proven, it must be sought, and beauty is better sensed by the soul than defined by rules. All the catechisms on art and politics that we bandy about smack of political and artistic infancy. Therefore, let the arguments continue, as that is doubtlessly the kind of laborious, irritating, and juvenile instruction our age still requires. But let those of us who feel within us a genuine urge not be bothered by the schoolyard din; let us instead complete our task while discreetly plugging our ears.

And then, when our current task has been accomplished, let us assess that done by the others, and let us not hastily exclaim, solely because it is done differently, that it is not done well. It is better to gain than to gainsay, and often one gains nothing for being so intent on criticizing everything.

We demand too much logic from our peers, and that only proves that we do not possess enough ourselves. We want every issue to be seen through our eyes, and the more an individual impresses us by the use of the higher faculties, the more we want to assimilate that person into our own frame of reference which, granting it may not be terribly inferior, is at least quite different. As philosophers, we would like a musician to find the keenest delight in Spinoza[24]; as musicians, we would like a philosopher to give us a rendition of the opera *William Tell*[25]; and when the artist who is a daring innovator in his own field rejects innovations in another, or, for that matter, when a thinker who can scarcely contain his desire to plunge into the uncharted realms of his beliefs recoils before the novelty of an artistic experiment, we call it inconsistency and would readily exclaim, "You there, artist! I condemn your works of art because you are not in my party or of my school; you, philosopher, I deny your wisdom because you understand nothing of mine."

Too often we judge in this manner, and too often published criticism contributes handily to this perfectly outrageous system of intolerance. This was especially noticeable a few years ago when numerous newspapers and magazines reflected many shades of opinion. One might then have said, "Tell me what newpaper you write for and I shall tell you which artist you are going to praise or criticize."

People have often said to me, "How can you co-exist with and speak to that friend of yours who thinks anything but the way you do? What concessions does he make to you, and what concessions are you forced to make to him?"

I have never made or demanded the least concession, and if I ever argued about anything, it was to teach myself while making others speak—to teach myself, but not necessarily in order to accept their solutions; instead, by examining their thought processes and searching out in them the source of their convictions, I came to understand just what factual contradictions the most organized human being contains within his apparent logic, and in turn, what true logic he harbors within his apparent contradictions.

Once an intellect reveals its powers, its needs, its aims—even its disabilities, along with its grandeur—I see no reason not to accept it fully, dark spots included, which, like those on the sun, may not be seen by the naked eye without a considerable amount of blinking.

Thus, I have, beyond the close friendship which binds me to certain extraordinary individuals, a great respect for matters which I would not myself accept as dogma, but which I see as the unavoidable, perhaps even necessary, conditions—the internal crackings of the whip, as it were—of their personal development. Though a great artist may deny in my presence some part of what constitutes the very life of my soul, I remain unconcerned; I know full well that by way of those places of my soul which are open to him, he will, through his ardor, help me recollect my own vital forces. Likewise, should a great philosopher criticize me for being an artist, he would only succeed in making me more of an artist by reviving my faith in higher truths through the very eloquence with which he explained them.

Our intellect is a box with compartments that communicate among themselves, thanks to a wonderful mechanism. Whenever a great intellect confides in us, it is as if he were allowing us to savor an entire bouquet of flowers, of which certain scents might be noxious to us individually, but which quicken and enchant us when they blend with scents that modify them.

These are some thoughts that come to mind concerning Eugène Delacroix, and they are equally applicable to a number of eminent personalities whom I have been lucky enough to know, without letting their argumentative and sometimes even derisive remarks upset me. I have been tenacious in resisting some of their pronouncements, but also tenacious in my affection for them and in my gratitude for the favor they did me of arousing a sense of self within me. Though they look on me as an incorrigible dreamer, they also know me to be a loyal friend.

In matters of theory, therefore, the great master of whom I speak may be melancholy and sullen, but on a person-to-person basis he is as much of a charmer and *bon enfant* as he is playful. Luckily for those whom he criticizes, he demolishes without fury and mocks without malice; for he has as much wit as he has genius, despite what one may infer from his paintings, where grandeur takes precedence over grace and where mastery has no use for prettiness. Delacroix's characters are stern; one enjoys looking them straight in the face. They call us to a region that lies above the one we live in. Whether they are gods, warriors, poets, or sages, the great figures of allegory and history that have been depicted by Delacroix capture our attention either with their fearsome bearing or their Olympian composure. It is imposssible, while viewing them, to imagine the pitiful studio model found in almost all the latest paintings, cloaked in a borrowed costume that was supposed to effect a transformation. It seems that though Delacroix did make men and women pose, he must somehow have blinked his eyes that they not appear excessively lifelike.

And yet these figures are real, albeit idealized in the direction of dramatic movement or majestic repose. They are just as real as the images that occur within us when we imagine the god of poetry or the heroes of antiquity. They are actually human, but not such commonplace human beings as it pleases the most common human being to imagine when he tries to comprehend them. They are truly living figures, but theirs is the kind of grandiose, sublime, even terrifying life only a genius can inspirit.

I am not referring to Delacroix's use of color. Only he might perhaps have the skill and the right to explain the one aspect of his art where even his most obstinate adversaries have found no grounds for debate; but to speak of color in painting is like attempting to convey the essence of music with words. Can Mozart's *Requiem* be described? One might well write a good poem while listening to it, but it would only be a poem, and not a translation; one medium cannot be translated into another. The arts are closely intertwined in the depths of our soul, but because they do not share the same language, they only communicate among themselves through mysterious analogies. They seek out, espouse, and fecundate one another amidst raptures in which each continues to express only itself.

"The beauty of this business," Delacroix once delightedly told me in one of his letters, "resides in those things that the spoken word is not capable of expressing. . . . I know you understand me," he added, "for a particular sentence in your letter tells me precisely how much you sense the limitations indispensable to each of the arts, limitations which your male colleagues sometimes overstep with admirable ease."

No matter which of the arts is in question, there is scarcely any way of analyzing the creative process, unless it is done by proceeding along the same level. When the shallow-minded wish to reduce the great procedures of the masters to their own level, they drift aimlessly without in the least penetrating the masterpiece in question; their efforts are to no avail.

And as for analyzing the methods of the masters—whether for blame or acclaim—the display of technical terms employed more or less skillfully by the critics in their discussions of painting and music remains no more than a tour de force that either fools or fails to fool the public. When the gambit fails—as often happens to those who discuss the profession, indiscriminately using terms which they do not understand—their display makes even the humblest amateur smile. When it succeeds, the public is none the wiser as to what it should rightfully be feeling, and students eager to capture the secrets of the masters learn nothing. In vain, you will explain to these critics the artist's method; to the naïve daubers who are awestruck by a bit of canvas and ask in amazement, "How is that done?" you will, in vain, reveal the scientific theory behind the craft. Had these methods been revealed to someone by the master himself, they would still be perfectly useless to him who is incapable of creating a similar work. If he has no talent, no medium whatsoever will serve his purpose. If he does have talent, he will find his medium on his own, or else will employ that of another, but in his own manner, having understood the means without your assistance. The only critical works on art that are useful are those which elevate and broaden the reader's sensibility by developing the capacity of his feeling for great things. Seen in that light, Diderot was a great critic,[26] and in our own day more than one critic has managed to write respectably on art. Other than that, there is only wasted effort and puerile pedantry.

I have before me an example of superior criticism. For those of you who may not have a copy at hand, this excerpt will illustrate what I mean:

"One cannot ignore the fact that fewer and fewer books are being printed that are directed at the most inspired part of the mind; a type of deadly chill is overtaking us little by little which will totally freeze the source of all veneration and poetic inspiration.... Are we to believe that masterpieces are not made for, nor appreciated by, the public at large, and that it reserves its greatest admiration for frivolous trifles? Could it be that the public feels an antipathy of some sort for whatever achievements stand out above the ordinary, and that its instincts naturally lead it toward what is coarse and short-lived? Could not every work which appears to isolate itself from the whims of fashion by virtue of its grandeur unwittingly possess the secret factor which displeases the public, and does not the public sense therein a kind of reproach for the inconstancy of its taste and the conceit of its opinions?"

After that declaration filled with pain and amazement, the critic I am quoting speaks of *The Last Judgment*[27] and, without using any trade terminology, without initiating us into techniques we have no need whatsoever of mastering, indeed, while remaining solely intent on communicating to us his own burning enthusiasm, takes us right to the core of Michelangelo's beliefs:

"Thus it is the style of Michelangelo," he says, "which alone seems appropriate to a subject of that nature. The kind of convention adhered to by this style, that is, the absolute avoidance at all costs of any triviality—at times risking turgidness and aiming for the impossible—was certainly appropriate in painting a tableau that transports us into a completely idealized sphere. How very true it is that our souls always surpass what art can express in this genre, and that poetry, which seems the least material in its means of expression, never gives us anything but an altogether too well-defined idea, if we compare works on a similar theme. When the *Apocalypse*[28] of Saint John depicts nature's final convulsions, the crumbling mountains, the stars falling from the heavens, even the greatest, most poetic mind cannot help but situate the scene being presented within a human framework. The comparisons used by the poet are drawn from material objects, which arrest our thoughts in mid-flight. Michelangelo, by contrast, projects, with a dozen or so symmetrically positioned clusters of people on one easily apprehended surface, what is an incomparably more devastating impression of the supreme catastrophe that will lead the lost human race to the feet of its judge. He does not owe the immense empire he plucks instantaneously from his imagination to any of the expedient sources that ordinary painters may employ; it is his style alone which sustains him in the regions of the sublime, and which whisks us there with him. . . . Michelangelo's Christ is neither a philosopher nor the hero of a novel; He is God Himself, about to reduce the world to ashes. Michelangelo, the painter of shapes, must have contrasts, shadows, light falling on the fleshy bodies in motion. *The Last Judgment* is the celebration of the flesh; hence we see it already traced on the bones of those who rise haggardly from the grave the instant the trumpet sounds to unseal their tombs and tear them from their centuries-old slumber. What a variety of lyric poses they assume as they open their eyelids at the break of this last baleful day, that once and for all rids the sepulcher of its dust and penetrates the very bowels of the earth where death has hoarded its victims! Some strain to raise the thick layer beneath which they have slept for so long; others, already free of their burden, remain prostrate, as though astonished at themselves. Further on, the avenging barge carries away the legions of the damned. There stands Charon, beating the dawdlers with his oar."[29]

Who actually wrote these beautiful lines? Don't we seem to be hearing Michelangelo himself speaking of his work and explaining its meaning? Isn't the style so altogether grand and resolute that it does not appear to belong to our century? Must it not be the master himself, as translated by some contemporary writer of the first order?

Not so! These lines have been written by a modern master who has neither inclination nor time to write. They were hastily scribbled one day, when the author was burning with indignation at the public's and critics' indifference to a beautiful reproduction of *The Last Judgment* by Sigalon,[30] which Parisians were being urged to view at the Palais de Beaux-Arts, yet continued flatly to ignore. These lines are signed "Eugène Delacroix"; the author, however, does not wish to hear the passage referred to in his presence, and seems to dread rereading it himself.

I shall not bemoan the absence of further comparable writings.[(5)] Instead, I shall only say, What a pity he wasn't able to add twelve more hours to his work-day, for none was long enough for painting! Only he, in my opinion, could communicate his own genius to the masses, while conveying to them the spirit of the masters whom he loved and understood so well.

Let us quote from his conclusion, for it will illustrate the process by which Delacroix became a painter equal to Michelangelo:

"Some have loudly claimed that the mere sight of Michelangelo's masterpiece would corrupt an art student's taste and induce a mannered style—as if anything could be more disastrous than the mannerisms of the Art Schools themselves. There are some, no doubt, for whom striking models lack appeal. The study of such a larger-than-life style, of such abstract art, if one may call it that, is comparable to those arduous regimens which only the hardy submit to. Faced with such grandeur and temerity, the simple-minded student will revert to his own teacher, seeing in the great painter's disdain for crude imitation only an inability to imitate; the schoolmaster, in turn, will ask himself if he should put aside tradition in the face of such contempt for all tradition; the sublime artist, however, moves on across the centuries surrounded by far worthier disciples. All the painters of renown march at his side and crown him with the rays of their own glory.... After art undergoes all the novel permutations to which it may be subjected both by whim and a need for change, the extraordinary style of the Florentine will always be a kind of magnetic pole toward which we shall have to turn again, in order to rediscover the road to all greatness and beauty."

And there you have his method! It consists of worshipping beauty first, then understanding it, and finally evoking it from within himself. There is no other way.

Delacroix's soul, with its thirst for great things, probably suffered mortal anguish because of the lack of intelligence that prevails in this century. It is fortunate that the charming good humor of his spirit spared him the kind of suffering that embitters. As for the kind that enervates, his temperament was too strong for him to acknowledge it. He solved the problem by soaring above it—a tremendous, victorious flight that left paradox and prattle far below— much as that fiery figure of Apollo, as if flung by him at the vaults of the Louvre, forgets the chimera he has just slain amid the splendor of the heavens.[31] He solved the problem without losing the youthfulness of his soul, the generosity and integrity of his instincts, the charm of his personality, or the modesty and good taste of his bearing.

Delacroix went through several phases of development as he went about impressing each of his illustrative sequences with a suitably profound sensibility. He was inspired by Dante, Shakespeare, and Goethe,[32] but once the Romantics had discovered in him their greatest exponent, they thought of him as belonging exclusively to their school. However, such creative fury could not be contained within such a closely defined sphere. His impetus implored both heaven and mankind to give it space, light, and panels large enough to contain its compositions; then, taking flight into the realm of its fullest idealism, he drew from the oblivion to which they were being relegated the allegories of ancient Olympus, and combined them—in his capacity of great poetic historian—with the examples set by the geniuses of recent centuries. Delacroix's searing interpretations enabled him to rejuvenate a world that had been lost to consciousness, or misrepresented by lifeless traditions. Surrounding his superhuman personifications, he created a world of light and effects which the word color cannot, perhaps, adequately convey, but which the public necessarily perceives on being possessed by the fear, thrill, or fascination that overtakes it on witnessing such virtuosity. This is where the master's emotional individuality bursts forth, visibly enriched by the collective emotions of modern times, whose wellspring lies hidden in the recesses of superior intellects and will continue to grow with each passing century.

Still, there will always be a number of hide-bound souls who rebuke Delacroix for not having offered their senses an interpretation of beauty, grace, voluptuous form, and tender expressiveness that accorded with their views. Time will tell whether their views were correct, and whether they were competent enough to discern the false from the true in what is itself the realm of fantasy. I doubt it. Those who truly understand Correggio, Raphael, Watteau, and Prudhon[33] also understand Delacroix. Grace has a throne of its own, and so does forcefulness. In any case, the graces are divinities of a thousand faces; they are lascivious or pure, according to the eye that regards them and according to the soul that puts them into words. The genius of Delacroix is stern, and whoever lacks a heightened sense of awareness will never fully enjoy it. In my opinion, the artist has become resigned to that.

Whatever the critics may say, however, Delacroix will leave behind a legacy great both in name and achievement. When we see his fragile, jittery-pale countenance, and hear him plaintively tell of the thousand persistent ailments that afflict him, we can only wonder that such a delicate constitution could so rapidly have produced such colossal works in the face of extraordinary adversity. Yet, there they are, soon to be followed—God willing—by many more; for the master is one of those who develop right up to the last instant; he is one whose each new masterpiece revises what we had thought was the last word.

Delacroix has not only been great in his art, but also in his artistic life, and my assessment does not even take into account his private virtues, his devotion to family, his kindness to less fortunate friends, in a word, his steadfast character. These are merits of a personal sort that friendship is reluctant to trumpet openly. The heartfelt effusions that appear in his wonderful letters would, at this juncture, form a beautiful chapter delineating him much better than I can. But should one's living friends be thus exposed, even if such revelations could only lead to the glorification of their beings? No, I do not believe they should. Friendship has a discretion all its own, much as love does. But in Delacroix, what demands public appreciation for an example well set is the integrity of his behavior; the meager income he was content to earn; the modest, protracted life of penury he accepted rather than make concessions in matters of artistic principle to the latest whims and fancies of the day (which are often simply those of the current social élite). His merit lies in the heroic perseverance with which—though an ailing, weak, and apparently broken man—he pursued his career, laughing at the scorn of fools, never paying back malice with malice, even though he possessed the kind of spell-binding wit and savoir vivre which could have made him an awesome adversary in that sort of ominously polite vanity contest. Maintaining his self-respect even in the smallest matters, he never snubbed the public, but continued to exhibit yearly amidst a crossfire of invective that would have deafened, or at least disheartened, any other person. Never resting, he sacrificed the most innocent pleasures—he has an admirable love and understanding for the other arts as well—to a rigorous work schedule that, for a long time, failed to improve either his standard of living or his career. Living from one day to the next, he had no desire for the ridiculous ostentation with which fashionable artists are wont to surround themselves; and yet, how well might he, whose tastes and physical makeup are so delicate, have adapted to a little added luxury and relaxation!

Throughout the ages and in all lands, people have spoken of great artists who surrendered nothing to vanity or greed, who sacrificed nothing to ambition, and forfeited nothing for the sake of revenge. To mention the name of Delacroix is to mention one of those very men whom the world is content to call honorable, not realizing what a difficult undertaking it is both for the craftsman who succumbs and the genius who struggles to uphold his honor.

There is no need for me to give a complete account of the relationship Delacroix and I share; suffice it to say that it has been one of unclouded friendship. Such a thing is both quite rare and quite exquisite, and between us it has found absolute integrity. I do not know of any flaws in the character of Delacroix. I have, at frequent intervals, lived close by him, in the informality of a country setting, without ever perceiving in him a single blemish, however small. And yet in the area of friendship, there is no one more sociable, more unaffected, or more unpretentious. It is so easy to be devoted to such a deserving person that you even perceive yourself to be flawless when you enjoy close relations with him. Furthermore, it is to him I owe what are unquestionably the greatest moments of pure delight that I, as an artist, have ever experienced. If other superior intellects initiated me into their discoveries and ecstasies within the sphere of a mutually shared ideal, I can honestly say that no other single artistic personality was ever more appealing or—if I may put it in such a way—more accessible, by virtue of his refreshing candor. The masterpieces we read, or see, or hear, are never better understood than when their power is reinforced, so to speak, by our esteem for an extraordinary talent. Delacroix is his own peer in music and poetry, as he is in painting, and everything he says in moments of revelation is, without his even knowing it, either fascinating or remarkable.

I do not propose to entertain the public with accounts of all my friends. To devote a chapter to each of them, aside from the fact that it might injure the timid modesty of certain persons who prefer to be withdrawn and inconspicuous, would be of interest only to me and a very limited number of readers. If I have mentioned Rollinat repeatedly, it is because this typical friendship gave me an opportunity to erect my humble altar to a religion of the soul that is contained, to a more or less pure degree, within each of us.

As for the famous, I do not ascribe to myself the right to open the sanctuary of their private lives, but I do consider it my duty to assess the outstanding totality of their lives as it relates to the mission they are fulfilling, and especially so if I find myself in a position to serve that function knowledgeably.

Let, therefore, those of my old friends who do not find their names in this segment of my autobiography not think they have been erased from my memory. Quite a few have remained dear to me and continue to occupy the sweet, honorable place in my heart they earned long ago, even though, with the passage of time, circumstances have forced them away from my environment.

You, David Richard,[34] are the one to mention out of this group, O paradigm of nobility and sweetness! O purest of souls! You deserve the esteem of a wider circle than that in which your truly Christian humility has always concealed itself. Charity has, in a manner of speaking, detached you from yourself, and both your patient studies and the generous effusions of your heart have led you into an apostolic style of life where my own heart has, with ceaseless admiration, pursued you.

For it is rare for souls inclined to such sentiments not to become themselves worthy of inspiring them in others. This simple axiom summarizes the entire life of David Richard. Endowed with both a delicate tenderness and a fervent faith, he saw in his friends (of which the illustrious Lamennais[35] heads the list) not supports or buttresses for his weaknesses, but natural replenishments for his dedication. I do not know if he himself ever received support or consolation. I certainly doubt whether he ever even considered uttering a complaint about any personal affliction. I do know, however, that he was always the one who listened, consoled, and soothed, drawing to himself everyone else's troubles and, then, either dispelling or palliating them by virtue of some mysterious force. I would have more to say about this force, if I dared speak of matters relating to the world of fantasy in connection with a man of such earnestness.

But why shouldn't I dare? I certainly contemplate doing it, and do not thereby feel my common sense veering in the direction of fantasy. No such dangers have surfaced in what David Richard has told me about phrenology and magnetism. He was himself always the first to call attention to any haphazard induction or unwarranted conclusion. He took very seriously those observations that abetted him in his quest to ascertain what part fatality plays in the destiny of mankind, but his spiritual inclinations kept him well within the realms of reason and religion that require us to reject the idea of invincible fatality.

Thus, after having zealously devoted itself to a search for a fatal determinant within the human organism, this noble intellect drew his inquiry to a halt just at the point where an atheism devoid of hope could have shaken a less reflective faith and less loving personality. He only immersed himself in the study of evil in order to seek a cure for it. He sought out imperfection in man for the sole purpose of extending pity, and illness for the purpose of healing. He remembered that hope is one of the three cardinal virtues, and standing on the very precipice of doubt, he lifted his eyes and prayed.

His friends were alarmed by an enthusiasm so penetrating and yet so tranquil. They often begged me to save him, if possible, from his mystical tendencies. Among those friends was Dr. Gaubert,[36] who became as much of a friend to me as did Dr. Richard. Gaubert was of the same temper, where virtue and goodness were concerned, but his enthusiasm was more expansive, and his intellect more given to absolutes.

I do not think it would have been possible for me to change Richard's convictions; I never even tried to do so, because I never found his soul to be in peril where these sensitive issues were concerned. I believe—if I understood Gaubert correctly (for Richard was not communicative where these matters were concerned)—that the debate turned on the essential point I touched on earlier: whether the destiny of an organism was predetermined or accidental; in other words, whether divine volition had predestined the range of a creature's instincts, as well as its irreversible damnation or salvation in this world, or, on the other hand, whether that same divine will had allowed the will of mankind to be tested by more or less trying, yet always surmountable, episodes of distress.

My readers will recall from the beginning of this manuscript that I lean toward the latter opinion. I have said that, in my view, we carry within us the eternal tempter, but that, by divine agency—called "grace" by the Christian community—we also harbor within us the ability to resist him. I thus share more the opinion of Richard, who believed in grace, than that of Gaubert, who believed only in certain phrenological permutations arrived at by diet and instruction.

I was not well enough educated, nor am I yet sufficiently so, to be out-spoken in either direction when dealing with men who have made these issues their life's work. My personal beliefs derive above all from my feelings, and they have always sufficed to determine my conduct. Thus, I found nothing in these two precious and beloved friends to impede my own spirit's progress along its proper course. Both men were agreed in singling out the deadly caus-es of good and evil as being part and parcel of every living being; what they differed on was the degree of curative effectiveness. Richard, believing that the supreme remedy lay in God, did not halt at the threshold of Catholic dogma as much as Gaubert might have wished, who—like me—was an enemy of the dogmas of eternal suffering in the afterlife and of absolute penance here on earth; he saw in our laws that demand penalties of incarceration and death little more than a translation of the religious concept of irreversible damnation.

It seemed to me that both tended toward pragmatic truth, one by desiring the laws to be more indulgent to the poor creatures deprived of a sense of responsibility for their actions, and the other by desiring virtue and faith to act upon the souls of the wayward or perverse.

If death had not robbed us of Gaubert in the midst of his career, he would have ultimately found some noble cause to which to dedicate his principles. Richard sought and attained his by devoting himself to a cure for insanity. He is now the chief medical officer at the Stephansfeld Asylum and continually seeks to calm, distract, console, and uplift his poor, deranged charges, and rekindle in them the spark of reason or morality.

I do not know how his views on magnetism[37] have evolved. Throughout the years in which we were able to keep in touch, he devoted himself at length to the study of this mysterious force, in which Gaubert had absolute faith. The latter had me observe some experiments which had me convinced for a while, but he himself discovered we had been duped. Personally, I must admit that, after being taken in so cunningly, I have acquired a skepticism that will be most difficult to cure.

Gaubert held fast to his beliefs to the end, admitting, as did his worthy friend, Dr. Frappart, that because sycophants and charlatans had taken over the lucrative business of being magnetic subjects, he had never been able to put his hands on a single decisive fact, but simultaneously protesting in the name of scientific logic that a fact is not necessarily proof. Frankly, that is a conclusion I have great difficulty in accepting. Science is, in this regard at least, something so new that it will be quite a while before it goes beyond the mere search for causes and the determination of how certain unusual facts came about. And if these occurrences seem impenetrable, which of nature's laws will command us, in the name of logic, to forego the proof? Does it follow that because magnetic attraction governs a certain order of substances, human thought can disengage itself from any organic function and take us into the realm of illusion?

I have given this a great deal of thought, without the least prejudice to the contrary; I have, in fact, been spurred on by that violent desire to abandon the positivist world and chart my course to that of mystery, to which the poetic imagination is so inclined. To delude myself was very thrilling at one time. My current opinion is that scientific officialdom is showing great irresponsibility in its disdainful refusal to undertake any attentive examination whatsoever of the magnetic phenomena. More often than not, I have found the excuses they give for not attempting such a study to be quite inadequate. Yet, I myself have never seen any evidence, and all things taken into consideration, the convictions I harbor do not warrant my speaking out in favor of magnetism, not under the many forms it has assumed in the process of becoming an object of profit and amusement, and still less so now that the tables try so much harder to move than in the past, when nothing of the sort was expected of them.

Nevertheless, human beings do show a kind of magnetism—the kind that certain animals exert on other species in order to attract and subject them. Great orators, great artists, even some among the common run of people who happen to be endowed with a stubborn, impulsive will, frequently bring this force to bear on those of their peers whose inclinations toward mysticism make them particularly vulnerable to it. But this force is far from absolute or irresistible; it fails entirely with a large number of subjects, even as it dominates completely a limited number of others. And even when this force is exercised by a superior person, and the majority succumb, even then it is powerless over a few recalcitrant individuals.

It is, thus, a limited power which needs the consent of others to function. No man comes into the world with absolute power to control his peers. God, who did not confer on man that right, also refuses him that power. Whatever greater powers of control some have been endowed with they owe entirely to providential design, which reserves that moral authority for those who are worthy of it.

Also, there are, in the exhilaration of suppressed passion, in the sustained strength of deep affection, and as well, perhaps, in the contests of strong minds, evidences of a magnetic intuition that neither heart nor mind refuses to admit; on the other hand, both heart and mind reject with disgust the prophecies of the charlatans and the forebodings of the streetcorner sibyls.

In the last analysis, I do seriously believe in "influences." I know of no other term for those sudden moods into which we are thrust unawares by certain persons who perhaps are not even aware of their power, these being usually the people we love, or find offensive, at first sight. Whether it is through an impression received in the course of a previous incarnation and of which we have lost recollection, or actually a fluid that emanates from these individuals, it is undeniable that encounters with them affect us either in beneficial or detrimental ways. I do not believe these suspicions to be products of the imagination, because I have never known the effects to be so. Nor am I referring to fantasies or preconceptions of a superficial or prejudiced nature. You do well to overcome these as soon as you perceive them to be ill-founded; some, however, are quite serious, but do not receive sufficient attention, though we invariably regret having spurned them when we no longer have the freedom to make that decision.

If this is a superstition, then it is one I must own up to, for it has been my experience to love all my life those people whom I loved at first sight. This was the case with David Richard, whom I have not seen in more than ten years, and it was also the case with my poor friend Gaubert, whom I shall not see again in this life. To see them was for me cause for true bliss, even physically, for I felt it in the ease with which I suddenly breathed—as though they were surrounding me with a purer atmosphere than I was accustomed to. Furthermore, no longer being able to see them has taken almost nothing away from the intellectual well-being their memories evoke in me, or from the serenity that overtakes my mind when I imagine I am talking to them.

For though I cannot unequivocally state that some souls are made for one another—too many differences in their abilities forbid them from following blindly the same path—there are, nonetheless, some that are suited to one another at some critical, dominant point. Using his phrenological parlance, Gaubert would tell me that protuberances of "affectivity" and "veneration" were what gave us a hold on one another. So be it! When such souls meet, each mutually senses and accepts the other without hesitation; they greet each other like old acquaintances; one has nothing new to inform the other of, yet they delight in conversing together as if they were meeting again after a long separation.

The admirable and unhappy woman of whom I spoke in the preceding chapter demanded of heaven saints and angels here on earth. I remember having often told her there were indeed some, but we did not always have the God-given sense to recognize them beneath the humble exterior, and sometimes tattered clothing, that concealed them. We have dreams of glory; we seek what is prestigious. Beauty, charm, wit, grace—all conspire to inebriate us, and off we run after a succession of meteoric cheaters, not suspecting that true saints are more often hidden in the crowd than exposed on pedestals. And whenever we do follow those beautiful lights that attract us like will-o'-the-wisps, they suddenly go out, and with them the enthusiasm they inspired in us. Such mistakes sometimes go under the rubric of passion. True saints do not engender such fanaticism. They inspire only feelings as sweet and angelic as themselves. They are too modest to want to tempt or dazzle anyone. They do not unsettle the mind; they do not torment the heart. They merely smile and give a blessing. Fortunate is the instinct that discovers them, and the intellect that esteems them.

Saints and angels! Why do we not wish to understand that these beautiful, incredible beings are already of this world in their latent state, much as the splendid butterflies inhabit their particular larvae. Such beings have neither fiery rays nor golden wings to distinguish them from the rest of mankind. Sometimes they even lack the deep luminous eyes that would brighten the pale countenance of my friend Gaubert. They are neither noticed nor admired in the world. They do not stand out anywhere, not on swift horses, not in the stage-boxes, not in the salons; nor do they stand out in the academies, assemblies, or clubs. Had they lived during the reign of Tiberius, they would only have appeared as martyrs in the arena, as did so many other loyal servants of God, of whom we might never have heard had not the opportunity for a great act of faith presented itself and sent to the heavenly archives both the holy names of obscure victims and the resplendence of their unprepossessing virtue.

Saints and angels! It is certain, as I see it, that Gaubert was a saint and that Richard was an angel; the latter was at peace and seemed to glide untroubled, and without fear, on the surface of his private radiance; the former was more agitated and more impatient. He would exhale scathing invectives against insanity or abnormality, both of which, despite study, he understood less and less as time wore on.

Because Gaubert felt a real tendersness toward me, he inspired in me the same feeling toward him. Though he was but a dozen or so years older, his bald head, hollow cheeks, frail health, and, above all, the simple austerity of his life and ideas—all these made him seem twenty years older, to me and and to his other friends. His type was that of the virtuous father, strict in his theories, but indulgent to the point of coddling, whenever his affections came into play. I mourned his death, not just out of respect and sorrow, but out of heartfelt self-ishness. Yet, all of us had heard him say a hundred times that we should not mourn our loved ones; instead, we were to thank God for having called them to Him, and extend our devotion beyond the grave by rejoicing in the knowledge that they had received their reward. He was right, but who can reason with the heart? Thus, if I have bitterly regretted his absence, that may be his fault. He had made himself too necessary, where I was concerned. I saw in him a haven from all discouragement and debility of the will, an embodiment of the law of duty, combined with the pleasures of ardent preaching and all the delights of fatherly solicitude which penetrate and soothe. Saints of a fiercely ascetic nature either capture the imagination or awaken the kind of pride we call emulation. Thus, it is only those with a similar pride whom they affect. Sweet, loving saints exert a greater attraction, and I, for my part, am fond only of these.

I shall have occasion to speak of Gaubert again, and of the kind brother who has survived him, at a later point in my story. But in connection with Richard and magnetism, I must first recount a particular phenomenon that I do not pretend to be able to explain.

I am, I believe, a very uncooperative subject where direct magnetic influence is concerned; I doubt whether I could be put to sleep, and even then, I do not think dreaming could be induced. Were I, nevertheless, to dream out loud, little more might be proven by that than is proven by those who make random predictions which later seem justified by random chance. Magnetic "passes" irritate my nerves and make me impatient. To put it bluntly, I no more believe in the fluid which travels from the palm of one person's hand to another person's brain than I do in the one that, through the fingertips, conjures the soul from a table or from a hat.

On the other hand, the extraordinary influence which the mere presence of a sympathetic or antipathetic person can exert on the nervous system is something I have personally experienced and must, perforce, believe in. The antipathy may be only of the physical kind, in fact, and still remain inexplicable. I have experienced it in relation to the violent migraines of which I have been a long-time sufferer. A mere chance meeting with certain people whom I had no further reason to hate, and who were causing me no aggravation, would immediately bring on an attack, or else make my headache doubly unbearable. And when, as soon as I saw them again, without even any recollection on my part—consequently, with no help from my imagination—these awful pains would seize me again suddenly, then I had to believe the "fluid" was playing some part in it.

The only curative fluid I have ever encountered was Richard's. On three or four occasions, a migraine or liver pain left me within minutes of coming into his presence; just for him to appear in the same room would have that effect. Neither his will-power nor my imagination had the least bit to do with it. Regardless of what is said about it, the imagination does not act unknown to itself, in clearheaded individuals.

I shall not comment further on that fact, but I am still convinced that certain individuals can act on certain others by means other than the emotions, the imagination, or the senses. Therefore, I say it is by means of the "fluid," since that is the accepted term. I believe one is always capable of contending with an excess of that influence, if it is harmful, but that one should not lightly deny its existence without first giving it some study. If it seems mysterious, it is only because a clear and specific explanation has not yet been found for it.

I ask the reader's forgiveness for having dwelled so long on such an insignificant matter that may relate only to me, and shall now conclude as follows: it is easy to traverse the cares of the world, in our own time, by summarily rejecting what offends our instincts, or by accepting blindly what flatters them. Personally, I feel it is my duty to report as impartially as possible not so much what has been said by those around me concerning this issue, but rather the exact impression made on me by those discussions. I have not wanted to speak of the mystery of electromagnetism with complete irreverence, nor did I want to go on without contributing some token of my own experience in support of what could or should be serious investigation.

Incidentally, I confer no more importance on my own opinion than what it truly deserves. If I am accountable to the public in this regard, it is above all because in some of my writings I permitted my imagination to stray into a world of its own dominion, a world whose depiction is usually of little consequence where realistic novels are concerned.[38] I must now depreciate the marvels I once assimilated without hesitation. One attractive feature of novels is that they are a kind of loose history of what is happening at any given moment in time in the minds of men, whether it be dramatic, humorous, or serious in nature. A historian is obliged to pass judgment on everything, but a novelist has more freedom and can, with no feeling of guilt, submit to the passing fancies of his imagination. He knows that, in fiction, these notions cannot misguide anyone, and that if they are later examined from a historical point of view, it is always possible to find in them the kind of enlightenment that is founded on appreciating the degree of emotional intensity radiated by an age that has itself experienced it. Part two of *Wilhelm Meister*, which seems no longer to take place in the real world, is very interesting to study as a manifestation of the new *Weltanschauung* [world view] that Goethe[39]—who, at the time, personified both rational and contemplative German thought—carried within him; I say this, by the way, without drawing any presumptuous comparisons between Goethe and the humble author of these pages.

As for any conclusive deductions regarding the taste for marvel that magnetism has brought into the world, that point has not yet been reached, and it will be quite some time before science will be able to make any such pronouncements with any substance to them. Yet, should nothing remain of these disputes but certain manuscripts, or the pages they have taken up in others, they will, nevertheless, have served to raise a multitude of questions of real interest and give the human mind practice in the struggle for progress.

For my part, I have at last come to understand—after torturing myself for some time with these problems—that there is no great shame in not being able to settle them satisfactorily. Each age has its own problems, and not in philosophy or politics are the least ones to be found. Thus, each age is hampered on its way by difficult issues in every field, and those who resolve them hurriedly often regret having taken a premature stand once they reach old age, when they find themselves contradicted by proven facts, or at least by probabilities that can no longer be taken lightly. Our weak spot lies in never daring to say "I don't know." We are afraid of being written off as ignorant or lazy. You can easily be neither one, however, and esteem yourself no greater than the age in which you live.

Admittedly, were people naïvely to acknowledge ignorance every time they felt it, little enough would be said, and even less would be written.

The impression that remains with me in connection with all that I have heard regarding certain very specious topics is that caring, intelligent people, who sincerely sought enlightenment, would always radiate light around them on other more important subjects. Thus, in studying the bony structure of the human cranium, Richard succeeded in shedding light on the human mind, via reflections of his subtle reason and fervent humanitarianism. Gaubert, in turn, would guide me through the catacombs, for days at a time, while speaking to me of life and death like a true metaphysician and philosopher.   *E.B.O.*

VI

Sainte-Beuve. —Luigi Calamatta. —Gustave Planche. —Charles Didier. —Why I do not say anything about certain others.

I do not think I am interrupting the progress of my account by dedicating a few more pages to my friends. The world of sentiments and ideas to which these friends introduced me is an essential part of my story, that of my moral and intellectual development. I have the deep conviction that I owe to others anything slightly good I have acquired in my soul. I was born with the taste and need for truth, but my mental constitution was not of the type to forego the kind of education that also appealed to my instincts, or find it ready-made in books. Especially my sensitivity, having hardly ever been checked, needed control. The enlightened friends and wise counsel came a little too late; by then the fire had smoldered too long under the ashes to be easily put out. But this painful sensitivity was often calmed, and always consoled, by wise and kindly affections.

When looked at one way, my partially cultivated mind could be considered a clean slate, but from another point of view it was a chaos. My ability to listen—a major blessing—let me at least receive from all who surrounded me a certain amount of clarity, as well as many subjects to reflect on. Among them were some superior men who led me to make great strides fairly quickly, and other men of less striking ability, who even appeared ordinary, but who were never so in my eyes; the latter helped me greatly to extricate myself from the maze of uncertainty in which my contemplation had wandered for so long.

Among the men of appreciable talent, Sainte-Beuve, with the abundant and precious resources of his conversation, was very salutary for me; at the same time, his friendship—somewhat easily offended, slightly capricious, but always precious to recapture—sometimes gave me the strength I lacked in my own affairs. Yes, he hurt me deeply by his dislikes and bitter attacks on people I admired, but I had neither the right nor power to modify his opinions, nor curb the sharpness of his arguments. And since, with regard to me, he was always generous and affectionate (I was told that his talk had sometimes betrayed me, but I no longer believe it) and since he had succored my spiritual and mental griefs with care and delicacy in times gone by, I see it as a duty to count him among my intellectual mentors and benefactors.

His literary style, however, did not serve me as a model, and in moments when my thought felt the need of a bolder expression, his delicate and adroit manner was more apt to hobble me than set me free. But when the feverish season is past, one comes back to that Vanloo-like form,[40] in order to recognize its true strength and beauty, in spite of the idiosyncracies and cachet of the school; beneath those charming strokes of studied elegance there is the genius of the master. As poet and critic, Sainte-Beuve is also a master. His thought is often complex, which makes it a little hard to grasp at first approach, but things which have real integrity are worth re-reading; then the clarity comes to life beneath the apparent obscurity. The single flaw of this writer is an excess of virtues. He knows so much, he understands so well, he sees and guesses so many things, his taste is so abundant, and his subject grips him from so many sides at once, that language may be for him insufficient, and the form always too confining for the subject.

In my opinion, he was dominated by a contradiction harmful not so much to his talent—he certainly proved that his talent did not suffer from it—but to his own happiness. By happiness I do not mean a fortuitous conjunction of events, which is in no man's power to call forth and control, but rather a certain source of faith and inner serenity, which however intermittent and troubled by outside contact, springs more or less eternal from the depths of the soul. The only happiness that God has granted us and of which we may, without being foolish, dare ask Him for continuance, is the feeling that amid the catastrophes of ordinary living, we stay in possession of pure, intimate joys that indeed become ideal for the one who savors them. In art as in philosophy, in love as in friendship, in all those abstract areas from which experience cannot remove the quality of feeling or dream, eventually age or early maturity brings us the benefit of being at peace with ourselves.

Probably that day has come for Sainte-Beuve, but at first I saw him as tormented as I was, and for as long, although he had infinitely more knowledge and reasoning power against suffering. He taught wisdom with convincing eloquence, and yet bore within him the turmoil of an unassuaged soul.

It seemed to me, then, that he wanted to solve the problem of human reason by complicating it. He saw happiness in the absence of illusion and entanglement, but then, just as quickly, he felt bored, disgusted, and depressed in the exercise of pure logic. He felt a need for grand emotions; he agreed that to avoid them through fear of disenchantment was the mark of a dupe, since inevitably the small emotions wear us down, a little at a time; but he wanted to control the great passion, while submitting to it. He wanted us to forgive our illusions for not being attainable, forgetting, it seems to me, that unless they were unattainable, they did not exist at all, and that friends, lovers, and philosophers who saw something to forgive in their ideals had already relinquished their idealism, and were quite simply going through the motions of virtue and wisdom.

I have always rebelled against the paradox of loving, or believing, as a form of duty. In point of fact, one can act as if one believes or loves—it is, in some cases, one's duty. But from the moment the belief, or the love, is no longer inspired, it is duty alone that one believes in and loves.

Sainte-Beuve was much too smart to give himself such an impossible assignment, but when he started to philosophize on the art of living, perhaps I was wrong, but I thought I saw him going around that vicious circle.

Too much heart for his mind and too much mind for his heart was how I summarized his eminent character for myself, and without daring to claim that I thoroughly understood him, I still imagine that this summary is the key to whatever was original and mysterious in his talent. Had this talent let itself grow weak, clumsy, or worn out by time, a more striking revenge would have been exacted; but by not giving in to change, it kept its excellent temper. Those who think they have glimpsed something more emotional and profound than an artist has deigned to express are letting themselves in for a certain amount of disappointment. They have had more ambition for this artist than he himself had. Likewise, the public cannot know that the works which charm and instruct it are often the overflow from a vase that has withheld the most precious part of its fluid. Besides, that is somewhat the story of us all. The soul always holds its greatest treasures in reserve, renderable only to God and presaged only by its outpourings of tenderness to its intimates. Frightening to contemplate would be the kind of genius that can spend itself in one fell swoop, for one fears it would exhaust itself in that supreme effort. The impossibility of complete self-expression is a godsend bestowed on human weakness, for if one could express the ultimate vision, it might at that moment cease to exist.

The occasion of a portrait that Buloz had had engraved to put on the frontispiece of one of my editions enabled me to make the acquaintance of Calamatta, an able and already reputable engraver, who lived poorly, but stylishly, with another Italian engraver, Mercuri, to whom we owe, among other things, the precious, small reproduction of *Les Moissonneurs* by Léopold Robert[41] These two artists were linked by a noble, brotherly friendship. My own timidity forbade all but a glance at, and swift greeting to, the shy Mercuri. Calamatta was more Italian in his manner; that is to say, more confiding and expansive. Him I quickly liked, and our friendship strengthened little by little over the duration of our lives.

Truthfully, I have met few friends as faithful, as tactful in their concern, who could be counted on to sustain a pleasant, sane relationship. When one can say of a man that he is a firm friend, one says an important thing about him, for it is rare to find a likable and lively person who is not in the least asinine, or a serious person who is not pedantic. Companionable amidst the laughter and bustle of an artist's life, Calamatta also has an introspective, and judicious side that one finds well attuned to matters of feeling. Many charming characters like his inspire confidence, but few deserve it as his does.

Engraving is at one and the same time a high art and a hard, exacting craft, whose method—enemy of inspiration—might better be renamed the genius of patience. The engraver must be an able craftsman before dreaming of being an artist. Certainly the role of craftsmanship is also immense in painting, and it takes on formidable difficulties particularly in mural painting. But there the emotions of a freely creating genius—which sparks itself—are so direct that the painter derives infinite pleasure. The engraver's pleasure is tempered by his fear of yielding to the desire to become a creator himself.[42]

I have heard much debate over this question: namely, whether the engraver must be an artist like Edelinck and Bervic, or like Marc-Antoine and

Audran;[43] that is to say, whether he is to copy faithfully the qualities and defects of his model, or whether he is to copy freely while giving play to his own genius; in a word, whether the engraving must be an exact reproduction, or an ingenious interpretation, of the work of the master.

I do not fancy myself a solver of difficult questions, especially outside my own field, but it seems to me that this one is analagous to translation. For my part, if I were charged with this function and had a choice, I would choose only masterpieces, and I would take pleasure in rendering them as faithfully as possible, because even the defects of the masters are attractive, or worthy of respect. On the other hand, if I were forced to translate a useful, but less well-written work, I would be tempted to rewrite it as best as I could, in order to make it as clear as possible. However, it is quite probable that a living author would not be very grateful for that service, for lesser talents generally prefer their defects to their strengths.

The misfortune of having done "too well" may befall engravers who interpret, and it is perhaps only the painter of genius who can forgive his copier for having had talent comparable to his own.

On the other hand, if one admitted, in principle, that every engraver is free to interpret as he likes the work he is reproducing, never mind how acceptable such freedom was, where would the interpreter stop, and what would happen to the useful and serious nature of the art, whose primary purpose is not only to popularize the work of painting, but, in addition, preserve intact for posterity the intentions of the masters, across time and events that destroy the originals?

Every science, every art, even every craft must have its precept. Nothing exists without a dominating idea which the work subserves, to which the will conscientiously adheres. In eras of decadence, when everyone does as he likes, without respect for anything or anyone, the arts decline and perish.

Hence, subjection and dependence are innate conditions from which engraving would be set free at its own risk. Without a doubt, the intelligent man who accepts, with a view to his livelihood, the task of reproducing a mediocre work, must be sorely tempted to correct the defects of the original, to modify a sorry or poor effect in order to make it more stimulating, to strengthen a lifeless or cold drawing, to soften a brutish one, to temper a vulgar expression, to ennoble a trivial sentiment. But the artist whose work is thus reinterpreted will have the right to damn the free translation, and if he is mistaken regarding the specific case, he will always be right in the abstract. For every intelligent translator, he can find ten who are not, and who ruin things thinking to make them better.

Besides, the public expects to see the work it recognizes and the conception that has been acclaimed. From the curious artist who wants to study the slightest detail to the historian who claims the expression of an era in all artifacts which that era has produced, the intelligent receiver of that public offering demands a faithful and literal translation.

So, it is rather a pity for engravers who are first and foremost artists. All their skill, insofar as they are engravers, must consist in looking for methods to render clearly the methods of painting, but if they want to invent, they should rightfully be told (and sometimes it is really too bad), "Save your inventing for your own creations, as did those who mastered both painting and engraving, and have spread their own ideas thereby."

Let us observe, however, that such masters (for example, Rembrandt) have never or almost never reproduced their own paintings; it was always, or almost always, on ad hoc drawings that they worked as engravers. Obviously, they envisioned and encountered an immense difficulty, perhaps insurmountable for the creative genius, at the prospect of translating themselves, and they had to leave to mere engravers—that is, to men who had devoted half their lives to the study of the craft—the responsibility of popularizing their major works.

After raising these questions and turning them over in his mind, Calamatta settled for an idea in which he found at least one absolute certainty: one must know how to draw very well in order to copy very well, for he who does not know how to draw well does not understand what he sees and cannot render it, however much concentration and will-power he brings to it. So, he seriously studied life drawing and, at the same time, pursued his work with the burin, which takes years to learn. Calamatta worked seven years in succession on *Le Voeu de Louis XIII* of Ingres.[44]

We are indebted to him for several remarkable portraits drawn by him, which his engraving then allowed him to disseminate. Among these, the one of Lammenais is noteworthy, where the resemblance is faithful and the expression striking.

But Calamatta's truly superior talent is in the passionately detailed and conscientiously copied renditions of the old masters. He has devoted the best of his power to reproducing the *Mona Lisa* of Leonardo da Vinci, which he is perhaps finishing at the moment I am writing, and the drawing of which has seemed to me a masterpiece. This woman's face, of a type said to be so difficult to reproduce, of a beauty so mystifying even to its contemporaries, whose expression the painter considered a miracle to grasp, surely deserves a permanent place in the arts. Her fugitive smile, that divine beaming of an unknown emotion, a great genius managed to fix on canvas, snatching thus from death's dominion an exquisite moment of life that reaches limitless beauty. But time destroys beautiful canvases as fatally (although more slowly) as it destroys beautiful bodies, whereas engraving preserves and immortalizes. One day, only reproductions will remain to attest that the masters and models lived, and when the remains of generations are nothing more than dust, the triumphant Mona Lisa will still be smiling her true and untranslatable smile, at young hearts who fall in love with her.

Among my friends who taught me by sustained example—the best lesson—that one must study, seek and always desire to love work more than oneself, and have no other aim but to leave behind the best of one's own effort, Calamatta was foremost. In this regard my soul holds for him a goodly share of that respect which is the essential basis of every enduring friendship.

I also owe a particular debt of gratitude as an artist to Gustave Planche, a purely critical, but very lofty mind. Melancholy by nature and seemingly sated early with the spectacle of things human, Gustave Planche has, nevertheless, neither a cold spirit nor a lukewarm heart. But a certain rigidity of mind, not sufficiently accessible to the play of varied emotions and spontaneity in the arts, focussed his line of vision in a single direction. For a long time he refused to admit beauty in anything except the grand or severe. What was simply graceful or pleasant was antipathetic to him. Thence stems a real injustice in several cases of his criticism, attributable to bad humor or prejudice, although no critic tried to be more honest than he.

Also, no critic has aroused more anger or desire for revenge. All this he has withstood patiently, pursuing his "executions" with apparent impassivity. But his inner strength was not really up to this role. The hostility he had provoked made him suffer, for his character was essentially more lenient than his pen; looking carefully, one can see that the typical cautions of hatred were not hidden behind that brittle, unbending facade. A quiet discussion easily brought him back from the excesses of his own logic. It is true that, taking up the pen again, swept along by some unfathomable penchant of his talent, he would end up discrediting what he had perhaps promised himself to spare.

I would have completely accepted his character, with all its drawbacks, if I had identified with the point of view he took as a critic. My differences in feeling about the works of art I sometimes defended against his attacks would not alone have prevented me from considering the severity of his judgments as proper expressions of his convictions.

But what I did not approve—and what I have approved less and less in the exercise of criticism in general, that of my friends included—was the haughty, disdainful tone, the cutting expression, in a word, the emotion that perverts the purpose and effect of this kind of teaching when it imbues it. I found Planche all the more at fault on this point, since his emotions were not misled by a malicious, envious, or vindictive personality. On the contrary, he used to speak about all beings very calmly, and he would, in conversation, do them much more justice, or show them much more indulgence, than he would in writing. Thus, it was obviously the result of a system worthy of awe but not at all charitable.

For criticism to be what it should—a form of teaching—it must show itself patient and generous, in order to be persuasive. It must know how to treat its subject with tact, for pride rebels against any kind of insult, especially a harsh one, in public. It is pointless to say that criticism is free and beholden only to itself; all things are beholden to God, who made charity the first of our duties and the strongest of our weapons. If the critics who judge us are stronger than we (which is not always the case), we shall easily be aware of it through their indulgence; when advice is cloaked in unpretentious explanations that bear proof, it has a value that mockery and disdain will never have.

I do not think we need ever yield to criticism, even the gentlest, unless it persuades us, but disinterested criticism, noble in sentiment and form, is always bound to be instructive, even when it contradicts us. It gives rise to a fresh perspective and a thorough discussion that can only be salutary for us. So, it is bound to find us grateful, when it has successfully taught the public and ourselves.

That was certainly Gustave Planche's intention, but he did not seize the proper means. He would wound the individual and provide the public with a source of scandal, which it found amusing on the surface, but took offense at on a deeper level. Besides, the moment the public perceives, or thinks it perceives, some grievance beneath a critique, it no longer judges anything but the grievance, and forgets to judge the work which stirred up the controversy.

Surely these quarrels diminished any discernment that Gustave Planche's knowledge and beautiful style might have spread, nor could the public's taste and understanding of the arts gain from them.

He was not the only one to whom this misfortune occurred. Judging by his personal character, he perhaps deserved it less than others, but by the harshness of his language and the persistence of his pitiless conclusions, he opened himself all the more to it.

The reproach I am allowing myself to address to him is surely disinterested, for no one has more constantly supported and encouraged me.

Besides, I have a very great predilection for the elevated and incisive side of his judgment that I find truly high-minded in several respects—painting and music particularly. I find him less fair in literature. He has withheld recognition to talents that the public has justly accepted. Against the prevailing taste for weird infatuations, his austere conscience has perhaps hardened to the point of exceeding objectivity and even rejecting those who deserve recognition.

Be that as it may, he has shown great moral courage, so great that there are those who say so and defend the man, his talent, and honesty against the enmity that the acerbic tone of his criticism earned him.

From the first steps in his career, he himself laid down his doctrine with the rigor of an uncontradictable mind. "Art is sick," he wrote in 1831. "One must treat it as such, console it and encourage it, as any capable doctor would do. We must encourage the convalescence hopefully, but so that fate does not play with our hopes . . . the patient must be strictly regulated, doggedly exercised, and consientiously criticized. . . . We must call on all its powers, and marshall all the means at the disposal of intelligence, to educate the public taste. . . . I have tried to make remarks on art that might be to the advantage of artists. What is my mission? Folly and vanity? That may well be. But go and tell painters and sculptors to write about the works of their contemporaries: they would be too afraid to hear accusations of envy and to risk the loss of all their friends."

Then, as if an explorer of new lands resolving to burn his vessels was suddenly made conscious of how his own harshness augmented the harshness of his task, he cries out, ending his first work on painting: " . . . I cannot deny my bitter sadness. What purpose will the thousands of words serve that I have these three months been sorting and dealing to the limit of my ability, that I try to impose on my fleeting thoughts so often impossible to grasp; so true, so obvious, so full of conviction as they come from my lips, so often false or exaggerated when they appear on paper?

"Let those who blame the sharp, disdainful, and sometimes bitter tone which reigns in this piece of work, if it is a work, reflect a moment and search in their own hearts; let them search in their memories, and let them ask themselves how many times, in order to transmit their everyday thoughts, in order to make people understand the passions they had in their hearts, how many times they have managed a sincere and faithful eloquence; let them dare count the tricks it has so often played on them, the innumerable betrayals of which they have been the victims, and then let them come and accuse me of presumption or trickery.

"Am I the one to be blamed? Is it my fault if the truth, to which my honor is committed, alters itself and mutilates itself on its way to the reader? Must I be blamed if sometimes irresistible necessities condemn me to say more or less than I would like to say, on pain of not being understood?"

These lines are very curious in that they seem to be a criticism of the critic himself. One senses in them a great nobility of intent, accompanied by frustration, a valiant resolution, along with remorse. One clearly sees in them a man who wants to avert from himself the reproach of partiality, but who scarcely knows other men if he imagines he can sway their anger by making an appeal to their supreme sense of fairness. He must have since smiled rather sadly, recalling the moment of naïveté in which he wrote those lines.

That moment of frustration passed, here are the interesting admissions which escaped from the pen of this most trenchant and least conciliatory of critics. Even harder on himself than on others, he cries out: "Austere criticism is an abyss that opens before you. Sometimes you feel faint and dizzy. From question to question, you finally arrive at the insoluble point: universal doubt. Now, this is quite simply the saddest of all notions. I know of none more discouraging or nearer despair. It is mean work (criticism), that does not even deserve the name of work. It is a sanctioned laziness, a perpetual and willful sloth; it is the painful raillery of impotence, the death-rattle of sterility; it is a cry from out of hell by way of agony."[6]

The rest of the chapter is as curious, and even more so. Not at all ingenuous or ill-considered, it is the voluntary sort of desperate confession by a young man who, ambitious to produce something great, is chafing in the wretched harness of criticism, worn probably against his will, on a day of uncertainty or discouragement. "Shame and unhappiness unto me," he says, "if I cannot ever fill a more glorious role."

Those laments were poorly considered, that viewpoint, false. The role of critic, understood, is a role just as great as that of creator; great philosophers are nothing other than critics of the ideas and asssumptions of their time. That has been sufficient not only for their glory, but also for the progress of their eras; for every movement toward perfection is composed of two equally important acts of the human will: to tear down and to rebuild. It is claimed that one is more difficult than the other, but if one rebuilds with difficulty, and often very badly, might it not be because one always begins laying the foundation on ruins, and if these ruins still serve as the base of the shaky building, is it not because the work of demolition—of criticism—has not gone deep enough? The conclusion is that one act is as rare and as difficult as the other.

Gustave Planche, mature and thinking more clearly, understood no doubt that he had been wrong to attack his vocation, for he continued in it, and he did much for the advancement of public taste—if not for his happiness or the greater pleasure of his adversaries—to which he has contributed importantly in spite of the shortcomings in his own attitude. If he has often failed to observe the niceties of tact, to acknowledge genius even when he thought it had gone astray, to encourage the conscientious and patient talent which is not genius, but which can grow under a favorable influence; if, in a word, he has made victims of his zeal and his despondency, of his moments of power and spleen, he has, nonetheless, included in his bitterest diatribes against individuals a host of excellent things from which the majority can profit, if they apply them carefully. He has shown, with a large number of artists and artworks, an unerring, enlightened taste, a connoisseur's feeling, expressed in an elegant, always concise manner, despite its rhetoric. His style has only the weakness of being a little too modeled and uniform. One might think it affected, as pompous as it is sometimes. But it is natural to that writer, who produces very rapidly and with great ease.

He was very useful to me, not only because he forced me, by his frank ridicule, to pay attention to the language, which I wrote much too casually, but in addition, because his conversation, unvaried but substantial and clear, taught me many things I had to learn, in order to begin my relatively modest achievement.

After a few months of what was for me a very pleasant and interesting relationship, I stopped seeing him for personal reasons; this should prejudice no one against his private character, which has never merited anything but my gratitude.

But since I am telling my own story, I must certainly say that our closeness had serious drawbacks for me. It surrounded me with violent enmities and bitterness. It is not possible to have as a friend such an "austere" critic (and I use without any sarcastic intent the word he always willingly applied to himself) without accusations of sharing his aversions and condemnations. First Delatouche, unwilling to patch things up with him, broke with me because of him. All whom Planche had hurt with his writings or words blamed me for having him at my place in their presence, and I was threatened with complete isolation through the abandonment by friends of longer standing than he, whom I should not sacrifice, they said, for a newcomer.

I felt very hesitant. He was unhappy by nature, and he had an attachment and devotion to me that seemed to soothe that nature. I would have found it cowardly to cast him off for the enemies his literary praise had earned me; one owes nothing to one's enemies. But I certainly felt that our connection was hurting me on a deeper level. His melancholy disposition, his universal disgust, his aversion to the mind's release through casual and pleasant productions in the arts, finally, the rigid reasoning and persistent analysis one had to withstand when speaking with him threw me into a kind of spleen to which I was only too disposed, at the time I knew him. I could see in him an eminent intellect that was generously trying to share its conquests with me, but which had amassed them at the price of the man's happiness, and I was still of an age when one needs the possibility of happiness more than knowledge.

It would have been cruel to quarrel with him about the cause of his depression, a total mystery which must in some way be linked to his constitution, and which I have never fathomed, no doubt because he never fathomed it himself. So, I did not try to broach the kind of deep discussion which ends up destroying the morale. Besides, I was not in a self-sacrificing mood. I felt depressed myself, for it was the time when I was writing *Lélia*. I carefully avoided telling Planche the basis of my own problem, so much did I fear his desperate solutions, for which there were no arguments, and talked with him only about the form and poetry of my novel.

These were not always to his taste, but if the work has defects, it is not the fault of his influence; it is indeed, on the contrary, the fault of my stubbornness.

I myself sensed very deeply—all the while struggling against religious doubt—that I could not get over this depression except through some unforeseen revelation of feeling or imagination. Consequently, I felt strongly that Planche's psychology was not applicable to my condition.

In those days, I used to have flashes of devoutness that I would hide from everyone with the greatest care, especially from him. Actually, not from everyone—I did recount them to Mme. Dorval, the only one who understood me. I remember several times, toward evening, having entered dark and silent churches, to lose myself in the contemplation of the idea of Christ and to pray again with mystic's tears, as in my youthful period of belief and exaltation.

But I could no longer meditate without agonizing over the question of divine justice and benevolence, in light of the evil and pain that reign on earth. Only the *Théodicée* of Leibnitz calmed me a little as I pondered what I had managed to understand and retain of it. He was my last anchor to salvation. I have always believed that the day I really understood him, I would be sheltered from every lapse of the spirit.

I also remember that, one day, Planche asked me whether I knew Leibnitz, and that I answered No, very quickly, not so much through modesty as out of fear of hearing him dispute and demolish him.

I would not, however, have driven Planche away for reasons of personal interest—even on so grave a matter as my peace of mind—barring some special circumstances, that he bore with very unselfish loyalty and without any grudge to our friendship. Nevertheless, people led me to understand that he had a few bad things to say about me. We had it out very briskly. He denied them on his honor. Eventually a lot of evidence spoke for his sincerity. But I did nothing more to promote our meeting. The last time was at Mme. Dorval's, and I do believe that was over ten years ago.

However, the bile that my regard for him had accumulated against me is still being produced, for in 1852, apropos a preface in which I had dared to say that "a serious critic, M. Planche, had alone in recent times properly judged Sedaine," journalists had me saying that "M. Planche, the only serious critic of the time, had been the only one to judge my play properly." This was a twisted interpretation, as you can see. But prejudice does not suffer close inspection. This gave rise to a little campaign of feuilletons against me. Here is the opportunity to mount a much more brilliant one, for I repeat that Planche is one of the most serious critics of this era; the most serious, alas! if one uses that word to mean the total absence of gaiety. For it is easy to see from his writings that he has not yet found in this wide world the tiniest joke.

If some of the blame for his continual vexation is his, let us not forget how often we say of a patient who becomes embittered and discouraged: "It's his own fault!" And in saying this, we are rather unwittingly cruel. When illness gets hold of us, however, we are more indulgent; we find it quite legitimate to yell and complain. Well, some intellects are chronically unwell due to an illusion which, it seems to us, they obstinately nurture, to their own detriment. Whether this illusion applies to the arts or sciences, to the past or present, it is, nonetheless, a fixed idea produced by a pronounced faculty for idealization, and considering its own inability to come to terms with itself, there is no room for advice or reproaches from outside.

Another melancholy character, another eminent mind, was Charles Didier.[45] He was one of my best friends; then our friendship cooled, we separated, and lost sight of each other. I do not know how he speaks of me today; I do know that I can speak of him as I wish.

I shall not say, as does Montesquieu, "Don't believe us when we speak of each other; we have quarreled." I feel stronger than that, at this time of summing up my life with the same calm and spirit of justice as if I were, being of sound mind, writing my last will.

So, I look into the past, and in it, between Didier and me, I see a few months of dissension and a few months of resentment. Then, on my part, long years of that forgetting which is my only revenge for the sorrows people have caused me, with or without premeditation. But short of those misunderstandings and crossed purposes, I see five or six years of perfect friendship. I reread letters containing admirable wisdom, devoted advice, truly disinterested consolation. And now that my time of forgetting is over, now that I am emerging from that enforced and perhaps needed respite from memory, those blessed years are here before me—the only good and useful things I have to note and preserve, in my heart.

Charles Didier was a man of genius, but with an ability far beneath his genius. He revealed himself in spurts, and I doubt that any of his works have afforded a complete outlet to the great fund of knowledge he had stored within him. It seemed to me his talent did not progress after *Rome souterraine*, which is a very beautiful book. He felt incapable of full literary expression, and because of it, suffered terribly. His life was marked by inner strife, a reality against which his imagination was perhaps not keen enough to react. The gaiety into which we sometimes would drag him, and to which he would allow himself to be drawn, used to do him more harm than good. He would pay for it the next day with a deeper uneasiness or despondency; the world of delightful frankness that the good nature and high spirits of others brought, and still bring to me would appear to him as foolish deception.

I used to call him "my bear," and sometimes "my white bear," because his still young and handsome face was singularly crowned with a beautiful head of hair, whitened before its time. This was a projection of his soul, still full of life at the core, but whose emergent force some trauma had paralyzed.

His harshly scolding manner did not bother any of us. We rather pitied this misanthropy, under which lay sterling qualities and amiable dedication; we respected it, even when he became peevish and too ready to accuse. He allowed himself to be led, and he was a man of sufficiently high esteem for one to be proud to have influenced him even a little.

In politics, religion, philosophy, and art his views were always straightforward and sometimes so beautiful that, during his rare effusions one sensed the superiority of his hidden side to his revealed one.

In the business of living, he was worth consulting, although his first reaction bore the imprint of too great a mistrust of men, things, and God Himself. This mistrust had the unfortunate effect of putting me on guard against his advice, which often would have been better for me to follow than my own instinct.

He was as preoccupied as I was, at the time, with examining social and religious ideas. I do not at all know to what conclusions he has come. I do not even know, from my distant perch, whether he has recently published any work. A few years ago, I heard of a legitimist pamphlet for which he was much reproached. I could not get hold of it then, and I have not read it yet. I could not help but think that, if this pamphlet purports to say what I have been told it does, its mode of expression did not reveal the author's true meaning, as often happens even to the cleverest writers. But if Charles Didier's point of view has changed completely, it would be even less conceivable to me that there was not still in him some disinterested conviction.

Here I shall close this portrait gallery of present and past friends, in order to postpone until later a new series of appreciations as they emerge in my memories. It will probably not be a completely exact chronology, for it will have to adjust to the pauses I make as I discuss my existence, but it will not be confused on purpose, nor in a way that may lead my memory into inaccuracy.

I am not committed, as I have said before, to speak of everyone I have ever known, or even everyone special. The omission of some should in no way make the reader question my esteem for them, and here I shall tell one of the principal motives for these omissions.

People about whom I was disposed to speak with all the decorum which taste requires, with all the respect due great intelligence, or all the regard to which every contemporary has a right, whoever he may be; people, in fact, who ought to have known me well enough not to worry, have imparted to me, or have had third parties express intense apprehensions about the parts I intended to give them in these memoirs.

To those people I had only one answer to give, and that was to promise not to assign them any part, good or bad, small or large, in my recollections. From the moment they doubted my discernment and good manners in a work like this, it was not my business to create confidence in my character as a writer, but rather to reassure them swiftly and absolutely by the promise of silence.

Not one of those whom I have already depicted has done my heart the wrong of questioning the judgments of my mind. And yet, I have not hidden the fact that a few misunderstandings, a few tiffs have occurred between two or three persons and me, nor have I wanted to examine or judge these passing disagreements for which I have to bear the blame of more outspokenness than sweetness. I have been all the better disposed to reject any suspicion in the past as they trusted me in my present revelations.

I think decidedly that people who have had such apprehensions have been wrong, and that they would have done better to put their trust in my retrospective judgment. *J.V.E.*

VII

I take up my narrative again. —I succeed in saying some extremely
delicate things, and I expressly say them without delicacy, thus
finding them more properly stated. —The opinion of my friend
Dutheil on marriage. —My opinion on love. —Marion Delorme. —
Two of Balzac's women. —Women's pride. —The pride of humanity
in general. —*Lettres d'un voyageur*: my plan in the beginning.
—How the traveller was me, and how he was not. —Physical and
emotional illnesses reacting on each other. —The self-concern of
youth. —The detachment of maturity. —Religious arrogance. —My
ignorance still depresses me. —If only I could relax and improve my
mind! —I love, therefore I believe. —Catholic arrogance, Christian
humility. —Liebnitz again. —Why my books have boring passages.
—New horizon. —Coming and going. —Solange and Maurice.
—Planet. —Departure plans and clauses of a will. —M. de Persigny.
—Michel (de Bourges).

I have already said that after my return from Italy in 1834, I had felt great
happiness in seeing my children again, my friends, my house. But this happiness was short-lived. For all intents and purposes, neither my children nor my
house belonged to me. Nor did my husband and I agree on the guidance of
these humble treasures. At school, Maurice was not receiving an education in
harmony with his instincts, his abilities, his health. Life at home was subject to
completely abnormal and dangerous influences. It was admittedly and
inevitably my fault, and being strongly opposed to daily quarrels and household disruptions, I was unable to find the strength in myself to overcome the
situation.

One of my friends, Dutheil, whose intention was to make my life more
endurable, told me that by becoming my husband's mistress I could become
mistress of my situation. This did not appeal to me in any way. Closeness without love is wretched to contemplate. A woman who courts her husband for the
purpose of subduing his will is doing something analagous to what prostitutes
do for bread and courtesans do for luxuries. Such reconciliations make the husband a despicable toy and a ridiculous fool.

Dutheil, playing devil's advocate, raised the question again and again.
Even though his words were often cynical, he was too intelligent not to under-

stand that, for my sake, it was necessary to idealize the objective. And so he invoked my love for my children and my concern for their future.

To this sacred consideration, I could only react with instinctive repugnance, but a reaction so intense and absolute that I really had to reflect, in order to ascertain the value my conscience should ascribe to it.

For most people, physical repugnance would be a sufficient excuse, but it was not sufficient for me. Duty can make us overcome such repugnance. We touch the infections of the sick—even those we don't like or don't know—in order to heal them.

Otherwise, my husband inspired neither disgust nor aversion in me. I only asked to love him as a brother, as I had felt inclined when our relationship began.

When a chaste young girl makes the decision to marry, she knows nothing at all about what marriage consists of, and can mistake love for what is not love. But at thirty, a woman can no longer entertain vague illusions; if she has courage and intelligence, she knows the price. And here I am speaking not so much of her physical being—which could resign itself to humility, if it could give itself up separately, as an object—but rather of her complete, indivisible being.

That is what I could not have made my husband understand, for he viewed it quite differently. But I did make Dutheil understand, for his brain easily comprehended the practicality as well as the refinement, and even the novelistic subtleties of the subject.

"Love is not the result of pure will," I told him. "Marriages by arrangement are an error we fall prey to, or a deception we practice on ourselves. We are not either body or mind; we are body and mind together. Where only one of these elements is present, there is no true love.

"If the body has functions in which the soul plays no part at all, such as eating and digesting—and even the pleasure of true gourmands, they say, is experienced through the imagination rather than the senses—can the union of two beings in love be likened to those functions? The mere thought of it is revolting. Didn't God, who made pleasure and sensual delight a condition of the coming together of all creatures, even plants, endow these creatures with judgment in proportion to their degree of perfection on the scale of being? Since man is more advanced, closer to perfection than the others, doesn't the feeling for this indispensable union, on a physical, intellectual, and moral level, exist for him already in the anticipation of his raptures?"

What I have just described is, I know, at best a commonplace. However, this incontestable truth is so rarely observed in practice that humans come together, and children are born by the thousands, without true love having presided one time in a thousand over the sacred act of reproduction.

Man perpetuates himself all the same, and if true love was the sole incentive, it would be necessary to return to the strange marital notions of Maréchal de Saxe to prevent depopulation.[46] But it is also true that the wish—nay, divine law—of Providence is transgressed every time a man and woman join their lips without uniting their hearts and minds. If the human race is still so far from the goal to which the beauty of its capabilities can aspire, then this is one of the most widespread and baleful causes.

People jokingly say that it is not so difficult to procreate: just put two people together. Well, I disagree. There must be three: a man, a woman, and God in both. If the thought of God is unfamiliar to their ecstasy, they will indeed make a child, but they will not make a human being. The true human being will only emanate from true love. Two bodies can join to produce a third, but thought alone can give life to thought. So, what are we? Beings who aspire to be human, and nothing more at this time—passive beings, incapable and unworthy of liberty and equality, because for the most part we are born of a passive act, devoid of choice.

By calling it an act of will do I yet do it too much honor? Where the heart and the mind do not reveal themselves, there is no true will. In that case, love is an act of servitude to which two slaves of matter subject themselves. "Fortunately," Dutheil replied, "mankind has no need for sublime aspirations in order to find its generative function easy and pleasant." I answered: "Unfortunately."

And be all that as it may, I added, when human beings, male or female, arrive at the understanding of perfect love, it is no longer possible—or, better stated, they are no longer permitted—to slide back and commit a purely animal act. No matter what the circumstance, the conscience must say No, even though the appetite may say Yes. And if one and the other find themselves perfectly in accord under all circumstances to say Yes or No simultaneously, how can we doubt the religious force of this inner declaration?

If you bring to bear considerations of pure utility—those so-called family interests in which selfishness parades as morality—you will merely circle the truth without penetrating it. You will say, in vain, that you sacrifice to a principle of virtue, not to a temptation of the flesh; you will not bend the law of God to this purely human principle. Man unknowingly commits constant sacrilege on earth, which divine wisdom can absolve in light of his ignorance, but he who has understood the ideal and crushes it under his feet will not be absolved. No personal or social reason within man's power is strong enough to permit him to transgress a divine law, when this law has been clearly revealed to his reason, his feelings, even his senses.

In the Victor Hugo drama, when Marion Delorme gives herself to Laffemas, whom she abhors, in order to save her lover's life, the sublimity of her devotion is only relative. The playwright understood very well that only a courtesan—a woman who had habitually devaluated herself—could accept the ultimate dishonor, out of love. On the other hand, in *La Cousine Bette*, when Balzac shows us a pure and respectabe woman tremblingly offer herself to an ignoble seducer in order to save her family from ruin, he traces with impeccable skill a feasible, but nonetheless odious, situation in which the heroine loses all our sympathy. Why does Marion Delorme retain it, in spite of her abasement? Because, unlike the legitimate wife and mother of a family, she does not have an awareness of the crime she is committing.

Balzac searched and dared everything. He went still further in another novel,[47] where he showed us a provocative woman seducing her husband, whom she does not love, to save him from another woman's trap. Balzac endeavored to relieve the guilt for this action by giving this heroine a daughter whose fortune the mother wants to preserve. Thus, maternal love above all pushes her to deceive her husband through something worse, perhaps, than infidelity—through a lie from her lips, her heart, and her senses.

I have not concealed from Balzac that this story, whose plot he claims is real, revolted me to the point of making me lose sight of the talent he displayed in telling it. It immediately struck me as immoral—me, the one they reproach for having written immoral books.

As I interrogated my conscience and my religion, I became yet more rigid in my observations. Not only do I regard the lie in sensual love as a mortal sin—and I find that expression quite apt, because it implies that certain mistakes kill our very soul—but I regard as a mortal sin also the illusion that the senses come to some sort of fruition in such unfulfilled love. I say, and I believe, that one must love with one's being, or live in complete chastity, no matter what the consequences. This will not impress men at all, I am well aware, but women, who have at their disposal a sense of shame and propriety, can accept this doctrine, no matter what their station in life, when they feel they are worthy of complying with it.

For those women who have not the least pride, I am at a loss what to say.

The word "pride," which I used so much in my writing at that time, comes back to me now with its true meaning. Because I forget so completely what I write, and feel so much distaste for rereading my work, it was necessary for me recently to receive a letter in which someone went to the trouble of transcribing a host of aphoristic sayings, taken from the *Lettres d'un voyageur* of September 1834 and January 1835, where I rediscovered a project I had promised myself to continue all my life. I am truly sorry not to have done it. Here was the plan, followed at the beginning of the series, from which I deviated along the way and which I seem eventually to have given up entirely. This apparent carelessness comes up especially in the diverse letters, or series of letters, I gathered under the same heading—*Lettres d'un voyageur*—letters which did not follow the original intention or manner of the first ones.

The intention and manner consisted, in my original concept, of understanding my successive moods in both an innocent and a contrived way at the same time. Obviously, this explanation is for those who do not remember these letters, or who do not know them, because those who are acquainted with them need no explanation.

I was full of things to say, and I wanted to say them to myself as well as to others. My identity was in the process of being created; I believed it to be quite formed, even though I could hardly envision its shape; it so deeply preoccupied me that, in spite of the weariness it had already spawned, I needed to examine and torment it, so to speak, like heated metal cast into a mold.

But as I felt, and still feel, that a soul in isolation has not the right to declare itself without having on hand some wise conclusion of use to others, and that I had no such conclusion, I wanted to generalize my own character while modifying it. I did not really feel that I had the right to speak as my real self, being only thirty years old and having lived such a sheltered life. I had barely cast a frightened glance at passion's dangers and life's dilemmas, and was still on the dizzying heights of first discoveries. An affirmation of my particular complaints might have taken precedence over my reflections on general ideas. It was permissible for me—a young woman still very immature in many regards—to philosophize in my way on life's troubles and speak of them as if I had drunk the dregs, but not to palm myself off as an experienced thinker, or one with a special destiny. Besides, to describe my real self would have been a chore too calculating for my exalted spirit. Hence, at the whim of my pen, and abandoning myself to utter fantasy, I created a very old, very experienced, and consequently very despairing persona for myself.

This third level of my supposed being, despair, was the only truthful one. In letting myself go to my darkest thoughts, I could enter the role of the old uncle, the old traveler whom I made speak. As for the framework in which I made him move, the milieu in which I myself existed was the best, since it was my impression of this milieu which I wanted to convey.

In a word, I wanted to make a proper novel of my life, yet not be my own self in it, but a persona analyzing and thinking about it. Furthermore, in being this character, I wanted to extend his point of view to an experience of unhappiness that I had not or could not have had.

I foresaw correctly that the fiction would not prevent the public from seeking and finding my real self behind the mask of an old man. Indeed, that was the case: an overly smart attorney, representing my husband during our marital separation trial, wanted to hold me responsible for all I had made the voyager say. Merely the fact that I wrote in the first person was enough for him to accuse me of all that the poor voyager accuses himself of, poetically and metaphysically. I had vices; I had committed crimes; wasn't that evident? The voyager, the old uncle, didn't he present his past life as a pit of intoxication and his present as a chasm of remorse? In truth, it was only four years before that I had left the fold—where the austerity of my daily life was easy to verify. Had I been able, in so few years, to acquire all the experience of good and evil that is attributed to my voyager, I would have been an amazing person. In any case, I would not have lived tucked in a garret as I did, surrounded by five or six people with sober or artistic temperaments like mine.

But it matters little what was attributed to me in *Lettres d'un oncle*, the title under which the sixth installment of *Lettres d'un voyageur* first appeared, and it is under that title that I promised myself to continue in the same vein. It might have been a good book—perhaps not beautiful, but interesting and lively, consequently more useful than the novels in which our personality is submerged beneath the fiction, perforce disseminating itself into sundry types and straying in fictitious situations.

I shall, in the future, return to the other letters in this collection; here I shall only concern myself with the one I just cited. I must say that something profoundly real existed for me beneath that fiction—namely, a disgust for life. The reader has seen this chronic pain, relived and combatted since early youth, forgotten and rediscovered like an angry traveling companion, who I thought had been left behind, but who suddenly turned up trailing along at my heels. The sadness was unremittingly present in Venice, and emerged still more bitterly on my return. I looked for its source where it did not exist—in outer circumstances that exerted immediate pressure. In good faith, I dramatized and exaggerated their importance; not the feeling—that was poignant in my heart—but the circumstances. Having been deceived by some of my illusions, I proceeded to divest myself of all my beliefs; having lost the calm and certainty of my previous convictions, I imagined that I no longer had the power to live.

I see the true cause very clearly today. It was physical and spiritual, like all causes of human suffering, where the soul does not suffer long before the body feels the effects, and vice versa. My body suffered the beginnings of hepatitis, which clearly manifested itself later and which was cured in time. I struggle with it still, for the enemy is in me, and makes itself felt at the very moment I think it to be dormant. I believe this sickness is, in fact, what the British call spleen, caused by an engorgement of the liver. Unknown to me, I had the germ, or predisposition, for it from my mother, who had it and died from it. I may die of it like her, as we all must die from some malady we carry in ourselves, in a latent form, from the moment of our birth. Any constitution, no matter how healthy, is invested with its own cause of destruction, either physical and activated by the moral and intellectual system, or moral and activated by the organism's functions.

Whether it was bile which made me melancholy, or melancholy which made me bilious, I shall not undertake to resolve, for such metaphysical and physiological dilemmas have ancient roots; it is certain that acute ailments of the liver have as symptoms, at least according to those who have suffered them, a profound sadness and the wish to die. Subsequent to the first onset of my sickness, I had had some years of happiness, but when the illness gripped me once again, I felt suddenly smitten by a desire for eternal repose, even though I was disposed to love life.

But if the physical illness is unrelated to the soul, the soul will resist, if not by an immediate show of will—for the illness often succeeds in deadening the will for a time—then by its general disposition and acquired beliefs. Since I no longer have those bitter doubts in which the thought of nothingness becomes irresistibly attractive, since this eternal repose of which I spoke has proved itself unnecessary for me, and finally, since I believe in something eternal beyond life, the fleeting thought of suicide has become easily conquered through reflection. And as for the black illusions of the world's unhappiness, produced by hepatitis, I would no longer take them seriously as I did during the time when I was ignorant that the cause lay in myself. I still suffer from them, but not as helplessly as in the past. I fight to push through the obscurity which brews in the imagination like a thunderstorm. Such times are reminiscent of those odd states our dreams occasionally conjure, when we reassure ourselves, as the apparitions mount, that we are dreaming, and we toss in our beds to wake up.

As for the spiritual cause of my despair considered independently from the physical cause, I have said it, and I shall say it again, for I write for those who suffer as I have suffered, and I could never overstate this point—I lived too much in myself, by myself, and for myself. I did not think of myself as selfish. Yet, if I was not a miser or coward in the strict sense of the word, I was selfish in my philosophy. That is very evident in *Lettres d'un voyageur*. One feels the ardent personality of youth in it, troubled, tenacious, sensitive— actually the word for it is arrogant.

Yes, arrogant. I was arrogant, then, and for some time thereafter. Many occasions demanded that kind of pride, whose origin is not in vanity. I have enough common sense to know that vanity is a form of madness; it has always inspired me with fear. It was not myself as a person that I wanted to love and respect. It was myself as a human creation, that is to say, a divine work, on a par with other human creations. But I did not want to let myself be spiritually debilitated by those who denied or scoffed at their own divinity.

I still have that kind of arrogance. I do not want to be counselled and persuaded to be what I believe is unworthy of human dignity. I resist with an obstinacy that can only come from belief, for my character is not at all forceful. Thus, belief is good for something. It sometimes remedies what the constitution lacks.

Arrogance, too, has its mad side that is nourished within the self and that joins man to God. As we sense ourselves becoming more intelligent, we feel closer to Him, and we are, but in a manner so commensurate with our misery that it does not satisfy our ambition. We want to comprehend God, and we brashly ask Him to reveal His secrets. As soon as the blind beliefs of religion as taught are no longer enough for us and we want to attain faith by deduction or induction—which is, I submit, our right and duty—we are in danger of arrogance. Especially we French—so ardent and quick to attack heaven, as if it were a stronghold—we do not know how to glide slowly and ascend gradually, on the wings of a patient philosophy and slow study. We ask, without humility, for grace—meaning enlightenment, serenity, and untroubled assurance—all at once. And when our shortcomings meet unforeseen obstacles requiring the slightest strain on our reasoning power, we become irritated and quite despairing.

This is the story of my life, the true story. All the rest has been but appearance. An extraordinary woman, whom I shall speak of later—Mme. Hortense Allart[48]—wrote to me not long ago about Sainte-Beuve: "He was always tormented by divine things." The words are expressive and apt, and summarized for me my own torment. Alas, yes! This search for abstract truth is a cross. But Sainte-Beuve's torment was less than mine, for he was scholarly, and I was never able to be so, not having time, memory, nor inclination to study the works of others. Well, knowledge of human works is hardly the divine light—it only receives a few fugitive rays from it. But it *is* a transmitting current, which I lack and will always lack. As long as I am forced to earn a living by working every day, I shall not be able to devote at least the several years needed to meditation and reading.

It will never happen; I shall die inside the thick cloud that envelops and oppresses me. I have pierced it only at moments. At times of inspiration more than of study, I have observed the divine ideal, as astronomers observe the sun's body, through fiery emissions which obscure it by their raging activity, and which spread open only to seal again. But that, perhaps, was enough, not for truth in a larger sense, but for the truth I need for my heart's satisfaction. It is enough for me to love the God I sense out there behind dazzling visions of the unknown, and for me to toss into His mysterious infinity the aspiration to infinity that He placed in me, which is an emanation from Him. Whatever path my thought may take—clairvoyance, reason, poetry—it will surely reach Him, and even in communication only with itself, my thought has still something from Him.

What shall I say to you, friendly hearts, who question me? I love; therefore, I believe. I feel that I love God with the disinterested love which Leibnitz tells us is the sole reality, and which cannot be satisfied here on earth, since we love our friends and lovers from the need to be happy, and others, such as our children, from the need to make them happy—both fundamentally the same, their happiness being necessary to ours. I feel that my pain and fatigue cannot alter the unalterable order, the serenity of the Author of all things. I sense He may not act to alleviate them by modifying exterior events around me, but I feel that when I nullify the person in myself that aspires to earthly joys, celestial joy pervades me, and absolute, joyous confidence inundates my heart with a feeling of well-being which is impossible to describe. Therefore, what should I do but believe?

But I have only truly felt this joy twice in my life: during adolescence, through the prism of Catholic faith; and at a mature age, under the influence of a total submission of my ego before God—which does not impede me, I admit, from seeking ceaselessly to understand Him, but which keeps me from denying Him at times when I do not understand Him.

Although my being has undergone changes and passed through phases of action and reaction, like that of all thinking beings, it is fundamentally bound to the need to believe, the thirst to know, the pleasure of loving.

Catholics, and I have known some very sincere ones, have railed against me that in these three terms there was one which would kill the other two. The thirst for knowledge is, according to them, the pitiless destroyer of the need to believe and the pleasure of loving.

These good Catholics are somewhat justified. As soon as you open the door to the mind's curiosity, the joys of the heart are bitterly disturbed and risk being swept away in the gale, for some time. But I still insist that the thirst for knowledge is inherent to human intelligence; that it is a divine right given to us; and that to refuse to exercise this right, to force oneself to destroy it, is to transgress a divine law. Among naïve believers, there are some who do not feel the thrill of their intelligence and who love God with their heart alone, like those lovers who love only with their senses. They, too, only know an unfulfilled love. They, too, are not yet at the state of human perfection. Being ignorant of their infirmity, they are not guilty, but they become so when they sense it, if they stubbornly persist in fulfillment through the senses alone.

Yet, Catholics would call what I am suggesting here the intimations of the demon of pride. I would respond to them: "Yes, let's talk of the demon of pride. I agree to use your poetic language. He exists in you as well as in me. In you, when he persuades you that your feeling is so grand and so beautiful that God accepts it without concerning Himself what form of worship your reason is following. You are lazy, not wanting to risk suffering should you encounter doubt in the deepening quest. And you have the vanity to believe that God exempts you from suffering, providing you adore Him as a fetish. You esteem yourselves too much. God would like more, but you are content.

"The demon of pride! He exists also in me every time I am annoyed at the sufferings I have borne on emerging from the easily blinding spell of the mysteries. He was present especially at the beginning of this quest, and he made me a skeptic for several years of my life. He was born in your house, my demon of pride; he came to me from Catholic teaching; he scorned my reason from the moment I wanted to use it. He said to me: 'Your heart alone has worth. Why have you let it languish?' And by dulling the weapon I needed, he cast me back into vagaries and tried to persuade me to believe only through my feelings.

"Thus, those whom you label free-thinkers, O Catholics, are not always sufficiently proud of their reasoning, while you are always excessively proud of your feelings."

But feeling without reasoning does evil as easily as good. Feeling without reasoning is demanding, imperious, selfish. At fifteen years of age, it was due to feeling without reasoning that I reproached God with a kind of impious anger for those hours of fatigue and languor during which He seemed to retract His grace from me. It was again through feeling without reasoning that at the age of thirty I wanted to die, saying God didn't love me or care about me, since He left me weak, ignorant, and unhappy on earth.

I am still ignorant and weak, but I am no longer unhappy, because I am less arrogant than in the past. I have recognized that my entire being—reason, feeling, instinct—comprised a character so finite, with actions so limited, that one must revert to Christian humility, saying: "I feel vividly, I understand very little, and I love a great deal." But one must reject Catholic orthodoxy when it says: "I pretend to feel and love without understanding anything."

I do not doubt it is possible, but it is not sufficient to accomplish the will of God, who wants man to understand as much as he is given to understand.

In summary, strive to love God by understanding Him, and strive to understand Him by loving Him; strive to believe what you do not understand, but strive to understand the better to believe. Thus counselled Leibnitz, the greatest theologian of the Enlightenment. For ten years, I have never failed to open to one of his pages without finding a passage in which he places within everyone's grasp the rule for a sound mind, that which I feel more and more capable of following.

I heartily ask to be pardoned for this chapter by those who are never tormented by divine things. I believe they are the vast majority; my insistence on religious ideas will, therefore, bore many people, but they were probably bored from the beginning of this work and long ago gave up reading it.

Furthermore, what has put me at ease, all my life, in writing books is the consciousness of how limited a popularity they must have. By limited popularity, I do not mean to imply they must, by their nature, redound just to an intelligent few. They have been better read and understood by those of the masses who have a feeling for the ideal in their aspirations, than by many artists who care only about the material world. But, whether of the masses or the few, I must surely satisfy only a small number. My editors have complained about it. "For God's sake," Buloz often wrote to me, "not so much mysticism!" Kindhearted Buloz did me the honor of seeing mysticism in my anxieties! Moreover, his whole world of readers thought, as he did, that I was becoming more and more tedious, and going beyond art's domain, by imbuing my characters with the preoccupations of my own brain. That may very well have been the case, but it is hard for me to see how I could have avoided writing with the blood of my own heart and the flame of my own thought.

People have often made fun of me in my presence, and I was not offended. What does it matter? I, too, enjoy laughing when the mood strikes; there is nothing which relaxes the soul intent on the spectacle of abstract things more than making fun of itself, at intervals. I have lived more often among gay people than serious ones, especially in my adulthood, and I like artistic characters, instinctive minds. Their daily behavior is much more relaxed than that of hardened intellectuals. When one is half artist, half mystic (I accept Buloz's label), as I am, one is not equipped to live with the apostles of pure reason, without risking insanity. But then, after days spent in forgetfulness of things dogmatic, one needs time to listen to, or read them.

That is why I inevitably wrote novels having parts which please some and displease others. Aside from the influence of actual sorrow, that is especially what explains the sorrow and the gaiety of *Lettres d'un voyageur*.

I am approaching the moment when my view opened on a new perspective—politics. I was led there, as I was prone to be, by the influence of my feelings. So, the three years of my life I am about to recount were a story of feelings.

Back to Nohant in September, then back to Paris with my children at the end of vacation, I returned in January 1835 again, to spend some time under my own roof. It was there I wrote the sixth installment of *Lettres d'un voyageur*, in a little less somber mood, but still very unhappy. Finally, I spent February and March in Paris, and in April I was again at Nohant.

These comings and goings fatigued my body and soul. I was miserable wherever I went. However, some health remained to my soul; those disconsolate letters provide me good evidence of that today. But while struggling to return peacefulness to my life at Nohant, I found such problems, and by the same token, my heart was so troubled, so torn by unacknowledged sorrow, that I felt a sudden need to flee. Where? I could not say. I did not want to know. It should be far, as far as possible, to make me forget. I felt sick, mortally sick. I was no longer sleeping, and it seemed to me, at moments, that my reason was on the verge of leaving me. I had cheerfully resolved to have my daughter with me, but I had to give up, for the moment, the pleasure of raising her myself. She had a completely different character than her brother, becoming as bored with my sedentary life as much as Maurice took pleasure in it. She already needed a series of distractions suited to her age and demanded by the excessive energy of her personality at that time. I took her to Nohant hoping the radical change would allow her to develop without a crisis. But when it came time to return to our garret, and she no longer had a half-dozen wild little neighbors to play with, her repressed physical vigor turned into open revolt. She was an enfant terrible, but so amusing that my friends spoiled her horribly. As for me, incapable of sustained strictness and overwhelmed by a blind tenderness for childhood, I did not know how to control her.

I hoped she would be calmer and happier with other children and under conditions in which discipline doled out in common would seem more bearable to an independent personality. I tried to board her in one of those charming little private schools in the Beaujon area, amid tranquil and cheerful gardens which seem destined to be inhabited by nothing but pretty little girls. The Misses Martin were two British sisters who were truly maternal toward their young pupils. There were only eight—an excellent opportunity to dote on them and watch over them with care.

My big girl got along very well in this new routine. She began to calm down and become civilized with her friends. But for a long time she stayed unruly with people outside, especially my friends, who got so much pleasure from enslaving themselves to her. She had a way of being so original and comical with them. Seeing that she disarmed them by making them laugh, the little conniver enjoyed herself to the fullest. She treated Emmanuel Arago, a good "older brother," even more irreverently than Maurice. Still childish enough himself to be amused by her, he was her favorite victim. One day, she was very friendly toward him, and showed him to the door of the garden at the boarding school: "Solange," he said to her, "what would you like me to bring you when I come back?"

"Nothing," she said to him, "but if you really love me you would do me a great favor."

"Pray, what is that, my dear."

"Just never come back to see me again."

Another time, she was staying with me, feeling a little sickly, and the doctor recommended a walk. She left willingly, in a carriage with Emmanuel, for the Luxembourg gardens, but along the way she changed her mind about walking. I had instructed Emmanuel to be firm; he held his own and told her that it was not customary to pass through the Luxembourg gardens in a carriage, and that she would have to walk whether she liked it or not. She appeared to submit, but arriving at the gate, when he took her in his arms to help her down, he noticed she was without shoes. She had deftly taken them off and thrown them into the street before arriving. "Now," she said to him, "let's see if you want me to walk barefoot."

When I was out with her, it often entered her mind to stop short and refuse either to walk or to get into a cab, which made passers-by gather around us. She was seven or eight years old when she was putting me through those paces, and I had to carry her forcibly from the bottom staircase to the attic, which was quite a chore. And the worst thing was that these bizarre moods had no cause that I could foresee or forestall. Even today she does not understand her behavior; it was as though her nature found it impossible to submit to the will of other people, and I could not get used permanently to breaking down this incomprehensible resistance.

So, I decided to separate from her for a time. Although it was soon proven to me that she accepted more readily the general, rather than the particular, rule and that she was happy in boarding school, I experienced great sorrow in seeing that her childhood happiness did not depend on me. As a result, I was even more prone to spoil her, in spite of my best resolutions.

For his part, Maurice was just the opposite. He neither wanted to live without me, nor was capable of it. My attic was the paradise of his dreams. Then, when it was time to say goodnight, the tears began in earnest, and I was no braver than he.

My friends criticized the way I indulged my children, and I knew very well that it was extreme. I surely did not do it for my own amusement, for it was tearing me apart. But how to overcome it? My very entrails felt as oppressed and tormented as did my heart and brain.

Planet advised me to take a strong resolve and leave France for at least a year. "Your stay in Venice was good for your children," he told me. "Maurice hasn't worked at school, and will not work, until he knows you're far away. He is still weak. Solange's wilfulness is due to a spurt of growth that you torment yourself about too much. By making you her victim, she is getting used to seeing you suffer, and that is not at all good for her. You're not happy, that is certain; you can come home to Nohant only as a guest. Your husband is already soured by your presence, and the time is coming when he will be angered by it. You're so distressed by your problems to the point of creating imaginary ones. Your writing proves you're turning against yourself and that you're obsessed by your own existence, your own destiny, by a conjunction of circumstances, distressing it is true, but not really so exceptional that your will-power could not overcome it, or deflect it. A time will come when you'll be able to, but before that, you must recover your emotional and physical health, which you're in the process of losing. You must get away from the scenes and causes of your suffering. You must get out of this circle of troubles and disappointments. Go write poetry in some beautiful country where you don't know anyone. You like solitude; you will never get enough of it here. Don't imagine you can live like a hermit in your garret. People will always besiege you. Solitude is bad over a long period of time, but there are times when it is necessary. This is one of those times. Obey the instinct that pushes you. Take flight! I know you; you will no sooner have escaped for several days than you will have become a believer again, and while you're away, I shall answer for you."

Planet has always been an excellent mind-doctor to his friends, persuasive by the attention which he lent to his counsel, and with which he applied himself to understand their true situations. Many friends make the error of judging you according to themselves, presenting a preconceived opinion to you, which no objection on your part can change, and which makes you feel you have not been understood. Ingenious in the art of consolation, Planet interrogates so minutely, and remains so open, that he succeeds in seeing himself as if he were you, and then he expounds with great decisiveness and clarity. People who knew Planet only superficially found him naïve and even silly, but for others of us from Berry, he was a true inspirer of courage and will. Speaking of this group, which never disbanded and of which I was a part, not one of us has not undergone, at least several times in his life, the extraordinary influence of Planet, the one among us who at first glance would seem to need the guidance of the others.

Thus, one beautiful morning, I was persuaded. After having arranged my affairs, for better or worse, to secure my resources, I left Paris without saying goodbye to anyone, or telling my plans to Maurice. I went to Nohant to take leave of my friends and beg them to watch over my children, should some accident cause my death while traveling, for I wanted to go far away to the East.

I knew very well that my friends would have no authority at all over my children as long as were minors. But they could exert some favorable influence on them as they grew. I even hoped that Mme. Decerfz would be a true mother to my daughter, and I wanted to sell my literary rights to create a little pension that might be put toward her education, should my husband consent to it. At the time of my daughter's marriage, this pension would have been turned over to her. It was a small thing, but it represented the cost of a girl's education at the best boarding schools. And so I left for Nohant, intending to make these arrangements, valid only in case of my death, as well as entreat my friends, in any case, to surround Maurice and Solange with a network of paternal care and continuing relationships—a duty I bequeathed them.

But before telling about what followed, I do not want to forget a particular event which took place in the winter of 1835. At Berry, I had a charming new friend, Mme. Rozane Bourgoing, wife of a civil servant in a recently established office at La Châtre. She was distinguished in all respects, exquisitely beautiful, and so friendly that she was soon accepted among us as if she had been born there.

Being called to Paris on business at the very time I was going back there (January, I think), she accepted one of the two tiny rooms in my garret, and spent two weeks there.

She said to me, one day, on receiving some letters from relatives who lived in Lyon: "They're giving me a really strange chore. A very prominent family is requesting my family to find out through me what their young man—whom I've never met—is up to in Paris, and other parts. His doings are a mystery even to his intimate friends. Damned if I know how to go about it. All I have is his address."

She resolved to invite him to come to see her, in order to talk to him about his family and sound him out on his plans and activities. I told her she could receive him in my home.

After his visit, she told me she was no wiser and that she had invited him to return in order to introduce him to me. She counted on me to make him talk more explicitly. I found this idea quite funny. If ever there was a person in this world inept at receiving confession, it was certainly I. But I could not refuse Rozane. I received the mysterious young man with her, and she even left us alone for a few minutes, hoping he would be less suspicious of me than of her.

I do not recall one word of the conversation, which revolved only around generalities, and without the help of Rozane—who has a precise recollection of the incident—I would not remember the conclusion I drew from it. But thanks to her, here it is, word for word, such as I gave it to her when he had left: "This young man is charming. He has a very remarkable mind, and his conscience seems to me quite at ease. If he travels—if he roams about the world—it will not be as some petty privateer, but rather as a political adventurer, a conspirator. He has devoted himself to the fortunes of the Bonaparte family. He still believes in that star. Happy is he who believes in something in this world!"

Well, I had not been far off in my guess. This young man was Fialin de Persigny.[49]

I return to describing my trip to the East, which took place only in my dreams.

I was at Nohant for several days when Fleury, leaving for Bourges, where Planet was living (he was editing an opposition newspaper there), suggested that I speak seriously about my situation and plans not only to that friend, but to the celebrated lawyer, Michel,[50] loyal friend to us all.

It is high time I spoke of that controversial figure whom I believe I understood very well, although it was not an easy thing to do. That was the time I began to undergo an influence of a kind completely exceptional in the lives of ordinary women—an influence which was precious to me for a long time and which, nonetheless, ceased suddenly and completely without destroying my affection. *M. S.*

VIII

Éverard. —His head, his face, his manners, his habits. —Patriots: enemies of cleanliness. —A nocturnal conversation on foot. —Sublimities and contradictions. —Fleury and I have the same dream at the same time. —From Bourges to Nohant. —Letters from Éverard. —The April lawsuit. —Lyon and Paris. —The lawyers. —A philosophical and political Pleiades. —Planet asks the social question. —The bridge of Saints-Pères. —A celebration at the royal palace. —Babouvist phantasmagory. —My morale. —Sainte-Beuve pokes fun. —An eccentric dinner. —A page from Louis Blanc. —Éverard sick and hallucinating. —I decide to leave. A crucial conversation. —Éverard wise and true. —Another page from Louis Blanc. —Two different points of view in the defense: I agree with Jules Favre.

What struck me immediately on seeing Michel for the first time, novice that I was in my study of phrenology, was the extraordinary shape of his head. He seemed to have two skulls soldered together, a sign that the eminent faculties of his soul were as prominent at the prow of this powerful vessel as those of his generous instincts were at the stern. Intelligence, reverence, enthusiasm, subtlety, and a great mind were balanced by familial love, friendship, domestic attachment, physical courage.[7] Éverard had a marvelous constitution, but Éverard was sick; Éverard was not supposed to live, indeed could not live. His chest, stomach, liver had been invaded. Despite a sober and austere life, he was worn-out, and from this extraordinary combination of faculties and qualities, each requiring its own key, the overall key was inevitably missing—mainspring of the most efficient human systems—good health.

It was precisely this lack of robustness which touched me deeply. How not to feel a tender concern for a beautiful soul at grips with the causes of its inevitable destruction, when that soul is ardently and courageously controlling its illness at every moment, and seems always in control of it. Éverard was only thirty-seven, but at first glance, he looked more like a little old man, thin, bald, and bent over; the time had not yet come when he would want to appear younger, wear a wig, dress fashionably, and step out in society. I was not to behold that vision; the transformation that he rejected as suddenly as he had assumed it was not accomplished under my eyes. Just as well. I prefer to retain the severe and simple image as it always appeared to me.

At first glance, Éverard seemed sixty, and, in effect, he was sixty; but at the same time, he seemed closer to forty when you looked more carefully at his beautiful pale face, his magnificent teeth, and at his near-sighted eyes, which showed admirable gentleness and candor through ugly spectacles. He thus appeared, and really was, peculiarly young and old at the same time.

This problematical condition was bound to be the cause of great unpredictability and contradiction in his character. His uniqueness was such that he could not be compared to anyone else. Verging on death from one moment to the next, life nevertheless abounded in him with an intensity tiring even for a mind most amazed and charmed by him—I mean my own.

This contrast paralleled another no less striking one in his habits. Born a peasant, he had retained the need for comfort and practicality in his clothing. Both at home and in town he wore a thick, shapeless great-coat and heavy clogs. He was cold in every season, everywhere, but being polite, he would not resort to keeping his cap or hat on indoors. Only he asked permission to put on a kerchief, whereupon he would pull out of his pocket three or four scarves which he knotted haphazardly one to the other, which he dropped while gesticulating, which he picked up and put back on again distractedly, sometimes coiffing himself, without realizing it, in the most fantastic or picturesque manner.

Beneath the outer garb, one could discern fine linen, always white and fresh, which betrayed the elegance of this Danube peasant. Certain provincial democrats blamed him for his secret sybaritism and extreme solicitude for his body. They were very wrong to do so. Cleanliness is a sign of sociability and deference for one's fellow man, and we must not proscribe a refined sense of cleanliness, because there is no such thing as being halfway clean. Not caring for oneself—a bad odor, teeth which are repugnant to look at, dirty hair—all are unbecoming habits we are wrong to accord scholars, artists, or patriots. We should chide them all the more for it, and they should allow it to themselves all the less, considering that the charm of dealing with them, or the excellence of their ideas, is inviting, but that even the most beautiful statement will lose in worth if it comes from a nauseating mouth. Finally, I am convinced that negligence of one's body must have some correspondence with negligence of one's mind, and should serve as a warning.

Éverard's brusque manners, over-familiarity, and acerbic frankness were only a facade and, admittedly, a mask to be worn before hostile people, or those he took at first sight to be hostile. By nature, he was sweet and obliging, graciousness itself; attentive to the smallest wish, the least discomfort of those he loved; tyrannical sounding, but freely affectionate, if one did not resist his theories on absolute authority.

His love for authority was undoubtedly not an act. It was at the very essence of his character and in no way diminished his goodness and the fatherly way he had of condescending. He wanted slaves, but only to make them happy, which would have been a fine and legitimate wish had he had relations only with weaklings. But as he wanted to make them strong, their happiness in being slaves would have ceased.

This simple reasoning never occurred to him, so true is it that the finest minds can be blind, in some cases, to the simplest insight, because they are absorbed by a ruling passion.

Having arrived at the inn at Bourges, I dined and sent Planet to tell Éverard I was there. He rushed to my side. He had just read *Lélia*, and he was raving about it. I told him all my troubles, my grief, and consulted him much less about the business at hand than about ideas. His mood was expansive, and from seven at night until four in the morning my two friends and I were virtually dizzy with admiration. We had said goodnight at midnight, but as there was a brilliant moon, and it was a magnificent spring night, Éverard proposed we take a walk through that beautiful, austere, and silent city, which seemed made to be viewed this way. We walked him back to his door; but he did not want to leave us there, and took us back to ours by way of the Hôtel Jacques Coeur, an admirable Renaissance palace, where we took a long pause. Then, he asked us to walk him back again; then, he returned again with us; and so it went until daybreak. We had made the trip nine times, and nothing, as you know, is as tiring as walking while talking, and stopping at each step, but we only felt our fatigue when he had left us.

What had he told us during that long night? All and nothing. He had let himself be prompted by our talk, which was only uttered to inspire his response, so curious had we been at first, and then so eager, to listen to him. He mounted from idea to idea to the most sublime vaultings toward Divinity, and when he had traversed all that space, he was truly transfigured. I believe that more eloquence never came from human lips; yet his awesome speech always used simple diction. At least it hastened to become natural and familiar again when it tore itself, smiling, from the grip of his enthusiasm. It was as if a myriad of musical ideas had lifted our souls to the heights of heavenly contemplation, then brought us back effortlessly, without a jar, by irresistible logic and gentle modulation, to earthly matters and the murmurs of the night.

I shall not recount the details he discussed with us. My *Lettres à Éverard* (sixth of the *Lettres d'un voyageur*), which are reasoned responses to his spontaneous preaching, can only give the reader an inkling. I was the passive subject of his impassioned declamations. Planet and Fleury had summoned me before his judge's bench so that I might plead my skepticism about earthly things and confess as well my foolish pride, which would fly off in worship of abstract perfection while forgetting the poor human beings here below. As my attitudes were more felt than reasoned, I was not very solid in my defense, and my resistance only served to indoctrinate me better. Nevertheless, I was aware of underlying contradictions in his own admirable teaching, that I should have been able to point out then and there, and to which I would have done well to pay more attention. But it was pleasant to let myself succumb to the charm of concrete ideas well thought-out and cleverly stated; to interrupt his argument by wrangling would have been self-defeating. Anyway, I did not have that kind of courage, nor did my friends, although one of them, Planet, had that perfectly sound common sense which *can* stand up to genius, and the other, Fleury, instinctively felt a secret distrust for Éverard's rhetoric.

But we were all three convinced, and the question of sincerity was of no consequence; we felt so exalted on leaving him that we could not and would not undermine our admiration and gratitude with doubt.

"I have never seen him this way," Planet told us. "For a year I have been living alongside him, and only this evening have I come to know him. He finally delivered himself entirely for you; he taxed his intellect and sensitivity to the limit. He may have just revealed himself to himself for the first time in his life, for he seems to have lived among us withdrawn, repressing a wish for utter abandon."

From this moment, Planet's attachment to Éverard became obsessive, and the same thing happened to several others who had doubted his sincerity until then, and believed only when they saw him open up before me. It was a remarkable modification in Éverard's existence and in his relations with friends that I brought about without realizing it. It brought true sweetness into his life, but was it truly good for him? No one can benefit from being too blindly worshipped.

After a few hours of unusually disturbed sleep, I and my Gaulois, Fleury, met again. He had had a frightful dream, and I was almost frightened myself listening to him recount it, for I had had nearly the same dream. A remark made lightly by Éverard had mysteriously lodged in a corner of our respective brains, precisely the remark which had least impressed us when it had been made.

It was certainly understandable that a remark could give rise to the same impression, or that the same cause could produce the same effect, in my friend's imagination and mine. However, we were both struck for an instant at the coincidence of having dreamed the same image at the same time, and little was needed for us both to consider it an omen in the manner of ancient soothsayers.

But soon our concern turned to laughter, also about the earnest exertions I had provoked in Éverard by my energetic resistance to his so-called humanitarian arguments for the guillotine. He surely did not believe a word of what he had said, for in political matters he was horrified by the death penalty, but he had carried logic to the point of absurdity. He would probably have laughed at his own extremism if, after having covered a world of ideas in our ensuing discussion, we had brought up again the paltry subject of a few heads, more or less, standing in the way of our accord.

We were right to tell ourselves that Éverard would not have wanted to kill even a fly to realize his utopia. Fleury, neverthless, remained struck by a dictatorial tendency, which he had recognized for the first time only on hearing it thwarted by my ideas on individual freedom.

Was Fleury's discomfort the effect of the allegorical dream that had visited us both, or his concern for a delicate friendship and the fear of having thrown me under a baneful influence, instead of the healing one I needed? What is certain is that the Gaulois was in a hurry to leave. He had made me a promise to be speedy when first climbing into the carriage, a promise he regretted when we arrived in Bourges. Now, he found we were not being harnessed up quickly enough. He was afraid Éverard would come to detain us longer.

Éverard, for his part, did think he would find us there and was astonished by our flight. Pushed by no particular anxiety, yet strongly determined to depart since early morning, I did indeed leave with Fleury, speaking of Éverard on the main road and admitting that, while I accepted the beautiful glimpse of his ideal republic, I needed to think about it and rest from his torrents of eloquence, which my nature would not submit to for too long without coming up for air.

But it was not, in fact, among my options, to inhale the morning air and the aroma of apple trees in bloom. Beatific reverie was not to the taste of my travelling companion. He was organized for argument, not for contemplation. He wanted to find some anchor in the struggles and successive solutions of humanity. He was not about to preach to me in Éverard's manner, but he wanted to preach to himself, comment on each of the master's words, accept or reject what appeared proper or false to him, and since he, too, had a distinguished mind and passion, it was impossible for me not to discuss Éverard, politics, or philosophy for eighteen leagues.

Nor did Éverard let me breathe. Hardly had I awakened after my rapid trip, when I received a letter inflamed with the same proselytism he seemed to have exhausted during our night's walk past the great moon-whitened buildings, on the resounding pavement of the old, sleeping city. The handwriting was illegible at first—as if wracked by a fever impatient to burn itself out—but once the first words came clear, all the rest followed. The style was as abbreviated as the remarks themselves were abundant, and as he used to write me very long letters, they were often themes that were not developed, and provided me a whole day of meditation after I had read them.

More letters followed in rapid succession, heedless of answers. His ardent mind had resolved to take mine over; all his energies were bent on this attempt. Abrupt directives and gentle persuasion—the two components of his extraordinary rhetoric—each in its turn bridged all the obstacles of mistrust by means both of burning enthusiasm and exquisite restraint; so much so that his imperious and unexpected manner of trampling social decorum, of posing as a keeper of your soul and a credulous apostle, left no opening for mockery, and never for a moment seemed ridiculous, because there was as much modesty, religious humility, and respectful tenderness in his cries of anger as in his cries of anguish.

"I know very well," he wrote me, after lyrical outbursts where the word *tu* was used in a most unaffected way, "that the malady of your mind derives from heartbreak. Love is a demanding passion. Extend this ardent and dedicated love, which will never receive its recompense in this world, to all humanity which is disparaged and in pain. Lavish not so much care on one creature! Alone, none of them merits it, but together, they deserve it in the name of the eternal author of creation!"

Such was, summed up, the theme he developed in his letters, which I answered under a changing spectrum of feeling, from a certain mistrust at the beginning to an almost total faith by the end. You could call these *Lettres à Éverard*—which passed almost immediately from his hands into those of the public—the swift chronicling of a swift conversion. This conversion was absolute in one sense, but quite incomplete in another. The rest of my account will explain how.

A great state of excitement then reigned in France. The Monarchy and the Republic were on the verge of playing their trump card in the great lawsuit which people called, for good reason, "the monster trial," even though the government, by a brutal series of denials of justice and violations of legality, had been able to keep it from attaining the proportions and consequences it could and should have had.

It was hardly possible to remain neutral in that vast debate, which no longer had the character of a conspiracy or surprise attack, but rather of a widespread protest in which all minds were stirring to ally themselves to one camp or the other. The cause of this trial—the events of Lyon—had had a more socialist character and a goal more generally shared than the revolts in Paris, which had preceded them. In Paris, at least in appearance, it had only been a question of changing the form of government. In Lyon, the problem of the organization of labor, together with the question of salaries, had been raised, and it had been fully probed. Elsewhere, people were solicited and somewhat dragged along by their political leaders, but in Lyon, they pulled these same leaders into a deeper and more serious struggle.

After the Lyon massacres, the idea of a civil war was no longer considered a favorable means to bring about democracy. Those in power had cannon and bayonets. From then on, despair alone could make people seek an end to suffering and misery by fighting. Conscience and reason advised other forms of struggle—reasoning and discussion. The reverberations of public speaking would have to shake public opinion. Indeed, it would take the opinion of all of France for that perfidious government—that system of provocation inaugurated by the politics of Louis-Philippe—to fall.

It was a beautiful hand to play: a simple, but far-reaching question of procedure could end in a lawful revolution. It could, at the very least, impart a backward movement to the aristocracy and erect a difficult barrier for them to cross. But the game was badly played by the democrats. They were the ones who had to draw back; the barrier was erected before them.

At first glance, however, it seemed that the uniting of legal talent from all the corners of the country, representing all sorts of intelligence from the provinces, would make for a vigorous resistance. The dream was, in the beginning, to form an elite corps—a small sacred battalion whose defenses were impossible to break because it represented a perfectly homogeneous mass. The strategy was based on speaking out and protesting, and almost all those called to the struggling ranks of democracy were brilliant orators and skillful debaters.

But people forgot that the most dedicated lawyers are, above all, artists, and while artists agree on certain rules of form, they differ from one another by what inspires them. At the beginning, they believed themselves to be very much in agreement on the political conclusion, but each one counted on his own means; people have difficulty in bending artists to one concerted effort —it is like discharging a cannon by the twelve-step method.

It came to a head when the differences between those partisans of democracy who espoused purely political and those who espoused purely socialist positions widened. Nevertheless, in Paris they were still in agreement against the common enemy. They were actually getting along better on that score than they had for a long time. The phalanx of provincial lawyers had just lined themselves up as equals, reserving special veneration for a pleiad of celebrities, chosen with enthusiasm from among the most important democratic names of the bar, politics and philosophy, science and literary art: Dupont, Marie, Garnier-Pagès, Ledru-Rollin, Armand Carrel, Buonarotti, Voyer d'Argenson, Pierre Leroux, Jean Reynaud, Raspail, Carnot, and so many others whose names were famous for their devotion to the cause or, later on, for their talent. Beside these already illustrious persons, the name of Barbès, as yet unknown, conferred on this select group a character no less sacred to posterity than Lamennais, Jean Reynaud and Pierre Leroux. A great man among the greatest, Barbès made up by his inspired virtue what he lacked in brilliance in learning.[51]

I have said they believed themselves to be totally in agreement at the start. For my part, I believed myself in agreement with Éverard, and I supposed that his friends were also in agreement with him. That was not the case. The majority of those whom he had brought from the provinces were at the most liberals, although they believed themselves to be radicals.

But Éverard had still not confided to anyone, no more to me than the others, his esoteric doctrine. His rhetorical fullness in no way affected his prudence, which, when it came to his plans, sometimes actually led him to the point of guile. He believed himself in possession of a great certainty, and sensing correctly that it went beyond the revolutionary tolerance of his followers, he insinuated the spirit of it gently, while leaving the precise meaning hidden.

Nevertheless, certain of his reservations and contradictions plagued me, although the others seemed oblivious to them, and that made me feel he harbored some hidden flaw. I spoke about it to Planet, who had gained no more insight than I, and who, more simply plagued for his own reasons, had the habit of saying on all occasions and subjects: "My friends, it is time to raise the social question!"

He would utter it so drolly, this chap Planet, that his proposal was always greeted by bursts of laughter, to the extent that, for us, his suggestion became a proverb. We said, "Let's raise the social question!" to say "Let's eat!" and when some garrulous character became boring, we suggested posing him the social question, to shut him up.

Nevertheless, Planet was right; despite some of his antics, his good sense always went straight to the point.

One magnificent evening, after we had been at the Théâtre-Français and were taking Éverard back to his dwelling near mine on Quai Voltaire, the social question was finally raised in all seriousness. I had always granted what we then called "equality of property," or "sharing of property," for lack of the simple word "communal," which became popular only later on. The proper words always filter down to the masses too late. Socialism had to be accused of wanting to return to agrarian law and all its brutal consequences in order to find phrases more apt to express its hopes.

I myself understood this sharing of earthly goods in a quite metaphorical way; by it I really meant the sharing in happiness due to all men; I could not imagine a literal division of property, which could not have made men happy unless they had been barbarians. How great, then, my stupefaction when Éverard, hedged in by my questions and the even more direct ones of Planet, finally explained his system to us.

We had stopped on the bridge of Saints-Pères. There was a ball or concert at the palace. We saw the lights reflected on the trees in the Tuileries gardens. We heard the sound of instruments, drowned from one moment to the next by the rolling carriage wheels on the Place du Carrousel, wafted on the night air heavy with spring perfume. The deserted embankment at the edge of the water, the silence and immobility which reigned on the bridge, contrasted with the blending sounds, the unseen movement. I had started to drift. I was no longer listening to the opening dialogue. I no longer cared about the social question. I was basking in the charming night, among the indistinct melodies, the soft gleams of moonlight mingling with the lights from the royal party.

The voice of Planet at my ear drew me from contemplation: "So, my good friend, you are inspired by old Buonarotti and would go as far as *babouvism*?"[52]

"What? What's that?" I broke in, quite astonished. "You want to revive that old business? You did leave Buonarotti's book at my place. I read it, it's beautiful. But such empirical methods could only have entered the desperate hearts of the men of that period, right after the fall of Robespierre. Today, they would be unresponsive; not on those roads would a civilized era wish to walk."

"Civilization!" Éverard cried out, enraged, hitting the sonorous railing of the bridge with his walking stick. "Yes! there you have the pompous word of the artists! Civilization! I tell you that to rejuvenate your corrupt society, this beautiful river must run red with blood, this damned palace be reduced to cinders, and this vast city wherein your glances are submerged a naked strand, where the poor man's family will push its plow and build its thatched roof cottage!"

Thereupon, my lawyer launched forth, and as my incredulous laughter heated his verve, he declaimed horribly and magnificently against the perversity of courts, the corruption of the big cities, the dissolution and enervation of the arts, luxury, industry—civilization, in brief. It was an appeal for the dagger and the torch; it was a curse on impure Jerusalem, with apocalyptic predictions; then, after these funereal pictures, he evoked the world of the future as he was dreaming it at that moment—the ideal of rustic life, the elevated principles of the golden age, the terrestrial paradise flourishing on the smoking ruins of the old world, by virtue of some fairy godmother.

As I was listening without contradicting, he stopped to question me. The palace clock struck two. "For two long hours you were pleading the case for death," I told him, "and I thought I was listening to old Dante on his return from hell. Now, I am delighting in your pastoral symphony. Why interrupt it so soon?"

"So," he shouted indignantly, "you are busy admiring my eloquence! You take pleasure in the sentences, the words, the images! You are listening to me as to a poem or an orchestra, that's all! You are no more convinced than that!"

I pleaded in turn, but artlessly, the case for civilization, especially the case for art, and then, spurred on by his disdain, I wanted to plead as well the

case for humanity, to make an appeal to the intelligence of my savage pedagogue, to the gentleness of his instincts, to the tenderness of his heart, which I
already knew to be so loving and impressionable. It was all useless. He was
mounted on his hobby, which was truly the pale horse of the vision. He was
beside himself. Ranting along, he descended onto the quay; he broke his walking stick on the walls of the old Louvre; such seditious statements poured from
his mouth that I failed to understand how he was neither noticed, overheard,
nor apprehended by the police. Only he in the whole world could act so eccen-
trically without appearing crazy and without growing ridiculous.

However, it made me depressed, and turning my back to him, I let him go
on arguing all alone, and set out again with Planet on the route to my dwelling.

He rejoined us on the bridge. He was both furious and distressed at not
having persuaded me. He followed me right to my door, wanting to prevent me
from returning home, begging me to listen to him still more, threatening never
to see me again if I left him that way. People might have called it a lovers'
quarrel, but only Babeuf's theories were at stake.

Only that, but Babeuf, nevertheless, was no light matter. Now that ideas
have gone beyond this grim doctrine it makes enlightened men smile, but it has
left its mark on the world: it stirred Bohemia under the name of Jan Huss; it
often dominated the ideals of Jean-Jacques Rousseau; it overwhelmed many
imaginations during the strife of last century's revolution; even during the
intellectual uprisings of 1848, it would merge, to some degree, with the spirit
of certain groups of that period, along with certain theories of dictatorship. In
brief, it became a cult, and since great shimmerings of truth and touching aspirations toward an ideal exist in every doctrine of renewal, it merited examination. And when it was reformulated at the foot of the scaffold on which
climbed the enthusiastic Gracchus and the stoic Darthé, already wounded by
their own hands, it continued to exert its seductive power.

Emmanuel Arago, pleading for Barbès in 1839, said: "Barbès is a *babouvist.*" It has not seemed to me since that time, in chatting with Barbès, that he
could ever have been a *babouvist* in the sense that Éverard had been in 1835.
You can be easily misled if you try to summarize and define the ideas of a man
in terms of his predecessor. Whatever you do, you cannot determine the exact
truth. Every doctrine is transformed in the minds of its followers, all the more
so when the followers become stronger than the master.

I do not want, here, to analyze or criticize Babeuf's doctrine. I only want
to show its possible effects. Since Éverard was the most implacable logician in
the universe in each aspect of his theory and in each phase of his conviction—never mind that he was the genius of illogic in the rest of his life—it is
surely worth noting that Babeuf's doctrine threw him into private delusions
and into a dream of colossal destruction.

I had spent the previous month reading Éverard and writing to him. I had
seen him during the interval; I had plied him with questions, and to make better
use of the little time we had, I had discussed nothing else. I had tried to build in
myself the edifice of his belief, in order to see if I could assimilate it fruitfully.
The reader must realize by now that I had already been converted to republican

sympathy and progressive ideas. What I had gained by listening to this man during his truly inspired moments was the ability to feel the vivid emotions that politics had never before awakened in me. I had always been detached from matters of action; I had observed streaming around me, with the force of a flooding river, the thousand accidents that go to make up our present history, and I had said: "I shall not drink from this water." Probably I should have continued refusing to merge my life with those bitterly agitating waves. Sainte-Beuve, who still exerted a little influence on me at that time through his clever mockery and sensible warnings, brought his talent as an appreciator and a critic to bear on practical things. From his lips, criticism exerted a great attraction on the reasonable, tranquil side of my mind. This sudden gathering of France's most diverse opinions, representing all the points on the republican horizon, amused him; they were blending, he said, like all of Dante's circles suddenly collapsed into one.

A dinner to which Liszt had invited Lamennais, Ballanche, the singer Nourrit, and me, had seemed to Sainte-Beuve the most fanciful thing imaginable. He wondered what we five could have found to say to each other. I answered that I could not enlighten him, since Lamennais paired off with Ballanche, Liszt with Nourrit, and I with the family cat.

But, nevertheless, let us today reread an informative page from Louis Blanc:

"And how now to represent the effect that so many surprising complications produced on our minds? The names of the defendants flew from mouth to mouth; people shared a stake in their risks, glorified their perseverance, wondered anxiously how far they would push the audacity of their resolutions. In salons even where their doctrines were abhorred, their daring touched the women's hearts. As prisoners they held an irresistible attraction for the public; though absent, they lived in everyone's thoughts. Is it surprising? They produced in the generous of this nation all sorts of powerful feelings—courage, defeat, misfortune. A stormy period, and yet regrettable! How the blood boiled furiously in our veins! How alive we felt! How good it was that God had made this French nation which would doubtlessly perish on the day when all these exalted emotions were lacking! Short-sighted politicians are alarmed by society's ardor. They are right: to wield power you have to be strong. And that is why mediocre statesmen insist on weakening a people. They tailor them to their own image; otherwise they could not lead them. Men of genius do not act that way. They do not take pains to extinguish the passions of a great people, they wish to strengthen them, and they know that lethargy is the final stage of a declining society."

This page seems to have been written for me, in that it so well sums up what was happening in and around me. I was, in miniature, the expression of this declining society, and the genius who, instead of offering me peace and happiness then and there, applied himself to my guidance, was Éverard, himself the expression of politic's bounteous malaise and certain ideas and errors of the moment.

In the few days since he and I had found each other again in Paris, the pace of life had quickened. I do not know whether the excitement which permeated the air would have found its way to my garret without him, but with him it entered in billows. He had introduced me to his close friend, Girerd de Nevers, and other defenders of the accused of April, chosen from the provinces neighboring Berry. Another of his friends, Degeorge d'Arras, also became a friend of mine; Planet, Emmanuel Arago, and two or three other common friends completed our night school. In the daytime, I received my other friends. Few of them knew Éverard, nor did they all share his ideas, but even the daytime hours were affected by discussions of public events, for this fever was contagious to all.

Éverard would come to fetch me at six o'clock, to dine outdoors at a quiet little restaurant, with our usual friends. We would go out all together in the evenings, sometimes on a boat on the Seine, sometimes along the boulevards, right up to the Bastille, overhearing the remarks, observing the movements of the crowd, which was excited and engrossed, but not as much as Éverard had imagined they would be on leaving the provinces.

In order not to stand out as the only woman among all these men, I sometimes had recourse to my boyish outfit, which permitted me to enter the famous session of May 20th, at the Luxembourg, unnoticed.

Éverard walked and spoke at a feverish pitch during these outings; no one could calm him or compel him to spare himself. Returning home, he would feel ill, and Planet and I often spent part of the night helping him combat a sort of terrifying agony. He was haunted, then, by lugubrious visions; courageous concerning his sickness, fearful before the images he awakened in himself, he used to beg us not to leave him alone with apparitions. That terrified me a bit myself. Planet, accustomed to seeing him like that, was not upset, and when he saw him dozing off, he would put him to bed, come back to chat with me softly in the next room, in order not to disturb his dozing, and take me back to my place when he sensed him sound asleep. Each time, Éverard would wake up after three or four hours, more active, more alive, more fiery than before, and, above all, more careless of the harm he was doing to himself; for each surge of vitality made the idea of a relapse seem impossible to him. He ran to attend heated meetings where the question of defending the accused was debated, and after intense discussions he would come back to his house to faint before dinner, if they had not already carried him back, passed out in a carriage. But then it was just a matter of a few instants of livid pallor and muffled groans. He would revive as if by a miracle of nature, or will, to speak and laugh with us; for in the midst of alternating exaltation and collapse, he would plunge into gaiety with the carefree abandon and innocence of a child.

To witness such contrasts moved me and drew me out of myself. My heart went out to this nature that resembled no other, and that, for the slightest concern, showed tremendous gratitude. The charm of his speech held me for hours at a time—me, whom talk tires enormously. And I was influenced also by a strong desire to share his political passion, his faith in general salvation, the invigorating hopes for a soon-to-be-realized social renewal that seemed destined to transform even the humblest among us into disciples.

But, I admit, after that harangue at the bridge of Saints-Pères—that antiso-

cial and antihumane invective with which he had entertained me—I felt myself
fall from heaven to earth, and that, shrugging my shoulders on rising, I again
took up my resolve to go off to hunt flowers and butterflies in Egypt or Persia.

Without too much reflection, I obeyed the instinct that pushed me toward
solitude, and I went to obtain my passport for foreign travel. On returning
home, I found Éverard waiting for me. "What's the matter?" he cried. "That's
not the calm face I know."

"It's the face of a traveler," I answered, "and I have definitely decided to
leave. Don't be upset. You are not one of those people to whom one is polite
out of social hypocrisy. I've had enough of all your republics. You each have
one, which isn't mine and which is no one else's either. This time it will come
to nothing. I'll come back to applaud and crown you at a better time, when you
have run out of utopias and have collected some sane ideas."

The dispute was a stormy one. He reproached me for my light-weight
mind and my dried-up heart. Pushed to the limit by his insults, I summed up
my feelings.

Who needed this demented will of his to dominate my convictions, and
impose on me those of others? Why, and how, had he been able to take advantage, to this extreme, literally, of the homage that my intelligence had rendered
his by listening to him without argument and admiring him? Yes, this admiration had been unreserved and sincere, but it did not have as a possible consequence the absolute abandoning of my ideas, instincts, and faculties. After all,
we didn't know each other totally, and we were perhaps not destined to understand completely, having come together from so far to discuss problems whose
solution he believed he had found. He had not given me that solution, nor did he
have it to give. I could not reproach him for that, but wasn't his personal anger
at my resistance to his general theories something of a tyrannical fantasy?

"In listening to me speak to you as a student attentive to a masters's
lessons, you thought you were my father," I told him. "You called me your
beloved son—your Benjamin; you created poetry with a biblical eloquence. I
heard you as in a grand and heavenly dream whose purity my memory will
always cherish. But one cannot always dream. To advance the reign of God
and the happiness of man in real life, one must do more than sing like an angel!
For me, this happiness lies rather in wisdom than in action. I want nothing in
life except the means to believe in God and love my fellow human beings. I
was sick, I was misanthropic. You made yourself strong to cure me; you affected me a great deal, surely. You fought very hard against my pride, and you
made me foresee an ideal of fraternity which warmed my glacial heart. In that,
you were truly Christian, and you converted me through my feelings. You
made me cry abundantly, as in the days when a sudden tenderness born of my
dreams would awaken my piety without warning. By myself I would not have
rediscovered, after so many uncertainties and so much spiritual fatigue, the
source of those invigorating tears. Your persuasiveness created the miracle I
was asking from you. Be blessed for that, and let me leave without regret. Let
me go now to meditate on the things you are seeking here, on the principles
which may perhaps be formulated and applied to the needs of the hearts and

minds of mankind. And don't tell me you have found them—that you hold them in your hand; it's not true. You don't hold anything, you are searching! You are no wiser than I, although you're a better person."

And as he appeared offended by my frankness, I went further:

"You are a true artist. You live only by your heart and your imagination. Your magnificent eloquence is a gift which forces you fatally toward argument. Your mind needs to dominate those who listen to the enraptured beliefs that reason has not yet ripened. It is at that point reality seizes me and distances me from you. I hear all this heartfelt poetry, all these soulful aspirations ending in sophistry, and that is exactly what I don't want to hear, what I'm sorry to have heard. Listen, my poor father, we idealists are indeed mad. The official world, the world of practicality, that sees only our odd behavior and opinions, treats us like dreamers. It is right. Let's not be upset about it. Let's accept its disdain. It does not understand that we are living out of a desire and hope whose goal is impersonal. It is mad in its own way; in our eyes it is utterly driven to pursue material goods and pleasures that we wouldn't want to touch with a pair of tongs. As long as society lasts, there will be lunatics who are too busy looking at the ground ever to imagine there is a sky above them, and lunatics who look too much at the sky to give their due to those who see only their feet. Therefore, the wisdom which should embrace the view of the finite and infinite, as they presently exist, is lacking to all. Let's not expect such wisdom from deluded positivists; by the same token, let's not pretend we have it to give to them before having found it ourselves.

"Such wisdom is the kind that politics cannot forego. If we forego it, we will act impulsively and end with chimeras or catastrophes. I sense that, in speaking to you in the midst of your fever for action, I cannot convince you; so I speak to you only to plead my right to withdraw from this conflict where I can't shed any light, and where I can't distinguish yours, shrouded as it still is in impenetrable mists."

When I had finished, Éverard, who had remained calm with great difficulty in order to hear me out, recovered his energy and conviction. He gave me such reasons that I felt myself vanquished:

"No one can find the light all by himself. Truth is no longer revealed to the thinker who has withdrawn to the summit. Nor is it revealed anymore to coteries in cloistral isolation, climbing their endless pinnacles of thought. It occurs through long, hard work and nothing else. To find, at present, the truth appropriate to societies being born, you must confront, you must weigh all opinions, you must communicate, discuss and consult one another, for better or worse, to arrive at a formula which can never be the absolute truth, for God alone possesses that, but which is the best possible expression of the human aspiration to the truth. That is why I live in a fever; that is why I eagerly digest all the ideas which strike me; that is why I speak until I am worn out, until I wander from the point; because to speak is to think aloud, and in thinking aloud, I proceed faster than in thinking silently. You others who listen to me, and you in particular, who listen more attentively than anyone else, you put too much stock in the fleeting lightning that streaks through my brain. You are not sufficiently committed to the necessity of following me as one follows a devoted and adventurous guide on a path, all the detours of which he doesn't yet know himself, but whose far-off goal his piercing vision and courage have apprehended. It is up to you to warn me of obstacles, to set me back on the path, when imagination or curiosity carries me away. That done, if you lose patience with my digressions, if you become tired of following a pilot uncertain of his course, look for a better one, but don't scorn him for not having been a god, and don't damn him for having shown you new shores leading more or less to the place where you wanted to go.

"As for you, I find you overly demanding and wrongheaded, a scholar without brains! As you admit, you know nothing, and as you stated, you wished to learn nothing. Then, suddenly, the fever to know took you overnight; you demanded visionary knowledge; you required absolute truth. Quickly, quickly, hand over God's secrets to Monsieur George Sand, who is in a big hurry!

"Well, then," he added after a volley of rancorless jokes that he snatched from the air like flies, "I am making a discovery—souls have a sex, and yours is female. Do you believe that still had not occurred to me? Reading *Lélia* and your first *Lettres d'un voyageur*, I saw you in my mind's eye as a young boy, a child poet, whom I made my son. My deepest regret is that I have no children of my own. To bring up those of my wife's first marriage was bittersweet for me. When I saw you for the first time, I was as surprised as if no one had told me you wear dresses and that, in real life, you have a woman's name. I wanted to hold on to my dream, simply to call you George, to address you as *tu*, as they do in the shade of Virgil's trees, and to look at you in the light of our little sun only long enough each day to know how your soul was faring. And in truth, I only knew you by the sound of your voice, which is muffled, and which doesn't remind me of the melodious flute of a woman's voice. Therefore, I have always spoken to you as to a boy who has read his philosophy and history. At present I see well—and you remind me—that you have the ambition and the imperiousness of undeveloped minds, of beings of pure feeling and imagination—of women, in short. I daresay your feeling is like an impatient logician who wants philosophical science to make all her strings vibrate at once, and gratify all her whims. But the logic of pure feeling is not sufficient in politics, and you demand the impossible—perfect harmony between the demands of action and those of our sensibility. Yes, that would be ideal, but it is still unrealizable on earth; so, you conclude that one should stand by with folded arms, and let it happen by itself.

"Fold your arms then and leave! Yes, indeed, you are free; but your conscience would not be, if it knew itself well. I don't have the right to ask for your affection. I did want to give you mine. Too bad for me; you didn't ask for it; you don't need it. Therefore, I shall not speak to you of me, but of yourself, and of something more important than yourself—duty.

"Your dream is of an individual freedom that does not fit in with the concept of duty in general. You worked hard to win this freedom for yourself. Then you lost it in your heart's abandon to earthly affections that held no satisfaction; now, you are gathering your resources in a life of austerity, which I approve, but the application of which extends wrongly to acts of your will and intelligence. You tell yourself that your body belongs to you and that the same is true for your soul. Well, that is a fallacy worse and more dangerous than all those for which you reproach me, since you are free to make it the law of your life, while my fallacies can only be realized through miracles. Think about this: if all the lovers of absolute truth said farewell to their country, their fellows, their duty—as you do—not only absolute truth, but even relative truth would no longer have one single follower. For truth does not mount on the rump behind those who flee, and gallop along with them. It isn't found in solitude, you poor dreamer! Its voice doesn't speak through plants or birds, or if it does, men can't understand such utterances. The divine philosopher whom you cherish knew it well when he said to his disciples: 'There where only three of you meet in my name, my spirit will be with you.'[53]

"Therefore, you will be forced to seek and pray among others. However little you find in joining them is something, and what you think you have found alone exists only for yourself, consequently does not exist. Go off, then, in pursuit of nothingness; I shall console myself over your departure with the certainty, despite my errors and those of others, that I seek and pursue something true and good."

Having delivered himself, he left me half-unaware of his departure, for I was absorbed in my own reactions to all he had said, of which my pen can render only the barest outline.

When I was ready to answer him, thinking he was in the next room, where he sometimes retired to take a five-minute rest from sudden exhaustion, I realized he had actually gone and locked me in. I looked everywhere for the key, which he had put in his pocket, and realized I had given the rest of the day off to the woman who served me and had a second key to the apartment. I attributed my capitivity to Éverard's distraction, and tried to think calmly again. After three hours he came back to free me, and when I pointed out his absent-mindedness, "Not at all," he said, laughing. "I did it on purpose. I was expected at a meeting, and seeing I still had not convinced you, I put you in solitary confinement to give you some time to think. I feared an act of rebellion, and that I'd no longer find you in Paris this evening. Now that you have reflected, here is your key, the key to freedom. Must I say goodbye and go out to dine without you?"

"No," I answered him. "I was wrong. I'm staying. Let's go out to eat, and let's hunt for something better than Babeuf for our intellectual nourishment."

I have reported this long conversation because it describes my life and the lives of a certain number of revolutionaries at that time. During this phase of the April lawsuit, laborious study was under way everywhere among us, sometimes wise and profound, sometimes naïve and untutored. When I think back on it, I am astonished by the progress that ideas have made in such a short time, and less awed by the enormous progress that remains to be made.

The true center of this social and philosophical lucubration was in the government prisons. "Then," said Louis Blanc, that admirable historian of our emotions, whom I cannot quote too often, "you saw these men—weighed down by the fact of their terrible detention—suddenly rise above the danger and above their fears to devote themselves to the study of the driest subjects. The Parisian committee for the defense had begun by distributing among the most capable members of the party the agenda for the science of government, assigning to one the philosophical and religious part, to another the administrative part; to this one the political economy, to another the arts. All gave the subject their fullest meditation, their most impassioned research. But not everyone on this intellectual course would run to the finish. Theoretical differences became manifest. Heated debates arose. The bodies of the captives belonged to the jailer, but their indomitable spirits were free to race through the unbounded realm of thought. In the darkness of their cells, they cared for the future of mankind; they kept up a dialogue with God; facing the scaffold, they were exalted, delirious with hope, as if they were marching to conquer the world. A moving and singular vision, whose memory it behooves us to cherish!

"That ignoble concerns filtered into this movement, that adherence sometimes gave way to petty or intense rivalries, that minds too weak to rise up with impunity may have been lost in the land of dreams, one cannot deny; but the all too inevitable cases of human failure need not detract from the general deed that we have just noted all that is solemn and grand."

If you want to judge the April lawsuit and all the acts attached to it in a just, detached, and truly philosophical way, you must reread in its entirety the very short, but dense, chapter of Louis Blanc's *Histoire de dix ans*. Men and matters are judged therein not only with the exact knowledge of the past that the historian must never alter or diminish in value, but with the rare equity of a great and generous mind which renders the moral, or supreme, truth of history amidst the apparent contradictions of the events and the men who experience them.

I shall not recount these events. That would be completely useless; they are recorded there in a manner that so well conforms to my feelings, my memory, and my conscience that I would not be able to add one thing.

A lost and unnoticed participant, yet living in response to this drama, I am here only as the biographer of a man who took an active part and, I should mention, an apparently problematic one, because he was hesitant, impressionable, and less a politician than an artist.

You know, reader, that a great debate arose among the defense—an ardent debate—insoluble under the pressure that the hasty actions of the peerage brought to bear. A portion of the accused agreed with the defense, not to be defended. It was not a question of winning the judicial case and being acquitted by government; it was a matter of making the common cause triumph in public opinion by pleading the sacred right of the people to take precedence over the established power, which stood for right through might. Another portion of the accused, those from Lyon, wished to be defended, not to proclaim their innocence of the act of which they were accused, but to teach France what had happened in Lyon—how the authorities had provoked the people, how they had treated the vanquished, how the accused had done what it was humanly possible to do to prevent civil war or render it noble, thereby softening its cruel results. It was a matter of deciding whether the authorities had had the right to declare a rebellion based on a few isolated provocations, possibly even carried out by mercenaries, in order to ride an army over a defenseless population. The defense had the facts, they wanted to tell them, and in my opinion, the real case lay there. They were strong enough to plead the case of the betrayed and mutilated; they were not strong enough to affirm the cause of human liberation.

Therefore, my opinions were closer to those of Jules Favre, who found himself in the position of adversary to Éverard in their secret meetings, and who was an adversary worthy of him. I did not know Jules Favre, I had never seen him, never heard him, but when Éverard, after having vehemently countered his arguments, came to report them to me, I decided Favre was correct. Éverard understood very well that my desire was not to contradict and irritate him, but he was bothered by my defection, and sensing that I dreaded having his utopias publicly exposed, he would shout: "To hell with the bridge of Saints-Pères and the social question!" *J.G.*

IX

An incriminating letter in the monster trial. —My draft rejected.
—The defection of the republican bar. —Trélat. —Éverard's speech.
—His condemnation. —Return to Nohant. —Plans for a settlement.
—The empty house in Paris. —Charles d'Aragon. —The Fieschi
affair. —Maurice's political opinions. —Lammenais. —Pierre
Leroux. —I am seized by homesickness. —The deserted house in
Bourges. —Éverard's contradictory nature. —I come back to Paris.

It was, above all, a question of bolstering the courage of certain
defendants—only a few, fortunately—who showed signs of weakening. I was
entirely in agreement with Éverard on this point, namely that whatever the
result of a division in the motives and ideas of the counsel for the defense
might be, fear or discouragement must not be visible, not even among a few of
the accused. He had me draft a piece in the form of a letter—the famous letter
that was to give a new dimension to the monster trial. His aim was to cause a
hopeless tangle in the prosecution's strategy. At times the idea tempted
Armand Carrel;[54] at others times it alarmed his cautious nature. But Éverard
pushed it forward, and although he could sometimes be very mistrustful of the
future, he now scarcely took time to reflect. He found my draft too sentimental,
and changed it. "It's not a question of shoring up wavering faith with homi-
lies," he told me. "Ideals do not count for very much with people. It is indignation and anger that stir them up. I want to make a violent attack on the peerage,
in order to exalt the defendants; moreover, I want to summon the entire republican bar." I pointed out to him that the republican bar would sign my draft and
would reject his. "They will all have to sign," he replied, "and if they don't,
we'll get along without them."

As a matter of fact, we got along without a great number, and it was a
great mistake to have provoked the defections. They were not all as reprehensible as they seemed to Éverard. Some had arrived not wanting an actual revolution, hoping only to contribute to a revolution of ideas; not thinking of profit or
glory, but of fulfilling a duty whose consequences had not been entirely
revealed to them. I knew several and could not possibly blame them, after they
had explained their reasons for abstaining.

The consequences of the letter are well known. It was fatal to the party
because it threw it into disarray; it was fatal to Éverard because it gave rise to a
speech which was controversial even in the ranks of his party. Inspired by generosity, he had taken on himself the full responsibility for the piece, which was

condemned by the Court of Peers. He would have done it even if Trélat had not set the example of sacrifice for him. For Trélat committed an act of heroic hostility before the court, while Éverard—before that same tribunal—strewed his profession of faith with antitheses. Let Louis Blanc tell it: "Then Michel de Bourges came forward. The purport of his speech was already known, and all waited in the midst of a solemn silence. He began in a brusque, deep voice. Leaning over the railing that served him as support, he first made it shake beneath the convulsive pressure of his hands, then, with an impetuous movement, he examined the length of it like the Roman Gaius Gracchus, whose too violent eloquence had to be moderated by a flute. Nevertheless, Michel de Bourges was not so daring nor so extreme as M. Trélat. He defended himself, something M. Trélat had not deigned to do, and the attacks he directed at the Peers were not totally devoid of caution. Always upholding the spirit of his message, he appeared disposed to take little account of the style; he acknowledged that, to judge by what he had seen during the three days, the Peers were worth more than their institution. As for the rest, and for what dealt with the very substance of the trial, he was unyielding."

I shall permit myself to add only a word to that excellent appraisal. As I saw it, Éverard did not defend himself, and I still suffer to think that, if he paid little heed to the style of his provocation, it was perhaps due to the criticism I had made of that same style. I thought—and I took the liberty of saying so to him—that the principal blunder of his party was their harsh language and the caustic tone of their arguments. They reverted too frequently to the vocabulary of the bitterest periods of the Revolution of 1789. They affected its use without considering that a choice of expressions redolent of the style of that time might, forty years later, appear offensive and, consequently, weak. I admired the originality of Éverard's speaking ability precisely because it gave color and new form to the ideas of the past. He was well aware that his power lay there, and he laughed wholeheartedly at the hackneyed phrases and trite oratory. But in writing, he sometimes fell back on them without realizing it, and when I pointed this out to him, he quietly agreed. However, we had not been in agreement on that point in drafting the letter. He had defended and upheld his version, but afterward, hearing it faulted by others, he became disgusted with it, and the artist prevailing by turns over the man of the party, he must have wished that a piece destined to create such a stir might have been a masterpiece of taste and eloquence. It is true that, had it been so, he would not have been accused and his goal would not have been attained.

Once he was no longer in the isolated situation in which the legal proceedings had placed each attorney, he was no longer forced to defend rigorously every expression in his letter. Since it was not signed by the entire party, it reverted to being his personal work, and perhaps he believed it was in bad taste to uphold it blindly.

I did not hear that speech, for I only attended the May 20th session. Nothing is more fleeting than a speech, and the stenography that preserves the words does not always preserve their spirit. In order to grasp perfectly all the nuances of the orator's thought at each peak of his improvisation, one would have to be able to set down his tone and photograph his facial expression. Éverard never prepared any of his political speeches; he drew his inspiration from the moment, and being under the influence of the nervous excitement that dominated and sustained his genius, he was not always in command of his words. This was not the only time he had been reproached for the unexpected turn of his thought and that it was judged more significant and conclusive than was consistent with his usual delivery.

Be that as it may, that speech, at the end of which he was carried home with an acute attack of bronchitis, gained numerous detractors for him among his fellow members. Éverard had offended beliefs and wounded egos during the stormy debates among party members themselves. He had bitter grudges held against him, and even some of the impartial were harsh with him. "Was it worth the trouble," they asked, "to have combatted so fiercely the opinion of those who wanted to adopt the defense's method, only to end by defending yourself, all alone, for a collective act?"

But wasn't it precisely because that cause no longer had a collective sense that Éverard was inevitably led to make so little of it? Wasn't there something naïve and grand in the modesty that made him confess to feeling no rancor or personal hatred? And was there anything hesitant in his peroration when he cried: "If I am penalized I shall put my fortune at the disposal of the Treasury, happy still to dedicate to the defense of the accused what I have earned in the practice of my profession. As for prison, I recall the words of that other republican who died nobly at Utica:[55] 'I would rather be in prison than sitting here at your side, O Caesar!'"

The decision which condemned Trélat to three years in prison and Michel to only a month became the subject of hostile remarks. Michel was jealous of Trélat's prison sentence, but not of the honor it earned the latter. He loved that noble nature dearly, and the parallel which was drawn between them, to the detriment of one, in no way diminished the affection and reverence he felt for the other. "Trélat is a saint," Éverard would say, "and I am not worthy of him." That was true, but to say it sincerely, under such circumstances, he himself had to have been very noble.

Éverard was quite seriously ill. The proof that he had not been as agreeable to the nobles as some of his adversaries claimed is that the Chamber of Peers treated him very brutally by summoning him to serve his prison term dead or alive. Without his knowledge, I lodged a complaint for him with M. Pasquier, who was quite willing to send the court-appointed doctor to verify his physical condition.

This doctor proceeded to interrogate Éverard in a rude manner, pretending that the illness was a subterfuge and the delay I requested a risk to the court. Éverard almost foiled the step I had taken, for on seeing the court doctor start off so offensively, he replied apruptly that he was not sick and refused to be examined. However, I managed to have his pulse taken, and the fever was so virulent that the monarchy's Aesculapius softened immediately, ashamed perhaps of such totally uncalled for and quite stupid abuse. Who, after all, condemned to a mere month in prison, would prefer flight? Through this miniature incident I saw how republicans were being persecuted, and I got an idea of the system used in the prisons to provoke those revolts that the authorities seemed eager to spark for the pleasure of punishing.

As soon as Éverard was better, I left with my daughter for Nohant. I no longer remember why Éverard's sentence was not to be served until the following November. Perhaps that delay was granted him out of consideration for his clients.

This time my stay at home was disagreeable—even difficult. I had to summon a great deal of will-power not to embitter our marital situation. My being there was positively a torture. Unhappily, my friends were forced to observe it; and the very ones who contributed to ruining my home life, my brother and one other, were aware that my position was untenable. They therefore recommended a settlement.

I was receiving three thousand francs as a substistence allowance for my daughter and me. It was very little especially as my work was not very lucrative and was, moreover, subject to human contingencies, such as the state of my health. However, it was possible, on the condition that, by spending six months of the year at home, I could set aside fifteen hundred francs a year to pay for my child's education. If my door was closed to me, my life would become precarious, and my husband would not—or should not—have a clear conscience.

He recognized that fact. My brother urged him to give me six thousand francs a year. He would have had about ten thousand left, including his own property—quite sufficient to live on at Nohant, alone, since that was what he wanted. M. Dudevant had yielded to this advice; he had, in effect, promised to double my allowance, but when it came to doing it, he told me it was impossible to live at Nohant with what he had left. In order to emerge from some financial difficulties into which he had gotten himself, he was required to furnish some explanations and ask for my signature. He had misused a portion of his small inheritance and had nothing left of it. He had bought some land that he could not pay for; he was worried and morose. After I signed, things went no better, according to him. He had not solved the problem he had given me to resolve several years before—his expenses exceeded our income. The wine cellar alone took a great portion of it, and for the rest, he was being robbed by the servants, who were allowed too many opportunites to do so. I pointed out to him several flagrant examples of knavery, believing I was helping him as well as myself. He was not at all grateful. Like Frederick the Great, he wished to be served by thieves. He forbade me to meddle in his affairs, criticize his management, or give orders to his servants. It seemed to me that all that was to some extent my concern, since he claimed he no longer had anything. I resigned myself to keeping quiet and waiting for him to see the light.

That was not long in coming. On a day when he was disgusted with everything around him, he told me that Nohant was ruining him, that he was undergoing personal difficulties, that he was bored in the midst of his leisure, and that he was ready to turn over the use and maintenance of it to me. He wanted to go to live in Paris or the Midi with the remainder of our income, which he assessed then at seven thousand francs. I accepted. He drew up the agreement and I signed without any discussion, but from then on he displayed such regret and annoyance over it that I departed for Paris, leaving him with the contract torn up and once again entrusting my fate to the providence of artists—work.

This took place in the month of April. My trip back to Nohant in June did not improve the situation. M. Dudevant's notion of leaving Nohant persisted; it was more firmly fixed when I returned, but since it was accompanied by resentment, I went away again without insisting on anything.

Éverard had returned to Bourges. In Paris I lived completely secluded for some time. I had a novel to write, and as I was dying from the heat in my garret on Quai Malaquais, I found a way to establish myself in a rather unusual workroom. The apartment on the ground floor was being renovated, and the work had been suspended for some reason. The spacious rooms of these fine premises were cluttered with stone and wood for the construction; the doors to the garden had been removed, and the enclosed garden itself, empty and abandoned, was awaiting its metamorphosis. So, I was afforded perfect solitude, shade, and cool fresh air. A carpenter's workbench made a desk more than sufficient for my writing necessities, and there I spent the most tranquil days I have ever been able to snatch; for nobody in the world knew where I was except for the porter, who had given me the key, and my chambermaid, who brought me my mail and my lunch. I only left my retreat to go to see my children at their respective boarding schools. I had again placed Solange with the Misses Martin.

I think that, like me, everybody longs for those rare, brief moments when external matters deign to arrange themselves in such a way as to leave us in absolute peace. The smallest nook then becomes a voluntary prison, and wherever it may be, it takes on an indefinable delight that gives us the feeling of having conquered and possessed time, silence, and ourselves. Everything was mine within those bare, devastated walls, soon to be covered with gilt and silk, but which no one would ever enjoy as I did. At least I told myself that the future occupants would perhaps never know an hour of the secure leisure and total reverie I savored there every day, from morning to night. Everything in that place was mine—the pile of planks that served me to rest on; the diligent spiders spinning their great webs, from cornice to cornice, with such skill; the mice mysteriously occupied in their meticulous investigations through the shavings. The garden's blackbirds, having come insolently to the threshold, would watch me, and suddenly motionless and wary, with a strange modulation, arrest their carefree, mocking song. I sometimes went down there in the evening, not to write again, but to breathe the air and muse on the steps of the landing. Thistles and mullein had pushed up among the loose stones; sparrows, aroused by my presence, rustled the leaves of the shrubbery, making the silence quiver, and the sounds of carriages and shouts from outside drifting in to me made me sense more fully the value of my freedom and the sweetness of my repose.

When my novel was finished, I again opened my door to a small group of friends. It was during this period, I believe, that I became friends with Charles d'Aragon, a person of most noble character, and also with M. Artaud, a scholarly and marvelously agreeable man. My other friends were republicans, but in spite of the unsettled times, no political dissension ever troubled the harmony and pleasant relationships in the garret.

One day, a great-hearted woman of whom I was fond, Mme. Julie Beaune, came to see me. "Paris is in an uproar," she told me. "They have just tried to kill Louis-Philippe." It was the Fieschi machine.[56] I was greatly disturbed; Maurice had just gone out with Charles d'Aragon, who had taken him expressly to see the king pass as they were on their way to visit the Comtesse de Montijo. I trembled that on their return they would find themselves involved in some fracas and was about to hurry there, when Aragon brought my schoolboy back to me safe and sound. While I was questioning Aragon about the incident, my son was telling me about a charming little girl with whom he claimed to have discussed politics. It was the future Empress of France. That childish tale reminds me of another. Maurice, a year later, wrote to me of the young prince who also attended Henri IV: "Montpensier invited me to his ball, in spite of my political opinions. I had a very good time there. He had us all join him in spitting on the heads of the national guardsmen." (While engaging in this diversion, the little prince and his young guests were on a gallery under which passed the bearskin hats.)

It was during the course of that year that I humbly approached two of the greatest intellects of our century, Lammenais and Pierre Leroux. I had planned to devote a long chapter to each of these distinguished men, but the limits of this work cannot be extended as I would like, and I would not want to curtail two subjects as far-reaching as those of their philosophy of history and their mission in the world of ideas. This work is the extensive and full preface to a book that will appear later on,[57] in which, no longer having to tell my own story in minute detail, I shall be able to take up more important personalities than my own.

I shall, therefore, limit myself to sketching some of the characteristics of the imposing figures I have met during the period of my existence contained in this book and to describing the impression they made on me.

I was searching, by that time, for a single religious and social truth. Thanks to Éverard, I had grasped that these truths are indivisible and must complement each other, but as yet I saw only a thick fog, weakly gilded by the light it hid from my eyes. One day, in the midst of the events of the monster trial, Liszt, who had been graciously received by Lammenais, got him to consent to climb up to my poet's loft. The Israelite child, Puzzi, Liszt's pupil—then a musician under his own name of Herman, today a discalced Carmelite going by the name of Frère Augustin—accompanied them.

Lammenais[58]—short, skinny, and sickly—had only a feeble breath of life in his chest. But what a ray of light in his head! His nose was too protuberant for his small stature and narrow face. Without that ill-proportioned nose, his face would have been handsome. The bright eyes darted flames; the straight forehead, furrowed by great vertical creases indicated intensity of will; the smil-

ing mouth and mobile features had an expression of austere tension—clearly a
head marked for a life of abnegation, contemplation, and preaching.

His whole being—unaffected manners, abrupt movements, awkward
bearing, open cheerfulness, excessive stubbornness, sudden jovialities—everything about him, even to his large, clean but shabby frock and blue stockings,
suggested the Breton clerk.

Only a short time was needed for one to be gripped with respect and
affection for that courageous and ingenuous soul. He revealed himself at once,
as golden and candid as nature.

When I first made his acquaintance, he had just arrived in Paris, and in
spite of so many past tribulations and more than half a century of griefs, he
was reentering the world of politics with all the illusions of a child about the
future of France. After a lifetime of study, controversy, and debate, he was to
leave his Brittany for good, to die actively in the whirl of events, and he was
beginning his campaign of glorious poverty by accepting the appointment as
counsel for the defense of the April accused.

It was fine and brave. He was full of faith, and he stated his faith concisely and forcefully; his words were fair, his reasoning quick, his images brilliant,
and every time he paused on one of the rhetorical horizons over which he successively traveled, he was totally there—past, present, and future, heart and
soul, body and belongings—with admirable guilelessness and gallantry. Within
his circle of friends, he summed up his ideas with a brilliance tempered by a
great store of natural humor. Those who had discovered him lost in meditation,
seeing only his sometimes distraught green eyes and his great nose sharp as a
sword, were afraid of him and declared his appearance to be diabolical. If they
had regarded him for three minutes, if they had exchanged three words with
him, they would have understood that they must cherish that goodness while
trembling before that power, and that everything in him had been meted out in
large portions—anger and sweetness, sadness and gaiety, indignation and
indulgence.

It was very well said[8] and understood, when on the day after his death,
just and upright minds grasped in the twinkling of an eye that illustrious career
of labor and suffering; posterity will forever express it, and it will be an honor
to have recognized and proclaimed it over Lammenais' still fresh grave: this
great thinker was, if not perfectly, at least remarkably, logical within himself, at
all stages of his development. What the narrow vision of some otherwise astute
critics led them, momentarily astonished, to label the evolution of a genius,
was in his case only the divine progress of an intellect that flowered within the
confines of tradition and was condemned by Providence to enlarge and shatter
it not without a thousand anguishes, compelled by a logic more powerful than
that of past beliefs—the logic of emotion.

That is what was instilled in me after I had heard him explain himself in a
quarter-hour of ingenuous, sublime conversation. Sainte-Beuve had tried in
vain to warn me, in his charming letters and witty conversation, against the
inconsistency of the author of the *Essai sur l'indifférence*. Sainte-Beuve apparently did not, then, have in mind the synthesis of his century. However, he had

followed its progress, and he had admired Lammenais' soaring flight, until the protestations in *L'Avenir*. When Lamennais embarked on political action, Sainte-Beuve was shocked to see that august name associated with so many that seemed to be protesting against his faith and doctrines.

Sainte-Beuve pointed out this contradiction with his customary gift, but to sense that that criticism bore only on appearances, you only needed to face him with the eyes of your soul, and listen with your heart to the hermit of La Chênaie. Instinctively you felt the spontaneity in that sincere heart on fire with justice and truth. A blend of absolute dogmatism and impetuousness, Lammenais never emerged from a previously held position through the door of pride, caprice, or curiosity. No! He was driven out by a great surge of offended tenderness, burning pity, and indignant charity. His heart very likely then said to his reason: "You thought to be there in the midst of truth. You had discovered this sanctuary, and you believed you could remain there always. You did not foresee anything beyond; you had made it your seat, drawn the curtain, closed the door. You were sincere, and to fortify yourself in what you believed to be good and permanent, as in a citadel, you had heaped up on your threshold all the arguments of your knowledge and dialectic. Well, you were mistaken! For, behold how unbeknownst to you, serpents lived beside you. Cold and silent they had slithered under your altar, and, lo, once warmed, they hiss and lift up their heads. Let us flee, for this place is cursed and truth would be profaned! Let us carry away our household gods, our work, our discoveries, our beliefs! But let us go farther, let us climb higher, let us follow those minds that rise up, casting off their irons; let us follow them in order to preserve a divine ideal while helping them rid themselves of the chains they drag behind them and cure themselves of the poison that infected them in the horrors of that prison."

And off they would go together, that great heart and that generous reason, which always deferred to each other. Together they constructed a new church—beautiful and buttressed by all the rules of philosophy. It was a marvel to see how the inspired architect made the letter of his former beliefs bend to the spirit of his new revelation. What had changed in it? Nothing, according to him. I have heard him say sincerely, at various periods in his life: "I defy anybody at all to prove to me that I am not as orthodox a Catholic today as I was while writing the *Essai sur l'indifférence*." And he was right, from his point of view. At the time he wrote that book, he had not envisioned the Pope standing beside the Czar blessing the victims.[59] If he had, he would have protested against the powerlessness of the Pope and against the indifference of the Church to religion. What had changed in the heart and conscience of that believer? Nothing. He never abandoned his principles, only the forced consequences of those principles.

Now, shall we say that there was in him a real inconsistency in his everyday relationships, his temper, his gullibility, his sudden suspicions, and his unexpected reversals? No, although we may sometimes have suffered from the ease with which he submitted to the passing influence of certain persons who exploited his affection for the benefit of their vanity or their grudges, we shall not say that his inconsistencies were real. They did not come from the depths of his emotions. They were on the surface of his personality, geared to the degree on the thermometer of his frail health. Nervous and irascible, he often lost his temper before having reflected, and his only fault was to believe too readily in wrongs he had not taken the time to verify. But for myself, although he might have attributed some to me, I confess I was never able to feel the slightest resentment toward him. Need I say it? I felt an almost maternal tenderness for that old man whom I recognized both as one of the fathers of my church and as one of the deities of my soul. By reason of the genius and virtue that shone in him, he was in my pantheon. By reason of the infirmities of his weak constitution, his vexations, his poutings, and his touchiness, he was, in my eyes, like an open-hearted child, but a child to whom one must say from time to time: "Watch out, you're going to be unjust. So keep your eyes open!"

And when I apply to such a man that admonishment for a child, it is not from the height of my poor reason, but from the depths of my tender heart, filled with affection for him even beyond the tomb. Truly, what can be more touching than to see a man of such genius and virtue unable to enter into full maturity as a personality due to his unusual degree of deference to others? Are you not moved when you see the Atlas lion dominated and led by the little dog that is the companion of his captivity? Lammenais seemed to be unaware of his power, and I believe he had not the least idea of what he meant to his contemporaries and to posterity. Strong as were his mission and ideal, so, too, was he modest about the importance of his inner life as an individual. He believed it to be worthless, and he went along submitting to whatever influences chanced his way. The least pedant might stimulate or upset him, and if need be, persuade him to act or abstain, even in his most personal behavior. He was willing to respond to all, to consult to the very last, to debate with them and sometimes listen to them, with the simple admiration of a pupil before a teacher.

From that touching weakness, that extreme humility, arose a few misunderstandings from which his true friends suffered. As for me, it was not with my personality that Lammenais' individuality ever collided, but with my socialist leanings. Having spurred me forward, he thought I progressed too quickly. I, on the other hand, found that he sometimes moved too slowly. Each of us was right from his own point of view—I under my small cloud, as he in his great sunshine—for in guilelessness and good will, I daresay we were matched. In His desire for humanity's welfare, God admits all mankind to the same communion.

I shall give an account elsewhere of my small disagreements with him, not only for the sake of relating them, but to show him in one aspect of his apostolic severity suddenly tempered by supreme impartiality and kindness. Suffice it to say for the present that, at the outset, in a few very brief, but thorough discussions, he was pleased to open up to me a system of social religion that made a great impression on me and was greatly beneficial; at the same time, his marvelous writings kindled the flame of my hope that had become almost extinguished.

For the moment, and for the same reason, I shall speak as concisely of

Pierre Leroux;[60] that is to say, in order not to half-tell about him, I shall say very little here and that little only as it related to me during the time I am describing.

It was a few weeks before or after the April trial. Planet was in Paris, preoccupied as always by the social question, and in the midst of the laughter that his favorite expression evoked around him, he took me aside and asked me, in all seriousness, to resolve this question for him once and for all. He wanted to judge the age, the events, and the men, even Éverard, his beloved master; he wanted to judge his own actions, his own instincts—in short, to find out where he was headed.

One day, when we had talked together for a long time, I asking him what precisely he was asking of me, and both of us acknowledging that we were not grasping clearly the connection between the actual revolution and the one we would like to foster, I had a brilliant idea. "I've heard Sainte-Beuve say," I told him, "that there are two men of superior intelligence who have delved into and clarified this problem particularly, in a direction that corresponds to my hopes and might allay my anxieties. Impelled by events of the time, they are more advanced than Lammenais, because they haven't been held back as he has by the impediments of Catholicism. They are in agreement on the points essential to their belief, and they are surrounded by a school of fellow believers who sustain the enthusiasm of their labors. These two are Pierre Leroux and Jean Reynaud. When Sainte-Beuve saw me torn by despair while writing *Lélia*, he told me to look to them for enlightenment, and he suggested bringing these learned mind doctors to me. But I didn't dare; I am too ignorant to understand them, too limited to judge them, and too timid to bare my inner doubts to them. However, it turns out that Pierre Leroux is also shy, for I have seen him, and I would be braver with him. But how to approach him, how to hold him for a few hours? Won't he laugh in our faces like the others if we put the social question to him?"

"Leave it to me," said Planet, "I'm certainly bold enough, and if I do make him laugh, it doesn't matter to me, provided he informs me. Write to him and ask him for me, as one of your friends—a miller, a simple countryman—for the republican 'catechism' in two or three hours of conversation. I certainly shall not be intimidated, and you'll seem to be listening for good measure."

I wrote, and Pierre Leroux came up to the garret to dine with the two of us. At first, being too astute not to have guessed the innocent trap I had set for him, he was quite self-conscious, and he stammered for some time before being able to express himself. No less modest than Lammenais, he was shy; Lammenais was not. But Planet's good-nature, straightforward questions, attentiveness, and quickness to understand put Leroux at ease, and after he had turned the question over for a bit, as he often did when talking, finally such perceptions and eloquence emerged from him that it was like great flashes of lightning from an imposing cloud. There is no instruction more valuable than his, if you do not pester him too much to formulate what he does not feel he has sufficiently done so for himself. He has a smooth, handsome face, a clear, penetrating gaze, a fond smile, a pleasing voice, and such emphatic expressions that this accord of purity and goodness grips your belief as much as the force of his reasoning. Even then, he was the best possible critic in the philosophy of history, and if he did not make you glimpse very clearly the motive of his philosophy, he at least made the past appear in such a strong light, and cast such a fair one on the future, that you felt as if his hand had snatched a blindfold from your eyes.

I did not feel particularly enlightened when he spoke to us about the "ownership of tools," a problem he was then turning over in his mind, which he has since elucidated in his writings. His philosophical language was too arcane for me, and I did not comprehend the wider implications of the words; but the logic of Providence appeared to me in his reasoning, and that was a great deal; it was a groundwork laid in the field of my inquiry. I promised myself I would study the history of mankind, but I did not, and only later, thanks to that noble intellect, was I at last able to grasp a few certainties.

In that first encounter with him, I was too disturbed by what was going on in my life. I was committed to produce a steady stream of love stories, without the aid of any philosophy, in order to earn sufficient means for the education of my daughter and for my obligations to others and myself. At the time, I was afraid of that life of labor for which I had accepted full responsibility. I was no longer permitted to stop for a moment to look over my work or to wait for inspiration, and I had fits of remorse thinking of all that time given over to a shallow occupation while my brain felt the need to surrender to salutary meditation. People who waste their time and who think artists produce with facility are surprised at how few moments those artists can reserve for themselves. They don't know that such mental gymnastics—if they don't impair your health—produce at least an excitation of the nerves, an obsession with imagery, and a spiritual lassitude that do not allow for carrying out any other type of work at the same time.

Ten times a day I would feel a sudden aversion for my profession, on hearing talk of serious works I would have liked to read, or of things that I would have liked to see for myself. Then, when I was with my children, I only wanted to live for and with them. And when my friends came, I reproached myself for not receiving them well enough and for sometimes being preoccupied in their midst. It seemed to me that all that was real in life was passing before me like a dream, and that only the imaginary world of the novel was pressing on me with sharp reality.

It was then I began to miss Nohant, from which, through weakness, I had banished myself, and which was closed to me through my own fault. Why had I torn up the agreement that assured me of half my income? At least I would have been able to rent a little house not far from mine to retire to with my daughter for half the year during Maurice's vacation. There I would have rested, looking out on the same horizons that had greeted my young eyes, among the friends of my childhood. I would have watched the smoke from Nohant's chimneys rising above the trees my grandmother had planted, far enough away not to be troubled by what was now going on under their shade, but near enough for me to imagine that I could still go there freely to read or dream.

Éverard, to whom I expressed this nostalgia and my distaste for Paris, advised me to settle in Bourges or its vicinity. I made a short trip there. One of his friends who was away loaned me his house, where I spent a few days alone in the company of Lavater,[61] whom I found in the library, and about whom I lovingly did a small work. That solitude in the midst of a dead city, in a poetic, deserted house seemed to me delightful. Éverard, Planet, and the mistress of the house, an excellent, care-worn woman, came to see me for an hour or two in the evening; then I spent half the night alone in a little courtyard filled with flowers, under the brilliant moon, savoring those scents of summer and that beneficent serenity that I had to win at sword's point. A man who did not know my name came from a nearby restaurant to bring me meals in a basket, which I received through the courtyard wicket. Once again I was forgotten by the world and plunged into forgetfuness of pressing problems.

But that pleasant retirement could not last. I could not take possession of that charming house, perhaps the only one in the whole city that would have suited me, because of its isolation in a quiet quarter and its neglected look, coupled with simple comfort. Besides, I needed to have my children with me, and such confinement would not have been good for them. From the moment I set foot on a street in Bourges, my presence would have been noticed throughout the city, and I could not accept the idea of a life of close relationships in a provincial city. I had no doubt I was approaching a situation of that kind, and I would not adapt to it very well.

In spite of Éverard's entreaties, I abandoned the idea of relocating in that area. The countryside seemed hideous to me: a flat plain, dotted with bogs and bereft of trees, lies spread out around the city like the countryside around Rome. One has to go a great distance to find forests and streams. And moreover, must I say it? Éverard—with Planet or with one or two friends—was delightful company; alone with me, he was too brilliant, he wore me out. He needed an interlocutor to reply to him. The others took that function on themselves, whereas I was only equipped to listen. When we were alone, my silence irritated him, and he viewed it as a sign of suspicion, or indifference to his ideas and political passions. His overbearing intellect bothered him strangely where I was concerned, for although my mind was easily persuaded, it refused to be dominated. With him, above all, my mind instinctively withdrew to an unassailable sanctuary—one of detachment from worldly things, insofar as they were futile or riotous. But once he had entangled me in a network of arguments employed by politicians—sometimes meant to outline for me excellent rules of leadership, sometimes meant to convince me of political necessities that to me seemed either culpable or puerile—I would be forced to answer him. And since it was not in my nature to debate, and painful for me to disagree with those whom I loved, as soon as I had spoken out clearly—which I myself found as astonishing and shattering as if I had been forced to speak in a dream—I would observe with terror the effect my words had on him. They upset him greatly; they threw him into profound disgust with his own existence, despair over the future, and crises of conscience.

That might have been good in a strong, moderate nature; it was bad in one that was only passionate and which swung rapidly from one extreme to the other.

He would cry out, then, that I had inexorable truth on my side, that I was more of a philosopher and more enlightened than he, that he was a wretched poet who was always being duped by wild dreams, and a great deal more besides. That impressionable brain, that mind—as naïve in humility as it was imperious in pride—knew no middle way for anything. He spoke of leaving his political career, his profession, and his business affairs and retiring to his small property to read the poets and philosophers, by the murmuring waters, in the willows' shade.

Then, I would have to bolster his morale, tell him he had pushed my logic to the point of absurdity, and remind him of the excellent reasons he had given to draw me out of my own apathy—reasons that had convinced me not to speak of the revolutionary mission and democratic achievement without respect.

We no longer quarreled over Babouvism. He had set aside that system to delve into another. He was rereading Montesquieu. For the moment, his politics had been moderated, for as I knew, he was always under the influence of a person or a book. A little later, he read Sénancour's *Obermann*, and for three months talked about retiring to the desert. Then, he was caught up by religious ideas and dreamed of the monastic life. Next, he became a Platonist, then an Aristotelian; finally, at the time I lost track of his infatuations, he had returned to Montesquieu.

In all those phases of conviction, he was a poet, a reasoner, an artist. His mind embraced all things. As excessive in vitality as he was in despondency, he had a period of stoicism during which he preached moderation to us with a vigor that was at once touching and comical.

One never tired of hearing him when he held to the teaching of ideas of a general nature, but when the discussion of those ideas touched him personally, our intimacy once again turned stormy, a fine storm certainly—full of grandeur, generosity, and sincerity—but one which I could not long sustain without weariness. That turbulence was his life; like the eagle, he soared through the tempest. For me it would have been death; I was a bird of lesser wingspan.

Above all, there was something about him to which I could never reconcile myself—his unpredictability. He would leave me in the evening, his thoughts calm and steady, and reappear the following day completely transformed, as though furious at having been subdued the night before. Then he would malign himself, declare himself ambitious in the narrowest sense of the word, mock my reservations and scruples of conscience, speak of political vengeance, and in attributing to himself hatreds and grudges, he would assume all manner of faults and even deep-seated vices which he did not have and to which he could never have lent himself. I would smile and let him go on. I regarded it as raving that would surely end, though it was troublesome while it lasted. The end did always come, leaving me astonished at the sudden and complete reversal of ideas, accompanied by oblivion of what he had just been thinking out loud. That was more disturbing, and I was forced to affirm what I had affirmed elsewhere—that the finest geniuses often border, as though unavoidably, on insanity. If Éverard had not been dedicated to sugared water as his only drink, even during meals, I would often have thought him drunk.

I was, by then, firmly enough attached to him to put up with all that without irritation, and care for him during his "attacks." A woman's friendship has a great deal of the maternal in it, and that sentiment has dominated my life more than I would have liked. In Paris I had tended Éverard through a serious illness. He had suffered greatly, and I had always found him admirably gentle, patient, and grateful for the smallest attentions. Such a bond creates great friendship. He would show me the most touching gratitude, and I had gotten quite used to fussing over his state of mind. Planet and I had spent several nights at his bedside, combatting his wracking fever with affectionate words that had more effect on that intellect than all the doctor's potions. I had reasoned away his delirium, calmed his worries, written his letters, brought his friends to him, and kept away the annoyances that might have reached him. Maurice, on his days of leave, had cared for him and pampered him as if he had been his grandfather. He adored my children, and they also loved him dearly.

Those were indeed pleasant bonds, and the purity of our attachment made them still more precious. It was a matter of indifference to me that the nature of our relationship might be misunderstood; our friends knew the truth, and their constant presence sanctified it even more. But it was a vain hope that an entirely fraternal pact would necessitate angelic tranquillity. Éverard did not have the placidity of Rollinat. Though chaste,[62] his emotions were not at all calm. He wanted exclusive possession of the soul, and he was as jealous of that possession as lovers and spouses are of the body. That constituted a kind of tyranny that could not be laughed away; you either had to submit or fight back.

I spent three years doing first one and then the other. My mind always protected itself from his influence when it was unreasonable; but my heart stood the weight and charm of his friendship, sometimes with joy, sometimes with bitterness. His heart contained stores of kindness that one was happy and proud to receive; his nature was always generous and incapable of descending to pettiness; but storms arose in his brain, which made one suffer cruelly watching him suffer, and realizing the impossibility of sparing him.

In order not to spend too much time on a situation that recurred frequently during those three years and—although less and less often—even after that, I shall sum up in a few words the subject of our disagreements. In the midst of his tumultuous fluctuations and torrents of conflicting ideas, Éverard harbored the gnawing worm of ambition. It has been said that he liked money and power. I never observed him to be instinctively cheap or mean. When he tortured himself over some loss of money, or when he was rejoicing over a success of that kind, it was with the legitimate emotion of a courageous invalid who fears the cessation of his strength, his work, and the fulfillment of his duties. Poor and debt-ridden, he had married a wealthy woman. If it was not a mistake, it was unfortunate. The woman had children, and the thought of depriving them for his personal needs was odious to Éverard. He longed to succeed, not only in order never to become a burden to them, but also, through a very understandable feeling of tenderness and pride, in order to leave them better off than they were when he adopted them.

His keenness for work, his worries when faced with a debt, and his concern over the investment of money earned by the sweat of his brow were all, therefore, motivated by a pressing reality. That is certainly not what one might impute to ambition in his case. But when a man commits himself to a role in politics, he must be able to sacrifice his fortune, and if he cannot do that, he is always accused of not wanting to do it.

Éverard's covetousness was on a higher plane. He had a thirst for power. Why would be impossible to say. It was simply a craving of his character. He was not extravagant, vain, or vindictive, and power meant only the need for action and the pleasure of commanding. He could never have profited from it monetarily. Once he had a well-established practice, he felt depressed and disgusted with his work. Once he was blindly obeyed, he felt sorry for his followers. In short, in all things, once he attained the avidly pursued goal, he found it beneath his aspirations.

But he thrived on the concerns of the statesman. Exceedingly clever in legal theory, powerful at intuiting cases he had not studied, quick to assimilate the most diverse notions, gifted with a memory as astonishing as Pierre Leroux's, and invincible in the deduction of factual matters, he felt as though his brilliant faculties were seizing him by the throat and choking him, unless they were active. The monotony of his profession exasperated him, while his subjection to the strain ended by ruining his health. He dreamed, therefore, of a revolution the way saints dream of heaven, and he did not realize that, in letting himself be devoured by that aspiration, he was wearing out his soul and rendering it incapable of confronting lesser perils and labors.

It was this fatal ambition that I tried in vain to calm. Undoubtedly it had its good side, and if fate had helped it along, it might have been purified in the crucible of experience and on the hearth of inspiration; but it fell back on itself without finding the nourishment it needed, at the right time, and he was destroyed by it, without noticeable benefit to the revolutionary cause.

He traversed the earth like a lost soul evicted from some better world and longing vainly for some grand existence in keeping with his grand desire. He disdained the portion of glory allotted him—one that would have intoxicated many others. Limited use of an immense talent was not sufficient for his vast dream. That is certainly pardonable—we all pardon him for it—but we cannot help regretting the powerlessness of our efforts to keep him longer among us.

Besides, it was not only from the point of view of his health that I tried to get him to have patience. I was thinking of his own ideal of justice and wisdom, which I felt was being compromised in the struggle between his instincts and his principles. While Éverard conceived of a world renewed by the moral progress of mankind, he accepted in theory what he called the necessities of pure politics: subterfuge, charlatanism, outright lies, insincere concessions, faithless alliances, and empty promises. Furthermore, he was one of those who say that the end justifies the means. I do not believe he ever conducted his personal life by those deplorable aberrations of the political mind, but I was distressed to see that he considered them pardonable and even inevitable.

Later on our differences deepened, and turned on the ideal itself. I had become a socialist, and Éverard was no longer one.

His ideas underwent still more changes after the February Revolution, which, in an untimely way, had surprised him in a phase of moderation only slightly dictatorial. It is not time to complete his story—too soon suspended by premature death. I must return to the account of my own vicissitudes.

Therefore, I left Bourges, saddened by his disturbed state, torn between the need to get away, and regret at leaving him in torment; but my duty was calling me elsewhere, and he realized that.   *M.C.*

X

Indecision. —I do not go to La Chênaie. —My brother's letter. —I do go to Nohant. —Great resolve. —The Vavray woods. —A dash to Châteauroux and Bourges. —The prison at Bourges. —The break in the wall. —A quarter hour in the dungeon. —Consultation, decision, and return. —Let's kidnap Hermione! —The Duteil family. —The Inn of La Boutaille and the gypsies. —First ruling. —The deserted house at Nohant. —Second ruling. —Reflections on separations. —The deserted house at La Châtre. —Bourges. —The Tourangin family. —Pleas. —Settlement. —Final return and possession of Nohant.

I did not really know which way to turn. The idea of going back to Paris was awful; staying away from my children had become intolerable for me. I had renounced the plan of leaving them behind to go on a long trip, and since then, strangely enough, I no longer wanted to leave them for a day. My deepest maternal feelings, numbed by anxiety, had revived at the same time that my mind had opened to ideas about society. I sensed a return of my mental well-being, and with it came an awareness of the true needs of my heart.

I could no longer work in Paris. I felt sick. Workmen had again taken over the ground floor; the unwelcome and the curious competed for my time with friends and my work. Politics, tense once more due to the Fieschi assassination attempt, became bitter to contemplate. The attempt was exploited to persecute our party. They arrested Armand Carrel, one of the most honorable men of our time. We were moving with giant steps toward the September laws.[63] The public was apathetic.

Not that the April lawsuit had given me great cause for hopefulness, but however realistic or pessimistic we were at the time, there had been in the air some ineffable breath of life which suddenly died down with a chill. The Republic was vanishing beyond the horizon for yet another stretch of time.

Lamennais had invited me to spend a few days at La Chênaie; I set off, but stopped midway, asking myself what on earth I—boring, tongue-tied, gauche as I felt—would do there. To dare ask him for an hour of his precious time was already a great deal, and in Paris he had granted me several, but I dared not go and take up entire days of his. I was wrong; I did not know the full extent of his kindness, his generosity, as I was to know it later. I feared the sustained pressure of not being able to follow his great mind, and that the least of his disciples might outdo me at carrying on a serious conversation. I did not know that his privacy afforded him respite from his strenuous mental endeavors; that no one conversed with such abandon and zest about things within everyone's grasp. Moreover, the splendid man made no demands on the minds of his interlocutors. It took very little to amuse him. Nonsense, trivia could make him laugh. And how he laughed! Like Éverard, he would laugh until it almost made him ill, but more often and more easily. Somewhere he wrote that tears are the lot of angels and laughter that of Satan. The sentiment may be apt for those poetic creatures, but among human beings when a righteous man laughs, it is as if his conscience is singing. People with true gaiety are always good, and he was the very proof of it.

So I did not go to La Chênaie. I retraced my steps, went back to Paris, and there received a letter from my brother telling me to go to Nohant. At that time, he was taking my side of the argument and urging my husband to give me back, without regret, my right to live there and receive the rent from my own land. "Casimir is fed up with the bother of running the property," he said, "and with the expenditures it causes him. He doesn't know how to cope with it. You, with your work, could get by there. He wants to go and live in Paris, or with his step-mother, in the Midi; receiving half of your income and living a bachelor's life, he will find himself wealthier than he is in your chateau," and so forth. My brother, who later took my husband's side against me, expressed himself very freely and decidedly on the situation at Nohant in my absence. "You mustn't abandon your own interests this way," he added. "You're doing your children an injustice."

At the time, my brother no longer lived at Nohant, but he made frequent trips back to the area.

I believed I should follow his advice, and I did in fact find M. Dudevant disposed toward leaving Berry and relinquishing to me the burden and the profits of the place. At the same time that he was firming his resolve to do this, he displayed so much spite toward me that I did not persist and went off once more, not having the heart to begin a struggle over money. A few weeks later, that struggle became necessary and inevitable. It took on more serious motives; it became a duty first to my children, then to my friends and associates, and perhaps also to the memory of my grandmother, whose eternal concern and last wishes were being too openly violated at the very place she had bequeathed to me for shelter and protection.

On October 19, 1835, I had gone to spend the last of Maurice's vacation at Nohant. Following a rage provoked by nothing—absolutely nothing, not even a word or a smile on my part—I went and shut myself into my little room. Maurice followed me there in tears. I calmed him by saying that it would not happen again. He accepted this as a vague expression of consolation one gives children, but to my mind the words were clear and definitive. I never wanted my children to witness a recurrence of what they had been unaware of until then. I did not want discord to make them lose the respect they owed their father or me.

A few days earlier, my husband had signed an informal contract effective the following November 11, by which I gave over to him more than half of my income. That contract, which left me the custody of my daughter and the right to live at Nohant, in no way insured me against a change of mind on his part. His manner and uncompromising way of speaking gave me proof that he considered null the promises twice made and twice signed. Marriage allowed him this right: under our laws, the husband is master, and the master is never obliged toward the one who is master of nothing.

When Maurice was in bed asleep, Duteil came to me to inquire about my frame of mind. He was openly critical of my husband's attitude. He wanted to bring about a reconciliation, which we both refused. I thanked him for his intercession, but I gave him no hint of the decision I had just reached. I needed Rollinat's opinion.

I spent the night reflecting. Feeling a full sense of my rights, as I did at that moment, my obligations appeared to me in all their rigor. I had delayed too long; I had indeed been weak and unheedful about my own lot. As long as it had only been a personal problem, from which my children's moral development did not suffer, I thought I could sacrifice and allow myself the inner satisfaction of leaving in peace a man whom I had not been born to make happy according to his tastes. For thirteen years he had enjoyed the comfort that belonged to me and that I had deprived myself of in order to satisfy him. I would like to have left that to him for life; he could have kept it. Even the day before, seeing him worried, I had told him, "You are having regrets about Nohant, I can see that very clearly, despite the distaste you've taken for managing it. Well, isn't it all for the best that I am relieving you of it? Do you believe that the front door will ever be closed to you?" He had answered, "I will never again set foot in a house where I am not the sole master." But the next day, he had again wanted to be the sole master.

He was no longer able, nor duty bound, to have given me a sense of security. I felt no resentment against him; I saw him as acting out of a predetermined motive; I had to separate my future from his or sacrifice more than I had already, that is to say, my dignity in the eyes of my children, or my life—by which I set no great store, but which I owed to them as well.

By morning, M. Dudevant had gone to La Châtre. No more was he sedentary, as he had been for so long. He was away for days and weeks at a time. He ought not have resented that at least I was there, during Maurice's vacation, to keep watch over the house and the children. I learned from the servants that nothing had changed in his plans: he was to leave for Paris the next day, the 21st, to take Maurice back to *collège*, and Solange to her boarding school. That had been the agreement; I was to rejoin them after a few days, but the new situation made me change my mind. I decided I would not see my husband again, neither in Paris nor at Nohant, nor even before his departure. I would have left the house entirely, had I not wished to spend the last day of his vacation with Maurice. Since there was no servant at my disposal, I harnessed a small horse to a broken cabriolet. I put my two children in this primitive vehicle and drove them to the Vavray Woods, a charming spot at that time, where seated on the moss in the shade of the old oaks, we could take in the whole sweep of the deeply melancholy Vallée Noire.

It was a beautiful day. Maurice had helped me unhitch the little horse, which grazed nearby. A soft autumn sun made the heather glow. Armed with knives and baskets, we were harvesting moss and jungermannes, which Malgache had asked me to gather there at random for his collection, not having the time himself, so he wrote me, to go that far to explore the area.

So, we were gathering some of everything, and my children—one of whom had not seen the domestic flare-up of the previous evening, the other who had already forgotten it, thanks to the natural insouciance of youth—were running around, shouting and giggling through the underbrush. Their gaiety, their joy and enthusiasm for the hunt, put me in mind of the happy times when I had run just like this at my mother's side, to help decorate our little grottoes. Alas! twenty years later I would have by my side another child, radiating strength, well-being and beauty, scampering about on the moss of the woods, gathering it into the folds of her skirt the way her mother had done, as I myself had done at the same spot, with the same little games, with the same fantasies of fairies and golden treasure. And that child now rests between my grandmother and my father.[64] So at this time—June 1855—it is painful to write, and the memory of that threefold past, without a future, chokes and weighs me down.

We had brought along a little basket for a light snack beneath the trees. We did not return until nightfall. The next day, the children went off with M. Dudevant, who had spent the night at La Châtre and did not ask to see me.

I was determined not to have further arguments with him; but I did not yet know by what means I would avoid this inevitable domestic necessity. My childhood friend, Gustave Papet, came to see me; I told him the whole story, and we left together for Châteauroux.

"I see no absolute remedy to this situation," Rollinat said to me, "aside from a legal separation. The outcome doesn't seem at all in doubt; the only question is whether you'll have the courage to do it. The legal formalities are brutal, and weak as I know you to be, you'll back down before the requirement of wounding and offending your adversary." I asked him if there were no way to avoid the scandal of open contestation; I had him explain the necessary steps, and when he was done, we recognized the fact that, assuming my husband allowed a decision by default, without a statement for the defense and without publicity, the position that he had established on his own by voluntary contract would remain unchanged for him, since that was my intention, with the essential advantage, for me, of making the covenant legal, which was to say, effective.

But Rollinat wanted to consult Éverard on all of this. We went back with him to Nohant that very day, and taking only time enough for dinner, set off again post-haste for Bourges, in the same cabriolet.

Éverard was paying his debt to the peerage. He was in prison. The city prison is the ancient chateau of the Ducs de Bourgogne. At night, it gave a strong impression of power and desolation. We won over one of the jailors, who brought us in through a break in the wall, and led us into the darkness through fantastic halls and stairways. There came a moment when, hearing the footsteps of an overseer, he pushed me through an open door which he then closed after me, while he shoved Rollinat elsewhere, and appeared alone as his superior passed.

I took from my pocket one of the matches I used for my cigarettes and looked about me. I was in a dreadfully gloomy cell situated at the foot of a turret. Two feet away, a subterranean stairway descended from ground level into the depths of the dungeons. I quickly put out the match, which could have betrayed me, and remained immobile, knowing the dangers of groping about this unprepossessing refuge.

I was left there a good quarter of an hour, which seemed like a very long time. At last my deliverer came to set me free, and we were able to go, at around two o'clock in the morning, to the apartment where Éverard, alerted by Gustave, was waiting for us in order to confer with me.

He approved of our having taken this step rapidly and in secret. Those of my friends on good terms with M. Dudevant should not know about it, in case it failed. He listened to the account of my whole marital life, and learning all the changes of heart I had had to endure, he declared himself, like Rollinat, in favor of a legal separation. My subsequent actions were laid out for me after thorough deliberation. I was to surprise my adversary by a petition to the presiding judge, so that, feeling more acutely the pressure of an accomplished fact, he would be more inclined to accept its consequences. We did not doubt he would accept them without argument, in order to avoid public knowledge of the causes for my determination. We did not anticipate that M. Dudevant would get bad counsel, and heed it.

To maintain my rights as plaintiff, I could not return to the conjugal domicile, and would have to stay with one of my friends at La Châtre until the presiding judge ruled on my temporary domicile. The oldest friend was Duteil, but would Duteil, also my husband's friend, wish to receive me under these circumstances? Concerning his wife and sister I had no doubts, and as for him, it was worth a try.

The jailor came to warn us that dawn was approaching and that we had to leave the same way we had come, without being seen, since prison rules forbade such nocturnal consultations. We left without incident. We got back on the road and went to pay Duteil a surprise visit at La Châtre. In a matter of thirty hours we had covered fifty-four leagues, in a broken-down wreck of a carriage, without a moment of mental relaxation.

"Here I am," I said to Duteil. "I'm coming to live with you, unless you send me away. I ask neither your counsel nor advice against M. Dudevant, who is your friend. I shall not call you as witness against him. As soon as I have obtained a ruling, I shall authorize you to become the mediator between us, which is to assure him the best possible conditions of existence on my part, those he had set up. So your role, which you may immediately reveal to him, is honorable and easy."

"You will stay with me," said Duteil with the heartfelt generosity that he exemplified on important occasions. "I'm so grateful for the preference you're showing me over your other friends that you can count on me forever, come what may. As for the proceedings you want to begin, let me talk them over with you."

"First give me something to eat, I'm dying of hunger, " I replied. "And after that I'll go to Nohant to fetch my slippers and my papers."

"I'll go along with you," he said, "and we'll talk on the way."

Somewhat refreshed by the lunch, I got back into the venerable carriage with him, and two hours later we were on our way back to his house. He had listened to me in silence, limiting himself to questions beyond the vagaries of procedure, not revealing his views. Finally, between the rows of poplars at the edge of the little town, he summed up his feelings this way: "I have relished being a guest in your husband's and your brother's company, but I never forgot, when you were there, that I was in your home and that I owed you boundless respect as mother of the household. That didn't prevent me sometimes from bothering you with my after-dinner babble and rowdiness during your working hours. You know very well it was done in spite of myself, and that a single word of reproach from you would sometimes sober me up as if by a miracle. Your mistake is to have spoiled me with too much kindness. So what happened? Just this, that even while I felt like your husband's comrade through twelve hours of revelry, every evening I spent a thirteenth hour of remorse, when I felt like your friend. After my wife and children, you are what I love most on earth. And if I have hesitated these last two hours to explain myself, it is because I dread the exhaustion and sadness of the struggle you are about to undertake. Neverthless, I believe that, if Casimir listens to my advice, it can be mild and remain restricted to the narrow confines of our little town. I see what counsel I must give him, in his own best interest, and I now think I have a good chance of persuading him. There you have it." And since we were scaling the little hump-back bridge at the entrance to the town, he snapped the whip at the horse and exclaimed with revived gaiety, "Come! Let's kidnap Hermione!"[65]

So, I settled down in his home for a few weeks, feeling that I had to live as if in a glass house, in the heart of La Châtre's gossip mill, to demolish all the stories that had been mounting ever since I existed, about the eccentricity of my character. These fantastic stories had grown by leaps and bounds since I had gone to Paris to try the artist's life. As I had absolutely nothing to hide and had never assumed any pose, it was very easy for me to remain myself. True, some minor resentments having to do with the notorious song[66] did persist for a time; a few fanatics on marital authority became even more rigid against my cause; but, in general, I saw all prejudice drop, and the days I spent at La Châtre would have been among the best of my life had my children been with me. Since I was fighting for them, I adopted a patient attitude. Very soon the Duteil family became my own. His beautiful and charming wife Agasta, his fine sister-in-law, Félicie—both of them tender-hearted and intelligent—were like sisters to me. M. and Mme. Desages (the latter was Duteil's sister) lived on the ground floor of the same house. Every evening there were fourteen of us gathered, seven of them children. (One of these children, Luc Desages, became the disciple and son-in-law of Pierre Leroux.) Charles and Eugénie Duvernet,

Alphonse and Laure Fleury, Planet (from then on a permanent resident at La Châtre), Gustave Papet (when he was not in Paris), and a few other members of the Duteil family came to join us often; for the children we organized charades, dressing-up, dances, and truly wonderful parlor games that delighted them. It was so good, the irrepressible laughter of those happy creatures. They put so much emotion and faith into the games. I myself was becoming a child again, "drawing all hearts in my wake."[67] Indeed, that was my vocation; I should have been a nanny or a schoolteacher.

At ten o'clock, the little pack of them went off to bed; at eleven, the rest of the family circle broke up. Félicie, as kind as an angel to me, prepared my work table and my small supper; she put her sister Agasta to bed, who was suffering from a serious nervous disorder and who, revived by the children's merriment, would fall back exhausted, as if at death's door. We would chat a bit with her to put her to sleep or, if she had fallen asleep on her own, in the company of Duteil and Planet, who liked to ramble on, and whom we had to send away to keep them from depriving me of my night's work. At midnight, I finally settled down to write until daybreak, occasionally lulled by strange howling.

Across the steep, narrow, dirty street, my window overlooked a classic sign, which had been swinging there since time immemorial: *A la boutaille.* Duteil, who claimed to have learned to read from that sign, said that the day the spelling mistake was corrected he would give up the ghost, because the whole physiognomy of Berry would be changed.[68]

The Inn of La Boutaille was run by an elderly sibyl, who rented rooms by the night, and this hovel was mainly frequented by travelling circus folk, suspect salesmen, and keepers of trained animals. Marmots, dancing dogs, hairless monkeys, and muzzled bears, in particular, held plenary sessions in the cellar, whose sunken windows faced the street. Those poor beasts, harassed by their exhausting travels and badly bruised by the blows that are inseparable from their classical education, lived there on good terms through a good part of the night. But toward dawn, hunger or boredom would take hold; they became restless, abused one another, climbed the bars of the window to howl, grimace, or growl, in the most lugubrious fashion.

This was prelude to some very curious scenes with which I often entertained myself by watching through the space between my shutters. The proprietress of La Boutaille, Mme. Gaudron, well aware of the types she was dealing with, got up first and most covertly to oversee the departure of her guests. They, on the other hand, planning to leave without paying, were groping in the dawn, making preparations, while one of them went down among the animals, inciting them to growl, in order to cover the furtive sounds of their comrades in flight.

The craftiness of these gypsies was marvelous to behold. I do not know through what keyhole they managed to slip away, but despite her watchful eye and keen ear, the old woman often found herself facing a whimpering urchin who claimed to be abandoned, along with the animals, by his callous comrades, and with no means to pay. What to do? Impound the animals and feed them until the police caught up with the delinquents? That was poor business. So, she could do nothing but let the pretended victim leave with the famished and menacing quadrupeds, which seemed little disposed to being held for ransom.

When the troop paid up honestly, the old woman was faced with another concern. She particularly dreaded those who behaved like gentlemen, not deigning to bargain. Then, she anxiously ferreted about their bundles, counted and recounted her pewter cutlery and her rags. The donkey's pack, when there was a donkey, was the particular object of her anxiety. She found a thousand excuses to detain that donkey, and at the last moment she artfully slipped her hand under the pack, to feel the chine. But despite all alarms and precautions, few days passed without the sound of her wailing about the losses, and cursing her clientele.

What beautiful Decamps, what fantastic Callots[69] I saw there by the wan moonlight, or the faint glow of a winter dawn, with the age-old sign banging in the wind, when the gypsies, pale as specters, got under way on the snow-covered pavement! Now a bronze-skinned woman, picturesque beneath her somber rags and carrying in her arms some poor child, rosy and beautiful, stolen or purchased along the way; now a little chimney sweep, uglier than his monkey; and now the strong man of the crossroads, dragging along behind him in a makeshift wheelbarrow his wife and numerous offspring. Most were frightening or freakish creatures; yet sometimes, by chance, a few more appealing figures stood out: sad, resigned clowns like the one idealized by Frédérick Lemaître; old mendicant musicians sawing away on the violin with a sort of unruly mastery; young girl gymnasts, ashen with fatigue, laughingly singing of springtime and love, in the arms of their fifteen-year-old lovers. Such misery, such unconcern, such tears or songs, on those dusty or icy roadways that led to God knows what shelter!

On February 16, 1836, the court handed down a ruling of separation in my favor. M. Dudevant did not appear, which led everyone to believe he accepted this solution. I could go and take possession of my legal domicile at Nohant. The ruling entrusted me with the care and education of my son and daughter.

I believed I was absolved from having to pursue the matter further. My husband wrote to Duteil in such a way as to make me hope this was so. I spent several weeks at Nohant awaiting his arrival in the region, for coming to terms and settling our affairs. Duteil undertook, on my behalf, to arrange all possible concessions, and in order to avoid any irritating meetings, I was to go to Paris the moment M. Dudevant arrived at La Châtre.

So I spent a few fine winter days at Nohant, during which, for the first time since my grandmother's death, I savored the pleasures of contemplation, no longer troubled by discord. As much for the sake of economy as out of justice, I had cleared the house of all servants used to taking over for me. I kept on only my grandmother's old gardener, who was housed with his wife in a lodge at the end of the courtyard. Thus, I was absolutely alone in the vast, silent house. I did not even receive friends from La Châtre, so as not to give rise to bitterness. It would not have been in good taste to put up the pot hooks so soon, as they say in Berry, and seem to be bruiting my victory.

The solitude was therefore absolute, and for once in my life I lived at

Nohant as in a *maison déserte*. The deserted house had long been one of my dreams. Until the day I could savor the sweetness of family life without trepidation, I comforted myself with the hope of possessing a house, be it a ruin or a cottage, in some unknown spot where I could disappear from time to time and work without the distraction of human voices.

At that time, which is to say at that moment—since like all the respites of my life it was brief—Nohant was the ideal of my fantasies. I amused myself by storing—or rather restoring—things. I hid everything that stirred painful memories, and I placed the old pieces of furniture the way they had been in my childhood. The gardener's wife came into the house only to do my room and bring me dinner. When it was cleared, I shut all the outside doors and opened all the inside ones. I lit many candles, and wandered through the suite of large rooms on the ground floor, from the little boudoir where I always slept to the spacious drawing room, illuminated in addition by a large fire. Then I put out all lights, and moving solely by the glow from the dying fire on the hearth, I enjoyed that mysterious darkness filled with melancholy thoughts, having recovered the tender, joyful memories of my early years. It amused me to feel a slight twinge of fear as I passed like a phantom before the mirrors tarnished by time, and the sound of my footsteps in the empty echoing rooms would give me an occasional chill, as if the ghost of Deschartres were creeping along behind me.

I went to Paris in March, if memory serves. M. Dudevant came to La Châtre and accepted a settlement that gave him infinitely better conditions than the ruling pronounced against him. But scarcely had he signed when he seemed bound to ignore it and lodge an objection. He handled it very poorly, embittered by the advice of my poor brother who, fickle as the wind (or, more likely, the wine), had turned against my victory, after furnishing me with all possible arms for combat. My husband's step-mother, Mme. Dudevant, invented, you might say, a necessity for him to pursue the battle. It happened that she detested me intensely for reasons unknown. Being on the brink of death, perhaps she felt an urge to detest someone—anyone. On the day of her death, this would become an urge to detest everyone—my husband especially. Be that as it may, she then set as a condition of his inheritance, so they told me, that her stepson resist any agreement whatsoever with me.

My husband, I repeat, handled it poorly. Wishing to stave off the separation, he decided to present to the court a petition dictated, or drafted more likely, by two servants I had fired and whom his renowned lawyer did not stop him from using as witnesses. The counsel of that lawyer has at times been disastrous. A recent event that has scarred my soul forever, without profit to his own glory, has cruelly proved that to me.[70]

As for his intervention in my marital affairs, it only served to embitter an outcome which could have been peaceful. The petition enlightened the judges beyond all necessity. It was not comprehensible to them that, in accusing me of causing such distress to him and myself, my husband wished to renew our union. They found the injury sufficient, and annulling their first decision on the grounds of faulty procedure, they upheld it on May 11, 1836, in exactly the same terms.

I had returned to Duteil's house at La Châtre; all through the night I had made plans and preparations for my departure. I had acquired, by loan, a sum of ten thousand francs, with which I was determined to take my children and flee to America, if the deplorable petition was taken under consideration. I now admit, without a qualm, my intention to resist the verdict, and I very openly venture to say that the rule governing legal separations is a law against which present conscience protests and one of the first that future wisdom will question.

The law's principal fault is the publicity it accords to debates. It forces one of the pair—the more dissatisfied, the more wounded of the two—to put up with an impossible existence, or else expose his or her innermost wounds. Shouldn't it be sufficient to reveal those wounds to magistrates of integrity, who would keep the secret, without being forced to publish the misdeeds of the one who committed them? Instead, witnesses are called; an inquiry is made; the indicated faults are published and posted. To shield children from influences which might be no more than temporarily harmful, one of the pair must heap on the court records a monument of blame against the other. And yet this is but the gentle, concealed part of such battles. Should the adversary resist, this must result in an outburst of pleas and a scandal in the papers. Therefore, a timid or generous wife must choose between respecting her husband or protecting her children. One of these duties will stand in opposition to the other. Will they then praise her—if maternal love does not win out—for having sacrificed her children's future to the demands of public morality, family sanctity? That sophism would be hard to sustain; if the duty of a mother is not more pressing than that of a wife, then at least it is equally so.

And if the husband asks for the separation, isn't his obligation more appalling still? A woman can articulate grounds of incompatibility sufficient to break the bond, without dishonoring the man whose name she bears. So for her to cite the wild living, the transports of anger, and the love affairs of her husband, within the marriage, in order to deliver herself from the pain resulting from infractions of the rule, is without a doubt too much to ask of her; actually public opinion allows a man to cleanse himself of such blemishes. Indeed, according to the prejudices and customs of our society, the more a man is known for his many conquests, the more he is met with congratulatory smiles. Particularly in the provinces, any man who has freely imbibed the pleasures of bed and board is accepted as a sporting fellow, and no more need be said. He is censured a bit for not having spared the pride of his legitimate wife; it is agreed that he was at fault for inveighing against her; but after all, it is the husband's right to act with absolute authority in the house; and if he has used the slightest tact, his sex would consider him more or less in the right; in fact, he might have strayed into considerable intemperance, and be no less the gentleman in all other regards.

Such is not the position of the woman accused of adultery. One kind of honor alone is attributed to a woman. Unfaithful to her husband, she is stigmatized and vilified, she is dishonored in the eyes of her children, she is liable to the loss of her civil rights—to imprisonment. This is what an outraged husband, wishing to shield his children from bad example, is forced to do, when asking for legal separation. He cannot complain either of injury or bad treatment. Since he is the stronger of the two and he has the rights, anyone would laugh in his face if he were to complain of being beaten. Therefore, he must invoke adultery, and morally kill the woman who bears his name. Perhaps it is in order to spare him the necessity of this moral murder that the law concedes him the right of real murder against her person.

What a solution to domestic misery! It is savage. It can kill the spirit of the child condemned to watch the prolongation of his parents' discord or to experience its outcome.

But this is still not the worst of it; the man is invested with many other rights. He may cast aspersions on the honor of his wife, have her put in prison, and then condemn her to return, in subordination to him, to submit to his pardon and his caresses. If he spares her this last outrage, the worst of all, he can cause her a life of malice and bitterness, reproach her for her faults at all hours, hold her eternally in the humiliation of servitude, in terror of his threats.

Imagine the role of the mother of a family, under the outrage of such misery! Visualize the attitude of her children, condemned to blush for her, or absolve her, while detesting the instigator of her punishment! Visualize the attitude of her parents, friends, servants! Imagine an implacable husband, a vindictive wife, and you have a tragic home. Imagine a husband who is irresponsible or good-natured, according to whim, a wife without consistency or dignity, and you have a ridiculous home. But never imagine a truly generous, moral husband capable of punishing in the name of honor, and of pardoning in the name of religion. Such a man as that can exercise his rigor and his clemency in the privacy of the household; he could never invoke the benefits of the law to inflict public shame that is beyond his power to erase.

Nonetheless, that legal path was followed by my husband's counselors, and later pleaded by a fine man, a provincial lawyer who, while perhaps not lacking in talent, was forced into absurdity, under the weight of an immoral and revolting system. I remember how—pleading in the name of religion, of authority, of orthodox principles, and wishing to evoke the sense of evangelical charity in Christ's image—he lent my husband the mantle of philosopher and prophet, his oratorical surge unable to rise quite enough to make him a god. I do indeed concur: to call on a god to approve of a husband taking revenge at the expense of his wife's reputation, prior to pardoning her for it, would have been a sacrilege.

Let us add that this supposedly legitimate revenge can rest on atrocious lies gathered in a moment of rage; the resentment of some menials has ways of embellishing a presumed fault with monstrous details. A husband authorized to submit defamations, and even attempt to prove them, would thereby risk either his honor or his reason.

No, a marital bond, once broken in the heart, cannot be retied by the hand of man. Love and faith, admiration and forgiveness are things too intimate and holy to allow more than God alone to witness and privacy to protect. The marital bond is broken from the moment it becomes unbearable to one of its members. A family and legal counsel should be called not to verify the grounds of the complaint, but rather the truth, degree, and persistence of the discontent. Let the test of time be imposed. Let a judicious delay guard against culpable whims or fleeting resentments. Surely one could never exert too much prudence in adjudicating on a family's future, but the decision should be based solely on incompatibilities that are certain in the judges' minds, unattested to by judicial formalities, and unknown to the public. Pleas out of hatred or revenge would vanish, and lawsuits would diminish.

The more the paths of deliverance are eased, the more the castaways of a marriage will bend every effort to save the vessel before abandoning it. If it is a sacred ark, as the spirit of the law proclaims, do not allow it to go down in stormy weather; do not allow its weary bearers to drop it into the mud; arrange things so that a husband and wife, forced to separate by the carefully considered need for dignity, may respect the bond they are breaking and imbue their children with respect for each of them.

Those are the reflections that crowded my mind on the eve of the day that was to decide my fate. My husband, irritated by the grounds pronounced at the trial, and holding against me and my counselors the extent to which the legal forms are indelicate and harsh, thought only of taking his revenge. Blinded, he did not realize that, in that respect, society was his sole enemy. He did not tell himself that I had articulated only the facts that were absolutely necessary, and furnished those proofs alone which were strictly required by the law. Yet he knew the Code better than I, having been received at the bar; but never had his thoughts—immobilized as they were by the weight of his authority—been willing to rise to a moral critique of the laws and consequently to foresee their pernicious consequences.

Hence, he was responding to an inquiry where no facts had been betrayed beyond those he liked to vaunt by imputations of which I would have trembled to merit the minutest part. His lawyer refused to read libel. The judges would have refused to hear it.

Thus, he went beyond the spirit of the law, which permits a husband offended by censure to justify by brutal complaint the harsh conduct of which he is accused. But the law which allows this means of defense in a trial in which the husband asks for separation to his advantage could not admit it as an act of revenge in a conflict in which he is rejecting the separation. That law pronounces all the more in favor of the woman who declares herself injured that this means is the worst of injuries; this is what occurred.

However, my mind was not at ease about the outcome of the debate. In the first moments of indignation, I would have liked for my husband to be required to give proof of the wrongs he was articulating. Éverard, who was to defend me, rejected the idea of such a debate. He was right, but my pride suffered, I admit, from the possibility of the slightest suspicion in the minds of the judges. This suspicion, I told myself, could perhaps gain sufficient weight in their minds for them to deny me, in the separation decree, the care and rearing of my son.

However, when I had thought it over, I recognized the lack of danger in my situation, whatever the outcome. Suspicion could not even enter the minds of my judges; the accusations too clearly bore the mark of insanity.

So, I fell sound asleep. I was exhausted from my own thoughts, which for the first time had taken in the general question of marriage in a rather lucid fashion. I swear that never before had I felt the sanctity of the marital pact and the causes of its fragility within our customs so intently as in this crisis in which I saw myself involved. At last I felt peaceful; I felt sure of the rectitude of my conscience and the purity of my ideals. I thanked God that, in the midst of my personal suffering, He had allowed me to maintain unwaveringly the idea and the love of truth.

At one o'clock in the afternoon, Félicie came into my room. "You can really sleep!" she exclaimed. "Well then, you should know that they are leaving the hearing, you have won your case, you have Maurice and Solange. Get up quickly to thank Éverard. He's at the door. He had the whole town in tears."

There were further attempts at dealing with M. Dudevant while I was on my way back to Paris, but his counsellors did not permit him to listen to reason. He brought an appeal before the court at Bourges. I went back to live at La Châtre.

Though I was spoiled and as happy as possible in the midst of the Duteil family, I suffered a bit from the noise of the children, who got up at the time I was falling asleep, and from the heat, rendered overpowering by the narrow street and the size of the house. Spending a summer in a town is bitterly painful for me. I had not even a poor little sprig of greenery to look at. Rozane Bourgoing offered me a room in her house, and it was agreed that the two families would gather every evening.

M. and Mme. Bourgoing, together with a young sister of Rozane's whom they treated as their child and who was almost as beautiful as Rozane, lived in a lovely house, with a small terraced garden, perched over a precipice. It was the old rampart of the town, and from there you could see the countryside, you were part of it. The Indre ran, dark and peaceful, beneath the curtain of magnificent trees, and off down a charming valley to lose itself in the greenery. Facing me, on the other shore, rose La Rochaille, a slope dotted with diluvian boulders and shaded by centuried walnut trees. A bit farther, you could glimpse Malgache's white cottage and reed huts; nearby, the landscape was dominated by the large square tower of the ancient chateau of the Lombaults.

Our little garden, completely filled with flowers, treated us to delicious aromas; the noise of the town was not too near. We would eat dinner outdoors, seated along a wide gable-end covered with honeysuckle, our feet on the paving stones of a small peristyle where violets found a way to sprout. Our friends would come and have a cup of coffee on the terrace balustrade, to the song of the nightingales and the sound of the millwheels in the river. My nights were exquisite. I had a large room on the ground floor, furnished with a small iron bed, a chair, and a table. When the friends had gone and the doors were closed, without disturbing anyone's sleep I could walk in the garden that was walled like a citadel, work for an hour, go in and out, count the sinking stars, greet the rising sun, take in a wide horizon and vast countryside at the same time, hear nothing but the song birds or the cries of the owls, and feel as though, at last, I was in the deserted house of my dreams. There I revised the last part of *Lélia* and added another volume to it. That is perhaps the place where, right or wrong, I felt myself most a poet.

From time to time I went to Bourges, or else Éverard would occasionally come to La Châtre. It was always with the intention of conferring on the case, but the case was the least of the things which we would talk about. My head was filled with my art, Éverard's with his politics, and Planet's with his socialism. Out of all that, Duteil and Malgache made a potpourri of imagination, wit, and gaiety. Fleury argued, with that mixture of common sense and enthusiasm that contended in his brain, at once practical and romantic. We loved each other too dearly to refrain from violent quarrels. What splendid violence, interspersed with sentimental declarations of affection and wild laughter! We could not separate; we forgot to sleep, and these allegedly restful days left us haggard with fatigue, but relieved of the surplus imagination and republican fervor that had built up within us during hours of solitude.

At last my unbearable case was called up in Bourges, where I went at the beginning of July, after having gone to Paris for Solange. Once again I wanted to be in a position to take her away in case of defeat. As for Maurice, I had taken measures to fetch him a bit later. I was still secretly in revolt against the law which I publicly invoked. This was extremely illogical, but the law was more so than I, the law that, in order to deny or accord me my rights as a mother, forced me to overcome all memory of marital amity, or see those memories outraged and repudiated in my husband's heart. Society can annul those maternal rights and, in general theory, grant precedence to those of the husband. Nature does not accept such decrees; never will a mother be persuaded that her children are hers less than her husband's. The children make no mistake about that either.

I knew the judges of Bourges to be predisposed against me and possessed of fantastic notions concerning me. So, the day I appeared dressed like everyone else in the city, those among the Bourgeois who had not seen me asked the others if it was true that I wore red trousers with pistols tucked into my belt.

M. Dudevant could clearly see that he had taken the wrong tack with his petition. He had been advised to assume the stance of a husband enraged by love and jealousy. It was a little late for that, and I think he drastically misplayed a role that went against his natural bent. He was urged to appear, at night, under my windows, and even at my door, as if to solicit a secret meeting; but his conscience rebelled against such a farce, and after walking up and down the street for a minute, I saw him going away with a laugh and a shrug. He was quite right.

I had been received as a guest by the Tourangin family, one of the city's most notable. Félix Tourangin, a rich industrialist and close relative of the Duteil family, had two daughters—one married, the other already grown—and four sons, of whom the youngest were still children. Agasta and her husband had gone with me. Rollinat, Planet and Papet had followed us. The others soon rejoined us; so I was surrounded by all of my Berry friends, for from then on I attached myself to the Tourangin family as if I had spent my whole life there. The father, Félix, called me his daughter; Elisa, an angel of kindness and a woman of the greatest merit and most appealing virtue, called me her sister. Together with her, I made myself a mother to the little brothers. Their other relatives often came to see us and demonstrated a most affectionate interest toward me, even M. Mater, the presiding judge, once my case was over. On the day of the proceedings, I also greeted Émile Regnault, of Sancerre, whom I had loved as a brother and who had espoused some now-forgotten cause against me. He came to make honorable amends for wrongs I no longer recalled.

Consistent with their adopted approach, my husband's lawyer, as I already said above, pleaded my husband's love, and while offering to give verbal proof of my crimes, generously offered me pardon after the insult. With marvelous eloquence Éverard brought out the cynical illogic of such a marital philosophy. If I was guilty, the first step should be to repudiate me, and if I was not, there was no need to play the generous one. In any case, generosity was difficult to accept after revenge. The entire facade of love crumbled in the light of the evidence. He read a letter of 1831, in which M. Dudevant told me: "I am going to Paris; I will not stay with you, because I do not wish to inconvenience you any more than I wish to be further inconvenienced by you." The prosecuting attorney read others in which his satisfaction at my absence was so clearly expressed that it left not much reason to count on this outdated affection which was being offered to me. And why was M. Dudevant defending himself against not having loved me? The more evil he said of me, the more one was inclined to absolve him. But to proclaim his affection and at the same time the alleged grounds that made me unworthy of it was to make one suspect a selfish motive on his part, a suspicion which he doubtless would not have wished to merit.

He sensed this, because without waiting for the ruling he dropped his appeal, and with the court acting on this withdrawal of suit, the decision at La Châtre took its full effect on the rest of my life.

We went back to the earlier agreement which he had offered me at Nohant, and which his unfortunate indecision had forced me to validate by a year of bitter struggles, needless, if he had been willing to adhere to it.

That earlier agreement, which formed the basis for the new one, charged him with paying for and overseeing Maurice's education. On that point, from the moment we were back in agreement, I no longer feared being separated from my son. But considering that Maurice's aversion to school could return, it was difficult for me to keep from expressing my reservations. Éverard, Duteil, and Rollinat remonstrated with me that any contract ought to entail reconciliation of heart and mind; that my husband was honor-bound to use a portion of the revenue I was giving him to pay for the education of our son; that Maurice was in good health, studying passably well, and seemed accustomed to the academic routine; that he was already twelve years old, and that within a very few years the direction of his ideas and choice of his career would pertain very little to his parents and very much to himself; that, in any case, his passion for me should in no way cause me anxiety, and that Mme. Dudevant, the Baroness, could not easily win out in her desire to win his heart and confidence away from me. It was all very good reasoning, to which I acceded, though regretfully. I had a foreboding of renewed struggle. In vain they tried to persuade me that childrearing in common was necessary—fortifying for the child's body and spirit. It did not seem to me that this suited Maurice, and I was not mistaken. But I gave in, fearing to mistake for the wisdom of maternal instinct a weakness of heart that could be dangerous to the object of my concern. M. Dudevant did not seem to raise any objection on the allocation of Maurice's vacations. He promised to send me the boy as soon as school let out, and he kept his word.

I kissed Elisa, a fine woman, and her family, who had so taken me to their hearts on first sight; Agasta who, on the morning of my trial had gone to hear mass on my behalf; the beautiful children and the gallant friends who had surrounded me with fraternal care. I left for Nohant, where I took up permanant residence on the feast day of Sainte-Anne, patroness of the village. There was dancing under the great elms, and the raucous, screeching sound of the cornemeuse, so dear to those raised on it, seemed a good omen.   *L. F.*

XI

Travelling in Switzerland. —Mme. d'Agoult. —Her salon at the
Hôtel de France. —Maurice gets sick. —Struggles and sorrows.
—I take him back to Nohant. —Letter from Pierret. —I go to Paris.
—My mother's illness. —Review of our relationship since my
marriage. —Her last moments. —Pierret. —I fly to Maurice.
—I run after Solange. —The Sub-Prefecture at Nérac. —Return to
Nohant. —New disputes. —Two fine children for fifty thousand
francs. —Work, weariness, and will. —The role of parents.

For all my legal troubles, I had not achieved the least degree of material
comfort. On the contrary, I was entering a period of serious financial difficulties that I could not avoid, as a result of both a system of management that I
would have to change in several respects, and also of debts I had been left
without hope of immediate compensation. But I did have the home of my
memories to shelter the future memories of my children. Are we really justified
in holding on so tightly to these dwellings filled with gentle and cruel images,
the history of our own lives written on all the walls in mysterious, indelible
characters, which at each shock to the soul, fill us with deep emotion, or childish superstition? I don't know. But that is the way we are all made. Life is so
short that we need, in order to take it seriously, to triple our notion of it, by
linking our existence in thought to the existences of the parents who preceded
us and the children who survive us.

Besides, I was not going to Nohant with the illusion of a final oasis. I was
well aware that I was bringing along my restless heart and my anxious mind.

Liszt was in Switzerland and had committed me to spending time there
with a person he had introduced me to, whom he saw often in Geneva where
she had been established for some time.[71] This was Comtesse d'Agoult, beautiful, gracious, witty, and endowed over and above all these attributes with superior intelligence. She, too, prevailed on me with extreme cordiality, and I
looked on this trip as a diversion for my spirit after the sickening materialism I
had just been immersed in. It was an especially fine outing for my children,
and a way to shield them from the bewilderment of their new situation, by taking them away, in this first moment of inner turmoil, from the gossip and talk
that might have reached their ears. So, as soon as the vacation brought Maurice
back, I left for Geneva with him, his sister, and Ursule.

After two months of interesting excursions and delightful encounters with my friends in Geneva, we all returned to Paris. I spent some time in a furnished apartment, since my garret on Quai Malaquais was nearly in ruins, and the proprietor had turned out the tenants in order to make urgent repairs. I had left that dear garret, already totally populated with my deceptive dreams and deep discouragement, with even more regret than the ground floor; my solitary workroom, risen from its rubble and become once more a luxurious apartment, had been taken over by an excellent woman, the beautiful Duchesse de Caylus, whose second husband was Louis de Rochemur. They had two adorable little girls, and where there are children I am easily attracted. I was pleasantly detained at their place, despite my unsociability, by a genuine sympathy— spontaneous and shared. So I used to see them quite often, the proximity suiting my sedentary habits. I would simply go downstairs. It was at their place that I met Lamartine for the first time; I met M. Berryer there also.[72]

At the Hôtel de France, where Mme. d'Agoult had persuaded me to stay with her, the living conditions were charming for a short while. She received many writers, artists, and a few society men of intelligence. It was at her place, or through her, that I met Eugène Sue, Baron d'Ekstein, Chopin, Mickiewicz, Nourrit, Victor Schoelcher, etc. My friends also became hers, and she met as well Lamennais, Pierre Leroux, Heinrich Heine, etc.[73] Although improvised in a hotel, her salon was a gathering of the elite, over whom she presided with exquisite grace and where she found her own high level among all those eminent specialists by the breadth of her mind and the variety of her faculties, both poetic and earnest.

Wonderful music was performed there, and in the intermissions you could improve your mind by listening to the conversation. She also entertained our mutual friend Mme. Marliani,[74] that passionate mind and maternal heart, whose excessive need to make real life bow before the ideal of her imagination and the demands of her sensibility was doomed to unhappiness.

This is not the place to go into a detailed appreciation of the various leading intellectuals I ran into from then on. I would have to describe each in a context that would take me too far off the course of my own history. Though that might be more interesting for me and others, I am, nevertheless, approaching the limit of space allotted to me, and I see that there remain, God willing, many rich subjects for a future work and perhaps a better book.

I had neither the means to live in Paris nor the taste for so busy a life, but I was forced to spend the winter there. Maurice got sick. The school routine, to which he had seemed adaptable for a year, became once more destructive to him, and after some minor indispositions which did not appear serious, the doctors recognized the beginning of an enlargement of the heart. I hastened to take him out to live with me; I wanted to bring him to Nohant. M. Dudevant, in Paris at the time, was opposed. I did not want to challenge paternal authority, whatever rights I could have had prevail. I owed it to my son, above all, not to teach him rebellion. I hoped to conquer his father through gentleness, and convince him through evidence.

This was difficult for him and terribly painful for me. People who have the good fortune to enjoy excellent health do not easily believe in illnesses they have no personal knowledge of. I wrote to M. Dudevant, I received him, I went to his place; from time to time, I entrusted Maurice to him, so that he could witness the illness for himself. He wouldn't hear of it. He believed in a conspiracy of excessive maternal tenderness indulging the weakness and laziness of childhood. He was cruelly mistaken. I had exerted every effort against Maurice's tears and my own terrors. I could see clearly that giving in to his father was making the child's health deteriorate. Besides, the headmaster refused to assume the responsibility for taking him back. Maurice's malady was aggravated by his father's distrust. What hurt his feelings most—he who had never lied—was being suspected of lying. Every aspersion on his courage, every doubt as to the reality of his illness drove a spur into that poor sick heart. He was visibly getting worse. He could no longer sleep. He was sometimes so weak I had to carry him to bed in my arms. A diagnosis signed by Levraud, the physician for the Collège Henri-IV, and Doctors Gaubert, Marjolin and Guersant (since I did not know the last two, they could not be suspected of complicity) did not convince M. Dudevant. Finally, after several weeks of terrors and tears, my child and I were united forever. M. Dudevant wanted to keep him an entire night at his place before he would be convinced of the fever and delirium. He was convinced so thoroughly that he wrote me as soon as it was morning to come get him. I ran. When he saw me, Maurice cried out, leaped on the tile floor in his bare feet, and clung to me for dear life. He wanted to leave without putting his clothes on.

We departed for Nohant as soon as the fever somewhat abated. I had been afraid to remove him from the care of Gaubert, who would come to see him three times a day. But Gaubert urged me to take him. The child was homesick. In his troubled dreams he would cry out "Nohant, Nohant!" in a heartrending voice. It was an obsession. He believed that as long as he was not there his father would take him back. "This child breathes only with your breath," Gaubert said to me, "you are his tree of life; you are the doctor he needs."

We made the trip with Solange, in short stages. Maurice recovered quickly some of his ability to sleep and eat. But acute rheumatism in all his joints and violent headaches often overcame him. He spent the rest of the winter in my room, and for six months we were not apart for so much as an hour. His classical education had to be interrupted. There was no way to put him back at his studies without possibly damaging his brain.

Mme. d'Agoult came to spend part of the year with me. Liszt, Charles Didier, Alexandre Rey, and Bocage came also.[75] We had a magnificent summer, and the great artist's piano playing was our special delight. But after this splendid sunny weather, dedicated to peaceful work and sweet leisure, came a very painful time.

One day, in the middle of dinner, I received a letter from Pierret saying, "Your mother has suddenly become victim of a very grave illness. She realizes it, and her fear of dying is making her condition worse. Don't come for a few days. We need that much time to prepare her for your arrival, as though it had nothing to do with her illness. Write to her as if you knew nothing, and invent some pretext for coming to Paris." The next day he wrote me, "Put it off a little longer, she suspects something. We have not given up hope of saving her."

Mme. d'Agoult was leaving for Italy. I put Maurice in the charge of Gustave Papet, who was living a half-league from Nohant. I left Solange with Mlle. Rollinat, who was seeing to her education at Nohant, and I rushed to my mother's.

Since my marriage, I had no more automatic subjects of argument with her, but her excitable disposition had not stopped making me suffer. She had come to Nohant and involuntarily delivered her unjust accusations and inexplicable irritability against the most inoffensive persons. And yet from that time on, following serious confrontations, I had finally gotten the upper hand. Besides, I always loved her with an instinctive passion which my all too justified causes of complaint could not destroy. My literary reputation produced in her the strangest alternations of joy and wrath. She would begin by reading the malevolent critics of certain newspapers, and their perfidious insinuations about my principles and morals. Immediately persuaded that all that was deserved, she would write me or rush over to heap reproaches on me, at the same time sending or bringing me a packet of insults which would never have reached me without her. I would ask her, then, if she had read the work thus incriminated. She never had read it before condemning it. After protesting that she would never open it, she would begin to read it. Then, just as quickly, she would become wrapped up in my work as blindly as a mother can. She would declare it sublime and the critics infamous. It would start all over with the next new work.

It was that way with everything, at every moment of my life. Wherever I went, wherever I stayed, whatever person old or young, male or female, she met at my place, what hat I had on my head, what shoes I had on my feet, called for criticism, a continuous crabbing that would degenerate into a serious quarrel and vehement reproaches if I did not hasten, just to satisfy her, to promise to change plans, acquaintances, and costumes to her liking. I risked nothing, since she would forget by the next day the reason for her vexation. But it took a lot of patience to encounter at each meeting a new, unpredictable outbreak. I had the patience, but I was heartsick to be able, only through perpetual storms, to rediscover her charming spirit and her bursts of affection.

For several years she had lived at 6 Boulevard Poissonnière, in a house that has been replaced by the house with the iron bridge. Almost always she lived by herself, since she could not keep a servant more than a week. She kept her little apartment in perfect order, meticulously clean, decorated with flowers and brilliant with daylight or sun. She thrived on the light and, in summer, kept her window open to the heat, dust, and noise of the boulevard—never having enough Paris in her room. "I am Parisian in my soul," she used to say. "Everything about Paris which puts others off I need and like. I'm never too hot or too cold. I prefer the dusty trees on the boulevard and the black gutters watering them to all those forests that scare you and those rivers where you can drown. Gardens don't please me anymore; they remind me too much of cemeteries. The silence of the countryside frightens or bores me. Paris always seems like being on a holiday to me. The busyness strikes me as gay and lifts me out of myself. You know very well that the day I'm forced to reflect, I'll die." Poor mother, she reflected a great deal during her last days!

Although several of my friends who had witnessed her rage or malice against me reproached me for being too soft-hearted toward her, I could not help being moved to the quick every time I went to see her. Sometimes I would pass beneath her window and craved to go up to her apartment. Then I would stop, fearful of the tempest that perhaps was waiting for me. But I nearly always gave in, and if I had been firm enough to go a week without seeing her, I set out with secret impatience to get there. I would observe the power of that natural instinct in me by the strange oppression I felt on seeing the door of her house. It was a little grillwork gate opening on a descending stairway. At the bottom lived a refreshment vendor who had, I think, the duties of a caretaker, because some voice always called out to me from the shop, "She's there. Go on up!" You crossed a little courtyard and went up one floor, then followed a hallway and climbed up three more floors. That gave time for reflection, and the reflection I always had in that dark corridor would be, "Let's see now. What kind of face is waiting for me up there? Good or bad? Smiling or upset? What can she think up today to enrage herself?"

But I would also recall the warm welcome she knew how to give me when I caught her in a good mood. What a sweet cry of joy! What a brilliant look in her eyes, what a tender maternal kiss! For that exclamation, that look, that kiss, I could certainly withstand two hours of bitterness. Then impatience would overtake me, I would find the stairway unbearable, I climbed rapidly; I would arrive more excited than breathless, my heart beating hard enough to break at the moment I pulled the bell. I listened through the door and already knew my fate; for when she was in a good mood, she recognized me by my ring, and I heard her cry out as she put her hand on the lock, "Ah, it's my Aurore!" But if she was feeling gloomy, she did not recognize my ring, or not wanting to say she had, she would call, "Who's there?"

That "Who's there?" would hit me like a rock on my chest, and it took quite some time before she would try to explain or could calm down. Finally, when I had managed to extract a smile, or when Pierret arrived highly disposed to take my side, the violent argument would turn into gaiety, and she was as happy as in her youth. At those times, she was so charming that all else had to be forgotten.

But on some days it was impossible to reach an understanding—precisely those when the welcome had been most cheerful, when the sound of the bell had awakened her most tender tones. It crossed her mind to keep me there for teasing, and as I saw the storm coming, I stole away, wearied or ruffled, going back down the stairs with as much impatience as I had climbed them.

To give an idea of these strange quarrels she would pick, it will be enough to relate this one, which proves among all the rest how little her heart had to do with these excursions of her imagination.

I was wearing a bracelet made of Maurice's hair—shades of silky blond— of a color and texture that could only have come from the head of a small child. Alibaud[76] had just been executed, and my mother had heard that he had long hair. I never saw Alibaud; I have heard he was very dark. But wouldn't you know my poor mother, whose head was full of that drama, imagined I was wearing a bracelet of his hair. "The proof is," she said, "that your friend Charles Ledru was that assassin's attorney." At that period I did not know the man even by sight, but there was no way to dissuade her. She wanted to make me throw that dear bracelet—the golden fleece of Maurice's babyhood—into the fire, and she had seen me wearing it ten times without paying attention. I was obliged to run out to keep her from snatching it. I often ran out laughing, but while laughing I felt tears on my cheeks. I could not get used to seeing her irritated and unhappy at times when I came bearing such affection. I was often heartsick from some secret bitterness, which she probably would not have been able to understand, but which an hour of her love could have dissipated.

The first letter I wrote when I resolved to fight my husband in the courts was to her. Her rush of sympathy for me was spontaneous and complete, and did not waver. In my trips to Paris during that struggle she never failed me. So, for nearly two years my poor mother became again for me what she had been in my childhood. She turned some of her teasing to Maurice, whom she would have liked to take charge of, and he resisted somewhat better than I might have hoped. But she adored him all the same, and I needed to see her indulge in these little scenes, to keep from suspecting the pleasant change in her attitude toward me. There were times when I would say to Pierret, "Mother is adorable now, but I find her a little less lively and gay. Are you sure she's not sick?"

"No indeed," he would reply. "On the contrary, she is feeling better. She has finally passed the age when one still feels the effects of a major crisis, and now you see her the way she was in her youth, just as loving, and almost as beautiful." That was true. When she was somewhat dressed up—and she dressed ravishingly—people on the boulevard stopped to watch her pass, unsure of her age and struck by the perfection of her features.

At the actual moment, at the end of July, when I arrived in Paris in response to the terrible news of her imminent death, I was, nevertheless, somewhat hopeful because of the most recent news. I rushed over, going down the boulevard stairway, and was stopped by the refreshment vendor, who called out, "Mme. Dupin isn't here anymore!" I thought it was his way of telling me she was dead, and her opened window, which I had taken for a good omen, struck me, now, as the sign of departure for eternity. "Calm down," he said, "she's no worse. She wanted to be cared for in a private hospital with a garden and more quiet. M. Pierret should have written you."

Pierret's letter had not reached me. I ran to the address indicated, supposing I would find my mother convalescing, since she had the pleasures of a garden on her mind.

I found her in a dreadful, stuffy little room, lying on a miserable bed, and so altered I hardly recognized her. She looked a hundred years old. She threw her arms around my neck, saying "I'm saved—you bring me life!" My sister, who was at her side, whispered to me that the choice of that dreadful room was due to a fantasy of the patient, not a necessity. Our poor mother imagined in her feverish moments that she was surrounded by thieves, and hid her money bag under her bolster, not wanting to stay in a better room for fear of revealing her resources to those imaginary brigands.

I had to enter into her fantasy for a while, but I gradually won out. The nursing home was beautiful and large. I rented the best apartment, opening on the garden, and she agreed to be moved there the next day. I brought Gaubert to see her. Since she liked his gentle, sympathetic face, he persuaded her to follow his prescriptions. But then he took me into the garden to tell me, "Don't raise your hopes. She can't recover. The liver is very badly tumefied, though the crises of horrible pain are over. She'll die without suffering. You can delay the fatal moment only a little, by lifting her spirits. As for physical treatment, cater to her every whim. She hasn't the strength to want anything specifically harmful. My own role is to prescribe insignificant things and act as if I counted on their effectiveness. She is as impressionable as a child. Keep her mind occupied with hope of a speedy recovery. Let her pass away quietly without being aware of it."

"After all," he added with his habitual serenity, he who was also terminally ill, and well aware of it, although he dutifully hid it from his friends, "it's no sin to die."

I alerted my sister, and from then on we had only one thought—to distract our poor invalid and lull her fears. She wanted to get up and go out. "That's dangerous," Gaubert said, "she can expire in your arms. But to keep her body in a state of inactivity which her mind finds unbearable is more dangerous yet. Do what she wants."

We got our poor mother dressed and carried her to a hired coach. She wanted to go to the Champs-Elysées. Once there, she was animated briefly by the life and vitality around her. "How nice all this is," she said, "those noisy coaches, those trotting horses, the fashionable women, the sunshine, the golden dust! You can't die in the midst of all this. No, in Paris one doesn't die." Her glance was still bright and her voice full. But as we approached the Arc de Triomphe, she became deathly pale and said to us, "I won't go that far. I've had enough." We were terrified. She seemed ready to exhale her last breath. I had the carriage stop. She livened up again. "Let's go home," she said. "On another day we'll go as far as the Bois de Boulogne."

She went out several more times. She was visibly growing weaker, but her fear of death was subsiding. Her nights were bad, disturbed by fever and delirium, but when day came she seemed reborn. She wanted to eat everything. My sister worried about her cravings and upbraided me for bringing her everything she asked for. I upbraided my sister for even thinking of contradicting her, and my sister was, in effect, reassured to see our poor invalid, surrounded by fruit and delicacies, just happy to see and touch them, saying "I'll taste them in a little while." She never did. She had savored them visually.

We took her down to the garden, and there, sunning in an armchair, she would fall into reverie, even meditation. She waited to be alone with me to tell me what was on her mind. "Your sister is devout," she said, "and I want you to know that I no longer am in the least, since I suppose I'm going to die. I don't want to see a priest's face, do you understand? If I must leave, I want it all smiles around me. After all, why should I fear going before God? I've always loved Him." And she added with childlike verve, "He can certainly reproach me for whatever He wishes, but not for not having loved Him. There I defy Him!"

I was not allowed to care for and console my dying mother without distractions. My brother, whose behavior was getting extraordinarily erratic and contradictory, wrote me, "I am warning you without your husband's knowledge that he is leaving for Nohant to carry off Maurice. Don't let him know I told you. That would get me in bad with him. But I think you ought to be on guard against his projects. You know best if your son is really too weak to go back to school."

Of course, given Maurice's state, it was out of the question for him to return to school, and I was afraid of the effect on his already shaken nerves that a painful surprise and an argument with his father might have.

I could not leave my mother. One of my friends took the next post, rushed to Ars, and brought Maurice to Fontainebleau, where I went, under an assumed name, to settle him at an inn. The same friend was willing to stay with him while I returned to my patient.

I arrived at the hospital at seven in the morning. I had travelled all night to gain time. I saw the window open. I remembered the open window on the boulevard, and I felt that all was over. I had kissed my mother, two nights before, for the last time, and she had said to me, "I feel really fine now, and I am having the most pleasant thoughts of my whole life. I'm beginning to like the countryside, which I couldn't bear before. That came to me just recently, while coloring lithographs to amuse myself. There was a beautiful view of Switzerland, with trees, mountains, chalets, cows, and waterfalls. That picture keeps coming back to me, and I see it even more beautiful than it was. I see it even better than nature. When I close my eyes, I see landscapes which you can't imagine and which you couldn't describe. It's all too beautiful, too grand! And it changes from one minute to the next, getting more and more beautiful. I really have to go to Nohant to make some grottoes and cascades in the little woods. Now that Nohant belongs only to you, I'll really like it. You're going to leave in two weeks aren't you? Well, I want to go with you."

That day, the heat was sweltering, and Gaubert had said to us, "Try to keep her from wanting to go out in a coach, unless it rains." When the heat got even worse, I pretended to go out to look for a coach and returned, saying it was impossible to find one.

"Actually, it makes no difference," she said. "I feel so good that I don't want to move. Go see Maurice. When you return, I am sure you will find me cured."

The next day she had not been restless in the least. At five in the afternoon, she said to my sister, "Do my hair. I want my hair to look nice." She looked at herself in the mirror. She smiled. The mirror fell out of her hand, and her soul slipped away. Gaubert wrote me immediately, but I missed his letter. I arrived to find her cured indeed—recovered from the frightful weariness and cruel task of living in this world.

Pierret did not weep. Like Deschartres at my grandmother's bedside, he seemed not to comprehend that two people could be separated forever. He accompanied her to the cemetery the next day, and returned laughing uproariously. Then he abruptly stopped laughing and melted in tears.

Poor Pierret, excellent man, he was never consoled. He went back to his beer and pipe at the Cheval Blanc. He was always cheerful, brusque, oblivious, noisy. He came to see me at Nohant the following year. On the surface he was still the same Pierret. But suddenly he said to me, "Let's talk a little about your mother. Do you remember . . . " and then he recalled again all the details of her life, all the singularities of her character, all the outbursts of which he had been the willing victim; he quoted her words, he recalled the inflections of her voice, and he laughed wholeheartedly. And then he picked up his hat and went out with a joke. I followed him closely, since I could see that he was overcome with nervous excitation, and I found him sobbing in a corner of the garden.

Immediately after my mother's death, I returned to Fontainebleau, where I spent a few days secluded with Maurice. He was doing well. The heat had alleviated his rheumatism. Gaubert, who came to see him there, did not find him cured, however. His heart still had irregular beats. It was still necessary to follow the regime—constant exercise, without the least mental exertion. We got up at daybreak and stayed out until nightfall, on little hired horses, alone together, looking for things to discover in that remarkable forest filled with unexpected vistas, natural variety, splendid flowers and marvelous butterflies for my young naturalist, who could devote himself to watching and chasing, and let study wait. He had had a penchant for that study, as well as for drawing, since he was born. To enjoy nature as he already knew how preserved him from the boredom of his forced inactivity.

But scarcely had I gotten over one crisis than a new alert took me by surprise. M. Dudevant had been to Berry and, not finding Maurice, had carried off Solange.

Could he have imagined that I had placed Maurice beyond his reach just to be spiteful? I intended to keep Maurice in hiding only long enough to avert the harmfil intention my brother had warned me about. I was still hoping to achieve what I did manage later—to reach an understanding with him on what was advantageous and necessary for the education and health of our son. If, instead of going to look for him clandestinely in my absence, he had openly come for him, I would have submitted Maurice to examination by doctors chosen by him, and he would have been convinced of the impossibility of putting him back in school.

Be that as it may, he thought he could commit an act of legitimate vengeance, for what was for me a source of terrible anxiety was, in his eyes, a desire to spite him. Where the soul is embittered, a person considers himself justified in imputing to others the wrongs he would inflict himself.

Never had M. Dudevant manifested the least desire to have Solange with him. He customarily said, "I don't meddle in the education of girls. I don't understand anything about it." Did he understand that of boys any better? No, his will was too rigid to bear with the innumerable trivialities, debilities, and compulsions of childhood. He had never tolerated contradiction, and what is a child but the living contradiction of all paternal plans? Besides, his military instincts did not incline him to put up with what is vexing and tedious in a child's nature for anyone but a mother.

So, he had no other plan in mind for Maurice than to make him first a schoolboy and later a soldier, and in taking away Solange, he had no other intention, so he told me later himself, than to make me come get her.

I should have told myself that, and kept calm. But the circumstances of the kidnapping were presented to me touchingly, and in reality, they had been more dramatic than need be. The governess had been struck, and my poor, terrified, little girl had been carried off by force, screaming so that the entire household was still upset. However, I had not turned Solange against her father, as he imagined. During his struggle with Marie-Louise Rollinat and her mother-in-law, who happened to be there, Solange threw herself at her father's knees, crying, "I love you, papa, I love you, don't take me away!" The poor child, knowing nothing, understood nothing.

The letters reporting this new adventure made me frantic. I ran to Paris, I entrusted Maurice to my friend Louis Viardot;[77] I went to the ministry and put my complaint on record. I was accompanied by another friend and the master clerk of my lawyer, M. Vincent, an excellent young man, full of courage and zeal, today a lawyer. I left by post, rushing towards Guillery day and night. During the two days of preparation, the minister, M. Barthe, had kindly made use of the telegraph, so I knew where my daughter was.

Mme. Dudevant had died the month before. She had not been able to keep my husband from his father's legacy. She left him some chores which were worth a dozen or so lawsuits, and the lands of Guillery, of which he had already taken possession. May God grant peace to that unhappy woman! She had been quite culpable toward me, much more than I care to say. We should forgive the dead. They become better, I hope, in a better world. In case the justified resentments of this world can delay their access to the next, for a long time now I have cried, "Open your doors to her, dear Lord."

And what do we know about repentance the day after death? The orthodox believers say that one instant of perfect contrition can wash the soul of all its impurities, even on the threshold of eternity. I am with them in that belief. But why do they claim that sorrow for sinning—that supreme expiation—ceases to be possible after the separation of soul and body? Do they mean that the soul loses its light and life while mounting to the tribunal where God has called it for judgment? Those Catholics are not consistent in the least who regard the miserable trial of this lifetime as definitive, since they admit a purgatory where one can weep, repent, and pray.

I arrived in Nérac; I ran to Sub-Prefect Haussmann,[78] today Prefect of the Department. I do not recall whether he was already the brother-in-law of my worthy friend, M. Artaud. The latter married Haussmann's sister. I do know that I went to request his aid and protection, and that he got into my carriage on the spot in order to rush to Guillery, that he had my daughter given to me without argument or fuss, that he took us back to the sub-prefecture with my travel companions, and that he did not allow us to return to the inn, nor leave before two days of rest—peaceful trips on the lovely Baise River, along the banks where tradition places the youthful amours of Florette and Henri IV.[79] He had me to dinner with old friends whom I was happy to see again, and I remember we talked a lot of philosophy, a neutral terrain compared to politics, where the young civil servant would not have been in agreement with us. He had a serious mind, eager to plumb the depths of the general problem, but his exquisite savoir vivre kept him from bringing up any sensitive issues.

I remember also that I was so little versed in modern philosophy at that time that I listened without having anything to say, and saying to my travel companion on our way back, "You discussed with M. Haussmann matters I don't understand at all. With respect to things present, I have only feelings and instincts. The science of new ideas has formulae that are strange to me and that I'll probably never learn. It's too late. In spirit I belong to a generation which has had its day." He assured me I was mistaken and that once I got immersed in a certain circle of discussion, I would never be able to tear myself away. He, too, was somewhat mistaken, but it is true that, before long, I did become keenly interested. Eight months had still to pass before I would have the tranquility needed for that kind of study.

Since M. Dudevant had inherited an income which he admitted was twelve thousand francs and was soon to double, it did not seem fair to me that he continued to have use of half my income. He judged otherwise, and it was necessary to dispute the matter further. I would not have given myself so much trouble over money, if I could have been certain of having enough for my two children's education. But literary work is so haphazard that I did not want to subject their existence to the chance and accidents of my calling; publishers, success, health—all can go bankrupt. I wanted to persuade my husband not to concern himself with Maurice, and he seemed so disposed. Since he thought he was too burdened to pay for his upkeep without my help, I proposed taking on the entire responsibility myself, and he finally accepted that solution by a definitive contract in 1838. On receipt of a sum of about fifty thousand francs which he demanded, he returned to me the use of the Narbonne town house, which I had inherited from my father, and much more precious, the guardianship of my two children to direct as I saw fit. I sold the rent coupon which had constituted part of my mother's pension. We signed an agreement for this exchange, both of us quite pleased with our lot.[9]

As for money, mine did not go far, considering the needs at hand. The Collège de Narbonne, a very old historical house, had been so poorly kept up that I had to spend nearly a hundred thousand francs to put it in good condition. I worked ten years for that amount, and to make the house my daughter's dowry.

But in the midst of these money shortages that my small pieces of property caused me, I did not lose heart. I had become both father and mother of the family. There is much work and worry when an inheritance is not adequate, and when one must exert absorbing effort, as is the case in writing for the public. I do not know what would have become of me if I had not had, along with the faculty of being able to stay up late, the love of my art, to keep me alive. I began to love it the day it became not a personal necessity for me, but an austere duty. It has not consoled me, but it has distracted me from many a pain and pulled me out of many a preoccupation.

But what diverse preoccupations for a head without a great range of resources were those extremes of life which I had to cope with simultaneously in my little sphere! Respect for art; obligations of honor; moral and physical care of children, which always comes before all else; details of the house; duties of friendship, charity, and kindness! How short are most days for keeping disorder from taking over the family, the house, business affairs, or the brain! I did my best, and I did only what will and faith make possible. I was not favored with one of those marvelous constitutions which takes in everything effortlessly and goes unwearied from the bed of a sick child to a legal consultation, and from a chapter of a novel to a record of accounts. I had, therefore, ten times, a hundred times more pain than showed. For several years, I allowed myself only four hours sleep. For many more years, I struggled against atrocious migraines, to the point of collapsing over my work, and still not everything always went as my dedication would have wished.

Thus, I conclude that marriage must be made as indissoluble as possible. For to sail a bark as fragile as family security on the restive waters of our society is not too much for a man *and* a woman, father *and* mother sharing the task, each according to his ability.

But the indissolubility of marriage is possible only on the condition that it is voluntary, and to make it voluntary, it must be made possible.

So, if to get us out of this vicious circle, you find something besides the insistence on equal rights between man and woman, you will have made a still better discovery. *M.G.R.*

XII

The death of Armand Carrel. —Émile de Girardin. —Éverard
summed up. —Departure for Majorca. —Frédéric Chopin. —The
monastery of Valldemosa. —*Les Préludes*. —Rainy day.
—Marseille. —Dr. Cauvières. —Sea voyage to Genoa. —Return to
Nohant. —Maurice's illness and recovery. —May 12, 1839.
—Armand Barbès. —His flaw and his transcendence.

At this point in my narrative, two issues recall two of the most
remarkable men of our time. The two are Carrel's death, which occurred
almost the same day as my lawsuit at Bourges, in 1836, and the marriage question, which I have just broached apropos of my own experience. I am thinking
of Émile de Girdardin[80]—Girardin the journalist and legislator; should I also
say Girardin the politician and philosopher? Perhaps the title of journalist
includes all the rest.

Up to that day, the nineteenth century had two great journalists: Armand
Carrel and Émile de Girardin. By a mysterious and poignant circumstance, one
killed the other. More striking yet, the vanquisher in that deplorable duel, still
young and to all appearances inferior to the vanquished with respect to talent,
came to surpass him in the progress in general ideas, which coincided with his
own. If Carrel had lived, would he have submitted to such progress? Let us
hope so, but let us be honest and admit that, had he remained the man he was
on the eve of his death, he would have seemed, and I speak here to those who
share my point of view, singularly reactionary.

Émile de Girardin never paused in his march forward, although he may
have appeared to be—may even perhaps have been—side-tracked from his
ascent by bursts of crossfire.

This seems so much the case that, without meaning to shock or to discover a paradox, we could envisage the incomprehensible workings of Providence
not in the sorrowful and regrettable death of Carrel, but in the heritage of his
genius continued by none other than his stricken adversary.

What role would Carrel have played in 1848? We often asked ourselves
that question at the time. My memories cast him as the born enemy of socialism. My friends' memories were in conflict with mine, and the result of our
discussions was that, having a great heart, he might have been illuminated by
some great light.

But it is certain that, in 1847, Émile de Girardin was what Armand Carrel
had been ten years earlier, with respect to the progression of his and other peo-

ple's minds during the intervening ten years. Since then, Girardin has gone beyond him—far beyond.

It is not a mere parallel that I wish to establish here between two characters very much opposed in their instincts, or two talents very different in their styles. It is a striking rapprochement, one that has often struck me, and which seems to me to have been brought about by the determinism of the situation.

Unless he had substantially changed, Carrel, under the Republic, would have run for president. Perhaps Carrel would have become president of the Republic. Girardin would probably have supported another candidate. But the question of the institution would not have divided them.

Up to that point, it was not obvious that Girardin had not yet gone further than Carrel. Nor did anyone in our ranks notice that Carrel had not gone futher than Girardin.

I did not know Carrel particularly well. I never spoke to him, although I had run into him often; but I shall remember all my life an hour of conversation between him and Éverard, when I was present without his knowing. I was reading in the embrasure of a window; the drapery had fallen of its own accord when he came in, covering me. They were discussing the masses. I was thunderstruck. Carrel had no notion of progress. They did not agree. Éverard influenced him; then was influenced by him in turn—the weaker, as often happens, pulling along the stronger.

Having explored many a horizon since that day, Éverard, in 1847, retreated, shutting himself up inside what would have been Carrel's limited horizon.

Seeing these great minds vacillate, the partisans took alarm, and were shocked or indignant. The more impatient cried defection, treason. Carrel's last days were poisoned by those unjust accusations. Éverard resisted and wrestled with their embittered suspicions until Carrel's end. Girardin, even more accused, insulted, and hated by every shade of party faction, was the only one who remained standing. In France, today, he is the champion of the boldest and most generous theories of liberty. Thus destiny worked, endowing him with strength superior to that of his adversaries.

From our political behavior we must be able to eliminate prejudice, impatience, and anger. The ideas we pursue will achieve their victory only through equitable and generous consciences. That a man like Carrel may be attacked and cursed by letters of reproach and impious threats; that so many others, equally innocent, may be accused of greed and lack of character—that, they say, is just the inevitable foam which rises on the flood tide of passion. They add that you have to be resigned to it, and that any revolution comes at this bitter price.

Not true. Let us not resign ourselves. Let us excuse those inevitable errors in the past, but never again accept them in the future. Let us say, once and for all, that no party, even our own, will govern long through hatred, violence, and insult. Let us no longer allow that republics can be stormy, and dictatorships vindictive. Let us no longer dream of progress, if it is on the condition that we march in mutual distrust and cruelty. Let us leave to the past its dark moments, its frenzy, its gross acts. Let us admit that men who have done great things, or who have merely had great ideas or sentiments, must not be accused lightly, and should not be accused at all, except after due deliberation. Let us have sufficient intelligence to appreciate these men from the point of view of a complete historical picture. Let us recognize their power and its limitations. To expect that a superior man will respond at every hour of his life to the ideal he has let us glimpse is to bring suit against God Himself, who has created man indecisive and limited. If, in a free state, we do not wish to vote for a man whose spirit one moment flagged, hesitated, or went astray, that is our right. But in meanwhile doing without him, let us still render him homage, realizing that perhaps tomorrow our destiny will need that man who took refuge in scruples or false prudence.[10]

When our political manners have progressed to that extent, when popularity struggles no longer employ as weapons insult, ingratitude, and calumny, rest assured we shall no longer see major defections. Defections are almost always reactions of wounded pride, acts of spite. Ah! I have seen it happen a hundred times. Many a man, who, if respected and spared, would have marched on the right path, violently left his co-religionists because of a cutting remark; the noblest characters are not immune to an attack on their honor, or merely a brutal criticism of their wisdom. I may not cite examples that are too close to us, but you have certainly seen them yourself, whatever your milieu. What harmful decisions have been reached, by a very slim margin, before your very eyes!

And isn't that part of human nature? You gradually become the enemy of the man who has declared himself your enemy. If he becomes enraged, no matter how patient you are, from the moment he is blind and unjust toward you, little by little you will consider him blind and unjust in everything. His very ideas become antipathetic at the same time as his language. You differ on a few points at the beginning, and suddenly the very beliefs that you held in common appear dubious, from the moment he gave them formulations that seemed to criticize or negate your own. You begin by playing with words, and you end with bloodshed. Duels often have no other cause, yet the public square is bloodied by duels from party to party.

Who bears the greatest guilt in these deadly conflagrations of history? The first person who said "raca" to his brother. If Abel had said that first to Cain, it is he God would have punished as the first murderer in the human race.

These reflections that distract me are not off the subject when I recall Carrel's death, Éverard's grief, and our party's hatred of Girardin. If we had been just; if we had acknowledged that Girardin could not have refused to fight with Carrel, something quite easy to recognize when examining the facts; if, after having treated Carrel as a cowardly mind, we had not treated his adversary as a murderer, it would not have taken twenty years to gain possession of our legitimate heritage—the welcome relief of the strength and great light that Émile de Girardin carried within him, and had had to carry alone, on the path leading to our common goals.

So much distrust and prejudice against him! I felt them myself, and not for the fact of the duel, where dangerously wounded himself, he bore off the still deeper wound of an irreparable sorrow. When impetuous voices around me cried, "No matter what, you don't kill Carrel! Carrel ought not have been killed!" I recalled that Girardin, having sustained the fire of Degouve-Denuncques,[81] had refused to aim at him, and that this act, worthy of the chivalrous Carrel, had been considered an insult, because it came from a political enemy. As for the cause of the duel, the witnesses would never have found it sufficient, if Carrel had not forced them by his obstinacy. Without a doubt, Carrel was embittered and wanted to wring a humiliation, rather than a reparation, for perhaps an imaginary wrong. As for the aftermath of the duel, it was heartrending and honorable for Girardin. He was insulted by Carrel's friends, but his only revenge was to wear mourning for Carrel.

So that was not the motive for our antipathy, and Éverard himself, weeping for Carrel, whom he cherished, affirmed the integrity of the adversary, after he regained his composure. But we thought we saw in that emerging, practical genius the born enemy of our utopias. And we were not mistaken. There was a gulf between us, then. Is it still there? Yes, on issues involving feelings, and on dreams of an ideal. For my part, after long reflection on the marriage question, I do not hesitate to say that M. de Girardin—though he touches on the vital questions of the family in a book that is admirable for its socialist politics and spirit of legislation—sheds no great light on the dogma of mother love, and indeed endangers it noticeably. He admits into the composition of the family only mother and children. I said above, and I shall say again, always and everywhere, there must be both father and mother.

But a discussion would lead us too far from the subject, and all this is a digression from my own story. I do not regret the digression, but I postpone to another setting an appreciation of Girardin, newly emergent in history, who appears so briefly in my narrative. Still, I wanted to devote a small space to him.

Carrel disappeared as though carried off by destiny, rather than immolated by an enemy. A great journalist—by definition, one who writes the history of his own times by daily synthesizing the past and the future, through times of inspiration as well as lapses in his genius—he let fall the torch he was bearing in the blood of his adversary and his own. His adversary washed away the blood with his tears, and picked up the torch. To hold it aloft was not easy after such a catastrophe. For a long time the light flickered, held in his benumbed fingers. The breath of passions could have dimmed it, or made it waver, but it was destined to live. We did not hail it as soon as we should, but it survived all the same. The mission of Carrel's heir was purified in the gale. At the dawn of catastrophe, his mission was chivalrous and generous. The moment came when Girardin alone among Frenchmen could show the courage and faith that Carrel surely would have been forced to lock in his heart, since Carrel would not have been able to resist seizing, once the moment arrived, the power for his own account. Girardin had the rare good fortune not to do likewise. That is sometimes a great honor.[11]

To get back to Éverard, three years had gone by since he had held sway over my spirit. This was no longer so, for reasons long forgotten. "Forgotten" is the right word, for clarity of memory is sometimes motivated by resentment.

I know, generally speaking, that the causes varied—on one hand, the caprices of his "ambition," to use his inveterate word to explain his violent and fleeting need to be active; on the other, the all too recurrent flare-ups of his character, often exacerbated by inaction or disappointment.

As for his ambition to have a seat in the Chamber of Deputies and exert influence there, I in no way disapproved. But I must confess that it spoiled Éverard a little. At those moments, when his altered face looked sixty, I cherished my old man with an almost filial affection, because at such moments he was gentle, simple, candid, completely imbued with divine ideals. Was he then most himself? That is what I could never ascertain. He was surely sincere. But what would he have been like if his constitution had been sound; that is to say, if a chronic illness had not made him continually alternate between fever and languor? His moments of sickly exaltation made him not antipathetic so much as alien to me; that was when he became youthful again and warmed to the petty combats of day-to-day politics, and I felt an unconquerable urge not to get too involved with him.

He would not forgive my indifference to what he then regarded as the consuming interest of his life, except after pouting and reproaching. To avoid the resumption of those quarrels, I encouraged neither his letters nor his visits. They became rarer and rarer. He was named deputy. His debut in the chamber, on some question of private property that I no longer remember exactly, established him more as a clever negotiator than a political orator. At that point, his effectiveness was effaced, as far as I was concerned. I did not want to torment him about it. I could await the revival of his true gift without anxiety. We went for months altogether without speaking or writing. I had settled at Nohant. His visits were further and further apart until the February Revolution. In our last conversations, we were no longer in agreement on basic issues. I had given further thought to my ideal. He seemed to have pushed his aside, to go back a century before the Revolution. You could not remind him of the bridge of Saints-Pères. He would have affirmed on oath that I had made it up, and that Planet had, too. He got exasperated when I tried to prove to him that I had maintained and improved my convictions, while he had let his regress and grow vague. He jeered somewhat bitterly at my socialism. Yet, he could easily shift to being tender and paternal. Then, I would predict that one day he would become a socialist again and that, outdistancing that position, he would reproach me for my moderation. This would certainly have happened if he had lived.

Neither absence nor death destroys great friendships. Mine for him endured and remains, in spite of everything. I never felt estranged from him, although he was so with me during the last years of his life. I shall tell why.

He wanted to be commissioner at Bourges under the provisional government. He was not appointed, and blamed me. He imputed to me an influence with the Minister of the Interior that I was far from having. M. Ledru-Rollin was not in the habit of consulting me on his political decisions. Some people said he was, but that was a bad joke. Éverard was naïve enough to believe provincial gossip.

But to be absolutely sincere, I did not hide from him that if I had had such influence, and if I had been consulted, or to put it better, if I had been the minister himself, I would not have acted otherwise. I pushed loyalty to the point of writing him, after Ledru-Rollin had made that decision and announced it afterwards in a conversation where I was present, that I had found his reasons serious and justified. As I said before, and told him myself, the Republic had taken Éverard by surprise when he himself was in a phase of marked antipathy for the ideas which were bound to bring the Republic to life. He could again have become the man of tomorrow; flexible and sincere as he was, we would hardly have minded his returning; and in any case, with a forcefulness like his we could have waited for him without compromising the future. But it is absolutely certain he was not the man for that day—the day of complete faith in, and limitless aspiration toward, the principles he had rejected the eve before.

I was not mistaken. Under the pressure of circumstances, Éverard was on one of the crests of the mountain when the violence of events made him come down without hope of ever climbing back up; a bitter death was waiting for him. I was told he never forgave my sincerity. Well, I believe just the opposite. I believe that, at a given moment known to him alone, his heart was just and his reason lucid. Today, when I envision his soul face to face, I am at peace.

There is another soul—no less beautiful and pure in its essence, no less sickly and troubled in this world—that reappears with a similar tranquility in my conversations with the dead, and in my expectation of that better world where we must all meet again in a brighter and holier light than that on earth.

I am speaking of Frédéric Chopin, who was my guest the last eight years of my retreat at Nohant, under the monarchy.

In 1838, as soon as Maurice had been definitively entrusted to me, I decided to find him a winter milder than ours. In that way, I hoped to spare him the return of the painful rheumatism of the preceding year. At the same time, I wanted to find a peaceful place where I could make him work a little, as well as his sister, and also work myself without strain. You save a lot of time when you do not have company; you are forced to stay up much less.

As I was making plans and preparations for leaving, Chopin, whom I saw every day and whose genius and character I loved dearly, told me on several occasions that, if he were in Maurice's place, he would soon be cured himself. I believed him, and that was a mistake. I did not include him in the trip in Maurice's place, but along with Maurice. His friends had long urged him to spend some time in the south of Europe. They thought he was consumptive. Gaubert examined him and swore that he was not: "You will in fact save him if you give him fresh air, exercise, and rest." The others, well aware that Chopin would never make up his mind to leave society and the Parisian scene unless someone beloved and devoted dragged him away, pressured me not to reject this desire of his, so apropos and completely unhoped for.

I was wrong, as it happened, to give in to their hopes and to my own solicitude. It was quite enough for me to handle, going alone to a foreign country with two children—one still sick, the other exuberantly healthy and boisterous—without taking on an additional emotional burden and a medical responsibility.

But Chopin was in a phase of health which was reassuring to everyone. Except for Grzymala,[82] who was not really deceived, we were all confident. However, I begged Chopin to examine his inner strengths, because for several years he had never envisioned without panic the prospect of leaving Paris, his doctor, his friends, his very apartment and piano. He was a man of imperious habit, and any change, regardless how small, was a dreaded event in his life.

I left with my children, saying that I would spend several days at Perpignan. If I did not find him there, or if he did not arrive within a reasonable delay, I would go on to Spain. I had chosen Majorca on the advice of persons who thought they knew the climate and resources of the country well, but who did not know them at all.

Mendizabal,[83] a mutual friend, as kind as he was eminent, was on his way back to Madrid and would accompany Chopin to the frontier, in case he followed through on his fantasy of making the trip.

So, off I went in November with my children and a chambermaid. I stopped the first evening at Plessis for the joy of embracing Angèle and that whole dear family which had opened its arms to me fifteen years earlier. I found the little girls grown up, beautiful married women. Tonine, my favorite, was both haughty and charming. Poor James was gout-ridden and used crutches. I kissed father and daughter for the last time! Tonine was to die following her first childbirth, her father shortly afterward.

We made an extensive detour, traveling for the sake of traveling. At Lyon we saw again our friend and eminent artist Mme. Montgolfier, Théodore de Seynes,[84] and others, and we went down the Rhone as far as Avignon. From there we went over to the Vaucluse, one of the most beautiful sights in the world, certainly justifying Petrarch's love, and his immortal lines.[85] After that, crossing the Midi to pay our respects to the Pont du Gard, we stopped a few days at Nîmes to give a kiss to our dear preceptor and friend, Boucoiran, and to meet Mme. d'Auribeau, a charming woman, who was to remain a friend. Then we reached Perpignan, where Chopin joined us the next day. He had stood the trip very well. He did not suffer too much from the sea travel to Barcelona, nor from Barcelona to Palma. The weather was calm, the sea excellent. We felt the heat increase from one hour to the next. Maurice tolerated the sea almost as well as I, Solange less well, but at the sight of the rugged coasts of the island, denticulated in the morning sunlight by the aloes and palm trees, she began to run on the deck, joyous and fresh as the morning itself.

I have little to say here of Majorca, having written a whole book on this trip.[86] I recounted there my anguish caused by the invalid whom I accompanied. As soon as winter came—and it announced itself suddenly, with torrential rains—Chopin suddenly presented all the signs of a pulmonary infection. I do not know what I would have done if Maurice had been gripped by rheumatism. We had no doctor who inspired confidence, and the simplest remedies were almost impossible to obtain. Even the sugar was often of poor quality and made one sick.

Thank God, Maurice, who confronted the wind and rain with his sister from morning to evening, recovered perfect health. Neither Solange nor I was afraid of the flooded paths or downpours. We had found a healthful and extraordinarily picturesque lodging in an abandoned Carthusian monastery, partly in ruins. I gave the children lessons in the morning. The rest of the day they ran and played while I worked. In the evening moonlight, together, we went through the cloister, or read in the cells. Our life in this romantic solitude would have been extremely pleasant, despite the savage countryside and the pilfering nature of its inhabitants, if the sad spectacle of the suffering Chopin and, on certain days, serious anxiety for his life had not effectively removed any pleasure or benefit from the trip.

The great artist was a detestable patient. What I had feared—but not sufficiently, unfortunately—happened. He allowed himself to become completely demoralized. He could endure suffering with courage enough, but he could not conquer the anxieties of his imagination. For him, the cloister was full of terrors and phantoms, even when he felt well. He did not say anything, so I had to guess. When I would return from my nocturnal explorations in the ruins with my children, I would find him, at ten in the evening, pale at his piano, his eyes haggard, his hair standing almost on end. It would take him several moments to recognize us.

He would then make an effort to laugh, and he would play us the sublime pieces he had just composed, or, to be more accurate, the terrible and harrowing music which had come to him unawares in that lonely hour of sorrow and fright.

That is where he composed the most beautiful of those brief pages that he modestly entitled *Préludes*. They are chef-d'oeuvres. Several bring to mind the visions of dead monks and echoes of funeral chants which besieged him. Others are melancholy and sweet. These came to him during hours of sunlight and health, to the noise of the children's laughter beneath the window, the distant sound of guitars, the song of birds under the wet foliage, the sight of little pale roses blooming in the snow.

Still others are mournful and sad, charming your ear, breaking your heart. There is one that came to him on a gloomy, rainy evening, which makes the soul frightfully despondent. Maurice and I had left him in a healthy state, that day, to go to Palma to buy some necessities for our encampment. The rains had come, the torrents had overflowed; we had made three leagues in six hours, returning in the midst of a flood, and we arrived well after nightfall, without shoes, abandoned by our cart driver, through unheard of risks.[12] We were rushing because we knew our patient would worry. His anxiety had been severe, to be sure, but it had frozen into calm despair, and he was playing a marvelous prelude while weeping. On seeing us come in, he rose, uttered a loud cry, then said with a wild expression and in a strange tone of voice, "Ah, just as I imagined, you have died!"

When he had gotten back his bearings and saw the state we were in, he was sick at the retrospective display of our dangers. He confessed to me later that, while waiting for us, he had seen all that in a dream and, no longer able to distinguish dream from reality, he had calmed himself and played the piano drowsily, persuaded that he had died himself. He saw himself drowned in a lake—heavy, icy drops falling rhythmically on his chest—and when I had him listen to the drops of water falling rhythmically on the roof, he denied having heard them. He was even angry at what I translated by the expression "imitative harmony." He vehemently protested—and he was right—against the naïveté of believing his notes to have been aural imitations. His genius, full of the mysterious harmonies of nature, translated them into sublime equivalents in his music, and not by a servile imitation of sounds.[13] His composition that evening was certainly full of raindrops resonating on the tiles of the monastery, but they were perhaps translated in his imagination and in his music into tears from heaven falling on his heart.

The genius of Chopin is the most profoundly feelingful that has ever existed. He made a single instrument speak the language of infinity. He was often able to condense in ten lines that a child could play poems of immense elevation, dreams of unequalled emotion. He did not need massive means to express his genius: neither saxophones nor ophicleides to fill the soul with terror; neither church organs nor human voices to fill it with faith and enthusiasm. He was not known to the masses, nor is he yet. There will have to be great progress in the appreciation of art for his works to become popular. The day will come when his music will be orchestrated without changing a note of the piano score, and when the whole world will know that a genius as vast, as complete, as knowing as that of the greatest masters whom he had assimilated contained an individuality even more exquisite than Sebastian Bach's, even more powerful than Beethoven's, even more dramatic than Weber's. He is all three together, yet he is still himself—more subtle in taste, more grandly austere, more painfully moving. Mozart alone is superior to him, because Mozart had, in addition, the calm that health confers and, as a consequence, an abundance of life.

Chopin realized his power and his weakness. His weakness was in the excess of that very power, when he could not control it. He could not, as could Mozart (and Mozart alone, moreover), make a flat-tint masterpiece. His music was full of nuances and the unforeseen. Sometimes—rarely—it was bizarre, mysterious, tortured. Although he had a horror of what could not be understood, his excessive emotion carried him away, without his being aware of it, to regions known to him alone. Perhaps I was a bad guide for him (he would consult me the way Molière consulted his housekeeper), because as a result of knowing him, I reached the point of being able to identify with every fiber of his being.

For eight years, his piano, initiating me daily into the secrets of its master's inspiration or meditation, revealed to me the raptures, perplexities, victories or torments of his genius. I understood him, therefore, as he understood himself, and a judge more unlike him might have forced him to be more intelligible for everyone.

In his youth, he had occasionally had cheerful and quite robust ideas. He wrote Polish songs and romances, none of them published, charmingly good-natured and sweet. Some of his last compositions are still like springs of crystal, reflecting a sunny sky. But they are rare and short, those tranquil ecstasies of his contemplation! The song of the lark in the sky and the easy floating of the swan on still waters are for him brief flashes of serene beauty. The cry of the lamenting, famished eagle on the cliffs of Majorca, the bitter blast of the north wind, and the dreary desolation of yews covered with snow saddened him much more keenly than the perfume of the orange trees, the grace of the vines, and the Moorish cantilena of the farm workers could gladden him.

His character was like this in everything. Responsive for a moment to gentle affections and a peaceful existence, he was hurt for days, for entire weeks, by the tactlessness of someone unimportant to him or by the petty exasperations of daily life. And, strange to say, a true wound did not crush him so much as a minor one. It seemed that he did not have the discrimination to appraise it, first, and then to feel it. The depth of his reaction was, thus, in no way in proportion to its cause. Where his deplorable health was concerned, he accepted its real dangers heroically, but he tormented himself to wretchedness over insignificant changes. This is the story of all creatures whose nervous system is excessively developed.

With his exaggerated sense of detail, horror of squalor, and need for refined comforts, he naturally found Majorca horrible after a few days of illness. He did not have the resources to start up again; he was too weakened. When he got better, the crosswinds ruled the coast, and for three weeks the steamboat could not leave port. It was the only embarkation possible, and barely possible at that.

Our stay at the monastery of Valldemosa was thus torture for him and torment for me. Sweet, cheerful, charming in society, Chopin sick, in exclusive intimacy, was cause for desperation. No one had a soul more noble, more refined, more disinterested; no interaction more true and sincere, no mind more brilliant in gaiety, no intelligence more serious and complete in its own domain. But in return, alas, no disposition was more uneven, no imagination more suspicious and frenzied, no self-esteem more impossible not to irritate, no demand of the heart more impossible to satisfy! And none of that was his own fault, really. It was due to his illness. His sensitivity was flayed alive: a crushed rose petal, the shadow of a fly made him bleed. Except for me and my children, everything beneath the Spanish sky was antipathetic and revolting. He was dying from impatience to leave, even more than from the inconveniences of staying.

At the end of the winter, we were finally able to get to Barcelona, and from there, still by boat, to Marseille. I left Valldemosa with mixed feelings of joy and sorrow. I would happily have spent two or three years there, alone with my children. We had a trunk full of good elementary texts which I had the time to teach them. The sky was getting to be magnificent, and the island an enchanted spot. Our romantic dwelling charmed us. Maurice was visibly getting stronger, and for us the privations were just something to laugh about. I would have had many long hours of uninterrupted work. I was reading good books of philosophy and history, when I was not being nurse, and the invalid himself would have been charming, if he had been able to get well. With what poetry his music filled that sanctuary, even in the midst of his most pain-ridden restlessness! And the monastery was so beautiful beneath its festoons of moss, and the flowering so splendid in the valley, the air so pure on our mountain, the sea so blue on the horizon! It was the most beautiful place I have ever lived in, and one of the most beautiful I have ever seen. And I scarcely had time to enjoy it. Not daring to leave the patient, I could only go out with my children for a brief period each day and, often, not at all. I was sick myself from fatigue and seclusion.

At Marseille we had to stop. I had Chopin examined by the famous Dr. Cauvière, who at first found his state seriously endangered, but who, however, became very hopeful seeing him get rapidly back on his feet. He predicted that Chopin would live a long time, if he received extensive care, and he was prodigal with his own. This worthy and amiable man, one of the leading physicians in France, the most charming, reliable, and devoted of friends, was providence for the fortunate and unfortunate in Marseille. A man of conviction and progress, he conserved to a very advanced age his beauty of face and soul. His physiognomy, simultaneously mild and lively, always lighted by a tender smile and brilliant glance, commanded respect and friendship equally. He has still one of the best physical constitutions in existence, free from infirmities, full of fire, young in heart and mind, as kind as he was brilliant, and always in possession of the faculties of a superior intelligence.

He was like a father to us. He bestirred himself unceasingly to make our stay pleasant. He took care of Chopin; he walked and spoiled the children; he filled my hours, if not with repose, at least with hope, confidence and intellectual well-being. I found him again this year (1855) at Marseille, fifteen years later, younger-seeming and more amiable still, if that is possible. He had just conquered cholera like a young man; loving, as in the beginning, the elect of his heart; believing in France, the future, truth, as the children of this century no longer do. Admirable old age, crowning an admirable life!

Seeing Chopin reborn with the springtime and responding to a very mild medication, he approved our plan to spend a few days in Genoa. It was a pleasure for me to see again with Maurice all the beautiful buildings and paintings that this charming city contains.

On the return trip, we had a squall at sea that left Chopin rather sick. We took a few days' rest at Marseille at the excellent doctor's.

Marseille is a magnificent city which, at the outset, annoys and displeases by the harshness of its climate and inhabitants. One gets used to them, however, because basically the climate is healthy and the inhabitants decent. It becomes clear how people can get used to the brutality of the mistral, the rages of the sea, and the burning rays of the implacable sun, when one realizes that this opulent city provides all the resources of civilization, in every possible degree, and that this stretch of Provence provides as many strange and beautiful spots as many somewhat overly praised spots in Italy.

I brought back to Nohant, without any mishap, Maurice recovered and Chopin on the way to recovery. At the end of a few days, it was Maurice's turn to be the sicker of the two. His heart was recovering too quickly. My friend Papet, who is an excellent physician and who, because of his fortune, practices medicine gratis for his friends and the poor, took it on himself to change the boy's regime radically. For two years he had been restricted to white meat and water tinged with red wine. Papet judged that such rapid growth required tonic, and after bleeding him, made him strong on a diet that was just the opposite. It was wise on my part to have trusted Papet, because from that moment on, Maurice was radically cured and attained strong, dependable health.

As for Chopin, Papet could not find any lingering symptom of a pulmonary infection, but only a chronic minor condition of the larynx, which he did not hope to cure, but in which he saw no grounds for serious alarm.[14]

Before going on, I must speak of a political event which took place in France, May 12, 1839,[89] while I was in Genoa, and of a man whom I place in the first ranks of my contemporaries, although I did not know him until much later—Armand Barbès.

Barbès' first bursts of enthusiasm, however, were those of heedless heroism, and, along with Louis Blanc, I do not hesitate to condemn the attempted coup of May 12. I shall go further and say that the unfortunate expression "the end justifies the means" contains something more serious than just a fatalistic saying would seem to. It can indeed be taken as a truism, if we grant that the lives of a certain number of men may be sacrificed to a principle benefiting humanity, on the condition of really advancing the power of that principle in the world. However, if the effort of valor and devotion must remain fruitless; if even in certain conditions and under the sway of certain circumstances it must, by failing, delay the hour of salvation, it is vain for it to be pure in intention; it becomes culpable in deed. It gives strength to the triumphant party; it shakes the faith of the vanquished. It makes innocent blood flow, the precious blood of the conspirators themselves, for the profit of a bad cause. It either makes the masses defiant, or strikes them with such stupefying terror that it is almost impossible to regain their confidence.

I am well aware that the end which will justify the means is God's secret, and that if, like the Ancients, one marched forth only after having consulted reputedly infallible oracles, one would have earned but little merit in risking one's fortune, liberty, and life. Besides, the oracle of modern times is the people: *Vox populi, vox Dei.* And it is a mysterious and deceptive oracle, often unaware itself of the source of its trances and revelations. But however difficult it may be to penetrate, the genius of the conspirator consists in assuring himself of that oracle.

The conspirator, therefore, is not up to his mission when he lacks wisdom, clairvoyance, and that special genius which divines the inevitable outcome of events. It is so grave a matter to throw a people—even a small fraction of them—into the bloody arena of revolution, that it is not permissible to give in to the instinct of sacrifice, enthusiasm, and martyrdom—to the illusions of the most sublime faith. Faith serves in its own domain. The miracles of faith do not leave that domain, and when man wishes to carry faith into the world of deeds, it is no longer sufficient that faith remain in a mystical state. Faith must be illuminated with worldly lights—special lights which require the knowledge and appreciation of the deed itself. Faith must become science, and a science as exact as that Napoléon brought to battles.

Such was the error of the leaders of the Société des Saisons. They counted on the miracle of faith, without taking into account the special enlightenment necessary in this kind of enterprise. They misjudged the people's state of mind, the means of resistance. Like the Roman Curtius, they rushed into the breach, without realizing that the people were in one of their periods of lassitude and disbelief, where for the sake of their self-love and out of respect for their future—indeed their immediate future—it would not do to expose them to their own acts of cowardice and atheism.

The end does not justify the means, but it does sanction great causes and, up to a certain point, imposes bad ones on human reason, the adherence of the people being in this case an obstacle against which one must know how to stand firm and wait. The fervor of noble, indignant souls must know how to be self-restraining at given moments of history and husband itself for the hour when it can set the sacred spark of a vast fire. It is then that a party can risk itself with a people, and even at the head of a people, to change their destiny. If a party fails despite the wisest precautions and most knowing efforts; if it is in a situation to render its defeat disastrous to the enemy; if, in a word, it expresses by its acts an immense, burning protest, its efforts are not lost, and those who survive will gather the fruit later. In such an instance, we still bless the losers of a good cause. This is when we absolve them of the misfortune attached to the crisis, recognizing that they did not act by chance. The amount of faith that survives such a disaster is proportionate to the chances their plan might have had to bear fruit. That is why we forgive an able, but vanquished, general who loses entire columns, in a battle in view of a probable victory, while we condemn an isolated hero who has a small escort slashed to pieces, with no chance of a useful result.

God forbid that I accuse Barbès, Martin Bernard, and other generous martyrs of that ilk, of having blindly made sacrifices to their unchecked boldness, their contempt for life, their egoistic need for glory! No, they were studious, modest minds. But they were young. They were exalted by the religion of duty. They hoped that their death would be fertile. They believed too much in the sustained excellence of human nature. They judged it by themselves. Ah, my friends, how beautiful your lives were, since to find fault in them, we must, in the name of cold reason, put on trial the most noble sentiments of which the soul of man is capable!

But Barbès' true grandeur was shown in his attitude toward his judges and was fulfilled in the long martyrdom of imprisonment. It was in prison that his soul rose to sainthood. From the silence of that humble and piously resigned soul emerged the most eloquent and pure teaching in virtue that this century has had the opportunity to witness. There—never an error, never a weakening in that absolute abnegation—in that calm, sweet courage, in those tender consolations he gave to hearts broken by suffering. Barbès' letters to his friends are worthy of the most beautiful ages of faith. Matured by reflection, he rose to the appreciation of the highest philosophies; but superior to the majority of those who teach, he assimilated stoical strength and united it with the humility of the true Christian. Thus, although not a creator in the sphere of ideas, he equalled the greatest thinkers of his time, without realizing it. In him, the words and thoughts of others became fertile; they germinated and grew in a heart so pure and fervent it became the mirror of truth, a touchstone for acute consciences, a rare and veritable subject of consolation for all those who are alarmed by the corruption of the times, the injustices of the parties, and dejection, in these days of trial and persecution. *M.G.R.*

XIII

I try the teaching profession and fail. —Indecision. —My brother's return. —Our quarters in Rue Pigalle. —My daughter at boarding school. —Square d'Orléans and my acquaintances. —A big meditation in the little Nohant woods. —Chopin's character developed. —Prince Karol. —Causes of suffering. —My son consoles me for everything. —My heart forgives everything. —My brother's death. —A few words about those who are gone. —Heaven. —The untold sorrows. —The future of the century. —Conclusion.

After the trip to Majorca, I thought about organizing my life in a way that would solve the difficult problem of making Maurice study without depriving him of fresh air and freedom of movement. That was possible at Nohant, and our readings could serve to replace his school Greek and Latin with ideas about history, philosophy, and art.

But Maurice loved painting, and I could not teach him that. Furthermore, I did not have enough confidence in myself where the other subjects were concerned to take our studies together very far. I studied and learned the night before what I explained to him the next day. I did not know anything systematically, and I was forced to invent a method for his studies at the same time that I introduced myself to the knowledge that that method was supposed to convey. At the same time as well, I had to find another method for Solange, whose mind required a completely different teaching approach, and one considering studies appropriate for her age.

All of this was beyond my power, unless I were to give up writing. I seriously considered it. By shutting myself away in the country the whole year, I hoped to live off Nohant, and to live quite satisfactorily, while devoting what spark of intelligence my soul possessed to the education of my children. However, I quickly discovered that teaching did not suit me, or to be more accurate, that I was not at all suited to the very special task of teaching. God had not made me articulate; I did not express myself clearly and precisely enough, not to mention that my voice gave out after fifteen minutes. Moreover, I did not have enough patience with my children; I might have taught someone else's children better. Perhaps one must not be too intensely involved with one's students. I exhausted myself with my efforts, and I often found a resistance in the children that made me despair. A young mother is not experienced enough in the preoccupations and listlessness of childhood. I did remember those characteristics in myself as a child, but remembering, too, that if someone had not overcome them in spite of me I might have remained passive or gone mad, I labored mightily to wear down their resistance, not knowing how to overcome it.

Later, I taught my granddaughter to read, and found the necessary patience, even though I loved her intensely, too, but I was a great deal older then.

During this period of indecision about how to organize my life in the best way possible for my adored children, my conscience pondered a serious question. I wondered if I should accept the idea of Chopin's having gotten used to living near me. I would have been quick to reject it, if I had known, then, for how short a time the solemn, retired life in the country would suit his mental and physical health. I still attributed his despair and abhorrence of Majorca to the heightening effects of the fever and our ruined monastery. Nohant offered more soothing surroundings, a less austere retreat, a congenial entourage, and resources in case of illness. Papet was an enlightened and affectionate doctor for him. Fleury, Duteil, Duvernet, and their families, Planet, and Rollinat in particular, were dear to him at first sight. They all loved him, too, and felt as inclined as I to spoil him.

My brother had returned to live in Berry. He established himself on the property of Montgivray, which his wife had inherited, about half a league from us. Poor Hippolyte had acted so strangely and irrationally toward me that he deserved a little sullenness in return, but I could not be sullen toward his wife, who had always behaved perfectly toward me, or toward his daughter, whom I cherished as if she had been mine, having partly raised her with the same care I had given Maurice. Moreover, my brother, when he acknowledged his faults, blamed himself so completely, so excessively, so energetically, issuing a thousand naïve witticisms, all the while swearing and crying profusely, that my resentment vanished within the hour. With anyone but him past behavior would have been inexcusable, and with him it would not be long before the future became intolerable, but what could I do? That's how he was! He was the companion of my early years, the bastard son born under a lucky star, the pampered child of our house. It would have been uncharacteristic for Hippolyte to play Antony.[90] The character in *Antony* is true in relation to the prejudices of certain families; anyway, what is beautiful is always more or less true. But one could easily invent a counterpart to Antony, and Dumas, the author of that tragedy, could have done so himself, with equal truth and beauty. In certain circles, the "love child" excites so much interest that he becomes, if not king of the family, at least its most independent and enterprising member. He is the one who dares everything, and to whom everyone yields out of a visceral need to compensate him for society's rejection. In actual fact, having no official status and having no legal claim to anything in my household, Hippolyte had, nevertheless, always managed to dominate there, with his boisterousness, bluff nature, and unruliness. He had driven me away for the simple reason that I did not want to cast him out. He had embittered and prolonged the struggle that brought me back, and had returned himself, pardoned and embraced, for a few tears he shed at the threshold of our paternal home. This was simply the beginning of a new series of repentances on his part and forgivenesses on mine.

His high spirits, unfailing gaiety, the originality of his witticisms, his genuine and enthusiastic effusiveness over Chopin's genius, his constant, respectful deference toward him alone—even during the inevitable and awful binges—found favor with this eminently aristocratic artist. Thus, everything went along very well, at first, and I eventually accepted the idea that Chopin might be able to rest and regain his health with us for a few summers, although his work would necessarily take him back to Paris during the winter.

Nevertheless, the prospect of this sort of family relationship with a friend who was new in my life gave me pause for thought. I was terrified at the task I was about to undertake, and that I had thought ended with the trip to Spain. If Maurice were to fall back into the state of apathy that had absorbed me, then farewell to the fatigue of lessons, it was true, but farewell, too, to the joys of my work. And which hours of my life could I devote to a second invalid much more difficult to care for and console than Maurice?

My heart was overwhelmed with a kind of dread in the presence of a new duty to be assumed. I was not deluded by passion. I felt a kind of maternal adoration for the artist—very vivid, very real—but which could not compete for a moment with instinctual love, the only chaste emotion that can also be passionate.

I was still young enough to have perhaps to struggle against love, against so-called passion, and feared this distinct possibility, given my age, my situation, and the destiny of women artists, especially those who abhor casual affairs. Determined never to submit to any influence that might distract me from my children, I saw a lesser, but still possible, danger even in the tender friendship I felt for Chopin.

Well, on reflection, this danger disappeared, and even took on the opposite characteristic, that of protection against the emotions which I no longer wished to experience. One more duty in a life already so full and overwhelmed with fatigue seemed to me one more chance for the austerity toward which I felt myself drawn with a kind of religious ardor.

If I had followed through with my project to shut myself away at Nohant all year long, to give up the arts and become a teacher to my children, Chopin would have been saved from the danger that threatened him without my knowing: that of becoming too attached to me. He did not yet love me so much that he could not have been dissuaded; his affection for me was not yet exclusive. He talked to me about a romance he had had in Poland, about loving entanglements he had later experienced in Paris, which he could resume, and especially about his mother, who was the true passion in his life, although he had become accustomed to living at a great distance from her. Since his profession was his only livelihood and was honor itself to him, he would be forced to leave me, and six months in Paris would find him, after a few days of discomfort and tears, returned to his habitual elegance, exquisite success, and intellectual flirtations. I had no reason to think otherwise.

But destiny was pushing us in the direction of an enduring relationship, and we both arrived there without realizing it.

Doomed to fail in my teaching enterprise, I resolved to place it in better hands and, for this purpose, took up permanent residence in Paris. I rented an apartment in Rue Pigalle, which consisted of two pavilions at the far end of a garden. Chopin moved to Rue Tronchet, but his lodgings were humid and cold. He once again developed a serious cough, and I saw myself obliged either to give up my role as sick nurse, or spend my time running back and forth. To spare me this, he came daily, his features distorted and his voice faint, to tell me that he was getting along marvelously. He would ask to dine with us, and he would leave each evening, shivering in his carriage. Seeing how much it distressed him to disturb our family life, I offered to rent him part of one of our buildings. He accepted joyfully. He set up his own apartment there, receiving his friends and giving his lessons, without disturbing me. Maurice had the apartment above his; I occupied the other pavilion with my daughter. The garden was pretty, and large enough to permit games and general merrymaking. The children had teachers of both sexes, who were doing their best. I saw as few people as possible, feeling quite contented with just my friends. My charming young relative Augustine; my sister's son Oscar, for whom I had assumed responsibility and whom I had placed in boarding school; the two lovely children of Mme. d'Auribeau, who had come to Paris for the same reason as myself—all these made up the darling circle of youth which joined my children from time to time and, to my great satisfaction, turned the house upside down.

We spent nearly a year this way, trying out this kind of school at home. Maurice got along rather well. He never developed any more interest in the classics than my own father had, but with Eugène Pettetan, Loyson and Zitardini, he acquired a taste for reading and understanding, and he was soon able to teach himself and discover on his own the horizons toward which his turn of mind carried him. He was also able to acquire some notions about drawing which he had thus far developed through instinct alone.

My daughter was a different story. Despite the excellent education given her in my home by Mlle. Suez, a Swiss woman of great learning and admirable gentleness, her impatient mind could not concentrate on anything. This was heartbreaking, for her intelligence, memory, and comprehension were remarkable. It was necessary to return her to classroom education, which she found more stimulating, and to boarding school, which restricted the number of distractions, and made them easier to overcome. She was not happy, however, at the first boarding school I found. I withdrew her immediately to take her to Mme. Bascans, at Chaillot, where she agreed that she was really better off than at home. At last, settled in a charming house, in a splendid setting, the object of tender care and private lessons with M. Bascans, a man of real merit, she was willing to admit that cultivating the mind could be something other than unrewarding vexation. For such had been the reasoning of this logician; she had maintained, until now, that human knowledge had been invented for the sole purpose of annoying little girls.

Having made the decision to separate myself from her once again (with more effort and regret than I wished to show her), I lived alternately at Nohant in summer and Paris in winter, without ever leaving Maurice, who always managed to amuse himself wherever he was. Chopin would come to spend three or four months each year in Nohant. I prolonged my stay there well into winter, and afterward I rejoined my "resident invalid," as he called himself, in Paris. He was anxious for my return, but he did not miss the country, which he never enjoyed for more than two weeks at a time, and which he tolerated for longer only because of his attachment to me. We had left our apartments in Rue Pigalle, which he came to find unpleasant, and had established ourselves on Square d'Orléans, where the enterprising Marliani had arranged a family life for all of us. She occupied a lovely apartment between our two. In order to visit one another—sometimes at her apartment, sometimes at mine, sometimes at Chopin's, when he felt inclined to play for us—we had only to cross a large, clean, sandy courtyard decorated with plants. We would all eat together at Marliani's, and share expenses. It was a good, economical arrangement and it allowed me to see all manner of people at Mme. Marliani's, to visit more intimately with friends in my own apartment, and to resume my work whenever I felt like retiring. Chopin, too, was delighted to have a beautiful, isolated drawing room where he could go to compose or dream. But he loved people, and rarely took advantage of his sanctuary, except to give lessons. Only at Nohant did he create and write. Maurice had his apartment and his studio above mine. Solange had a pretty little room near mine, where she loved to lord it over Augustine on the days when she visited. She would imperiously banish her brother and Oscar, claiming that the boys were bad-mannered and smelled of cigar. That did not prevent her from climbing up to the studio a moment later to enrage them. Thus, they spent their time insulting and chasing one another from their respective rooms, only to come back to knock at the door and begin it all again. Another child—mocked for his shyness at first, but soon teasing and mocking in return—added to the comings and goings, the pranks, and the bursts of laughter that drove the neighborhood to despair. It was Eugène Lambert, one of Maurice's classmates at Delacroix's painting studio. He was a boy of great wit, heart, and aptitude, who became my child almost as much as my own, and who, invited to Nohant for a month, has by now spent a dozen summers there, not to mention several winters.

I eventually brought Augustine to live with us, as family life became more precious and necessary to me each day.[15]

If I had to speak in detail of all the dear and illustrious friends who surrounded me during these eight years, I would begin another volume. But isn't it sufficient to name, in addition to those I've already mentioned, Louis Blanc, Godefroy Cavaignac, Henri Martin, and the greatest female singer of our era, possessing as well a noble heart, Pauline Garcia, daughter of an artistic genius, sister of La Malibran, and wife of my good friend Louis Viardot, an unpretentious scholar, man of taste, and above all a good and upright man.[92]

Among those whom I frequented with equal esteem but less intimacy, I shall mention Mickiewicz, Lablache, Alkan the Elder, Soliva, E. Quinet, Général Pépé, and others. And without creating categories of talent or celebrity, I want to remember the faithful friendship of Bocage, that great artist; and the touching friendship of Agricol Perdiguier, that noble artisan; the friendship of Ferdinand François, a pure and stoic soul; that of Gilland, a proletarian writer of great talent and great faith; that of Étienne Arago, so true and so charming; and that of Anselme Petétin, so melancholy and sincere; that of M. de Bonnechose, the best and most likable of men and invaluable friend of Mme. Marliani; that of M. de Rancogne, a charming, unpublished poet, a gay and sensitive old man, whose wit was like a rose and whose heart bore not a thorn; that of Mendizabal, the playful, affectionate father of our precious childhood; that of Dessaüer, eminent artist, pure and worthy character;[16] finally that of Hetzel, who was not less precious to me for having come late into my life; and that of Dr. Varennes, one of the oldest and most mourned of friends.[93]

Alas! Death or absence has severed most of these relationships without clouding my memories or dulling my sympathies. Among those of whom I never lost sight I mention Captain d'Arpentigny, one of the most original and far-reaching minds that exist; and Mme. Hortense Allart,[94] a writer of lofty sentiment and poetic form, an erudite woman "all pretty and pink," as Delatouche used to say—a courageous, independent spirit, a brilliant, serious woman who brought as much serenity to her life in seclusion as she brought grace and brilliance to society, a strong and tender mother, with a woman's compassion and a man's firmness.

I also saw that impassioned mind, that woman who had the illusions of a child and the soul of a hero, that madwoman, that martyr, that saint—Pauline Roland.[95]

I mentioned Mickiewicz, a genius equal to Byron, a soul led to dizzying rapture through love for his country and the sanctity of its customs. I mentioned Lablache, the greatest comic actor and the most perfect singer of our time; in private life he was a lovable wit and a respectable family man. I mentioned Soliva, a truly talented lyric composer, an admirable teacher, a worthy character, a playful and serious artist. Finally, I mentioned Alkan, celebrated pianist, full of original ideas, an erudite musician, a man of heart. As for Edgar Quinet, everyone who reads him may know him: a great heart and vast intelligence; his friends are familiar as well with his artless modesty and with the gentleness of his dealings with others. Finally, I mentioned Général Pépé, a pure, heroic soul, one of those characters who reminds you of the men in Plutarch. I have not mentioned Mazzini,[96] or the others who remained my friends, both in the political world and in private life, since I did not really know them until later.

At this time, through my varied associations, I was already in contact with the extremes of society, from wealth to abject poverty, from the most reactionary beliefs to the most revolutionary ones. I enjoyed being aware of and understanding the various machinations that cause humanity to function and that determine its vicissitudes. I watched attentively; I often misjudged; now and then I saw clearly.

After the disappointments of my youth, too many illusions came to govern me. My morbid skepticism was succeeded by too much ingenuousness and good will. I was duped a thousand times by a dream of an archangelical fusion of opposing forces in the great battle of ideas. I am still sometimes quite capable of similar wishfulness, the result perhaps of a full heart, yet I ought to be well cured of it, for my heart has bled a great deal.

The life I am recounting now was as good as possible, on the surface. The sun shone for me on my children, on my friends, on my work. But the life I am not recounting was clouded with terrible sorrow.

I remember a day when, revolted by nameless injustices which, in my private life, came at me from all sides at once, I went off to cry in the woods in my garden at Nohant, at the place where my mother and I used to make pretty little rock gardens for me. I was about forty years old then, and although subject to severe neuralgia, I felt physically a great deal stronger than I had as a child. I was taken by a sudden fancy, in the midst of dark thoughts, to pick up a huge rock, perhaps one of those I had seen my robust little mother carry. I lifted it without effort, and then let it fall in despair, saying to myself: "Oh my God, I may have forty more years to live!"

A horror of life, a thirst for repose, that I had fought off for a long time, came back, this time with a vengeance. I sat down on that rock and I poured out my sorrows in a flood of tears. But a great revolution took place inside me: after two hours of exhausted weeping, there followed two or three hours of meditation and restored equanimity, which I remember clearly as a decisive moment in my life.

Resignation is not in my nature. It is a state of sadness mixed with flittering hopes that is unknown to me. I have witnessed this state of mind in others, but I have never been able to experience it. My constitution apparently refuses to accept it. I have to feel absolute despair in order to restore my courage. Only when I am at the point of telling myself "All is lost!" can I begin to accept everything. I even admit that the word "resignation" irritates me. The way I think of it—right or wrong—it is an absurd laziness that attempts to evade the inexorable logic of misfortune; it is an indolence of soul that prompts us to seek our own salvation, to offer a calloused back to the blows of iniquity, to become inert, without horror for the suffering we submit to, and consequently without pity for those who inflict it on us. It seems to me that those who are resigned are full of scorn for the human race. No longer struggling to raise the rocks that crush them, they tell themselves that all is rock and they alone are the children of God.[17]

Another solution presented itself to me. To endure everything without hate or resentment, while combatting it with faith; no ambition, no dream of personal happiness for myself in this world, but much hope and effort for the happiness of others. This appeared to me the logical conclusion, in light of my nature. I could live without personal happiness, having no personal desires. But I did feel affection for others and the passionate need to express that feeling. I needed to cherish, or die. To cherish while being hardly, or poorly, cherished oneself is to be unhappy, but one can be unhappy and live. What keeps one from living is to not use one's own life, or to use it in a way that is contrary to its requisites.

Faced with this resolution, I wondered whether I would have the strength to follow it. I did not have a high enough opinion of myself to dream of rising to the level of virtue. Moreover, you see, in the period of skepticism in which we live, a great insight has emerged: that virtue is itself only an insight, one that pervades the soul, I would add—considering my belief—with the help of God. But whether one accepts or rejects the concept of divine aid, reason clearly shows us that virtue is the result of truth illuminating our consciousness, thereby forming a conviction which governs the heart and the will.

Thus eliminating from my private vocabulary the proud word "virtue," which seemed antiquated to me, and contenting myself with contemplating an inner conviction, I managed to tell myself, rather wisely I believe, that one does not go back on a formed conviction, and that in order to persevere in a decision made in light of that conviction, one has only to look inside oneself each time one's ego attempts to go against it.

No doubt I could be agitated, troubled, even torn by this imbecilically human ego, for the soul does not keep a constant vigil; it falls asleep and dreams. But it also seemed certain that, knowing the truth, that is, the impossibility of finding happiness through egotism, I would find the strength to keep my soul watchful.

Having thus calculated my chances with great religious ardor and with a genuine impulse toward God, I felt very peaceful, and I have kept this inner tranquility throughout my life. I have kept it not without disturbance, interruption, or lapses—my physical equilibrium succumbing at times to the rigors of my will—but I have always found it again with certainty, deep in the rhythm of my life.

I have found it again especially through prayer. By prayer I do not mean a chosen arrangement of words cast toward heaven, but a silent conversation with an ideal of luminous perfection.

Of all the sorrows I could no longer to submit to but had to combat, the sufferings of my resident invalid were not the least.

Chopin always wanted Nohant, but could never tolerate Nohant. He was a man of the world par excellence, not of the official or populous gathering, but of intimate society—salons of twenty people—just when the crowd is leaving and the habitués gather around the artist to draw his purest inspiration from him with their friendly importuning. It was only then he exerted all his talent. It was then, too, having plunged his listeners deep into meditation or poignant sadness—for his music sometimes filled one's soul with an awful despondency, especially when he improvised—suddenly, as if to cancel this effect and the memory of its pain, he would turn and steal a look in the mirror, arrange his hair and his tie, and all at once mimic a phlegmatic Englishman, an impertinent oldster, a sentimental English lady, or a mercenary Jew. They were always pathetic types, however comic, but so perfectly rendered that one never tired of wondering at his gift.

All these expressions drawn from himself—sublime, delightful, or bizarre —made him the center of elite gatherings, where they literally fought over him. His noble character, his disinterestedness, his pride, his enlightened arrogance—enemy of all crass vanity and insolent boasting—the sureness of his dealings with people, and the exquisite delicacy of his savoir vivre made him a friend as genuine as he was agreeable.

To tear Chopin away from such a life, to engage him in a simple, chang-less, constantly creative existence, he who had grown up in the lap of royalty, would have been to deprive him of what gave him fervor—an artificial fervor, it is true, for like a painted lady, he shed his power and animation when he returned home at night and gave himself over to fever and insomnia— but a life, though perhaps shorter, that would have been more lively than one of retreat and intimacy, limited to the unvarying circle of a single family. In Paris, he moved through several circles each day, or at least he chose a different one as his milieu each evening. Hence, he had twenty or thirty salons, in turn, to charm and enliven by his presence.

Chopin was not exclusive in his affections; he was so only in what he required. His soul, readily influenced by every grace, every smile, surrendered itself with extraordinary ease and spontaneity. It is true that it withdrew quite as easily: an awkward word, an ambiguous smile disturbed him extremely. He would fall madly in love with three different women during a single evening's festivities, and then would go off alone, with no thought for any of them, leav-ing each convinced that she alone had captivated him.

He was the same in friendship, becoming enthused at the first meeting, disenchanting himself, recovering endlessly, thriving on infatuation for those who were its object, or on secret discontent which would poison even his warmest feelings. A story he told me about himself proved how little he mea-sured what he gave of his own heart against what he required from others.

He had become deeply enamored of the granddaughter of a famous musi-cian, and was thinking of asking for her hand in marriage at the same time that he was considering another love match in Poland. His loyalty was pledged to neither, and his inconstant soul floated from one passion to the other. The young Parisian woman received him warmly, and everything was going along perfectly when, one day, he arrived at her home with another musician who, at the time, was better known in Paris than he. The young woman took it into her head to offer a chair to the other musician before seating Chopin. He never saw her again and forgot her immediately.

It was not that his heart was unresponsive. Far from that, it was ardent and devoted, but not continuously to one particular person. It gave itself alter-nately to five or six affections which vied within him for first place.

An artistic type of such vacillation was not meant to live long in this world. He was devoured by dreams of an ideal and fortified by none of the cus-tomary worldly tolerance afforded by philosophy or compassion. He was never willing to compromise with human nature. He in no way accepted things as they were. Therein lay his vice and his virtue, his greatness and his misery. Unforgiving of the slightest flaw, he had enormous enthusiasm for the least spark of talent, his impassioned imagination doing everything possible to see it as the full blaze of genius.

As a result, it was both sweet and bitter to be his favorite, for he held you accountable, with interest, for the merest glimmer of light, and overwhelmed you by his disillusionment at the briefest passing shadow.

Some have claimed, because they thought they recognized a few of his characteristics, that in one of my novels[98] I described and analyzed him in great detail. They were wrong. Proceeding on this same basis, too convenient and not reliable, Liszt himself was unwittingly led astray in his *Vie de Chopin*, overly exuberant in style, but also filled with some very good things and some very beautiful pages.

I outlined in the character Prince Karol a man of resolute temperament, exclusive in his feelings and demands. Chopin was not such a man. Nature does not create things the way art does, however realistic the latter succeeds in being. Nature has caprices and inconsistencies, not real perhaps, but very mysterious. Art corrects these inconsistencies only because it is too limited to convey them.

Chopin was a combination of those magnificent inconsistencies that only God can create, and that have their own peculiar logic. He was modest by principle and gentle by habit, but he was imperious by instinct and full of an unconscious arrogance—from whence came a hurtfulness he did not intend, and which was not truly focused on any particular object.

Moreover, Prince Karol was not an artist. He was a dreamer and nothing more. Not being a genius, he did not have the prerogatives of genius. He was, therefore, a character who was so far from being the portrait of a great artist that Chopin, who read the manuscript on my desk daily, had not the least inclination to see himself in it, suspicious as he was.

Nevertheless, people have told me that, later, in reaction, he imagined himself Karol. Enemies—and I had some who were close to him and called themselves his friends, as though that gave them the right to make him suffer—enemies made him believe that this novel was an exposé of his character. By that point, his memory had no doubt begun to fail; he had forgotten the book. If only he had reread it!

The story was so little like ours. It was quite the opposite. There was neither that ecstasy nor that same suffering between us. Our story was nothing like a novel; its basis was too simple and too serious for us ever to have quarreled about each other. I accepted everything about Chopin's life as it existed outside my own. Having neither his tastes, nor his ideas outside art, nor his political principles, nor his appreciation of material things, I never attempted to change him in any way. I respected his individuality as I respected that of Delacroix and of my other friends who were committed to different paths than my own.

For his part, Chopin accorded me, I might say honored me with a kind of friendship that was exceptional in his life. He was always the same toward me. He doubtless had few illusions about me, since he never lowered his opinion of me. That is what allowed the harmony between us to last such a long time.

A stranger to my studies, to my pursuits, and consequently, to my convictions; entrapped as he was by Catholic dogma, he said of me, as did Mother Alicia, in the last days of her life:[18] "What's the difference, as long as she loves God!"

Thus, we never addressed a single mutual reproach to each other, except for one time, which was, alas! the first and last. Such lofty affection had to be torn asunder, not worn down in minor skirmishes.

But if Chopin was all devotion, kind attention, obliging charm, and deference personified with me, he had not, for all that, renounced the acerbity of his character for those who surrounded me. With them, the capriciousness of his heart, generous and moody by turn, gave itself free rein, moving from infatuation to aversion, and back again. Nothing ever showed itself of his inner life; his lips never betrayed the sufferings of that inner being which his artistic masterpieces expressed indirectly and mysteriously. In any event, he maintained such reserve during our seven years that I was the only one who could divine his suffering, relieve it, and delay its outbursts.

Why didn't some series of events outside us separate us from one another before the eighth year!

My affection had managed to achieve the miracle of making him a little calmer and a little happier, only because God willed him to retain a little of his health. Nevertheless, he declined visibly, and I no longer knew what remedies to employ to combat his growing nervous irritability. The death of his friend Dr. Matuszynski and, then, that of his own father were two terrible blows for him. Catholic dogma endows death with an awful dread. Chopin, instead of dreaming of a better world for those departed souls, had only terrifying visions, and I was obliged to spend many nights in the room next to his, always prepared to get up from my work a hundred times a night to chase the phantoms from his sleep or his insomnia. The image of his own death appeared to him, escorted by all the superstitions of Slavic fantasy. As a Pole, he lived in a nightmare of legends. Specters called to him, clutched at him, and instead of glimpsing his father and his friend smiling at him through beams of holy light, he found himself shoving away their fleshless visages, and struggling against their icy grasps.

Nohant had become antipathetic to him. He was still briefly elated on his return in the spring, but as soon as he set to work, everything around him turned gloomy. His creativity was spontaneous, miraculous; he found it without seeking it, without expecting it. It arrived at his piano suddenly, completely, sublimely, or it sang in his head during a walk, and he would hasten to hear it again by recreating it on his instrument. But then would begin the most heartbreaking labor I have ever witnessed. It was a series of efforts, indecision, and impatience to recapture certain details of the theme he had heard. What had come to him all of a piece, he now over-analyzed in his desire to transcribe it, and his regret at not finding it again "neat," as he said, threw him into despair. He would shut himself up in his room for days at a time, weeping, pacing, breaking his pens, repeating or changing a single measure a hundred times writing it and erasing it with equal frequency, and beginning again the next day with desperate perseverance. He would spend six weeks on a page, only to end up writing it just as he had done in his first outpouring.

For a long time, I had had enough influence over him to make him trust his first burst of inspiration. But when he was no longer inclined to believe me, he reproached me gently for having spoiled him and for not having been exacting enough with him. I tried to distract him, to take him on walks. Sometimes, taking my whole brood in a country wagon, I would tear him away from his agony in spite of himself. I would lead him to the banks of the Creuse, and after two or three days, lost in the sun or the rain, on awful roads, we would arrive, laughing and famished, at some magnificent sight, where he seemed to find rebirth. The fatigue broke him the first day, but he slept! The last day, returning to Nohant, he would be completely restored and rejuvenated, and he would find the solution to his work without too much effort. But it was not always possible to convince him to leave his piano, which was more often a torment than a joy to him, and little by little he began to show his temper when I disturbed him. I didn't dare insist. Chopin was terrifying when angry, and when, as with me, he contained himself, he looked ready to suffocate and die.

My life, always active and gay on the surface, had inwardly become more painful than ever. I despaired at not being able to inspire in others that happiness I had been unable to find for myself, because of several sources of deep sorrow that I had forced myself to struggle against.[99] Chopin's friendship had never been a refuge for me in times of sadness. He had quite enough of his own misfortunes to bear. Mine would have crushed him, and, too, he was only vaguely aware of them and did not understand them at all. He would have evaluated everything from a very different point of view than my own. My real strength came to me from my son, who was now old enough to share the most serious concerns of life with me, and who sustained me with his equanimity, his precocious reasoning, and his unfailing good spirits. He and I do not have the same ideas about everything, but we do have great similarities in the ways we are made, thus a great many of the same tastes and needs. In addition, we share a natural bond of affection so strong that no disagreement between us can last longer than a day, nor can it stand up against a moment's face-to-face explanation. If we do not live within the very same sphere of ideas and feelings, at least there is always a great door standing wide open in the wall between us, a passage affording enormous affection and absolute confidence.

After the last relapse of our invalid, he had become extremely gloomy, and Maurice, who had loved him tenderly until then, was suddenly, unexpectedly hurt by him over a trivial subject. They embraced a moment after, but a pebble had disturbed the peaceful lake, and more came to trouble the surface, one by one. Chopin was often irritated without reason and sometimes irritated by good intentions. I saw the breach grow and spread to my other children, though rarely to Solange, whom Chopin preferred for the reason that she alone had not spoiled him. But it did to Augustine, with a frightening bitterness, and even to Lambert, who was never able to understand it. Augustine, the most gentle and certainly the least offensive of us all, was consternated—he had been so good to her at first. All of this was tolerated; but finally, one day, Maurice, weary of the pinpricks, spoke of leaving the circle. That could not and should not be. Chopin was not able to accept my legitimate and necessary intervention. He bowed his head and declared that I no longer loved him.

What blasphemy after eight years of maternal devotion! But that wounded heart was not conscious of its delusion. I thought that a few months' silence and distance would heal the wound and revive his friendship and fair-mindedness. But the February Revolution arrived, and Paris instantly became odious to a spirit incapable of adjusting to any sort of social upheaval. Free to return to Poland, certain of being tolerated there, he had preferred to languish for ten years far from his family, whom he adored, rather than suffer the sight of his country transformed. He had fled from tyranny as he now fled from freedom.

I saw him again briefly in March 1848. I clasped his trembling, icy hand. I wanted to talk to him; he vanished. It was my turn to say he no longer loved me. I spared him that pain, and left everything to Providence and the future.

I was not to see him again. Wicked hearts came between us. There were good ones as well, who did not know how to deal with him. There were frivolous ones, who preferred not to get involved in delicate situations; Gutmann was not there.[19]

People have told me he called for me, missed me, loved me like a child, until the end. They thought they should hide this from me until now. They also thought they should hide from him the fact that I was ready to run to him. They acted rightly, if the emotion of seeing me again would have shortened his life by a day or even an hour. I am not one of those who believe that things are resolved in this world. Perhaps they only begin here, and surely they do not end here. Life here on earth is a veil that sickness and suffering thickens for certain souls, a veil which lifts now and then only for the heartiest constitutions, but which death tears aside for all of us.

As sick nurse, for such was my mission during a good portion of my life, I have had to accept without too much astonishment, and certainly without resentment, the elation and depression of the soul in the grips of fever. At the bedsides of the sick, I have learned to respect what is genuinely their healthy free will and pardon what is the agitation of their distress.

I have been repaid for my years of vigil, anguish, and devotion with years of tenderness, trust, and gratitude, which cannot be cancelled out in God's sight because of an hour's unfairness or frenzy. God's punishment? No! God hardly noticed that hour of suffering that I, too, wish to forget. I endured it, not with cold stoicism, but with tears of pain and with rapture, in the privacy of prayer. And because I have said to those absent through life or through death, "Be blessed" I hope to find that same benediction in the hearts of those who close my eyes.

About the time I lost Chopin, I also lost my brother, more sadly yet. His reason had been deteriorating for some time; drunkenness had ravaged his fine constitution, and caused him to fluctuate between idiocy and madness. He had spent his final years alternately falling out and making up with me, my children, his own family, and all his friends. As long as he continued to visit me, I prolonged his life by adding water to the wine we served him, without his knowledge. His taste was so dulled that he did not notice, and even if he made up for quality with quantity, at least his drunkenness was less stupefying and less exacerbated. But I could only postpone that fatal moment when his nature no longer had the strength to respond and he was unable to regain his lucidity even when sober. He spent his last month enraged at me and writing me unimaginable letters. The February Revolution, which he could no longer understand from whatever viewpoint he assumed, had delivered a final blow to his unsteady faculties. At first an impassioned republican, he reacted as so many others did, who, unlike him, had no bouts of insanity as their excuse: he grew fearful and began to imagine that the common people wanted to take his life. The people! The common folk from whence he came, as I did on the maternal side, with whom he made the rounds more often than mere friendliness required, became a source of dread for him. He wrote me that he had learned from a reliable source that my political friends wanted to assassinate him. My poor brother! This delusion passed, he had a succession of others, without interruption, until his unsettled imagination faded, in turn, and gave way to the stupor of an agony no longer aware of itself. His son-in-law survived him by only a few years. His daughter, the mother of three beautiful children, still young and pretty herself, lives near me at La Châtre. She is a gentle and courageous soul who has already suffered a great deal, but who will never shirk her duties. My sister-in-law, Emily, lives even closer to me, in the country. A longtime victim of the aberrations of one she loved, she is now resting from her prolonged fatigue. She is a stern and perfect friend, an upright soul and a mind nourished on good reading.

Ursule is still here, too, in this little town where I have cultivated so many dear and lasting relationships for so long. But, alas! death or exile has brought down many around us. Duteil, Planet and Néraud are no longer. Fleury was deported, like so many others, because of his opinions, even though he would not have been in a position to act against the current government. I won't even mention my friends in Paris, or in the rest of France. It is as if a circle of isolation has been drawn around me. Those who have by a miracle escaped this system of banishments, often decreed by the emotional reaction and personal grudges of the provinces, live as I do, on hopes and regrets.

As I end my story, let me describe the present circumstances of those of my childhood friends who have played a role in it. The Duvernet family still lives in the charming countryside that I have visited since my childhood. Mama Decerfz is also at La Châtre, mourning for her exiled children. Rollinat is still at Châteauroux; he comes to see us whenever he has a day of leisure.

It is rather natural that after having lived for a half-century you find yourself deprived of some of those for whom you have had great feeling; but we are passing through a period when violent moral tremors have shaken all of us and thrown every family into mourning. In recent years especially, the revolutions which bring in their wake horrible days of civil war; which arouse self-interest and incite the passions; which seem inevitably to summon the great endemic social ills after crises of anger and pain, after the banishment of some and the tears or the terror of others—these revolutions, which make major wars imminent, and which, following one after the other, destroy the souls of some and reap the lives of other, have set one half of France mourning the other half.

For my part, it is no longer by dozens but by hundreds that I count the bitter losses I have suffered in recent years. My heart is a cemetery. And if I do not feel myself drawn to the tomb which has already swallowed up half of my life in a kind of virulent whirlpool, it is because that half is peopled for me with so many beloved beings that it sometimes becomes confused with my present life to the point of deluding me. This delusion is not without a certain austere charm, and my thoughts now converse as often with the dead as with living.

Sacred promise of heaven where we shall find and recognize one another again, you are not a vain dream! If we cannot aspire to the pure bliss of those spirits who visit our land of chimeras; if we must always foresee beyond this life work, duty, hardships and a time-bound body, at least our reason permits, and our heart suggests, that we may expect an evolution of human progress by virtue of our good intent. The saints of all religions, who cry out to us from the far reaches of antiquity, to separate ourselves from matter in order to elevate ourselves up through the celestial heirarchy of spirits, have not misled us as to the essentials of faith admissible to modern reason. Today we believe that immortality results from the condition that we constantly take on new organs to extend our being, which is probably denied the right to become pure spirit; but we may consider this earth a place of passage, and count on a more gentle awakening in the cradle that awaits us elsewhere. From world to world, we can, by disengaging ourselves from the bestiality which opposes our spirituality here on earth, prepare ourselves to assume a purer body, more appropriate to the needs of the soul, less battered and shackled by the infirmities of our present life. And certainly the first of our legitimate aspirations, since it is a noble one, is to retain in that future life the power to remember, to a certain extent, our preceding existence. It would not be very pleasant to recall every detail, all the worries, all the pain. As for this life, memory is often a nightmare, but to remember the purifying highpoints of the ordeals through which we triumphed would be a reward, and the heavenly crown would be to embrace our friends, recognized by us and recognizing us in return. Oh, the hours of supreme joy and ineffable emotion when a mother reclaims her child and when friends reclaim the objects of their love! Let us love each other in this world, those of us who are still here; let us love each other truly enough to be allowed to find each other again on the shores of eternity, with the ecstasy of a family reunited after a lengthy pilgrimage.

During the years whose principal events I have just retraced, I locked away in my breast other even more poignant sorrows, whose revelation, assuming I could speak of them, would have served no useful purpose in this book. These misfortunes were, so to speak, outside my life, since no influence on my part could have averted them, and since I personally was not responsible for bringing them within my sphere. In certain respects, we create our own lives; in other respects, we endure the one others subject us to. I have recounted, or alluded to everything that touched my existence through my own choices, or everything that found its way there drawn by my instincts. I have told how I passed through and submitted to the various necessities of my temperament. This is all I wanted to say and all I ought to have said. As for the afflictions that other temperaments have necessarily visited on me, that is the role of secret martyr we are all forced to play, whether in public or private life, and that we must endure in silence.

The things I have not recounted, then, are those that I could not excuse, because I could not yet explain them to myself. In every affectionate relationship where I erred, however slight my wrongs appeared to me, they were sufficient to help me understand and forgive those who behaved similarly toward me. But in those cases where my unbounded devotion was suddenly repaid with ingratitude or aversion, where my tenderest concern found itself powerless before an implacable object, in no way understanding those formidable mishaps of life, not wanting to blame God, and sensing that the bewilderment and social disillusionment of this century were primary causes, I fell back on my submission to heaven's decree; otherwise, I would have had to curse or repudiate it.

This is when the terrible question always returns: Why did God, when making man perfectible and capable of understanding the beautiful and the good, make him so slow to reach perfection, so problematically attached to the good and the beautiful?

Supreme wisdom answers us through the mouths of all the philosophers, "This slowness from which you suffer is not perceptible in the immense duration of the laws of the universe. He who lives in eternity has no need to measure time, but you whose notion of eternity is dim are overwhelmed by time's poignant pressures."

Yes, without doubt, the succession of our bitter and unsettled days oppresses us and, in spite of ourselves, diverts our minds from the contemplation of eternity. Do not be too ashamed of that weakness. It has its source in the depths of our sensibilities. Considering our troubled society and our civilization in travail, this sensibility and its weakness are perhaps our greatest strength. They provide the heartbreaks and also the ethics of our lives. He who receives the blows that befall him with perfect strength and calm has not found true wisdom, for he has no reason not to regard with the same disdainful stoicism the wounds which make his brothers bleed and cry. Let us suffer, then, and let us complain when our complaint can be useful; when it cannot, let us keep silent, but let us inwardly weep. God Himself, who sees our tears unknown to us, and who, in His immutable serenity, seems not to notice, created us with this capacity to suffer, in order to teach us to lose the desire to make others suffer.

Just as the physical world in which we live formed and fertilized itself through the influence of volcanos and rains until it became appropriate for the use of man, the moral world in which we suffer forms and fertilizes itself through the influence of burning ideals and saintly tears until it is worthy to serve our needs. Our days are consumed and fade away in the midst of such torments. If we feel deprived of hope and confidence, they seem frightening and sterile, but illuminated by faith in God and warmed by love of humanity, they become acceptable—even bitter-sweet.

Sustained by these notions, which are so simple and yet so slowly acquired with real conviction, for in my youth the strivings of my sense of justice were hindered by excessive sensitivity, I pass through the end of this period of my story without too greatly deviating from my conscious choice to give up my self-concern. Whenever I discovered it anew, grumbling within me, disturbed over little things and too eager for repose, I at least knew how to give it up again without great effort, as soon as a clear occasion to do so in a useful way rendered me the lucid use of my inner strength. If I was not possessed of virtue, at least I was, and still am, I hope, on the path that leads to it. Not being flawless, I am not writing for saints. But those who, like me, lacking but infatuated with a fond ideal, want to pass through the brambles of life without leaving their whole fleece behind, may find help in my humble experience, and some consolation in seeing that their sorrows are like those of one who feels, remembers, and recounts, and who calls to them: "Let's help one another not to despair."

And yet, this century—this sad, great century in which we live—seems to be adrift; it veers on the edge of the abyss, and I hear voices ask, "Where are we going? You, who keep looking toward the horizon, what do you see there? Are we in a rising, or falling, tide? Will we come to rest in the Promised Land, or be drawn into the vortex of chaos?"

I have no answer to these cries of distress. I am not informed by prophetic light, and the cleverest reasoners—those who systematically take into account the odds of politics, economics, and trade—always find themselves thwarted by the unexpected, because the unexpected is the benevolent or destructive genius of mankind, which at times sacrifices its material interest in favor of its moral greatness, and at other times its moral greatness in favor of its material interest.

It is quite true that jealous, uneasy concern for material interests dominates the present state of things. After major crises, such preoccupations are natural, and the motto of threatened individuality—every man for himself—if not glorious, is at least understandable. Let us not be too irritated by it, for everything that does not have a feeling of collective providence as its object fits, nonetheless, in the scheme of that providence. It is obvious that the worker who says, "Work above all and despite all," is yielding to the necessities of the moment and is considering only the moment in which he is living; but through his willingness to work he furthers the notions of dignity and independence. And so it is with all workers at all levels of society. Industrialism tends to free itself from all kinds of servitude and transform itself into a positive force, reserving the right later to moralize and establish itself as a legitimate force through fraternal association.

That is the moment we have anticipated and when we wonder if, after the ephemeral blaze of glory of the last thrones, the nations of Europe will become aristocratic or democratic republics. There appears the abyss—a general conflagration or separate struggles at all points. When you have breathed the atmosphere of Rome for only an hour, you see that cornerstone of the great edifice of the Old World so ready to be dislodged that you can almost feel the quake of volcanic, human earth.

But what will be the outcome? Over what hot lava or polluted mud shall we have to make our paths? But why torment ourselves? Humanity tends to seek its own level; it wants to, it has to, it shall. God helps us, and always will, through invisible action which is always the product of those properties of human strength and divine ideal that humanity is permitted to glimpse. That formidable mishaps will impede our efforts, alas! is to be expected, to be accepted in advance. Why not envisage life in general the way we view our individual lives? A great deal of fatigue and suffering, a little hope and goodness. Doesn't the life of a century sum up the life of a man? Which of us has managed to succeed, once and for all, in fully realizing our good or evil desires?

Let us not seek, like ineffectual augurs, the key to human destiny in a particular ordering of facts. Such searches are in vain; our commentaries are useless. I do not believe that augury should be the aim of the sages of our era. What they ought to seek is to illuminate their reason, to study the social problem, and to vivify themselves through this study while making it prevail through some lofty and sublime sentiment. Oh, Louis Blanc, your life's work should often pass before our eyes! In the midst of days of crises that make you an exile and a martyr, you seek in the history of the men of our time the spirit and will of Providence. More capable than all the others of explaining the causes of revolutions, you are more capable still of grasping and explaining their goal. There lies the power of your eloquence. There lies the sacred fire of your art. Your writings are of the sort that one reads in order to learn facts, and that force one to master those facts by inspiring one with a sense of justice and enthusiasm for the eternally true.

And you as well, Henri Martin, Edgar Quinet, Michelet, you lift our hearts as soon as you place the historical facts before our eyes. You do not touch the past without availing us of the thoughts that should guide us in the future.

And you, Lamartine, as well. Although, by our lights, you are too tied to civilizations that have had their day, you scatter those flowers of civilization on our future through your charm and abundant genius.

For each to prepare himself for the future, is, therefore, the work of men whom the present prevents from preparing in common. Initiation to public life is doubtless quicker under the reign of freedom; the impassioned or peaceful discussions in a group and the mild or fiery exchanges of emotions in a forum enlighten the masses quickly; occasionally they mislead them, but nations are not lost because they gather and meditate, just as the education of societies continues no matter what the politics of the time.

In summary, the century is great, albeit sick, and if the men of today are not doing such great things as at the end of the last century, they are conceiving and ably preparing for still greater things. They already feel deeply that they must.

And you and I, reader, have our moments of defeat and despair, when it seems to us that the world marches onward in folly to worship the gods of the Roman decadence. But if we examine our hearts, we find them as full of innocence and charity as in the early days of our childhood. Then, let us all look into ourselves, and let us tell one another that it is not our business to discover the secrets of heaven in the pageant of ages past, but rather to keep those secrets from dying fruitless in our souls. *S.A.H.*

Conclusion

I had had no happiness in that entire phase of my existence. There is no happiness for anyone. This world was not created for permanent satisfactions of any kind.

I had had moments of happiness, that is to say delights, in maternal love, in friendship, in reflection, and in reverie. These were quite enough to thank God for. I had tasted the only sweets I could have craved.

When I started to write the account that I leave off here, I had just been filled to brimming by pain deeper than could be told. However, I was calm and mistress of my will in the sense that, with memories crowding before me under a thousand shapes that could vary according to how I esteemed them, I felt my conscience sane enough and my religion stable enough to help me seize the veritable hour in which the past would reveal itself to me.

Now that the final page of the story of my life is in view, more than seven years after I penned the first page, I am again undergoing unbearable personal suffering.

My life—twice deeply disrupted, in 1847 and again in 1855—has refused the lure of the grave; and my heart—twice broken, a hundred times aggrieved—has refused the dread poison of doubt.

Shall I attribute these victories of faith to my own reasoning or will-power? No, there is nothing strong in me except the need to love.

But I did receive help, and I did not disregard it, I did not refuse it. This help God sent me, but it was not made manifest through miracles. Poor humans, we do not deserve them; we would not be equal to them; our weak minds fail us if we merely imagine the faces of angels in the flaming nimbus of Divinity. But grace came to me, as it comes to all, as it can and should come, through the exchange and refinement of truths. Leibnitz first, then Lamennais, then Lessing, then Herder explicated by Quinet,[100] then Pierre Leroux, then Jean Reynaud, then Leibnitz again—those are the main markers that stopped me from drifting too far in my various attempts at philosophy. From these luminaries I did not absorb everything in equal doses, nor have I even retained everything I absorbed. The proof is that, given a distance from the various stages of my inner life, I have been able to create for myself a fusion of these great sources of truth, searching ceaselessly and imagining sometimes to have found the place where they are united, in spite of the lacunae that separate them. One belief made wholly of sublime sentiment—the doctrine of Jesus—summarizes further their essential points, notwithstanding the gap of centuries. The more we examine the great philosophical revelations, the more our minds may be enlightened by the heavenly revelations of our hearts when we examine the evangelical doctrine.

This is perhaps not a very advanced conception in the opinion of my century. The times are not going in that direction for the moment. No matter, the day will come.

Earth of Pierre Leroux, Heaven of Jean Reynaud, Universe of Leibnitz, Charity of Lamennais, you all mount together toward the godhead of Jesus; and whoever reads you without exaggerating the subtleties of metaphysics and without being steeled in the armor of argument will emerge from your radiance more lucid, loving, and wise. The help of each master's wisdom comes at the right moment in this world where there is no definitive conclusion. When, with the youth of my time, I shook the keystone of the mysteries, Lamennais aptly came to shore up the sacred parts of the temple. When, indignant after the September Laws, we were again ready to overturn the sanctuary, Leroux came—eloquent, ingenious—to promise us the reign of heaven on the very earth we cursed. And in our time, as we still despair, the already great Reynaud has raised himself to even greater heights to extend to us, in the name of science and faith, in the name of Leibnitz and Jesus, the concept of an infinity of worlds as a homeland that beckons us.

I have said that the help of God has sustained me as the intermediary of the teachings of genius; I wish to add, in ending, the equally divine help sent to me as the intermediary of the heart's affections.

Be blessed filial friendship, friendship of my son, who has responded to every fiber of my maternal feeling; be blessed hearts tested by common suffering, who have each day rendered more dear the task of living for you and with you!

Be blessed also, poor angel torn from my breast and ravished by death to my endless torment. Adored child,[20] you have gone to rejoin Georges, adored by Marie Dorval, in the heaven of love. Marie died of her pain, while I remain standing, alas!

Alas, and thanks, my God! Since my pain is the crucible where love is purified, and since I am truly loved by a few, I can still refuse to falter on the road where charity to all commands us to walk.

June 14, 1855.

T.J./A.S.

Author's Notes

Part One

Chapter i

(1) This first part of the work was written in 1847.

(2) One would have called it "sensibility" in the last century, "charity" prior to that, and "fraternity" fifty years ago.

(3) Here are the facts as I have found them in my grandmother's notes: "Franceuil, my husband, said one day to Jean-Jacques, 'Let's go to the Français, shall we?' 'Let's go,' said Rousseau. 'That's always good for yawning away an hour or two.' This was perhaps the only witty rejoinder he made in his life, and not enormously witty at that. Perhaps it was the same night that Rousseau stole three livres, ten sous from my husband. It has always seemed to us that there had been affectation in his showing off this swindle; Franceuil had no recollection of it, and it even occurred to him that Rousseau had invented it in order to show the sensitivity of his conscience and prevent us from suspecting those crimes to which he did not confess. Besides, Jean-Jacques, if it had been the case, you would have to crack your whip a bit harder today to make our ears stand up!"

(4) It appears that this prodigious tale is really most ordinary, for since I have written this volume, we⁶ have seen other examples. A brood of redstarts, raised by us and hardly beginning to know how to feed, nourished tenderly all the little birds of its kind that we placed in the same cage.

Chapter ii

(5) Here is the rather curious anecdote as told by Voltaire in *Histoire de Charles XII*: " . . . Augustus preferred to accept harsh conditions from a conqueror rather than from his subjects. He decided to sue for peace with the King of Sweden, and wanted to enter into a secret treaty with him. He was obliged not to divulge this course of action to the Senate, whom he regarded as a still more intractable foe. It was a ticklish affair, so he relied on the services of the Countess von Königsmarck, a Swedish lady of high birth to whom he was then attached. It is she whose brother met an untimely death, and whose son commanded the French armies with singular success to the glory of France. This woman, celebrated in European society for her wit and beauty, was more capable than any minister of bringing a negotiation to a successful conclusion. Besides, since she owned some property in Charles XII's realm and had long been a member of his court, she had a plausible pretext for venturing to find this prince. She therefore came to the Swedish camp in Lithuania, and first approached Count Piper, who thoughtlessly promised her an audience with his master. Among the achievements that made the

Countess one of the most delightful persons in Europe was her special gift for speaking the languages of several countries she had never visited, with as much elegance as though she were a native. She would even amuse herself sometimes by writing French poetry which might have been mistaken for that of someone born at Versailles. She composed one for Charles XII that ought not go unmentioned in our story. She began by introducing the gods of antiquity, who all praised the king's virtues, and ended with these lines:

> At last each god on proclaiming his glory,
> Did grant him prior place in the temple of Mem'ry;
> Yet Venus and Bacchus said not a word.

This fine wit and charm were wasted on a man such as the King of Sweden. He steadfastly refused to see her. So, she decided to intercept him on the road during one of his frequent excursions on horseback. She actually did encounter him one day on a very narrow lane, and thereupon alighted from her carriage. The king bowed to her without a word, turned his horse around, and rode off in the direction from whence he had come. As a result, the Countess von Königsmark only obtained from her journey the satisfaction of knowing that the King of Sweden feared no one but her."

(6) Her real name was Marie Rinteau, and her sister's name was Geneviève. The name they went by, Mlles. Verrières, was assumed.

(7) Extract from the *Collection de décisions nouvelles et de notions relatives à la jurisprudence actuelle*, by J. B. Denisart at Châtelet de Paris, Vol. III, p. 704, Paris, 1771.

(8) M. Antoine de Horn, Chevalier de Saint-Louis, King's Lieutenant for the Province of Schelestadt.

(9) The Dauphine died in 1767; my grandmother, therefore, was nineteen years old when she went to live with her mother.

(10) He was sending her his translation of *The Twelve Caesars* by Suetonius.

(11) It would appear that there was some opposition, but I don't know from what quarter, for they went to England to be married in the chapel of the French Embassy, and had their union ratified in Paris afterward.

(12) This work was hardly circulated. Mme. de Pompadour, patron of Montesquieu, persuaded M. Dupin to destroy his work, even though it was already printed and published. However, I happily own a copy. Without prejudice or family conceit, I can say it is a very fine work, a condensed critical analysis, which points out all the contradictions in *L' Esprit des lois*, and here and there offers much more penetrating insights on the formation of laws and moral codes of nations.

(13) I have made a slight error here which has been brought to my attention by my cousin, M. de Villeneuve, who inherited Chenonceaux and the legend of Mme. Dupin. Abbé de Saint-Pierre died in Paris very shortly after having taken gravely ill at Chenonceaux. (Note of 1850.)

(14) I write this in July 1847. Who knows whether, before these memoirs are published, a social upheaval will not have given rise to a great many very courageous thinkers?

Chapter iii

(15) Maurice-François-Élizabeth, born on January 13, 1778. His godfather was Marquis de Polignac.

(16) Here is a piece of information given to me by my cousin, René de Villeneuve: "The Lambert mansion was inhabited by our family and by a personal friend of Mme. Dupin de Chenonceaux, beautiful and charming Princesse de Rohan-Chabot. It was really a palace. In one night, M. de Chenonceaux, son of M. and Mme. Dupin, that ungrateful pupil of Jean-Jacques, married for only a little while to Mlle. de Rochechouart, lost seven hundred thousand francs gambling. The next day this debt of honor had to be paid. The Lambert mansion was mortgaged, and other items were sold. Out of those splendors, out of those celebrated paintings, all I have left is a very beautiful picture by Lesueur, depicting three muses, one of them playing the bass viol. He painted it twice, the other copy is at the Museum. M. de Chenonceaux, our great-uncle, and our grandfather, Francueil, spent seven to eight million in their time. My father, married to your father's sister, was at the same time the nephew of Mme. Dupin de Chenonceaux and her only heir. That is why I have been the owner of Chenonceaux for forty-nine years." Elsewhere I shall discuss with what devoted care and understanding for art M. and Mme. Villeneuve have preserved and restored this château, one of the masterpieces of the Renaissance.

(17) 1847.

(18) Here are the terms of this decree, whose purpose was to restore confidence by means of terror:
"First Article. —Any gold or silver metal, coined or uncoined, diamonds, jewels, gold and silver braid, and all other furniture or valuables which are or will be discovered hidden in the ground, in basements, in the interior of walls, in roof timbers, under flooring or paving stones, in fireplaces or chimneys, and other secret hiding places, are to be seized and confiscated for the benefit of the Republic.
"Article Two. —Any informant who brings about the discovery of objects of this nature will receive a twentieth of their value in promissory notes. . . .
"Article Six. —The gold and silver, china, jewels, and other effects of whatever nature shall be sent immediately with an inventory to the committee of city inspectors, who will without delay place the coined pieces in the national treasury and the silver in the Mint.
"Article Seven. —The jewels, furniture, and other effects shall be sold at auction, with all possible haste, by the same committee, who will put the receipts in the treasury and account for it at the national Convention." (23 Brumaire, year II [Nov. 13, 1793]).

(19) She had spent a large part of her voluntary retreat in this convent before marrying her second husband.

Chapter iv

(20) *L'Inconnu, roman inconnu* [*The Unknown Man: An Unknown Novel*] by Maurice Sand.

(21) This was M. Hékel, author of a work on diplomacy and international law. He visited my grandmother's house on a regular basis and had taken a great liking to young Maurice. The mount refers to Montagne Sainte-Geneviève.

(22) The Abbé de Beaumont, his uncle, son of the Duc de Bouillon and Mlle. Verrières.

(23) The lodging was on the ground floor. The man was standing in the street.

(24) *Le Devin du village* by J.-J. Rousseau. My grandfather did the recitatives.

(25) His mother's favorite dog.

(26) One might believe that such sentiments coming from a child who was a victim of the Revolution are a pretense designed to pass censorship and reassure the examiners of the worthiness of his mother's case, or to one day serve as mitigating evidence in a legal action. But it is nothing of the sort. These expressions are sincere and ingenuous. My father's entire life attests to this fact, and all his subsequent letters furnish further testimony of it. Besides, it is not surprising that a child brought up in the philosophical enlightenment of the eighteenth century should have maintained these principles during and after the Revolution. My grandmother also maintained them, as we shall see.

(27) Until this letter, he has signed Maurice. Here he assumes a family name; he may feel he is now a grown man because he studies battles, and dreams of his own.

(28) I have already mentioned that this friend from the mount was M. Hékel, a man of letters and one especially noted for the virtues of his heart and the sincerity of his opinions. But this pen name, "friend from the mount," which my father employed to identify him—apparently because M. de Hékel had been implicated by that time—does not at all mean he shared the political viewpoint of the "montagnards." Far from it, M. Hékel was a faithful partisan of the Royalist party. I have several of his letters which show him to be a pedantic, virtuous man, a fine talker but short on ideas. However, he showed great wit and ardor in his conversation, and my father always admired not only his character, but also his company, although nothing could have been more different than their way of looking at things and their way of living.

(29) This is a case of reactionary slander. Of all the terrorists, Robespierre was the most humane, the most opposed both by nature and conviction to the apparent necessity for the reign of Terror and its inevitable, systematic use of the death penalty. By now this has been proven conclusively, and in this respect, the testimony of M. de Lamartine cannot be challenged. The reaction on the part of those involved in 9 Thermidor is one of the most cowardly that history has recorded. This is again sufficiently proven. With but few exceptions, these instigators failed to exhibit any strength of mind nor any pang of conscience in sacrificing Robespierre. Most of them found him too weak and too merciful on the eve of his death, and afterward they attributed their own crimes to him in order to gain popularity. Let us once and for all be fair in our judgment and no longer be afraid to say it: Robespierre is the greatest figure of the Revolution and one of the greatest in history. This is not to say that he didn't have his faults, commit blunders, and was consequently guilty of crimes for which he can be reproached; carried along down that steep slope, he accepted the unfortunate theories of the moment, although he was vastly superior to the men who applied them. But in what stormy political career can history show us one *single* man innocent of some mortal sin against humanity? Would it be Richelieu, Caesar, Mahomet, Henry IV, Maréchal de Saxe, Peter the Great, etc., etc.? What great minister, prince, captain, lawmaker has not committed the most chilling deeds that shock one's conscience? Why then should Robespierre be the scapegoat for all the crimes committed or suffered by our unfortunate people during their hour of fatal conflict?

Chapter v

(30) 1847.

(31) Jourdan was then commander of the army at Sambre-et-Meuse; Moreau, of the army of the Rhine-and-Moselle. They fought on the Rhine against Archduke Charles. The fourth defeat of Jourdan, which ended the campaign, was glorious for our troops.

Chapter vi

(32) That is to say, "unravelled." This was an activity for girls or women, which consisted of picking out the gold from the silk, in order to sell it.

(33) The following is an extract from the list of births and baptisms in the Protestant parish registry at the Church of Saints-Côme-et-Damien in Goslar:"On October 28, 1696, a woman of rank who is not further identified gave birth to a son in the house of (the widow) R. Henry Christoph, the child being baptised the 30th of the same month, in the evening, in the house, by Archdeacon Mag. J. S. Alburg, and christened with the name of Mauritius. His godparents were Messrs. Doctor Trumph, R.N. Dusings, and R. Henry Winckel."

(34) By the general.

(35) That is, frowned on at court.

Chapter vii

(36) German thought goes further than ours. In action they remain behind. I believe their spirit has greater scope, their character less grandeur.

(37) I am writing at the beginning of 1848.

(38) M. Lamartine,[48] for all his pure intentions and wonderful talent, resolved nothing. He was a generous and sincere advocate of all parties. He in no way could, and perhaps in no way should, have come to a conclusion concerning this doctrine.

(39) If you want to know why they called the devil Hercules, consult the spirit of the times. He is the only god invoked by Robert's robbers.

(40) I shall speak elsewhere of M. Delatouche, to whom I owe such good advice and encouragement for my first steps in a literary career.

Chapter viii

(41) Abbé de Beaumont, his uncle.

(42) Montauciel, in the opera *Le Déserteur*, by Grétry.

(43) This Alphonse Fleury was exiled on December 2, for reasons of political

dissidence, after the most honorable and most generous conduct under the Republic. (Note of 1853.)

(44) This inlaid cabinet is the one which was broken open by Deschartres and my father in '93, in order to purloin the papers which could have spelled the death sentence for my grandmother. I still have this chest with its twenty-three pigeon holes, some of which still had until a short time ago traces of the sealing wax of the Republic. I learned of its identity only recently, upon discovering the report of the incident and my father's letter, above. Pieces of furniture have their own story, and if they could speak, what things they would tell us!

(45) The father of my childhood friend.

Chapter ix

(46) Count Durosnel, born in Paris and son of the chief clerk in the cavalry office of the war ministry. His taste for arms and his excellent education led him to advance rapidly in his military career. He was promoted successively through the ranks up to that of brigadier general, which he obtained December 24, 1805, for his fine conduct at Austerlitz. He distinguished himself equally well at Iena and led a courageous charge which proved very effective. After this success, he was sent to the Oder to intercept the convoys, in which he succeeded. He distinguished himself as well in the campaigns of 1807, 1808, and 1809 and was made a major general during the last of these campaigns, in which he was believed killed, but in which he was only wounded and taken prisoner. Named governor of Dresden after its capture in 1813, he remained there until the capitulation, and in 1815 was appointed by Bonaparte deputy commander of the Paris national guard, etc. (See *La Biographie moderne de 1815*.)

Chapter x

(47) We shall see later on that this feigned uncertainty on the general's part was a little "staged" by my father, who was planning to rejoin the war squadrons, and did not wish to be taken by the general outside the theater of operations of the ensuing conflict.

(48) He was deceiving her; he was forced to deceive her.

Chapter xi

(49) It is a saber surrounded with laurels, with the motto: "He wishes to earn them."

Chapter xiii

(50) 18 Brumaire.[73]

(51) The fort at Bard.

Chapter xiv

(52) "I find myself" is rather an understatement, considering that he was there without orders, without a horse, and *just for the fun of it.*

Part Two

Chapter i

(1) This was the moment of the negotiations between Cobentzel and Joseph Bonaparte at Lunéville. Bonaparte, wanting to obtain essential conditions, threatened to renew hostilities; Cobentzel held his ground, making some concessions, however, from time to time, in order to benefit from the winter, hoping that that season would arrest our troops.

Chapter ii

(2) Father of Alexandre Dumas.

(3) She was not mistaken, but she never knew it.

(4) It was the time when French roads were infested with all sorts of cutthroats, chauffeurs, Chouans [insurgent royalists in Brittany], deserters, cast-offs of all parties, but particularly of the Royalist party.

(5) Général Brune.

Chapter iv

(6) Dupont.

(7) Bonaparte was then in Lyon, presiding over the Italian negotiations.

(8) The most rarified society of the old regime. I have changed the initials and left out the first names, so it would be useless for the reader to try to find out to whom my father's criticisms should be applied.

(9) The widow of Général de La Marlière, who was involved in the Custine case, and went to the guillotine.

(10) I believe she is the same one who had been married to M. de Wismes, prefect of Angers, whose daughters went to the convent with me.

(11) Général Lejeune, painter of historical subjects. I have his lovely pencil drawing of my father, a very good likeness.

(12) That "very reliable" person lost or stole the shawl; it is true that my father did not "know" her.

(13) M. de Vitrolles told me that something unusual happened during this musical training, perhaps begun too late. Before he learned anything at all, my father had a head full of charming melodies, and his musical ideas overflowed. As soon as he acquired the knowledge needed to express them, his imagination cooled, and his natural genius left him without his realizing it.

(14) The tutor's honorarium and the maid's salary were in arrears since 1792.

(15) He was much mistaken about the income from Nohant.

(16) I think I can name them, seeing as his humor is not bitter.

(17) His mare.

(18) "The custom of the legate *a latere* is to have the golden cross carried in advance. This is a sign of the extraordinary power that the Holy See delegates to such representatives. Wishing, in accordance with the views of his court, that the exercise of the cult be as public and as visible as possible in France, Cardinal Caprara asked that, as customary, the golden cross be carried before him by an officer on horseback, dressed in red. But that spectacle was feared as too excessive for the Parisian people. A compromise was reached, and it was agreed that the cross would be carried in one of the carriages preceding the legate's." M. Thiers, *Histoire du Consulat et de l'Empire*, Vol. III, Book XIV.

(19) This narrative of my father cannot be accused of partiality. It conforms with history. The people were indifferent to this restoration of Catholic ritual. The army was hostile to it. The bourgeoisie made fun of it, as did the Voltairian members of the nobility.

(20) Apolline de Guibert and Laure de Ségur are the wives of René and Auguste de Villeneuve.

(21) Bonaparte had been proclaimed Consul for life.

(21a) My mother was among them. She had a broken rib, which explains my father's irritation.

Chapter v

(22) 1847.

(23) Louis-Phillippe; this was written in 1847.

Chapter vi

(24) Despite the natural good will and flexibility of his character, my father is experiencing growing constraint and antipathy toward his general. I would have eliminated his somewhat facetious comments, as I have those regarding many others whose portraits and critiques I have in hand, except for the fact that Général Dupont was a person history was to judge more severely later on than my father could do in 1801. By a strange coincidence, or rather by a natural consequence of the connections between

those in his circle, my father twice found himself associated with generals who were among the first to betray France in 1814—Harville and Dupont—one as general, the other as senator.

(24a) Miémié is Mlle. Roumier, the elderly nursemaid whom he loved so much. No sooner had she received her back wages than she wanted to return to live with her family. In spite of regrets on both sides, she went through with that resolution.

(25) Deschartres had become my grandmother's tenant farmer.

(26) Duc de Vicence.

(27) Ordener Senior was head of the consular guard in 1802.

(28) That happened notably in Zurich, during the 1799 campaign. The soldiers were rebelling because their pay was in arrears.

(29) Auguste de Villeneuve, his nephew.

(30) It would be useless for the reader to look for the names that these initials stand for. I am changing the initials on purpose, not wishing to "disturb" anyone needlessly.

(31) For all his apparent facetiousness, my father was a good judge of character. M. de Vitrolles is one of the rare *human beings* in the royalist party, indeed known for his wit and integrity.

(32) Mlle. Dupin, daughter from my grandfather's first marriage, had been married to M. de Villeneuve, and then made a second marriage with M. de Villeleroux.

Chapter vii

(33) M. Thiers affirms that the soldiers were very well housed in huts and that they had everything they needed. That must indeed have been Bonaparte's intention. But the facts do not always conform to the outlay of "cash" and to the plans on paper, which are the stuff of official history; if they did, we would have to reverse the proverb, "Soldiers die, records remain."

(34) Printed at the head of the letter.

(35) Bisson, the youngster of the troop, distinguished himself early because of his heroic bravura. In charge of defending Catelet on the Sambre with sixty grenadiers and fifty dragoons, attacked by six thousand men and seven cannon, he positioned his grenadiers as sharpshooters before the two main river crossings in advance of the bridge to the city, which he had had cut off, and his dragoons in three platoons on the right bank. When they saw the sharpshooters, the enemy thought there was a large army in place and started attacking in formation. However, Bisson was there all alone with two drummers stationed at different points, to foster the enemy's error. This maneuver gave Général Legrand time to arrive with a brigade and retain an advantageous position. At the Missenheim campaign, Bisson and four hundred seventeen men held at bay three thousand infantry and twelve hundred horsemen. He distinguished himself at Marengo, etc., and died in Mantua in 1811.

Chapter viii

(36) I am writing this on June 2, 1848, ignorant as to what the outcome will be of the plan presented at the National Assembly by Minister Crémieux.

(37) Meaning Sophie.

(38) I don't know what happened to my great-uncle's melodrama; I don't even know what it was called.

(39) My uncle by recent marriage to my Aunt Lucie.

Chapter ix

(40) At the ceremony of the Condordat, they did not dare display this cross and this pedant to the people of Paris. They put them into a carriage; this had been the subject of a serious discussion between the First Consul and the papal legate, so "popular" was the Catholic restoration. At the coronation, the cross so visibly carried raised not a murmur, but the bearer caused much laughter because of his obesity.

(41) Twelve years later, I again saw at my Great-Uncle Beaumont's this same Marquis de Seulé, in every way similar to the portrait my father draws, and still dressed as before the Revolution; he was a type. At eighty years of age he was still frisky and a flirt. He would strike a pose and then look at people's expressions to see if they were noticing the shape of his leg. His wore sequined jackets and still composed quatrains.

(42) That of the Dauphin, father of Louis XVI.

(43) Marmontel was mistaken, since an official decree had been needed to rectify this document.

(44) This Mme. de Chalut, who had been Mlle. Varanchon, favorite lady in waiting of the first and second Dauphines, was married under the latter's auspices, and her husband was named farmer general. She, along with the Marquis de Polignac, held my father at the baptismal font.

(45) I wear this ring all the time.

Chapter x

(46) During this glorious affair, the Austrians had plundered the baggage of the Dupont division at Albeck, collecting, as writes M. Thiers, some vulgar trophies, sad consolation for a defeat of twenty-five thousand men fighting against six thousand.

(47) At that time he also received the Cross of the Legion of Honor.

(48) The three children were Caroline, myself, and a son born in 1806, who did not survive. I have no recollection of him.[38]

(48a) *Histoire de Napoléon,* by M. Élias Regnault.

Chapter xiii

(49) To capture the right sound, one would have to change a letter and pronounce it *orbluces*.

Chapter xiv

(50) 1848.

Chapter xv

(51) If carried to an extreme, this point of view would, of course, be open to question. At present, we are seeing the emergence of the school of Realism, which will be a step forward if it does not exceed its purpose and become too systematic. But in the works I have read, those of M. Champfleury,[55] among others, the realism is still sufficiently poeticized so as not to contradict the theory I outline above. I am glad for this opportunity to mention that I find M. Champfleury's style ravishing, realistic or not. (Note of 1854.)

Part Three

Chapter ii

(1) And almost all of them are, I am happy to say.

(2) Since then, I have made an observation that unfortunately seems true: most women cheat at cards and are dishonest in business. I have observed these tendencies in wealthy, pious, respected women. I cannot help but mention this, because it is true, and to point out an evil is to combat it. Does the tendency toward duplicity, which can be seen even in young girls who play cards for no money, stem from an innate need to deceive or from a nervous unwillingness to submit to the laws of chance? Doesn't it rather grow out of an incomplete moral education? The world has a double standard of honor: honor for men depends on physical bravery and reliability in money transactions; honor for women depends only on modesty and marital fidelity. If I were to take the liberty here to tell men that a little chastity and fidelity would not harm them, they would certainly shrug their shoulders. But would they deny that an honorable woman who is at the same time as honorable as a man would doubly merit their respect and confidence?

(3) Mme. de Pardaillan was the friend of the dowager Duchesse d'Orléans.

Chapter iii

(4) 1848.[7]

(5) The Berrichon likes reflexive verbs. He will say, "That man doesn't know what he wishes *himself*, he doesn't know what to make *himself*, or invent *himself*."

Chapter iv

(6) *Aveuglat* is a sort of blind man's bluff. *Cob* and *évalines* are ways of playing with knuckle-bones using a large marble. *Traîne-balin* is, I believe, called *petits pac-quets* in Paris. *Marelle* [hopscotch] must be known in a number of provinces; it is explained in Esmangard's notes to *Gargantua*. A serious antiquarian from Berry has gone to the trouble of composing a work on the etymology of the word *évaline*. He has not made so bold as to do the same for *cob*. It was doubtless all becoming too arduous and grave.

Chapter v

(7) I believe it was *La Mort d'Abel*, whose author I do not recall.

Chapter vii

(8) Baron Pétiet has asked me to rectify some lapses in memory concerning his career. I have confused him with his brother, the general, who is at present a deputy in the Legislative Assembly. The one who was Général Colbert's aide-de-camp and broth-er-in-law in 1815, was only twenty-one at the time; he had been first page to the Emper-or, seen action, and had already been wounded six times. He left the service in 1830.

Chapter viii

(9) I have no doubt that my grandmother would have come up with better rea-sons, had her moral and intellectual powers still been in full force. She certainly must have taken care of the formation of my father's character more efficiently. But no mat-ter how much I search my memory for a trace of her truly philosophical teaching, I can-not find it. I think I can affirm that, during one phase of her life, prior to the Revolu-tion, she had preferred Rousseau to Voltaire, but the older she grew, the more Voltairian she became. It was inevitable that the spirit of bigotry prevalent during the Restoration pushed this reaction to its extreme in the philosophical intellects dating from the pre-ceding century. Well, we know how poorly grounded and lacking in morality is Voltaire's philosophy of history.

(10) There were, among other metaphors, a moon which "tilled the clouds, seated in her silver skiff."

(11) Nor is that attraction to mystery a phenomenon peculiar to me. Let all moth-ers recall their own childhood, which they forget when raising their daughters. The condition of soul-searching is inherent to childhood and especially to girlhood. That tendency must neither be brutally thwarted nor allowed to develop too far. I have seen mothers so insensitive and jealous in their surveillance that they always suspected some impurity in their daughter's chaste daydreams and threw stones and filth into that pure and quiet lake which as yet only reflected heaven. I have seen others who let it be mud-died from the outside, without suspecting a thing. It is certainly difficult, at times

almost impossible, to see to the bottom of those still waters, and for this very reason they deserve our constant attention.

(12) He became even more fantastic when he recited the swineherd's song—a strange chant that must have gone back to antiquity, like those of the herdsmen of our country. It would be impossible to translate it musically, because it is a series of phrases of bizarre intonation, without any fixed rhythm, broken up with a mixture of shouts and herd calls that form connections between them. It is sad, jeering, and in essence as frightening as the Sabbath of the Gallic divinities. Like all the songs preserved through oral tradition, there are an infinite number of versions, which are modified at the herder's whim, but always keeping their primitive coloring. Most often the words are improvised. However, one always hears them come back to these three hallowed lines:

> When the swine have acorns,
> The masters have money,
> The swineherds white bread....

And these:

> May death and the devil
> Carry off all pigs!
> The big and the little,
> The sow and the kids.

Elsewhere[22] I shall speak of the "Song of the Oxen," something superb and also from antiquity.

Chapter ix

(13) The *pastural* is one of the last vestiges of nomadic pastoral life, and exists almost nowhere else but in the central part of France. It is a vast enclosure abandoned to nature's caprices from time immemorial. Usually the soil is excellent and the clearing or farming of these lands would be very profitable, but farmer and sharecropper will not hear of it. They seem to think their cattle cannot prosper without that pasturage which is, nevertheless, very sparse and interferes with the locomotion of the livestock. Pasturals are large fields closed in by impenetrable hedges full of brushwood, with a cultivated hollow dug in one corner. One can study the original soil there, because these areas have probably never been cleared. They are virginal from the point of view of cultivation, and the vegetation, although abundant, does not develop past a certain point; the bushes remain low; briars and black brambles abound; the grass that grows there is neither luxuriant nor nourishing; the livestock thus do not even have the advantage of cool or shade. True, it is a means, in the absence of man-made pastures, of keeping the cattle outside all summer, night and day. Natural pastures are mowed late in the season; moreover, they must be left free from pasturing during one other part of the summer if one wants to have a second growth. But why does the peasant in our region prefer the *pastural* to the man-made pasture? Because it was his father's custom, and it would take too much effort to change it.

Chapter x

(14) I am told that some biased critics object to the frankness with which I speak of my relatives, particularly my mother. It is easy to object and I expected it. There are

always certain readers who misconstrue what they read—the kind who either cannot or will not understand the true morality of human affairs. Since I don't write for them, it would be useless to respond to them; their point of view is opposed to mine; but I ask those who do not automatically hate my work to reread this page and reflect on it. If there are among them a few who have suffered like me, for the same reasons, I believe I shall have calmed the anguish of their innermost doubts and healed their wound by an assessment superior to that of the champions of false morality.

Chapter xi

(15) The entire convent disappeared in the projects of urban renewal under the last Empire. Rue des Fossés-Saint-Victor, which, in relation to the high ground of the convent gardens, was a sort of moat, has been leveled. The community of English nuns was set up outside the walls of Paris. (Note of 1874.)

(16) She was given this title only in English.

Chapter xii

(17) 1848.

(18) He was the confessor of some of the resident pupils and nuns, but not mine. This Abbé de Villèle, brother of the Minister, has since become the Archbishop of Bourges.

Chapter xiii

(19) That is no reason not to remember the good deed he did since these lines were written. Sub-Prefect in Nérac, M. de Pompignan went down into a noxious mine-shaft, where no one else dared go, to bring up some poor asphyxiated workers. Twice he lost consciousness but went down again with renewed courage. Although successful in his efforts, he almost paid for his admirable bravery with his life.

Chapter xiv

(20) From time to time, the priests who said mass, sometimes in our chapel, other times in the Scottish chapel, brought with them some pious pupil who was proud to be altar boy. I remember having often seen, wearing the purple robe and white surplice, the brother of one of our most beautiful classmates. He, too, was one of the best-looking boys from the nearby school, the same one who was later known in society as "handsome Dorsay." I came to know him shortly before his death, at a time when he was filled with generous concern for political victims. Even on his death bed he was noble, generous Dorsay. His sister, Ida, who was as beautiful and kind, had already left the convent by the time I entered, but she often returned to see her old friends. She married the Comte de Guiche; she is now Duchesse de Grammont.

Part Four

Chapter i

(1) He may have been of English origin, as the name, Whitehead, would indicate.

Chapter ii

(2) Dormitory was the word not only for the communal bedroom of the lower class, but also for the long, dark, narrow corridors that separated the double rows of closed cells.

Chapter iii

(3) I later met the beautiful and truly angelic person referred to. She had married M. de Rochemur, her second husband. She recounted to me the entire story of her marriage to the Duc de Caylus. Ah! my cousin René, if you had only heard her describe the "perfect happiness" of her first marriage!

Chapter iv

(4) Translated by the Jesuit, Gonnelieu, 17—.

(5) At that time, I believed, as did many others, that Thomas à Kempis was the author of *L'Imitation*. The evidence furnished by Henri Martin on the legitimate authorship by Jean Gerson seems so conclusive to me now I do not hesitate to accept it.

(6) From Fontenelle's *Éloge de Leibnitz*

Chapter vi

(7) In one of these letters she recounts how Clary de Faudoas almost set fire to her cell when she was celebrating the birth of the little duke (Henri V) by burning candles. I cite this small fact as a historical marker [September 29, 1820] in my narrative.

Chapter vii

(8) In the first draft of the will, it had been fifteen hundred francs. He had had it reduced to one thousand after much insistence and even anger.

(9) Mlle. de Guibert and Mlle. de Ségur.

Chapter ix

(10) This part was written in 1853 and 1854.

Chapter xi

(11) The main market for cork is not in the form of bottle stoppers, which are made from scraps and waste. It is shipped off as sheets of bark, having been straightened and flattened, and is used to line every luxury accommodation in Russia, between the walls and the hangings. Hence it is a very expensive product since it grows within a very limited area.

Chapter xii

(12) A few years ago, I would willingly have allowed, as a future principle, a state religion that included freedom of discussion, with a set of rules for that discussion. I confess that I have since wavered in this belief. I have not really accepted, without inner reservations, the doctrine of absolute freedom, but I have found in the socialist works of Émile de Girardin[54] such a strong demonstration of the right to individual freedom that I still need to discover how freedom with regard to morality will escape its own excesses, if we grant to man, from earliest childhood, the right of absolute disbelief. When I say "discover," I am boasting. What can one discover all by oneself? Only skepticism. I should have said "to wait and see." Doubts are resolved over time, through the collective work of superior minds, and that work is always collective, in spite of apparent divergences. It is only a question of having patience until the light goes on. What slows it down a lot is the passionate pride with which we need to commit ourselves, in this world, to a particular form of the truth. It is good we have this passion, but it is also good that at certain times we have the honesty to say, "I don't know."

Chapter xiii

(13) Yes, it is the same thing. We may sometimes resist the duty of defending our rights by an unpremeditated act of generosity. I have often done this, perhaps through weakness, and the result has never been good for others. Impunity worsened their ill will and made them more guilty—consequently more unhappy. I would have been wiser coolly to ascertain how legitimate was the right in question, and find a means to be generous as well as fair.

(14) By Alfred de Bougy.

Chapter xiv

(15) Besides, sanctuaries conceal explosives in their own bosoms. I have since learned, on rereading these lines, that Sister Hélène broke with the convent a long time ago and went to live in England, taking Poulette with her; and Poulette—after fifty years of claustral life with the English, Poulette, so lively and beloved, Poulette who seemed the foundation and keystone of the monasterial arch—went to die far away, estranged from all the sisters, estranged from Hélène as well, whose quarrel she had taken up.

(16) She pretended that the original name had been O'Wen.

Chapter xv

(17) One more reason to speak about the living only with caution.

(18) *Le Figaro* was a small newspaper at the time, and did not have many subscribers. (Note of 1874.)

Part Five

Chapter i

(1) I believe it was in May 1832.

Chapter ii

(2) In pointing out this fact, I do not mean to say that compulsory charity is a social solution. This will be seen in a moment.

Chapter iii

(3) Géraldy, the singer, was in Venice during the same period, and suffered at the same time as Alfred de Musset from no less serious an illness. As for Léopold Robert, who settled there and blew his brains out not long after I left, I do not doubt that the Venetian atmosphere, too exciting for certain constitutions, did much to augment the depression that took hold of him. For some time I lived opposite the house he occupied, and I saw him pass every day in a boat he rowed himself. Dressed in a black velvet shirt and magistrate's cap, he brought to mind the painters of the Renaissance. His face was pale and sad, his voice rough and grating. I really wanted to see his painting of the Chioggian fishermen, which people spoke of as some mysterious marvel, for he kept it hidden with a kind of angry and bizarre possessiveness. Familiar with his hours, I would have been able to take advantage of his excursions to sneak into his studio, but I was told that, if he found out his landlady had been disloyal, he would lose his mind. I was thoughtful enough not to cause him a fit of temper, but this led me to conclude from what I heard from those who knew him that his was already an advanced case of madness.

(4) Alas! as I now reread this page, a third has left this world as well. My dear Malgache will not receive the flowers I have just picked for him in the Apennines.

Chapter v

(5) He wrote a handful more which posterity will no doubt carefully collect, among them a tract entitled *Questions sur le beau*.

Chapter vi

(6) *Salon de 1831*, by M. Gustave Planche, Paris, 1831.

Chapter viii

(7) For this narrative I shall confer on him the pseudonym, Éverard, that I used in *Lettres d'un voyageur*. It has always given me pleasure to rebaptize my friends with a name of my choosing, the origin of which I do not always remember.

Chapter ix

(8) This great man who was so misunderstood, so maligned in his lifetime, insulted even on his death-bed, by the pamphleteers, and borne to the common grave under the eyes of the police—as if the tears of the people could resurrect his body—this priest of God, crucified for sixty years, has, nevertheless, been buried with honor and reverence by writers in the serious press. When I have the honor of giving him a more complete tribute than that found in these pages, I shall certainly not be able to put it better than did Paulin Limayrac, and before him, some time before the death of the master, Alexandre Dumas. That chapter in the memoirs of the author of *Antony* is both excellent and lavish; it proves that genius can touch on everything, and that the prolific novelist, the dramatic and lyric poet, the witty critic, the artist full of fantasy and surprise—all the types that make up Alexandre Dumas—did not hinder the development of the philosophical writer in him, as was evidenced with equal power, when the opportunity presented itself.

Chapter xi

(9) Since that time, our relationship has been good. He came to Nohant for the marriage of my daughter.

Chapter xii

(10) That is how we should judge Lamartine.

(11) As I am correcting these proofs, I have been afflicted by a sad piece of news. Mme. de Girardin is dead. I saw her ill a month ago, but still radiating beauty, intelligence, grace, and kindness—because she was really and truly kind. We all knew of her genius, but only her friends knew of the delicacy of her affection, the exquisite strain of her motherliness, which her dramatic works have just revealed. I myself profoundly appreciated this. She wept with us over the most sorrowful of losses, the death of an adored child, and wept so instinctively, so emotionally—she who had never been a mother. It is not intelligence alone that reveals to a woman what mothers must suffer. It is the genius of tenderness; Mme. de Girardin had such genius to crown her admirable character.

(12) See *Un hiver dans le midi de l'Europe.*[87]

(13) I gave a definition of this distinction in *Consuelo.* This fully satisfied him and should, as a consequence, be clear.[88]

(14) It was at that time that I lost my friend Gaubert. In 1837, Papa Duris-Dufresne had already died grievously and tragically. He had dined with my husband the night before. "Someone from Châteauroux had met him at eleven in the morning, October 29. He was elated, for he was going to become a grandfather; he had just bought sugar almonds. After that, there is no trace of his movements. His body was found in the Seine. Was he murdered? There is no evidence of it. He had not been robbed. His gold earrings were still in place." (Letter from Malgache, 1837.) This deplorable end has remained a mystery. My brother, who had seen him two days earlier, had heard him say apropos of political events, "All is finished, all is lost!" He seemed deeply affected, but resilient and energetic; he had recovered his gaiety in a few minutes.

Chapter xiii

(15) This beautiful, sweet child was always a consoling angel for me. But despite her virtues and affection, she also caused me a great deal of sorrow. Her guardians fought me for her, although I had strong reasons for assuming exclusive responsibility of protecting her. Once she reached majority, she did not want to leave me. This led to an unspeakable battle and vile extortion on the part of people whom I shall not name. I was threatened with libel if I did not give them forty thousand francs. I let the libels appear—an infamous collection of ridiculous lies that the authorities chose to ban. Nor was this the most painful moment of martyrdom I ever underwent for that worthy and innocent child: there was a backlash of slanderous attacks on her, and to protect her against everyone, I was forced, more than once, to break my own heart and my fondest attachments.[91]

(16) Heinrich Heine has attributed to me some outrageous feelings against Dessaüer. Genius has its delusions.

(17) This was Lamennais' opinion as well: Silvio Pellico[97] was for him a model of resignation, which filled him with anger.

(18) That dearly beloved soul returned to God on January 20th, 1855.

(19) Gutmann, his most perfect student, today a true master himself, always a noble heart, was forced to be absent during Chopin's last illness, and returned only to hear his final sigh.

(20) Jeanne Clésinger, my granddaughter.

Editor's Notes

Part One

Chapter i

1. When France was declared a republic, in 1792, a new official calandar was created starting with Year I.

2. *Indiana*. [1832]

3. Louis XVIII was restored to the throne in 1814 and ruled until 1824, when his brother Charles X became king until he was overthrown in the revolution of 1830; each was therefore on the throne during the period of her life covered in the autobiography.

4. The kind of tennis referred to by Sand is not lawn, but court tennis, a royal game of ancient history, played indoors on a smaller court, walled and roofed, and with smaller rackets or, in former times, no rackets at all. The game reached its heyday in France in the sixteenth and seventeenth centuries; by the nineteenth century it had lost some of its popularity, witness the fact that courts were demolished to make way for other urban structures.

5. Georges-Louis de Buffon (1707–1788), French naturalist and writer.

6. GS uses the first person plural from time to time to refer to herself and members of her household.

Chapter ii

7. On the revolutionary calendar 9 Thermidor was equivalent to July 27, 1794, marking the end of the Terror after the fall of Robespierre.

8. Jean de La Harpe (1739–1803), French writer and critic.

9. *Le Devin du Village* is by J.-J. Rousseau; *Les Sauvages* was composed by Jean-Philippe Rameau (1683–1764); Grétry (1741–1813) was a French composer; Michel-Jean Sedaine (1719–1797) was a French playwright who parted with the classical tradition of writing tragedy or comedy; he wrote "dramas."

10. From Mozart's *Don Giovanni*, libretto by Abbé Da Ponte.

11. This activity is elucidated in I, vi.

12. (1651–1739), wealthy financier under Louis XIV and Louis XV.

13. Claude-Henri de Saint-Simon (1760–1825), French founder of socialism, he advocated equality of men and women on every level.

14. Pierre Bayle (1647–1706), erudite French writer whose enlightened point of view presaged that of Voltaire.

Chapter iii

15. Marie-Antoinette.

16. Jacques Necker (1732–1804), Swiss banker, served the French government, in 1777 and 1788, in financial reform. He was the father of Germaine Necker, later Mme. de Staël. Victor Mirabeau (1715–1789), was a French economist; his son, Honoré-Gabriel (1749–1791) was eloquent on behalf of the Revolution.

17. *Psalms*, 69:10,

18. GS is perhaps referring to this queen's tendency to free herself of court formalities as well as her habits of spending and socializing.

19. July 27-28, 1794; the fall of Robespierre.

Chapter iv

20. Jean-Sylvain Bailly (1736–1793), Mayor of Paris; Gilbert Motier, Marquis de La Fayette (1757–1834), in charge of the national guard. His name comes up again in IV, xv.

21. Louise Contat (1760–1813) often played the role of the coquette at the Comédie-Français.

22. GS does indeed mean her son Maurice (not her father), who was part of her household when she was writing her autobiography.

23. There have in fact been innumerable changes in her citations from these letters, as the notes of Georges Lubin, editor of the French edition, amply testify. Besides omissions of various kinds, GS often combines several letters under one date and sometimes alters the content to emphasize aspects of the persons involved and the themes. In general, the changes seem to have been made in order to augment and render consistent what is novelistic in the content. In a number of cases, such as Letter I, no original has been found.

24. It would seem that they had agreed to look at the Panthéon dome at the same time.

25. The gardener to whom Boileau dedicated Epistle xi; not to be confused with Mme. Dupin's footman, who will appear shortly.

26. Maurice's parody of La Fontaine, "The Tortoise and the Two Ducks," *Fables.*, Book x.

27. Inauguration of a new revolutionary cult marking the beginning of the Reign of Terror.

28. Source unknown. Perhaps the hero of a contemporary play.

29. Boileau, *Art poétique*, II, v, 149-50.

30. The fall of Robespierre and his followers.

Chapter v

31. This is, perhaps, how the grandmother was referred to in the legal documents.

32. A district in western France where a Royalist insurrection arose among the peasants and spread from 1793–1795; Palluau is a town in that area.

33. E. T. A. Hoffmann (1776–1822), German story writer and musician, known for tales of fantasy.

34. A five-person governing body, in power from 1795–1799, in accordance with the newly adopted constitution, which also stipulated a two-house legislature.

35. Virtuoso dancer and star of the Paris Opéra from his debut in 1772 until 1816.

36. Details of this coiffure will soon appear in one of Maurice's letters.

37. *Merveilleux* and *incroyable* were names given to those who wore very extreme costumes.

38. An allusion not to Rabelais' Panurge, but to a character in a contemporary opera by Grétry.

39. Character in Beaumarchais, *Le Mariage de Figaro*.

Chapter vi

40. Maurice de Saxe (1696–1750), illegitimate son of Augustus II of Saxony (King of Poland) and Aurora Königsmarck, a Swedish countess; known for his strength, bravery, and excessive style of living, he ultimately became a field marshal in the French army.

41. Baron de Grimm (1723–1807), man of letters and social critic, places the blame for the marshal's death on Mme. Favart (1727–1772), wife of the playwright, and a noted actress of the time.

42. A very popular French actress of the time (1692–1738), her salon was frequented by Voltaire and other notables of French letters. When mistress of Maurice de Saxe, she sold her jewels and plate to finance his ill-starred adventures as Duke of Courland.

Chapter vii

43. Paul Barras (1755–1829), member of the Convention, then of the Directoire.

44. A confederation founded by Duc de Guise in 1576 for the ostensible purpose of defending the Catholic church against Calvinists. The massacre of French protestants had occurred four years earlier, on the eve of St. Bartholomew's Day, Aug. 24, 1572.

45. Name given to that post-revolutionary group of Convention members who occupied the highest benches in the chamber and voted for the most extreme measures.

46. During the Reign of Terror, the former was responsible for the drownings at Nantes; the latter was purveyor of the guillotine.

47. Annual prizes for valor and literature awarded in the name of the eighteenth-century philanthropist, Baron de Montyon.

48. Alphonse Lamartine (1790–1869), French lyric poet who became active in republican politics and held office in the 1848 provisionary government.

49. Under the revolutionary calendar, every month was divided into three periods of ten days each known as *décades*.

50. Henri de La Tour d'Auvergne (1611–1675), known as Turenne, was a French field marshal whose bravery was reputedly matched by his modesty and reflective character. He was the ancestor of the M. de La Tour d'Auvergne (1748–1800) of whom Maurice speaks, illegitimately descended from his nephew; Maurice's subject was First Grenadier of France, was also famous for his bravery, and considered to be the epitome of the republican hero and patriot.

51. A card game now obsolete in which the object was to avoid winning tricks.

52. A military detachment whose reputation was so fierce that in 1793 they were able to capture fortifications in Spain without striking a blow.

Chapter viii

53. Maurice may be referring to a character in a contemporary play or opera which remains obscure to the editor.

54. Maurice's "flying bridge" would seem to defy current principles of engineering; however, rope or cable ferries do exist whereby a cable, supported by towers on each bank and suspended across the river, guides boats across the river by means of pulleys to which each boat attaches its own ropes from bow and stern. When the angle of the boat is adjusted via these ropes, the pressure of the current forces the boat across the river. (Courtesy of Herbert Beller, C.E.)

Chapter ix

55. Names of botanicals thought at the time to be helpful in treating kidney ailments.

56. *A great Dane* hardly seems a likely translation for *un grand danois*, as Maurice writes. This puzzling item is probably the fan Maurice refers to later.

57. Maurice is making reference to a scene in Beaumarchais, *Le Mariage de Figaro*.

Chapter x

58. Voltaire, *La Tactique*.

59. Under the Directoire, clothing fashions became extremely foppish and bizarre, giving rise to a series of names, such as *incroyable* and *merveilleux*, to describe those who wore them.

60. In Molière, *Les Précieuses ridicules*, Act I, Mascarille, his hand on the top button of his breeches, offers to show the two ladies his wound, but they decline.

61. An allusion to an opera of the time, music by Grétry, *Panurge dans l'île des lanternes*.

62. Franz II of Austria.

63. In Molière, *La Comtesse d'Escarbagnas*, a character named Tibaudier (not Thibaudier) makes a similar remark, implying that he is adept at both horsemanship and penmanship.

64. GS will soon explain the "misdeeds."

65. Source unknown.

66. A light-weight hunting carriage.

Chapter xi

67. To the spa at Néris.

68. In Grétry's opera, *Le Déserteur*.

69. The German system of *schlagen* [beating] had earlier been incorporated in French military training practice.

Chapter xii

70. *Le Caravane du Caire, où l'heureux esclavage*, an opera of the time, by Grétry.

71. Emigrés.

72. The last of the Roman Stoics.

Chapter xiii

73. The Directoire is overthrown and the Consulate established, with Napoléon as First Consul.

74. The coup d'état of the Directoire, August 1795.

75. An indulgent epicure, sixteenth-century creation of the poet Roger de Collerye.

76. Napoléon.

77. Reference to a play by Révéroni Saint-Cyr, *Élisa ou le voyage au Mont-Bernard*, with music by Chérubini.

Chapter xiv

78. Light, two-wheeled, one-horse carriages.

Part Two

Chapter i

1. GS has interpolated such veiled hints in anticipation of Maurice's coming relationship with Sophie, his wife-to-be, who makes her appearance in Letter VII in the next chapter.

2. Molière's bourgeois gentleman.

Chapter ii

3. Warrior of ancient Rome.

4. In his notes, GL provides a part omitted from Maurice's letter from which it is clear the latter was under the impression that the young woman in question was married to the division storekeeper, Collin, who had already seen active service in the early years of the Revolution as a brigade chief.

5. GL deems this phrase of GS an "acute exaggeration" considering that Maurice was a prisoner of war for only two months.

6. An example of a phrase that would seem to be of GS's creation, since it does not, as GL informs us, exist in the original.

Chapter iii

7. Collin.

8. Paul de Gondi, Cardinal de Retz (1613–1679), a French churchman whose interest in political and literary matters overrode his clerical ones.

Chapter iv

9. Maurice became the owner of a building on Rue de la Harpe, formerly a school, by way of settlement of the legal proceedings with his nephews.

10. The Belvedere is considered the most famous statue of Apollo, copy of an original Greek bronze; Antinoüs was a beautiful youth loved by the Roman Emperor Hadrian, commemorated in many statues that depict him as an ideal type.

11. Main character in a comedy-ballet of the same name, by Molière.

12. The notes of GL confirm the existence of three children as per a letter, in 1807, of Maurice to his wife.

13. From La Fontaine, *Fables, "The Wolf and the Dog."*

14. Masonic designations of rank.

15. Napoléon.

Chapter v

16. A hero from Tasso, *Jerusalem Delivered.*

Chapter vi

17. This reference is to the Royalist conspiracy, early in 1804, to assassinate Napoléon; young Duc d'Enghein was summarily tried and shot, though his connection with the conspiracy was never proven; the others were executed, except Moreau, who was banished.

18. Mme. de Guibert is René de Villeneuve's mother-in-law and, at this time, thought to be secretly married to Bertrand Barère, member of the National Convention; her first husband, whom she still appears to be mourning, had died in 1790.

19. Son of Josèphine prior to her marriage to Napoléon.

20. Their stepfather.

Chapter vii

21. Maurice is, as usual, making fun of his tutor; the possessive adjective *leur* does not change in the feminine.

22. Matter of a thirteenth-century tale of courtly love that the trouvères used to tell.

23. Grammarians.

24. The pedant in Molière, *Les Femmes Savantes.*

25. London.

26. She was born on 12 Messidor, or July 1, 1804, a correction she makes later.

27. See note 26.

Chapter viii

28. King of France from 1830 to 1848, he was at first supported by liberal factions whose increasing disillusionment culminated in the revolution of 1848, in which GS took an active part.

29. See note 26.

30. See note 26.

31. Or, July 1, 1804, by all lights the correct date.

32. Characters from Racine.

Chapter ix

33. Thus Nero confides his jealousy of Brittanicus in Racine's tragedy.

34. Unidentified.

35. Jean-François Marmontel (1723–1799), French writer of plays, fiction, moral tales, and social criticism.

36. GL informs us that no record of this has been found.

37. Prince Murat, brother-in-law of Napoléon and field marshal of France, will become Maurice's commanding officer in the Austrian and Spanish campaigns.

Chapter x

38. GL's notes state that inquiries regarding the existence of the son have been fruitless.

39. GS is relying on Regnault, *Histoire de Napoléon*, for this citation and the ones that follows.

Chapter xii

40. The child, Maria, frees the toy Nutcracker from his enchantment, and marries him, transformed as the fairy-tale prince.

41. Revolt by the Spanish people against their French invaders, which the French suppressed.

42. The Infanta, daughter of Charles IV and Maria Louisa.

43. Napoléon.

44. The governing minister of Spain, who was a favorite of King Charles, as well as the known lover of the Queen.

Chapter xiii

45. Etruria is the ancient name for Tuscany.

46. Ancient name for Portugal.

47. Godoy.

48. Identified in GL's notes as a fictive ambassador of King Merlin, from the fairy tales of Mme. Aulnoy.

49. The words "sentiment" and "sentimental" have positive connotations for GS, typical of her time, and are often used to refer to the "finer" human feelings such as empathy for others.

50. This kind of congenital malformation is known to the opthalmological profession. Dr. Nan Haworth informed the editor that, historically, doctors would try to displace the obscuring lens from the line of vision by applying pressure to the eye, a method known as "couching," which may elucidate the behavior of the Spanish doctor described in the coming chapter.

Chapter xiv

51. A spa in the Pyrenees, on the French side, where the prince would be going to "take the waters," cf. Maurice's coming reference to the waters of Nohant.

52. Where Jesus performed the miracle of turning water into wine. (*John* 2:1, 11; 4:46, 54; 21:2.)

53. See note 50.

Chapter xv

54. See Chapter LXXVI in the translation reprinted by Da Capo Press in 1979.

55. Jules Husson-Fleury, called Champfleury (1821–1889), French novelist and theoretician of Realism, with whom GS corresponded on the subject.

56. Jean-Gaspard Lavater (1741–1801), Swiss philosopher and theologian, proposed a theory of character analysis using a person's physical features.

57. GS continues this discussion in Part V, Chapter xiii.

58. Glück and Piccini were 18th-century composers who represented rival schools—the German and Neopolitan, respectively; Leo, Hasse, and Durante were their forerunners.

Part Three

Chapter i

1. Eugène Sue (1804–1857), French novelist and contemporary of GS, who also shared her concerns with regard to poor country folk.

Chapter ii

2. GS is reminded of Orgon's words of praise for Tartuffe, in Molière's play, Act I, Scene v.

3. A collection of caricatures by an illustrator who lived in Paris (1804–1866).

4. The notes of GL inform us that *Ma tante Aurore*, by Boieldieu, was a popular comic opera of the time.

5. Considering the description she goes on to give, GS would have more accurately called it "matriarchal."

6. This relationship has been referred to by Maurice in Part II, Chapter vi; also see note 18.

Chapter iii

7. GS is reminding the reader of the time of her writing.

8. According to GL's notes, Frederick Stapss, son of a German pastor, approached Napoléon, and was found to be armed with a kitchen knife; he was imprisoned and executed at the age of seventeen. Dominique Ernst Von Sahla, an eighteen-year-old Prussian prince, came to Paris bearing twelve pistols, in order to kill the emperor; released after three years in prison, he returned once more during Napoléon's coup of the Hundred Days, armed with explosives, but only wounded himself.

Chapter iv

9. These were manuals of sorcery and magic long popular among French peasants.

10. Name applied by ancient writers to the wooded mountain system in mid-Germany.

11. Daughter of Empress Josephine by a first marriage, Eugénie-Hortense became Queen of Holland when, at Napoléon's behest, she was married to his brother, Louis.

12. GS is referring to the events following the death of her grandmother in December 1821, when her mother came to dispute her guardianship with René de Villeneuve.

13. Declining battle, the Russians allowed the French to invade to the gates of Moscow, then set fire to that city, as ordered by the governor, Rostopchin.

Chapter v

14. Marie-Josèphe de Saxe, niece of the Maréchal de Saxe, had married the dauphin, Louis; Kings Louis XVI, Louis XVIII and Charles X were their sons.

Chapter vi

15. Devoted companion of Virgil's Aeneas.

16. One of Molière's sensible woman servants, this one from *Le Bourgeois gentilhomme*.

Chapter vii

17. Minister of Commerce and Finance under Louis XIV.

18. In contrast to the 1799 uprising in the Vendée, inspired by royalist sentiment.

19. Royalists.

20. Louis XVIII.

Chapter viii

21. *Essays*, Book I, Chapter xxvi, "On the Education of Children."

22. See the second prefatory chapter of *La Mare au Diable [The Devil's Pool]* [1846].

Chapter ix

23. "'And let fall some of the handfuls of purpose for her, and leave them that she may glean them, and rebuke her not.' And when she was risen up to glean, Boaz commanded his young men saying, 'Let her glean even among the sheaves and reproach her not.'" (*Ruth*, 2: 16–17.)

24. Sacred bull of the Egyptians, offspring of Osiris and Phtah.

25. La Fontaine, *Fables*, VII, 1, "The Animals Sick with the Plague."

26. Grammarians.

27. Possibly La Fontaine again, *Fables*, VI, 18, "The Carter in the Mire."

28. GS is referring to a series of articles she published in the early 1850's, under the title *Les Visions de la nuit dans les campagnes*.

29. Primarily in *La Mare au diable [The Devil's Pool]* [1846] and *Les Maîtres sonneurs [The Master Bagpipers]* [1853].

Chapter xii

30. Louis-Marie de Salgues de Lescure was in charge of the royalist forces who began the uprising in the Vendée. He was killed in battle with the republican forces, known as the Bleus, in 1793.

31. Royalist insurgents of Brittany and western France.

32. One of Louise's five sisters.

33. GS is referring to Louise's brother, Henri, whose political loyalties had shifted from monarchy, to republic, to empire.

34. One of the three Furies.

35. These remarks of the English girls are given here verbatim, as GS writes them in English.

Part Four

Chapter i

1. The Revolutionary government had abolished religious vows along with orders in 1790; Napoléon had reinstated certain charitable orders, limiting religious vows to a maximum of five years at a time.

Chapter ii

2. *Le Lutrin*, I, v, 12.

3. This comment of Sister Teresa is in English, to which GS adds a footnote for her French readers, giving the translation into French: "*Elle est dans ses vapeurs.*" A more current rendering into English might be: "She has her period."

4. Jules Michelet (1798–1874), historian and man of letters known for his vivid portrayal of the past. GS perhaps has in mind *Le prêtre, la femme, et la famille*.

5. *Matthew*, IV, 1-2.

6. GS is alluding to Phèdre describing the charms of Hippolyte, in Racine's tragedy, Act II, Sc. v.

7. See II, xvi.

8. GL's notes describe this as a fairy play in five acts, which was a huge success when first put on in 1839, thanks to its many magical transformations and tricks.

Chapter iii

9. A contemporary opera by Jean-Simon Mayr (1763–1846), starring the remarkable Italian soprano, Angelica Catalani (1780–1849), who for nearly thirty years sang at all the great opera houses. The reference in the next sentence is to the Italian singer, Filippo Galli (1783–1853).

10. Three 18th c. operas, the first two by Glück, the third by Sacchini.

11. Louis Carrogis, called Carmontelle (1717–1806), French artist and writer.

12. Named for an Italian revolutionary hero who had served in Napoléon's army and went on to fight for unification of Italy on various occasions.

Chapter iv

13. Eighteenth-century writers of romantic fiction.

14. A work by the forerunner of Romanticism, François-René de Chateaubriand (1768–1848), which explained Christianity by way of its instinctive appeal to the emotions and senses as the most poetical of religions, hence the most favorable to art.

15. Jean Gerson (1363–1429), French theologian and scholar, Chancellor of the University of Paris hence strongly influential with the Popes of Rome and Avignon, by which power he directed the trial against Jan Huss for the murder of the Duc d'Orléans. His intention was to simplify theology by a return to the Scriptures, along with a de-emphasis of art and romance. His authorship of the work from which GS quotes is disputed.

16. Blaise Pascal (1623–1662), French mathematician and scientist, wrote a series of letters, *Les Provinciales*, in defense of the Jansenist Antoine Arnauld, who had attacked the Jesuits for minimizing the evangelical spirit of Catholicism by their emphasis on reason, self-sufficiency, and ceremony. Though his letters did not save Arnauld from exile, Pascal's literary efforts were admired for their technique of using the words of the Jesuits themselves, including those of Escobar, to dispute them.

17. Gabriell Bonnot de Mably (1709–1785), French political philosopher whose theories were influential on such revolutionaries as Marat and Babeuf.

18. Gottfried Leibnitz (1646–1716), German metaphysician who attempted to resolve the problem of the relationship between mind and body through his theory of the "monad," which consitutes every entity, and "pre-established harmony," which accounts for the relationships between monads. GS will shortly be referring to the preface to his *Essais de Théodicée sur la bonté de Dieu, la liberté de l'homme et l'origine du mal.*

19. Fontenelle (1657–1757), Frenchman of letters, who wrote his eulogy to Leibnitz in 1722.

Chapter v

20. Louise d'Épinay (1726–1783), French woman writer unusually educated and liberated for her time, left more of a mark on history through her friendships with such eighteenth-century men of letters as Rousseau, Diderot, Voltaire, and Baron Von Grimm than through her writing. The correspondence here referred to is in her three volumes of *Mémoirs et Correspondance*.

21. The young man was Stéphane Ajasson de Grandsagne. According to the notes of GL, all evidence points to an intimate friendship between Aurore and Stéphane in 1820-21, and to his later being father of her second child.

22. Jean de La Bruyère (1645–1696), French moralist noted for the incisive and lively picture of his time contained in *Caractères*.

23. Nicolas de Malbranche (1638–1715), French metaphysician who founded a theory of moral behavior on the idea of order, in *Recherche de la vérité*.

24. GS has had recourse, in Part III, Chapter ii, to this expression by which Molière has Orgon describe Tartuffe (Act I, Sc. v).

25. The first and third citations are from *Matthew* 18:6 and 10:16-23, respectively; the second from *John* 8:7.

Chapter vi

26. The first edition of *Le Génie* (1802) contained the romantic piece of fiction, *René*, which Chateaubriand intended as an illustration of *Le Génie*'s chapter on the emptiness of passion; based on the author's own melancholy adolescence, the character René embodies the tortured soul whose abundant and powerful passions he knows in advance will never be satisfied and whose knowledge of the impossibility of happiness in reaching any ideal leads him to thoughts of suicide.

27. Gilbert and Millevoie were French 18th century poets; Edward Young was their English predecessor.

28. GS again voiced her attraction to the melancholy Jacques of *As You Like It*, whom she likened to Molière's misanthrope, Alceste, when she adapted that play for a French audience, in 1854.

29. GL's notes inform us that, as in the letters of her father previously presented, GS has taken the liberty of partially rewriting them. From the example he gives in his notes, it would seem that her purpose has been to unify and polish the style, as well as elaborate on details, rather than censor the content.

30. A tale based on the heroic captain, by the name of Gaston de Foix, who fought in the army of Louis XII and was killed in battle in 1512.

Chapter vii

31. There would indeed have been a noticeable contrast between the chatty, eighteenth-century French poetry of Gresset and the somber, impressionistic poems of MacPherson, who invented the persona of Ossian, a third-century Scottish bard.

32. GS is referring to the court of Louis XVIII, who, the reader will recall, became king in 1814, after Tallyrand had paved the way following the fall of Napoléon.

Chapter viii

33. Charles-Victor d'Arlincourt (1788–1856), prolific French writer of pseudo historical novels and romances.

34. Lazare Carnot (1753–1823), exiled under the new monarchy, had been

Minister of War under Napoléon, though he remained committed to republican ideals, which he had already served as a member of the Convention.

Chapter ix

35. Giuditta Négri (1797–1865), renowned Italian singer; when staying in Venice in 1834, GS will recognize her again (See V, iii.).

36. GS' description of Louis-Phillipe, who was to replace Charles X as king of France after the Revolution of 1830, and rule until the Revolution of 1848, would have had special significance for her contemporaries.

Chapter x

37. Apparently no relation to GS' cousins.

38. Thursday after Trinity Sunday—the eighth Sunday after Easter—which celebrates the Eucharist.

39. Tasso, *Jerusalem Delivered*, IV, iii.

40. Virgil, *Georgics*, II, 458-459.

41. A Latin epic by Statius, narrating the story of the seige of Boetian Thebes.

42. GS is here referring to Aurélien de Sèze, a young lawyer from Bordeaux, five years older than she, with whom she carried on an ardent correspondence, some of whose traits are recognizable in the libertine character, Raymon, in her first novel, *Indiana* [1832].

Chapter xi

43. Pantagruel, Manduce, Panurge, and Thélème are inventions of François Rabelais, sixteenth-century French writer, doctor, and monk, whose major literary works, *Gargantua* and *Pantagruel*, are noted for gigantism.

44. GL refers us for clarification to the letter GS wrote to Casimir on Nov. 15, 1825, in which she confessed her infatuation with Aurélien de Sèze.

45. *L'Ésprit des lois* was the major work of Charles Montesquieu (1689–1755), born at La Brède, from which emerges a temperate, humanizing interpretation of law, examined in light of politics, religion, customs, economics, climate, and war.

46. GL finds no evidence for this claim that Casimir's paternal line stems from the Scottish banker, John Law (1671–1729).

47. Josèph de Villèle (1773–1854), leader of the ultra-royalist party during the Restoration, from 1821 to 1828.

48. François Duris-Dufresne (1769–1837), the liberal candidate for deputy from La Châtre, who was successfully elected.

49. Alexis Pouradier-Duteil, friend and compatriot of GS, who will play an active role in her coming separation from Casimir.

50. Aurélien de Séze was present and signed the birth certificate, although GL's notes speculate that Stéphane de Grandsagne (see IV, v) may have been the father of Solange.

51. GS had met Jules Sandeau in July, 1830, a law student with whom she was to collaborate on her first published novel, *Rose et Blanche*.

Chapter xii

52. Aurélien de Séze is the one to whom GS is referring.

53. Jules Néraud, lifetime friend of GS, lawyer by profession and botanist by preference, so nick-named because of his travels to Madagascar, among other places.

54. Émile de Girardin (1804–1881), French journalist, married to the writer of poetry, novels, and plays, Delphine Gay (1804–1855).

55. *La Marraine [The Godmother]*, unpublished.

56. Rabelais, *Pantagruel*, IV, 18.

57. Duteil.

58. Operas by Karl Maria von Weber and Gioachino Rossini, respectively.

59. On July 19, 1830, Jules-Armand Polignac, minister of foreign affairs toward the end of the reign of Charles X, signed the so-called *Ordonnances*, which brought on the Revolution of 1830.

Chapter xiii

60. GS is referring to the Paris evoked in Hugo's novels; the novelist himself was only two years older than she.

61. Gabriel-Rigodin Planet, law student at the time, was to become an important adjunct to Michel de Bourges in attaining GS' legal separation.

62. Henri de Latouche, the literary mentor to the Berrichon group, to whom GS dedicated the first edition of *Lélia*, will be discussed further in IV, xvi and V, i.

63. Deputy from La Châtre already referred to in IV, ii.

64. The renowned general and statesman.

65. Another of the young Berrichon lawyers, who became a close friend and confidant, and to whom GS dedicated the 1875 edition of her autobiography.

66. From Montaigne, *Essays*, I, 27, "On Friendship," regarding Montaigne's friendship with Étienne de La Boétie.

67. On the subject of homosexuality, GS' opinions obviously reflect the prejudice of her time; it is the editor's impression that, if she were writing today, her ideas would be more liberal.

68. Montaigne, *op. cit.*

Chapter xiv

69. Jules Sandeau, seven years her junior, met GS in the Berry region when on vacation from his law studies in Paris. Their collaboration on a novel, *Rose et Blanche* [1831], was the factor that precipitated her move to Paris.

70. *Indiana* [1832] became the first novel GS published under her own pseudonym.

71. In 1819, a young German patriot, Karl Sand, had killed Auguste Kotzebue, German playwright and known Russian agent, for which he was executed; he was considered a hero by young enthusiasts for liberty.

72. An insurrection early in June, 1832, in which republican forces came close to overthrowing Louis-Phillippe.

73. Duc de Reichstadt was the title given to the son of Napoléon I; Duc de Bordeaux, the title of the grandson of Charles X.

74. *Valentine* was GS' second novel, published in 1832.

Chapter xv

75. Marquis de La Fayette had taken an active part in the American and French Revolutions, then tempered his political liberalism somewhat in light of the Terror, and was imprisoned. He remained inactive during Napoléon's reign but re-emerged on the liberal side when the Restoration took place. He again took command of the National Guard during the Revolution of 1830.

76. Character in Molière's *Les Femmes Savantes*, who personifies down-to-earth common sense.

77. The teacher to whom the heroine of *Consuelo* [1842] owes her training as a singer.

78. Honoré de Balzac (1799–1850), renowned and prolific novelist, author of *La Comédie Humaine*, a series of novels noted for acute observation and skillful narration.

79. Followers of a political and social doctrine, propounded by Claude-Louis Saint-Simon (1760–1825), which antedated socialism *per se*, but promoted the notion of individual labor in a communal context, and questioned the need for marriage bonds. GS' heroine, Indiana, eventually escapes a suffocating marriage and embarks on a less conventional relationship, with her cousin Ralph, in an exotic island setting, off the coast of Madagascar, outside the bounds of traditional society.

80. Part III, Chapters viii and ix.

Part Five

Chapter i

1. Under the leadership of François Buloz (1803-1877) the *RDM* came to represent the best of nineteenth-century French literature.

2. The term *collège* generally refers to a private, or preparatory, school where one begins a classical education, equivalent to the English grammar school, or what are now considered secondary schools. Maurice was not quite ten years old.

3. Charles-Augustin Sainte-Beuve (1804-1869) was a poet and novelist before he became a literary critic and historian, for which he is better known.

Chapter ii

4. Two notoriously poor, but gifted, poets, who died of poverty, according to GL's notes.

5. An early prototype of the romantic hero, created by Étienne de Sénancourt (1770–1846) in the novel by the same name; Chateaubriand's hero, René, has been referred to in Part IV, Chapter vi.

6. In June 1833, GS met Alfred de Musset, who, at the age of 23, was an acclaimed poet of the romantic school. They spent a week in Fontainebleau in August and left for Italy in December.

Chapter iii

7. Henri Beyle (1783–1842), French writer, author of *La Chartreuse de Parme* and *Le Rouge et le noir*, was considered an eccentric stylist but astute in his depiction of human passion. As a young man, he fell in love with Italy, and lived there until he was expelled for suspected espionage, but after the July 1830 Revolution, when his appointment as consul at Trieste was disputed, he was sent to Civitavecchia, a suburb of Rome, where he then longed for Paris, the city of conversation.

8. Although GS fails to mention it until later, Alfred de Musset has been her companion since the beginning of the trip.

9. Dr. Pietro Pagello was called in to treat the patient, and became a cause for jealousy on Musset's part, leading to his departure for Paris at the end of March 1834, whereupon the doctor became GS's escort and returned with her to Paris in August.

10. The General who led the 1848 revolution in Venice, and whom GS has mentioned several times already. See IV, iii, note 12.

11. Though his reputation for political morality was questionable, Charles Maurice de Talleyrand-Périgord (1754–1838) had a long career as minister and diplomat from the time of the Revolution, and played an influential role during the Directoire, in the signing of the Concordat, bringing Napoléon to power and in his demise, in the Restoration of the monarchy, and in the acceptance of the throne by Louis-Phillipe during the July 1830 Revolution.

12. GS reached the apex of her political activism in March and April of 1848, when in response to the requests of the revolutionary government, she wrote a series of articles for the official *Bulletin de la République*, the sixteenth of which was considered too radically explosive, and provoked a demonstration against her at Nohant.

Chapter iv

13. Marie Dorval (1798–1849), French actress, whose reputation was based mainly on her striking performances in melodrama.

14. Dramas by Dumas and Hugo, respectively.

15. Comic opera, music by Méhul.

16. Comedy by Beaumarchais.

17. Melodrama by Boirie, Carmouche, and Poujol.

18. Drama by Rougemont, Laffitte, and Lagrange.

19. *Angelo* by Hugo, *Chatterton* by Alfred de Vigny, *Marie-Jeanne* by D'Ennery and Maillan.

20. Mlle. Mars (1779–1847) was a popular French actress who starred in neo-classic as well as romantic comedy.

21. Élisa Félix (1820–1858) French tragedien who gained international acclaim under the name Rachel.

22. Marie Dorval's relationship with her son-in-law, René Luguet, may very well have provided GS with the main characters for *François le champi* [1848], her novel about a foundling who eventually rescues his adoptive mother from poverty and death, and marries her.

Chapter v

23. Eugène Delacroix (1798–1863), leading painter of the French Romantic school.

24. Baruch Spinoza (1632–1677), Dutch philosopher whose primary concerns were ethics and a pantheistic view of the universe.

25. An opera by Gioachino Rossini (1792–1868), noted Italian composer.

26. Denis Diderot (1713–1784), man of letters, science, and philosophy, as well as a disseminator of eighteenth-century ideas via the *Encyclopédie*, of which he was principal editor.

27. The immense fresco illustrating the Old and New Testaments, with which the Florentine artist, Michelangelo Buonarotti (1475–1564) decorated the ceiling of the Sistine Chappel in Rome, working from 1508 to 1541.

28. The Revelation according to Saint John, in the *New Testament*.

29. Allusion to Dante's *Inferno*, Canto III.

30. Xavier Sigalon (1788–1837)· French painter of historical subjects.

31. GS is referring to the center panel on the ceiling of the Galerie d'Apollon.

32. Delacroix used scenes from *Hamlet* and *Faust* for a series of lithographs, and painted *La Barque de Dante* from the *Inferno*.

33. The first two represent Italian Renaissance painting, the third, French Renaissance, and the last, Pierre-Paul Prud'hon (1758–1823) was a French predecessor of Delacroix. He pays tribute to all in his *Journal*.

34. A Swiss doctor (1806–1859), who became director of a hospital for the insane in northeastern France.

35. Abbé Felicité de Lammenais (1782–1854), French theologian and iconoclast thinker, whose strong belief in tradition did not preclude a belief in progress and revolutionary ideas.

36. Pierre-Marcel Gaubert (1796–1839), a medical doctor who treated GS and her family, and in whom she had great trust, according to GL.

37. A theory that emerged early in the history of psychology, now identified with mesmerism, by which one person can influence another through animal magnetic forces.

38. *Consuelo* [1842] would be an example.

39. Johann Wolfgang Goethe (1749–1832), published *Die Wanderjahre* in 1821, at least twenty years after *Wilhelm Meisters Lehrjahre*.

Chapter vi

40. The foremost exponent of the Vanloo school was Carle Vanloo (1705–1765), a French painter of Flemish origin, considered a born painter with almost excessive facility, who typified the rococo style.

41. Luigi Calamatta (1801–1869) and Paolo Mercuri (1804–1884) were Italian engravers; the former had a daughter, Lina, who married GS' son, Maurice. Léopold Robert (1794–1835), Swiss painter of the French school, was referred to in a note of GS in Part V, Chapter iii.

42. In the eighteenth and ninetheenth centuries, line engravers were, by and large, employed in reproducing the paintings of others.

43. Gerard Edelinck (1649–1707), Flemish engraver; Charles Clémont Bervic (1756–1822), French engraver; Raimondi Marcantonio (1480–1530), Italian engraver; Gérard Audran (1640–1703), French engraver.

44. Jean-Auguste-Dominique Ingres (1780–1867), French painter noted for the perfection of his technique. In *The Vow of Louis XIII* [1824], a religious painting which represents the culmination of his Raphaelesque manner, Ingres finally received universal approval.

45. GL's notes inform us that Didier was born in 1805, and died a suicide in 1864. Though he made writing a profession, he never achieved fame. His best known novel was *Rome souterraine* [1833].

Chapter vii

46. See Part I, Chapter vi.

47. *Une double famille.*

48. Hortense Allart (1801–1879), French woman writer, as liberated in her life style as GS was, who wrote books on politics and history as well as novels.

49. Fialin de Persigny (1808–1872), French statesman, strongly devoted to restoring the Empire. During the reign of Napoléon III, 1852–1870, he acted as minister of the interior, senator, and then ambassador to England.

50. Michel de Bourges (1797–1853) had strong republican roots and gave them eloquent expression as one of an army of defending attorneys in the April 1835 mass trial of thousands of insurgents from all over France before the chamber of peers. Later he was successful in the prosecution of GS's suit for separation. His political career culminated in 1849, when he was briefly seated in the national assembly.

Chapter viii

51. All names of eloquent, committed republicans, radical to varying degrees, who starred in the line for the defense, in the mass trial in April, 1835.

52. A radical doctrine of equality which would divide all forms of wealth, by force if necessary, among all, put forth by François-Noël Babeuf, called Gracchus (1760–1797). He was put to death when he, along with his disciple Darthé, challenged the direction of the Directoire.

53. *Matthew*, 18:20.

Chapter ix

54. Armand Carrel (1800–1836), French journalist, editor-in-chief of the *National*, had been active in opposing the July Monarchy (1830), when Louis-Philippe was established as king. In Part V, Chapter xii, GS discusses his premature death as well as his political role.

55. Cato of Utica.

56. Giuseppe Fieschi (1790–1836) had organized an infernal machine to attempt to assassinate the king on July 28, 1835.

57. An unkept promise.

58. Cf. note 35.

59. An allusion to the Russian invasion of Poland in 1832.

60. Pierre Leroux (1797–1871), French philosopher and economist, founder of the *Globe*, official organ of the Saint-Simonian community. His manifesto of Humanitarianism was most influential in several of the novels of GS, with whom he established the *Revue indépendante* in 1841. After the revolution of 1848, he was elected to the Assemby as a somewhat mystical spokesman for the radical Socialist wing.

61. Jean-Gaspard Lavater (1741–1801), Swiss philosopher and theologian, who invented the theory of physiognomy, or the art of judging character by facial traits.

62. GL finds it regrettable that GS so insistently uses words like "purity," "fraternal," and "chaste" to describe a relationship that is known to have been sexual; however, it seems to this editor, had GS done otherwise, it would have been tantamount to an admission of adultery. Considering that Michel had only recently died, and his wife and her children might still have been affected by such an admission, Sand's disclaimers seem protective rather than dishonest. In Chapter x, following this one, her remarks on adultery as a moral killer of women further elucidates her avoidance of an admission.

Chapter x

63. Curtailing freedom of the press.

64. GS is referring to her granddaughter, Jeanne-Gabrielle Clésinger, who had died at the age of five-and-a-half, on January 14, 1855.

65. An allusion to Racine's *Andromaque*, III, 1.

66. See Part IV, Chapter xi.

67. See Part IV, note 6.

68. The correct spelling would be: *A la bouteille [At the bottle]*.

69. French painters who used itinerant performers as their subjects, the first, Alexandre-Gabriel Decamps, a contemporary (1803–1860), the second, Jacques Callot, a predecessor (1593–1635).

70. The notes of GL inform us that, in 1855, this same attorney, then representing her son-in-law, Auguste Clésinger, was indirectly to blame for her granddaughter's death.

Chapter xi

71. Franz Liszt (1811–1886), Hungarian pianist and composer, and Marie d'Agoult (1805–1876), French writer under the name Daniel Stern, were living together; she had recently given birth to the first of their three children.

72. Alphonse Lamartine (1790–1869), French lyric poet as well as republican

political figure, deputy in 1834, member of the provisionary government of 1848. Antoine Berryer (1790–1868), renowned attorney and speaker for the legitimist party.

73. Eugène Sue (1804–1857), French novelist; Ferdinand d'Eckstein (1790–1861), convert to Catholicism and frequenter of literary salons; Frédéric Chopin (1810–1849), Polish pianist and composer; Adam Mickiewicz (1798–1855), Polish poet; Adolphe Nourrit (1802–1839), French singer; Victor Schoelcher (1804–1893), French journalist and abolitionist; Heinrich Heine (1797–1856), German poet.

74. Charlotte de Folleville (1790[?]–1850) married to the Consul-General of Spain, Emmanuel Marliani, became a close friend and confidant of GS, whose social views she shared.

75 Alexander Rey (1812–1904), French journalist and political figure, deputy in 1848, prefect in 1876, was briefly tutor for Maurice; Pierre-François Touzé (1799–1862), French actor called Bocage.

76. Louis Alibaud (1810–1836), member of the Fieschi machine which had failed in its attempt to assassinate Louis-Philippe.

77. Louis Viardot (1800–1883), lawyer, journalist, and director of the Théatre-Italien, married Pauline Garcia, a singer who became a close friend of GS. Viardot, too, was a founder of Pierre Leroux's *Revue indépendante*.

78. Georges-Eugène Haussmann (1809–1891), later Baron, is noted for overseeing major public works in the modernization of the city of Paris.

79. According to legend, Florette, daughter of the gardener, was seduced by King Henri, and drowned herself in the river.

Chapter xii

80. Émile de Girardin (1806–1881), French journalist, who adhered to different degrees of socialism at different times and founded numerous newspapers, had recently published a work in which he addressed "the marriage question." He was married to Delphine Gay (1804–1855), who in her youth had been a writer of witty poetry, then became a columnist under the pen name of Vicomte de Launay, and a successful playwright.

81. A member of Carrel's dueling party.

82. Albert Grzymala (1793–1870), Polish patriot, émigré and loyal friend of Chopin.

83. Juan de Dios Alvarez y Mendizibal (1790–1853) was president of the ministerial counsel of Spain, and after, Minister of Finance.

84. Both were part of the active community of music lovers and players at Lyon.

85. *Chiave, fresche, et dolce acque* . . . [Clear, fresh, and gentle waters . . .] *Canzone*, CXXVI.

86. *Un hiver à Majorque* [1842].

87. The title of *Un Hiver à Majorca*, when it first appeared in serial form.

88. Music is a pervasive theme in *Consuelo*, but Chapters 52 and 56 (translation reissued by Da Capo Press, 1979) are particularly apt here.

89. A short-lived insurrection was the work of the Société des Saisons, under the leadership of Armand Barbès (1809–1870) and Martin Bernard (1808–1883).

Chapter xiii

90. The illegitimate son in Dumas' play by that name.

91. Solange resented the presence of this so-called adopted sister and was instrumental in breaking a first marriage engagement arranged by GS.

92. Louis Blanc (1811–1882) and Henri Martin (1810–1883) were historians and political figures whom GS often quotes as authorities; Godefroy Cavaignac (1801–1845) was a staunch republican and journalist; Pauline (1821–1910) and Maria (1808–1836) (La Malibran) Garcia were noted singers of Spanish origin, the former a model for Consuelo.

93. Lablanche, Alkan, Soliva, and Dessaüer were musicians; Edgar Quinet (1803–1875), historian and political figure; Perdiguier and Gilland, proletarian writers; Ferdinand François, Étienne Arago, and Anselme Petétin, journalists and political figures; Pierre-Jules Hetzel (1814–1886), publisher of GS' works.

94. Cf. Part V, Chapter vii, note 48.

95. Pauline Roland (1805–1852), advanced social thinker and activist, was arrested after the 1848 coup and died on her return from exile.

96. Giuseppe Mazzini (1808–1872), an Italian patriot who fought for his country's independence from the distance of perpetual exile.

97. Silvio Pellico (1789–1854), an Italian author who wrote as a martyr, when imprisoned for political crimes.

98. In the character of Prince Karol, in *Lucrezia Floriani* [1846].

99. Solange was a focal point of this sorrow, intent as she was to marry a man Chopin and GS disliked; also, Chopin seems to have been infatuated with the young woman.

100. Gotthold Ephraïm Lessing (1729–1781), German playwright and social critic: Johann-Gottfried Herder (1744–1803), German philosopher, whose *Ideas on the Philosophy of the History of Humanity* was translated by Quinet.